Autodesk Inventor 2026

A Power Guide for Beginners and Intermediate Users

CADArtifex

A premium provider of learning products and solutions

www.cadartifex.com

Autodesk Inventor 2026: A Power Guide for Beginners and Intermediate Users
Author: Sandeep Dogra
Email: info@cadartifex.com

Published by
CADArtifex
www.cadartifex.com

ISBN: 978-9394074569

www.cadartifex.com

Dedication

First and foremost, I would like to thank my parents for being a great support throughout my career and while writing this book.

Heartfelt gratitude goes to my wife and my sisters for their patience and endurance in supporting me to take up and successfully accomplish this challenge.

I would also like to acknowledge the efforts of the employees at CADArtifex for their dedication in editing the contents of this book.

Contents at a Glance

Table of Contents

Part 4. Creating Animation and Exploded Views

Part 5. Creating Drawings

Preface

Autodesk Inventor is a product of Autodesk Inc., one of the biggest technology providers for engineering, architecture, construction, manufacturing, media, and entertainment industries, offering robust software tools for 3D design that let you design, visualize, simulate, and publish your ideas before they are built or created. Autodesk is a leader in developing software for creators. Moreover, Autodesk continues to develop a comprehensive portfolio of state-of-the-art CAD/CAM/CAE software for global markets.

Autodesk Inventor is a feature-based, parametric solid-modeling mechanical design and automation software which allows you to convert 2D sketches into 3D models by using simple but highly effective modeling tools. Autodesk Inventor provides a wide range of tools that allow you to create real-world components and assemblies. These components and assemblies can be used for generating 2D engineering drawings for production, validating designs by simulating their real world conditions, visualization, and documentation. It also enables you to create photorealistic renderings, animations, and so on, in addition to creating rapid prototypes of your design. Autodesk Inventor helps in reducing development costs while maximizing efficiency and quality.

Autodesk Inventor 2026: A Power Guide for Beginners and Intermediate Users has been designed for both instructor-led courses and self-paced learning. This textbook aims to assist engineers and designers interested in learning Autodesk Inventor to create 3D mechanical designs. It is an excellent guide for new Inventor users and a valuable teaching aid for classroom training.

The textbook consists of 14 chapters and a total of 794 pages, covering major environments of Autodesk Inventor, such as the Sketching environment, Part modeling environment, Assembly environment, Presentation environment, and Drawing environment. It teaches you how to use Autodesk Inventor mechanical design software to build parametric 3D solid components and assemblies, as well as create animations and 2D drawings.

This textbook not only focuses on the usage of the tools and commands of Autodesk Inventor but also on the concept of design. Each chapter contains tutorials that provide step-by-step instructions for creating mechanical designs and drawings with ease. Additionally, every chapter ends with hands-on test drives that allow users to experience the user-friendly and powerful technical capabilities of Autodesk Inventor.

Who Should Read This Textbook

This textbook is written to benefit a wide range of Autodesk Inventor users, varying from beginners to advanced users as well as Autodesk Inventor instructors. The easy-to-follow chapters of this textbook allow easy comprehension of different design techniques, Autodesk Inventor tools, and design principles.

What Is Covered in This Textbook

Autodesk Inventor 2026: A Power Guide for Beginners and Intermediate Users textbook is designed to help you learn everything you need to know to start using Autodesk Inventor with straightforward, step-by-step tutorials. This textbook covers the following topics:

Chapter 1, ***"Introduction to Autodesk Inventor,"*** introduces Autodesk Inventor user interface, different Inventor environments, and methods for identifying Inventor files. It also explains how to create a project, invoke a Marking Menu, customize the color scheme, choose the user interface theme, export files to other CAD formats, save files, and open existing files.

Chapter 2, ***"Drawing Sketches with Autodesk Inventor,"*** discusses how to invoke the Part modeling and the Sketching environments. It explains how to specify the units as well as grids and snap settings. Besides, this chapter introduces methods for drawing lines, rectangles, circles, ellipses, arcs, slots, polygons, and splines by using the respective sketching tools. It also discusses how to edit a spline.

Chapter 3, ***"Editing and Modifying Sketches,"*** introduces various editing and modifying operations such as trimming unwanted sketch entities, extending sketch entities, splitting sketch entities, and offsetting sketch entities. It also explains how to create 2D fillets, chamfers, construction and centerline entities, pattern sketch entities, and mirror sketch entities in addition to methods for copying, rotating, scaling, and stretching sketch entities.

Chapter 4, ***"Applying Constraints and Dimensions,"*** introduces various constraints and different methods for applying them. The chapter discusses how to control the display of constraints in the drawing area, apply different dimensions, control dimension settings, and edit dimensions. It also discusses working with different states of a sketch and displaying available degrees of freedom of the sketch entities.

Chapter 5, ***"Creating Base Feature of Solid Models,"*** discusses how to create extrude and revolve base features by using the Extrude and Revolve tools. The chapter describes how to navigate a model by using mouse buttons, ViewCube, and navigation tools such as Navigation Wheel, Pan, Zoom, and Orbit. Further, it explains changing the visual style of a model to realistic, shaded, shaded with edges, and shaded with hidden edges.

Chapter 6, ***"Creating Work Features,"*** explains that the three default planes: Front, Top, and Right may not be enough for creating models having multiple features. Therefore, this chapter discusses how to create additional work planes. Additionally, it also elaborates on creating work axes, work points, and a user coordinates system.

Chapter 7, ***"Advanced Modeling - I,"*** introduces advanced options for creating extrude and revolve features. It discusses how to work with a sketch having multiple profiles. It explains how to project geometries of existing features onto the sketching plane, intersecting edges of a model onto the sketching plane, 2D sketch onto a face of a model, and geometries of a DWG file onto the sketching plane. The chapter also elaborates on creating a section view, editing a feature and its sketch, displaying earlier state of a model, reordering features of a model, measuring the distance between the entities, assigning an appearance, applying a material, assigning the finishes and manufacturing data, and calculating physical properties of a model.

Chapter 8, ***"Advanced Modeling - II,"*** discusses how to create sweep features, loft features, coil features, emboss features, mark features, and rib features. It also discusses the methods for applying an image on a face of a model and creating a shell feature.

Chapter 9, ***"Patterning and Mirroring,"*** introduces methods for creating rectangular patterns, circular patterns, and sketch driven patterns. It also discusses about suppressing and unsuppressing features and pattern occurrences, as well as mirroring a feature or a body about a mirroring plane.

Chapter 10, "***Advanced Modeling - III,***" discusses how to create simple, clearance, tapped, and taper tapped holes as per the standard specifications by using the **Hole** tool. It also explains how to create threads, different types of fillets, and chamfers, splitting a face and a solid body, as well as creating 3D Sketches and curves.

Chapter 11, "***Working with Assemblies - I,***" discusses how to create assemblies by using the bottom-up assembly approach. The chapter introduces the procedures for inserting components into the Assembly environment, working with degrees of freedom, and applying various constraints. The application of various joints such as rigid, rotational, slider, cylindrical, and ball have been described. Besides, methods for editing constraints and joints, deleting constraints and joints, as well as moving and rotating individual components of an assembly have also been described.

Chapter 12, "***Working with Assemblies - II,***" discusses how to create assemblies by using the top-down assembly approach. It also explains editing individual components of an assembly, patterning, mirroring, and copying components of an assembly, and creating the Bill of Material (BOM) of an Assembly.

Chapter 13, "***Creating Animation and Exploded Views,***" discusses how to create animation of an assembly in the Presentation Environment. The chapter explains how to capture actions and tweaks on the Timeline and discusses methods for editing time and properties of a tweak, deleting a tweak, creating a snapshot view, editing a snapshot view, renaming a snapshot view, deleting a snapshot view, publishing a snapshot view to a raster image, creating an exploded view in a drawing file, creating a new storyboard, and creating a new scene. Besides, the chapter also describes how to play an animation of a storyboard and publish it to a video file.

Chapter 14, "***Working with Drawings,***" discusses how to create 2D drawings of components and assemblies in the Drawing environment, with a focus on editing sheet size, title block, and drafting standards. The chapter introduces the concept and definition of angle of projections, creating various types of drawing views such as base view, projected views, and section view, deleting a drawing view, applying dimensions, adding texts/notes, adding surface finish symbols, adding weld symbols, adding hole and thread notes, adding parts list / Bill of Materials (BOM), and editing the parts list. Besides, it also discusses how to add balloons to the components of an assembly.

Icons/Terms used in this Textbook

The following icons and terms are used in this textbook:

Note

Note: Notes highlight information requiring special attention.

Tip

Tip: Tips provide additional advice, which increases the efficiency of the users.

Flyout

A flyout is a list in which a set of tools are grouped together, see Figure 1.

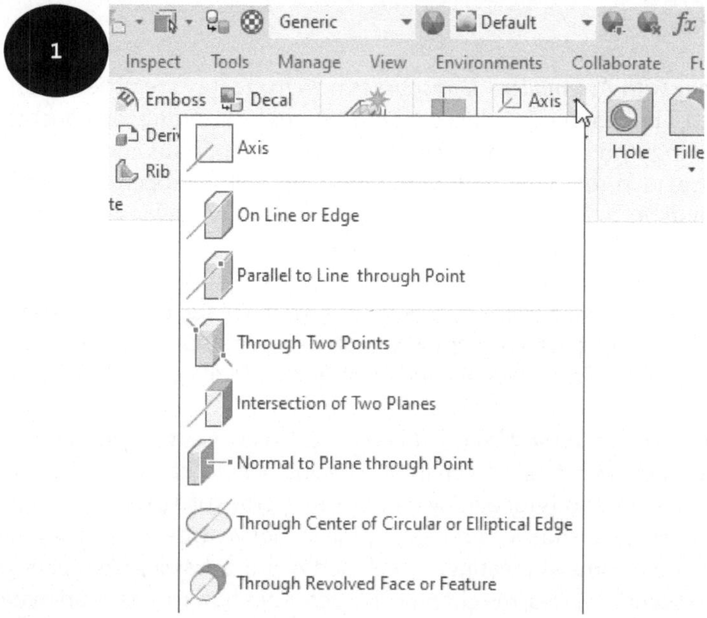

Drop-down List

A drop-down list is a list in which a set of options are grouped together, see Figure 2.

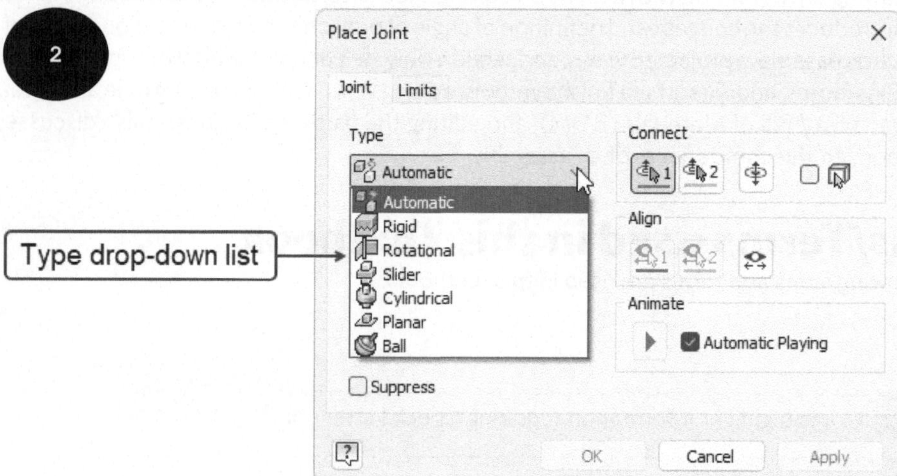

Selector
A Selector allows you to select a geometry as an input for performing a specific operation, see Figure 3.

Button
A Button appears as a 3D icon and is used for confirming or discarding an action, see Figure 3.

Field
A Field allows you to enter a new value, or modify an existing value, as per your requirement, see Figure 3.

Rollout
A rollout is an area in which buttons, fields, selectors, check boxes, etc. are available to specify various parameters, see Figure 3. A rollout can either be in the expanded or collapsed form. You can expand or collapse a rollout by clicking on the arrow available on its title bar.

Check box
A check box allows you to turn on or off the uses of a particular option, see Figure 3.

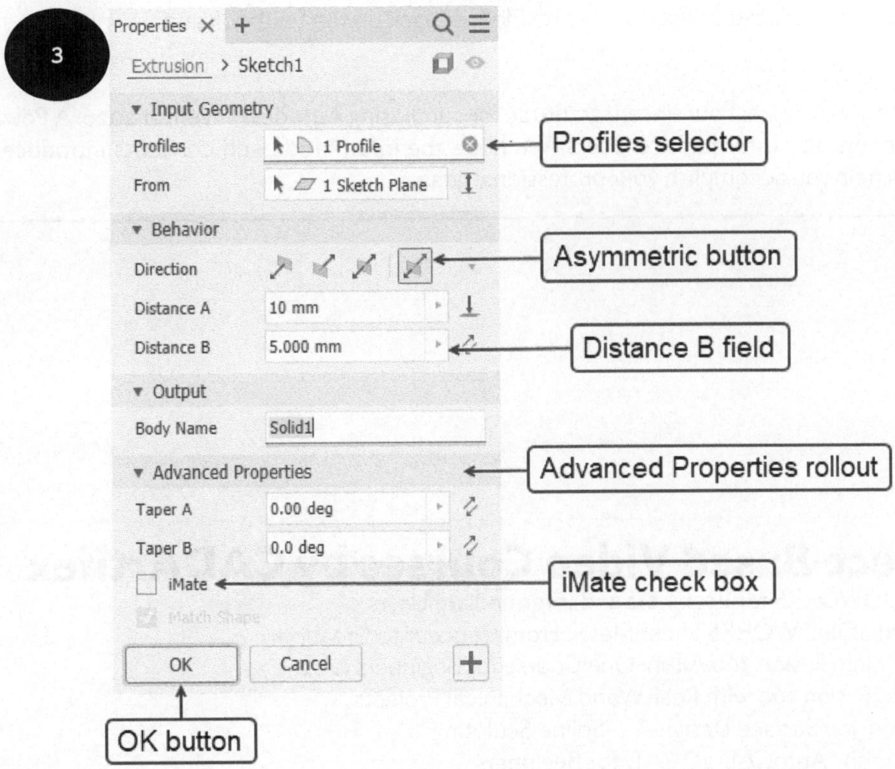

How to Download Online Resources

Students and faculty members can **download all parts/models** used in the illustrations, Tutorials and Hands-on Test Drives (exercises) of the textbook. In addition, faculty can also download PowerPoint Presentations (PPTs) of each chapter of the textbook.

To download the free online teaching and learning resources of the textbook, log on to our website (*cadartifex.com/login*). If you are a new user, you need to first register (*cadartifex.com/register*) for downloading the online resources of the textbook.

Interactive Support for Your Learning

In the book, you'll find QR codes next to key tutorial steps for certain tutorials. Scan these codes to access video demonstrations, designed to help you through any challenging parts of the process.

How to Contact the Author

We value your feedback and suggestions. You can email us at info@cadartifex.com. You can also visit our website at www.cadartifex.com to provide feedback on the textbook and download free learning resources.

We would like to express our sincere gratitude for purchasing **Autodesk Inventor 2026: A Power Guide for Beginners and Intermediate Users**. We hope the information and concepts introduced in this textbook help you accomplish your professional goals.

CHAPTER

1

Introduction to Autodesk Inventor

In this chapter, the following topics will be discussed:

- Installing Autodesk Inventor
- Getting Started with Autodesk Inventor
- Starting a New Inventor File
- Identifying Inventor Files
- Creating and Accessing a Project
- Invoking a Marking Menu
- Customizing the Color Scheme
- Choosing the User Interface Theme
- Exporting Files to Other CAD Formats
- Saving Files
- Opening Existing Files

Welcome to the world of Computer Aided Design (CAD) with Autodesk Inventor. Autodesk Inventor is a product of Autodesk Inc., one of the biggest technology providers for engineering, architecture, construction, manufacturing, media, and entertainment industries, offering robust software tools for 3D design that let you design, visualize, simulate, and publish your ideas before they are built or created. Autodesk is a leader in developing software for creators. Moreover, Autodesk continues to develop a comprehensive portfolio of state-of-the-art CAD/CAM/CAE software for global markets.

Autodesk Inventor is a feature-based, parametric solid-modeling mechanical design and automation software that allows you to convert 2D sketches into 3D models by using simple but highly effective modeling tools. Autodesk Inventor provides a wide range of tools that allow you to create real-world components and assemblies. These components and assemblies can be used for generating 2D engineering drawings for production, validating designs by simulating their real world conditions, visualization, and documentation. Autodesk Inventor helps in reducing development costs while maximizing efficiency and quality.

Installing Autodesk Inventor

If you do not have Autodesk Inventor installed in your system, you first need to get it installed. However, before you start installing it, you need to evaluate the system requirements and ensure that you have a system capable of running Autodesk Inventor adequately. Below are the system requirements for installing Autodesk Inventor 2026.

1. **Operating Systems**: 64-bit Microsoft® Windows® 10 and Windows®11
2. **Memory**: 16 GB RAM for less than 500-part assemblies (32 GB RAM or more recommended)
3. **Disk Space**: 40 GB (Installer plus full installation)
4. **CPU**: 2.5 GHz or greater (3.0 GHz or greater, 4 or more cores recommended)
5. **Graphics**: 1 GB GPU with 29 GB/S Bandwidth and DirectX 11 compliant (8 GB GPU with 106 GB/S Bandwidth and DirectX 11 compliant recommended)

For more information about the system requirements for Autodesk Inventor, visit the Autodesk website at *autodesk.com/support/technical/article/caas/sfdcarticles/sfdcarticles/System-requirements-for-Autodesk-Inventor-2026.html*

Once the system is ready, install Autodesk Inventor by using the downloaded Inventor software setup files. You can download the setup files by logging in to your Autodesk account.

Getting Started with Autodesk Inventor

Once Autodesk Inventor 2026 is installed on your system, double-click on the **Autodesk Inventor Professional 2026** icon on the desktop of your system. The system prepares for start-up by loading all the required files of Inventor. Once all the required files have been loaded, the startup user interface of Autodesk Inventor appears, see Figure 1.1.

1.1

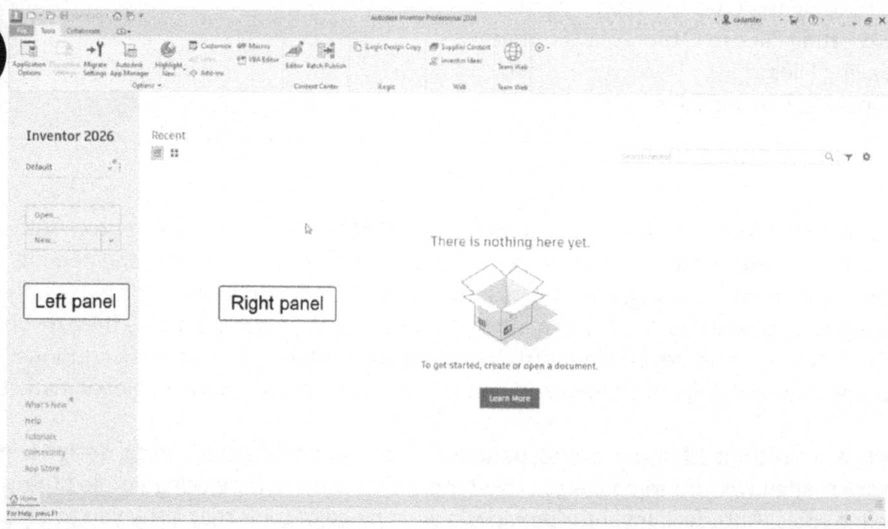

The left panel of the start up user interface of Autodesk Inventor 2026 provides quick access to existing projects, start a new file, open an existing file, and define a new project. It also provides quick access to Autodesk Inventor learning resources such as What's New, Help Document, Tutorial Gallery, Autodesk Community, and so on. The right panel of the startup user interface of Autodesk Inventor 2026 displays recently used files as thumbnails or as a list view.

Note: When you start Autodesk Inventor 2026, the **Sign in** page appears in the default browser if you are not already logged in to your Autodesk account, see Figure 1.2. In this page, enter your E-mail ID and then click on the **NEXT** button. The **Welcome** page appears in the browser. Enter the password and then click on the **SIGN IN** button on the **Welcome** page to log in to your Autodesk account. Next, you can click on the **Go to product** button on the message page that appears in the browser to open AutoCAD. If AutoCAD not open, you need to open it manually.

1.2

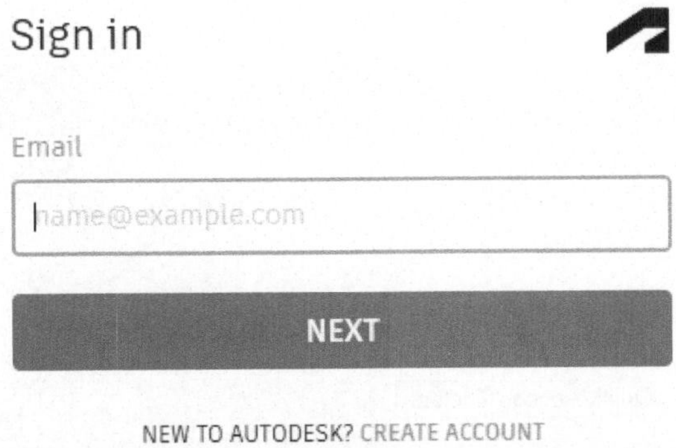

Starting a New Inventor File

In Autodesk Inventor, you need to invoke different environments such as **Part**, **Assembly**, **Drawing**, and **Presentation** for creating a 3D solid part, an assembly, a 2D drawing, and a presentation, respectively. You can invoke these environments by using the respective option of the **New** drop-down list available in the left panel of the startup user interface, see Figure 1.3. You can also invoke the required environment by using the **New** tool available in the **Quick Access Toolbar**, see Figure 1.4. The methods for invoking different environments of Autodesk Inventor are discussed next.

1.3

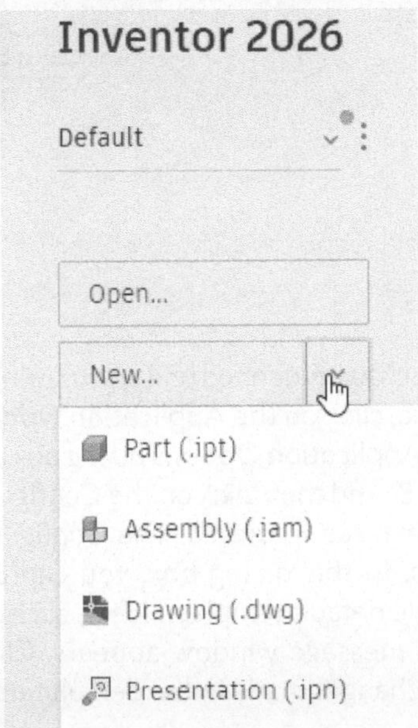

1.4

Invoking the Part Modeling Environment

To invoke the Part modeling environment for creating a 3D solid part, click on the down arrow next to the **New** tool in the left panel of the startup user interface of Autodesk Inventor and then click on the **Part (.ipt)** option in the **New** drop-down list that appears, see Figure 1.5. The Part modeling environment is invoked with a default template. Figure 1.6 shows the user interface of the Part modeling environment.

1.5

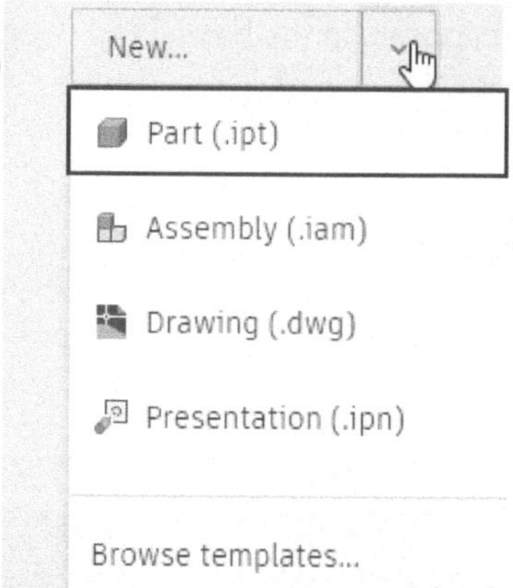

1.6

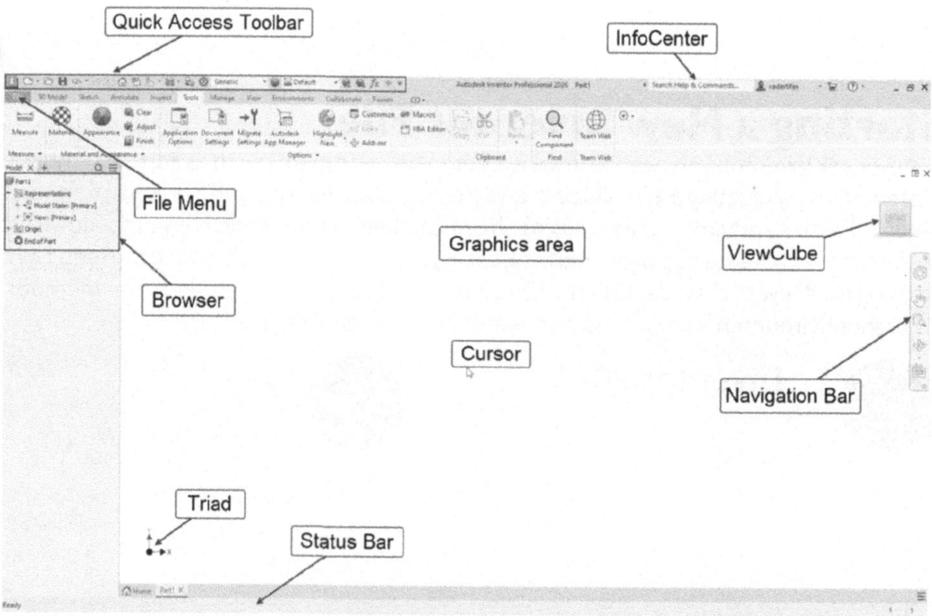

Note: A template contains some properties of the file such as predefined unit and drawing standard. To change the properties of the default template, click on the **Application Options** tool in the **Tools** tab of the **Ribbon**, see Figure 1.7. The **Application Options** dialog box appears. In this dialog box, click on the **File** tab (see Figure 1.8) and then click on the **Configure Default Templates** button in the **Default Templates** area, see Figure 1.8. The **Configure Default Templates** dialog box appears, see Figure 1.9. In this dialog box, you can define the measurement units and drawing standard for the default template. Next, click on the **OK** button. The **Autodesk Inventor Professional** message window appears. Click on the **Overwrite** button in this window to accept the changes made in the default template.

1.7

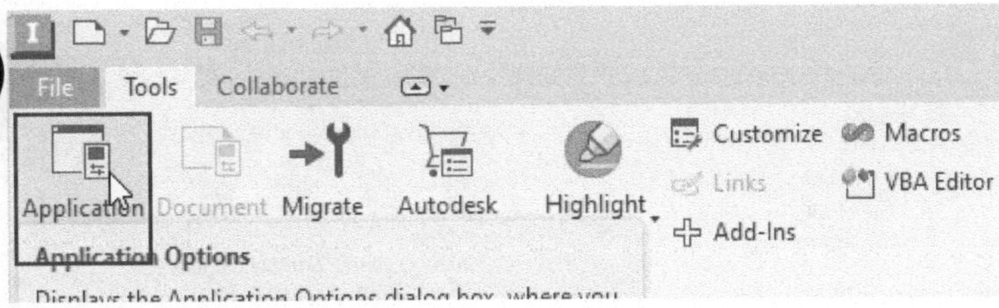

1.8

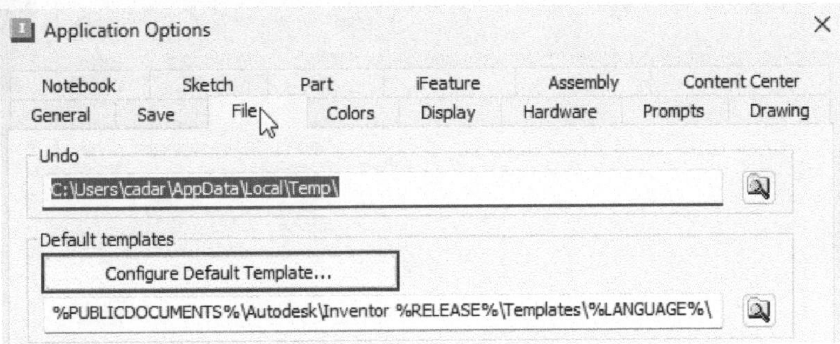

1.9

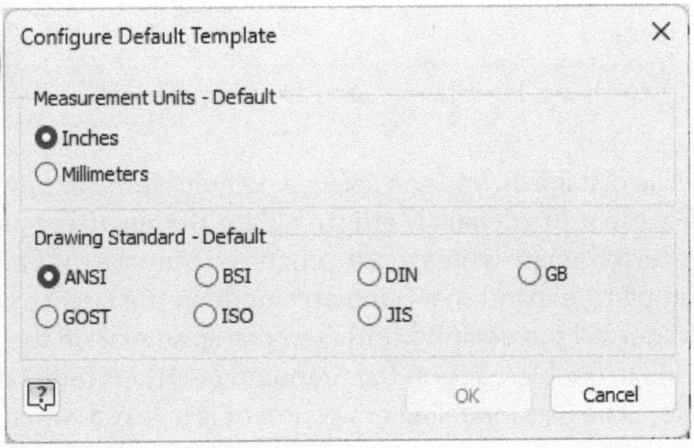

Alternatively, to invoke the Part modeling environment, click on the **New** tool in the left panel of the startup user interface (see Figure 1.10) or in the **Quick Access Toolbar** (see Figure 1.11). The **Create New File** dialog box appears, see Figure 1.12. You can also press the CTRL + N keys to invoke the **Create New File** dialog box.

1.10

1.11

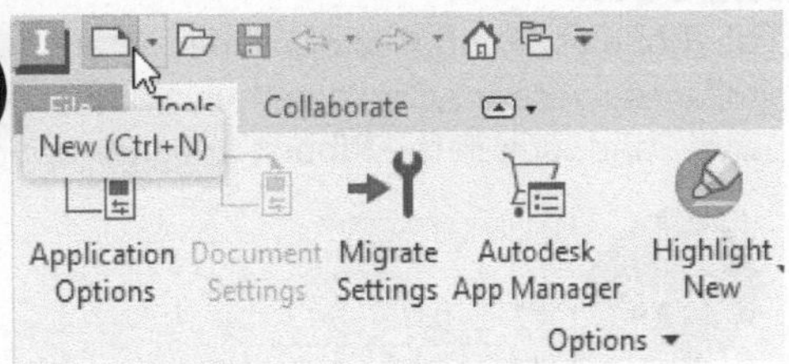

1.12

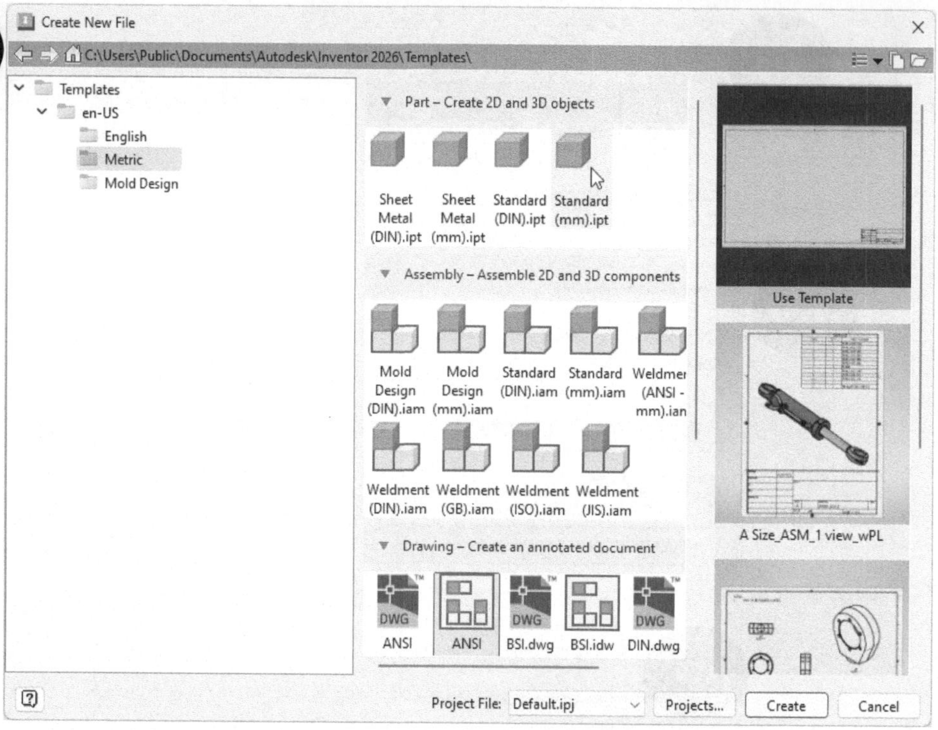

In the **Create New File** dialog box, you can select a default Metric or English template for invoking the Part modeling environment. In a default Metric template, the length is measured in millimeters whereas, in an English template, the length is measured in inches. To invoke the Part modeling environment with a default Metric template, expand the **Templates** node in the **Create New File** dialog box and then select the **Metric** folder. All the default Metric templates appear on the right panel of the dialog box, refer to Figure 1.12. Next, double-click on the **Standard (mm).ipt** template (*.ipt* is the file extension of the Inventor part file). The Part modeling environment is invoked with the default Metric template.

The various user interface components of the Part modeling environment such as **Ribbon**, **Browser**, **ViewCube**, and **Navigation Bar** are discussed next.

Ribbon

The **Ribbon** is composed of a series of tabs such as **3D Model**, **Sketch**, and **Annotate** in which a set of similar tools are grouped together in different panels, see Figure 1.13. Note that the availability of tabs, panels, and tools in the **Ribbon** depends upon the currently invoked environment of Inventor.

1.13

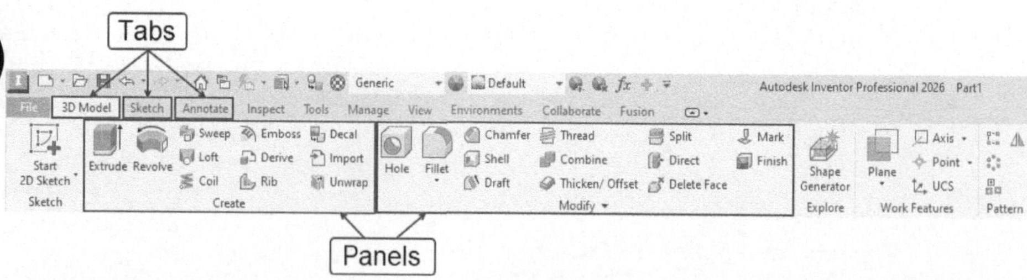

By default, the **Ribbon** is docked horizontally at the top of the graphics area. You can also dock the **Ribbon** vertically to the left or right of the graphics area. For doing so, right-click anywhere on the **Ribbon**. A shortcut menu appears. In this shortcut menu, move the cursor over the **Docking Positions** and then select the required option in the cascading menu that appears, see Figure 1.14. You can also undock the **Ribbon** such that it can float within the graphics area by clicking on the **Undock Ribbon** option in the shortcut menu that appears when you right-click on the **Ribbon**.

1.14

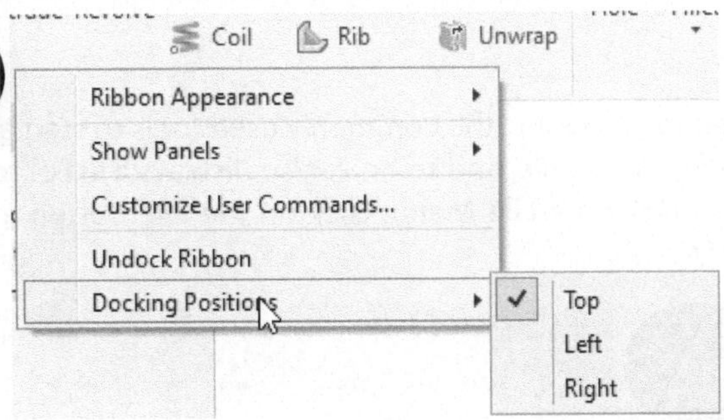

In Autodesk Inventor, you can also add a custom panel with user defined tools in each tab of the **Ribbon**. For doing so, right-click anywhere on the **Ribbon** and then click on the **Customize User Commands** option in the shortcut menu that appears. The **Customize** dialog box appears, see Figure 1.15. Ensure that the **Ribbon** tab is selected in the **Customize** dialog box. Next, select the required tab in the **Choose tab to add custom panel to** drop-down list of the right panel in the dialog box. After selecting the required tab, select a tool on the left panel of the dialog box and then click on the **Add** button >>. The selected tool gets added to the right panel of the dialog box. Similarly, you can add multiple tools to the right panel of the dialog box. Next, click on the **Apply** button and then the **OK** button in the dialog box. All selected tools get added in the **User Commands** panel, at the end of the selected tab in the **Ribbon**.

1.15

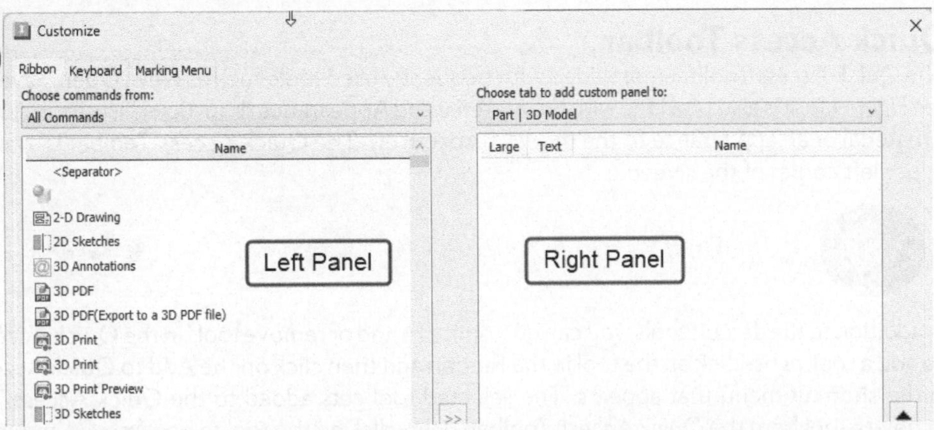

You can also change the appearance of the **Ribbon** to **Normal**, **Test Off**, **Small**, **Compact**, or **Large**. For doing so, right-click anywhere on the **Ribbon** and then move the cursor over the **Ribbon Appearance** option in the shortcut menu that appears, see Figure 1.16. A cascading menu appears. In this cascading menu, select the required option to define the appearance of the **Ribbon**. By default, the **Normal** option is selected as the appearance of the **Ribbon**. The **Reset Ribbon** option in the cascading menu is used for resetting the **Ribbon** to the default settings.

1.16

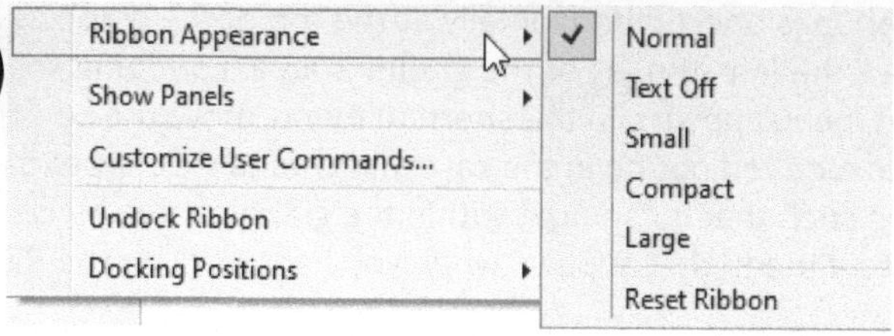

File Menu

The **File Menu** is used for accessing the commonly used tools to start a new file, open an existing file, save a file, export a file, share a file, and so on. It also displays a list of recently used files in its **Recent Documents** area. To invoke the **File Menu**, click on the **File** button at the upper left corner of the **Ribbon**, see Figure 1.17.

1.17

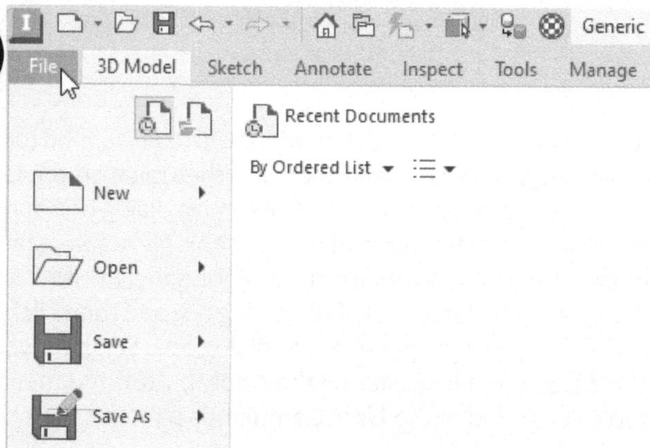

Quick Access Toolbar

The **Quick Access Toolbar** is provided with frequently used tools such as **New**, **Open**, **Save**, and **Undo**, see Figure 1.18. It is also provided with the **Material** and **Appearance** drop-down lists for quickly assigning a material or an appearance to the model, respectively. The **Quick Access Toolbar** is available at the upper left corner of the screen.

1.18

In addition to the default tools, you can customize to add or remove tools in the **Quick Access Toolbar**. To add a tool, right-click on the tool in the **Ribbon** and then click on the **Add to Quick Access Toolbar** in the shortcut menu that appears. The selected tool gets added to the **Quick Access Toolbar**. To remove a tool from the **Quick Access Toolbar**, right-click on the tool to be removed and then click on the **Remove from Quick Access Toolbar** in the shortcut menu that appears.

InfoCenter

The **InfoCenter** is available at the upper right corner of the Inventor window, see Figure 1.19. It is used for accessing help documents for finding information related to a topic. Also, it provides tools to access the Autodesk App Store, Sign In/Sign Out to Autodesk account, account details, search a tool, and so on.

Browser

The **Browser** appears on the left side of the graphics area and keeps a record of all features or operations used for creating a model, see Figure 1.20. Note that the first created feature appears at the top and the next created features appear one after the other in the **Browser**. You can drag the **End of Part** up or down in the **Browser** to step upward or downward through the regeneration order of the features. Note that the features present after the **End of Part** get suppressed and do not appear in the graphics area.

1.19

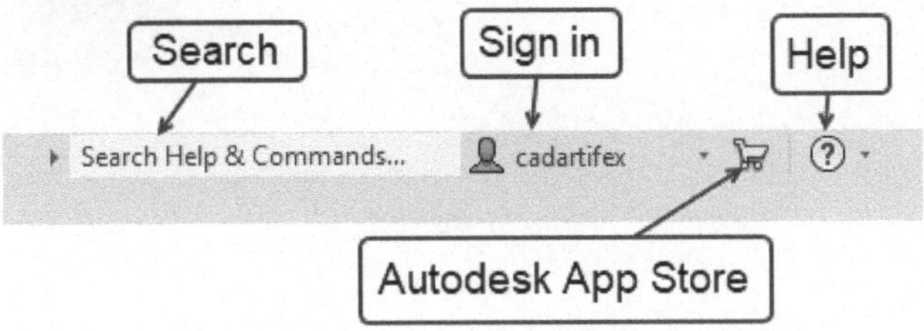

1.20

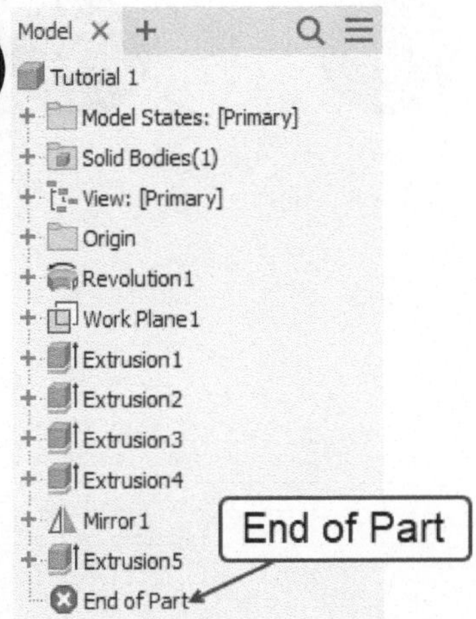

Note: The **Origin** folder in the **Browser** contains three default planes, three default axes, and a center point.

ViewCube

The **ViewCube** is available at the upper right corner of the graphics area and is used for navigating the model, see Figure 1.21. You can orbit or switch between the standard and isometric views of a model by using the **ViewCube**. You will learn to navigate a model by using the **ViewCube** in Chapter 5.

1.21

Navigation Bar

The **Navigation Bar** is used for accessing navigation tools such as **Zoom**, **Orbit**, and **Pan**, see Figure 1.22. It is available to the right of the graphics area. The various navigation tools of the **Navigation Bar** are discussed in Chapter 5.

Tip: You can turn on or off the display of **ViewCube** and **Navigation Bar** in the graphics area. For doing so, click on the **View** tab in the **Ribbon** and then invoke the **User Interface** flyout in the **Windows** panel, see Figure 1.23. Next, select or clear the respective check boxes in the **User Interface** flyout.

1.22

1.23

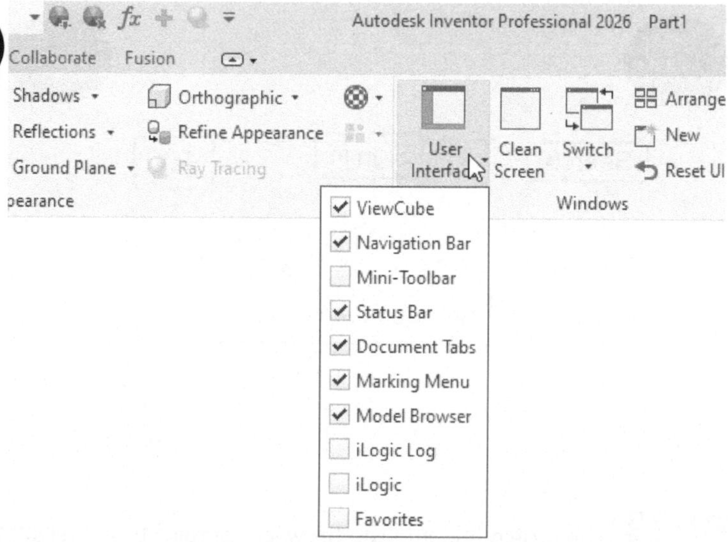

Status Bar

The **Status Bar** is available at the bottom of the graphics area and provides information about the action to be taken based on the currently active tool. It also displays the current state of the sketch being created, the coordinate system, and so on.

Invoking the Assembly Environment

To invoke the Assembly environment for creating an assembly, click on the down arrow next to the **New** tool in the left panel of the startup user interface of Autodesk Inventor and then click on the **Assembly (.iam)** option in the **New** drop-down list that appears, see Figure 1.24. The Assembly environment is invoked with the default template, see Figure 1.25. Note that the method for editing properties such as unit and drawing standard of the default template is the same as discussed earlier.

1.24

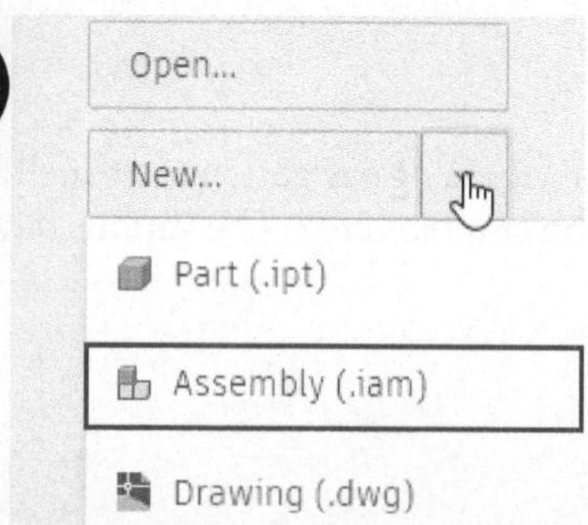

1.25

Alternatively, to invoke the Assembly environment, click on the **New** tool in the left panel of the startup user interface (see Figure 1.26) or in the **Quick Access Toolbar** (see Figure 1.27). The **Create New File** dialog box appears, see Figure 1.28. You can also press the CTRL + N keys to invoke the **Create New File** dialog box.

1.26

1.27

1.28

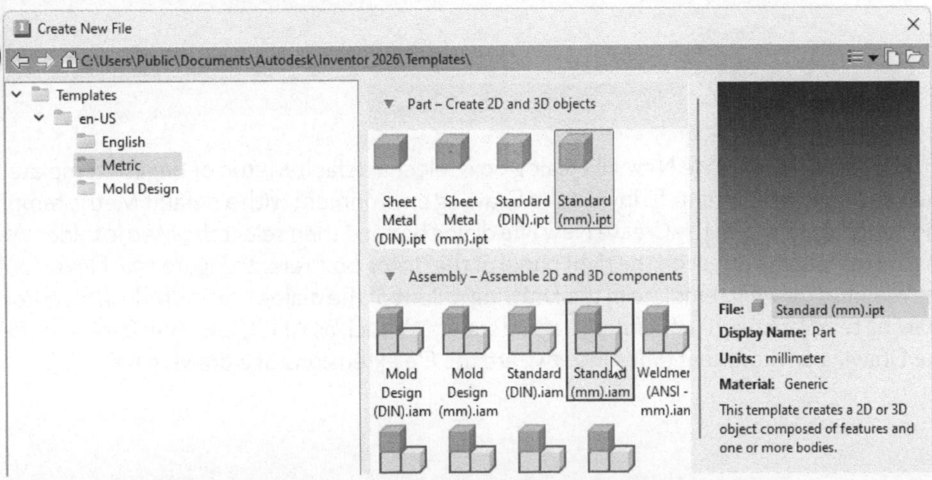

In the **Create New File** dialog box, you can select a default Metric or English template for invoking the Assembly environment. Expand the **Templates** node in the **Create New File** dialog box and then select the **Metric** folder. All the default Metric templates appear on the right panel of the dialog box, refer to Figure 1.28. Next, double-click on the **Standard (mm).iam** template (*.iam* is the file extension of the Inventor assembly file). The Assembly environment is invoked with the default Metric template. After invoking the Assembly environment, you can create an assembly by assembling two or more than two components. Figure 1.29 shows an assembly. You will learn more about creating assemblies in later chapters.

1.29

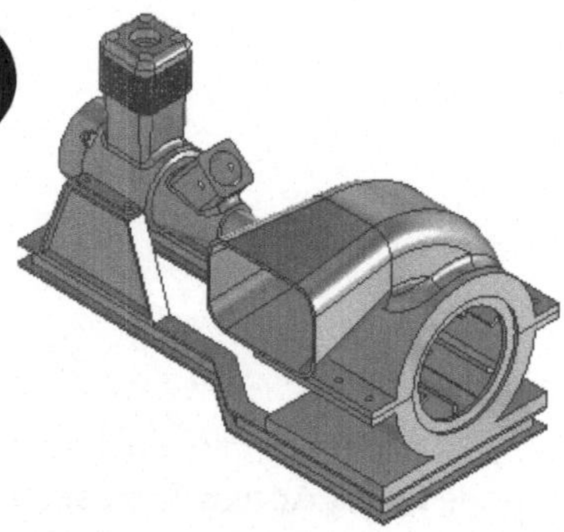

Invoking the Drawing Environment

To invoke the Drawing environment for creating a 2D drawing of a part or an assembly, click on the **New** tool in the left panel of the startup user interface (see Figure 1.30) or in the **Quick Access Toolbar** (see Figure 1.31). The **Create New File** dialog box appears, see Figure 1.32. You can also press the CTRL + N keys to invoke the **Create New File** dialog box.

1.30

1.31

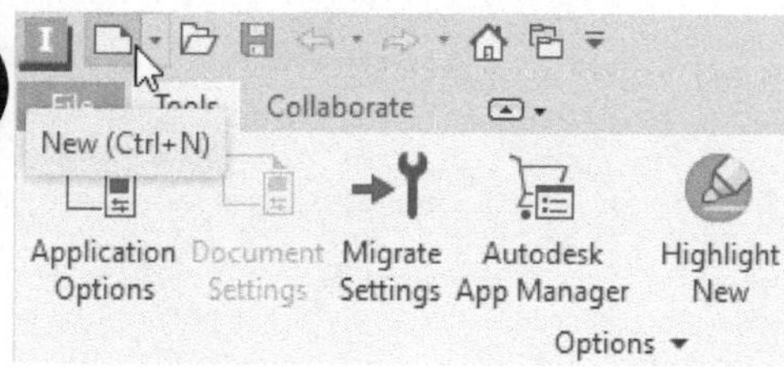

After invoking the **Create New File** dialog box, select a default Metric or English template for invoking the Drawing environment. To invoke the Drawing environment with a default Metric template, expand the **Templates** node in the **Create New File** dialog box and then select the **Metric** folder. All the default Metric templates appear on the right panel of the dialog box, refer to Figure 1.32. Next, double-click on the required drawing template in the **Drawing** rollout of the dialog box. Autodesk Inventor has various drawing templates with predefined drafting standards such as **ANSI**, **ISO**, **BSI**, **DIN**, and **JIS** for invoking the Drawing environment (*.idw* and *.dwg* are the file extensions of a drawing file).

1.32

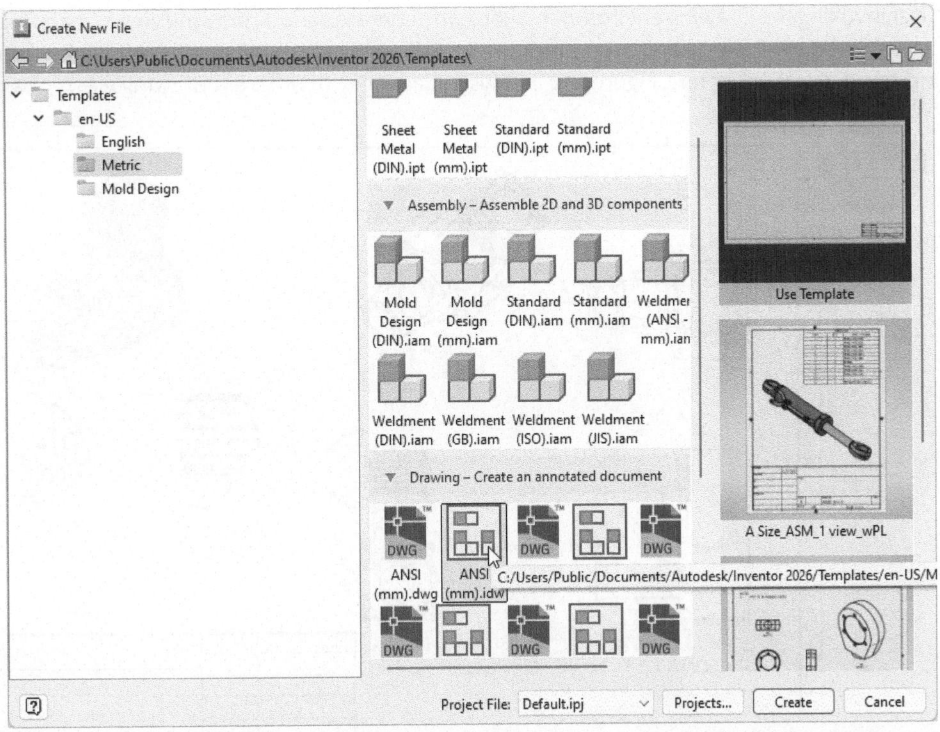

Alternatively, to invoke the Drawing environment, click on the down arrow next to the **New** tool in the left panel of the startup user interface and then click on the **Drawing (.dwg)** option in the **New** drop-down list that appears, see Figure 1.33. The Drawing environment gets invoked with the default template. Note that the method for editing the properties such as unit and drawing standard of the default template is the same as discussed earlier. The Drawing environment is invoked with the default template.

1.33

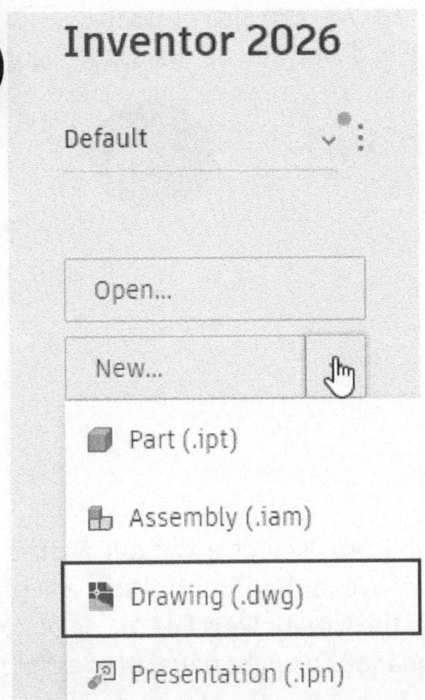

After invoking the Drawing environment, you can generate various drawing views of a component or an assembly. You will learn about generating various drawing views, applying dimensions, creating BOM, and so on in later chapters. Figure 1.34 shows a drawing with different drawing views of a component.

1.34

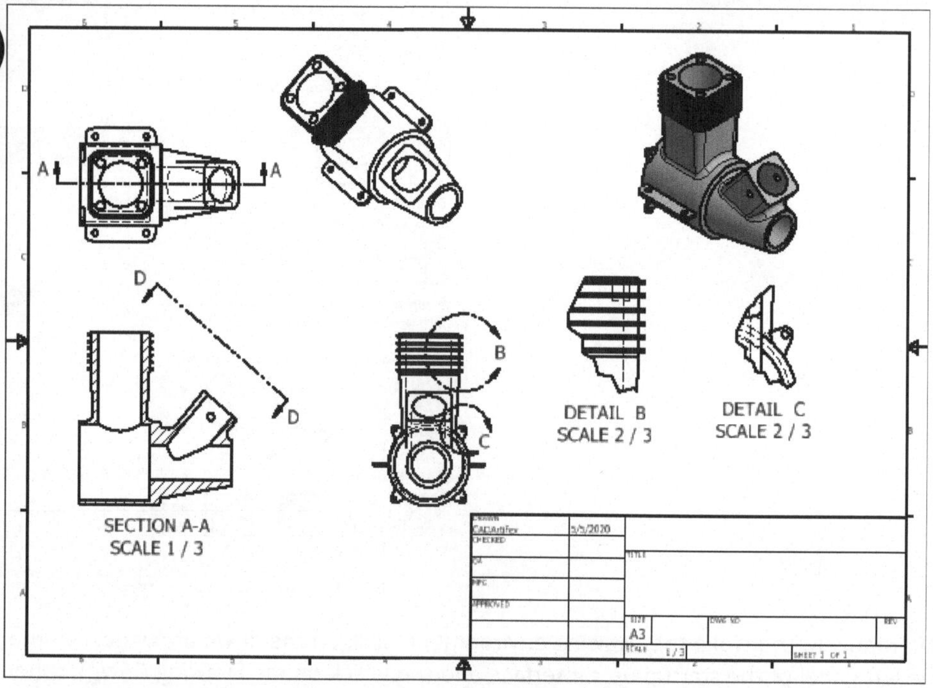

Invoking the Presentation Environment

To invoke the Presentation environment for creating an animation and an exploded view of a design, click on the **New** tool in the left panel of the startup user interface (see Figure 1.35) or in the **Quick Access Toolbar** (see Figure 1.36). You can also press the CTRL + N keys to invoke the **Create New File** dialog box. The **Create New File** dialog box appears, see Figure 1.37.

1.35

1.36

In the **Create New File** dialog box, select a default Metric or English template for invoking the Presentation environment. To invoke the Presentation environment with a default Metric template, expand the **Templates** node in the **Create New File** dialog box and then select the **Metric** folder. All the default Metric templates appear on the right panel of the dialog box, see Figure 1.37. Next, scroll down in the dialog box and then double-click on the **Standard (mm).ipn** template, see Figure 1.37 (*.ipn* is the file extension of the Inventor presentation file). The Presentation environment is invoked and the **Insert** dialog box appears. Also, you are prompted to select an assembly file for creating its animation and exploded views. Browse to the location where the assembly file is saved and then select it for creating its animation and exploded views. Next, click on the **Open** button in the dialog box. The selected assembly gets opened in the Presentation environment, see Figure 1.38.

1.37

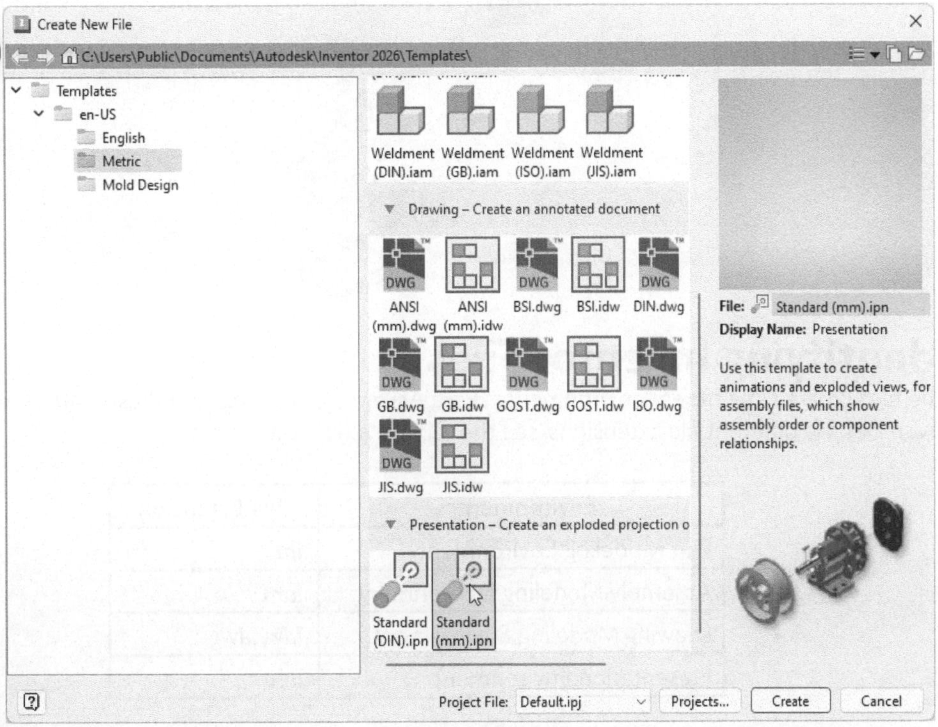

1.38

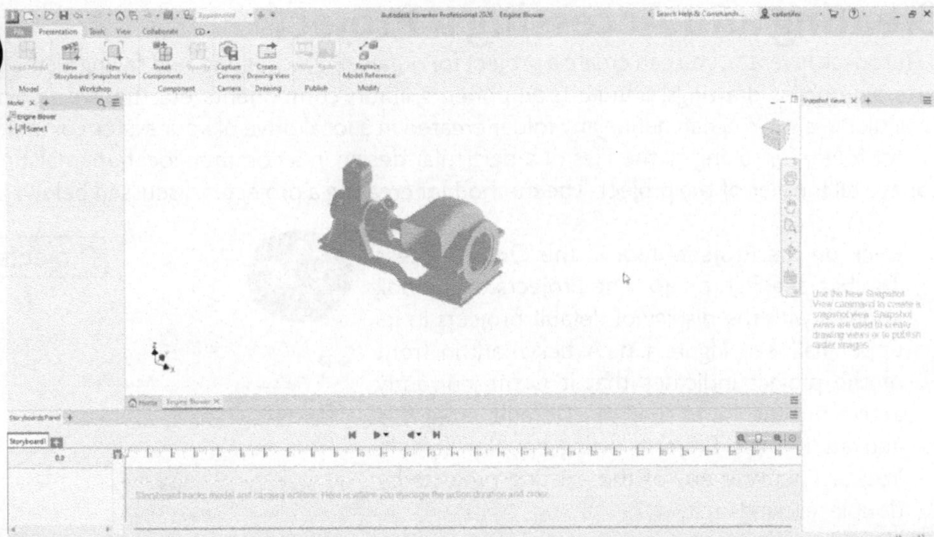

After invoking the Presentation environment, you can create an animation and exploded view of the assembly. You will learn about the same in later chapters. Figure 1.39 shows the exploded view of an assembly in the Presentation environment.

1.39

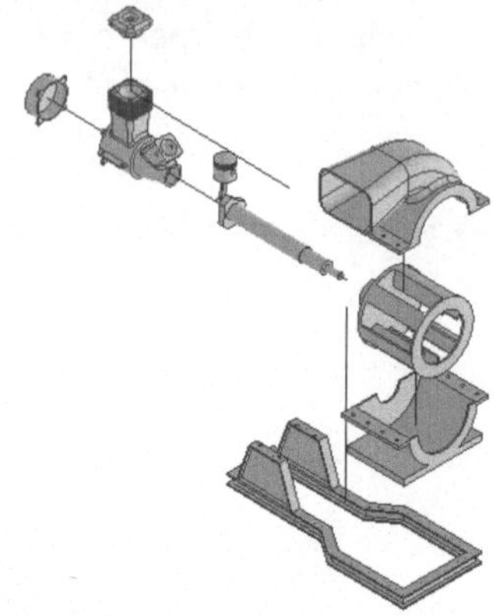

Identifying Inventor Files

The files created in different environments (Part, Assembly, Drawing, and Presentation) of Autodesk Inventor have different file extensions, see the table given below:

Environments	File Extension
Part Modeling Environment	*.ipt*
Assembly Modeling Environment	*.iam*
Drawing Modeling Environment	*.idw, .dwg*
Presentation Environment	*.ipn*

Creating and Accessing a Project

In Autodesk Inventor, you can create a project for organizing, accessing, and saving all the files such as parts, assemblies, drawings, standard components, library components, etc, that are associated with a particular design. You can define any folder created in a local drive of your system or in a vault as the project folder for saving all the files of a particular design in a common location, making it easier to manage all the files of the project. The method for creating a project is discussed below:

1. Click on the **Projects** tool in the **Quick Access Toolbar**, see Figure 1.40. The **Projects** dialog box appears with the display of default projects in its upper half, see Figure 1.41. A tick-mark in front of the project indicates that it is the currently active project. Note that the **Default** project is activated in the **Projects** dialog box, by default. You can activate any of the existing projects by double-clicking on it.

1.40

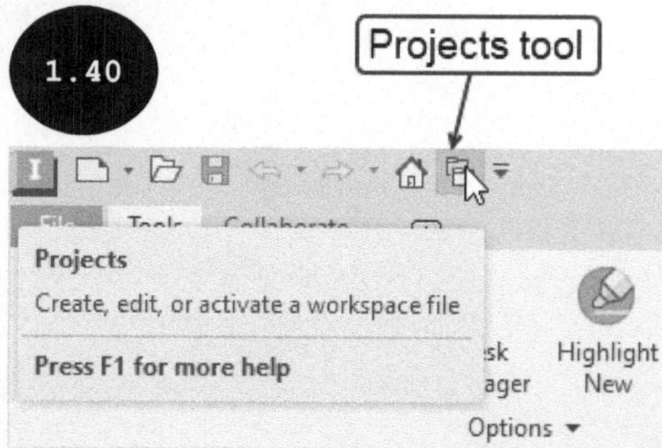

1.41

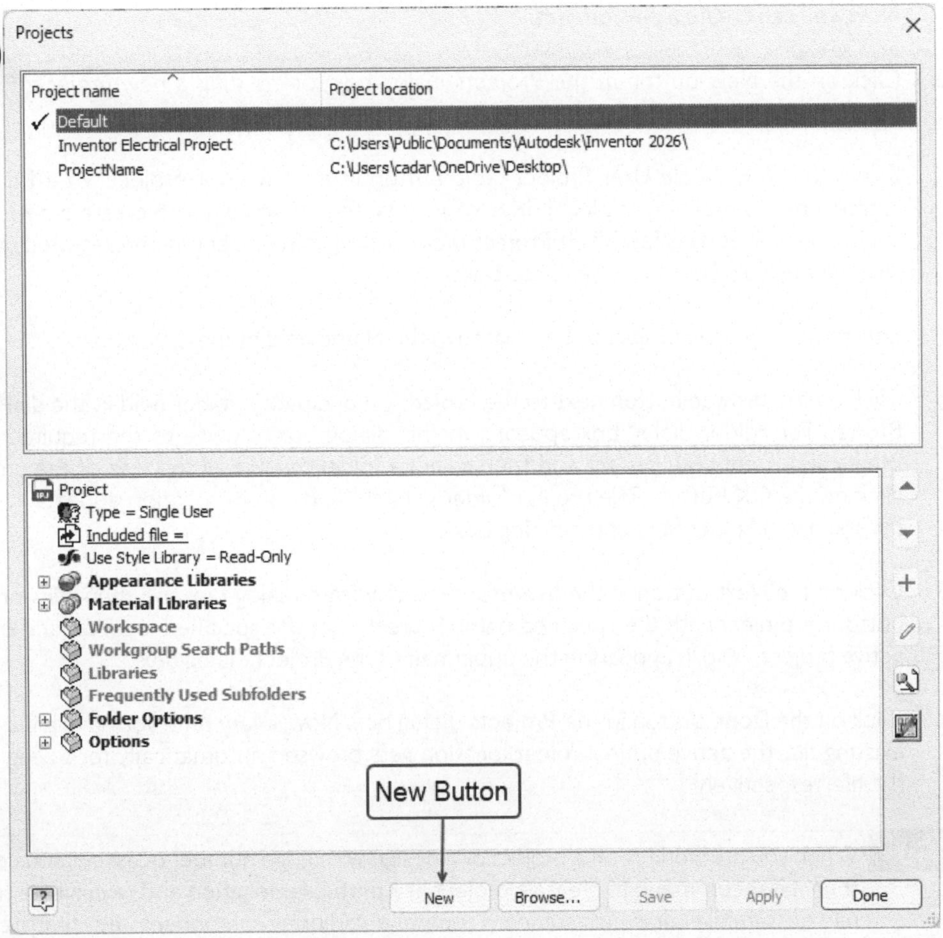

Tip: You can also invoke the **Projects** dialog box by clicking on the **Projects and Settings** icon (*three vertical dots*) in the left panel available next to the **Projects** drop-down list in the startup user interface (see Figure 1.42), and then click on the **Settings** option that appears.

1.42

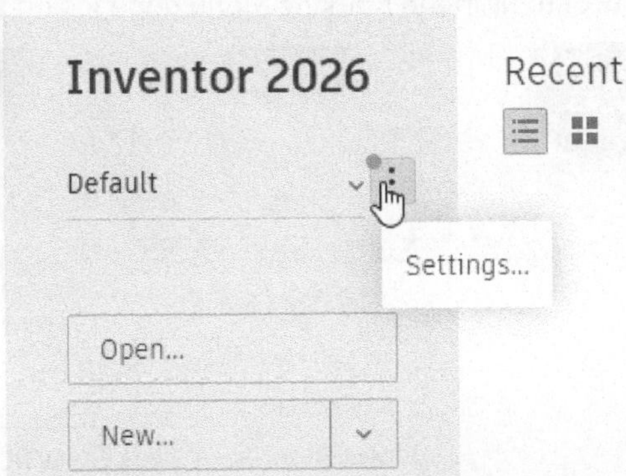

Now, you can create a new project.

2. Click on the **New** button in the **Projects** dialog box for creating a new project. The **Inventor project wizard** dialog box appears.

3. Select the **New Single User Project** radio button in the **Inventor project wizard** dialog box to create a new project on the local drive of your system. If you want to create a new project in a vault, then select the **New Vault Project** radio button. After selecting the required radio button, click on the **Next** button in the dialog box.

4. Enter a name for the project to be created in the **Name** field of the dialog box.

5. Click on the **Browse** button next to the **Project (Workspace) Folder** field in the dialog box. The **Browse For Folder** dialog box appears. In this dialog box, browse to the required location in the local drive of your system and then select a folder to save all the files of the project. Next, click on the **OK** button. The project folder gets defined and its location appears in the **Project (Workspace) Folder** field of the dialog box.

6. Click on the **Next** button in the **Inventor project wizard** dialog box and then click on the **Finish** button. A project with the specified name is created at the specified location and becomes an active project. Also, it appears in the upper half of the **Project** dialog box.

7. Click on the **Done** button in the **Projects** dialog box. Now, every time you save a file or open an existing file, the active project folder location gets browsed automatically for saving or opening the file, respectively.

Tip: When you are working on a project or a design with large number of associated components then it is recommend to create a project at a particular location and save all the files such as parts, assemblies, drawings, standard components, library components, etc, that are associated with it in the specified project folder.

Invoking a Marking Menu

The Marking Menu gets invoked when you right-click in the graphics area. It provides quick access to the most frequently used tools in the Wheel and some other tools in the Overflow menu, see Figure 1.43. Note that the availability of tools in the Marking Menu depends on the active workspace.

1.43

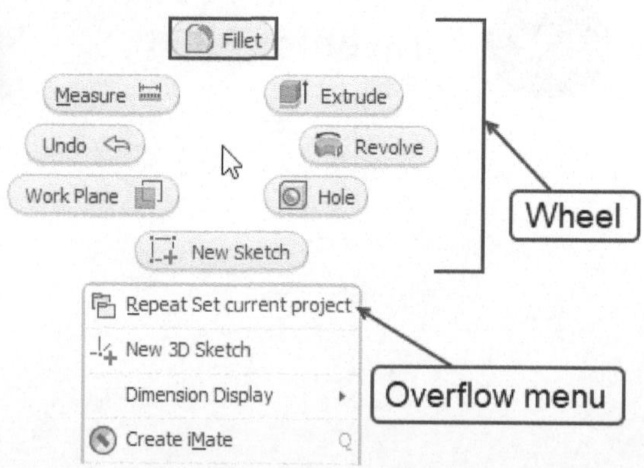

Customizing the Color Scheme

In Autodesk Inventor, you can customize the color scheme of the graphical elements such as Grids, Sketch preview, Selection highlight, Drafting 2D screen, as well as the background color of the graphics area. For doing so, click on the **Tools** tab in the **Ribbon** and then click on the **Application Options** tool in the **Options** panel, see Figure 1.44. The **Application Options** dialog box appears.

1.44

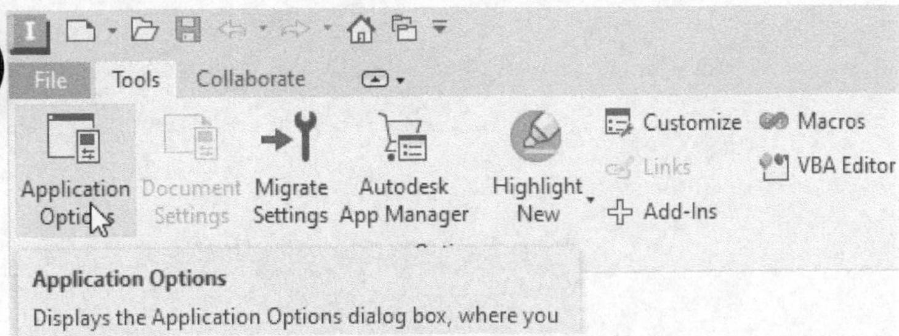

In the **Application Options** dialog box, click on the **Colors** tab. The options to specify color scheme appear in the dialog box. In the **In-canvas Color Scheme** area of the **Color** tab, you can select a pre-defined color scheme to be used. In this textbook, the **Presentation** color scheme is used with a single white background color. To use this setting, select the **Presentation** color scheme in the **In-canvas Color Scheme** area and then select the **1 Color** option in the **Background** drop-down list. Next, click on the **Apply** button to apply the change. You can also customize a pre-defined color scheme. For doing so, select a color scheme to be customized and then click on the **Customize Schemes** button. The **Color Scheme Editor** dialog box appears, see Figure 1.45. By using this dialog box, you can customize the selected color scheme by editing its graphical elements, as required.

1.45

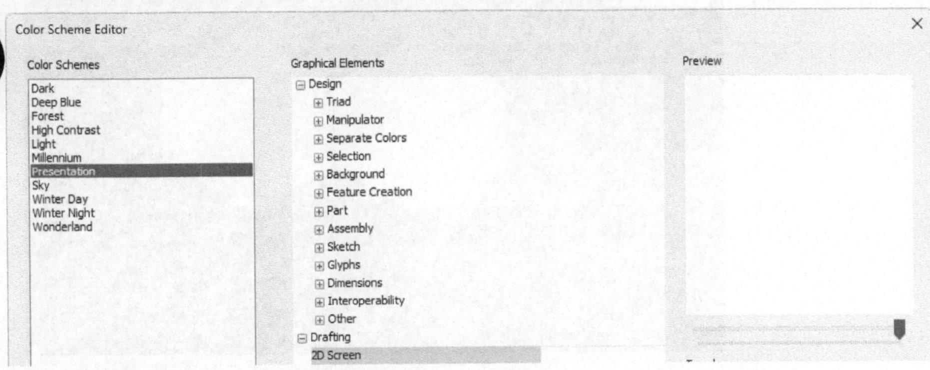

Choosing the User Interface Theme

Autodesk Inventor is provided with two color themes: Dark color theme and Light color theme. The Dark color theme is the default color theme of Autodesk Inventor. As a result, the **Ribbon**, **Browser**, and several other user interface components of Inventor appear in the Dark color theme, by default, see Figure 1.46. To choose the Light color theme, click on the **Tools** tab in the **Ribbon** and then click on the **Application Options** tool to invoke the **Application Options** dialog box. In this dialog box, click on the **Colors** tab and then select the **Light** option in the **UI Theme** drop-down list, see Figure 1.47. Click on the **Apply** button in the **Application Options** dialog box to apply the Light color theme. Next, click on the **OK** button to close the dialog box. In this textbook, the Light color theme is used for all screenshots to ensure better image clarity.

1.46

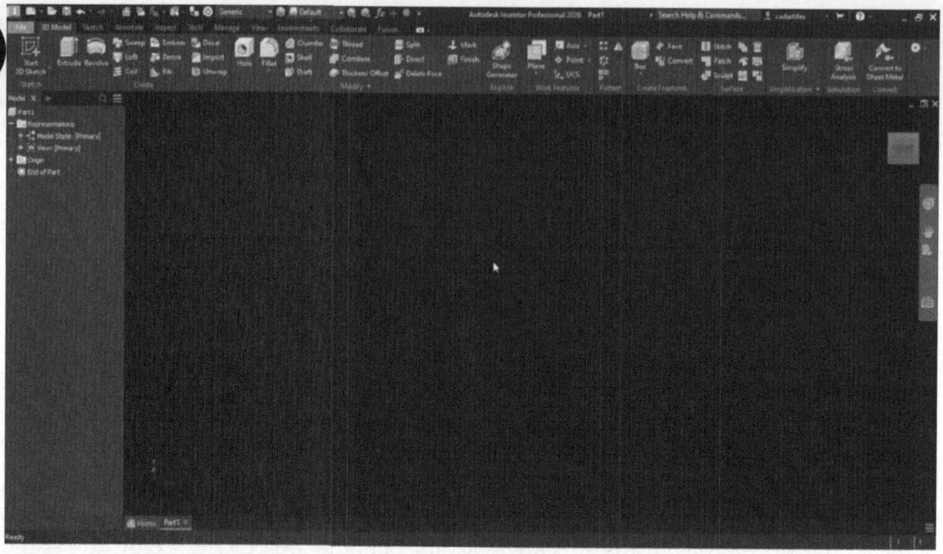

1.47

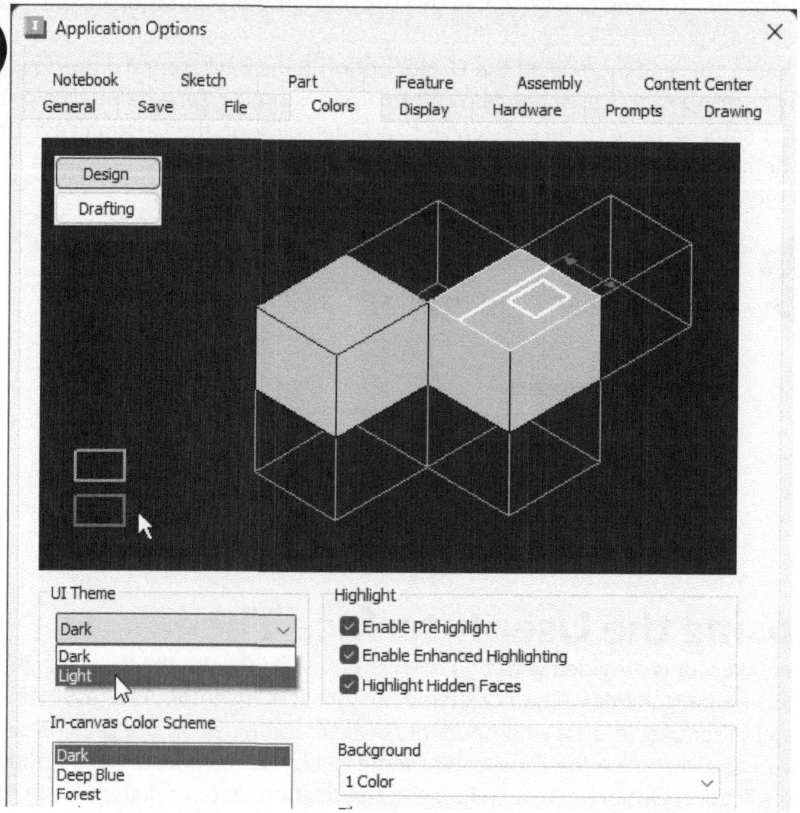
Application Options
Notebook
Sketch
Part
iFeature
Assembly
Content Center
General
Save
File
Colors
Display
Hardware
Prompts
Drawing
Design
Drafting
UI Theme
Dark
Dark
Light
Highlight
Enable Prehighlight
Enable Enhanced Highlighting
Highlight Hidden Faces
In-canvas Color Scheme
Dark
Deep Blue
Forest
Background
1 Color

Exporting Files to Other CAD Formats

In Autodesk Inventor, you can also export Inventor files to other CAD formats or neutral file formats. For doing so, click on the **File > Export > CAD Format** in the **File Menu,** see Figure 1.48. The **Save As** dialog box appears. In this dialog box, select the required file format such as **AutoCAD DWG Files (*.dwg), CATIA V5 Part Files (*CATPart), IGES Files (*.igs;*.iges),** or **STEP Files (*.stp;*.ste;*.step;*.stpz)** in the **Save as type** drop-down list. Next, browse to the required location and then click on the **Save** button. The Inventor file gets exported to the selected CAD format.

1.48

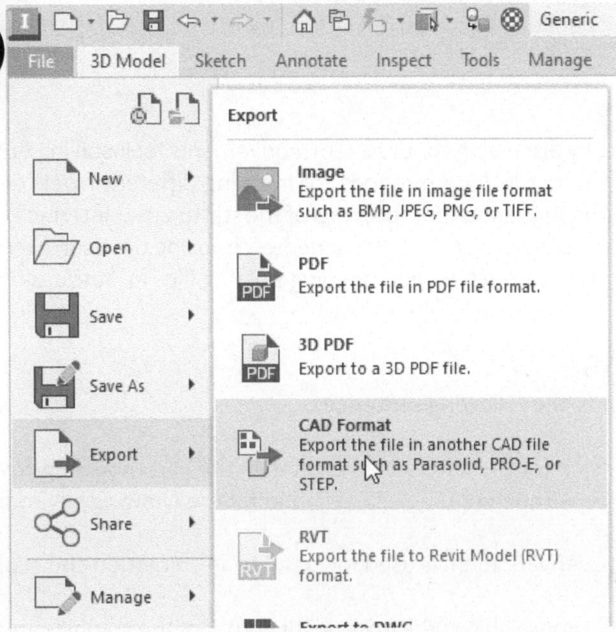

Saving Files

To save a file created in any of the environments of Autodesk Inventor, click on the **Save** tool in the **Quick Access Toolbar** or click on **File** > **Save** in the File Menu. The **Save As** dialog box appears. You can also press CTRL + S to invoke the **Save As** dialog box. In this dialog box, enter the name of the file in the **File name** field of the dialog box and then browse to the location where you want to save the document. Next, click on the **Save** button.

Tip: You can also save a copy of an object or a file with a different name by using the **Save As** tool. For doing so, click on the **File** > **Save As** > **Save As** in the File Menu and then specify a new name for the file and location to save the file in the **Save As** dialog box that appears. Next, click on the **Save** button in the dialog box.

Opening Existing Files

To open an existing Inventor file, click on the **Open** tool in the left panel of the startup user interface or press the CTRL + O keys. The **Open** dialog box appears. Alternatively, click on the **Open** tool in the **Quick Access Toolbar** or click on **File > Open** in the File Menu. In the **Open** dialog box, ensure that the **Autodesk Inventor Files (*.iam;*.dwg;*.idw;*.ipt;*.ipn;*.ide)** file extension is selected in the **Files of type** drop-down list. You can select the file extension in this drop-down list depending upon the file to be opened. After selecting the required file extension, browse to the location where the Inventor file is saved and then click on the file to be opened. Next, click on the **Open** button in the dialog box. The selected file gets opened in Autodesk Inventor.

Summary

The chapter begins by discussing about system requirements for installing Autodesk Inventor. The topics described in the chapter include methods for invoking different Inventor environments, identifying Inventor files, identifying various components of the startup user interface, creating a project, invoking the Marking Menu, customizing the color scheme, choosing the user interface theme, exporting files to other CAD formats, saving files, and opening existing files in Autodesk Inventor.

Questions

Complete and verify the following sentences:

- The file extension for the documents created in the Part modeling environment is _______, for the Assembly environment is ________, and for the Drawing environment is _________.
- The ________ environment is used for creating an animation and exploded view of an assembly.
- The ________ is available at the upper right corner of the graphics area and is used for navigating the model.
- The features of a model present after the ________ in the **Browser** get suppressed and do not appear in the graphics area.
- The ________ tool is used for saving a copy of an object or a file with a different name.
- In Autodesk Inventor, you cannot open files created in other CAD applications. (True/False)
- The Browser is used for keeping a record of all operations/features in an order. (True/False)

CHAPTER

2

Drawing Sketches with Autodesk Inventor

In this chapter, the following topics will be discussed:

- Invoking the Part Modeling Environment
- Invoking the Sketching Environment
- Working with the Selection of Planes
- Specifying Units
- Specifying Grids and Snap Settings
- Creating a Line Entity
- Creating an Arc by using the Line Tool
- Creating a Circle
- Creating an Ellipse
- Creating an Arc
- Creating a Rectangle
- Creating a Slot
- Creating a Polygon
- Creating a Spline
- Editing a Spline

Autodesk Inventor is a feature-based, parametric, solid modeling mechanical design and automation software. Before you start creating solid 3D components in Autodesk Inventor, you need to understand the software. To design a component in this software, you need to create all its features one by one, see Figures 2.1 and 2.2. Note that the features are divided into two main categories: Sketch based features and Placed features. A feature created using a sketch is known as a sketch based feature, whereas a feature created on an existing feature without using a sketch is known as a placed feature. Of the two categories, the Sketch based feature is the first feature to be designed for any real world component. Therefore, it is important to first learn how to draw a sketch.

Figure 2.1 shows a component consisting of an extrude feature and a chamfer. Of these two features, the extrude feature is created using a sketch, see Figure 2.2. Therefore, this feature is known as a sketch based feature. On the other hand, the chamfer is a placed feature because no sketch is used for creating this feature.

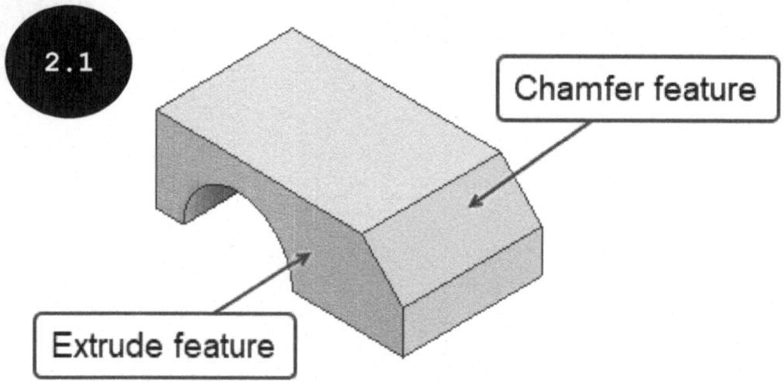

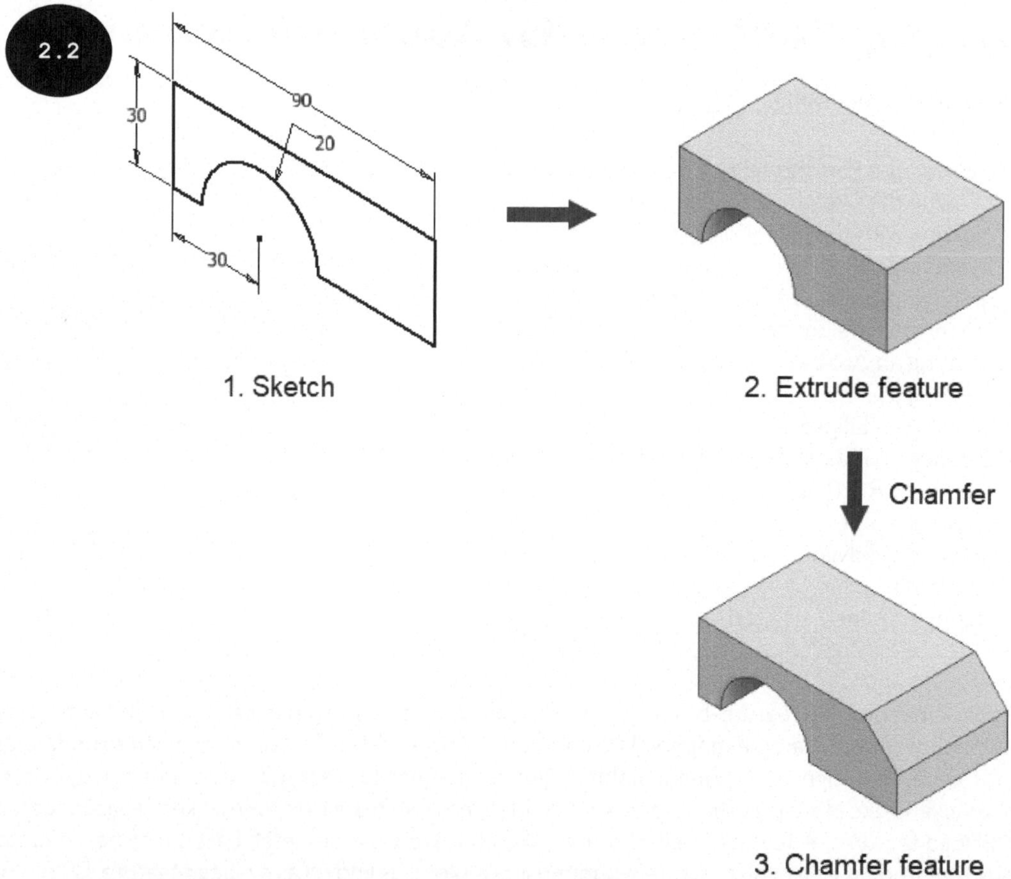

As the first feature of any component is a sketch based feature, you need to first learn how to create sketches in the Sketching environment. In Autodesk Inventor, the Sketching environment can be invoked within the Part modeling environment.

Invoking the Part Modeling Environment

Start Autodesk Inventor by double-clicking on the **Autodesk Inventor Professional 2026** icon on your desktop. After loading all the required files, the startup user interface of Autodesk Inventor appears, see Figure 2.3. The startup user interface of Autodesk Inventor allows you to start a new file, open an existing file, define a new project, access Autodesk Inventor learning resources such as What's new, Tutorials, Help file, and so on.

2.3

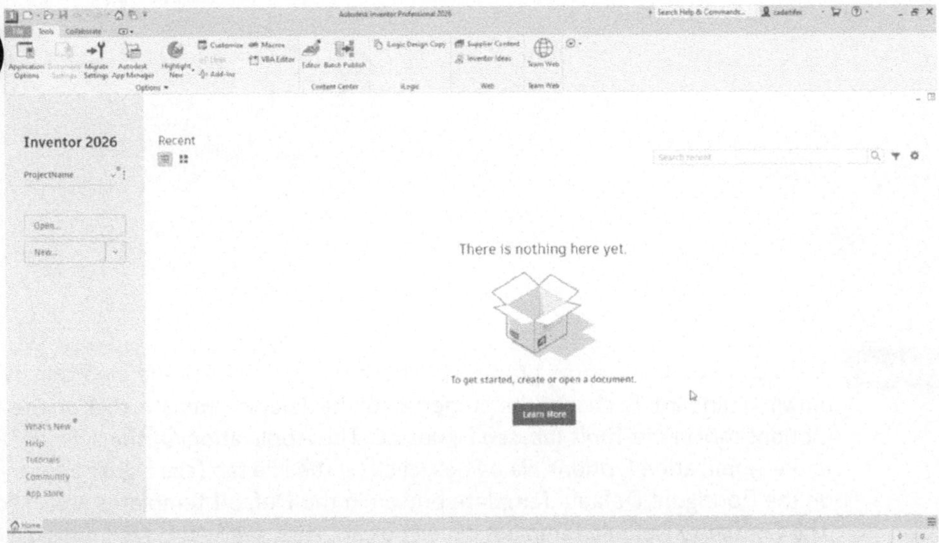

To invoke the Part modeling environment, click on the arrow next to the **New** tool in the left panel of the startup user interface and then click on the **Part** option in the drop-down menu that appears, see Figure 2.4. The Part modeling environment is invoked with a default template, see Figure 2.5.

2.4

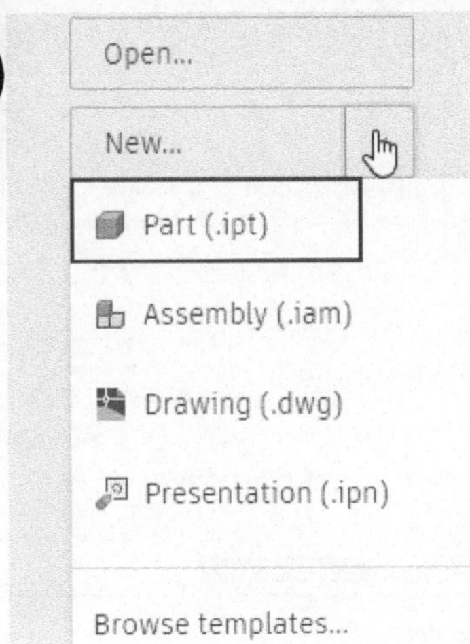

2.5

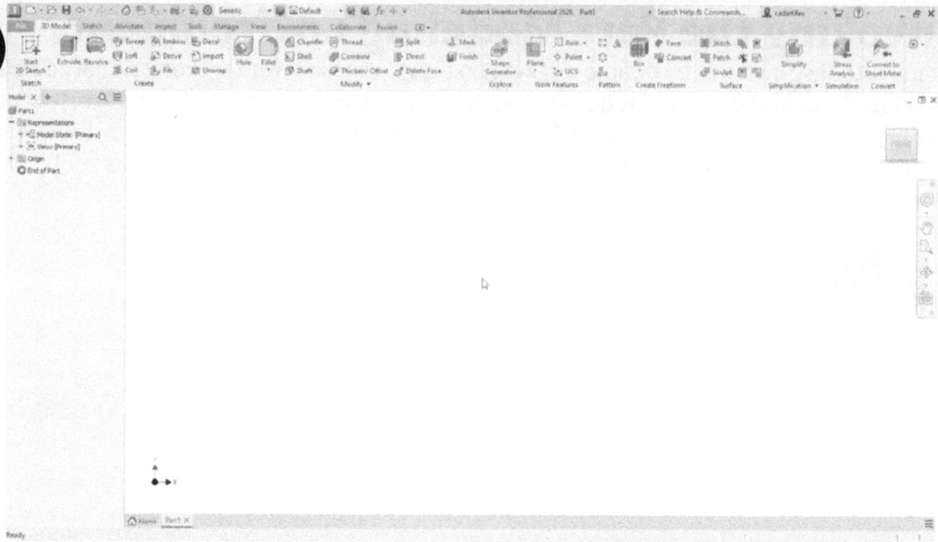

Note: A template contains some properties of the file such as a predefined unit system and a drawing standard. To change the properties of the default template, click on the **Application Options** tool in the **Tools** tab, see Figure 2.6. The **Application Options** dialog box appears. In the **Application Options** dialog box, click on the **File** tab (see Figure 2.7), and then click on the **Configure Default Template** button in the **Default templates** area, see Figure 2.7. The **Configure Default Template** dialog box appears, see Figure 2.8. In this dialog box, you can define the measurement units and the drawing standard for the default template.

2.6

2.7

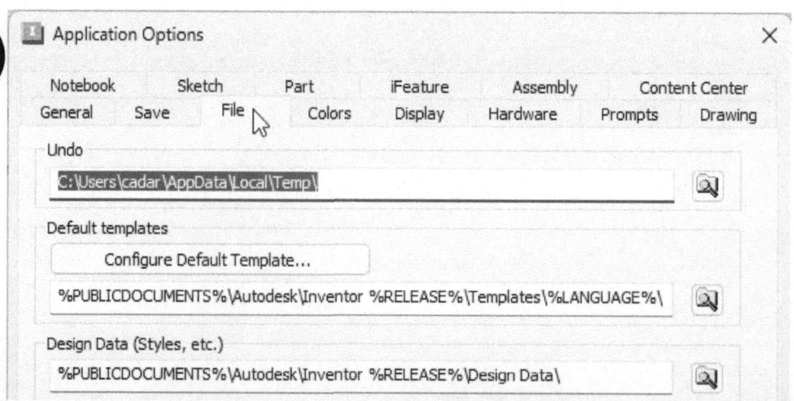

Invoking the Part Modeling Environment

Start Autodesk Inventor by double-clicking on the **Autodesk Inventor Professional 2026** icon on your desktop. After loading all the required files, the startup user interface of Autodesk Inventor appears, see Figure 2.3. The startup user interface of Autodesk Inventor allows you to start a new file, open an existing file, define a new project, access Autodesk Inventor learning resources such as What's new, Tutorials, Help file, and so on.

2.3

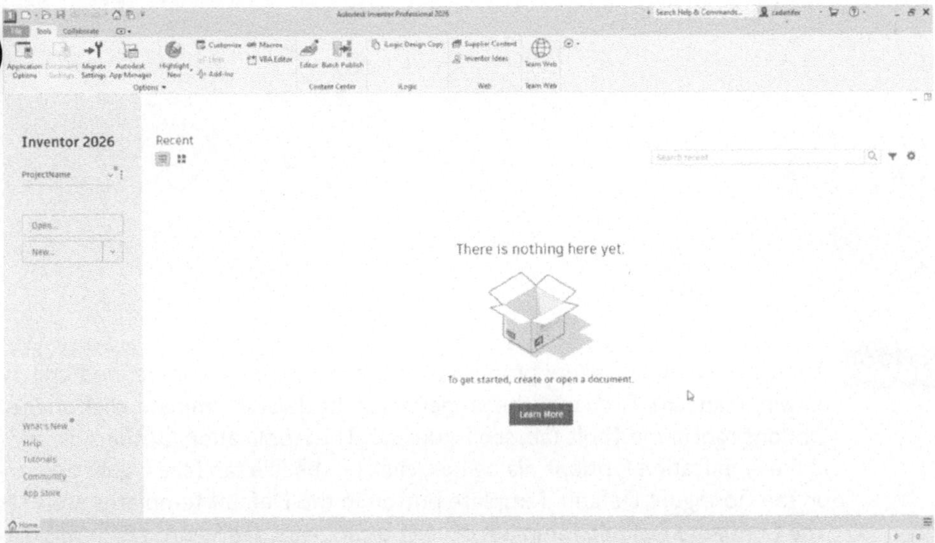

To invoke the Part modeling environment, click on the arrow next to the **New** tool in the left panel of the startup user interface and then click on the **Part** option in the drop-down menu that appears, see Figure 2.4. The Part modeling environment is invoked with a default template, see Figure 2.5.

2.4

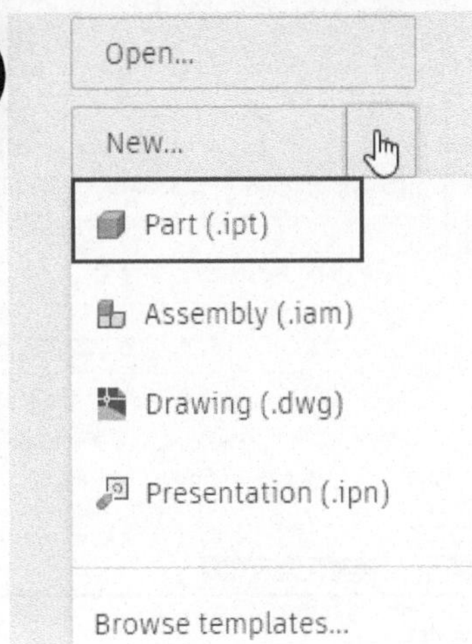

2.5

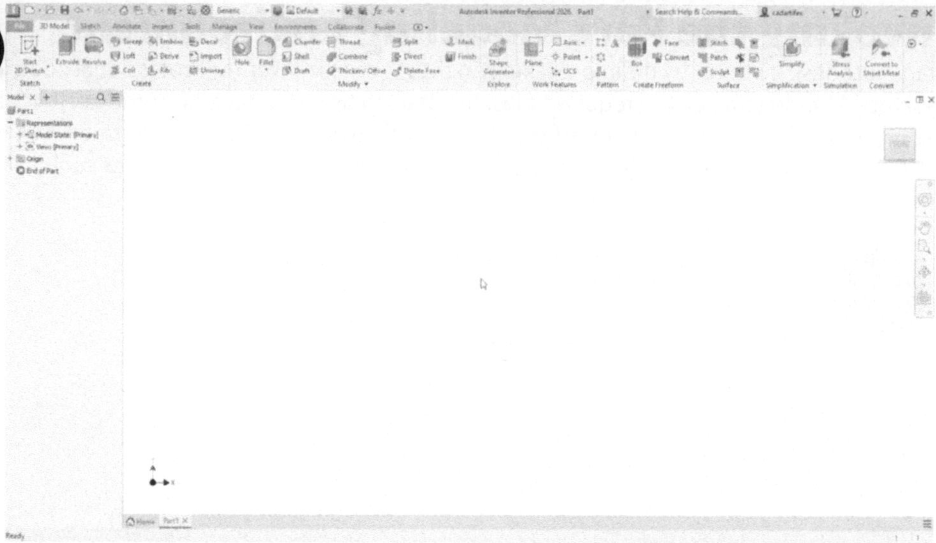

Note: A template contains some properties of the file such as a predefined unit system and a drawing standard. To change the properties of the default template, click on the **Application Options** tool in the **Tools** tab, see Figure 2.6. The **Application Options** dialog box appears. In the **Application Options** dialog box, click on the **File** tab (see Figure 2.7), and then click on the **Configure Default Template** button in the **Default templates** area, see Figure 2.7. The **Configure Default Template** dialog box appears, see Figure 2.8. In this dialog box, you can define the measurement units and the drawing standard for the default template.

2.6

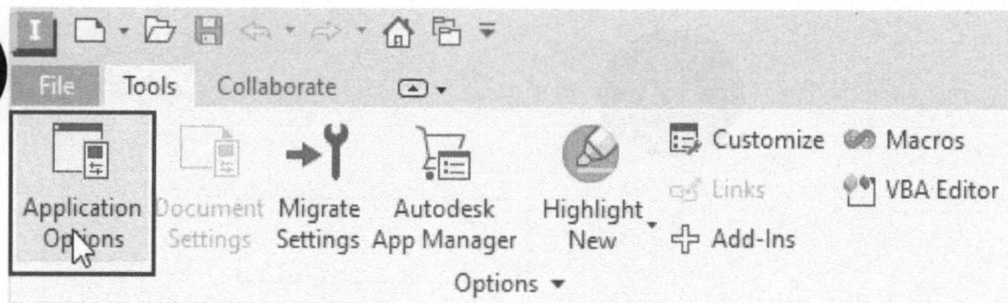

2.7

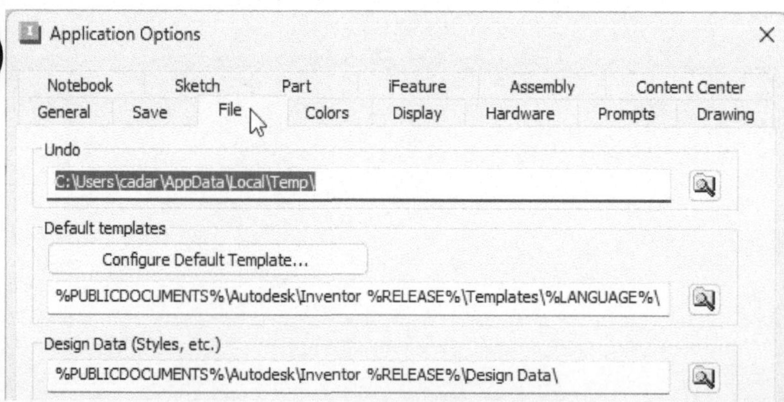

2.8

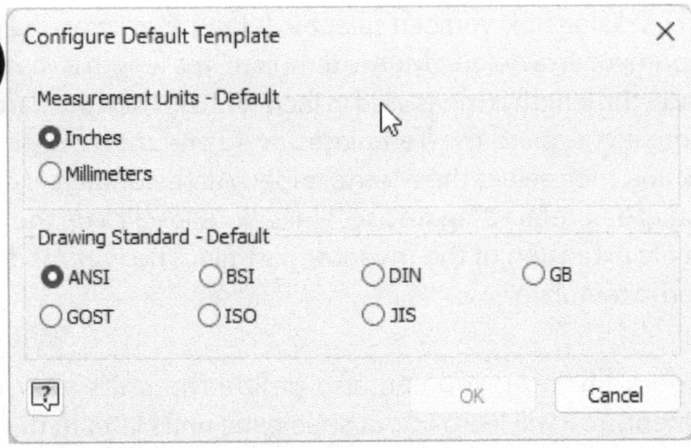

Alternatively, to invoke the Part modeling environment, click on the **New** tool in the left panel of the startup user interface (see Figure 2.9) or press the CTRL + N key. The **Create New File** dialog box appears, refer to Figure 2.10.

2.9

2.10

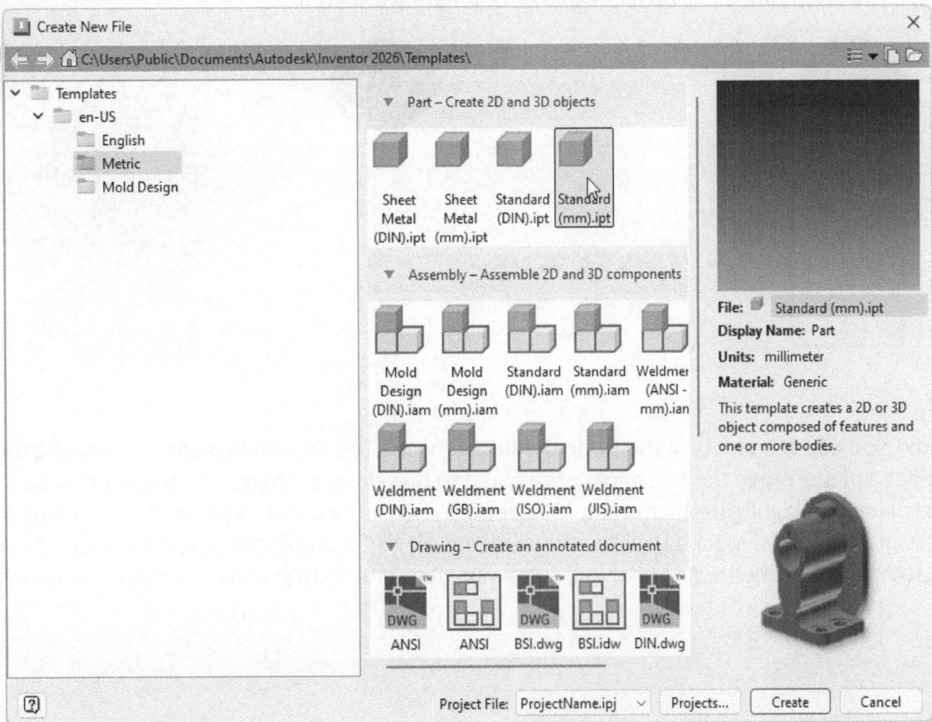

In the **Create New File** dialog box, you can select a default Metric or English template for invoking the Part modeling environment. In a default Metric template, the length is measured in millimeters, whereas in an English template, the length is measured in inches. To invoke the Part modeling environment with a default Metric template, expand the **Templates** node and then the **en-US** sub-node in the **Create New File** dialog box and then select the **Metric** folder. All the default Metric templates appear on the right panel of the dialog box, refer to Figure 2.10. Next, double-click on the **Standard (mm).ipt** template. Note that *.ipt* is the file extension of the Inventor part file. The Part modeling environment is invoked with the default Metric template.

Note: In Autodesk Inventor, you can also define the units after invoking the Part modeling environment. You will learn about specifying units later in this chapter.

In this textbook, the metric unit system and ANSI standard have been used as the default unit system.

The various components of the Part modeling environment such as **Ribbon**, **Browser**, **ViewCube**, and **Navigation Bar** have been discussed in Chapter 1. After invoking the Part modeling environment, you can invoke the Sketching environment for creating the sketch of the first feature of a model.

Invoking the Sketching Environment

After invoking the Part modeling environment, you need to invoke the Sketching environment for creating a sketch of the first feature of a model. For doing so, click on the **Start 2D Sketch** tool in the **Sketch** panel of the **3D Model** tab (see Figure 2.11) or press the S key. The three default planes: Front, Top, and Right, which are mutually perpendicular to each other appear in the graphics area, see Figure 2.12. Also, you are prompted to select a plane for creating a sketch.

2.11

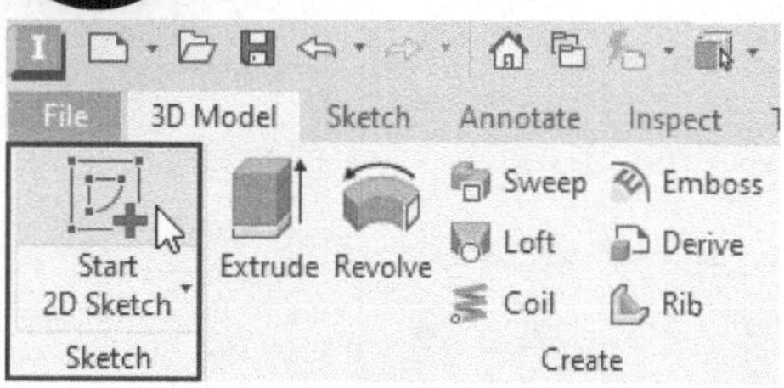

2.12

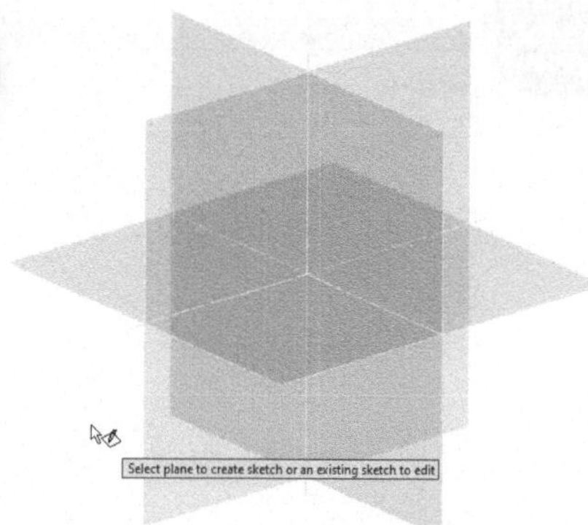

Now, you can select any of the three default planes as the sketching plane for creating the sketch. To select a plane, move the cursor over the plane to be selected. Next, click the left mouse button when the plane gets highlighted in the graphics area. As soon as you select a plane, the Sketching environment gets invoked, see Figure 2.13. Also, the selected plane becomes the sketching plane for drawing the sketch, and it is oriented normal to the viewing direction so that you can create the sketch easily.

Note that the Sketching environment also displays a yellow colored point with two perpendicular axes at the center of the graphics area. This yellow colored point represents the origin (0,0) of the Sketching environment and the perpendicular axes represent the X axis and Y axis of the sketching plane, refer to Figure 2.13.

2.13

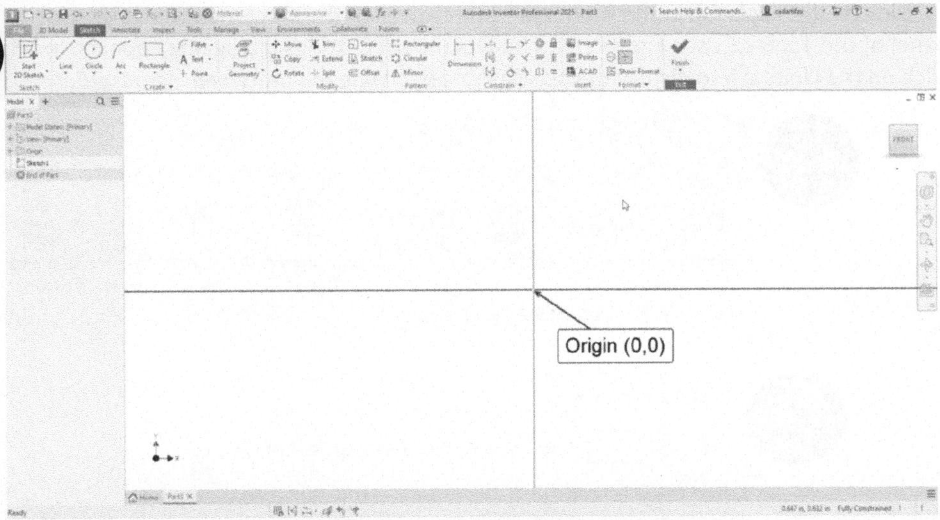

Working with the Selection of Planes

As discussed earlier, to invoke the Sketching environment, you need to select a plane as the sketching plane. Selection of an appropriate plane is very important for defining the right orientation of a model. Figure 2.14 shows the isometric view of a model having length 200 mm, width 100 mm, and height 40 mm. To create this model with the same orientation, you can select the Top plane as the sketching plane and then draw a rectangular sketch of 200 mm X 100 mm. However, if you select the Front plane as the sketching plane for creating this model, then you need to draw a rectangular sketch of 200 mm X 40 mm. Likewise, if you select the Right plane as the sketching plane, then you need to draw a rectangular sketch of 100 mm X 40 mm.

2.14

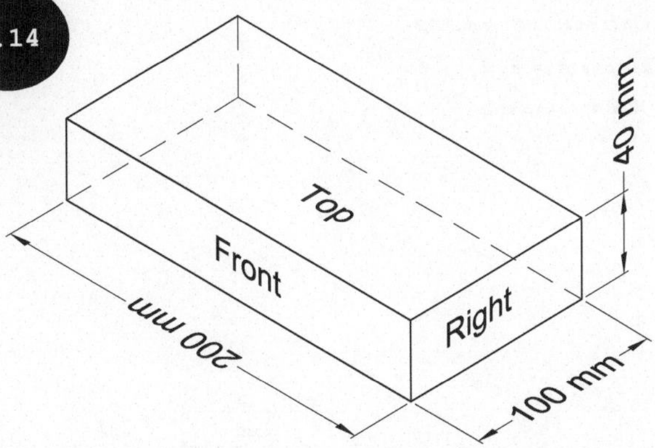

Once the Sketching environment has been invoked, you can start drawing the sketch by using different sketching tools in the **Sketch** tab of the **Ribbon**. However, before you start drawing the sketch, it is important to understand the specification of units, grids, and snaps settings.

Specifying Units

As discussed earlier, you can invoke the Part modeling environment with a default template (Metric or English), which contains a predefined unit system and drawing standard for creating a design. However, you can further modify the default unit system at any point of your design for any particular file. For doing so, click on the **Tools** tab in the **Ribbon** and then click on the **Document Settings** tool in the **Options** panel of the **Tools** tab, see Figure 2.15. The **Document Settings** dialog box appears. In this dialog box, click on the **Units** tab to display the options for specifying the units, see Figure 2.16.

2.15

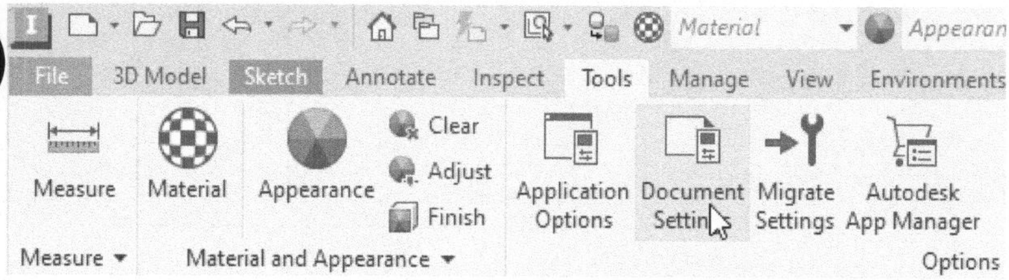

2.16

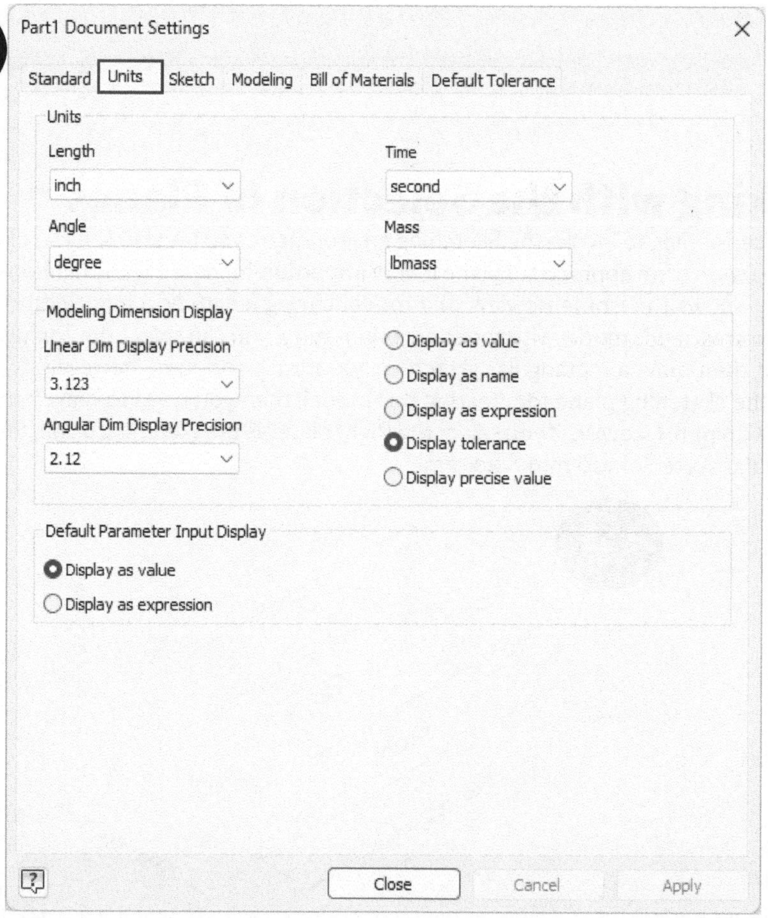

Now, you can define the required unit of length, time, mass, and angle measurements by selecting the required option in the respective drop-down list of the **Units** area in the dialog box, see Figure 2.16. You can also specify the dimensional precision for linear and angular dimensions by selecting the required option in the respective drop-down list of the **Modeling Dimension Display** area in the dialog box. Once you have defined units for the currently opened file, click on the **Apply** button to accept the changes made in the dialog box. Next, click on the **Close** button to exit the dialog box.

Specifying Grids and Snap Settings

Grids help you to specify points in the drawing area for creating sketch entities correctly and act as reference lines. By default, the display of grids is turned off in the drawing area. You can turn on the display of grids in the drawing area and specify snap settings to restrict the movement of the cursor at specified intervals.

To turn on the display of grids in the drawing area, click on the **Tools** tab in the **Ribbon** and then click on the **Application Options** tool in the **Options** panel of the **Tools** tab, see Figure 2.17. The **Application Options** dialog box appears. In this dialog box, click on the **Sketch** tab to display options related to Sketching environment, see Figure 2.18. Next, select the **Grid lines**, **Minor grid lines**, and **Axes** check boxes in the **Display** area of the dialog box to turn on the display of grid lines, minor grid lines, and axes in the drawing area, respectively.

2.17

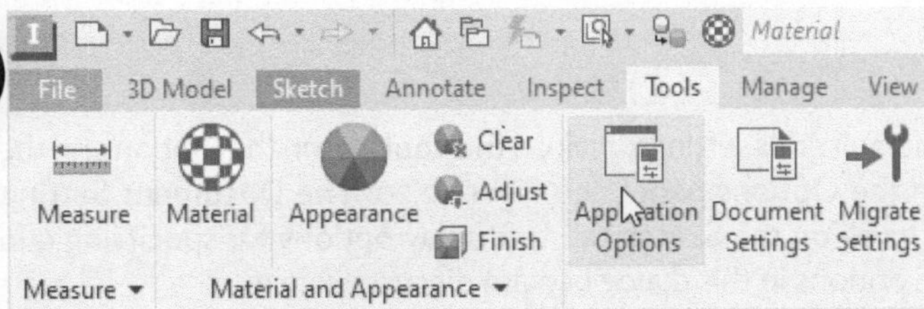

2.18

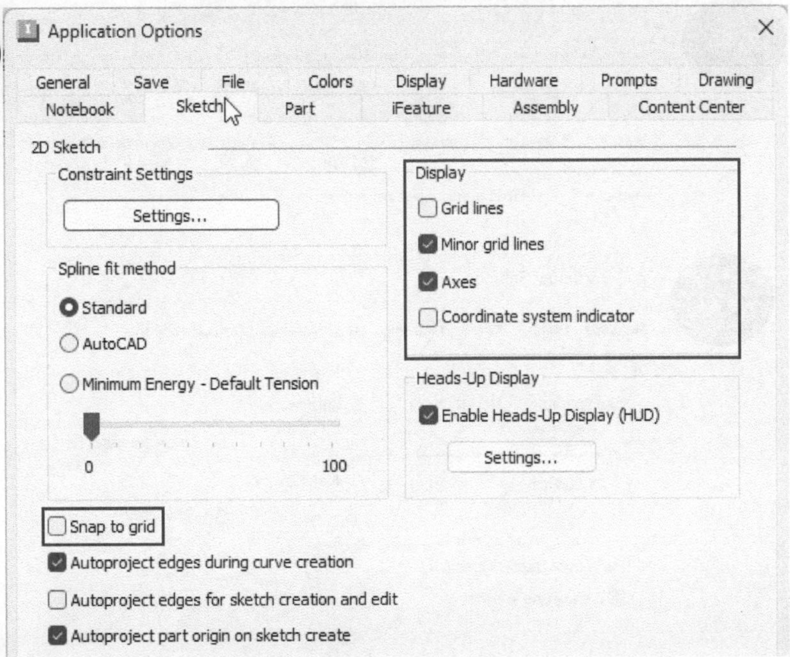

You can also turn on the snap settings such that the cursor snaps to the grid lines in the drawing area while creating sketch entities. For doing so, select the **Snap to grid** check box in the dialog box, refer to Figure 2.18. Next, click on the **Apply** button in the dialog box to accept the changes made and then click on the **Close** button to exit the dialog box. The grid lines appear in the drawing area with default grids settings, see Figure 2.19.

2.19

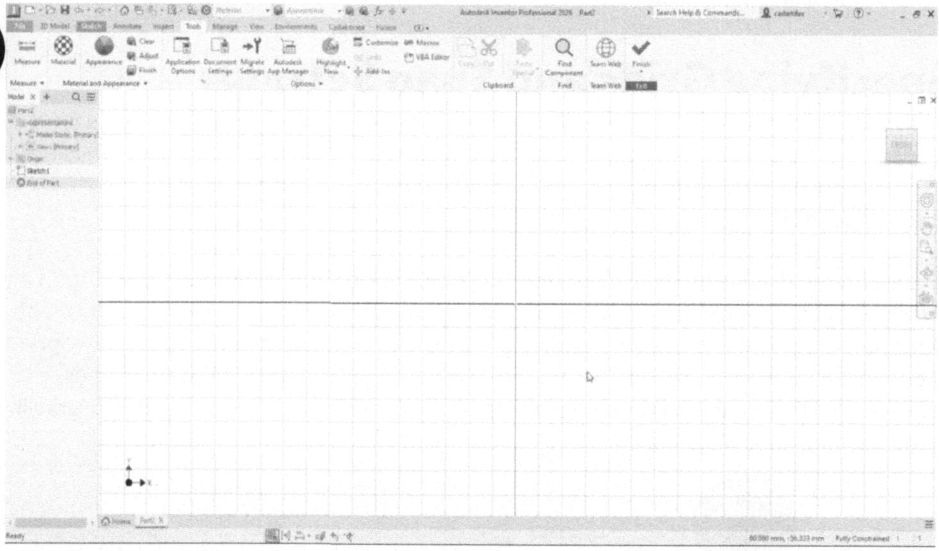

To change the default grids settings, click on the **Tools** tab in the **Ribbon** and then click on the **Document Settings** tool in the **Options** panel, see Figure 2.20. The **Document Settings** dialog box appears. In this dialog box, click on the **Sketch** tab to display options for specifying grids and snap settings, see Figure 2.21. The options in this dialog box are discussed next.

2.20

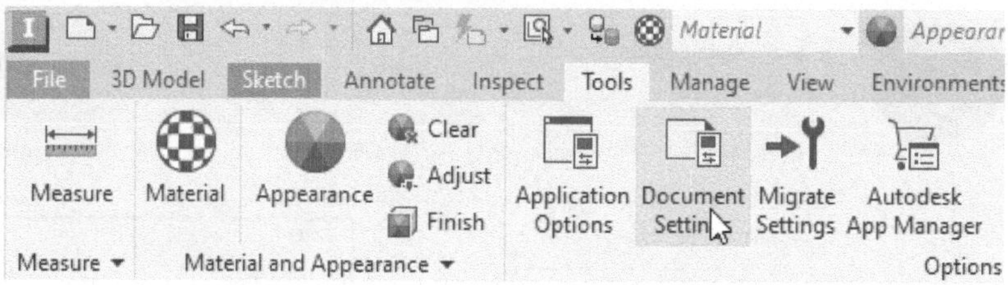

2.21

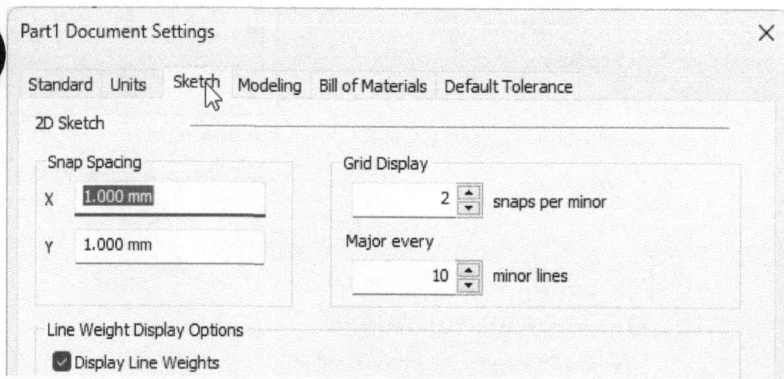

Snap Spacing

The X field of the **Snap Spacing** area of the dialog box is used for defining the snap spacing in the X direction and the Y field is used for defining the snap spacing in the Y direction. For example, if you enter **2** in the X field and **2** in the Y field in this area, then the cursor will snap to an incremental distance of 2 mm in X and Y directions while creating sketch entities.

Grid Display

The **snaps per minor** field of the **Grid Display** area of the dialog box is used for specifying the number of snap points between each grid. For example, if you enter **2** in the **snaps per minor** field, then the cursor will snap twice between each grid with the incremental distance that is specified in the X and Y fields of the **Snap Spacing** area of the dialog box.

The **Major every minor lines** field of this area is used for defining the number of minor grid lines between two major grid lines. Note that the value entered in this field defines the number of divisions or grids between two major grid lines. For example, if you enter **5** in the **Major every minor lines** field, then two major grid lines will be divided into 5 smaller grids horizontally and vertically.

Note: The major grid lines are darker in color, whereas the minor grid lines are lighter and are displayed inside the major grid lines.

After defining the grids and snap settings, click on the **Apply** button in the dialog box to accept the changes made and then click on the **Close** button to exit the dialog box. The display of grids in the drawing area gets modified as per the settings specified in the dialog box.

Creating a Line Entity

A line is defined as the shortest distance between two points. You can draw a line by using the **Line** tool. The method for creating a line is discussed below:

1. Click on the **Line** tool in the **Create** panel of the **Sketch** tab, see Figure 2.22. Alternatively, press the **L** key. You are prompted to specify the start point of the line. Also, the coordinates of the current location of the cursor appear in the Pointer Input boxes in the drawing area, see Figure 2.23.

2.22

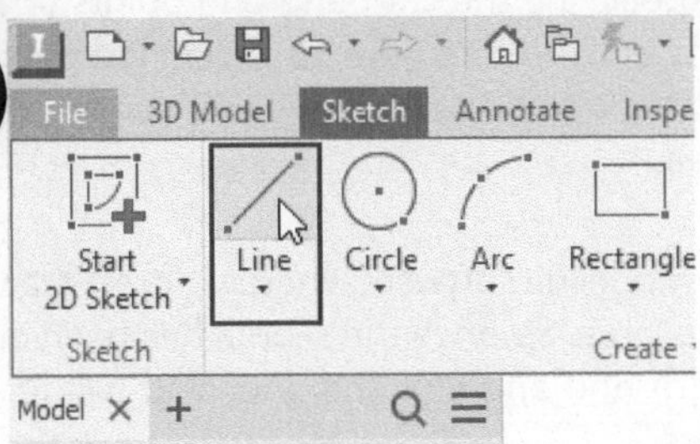

2.23

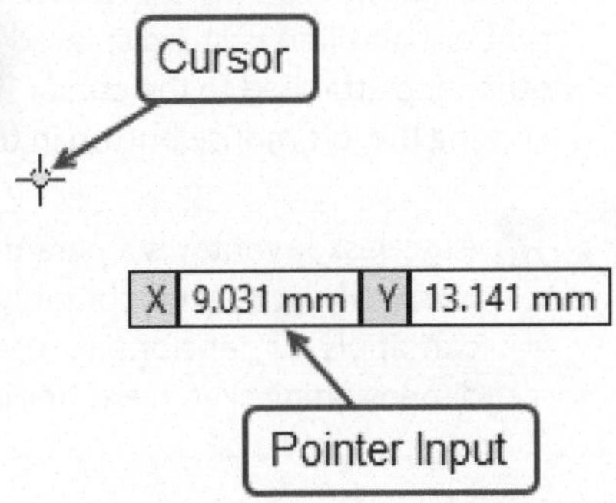

2. Click to specify the start point of the line in the drawing area. Alternatively, you can also specify the X and Y coordinates in the Pointer Input boxes to define the start point of the line in the drawing area.

Tip: You need to press the TAB key to switch between the boxes of the Pointer Input for specifying the coordinates. After specifying the coordinates in the Pointer Input boxes, you need to press the ENTER key.

3. Move the line cursor away from the start point. A rubber band line appears with one of its ends fixed at the start point and the other end attached to the cursor. Notice that as you move the cursor, the length and angle of the line changes and appears in the Dimension Input boxes, see Figure 2.24.

Note: If you move the cursor horizontally or vertically after specifying the start point of the line, the symbol of horizontal or vertical constraint appears near the cursor, respectively, see Figure 2.25. The symbol of constraint indicates that if you click the left mouse button to specify the second point of the line, the corresponding constraint will be applied. You will learn more about constraints in later chapters.

2.24

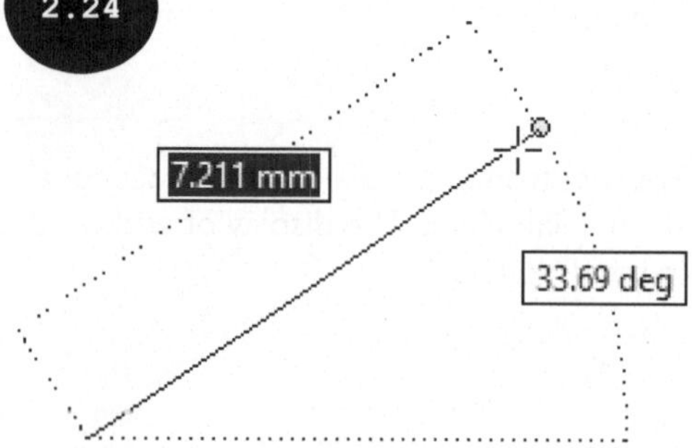

2.25

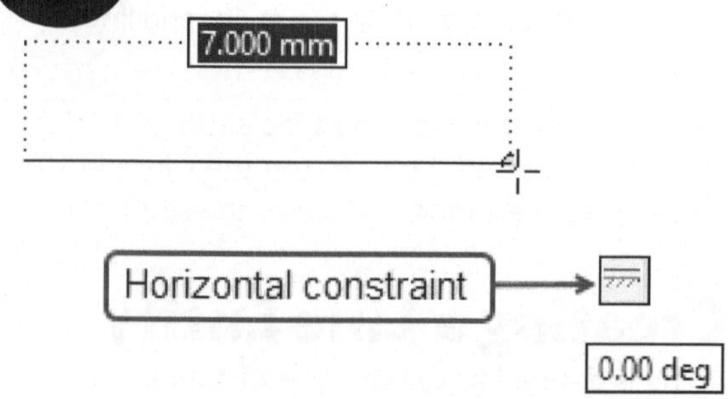

4. Click the left mouse button anywhere in the drawing area to specify the second point of the line. A line between the specified points is drawn. Alternatively, you can also specify the length and angle of the line in the Dimension Input boxes to create a line of specified parameters. You can press the TAB key to switch between the boxes of the Dimension Input for specifying the length and angle values of the line. Notice that after specifying the start and end points of a line, the rubber band line is still displayed with one of its ends fixed to the last specified point and the other end attached to the cursor. This indicates that a chain of continuous lines can be drawn by clicking the left mouse button in the drawing area.

Tip: Autodesk Inventor is a parametric 3D solid modeling software where you can draw a sketch by specifying points arbitrarily in the drawing area. So once the sketch has been drawn, you can apply dimensions to specify the length and angle of the line. You will learn about dimensioning sketch entities in later chapters.

5. Once all the line entities have been drawn, right-click in the drawing area and then click on the **OK** option in the Marking Menu that appears to exit the **Line** tool, see Figure 2.26. Alternatively, press the ESC key to exit the **Line** tool.

2.26

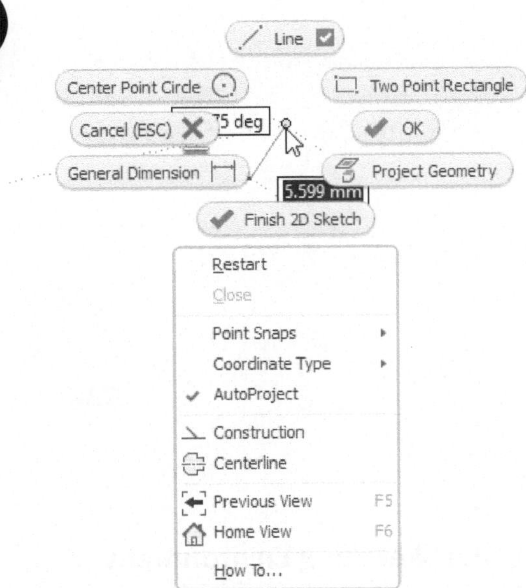

Note: If you have created two or more than two continuous lines, then you can create a close sketch automatically by joining the last and first specified point. For doing so, after creating two or more than two continuous lines, right-click in the drawing area and then click on the **Close** option in the Marking Menu that appears.

Tutorial 1

Draw a sketch of the model shown in Figure 2.27. The dimensions and the 3D model shown in the figure are for your reference only. You will learn about applying dimensions and creating 3D models in later chapters. All dimensions are in mm.

2.27

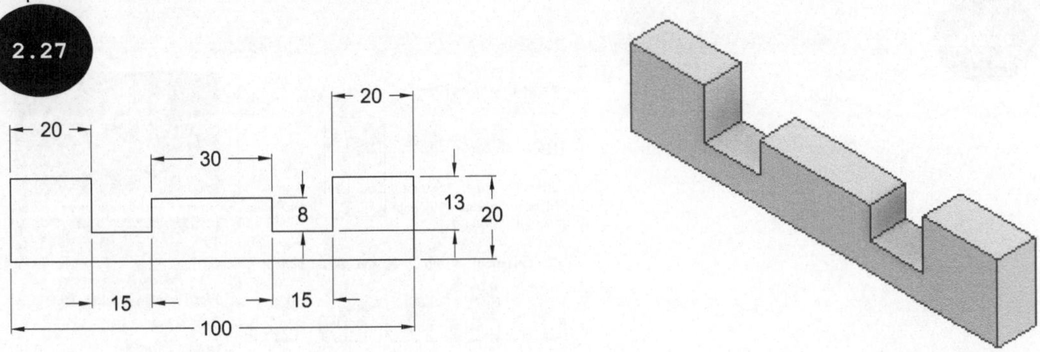

Section 1: Starting Autodesk Inventor

1. Start Autodesk Inventor by double-clicking on the Autodesk Inventor icon on your desktop. The startup user interface of Autodesk Inventor appears, see Figure 2.28.

2.28

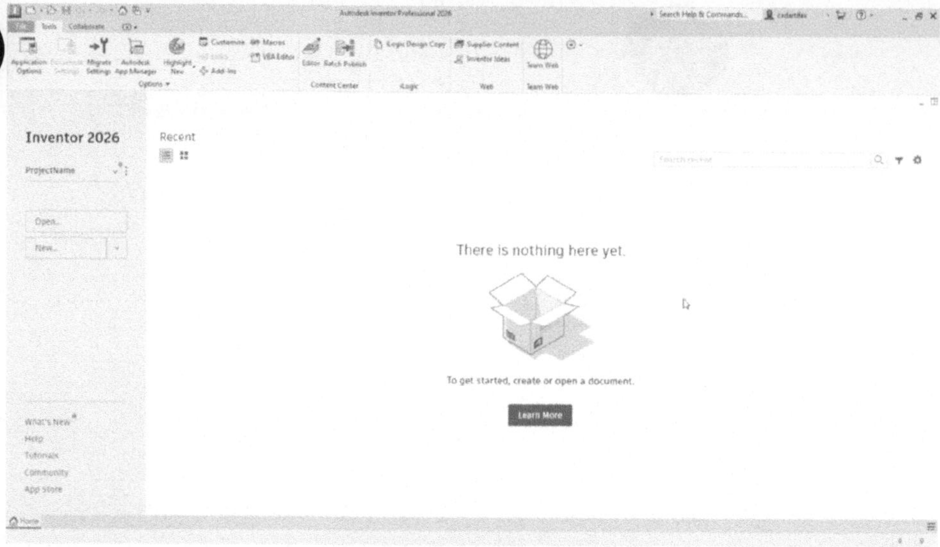

Section 2: Invoking the Sketching Environment

1. Click on the **New** tool in the left panel of the startup user interface (see Figure 2.29) or press the CTRL + N keys. The **Create New File** dialog box appears, see Figure 2.30.

2.29

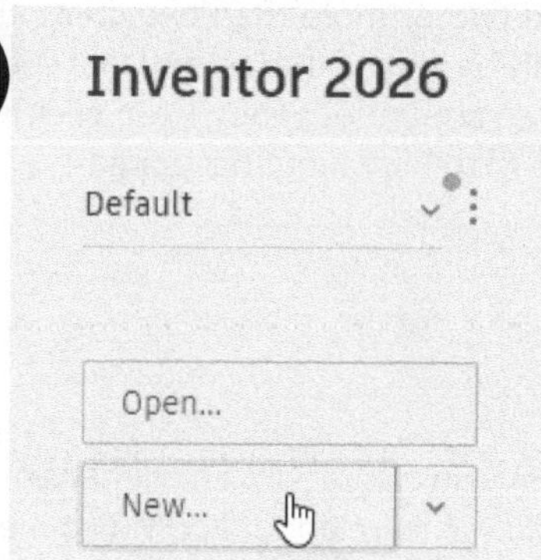

2.30

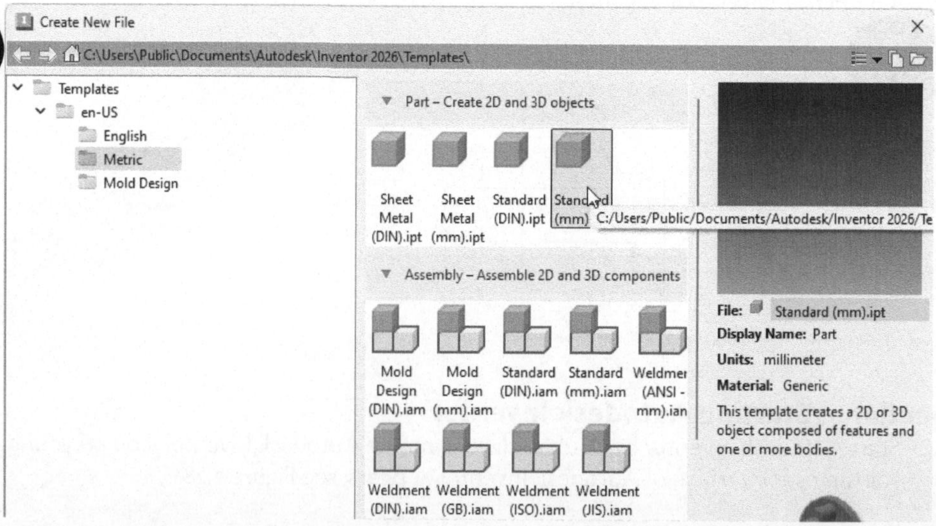

2. Expand the **Templates** node and then the **en-US** sub-node in the **Create New File** dialog box, refer to Figure 2.30. Next, click on the **Metric** folder. All the default Metric templates appear on the right panel of the dialog box.

3. Double-click on the **Standard (mm).ipt** template in the right panel of the dialog box. The Part Modeling environment is invoked with a Metric template.

4. Click on the **Start 2D Sketch** tool in the **Sketch** panel of the **3D Model** tab in the **Ribbon**, (see Figure 2.31) or press the S key. The three default planes: Front (XY Plane), Top (XZ Plane), and Right (YZ Plane), which are mutually perpendicular to each other appear in the graphics area, see Figure 2.32. Also, you are prompted to select a plane for creating a sketch.

5. Move the cursor over the Front plane (XY Plane) and then click the left mouse button when the plane gets highlighted in the graphics area, see Figure 2.32. The Sketching environment is invoked and the Front plane is oriented normal to the viewing direction, see Figure 2.33.

2.31

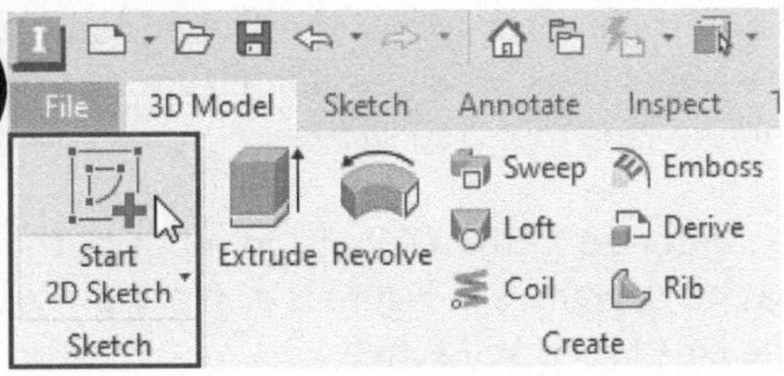

2.32

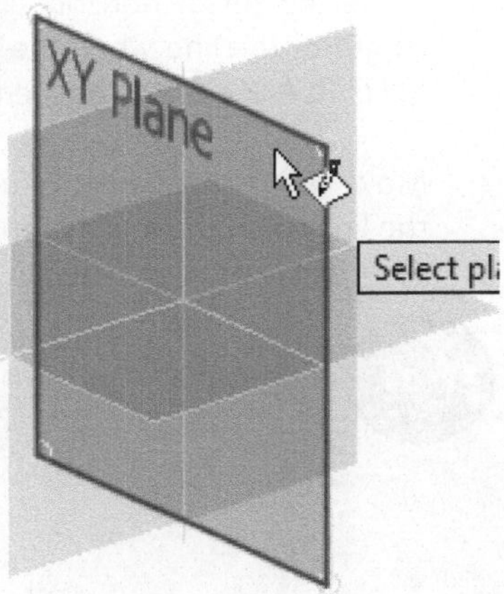

2.33

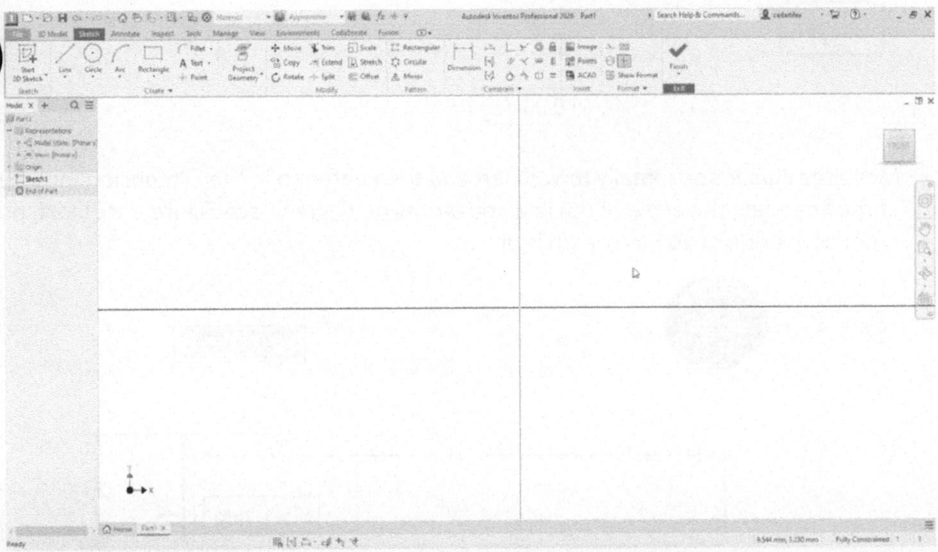

Note: In this Tutorial, the display of grids, axes, and the coordinate system in the drawing area have been turned off. For doing so, click on the **Application Options** tool in the **Options** panel of the **Tools** tab in the **Ribbon** and then click on the **Sketch** tab in the **Application Options** dialog box that appears. Next, clear the **Grid lines**, **Minor grid lines**, **Axes**, and **Coordinate system indicator** check boxes in the **Display** area of the dialog box.

Section 3: Drawing the Sketch

1. Click on the **Line** tool in the **Create** panel of the **Sketch** tab or press the **L** key. The Line tool gets activated and you are prompted to specify the start point of the line.

2. Move the cursor to the origin and then click to specify the start point of the line when the cursor snaps to the origin. Alternatively, you can specify coordinates (0,0) in the Pointer Input by pressing the TAB key.

3. Move the cursor horizontally toward right and then enter **100** in the Dimension Input as the length of the line when the angle of the line appears as 0 degree, see Figure 2.34. Next, press ENTER. A line of 100 mm length is drawn and the **Line** tool is still active.

4. Move the cursor vertically upward and then enter **20** in the Dimension Input as the length of the line when the angle of the line appears as 90 degrees, see Figure 2.35. Next, press ENTER. A vertical line of 20 mm length is drawn and the **Line** tool is still active.

2.34

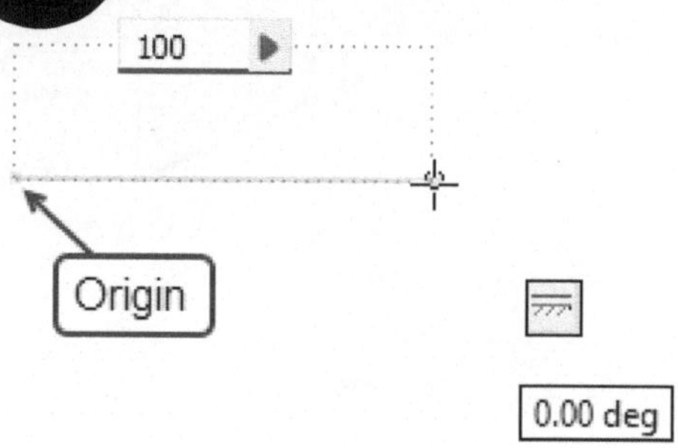

2.35

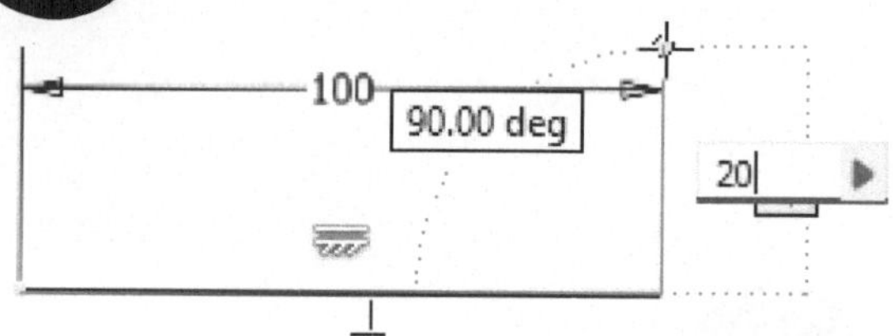

5. Move the cursor horizontally toward left and then enter **20** in the Dimension Input as the length of the line when the angle of the line appears as 90 degrees, see Figure 2.36. Next, press ENTER. A horizontal line of 20 mm length is drawn.

2.36

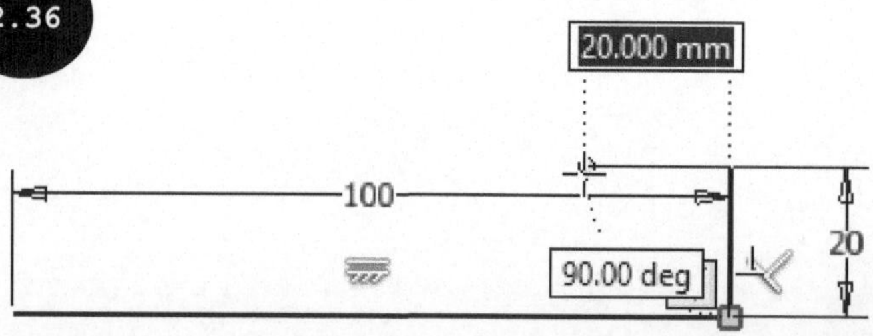

6. Move the cursor vertically downward and then enter **13** in the Dimension Input as the length of the line. Next, press ENTER. A vertical line of 13 mm length is drawn.

7. Move the cursor horizontally toward left and then enter **15** in the Dimension Input as the length of the line. Next, press ENTER. A horizontal line of 15 mm length is drawn.

8. Move the cursor vertically upward and then enter **8** in the Dimension Input as the length of the line. Next, press ENTER. A vertical line of 8 mm length is drawn.

9. Move the cursor horizontally toward left and then enter **30** in the Dimension Input as the length of the line. Next, press ENTER. A horizontal line of 30 mm length is drawn.

10. Similarly, draw the remaining sketch entities one after the other. Figure 2.37 shows the sketch after all the sketch entities have been drawn.

2.37

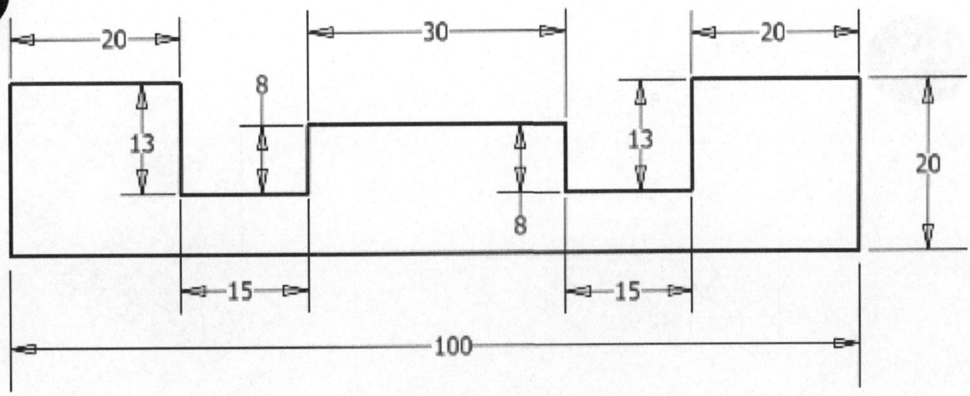

Note: When you specify length and angle values in the Dimension Input for creating a line entity, the dimensions get applied on the entity, by default. This happens because, the **Create dimensions from input values** check box is selected in the **Constraint Settings** dialog box. To invoke this dialog box, click on the **Application Options** tool in the **Options** panel of the **Tools** tab in the **Ribbon** and then click on the **Sketch** tab in the **Application Options** dialog box that appears. Next, click on the **Settings** button in the **Constraint Settings** area of the dialog box. The **Constraint Settings** dialog box appears. In this dialog box, the **Create dimensions from input values** check box is selected in the **Dimension** area, by default. As a result, the dimensions get applied automatically on entering the length and angle values in the Dimension Input while creating an entity.

11. Right-click in the drawing area. A Marking Menu appears. In this Marking Menu, click on the **OK** option to exit the **Line** tool.

Tip: After creating the sketch, you can change the default placement location of the dimensions by dragging them to the new location in the drawing area, as required.

12. Click on the **Finish Sketch** tool in the **Exit** panel of the **Ribbon** to exit the Sketching environment.

13. Click on the **Save** button in the **Quick Access Toolbar**. The **Save As** dialog box appears. Next, browse to the required location in the local drive of your system and create a folder with the name Autodesk Inventor. Next, create another folder with the name **Chapter 2** inside the Autodesk Inventor folder.

14. Enter **Tutorial 1** in the **File name** field of the dialog box and then click on the **Save** button. The sketch is saved in the specified location (>:*\Autodesk Inventor\Chapter 2*).

Hands-on Test Drive 1

Draw a sketch of the model shown in Figure 2.38. The dimensions and the 3D model shown in the figure are for your reference only. You will learn about applying dimensions and creating 3D models in later chapters. All dimensions are in mm.

2.38

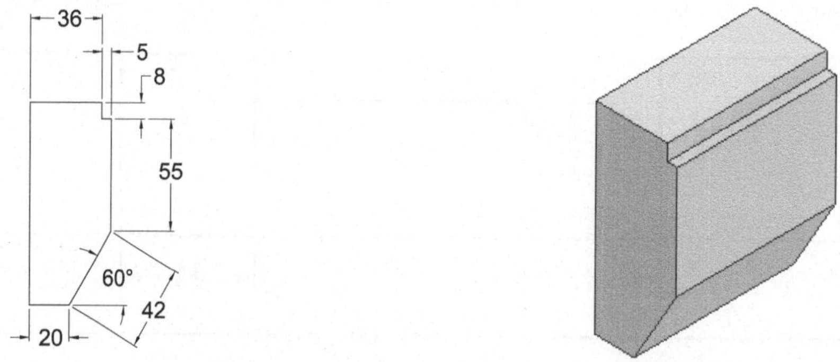

Creating an Arc by using the Line Tool

In Autodesk Inventor, you can also draw a tangent or perpendicular arc by using the **Line** tool. In order to do this, at least one line or arc entity has to be drawn in the drawing area. The method for drawing an arc by using the **Line** tool is discussed below:

1. Invoke the Sketching environment.

2. Invoke the **Line** tool and then draw a line by specifying two points in the drawing area. Once the line is drawn, do not exit the **Line** tool.

3. Move the cursor to the last specified point as the start point of the arc and then drag the cursor by pressing and holding the left mouse button. The arc mode is activated and the preview of a tangent arc appears in the drawing area, see Figure 2.39.

2.39

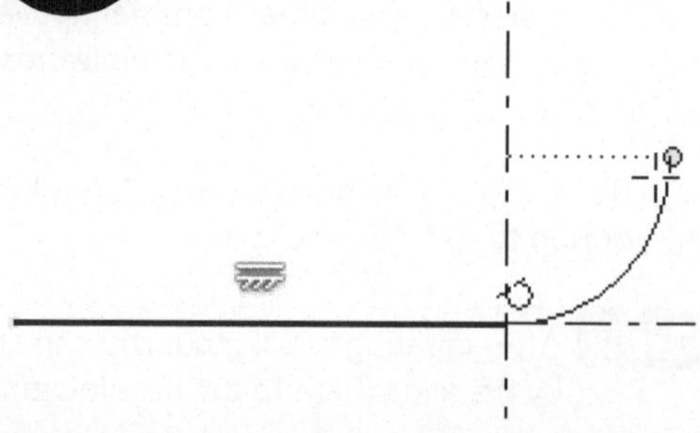

Note: The creation of arc (tangent or perpendicular) depends upon how you move the cursor from the last specified point in the drawing area. Figure 2.40 shows the possible movements of the cursor and the creation of arcs in the respective movements.

2.40

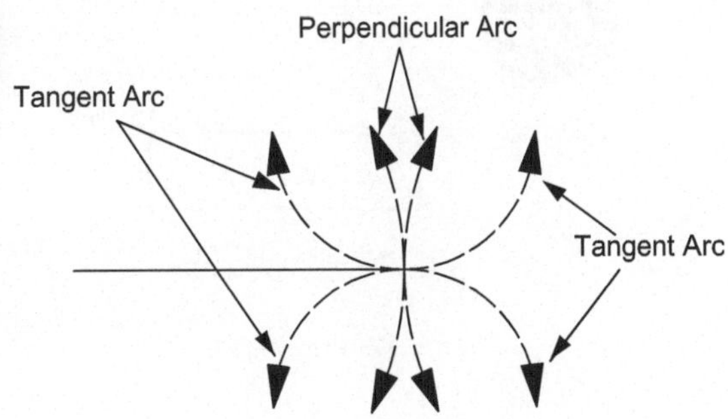

4. Release the left mouse button to specify the endpoint of the arc. An arc is drawn and the line mode is activated again. You can continue with the creation of line entities or drag the cursor for drawing an arc.

5. Once you have created all entities, right-click in the drawing area and then click on the **OK** option in the Marking Menu that appears to exit the **Line** tool.

Tutorial 2

Draw a sketch of the model shown in Figure 2.41, by using the **Line** tool. The dimensions and the 3D model shown in this figure are for your reference only. All dimensions are in mm. You will learn about applying dimensions and creating 3D models in later chapters.

2.41

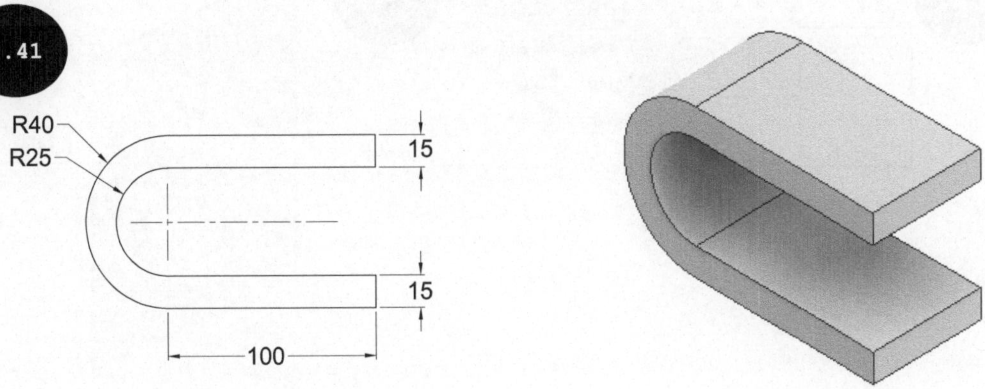

Section 1: Starting Autodesk Inventor

1. Start Autodesk Inventor by double-clicking on the Autodesk Inventor icon on your desktop. The startup user interface of Autodesk Inventor appears.

Section 2: Invoking the Sketching Environment

1. Click on the arrow next to the **New** tool in the left panel of the startup user interface and then click on the **Part** option in the drop-down menu that appears, see Figure 2.42. The Part modeling environment is invoked with the default template.

2.42

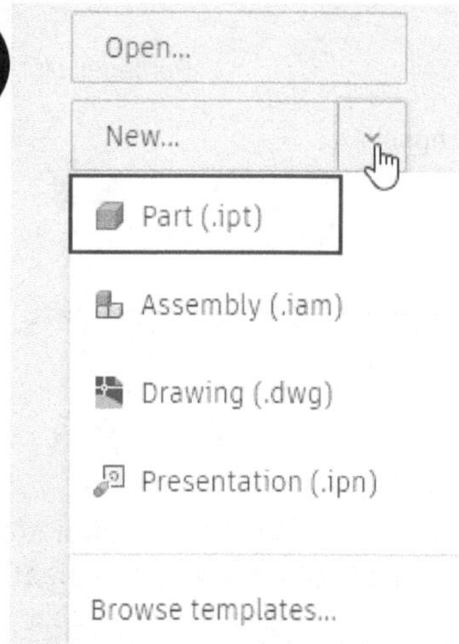

2. Click on the **Start 2D Sketch** tool in the **Sketch** panel of the **3D Model** tab in the **Ribbon** (see Figure 2.43) or press the S key. The three default planes: Front (XY Plane), Top (XZ Plane), and Right (YZ Plane), which are mutually perpendicular to each other appear in the graphics area. Also, you are prompted to select a plane for creating a sketch.

3. Move the cursor over the Front plane (XY Plane) and then click the left mouse button when the plane gets highlighted in the graphics area, see Figure 2.44. The Sketching environment is invoked and the Front plane is oriented normal to the viewing direction.

2.43

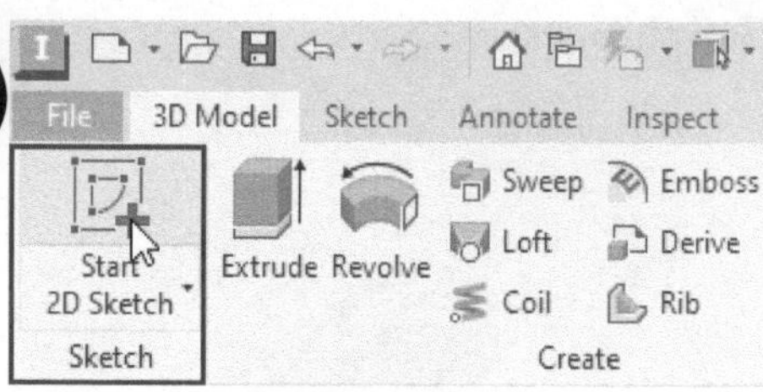

2.44

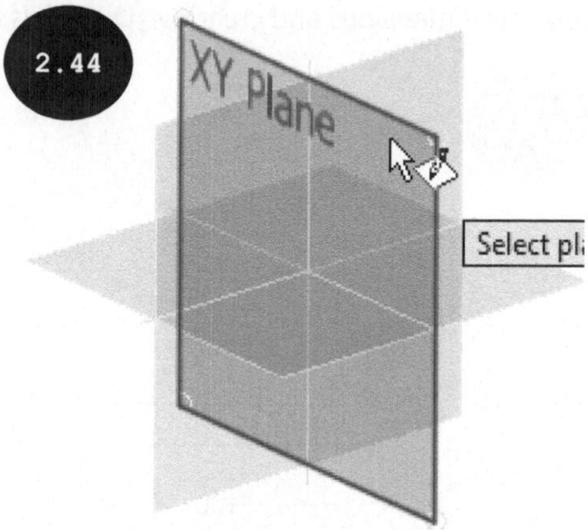

Note: It is evident from Figure 2.41 that all the sketch entities are multiples of 5. Therefore, you can set the snap settings such that the cursor snaps to an increment of 5 mm only.

Section 3: Specifying Units, Grids, and Snap Settings

1. Click on the **Tools** tab in the **Ribbon** and then click on the **Document Settings** tool in the **Options** panel, see Figure 2.45. The **Document Settings** dialog box appears, see Figure 2.46.

2.45

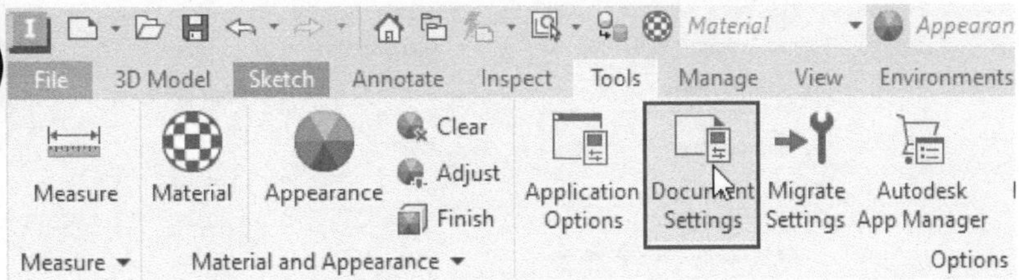

2. Click on the **Units** tab in the **Document Settings** dialog box to display the options for setting units for the current drawing.

3. Ensure that **millimeter** option is selected in the **Length** drop-down list as the unit of the current drawing, see Figure 2.46.

2.46

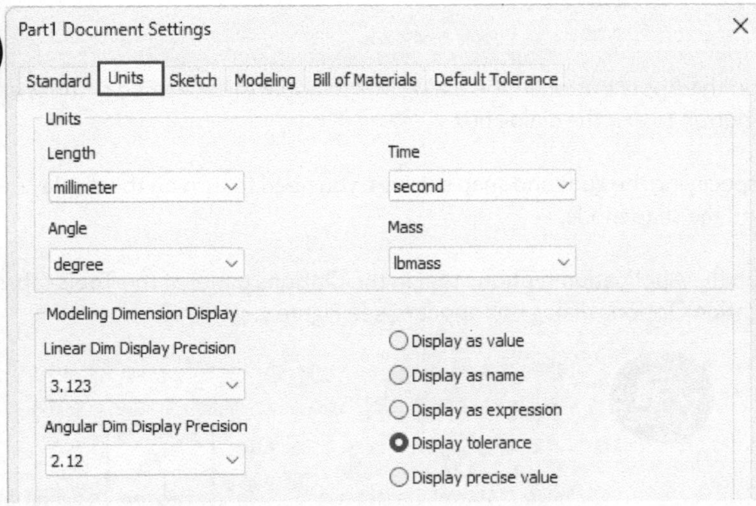

Now, you need to specify the grids and snap settings such that the cursor snaps to an increment of 5 mm.

4. Click on the **Sketch** tab in the **Document Settings** dialog box. Next, specify **5 mm** in the X and Y fields of the **Snap Spacing** area in the dialog box to snap the cursor to an incremental distance of 5 mm in X and Y directions, see Figure 2.47.

5. Enter **1** in the **snaps per minor** field of the **Grid Display** area in the dialog box as the number of snap points between each grid, see Figure 2.47.

6. Enter **5** in the **Major every minor lines** field in the **Grid Display** area as the number of minor lines between two major grid lines, see Figure 2.47.

2.47

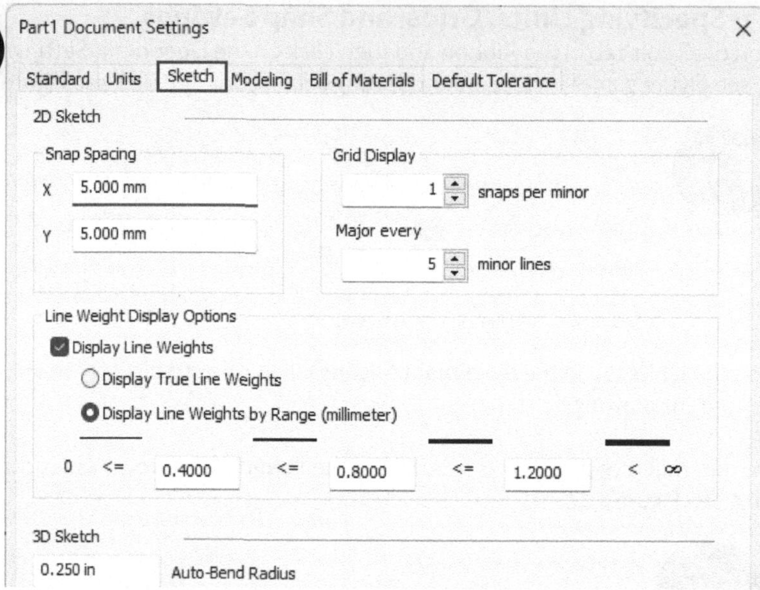

7. Click on the **Apply** button in the dialog box to apply the specified settings and then click on the **Close** button to exit the dialog box.

   After specifying the grids and snap settings, you need to turn on the display of grids in the drawing area and the snap mode.

8. Click on the **Application Options** tool in the **Options** panel of the **Tools** tab, see Figure 2.48. The **Application Options** dialog box appears, see Figure 2.49.

2.48

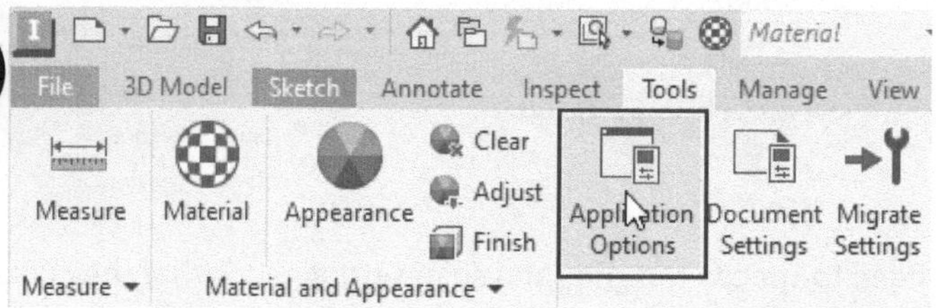

9. Click on the **Sketch** tab in the **Application Options** dialog box to display options related to the Sketching environment, see Figure 2.49.

10. Select the **Grid lines**, **Minor grid lines**, and **Axes** check boxes in the **Display** area of the dialog box to turn on the display of grid lines, minor grid lines, and axes in the drawing area, see Figure 2.49.

    Now, you need to turn on the snap mode.

11. Select the **Snap to grid** check box in the **Sketch** tab of the dialog box, see Figure 2.49.

2.49

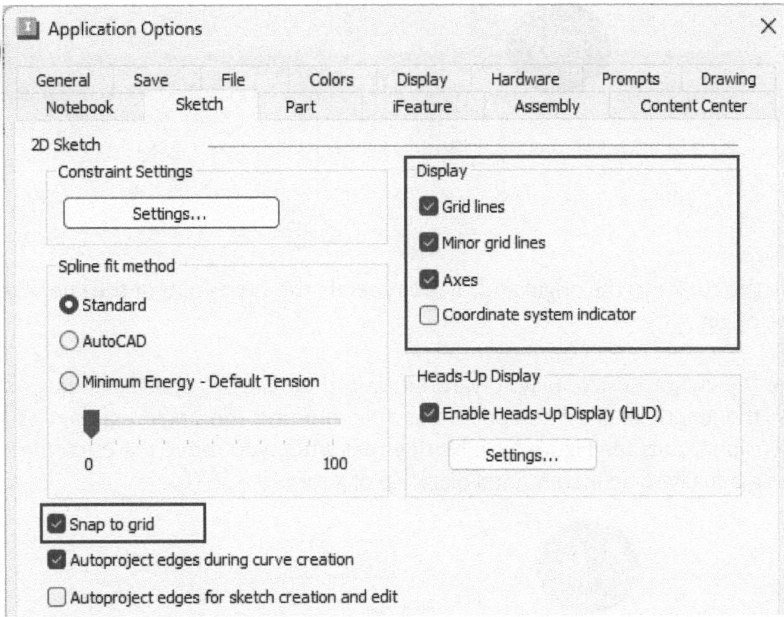

12. Click on the **Apply** button in the dialog box to apply the specified settings and then click on the **Close** button to exit the dialog box. The grids appear in the drawing area as per the specified settings, see Figure 2.50.

2.50

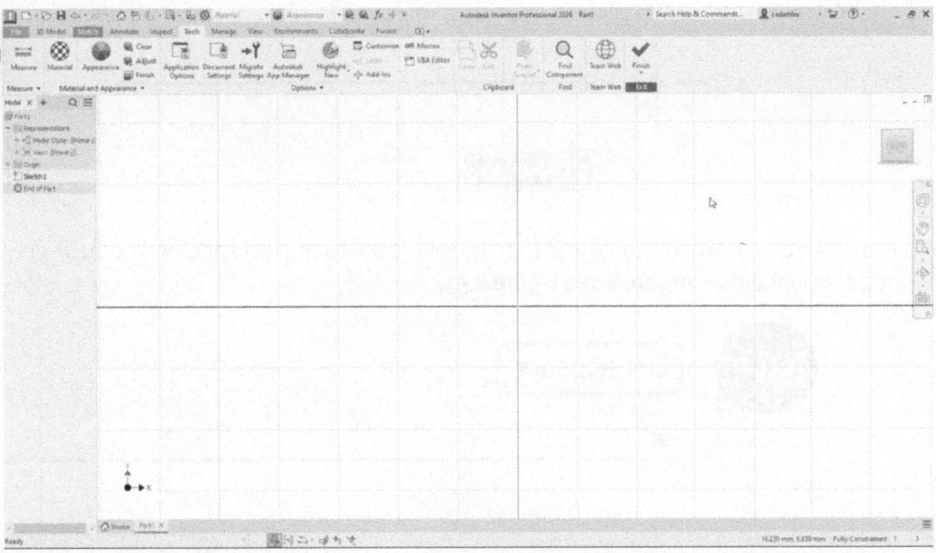

Once the units, grids, and snap settings have been specified, you can start creating the sketch by using the **Line** tool.

Section 4: Drawing the Sketch

1. Click on the **Sketch** tab in the **Ribbon** to display the sketching tools and then click on the **Line** tool, see Figure 2.51. The **Line** tool gets activated. Alternatively, press the **L** key to activate the **Line** tool.

2.51

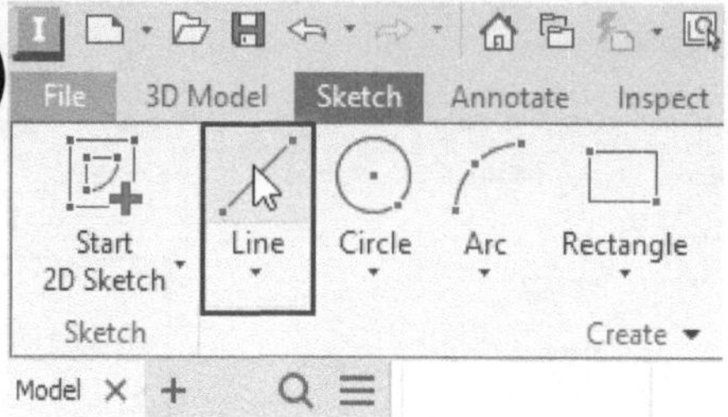

2. Move the cursor to the origin and click to specify the start point of the line when the cursor snaps to the origin.

3. Move the cursor horizontally toward left and then click to specify the second point of the line when the length of the line appears as 100 mm and the angle appears as 180 degrees in the Dimension Input, see Figure 2.52. Notice that when you move the cursor in the drawing area, it snaps gradually to an incremental distance of 5 mm.

2.52

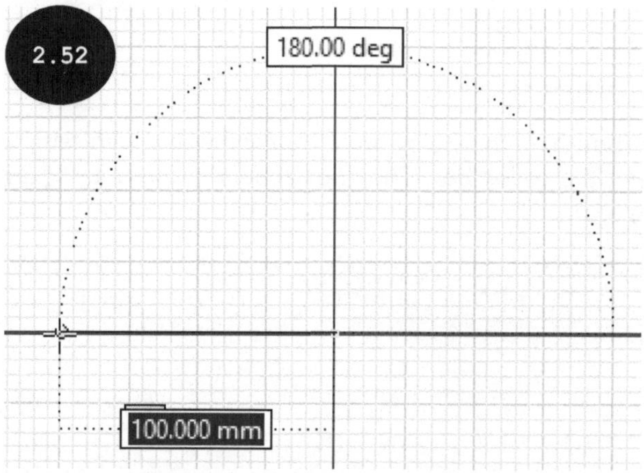

4. Move the cursor to a distance and then move it back to the last specified point. A gray colored dot appears in the drawing area, see Figure 2.53.

2.53

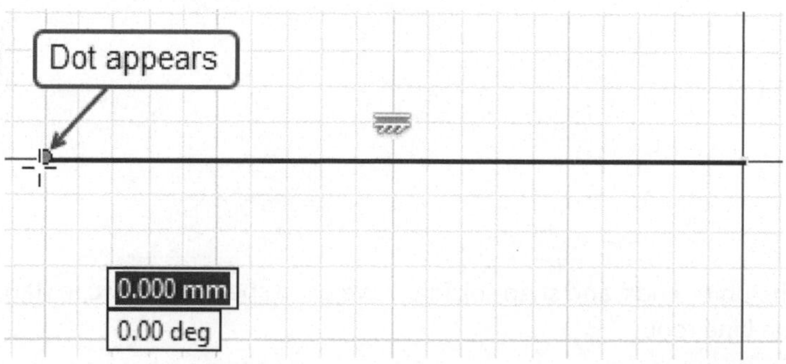

5. Drag the cursor by pressing and holding the left mouse button from the last specified point in the upward direction. The arc mode is activated and a preview of the tangent arc appears in the drawing area, see Figure 2.54.

2.54

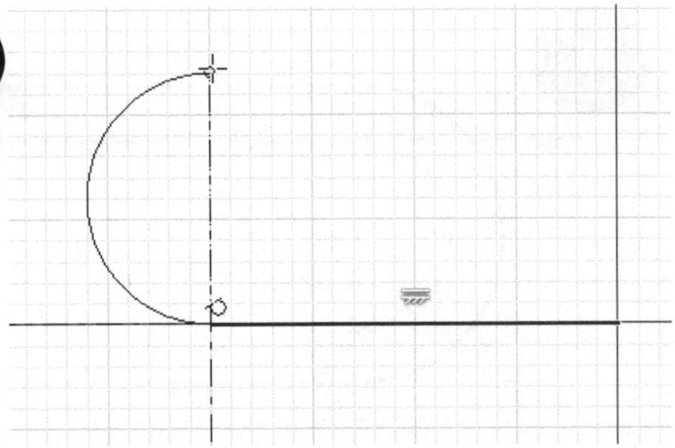

Note: In Figures 2.53 and 2.54, the display of axes is turned off for clarity of image.

6. Release the left mouse button to specify the endpoint of the tangent arc when the radius of the arc appears as 40 mm in the Status Bar at the lower right corner of the screen, see Figure 2.55. The tangent arc is created and the preview of a line appears attached to the cursor.

2.55

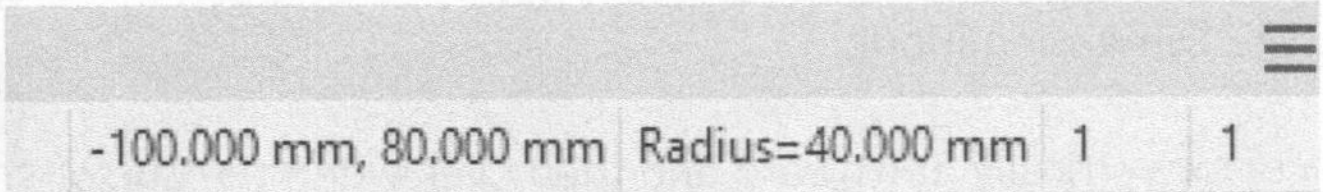

7. Move the cursor horizontally toward right and click when the length of the line appears as 100 mm in the Dimension Input, see Figure 2.56.

2.56

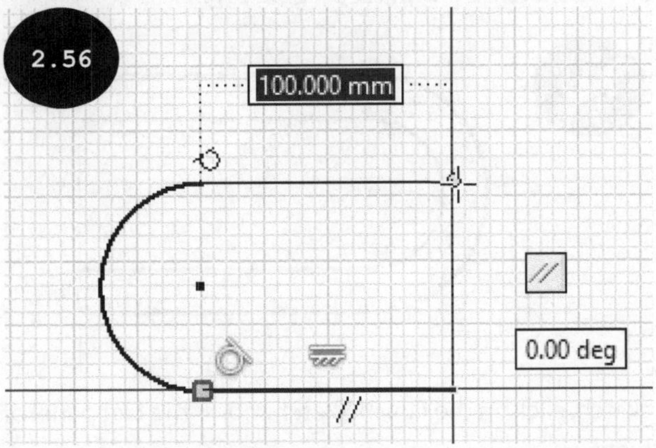

8. Move the cursor vertically downward and click when the length of the line appears as 15 mm.
9. Move the cursor horizontally toward left and click when the length of the line appears as 100 mm.
10. Move the cursor to the last specified point. A gray colored dot appears in the drawing area. Next, drag the cursor by pressing and holding the left mouse button in the downward direction. The preview of a tangent arc appears, see Figure 2.57.

2.57

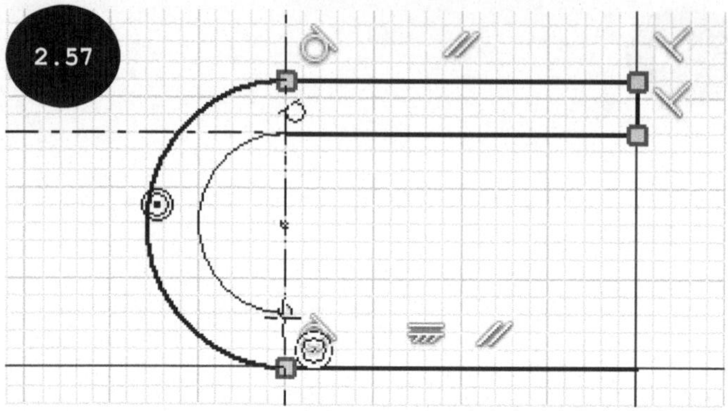

11. Release the left mouse button to specify the endpoint of the tangent arc when the radius of the arc appears as 25 mm in the Status Bar at the lower right corner of the screen, see Figure 2.58. The tangent arc is created and the preview of a line appears attached to the cursor.

2.58

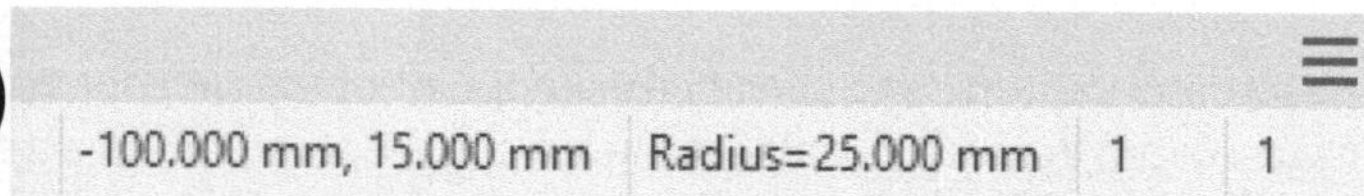

12. Move the cursor horizontally toward right and then click when the length of the line appears as 100 mm in the Dimension Input.

13. Move the cursor vertically downward and then click when the cursor snaps to the start point of the first sketch entity.

14. Right-click in the drawing area and then click on the **OK** option in the Marking Menu that appears to exit the **Line** tool. The sketch is drawn, see Figure 2.59.

2.59

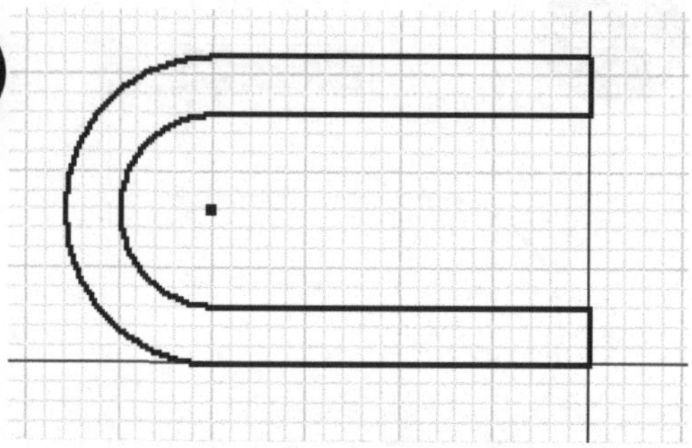

15. After creating the sketch, click on the **Finish Sketch** tool in the **Exit** panel of the **Ribbon** to exit the Sketching environment.

16. Click on the **Save** tool in the **Quick Access Toolbar**. The **Save As** dialog box appears. Next, browse to the Chapter 2 folder of the Autodesk Inventor folder. You need to create these folders in the local drive of your system, if not created earlier.

17. Enter **Tutorial 2** in the **File name** field of the dialog box and then click on the **Save** button. The sketch is saved in the specified location.

Hands-on Test Drive 2

Draw a sketch of the model shown in Figure 2.60. The dimensions and the 3D model shown in the figure are for your reference only. Draw all entities of the sketch by using the **Line** tool. As all the dimensions of the sketch are multiples of 5, you can set the snap settings such that the cursor snaps to an increment of 5 mm. All dimensions are in mm.

2.60

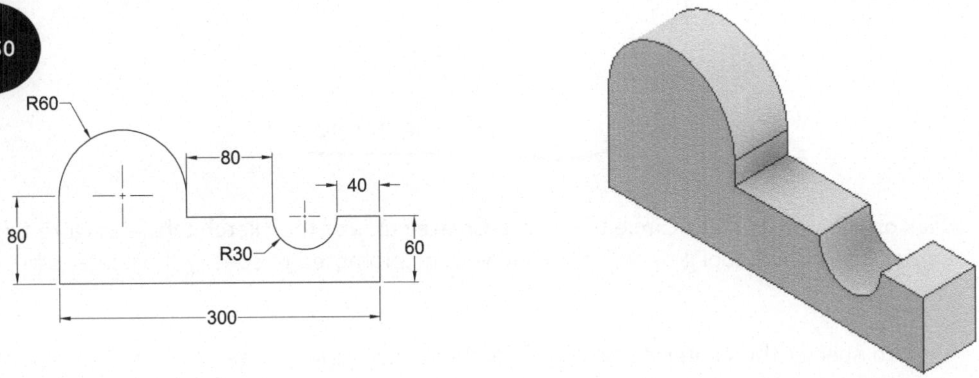

Creating a Circle

In Autodesk Inventor, you can draw a circle by using the **Center Point Circle** and **Tangent Circle** tools available in the **Circle** flyout of the **Create** panel in the **Ribbon**, see Figure 2.61. To invoke the **Circle** flyout, click on the arrow next to the **Circle** tool in the **Create** panel of the **Ribbon**, see Figure 2.61. The tools for drawing a circle are discussed next.

2.61

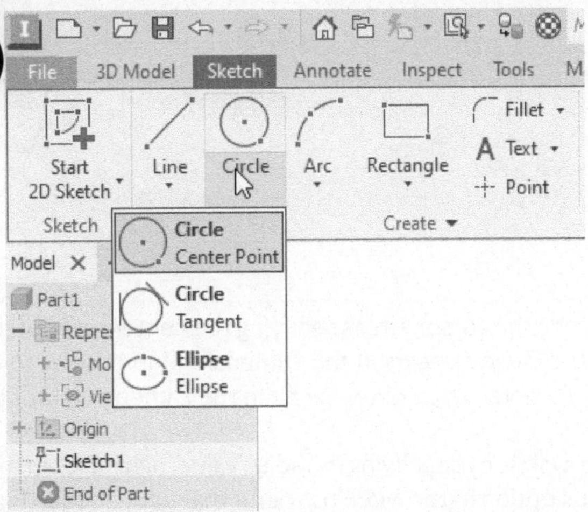

Creating a Circle by using the Center Point Circle Tool

The **Center Point Circle** tool is used for drawing a circle by specifying its center point and a point on its circumference, see Figure 2.62. The method for drawing a circle by using the **Center Point Circle** tool is discussed below:

2.62

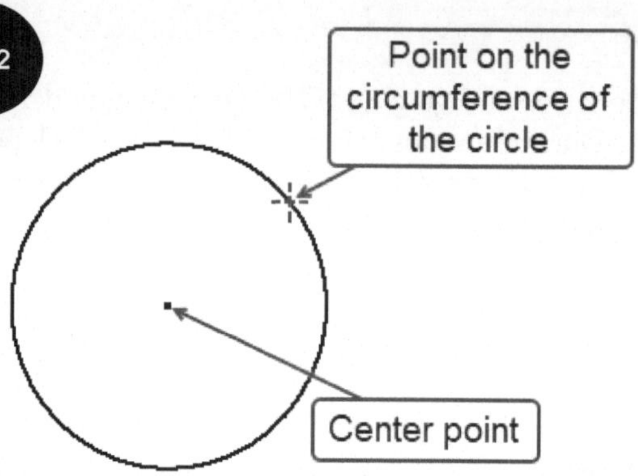

1. Click on the **Center Point Circle** tool in the **Create** panel of the **Sketch** tab, see Figure 2.63. The **Center Point Circle** tool gets activated and you are prompted to specify the center point of the circle.

2. Click to specify the center point of the circle in the drawing area. You can also specify the coordinates (X,Y) in the Pointer Input to specify the center point of the circle.

3. Move the cursor to a distance in the drawing area. A preview of the circle appears, see Figure 2.64. Also, you are prompted to specify a point on the circumference of the circle.

2.63

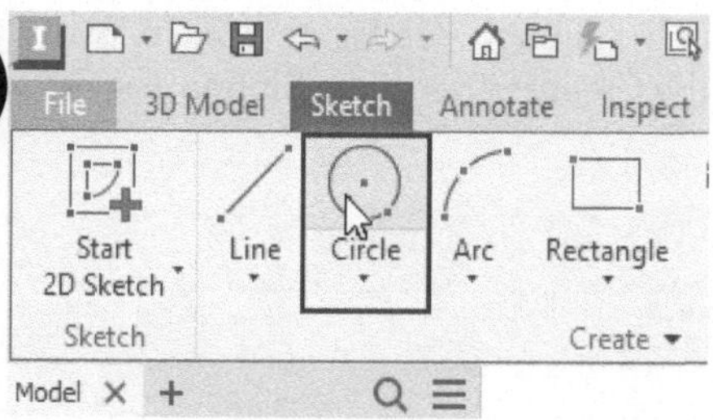

2.64

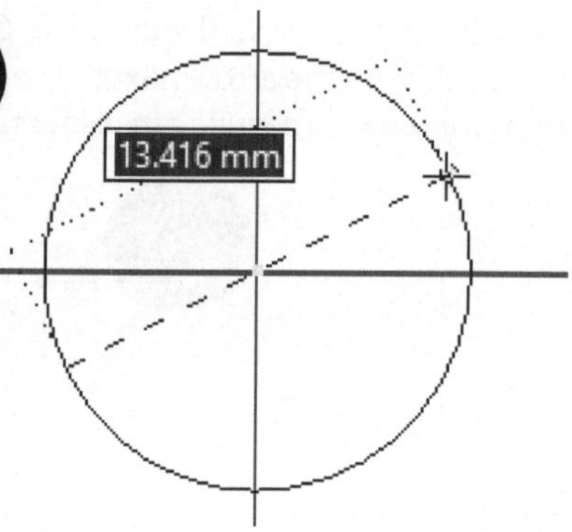

Note: As you move the cursor after specifying the center point of the circle, the current diameter value of the circle appears in the Dimension Input, refer to Figure 2.64. You can enter the required diameter value of the circle in the Dimension Input for creating the circle.

To create a circle by specifying its radius value, right-click in the drawing area and then select the **Radius** option in the Marking Menu that appears, see Figure 2.65.

2.65

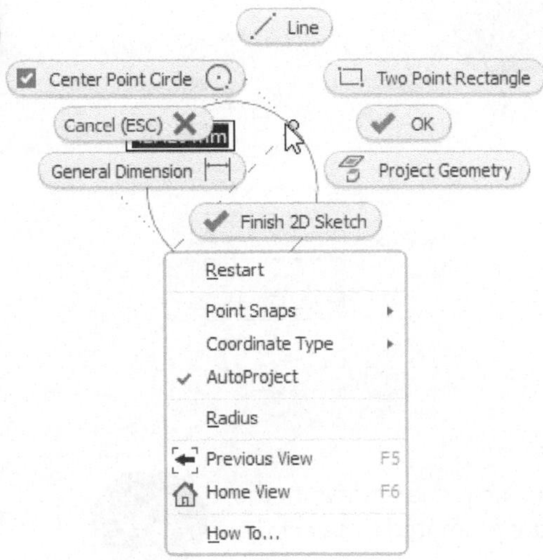

4. Click to specify a point in the drawing area. A circle is drawn and the **Center Point Circle** tool is still active.

5. Press the ESC key to exit the **Center Point Circle** tool or right-click in the drawing area and then click on the **OK** option in the Marking Menu to exit the tool.

Creating a Circle by using the Tangent Circle Tool

The **Tangent Circle** tool is used for drawing a circle that is tangent to three line entities, see Figure 2.66. The method for drawing a circle by using the **Tangent Circle** tool is discussed below:

2.66

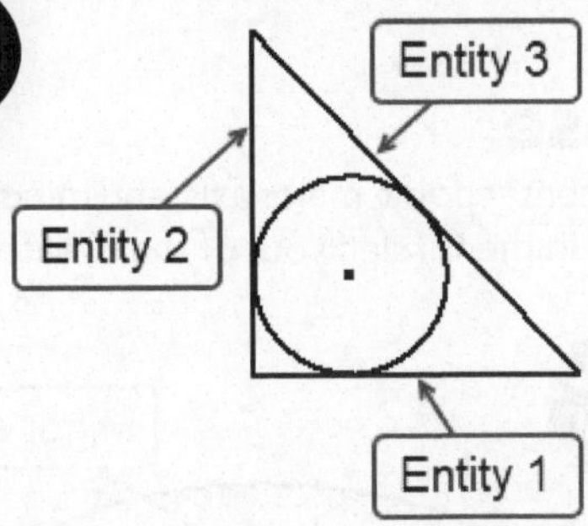

1. Invoke the **Circle** flyout in the **Create** panel of the **Sketch** tab and then click on the **Tangent Circle** tool, see Figure 2.67. The **Tangent Circle** tool gets activated and you are prompted to select the first line entity.

2.67

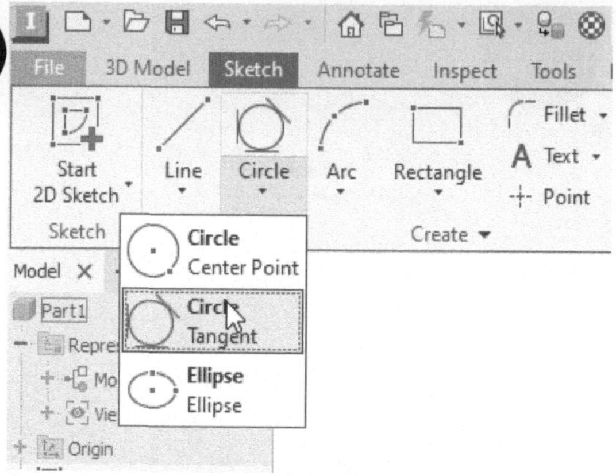

2. Click to select the first line entity in the drawing area. You are prompted to select the second line entity.

3. Click to select the second line entity in the drawing area. You are prompted to select the third line entity.

4. Click to select the third line entity in the drawing area. A circle tangent to the selected entities is drawn, see Figure 2.68.

2.68

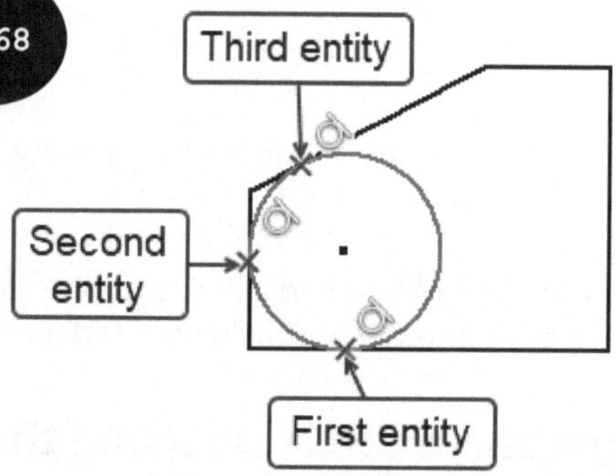

5. Press the ESC key to exit the **Tangent Circle** tool or right-click in the drawing area and then click on the **OK** option in the Marking Menu to exit the tool.

Creating an Ellipse

An ellipse is drawn by defining its center point, major axis, and minor axis, see Figure 2.69. You can draw an ellipse by using the **Ellipse** tool in the **Circle** flyout of the **Create** panel. The method for creating an ellipse is discussed below:

2.69

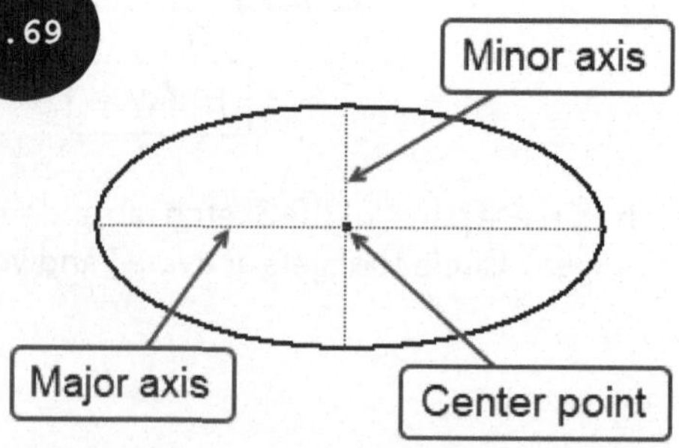

1. Invoke the **Circle** flyout in the **Create** panel and then click on the **Ellipse** tool, see Figure 2.70. The **Ellipse** tool gets activated and you are prompted to specify the center point of the ellipse.

2.70

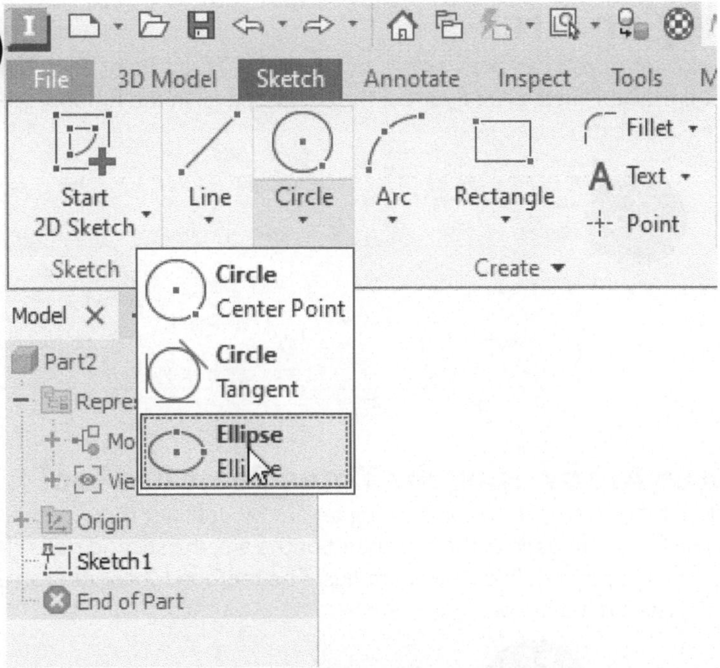

2. Click to specify the center point of the ellipse in the drawing area.

3. Move the cursor away from the specified center point and then click to define the major axis of the ellipse in the drawing area.

4. Move the cursor to a distance in the drawing area. A preview of the ellipse appears, see Figure 2.71. Also, you are prompted to specify a point on the ellipse.

2.71

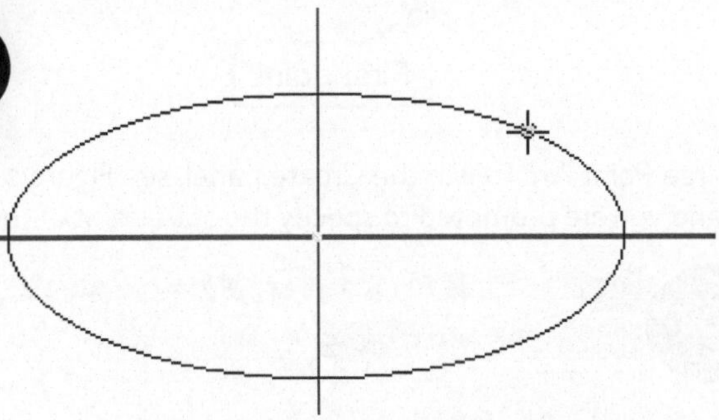

5. Click to specify a point on the ellipse to define the minor axis of the ellipse. The ellipse is drawn.

6. Right-click in the drawing area and then click on the **OK** option in the Marking Menu that appears to exit the **Ellipse** tool.

Creating an Arc

In Autodesk Inventor, you can draw an arc by using the **Three Point Arc**, **Tangent Arc**, and **Center Point Arc** tools available in the **Arc** flyout of the **Create** panel in the **Ribbon**, see Figure 2.72. The tools for drawing an arc are discussed next.

2.72

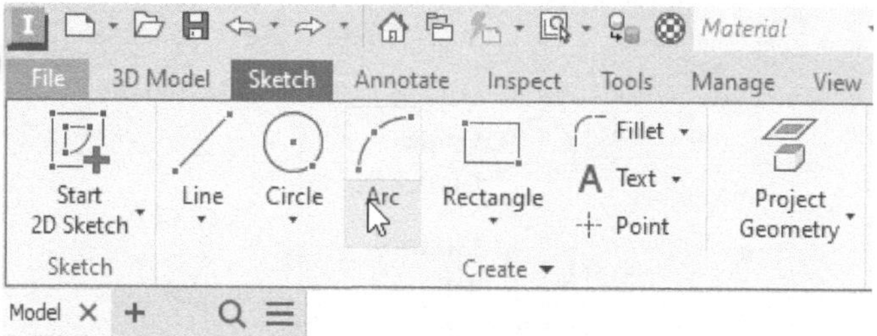

Creating an Arc by using the Three Point Arc Tool

The **Three Point Arc** tool is used for drawing an arc by defining three points on its arc length, see Figure 2.73. The first point defines the start point of the arc, the second point defines the endpoint of the arc, and the third point defines the arc radius. The method for creating an arc by using the **Three Point Arc** tool is discussed below:

2.73

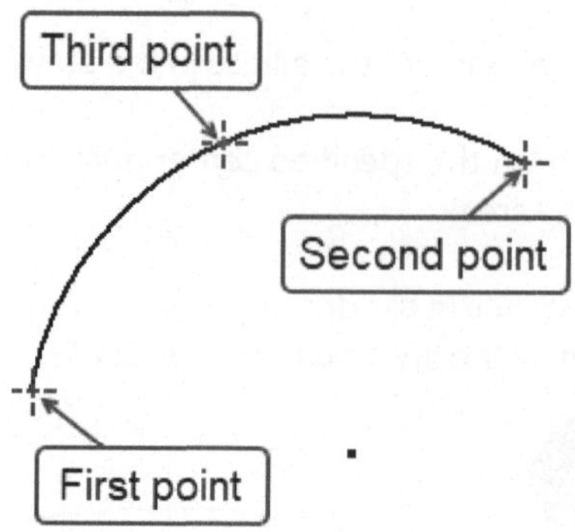

1. Click on the **Three Point Arc** tool in the **Create** panel, see Figure 2.74. The **Three Point Arc** tool gets activated and you are prompted to specify the start point of the arc.

2.74

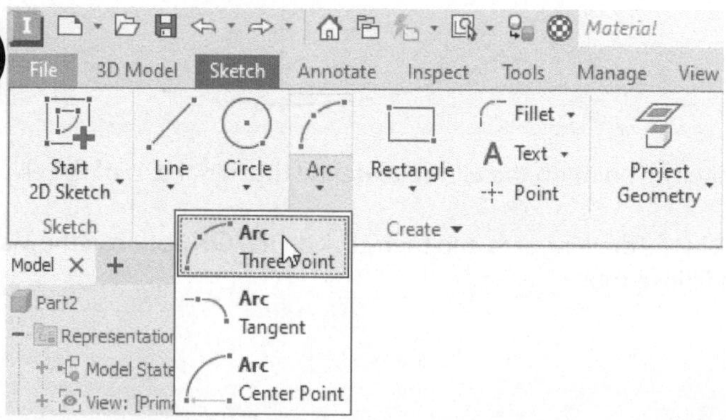

2. Click to specify the start point of the arc in the drawing area. You are prompted to specify the endpoint of the arc.

3. Move the cursor to a distance and then click to specify the endpoint of the arc in the drawing area. A preview of the arc appears, see Figure 2.75. Also, you are prompted to specify a point on the arc length.

4. Click to specify a point on the arc length to define the arc radius. An arc is drawn by specifying three points. Press ESC to exit the tool.

2.75

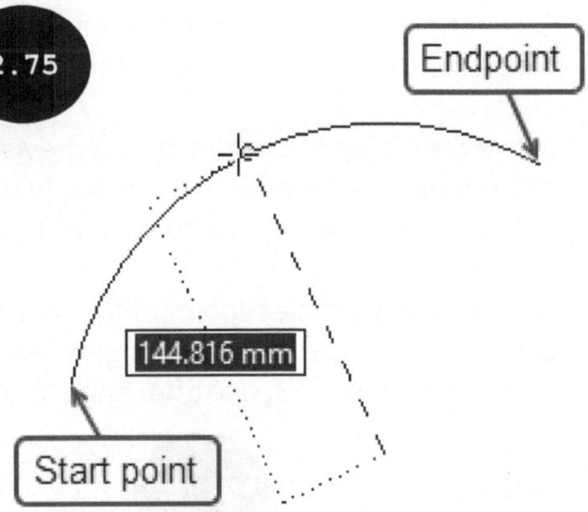

Creating an Arc by using the Tangent Arc Tool

The **Tangent Arc** tool is used for drawing an arc tangent to an existing entity, see Figure 2.76. You can draw an arc tangent to a line, an arc, or a spline by using the **Tangent Arc** tool. The method for creating a tangent arc is discussed below:

2.76

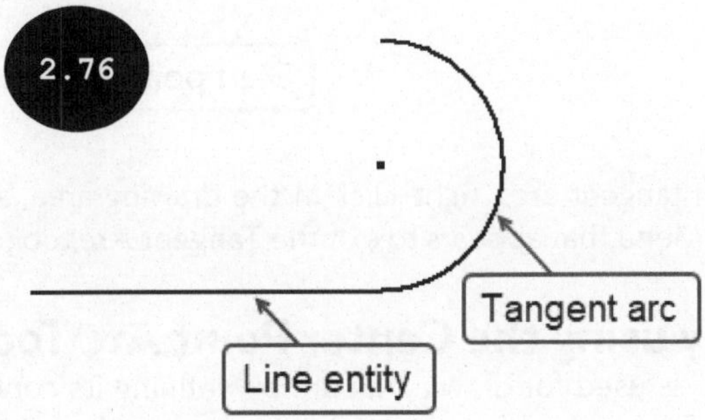

1. Invoke the **Arc** flyout in the **Create** panel and then click on the **Tangent Arc** tool, see Figure 2.77. The **Tangent Arc** tool gets activated and you are prompted to specify a start point.

2.77

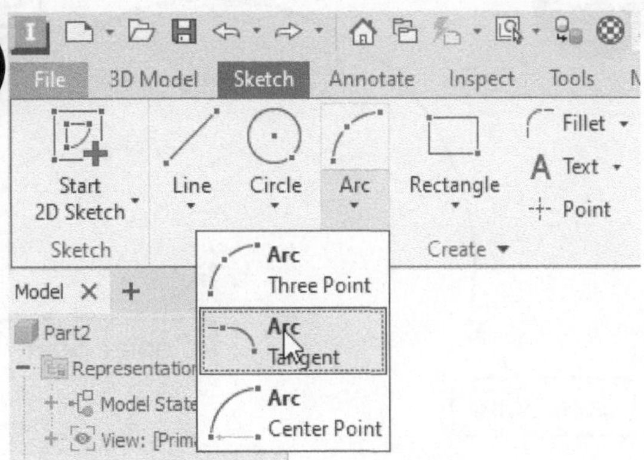

2. Move the cursor to the endpoint of an existing entity (line, arc, or spline) in the drawing area and then click to specify the start point of the tangent arc when the cursor snaps to it.

3. Move the cursor to a distance. The preview of a tangent arc appears in the drawing area such that its endpoint is attached to the cursor. Note that the tangency of arc depends upon how you move the cursor from the specified start point in the drawing area.

4. Click to specify the endpoint of the tangent arc in the drawing area, see Figure 2.78. The tangent arc is drawn. Note that the **Tangent Arc** tool remains activated. As a result, you can continue creating tangent arcs, one after another, by specifying the start point and endpoint.

2.78

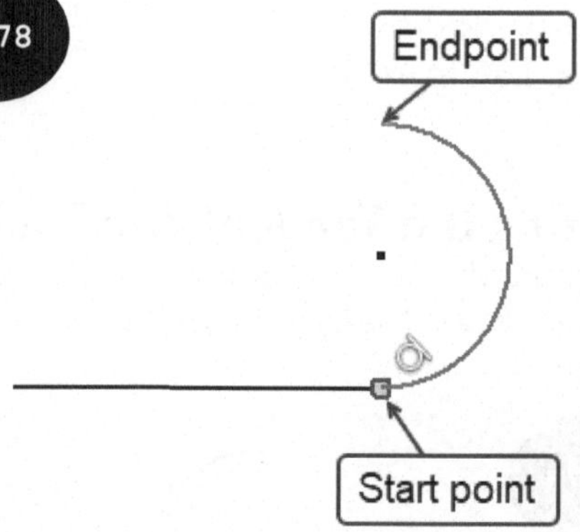

5. Once you have drawn tangent arcs, right-click in the drawing area, and then click on the **OK** option in the Marking Menu that appears to exit the **Tangent Arc** tool, or press the ESC key.

Creating an Arc by using the Center Point Arc Tool

The **Center Point Arc** tool is used for drawing an arc by defining its center point, start point, and endpoint, see Figure 2.79. The method for creating an arc by specifying its center point, start point, and endpoint is discussed below:

2.79

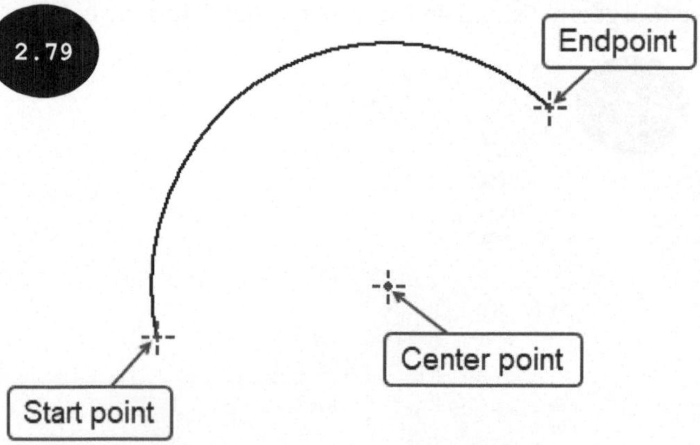

1. Invoke the **Arc** flyout in the **Create** panel and then click on the **Center Point Arc** tool (see Figure 2.80) or press the A key. The **Center Point Arc** tool gets activated and you are prompted to specify the center point of the arc.

2. Click to specify the center point of the arc in the drawing area. The preview of a construction circle appears in the drawing area and you are prompted to specify the start point of the arc.

2.80

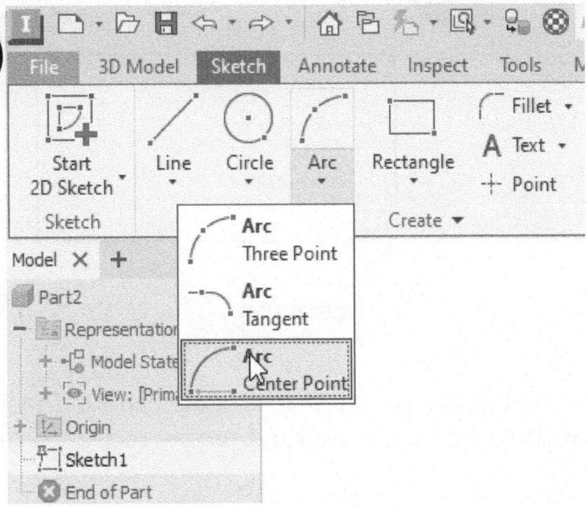

3. Click in the drawing area to define the start point of the arc. Next, move the cursor clockwise or anti-clockwise. The preview of an arc appears in the drawing area.

4. Click to specify the endpoint of the arc in the drawing area. An arc is drawn by specifying its center point, start point, and endpoint.

5. Press the ESC key to exit the **Centre Point Arc** tool or right-click in the drawing area and then click on the **OK** option in the Marking Menu to exit the tool.

Creating a Rectangle

In Autodesk Inventor, you can draw a rectangle by using the **Two Point Rectangle**, **Three Point Rectangle**, **Two Point Center Rectangle**, and **Three Point Center Rectangle** tools available in the **Rectangle** flyout of the **Create** panel in the **Sketch** tab, see Figure 2.81. Note that in the **Rectangle** flyout, the tools for drawing slots and polygons are also available. You will learn about drawing slots and polygons later in this chapter. The tools for drawing a rectangle are discussed next.

2.81

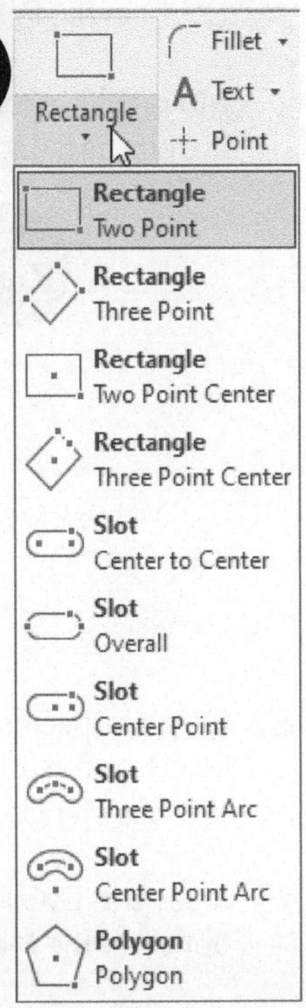

Creating a Rectangle by using the Two Point Rectangle Tool

The **Two Point Rectangle** tool is used for drawing a rectangle by specifying two diagonally opposite corners of a rectangle. The first corner defines the position of the rectangle and the second corner defines the length and width of the rectangle, see Figure 2.82. The method for creating a rectangle by specifying two diagonally opposite corners is discussed below:

2.82

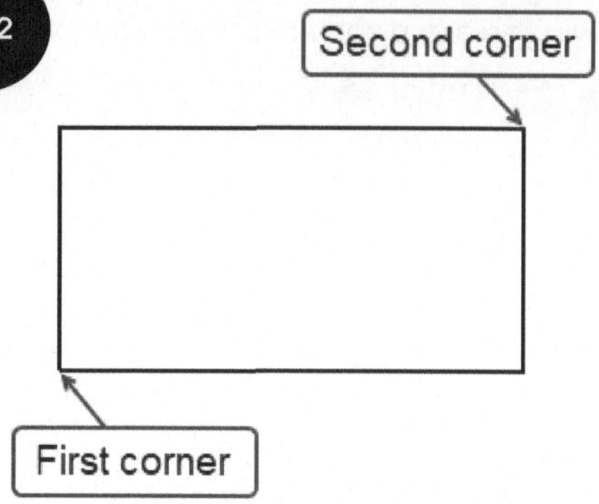

1. Click on the **Two Point Rectangle** tool in the **Create** panel of the **Sketch** tab, see Figure 2.83. The **Two Point Rectangle** tool gets activated and you are prompted to specify the first corner of the rectangle.

2.83

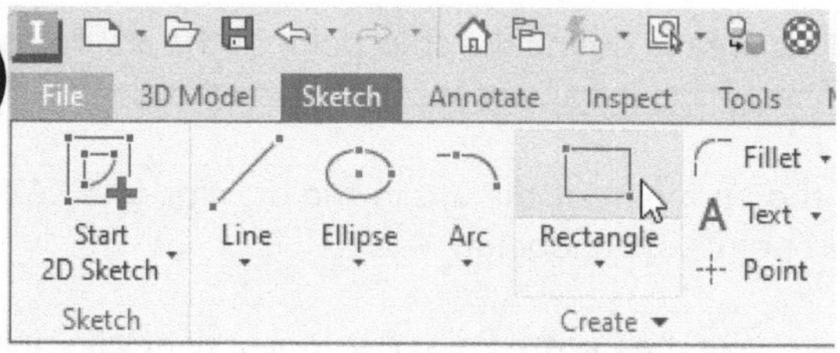

2. Click to specify the first corner of the rectangle in the drawing area. You can also enter coordinates (X, Y) in the Pointer Input for specifying the first corner of the rectangle.

3. Move the cursor away from the first specified corner. The preview of a rectangle appears and you are prompted to specify the diagonally opposite corner of the rectangle, see Figure 2.84.

2.84

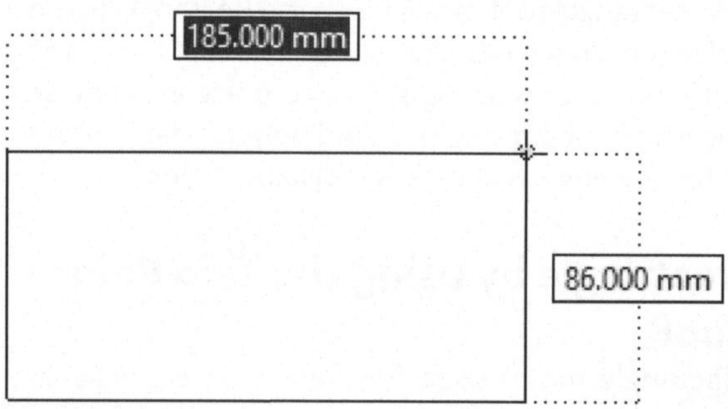

4. Click to specify the second corner of the rectangle in the drawing area. You can also enter the length and width values of the rectangle in the Dimension Input for specifying the second corner of the rectangle. A rectangle is drawn by specifying two diagonally opposite corners.

5. Press the ESC key to exit the tool or right-click in the drawing area and then click on the **OK** option in the Marking Menu to exit the **Two Point Rectangle** tool.

Creating a Rectangle by using the Three Point Rectangle Tool

The **Three Point Rectangle** tool is used for drawing a rectangle by specifying three corners. The first two corners define the width and orientation of the rectangle and the third corner defines the length of the rectangle, see Figure 2.85. The method for creating a rectangle by specifying three corners is discussed below:

2.85

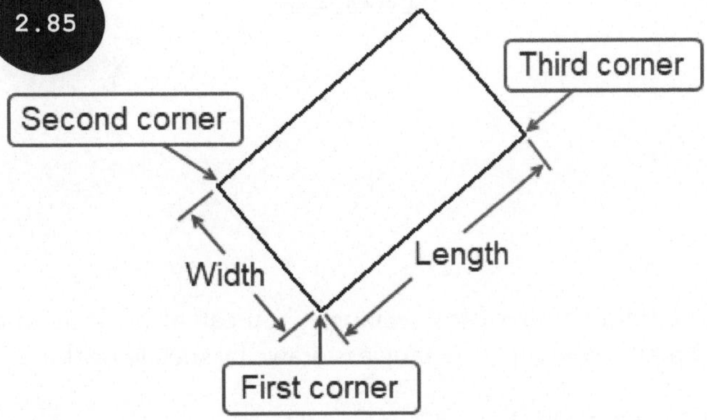

1. Invoke the **Rectangle** flyout and then click on the **Three Point Rectangle** tool, see Figure 2.86. The **Three Point Rectangle** tool gets activated and you are prompted to specify the first corner of the rectangle.
2. Click to specify the first corner of the rectangle in the drawing area. You can also enter coordinates (X, Y) in the Pointer Input for specifying the first corner of the rectangle.
3. Move the cursor to a distance in the drawing area. A rubber band line appears attached to the cursor with the display of width and angle values in the Dimension Input, see Figure 2.87. Also, you are prompted to specify the second corner of the rectangle.

2.86

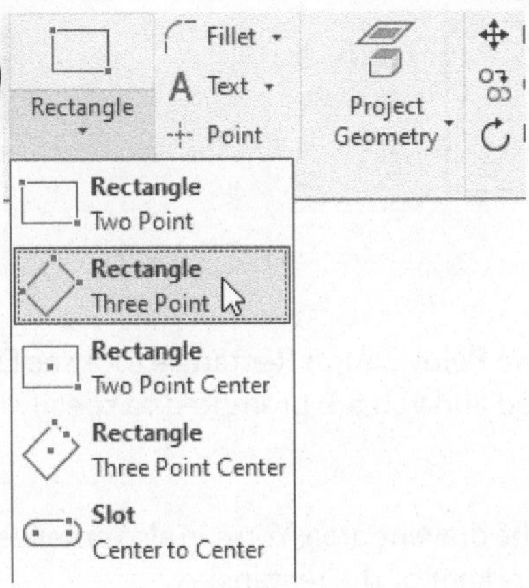

2.87

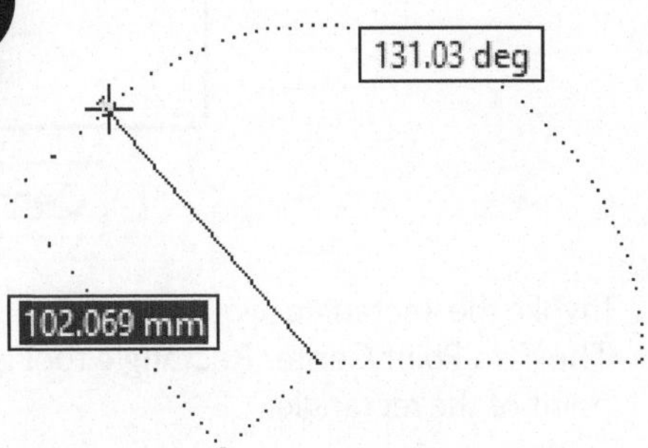

4. Click to specify the second corner of the rectangle in the drawing area. You can also specify the width and angle values of the rectangle in the Dimension Input to define the second corner of the rectangle. Note that you need to press the TAB key to switch between the width and angle values in the Dimension Input.

5. Move the cursor to a distance in the drawing area. The preview of a rectangle appears with the display of length value in the Dimension Input, see Figure 2.88. Also, you are prompted to specify the third corner of the rectangle.

2.88

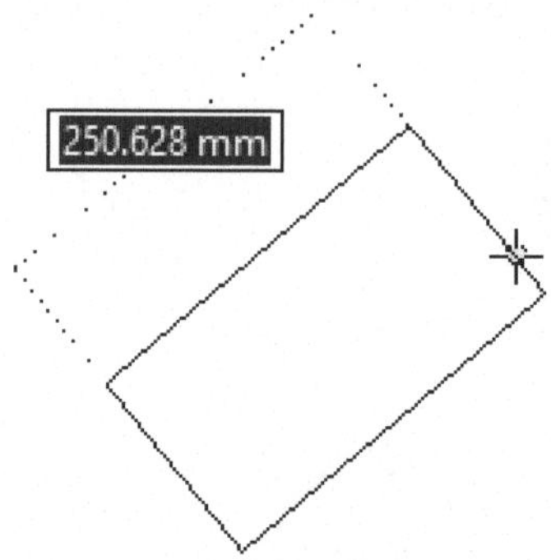

6. Click to specify the third corner of the rectangle. You can also specify the length value of the rectangle in the Dimension Input. A rectangle is drawn by specifying three corners.

7. Press the ESC key to exit the tool.

Creating a Rectangle by using the Two Point Center Rectangle Tool

The **Two Point Center Rectangle** tool is used for drawing a rectangle by specifying a center point and a corner point, see Figure 2.89. The method for creating a rectangle by specifying a center point and a corner point is discussed below:

2.89

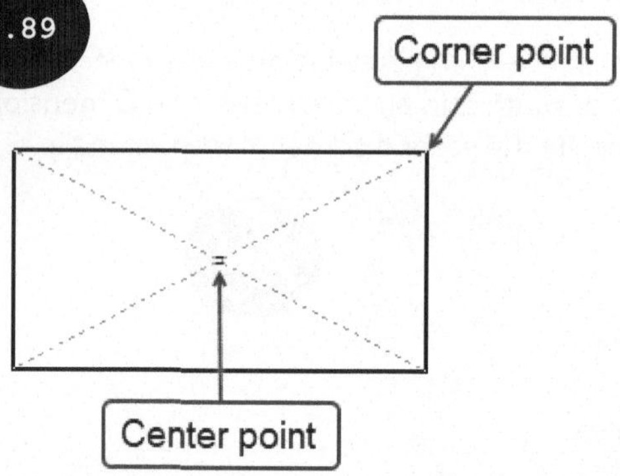

1. Invoke the **Rectangle** flyout and then click on the **Two Point Center Rectangle** tool, see Figure 2.90. The **Two Point Center Rectangle** tool gets activated and you are prompted to specify the center point of the rectangle.

2. Click to specify the center point of the rectangle in the drawing area. You can also enter coordinates (X, Y) in the Pointer Input for specifying the center point of the rectangle.

3. Move the cursor to a distance in the drawing area. The preview of a rectangle appears (see Figure 2.91) and you are prompted to specify a corner of the rectangle.

2.90

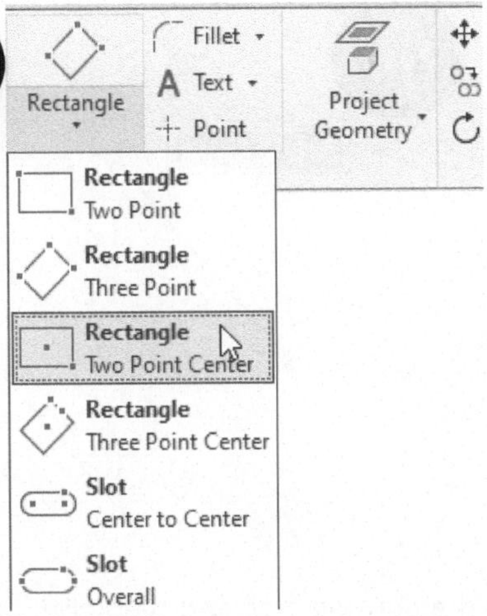

2.91

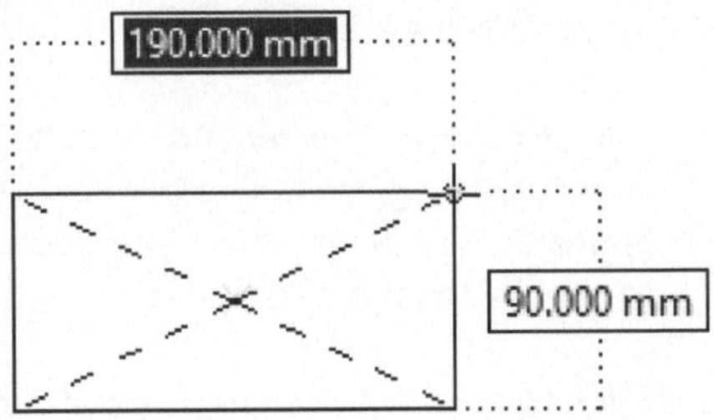

4. Click to specify a corner of the rectangle in the drawing area. You can also enter the length and width values of the rectangle in the Dimension Input. A rectangle is drawn by specifying a center point and a corner.

5. Press the ESC key to exit the tool or right-click in the drawing area and then click on the **OK** option in the Marking Menu to exit the **Two Point Center Rectangle** tool.

Creating a Rectangle by using the Three Point Center Rectangle Tool

The **Three Point Center Rectangle** tool is used for drawing a rectangle by specifying three points. The first point defines the center of the rectangle, the second point defines the width and orientation of the rectangle, and the third point defines the length of the rectangle, see Figure 2.92. The method for creating a rectangle by specifying three points is discussed below:

2.92

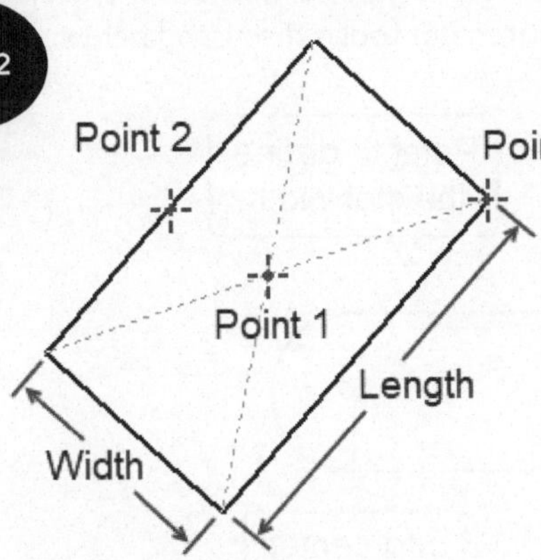

1. Invoke the **Rectangle** flyout and then click on the **Three Point Center Rectangle** tool. You are prompted to specify the center point of the rectangle.

2. Click to specify the center point (first point) of the rectangle in the drawing area. You can also enter coordinates (X, Y) in the Pointer Input for specifying the center point of the rectangle.

3. Move the cursor to a distance in the drawing area. An inference line appears attached to the cursor and you are prompted to specify the second point in the drawing area.

4. Click to specify the second point of the rectangle in the drawing area. The preview of a rectangle appears, (see Figure 2.93) and you are prompted to specify the third point.

5. Click to specify the third point of the rectangle in the drawing area. A rectangle is drawn by specifying three points.

2.93

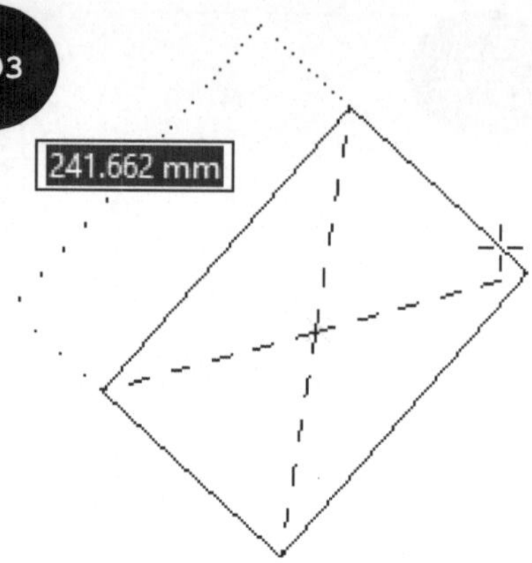

6. Press the ESC key to exit the tool or right-click in the drawing area and then click on the **OK** option in the Marking Menu to exit the **Three Point Center Rectangle** tool.

Creating a Slot

In Autodesk Inventor, you can draw straight and arc slots by using the slot tools in the **Rectangle** flyout, see Figure 2.94. The various tools for drawing slots are discussed next.

2.94

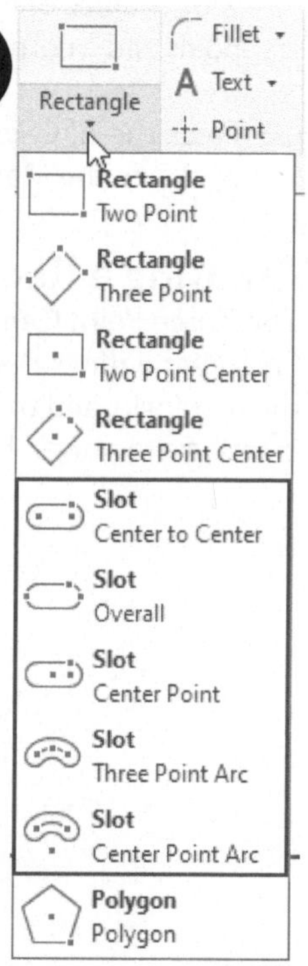

Creating a Slot by using the Center to Center Slot Tool

The **Center to Center Slot** tool is used for drawing a straight slot by specifying centers of both the slot arcs as start and end centers and a point to define the slot width, see Figure 2.95. The method for creating a slot by using the **Center to Center Slot** tool is discussed below:

2.95

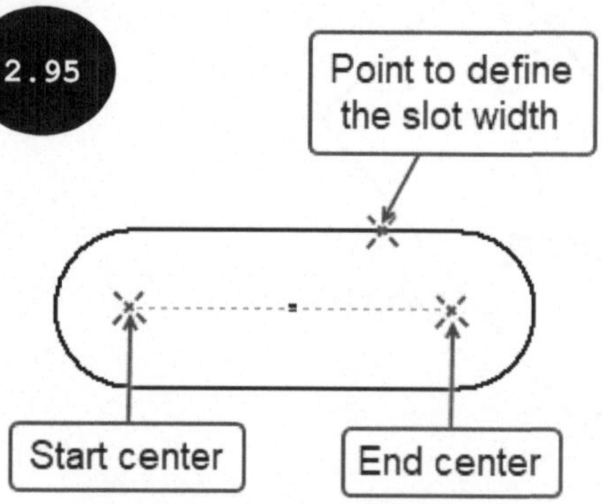

1. Invoke the **Rectangle** flyout and then click on the **Center to Center Slot** tool, see Figure 2.96. You are prompted to specify the start center of the slot.

2. Click to specify the start center point of the slot in the drawing area. You can also enter coordinates (X, Y) in the Pointer Input for specifying the start center of the slot.

3. Move the cursor to a distance in the drawing area. A straight rubber band line with its one end attached to the cursor appears. Also, you are prompted to specify the end center point of the slot.

4. Click to specify the end center point of the slot anywhere in the drawing area. You can also enter the distance and angle values in the Dimension Input for specifying the end center point of the slot.

5. Move the cursor to a distance in the drawing area. The preview of the slot appears, see Figure 2.97. Also, you are prompted to specify a point on the slot to define its width.

2.96

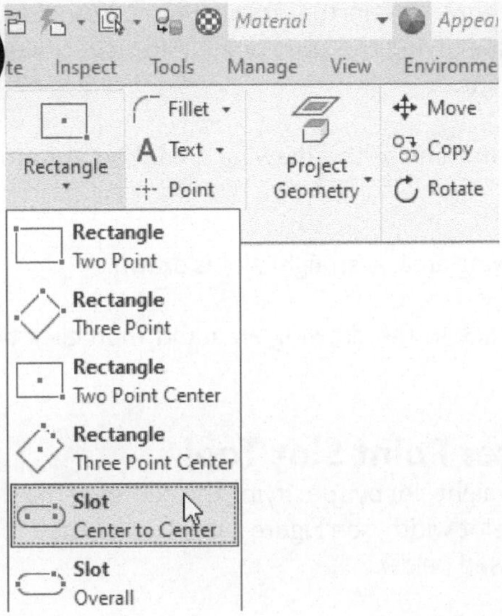

2.97

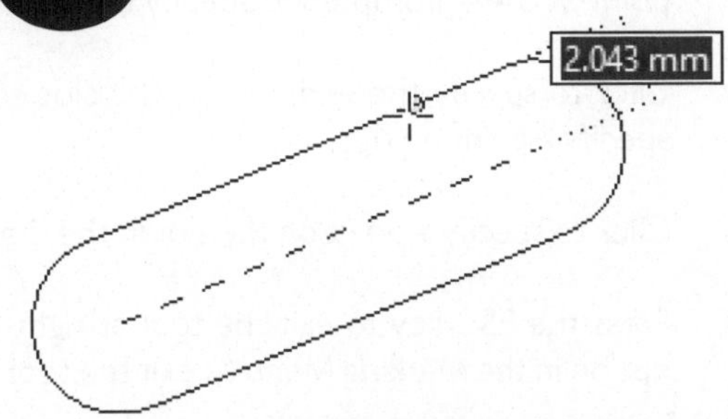

Tip: You can also specify the diameter or radius value of the slot arc. For doing so, when you are prompted to specify a point on the slot, right-click in the drawing area to display the Marking Menu. Next, click on the **Diameter** or **Radius** option in the Marking Menu to create a slot by specifying diameter or radius of the slot arc, respectively.

6. Click to specify a point on the slot in the drawing area. A straight slot is drawn by specifying centers of both the slot arcs and a point on the slot.

7. Press the ESC key to exit the tool or right-click in the drawing area and then click on the OK option in the Marking Menu to exit the tool.

Creating a Slot by using the Overall Slot Tool

The **Overall Slot** tool is used for drawing a straight slot by specifying start and end points of the slot center line, and a point on the slot to define the slot width, see Figure 2.98. The method for creating a slot by using the **Overall Slot** tool is discussed below:

2.98

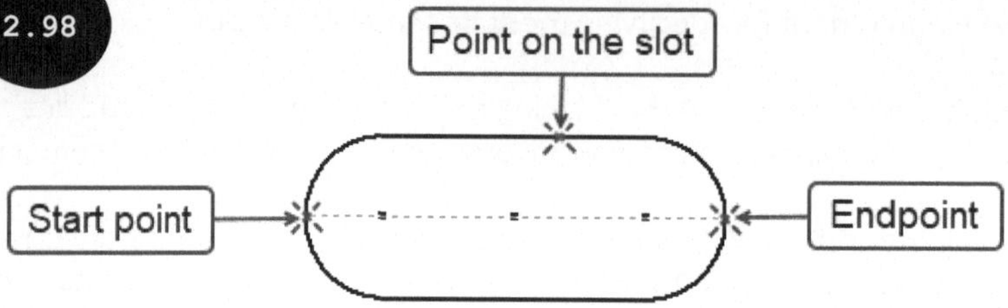

1. Invoke the **Rectangle** flyout and then click on the **Overall Slot** tool. You are prompted to specify the start point of the slot center line.

2. Click to specify the start point of the slot center line in the drawing area. You can also enter coordinates (X, Y) in the Pointer Input for specifying the start point. After specifying the start point, you are prompted to specify the endpoint.

3. Click to specify the endpoint of the slot center line in the drawing area. You are prompted to specify a point on the slot.

4. Click to specify a point on the slot in the drawing area. A straight slot is drawn.

5. Press the ESC key to exit the tool or right-click in the drawing area and then click on the **OK** option in the Marking Menu to exit the tool.

Creating a Slot by using the Center Point Slot Tool

The **Center Point Slot** tool is used for drawing a straight slot by specifying the center of the slot, center of a slot arc, and a point on the slot to define the slot width, see Figure 2.99. The method for creating a slot by using the **Center Point Slot** tool is discussed below:

2.99

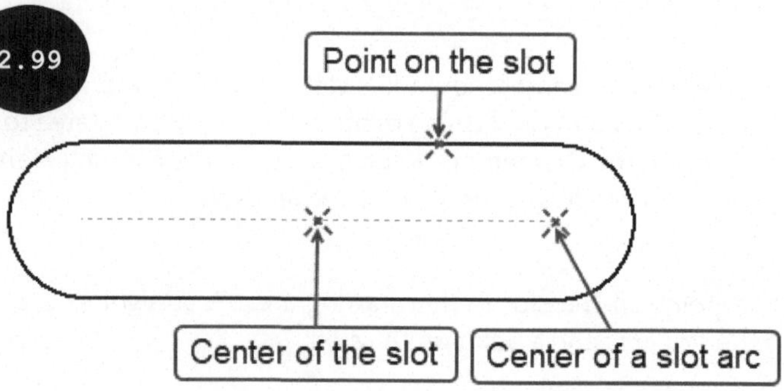

1. Invoke the **Rectangle** flyout and then click on the **Center Point Slot** tool. You are prompted to specify the center of the slot.

2. Click to specify a center point of the slot in the drawing area. You can also enter coordinates (X, Y) in the Pointer Input for specifying the center point. After specifying the center point, you are prompted to specify the second point as the center of a slot arc.

3. Click to specify the second point as the center of the slot arc in the drawing area. You are prompted to specify a point on the slot.

4. Click to specify a point on the slot in the drawing area. A center point slot is drawn.

5. Press the ESC key to exit the tool.

Creating a Slot by using the Three Point Arc Slot Tool

The **Three Point Arc Slot** tool is used for drawing an arc slot by specifying three points on the slot center arc, see Figure 2.100. The method for creating a slot by using the **Three Point Arc Slot** tool is discussed below:

1. Invoke the **Rectangle** flyout and then click on the **Three Point Arc Slot** tool. You are prompted to specify the start point of the center arc.

2. Click to specify the start point (first point) in the drawing area. You are prompted to specify the endpoint of the center arc.

3. Click to specify the endpoint (second point) in the drawing area. You are prompted to specify a point on the center arc.

4. Click to specify a point (third point) on the slot center arc in the drawing area. Next, move the cursor to a distance. The preview of an arc slot appears, see Figure 2.101. Also, you are prompted to specify a point on the slot to define its width.

2.100

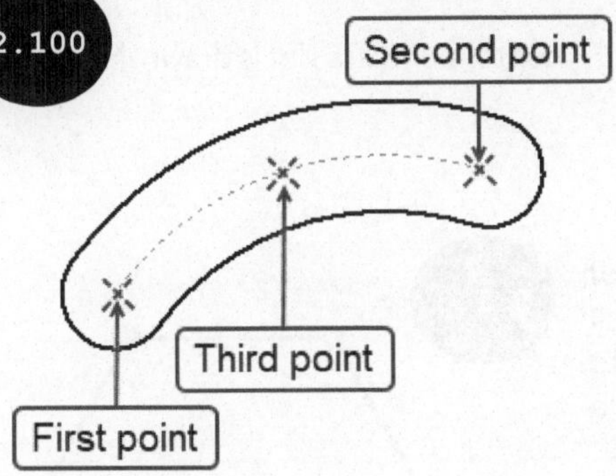

2.101

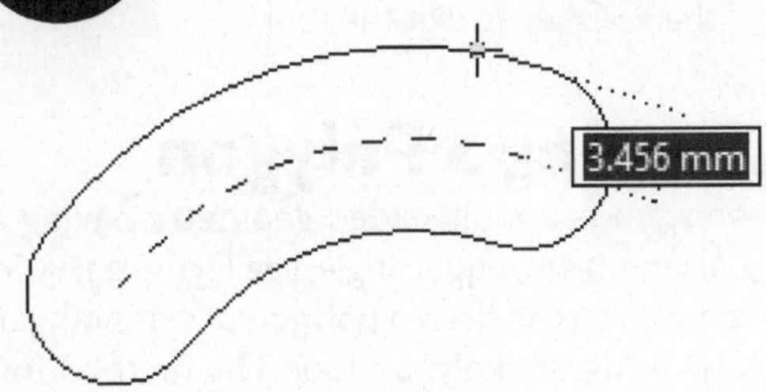

5. Click to specify a point on the slot in the drawing area. A three point arc slot is drawn.

6. Press the ESC key to exit the tool or right-click in the drawing area and then click on the **OK** option in the Marking Menu to exit the tool.

Creating a Slot by using the Center Point Arc Slot Tool

The **Center Point Arc Slot** tool is used for drawing an arc slot by specifying the center point, start point, and endpoint of the slot center arc, see Figure 2.102. The method for creating a slot by using the **Center Point Arc Slot** tool is discussed below:

2.102

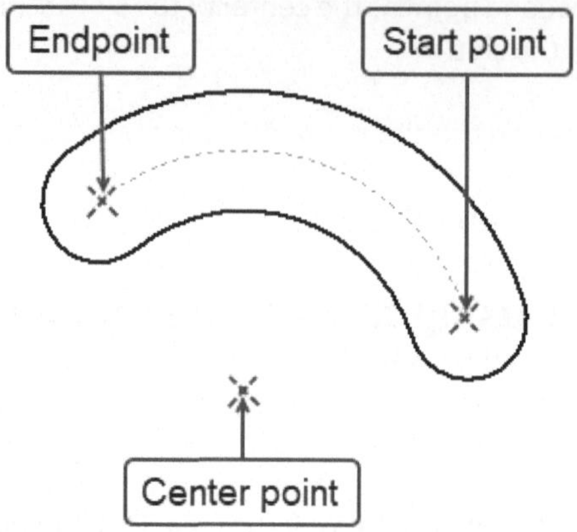

1. Invoke the **Rectangle** flyout and then click on the **Center Point Arc Slot** tool. You are prompted to specify the center point of the slot center arc.

2. Click to specify the center point of the slot center arc in the drawing area. You are prompted to specify the start point of the center arc.

3. Click to specify the start point of the center arc in the drawing area. You are prompted to specify the endpoint of the center arc.

4. Click to specify the endpoint of the center arc in the drawing area. You are prompted to specify a point on the slot to define the width of the slot.

5. Click to specify a point on the slot in the drawing area. A center point arc slot is drawn. Next, press the ESC key to exit the tool.

Creating a Polygon

A polygon is a multi-sided geometry having all sides of equal length and equal angle, see Figure 2.103. In Autodesk Inventor, you can draw a polygon of sides ranging from 3 to 120 by using the **Polygon** tool. The method for creating a polygon is discussed below:

2.103

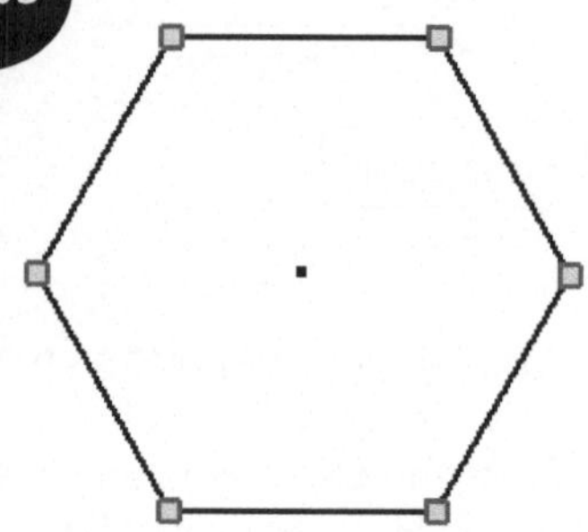

1. Invoke the **Rectangle** flyout and then click on the **Polygon** tool, see Figure 2.104. The **Polygon** dialog box appears, see Figure 2.105. Also, you are prompted to specify the center of the polygon. The options of the **Polygon** dialog box are discussed below:

2.104

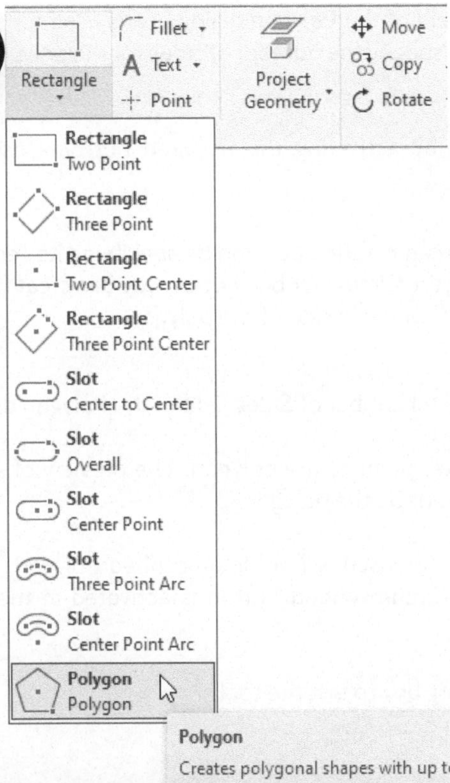

2.105

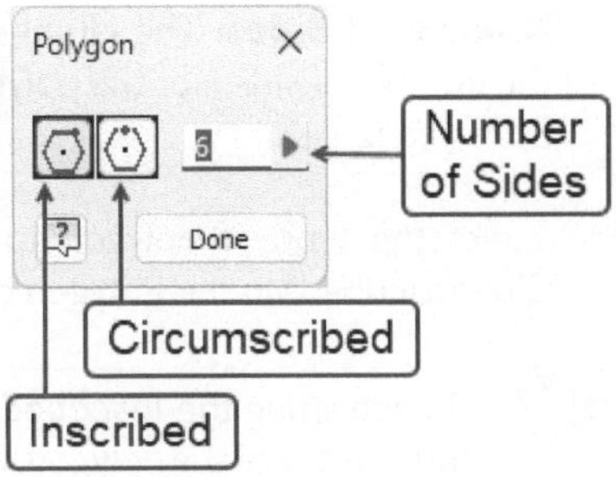

Inscribed: The **Inscribed** button of the **Polygon** dialog box is used for drawing a polygon which is created inside an imaginary circle such that the vertex between two edges of the polygon determines its size and orientation, see Figure 2.106. You can draw an inscribed polygon by specifying the center point, number of polygon sides, and a vertex of the polygon.

Circumscribed: The **Circumscribed** button is used for drawing a polygon which is created outside an imaginary circle such that the midpoint of an edge segment of the polygon determines its size and orientation, see Figure 2.107. You can draw a circumscribed polygon by specifying the center point, number of polygon sides, and the midpoint of any side of the polygon.

2.106

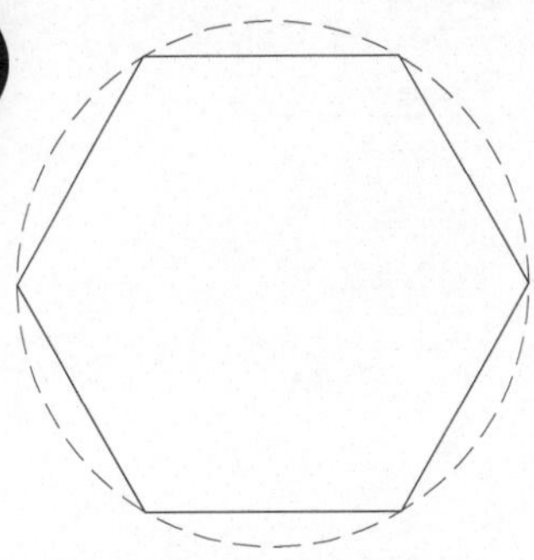

Inscribed Polygon

2.107

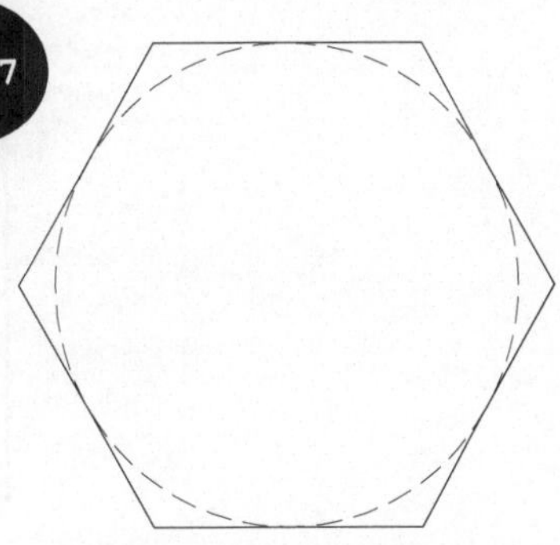

Circumscribed Polygon

Number of Sides: The **Number of Sides** field of the **Polygon** dialog box is used for specifying the number of sides for the polygon. You can specify the number of sides for the polygon ranging from 3 to 120.

2. Select the type of polygon to be created by activating the required button (**Inscribed** or **Circumscribed**) in the **Polygon** dialog box.

Tip: On activating the **Inscribed** button, you can create a polygon by specifying its center point and a vertex of the polygon. On activating the **Circumscribed** button, you can create a polygon by specifying its center point and the midpoint of a side of the polygon.

3. Enter the number of sides of the polygon in the **Number of Sides** field of the **Polygon** dialog box.
4. Click in the drawing area to specify the center point of the polygon. The preview of a polygon appears and you are prompted to specify a point on the polygon.
5. Click to specify a point in the drawing area. An inscribed or circumscribed polygon is created depending upon whether the **Inscribed** or **Circumscribed** button is activated in the **Polygon** dialog box.
6. Click on the **Done** button in the **Polygon** dialog box to exit the tool.

Creating a Spline

A Spline is defined as a curve having a high degree of smoothness and is used for creating free form features. You can draw a spline by specifying two or more than two control vertices or points in the drawing area. In Autodesk Inventor, you can also draw a spline by defining mathematical equations. The tools for drawing different types of splines are available in the **Line** flyout, see Figure 2.108. All these tools are discussed below:

2.108

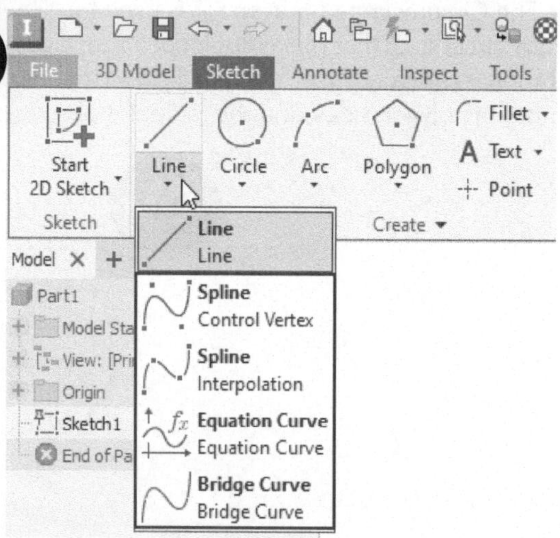

Creating a Spline by using the Control Vertex Spline Tool

The **Control Vertex Spline** tool is used for drawing a spline such that it passes near a set of control vertices that influence the shape of the spline, see Figure 2.109. The method for drawing a spline by using the **Control Vertex Spline** tool is discussed below:

2.109

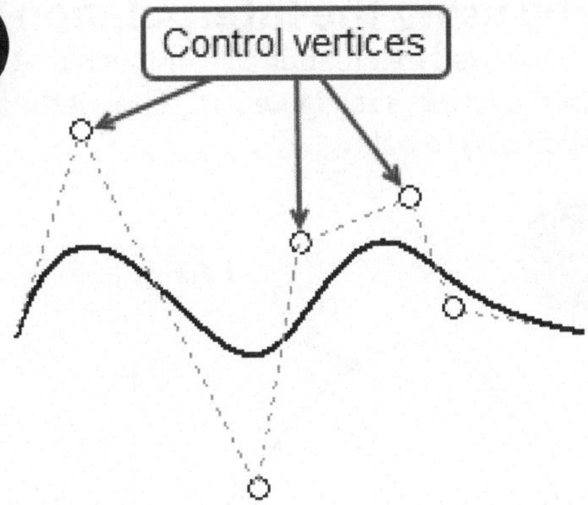

1. Click on the arrow below the **Line** tool in the **Create** panel and then click on the **Control Vertex Spline** tool in the flyout that appears, refer to Figure 2.108. The **Control Vertex Spline** tool gets activated and you are prompted to specify the first control vertex in the drawing area.

2. Click to specify the first control vertex in the drawing area. You are prompted to specify the next control vertex.

3. Click to specify the second control vertex in the drawing area. You are prompted to specify the next control vertex. Also, the preview of a spline appears such that it passes near the specified control points.

4. Similarly, continue specifying all the control vertices one after the other in the drawing area by clicking the left mouse button. Figure 2.110 shows the preview of a spline passing near the specified control vertices.

2.110

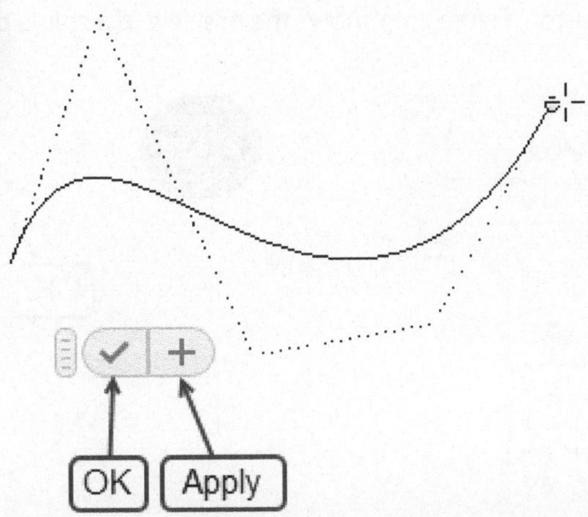

5. After specifying all the control vertices, click on the **OK** button that appears in the drawing area to finish the creation of spline and exit the tool, refer to Figure 2.110. Alternatively, click on the **Apply** button that appears in the drawing area to finish the creation of spline and continue with creating more splines.

Creating a Spline by using the Interpolation Spline Tool

The **Interpolation Spline** tool is used for creating a spline such that it passes through a set of fit points that influence the shape of the spline, see Figure 2.111. The method for drawing a spline by using the **Interpolation Spline** tool is discussed below:

2.111

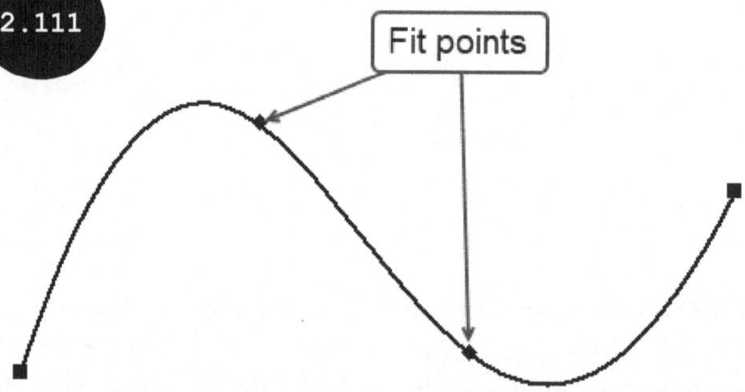

1. Click on the arrow below the **Line** tool in the **Create** panel and then click on the **Interpolation Spline** tool in the flyout that appears, see Figure 2.112. The **Interpolation Spline** tool gets activated and you are prompted to specify the first point in the drawing area.

2. Click to specify the first point in the drawing area for creating the spline. You are prompted to specify the next point.

3. Click to specify the second point in the drawing area. You are prompted to specify the next point. Also, a preview of the spline appears such that it passes through the specified fit points.

4. Similarly, continue to specify all the fit points one after the other in the drawing area by clicking the left mouse button. Figure 2.113 shows the preview of a spline passing through the specified fit points.

2.112

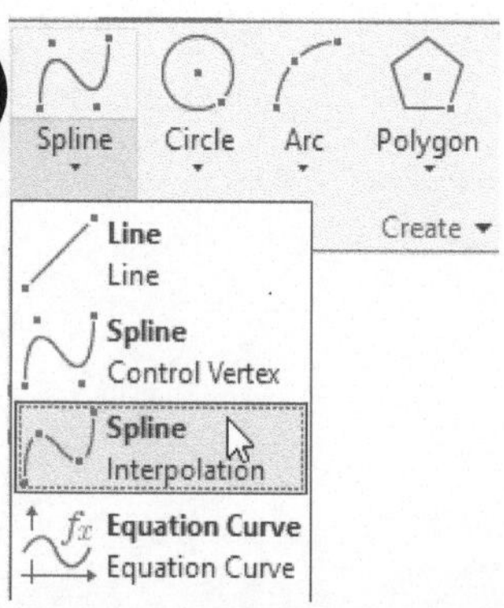

2.113

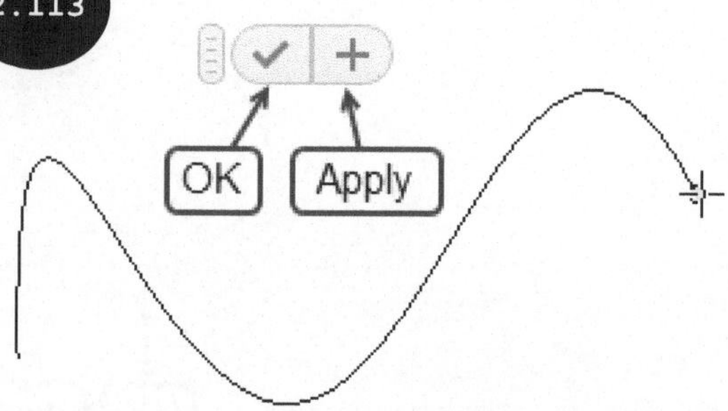

5. After specifying all the fit points, click on the **OK** button that appears in the drawing area to finish the creation of spline and exit the tool, refer to Figure 2.113. Alternatively, click on the **Apply** button that appears in the drawing area to finish the creation of spline and continue with creating more splines.

Creating an Equation Driven Spline

In Autodesk Inventor, you can also create an equation driven spline by using the **Equation Curve** tool. The method for drawing a spline by using the **Equation Curve** tool is discussed below:

1. Click on the arrow below the **Line** tool in the **Create** panel and then click on the **Equation Curve** tool in the flyout that appears. A Mini-Toolbar appears in the drawing area, see Figure 2.114.

2.114

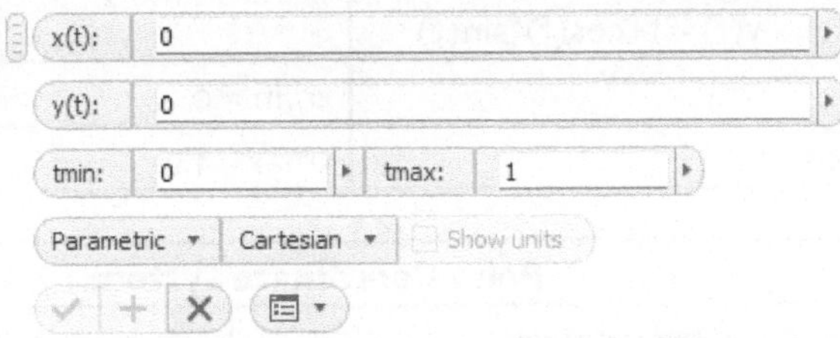

Parametric: By default, the **Parametric** option is selected in the Mini-Toolbar as the type of curve to be created. As a result, you can create a spline by defining two equations in the **x(t)** and **y(t)** or **r(t)** and **θ(t)** fields of the Mini-Toolbar, respectively. Note that the availability of fields "**x(t)** and **y(t)** or **r(t)** and **θ(t)**" depends upon the type of coordinate system (**Cartesian** or **Polar**) selected in the Mini-Toolbar for creating an equation driven spline.

When the **Cartesian** option is selected, the first **x(t)** equation calculates the X coordinates and the second **y(t)** equation calculates the Y coordinates of the control points as a function of 't'. When the **Polar** option is selected, the first **r(t)** equation calculates the r (radial distance) and the second **θ(t)** equation calculates the θ (angle from a fixed direction) of the control points as a function of 't'.

Explicit: On selecting the **Explicit** option in the Mini-Toolbar as the type of curve, you can create a spline by defining only one equation in the **y(x)** or **r(a)** field of the Mini-Toolbar. Note that the availability of fields "**y(x)** or **r(a)**" depends upon the type of coordinate system (**Cartesian** or **Polar**) selected in the Mini-Toolbar, respectively.

When the **Cartesian** option is selected, the **y(x)** equation calculates the Y coordinates of the control points as a function of 'x'. When the **Polar** option is selected, the **r(a)** equation calculates the r (radial distance) of the control points as a function of 'a'.

2. Select the type of curve (**Parametric** or **Explicit**) to be created in the Mini-Toolbar.

3. Select the type of coordinate system (**Cartesian** or **Polar**) in the Mini-Toolbar for creating a spline.

4. After selecting the type of curve and coordinate system, enter the equations for creating the spline in the respective fields of the Mini-Toolbar. Also, enter the minimum and maximum values of the function 't', 'x', or 'a' in the respective fields of the Mini-Toolbar depending on the type of curve and coordinate system selected, refer to the tables below:

Cartesian Coordinate System	
Parametric	**Explicit**
Enter equations for 'x' and 'y' as the functions of 't' in the x(t) and y(t) fields	Enter an equation for 'y' as a function of 'x' in the y(x) field
For example: x(t) = 80*sin(t)^2 y(t) = t+cos(t)*sin(t)	For example: y(x) = 20*sin(1rad*x/10)
tmin = 0	xmin = 0
tmax = 140	xmax = 140

Polar Coordinate System	
Parametric	**Explicit**
Enter equations for 'r' and 'θ' as the functions of 't' in the r(t) and θ(t) fields	Enter an equation for 'r' as a function of 'a' in the r(a) field
For example: r(t) = 80*sin(t)^2 θ(t) = t*50	For example: r(a) = 50*sin(5*a/10)
tmin = 0	amin = 0
tmax = 30	amax = 140

5. Click on the **OK** button in the Mini-Toolbar. An equation driven spline is created in the drawing area. Figure 2.115 shows a spline created by specifying **Parametric** as the curve type, **Cartesian** as the coordinate system, equations as **x(t) = 80*sin(t)^2** and **y(t) = t+cos(t)*sin(t)**, and minimum and maximum values of the function 't' as **tmin = 0**, and **tmax = 140**.

2.115

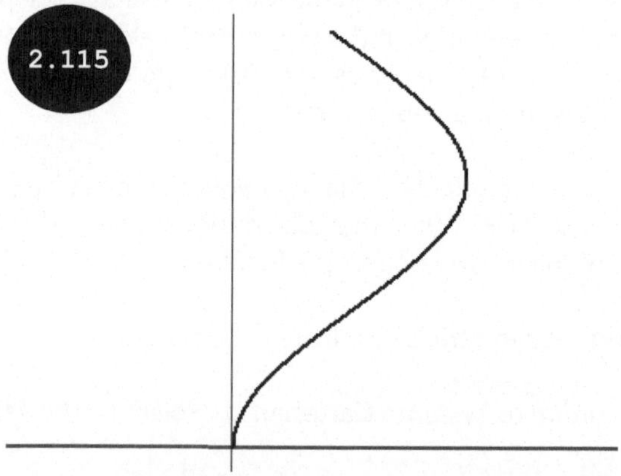

Creating a Bridge Curve

A bridge curve is a smooth (G2) continuous curve. You can create a bridge curve between two existing lines, arcs, splines, or projected curves by using the **Bridge Curve** tool. The method for creating a bridge curve between two existing curves is discussed below:

1. Click on the arrow below the **Line** tool in the **Create** panel and then click on the **Bridge Curve** tool in the flyout that appears. The **Bridge Curve** tool gets activated and you are prompted to select the first curve.

2. Click to select the first curve in the drawing area, see Figure 2.116. You can select a line, an arc, a spline, or a projected curve as the first curve. You are prompted to select the second curve.

3. Click to select the second curve in the drawing area, see Figure 2.116. You can select a line, an arc, a spline, or a projected curve as the second curve. A bridge curve is created between the selected curves, see Figure 2.116.

2.116

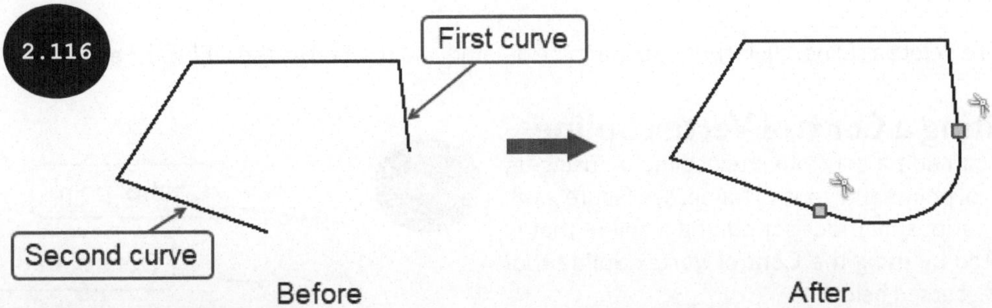

Editing a Spline

Editing a spline is important in order to achieve its complex shape and maintain a high degree of smoothness and curvature. You can edit an interpolation spline and a control vertex spline created by using the **Interpolation Spline** tool and **Control Vertex Spline** tool, respectively. The methods for editing both these splines are discussed below:

Editing an Interpolation Spline

You can edit an interpolation spline by using its fit points and tangent handle. For doing so, click on a fit point of an interpolation spline in the drawing area. The selected fit point gets highlighted and the tangent handles appear at each fit point of the spline in light gray color, see Figure 2.117. The various methods for editing a spline created by using the **Interpolation Spline** tool are discussed below:

2.117

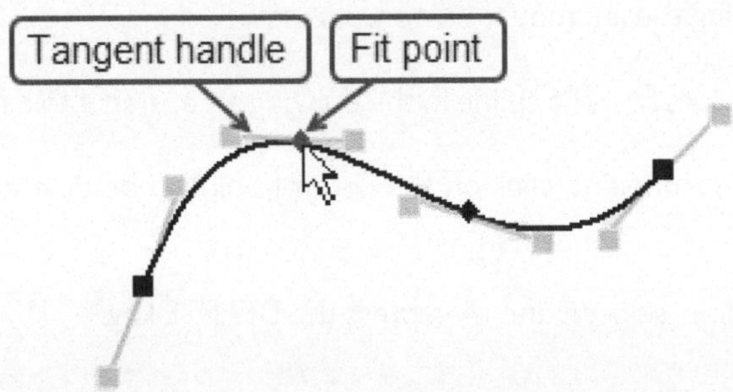

- To change the location of a fit point, press and hold the left mouse button on the fit point to be edited and then drag it to the required location in the drawing area.
- To edit the tangency or to resize the spline, drag the endpoints of the tangent handle.
- To edit the shape of the spline, right-click on a tangent handle and then click on the **Activate Handle** option in the Marking Menu that appears. Next, drag the tangent handle to change the shape of the spline.
- To add an additional fit point in a spline, right-click on the spline and then click on the **Insert Point** option in the Marking Menu that appears. Next, click on the spline at the required location to add a new fit point. A fit point gets added at the specified location on the spline. Similarly, you can also add multiple fit points one by one.
- To delete an existing fit point of a spline, select the fit point to be deleted and then press the DELETE key.
- To delete a spline, click on the spline to be deleted and then press the DELETE key.

Editing a Control Vertex Spline

You can edit a control vertex spline by using its control points and control frame, see Figure 2.118. The various methods for editing a spline that is created by using the **Control Vertex Spline** tool are discussed below:

2.118

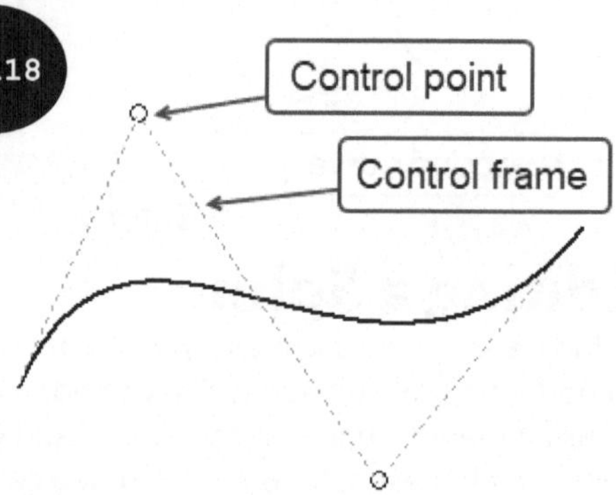

- To change the location of a control point, press and hold the left mouse button on the control point to be edited and then drag it to the required location in the drawing area.
- To change the shape of the spline, drag the control frame.
- To resize the shape of the spline, drag the endpoints of the spline.
- To add an additional control point, right-click on the spline and then click on the **Insert Vertex** option in the Marking Menu that appears. Next, click on the control frame of the spline. A control point gets added on the selected frame of the spline. You can add multiple control points on a frame by clicking the left mouse button.
- To change the location of a spline in the drawing area, drag it to a new location.
- To delete a control point, click on the control point to be deleted and then press the DELETE key.
- To delete a spline, select it and then press the DELETE key.

Tip: You can also convert an interpolation spline into a control vertex spline or vice-versa. For doing so, right-click on an interpolation spline and then click on the **Convert to CV Spline** option in the Marking Menu that appears. The selected interpolation spline gets converted to control vertex spline. Similarly, you can convert a control vertex spline into an interpolation spline by clicking on the **Convert to Interpolation** option in the Marking Menu.

Tutorial 3

Draw the sketch of the model shown in Figure 2.119. The dimensions and the 3D model shown in the figure are for your reference only. All dimensions are in mm. You will learn about applying dimensions and creating the 3D model in later chapters.

2.119

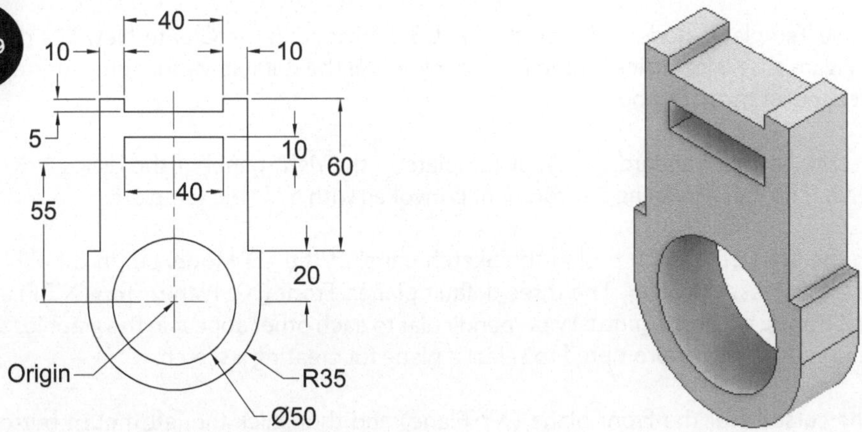

Section 1: Starting Autodesk Inventor

1. Start Autodesk Inventor by double-clicking on the Autodesk Inventor icon on your desktop. The startup user interface of Autodesk Inventor appears.

Section 2: Invoking the Sketching Environment

1. Click on the **New** tool in the left panel of the startup user interface (see Figure 2.120) or press the CTRL + N keys. The **Create New File** dialog box appears, see Figure 2.121.

2.120

2.121

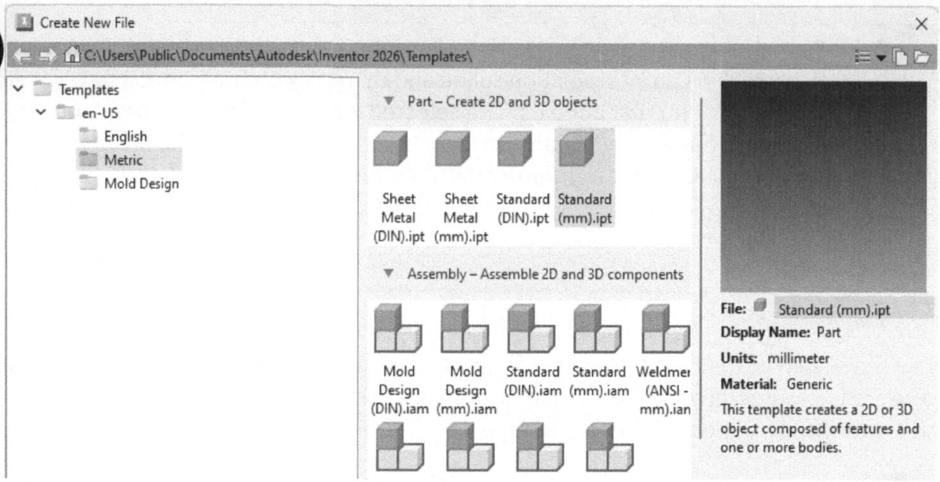

2. Expand the **Templates** node and then the **en-US** sub-node in the **Create New File** dialog box, refer to Figure 2.121. Next, click on the **Metric** folder. All the default Metric templates appear on the right panel of the dialog box.

3. Double-click on the **Standard (mm).ipt** template in the right panel of the dialog box, refer to Figure 2.121. The Part Modeling environment is invoked with a Metric template.

4. Click on the **Start 2D Sketch** tool in the **Sketch** panel of the **3D Model** tab in the **Ribbon**, see Figure 2.122 or press the S key. The three default planes: Front (XY Plane), Top (XZ Plane), and Right (YZ Plane), which are mutually perpendicular to each other appear in the graphics area, see Figure 2.123. Also, you are prompted to select a plane for creating a sketch.

5. Move the cursor over the Front plane (XY Plane) and then click the left mouse button when the plane gets highlighted in the graphics area, see Figure 2.123. The Sketching environment is invoked and the Front plane is oriented normal to the viewing direction.

2.122

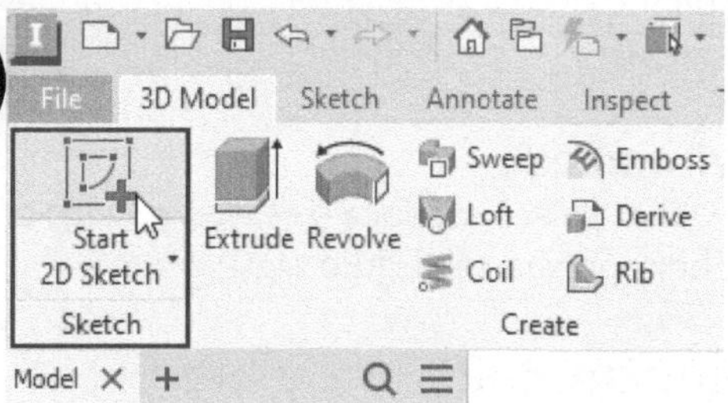

2.123

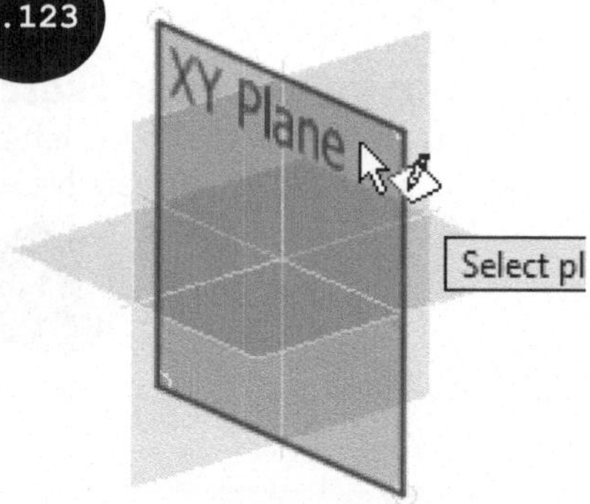

Note: It is evident from Figure 2.119 that all the sketch entities of this tutorial are multiples of 5 mm. Therefore, you can set the snap settings such that the cursor snaps to an increment of 5 mm.

Section 3: Specifying Grids and Snap Settings

1. Click on the **Tools** tab in the **Ribbon** and then click on the **Document Settings** tool in the **Options** panel, see Figure 2.124. The **Document Settings** dialog box appears.

2.124

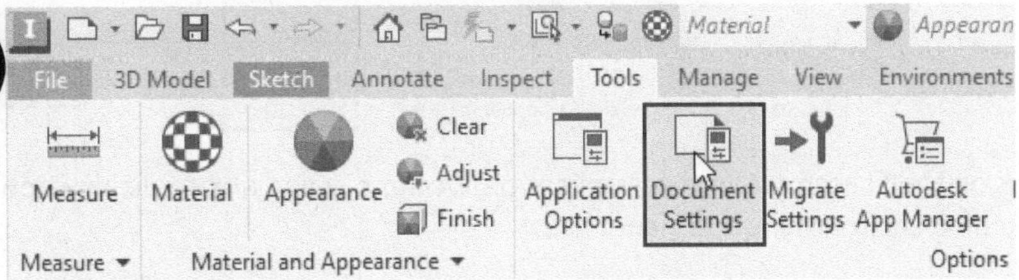

Now, you need to specify the grids and snap settings such that the cursor snaps to an increment of 5 mm.

2. Click on the **Sketch** tab in the **Document Settings** dialog box, see Figure 2.125. Next, specify **5 mm** in the **X** and **Y** fields of the **Snap Spacing** area in the dialog box to snap the cursor to an incremental distance of 5 mm in X and Y directions, see Figure 2.125.

3. Enter **1** in the **snaps per minor** field of the **Grid Display** area in the dialog box as the number of snap points between each grid, see Figure 2.125.

4. Enter **5** in the **Major every minor lines** field in the **Grid Display** area as the number of minor lines between two major grid lines, see Figure 2.125.

2.125

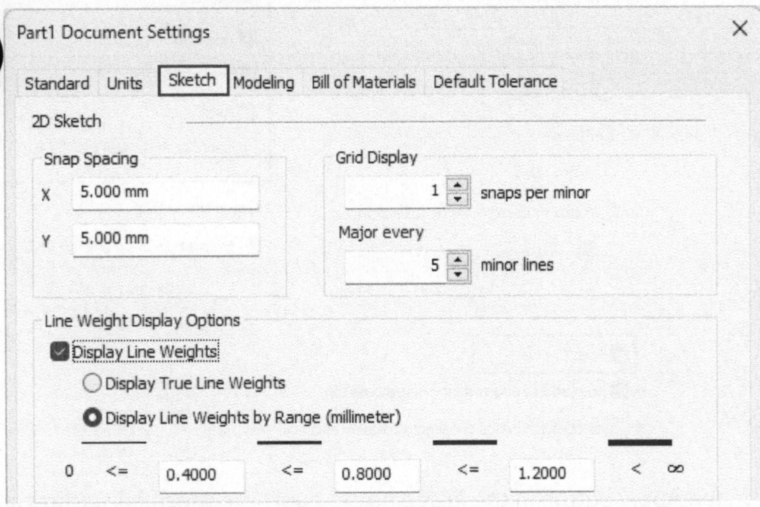

5. Click on the **Apply** button in the dialog box to apply the specified settings and then click on the **Close** button to exit the dialog box.

After specifying the grids and snap settings, you need to turn on the display of grids in the drawing area and activate the snap mode.

6. Click on the **Application Options** tool in the **Options** panel of the **Tools** tab, see Figure 2.126. The **Application Options** dialog box appears.

2.126

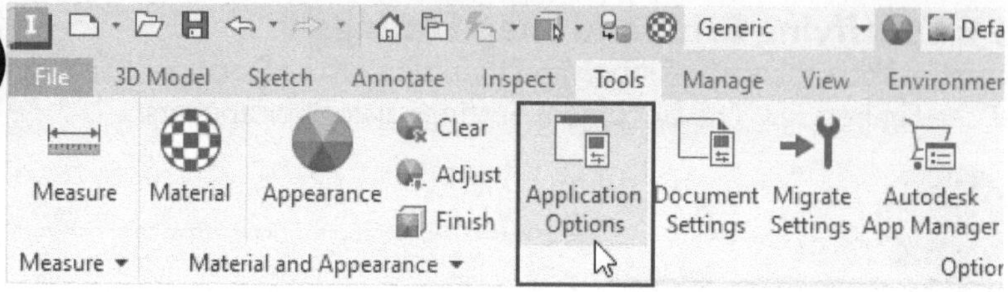

7. Click on the **Sketch** tab in the **Application Options** dialog box to display options related to the Sketching environment, see Figure 2.127.

8. Select the **Grid lines**, **Minor grid lines**, and **Axes** check boxes in the **Display** area of the dialog box to turn on the display of grid lines, minor grid lines, and axes in the drawing area, see Figure 2.127.

   Now, you need to activate the snap mode.

9. Select the **Snap to grid** check box in the **Sketch** tab of the dialog box to activate the snap mode, see Figure 2.127.

2.127

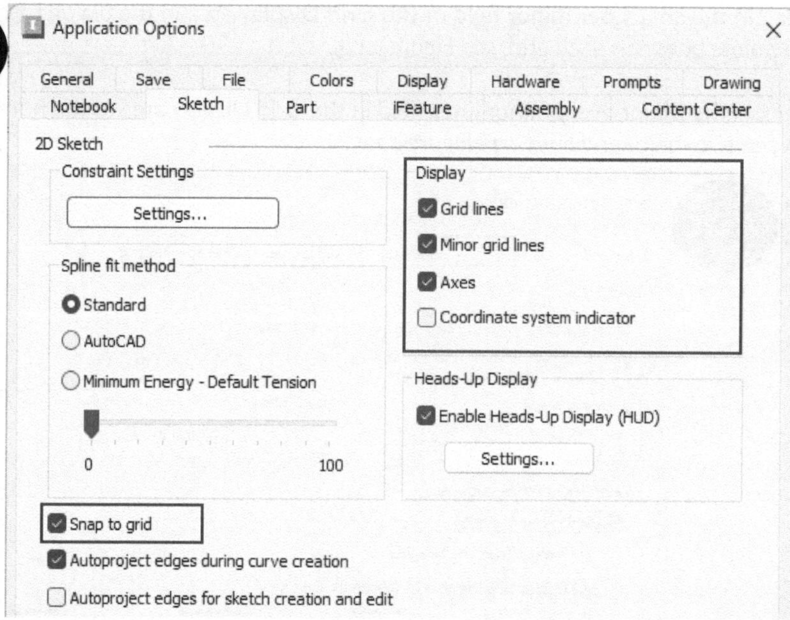

10. Click on the **Apply** button in the dialog box to apply the specified settings and then click on the **Close** button to exit the dialog box. The grids appear in the drawing area as per the specified settings, see Figure 2.128.

2.128

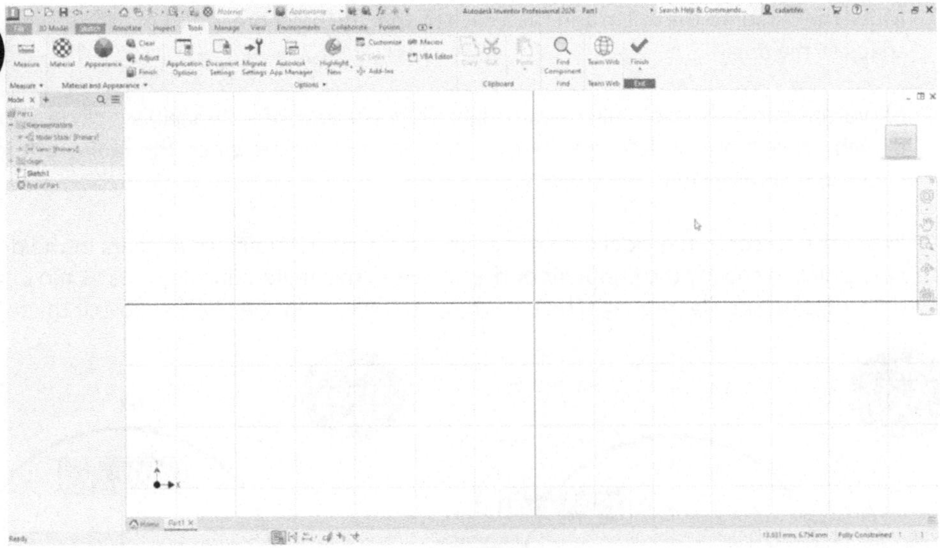

Section 4: Drawing the Sketch

2.129

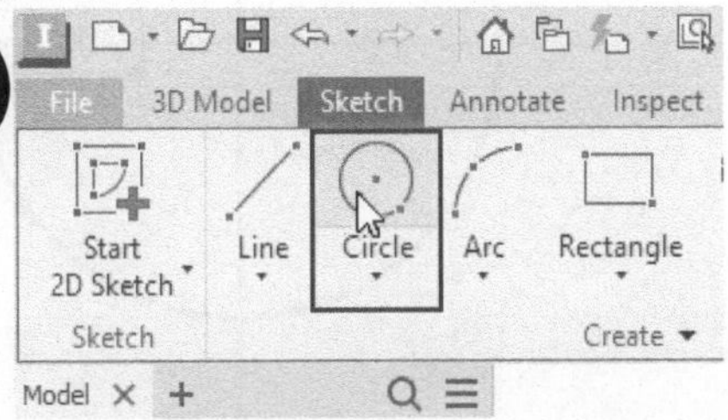

1. Click on the **Sketch** tab in the **Ribbon** and then click on the **Center Point Circle** tool, see Figure 2.129. The **Center Point Circle** tool gets activated and you are prompted to specify the center point of the circle.

2. Move the cursor to the origin and click to specify the center point of the circle when the cursor snaps to the origin.

3. Move the cursor horizontally toward right and then click to specify a point when the diameter of the circle appears as 50 mm, see Figure 2.130. A circle of diameter 50 mm is drawn. Next, press the **ESC** key to exit the **Center Point Circle** tool.

4. Invoke the **Arc** flyout and then click on the **Center Point Arc** tool (see Figure 2.131) or press the A key. You are prompted to specify the center point of the arc.

2.130

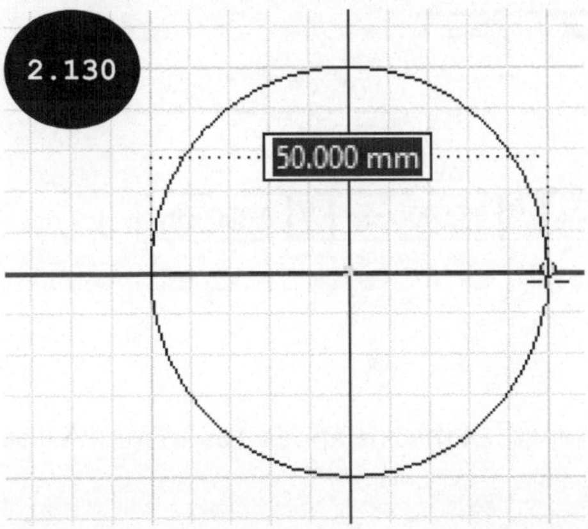

2.131

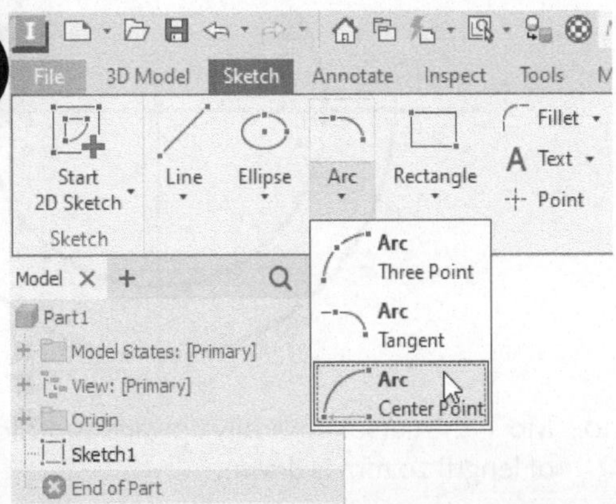

5. Move the cursor to the origin and then click to specify the center point of the arc when the cursor snaps to the origin.

6. Move the cursor horizontally toward right. The preview of an imaginary circle appears in the drawing area. Next, click to specify the start point of the arc when the radius of the imaginary circle appears as 35 mm, see Figure 2.132.

7. Move the cursor in the clockwise direction. The preview of an arc appears in the drawing area. Next, click to specify the endpoint of the arc when the angle value appears as 180 degrees in the drawing area, see Figure 2.133. The arc is drawn. Next, press the ESC key to exit the tool.

2.132

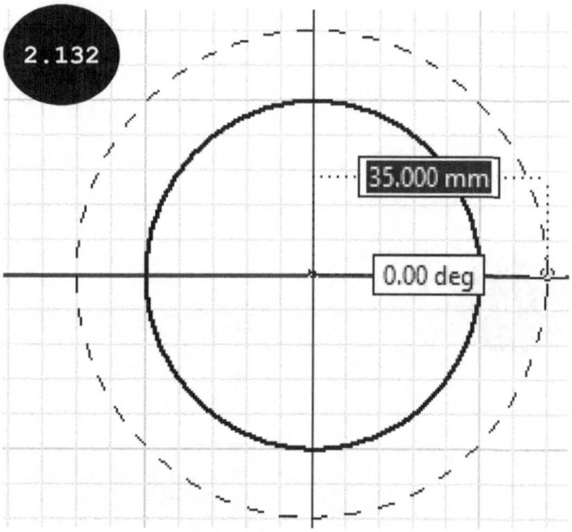

2.133

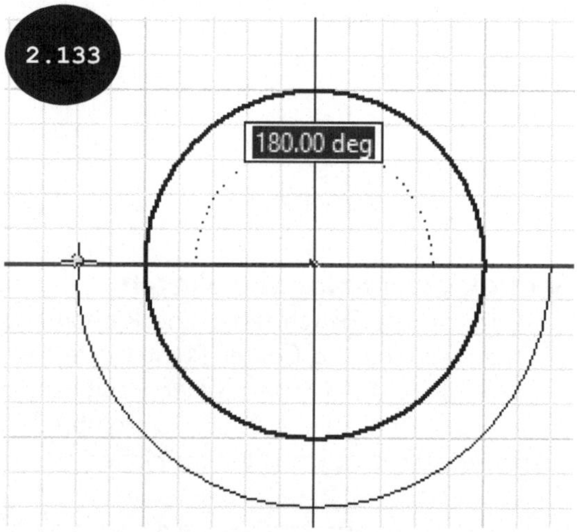

8. Click on the **Line** tool in the **Create** panel of the **Sketch** tab or press the **L** key. The **Line** tool gets activated and you are prompted to specify the start point of the line.

9. Move the cursor to the start point of the previously drawn arc and then click the left mouse button when the cursor snaps to it, see Figure 2.134.

2.134

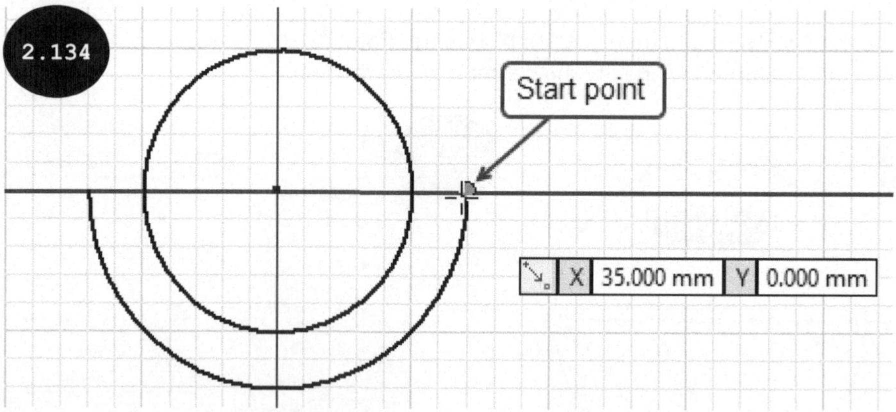

10. Move the cursor vertically upward and click when the length of the line appears as 20 mm. A line of length 20 mm is drawn.

11. Move the cursor horizontally toward left and click when the length of the line appears as 5 mm.
12. Move the cursor vertically upward and click when the length of the line appears as 60 mm, see Figure 2.135.
13. Move the cursor horizontally toward left and click when the length of the line appears as 10 mm.
14. Move the cursor vertically downward and click when the length of the line appears as 5 mm.
15. Move the cursor horizontally toward left and click when the length of the line appears as 40 mm.
16. Move the cursor vertically upward and click when the length of the line appears as 5 mm.
17. Move the cursor horizontally toward left and click when the length of the line appears as 10 mm.
18. Move the cursor vertically downward and click when the length of the line appears as 60 mm.
19. Move the cursor horizontally toward left and click when the length of the line appears as 5 mm.
20. Move the cursor vertically downward and click when the cursor snaps to the endpoint of the arc. The sketch appears similar to the one shown in Figure 2.136. Next, press the **ESC** key to exit the **Line** tool.

2.135

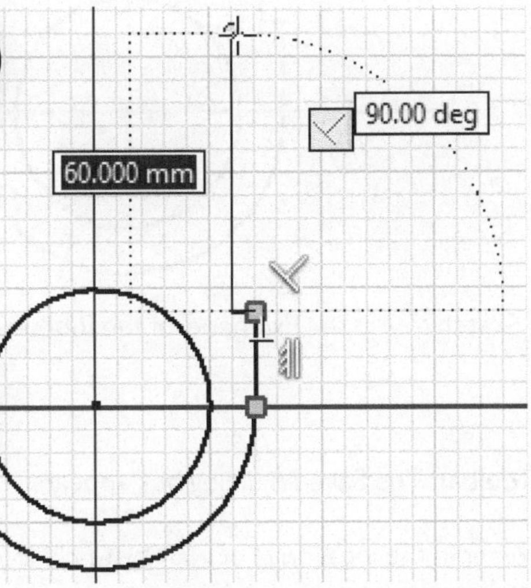

2.136

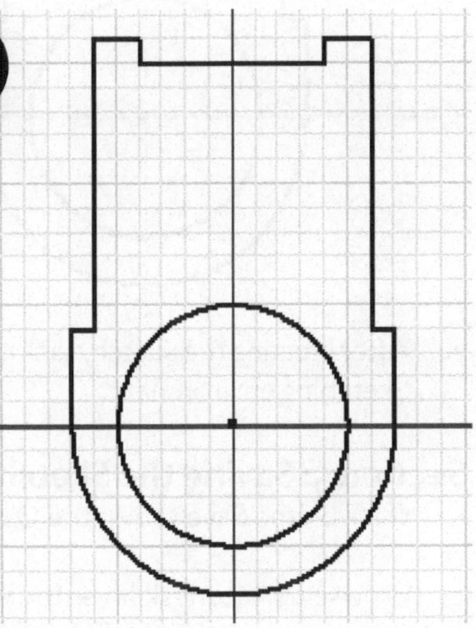

21. Click on the **Two Point Rectangle** tool in the **Create** panel of the **Sketch** tab, see Figure 2.137. You are prompted to specify the first corner of the rectangle in the drawing area.

2.137

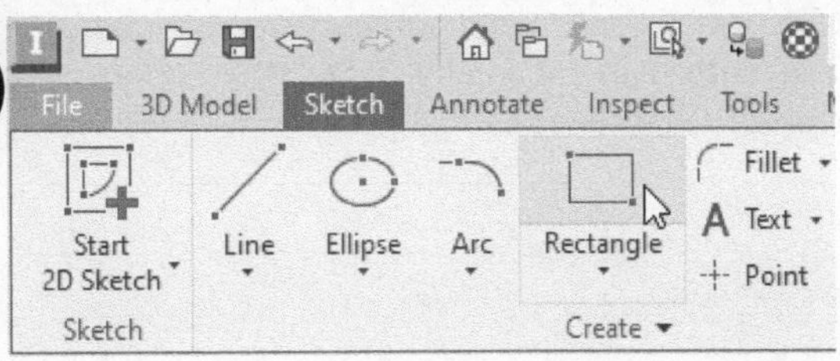

22. Press the TAB key to activate the Pointer Input and then enter **-20** as the X coordinate in the X box. Again, press the TAB key and then enter **65** as the Y coordinate. Next, press the ENTER key. The first corner of the rectangle is specified in the drawing area and you are prompted to specify the second corner of the rectangle.

Tip: As Autodesk Inventor is a parametric 3D modeling software, you can draw a sketch by specifying points arbitrarily in the drawing area. Once the sketch has been drawn, you need to apply dimensions to drive the entities of the sketch. You will learn about dimensioning sketch entities in later chapters.

23. Move the cursor toward the right and click to specify the second corner of the rectangle when the length 40 mm and width 10 mm appear in the Dimension Input, see Figure 2.138. Next, press the **ESC** key to exit the tool. Figure 2.139 shows the final sketch of Tutorial 3.

2.138

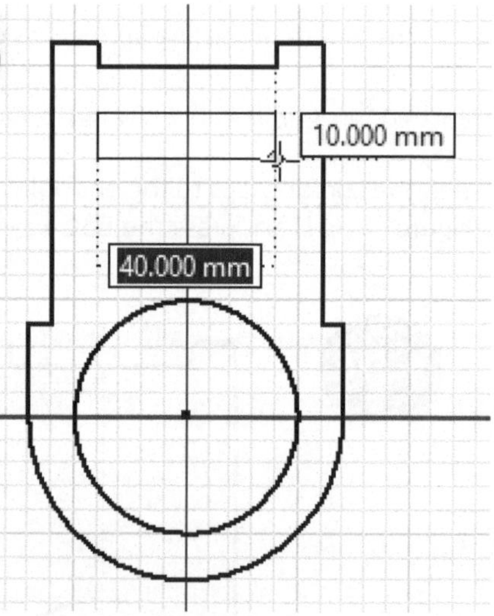

2.139

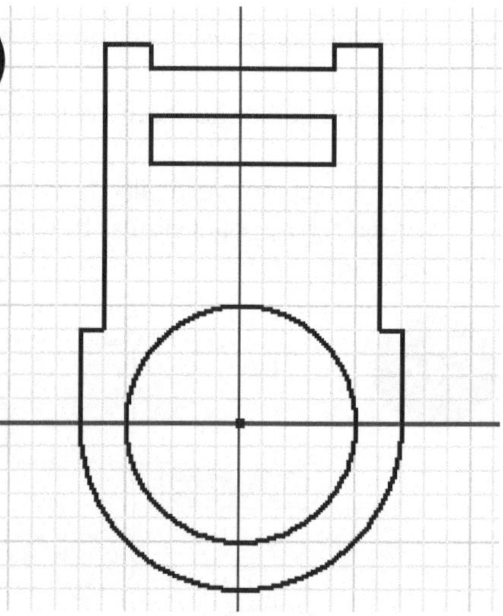

24. After creating the sketch, click on the **Finish Sketch** tool in the **Exit** panel of the **Ribbon** to exit the Sketching environment.

Section 5: Saving the Sketch

1. Click on the **Save** tool in the **Quick Access Toolbar**. The **Save As** dialog box appears.

2. Browse to **Autodesk Inventor > Chapter 2** folder in the local drive of your system. Note that you need to create these folders, if not created earlier.

3. Enter **Tutorial 3** in the **File name** field of the dialog box.

4. Click on the **Save** button in the dialog box. The sketch is saved in the specified location (>:\Autodesk Inventor\Chapter 2).

Tutorial 4

Draw a sketch of the model shown in Figure 2.140. The dimensions and the model shown in the figure are for your reference only. All dimensions are in mm. You will learn about applying dimensions and creating the 3D model in later chapters.

2.140

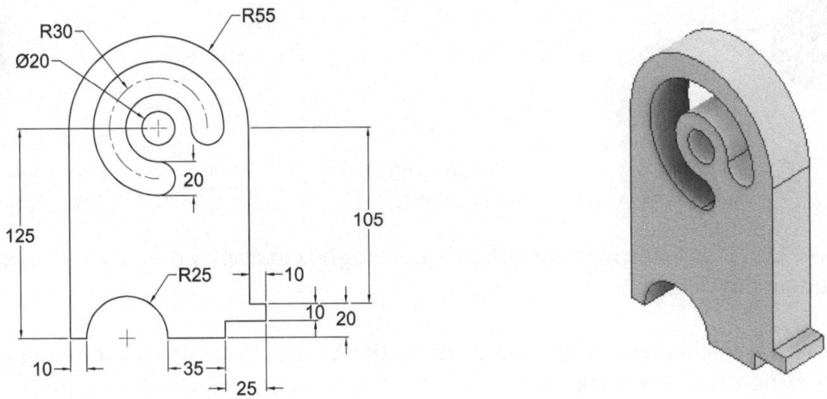

Section 1: Starting Autodesk Inventor

1. Start Autodesk Inventor by double-clicking on the Autodesk Inventor icon on your desktop. The startup user interface of Autodesk Inventor appears.

Section 2: Invoking the Sketching Environment

1. Click on the arrow next to the **New** tool in the left panel of the startup user interface and then click on the **Part** option in the drop-down menu that appears, see Figure 2.141. The Part modeling environment is invoked with the default template.

2.141

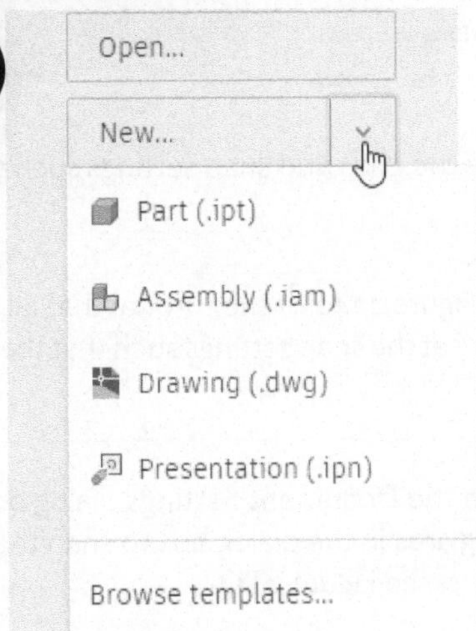

2. Invoke the Sketching environment by selecting the Front (XY) plane as the sketching plane using the **Start 2D Sketch** tool.

Section 3: Specifying Units, Grids, and Snap Settings

Now, you need to specify the units, grids, and snap settings in the Sketching environment.

1. Click on the **Tools** tab in the **Ribbon** and then click on the **Document Settings** tool in the **Options** panel, see Figure 2.142. The **Document Settings** dialog box appears.

2.142

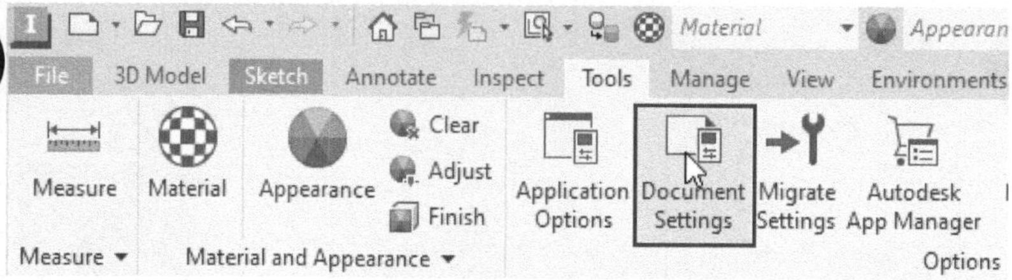

2. Click on the **Units** tab in the **Document Settings** dialog box to display the options for setting units for the current drawing.

3. Ensure that the **millimeter** option is selected in the **Length** drop-down list as the unit of the current drawing, see Figure 2.143.

2.143

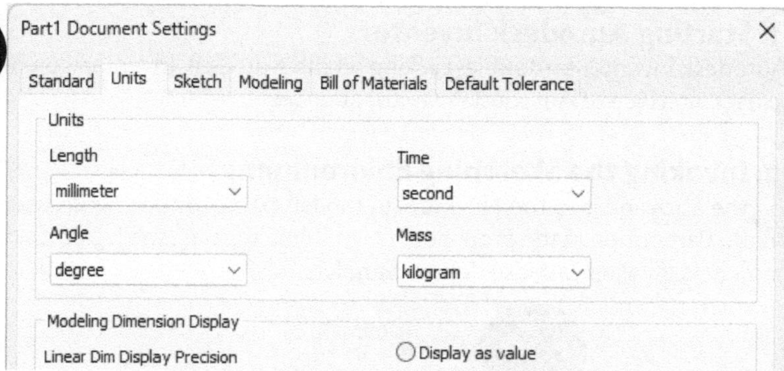

Now, you need to specify the grids and snap settings such that the cursor snaps to an increment of 5 mm.

Note: It is evident from Figure 2.140 of the tutorial that all the sketch entities are multiples of 5. Therefore, you can set the snap settings such that the cursor snaps to an increment of 5 mm only.

4. Click on the **Sketch** tab in the **Document Settings** dialog box. Next, specify **5 mm** in the **X** and **Y** fields of the **Snap Spacing** area in the dialog box to snap the cursor to an incremental distance of 5 mm in X and Y directions, see Figure 2.144.

5. Enter **1** in the **snaps per minor** field of the **Grid Display** area in the dialog box as the number of snap points between each grid, see Figure 2.144.

6. Enter **5** in the **Major every minor lines** field in the **Grid Display** area as the number of minor lines between two major grid lines, see Figure 2.144.

2.144

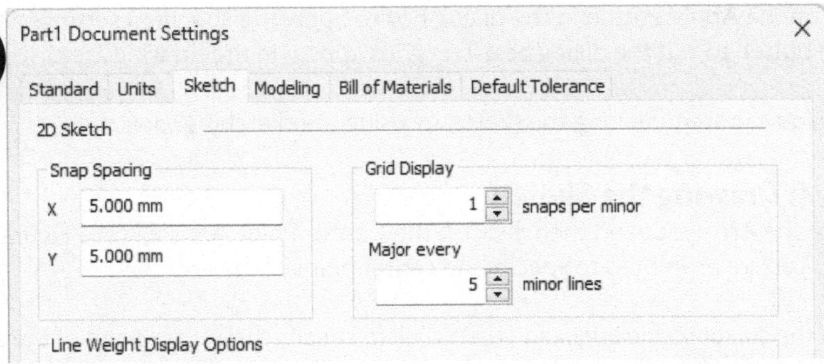

7. Click on the **Apply** button in the dialog box to apply the specified settings and then click on the **Close** button to exit the dialog box.

   After specifying the grids and snap settings, you need to turn on the display of grids in the drawing area and activate the snap mode.

8. Click on the **Application Options** tool in the **Options** panel of the **Tools** tab, see Figure 2.145. The **Application Options** dialog box appears.

9. Click on the **Sketch** tab in the **Application Options** dialog box, see Figure 2.146.

2.145

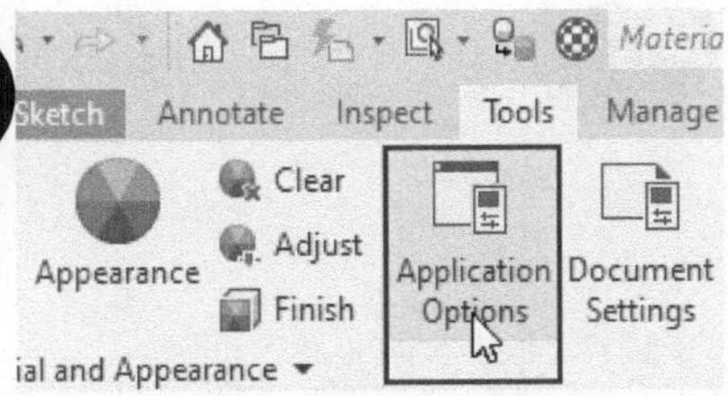

10. Select the **Grid lines, Minor grid lines**, and **Axes** check boxes in the **Display** area of the dialog box, see Figure 2.146.

11. Select the **Snap to grid** check box in the dialog box to activate the snap mode, see Figure 2.146.

2.146

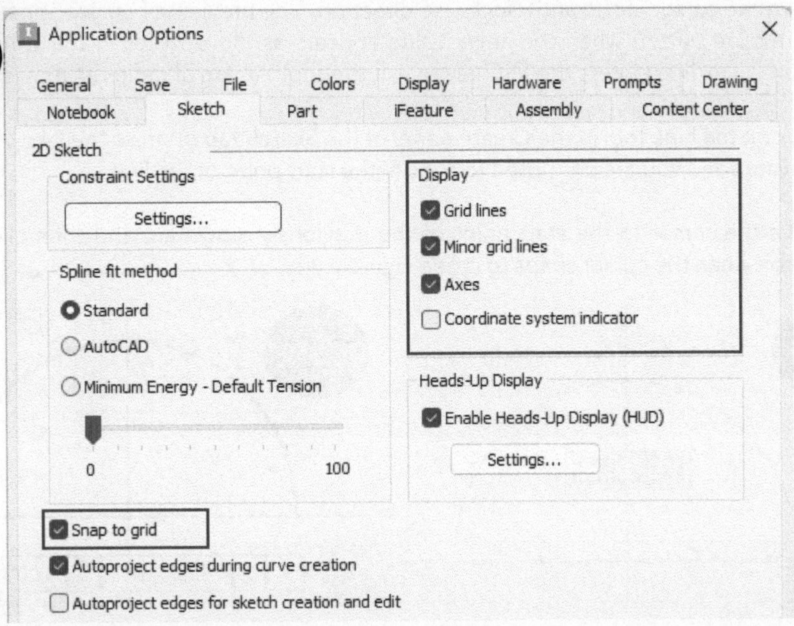

12. Click on the **Apply** button in the dialog box to apply the specified settings and then click on the **Close** button to exit the dialog box. The grids appear in the drawing area.

    Now, you can start creating the sketch by using the sketching tools.

Section 4: Drawing the Sketch

1. Invoke the **Arc** flyout and then click on the **Center Point Arc** tool (see Figure 2.147), or press the A key. You are prompted to specify the center point of the arc.

2. Move the cursor to the origin and then click to specify the center point of the arc when the cursor snaps to the origin.

3. Move the cursor horizontally toward right. The preview of an imaginary circle appears in the drawing area. Next, click to specify the start point of the arc when the radius of the imaginary circle appears as 25 mm in the Dimension Input, see Figure 2.148.

2.147

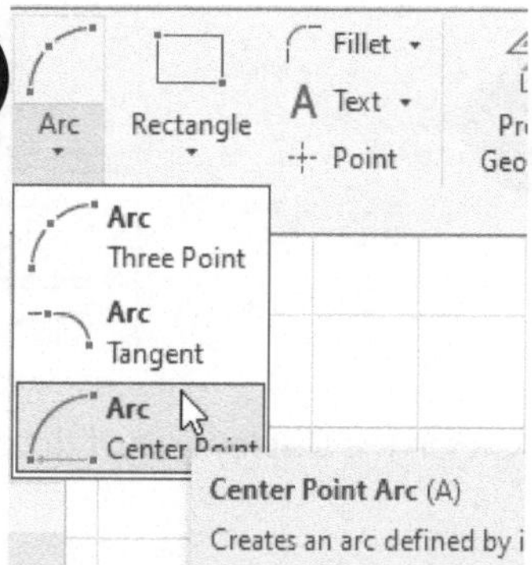

2.148

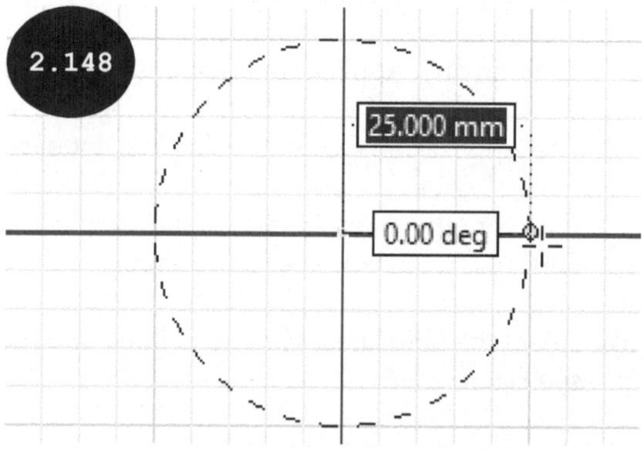

4. Move the cursor in the anti-clockwise direction. The preview of an arc appears. Next, click the left mouse button when the angle value appears as 180 degrees in the Dimension Input, see Figure 2.149. Next, press the ESC key to exit the tool. An arc of radius 25 mm is drawn.

5. Click on the **Line** tool in the **Create** panel of the **Sketch** tab or press the **L** key. The **Line** tool gets activated and you are prompted to specify the start point of the line.

6. Move the cursor to the start point of the previously drawn arc and then click the left mouse button when the cursor snaps to it, see Figure 2.150.

2.149

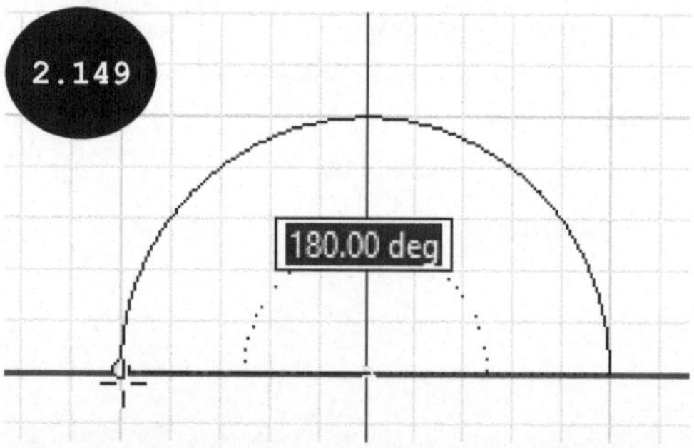

2.150

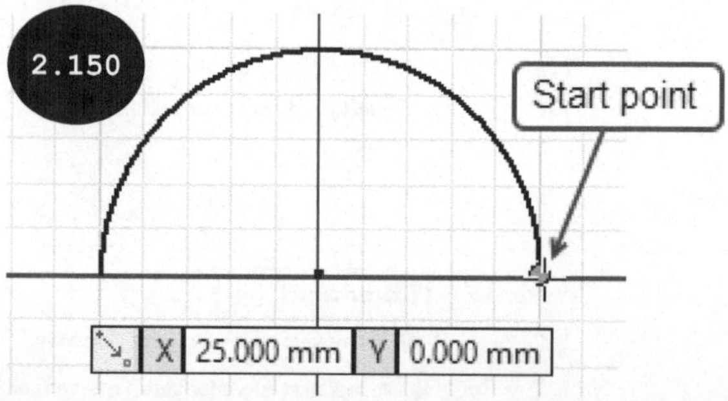

7. Move the cursor horizontally toward right and click when the length of the line appears as 35 mm in the Dimension Input, see Figure 2.151.

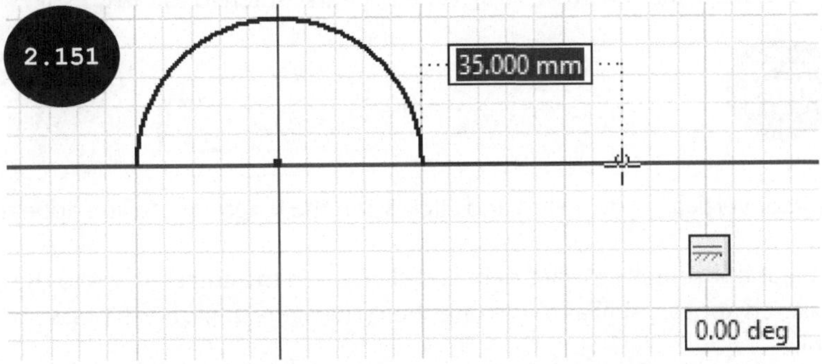

8. Move the cursor vertically upward and click when the length of the line appears as 10 mm.

9. Move the cursor horizontally toward right and click when the length of the line appears as 25 mm.

10. Move the cursor vertically upward and click when the length of the line appears as 10 mm.

11. Move the cursor horizontally toward left and click when the length of the line appears as 10 mm.

12. Move the cursor vertically upward and click when the length of the line appears as 105 mm.

13. Move the cursor to a distance and then move it back to the last specified point. A gray colored dot appears in the drawing area, see Figure 2.152.

14. Drag the cursor by pressing and holding the left mouse button from the last specified point to a small distance in the upward direction and then toward the left. The arc mode is activated and the preview of a tangent arc appears in the drawing area, see Figure 2.153.

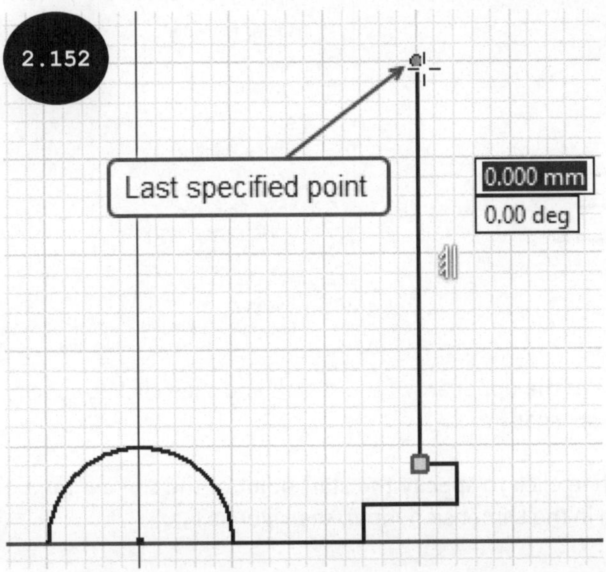

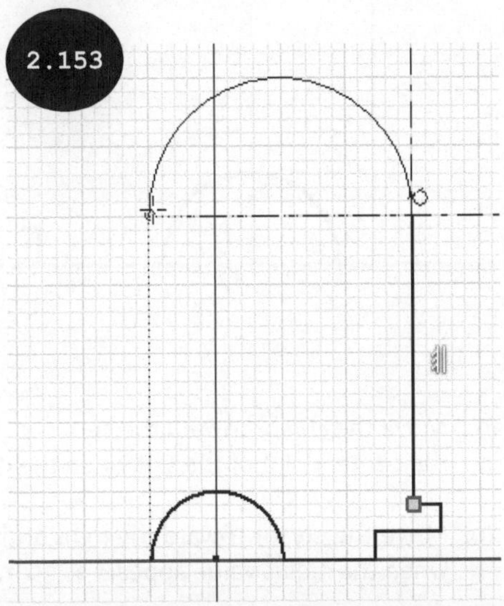

15. Release the left mouse button to specify the endpoint of the tangent arc when the radius of the arc appears as 55 mm in the Status Bar at the lower right corner of the screen, see Figure 2.154. A tangent arc is created and the preview of a line appears attached to the cursor.

2.154

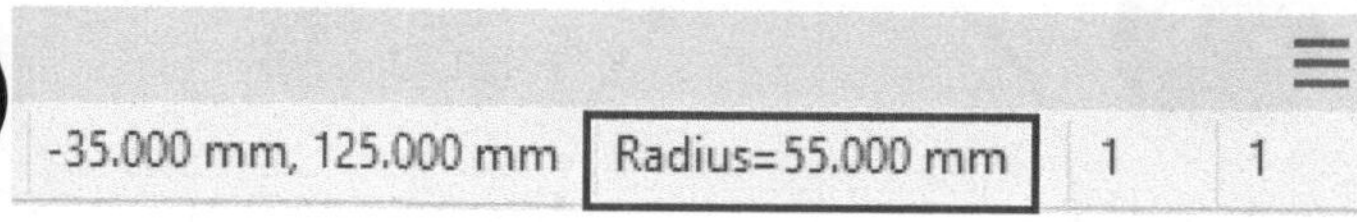

16. Move the cursor vertically downward and click when the length of the line appears as 125 mm.

17. Move the cursor horizontally toward right and click when the cursor snaps to the endpoint of the first arc. A sketch appears similar to the one shown in Figure 2.155. Next, press the **ESC** key to exit the **Line** tool.

Now, you need to create the inner slot and circle of the sketch.

18. Invoke the **Rectangle** flyout and then click on the **Center Point Arc Slot** tool, see Figure 2.156. You are prompted to specify the center point of the slot.

2.155

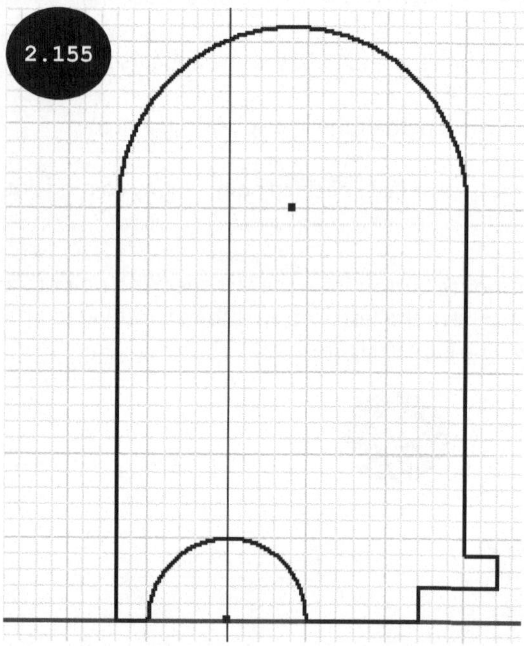

2.156

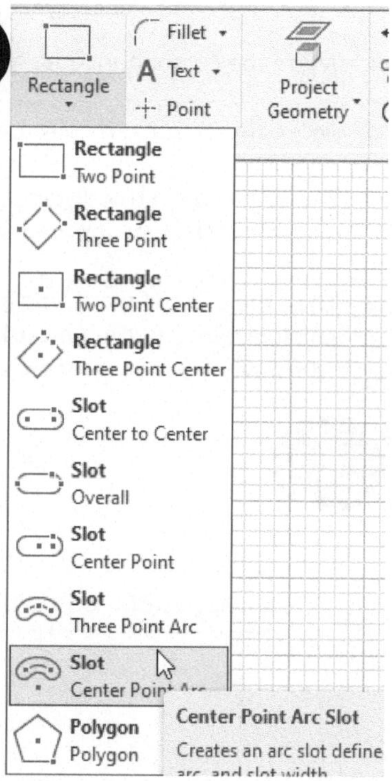

19. Move the cursor toward the center point of the upper arc of the sketch and then click to specify the center point of the slot when the cursor snaps to it.

20. Move the cursor toward the right and then click to specify the start point of the slot center arc when the radius value appears as 30 mm in the Dimension Input, see Figure 2.157.

21. Move the cursor in an anti-clockwise direction up to 270 degrees and then click to specify the endpoint of the slot center arc, see Figure 2.158. The preview of an arc slot appears, see Figure 2.159.

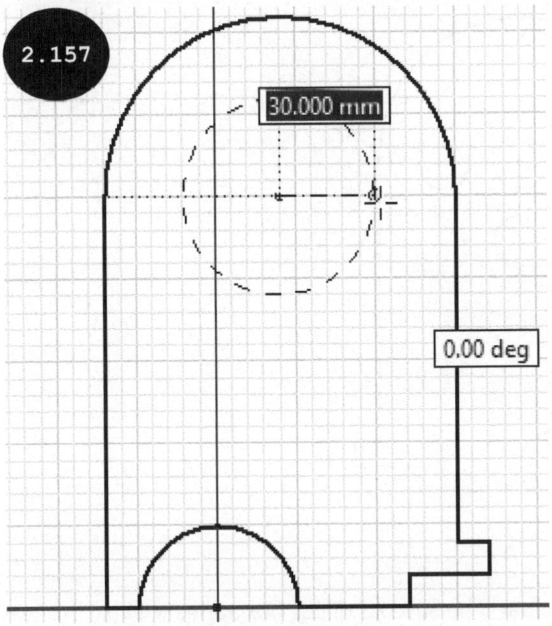

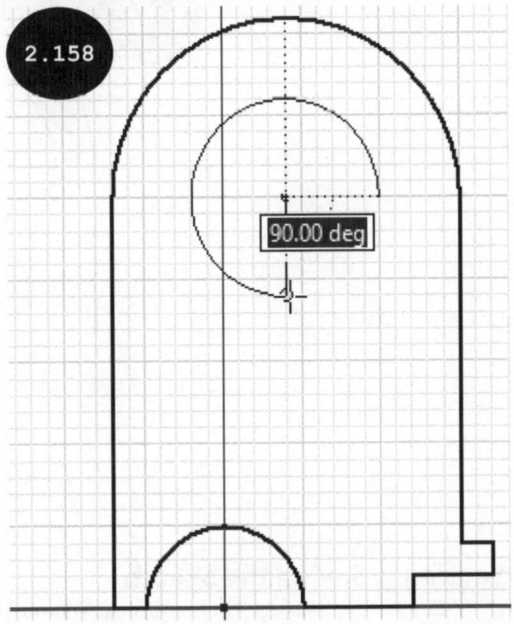

22. Move the cursor vertically downward and then click to specify a point when the width of the slot appears as 20 mm in the Dimension Input, see Figure 2.159. An arc slot is drawn. Next, press the ESC key to exit the tool.

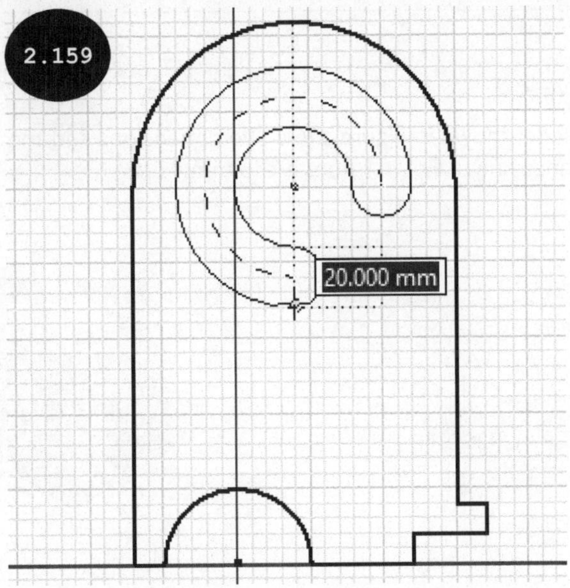

23. Create a circle of diameter 20 mm at the center of the arc slot. Figure 2.160 shows the final sketch of Tutorial 4.

24. Click on the **Finish Sketch** tool in the **Exit** panel to exit the Sketching environment.

2.160

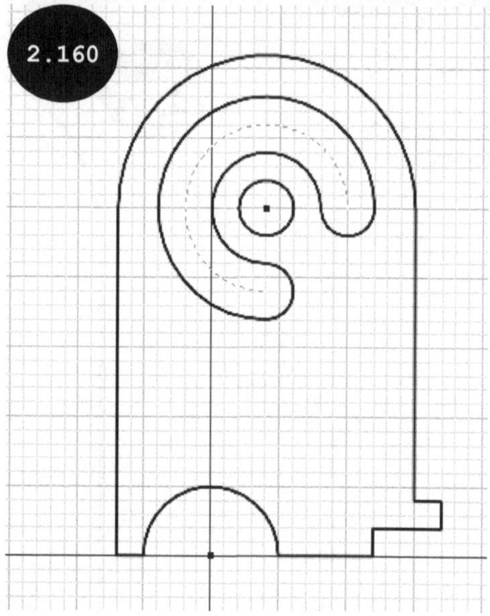

Section 5: Saving the Sketch

1. Click on the **Save** tool in the **Quick Access Toolbar**. The **Save As** dialog box appears. Next, browse to **Autodesk Inventor > Chapter 2** folder in the local drive of your system.

2. Enter **Tutorial 4** in the **File name** field of the dialog box and then click on the **Save** button. The sketch is saved in the specified location (>:\Autodesk Inventor\Chapter 2).

Hands-on Test Drive 3

Draw a sketch of the model shown in Figure 2.161. The dimensions and the 3D model shown in the figure are for your reference only. All dimensions are in mm.

2.161

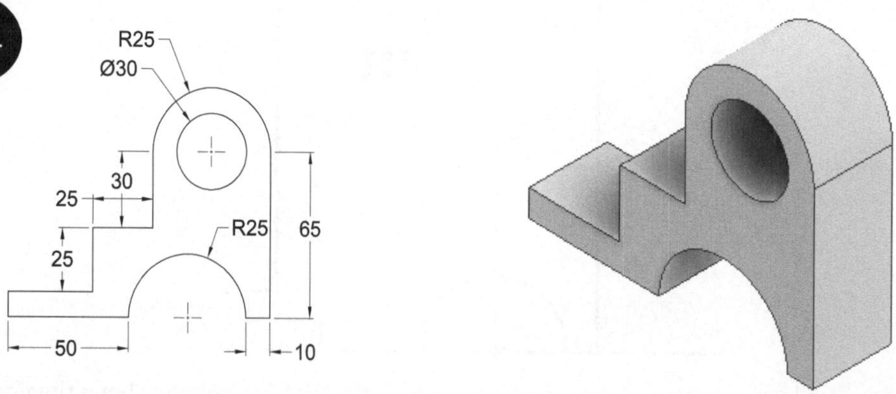

Hands-on Test Drive 4

Draw a sketch of the model shown in Figure 2.162. The dimensions and the 3D model shown in the figure are for your reference only. All dimensions are in mm.

2.162

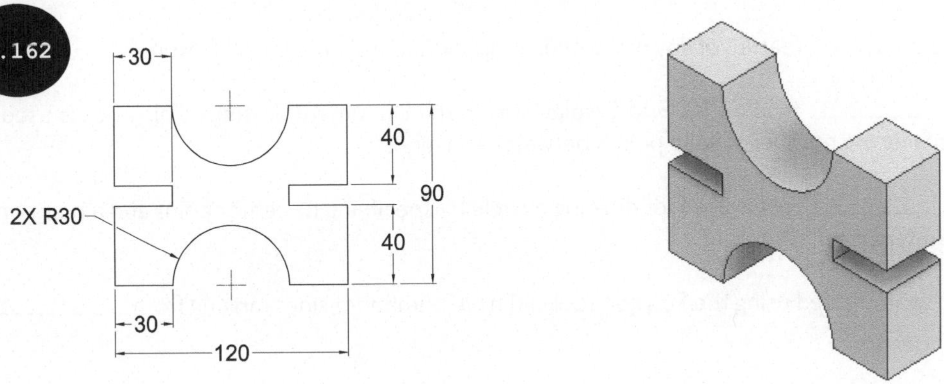

Hands-on Test Drive 5

Draw a sketch of the model shown in Figure 2.163. The dimensions and the 3D model shown in the figure are for your reference only. All dimensions are in mm.

2.163

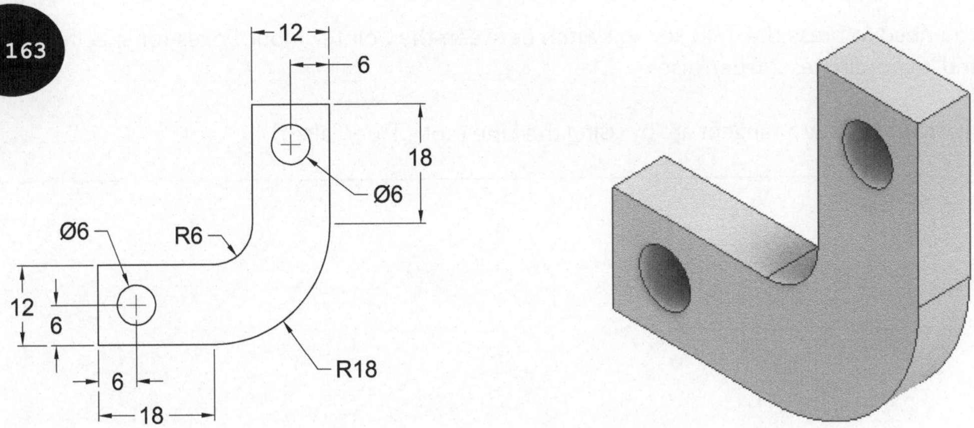

Summary

In this chapter, you have learned that the Sketching environment is invoked within the Part modeling environment. To invoke the Sketching environment, you need to select a plane as the sketching plane. After invoking the Sketching environment, the chapter discussed specifying units, grids, and snap settings. It also discussed in detail about various methods for creating lines, arcs, circles, ellipses, rectangles, slots, polygons, and splines in addition to the method for editing a spline.

Questions

Complete and verify the following sentences:

- Features are divided into two main categories: _________ and _________ .
- The _________ feature of any real world component is a sketch based feature.
- The _________ field of the **Grid Display** area in the **Document Settings** dialog box is used for specifying the number of snap points between each grid.
- The _________ tool is used for drawing a circle by specifying its center point and a point on its circumference.
- A polygon created using the **Polygon** tool can have number of sides ranging from _________ to _________.
- To draw an ellipse, you need to define its _________, _________, and _________.
- In Autodesk Inventor, you can also create an equation driven spline by using the _________ tool.
- The _________ tool is used for drawing a circle that is tangent to three line entities.
- You need to press the TAB key to switch between the Pointer Input boxes for specifying the X and Y coordinates. (True/False)
- You cannot draw a tangent arc by using the **Line** tool. (True/False)

CHAPTER

3

Editing and Modifying Sketches

In this chapter, the following topics will be discussed:

- Trimming Sketch Entities
- Extending Sketch Entities
- Splitting Sketch Entities
- Offsetting Sketch Entities
- Creating a 2D Fillet
- Creating a 2D Chamfer
- Patterning Sketch Entities
- Creating Construction and Centerline Entities
- Mirroring Sketch Entities
- Moving a Sketch Entity
- Creating a Copy of Sketch Entities
- Rotating an Entity
- Scaling Sketch Entities
- Stretching Sketch Entities

Editing and modifying a sketch plays an important role in giving the sketch a desired shape. In Autodesk Inventor, various editing operations such as trimming unwanted sketched entities, extending sketch entities, splitting, mirroring, patterning, moving, copying, and rotating sketch entities can be performed in the Sketching environment. In addition to various editing operations, you will also learn about creating fillets and chamfers in a sketch. The various editing operations are discussed next.

Trimming Sketch Entities

You can trim the unwanted sketch entities up to their nearest intersection or an intersection with defined boundaries by using the **Trim** tool of the **Modify** panel in the **Sketch** tab, see Figure 3.1. The different methods for trimming sketch entities are discussed below:

3.1

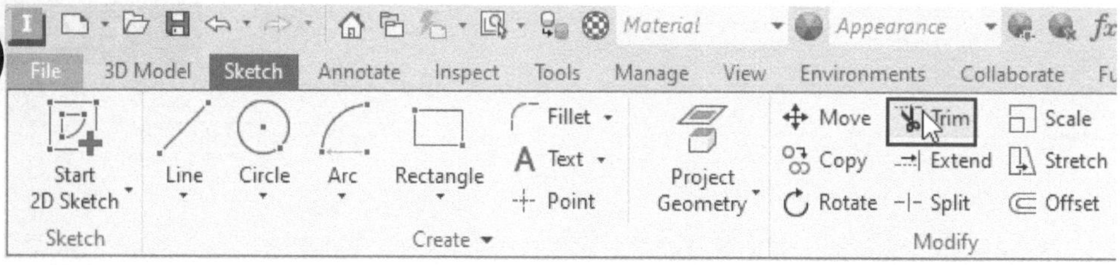

Trimming Sketch Entities Up to their Nearest Intersection

1. Click on the **Trim** tool in the **Modify** panel of the **Sketch** tab, (refer to Figure 3.1), or press the X key. The **Trim** tool gets activated and you are prompted to select a portion of a curve to be trimmed.

2. Move the cursor over the portion of the entity to be trimmed and pause. The entity gets highlighted and the portion of the entity to be trimmed appears as a dashed entity up to its nearest intersection in the drawing area, see Figure 3.2.

3. Click the left mouse button to trim the portion of the entity. The entity gets trimmed up to its nearest intersection, see Figure 3.3.

3.2

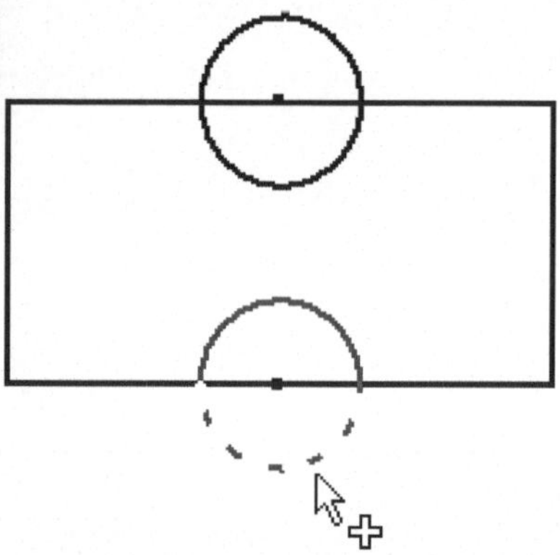

3.3

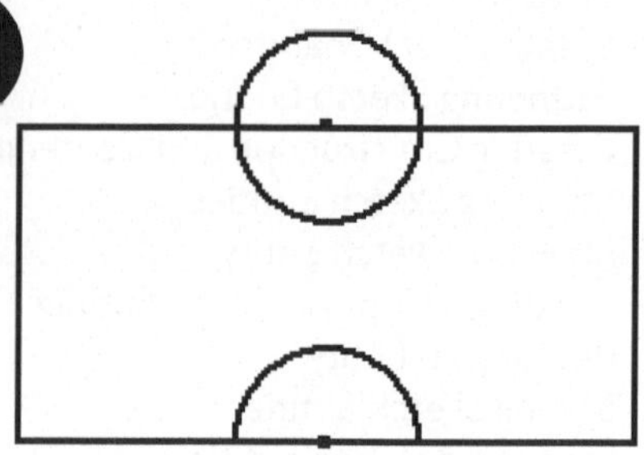

Tip: If an entity does not have a point of intersection with any other entity, then the selected entity will get deleted by using the **Trim** tool.

4. You can continue trimming entities one by one, in a similar way by clicking the left mouse button. Figure 3.4 shows the sketch after trimming the unwanted entities of the sketch.

3.4

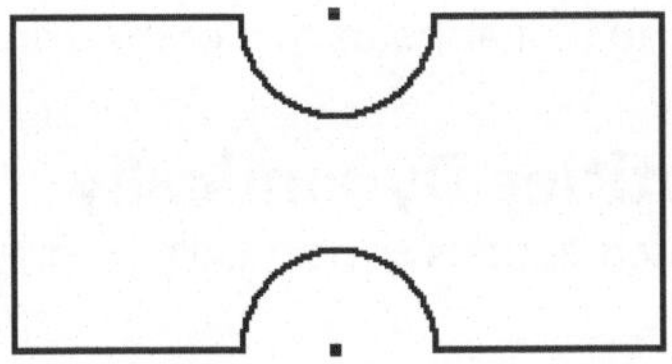

5. Press the ESC key to exit the **Trim** tool or right-click in the drawing area and then click on the **OK** button in the Marking Menu that appears to exit the **Trim** tool.

Trimming Sketch Entities by Defining Boundaries

In Autodesk Inventor, you can also define boundaries as cutting edges for trimming the sketch entities by using the **Trim** tool.

1. Click on the **Trim** tool in the **Modify** panel of the **Sketch** tab or press the X key. You are prompted to select a portion of a curve to be trimmed.

2. Press and hold the CTRL key and then select two sketch entities to be used as boundaries for trimming the sketch entities, see Figure 3.5.

3. Release the CTRL key and then move the cursor over the portion of the entity to be trimmed and pause. The entity gets highlighted and the portion of the entity to be trimmed appears as a dashed entity up to its intersection with defined boundaries, see Figure 3.6.

3.5

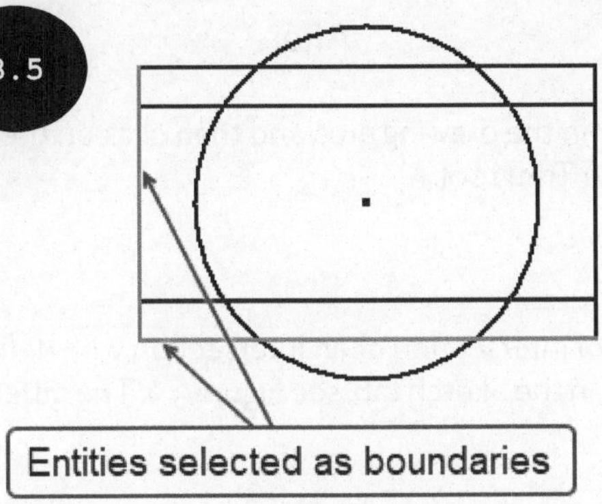

3.6

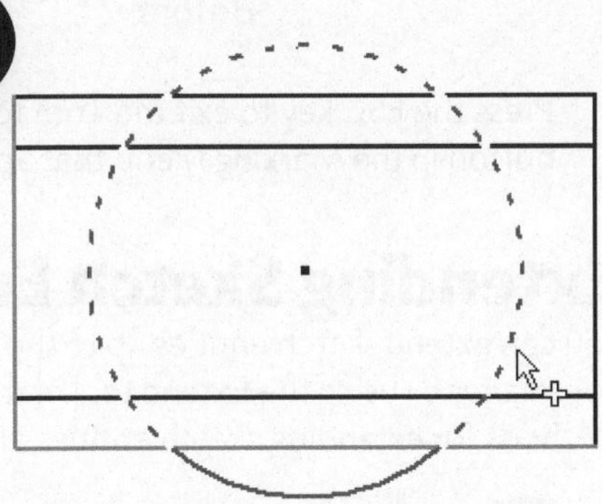

4. Click the left mouse button to trim the portion of the entity. The entity gets trimmed up to its intersection with defined boundaries, see Figure 3.7.

3.7

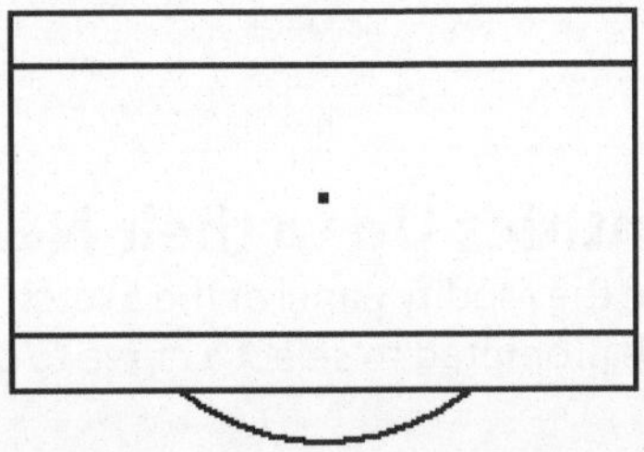

5. Press the ESC key to exit the **Trim** tool or right-click in the drawing area and then click on the **OK** button in the Marking Menu that appears to exit the **Trim** tool.

Trimming Sketch Entities Dynamically

You can also trim the sketch entities dynamically by dragging the cursor over the entities to be trimmed.

1. Click on the **Trim** tool in the **Modify** panel of the **Sketch** tab or press the X key. You are prompted to select the portion of a curve to be trimmed.

2. Drag the cursor over the entities to be trimmed by pressing and holding the left mouse button. A light colored tracing line following the cursor appears and the sketch entities coming across the tracing line get trimmed from their nearest point of intersection, see Figure 3.8.

3.8

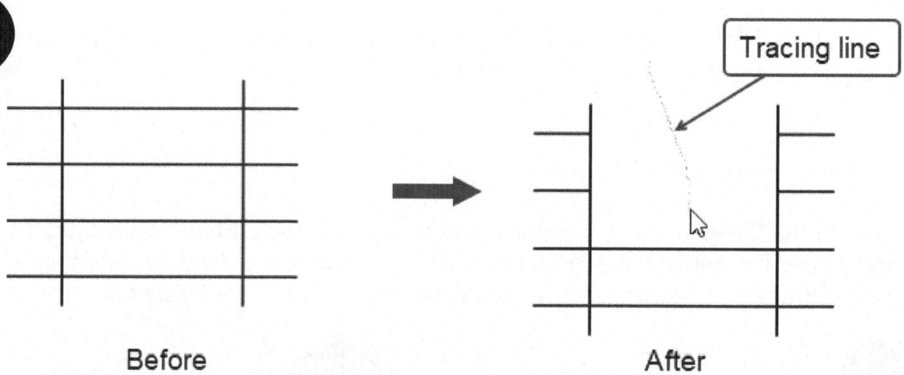

3. Press the ESC key to exit the **Trim** tool or right-click in the drawing area and then click on the **OK** button in the Marking Menu that appears to exit the **Trim** tool.

Extending Sketch Entities

You can extend sketch entities up to their nearest point of intersection or an intersection with defined boundaries by using the **Extend** tool of the **Modify** panel in the **Sketch** tab, see Figure 3.9. The different methods for extending sketch entities are discussed below:

3.9

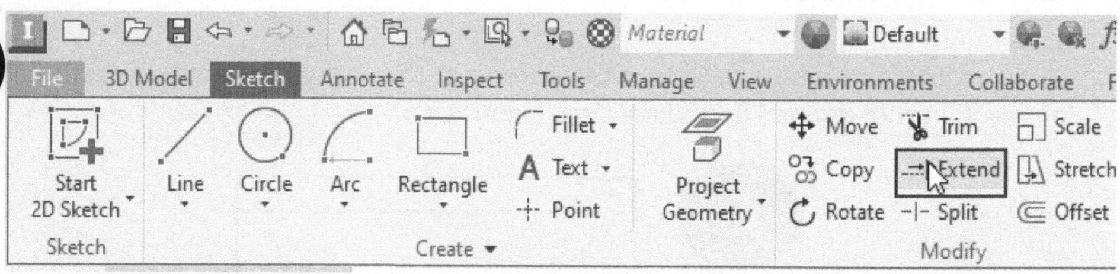

Extending Sketch Entities Up to their Nearest Intersection

1. Click on the **Extend** tool in the **Modify** panel of the **Sketch** tab, refer to Figure 3.9. The **Extend** tool gets activated and you are prompted to select a curve to be extended.

2. Move the cursor over the entity to be extended. A preview of the extended line appears up to its next intersection in the drawing area, see Figures 3.10 and 3.11. It is evident from Figure 3.11 that you can also extend an entity up to an imaginary intersection created with its nearest intersecting entity.

3.10

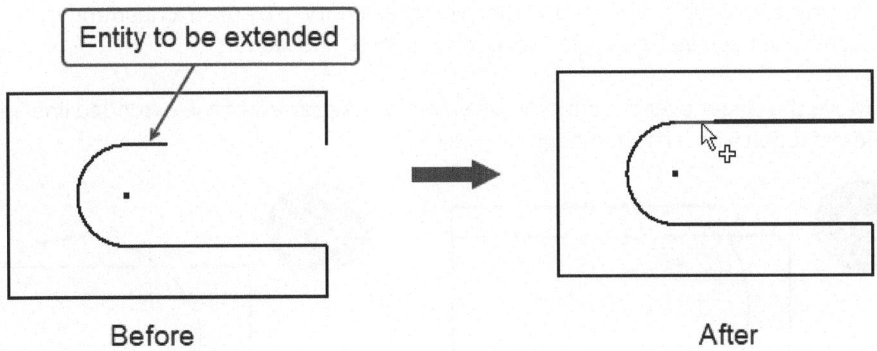

3.11

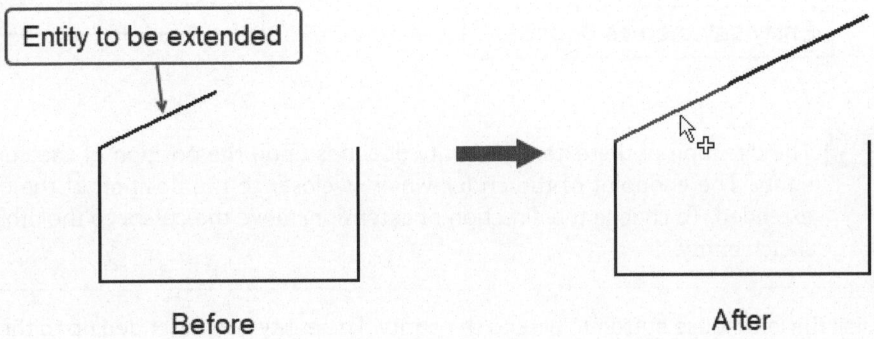

Note: The direction of the extended entity depends upon the position of the cursor over the entity. The endpoint of the entity, which is closer to the position of the cursor will be extended. To change the direction of extension, move the cursor to the other side of the sketch entity.

3. Click the left mouse button when the preview of the extended line appears. The selected entity is extended up to the next intersection.

4. Similarly, you can continue extending entities one by one, up to their next intersection by clicking the left mouse button.

Tip: You can also drag the cursor over the entities to be extended up to their nearest intersection.

5. Press the ESC key to exit the **Extend** tool.

Extending Sketch Entities by Defining Boundaries

You can also define boundaries for extending the sketch entities by using the **Extend** tool.

1. Click on the **Extend** tool in the **Modify** panel of the **Sketch** tab.

2. Press and hold the CTRL key and then select an entity to be used as a boundary for extending the sketch entities, see Figure 3.12. Next, release the CTRL key.

3. Move the cursor over the entity to be extended. A preview of the extended line appears up to its intersection with a defined boundary, see Figure 3.13.

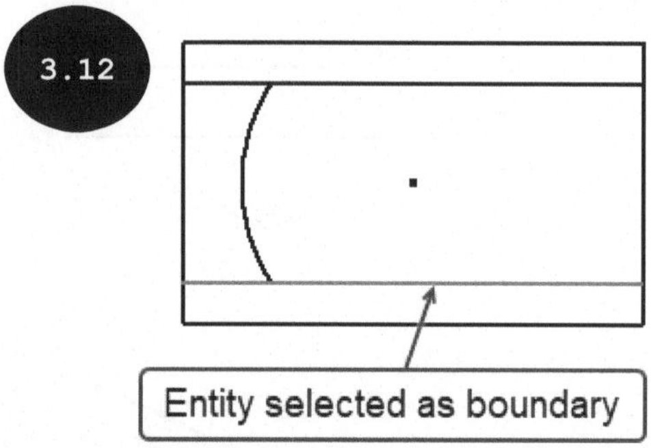

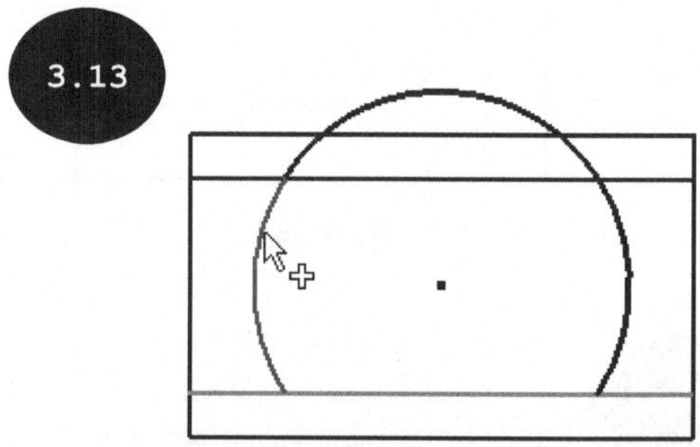

Note: The direction of the extended entity depends upon the position of the cursor over the entity. The endpoint of the entity, which is closer to the position of the cursor will be extended. To change the direction of extension, move the cursor to the other side of the sketch entity.

4. Click the left mouse button to extend the entity. The entity gets extended up to the intersection with defined boundaries.

5. Press the ESC key to exit the **Extend** tool.

Note: In Autodesk Inventor, while working with the **Trim** or **Extend** tool, you can temporarily switch from one tool to another by pressing the SHIFT key. For example, if you are working with the **Trim** tool for trimming sketch entities then on pressing the SHIFT key, you can temporarily switch to the **Extend** tool for extending sketch entities and vice-versa.

Splitting Sketch Entities

In Autodesk Inventor, you can split a sketch entity into two or more than two segments at its intersection with other entities by using the **Split** tool in the **Modify** panel of the Sketch tab. The method for splitting an entity is discussed below:

1. Click on the **Split** tool in the **Modify** panel of the **Sketch** tab, see Figure 3.14. The **Split** tool gets activated and you are prompted to select a curve to be split.

3.14

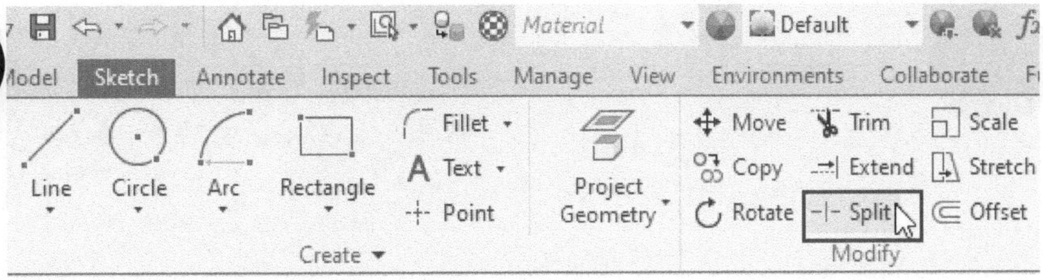

2. Move the cursor over the entity to be split and then pause the cursor over it. The intersection points of the selected entity are highlighted in the drawing area, see Figures 3.15 and 3.16. It is evident from Figure 3.16 that you can also split an entity at an imaginary intersection created with another sketch entity.

3.15

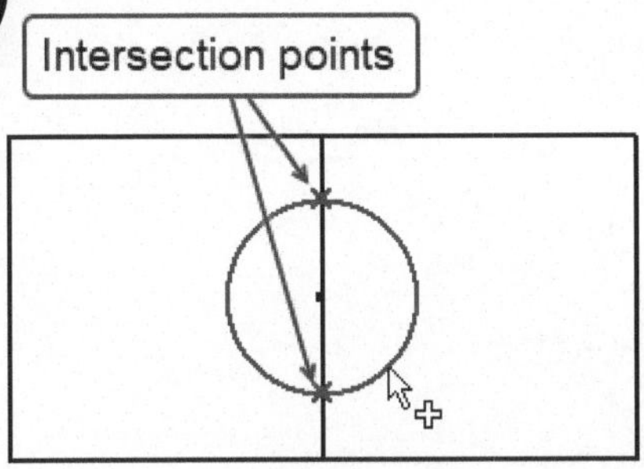

3.16

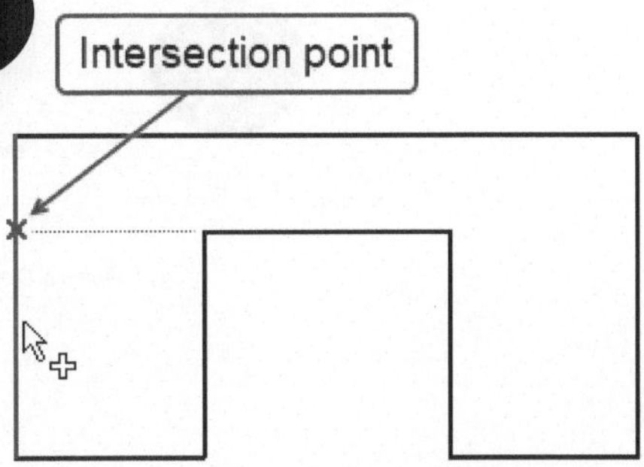

Note: If an entity does not have any intersection with other sketch entities, then it cannot be split.

3. Click the left mouse button when the intersection points get highlighted in the drawing area. The selected entity gets split into two segments at its intersection points.

4. Similarly, you can continue splitting the sketch entity at its nearest intersection by clicking the left mouse button.

5. Press the ESC key to exit the **Split** tool or right-click in the drawing area and then click on the **OK** button in the Marking Menu that appears to exit the tool.

Offsetting Sketch Entities

You can offset sketch entities at a specified offset distance by using the **Offset** tool of the **Modify** panel in the **Sketch** tab. The method for offsetting an entity at a specified offset distance is discussed below:

1. Click on the **Offset** tool in the **Modify** panel of the **Sketch** tab, see Figure 3.17. The **Offset** tool gets activated and you are prompted to select a curve to be offset.

3.17

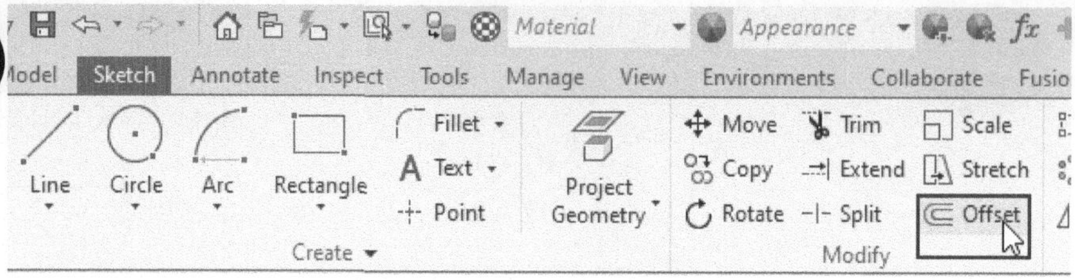

2. Right-click in the drawing area. The Marking Menu appears with the **Loop Select** option selected, by default, see Figure 3.18. As a result, on selecting an entity to be offset in the drawing area, all the contiguous entities (closed or open loop) of the selected entity get automatically selected in the drawing area. If you want to offset an individual sketch entity, then you need to clear the **Loop Select** option by clicking on it.

3.18

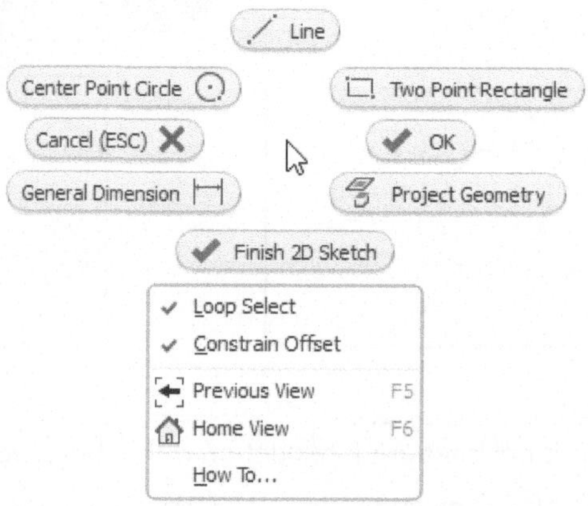

3. Ensure that the **Loop Select** option is selected in the Marking Menu to offset entities of the sketch as a loop.

4. Click on an entity of the sketch in the drawing area. The preview of an offset loop appears in the drawing area, see Figure 3.19.

5. Enter the required offset distance value in the Dimension Input box that appears in the drawing area and then press ENTER. You can also move the cursor to the required location in the drawing area and then click to specify the position of the offset loop. An offset loop gets created.

Note: To offset an individual sketch entity, clear the **Loop Select** option in the Marking Menu that appears on right-clicking in the drawing area and then select an entity to be offset in the drawing area. Next, press ENTER. The preview of an offset entity appears in the drawing area, see Figure 3.20. Move the cursor to the required location and then click to specify the position of the offset entity or enter an offset distance value in the Dimension Input box. The selected entity gets offset at the specified offset distance.

3.19

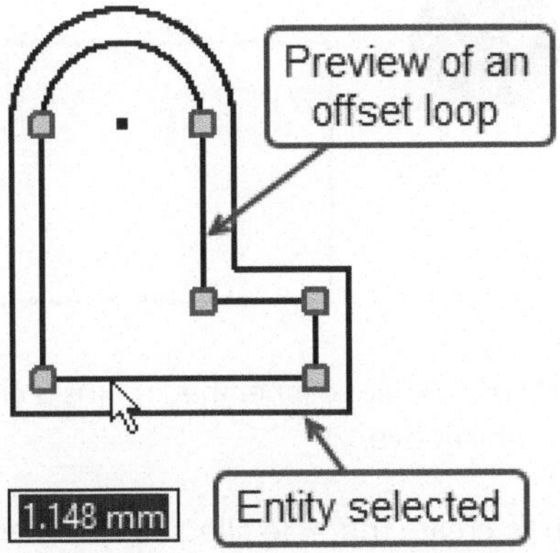

3.20

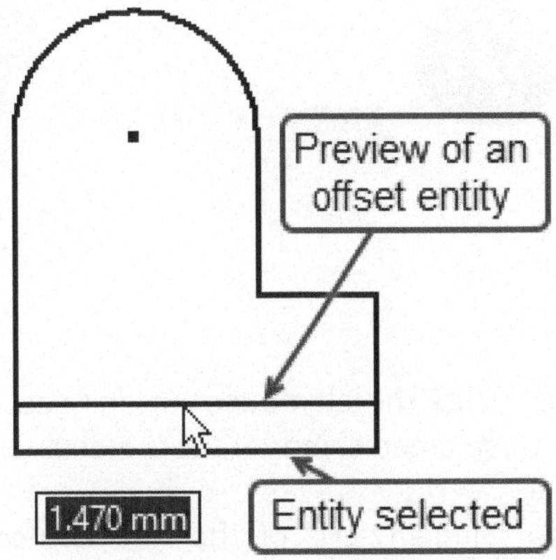

6. Press the ESC key to exit the **Offset** tool or right-click in the drawing area and then click on the **OK** button in the Marking Menu that appears to exit the tool.

Creating a 2D Fillet

A 2D fillet is used for removing a corner at the intersection of two sketch entities by creating an arc of constant radius, see Figure 3.21. In the Sketching environment, you can create a 2D fillet by using the **Fillet** tool of the **Create** panel in the **Sketch** tab. The method for creating a fillet is discussed below:

3.21

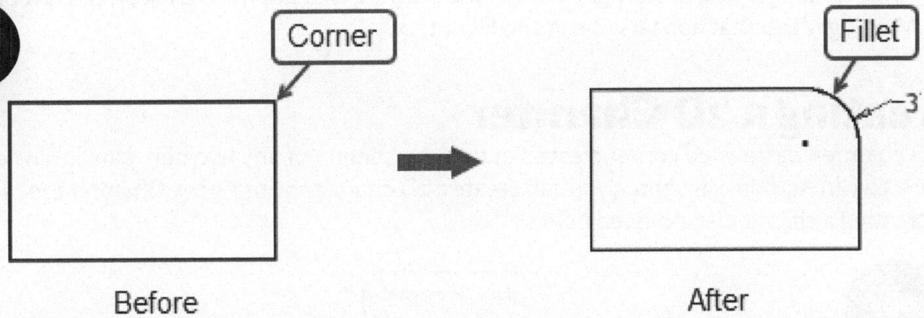

1. Click on the **Fillet** tool in the **Create** panel of the **Sketch** tab, see Figure 3.22. The **2D Fillet** dialog box appears, see Figure 3.23. Also, you are prompted to select lines, arcs, or a corner to create a fillet.

3.22

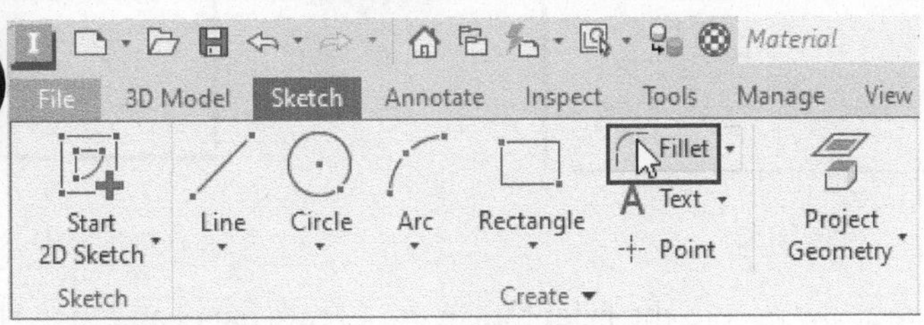

2. Enter the fillet radius in the **Radius** field of the **2D Fillet** dialog box.

3. Move the cursor over the corner/vertex of the sketch to be filleted. The preview of a fillet appears in the drawing area, see Figure 3.24. Alternatively, you can select two line entities or arc entities one by one for creating a fillet of specified radius at their intersection.

3.23

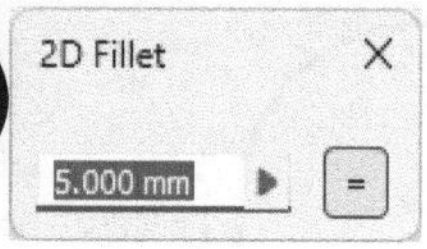

3.24

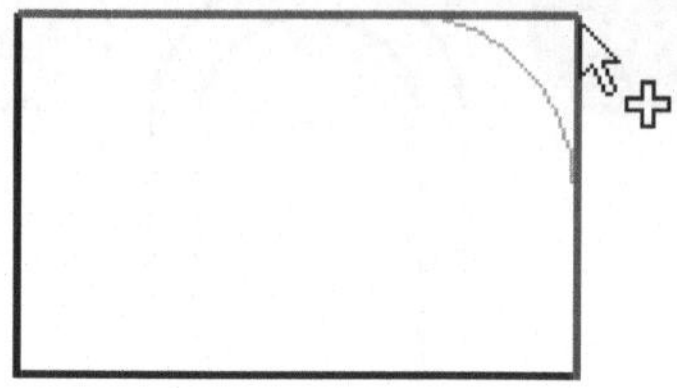

4. Click the left mouse button to accept the fillet preview. A fillet of specified radius is created at the selected corner of the sketch and the **Fillet** tool is still active.

5. Similarly, click on the other corners of the sketch to create multiple fillets of specified radii.

Note: By default, the **Equal to Parameters** button is activated in the **2D Fillet** dialog box. As a result, on creating multiple fillets, the radius dimension is applied to one of the fillets and an equal relation is applied among all the remaining fillets. However, if the **Equal to Parameters** button is deactivated, then the fillet radius is applied to all the fillets created in the drawing area. You can activate or deactivate the **Equal to Parameters** button by clicking on it in the **2D Fillet** dialog box.

6. After creating all the fillets, right-click in the drawing area and then click on the **OK** button in the Marking Menu that appears to exit the **Fillet** tool.

Creating a 2D Chamfer

A 2D chamfer is a beveled corner created at the intersection of any two non-parallel line entities, see Figure 3.25. In Autodesk Inventor, you can create a 2D chamfer by using the **Chamfer** tool. The method for creating a chamfer is discussed below:

3.25

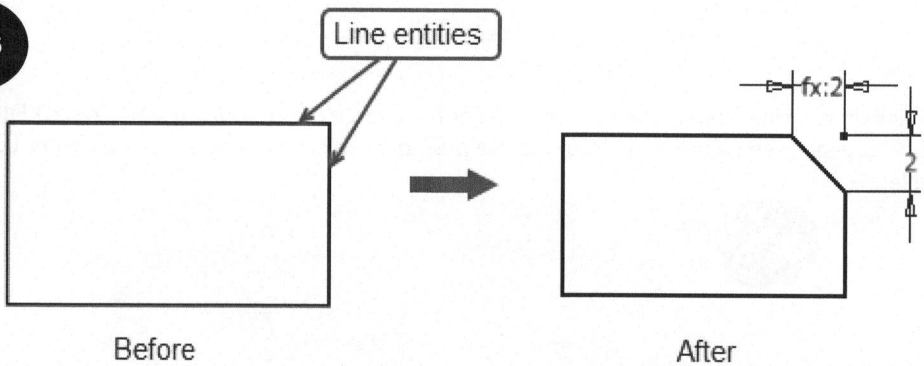

1. Click on the arrow next to the **Fillet** tool in the **Create** panel and then click on the **Chamfer** tool in the flyout that appears, see Figure 3.26. The **2D Chamfer** dialog box appears, see Figure 3.27. The options in this dialog box are used for creating different types of chamfers and are discussed below:

3.26

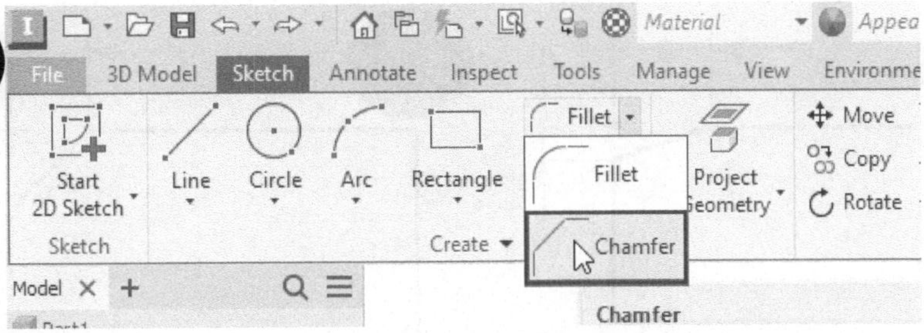

3.27

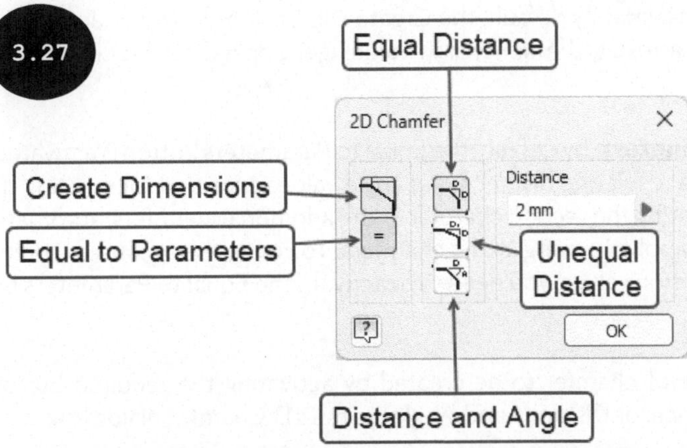

Equal Distance: The **Equal Distance** button of the **2D Chamfer** dialog box is used for creating a chamfer at an equal distance from the intersection of both the selected line entities, see Figure 3.28. You can specify a distance value in the **Distance** field of the dialog box.

3.28

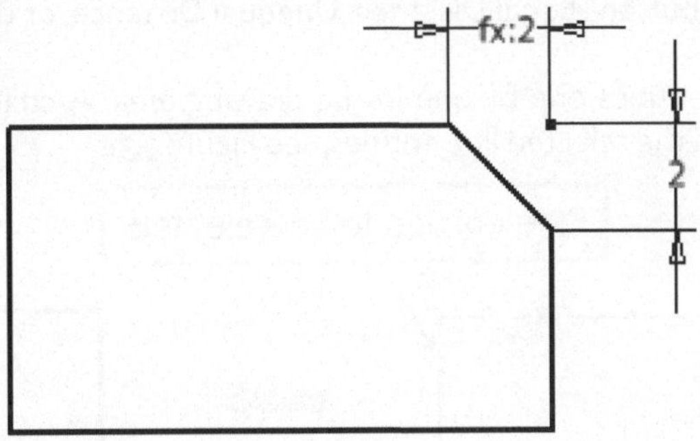

Unequal Distance: The **Unequal Distance** button is used for creating a chamfer by specifying different distance values from the intersection of each selected line entity in the **Distance 1** and **Distance 2** fields of the dialog box, see Figure 3.29. Note that the **Distance 1** and **Distance 2** fields appear in the dialog box when the **Unequal Distance** button is activated.

Distance and Angle: The **Distance and Angle** button is used for creating a chamfer by specifying an angle from the first selected line entity and the distance from its intersection with the second selected line entity, see Figure 3.30. You can specify the angle and distance values in the **Distance** and **Angle** fields that appear in the dialog box on activating the **Distance and Angle** button.

3.29

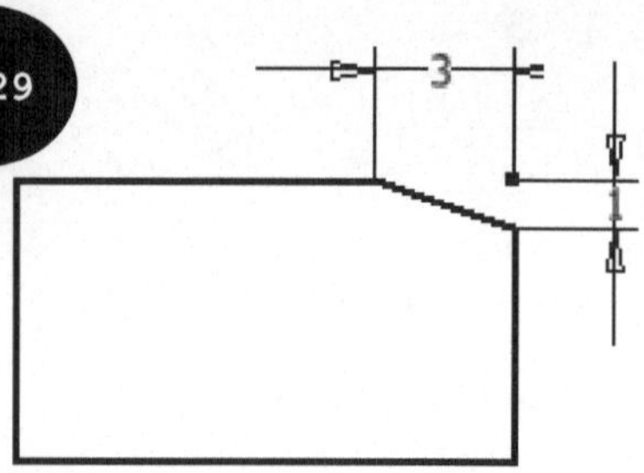

3.30

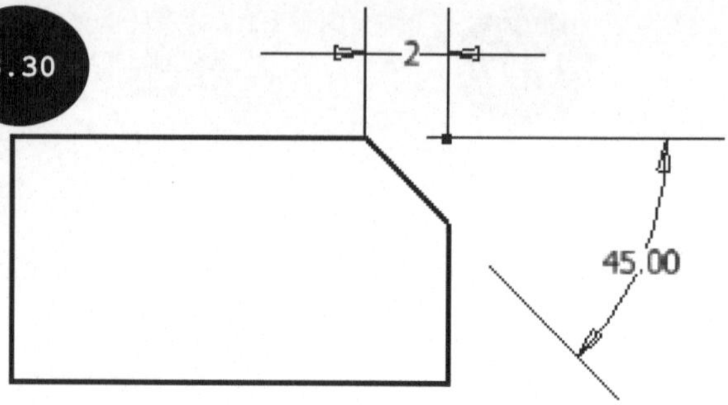

Create Dimensions: By default, the **Create Dimensions** button is activated in the **2D Chamfer** dialog box. As a result, the dimension values get applied to the chamfer in the drawing area, automatically.

Equal to Parameters: By default, the **Equal to Parameters** button is activated in the **2D Chamfer** dialog box. As a result, the distance and angle values specified for creating the first chamfer will be used for creating the second chamfer or the additional chamfers, automatically. Also, an equal relation will be applied among all the chamfers. To create the second or additional chamfers with different dimension values, you need to deactivate the **Equal to Parameters** button by clicking on it.

2. Select the type of chamfer to be created by activating the required button (**Equal Distance**, **Unequal Distance**, or **Distance and Angle**) in the **2D Chamfer** dialog box.

   After selecting the type of chamfer to be created, the respective fields for specifying the chamfer parameters appear in the dialog box.

3. Specify the chamfer parameters in the respective fields of the dialog box depending upon the type of chamfer button (**Equal Distance**, **Unequal Distance**, or **Distance and Angle**) activated.

4. Select two line entities one by one in the drawing area. A chamfer of specified parameters is created between the selected line entities, see Figure 3.31.

3.31

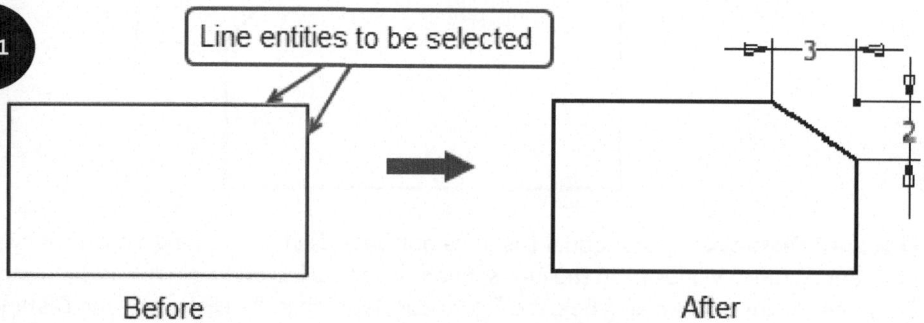

Tip: Instead of selecting two line entities of a sketch individually, you can also select a vertex that is created at the intersection of two sketch entities for creating a chamfer.

5. Click on the **OK** button in the **2D Chamfer** dialog box to exit the tool.

Patterning Sketch Entities

In Autodesk Inventor, you can create rectangular and circular patterns of sketch entities by using the **Rectangular Pattern** and **Circular Pattern** tools, respectively. Both the tools are discussed below:

Creating a Rectangular Pattern

The **Rectangular Pattern** tool is used for creating multiple instances or duplicate copies of an existing sketch entity, rectangularly in one or two linear directions, refer to Figure 3.32.

3.32

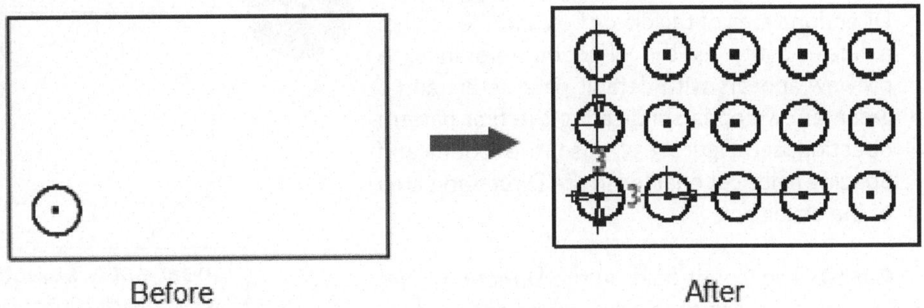

The method for creating a rectangular pattern is discussed below:

1. Click on the **Rectangular Pattern** tool in the **Pattern** panel of the **Sketch** tab, see Figure 3.33. The **Rectangular Pattern** dialog box appears, see Figure 3.34. Also, you are prompted to select a geometry to be patterned.

3.33

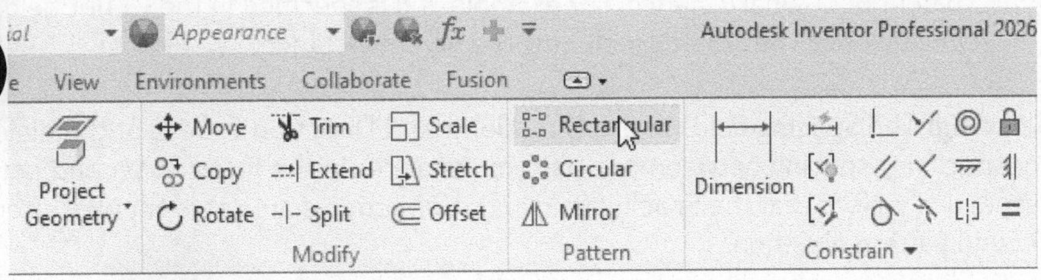

3.34

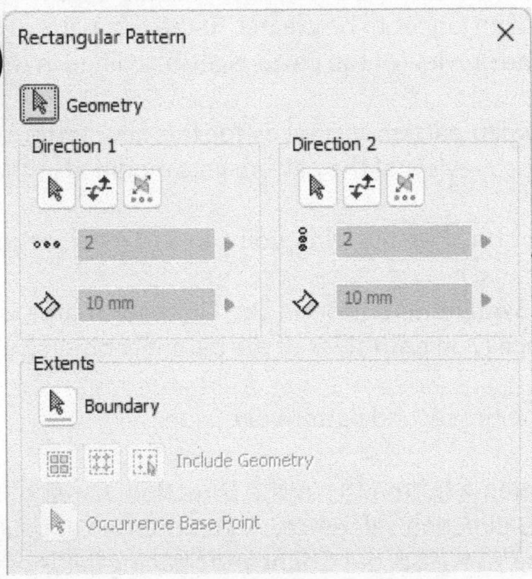

Geometry: By default, the **Geometry** button is activated in the **Rectangular Pattern** dialog box and is used for selecting a geometry to be patterned. You can select a single or multiple geometries to be patterned.

2. Select one or more entities in the drawing area to be patterned.

   Now, you need to define the pattern directions.

3. Click on the **Direction 1** button in the **Direction 1** area of the dialog box and then select a linear entity as the direction reference. A preview appears with default parameters and a green arrow appears indicating the first pattern direction, see Figure 3.35. Also, the **Count** and **Spacing** fields get enabled in the **Direction 1** area of the dialog box.

3.35

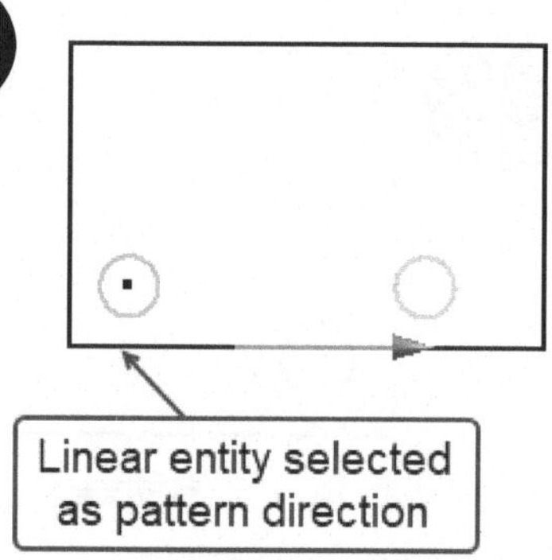

Count: The **Count** fields in the **Direction 1** and **Direction 2** areas of the dialog box are used for specifying number of pattern instances to be created in the first and second pattern directions, respectively. Note that the **Count** field in the **Direction 2** area gets enabled after you define the second pattern direction.

Note: The number of pattern instances specified in the **Count** field is counted along with the parent or original instance. For example, if 6 is specified in the **Count** field, then 6 pattern instances will be created including the parent instance.

Spacing: The **Spacing** fields in the **Direction 1** and **Direction 2** areas of the dialog box are used for specifying spacing between two pattern instances in the first and second pattern directions, respectively. Note that the **Spacing** field in the **Direction 2** area gets enabled after you define the second pattern direction.

4. Enter the number of instances to be created in the first pattern direction in the **Count** field of the **Direction 1** area. The preview of the pattern gets modified in the drawing area.

5. Enter spacing between pattern instances for the first pattern direction in the **Spacing** field of **Direction 1** area. The preview of the pattern gets modified in the drawing area.

6. Click on the **Flip** button in the **Direction 1** area to reverse the first pattern direction, if needed.

   Symmetric: The **Symmetric** button in the **Direction 1** area is used to define the first pattern direction symmetrically on both sides of the parent geometry.

   Now, you can define the second pattern direction.

7. Click on the **Direction 2** button in the **Direction 2** area of the dialog box and then select a linear entity as the direction reference. A green arrow appears indicating the second pattern direction, see Figure 3.36. Also, the **Count** and **Spacing** fields of the **Direction 2** area get enabled.

3.36

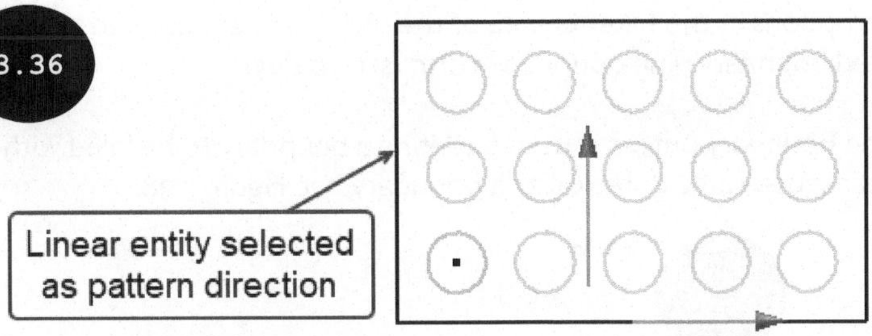

8. Click on the **Flip** button in the **Direction 2** area to reverse the second pattern direction, if needed.

   Symmetric: The Symmetric button in the **Direction 2** area is used to define the second pattern direction symmetrically on both sides of the parent geometry.

9. Enter the number of instances to be created for the second pattern direction in the **Count** field of the **Direction 2** area.

10. Enter the spacing between pattern instances in the second pattern direction in the **Spacing** field of the **Direction 2** area.

    In Autodesk Inventor, you can also suppress or remove pattern instances that are not required to be a part of the pattern.

11. Expand the **Rectangular Pattern** dialog box by clicking on the double arrow at the lower right corner of the dialog box for displaying advanced options. Figure 3.37 shows the expanded **Rectangular Pattern** dialog box. The advanced options in this dialog box are discussed below:

3.37

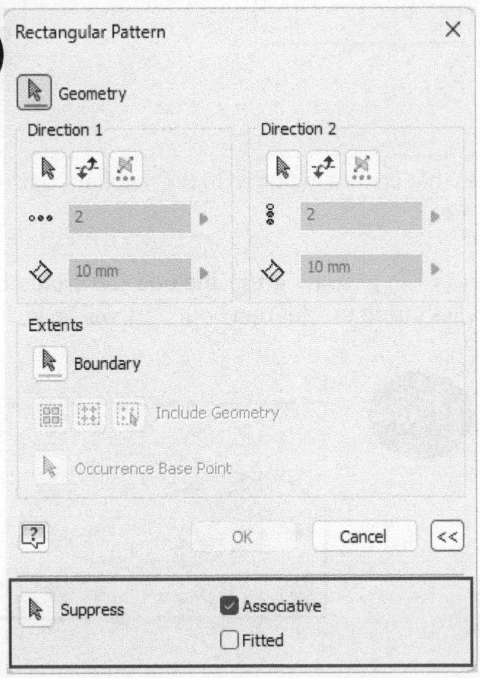

Extents: The options in the **Extents** area of the dialog box are used to create pattern instances within a defined boundary. The options are discussed below:

Boundary: The **Boundary** button is used to define a boundary to be filled with pattern instances. You can select a closed area or region as a boundary, see Figure 3.38.

3.38

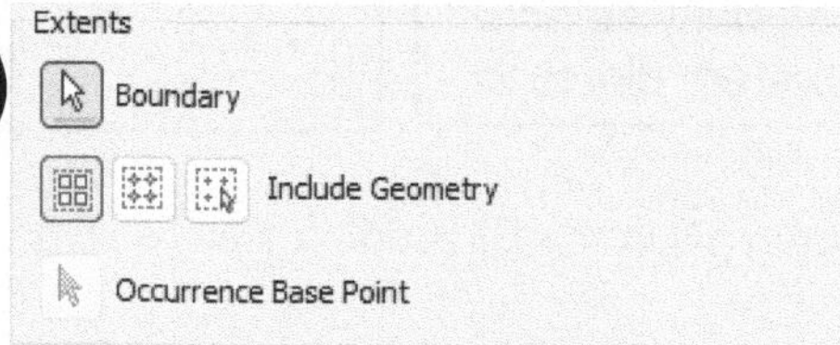

Note that upon selecting a boundary, the **Include Geometry**, **Include Centroids**, and **Include using occurrence base points** buttons become enabled in the **Extents** area of the dialog box. These buttons are discussed below:

Include Geometry : By default, this button is activated. As a result, all the pattern instances that lie completely inside the defined boundary will be included in the resultant pattern, see Figure 3.39.

3.39

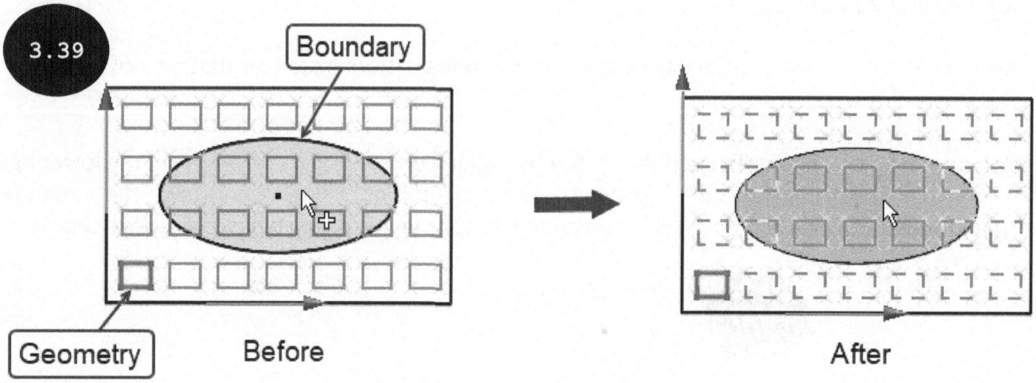

Note: The instances that are not included in the resultant pattern appear as reference entities in the drawing area.

Include Centroids : On activating the **Include Centroids** button, all the pattern instances whose center point lies inside the defined boundary will be included in the resultant pattern, see Figure 3.40.

3.40

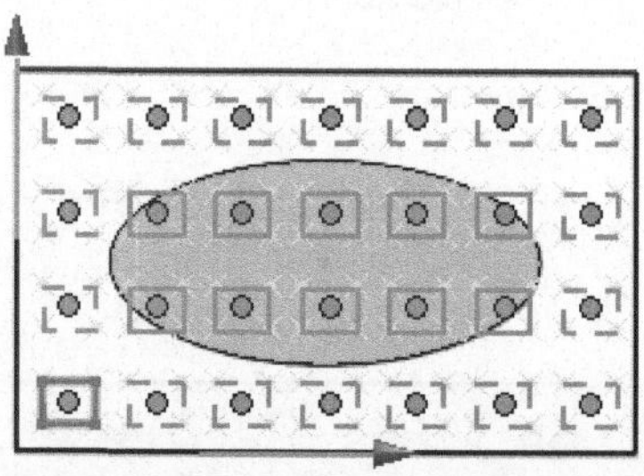

Include using occurrence base points: On activating the **Include using occurrence base points** button, the **Occurrence Base Point** button gets enabled to define a base point on the parent geometry. In doing so, all the pattern instances with defined base points lying inside the boundary will be included in the resultant pattern, see Figure 3.41.

3.41

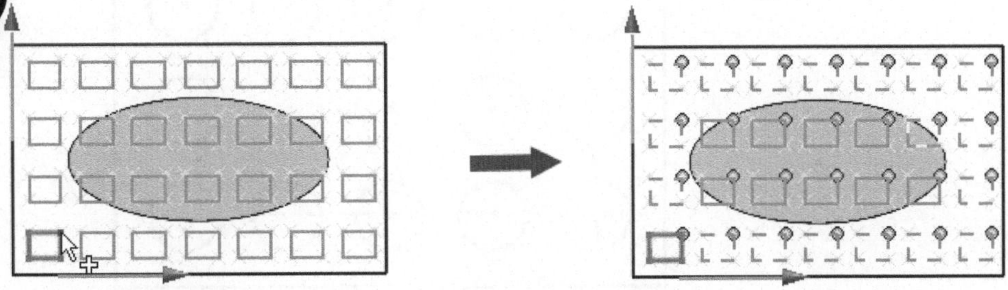

Before After

Suppress: On activating the **Suppress** button in the dialog box, you can select the pattern instances to be suppressed or removed from the resultant pattern. A preview of the suppressed instances appears as reference entities in the drawing area, see Figure 3.42. To recall or include the suppressed instances of the pattern, select them again in the preview of the pattern.

3.42

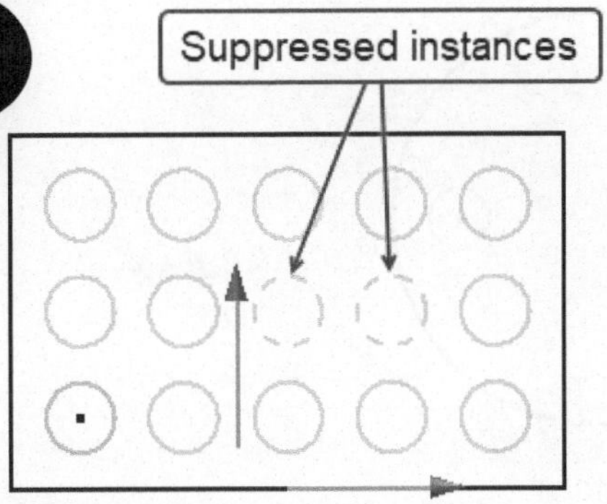

Associative: By default, the **Associative** check box is selected. As a result, the pattern gets updated automatically if any change is made in a pattern instance or parameters such as spacing and count.

Fitted: By default, the **Fitted** check box is cleared. As a result, the distance value specified in the **Spacing** field is used as the spacing between two consecutive pattern instances. If you select the **Fitted** check box, then all the pattern instances get equally fitted within the distance value specified in the **Spacing** filed. In other words, the distance value specified in the **Spacing** field of the dialog box is used as the overall spacing between first and last pattern instances when the **Fitted** check box is selected.

12. If needed, suppress the pattern instances that are not required in the resultant pattern by using the **Suppress** button.

13. Click on the **OK** button in the dialog box. A rectangular pattern is created in the first and second pattern directions as per the specified parameters. Figure 3.43 shows a rectangular pattern where two pattern instances have been suppressed.

3.43

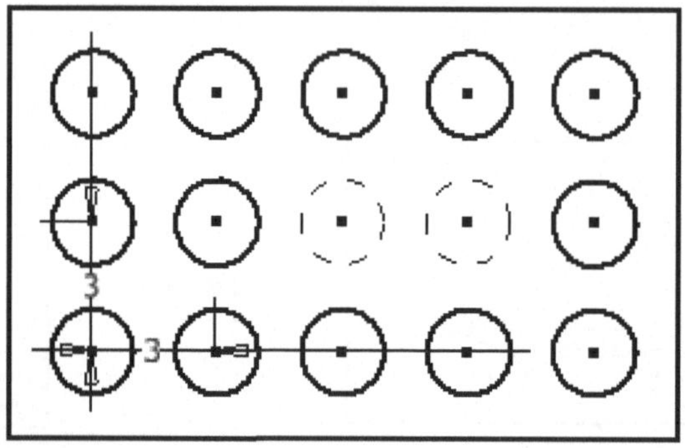

Creating a Circular Pattern

The **Circular Pattern** tool is used for creating multiple instances or duplicate copies of an existing sketch entity in a circular manner about a center point, see Figure 3.44. The method for creating a circular pattern is discussed below:

3.44

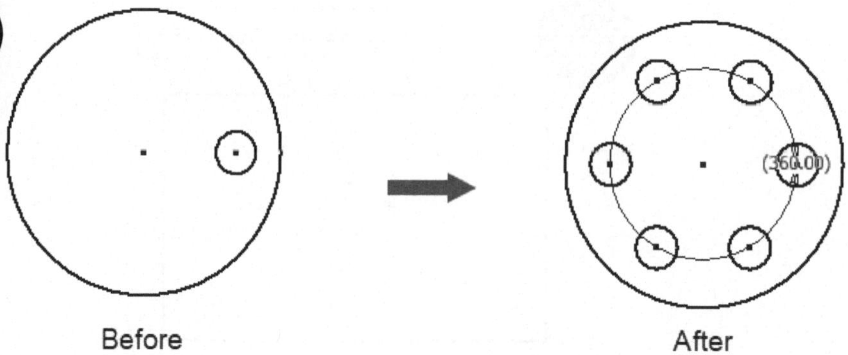

1. Click on the **Circular Pattern** tool in the **Pattern** panel of the **Sketch** tab, see Figure 3.45. The **Circular Pattern** dialog box appears, see Figure 3.46. Also, you are prompted to select a geometry to be patterned.

3.45

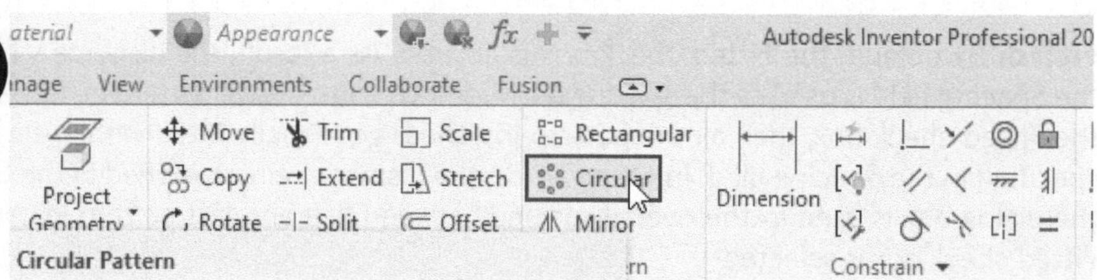

3.46

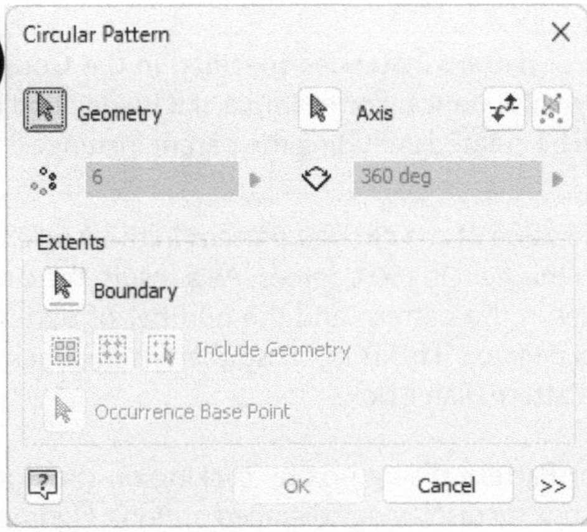

Geometry: By default, the **Geometry** button is activated in the **Circular Pattern** dialog box and is used for selecting a geometry to be patterned. You can select a single or multiple geometries to be patterned.

2. Select one or more entities in the drawing area to be patterned by clicking the left mouse button, see Figure 3.47.

3. Click on the **Axis** button in the dialog box to define an axis of rotation for the circular pattern.

4. Click on a point or a circular entity to define the axis of rotation. The preview of a circular pattern appears with default parameters, see Figure 3.48. Also, an arrow appears indicating the direction of pattern.

3.47

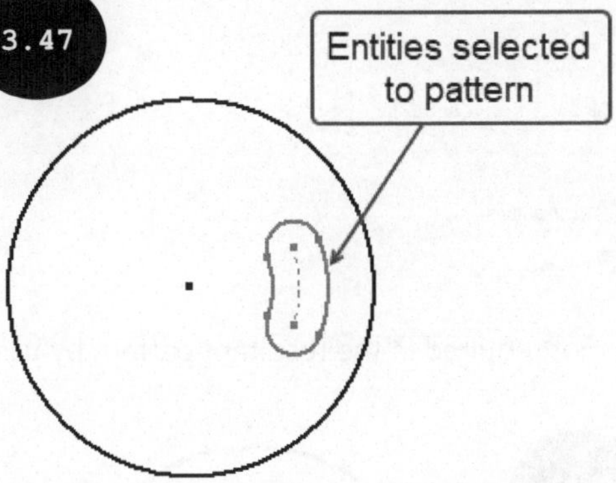

3.48

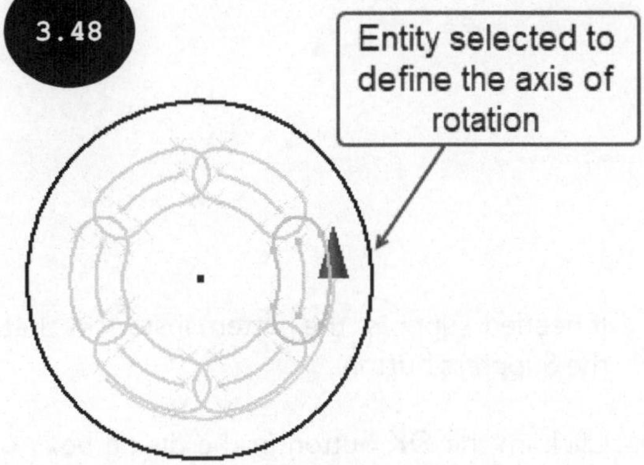

5. Click on the **Flip** button to reverse the direction of pattern, if needed.

   Symmetric: The **Symmetric** button in the **Circular Pattern** dialog box is used to define the pattern direction symmetrically on both sides of the parent geometry.

6. Enter the number of pattern instances to be created in the **Count** field of the dialog box.

Note: The number of pattern instances specified in the **Count** field is counted along with the parent or original instance. For example, if 4 is specified in the **Count** field, then 4 pattern instances will be created including the parent instance.

7. Enter the total angle value of the circular pattern in the **Angle** field of the dialog box. By default, the value entered in this field is 360 degrees. As a result, the circular pattern is created such that it covers 360 degrees in the pattern and the number of pattern instances are equally adjusted within the total 360 degrees. This is because the **Fitted** check box is selected by default in this expanded **Circular Pattern** dialog box.

8. Expand the **Circular Pattern** dialog box by clicking on the double arrow >> at the lower right corner of the dialog box for displaying advanced options. Figure 3.49 shows the expanded **Circular Pattern** dialog box. All these advanced options are same as discussed earlier.

   Extents: The options in the **Extents** area of the dialog box are used to create pattern instances within a defined boundary. These options are the same as discussed earlier.

3.49

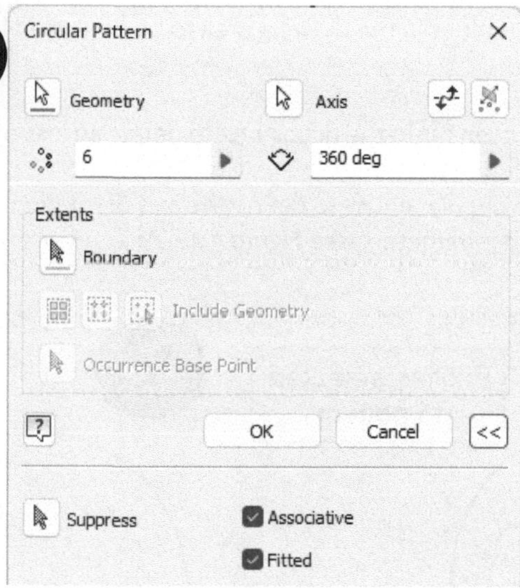

9. If needed, suppress the pattern instances that are not required in the resultant pattern by using the **Suppress** button.

10. Click on the **OK** button in the dialog box. A circular pattern is created as per the specified parameters. Figure 3.50 shows a circular pattern.

3.50

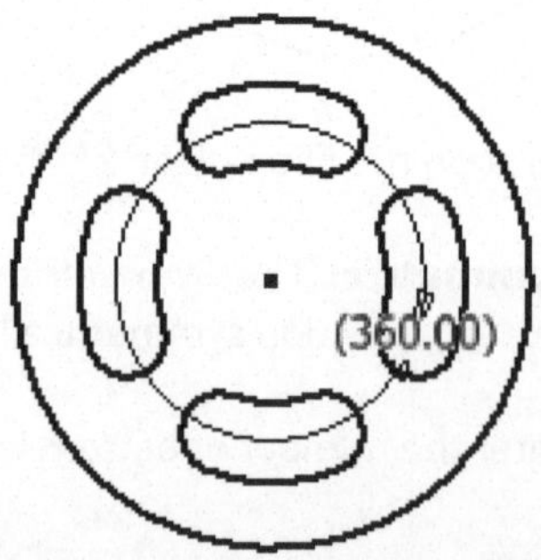

Creating Construction and Centerline Entities

In Autodesk Inventor, you can activate the construction and centerline modes for creating the respective entities in the drawing area by using the **Construction** and **Centerline** tools of the **Format** panel, respectively, see Figure 3.51.

3.51

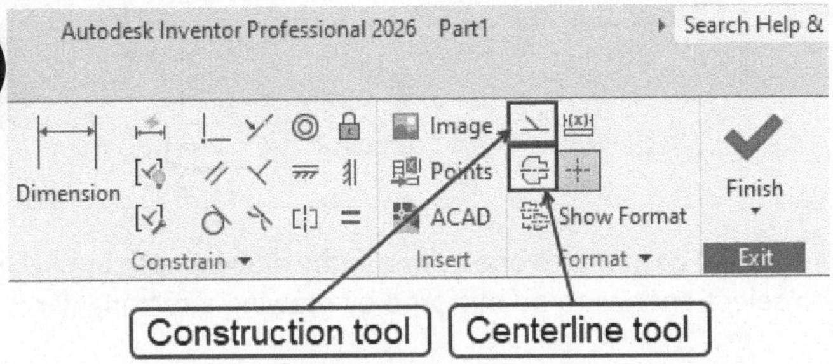

To create construction entities, click on the **Construction** tool in the **Format** panel of the **Sketch** tab. The construction mode gets activated. Now, the sketch entities you create in the drawing area by using the sketching tools will act as construction entities and can only be used as reference. Figure 3.52 shows a circle created by using the **Center Point Circle** tool after activating the **Construction** tool.

Similarly, you can create a centerline by activating the **Centerline** tool in the **Format** panel. Figure 3.53 shows a line created by using the **Line** tool after activating the **Centerline** tool.

3.52

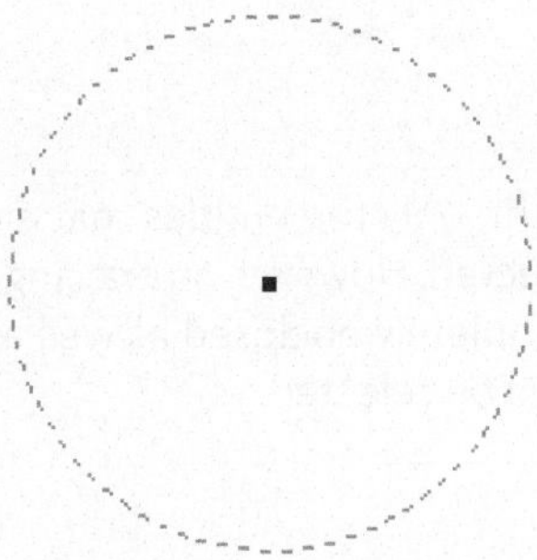

3.53

Note: You can also convert existing solid sketch entities into construction entities. For doing so, select entities to be converted and then click on the **Construction** tool in the **Format** panel. The selected entities get converted into construction entities.

Mirroring Sketch Entities

In Autodesk Inventor, you can mirror sketch entities about a mirroring line by using the **Mirror** tool of the **Pattern** panel in the **Sketch** tab. You can select a line or a centerline as the mirroring line. The method for mirroring sketch entities is discussed below:

1. Click on the **Mirror** tool in the **Pattern** panel of the **Sketch** tab, see Figure 3.54. The **Mirror** dialog box appears, see Figure 3.55. Also, you are prompted to select a geometry to be mirrored, since, the **Select** button is activated in the **Mirror** dialog box by default.

3.54

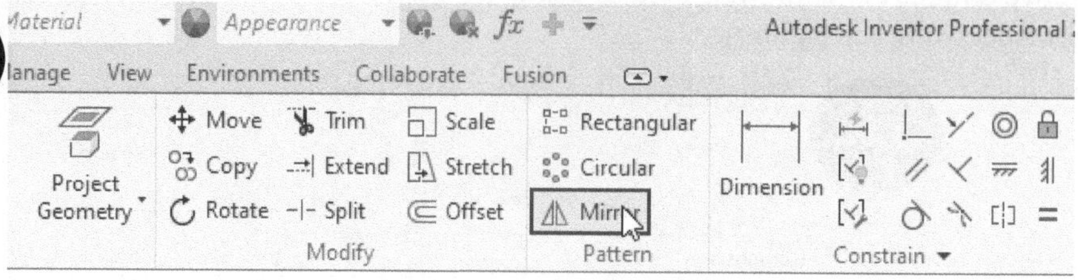

2. Select the entities to be mirrored one by one in the drawing area by clicking the left mouse button. You can also select entities to be mirrored by drawing a rectangular window around them, see Figure 3.56.

3.55

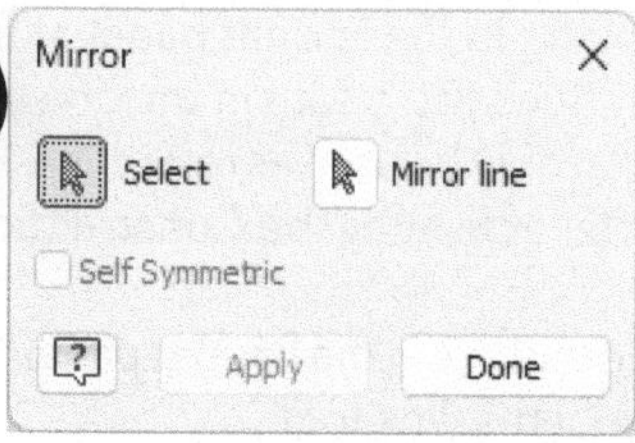

3.56

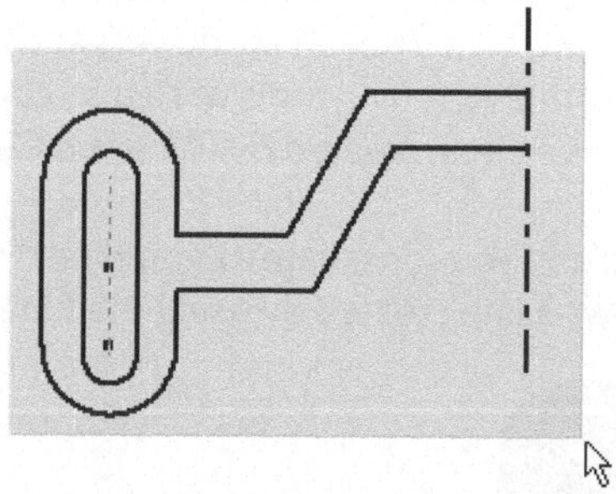

Note: On drawing a rectangular window from left to right, only the entities that are completely enclosed within the rectangular window will be selected. However, on drawing a rectangular window from right to left, all entities that are completely enclosed as well as the entities that are partially inside the rectangular window will be selected.

Now, you need to select a mirroring line.

3. Click on the **Mirror line** button in the dialog box. You are prompted to select a mirroring line.

4. Select a line or a centerline as the mirroring line in the drawing area, refer to Figure 3.57.

5. Click on the **Apply** button and then the **Done** button in the dialog box. A mirror image of the selected entities is created, see Figure 3.57.

Note: When you mirror entities, a symmetric constraint is applied between the original entities and the mirrored entities with respect to the mirroring line. As a result, on modifying the original entities, the mirrored entities get automatically modified and vice-versa. You will learn more about constraints in later chapters.

3.57

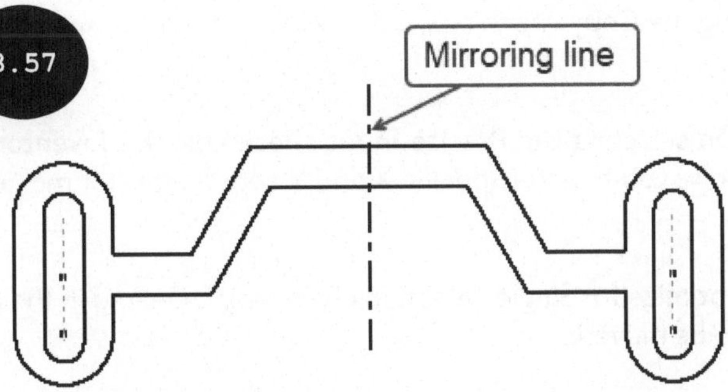

Moving a Sketch Entity

You can move a sketch entity from one position to another in the drawing area by using the **Move** tool of the **Modify** panel in the **Sketch** tab. The method for moving an entity is discussed below:

1. Click on the **Move** tool in the **Modify** panel, see Figure 3.58. The **Move** dialog box appears, see Figure 3.59. You are then prompted to select a geometry to be moved. The options in the **Move** dialog box are discussed below:

3.58

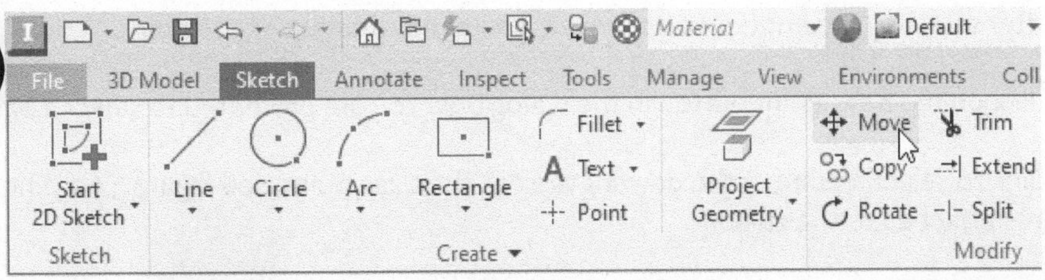

3.59

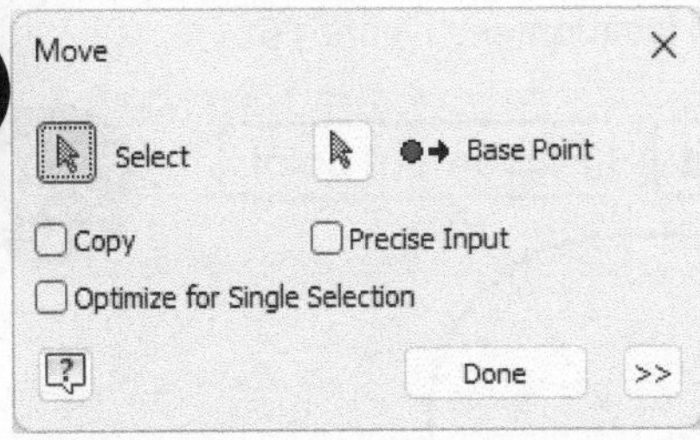

Select: The **Select** button in the **Move** dialog box is used for selecting sketch entities to be moved from one position to another in the drawing area. By default, the **Select** button is activated in the dialog box.

Base Point: The **Base Point** button is used for selecting a base point which acts as a reference point for moving the selected entities.

Optimize for Single Selection: By default, the **Optimize for Single Selection** check box is cleared. As a result, you are allowed to make multiple selections for entities to be moved. However, if you select the **Optimize for Single Selection** check box, then on making a single selection in the drawing area, you will be automatically switched to the base point selection mode.

Copy: On selecting the **Copy** check box, a duplicate copy of the selected entities moves to the specified location.

Precise Input: On selecting the **Precise Input** check box, the **Inventor Precise Input** toolbar appears, which allows you to enter specific X and Y coordinates for moving the entities to a new location.

2. Ensure that the **Optimize for Single Selection** check box is cleared in the dialog box for selecting multiple entities to be moved.

3. Select one or more entities to be moved, see Figure 3.60. You can select entities one by one by clicking the left mouse button or by drawing a rectangular window around the entities.

Note: On drawing a rectangular window from left to right, only the entities that are completely enclosed within the rectangular window will be selected. However, on drawing a rectangular window from right to left, all entities that are completely enclosed as well as the entities that are partially inside the rectangular window will be selected.

After selecting the entities to be moved, you need to select a base point.

4. Click on the **Base Point** button in the dialog box. You are prompted to select a base point.

5. Click to select a point in the drawing area as the base point, see Figure 3.60. The selected entity gets attached to the cursor.

6. Click to specify a placement point in the drawing area, see Figure 3.60. The selected entity gets moved to the specified location, see Figure 3.61.

3.60

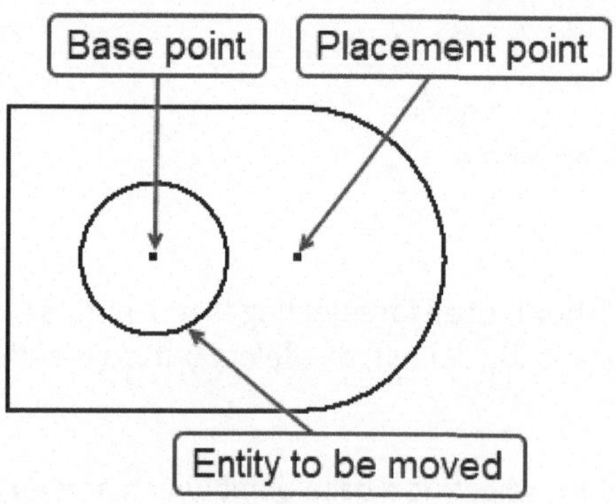

3.61

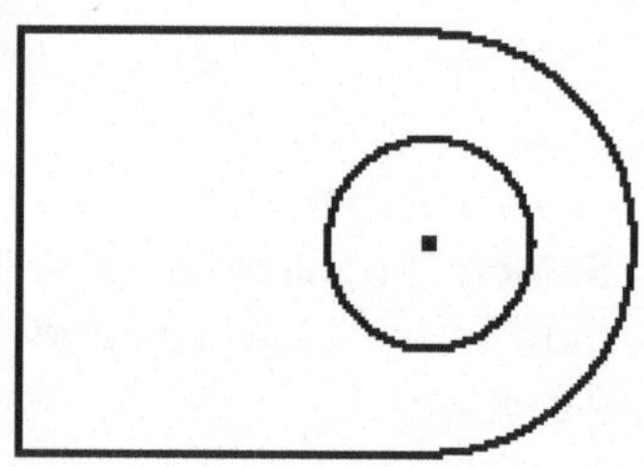

7. Click on the **Done** button in the dialog box.

Note: While moving entities, you can also control the behavior of the dimensions and constraints that are applied to the selected entities. For doing so, expand the **Move** dialog box by clicking on the double arrows available at the lower right corner of the dialog box. Figure 3.62 shows the expanded **Move** dialog box.

By default, the **Prompt** option is selected in the **Relax Dimensional Constraints** and **Break Geometric Constraints** areas of the expanded **Move** dialog box. As a result, if the move operation fails due to the applied dimensions and constraints of the selected entities, then a dialog box appears indicating the problem and also provides possible solutions.

On selecting the **Never** option in the **Relax Dimensional Constraints** and **Break Geometric Constraints** areas, the dimensions and constraints that are applied to the selected entities will not be ignored while performing the move operation.

On selecting the **Always** option in the **Relax Dimensional Constraints** and **Break Geometric Constraints** areas, the applied dimensions get modified based on the new location and the constraints associated with the selected entities get deleted.

On selecting the **If No Equation** option, the dimensions that are a function of any other dimension will not be ignored while performing the move operation. This option is only available in the **Relax Dimensional Constraints** area of the expanded **Move** dialog box.

3.62

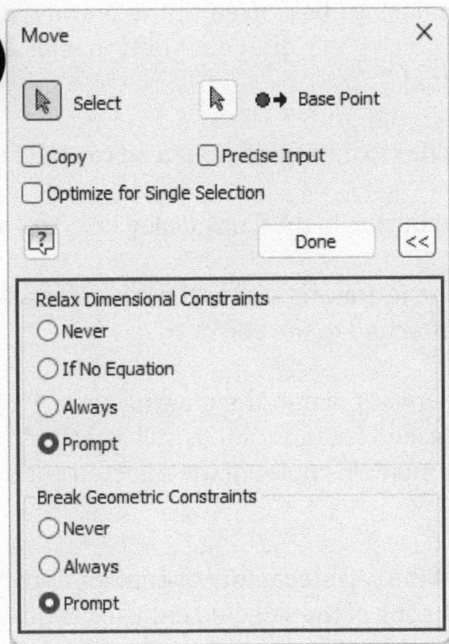

Creating a Copy of Sketch Entities

You can create a copy of a set of sketch entities by using the **Copy** tool. The method for creating a copy of entities is discussed below:

1. Click on the **Copy** tool in the **Modify** panel of the **Sketch** tab. The **Copy** dialog box appears, see Figure 3.63. Also, you are prompted to select the geometry to be copied.

3.63

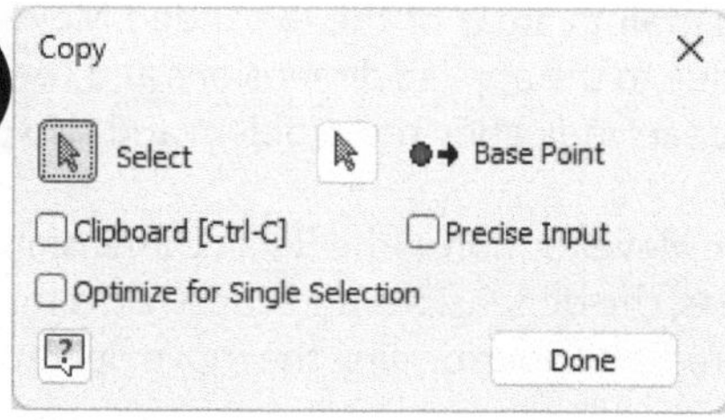

Note: All the options in the **Copy** dialog box are same as discussed earlier except the **Clipboard [Ctrl-C]** check box. On selecting the **Clipboard [Ctrl-C]** check box, you can copy the selected entities to the clipboard and paste into a different sketch.

2. Ensure that the **Optimize for Single Selection** check box is cleared in the dialog box for selecting multiple entities to be copied.

3. Select one or more entities to be copied in the drawing area, see Figure 3.64. You can select entities one by one by clicking the left mouse button or by drawing a rectangular window around the entities to be selected.

   After selecting the entities to be copied, you need to select a base point.

4. Click on the **Base Point** button in the **Copy** dialog box. You are prompted to select a base point.

5. Click to select a point in the drawing area as the base point, see Figure 3.64. A copy of the selected entity or entities gets attached to the cursor.

6. Click to specify a placement point in the drawing area. A copy of the selected entity or entities gets created in the specified location, and is still attached to the cursor. This indicates that you can continue to create multiple copies of the selected entities by specifying placement points in the drawing area.

7. After creating a copy of the selected entity or entities, click on the **Done** button in the dialog box or press the ESC key. A copy of the selected entity or entities is created, see Figure 3.65.

3.64

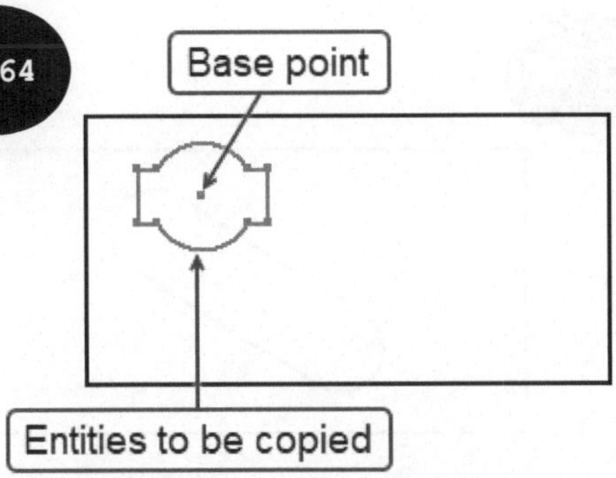

3.65

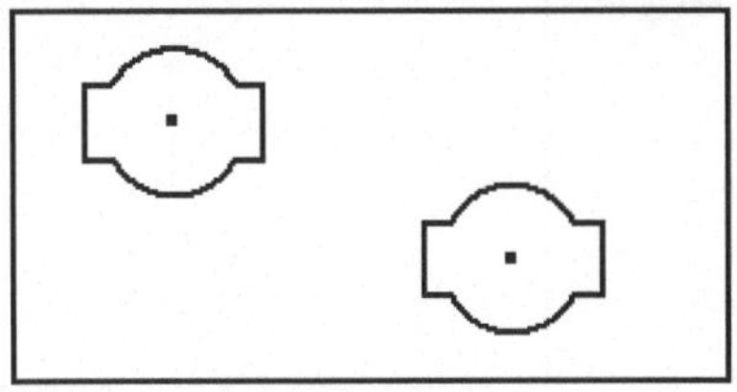

Rotating an Entity

You can rotate one or more sketch entities at an angle by using the **Rotate** tool. The method for rotating an entity is discussed below:

1. Click on the **Rotate** tool in the **Modify** panel of the **Sketch** tab. The **Rotate** dialog box appears, see Figure 3.66. Also, you are prompted to select the geometry to be rotated.

3.66

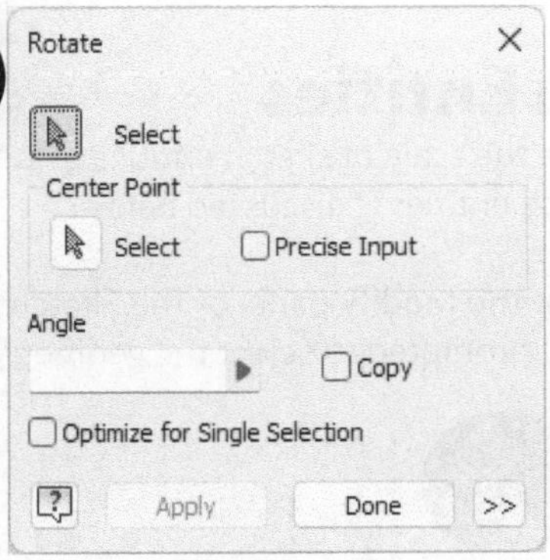

2. Select one or more entities to be rotated in the drawing area, see Figure 3.67. You can select entities one by one by clicking the left mouse button or by drawing a rectangular window around the entities to be selected.

   After selecting the entities to be rotated, you need to select a center point of rotation.

3. Click on the **Center Point** button in the **Rotate** dialog box. You are prompted to select a center point.

4. Click to select a point in the drawing area as the center point for rotating the selected entities, see Figure 3.67. The preview appears in the drawing area such that, as you move the cursor, the selected entities rotate around the specified center point.

5. Enter the angle of rotation in the **Angle** field of the dialog box and then click on the **Apply** button in the dialog box. The selected entities get rotated at the specified angle around the center point in the drawing area, see Figure 3.68. Alternatively, you can also click arbitrarily in the drawing area to specify the angle of rotation.

3.67

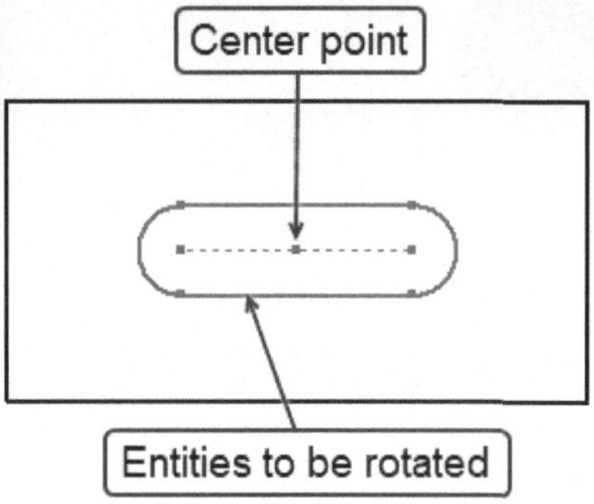

3.68

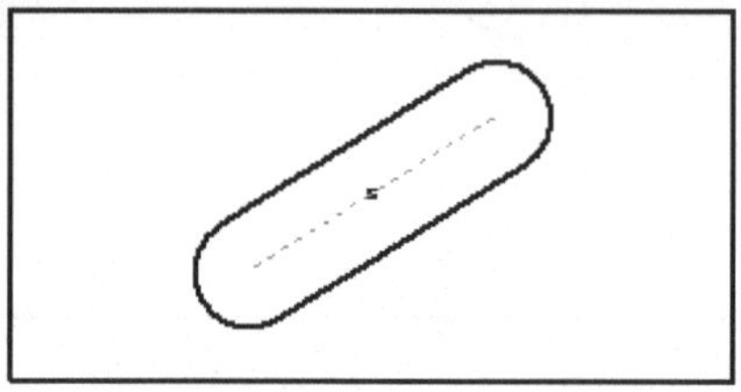

6. Press the ESC key or click on the **Done** button to exit the dialog box.

Tip: While rotating the entities, you can also control the behavior of the dimensions and constraints that are applied to the selected entities by using the options available in the expanded **Rotate** dialog box. You can expand the dialog box by clicking on the double arrow available at its lower right corner. The options are the same as discussed earlier.

Scaling Sketch Entities

You can increase or decrease the scale of sketch entities by using the **Scale** tool of the **Modify** panel. The method for scaling sketch entities is discussed below:

1. Click on the **Scale** tool in the **Modify** panel of the **Sketch** tab. The **Scale** dialog box appears, see Figure 3.69. Also, you are prompted to select the geometry to be scaled.

3.69

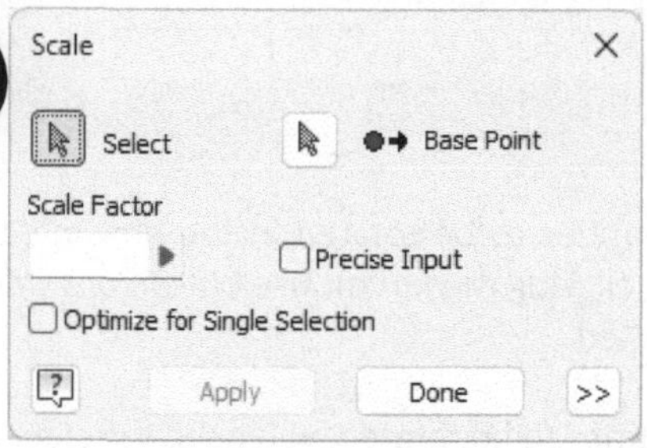

2. Select one or more entities to be scaled in the drawing area, see Figure 3.70. You can select entities one by one by clicking the left mouse button or by drawing a rectangular window around the entities to be selected.

   After selecting the entities to be scaled, you need to select a base point.

3. Click on the **Base Point** button in the **Scale** dialog box. You are prompted to select a base point.

4. Click to select a base point in the drawing area as a reference point for scaling the selected entities, see Figure 3.70. The **Autodesk Inventor Professional** dialog box appears which informs you that

the selected geometry being edited is constrained to another geometry, see Figure 3.71. Note that this dialog box appears, if the selected entities to be scaled have constraints with other entities of the sketch.

3.70

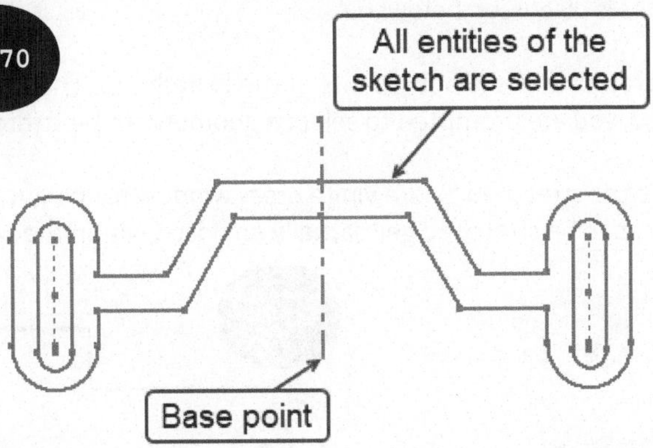

3.71

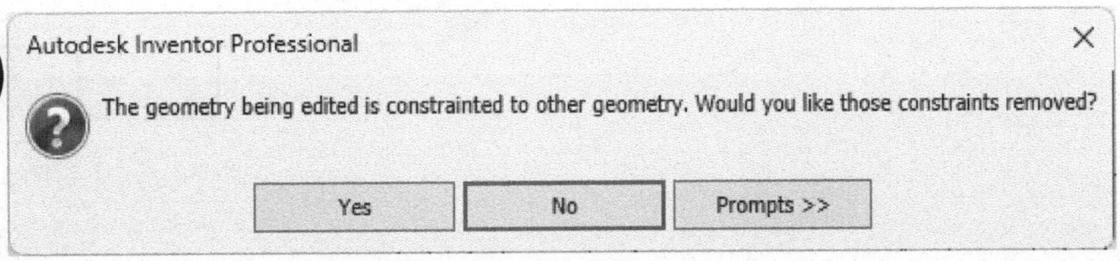

5. Click on the **No** button in the dialog box to retain the applied constraints. If you click on the **Yes** button, the applied constraints will be removed. The preview appears in the drawing area such that as you move the cursor, the selected entities get scaled, dynamically, see Figure 3.72.

3.72

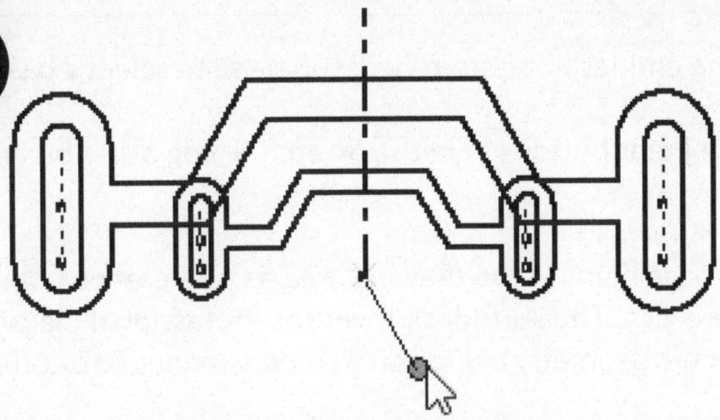

6. Enter the scale factor in the **Scale Factor** field of the **Scale** dialog box for scaling the selected entities. Next, click on the Apply button. The selected entities get scaled at the specified scale factor.

7. Press the ESC key or click on the **Done** button to exit the dialog box.

Tip: While scaling entities, you can also control the behavior of the dimensions and constraints that are applied to the selected entities by using the options available in the expanded **Scale** dialog box. You can expand the dialog box by clicking on the double arrow available at its lower right corner. The options are the same as discussed earlier.

Stretching Sketch Entities

You can stretch entities of a sketch by using the **Stretch** tool of the **Modify** panel. The method for stretching sketch entities is discussed below:

1. Click on the **Stretch** tool in the **Modify** panel of the **Sketch** tab. The **Stretch** dialog box appears, see Figure 3.73. Also, you are prompted to select a geometry to be stretched.

2. Select the entities to be stretched by drawing a cross window from right to left in the drawing area such that the entities to be stretched get partially enclosed within the window, see Figure 3.74.

3.73

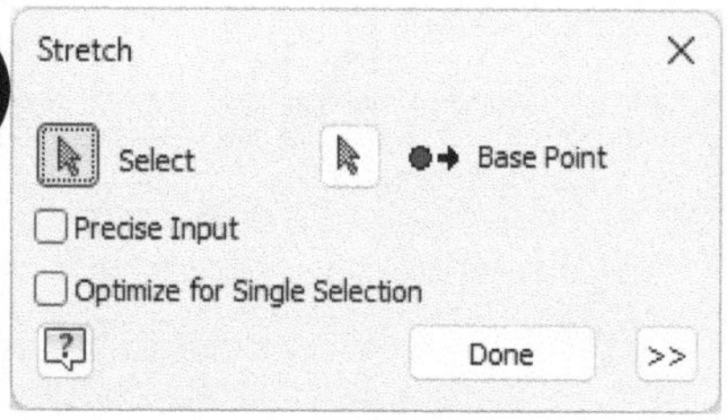

3.74

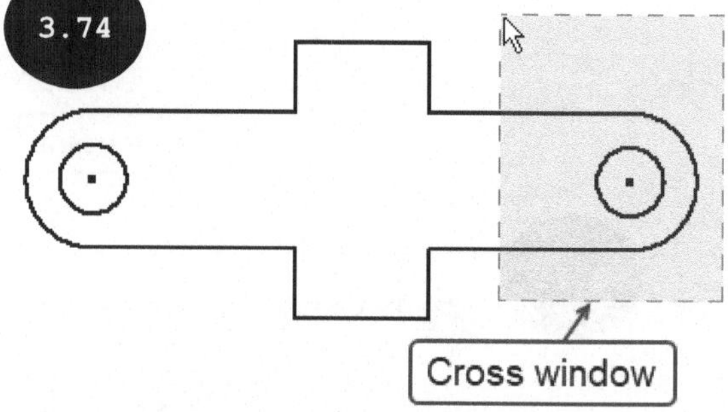

Note: You can only stretch objects that are partially enclosed by the boundary of the cross window. The objects that are completely enclosed within the boundary will move rather than being stretched.

After selecting the entities to be stretched, you need to select a base point.

3. Click on the **Base Point** button in the **Stretch** dialog box. You are prompted to select a base point.

4. Click to select a base point in the drawing area as a reference point for stretching the selected entities, see Figure 3.75. The **Autodesk Inventor Professional** dialog box appears which informs you that the selected geometry being edited is constrained to another geometry.

5. Click on the **No** button in the **Autodesk Inventor Professional** dialog box to retain the applied constraints. If you click on the **Yes** button, the applied constraints will be removed. The preview appears in the drawing area such that as you move the cursor, the selected entities get stretched, dynamically, see Figure 3.76.

3.75

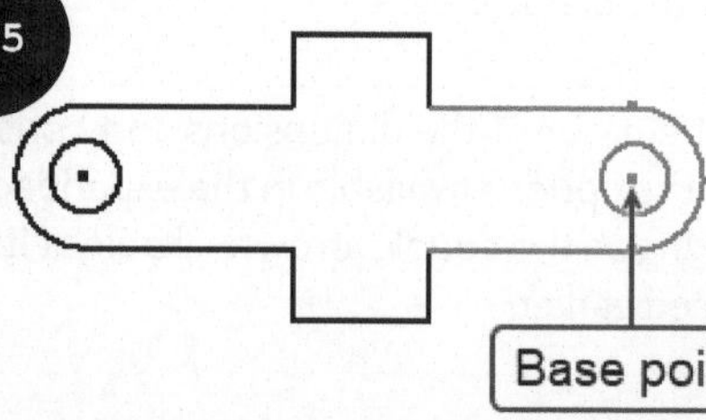

3.76

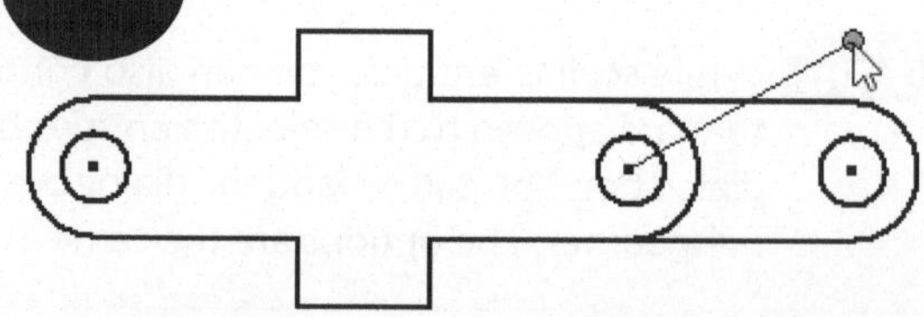

6. Click to specify a new position for the stretched entities in the drawing area. The entities get stretched.

7. Press the ESC key or click on the **Done** button to exit the dialog box.

Tutorial 1

Draw the sketch of the model shown in Figure 3.77. The dimensions and the 3D model shown in the figure are for your reference only. You will learn about applying dimensions and creating the 3D model in later chapters. All dimensions are in mm.

3.77

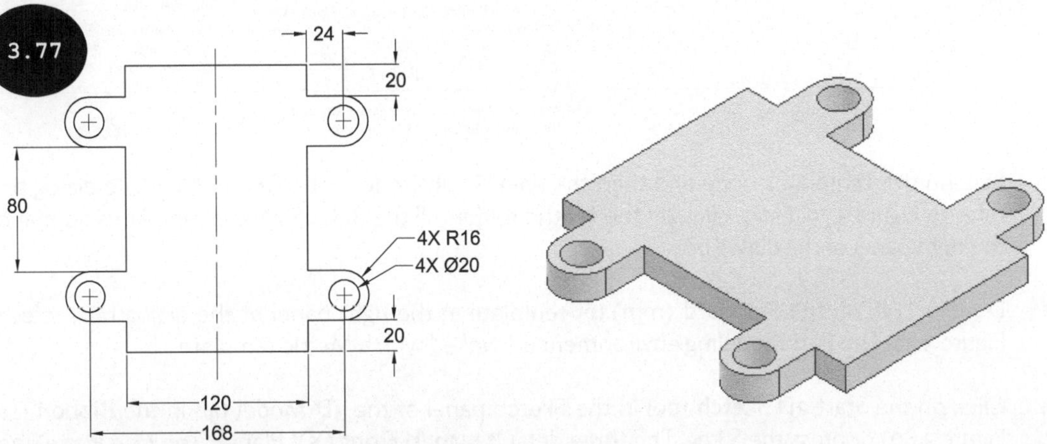

Section 1: Starting Autodesk Inventor

1. Start Autodesk Inventor by double-clicking on the Autodesk Inventor icon on your desktop. The startup user interface of Autodesk Inventor appears.

Section 2: Invoking the Sketching Environment

1. Click on the **New** tool in the startup user interface of Autodesk Inventor (see Figure 3.78) or press the CTRL + N keys. The **Create New File** dialog box appears, see Figure 3.79.

3.78

3.79

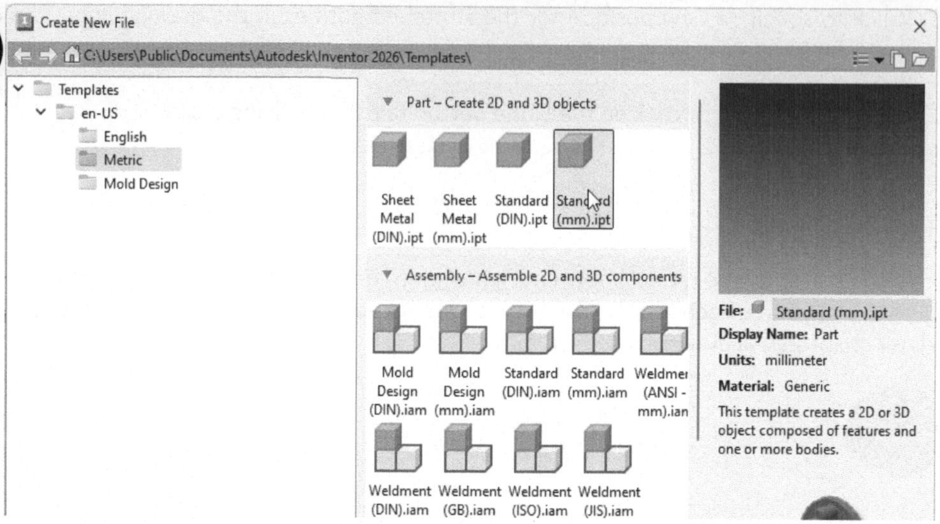

2. Expand the **Templates** node and then the **en-US** sub-node in the **Create New File** dialog box, refer to Figure 3.79. Next, click on the **Metric** folder. All the default Metric templates appear on the right panel of the dialog box.

3. Double-click on the **Standard (mm).ipt** template in the right panel of the dialog box, refer to Figure 3.79. The Part Modeling environment is invoked with a Metric template.

4. Click on the **Start 2D Sketch** tool in the **Sketch** panel of the **3D Model** tab in the **Ribbon** (see Figure 3.80) or press the S key. The three default planes: Front (XY Plane), Top (XZ Plane), and Right (YZ Plane), which are mutually perpendicular to each other appear in the graphics area. Also, you are prompted to select a plane for creating a sketch.

3.80

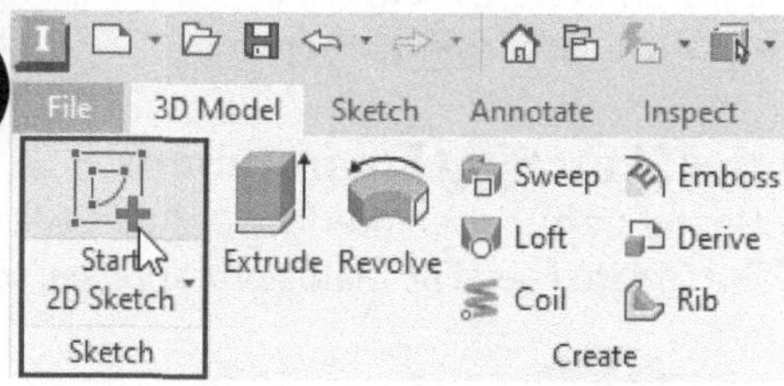

5. Move the cursor over the Top plane (XZ Plane) and then click the left mouse button when the plane gets highlighted in the graphics area. The Sketching environment is invoked and the Top plane is oriented normal to the viewing direction.

Note: It is evident from Figure 3.77 that all the sketch entities of this tutorial are multiples of 2. Therefore, you can set the snap settings such that the cursor snaps to an increment of 2 mm.

Section 3: Specifying Grids and Snap Settings

1. Click on the **Tools** tab in the **Ribbon** and then click on the **Document Settings** tool in the **Options** panel, see Figure 3.81. The **Document Settings** dialog box appears.

3.81

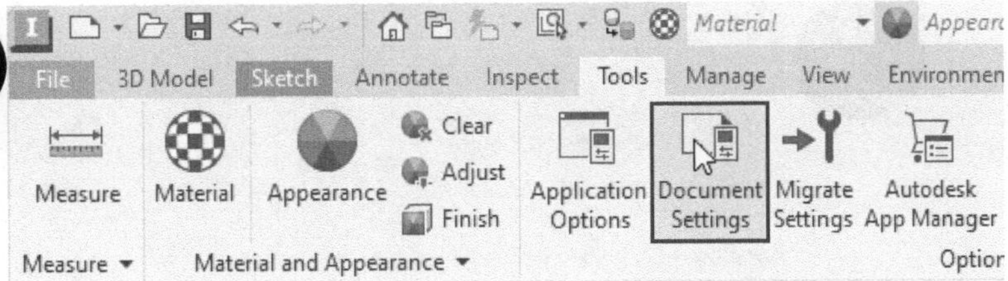

Now, you need to specify the grids and snap settings such the cursor snaps to an increment of 2 mm.

2. Click on the **Sketch** tab in the **Document Settings** dialog box, see Figure 3.82. Next, specify **2 mm** in the X and Y fields of the **Snap Spacing** area in the dialog box to snap the cursor to an incremental distance of 2 mm in X and Y directions.

3. Enter **1** in the **snaps per minor** field of the **Grid Display** area in the dialog box as the number of snap points between each grid, see Figure 3.82.

4. Enter **5** in the **Major every minor lines** field in the **Grid Display** area as the number of minor lines between two major grid lines, refer to Figure 3.82.

3.82

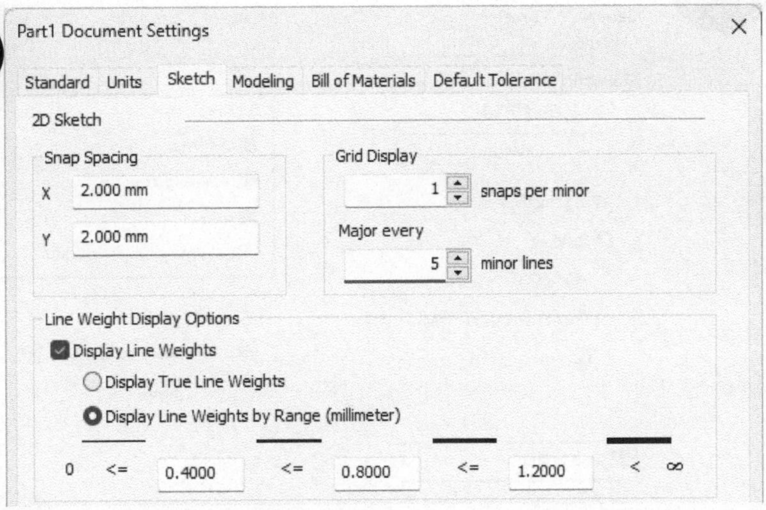

5. Click on the **Apply** button in the dialog box to apply the specified settings and then click on the **Close** button to exit the dialog box.

   After specifying the grids and snap settings, you need to turn on the display of grids in the drawing area and activate the snap mode.

6. Click on the **Application Options** tool in the **Options** panel of the **Tools** tab, see Figure 3.83. The **Application Options** dialog box appears.

3.83

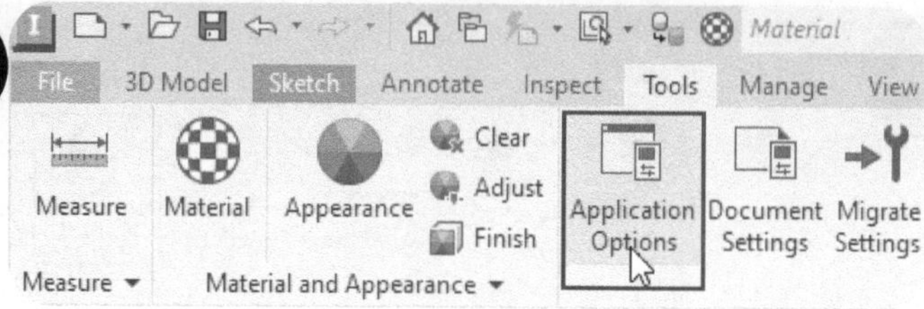

7. Click on the **Sketch** tab in the **Application Options** dialog box to display options related to the Sketching environment, see Figure 3.84.

8. Select the **Grid lines**, **Minor grid lines**, and **Axes** check boxes in the **Display** area of the dialog box to turn on their display in the drawing area, see Figure 3.84.

   Now, you need to activate the snap mode.

9. Select the **Snap to grid** check box in the **Sketch** tab of the dialog box to activate the snap mode, see Figure 3.84.

3.84

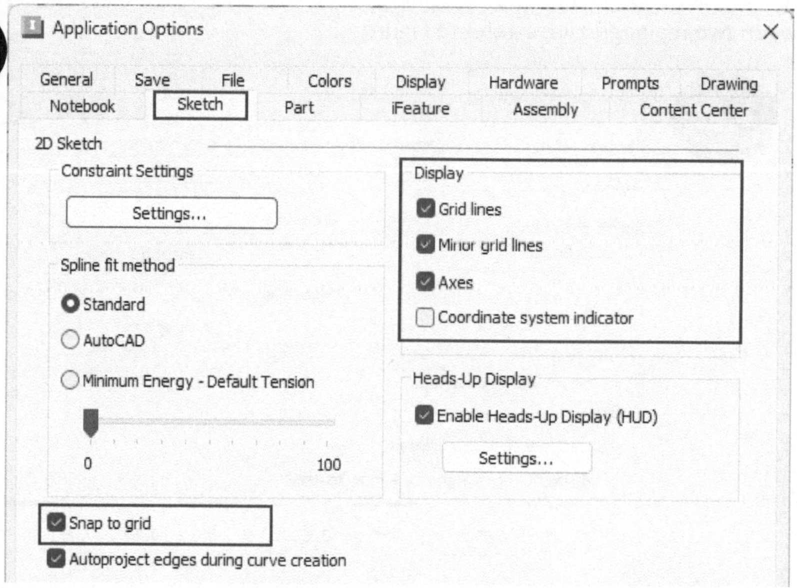

10. Click on the **Apply** button in the dialog box to apply the specified settings and then click on the **Close** button to exit the dialog box. The grids appear in the drawing area as per the specified settings.

Section 4: Drawing the Sketch

As the sketch of this tutorial is symmetric about its center line, you can create the right half of the sketch and then mirror it to create the left half.

1. Click on the **Sketch** tab in the **Ribbon** to display the sketching tools and then click on the **Line** tool, see Figure 3.85. The **Line** tool gets activated and you are prompted to specify the start point of the line.

3.85

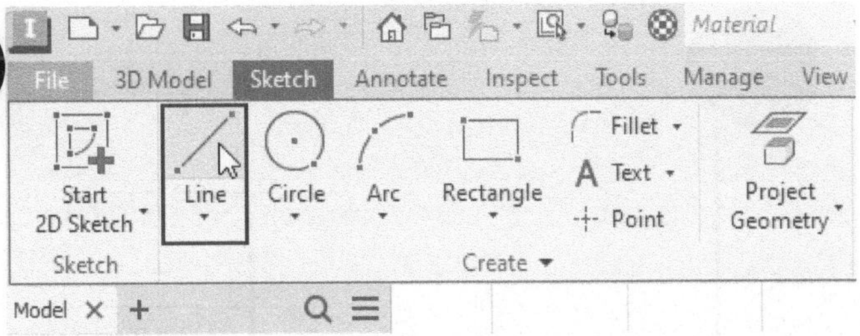

2. Move the cursor to the origin and then click to specify the start point of the line when the cursor snaps to the origin.

3. Move the cursor horizontally toward right and then click to specify the endpoint of the first line when the length of the line appears as 60 mm in the Dimension Input, see Figure 3.86.

3.86

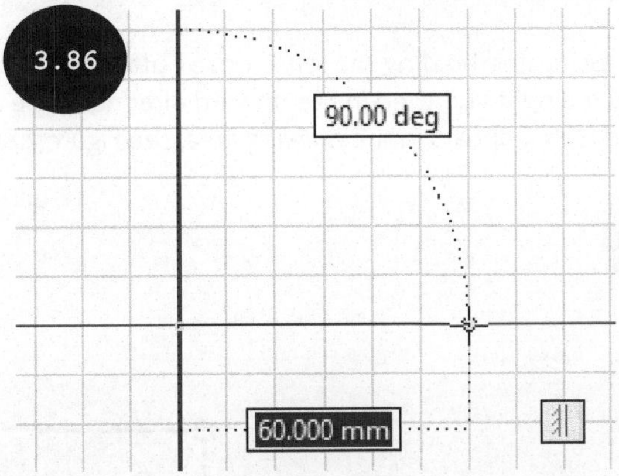

4. Move the cursor vertically upward and then click to specify the endpoint of the second line entity when the length of the line appears as 20 mm, see Figure 3.87.

3.87

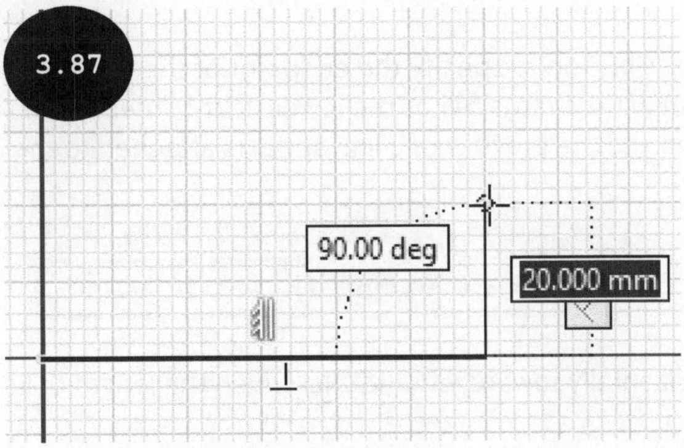

5. Move the cursor horizontally toward right and click to specify the endpoint of the line when the length of the line appears as 24 mm, see Figure 3.88.

3.88

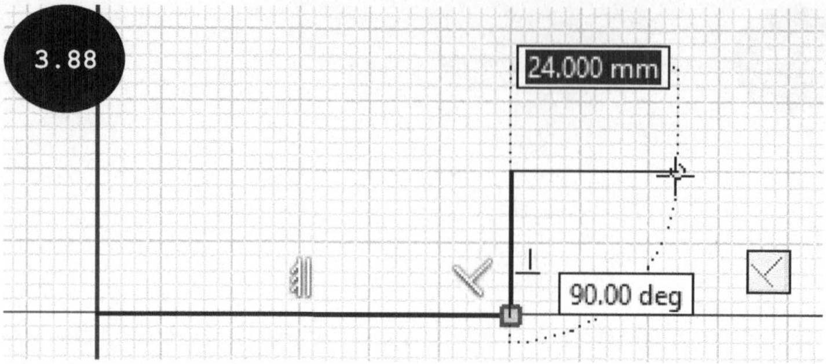

Now, you need to create an arc of radius 16 mm.

6. Move the cursor to a distance and then move it back to the last specified point. A gray colored dot appears in the drawing area.

7. Drag the cursor by pressing and holding the left mouse button from the last specified point to a small distance toward the right and then in the upward direction. The arc mode is activated and the preview of a tangent arc appears in the drawing area, see Figure 3.89.

3.89

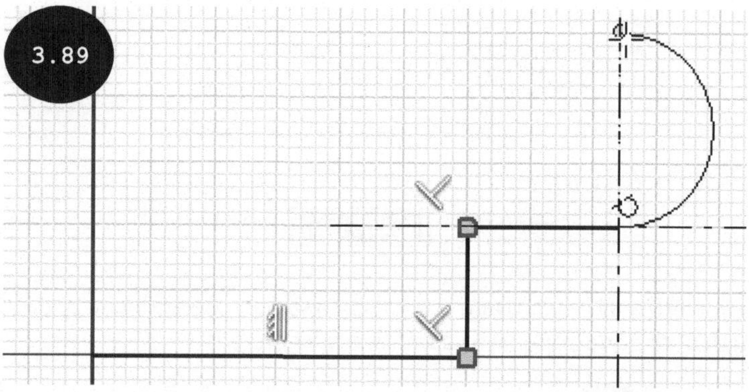

8. Release the left mouse button to specify the endpoint of the tangent arc when the radius of the arc appears as 16 mm in the Status Bar at the lower right corner of the screen, see Figure 3.90. A tangent arc is created and the preview of a line appears attached to the cursor.

3.90

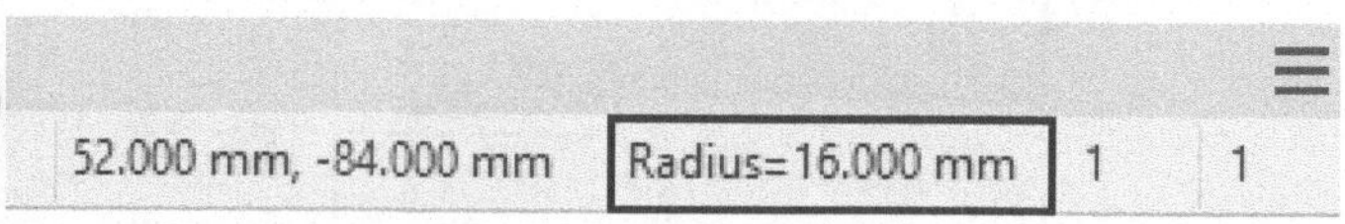

9. Move the cursor horizontally toward left and click when the length of line appears as 24 mm.

10. Move the cursor vertically upward and click when the length of the line appears as 80 mm.

11. Move the cursor horizontally toward right and then click when the length of the line appears as 24 mm, see Figure 3.91.

12. Drag the cursor from the last specified point and create a tangent arc of radius 16 mm, see Figure 3.92. In this figure, the preview of a tangent arc of radius 16 mm appears.

3.91

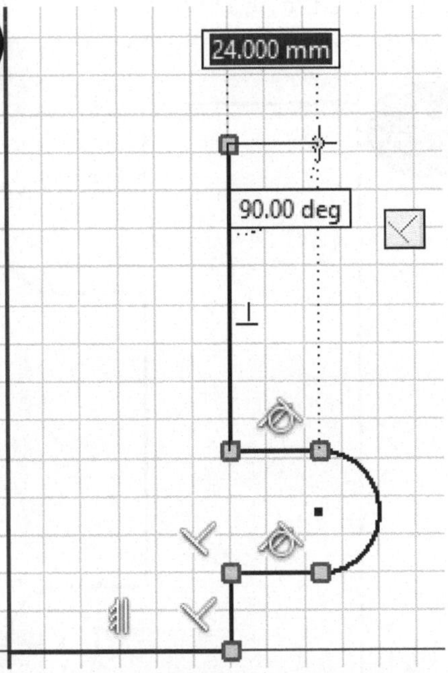

3.92

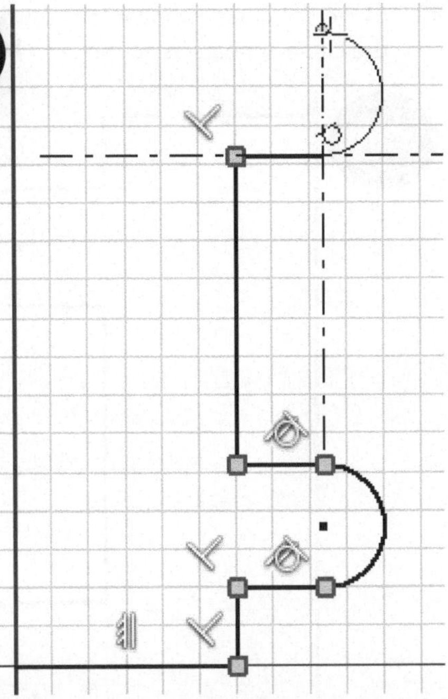

13. Move the cursor horizontally toward left and click when the length of the line appears as 24 mm.

14. Move the cursor vertically upward and click when the length of the line appears as 20 mm.

15. Move the cursor horizontally toward left and then click when the length of the line appears as 60 mm. Next, press the ESC key to exit the **Line** tool. The sketch appears similar to the one shown in Figure 3.93.

3.93

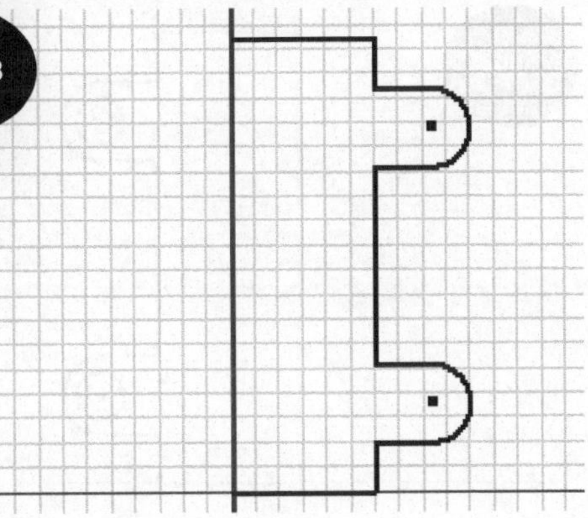

Now, you need to create two circles of diameter 20 mm.

16. Click on the **Center Point Circle** tool in the **Create** panel of the **Sketch** tab or press CTRL + SHIFT + C. You are prompted to specify the center point of the circle.

17. Move the cursor toward the center point of the lower arc of the sketch and then click the left mouse button when the cursor snaps to it, see Figure 3.94.

18. Move the cursor horizontally toward left and click the left mouse button when the diameter of the circle appears as 20 mm, see Figure 3.95. A circle of diameter 20 mm is created.

3.94

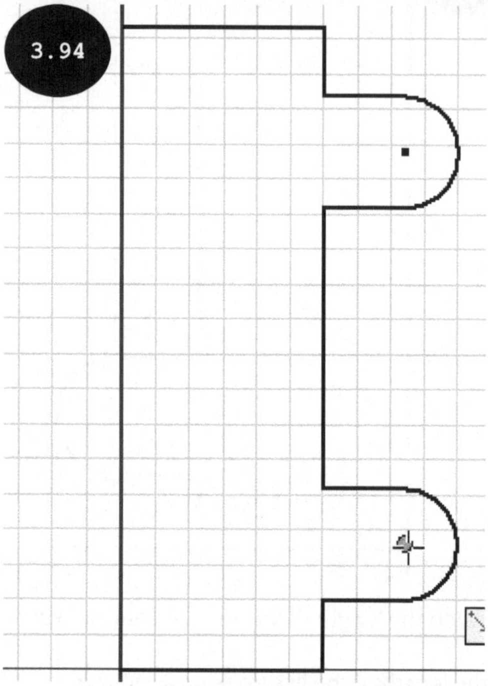

3.95

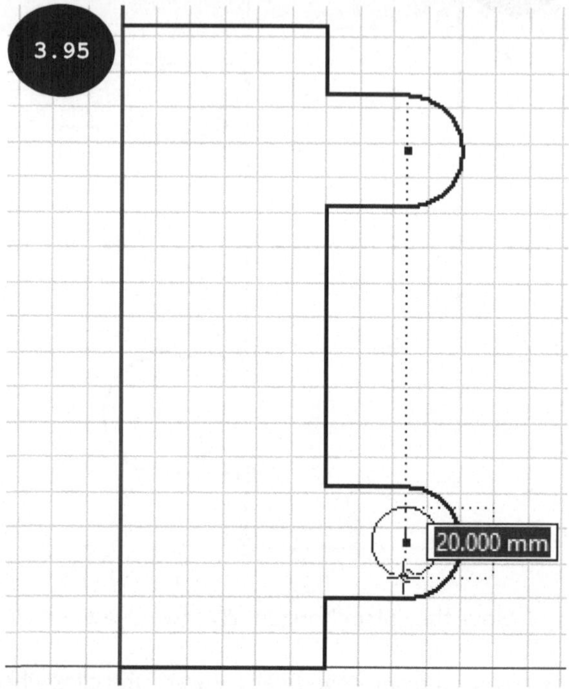

19. Similarly, create another circle of diameter 20 mm at the center point of the upper arc of the sketch. Next, press the ESC key to exit the **Center Point Circle** tool. The right half of the sketch is created, see Figure 3.96.

3.96

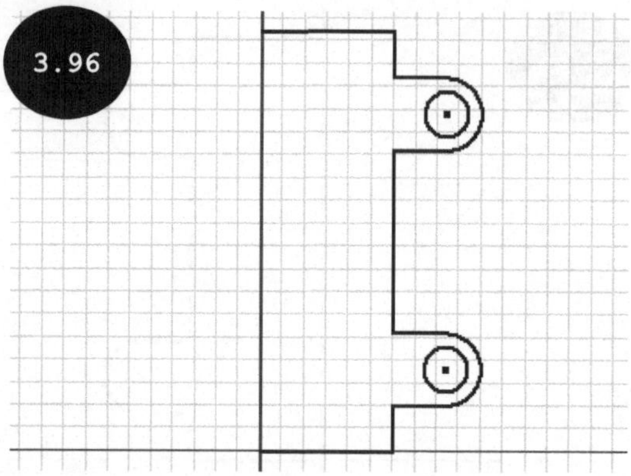

Section 5: Drawing the Centerline

Now, you need to create a centerline for mirroring the sketch.

1. Press the **L** key to invoke the **Line** tool.

2. Click on the **Centerline** tool in the **Format** panel of the **Sketch** tab to activate the centerline mode, see Figure 3.97.

3.97

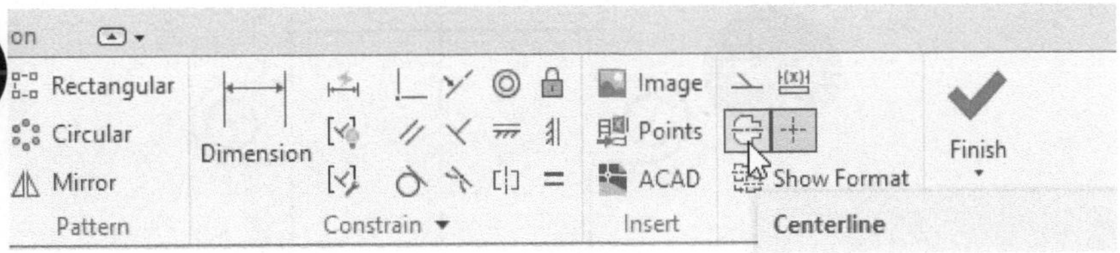

3. Click to specify the start point of the centerline at the origin.

4. Move the cursor vertically upward and then click to specify the endpoint of the centerline anywhere outside the top most entity of the sketch. A vertical centerline is created, see Figure 3.98. Next, press the ESC key to exit the tool.

5. Click on the **Centerline** tool in the **Format** panel of the **Sketch** tab again to deactivate the centerline mode.

Section 6: Mirroring Sketch Entities

After creating the centerline, you need to mirror the sketch.

1. Click on the **Mirror** tool in the **Pattern** panel of the **Sketch** tab. The **Mirror** dialog box appears and you are prompted to select the sketch to be mirrored.

2. Select all the sketch entities one by one, except the centerline, by clicking the left mouse button or by drawing a window around the entities to be selected, see Figure 3.99. You can do this by dragging the cursor from left to right.

3.98

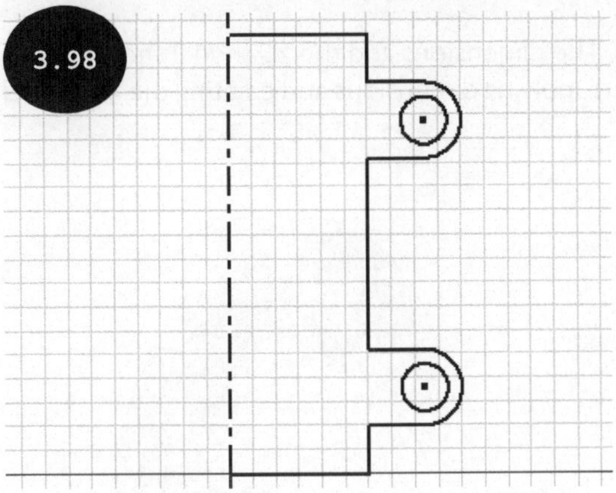

3.99

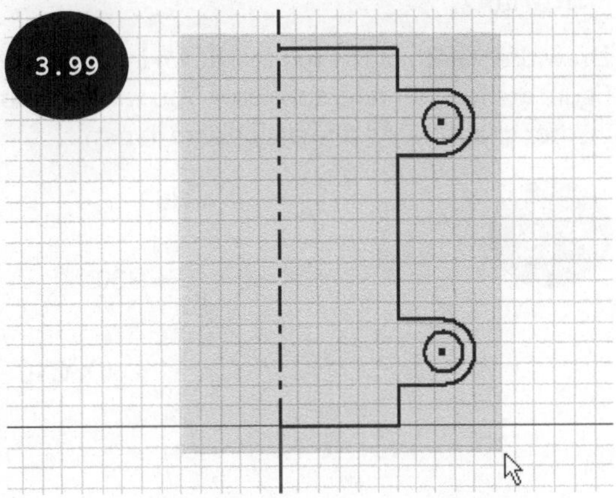

3. Click on the **Mirror line** button in the dialog box. You are prompted to select a mirroring line.

4. Click to select the vertical centerline of the sketch as the mirroring line in the drawing area.

5. Click on the **Apply** button and the **Done** button in the dialog box. The mirror image of the right half of the sketch is created. Figure 3.100 shows the final sketch.

3.100

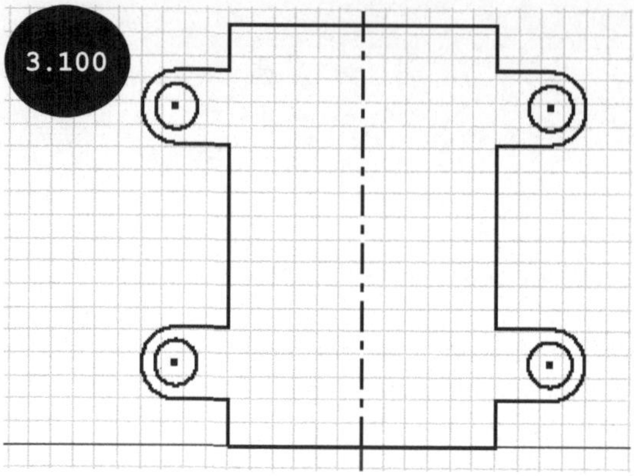

6. After creating the sketch, click on the **Finish Sketch** tool in the **Exit** panel of the **Ribbon**.

Section 7: Saving the Sketch

1. Click on the **Save** tool in the **Quick Access Toolbar**. The **Save As** dialog box appears. Next, browse to **Autodesk Inventor > Chapter 3** folder in the local drive of your system. Note that you need to create Chapter 3 folder inside the Autodesk Inventor folder.

2. Enter **Tutorial 1** in the **File name** field of the dialog box and then click on the **Save** button. The sketch is saved in the specified location (>:\Autodesk Inventor\Chapter 3).

Tutorial 2

Draw the sketch of the model shown in Figure 3.101. The dimensions and the 3D model shown in this figure are for your reference only. You will learn about applying dimensions and creating the 3D model in later chapters. All dimensions are in mm.

3.101

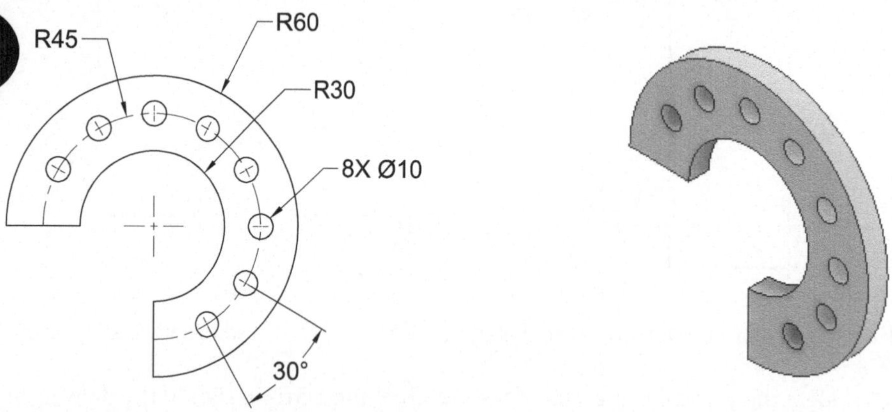

Section 1: Starting Autodesk Inventor

1. Start Autodesk Inventor by double-clicking on the Autodesk Inventor icon on your desktop. The startup user interface of Autodesk Inventor appears.

Section 2: Invoking the Sketching Environment

1. Click on the **New** tool in the startup user interface of Autodesk Inventor or press the CTRL + N keys. The **Create New File** dialog box appears, see Figure 3.102.

3.102

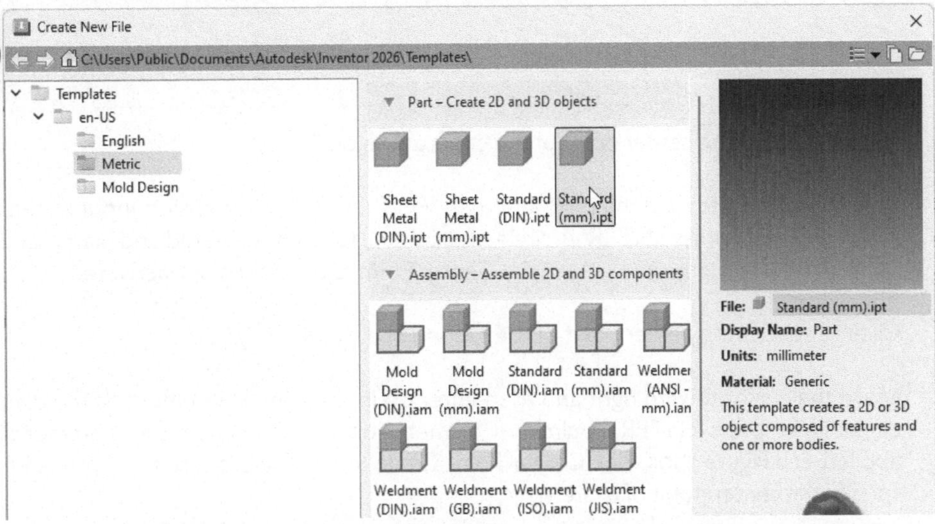

2. Expand the **Templates** node and then the **en-US** sub-node in the dialog box. Next, click on the **Metric** folder. All the default Metric templates appear on the right panel of the dialog box.

3. Double-click on the **Standard (mm).ipt** template in the right panel of the dialog box, refer to Figure 3.102. The Part Modeling environment is invoked with a Metric template.

4. Click on the **Start 2D Sketch** tool in the **Sketch** panel of the **3D Model** tab in the **Ribbon**, (see Figure 3.103) or press the S key. The three default planes: Front (XY Plane), Top (XZ Plane), and Right (YZ Plane) appear in the graphics area.

3.103

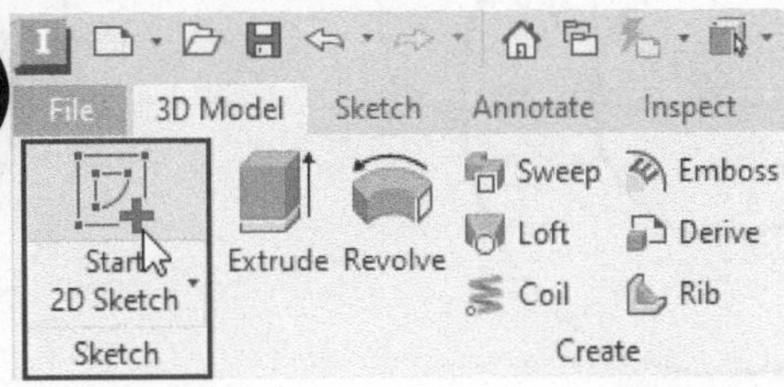

5. Move the cursor over the Front plane (XY Plane) and then click the left mouse button when the plane gets highlighted in the graphics area. The Sketching environment is invoked and the Front plane is oriented normal to the viewing direction.

Note: In this tutorial, the display of grids and snap settings is turned off.

Section 3: Drawing the Sketch

1. Click on the **Center Point Circle** tool in the **Create** panel of the **Sketch** tab, see Figure 3.104. The **Center Point Circle** tool gets activated and you are prompted to specify the center point of the circle.

3.104

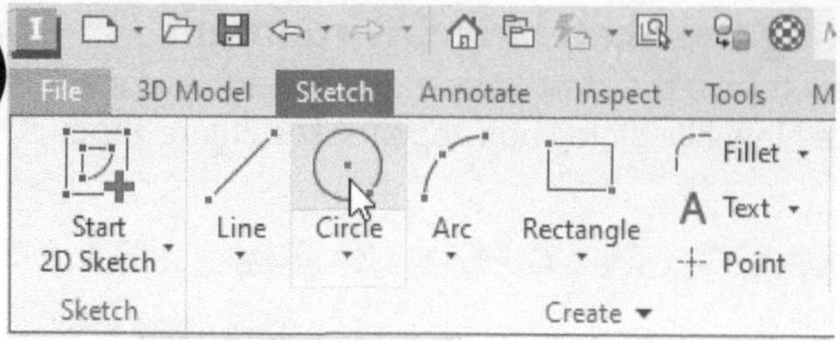

2. Click to specify the center point of the circle at the origin.

3. Move the cursor toward the right and then enter **120** in the Dimension Input as the diameter of the circle. Next, press ENTER. A circle of diameter 120 mm is created and diameter dimension is applied, refer to Figure 3.105. Also, the **Center Point Circle** tool is still activated.

4. Click to specify the center point of the second circle at the origin.

5. Move the cursor toward right and then enter **60** in the Dimension Input as the diameter of the circle. Next, press ENTER. A circle of diameter 60 mm is created and diameter dimension is applied, see Figure 3.105. The **Center Point Circle** tool is still activated and you are prompted to specify the center point of a circle.

6. Click to specify the center point of the third circle at the origin.

7. Move the cursor toward right and then enter **90** in the Dimension Input as the diameter of the circle. Next, press ENTER. A circle of diameter 90 mm is created and diameter dimension is applied, see Figure 3.106.

3.105

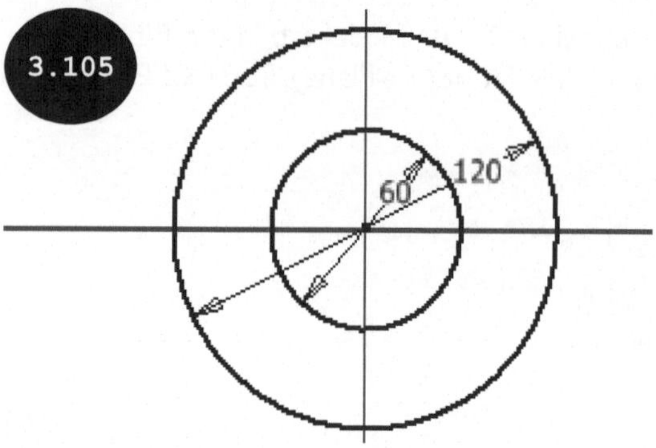

3.106

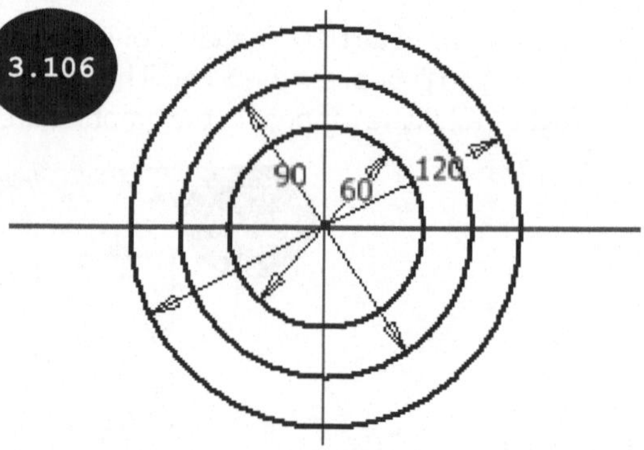

8. Press the ESC key to exit the **Center Point Circle** tool.

Tip: When you enter dimension values in the Dimension Input for creating sketch entities, the dimensions get applied by default, since the **Create dimensions from input values** check box is selected in the **Constraint Settings** dialog box. To invoke this dialog box, click on the **Application Options** tool in the **Options** panel of the **Tools** tab in the **Ribbon** and then click on the **Sketch** tab in the **Application Options** dialog box that appears. Next, click on the **Settings** button in the **Constraint Settings** area of the dialog box. The **Constraint Settings** dialog box appears. In this dialog box, the **Create dimensions from Input values** check box is selected in the **Dimension** area, by default.

After creating a circle of diameter 90 mm, you need to convert it into a construction circle.

9. Select a circle of diameter 90 mm in the drawing area and then click on the **Construction** tool in the **Format** panel of the **Sketch** tab, see Figure 3.107. The construction mode gets activated and the circle of diameter 90 mm is converted into a construction circle, see Figure 3.108.

3.107

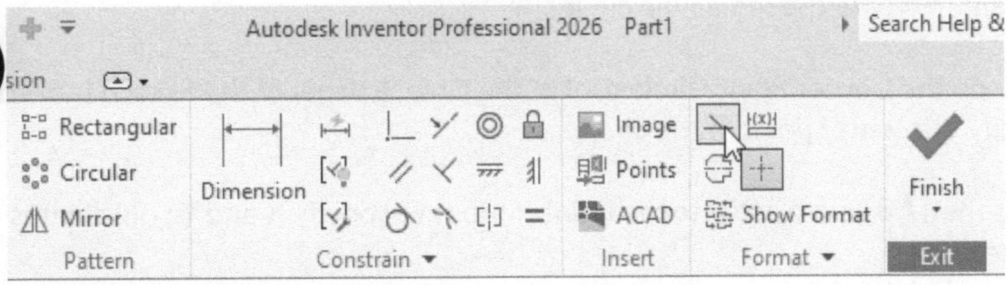

10. Press the ESC key to exit the current selection set.

11. Click on the **Line** tool in the **Create** panel of the **Sketch** tab or press the **L** key. The **Line** tool gets activated and you are prompted to specify the start point of the line.

12. Specify the start point of the line at the origin. You are prompted to specify the endpoint of the line.

13. Move the cursor horizontally toward left and then click to specify the endpoint of the line when the cursor snaps to the outer circle and the length of the line appears as 60 mm in the Dimension Input, see Figure 3.109. A horizontal line is created and the **Line** tool is still activated.

3.108

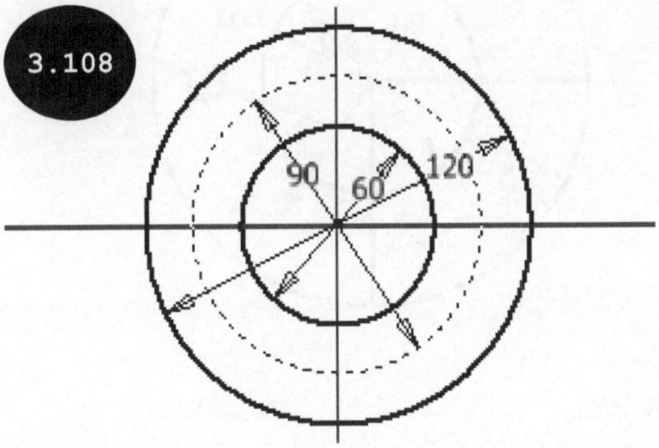

3.109

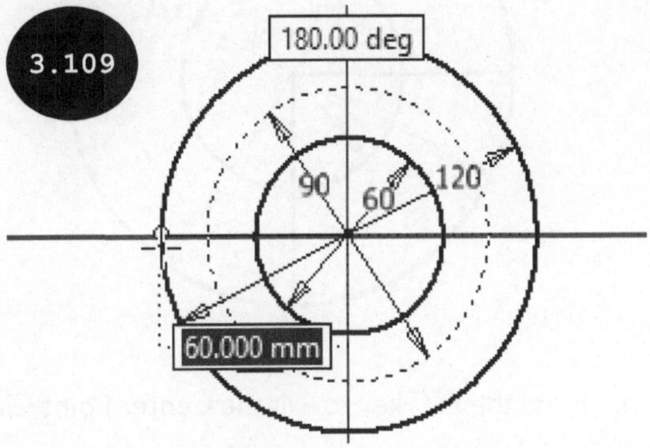

14. Move the cursor to the origin and click to specify the start point of another line when the cursor snaps to the origin.

15. Move the cursor vertically downward and click to specify the endpoint of the line when the length of the line appears as 60 mm and the cursor snaps to the outer circle. A vertical line of length 60 mm is created, see Figure 3.110.

Note: In Figure 3.110, the display of axes is turned off for the clarity of image. For doing so, click on the **Application Options** tool in the **Options** panel of the **Tools** tab to display the **Application Options** dialog box. Next, click on the **Sketch** tab in the **Application Options** dialog box and then clear the **Axes** check box.

16. Press the ESC key to exit the **Line** tool.

    Now, you need to create a circle of diameter 10 mm. It is evident from Figure 3.101, that the circles of diameter 10 mm are eight in count. As the diameter of all the circles is same and the circles are on the same PCD (Pitch Circle Diameter), you can create one circle and then create a circular pattern to create the remaining circles.

17. Click on the **Center Point Circle** tool in the **Create** panel of the **Sketch** tab. You are prompted to specify the center point of the circle.

18. Press the TAB key to activate the Pointer Input to specify X and Y coordinates of the center point of the circle.

19. Enter **45** as the X coordinate and then press the TAB key. Next, enter **0** as the Y coordinate in the Pointer Input and then press ENTER. The center point of the circle is specified and you are prompted to specify the diameter of the circle.

20. Enter **10** as the diameter of the circle in the Dimension Input. A circle of diameter 10 mm is created, see Figure 3.111.

3.110

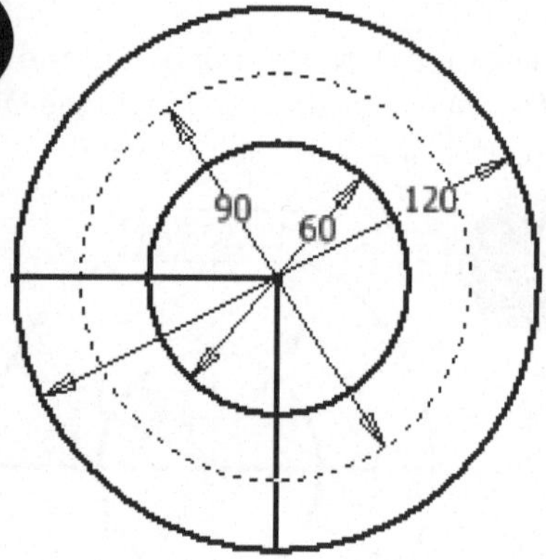

3.111

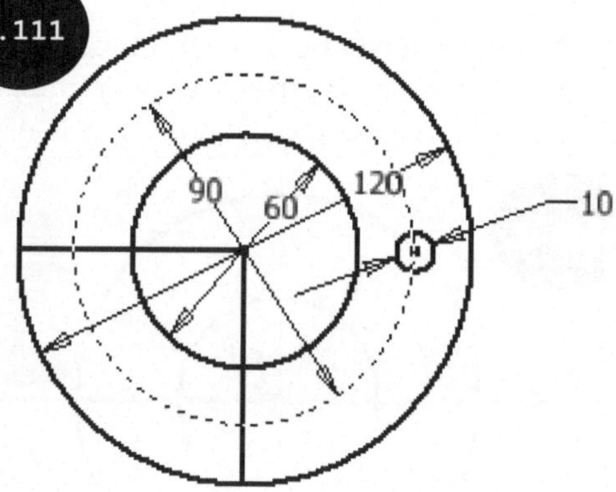

21. Press the ESC key to exit the **Center Point Circle** tool.

Section 4: Trimming Sketch Entities

Now, you need to trim the unwanted entities of the sketch.

1. Click on the **Trim** tool in the **Modify** panel of the **Sketch** tab or press the **X** key. You are prompted to select a portion of the curve to be trimmed.

2. Move the cursor over the portion of the outer most circle to be trimmed, see Figure 3.112. The circle gets highlighted in red and the portion to be trimmed appears as a dashed entity.

3. Click to trim the portion of the outer circle. The selected portion of the circle is trimmed, see Figure 3.113.

3.112

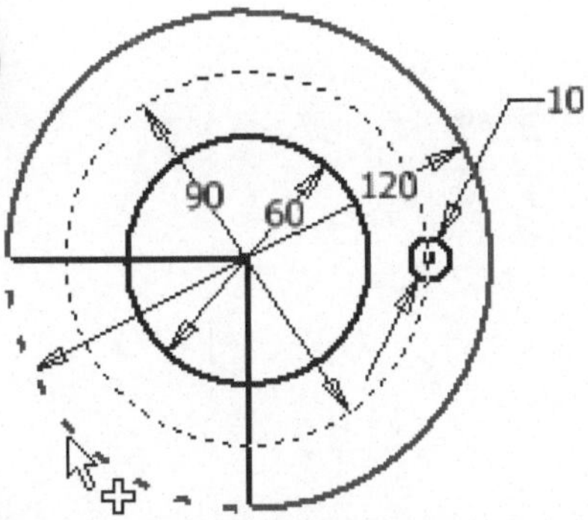

3.113

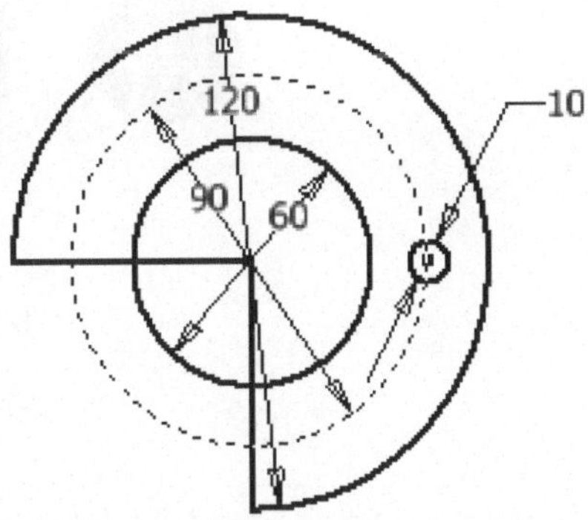

4. Similarly, trim the other unwanted portions of the sketch. Figure 3.114 shows entities to be trimmed and Figure 3.115 shows the sketch after trimming all the unwanted entities.

3.114

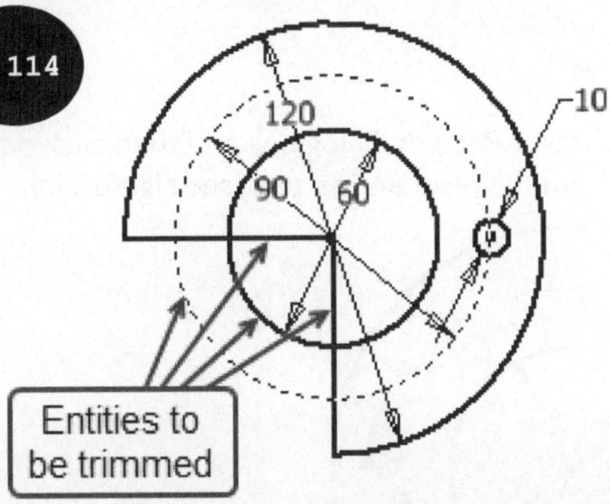

3.115

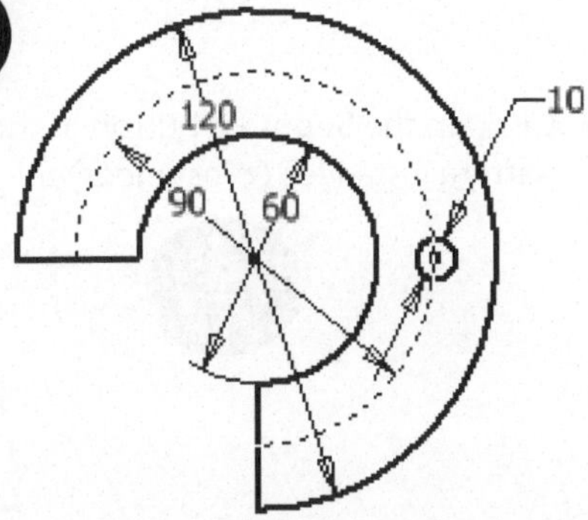

Section 5: Creating the Circular Pattern

Now, you need to create a circular pattern.

1. Click on the **Circular Pattern** tool in the **Pattern** panel of the **Sketch** tab. The **Circular Pattern** dialog box appears. Also, you are prompted to select a geometry.

2. Select a circle of diameter 10 mm in the drawing area as the geometry to be patterned.

3. Click on the **Axis** button in the **Circular Pattern** dialog box and then select the outer circle of the sketch to define the axis of revolution. A preview of the circular pattern appears with default parameters.

4. Enter **12** in the **Count** field of the dialog box as the number of instances to be created.

5. Ensure that **360 deg** is entered in the **Angle** field of the dialog box as the total angle of revolution.

6. Click on the double arrow >> at the lower right corner of the **Circular Pattern** dialog box. The dialog box gets expanded and additional options appear, see Figure 3.116.

7. Ensure that the **Associative** and **Fitted** check boxes are selected in the expanded **Circular Pattern** dialog box, see Figure 3.116.

3.116

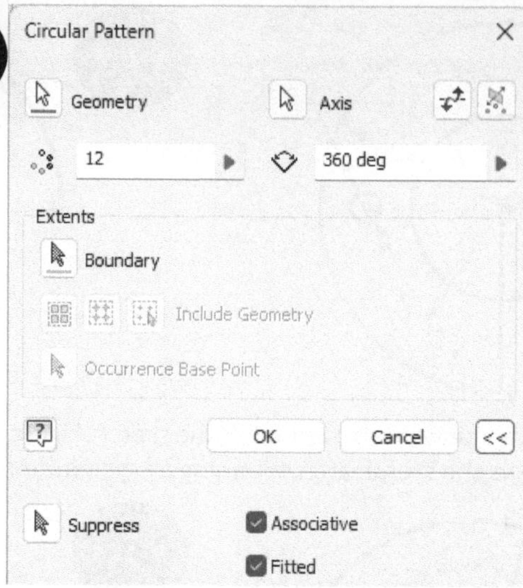

8. Click on the **Suppress** button in the expanded **Circular Pattern** dialog box and then click on the pattern instances (4 instances) to remove them from the resultant pattern, see Figure 3.117.

3.117

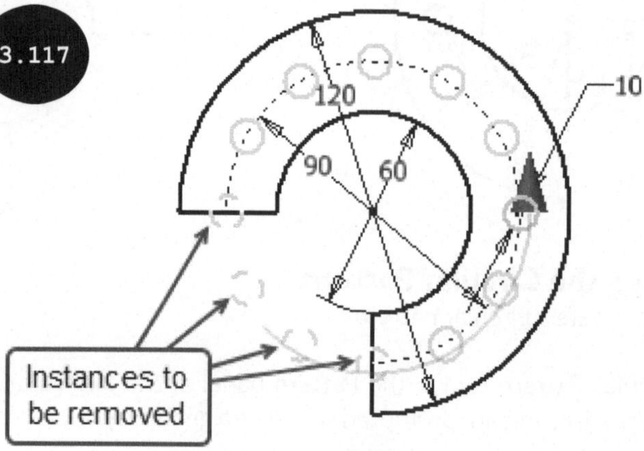

9. Click on the **OK** button in the **Circular Pattern** dialog box. The circular pattern is created, see Figure 3.118. Note that the instances that are removed from the pattern appear as reference entities only.

10. After creating the sketch, click on the **Finish Sketch** tool in the **Exit** panel of the **Ribbon**.

3.118

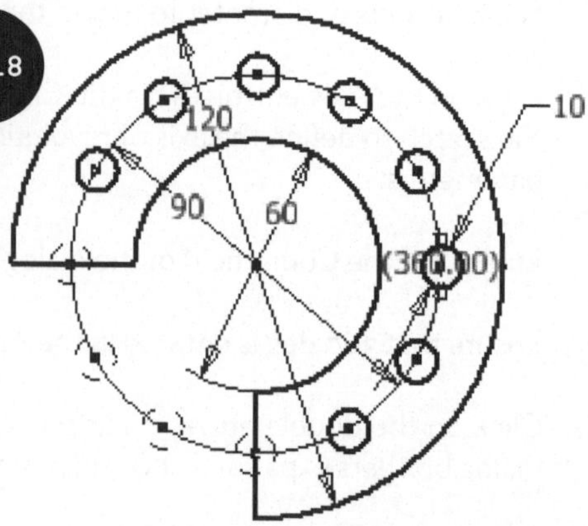

Section 6: Saving the Sketch

1. Click on the **Save** tool in the **Quick Access Toolbar**. The **Save As** dialog box appears. Next, browse to **Autodesk Inventor > Chapter 3** folder in the local drive of your system. Note that you need to create these folders, if not created earlier.

2. Enter **Tutorial 2** in the **File name** field of the dialog box and then click on the **Save** button. The sketch is saved in the specified location (>:\Autodesk Inventor\Chapter 3).

Hands-on Test Drive 1

Draw a sketch of the model shown in Figure 3.119. The dimensions and the 3D model are for your reference only. All dimensions are in mm.

3.119

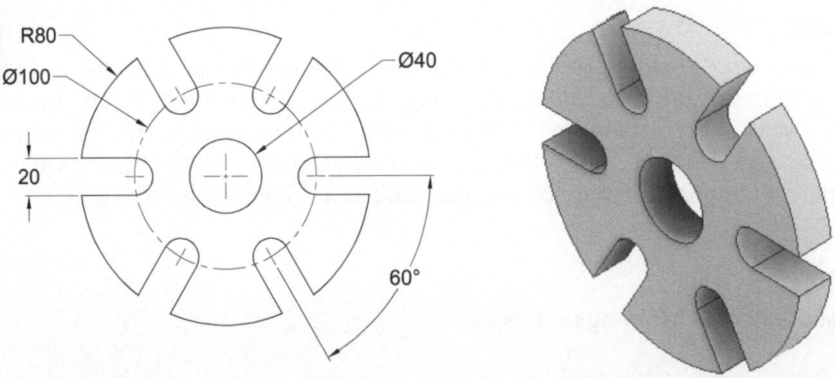

Hands-on Test Drive 2

Draw a sketch of the model shown in Figure 3.120. The dimensions and the 3D model are for your reference only. All dimensions are in mm.

3.120

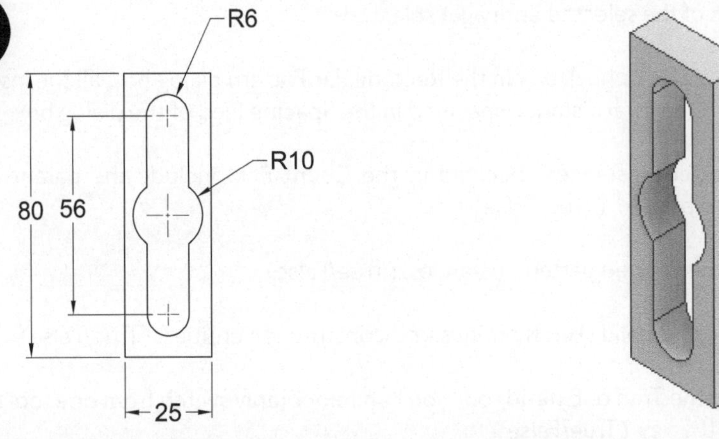

Hands-on Test Drive 3

Draw a sketch of the model shown in Figure 3.121. The dimensions and the 3D model are for your reference only. All dimensions are in mm.

3.121

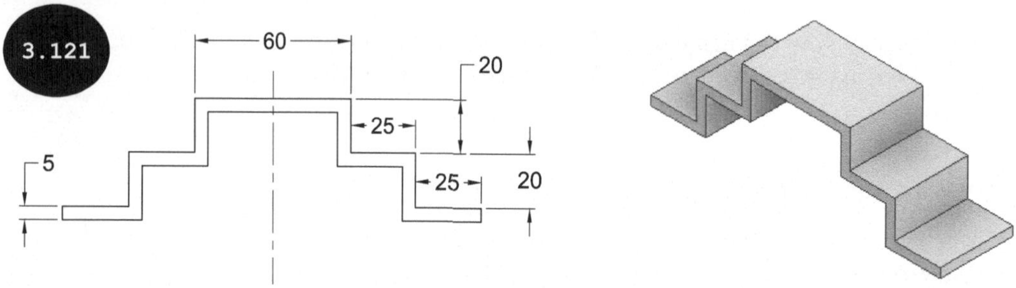

Summary

In this chapter, you have learned about editing and modifying sketch entities that include trimming, extending, splitting, offsetting, patterning, mirroring, moving a sketch entity, creating a copy of sketch entities, rotating an entity, scaling, and stretching sketch entities by using the respective tools. This chapter also discussed in detail the methods for creating 2D fillets and 2D chamfers in the Sketching environment, in addition to creating construction entities and centerline in the sketch.

Questions

Complete and verify the following sentences:

- The _________ tool is used for offsetting sketch entities at a specified offset distance.
- You can rotate sketch entities at an angle by using the _________ tool.
- You can stretch the entities of a sketch by using the _________ tool.
- While offsetting sketch entities, if you select the _______ option in the Marking Menu, all the contiguous entities of the selected entity get selected.
- On selecting the _______ check box in the **Rectangular Pattern** dialog box, all the instances get equally fitted within the total distance specified in the **Spacing** filed of the dialog box.
- The number of pattern instances specified in the **Count** field include the parent or original instance selected to pattern. (True/False)
- You cannot recall the skipped pattern instances. (True/False)
- You can convert existing solid sketch entities into construction entities. (True/False)
- While working with the **Trim** or **Extend** tool, you can temporarily switch from one tool to another by pressing the SHIFT key. (True/False)

CHAPTER

4

Applying Constraints and Dimensions

In this chapter, **the following topics will be discussed:**

- Working with Constraints
- Applying Constraints
- Controlling the Display of Constraints
- Controlling Constraint Settings
- Applying Dimensions
- Controlling Dimension Settings
- Modifying/Editing Dimensions
- Working with Different States of a Sketch
- Displaying Available Degrees of Freedom

Once you are done with creating a sketch, you need to make the sketch fully constrained by applying the required constraints and dimensions. A fully constrained sketch is a sketch, in which all degrees of freedom are fixed, thereby making it a stable sketch. This means that the entities of the sketch cannot change their shape, size, or position upon being dragged. You will learn about fully constrained sketches later in this chapter. Before that, you need to understand constraints and dimensions.

Working with Constraints

The constraints are used to restrict some of the degrees of freedom of a sketch. You can apply constraints on a sketch entity, between sketch entities, and between sketch entities and planes, axes, edges, or vertices. Some constraints such as horizontal, vertical, and coincident are applied automatically while drawing sketch entities. For example, while drawing a line, if you move the cursor horizontally toward left or right, a symbol of horizontal constraint appears near the cursor, see Figure 4.1. This indicates that if you specify the endpoint of the line, a horizontal constraint will be applied to the line. Likewise, if you move the cursor vertically upward or downward, a symbol of vertical constraint appears near the cursor, see Figure 4.2. This indicates that if you specify the endpoint of the line, a vertical constraint will be applied to the line.

4.1

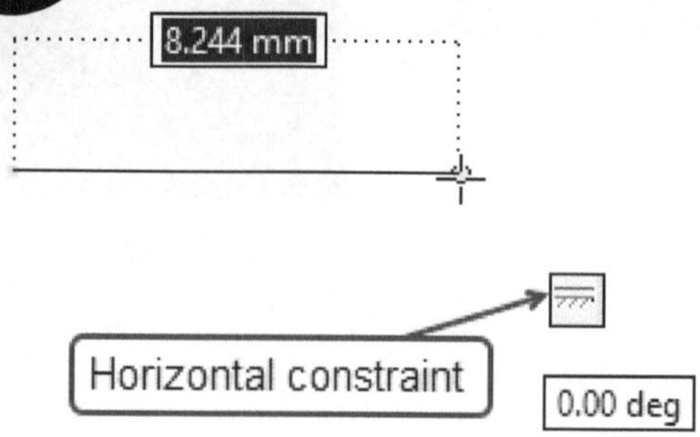

4.2

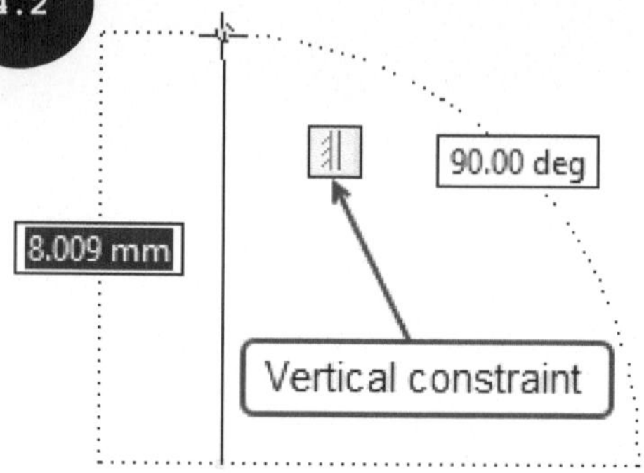

Tip: You can temporarily disable automatic application of constraints to the sketch entities while drawing them by pressing and holding the CTRL key.

In addition to the automatically applied constraints, you can also apply constraints manually. The methods for applying various types of constraints are discussed next.

Applying Constraints

In Autodesk Inventor, the tools for applying various types of constraints are available in the **Constrain** panel of the **Sketch** tab in the **Ribbon**, see Figure 4.3. Various types of constraints are discussed below:

4.3

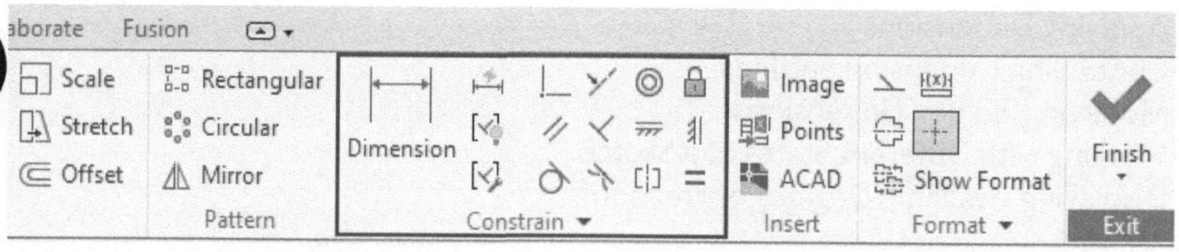

Applying Horizontal Constraint

Horizontal constraint is used for changing the orientation of an entity to horizontal and then forcing the entity to remain horizontal. This constraint can be applied to a line, centerline, or between two points. To apply a horizontal constraint, click on the **Horizontal Constraint** tool in the **Constrain** panel of the **Sketch** tab and then click on an entity or two points one by one. The selected entity or points become horizontal. After applying the constraint, press the ESC key to exit the tool.

Applying Vertical Constraint

Vertical constraint is used for changing the orientation of an entity to vertical and then forcing the entity to remain vertical. This constraint can be applied to a line, centerline, or between two points. To apply this constraint, click on the **Vertical Constraint** tool in the **Constrain** panel and then click on an entity or two points one by one. The selected entity or points become vertical. After applying the constraint, press the ESC key to exit the tool.

Applying Coincident Constraint

Coincident constraint is used for making two points/vertices coincide with each other, see Figure 4.4. You can also coincide a point to lie on a line/arc/circle/ellipse by applying the coincident constraint.

To apply this constraint, click on the **Coincident Constraint** tool in the **Constrain** panel of the **Sketch** tab and then click on two points one by one. The selected points become coincident with each other. After applying the constraint, press the ESC key to exit the tool.

4.4

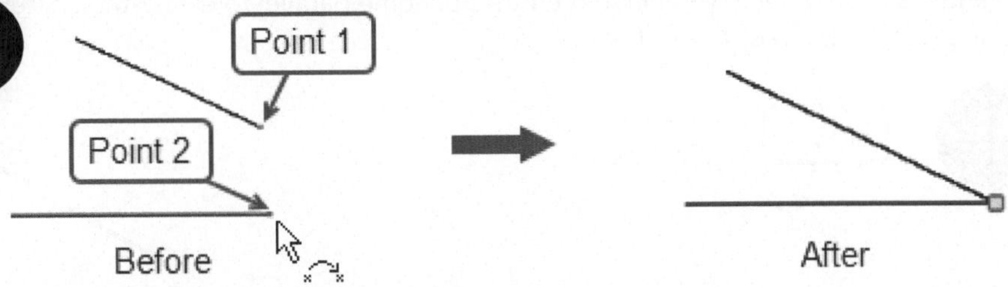

Applying Collinear Constraint

Collinear constraint is used for making two lines collinear to each other, see Figure 4.5. You can also make a line collinear to a linear edge. To apply this constraint, click on the **Collinear Constraint** tool in the **Constrain** panel and then click on two lines one by one. The selected lines become collinear to each other. After applying the constraint, press the ESC key to exit the tool.

4.5

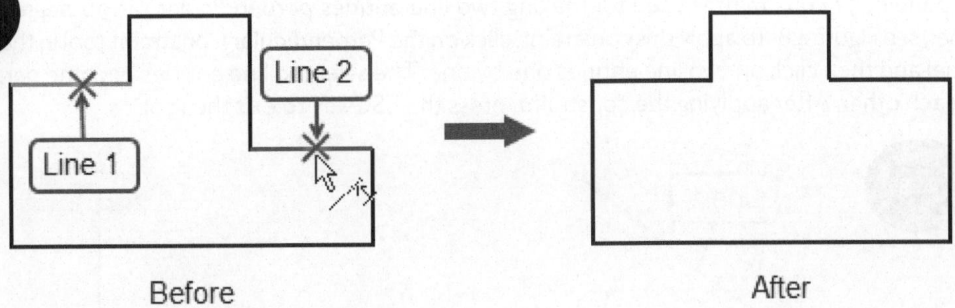

Applying Concentric Constraint

Concentric constraint is used for making two arcs, two circles, two ellipses, or a combination of these entities concentric to each other such that the selected entities share the same center point, see Figure 4.6. To apply this constraint, click on the **Concentric Constraint** tool in the **Constrain** panel and then click on two arcs, two circles, or two ellipses one by one. The selected entities become concentric to each other and share the same center point. Press the ESC key to exit the tool.

4.6

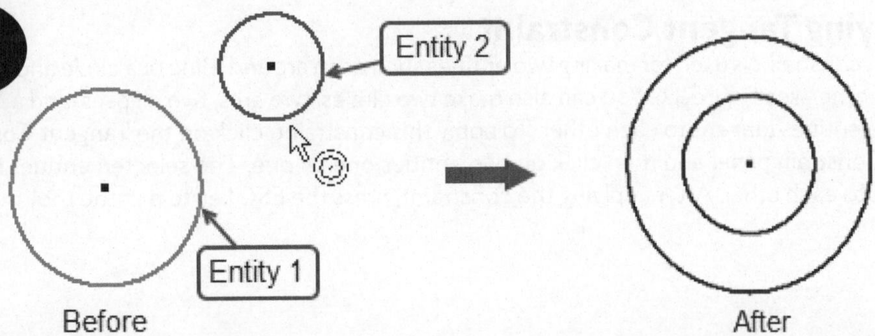

Applying Parallel Constraint

Parallel constraint is used for making two line entities parallel to each other, see Figure 4.7. To apply the parallel constraint, click on the **Parallel Constraint** tool in the **Constrain** panel and then click on two line entities one by one. The selected entities become parallel to each other. After applying the constraint, press the ESC key to exit the tool.

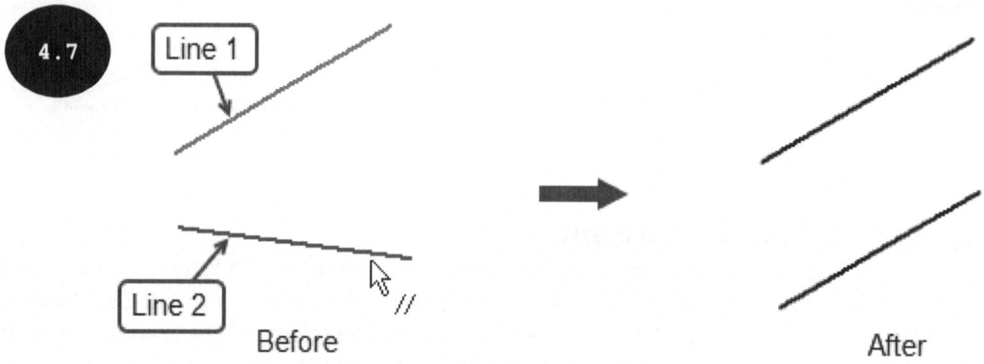

Applying Perpendicular Constraint

Perpendicular constraint is used for making two line entities perpendicular (at 90 degrees) to each other, see Figure 4.8. To apply this constraint, click on the **Perpendicular Constraint** tool in the **Constrain** panel and then click on two line entities one by one. The selected line entities become perpendicular to each other. After applying the constraint, press the ESC key to exit the tool.

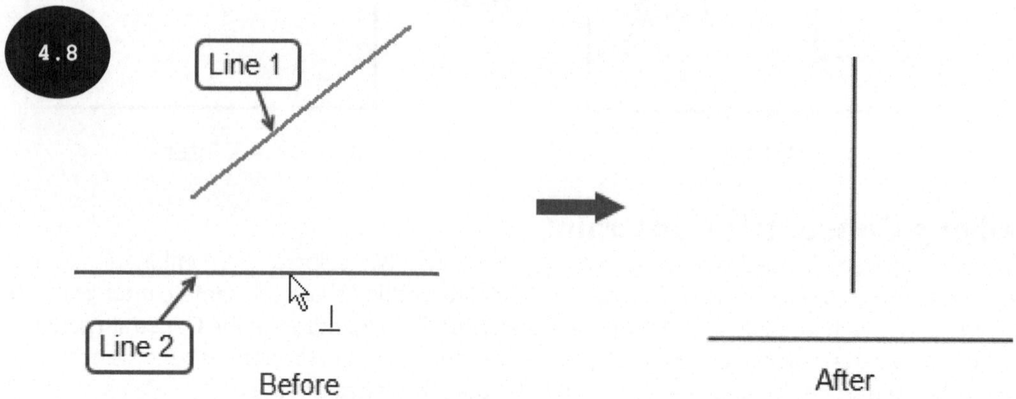

Applying Tangent Constraint

Tangent constraint is used for making two entities such as an arc and a line or a circle and a line tangent to each other, see Figure 4.9. You can also make two circles, two arcs, two ellipses, and a combination of these entities tangent to each other. To apply this constraint, click on the **Tangent Constraint** tool of the **Constrain** panel and then click on two entities one by one. The selected entities become at a tangent to each other. After applying the constraint, press the ESC key to exit the tool.

4.9

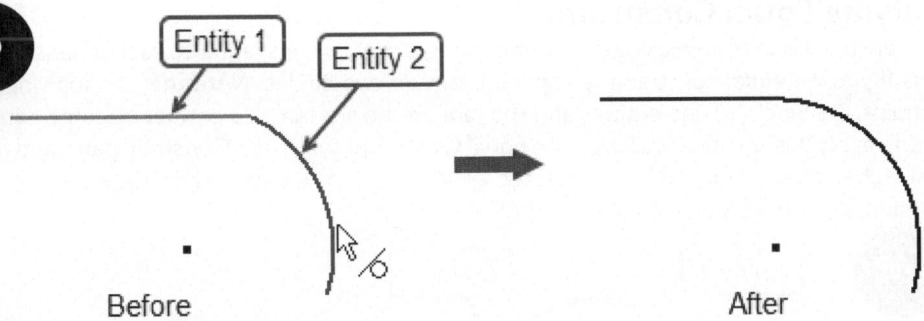

Applying Smooth Constraint

Smooth constraint is used for applying a curvature continuity (G2) at the transition point between a spline and a line, arc, or spline, see Figure 4.10. In this figure, the smooth constraint is applied between a spline and a line. To apply this constraint, click on the **Smooth (G2) Constraint** tool in the **Constrain** panel and then click on a spline and a line, arc, or spline. The curvature continuity (G2) is applied between the selected entities. After applying the constraint, press the ESC key to exit the tool.

4.10

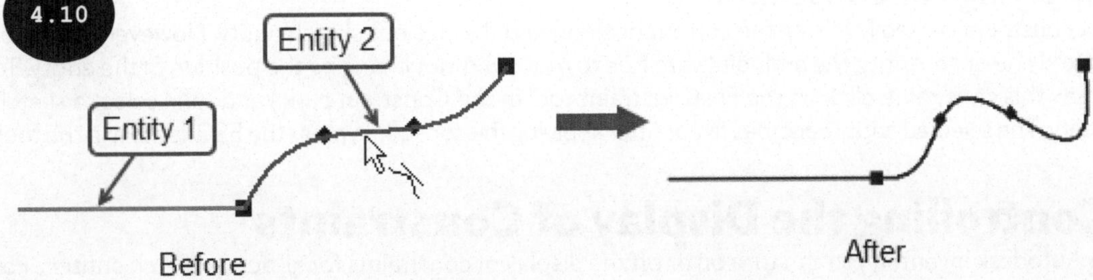

Applying Symmetric Constraint

Symmetric constraint is used for making two points, two lines, two arcs, two circles, or two ellipses symmetric about a symmetry line, see Figure 4.11. In this figure, the symmetric constraint is applied between two circles about a symmetry line. To apply this constraint, click on the **Symmetric Constraint** tool in the **Constrain** panel. Next, select the two sketch entities one by one and then select a symmetry line. The selected sketch entities become symmetric about the selected symmetry line. After applying the constraint, press the ESC key to exit the tool.

4.11

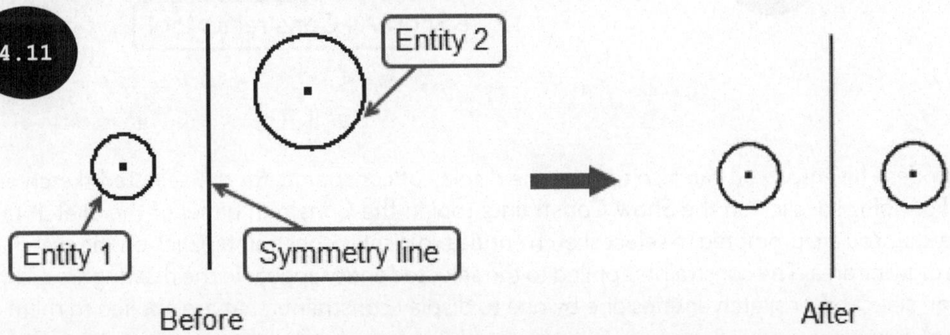

Applying Equal Constraint =

Equal constraint is used for making two entities (arcs, circles, or lines) equal to each other, see Figure 4.12. In this figure, an equal constraint is applied between two circles. Note that on applying the equal constraint, the length of line entities and the radii of the arc or circle entities become equal to each other. To apply this constraint, click on the **Equal Constraint** tool in the **Constrain** panel and then select two sketch entities one by one. The selected entities become equal to each other. After applying the constraint, press the ESC key to exit the tool.

4.12

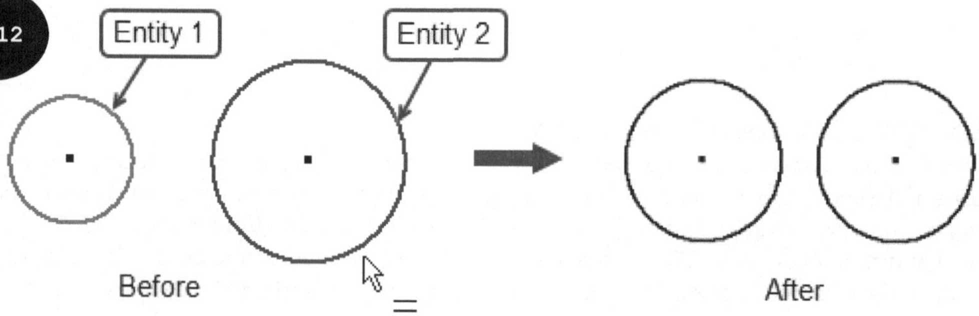

Applying Fix Constraint

Fix constraint is used for fixing the current position and the size of a sketch entity. However, in case of a fixed line or arc entity, the endpoints are free to move without changing the position of the entity. To apply this constraint, click on the **Fix Constraint** tool in the **Constrain** panel and then select a sketch entity. The selected entity becomes fixed. After applying the constraint, press the ESC key to exit the tool.

Controlling the Display of Constraints

In Autodesk Inventor, you can turn on or off the display of constraints for all active sketch entities. For doing so, click on the **Show All Constraints** or **Hide All Constraints** tool in the Status Bar, see Figure 4.13. Note that the availability of the tool (**Show All Constraints** or **Hide All Constraints**) in the Status Bar depends on whether the constraints are currently turned on or off in the drawing area. You can also press the F8 key to turn on the display of constraints for all sketch entities in the drawing area and the F9 key to turn off the display of constraints for all sketch entities. Alternatively, right-click in the drawing area and then click on the **Show All Constraints** or **Hide All Constraints** option in the Marking Menu that appears to turn on or off the display of constraints in the drawing area.

4.13

In Autodesk Inventor, you can also turn on the display of constraints for the selected sketch entities only. For doing so, click on the **Show Constraints** tool in the **Constrain** panel of the **Sketch** tab, see Figure 4.14. You are prompted to select sketch entities to display constraints. Click on the sketch entity in the drawing area. The constraints applied to the selected entity appear in the drawing area. Similarly, you can select other sketch entities one by one to display constraints that are applied to them in the drawing area.

4.14

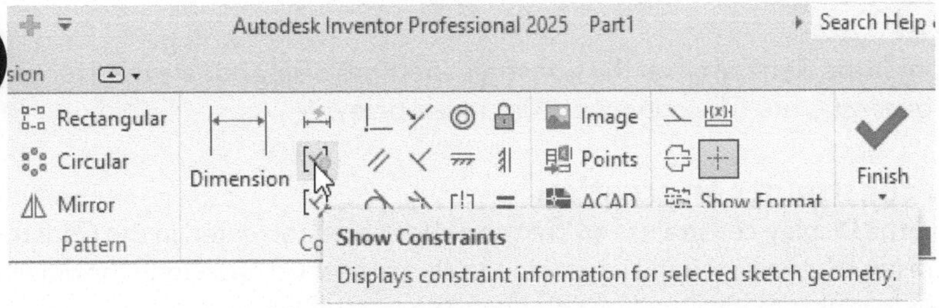

Note: You can also delete an already applied constraint by selecting it in the drawing area and then pressing the DELETE key.

Controlling Constraint Settings

In Autodesk Inventor, you can control the default constraint settings such as displaying constraints in the sketch, applying constraints automatically while creating sketch entities, and so on. For doing so, click on the **Constraint Settings** tool in the **Constrain** panel, see Figure 4.15. The **Constraint Settings** dialog box appears, see Figure 4.16. The options in this dialog box are discussed below:

4.15

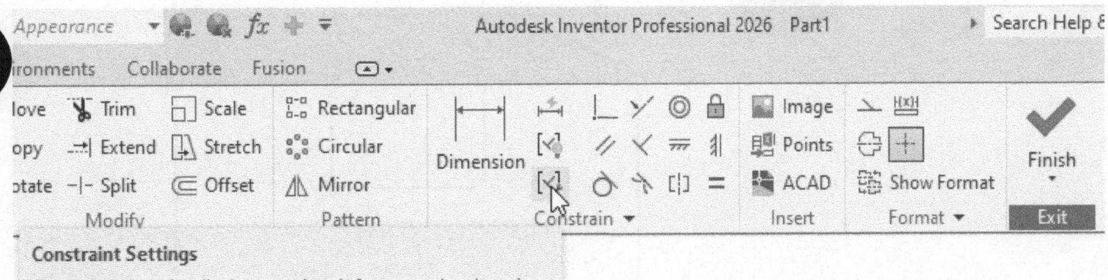

4.16

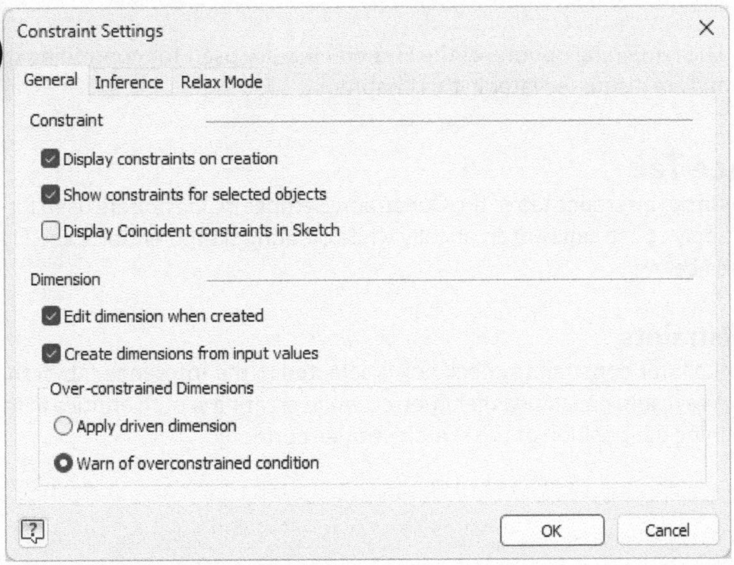

General Tab

The options in the **General** tab of the **Constraint Settings** dialog box are used for controlling the display settings for constraints. The options are discussed below:

Display constraints on creation

By default, the **Display constraints on creation** check box is selected in the **Constraint Settings** dialog box. As a result, when a constraint is applied to a sketch entity, it appears in the drawing area temporarily and gets hidden automatically when you finish the current command.

Show constraints for selected objects

By default, the **Show constraints for selected objects** check box is selected. As a result, when you select a sketch entity, the constraints that are applied to it, appear or get highlighted in the drawing area.

Display Coincident constraints in Sketch

On selecting the **Display Coincident constraints in Sketch** check box, the glyphs of coincident constraints applied between sketch entities appear in the drawing area, see Figure 4.17.

4.17

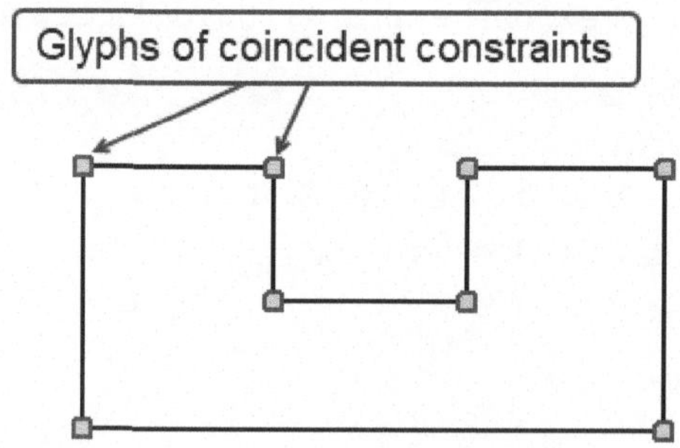

Note: The remaining options of the **General** tab are used for controlling the dimension settings and are discussed later in this chapter.

Inference Tab

The options in the **Inference** tab of the **Constraint Settings** dialog box are used for controlling constraint settings to apply constraints automatically while creating sketch entities, see Figure 4.18. The options are discussed below:

Infer constraints

By default, the **Infer constraints** check box is selected in the **Inference** tab of the **Constraint Settings** dialog box. As a result, constraints get inferred while creating sketch entities in the drawing area which helps in defining the position of the sketch entities correctly.

4.18

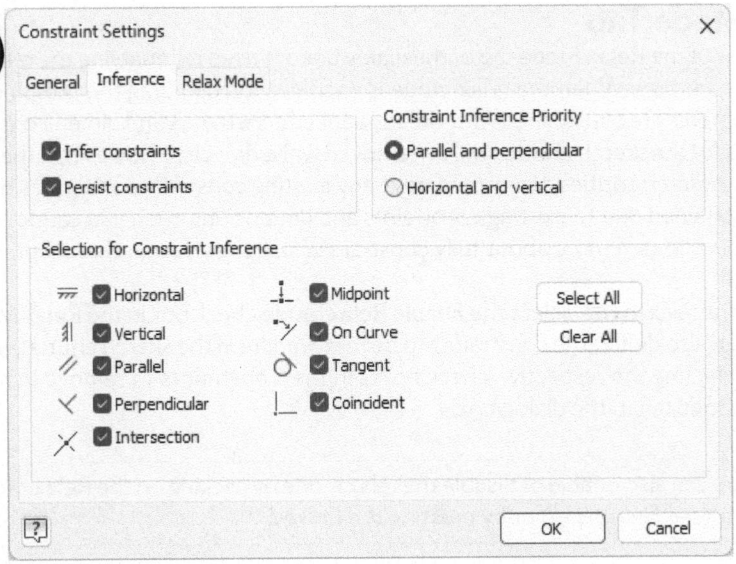

Persist constraints

By default, the **Persist constraints** check box is selected. As a result, the inferred constraints are applied automatically while creating sketch entities in the drawing area. Note that this check box is enabled only when the **Infer constraints** check box is selected. Also, you can define the type of constraints to be applied automatically by selecting the respective check boxes of the constraints in the **Selection for Constraint Inference** area of the **Inference** tab in the dialog box.

Tip: If the **Infer constraints** check box is selected and the **Persist constraints** check box is cleared, then none of the constraints will be applied automatically while creating the sketch entities except the coincident constraint, unless the coincident check box is cleared in the **Selection for Constraint Inference** area of the **Inference** tab in the dialog box.

Constraint Inference Priority

By default, the **Parallel and perpendicular** radio button is selected in the **Constraint Inference Priority** area of the **Inference** tab in the dialog box. As a result, the constraints that define relationships between sketch entities as parallel and perpendicular are the preferred constraints to be applied first, automatically.

On selecting the **Horizontal and vertical** radio buttons, the constraints that define the orientation of the sketch entities as horizontal and vertical become the preferred constraints to be applied first, automatically.

Selection for Constraint Inference

The **Selection for Constraint Inference** area of the **Inference** tab is used for selecting the constraints to be applied automatically while creating the sketch entities. For doing so, select the check boxes of the constraints to be applied automatically in the **Selection for Constraint Inference** area of the dialog box. The **Select All** button is used for selecting all the constraints to be applied automatically and the **Clear All** button is used for clearing the selection of all the constraints.

Relax Mode Tab

The options of the **Relax Mode** tab of the dialog box are used for enabling the relax mode and defining the relative settings. When the relax mode is enabled, you can drag the sketch entities freely even if their movements are constrained with already applied constraints and dimensions. Also, any conflicting constraints for the sketch entities will be removed while dragging. However, if the relax mode is turned off, dragging sketch entities does not remove any existing constraints or dimensions. Also, if the sketch is fully constrained due to existing constraints and dimensions, then you cannot even drag the sketch entities. You will learn more about fully constrained sketches later in this chapter.

To enable the relax mode, select the **Enable Relax Mode** check box in the **Relax Mode** tab of the dialog box. You can also define the constraints to be removed from the sketch entities while dragging in relax mode by selecting the respective check boxes in the **Constraints to remove in relax dragging** area of the **Relax Mode** tab in the dialog box.

Tip: You can also enable or disable the relax mode by clicking on the **Relax Mode** tool in the Status Bar (see Figure 4.19) or by pressing the F11 key.

4.19

Applying Dimensions

Once a sketch has been drawn and the required geometric constraints have been applied, you need to apply the required dimensions to the sketch. As Autodesk Inventor is a parametric software, the parameters of sketch entities such as length and angle are controlled or driven by dimension values. On modifying a dimension value, the respective sketch entity also gets modified accordingly. In Autodesk Inventor, you can apply dimensions by using the **General Dimension** tool. You can activate the **General Dimension** tool by using one of the following methods:

- Click on the **General Dimension** tool in the **Constrain** panel of the **Sketch** tab, see Figure 4.20.

4.20

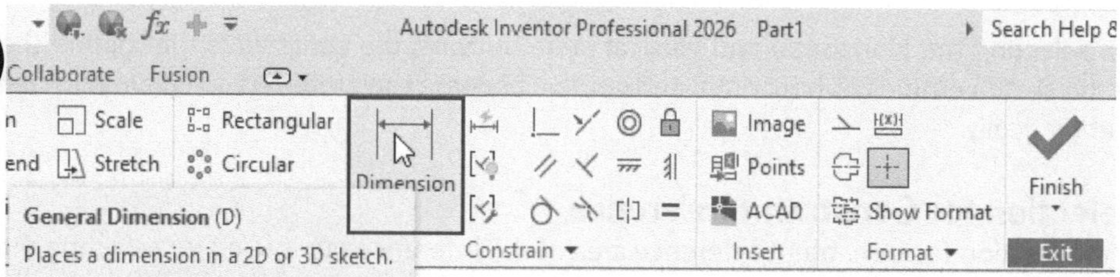

- Right-click in the drawing area and then click on the **General Dimension** option in the Marking Menu that appears, see Figure 4.21.

4.21

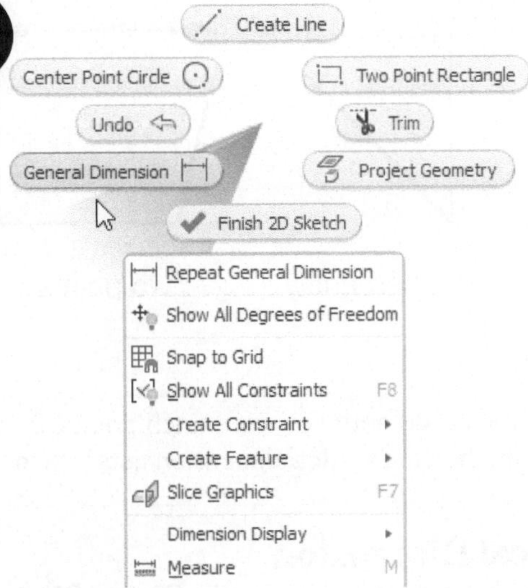

- Press the **D** key.

The **General Dimension** tool is used for applying dimension, depending upon the type of entity selected. For example, if you select a circle, the diameter dimension is applied, and if you select a line, the linear dimension is applied. You can apply horizontal, vertical, aligned, angular, diameter, radius, and linear diameter dimensions by using this tool. The methods for applying dimensions by using the **General Dimension** tool are discussed next.

Applying a Horizontal Dimension

1. Click on the **General Dimension** tool in the **Constrain** panel of the **Sketch** tab or press the **D** key. The **General Dimension** tool gets activated and you are prompted to select a geometry.

2. Select the required sketch entity or entities for applying the horizontal dimension. You can select a horizontal sketch entity, an inclined sketch entity, two points, or two vertical entities, refer to Figure 4.22. The current dimension value of the selected entity or entities appears attached to the cursor.

3. Move the cursor vertically up or down and then click to specify the placement point for the horizontal dimension. The **Edit Dimension** dialog box appears.

Note: The **Edit Dimension** dialog box appears on specifying the placement point only if the **Edit dimension when created** check box is selected in the **Constraint Settings** dialog box. To invoke this dialog box, click on the **Constraint Settings** tool in the **Constrain** panel of the **Sketch** tab. Alternatively, while applying a dimension, right-click in the drawing area and then select the **Edit Dimension** option in the Marking Menu that appears.

4. Enter the required dimension value in the **Edit Dimension** dialog box and then press ENTER or click on the green tick-mark button in the dialog box. The horizontal dimension is applied, refer to Figure 4.22.

4.22

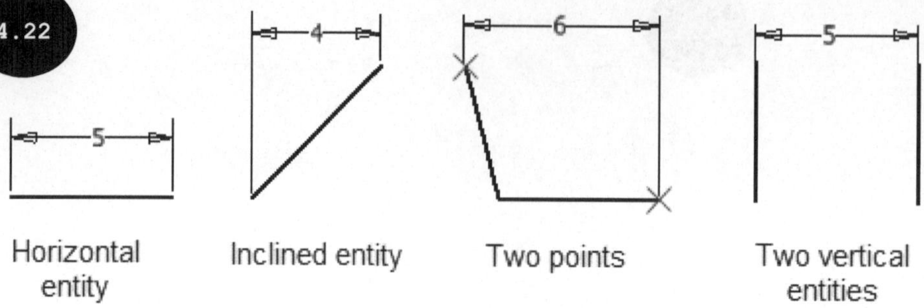

Tip: After selecting an inclined entity or two sketch points, if you move the cursor horizontally toward right or left, then the vertical dimension gets attached to the cursor.

Applying a Vertical Dimension

Similar to applying a horizontal dimension by using the **General Dimension** tool, you can apply a vertical dimension to a vertical sketch entity, an inclined sketch entity, between two points, or between two horizontal sketch entities, see Figure 4.23. Note that, to apply a vertical dimension, you need to move the cursor horizontally toward right or left after selecting one or more entities.

4.23

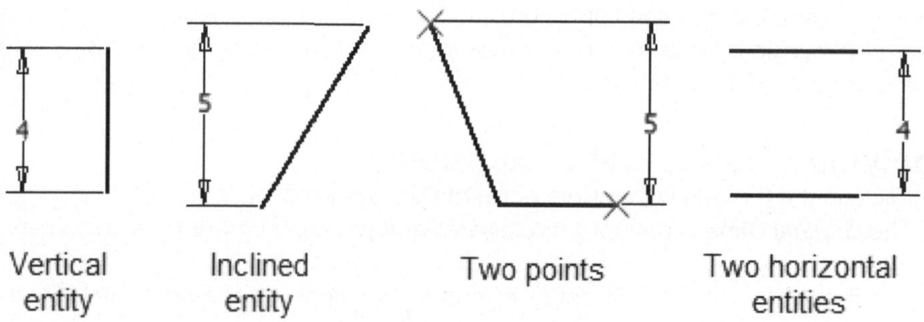

Applying an Aligned Dimension

An aligned dimension is generally used for measuring the aligned length of an inclined line. The method for applying an aligned dimension is discussed below:

1. Invoke the **General Dimension** tool by pressing the D key.

2. Select an inclined sketch entity or two points for applying an aligned dimension.

3. Right-click in the drawing area and then click on the **Aligned** option in the Marking Menu that appears, see Figure 4.24. The aligned dimension appears attached to the cursor.

4.24

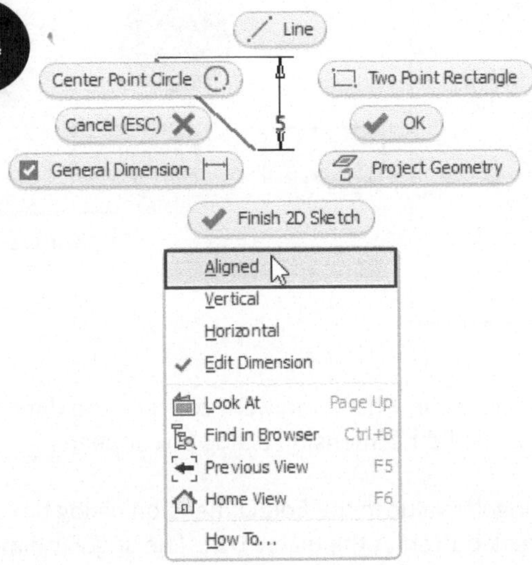

4. Click to specify the placement point for the aligned dimension in the drawing area. The **Edit Dimension** dialog box appears.

5. Enter the required dimension value in the **Edit Dimension** dialog box and then press ENTER or click on the green tick-mark button in the dialog box. The aligned dimension is applied, refer to Figure 4.25.

4.25

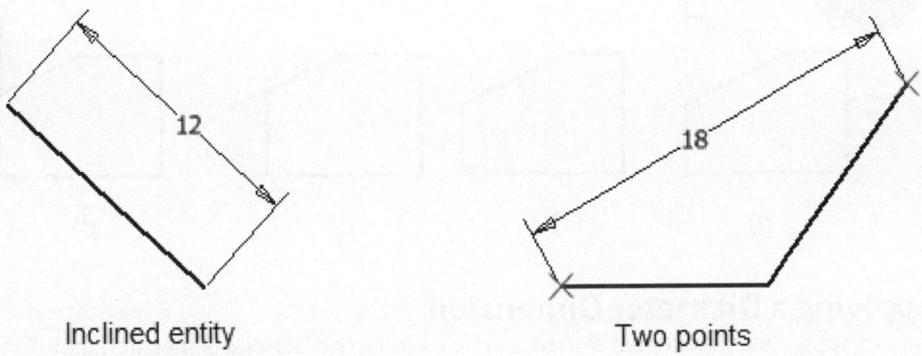

Applying an Angular Dimension

You can apply an angular dimension for dimensioning angles between two non-parallel line entities or three points by using the **General Dimension** tool. The method for applying angular dimension is discussed below:

1. Invoke the **General Dimension** tool by pressing the D key.

2. Select two non-parallel line entities or three points one by one in the drawing area. The angular dimension between the selected entities or points gets attached to the cursor, refer to Figures 4.26 and 4.27.

4.26

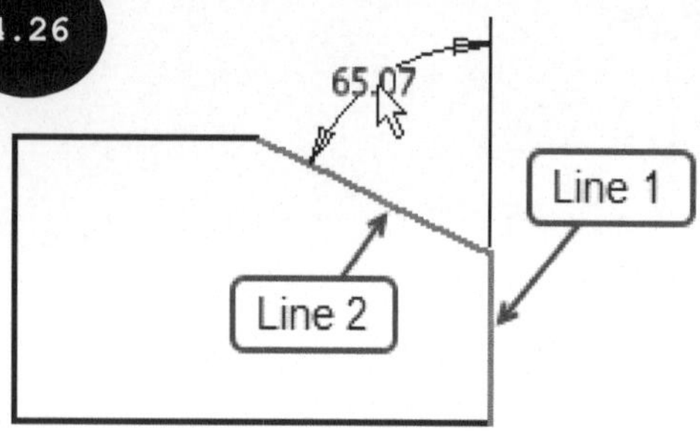

4.27

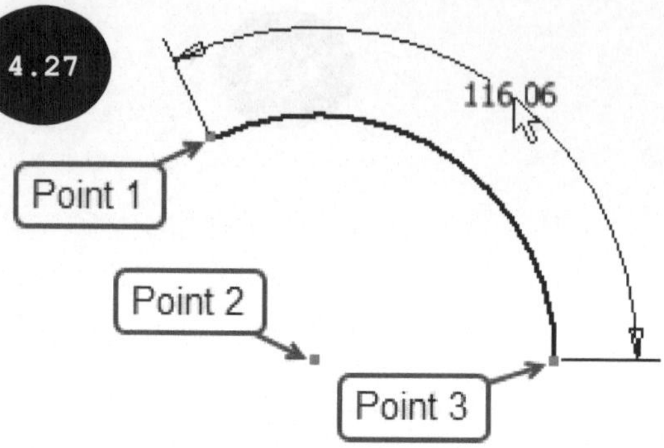

3. Move the cursor to a location where you want to place the dimension and then click to specify the placement point. The **Edit Dimension** dialog box appears.

4. Enter the required angular value in the **Edit Dimension** dialog box and then press ENTER or click on the green tick-mark button in the dialog box. The angular dimension is applied between the selected entities or points.

Note: An angular dimension is applied between the two selected entities depending upon the location of the placement point in the drawing area, refer to Figure 4.28.

4.28

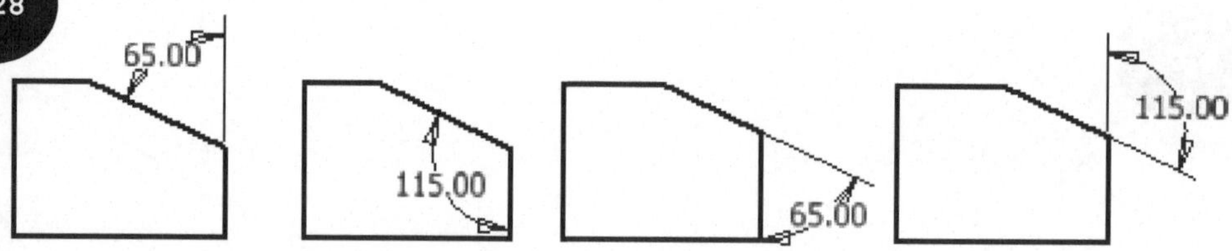

Applying a Diameter Dimension

You can apply a diameter dimension to a circle by using the **General Dimension** tool. The method for applying a diameter dimension to a circle is discussed below:

1. Invoke the **General Dimension** tool by pressing the D key.

2. Select a circle in the drawing area. The diameter dimension gets attached to the cursor.

3. Move the cursor to the required location and then click to specify a placement point in the drawing area. The **Edit Dimension** dialog box appears.

4. Enter the diameter value in this dialog box and then press ENTER or click on the green tick-mark button in the dialog box. The diameter dimension is applied to the circle, see Figure 4.29.

4.24

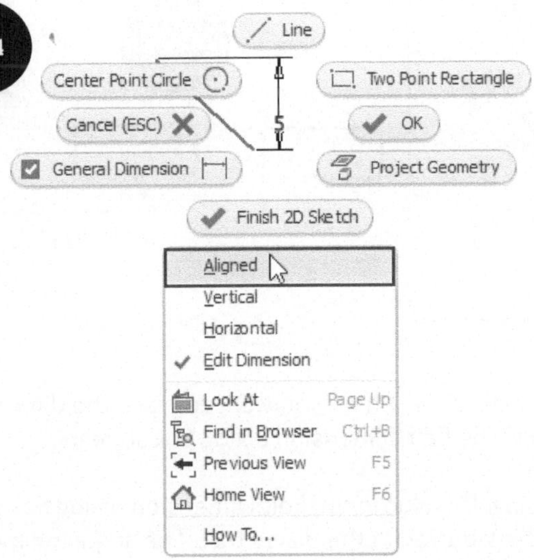

4. Click to specify the placement point for the aligned dimension in the drawing area. The **Edit Dimension** dialog box appears.

5. Enter the required dimension value in the **Edit Dimension** dialog box and then press ENTER or click on the green tick-mark button in the dialog box. The aligned dimension is applied, refer to Figure 4.25.

4.25

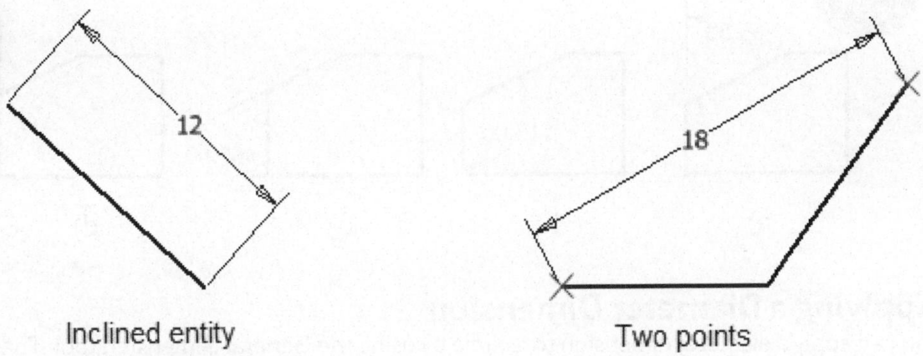

Applying an Angular Dimension

You can apply an angular dimension for dimensioning angles between two non-parallel line entities or three points by using the **General Dimension** tool. The method for applying angular dimension is discussed below:

1. Invoke the **General Dimension** tool by pressing the D key.

2. Select two non-parallel line entities or three points one by one in the drawing area. The angular dimension between the selected entities or points gets attached to the cursor, refer to Figures 4.26 and 4.27.

4.26

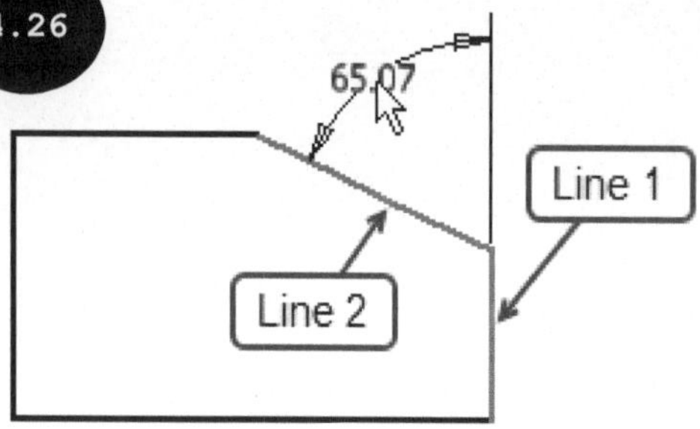

4.27

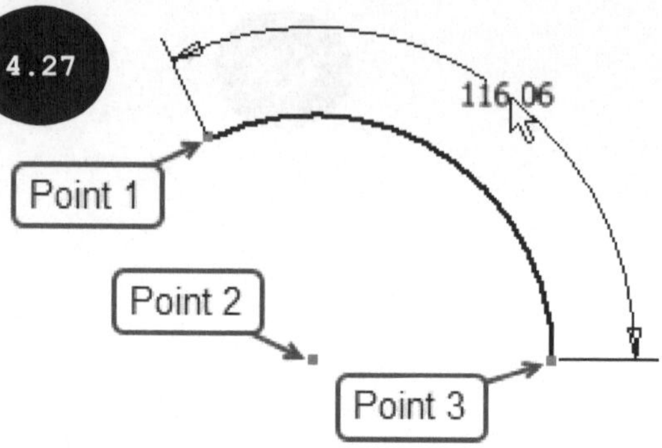

3. Move the cursor to a location where you want to place the dimension and then click to specify the placement point. The **Edit Dimension** dialog box appears.

4. Enter the required angular value in the **Edit Dimension** dialog box and then press ENTER or click on the green tick-mark button in the dialog box. The angular dimension is applied between the selected entities or points.

Note: An angular dimension is applied between the two selected entities depending upon the location of the placement point in the drawing area, refer to Figure 4.28.

4.28

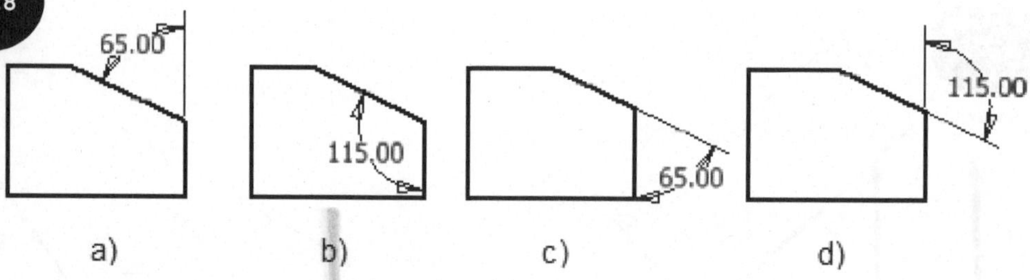

Applying a Diameter Dimension

You can apply a diameter dimension to a circle by using the **General Dimension** tool. The method for applying a diameter dimension to a circle is discussed below:

1. Invoke the **General Dimension** tool by pressing the D key.

2. Select a circle in the drawing area. The diameter dimension gets attached to the cursor.

3. Move the cursor to the required location and then click to specify a placement point in the drawing area. The **Edit Dimension** dialog box appears.

4. Enter the diameter value in this dialog box and then press ENTER or click on the green tick-mark button in the dialog box. The diameter dimension is applied to the circle, see Figure 4.29.

Note: By default, the diameter dimension is applied to a circle. However, you can also apply a radius dimension to a circle. For doing so, after selecting a circle to apply dimension, right-click in the drawing area and then click on the **Dimension Type > Radius** in the Marking Menu that appears. The radius dimension gets attached to the cursor. Next click to specify the placement point in the drawing area. The **Edit Dimension** dialog box appears. Enter the radius value in this dialog box and then press ENTER. The radius dimension is applied to the circle, see Figure 4.30.

4.29

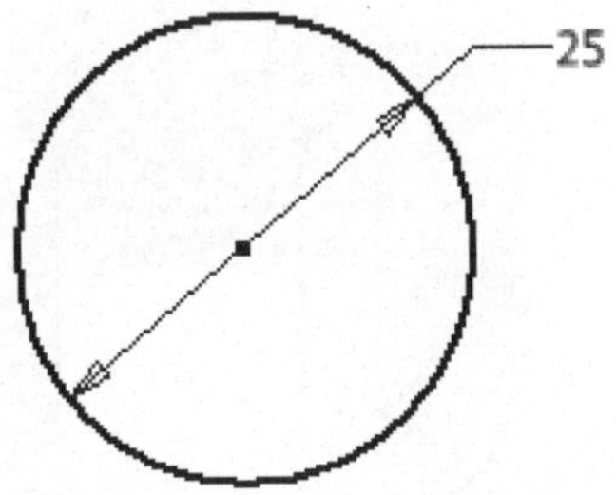

4.30

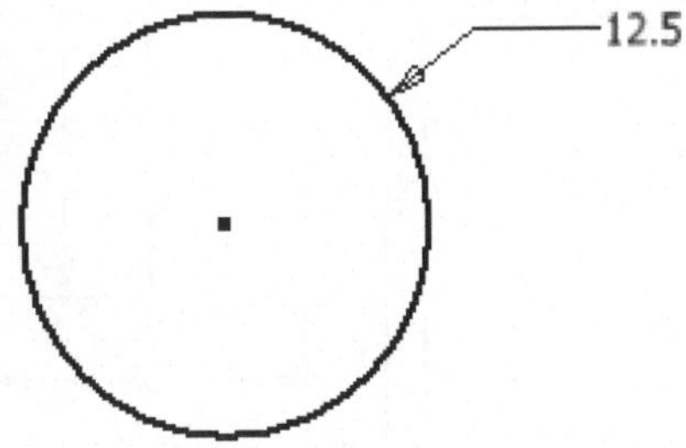

Applying a Radius Dimension

You can apply a radius dimension to an arc by using the **General Dimension** tool. The method for applying a radius dimension is discussed below:

1. Invoke the **General Dimension** tool and then select an arc in the drawing area. The radius dimension gets attached to the cursor.

2. Move the cursor to the required location and then click to specify a placement point in the drawing area. The **Edit Dimension** dialog box appears.

3. Enter the radius value in this dialog box and then press ENTER. The radius dimension is applied to the selected arc, see Figure 4.31.

4.31

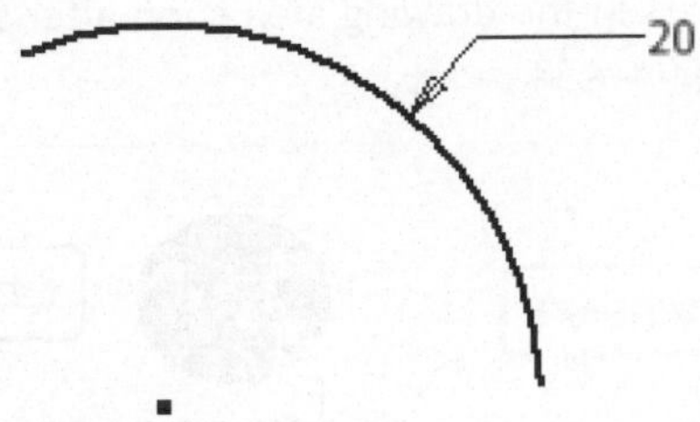

Note: By default, the radius dimension is applied to an arc. However, you can also apply the diameter dimension to an arc. For doing so, after selecting the arc to apply dimension, right-click in the drawing area and then click on the **Dimension Type > Diameter** in the Marking Menu that appears. The diameter dimension gets attached to the cursor. Next click to specify the placement point in the drawing area. The **Edit Dimension** dialog box appears. Enter the diameter value in this box and then press ENTER. The diameter dimension is applied to the selected arc.

Applying a Linear Diameter Dimension

You can apply a linear diameter dimension to a sketch of a revolved feature, see Figure 4.32. The method for applying a linear diameter dimension is discussed below:

4.32

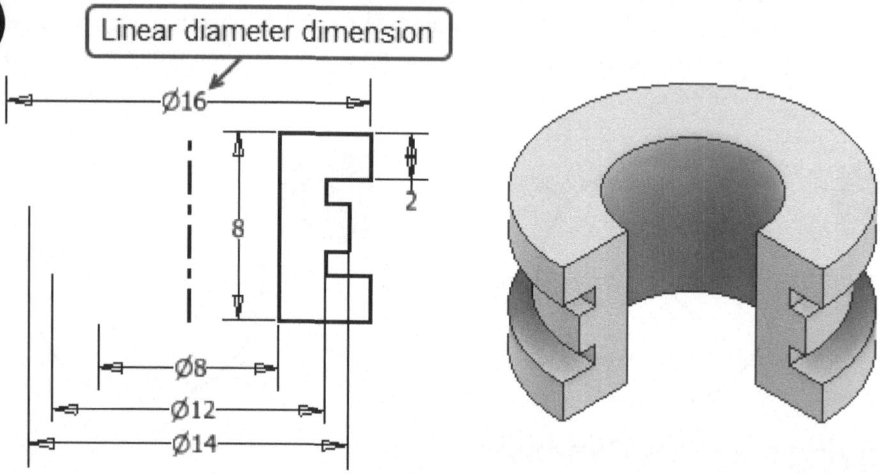

1. Invoke the **General Dimension** tool by pressing the D key. You are prompted to select a geometry.
2. Select a line or a centerline (entity 1) as the revolving axis of the sketch, refer to Figures 4.33 and 4.34. In Figure 4.33, a line is selected as the revolving axis, whereas in Figure 4.34, a centerline is selected as the revolving axis of the sketch.
3. Select a linear entity of the sketch (entity 2). A linear dimension between the selected entities is attached to the cursor, see Figure 4.33.

Note: If you select a centerline (entity 1) as the revolving axis of the sketch then the linear diameter dimension appears in the drawing area soon after selecting a linear entity of the sketch (entity 2), see Figure 4.34.

4.33

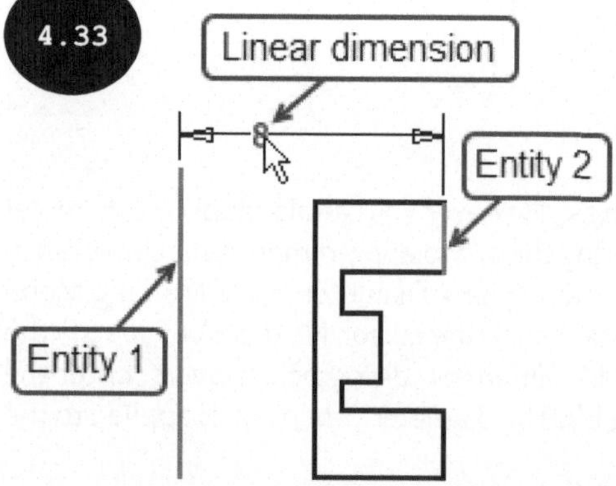

4.34

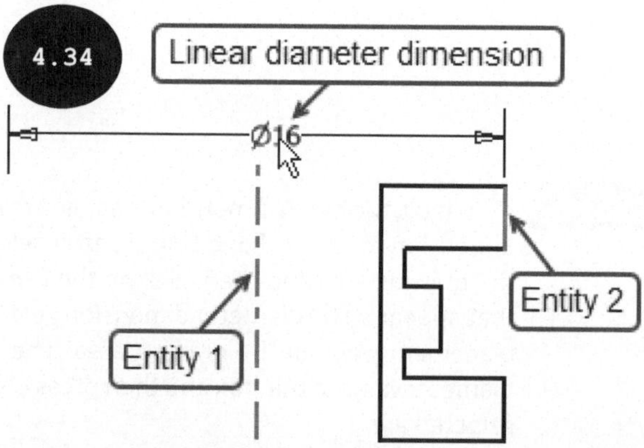

4. Right-click in the drawing area and then click on the **Linear Diameter** option in the Marking Menu that appears, see Figure 4.35. A linear diameter dimension appears in the drawing area.

4.35

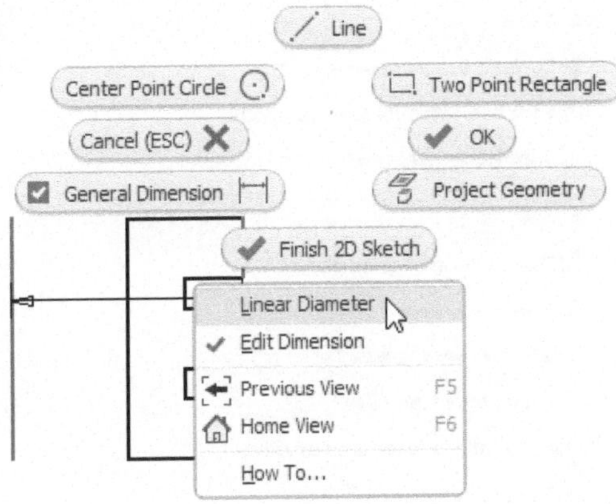

Note: If you select a centerline as the revolving axis of the sketch then you can skip step 4 discussed above.

5. Move the cursor to the required location and then click to specify a placement point in the drawing area. The **Edit Dimension** dialog box appears.

6. Enter the linear diameter value in this dialog box and then press ENTER. The linear diameter dimension is applied.

7. You can apply all the linear diameter dimensions in a similar manner and then press the ESC key to exit the tool.

Controlling Dimension Settings

In Autodesk Inventor, you can control the default dimension settings by using the **Constraint Settings** dialog box. For doing so, click on the **Constraint Settings** tool in the **Constrain** panel, see Figure 4.36. The **Constraint Settings** dialog box appears, see Figure 4.37. The options of this dialog box that are used for controlling the constraint settings are discussed earlier in the chapter and the options that are used for controlling dimension settings are discussed below:

4.36

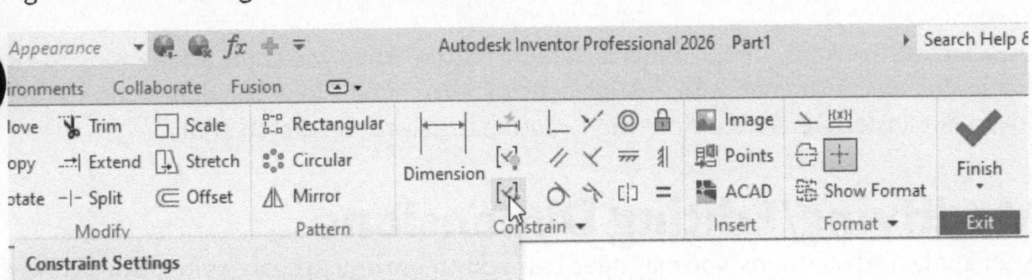

4.37

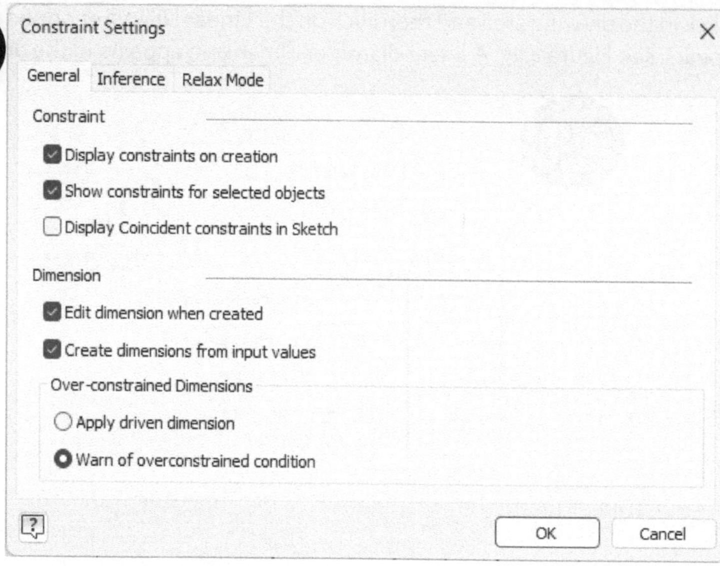

Edit dimension when created

By default, the **Edit dimension when created** check box is selected in the **Dimension** area of the **Constraint Settings** dialog box. As a result, when you apply a dimension to a sketch entity, the **Edit Dimension** dialog box appears automatically with the current dimension value of the selected entity. In this dialog box, you can enter the required dimension value and then press ENTER. You need to select this check box, if not selected.

Create dimensions from input values

By default, the **Create dimensions from input values** check box is selected. As a result, when you enter dimension values in the Dimension Input while creating sketch entities, the respective dimensions get applied automatically to the sketch entities in the drawing area.

Over-constrained Dimensions

By default, the **Warn of overconstrained condition** radio button is selected in the **Over-constrained Dimensions** area of the dialog box. As a result, when you apply a dimension to a sketch entity that is already constrained with existing constraints or dimensions, the **Autodesk Inventor Professional** warning window appears which informs you that adding this dimension will over-constrain the sketch. You can click on the **Accept** button in this window to apply this dimension as the driven dimension (reference dimension).

On selecting the **Apply driven dimension** radio button, when you apply a dimension to a sketch entity that is already constrained with existing constraints or dimensions, the dimension will be applied as a driven dimension (reference dimension), automatically to the sketch entity.

Modifying/Editing Dimensions

After applying dimensions, you may need to modify them due to changes in the design, revisions in the design, and so on. To modify an already applied dimension, double-click on the dimension value to be modified. The **Edit Dimension** dialog box appears with the display of the current dimension value, see

Figure 4.38. Enter the new dimension value in this box and then press ENTER. The selected dimension value gets modified and the length of the entity is changed, accordingly.

4.38

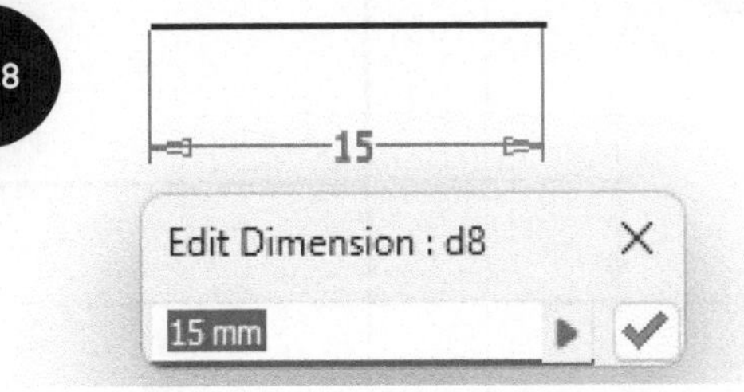

Note: If the **General Dimension** tool is activated then the **Edit Dimension** dialog box appears when you single click on the dimension to be edited.

Working with Different States of a Sketch

In Autodesk Inventor, a sketch can be either Under Constrained or Fully Constrained. Both these states of a sketch are discussed below:

Under Constrained Sketch

An under constrained sketch is a sketch in which all degrees of freedom are not fixed. This means that the entities of the sketch can change their shape, size, and position upon being dragged. Figure 4.39 shows a rectangular sketch in which the length of the rectangle is defined as 10 mm. However, the width and the position of the rectangle with respect to the origin are not defined. This means that the width and position of the rectangle can be changed by dragging the respective entities of the rectangle. Note that the entities of an under-constrained sketch appear in black color in the drawing area.

4.39

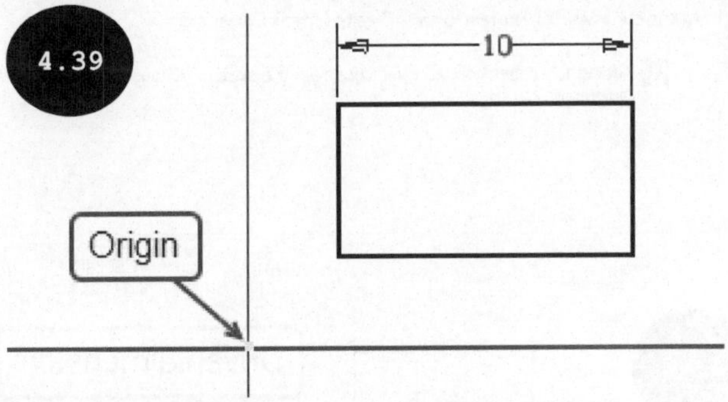

Fully Constrained Sketch

A fully constrained sketch is a sketch in which all degrees of freedom are fixed. This means that the entities of the sketch cannot change their shape, size, and position upon being dragged. Figure 4.40 shows a rectangular sketch in which the length, width, and position of the sketch are defined. Note that the entities of a fully constrained sketch appear in dark blue. Also, the status of the sketch appears as Fully Constrained in the Status Bar at the lower right corner of the screen.

4.40

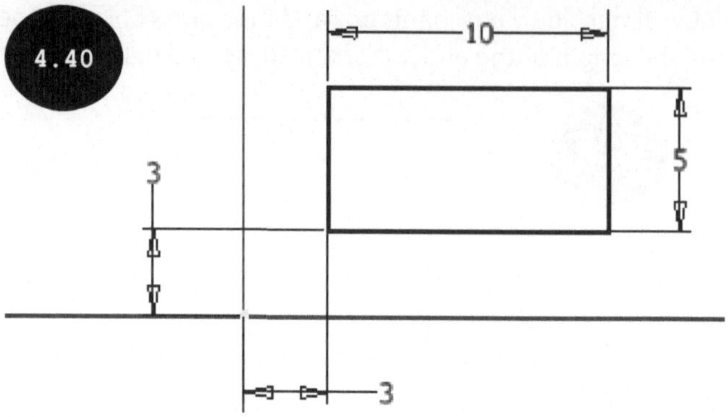

Tip: The sketch shown in Figure 4.40 is a fully constrained sketch as all its entities are dimensioned and the required constraints have been applied. The constraints applied in this sketch are horizontal to the horizontal entities and vertical to the vertical entities. Horizontal and vertical constraints are applied automatically to the entities while drawing them.

Note: When you apply a dimension to a fully constrained sketch or a sketch entity that is already constrained with existing dimensions and constraints, the **Autodesk Inventor Professional** warning window appears, see Figure 4.41. It informs you that adding this dimension will over-constrain the sketch and suggests to apply it as a driven dimension. Click on the **Accept** button to apply the dimension as a driven dimension. The newly applied dimension becomes a driven dimension and acts as a reference dimension only. As a result, the sketch does not become over-constrained. Figure 4.42 shows a sketch with driven dimension applied on a horizontal entity.

4.41

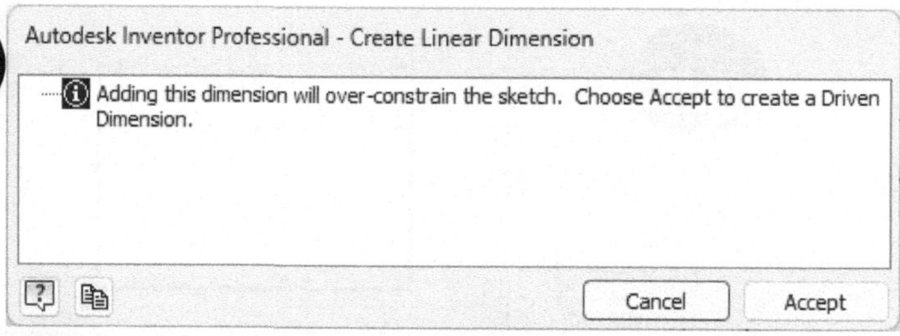

4.42

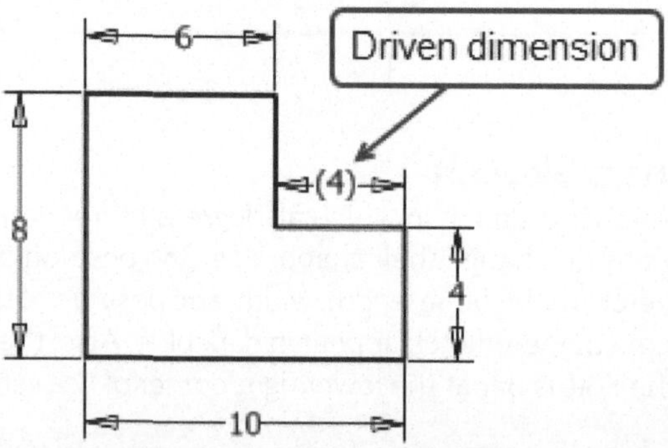

Displaying Available Degrees of Freedom

In Autodesk Inventor, you can display the available degrees of freedom of the sketch entities that are not constrained by dimensions and constraints in the drawing area. For doing so, click on the **Show All Degrees of Freedom** tool in the Status Bar, see Figure 4.43. All the available or free degrees of freedom of the sketch appear in the drawing area, see Figure 4.44.

4.43

4.44

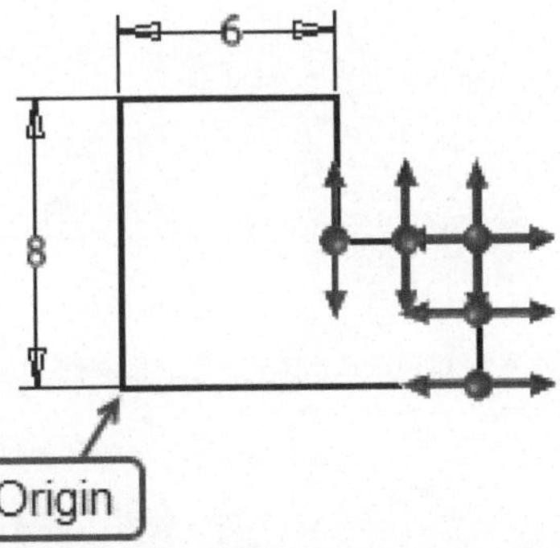

You can also display the available degrees of freedom of a particular sketch entity. For doing so, select the sketch entity in the drawing area and then right-click to display the Marking Menu. Next, select the **Display Degrees of Freedom** option in the Marking Menu. The available degrees of freedom of the selected entity appear in the drawing area.

Tutorial 1

Draw the sketch shown in Figure 4.45 and make it fully constrained by applying all dimensions and constraints. The 3D model shown in this figure is for your reference only. You will learn about creating the 3D model in the later chapters. All dimensions are in mm.

4.45

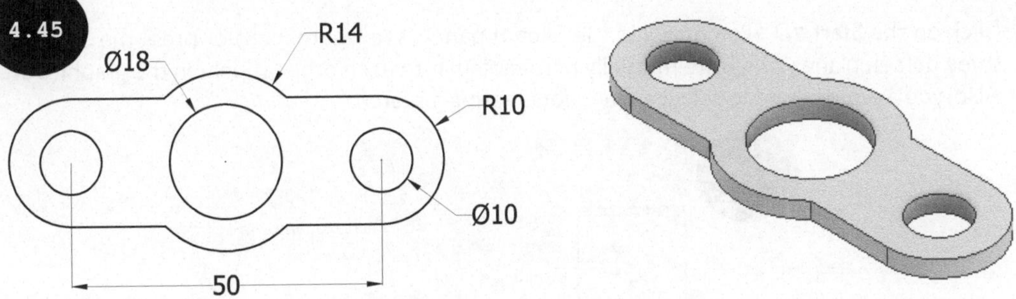

Section 1: Starting Autodesk Inventor

1. Start Autodesk Inventor by double-clicking on the Autodesk Inventor icon on your desktop. The startup user interface of Autodesk Inventor appears.

Section 2: Invoking the Sketching Environment

1. Click on the **New** tool in the startup user interface of Autodesk Inventor (see Figure 4.46) or press the CTRL + N keys. The **Create New File** dialog box appears, see Figure 4.47.

4.46

4.47

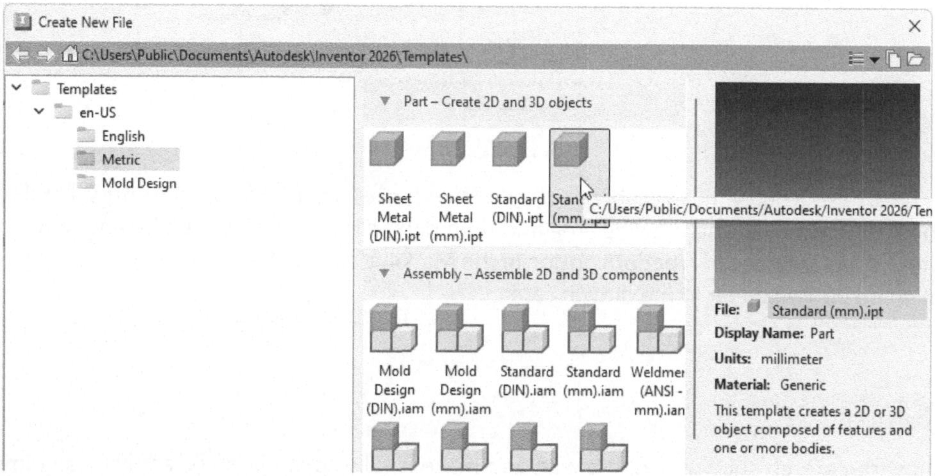

2. Double-click on the **Standard (mm).ipt** template in the right panel of the dialog box, refer to Figure 4.47. The Part Modeling environment is invoked with a Metric template.

3. Click on the **Start 2D Sketch** tool in the **Sketch** panel (see Figure 4.48) or press the S key. The three default planes which are mutually perpendicular to each other appear in the graphics area. Also, you are prompted to select a plane for creating a sketch.

4.48

4. Move the cursor over the Top plane (XZ Plane) and then click the left mouse button when the plane gets highlighted in the graphics area. The Sketching environment is invoked and the Top plane is oriented normal to the viewing direction.

5. Ensure that the direction of the X axis of the triad that appears at the lower left corner of the screen is toward right and the direction of the Z axis of the triad is downward, see Figure 4.49. You can change the direction of the X and Z axes of the triad by using the rotational arrows of the ViewCube that appear in the upper right corner of the screen, see Figure 4.49. This helps to get the right orientation of the final model.

4.49

Section 3: Creating the Sketch

Now, you can create the sketch by using the sketching tools. In this tutorial, you will turn off the grids and snap settings for creating sketch entities by specifying points arbitrarily in the drawing area and then applying the required dimensions.

1. Click on the **Tools** tab in the **Ribbon** and then click on the **Application Options** tool in the **Options** panel of the **Tools** tab. The **Application Options** dialog box appears.

2. Click on the **Sketch** tab in the **Application Options** dialog box and then clear the **Grid lines, Minor grid lines,** and **Axes** check boxes in the **Display** area of the dialog box to turn off the display of grid lines, minor grid lines, and axes. Also, clear the **Snap to grid** checkbox in the dialog box to turn off the snap mode.

3. Click on the **Apply** button in the dialog box and then the **Close** button.

4. Click on the **Center Point Circle** tool in the **Create** panel of the **Sketch** tab, see Figure 4.50. The **Center Point Circle** tool gets activated and you are prompted to specify the center point of a circle.

4.50

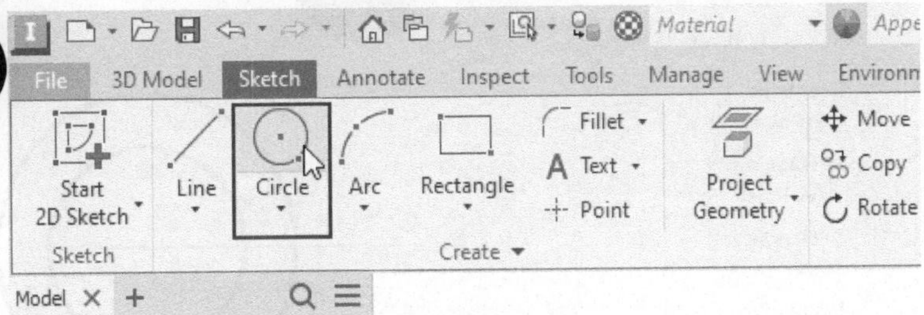

5. Click to specify the center point of a circle at the origin.

6. Move the cursor toward right and then click to specify a point when the diameter of the circle appears close to 28 mm in the Dimension Input, see Figure 4.51. A circle of diameter close to 28 mm is created and the **Center Point Circle** tool is still active.

7. Click to specify the center point of the second circle at the origin.

8. Move the cursor toward right and then click to specify a point when the diameter of the circle appears close to 18 mm in the Dimension Input, see Figure 4.52. A circle of diameter close to 18 mm is created and the **Center Point Circle** tool is still active.

4.51

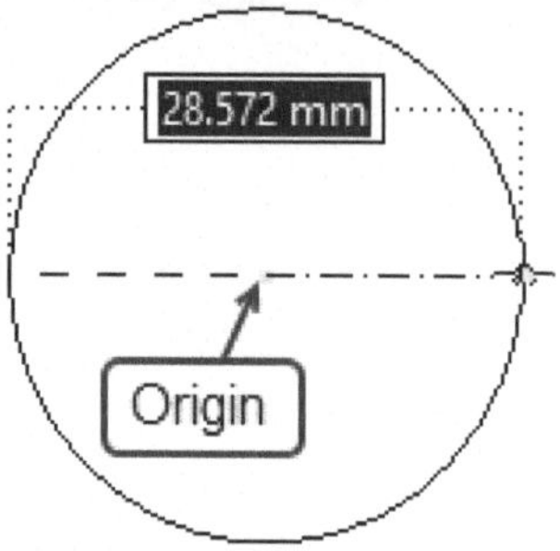

4.52

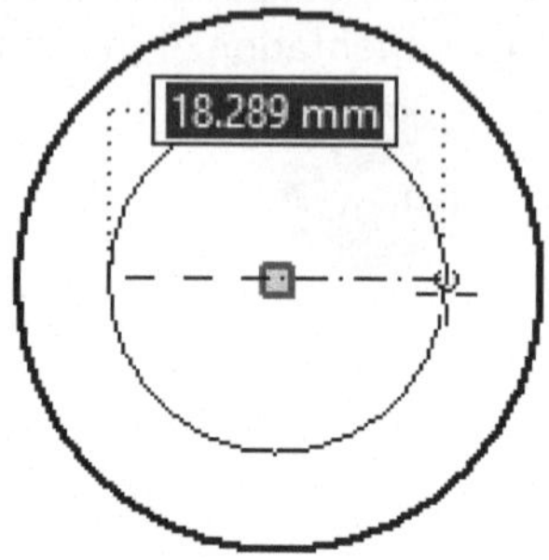

Note: As the sketch of this tutorial is being created by specifying points arbitrarily in the drawing area, the dimension values shown in the figures may be different in your case.

9. Press the ESC key to exit the **Center Point Circle** tool.

10. Invoke the **Rectangle** flyout in the **Create** panel and then click on the **Center Point Slot** tool, see Figure 4.53. You are prompted to specify the center of the slot.

11. Move the cursor to the origin and then click to specify the center point of the slot when the cursor snaps to the origin.

12. Move the cursor horizontally toward right and click when the half length of the slot appears close to 25 mm (50/2 = 25) in the Dimension Input, see Figure 4.54. Next, move the cursor to a distance in the drawing area. A preview of the slot appears.

4.53

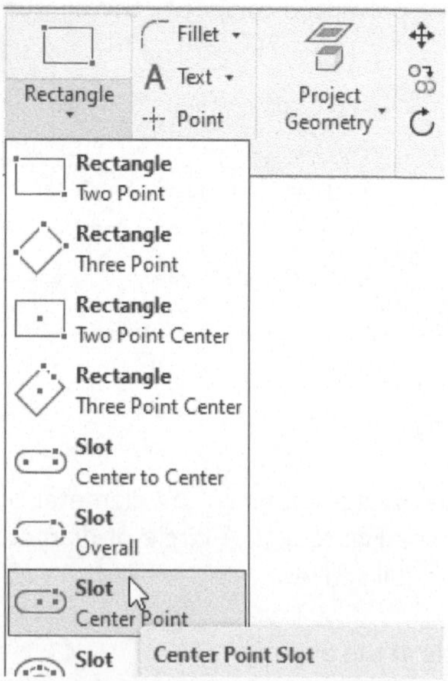

4.54

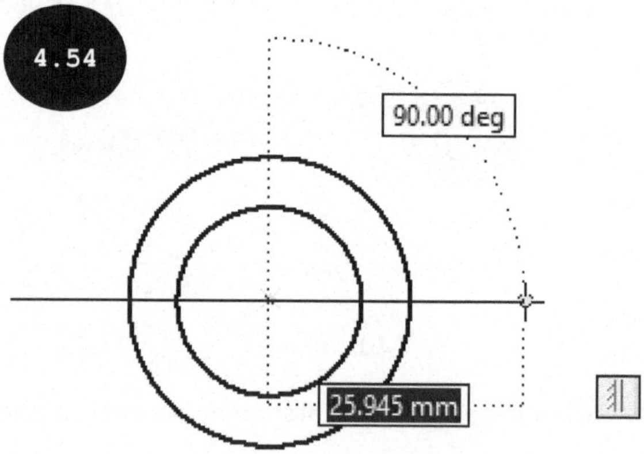

Tip: While drawing sketch entities, you may need to zoom into or zoom out of the drawing display area by scrolling the middle mouse button.

13. Click the left mouse button when the width of the slot appears close to 20 mm in the Dimension Input, see Figure 4.55. The slot is created.

4.55

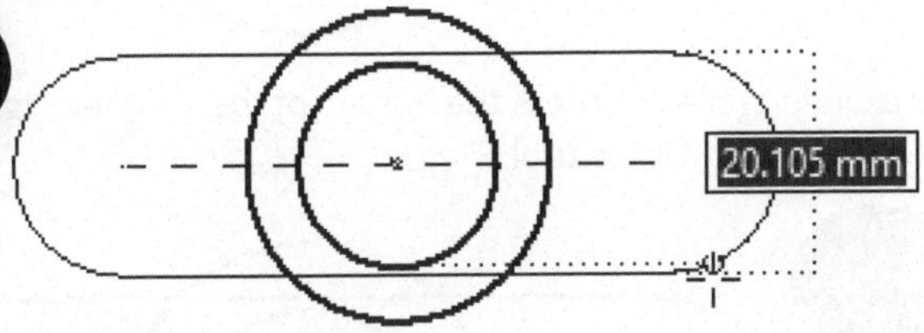

14. Press the ESC key to exit the **Center Point Slot** tool.

15. Click on the **Center Point Circle** tool in the **Create** panel of the **Sketch** tab, see Figure 4.56. You are prompted to specify the center point of the circle.

4.56

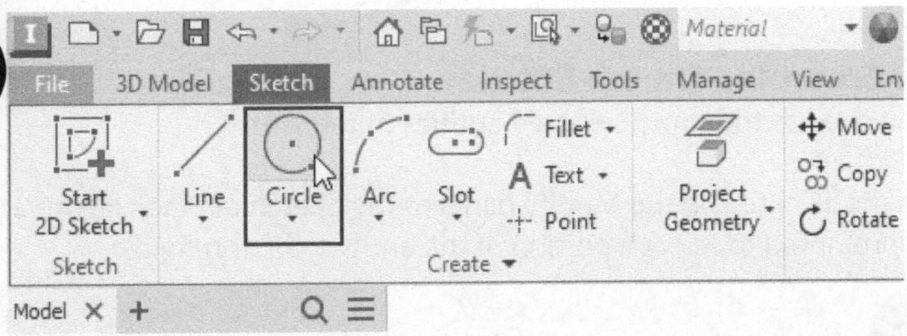

16. Click to specify the center point of the circle when the cursor snaps to the center point of the right slot arc, see Figure 4.57.

4.57

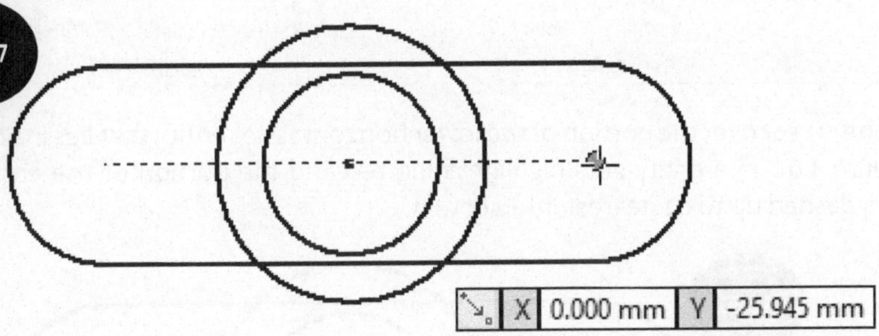

17. Move the cursor horizontally toward right and click when the diameter of the circle appears close to 10 mm, see Figure 4.58. A circle of diameter close to 10 mm is created and the **Center Point Circle** tool is still active.

4.58

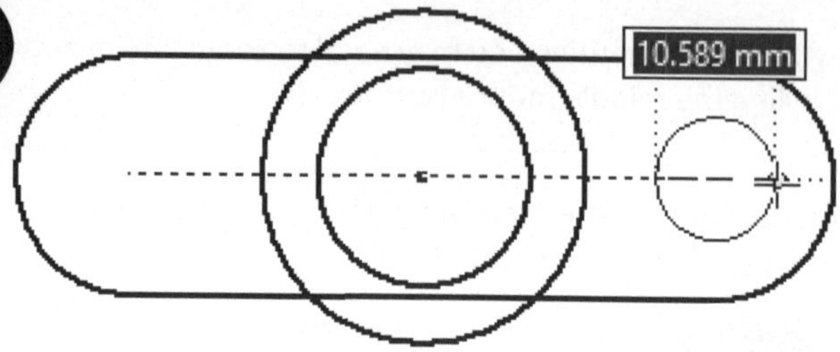

18. Similarly, create a circle at the center of the left arc of the slot, see Figure 4.59. Next, press the ESC key to exit the **Center Point Circle** tool.

4.59

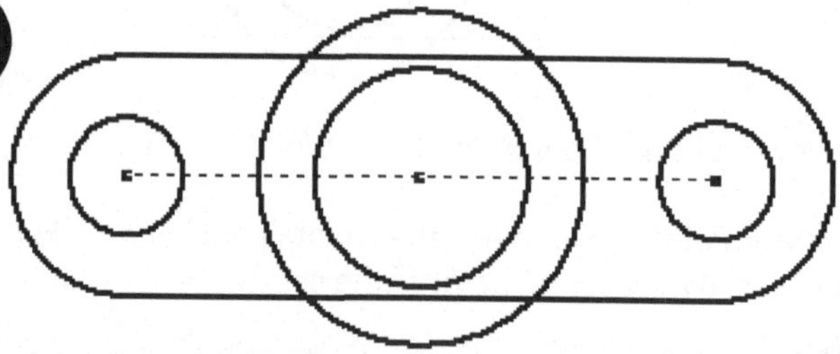

Section 4: Trimming Sketch Entities

Now, you need to trim the unwanted entities of the sketch.

1. Click on the **Trim** tool in the **Modify** panel of the **Sketch** tab (see Figure 4.60) or press the X key. You are prompted to select a portion of the entity to be trimmed.

4.60

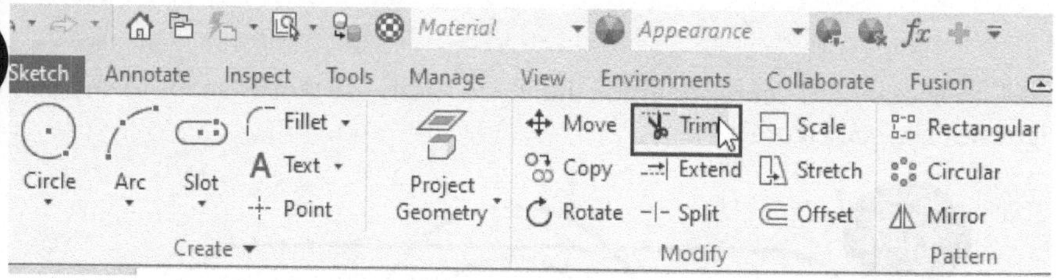

2. Move the cursor over the portion of the lower horizontal slot entity that lies inside the outer circle, see Figure 4.61. The entity gets highlighted in red and the portion of the entity to be trimmed appears dashed up to its nearest intersection.

4.61

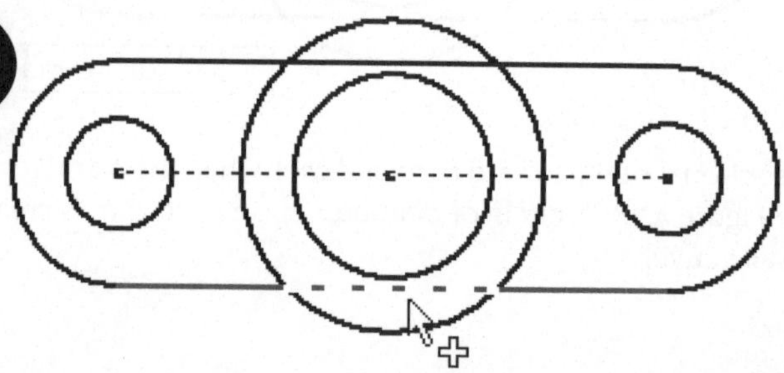

3. Click the left mouse button when the portion of the entity to be trimmed appears as dashed. The selected entity gets trimmed up to its nearest intersection, see Figure 4.62. Also, the **Trim** tool is still active.

4.62

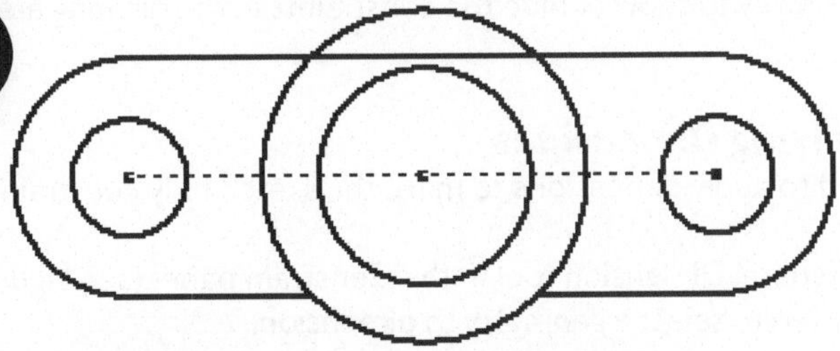

4. Similarly, click on the other unwanted entities of the sketch one by one to trim them. Figure 4.63 shows the sketch after trimming all the unwanted entities.

4.63

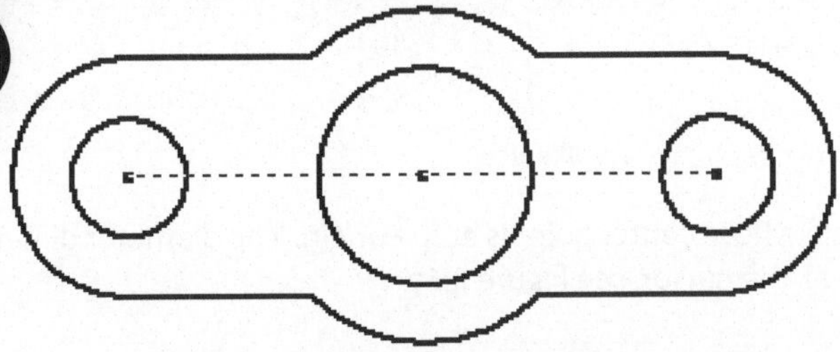

5. Once you have completed the trimming operation, press the ESC key to exit the tool.

Section 5: Applying Constraints

After creating the sketch, you need to make it fully constrained by applying proper constraints and dimensions to the sketch entities.

1. Click on the **Equal** tool in the **Constrain** panel of the **Sketch** tab and then select two circles of diameter close to 10 mm one by one, see Figure 4.64. An equal constraint is applied between the selected circles and the **Equal** tool is still active.

2. Select two arcs of radius close to 14 mm one by one, see Figure 4.65. An equal constraint is applied between the selected arcs and the **Equal** tool is still active.

4.64

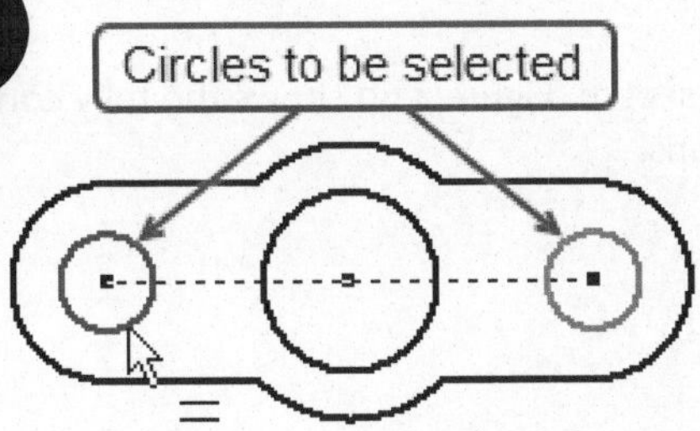

4.65

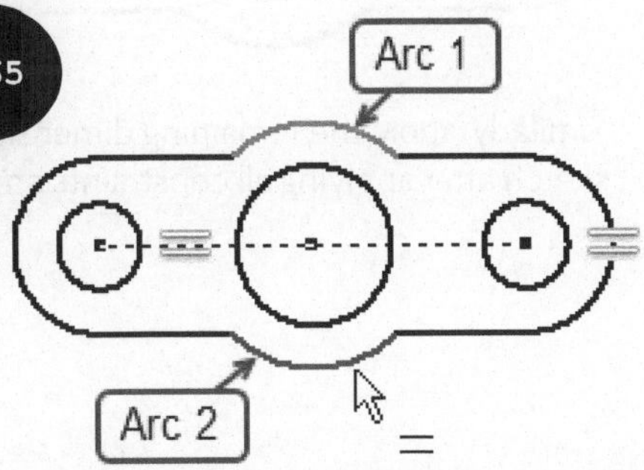

3. Press the ESC key to exit the **Equal** tool.

Tip: You can turn on or off the display of the applied constraints in the drawing area by clicking the **Show All Constraints** or **Hide All Constraints** tool in the Status Bar. You can also press the F8 or F9 key to show or hide the constraints in the drawing area.

Section 6: Applying Dimensions

Now, you need to apply dimensions to make the sketch fully constrained.

1. Click on the **General Dimension** tool in the **Constrain** panel (see Figure 4.66) or press the D key. You are prompted to select a geometry to dimension.

4.66

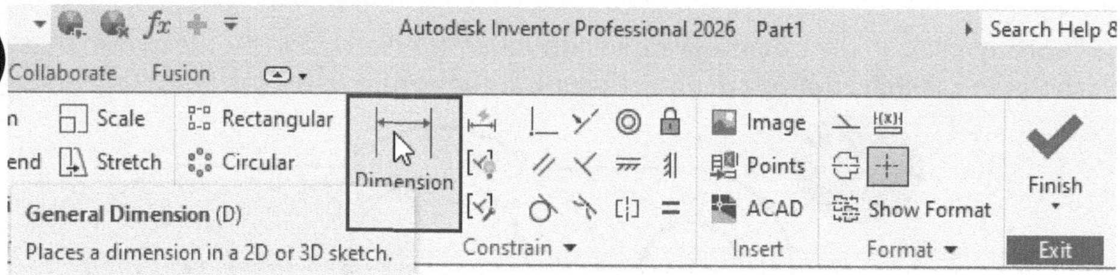

2. Select the circle whose center point is at the origin. The diameter dimension of the selected circle gets attached to the cursor, see Figure 4.67.

3. Move the cursor to the location where you want to place the dimension in the drawing area and then click to specify the placement point. The **Edit Dimension** dialog box appears.

4. Enter **18** in the **Edit Dimension** dialog box as the diameter of the circle and then click on the green tick-mark button. The diameter of the circle is modified to 18 mm and the diameter dimension is applied, see Figure 4.68.

4.67

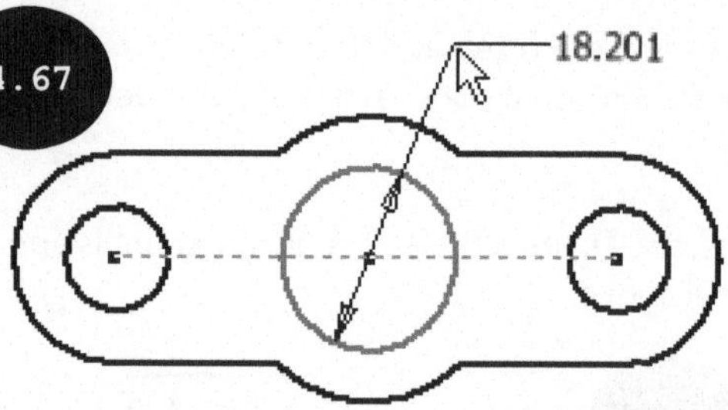

4.68

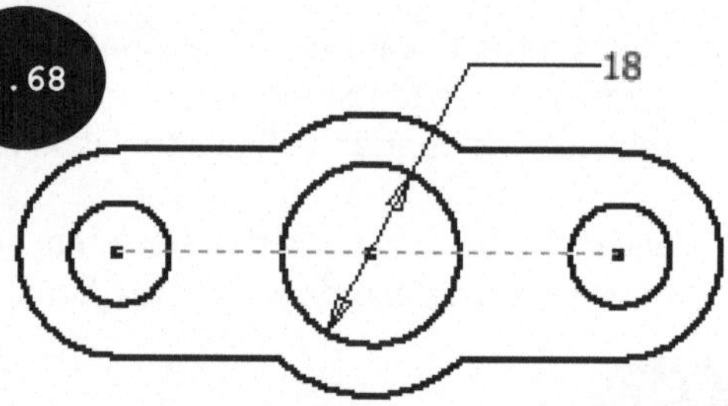

5. Similarly, apply the remaining dimensions to the sketch. Figure 4.69 shows the fully constrained sketch after applying all constraints and dimensions.

4.69

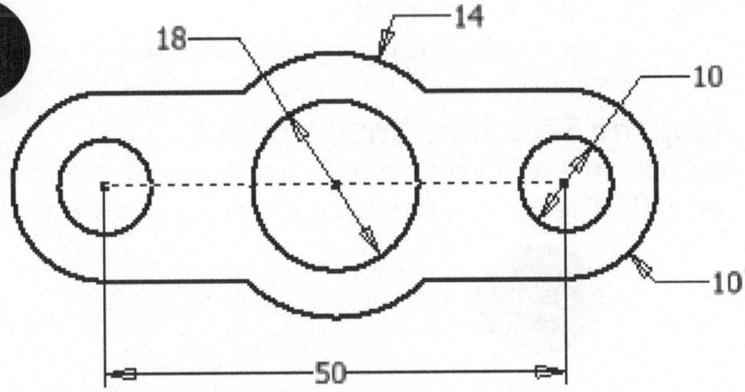

6. After creating the sketch, click on the **Finish Sketch** tool in the **Exit** panel of the **Ribbon** to exit the Sketching environment.

Section 7: Saving the Sketch

1. Click on the **Save** tool in the **Quick Access Toolbar**. The **Save As** dialog box appears. Next, browse to **Autodesk Inventor > Chapter 4** folder in the local drive of your system. Note that you need to create Chapter 4 folder inside the Autodesk Inventor folder.

2. Enter **Tutorial 1** in the **File name** field of the dialog box and then click on the **Save** button. The sketch is saved in the specified location (>:\Autodesk Inventor\Chapter 4).

Tutorial 2

Draw the sketch, shown in Figure 4.70, and make it fully constrained by applying all the required dimensions and constraints. The 3D model shown in the figure is for your reference only. You will learn about creating a 3D model in later chapters. All dimensions are in mm.

4.70

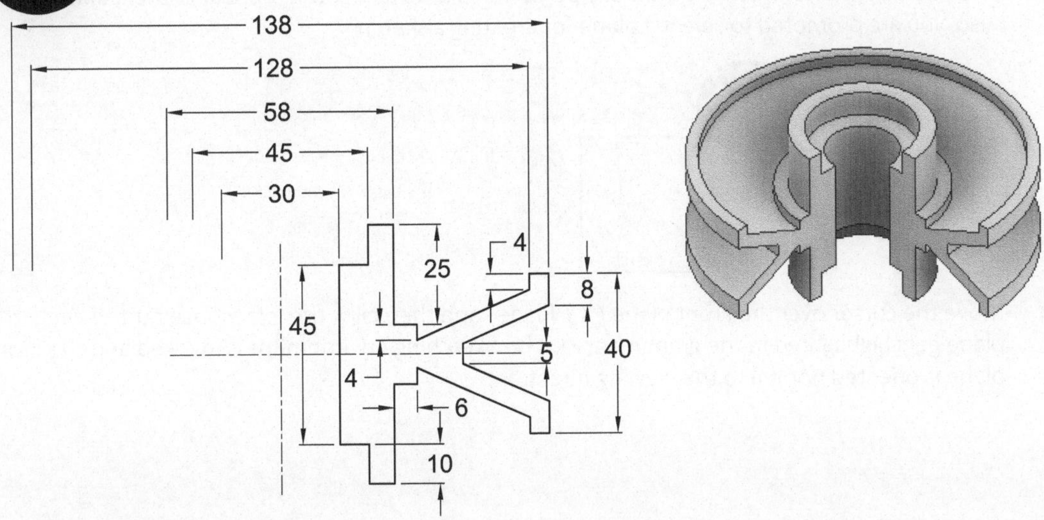

Section 1: Starting Autodesk Inventor

1. Start Autodesk Inventor by double-clicking on the Autodesk Inventor icon on your desktop.

Section 2: Invoking the Sketching Environment

1. Click on the **New** tool in the startup user interface of Autodesk Inventor (see Figure 4.71) or press the CTRL + N keys. The **Create New File** dialog box appears, see Figure 4.72.

4.71

4.72

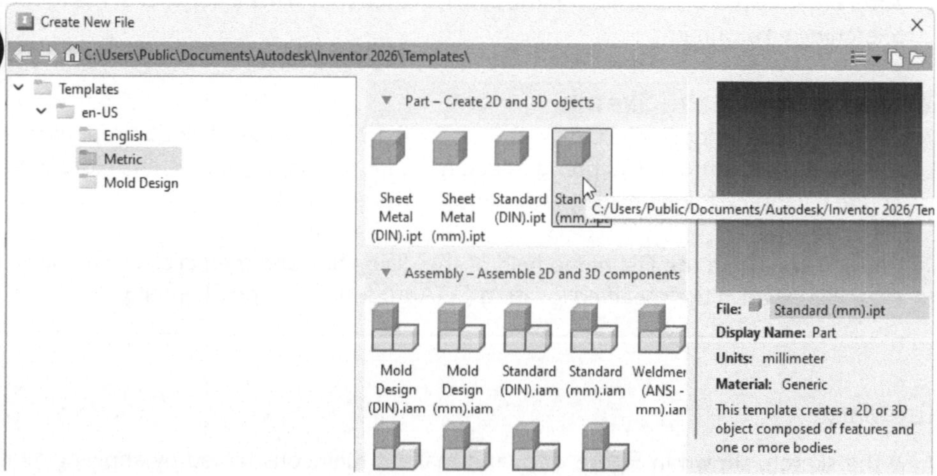

2. Double-click on the **Standard (mm).ipt** template in the right panel of the dialog box, refer to Figure 4.72. The Part Modeling environment is invoked with a Metric template.

3. Click on the **Start 2D Sketch** tool in the **Sketch** panel (see Figure 4.73) or press the S key. The three default planes which are mutually perpendicular to each other appear in the graphics area. Also, you are prompted to select a plane for creating a sketch.

4.73

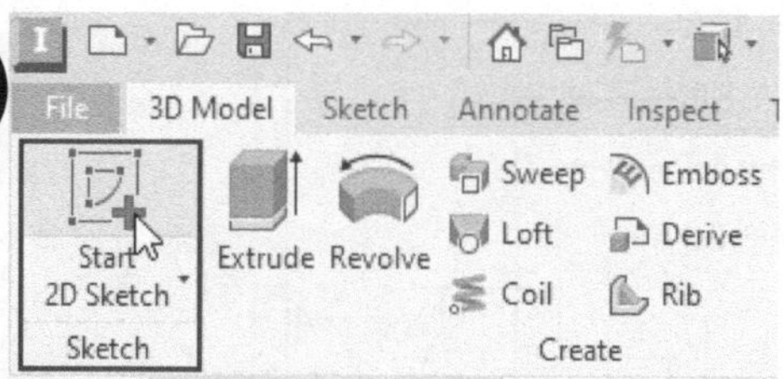

4. Move the cursor over the Front plane (XY Plane) and then click the left mouse button when the plane gets highlighted in the graphics area. The Sketching environment is invoked and the Front plane is oriented normal to the viewing direction.

Section 3: Creating the Sketch

Now, you need to create the sketch by using the sketching tools.

Note: Ensure that the snap mode and the display of grids are turned off. As Autodesk Inventor is a parametric software, in this tutorial, you can turn off the snap mode and create the sketch entities by specifying points arbitrarily in the drawing area and then applying required dimensions.

1. Click on the **Line** tool in the **Create** panel and then click on the **Centerline** tool in the **Format** panel of the **Sketch** tab to activate the centerline mode.

2. Create a vertical and a horizontal centerline of any length starting from the origin, one by one, see Figure 4.74.

4.74

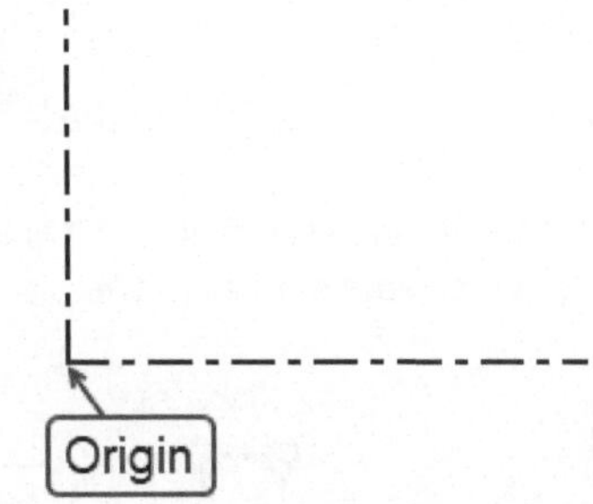

3. After creating the centerlines, click on the **Centerline** tool again in the **Format** panel to deactivate the centerline mode.

4. Press the L key to invoke the **Line** tool.

5. Move the cursor over the horizontal centerline (see Figure 4.75) and then click to specify the start point of the line on it at a distance from the origin.

6. Move the cursor vertically upward and then click to specify the endpoint of the line when the length of the line appears close to 22.5 mm near the cursor, see Figure 4.76. A vertical line of length close to 22.5 mm is created.

4.75

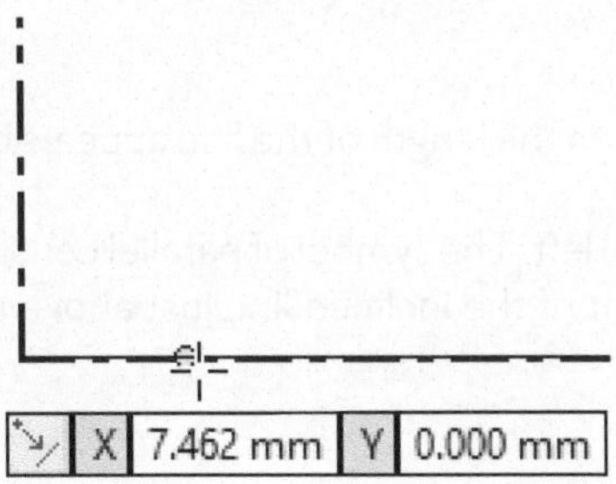

4.76

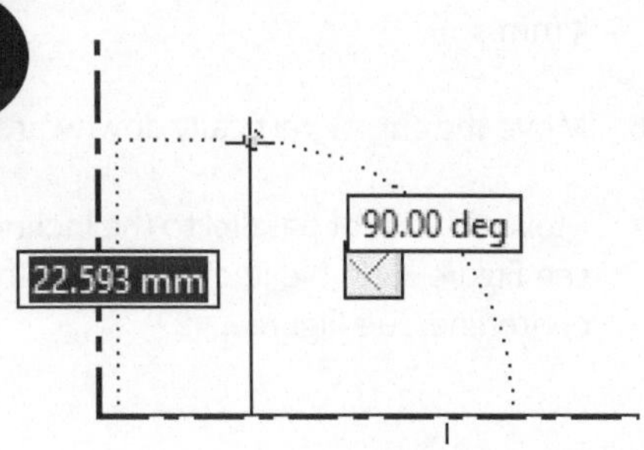

7. Move the cursor horizontally toward right and click to specify the endpoint of the second line when the length of the line appears close to 7.5 mm. A horizontal line of length close to 7.5 mm is created.

8. Move the cursor vertically upward and click to specify the endpoint of the line when the length of the line appears close to 10 mm. A vertical line of length close to 10 mm is created.

9. Move the cursor horizontally toward right and click when the length of the line appears close to 6.5 mm. A horizontal line of length close to 6.5 mm is created.

10. Move the cursor vertically downward and click when the length of the line appears close to 25 mm.

11. Move the cursor horizontally toward right and click when the length of the line appears close to 6 mm.

12. Move the cursor vertically downward and click when the length of the line appears close to 4 mm.

13. Move the cursor toward right at an angle (see Figure 4.77) and then click to specify the endpoint of the inclined line when the line appears similar to the one shown in Figure 4.77.

4.77

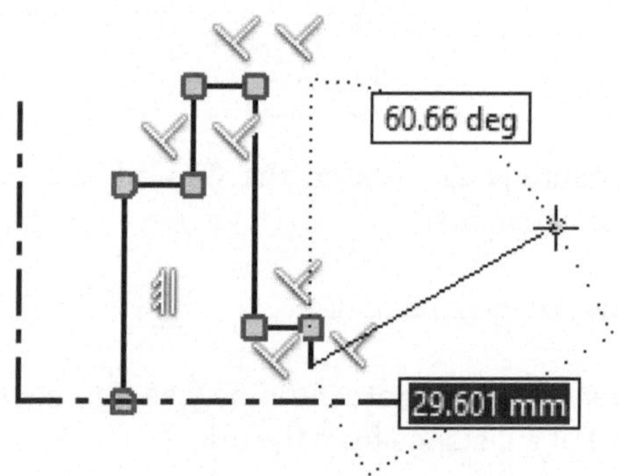

14. Move the cursor vertically upward and click when the length of the line appears close to 4 mm.

15. Move the cursor horizontally toward right and click when the length of the line appears close to 5 mm.

16. Move the cursor vertically downward and click when the length of the line appears close to 8 mm.

17. Move the cursor parallel to the inclined line toward left. The symbol of parallel constraint appears, see Figure 4.78. Next, click to specify the endpoint of the inclined line just above the horizontal centerline, see Figure 4.78.

4.78

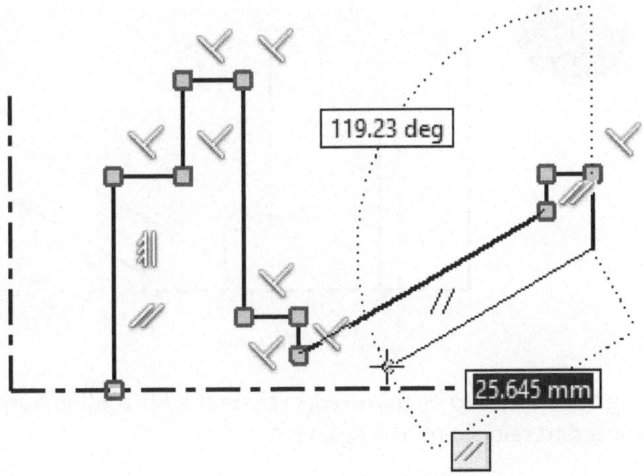

18. Move the cursor vertically downward and then click the left mouse button when the cursor snaps to the horizontal centerline. Next, press the ESC key to exit the **Line** tool. Figure 4.79 shows the sketch after creating its upper half.

4.79

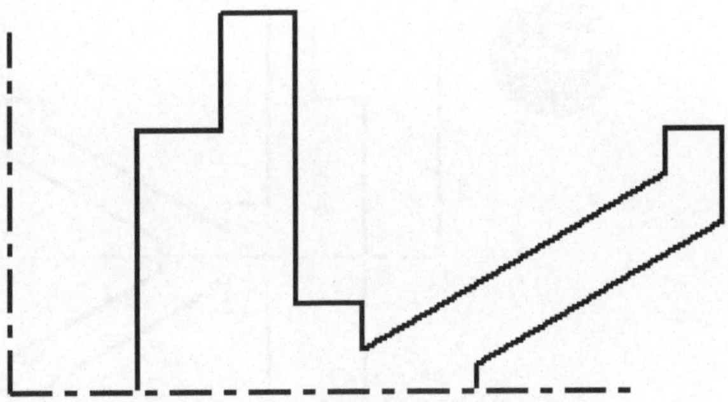

Section 4: Mirroring Sketch Entities

After creating the upper half of the sketch, you need to mirror it to create the lower half.

1. Click on the **Mirror** tool in the **Pattern** panel of the **Sketch** tab of the **Ribbon**. The **Mirror** dialog box appears, see Figure 4.80. Also, you are prompted to select entities to be mirrored.

4.80

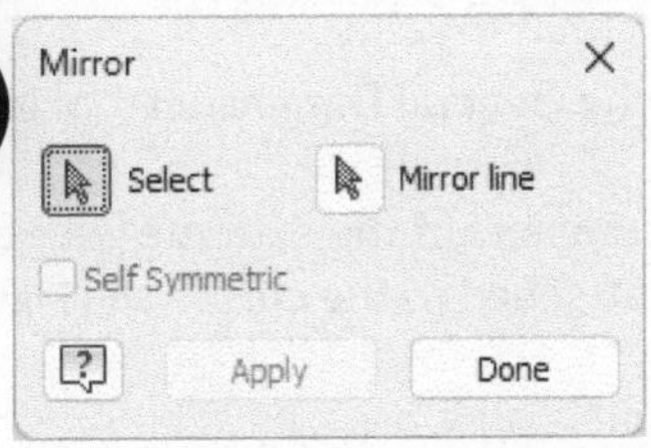

2. Select all the sketch entities except the vertical and horizontal centerlines as the entities to be mirrored. You can select the entities one by one by clicking the left mouse button or by drawing a window from left to right around the entities to be selected, see Figure 4.81. You can draw a window by dragging the cursor.

4.81

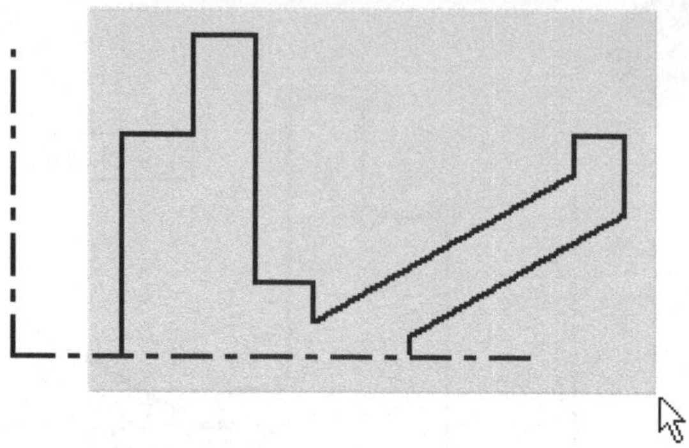

3. After selecting the entities to be mirrored, click on the **Mirror line** button in the **Mirror** dialog box. You are prompted to select a mirroring line.

4. Select the horizontal centerline as the mirroring line in the drawing area.

5. Click on the **Apply** button and then the **Done** button in the **Mirror** dialog box. A mirror image of the selected entities is created, see Figure 4.82.

4.82

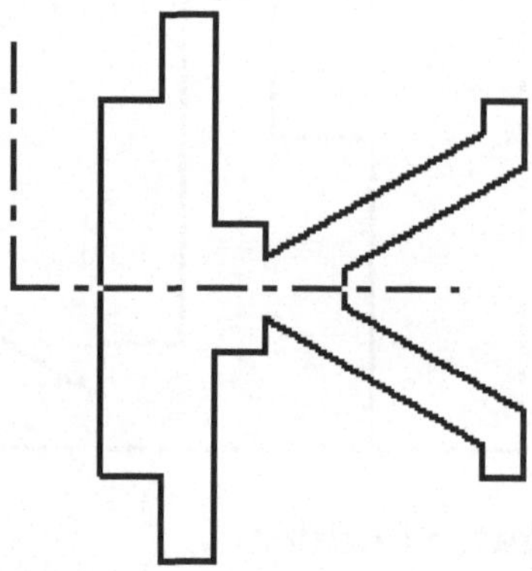

Section 5: Applying Dimensions

Now, you need to apply dimensions to make the sketch fully constrained. Constraints such as horizontal, vertical, and parallel are already applied to the sketch entities while drawing them.

1. Press the **D** key to invoke the **General Dimension** tool for applying dimensions.

2. Click to select both the endpoints of the extreme left vertical line of the sketch one by one. The linear dimension appears attached to the cursor, see Figure 4.83.

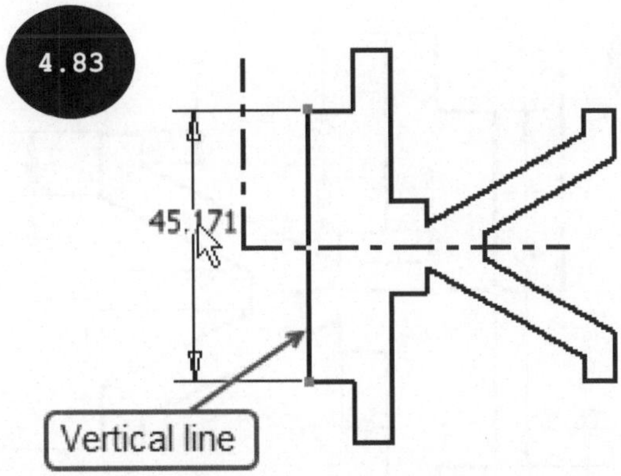

3. Move the cursor toward left to a distance and then click to specify the placement point. The **Edit Dimension** dialog box appears.

4. Enter **45** in the **Edit Dimension** dialog box and then press ENTER. The length of the line is modified and the dimension is applied, see Figure 4.84. Also, the **General Dimension** tool remains active.

5. Click on the next vertical line, see Figure 4.85. The linear dimension is attached to the cursor. Next, move the cursor toward left to a distance and then click to specify the placement point. The **Edit Dimension** dialog box appears.

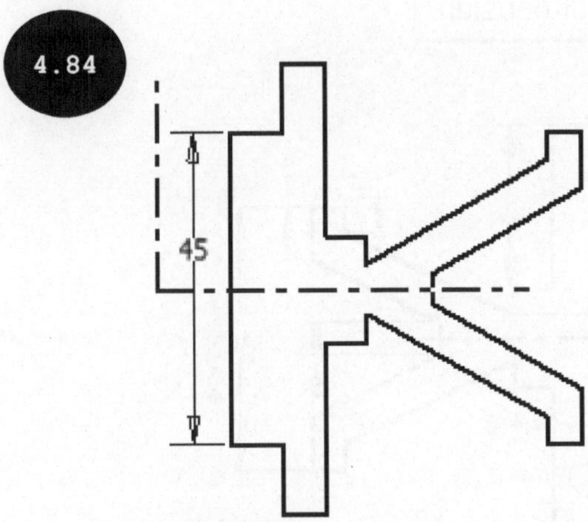

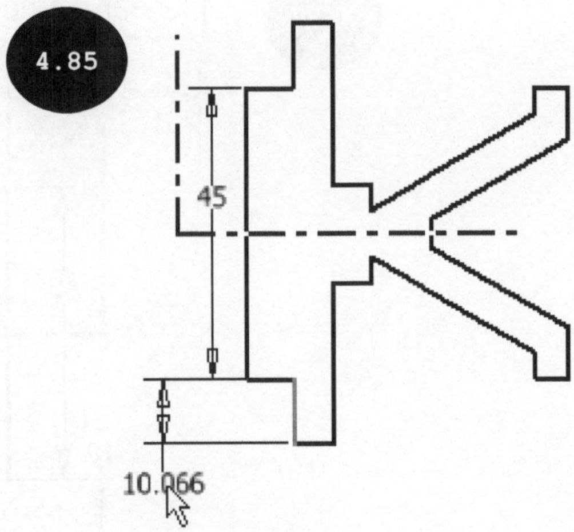

6. Enter **10** in the **Edit Dimension** dialog box and then press ENTER. The length of the line is modified to 10 mm and the linear dimension is applied. Also, the **General Dimension** tool remains active.

7. Similarly, apply the remaining linear dimensions to the sketch entities, see Figure 4.86.

4.86

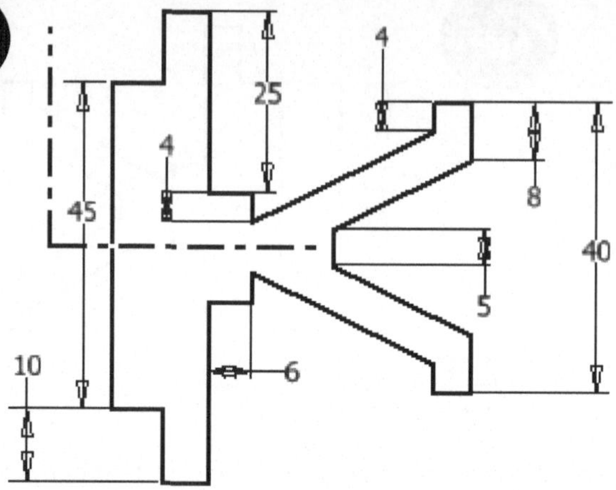

After applying the linear dimensions, you need to apply the linear diameter dimensions.

8. Ensure that the **General Dimension** tool is activated.

9. Select the vertical centerline and then select the extreme left vertical line of the sketch. The linear diameter dimension appears attached to the cursor, see Figure 4.87.

4.87

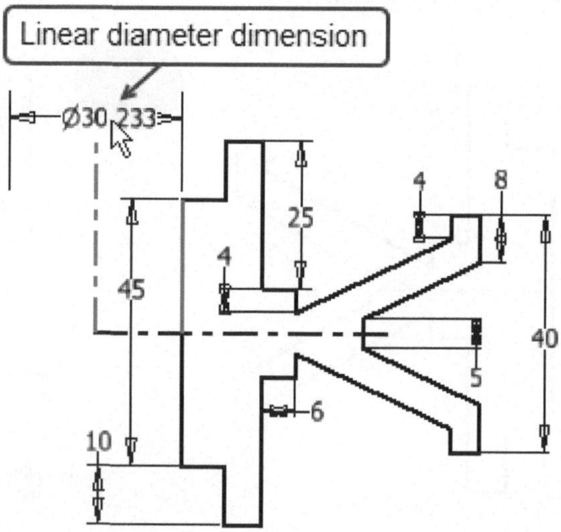

10. Click to specify the placement point for the linear diameter dimension in the drawing area. The **Edit Dimension** dialog box appears.

11. Enter **30** in the **Edit Dimension** dialog box and then press ENTER. The linear diameter dimension is applied, see Figure 4.88.

4.88

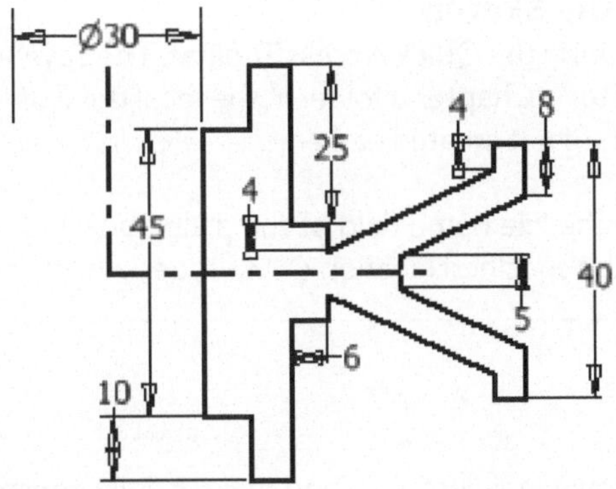

12. Similarly, apply the remaining linear diameter dimensions to the sketch, see Figure 4.89.

13. Press the ESC key to exit the **General Dimension** tool. Figure 4.89 shows the fully constrained sketch after applying all the dimensions.

Note: In the Status Bar at the lower right corner of the screen, the status of the sketch appears as **2 dimensions needed.** This status appears because of the unconstrained length of the vertical and horizontal centerlines of the sketch.

14. After creating the sketch, click on the **Finish Sketch** tool in the **Exit** panel of the **Ribbon** to exit the Sketching environment.

4.89

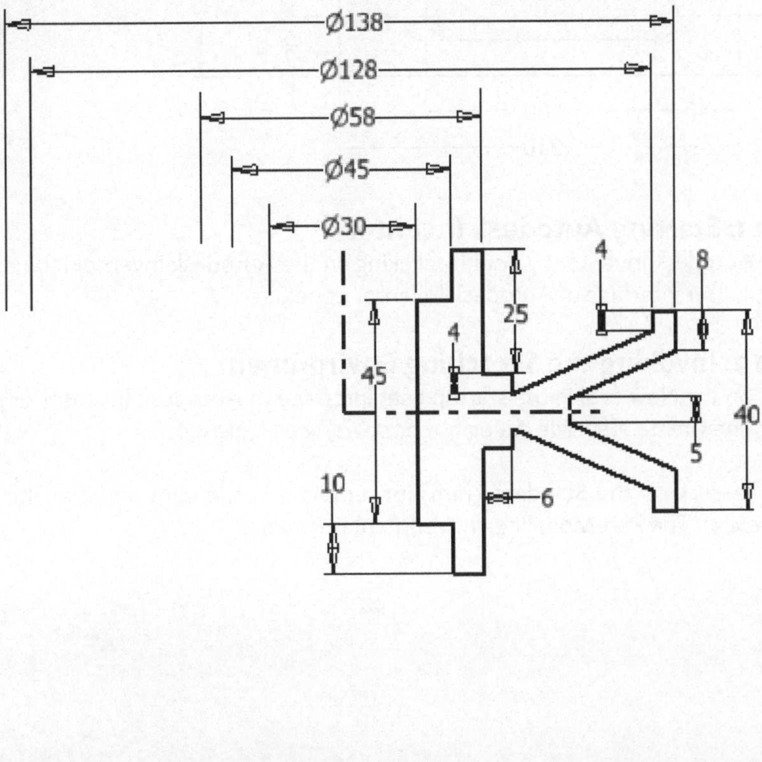

Section 6: Saving the Sketch

1. Click on the **Save** tool in the **Quick Access Toolbar**. The **Save As** dialog box appears. Next, browse to **Autodesk Inventor > Chapter 4** folder in the local drive of your system. Note that you need to create these folders, if not created earlier.

2. Enter **Tutorial 2** in the **File name** field of the dialog box and then click on the **Save** button. The sketch is saved in the specified location (>:\Autodesk Inventor\Chapter 4).

Tutorial 3

Draw the sketch, as shown in Figure 4.90 and make it fully constrained by applying all the required dimensions and constraints. The 3D model shown in the figure is for your reference only. You will learn about creating the 3D model in later chapters. All dimensions are in mm.

4.90

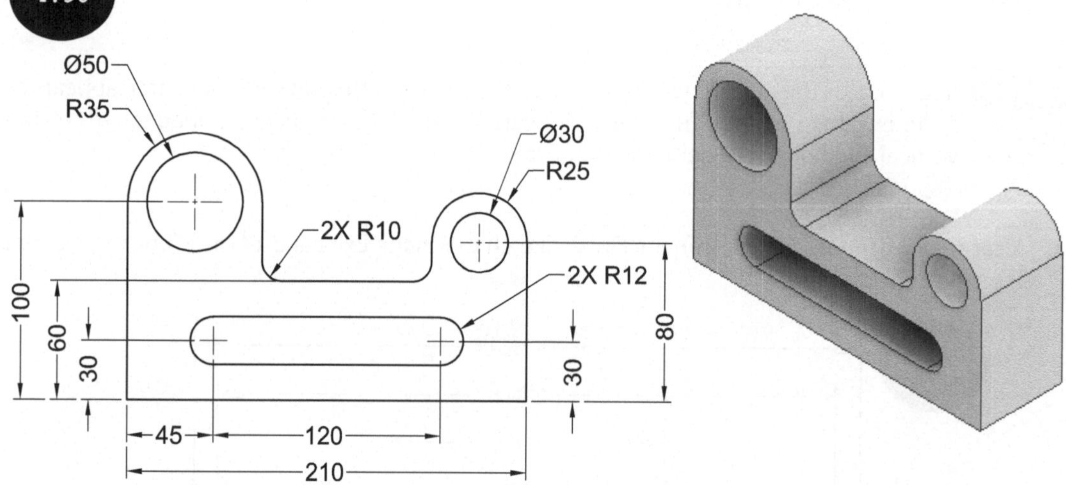

Section 1: Starting Autodesk Inventor

1. Start Autodesk Inventor by double-clicking on the Autodesk Inventor icon on your desktop. The startup user interface of Autodesk Inventor appears.

Section 2: Invoking the Sketching Environment

1. Click on the **New** tool in the startup user interface of Autodesk Inventor or press the CTRL + N keys. The **Create New File** dialog box appears, see Figure 4.91.

2. Double-click on the **Standard (mm).ipt** template in the right panel of the dialog box, refer to Figure 4.91. The Part Modeling environment is invoked.

4.91

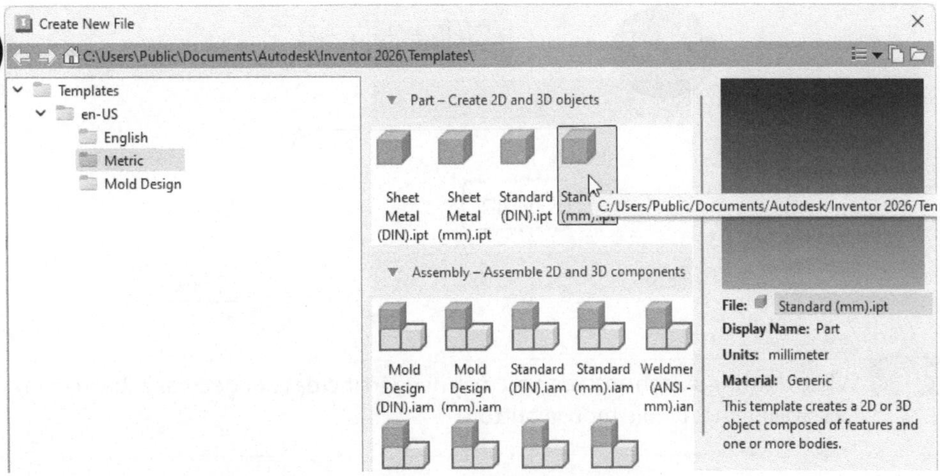

3. Click on the **Start 2D Sketch** tool in the **Sketch** panel (see Figure 4.92) or press the S key. The three default planes appear in the graphics area. Also, you are prompted to select a plane for creating a sketch.

4.92

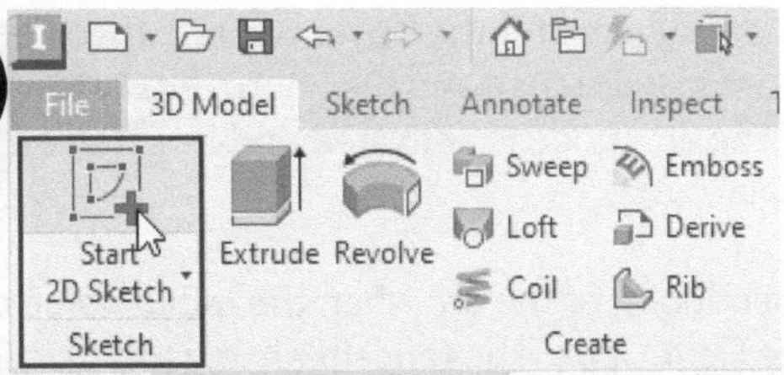

4. Move the cursor over the Front (XY Plane) and then click the left mouse button when the plane gets highlighted in the graphics area. The Sketching environment is invoked and the Front plane is oriented normal to the viewing direction.

Section 3: Creating the Sketch

Now, you need to create the sketch by using the sketching tools.

Note: Ensure that the snap mode and the display of grids are turned off. As Autodesk Inventor is a parametric software, in this tutorial, you can turn off the snap mode and create the sketch entities by specifying points arbitrarily in the drawing area and then applying required dimensions.

1. Invoke the **Line** tool by pressing the L key. You are prompted to specify the start point of the line.

2. Click to specify the start point of the line at the origin.

3. Move the cursor horizontally toward right and click to specify the endpoint of the line when a length close to 210 mm appears and a symbol of horizontal constraint appears near the cursor, see Figure 4.93. A horizontal line of length close to 210 mm is created. Also, the horizontal relation is applied to the line.

4.93

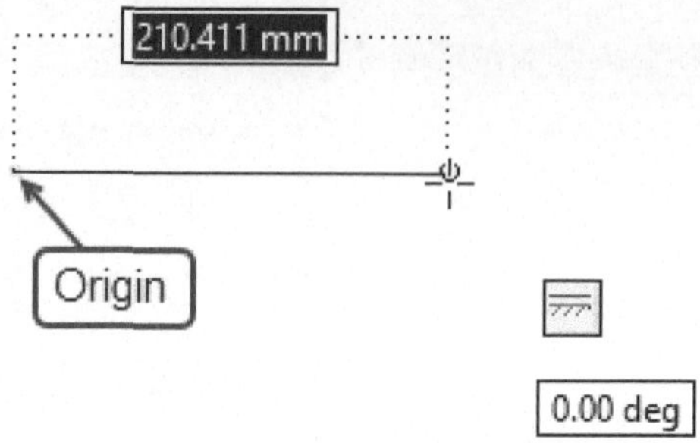

Tip: While drawing sketch entities, you may need to increase or decrease the drawing display area by scrolling the middle mouse button.

4. Move the cursor vertically upward and create a vertical line of length close to 80 mm.

   Now, you need to create a tangent arc.

5. Move the cursor to a distance and then over the last specified point in the drawing area. Next, drag the cursor upward to a distance and then horizontally toward left by pressing and holding the left mouse button. The arc mode is activated and the preview of the tangent arc appears in the drawing area, see Figure 4.94.

6. Click to specify the endpoint of the arc when the radius value of the arc appears close to 25 mm in the Status Bar, see Figure 4.94. The tangent arc of radius close to 25 mm is created and the line mode is activated again.

7. Move the cursor vertically downward and create a vertical line of length close to 20 mm.

8. Move the cursor horizontally toward left and create a horizontal line of length close to 90 mm.

9. Move the cursor vertically upward and create a vertical line of length close to 40 mm.

10. Create a tangent arc of radius close to 35 mm at an angle of 180 degrees, see Figure 4.95. Also, ensure that the endpoint of the tangent arc is aligned to the start point of the first line entity, see Figure 4.95.

4.94

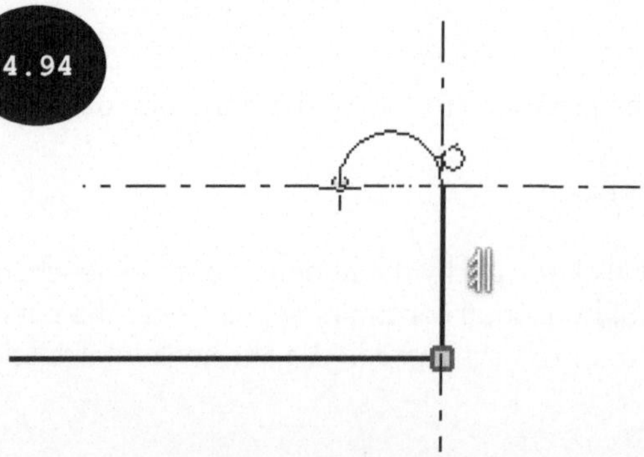

4.95

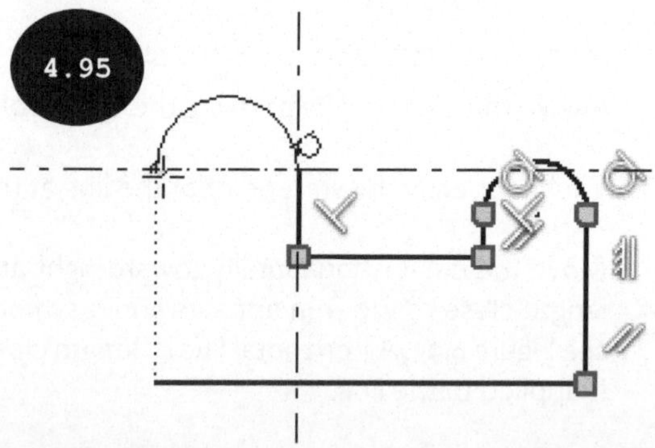

11. Move the cursor vertically downward and click to specify the endpoint of the line when the cursor snaps to the start point of the first line entity, see Figure 4.96.

4.96

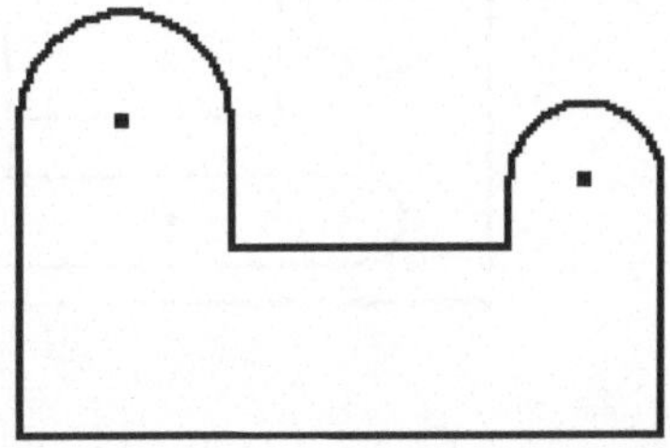

12. Press the ESC key to exit the **Line** tool.

    Now, you need to create circles of the sketch.

13. Click on the **Center Point Circle** tool in the **Create** panel of the **Sketch** tab. You are prompted to specify the start point of the circle.

14. Create two circles of diameter close to 50 mm and 30 mm, respectively, see Figure 4.97. Next, exit the **Center Point Circle** tool.

15. Invoke the **Rectangle** flyout in the **Create** panel of the **Sketch** tab and then click on the **Center to Center Slot** tool. You are prompted to specify the start center point of the slot.

16. Create a straight slot similar to the one shown in Figure 4.98 and then exit the tool. You can create a slot for any parameters, as later in this tutorial, you will need to apply dimensions in order to make the sketch fully constrained.

4.97

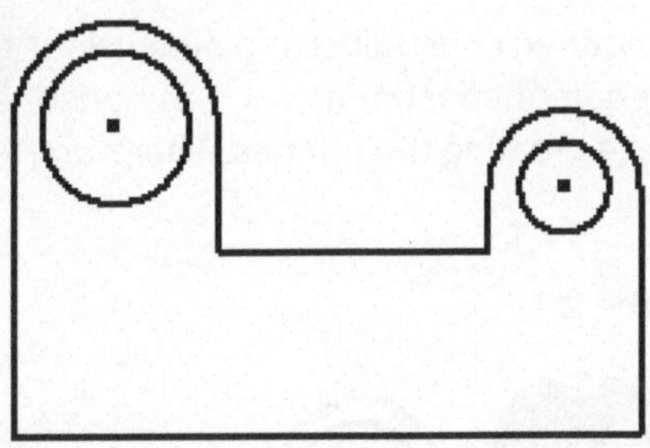

4.98

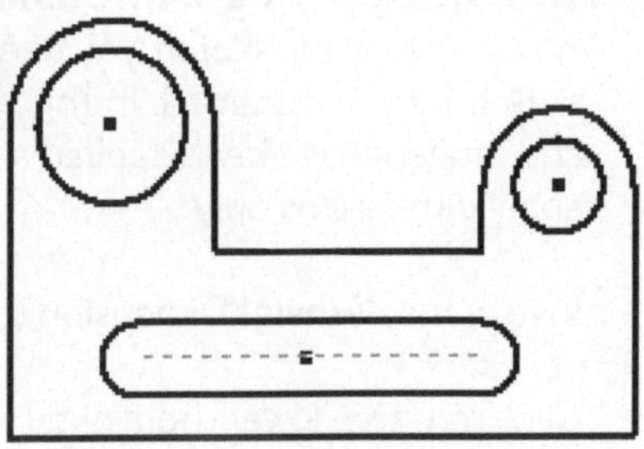

    Now, you need to create fillets in the sketch.

17. Click on the **Fillet** tool in the **Create** panel of the **Sketch** tab. The **2D Fillet** dialog box appears.

18. Enter **10** in the **Radius** field of dialog box. Also, ensure that the **Equal to Parameters** button is activated in the **2D Fillet** dialog box.

19. Move the cursor over the upper right vertex of the sketch, see Figure 4.99. A preview of the fillet appears. Next, click the left mouse button to accept the fillet preview. A fillet of radius 10 mm is created.

4.99

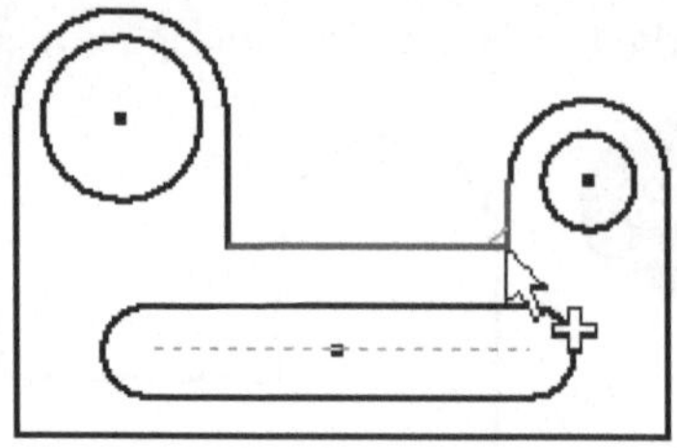

20. Move the cursor over the upper left vertex of the sketch, see Figure 4.100. A preview of the fillet appears. Next, click the left mouse button to accept the fillet preview. A fillet of radius of 10 mm is created, see Figure 4.101.

4.100

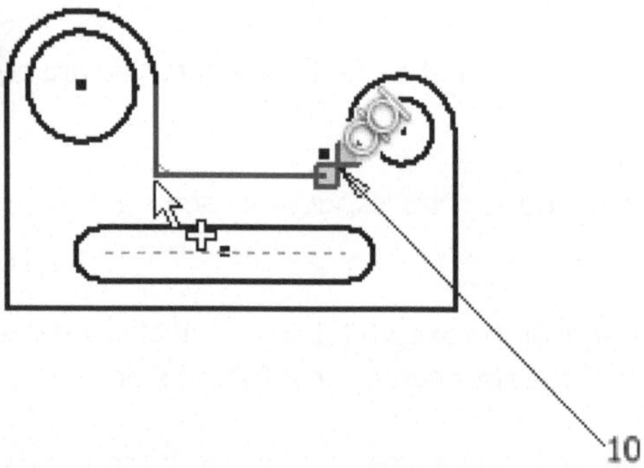

4.101

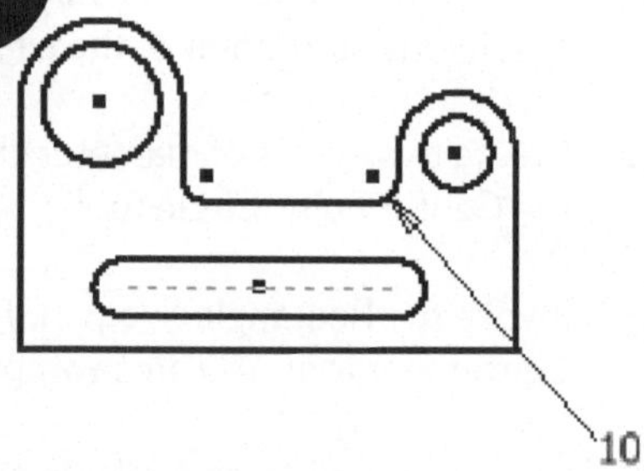

21. Press the ESC key to exit the **Fillet** tool.

Section 4: Applying Dimensions

After creating the sketch, you need to apply the required constraints and dimensions to make the sketch fully constrained. In this sketch, all the required constraints such as horizontal, vertical, and tangent have been applied automatically while creating the entities. Therefore, you need to apply dimensions only.

1. Invoke the **General Dimension** tool by pressing the D key.

2. Click on the lower horizontal line of the sketch. The linear dimension gets attached to the cursor, see Figure 4.102.

3. Click to specify the placement point for the attached linear dimension in the drawing area. The **Edit Dimension** dialog box appears.

4.102

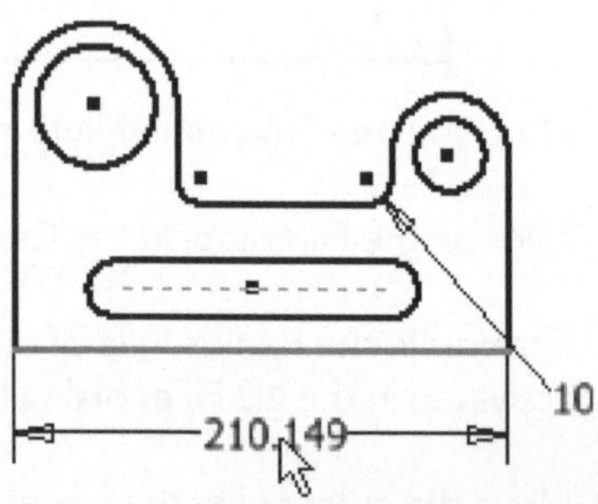

4. Enter **210** in the **Edit Dimension** dialog box and then click on the green tick mark button ✔. The length of the line is modified to 210 mm and the linear dimension is applied, see Figure 4.103.

4.103

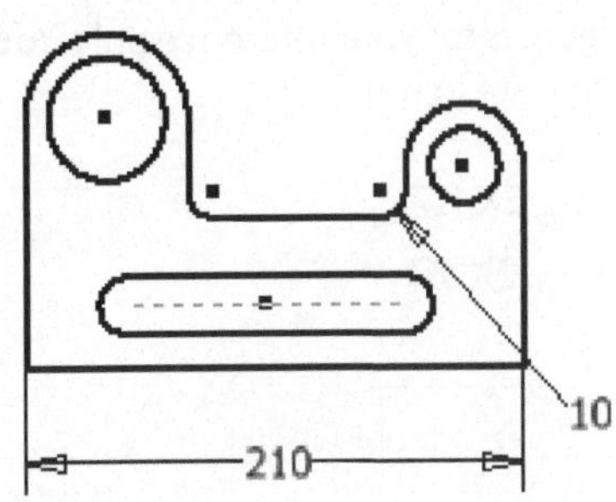

5. Similarly, apply the remaining dimensions to the sketch by using the **General Dimension** tool, see Figure 4.104. Next, press the ESC key to exit the tool.

4.104

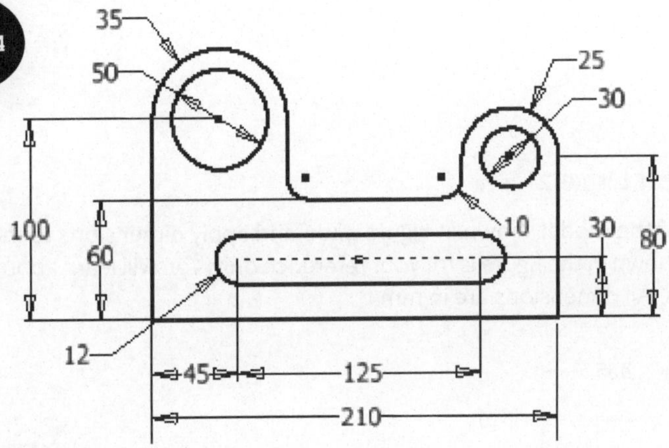

Tip: After placing a dimension in the required location, you may need to further change its location in order to place other dimensions. To change the location of an existing dimension, press and hold the left mouse button over the dimension and then drag it to the new location. Next, release the left mouse button.

6. After creating the sketch, click on the **Finish Sketch** tool in the **Exit** panel of the **Ribbon** to exit the Sketching environment.

Section 5: Saving the Sketch

1. Click on the **Save** tool in the **Quick Access Toolbar**. The **Save As** dialog box appears. Next, browse to **Autodesk Inventor > Chapter 4** folder in the local drive of your system. Note that you need to create these folders, if not created earlier.

2. Enter **Tutorial 3** in the **File name** field of the dialog box and then click on the **Save** button. The sketch is saved in the specified location (>:\Autodesk Inventor\Chapter 4).

Hands-on Test Drive 1

Draw a sketch of the model shown in Figure 4.105 and apply dimensions to make it fully constrained. The 3D model shown in the figure is for your reference only. You will learn about creating the 3D model in later chapters. All dimensions are in mm.

4.105

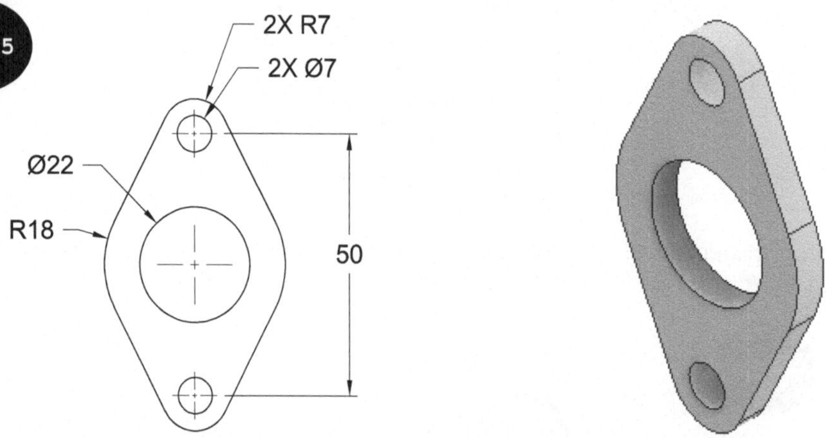

Hands-on Test Drive 2

Draw a sketch of the model shown in Figure 4.106 and apply dimensions to make it fully constrained. The 3D model shown in the figure is for your reference only. You will learn about creating the 3D model in later chapters. All dimensions are in mm.

4.106

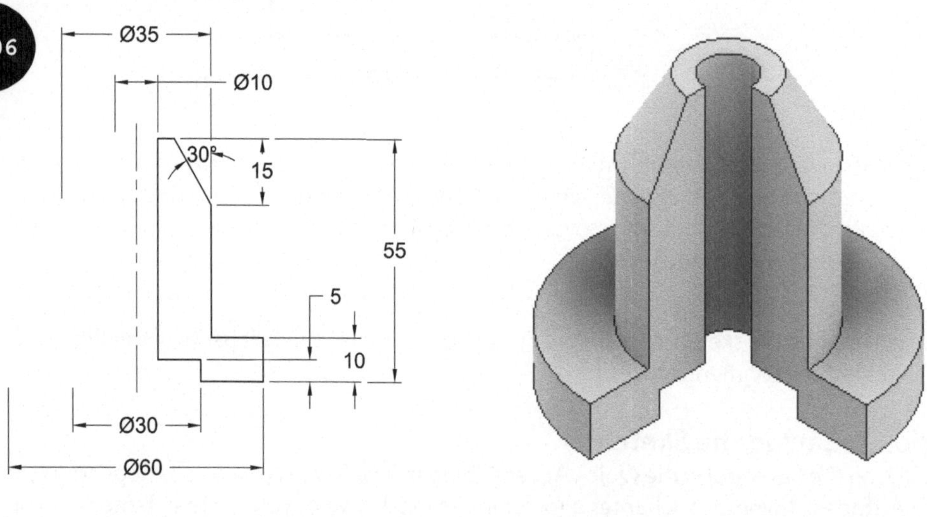

Hands-on Test Drive 3

Draw a sketch of the model shown in Figure 4.107 and apply dimensions to make it fully constrained. The 3D model shown in the figure is for your reference only. You will learn about creating the 3D model in later chapters. All dimensions are in mm.

4.107

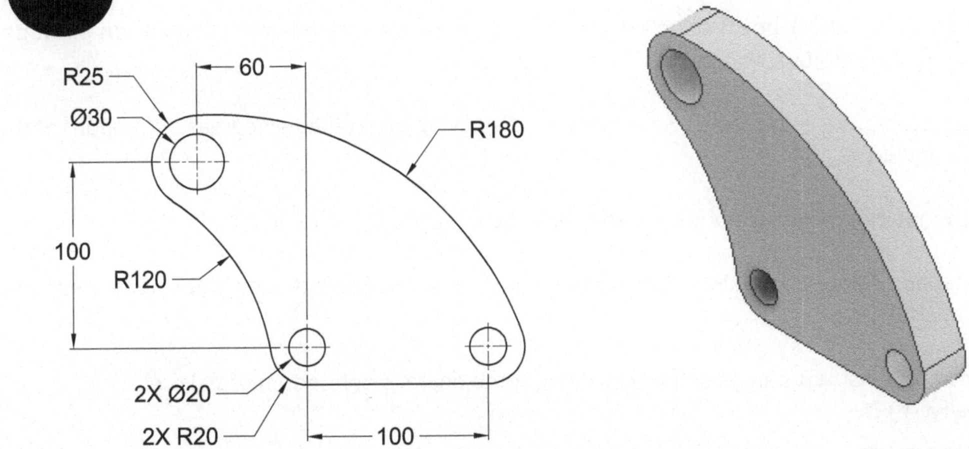

Summary

In this chapter, you have learned about creating fully constrained sketches by applying geometric constraints and dimensions. The chapter discussed in detail the application of various types of constraints and dimensions. It also explored concepts of displaying constraints, constraint settings, dimension settings, modifying or editing dimensions, working with different states of a sketch, and displaying available degrees of freedom for a sketch.

Questions

Complete and verify the following sentences:

- The _________ constraint is used for coinciding a sketch point onto a line, an arc, or an elliptical entity.
- You can turn on or off the display of all the applied constraints of a sketch by using the _________ or _________ tool, respectively.
- The _________ dimension is applied to a sketch representing a revolve feature.
- All degrees of freedom of a _______ sketch are fixed.
- You can temporarily disable applying constraints automatically to the sketch entities while drawing them by pressing and holding the _______ key.

- The _______ constraint is used for applying a curvature continuity (G2) at the transition point between a spline and a line, arc, or spline.
- When the _______ mode is enabled, you can drag the sketch entities freely even if their movements are constrained with already applied constraints and dimensions.
- You can also enable or disable the relax mode by clicking on the _______ tool in the Status Bar.
- If the _______ check box is selected, the dimension values entered in the Dimension Input get applied to the resultant sketch entities, automatically.
- The _______ tool in the Status Bar is used for displaying the available degrees of freedom of the sketch entities.
- You cannot modify dimensions once they have been applied. (True/False)
- You cannot delete constraints that have already been applied between the selected entities. (True/False)
- Geometric constraints are used for restricting some degrees of freedom of a sketch. (True/False)

CHAPTER

5

Creating Base Features of Solid Models

In this chapter, the following topics will be discussed:

- Creating an Extrude Feature
- Creating a Revolve Feature
- Navigating a 3D Model in the Graphics Area
- Changing the Visual Style of a Model

Once a sketch has been created and fully constrained, you can convert it into a solid feature by using the feature modeling tools, see Figure 5.1.

5.1

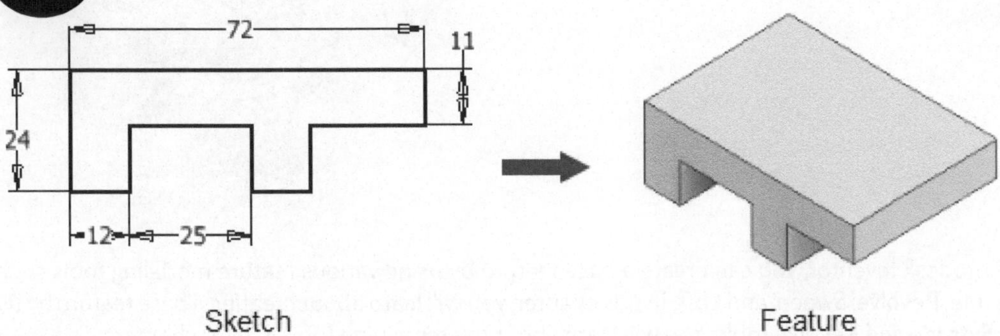

In Autodesk Inventor, the feature modeling tools are available in the **Create** panel of the **3D Model** tab in the Part modeling environment, see Figure 5.2. To create a 3D solid model, you need to create all its features one by one using the feature modeling tools, see Figure 5.3. The first created feature of a model is known as the base feature, first feature, or the parent feature of the model.

5.2

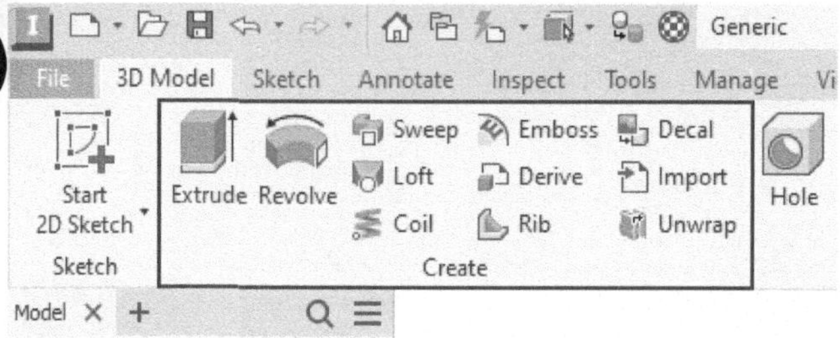

5.3

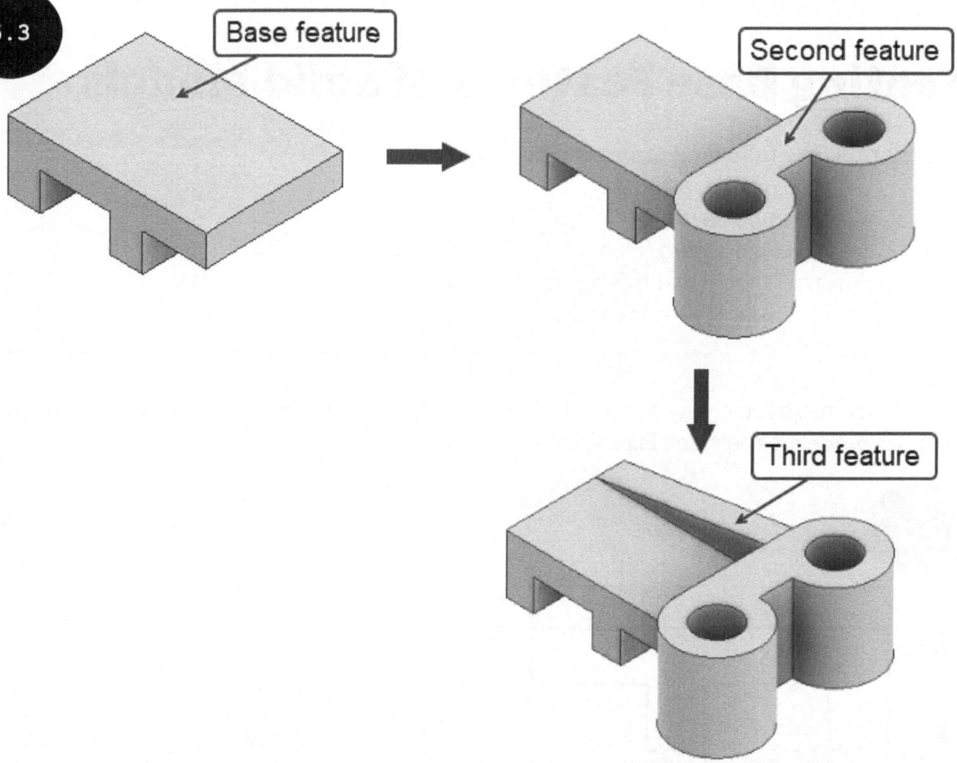

In Autodesk Inventor, you can create a base feature by using various feature modeling tools such as **Extrude**, **Revolve**, **Sweep**, and **Loft**. In this chapter, you will learn about creating a base feature by using the **Extrude** and **Revolve** tools. You will learn about the remaining tools in later chapters.

Creating an Extrude Feature

An extrude feature is created by adding or removing material, normal to the sketching plane. Note that the sketch of the extruded feature defines its geometry. The base extrude features are essentially created by adding material. Figure 5.4 shows different base extrude features that are created from their respective sketches. In Autodesk Inventor, you can create an extrude feature by using the **Extrude** tool of the **Create** panel of the **3D Model** tab in the **Ribbon**.

5.4

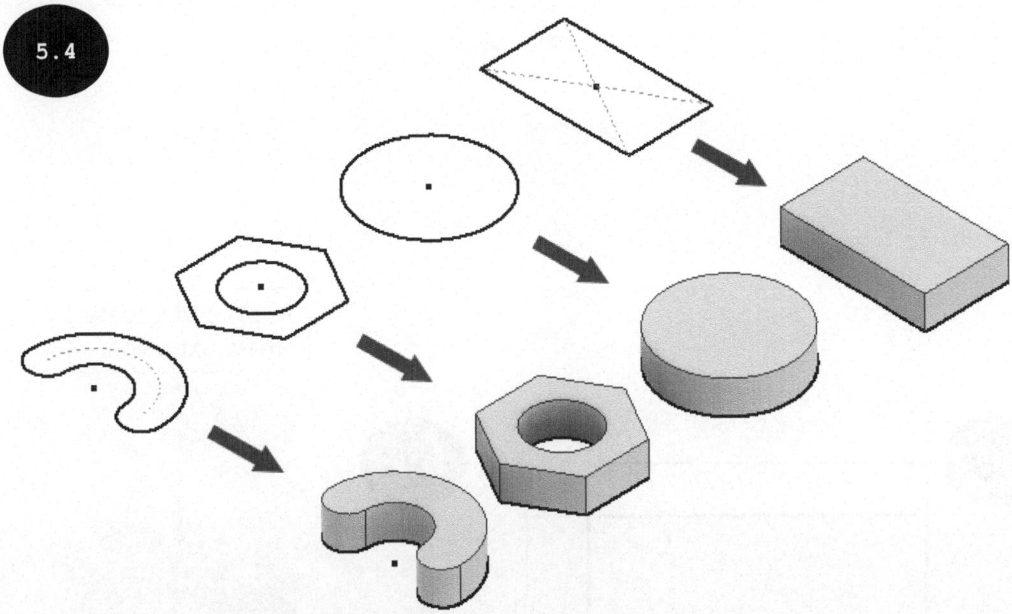

After creating the sketch using the sketching tools, exit the Sketching environment by clicking on the **Finish Sketch** tool in the **Exit** panel of the **Sketch** tab. Next, click on the **Extrude** tool in the **Create** panel of the **3D Model** tab, see Figure 5.5. The **Extrusion** property panel appears, see Figure 5.6. Also, a preview of the extruded feature appears in the graphics area with the default extrusion parameters, see Figures 5.7 and 5.8. Figure 5.7 shows a rectangular sketch created on the Top Plane in the Sketching environment and Figure 5.8 shows the preview of the resultant extrude feature. Note that the preview of the extrude feature appears in the graphics area only if the sketch to be extruded has a single profile.

5.5

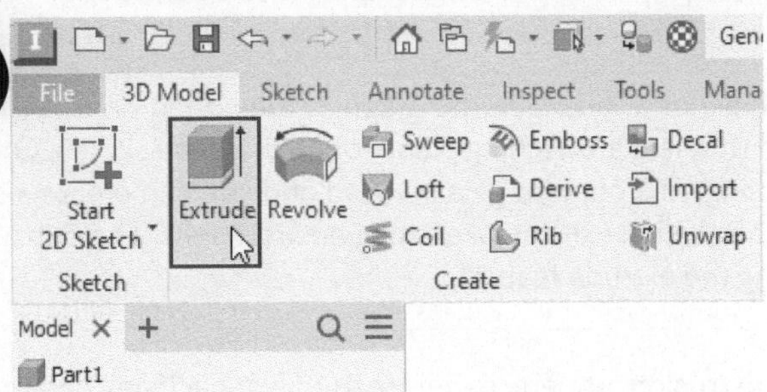

5.6

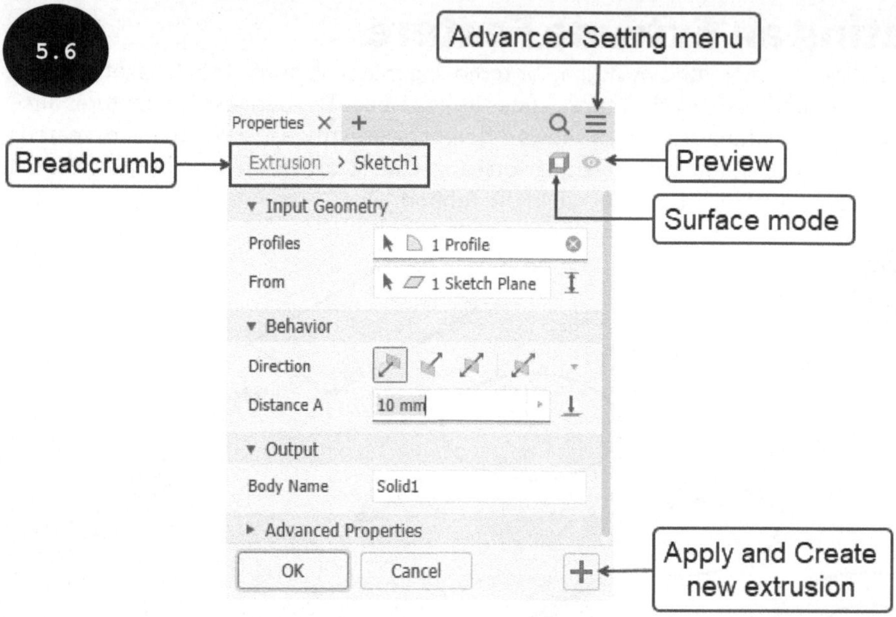

5.7

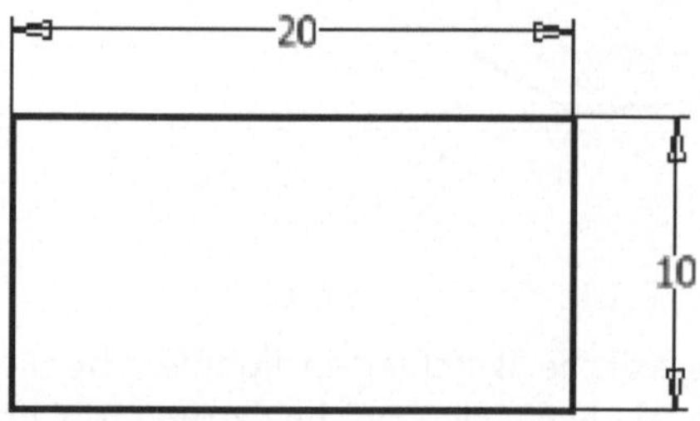

5.8

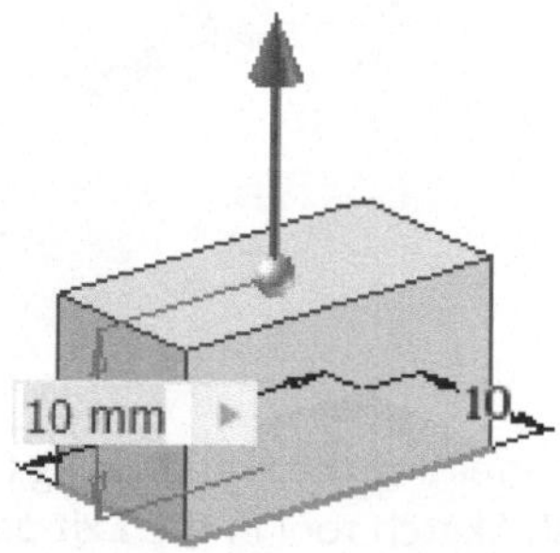

Note: On invoking the **Extrusion** property panel, if the sketch has only one profile then it will be selected automatically and the preview of the feature appears in the graphics area. However, if the sketch has more than one profile then it will not be selected automatically and you will be prompted to select a sketch profile to be extruded.

Tip: If a sketch is not available in the graphics area, then on invoking the **Extrude** tool, you are prompted to select a sketching plane for creating the sketch. On selecting a sketching plane, the Sketching environment gets invoked and you can create a sketch to be extruded. After creating the sketch, exit the Sketching environment. The **Extrusion** property panel appears for creating the extrude feature.

The options in the **Extrusion** property panel are used for specifying parameters for the extrude feature. Some of the options in this property panel are discussed below:

Breadcrumb

The **Breadcrumb** displays the feature hierarchy (current or active feature and its associated sketch). It helps to quickly switch between environments from editing the feature to editing the associated sketch. For example, to edit the associated sketch of the feature, click on the name of the sketch in the **Breadcrumb**, see Figure 5.9. The Sketching environment gets invoked. Now, you can edit the sketch, as required, and then switch back to the feature mode by clicking on the name of the feature in the **Breadcrumb**. Note that the active mode (feature or sketch) appears in blue.

5.9

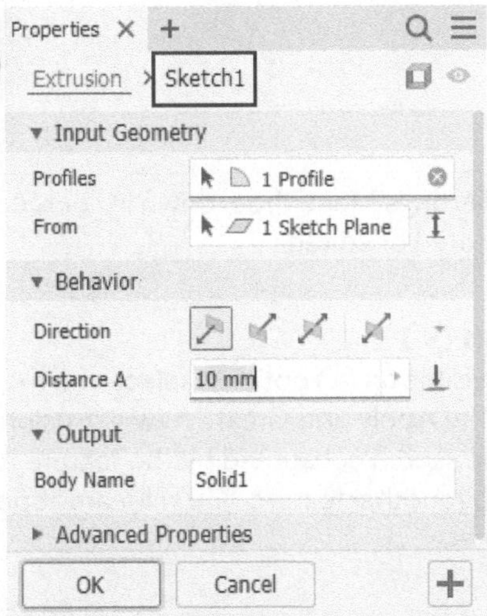

In **Breadcrumb**, you can also change or edit the default name of the feature or sketch by entering a new name in the **Edit Name** field that appears on clicking its default name. You can edit the default name of the feature or sketch that is activated and that appears in blue.

Surface mode

By default, the **Solid** mode is activated in the **Extrusion** property panel. As a result, a solid feature is created. You can switch to the surface mode for creating a surface feature by clicking on the **Surface mode** button in the **Extrusion** Property panel. Note that to switch back to the solid mode, you need to click on the **Surface mode** button again. Its a toggle button to switch between the solid and surface modes. Note that a surface feature has zero thickness and no mass properties.

Preview

The **Preview** button is used to turn on or off the visibility of the feature preview in the graphics area. By default, the visibility of the feature preview is turned on. As a result, a preview of the feature appears in the graphics area. Note that you cannot turn off the preview of a base feature in the graphics area.

Advanced Settings Menu

The options of the **Advanced Settings Menu** drop-down list are used for keeping a sketch visible, showing or hiding preset, and getting access to help document. To invoke this drop-down list, click on the **Advanced Settings Menu** button at the top right corner of the property panel, see Figure 5.10. The options are discussed below:

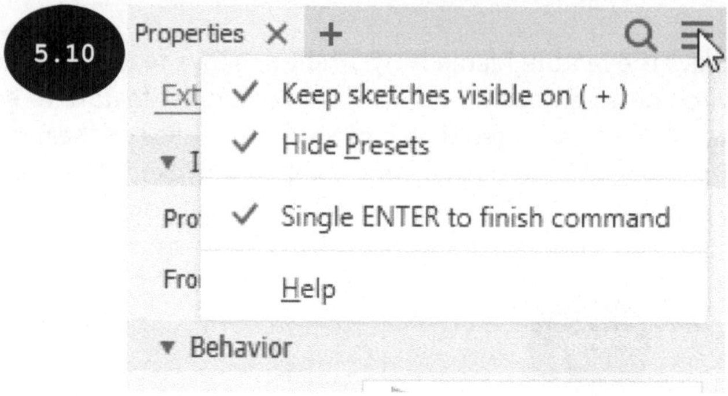

Note: The **Advanced Settings Menu** drop-down list only contains options that are related to the feature being created or edited.

Keep sketch visible on (+)

By default, the **Keep sketch visible on (+)** option is selected in the **Advanced Settings Menu** drop-down list. As a result, on clicking the **Apply and Create new extrusion** button + in the property panel, the feature gets created and the sketch consumed by the feature remains visible in the graphics area so that it can be used for creating another feature. You will learn about the **Apply and Create new extrusion** button + later in this chapter.

Hide Presets

A preset is defined as a pre-defined set of feature parameters or definitions. You can use a preset to quickly create a feature with pre-defined feature parameters. By default, the **Hide Presets** option is selected, refer to Figure 5.10. As a result, the options for selecting an existing preset or creating a new preset are turned off in the **Extrusion** property panel. To turn on the display of preset options, click on the **Hide Presets** option in the **Advanced Settings Menu** drop-down list. Figure 5.11 shows the **Extrusion** property panel with the display of preset options turned on. The options are discussed below:

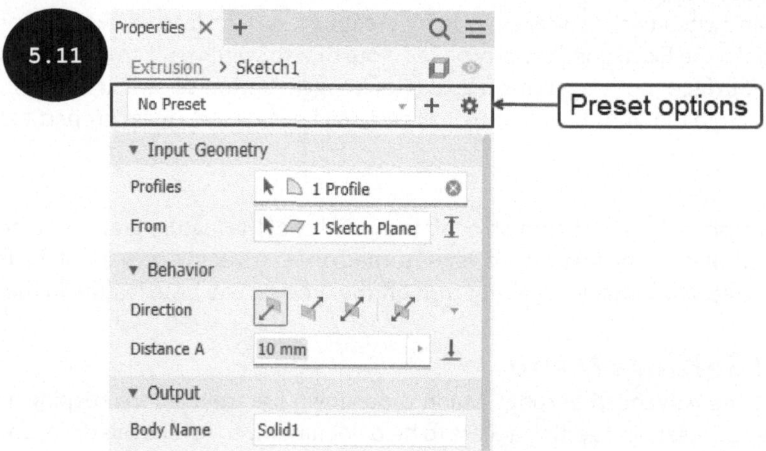

Preset Drop-down List

The **Preset** drop-down list is used for selecting an existing preset for creating a feature with pre-defined parameters, see Figure 5.12. By default, the **No Preset** option is selected in the **Preset** drop-down list. As a result, the **Extrusion** property panel is seeded with default parameters. The **Last Used** option is used for creating a feature with the most recently used parameters.

5.12

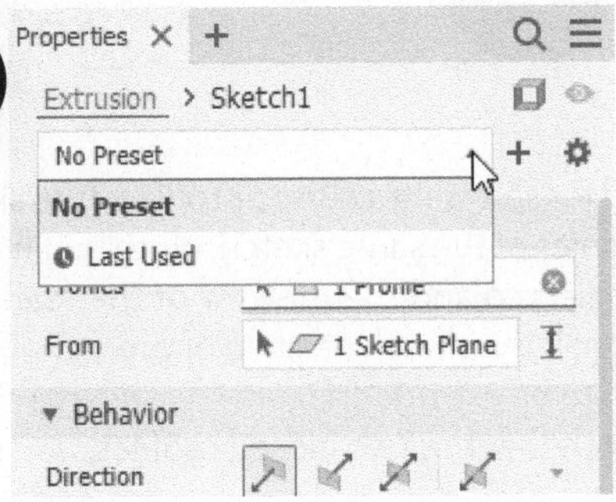

Create new preset

The **Create new preset** button + is used for creating a new preset with the currently specified parameters in the property panel. For doing so, define the parameters in the property panel, as required and then click on the **Create new preset** button +. A new preset gets created and its default name appears in an edit field, see Figure 5.13. Enter a new name for the preset or accept the default name and then click on the tick-mark that appears in the property panel.

5.13

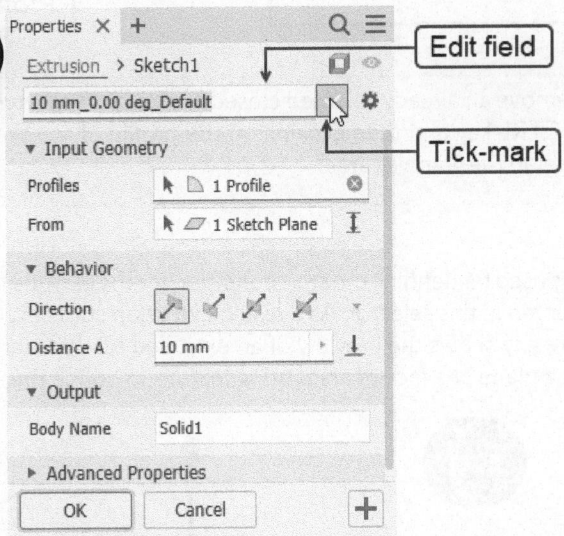

Preset Settings

On clicking the **Preset Settings** button ⚙ in the property panel, a flyout appears with additional options to save the current parameters as a preset, rename the selected preset, delete the selected preset, define the sort order for the preset, and so on.

Help

The **Help** option in the **Advanced Settings Menu** drop-down list is used for accessing the help document for the currently active tool.

Input Geometry

The options of the **Input Geometry** rollout are used for selecting profiles of a sketch to be extruded and a start condition for the feature, see Figure 5.14. The options in this rollout are discussed below:

5.14

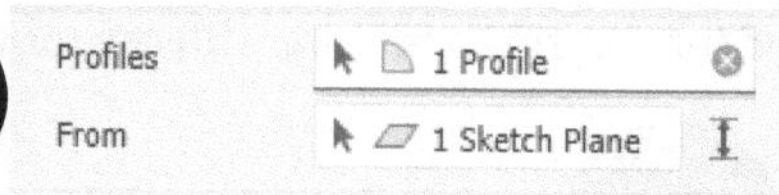

Profiles

The **Profiles** selector is used for selecting a closed profile of the sketch to be extruded. You can select a single profile or multiple profiles of the same sketch. Note that if the sketch has only one closed profile then it gets automatically selected and the preview of the feature appears in the graphics area with default parameters. However, if the sketch has two or more than two closed profiles then you need to select a profile of the sketch to be extruded. Figure 5.15 shows a sketch that has only one closed profile and Figure 5.16 shows a sketch that has two closed profiles.

5.15

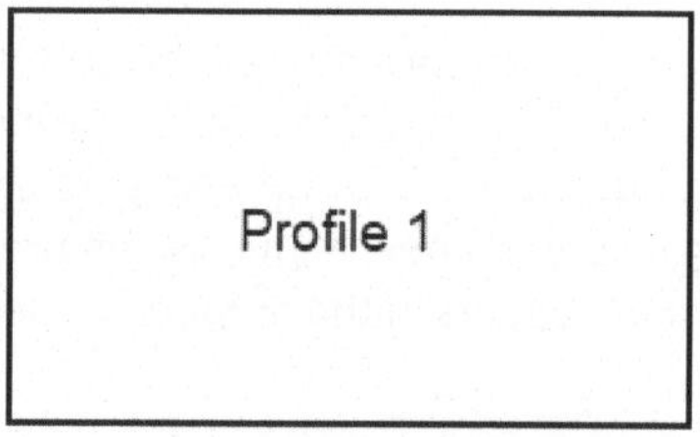

5.16

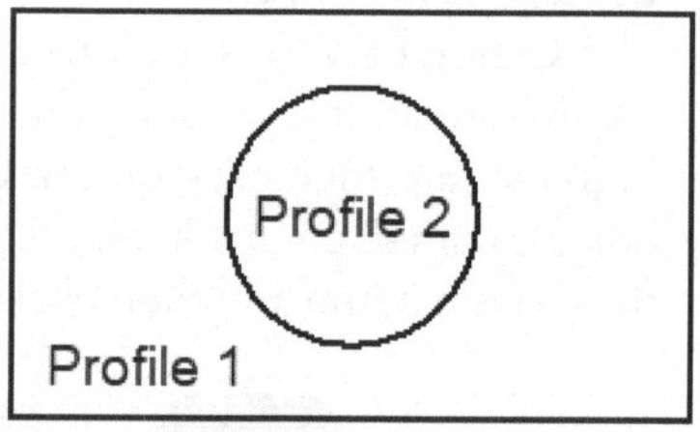

Tip: You can remove an already selected closed profile of the sketch by pressing and holding the SHIFT or CTRL key and then clicking on the profile of the sketch to be removed from the selection set in the graphics area.

From

The **From** selector is used for defining the start condition for the extrude feature. By default, the **Sketch Plane** option is selected in this selector. As a result, extrusion starts exactly from the sketching plane of the sketch. Figure 5.17 shows the preview of an extruded feature starting from its sketching plane. You can also select a plane or a face of an existing feature to define the start condition for a feature.

5.17

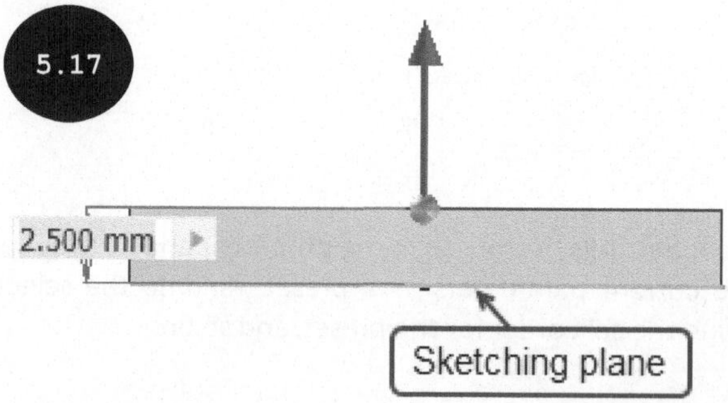

Note: You will learn more about selecting a plane or a face to define the start condition for an extrude feature in later chapters while creating the second and further features of a model.

Behavior

The options in the **Behavior** rollout of the **Extrusion** property panel are used for defining the direction and depth of extrusion, see Figure 5.18. These options are discussed below:

5.18

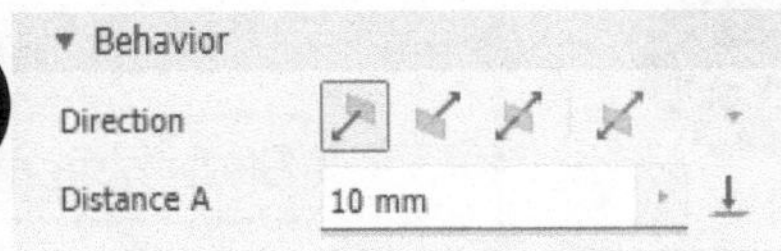

Default

The **Default** button in the **Behavior** rollout is used for defining the direction of extrusion on one side of the sketching plane that is the default direction of extrusion. After defining the direction of extrusion, you can specify the depth of extrusion in the **Distance A** field of the **Behavior** rollout. You can also drag the handle available in the preview of the extrude feature to define the depth of the extrusion in the graphics window.

Flipped

The **Flipped** button is used for reversing the default direction of extrusion to the other side of the sketching plane.

Symmetric

The **Symmetric** button is used for extruding the sketch profile symmetrically on both sides of the sketching plane, see Figure 5.19. Note that on selecting the **Symmetric** button, the distance value specified in the **Distance A** field is measured as the total length of the extrusion. For example, if the specified distance value is 10 mm then the resultant feature will be created by adding 5 mm material on each side of the sketching plane.

5.19

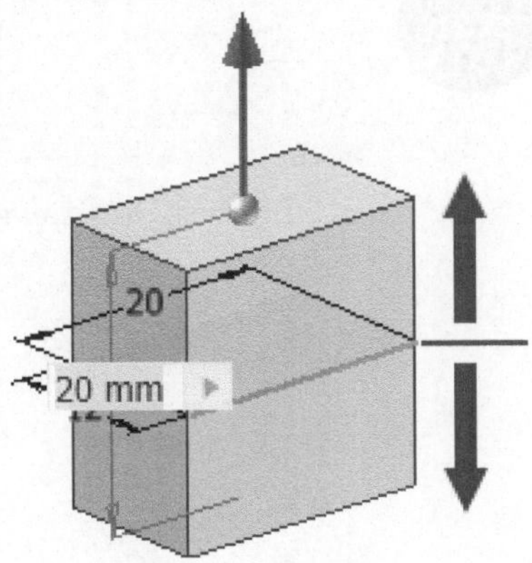

Asymmetric

The **Asymmetric** button is used for extruding the sketch profile asymmetrically with different depths of extrusion on both sides of the sketching plane, see Figure 5.20. On selecting the **Asymmetric** button, the **Distance A** and **Distance B** fields become available in the rollout, which are used for specifying different depths of extrusion on both sides of the sketching plane. You can also invert the distance values specified in the **Distance A** and **Distance B** fields by clicking on the **Flip direction** button that appears on the right of the **Distance B** field in the **Behavior** rollout.

5.20

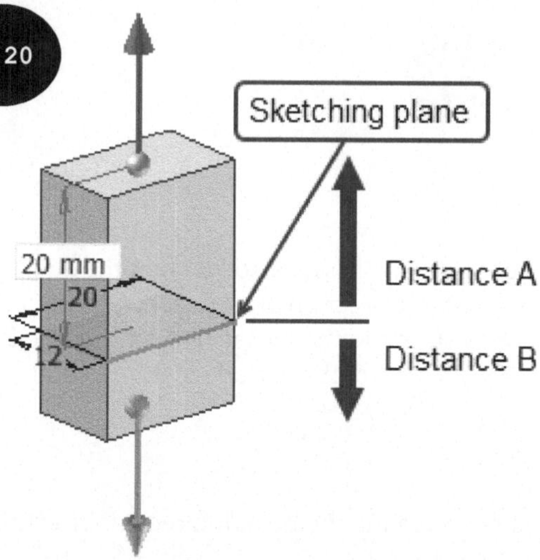

Tip: In the **Behavior** rollout, you can change the display style of direction options from icons/buttons to drop-down list. For doing so, click on the arrow next to the **Asymmetric** button and then click on the **Dropdown** option in the flyout that appears, see Figure 5.21. Similarly, to change the display style from drop-down list to icons, you need to select the **Icons** option in the drop-down list.

5.21

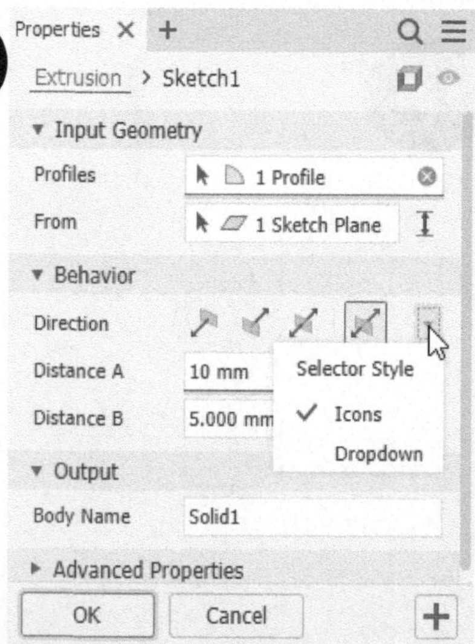

Note: The **To** option  of the **Behavior** rollout is discussed in later chapters while creating the second or further features of a model. Also, options such as **Through All** and **To Next** are not available in the **Behavior** rollout while creating a base feature and are discussed in later chapters.

Output

In the **Body Name** field of the **Output** rollout, you can specify a name for the solid body (model) being created. By default, the name of a solid body appears as *Solid1, Solid2, ... or Solid(n)* in this field. Note that the **Body Name** field is available only while creating a base feature of a model. While creating the second or further features of a model, the **Output** rollout displays options for selecting the type of boolean operation to be performed for creating the feature. You will learn about different types of boolean operations in later chapters.

Advanced Properties

By default, the **Advanced Properties** rollout is collapsed in the property panel. To expand this rollout, click on its title bar, see Figure 5.22. The **Taper A** field in the expanded **Advanced Properties** rollout is used for adding tapering in one direction of the extrude feature. By default, 0 (zero) is entered in this field. As a result, the resultant extrude feature is created without any tapering in it. You can enter the required taper angle from 0 to 89 degrees in this field. Figure 5.23 (a) shows the preview of an extrude feature having a taper angle value set to 15 degrees. To reverse the taper direction from the outward to the inward side of the sketch or vice-versa, click on the **Flip direction** button available to the right of the **Taper A** field in the rollout. You can also enter a positive or a negative taper angle to flip the taper direction from outward to the inward side of the sketch, respectively. Note that a positive taper angle tapers outward, whereas a negative taper angle tapers inward, see Figure 5.23 (b).

5.22

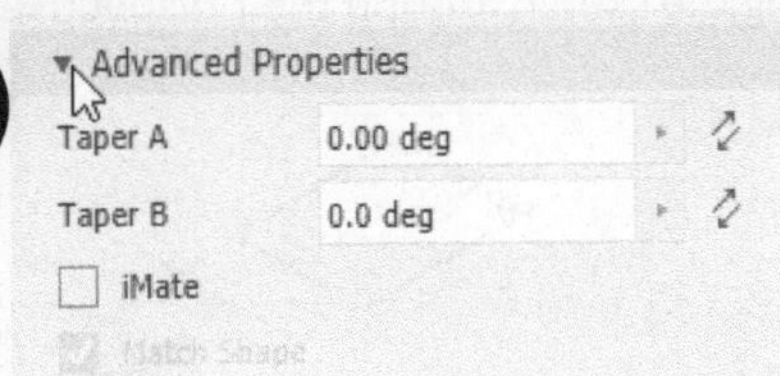

5.23

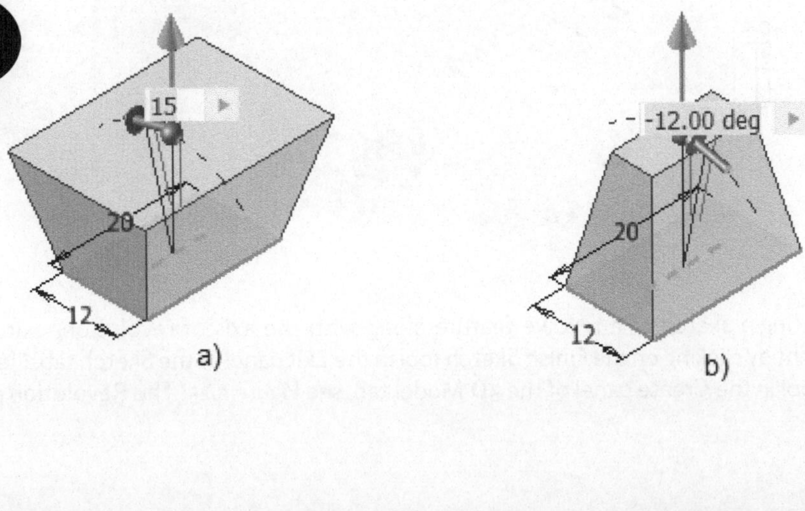

a) b)

The **Taper B** field in the **Advanced Properties** rollout is enabled only when the **Asymmetric** button is selected in the **Behavior** rollout and is used for specifying the taper angle in the second direction of the extrude feature.

Tip: You can also drag the manipulator handle that appears along with the preview of the extrude feature in the graphics area to set the taper angle, dynamically.

Apply and Create new extrusion

The **Apply and Create new extrusion** button of the property panel is used for creating the extrude feature as per the current specified parameters and begin creating another extrude feature using the same parameters. Note that the property panel remains visible for creating another extrude feature if the **Keep sketch visible on (+)** option is selected in the **Advanced Settings Menu** drop-down list of the property panel, as discussed earlier. You can further change the parameters in the property panel to create another extrude feature.

After specifying all the required parameters, click on the **OK** button in the **Extrusion** property panel to create the extrude feature as per the currently specified parameters and close the property panel.

Creating a Revolve Feature

A revolve feature is a feature created such that the material is added or removed by revolving the sketch around an axis of revolution. Note that the sketch to be revolved should be on either side of the axis of revolution. You can use a line, a construction line, or a centerline as the axis of revolution. In Autodesk Inventor, you can create a revolve feature by using the **Revolve** tool. Note that the base revolve features are essentially created by adding material. Figure 5.24 shows sketches and the resultant base revolve features created by revolving the sketch around their respective axes of revolution.

5.24

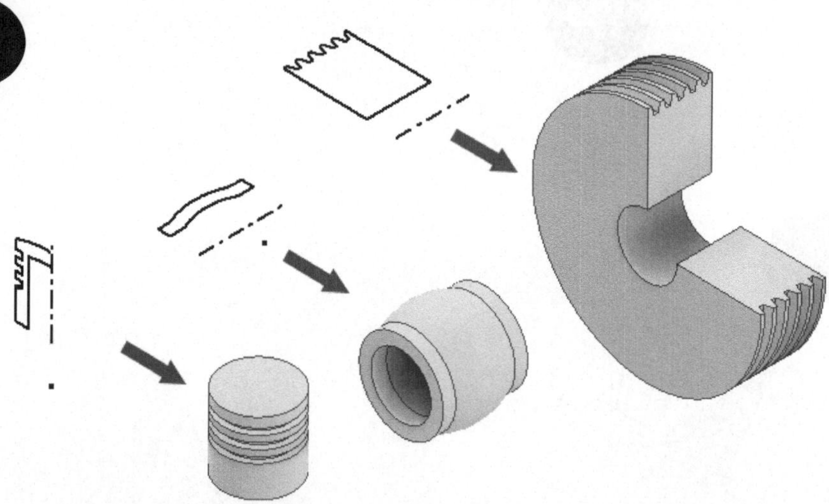

After creating a sketch of a revolve feature along with the axis of revolution, exit the Sketching environment by clicking on the **Finish Sketch** tool in the **Exit** panel of the **Sketch** tab. Next, click on the **Revolve** tool in the **Create** panel of the **3D Model** tab, see Figure 5.25. The **Revolution** property panel appears, see Figure 5.26. Also, the preview of the revolve feature appears, see Figure 5.27. Note that on invoking the **Revolution** property panel, the preview of the revolve feature appears automatically if the sketch has only one profile and one centerline.

Note: If the sketch to be revolved has only one profile and one centerline then the profile and the centerline will automatically be selected. Also, the preview of the resultant revolve feature appears in the graphics area. However, if the sketch has two or more than two profiles or centerlines, or does not have any centerline, then on invoking the **Revolve** tool, the preview of the revolve feature does not appear and you are prompted to select a profile and an axis of revolution.

5.25

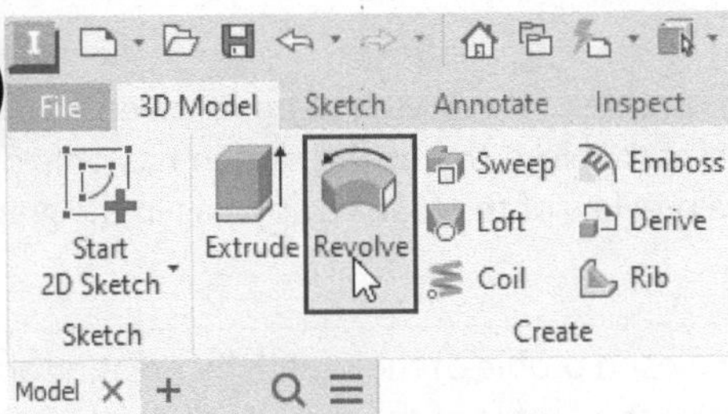

5.26

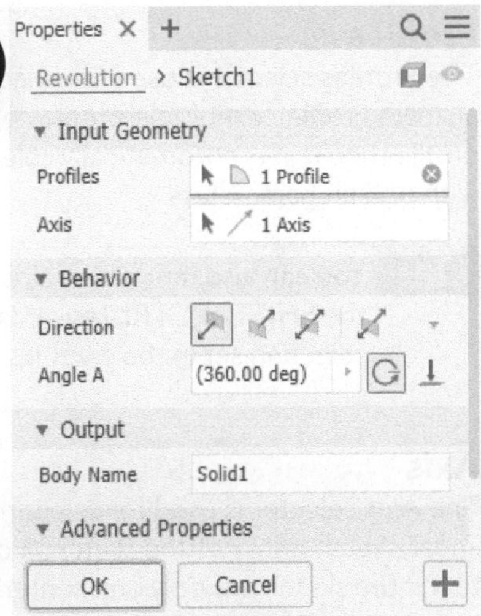

5.27

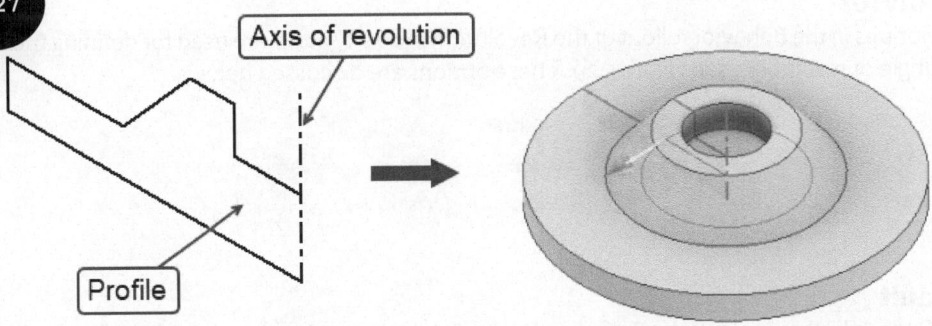

Tip: If a sketch is not available in the graphics area then on invoking the **Revolve** tool, you are prompted to select a sketching plane for creating the sketch. On selecting a sketching plane, the Sketching environment gets invoked and you can create a sketch to be revolved. After creating the sketch, exit the Sketching environment. The **Revolution** property panel appears for creating the revolve feature.

Some of the options in the **Revolution** property panel are same as discussed earlier and the remaining options are discussed below:

Input Geometry

The options in the **Input Geometry** rollout are used for selecting profiles of a sketch to be revolved and an axis of revolution, see Figure 5.28. The options of this rollout are discussed below:

5.28

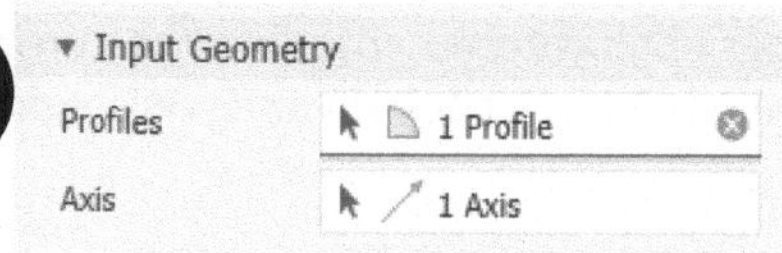

Profiles

The **Profiles** selector is used for selecting a closed profile of the sketch to be revolved. You can select a single profile or multiple profiles of the same sketch. Note that if the sketch has only one closed profile then it gets automatically selected and the preview of the feature appears in the graphics area with default parameters.

Tip: You can also remove an already selected closed profile of the sketch by pressing and holding the SHIFT or CTRL key and then clicking on the profile of the sketch to be removed from the selection set in the graphics area.

Axis

The **Axis** selector is used for selecting an axis of revolution of the revolved feature. You can select a linear sketch entity of the sketch, a centerline, or a construction line as the axis of revolution. Note that if the sketch has only one centerline, then it is automatically selected as the axis of revolution on invoking the **Revolution** property panel.

Behavior

The options in the **Behavior** rollout of the **Revolution** property panel are used for defining the direction and angle of revolution, see Figure 5.29. These options are discussed below:

5.29

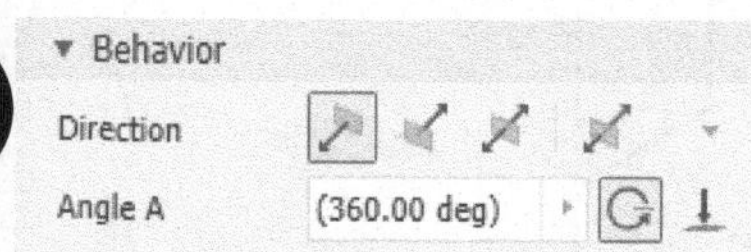

Default

The **Default** button in the **Behavior** rollout is used for defining the direction of revolution on one side of the sketching plane which is the default direction of revolution around the axis of revolution. After defining the direction of revolution, you can specify the angle of revolution in the **Angle A** field of the **Behavior** rollout, as required. By default, 360 degrees is specified as the angle of revolution in the **Angle A** field, since, the **Full** button to the right of the **Angle A** field is activated, by default. You can also drag the handle available in the preview of the revolve feature to define the angle of revolution in the graphics window.

Flipped

The **Flipped** button is used for reversing the default direction of revolution to the other side of the sketching plane.

Symmetric

The **Symmetric** button is used for revolving the sketch profile symmetrically on both sides of the sketching plane around the axis of revolution, see Figure 5.30. Note that on selecting the **Symmetric** button, the angle value specified in the **Angle A** field is measured as the total angle of the revolution. For example, if the specified angle value is 240 degrees, then the resultant revolve feature will be created by adding material up to an angle of 120 degrees on each side of the sketching plane.

5.30

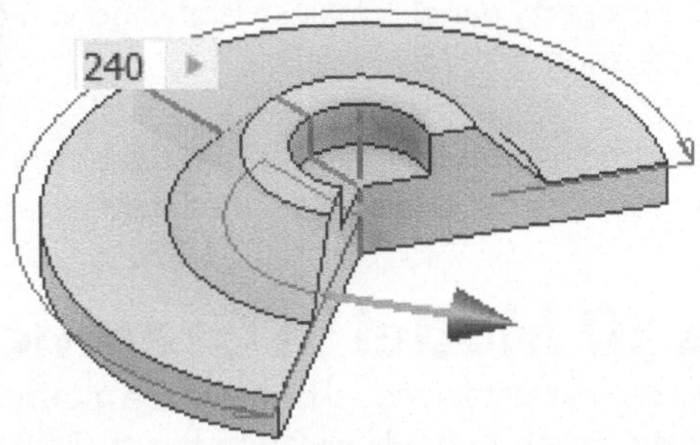

Asymmetric

The **Asymmetric** button is used for revolving the sketch profile asymmetrically with different angles of revolution on both sides of the sketching plane, see Figure 5.31. On selecting the **Asymmetric** button, the **Angle A** and **Angle B** fields become available in the rollout, which are used for specifying different angles of revolution on both sides of the sketching plane. You can also invert the angle values specified in the **Angle A** and **Angle B** fields by clicking on **Flip direction** button that appears to the right of the **Angle B** field in the rollout.

5.31

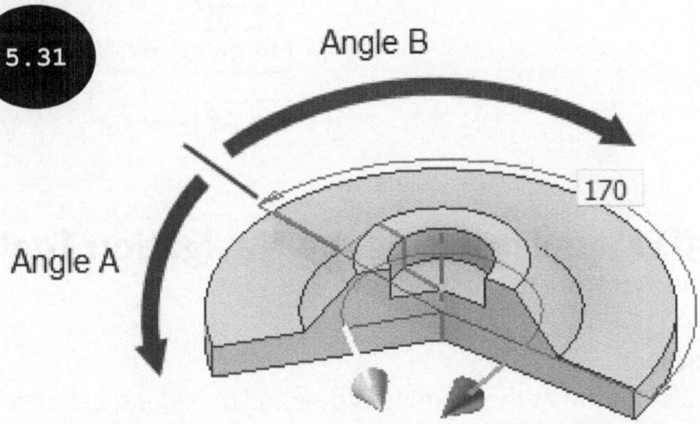

Note: The **To** and **To Next** options of the **Behavior** rollout are discussed in later chapters while creating the second or further features of a model. Note that the **To Next** option is not available while creating a base feature of a model. It appears in the rollout on creating the second or further features of a model.

Output

In the **Body Name** field of the **Output** rollout, you can specify a name for the solid body (model) being created. By default, the name of a solid body appears as *Solid1, Solid2, ... or Solid(n)* in this field. Note that the **Body Name** field is available only while creating a base feature of a model. While creating the second or further features of a model, the **Output** rollout displays options for selecting the type of boolean operation to be performed for creating the feature. You will learn about different types of boolean operations in later chapters.

Apply and Create new revolution

The **Apply and Create new revolution** button of the property panel is used for creating the revolve feature as per the currently specified parameters and creating another revolve feature using the same parameters. Note that the property panel remains visible and you can further change parameters in the property panel to create another revolve feature.

After specifying all the required parameters, click on the **OK** button in the **Revolution** property panel to create the revolve feature as per the current specified parameters and close the property panel.

Navigating a 3D Model in Graphics Area

In Autodesk Inventor, you can navigate a model by using the mouse buttons and the navigation tools. You can access the navigation tools in the **Navigation Bar** available on the right side of the graphics area, see Figure 5.32. You can also navigate a model by using the ViewCube. Different methods for navigating a 3D model are discussed below:

5.32

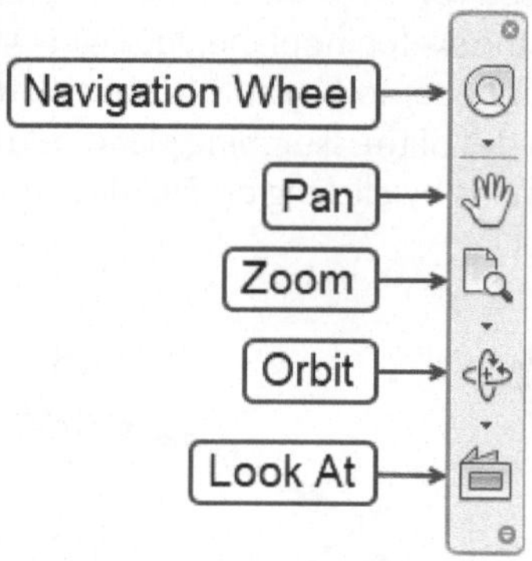

Navigating a 3D Model by Using the Navigation Tools

The different navigation tools are discussed below:

Navigation Wheel

Navigation Wheel is also known as the Steering Wheel and provides quick access to many commonly used navigation tools such as **Pan**, **Zoom**, and **Orbit** in a single interface. Navigation Wheel is divided into different wedges and each wedge represents a navigation tool. Figure 5.33 shows the Full Navigation Wheel. You can invoke different types of Navigation Wheels such as Full Navigation Wheel, Mini Full Navigation Wheel, Mini View Object Wheel, or Mini Tour Building Wheel by using the **Wheel** flyout, see Figure 5.34. For doing so, click on the arrow at the bottom of the **Navigation Wheel** tool in the **Navigation Bar** and then click on the required option in the **Wheel** flyout that appears, see Figure 5.34.

5.33

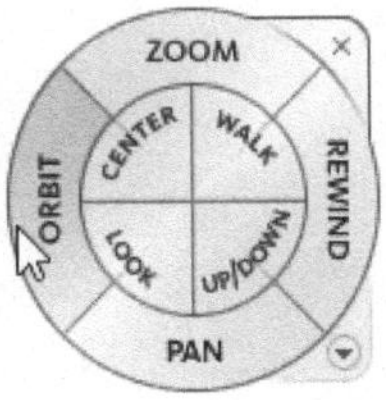

5.34

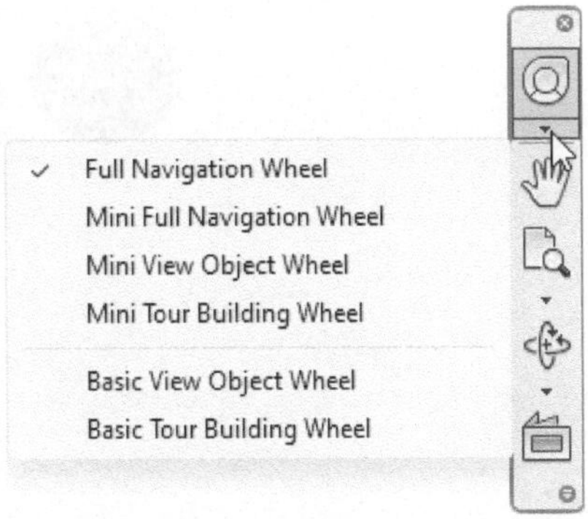

Note: If the **Navigation Bar** is not available on the right side of the graphics area, click on the **View** tab in the **Ribbon** and then in the **Windows** panel, invoke the **User Interface** flyout, see Figure 5.35. Next, ensure that the **Navigation Bar** check box is selected in it.

5.35

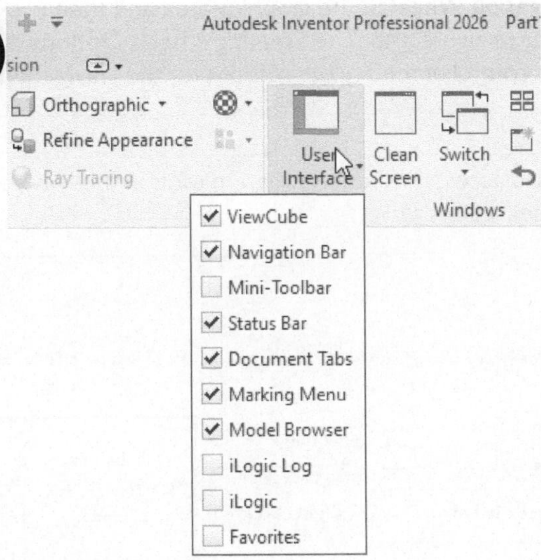

To invoke the Navigation Wheel, click on the **Navigation Wheel** tool in the **Navigation Bar**. The Navigation Wheel appears depending on the option selected in the **Wheel** menu. Note that the Navigation Wheel follows the cursor as you move in the graphics area. Now, you can press and hold the left mouse button on the required wedge of the Navigation Wheel to perform the respective navigation operation. For example, press and hold the left mouse button on the **Zoom** wedge of the Navigation Wheel and then drag the cursor upward or downward to zoom out or zoom into the view of the model, dynamically in the graphics area. Similarly, to move the view of the model, press and hold the left mouse button on the **PAN** wedge and then drag the cursor in the graphics area.

To close the Navigation Wheel, right-click in the graphics area and then click on the **Close Wheel** option in the menu that appears, see Figure 5.36. This menu also provides options to switch between different types of Navigation Wheel. You can press the ESC key or the CTRL + W to close the Navigation Wheel.

5.36

Tip: You can control or modify the default settings for the Navigation Wheel. For doing so, right-click on the **Navigation Wheel** in the graphics area and then click on **Options** in the menu that appears, refer to Figure 5.36. The **SteeringWheels Options** dialog box appears. In this dialog box, you can control or modify the settings for the Navigation Wheel.

Note: You can also access different navigation tools in the **Navigate** panel of the **View** tab in the **Ribbon**, see Figure 5.37.

5.37

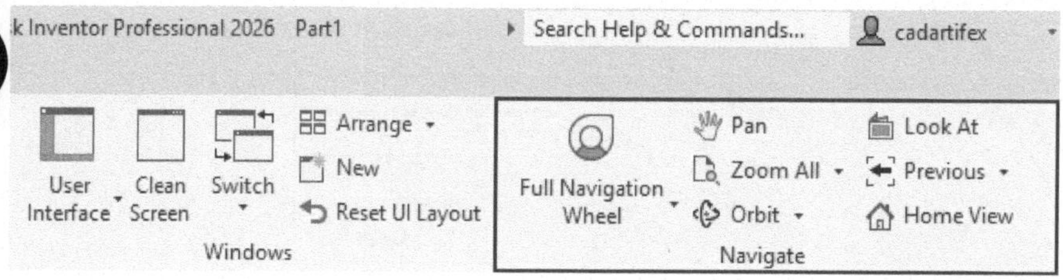

Pan

The **Pan** tool is used for panning/moving a 3D model in the graphics area. To use this tool, click on the **Pan** tool in the **Navigation Bar**, see Figure 5.38. Next, drag the cursor in the graphics area by pressing and holding the left mouse button to move the model. You can also access the **Pan** tool in the **Navigate** panel of the **View** tab in the **Ribbon**.

Zoom

Autodesk Inventor has many powerful tools to zoom into or zoom out of a 3D model in the graphics area for better control over it. These tools are available in the **Zoom** flyout of the **Navigation Bar**, see Figure 5.39. To invoke the **Zoom** flyout, click on the arrow at the bottom of the zoom tool in the **Navigation Bar**. All these tools are discussed below:

5.38

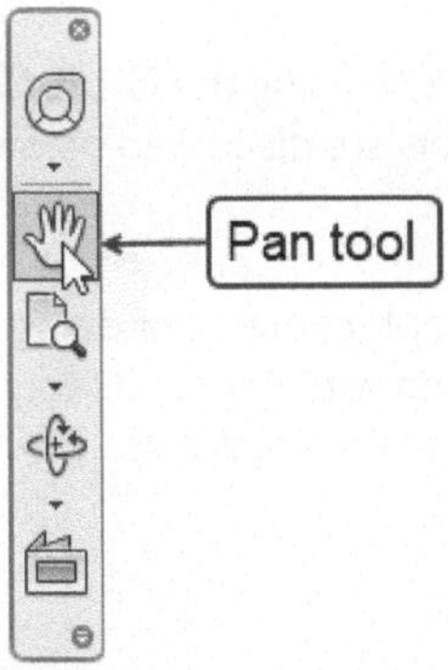

5.39

Zoom

The **Zoom** tool is used for zooming in or zooming out of the view of a 3D model in the graphics area, dynamically. In other words, you can dynamically enlarge or reduce the view of the 3D model by using the **Zoom** tool. To invoke the **Zoom** tool, click on the arrow at the bottom of the zoom tool of the **Navigation Bar**. The **Zoom** flyout appears, refer to Figure 5.39. In this flyout, click on the **Zoom** tool.

After invoking the **Zoom** tool, press and hold the left mouse button in the graphics area and then drag the cursor upward or downward. On dragging the cursor upward, the view of the 3D model starts reducing, and on dragging the cursor downward, the view of the 3D model starts enlarging. Note that in the process of enlarging or reducing the view of the 3D model, the scale of the model remains the same; only the viewing distance changes to enlarge or reduce the view.

Zoom All

The **Zoom All** tool is used for zooming the model in the graphics area such that all visible objects of the model fit completely inside the graphics area. To invoke the **Zoom All** tool, click on the arrow at the bottom of the zoom tool in the **Navigation Bar** and then click on the **Zoom All** tool in the **Zoom** flyout that appears, refer to Figure 5.39.

Zoom Window

The **Zoom Window** tool is used for zooming a particular portion or an area of a 3D model. You can specify a portion or an area of a model to be zoomed into by drawing a rectangular window around it. To invoke the **Zoom Window** tool, invoke the **Zoom** flyout in the **Navigation Bar** and then click on the **Zoom Window** tool. Next, define a rectangular window by dragging the cursor around the portion or area of the model to be zoomed. The area inside the defined rectangular window gets enlarged.

Zoom Selected

The **Zoom Selected** tool is used for zooming into or out of a selected entity or geometry of the model in the graphics area. To invoke the **Zoom Selected** tool, invoke the **Zoom** flyout in the **Navigation Bar** and then click on the **Zoom Selected** tool. You are prompted to select an entity of the model to be zoomed. Click to define the entity of the model. The selected entity of the model gets zoomed in the graphics area.

Orbit

In Autodesk Inventor, you can rotate a 3D model in the graphics area by using the **Orbit**, **Constrained Orbit**, and **Rotate at Angle** tools of the **Navigation Bar**. All these tools are discussed below:

Orbit

The **Orbit** tool is used for rotating the model freely inside the graphics area. For doing so, click on the **Orbit** tool in the **Navigation Bar**, see Figure 5.40. A circular rim with lines at its four quadrants and a cross mark at its center appears in the graphics area around the model, see Figure 5.41.

5.40

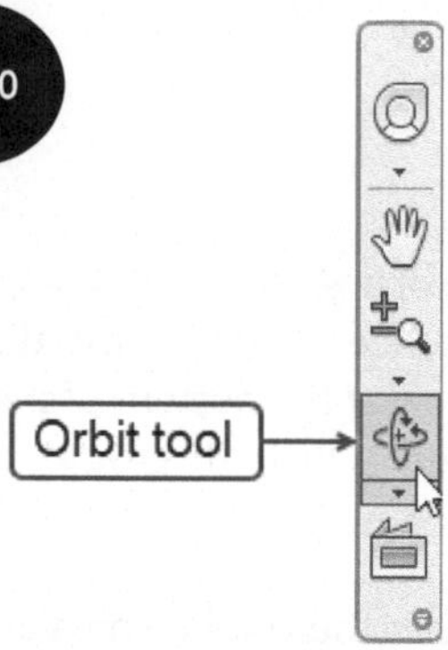

5.41

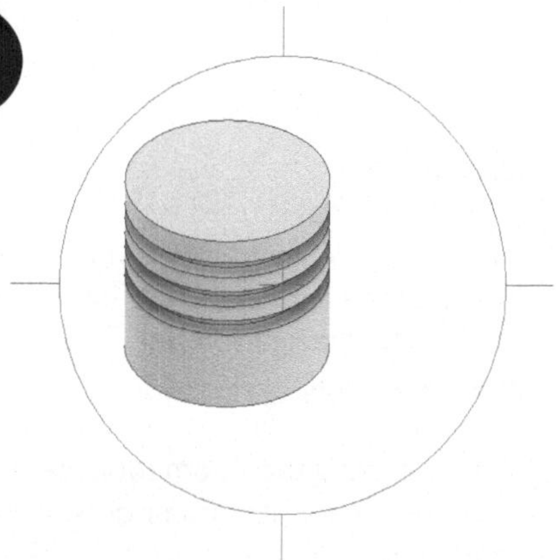

To rotate a model freely, drag the cursor after pressing and holding the left mouse button inside the circular rim in the graphics area. Alternatively, drag the cursor after pressing and holding the SHIFT key and the middle mouse button.

To rotate a model around the vertical axis, move the cursor over the horizontal line at the right or left quadrant of the circular rim. The cursor icon changes to a horizontal elliptical arrow. Next, drag the cursor by pressing the left mouse button to rotate the model about the vertical axis. Similarly, you can rotate the model around the horizontal axis by dragging the cursor after positioning it over a vertical line at the top or bottom quadrant of the circular rim.

Constrained Orbit

The **Constrained Orbit** tool is used for rotating the model about axes in the model space by constraining the view of the model along a plane. To invoke the **Constrained Orbit** tool, click on the arrow at the bottom of the **Orbit** tool in the **Navigation Bar** and then click on the **Constrained Orbit** tool in the flyout that appears, see Figure 5.42. A circular rim with lines at its four quadrants and a cross mark at its center appears in the graphics area around the model. Next, drag the cursor after pressing and holding the left mouse button from left to right or top to bottom inside the circular rim. You can also rotate the model around the vertical or horizontal axes by using the horizontal or vertical lines of the circular rim present in the graphics area, respectively.

Rotate at Angle

The **Rotate at Angle** tool is used for rotating the model by increments of an angle. To invoke this tool, click on the arrow at the bottom of the **Orbit** tool in the **Navigation Bar** and then click on the **Rotate at Angle** tool in the flyout that appears, see Figure 5.42. The **Incremental View Rotate** dialog box appears, see Figure 5.43. Specify the required incremental angle value in the **Increment** field of the dialog box. Next, rotate the model in the down, up, left, right, counterclockwise, or clockwise directions by clicking on the **Down**, **Up**, **Left**, **Right**, **Counterclockwise**, or **Clockwise** buttons, respectively, available to the right of the **Increment** field. To return to the original view, click on the **Reset** button in the dialog box. After rotating the model, click on the **OK** button to exit the dialog box.

5.42

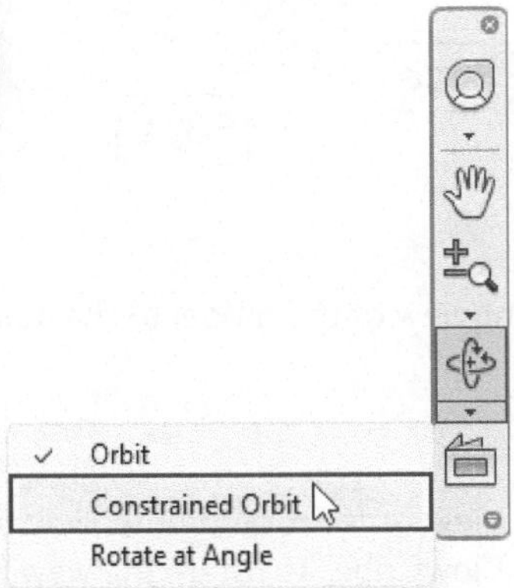

5.43

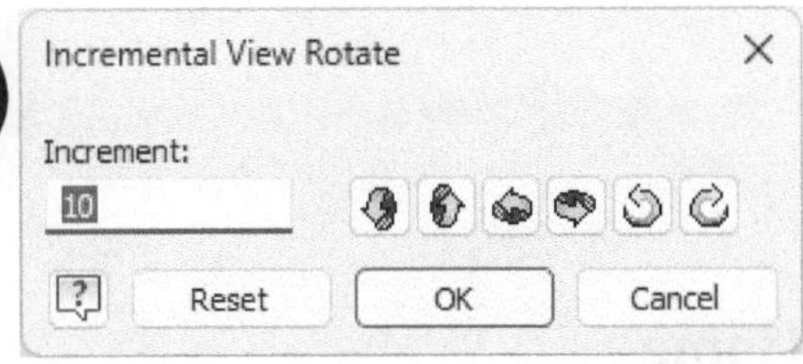

Look At

The **Look At** tool is used for displaying the selected planar face of a 3D model normal to the viewing direction. To invoking this tool, click on the **Look At** tool in the **Navigation Bar** and then click on the planar face of the model. The selected face becomes normal to the viewing direction in the graphics area.

Navigating a 3D Model by Using the Mouse Buttons

In Autodesk Inventor, you can navigate a 3D model in the graphics area by using the mouse buttons. The methods for navigating a 3D model by using the mouse buttons are discussed below:

- To pan a 3D model, press and hold the middle mouse button and then drag the cursor in the graphics area.
- To zoom into or out of the view of a 3D model, scroll up or down the wheel of the mouse.
- To rotate or orbit a 3D model, press and hold the middle mouse button plus the SHIFT key and then drag the cursor in the graphics area.

Navigating a 3D Model by Using the ViewCube

ViewCube is available at the upper right corner of the graphics area, see Figure 5.44. It is used for changing the view or orientation of a model.

By using the ViewCube, you can switch between standard and isometric views. By default, it is in the inactive state. When you move the cursor over the ViewCube, it becomes active and works as a navigation tool. You can navigate a model by using the ViewCube components, see Figure 5.45. The various ViewCube components are discussed below:

5.44

5.45

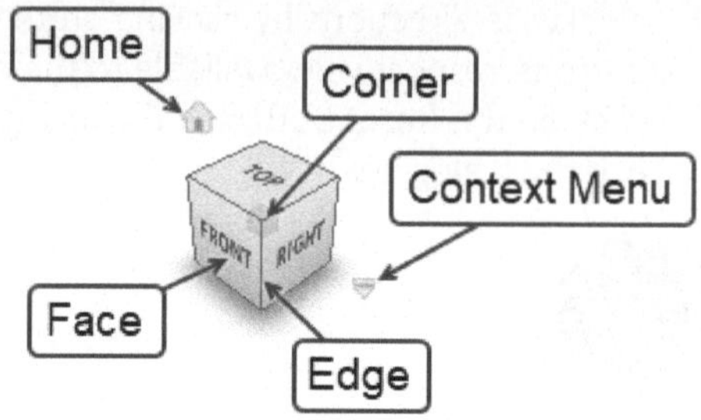

Home

The Home icon of ViewCube is used for bringing the current view of the model to the default home or isometric view.

Corner

A corner of the ViewCube is used for getting an isometric view or for rotating the view freely in all directions. To get an isometric view, click on a corner of the ViewCube. To rotate the view freely in all directions, drag a corner of the ViewCube by pressing and holding the left mouse button.

Edge

An edge of the ViewCube is used for getting an edge-on view or for rotating the view freely in all directions. To get an edge-on view, click on an edge of the ViewCube. To rotate the view freely in all directions, drag an edge by pressing and holding the left mouse button.

Face

A face of the ViewCube is used for getting an orthogonal view such as a top, front, or right. For example, to get the top view of a model, click on the top face of the ViewCube.

Context Menu

Context Menu is provided with additional options for controlling the view of a model or the ViewCube settings. To invoke the Context Menu, click on the arrow available at the bottom of the ViewCube. The Context Menu appears, see Figure 5.46. Alternatively, you can also invoke the Context Menu by right-clicking on the ViewCube. Some of the options of the Context Menu are discussed below:

Go Home

The **Go Home** option is used for bringing the current view of the model to the default home view.

Orthographic

By default, the **Orthographic** option is selected. As a result, the orthographic views of the model appear in the graphics area.

Perspective

The **Perspective** option is used for displaying the perspective views of the model in the graphics area.

Set Current View as Home

In Autodesk Inventor, you can set the current view of a model as the Home view with a fixed distance or fit to view. For doing so, move the cursor over the **Set Current View as Home** option in the Context Menu. A cascading menu appears with the **Fixed Distance** and **Fit to View** options, see Figure 5.47. The **Fixed Distance** option is used for setting the current view of the model as the Home view with the fixed view distance as it is currently set for the model. The **Fit to View** option is used for setting the current view of the model as the Home view with the fit to view distance. This means that the view of the model adjusts automatically and fits in the graphics area.

5.46

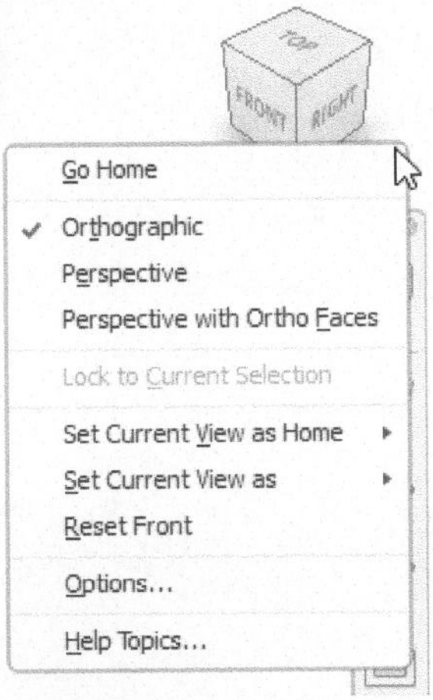

5.47

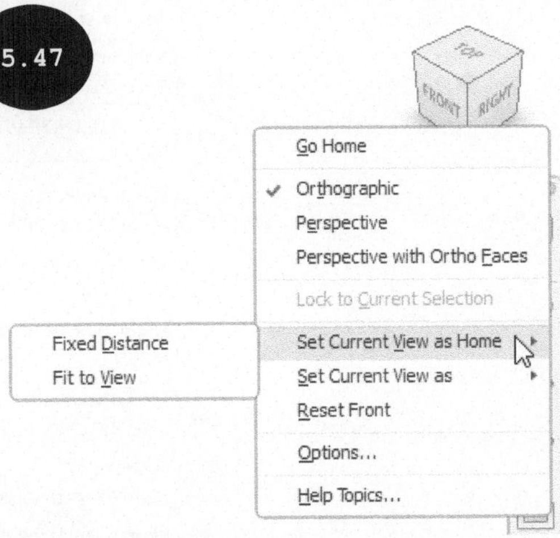

Set Current View as

You can set the current view of the model as the Top or Front view. For doing so, move the cursor over the **Set Current View as** option in the Context Menu. A cascading menu appears with the Top and Front options. Click on the required option in this menu.

Reset Front

The **Reset Front** option of the Context Menu is used for resetting the Front view of the model to the default settings.

Options

The **Options** option of the Context Menu is used for invoking the **ViewCube Options** dialog box. By using this dialog box, you can control the default settings of the ViewCube.

Changing the Visual Style of a Model

You can change the visual or display style of a model to realistic, shaded, shaded with edges, shaded with hidden edges, wireframe, wireframe with hidden edges, wireframe with visible edges only, monochrome, watercolor, sketch illustration, or technical illustration. The tools for changing the visual style of the model are available in the **Visual Style** flyout of the **Appearance** panel in the **View** tab of the **Ribbon**, see Figure 5.48. These tools are discussed below:

5.48

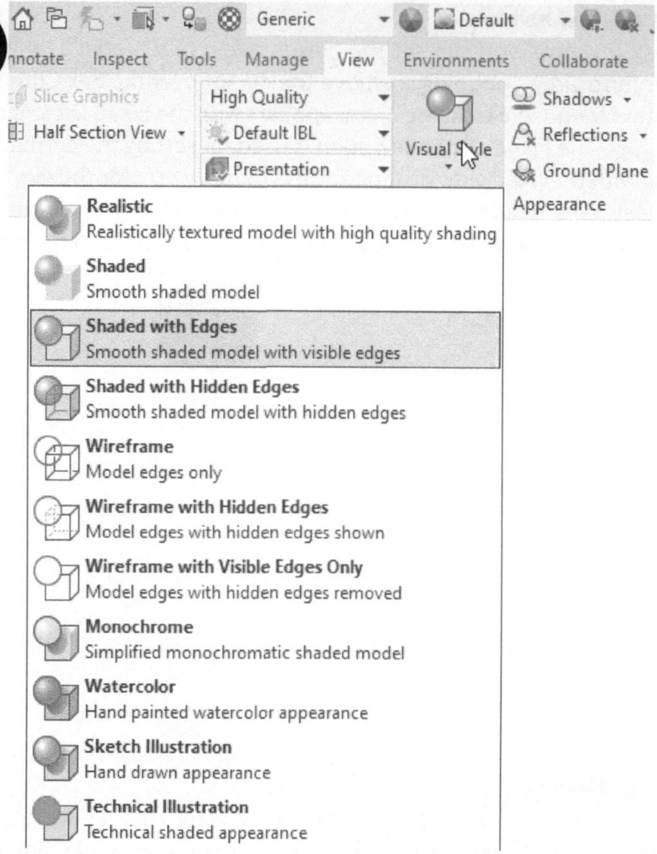

Realistic

The **Realistic** tool of the **Visual Style** flyout is used for displaying the faces of a model in high-quality shaded mode with realistic appearances. In this style, the display of visible and hidden edges of the model is turned off.

Shaded

The **Shaded** tool is used for displaying the faces of the model in smooth shaded mode with standard appearances, see Figure 5.49. In this style, the display of visible and hidden edges of the model is turned off.

Shaded with Edges

The **Shaded with Edges** tool is used for displaying smooth shaded model with visible edges in black, see Figure 5.50. In this style, the display of the visible edges of the model is turned on.

5.49

5.50

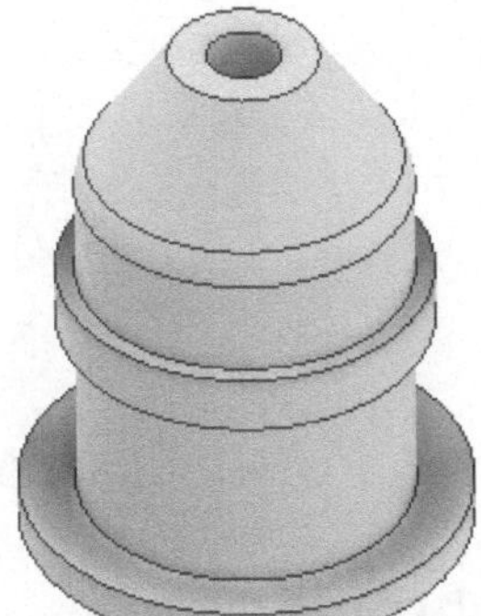

Shaded with Hidden Edges

The **Shaded with Hidden Edges** tool is used for displaying a smooth shaded model with visible and hidden edges, see Figure 5.51. In this style, the display of visible and hidden edges of the model is turned on. Note that the visible edges appear as solid black lines, whereas the hidden edges appear as dotted white lines.

Wireframe

The **Wireframe** tool is used for displaying the model edges only, such that the visible and hidden edges of the model appear as solid lines with shading turned off, see Figure 5.52.

5.51

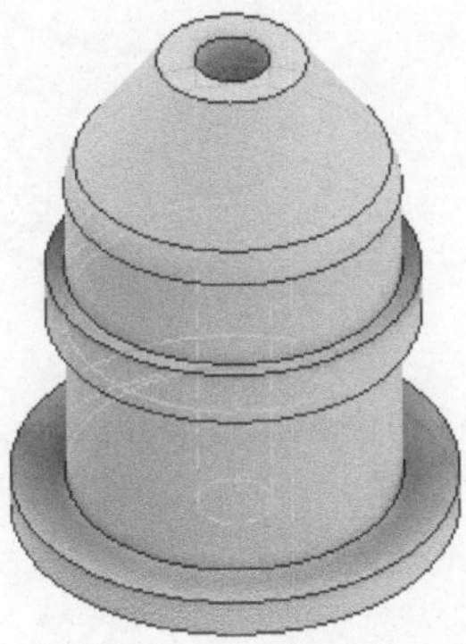

5.52

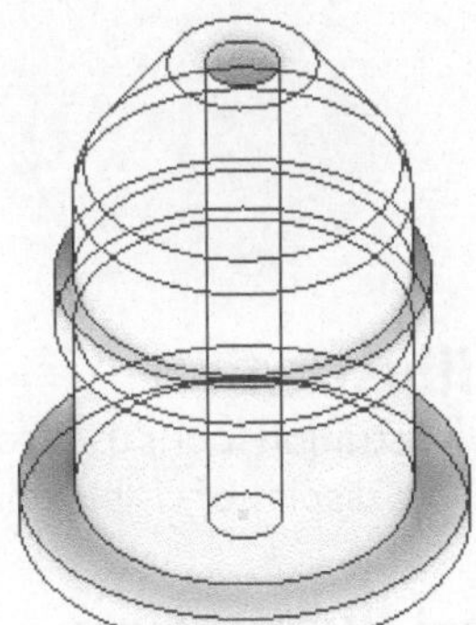

Wireframe with Hidden Edges

The **Wireframe with Hidden Edges** tool is used for displaying the model edges only, such that the visible edges of a model appear as solid lines and hidden edges of the model appear as dotted lines with shading turned off, see Figure 5.53.

Wireframe with Visible Edges Only

The **Wireframe with Visible Edges Only** tool is used for displaying only the visible edges of a model, such that the visible edges of the model appear as solid lines with shading turned off, see Figure 5.54. In this style, the display of hidden edges of the model is turned off.

5.53

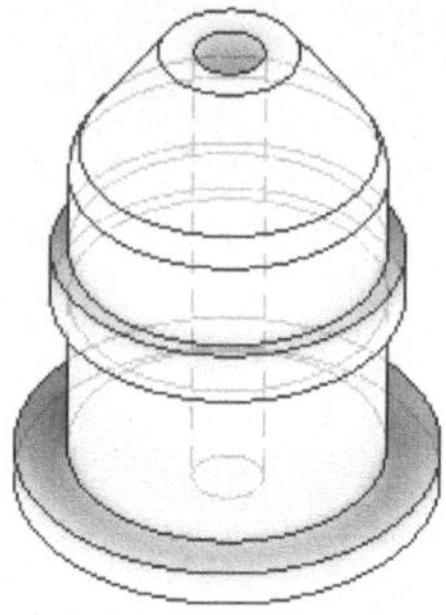

5.54

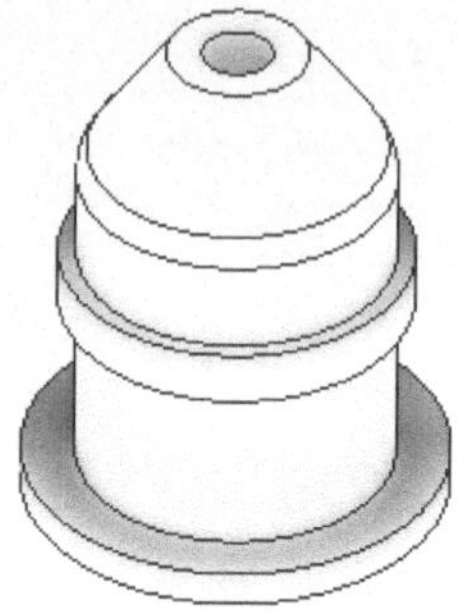

Monochrome

The **Monochrome** tool is used for displaying a simplified monochromatic shaded model with standard appearances, see Figure 5.55. In this style, the display of visible and hidden edges of the model is turned off.

Watercolor

The **Watercolor** tool is used for displaying a model with hand painted watercolor appearances, see Figure 5.56. In this style, the display of visible and hidden edges of the model is turned off.

5.55

5.56

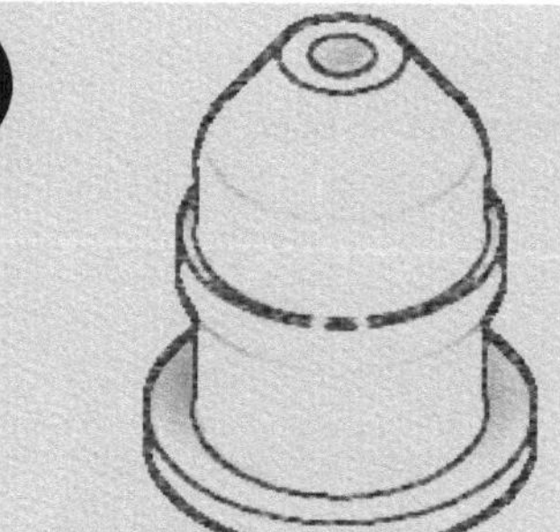

Sketch Illustration

The **Sketch Illustration** tool is used for displaying a model with hand drawn appearances, see Figure 5.57. In this style, the display of visible edges of the model is turned on.

Technical Illustration

The **Technical Illustration** tool is used for displaying a model with technical shaded appearances, see Figure 5.58. In this style, the visible components of an assembly appear with shaded appearances.

5.57

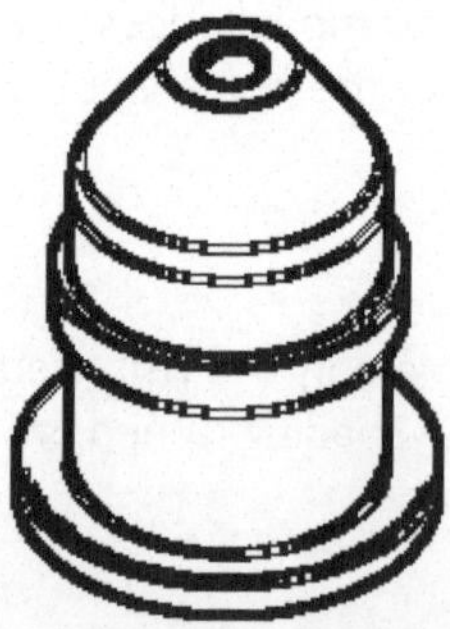

5.58

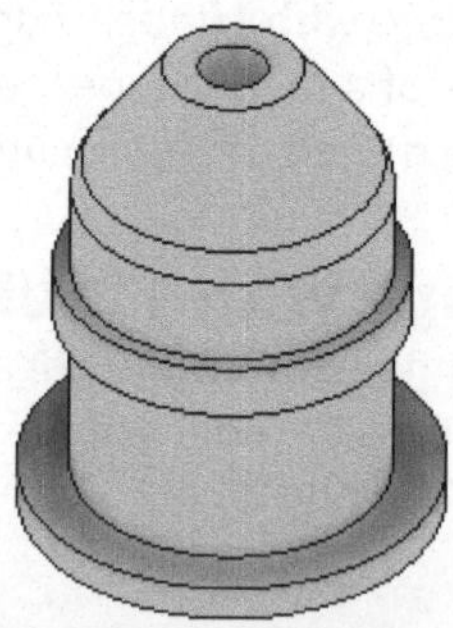

Tutorial 1

Create an extruded model as shown in Figure 5.59. The depth of extrusion is 15 mm. All dimensions are in mm.

5.59

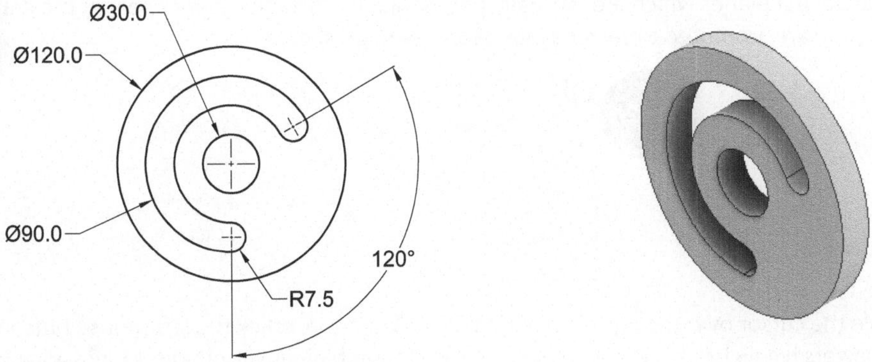

Section 1: Starting Autodesk Inventor

1. Start Autodesk Inventor by double-clicking on the Autodesk Inventor icon on your desktop. The startup user interface of Autodesk Inventor appears.

Section 2: Invoking the Sketching Environment

1. Click on the **New** tool in the startup user interface of Autodesk Inventor (see Figure 5.60) or press the CTRL + N keys. The **Create New File** dialog box appears, see Figure 5.61.

5.60

5.61

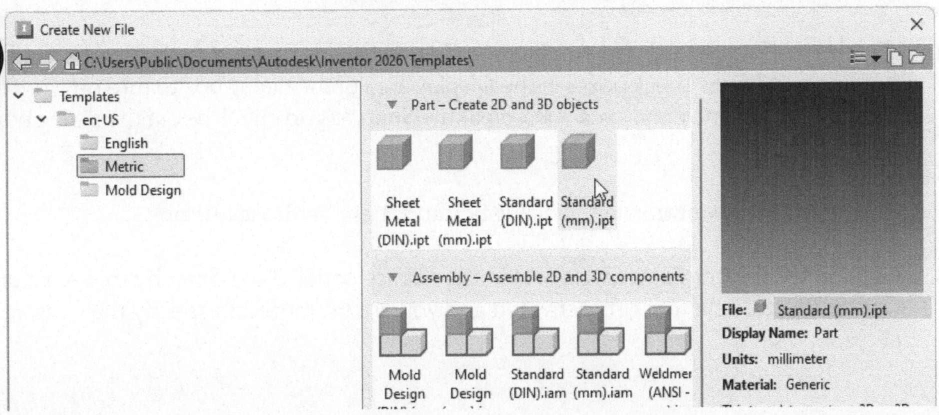

2. Double-click on the **Standard (mm).ipt** template in the right panel of the dialog box, refer to Figure 5.61. The Part Modeling environment is invoked with a Metric template.

3. Click on the **Start 2D Sketch** tool in the **Sketch** panel (see Figure 5.62) or press the S key. The three default planes which are mutually perpendicular to each other appear in the graphics area. Also, you are prompted to select a plane for creating a sketch.

5.62

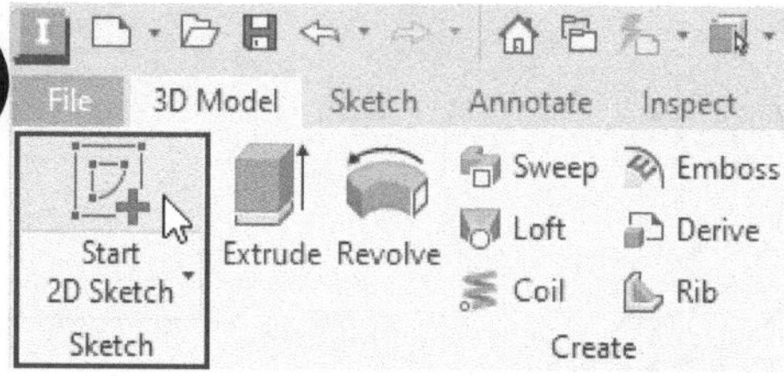

4. Move the cursor over the Front plane (XY Plane) and then click the left mouse button when the plane gets highlighted in the graphics area. The Sketching environment is invoked and the Front plane is oriented normal to the viewing direction.

Section 3: Creating the Sketch

Now, you need to create the sketch by using the sketching tools. In this tutorial, you will turn off the grids and snap settings for creating sketch entities by specifying points arbitrarily in the drawing area and then applying the required dimensions.

1. Click on the **Tools** tab in the **Ribbon** and then click on the **Application Options** tool in the **Options** panel, see Figure 5.63. The **Application Options** dialog box appears.

5.63

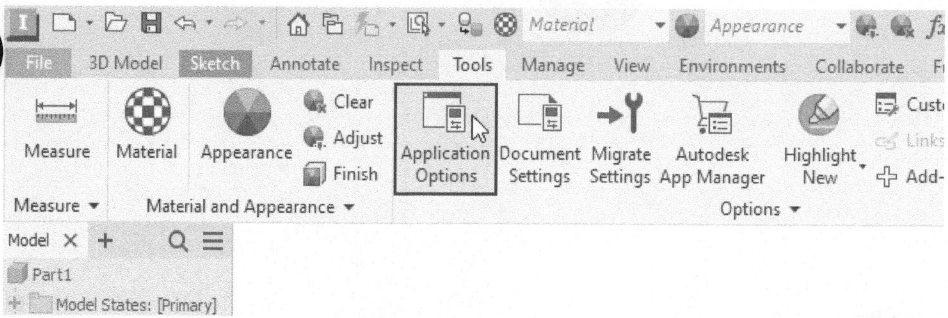

2. Click on the **Sketch** tab in the **Application Options** dialog box and then clear the **Grid lines, Minor grid lines**, and **Axes** check boxes in the **Display** area of the dialog box to turn off the display of grid lines, minor grid lines, and axes. Also, clear the **Snap to grid** check box in the dialog box to turn off the snap mode.

3. Click on the **Apply** button in the dialog box and then the **Close** button.

4. Click on the **Center Point Circle** tool in the **Create** panel of the **Sketch** tab, see Figure 5.64. The **Center Point Circle** tool gets activated and you are prompted to specify the center point of the circle.

5.64

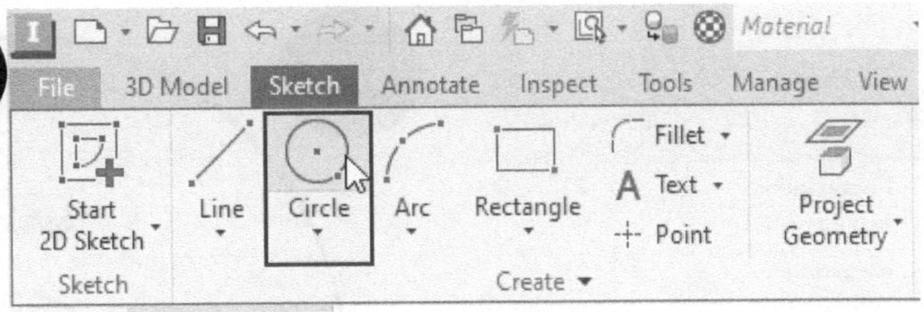

5. Click to specify the center point of the circle at the origin.

6. Move the cursor toward right and then click to specify a point when the diameter of the circle appears close to 30 mm in the Dimension Input, see Figure 5.65. A circle of diameter close to 30 mm is created and the **Center Point Circle** tool is still active.

7. Click to specify the center point of the second circle at the origin.

8. Move the cursor toward the right and then click to specify a point when the diameter of the circle appears close to 120 mm in the Dimension Input, see Figure 5.66. A circle of diameter close to 120 mm is created and the **Center Point Circle** tool is still active.

5.65

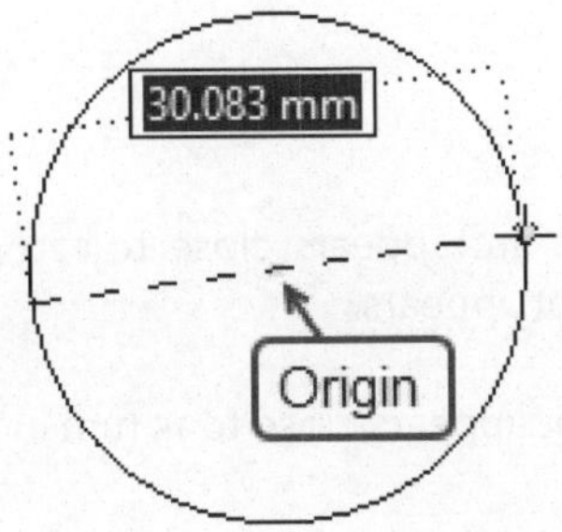

5.66

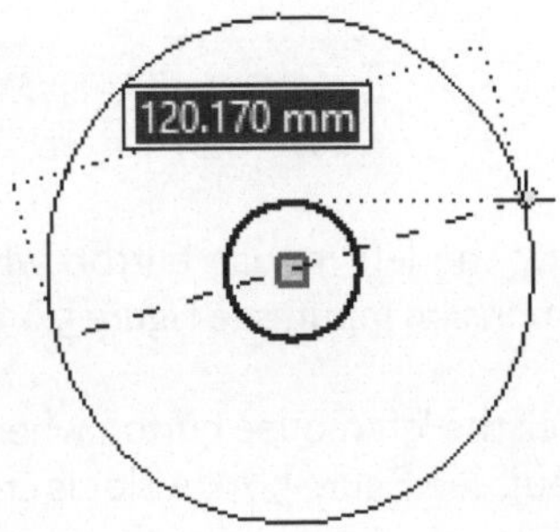

9. Press the ESC key to exit the **Center Point Circle** tool.

10. Invoke the **Rectangle** flyout in the **Create** panel and then click on the **Center Point Arc Slot** tool, see Figure 5.67. You are prompted to specify the center of the slot.

11. Move the cursor to the origin and then click to specify the center point of the slot when the cursor snaps to the origin.

12. Move the cursor at an angle toward the right and then click when the radius of an imaginary circle appears close to 37.5 mm and the angle value appears close to 30 degrees from the X-axis in the Dimension Input, see Figure 5.68. Next, move the cursor anti-clockwise in the drawing area. The preview of an arc appears.

5.67

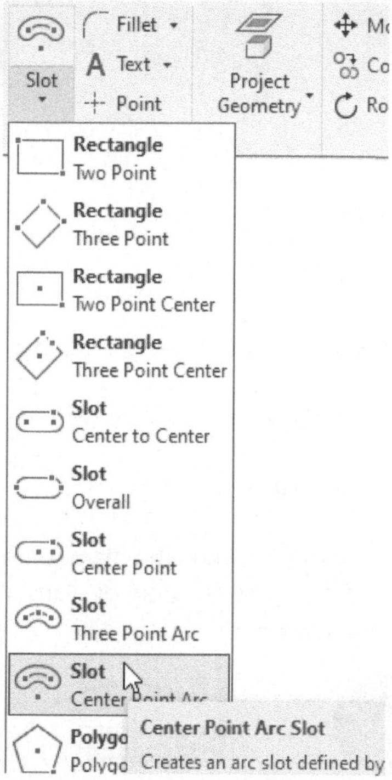

5.68

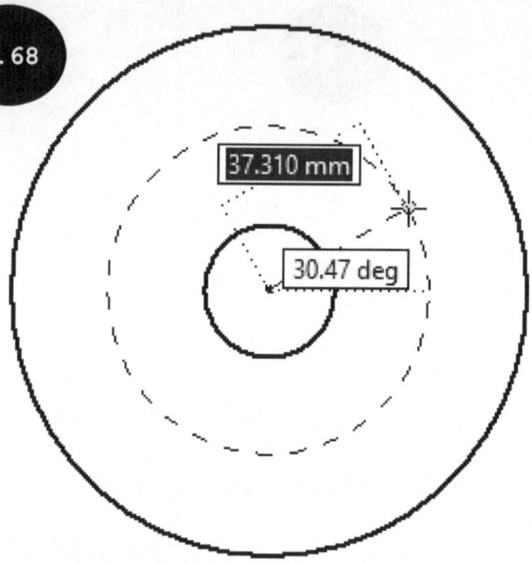

13. Click the left mouse button when the angle of the arc appears close to 120 degrees in the Dimension Input, see Figure 5.69. The preview of a slot appears.

14. Click the left mouse button when the width of the slot appears close to 15 mm in the Dimension Input, see Figure 5.70. A slot is created.

5.69

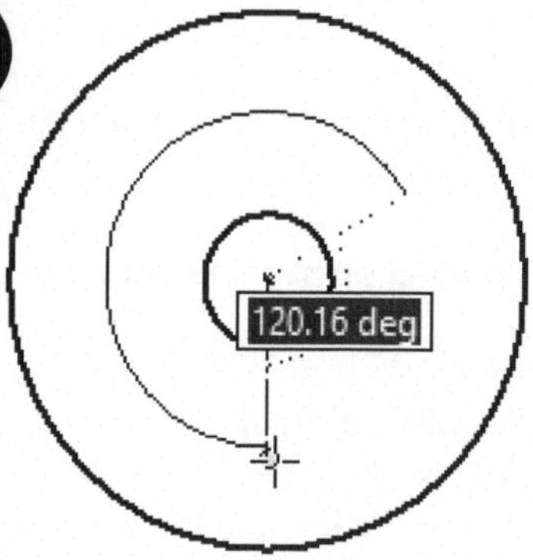

5.70

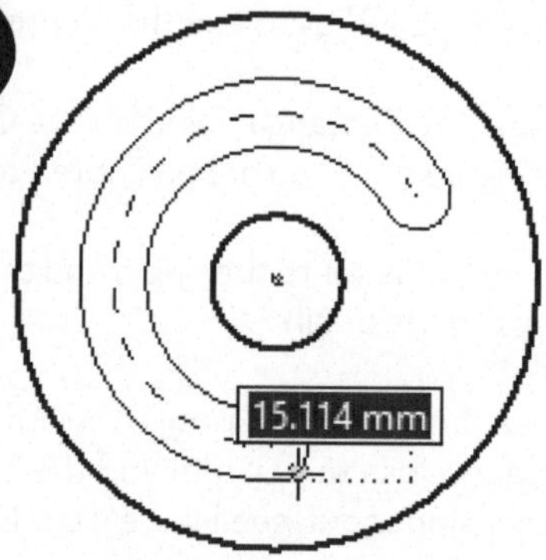

Section 4: Applying Constraints

After creating the sketch, you need to make it fully constrained by applying proper constraints and dimensions to the sketch entities.

1. Click on the **Vertical Constraint** tool in the **Constrain** panel of the **Sketch** tab.

2. Select the center point of the lower slot arc and the origin one by one, see Figure 5.71. A vertical constraint is applied between the selected slot arc and the origin.

5.71

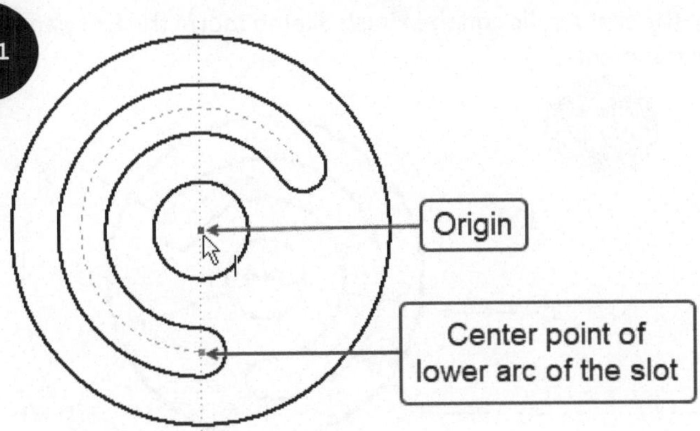

3. Press the ESC key to exit the **Vertical Constraint** tool.

Section 5: Applying Dimensions

Now, you need to apply dimensions to make the sketch fully constrained.

1. Click on the **General Dimension** tool in the **Constrain** panel, (see Figure 5.72), or press the D key. You are prompted to select a geometry to dimension.

5.72

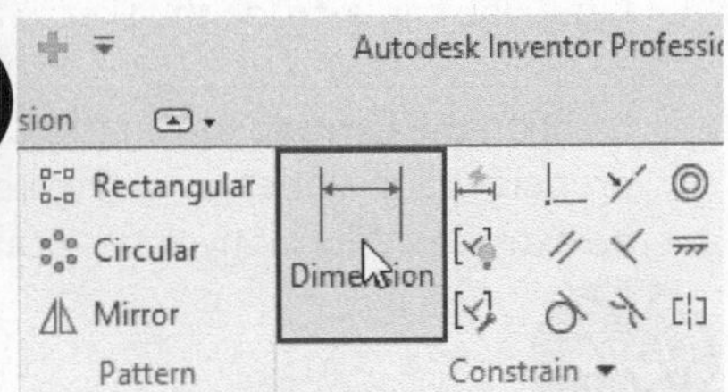

2. Select the inner circle of the sketch. The diameter dimension of the selected circle gets attached to the cursor, see Figure 5.73.

3. Move the cursor to the location where you want to place the dimension in the drawing area and then click to specify the placement point. The **Edit Dimension** dialog box appears.

4. Enter **30** in the **Edit Dimension** dialog box as the diameter of the circle and then click on the green tick-mark ☑ button. The diameter of the circle is modified to 30 mm and the diameter dimension is applied, see Figure 5.74.

5.73

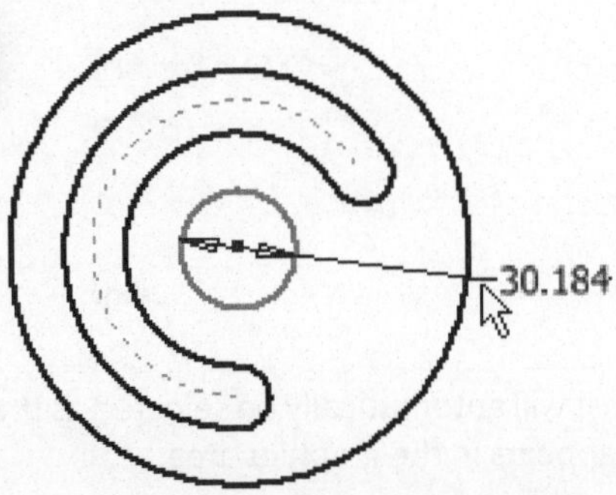

5.74

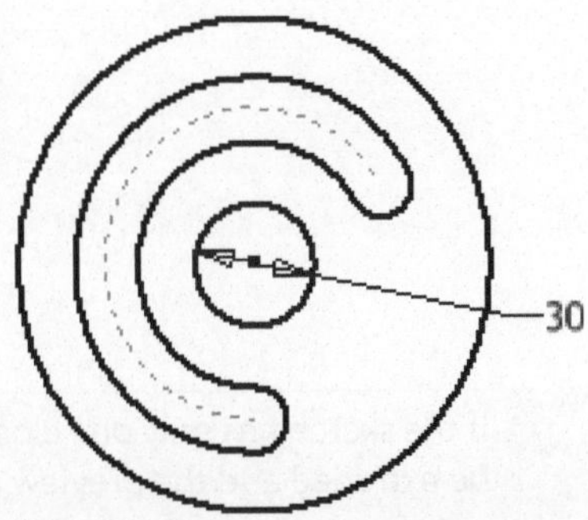

5. Similarly, apply the remaining dimensions to the sketch. Figure 5.75 shows the fully constrained sketch after applying all constraints and dimensions.

6. After creating the sketch, click on the **Finish Sketch** tool in the **Exit** panel of the **Ribbon** to exit the Sketching environment.

5.75

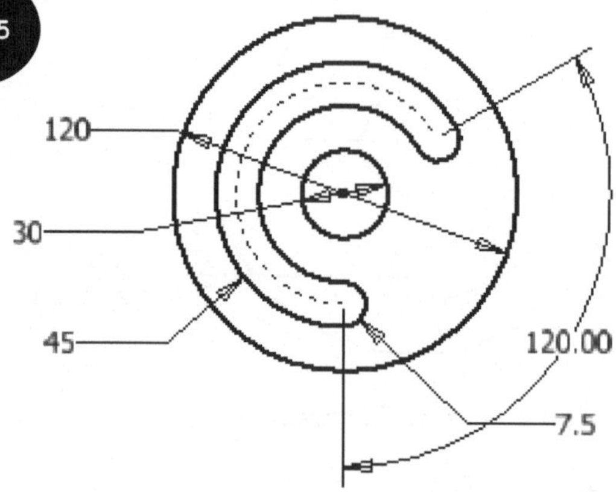

Section 6: Extruding the Sketch

Now, you can extrude the sketch and convert it into a feature.

1. Click on the **Extrude** tool in the **Create** panel of the **3D Model** tab, see Figure 5.76. The **Extrusion** property panel appears, see Figure 5.77. Also, you are prompted to select a profile of the sketch to be extruded. Alternatively, you can press the **E** key to invoke the **Extrusion** property panel.

5.76

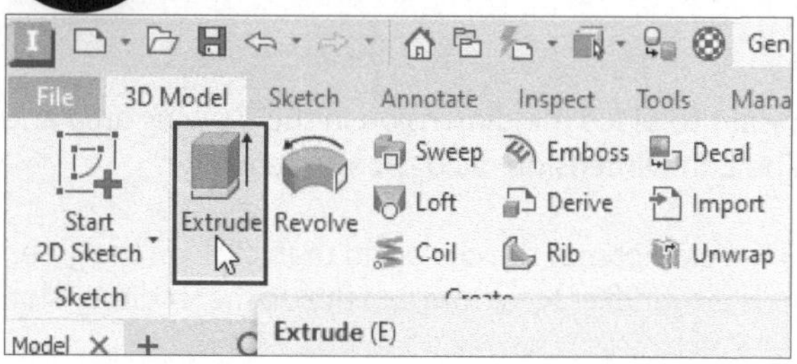

5.77

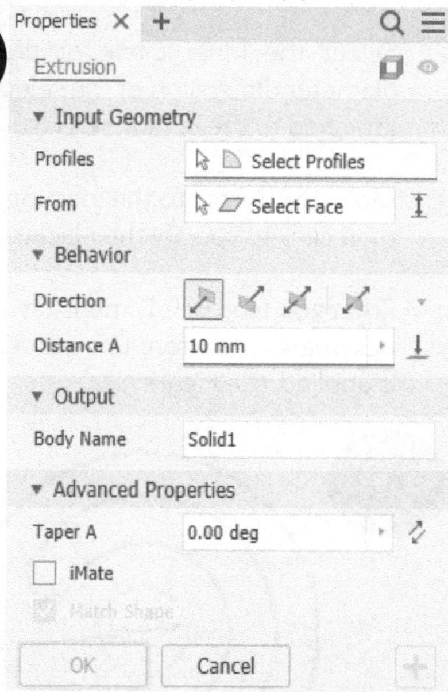

Tip: If the sketch has only one closed profile then it will automatically be selected as the profile to be extruded and the preview of the feature appears in the graphics area.

2. Move the cursor over the outer closed profile of the sketch and then click when it gets highlighted in the graphics area, see Figure 5.78. The preview of an extrude feature appears with the default depth of extrusion.

3. Enter **15** in the **Distance A** field of the **Behavior** rollout in the **Extrusion** property panel. The depth of the extrusion changes to 15 mm, see Figure 5.79.

5.78

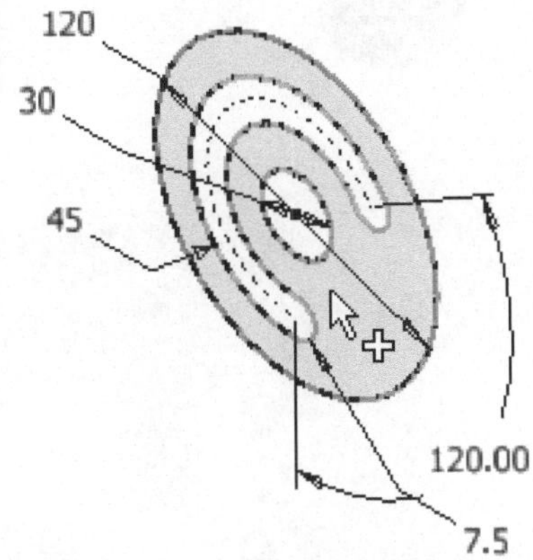

5.79

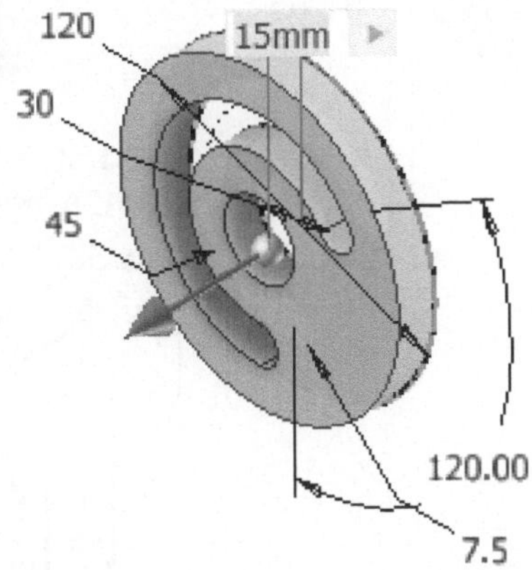

4. Click on the **OK** button in the property panel. The extrude feature is created, see Figure 5.80.

5.80

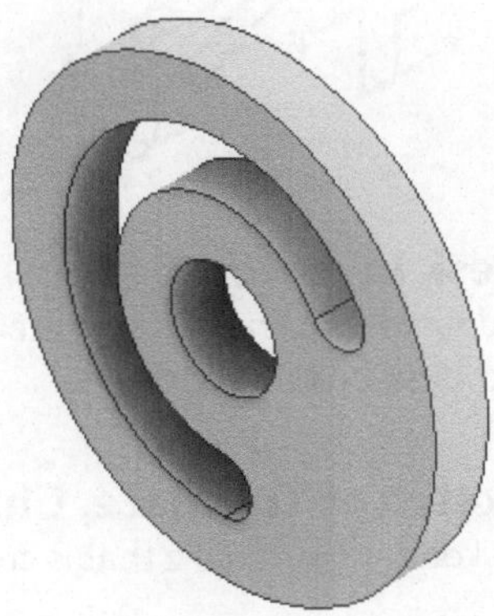

Section 7: Saving the Model

Now, you need to save the model.

1. Click on the **Save** tool in the **Quick Access Toolbar**. The **Save As** dialog box appears. Next, browse to the **Autodesk Inventor > Chapter 5** folder in the local drive of your system. Note that you need to create Chapter 5 folder inside the Autodesk Inventor folder.

2. Enter **Tutorial 1** in the **File name** field of the dialog box and then click on the **Save** button. The model is saved in the specified location (>:\Autodesk Inventor\Chapter 5).

Tutorial 2

Open the sketch created in Tutorial 2 of Chapter 4 (see Figure 5.81), and then revolve it around the vertical centerline at an angle of 270 degrees, see Figure 5.82. Also, change the visual style of the model to 'wireframe with visible edges only'. All dimensions are in mm.

5.81

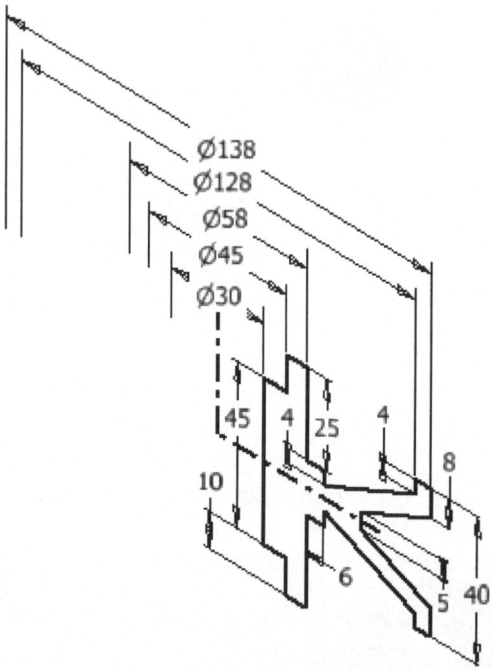

5.82

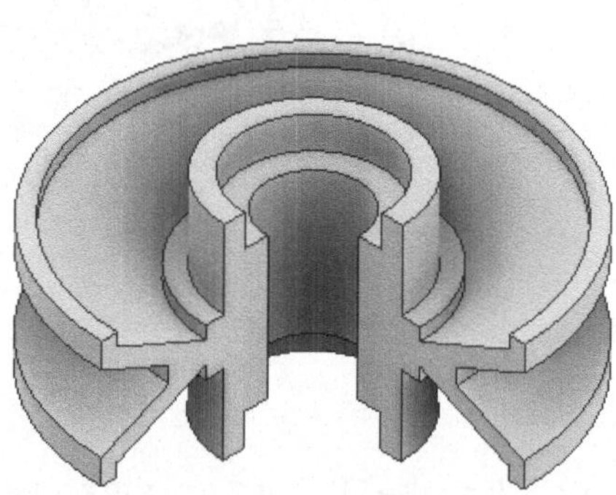

Section 1: Starting Autodesk Inventor

1. Start Autodesk Inventor by double-clicking on the Autodesk Inventor icon on your desktop. The startup user interface of Autodesk Inventor appears.

Section 2: Opening the Sketch of Tutorial 2, Chapter 4

Now, you need to open the sketch of Tutorial 2 that is created in Chapter 4.

1. Click on the **Open** tool in the left panel of the startup user interface of Autodesk Inventor. The **Open** dialog box appears. You can also invoke the **Open** dialog box by pressing CTRL + O.

2. Browse to the Chapter 4 folder of the Autodesk Inventor folder in the local drive of your computer and then select the **Tutorial 2** file.

3. Click on the **Open** button in the dialog box. The sketch of Tutorial 2 created in Chapter 4 is opened in the current session of Autodesk Inventor, see Figure 5.83.

5.83

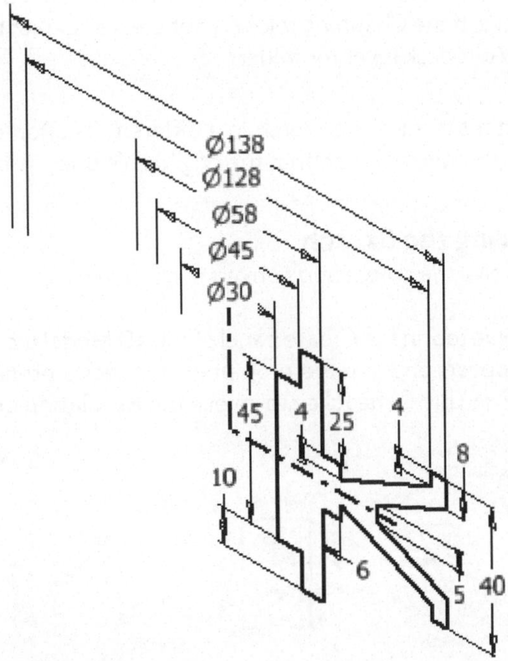

Section 3: Saving the Sketch

Now, you need to save the sketch with the name "Tutorial 2" in Chapter 5 folder.

1. Click on **File > Save As** in the **File Menu**, see Figure 5.84. The **Save As** dialog box appears.

5.84

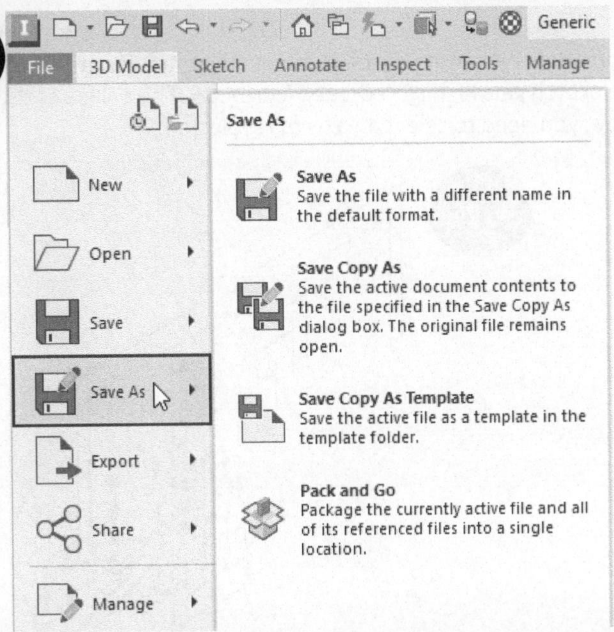

2. Browse to the Chapter 5 folder of the Autodesk Inventor folder and then save the sketch in it with the name Tutorial 2. If the Chapter 5 folder is not created earlier then you need to first create this folder inside the Autodesk Inventor folder.

Note: It is important to save the sketch in a different location or with a different name before making any modification, so that the original file does not get modified.

Section 4: Revolving the Sketch

Now, you can revolve the sketch and convert it into a feature.

1. Click on the **Revolve** tool in the **Create** panel of the **3D Model** tab, see Figure 5.85. The **Revolution** property panel appears and you are prompted to select a profile of the sketch to be revolved. Alternatively, you can press the **R** key to invoke the **Revolution** property panel.

5.85

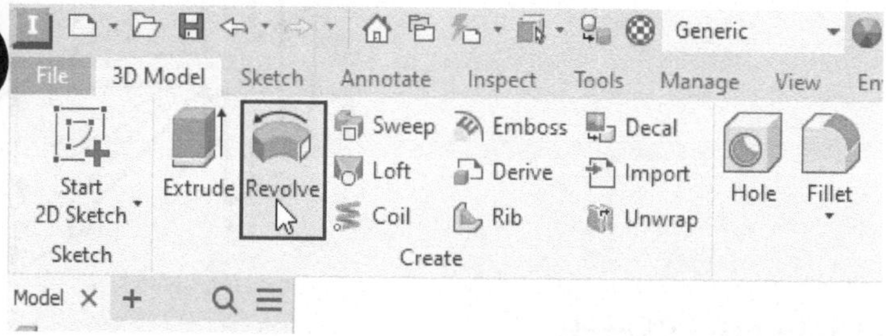

Tip: If the sketch to be revolved has only one profile and one centerline then the profile and the centerline will automatically be selected. Also, the preview of the resultant revolve feature appears in the graphics area.

2. Move the cursor over an entity of the sketch in the graphics area and then click when the closed profile of the sketch gets highlighted, see Figure 5.86. The profile of the sketch to be revolved gets selected. Now, you need to select an axis of revolution.

5.86

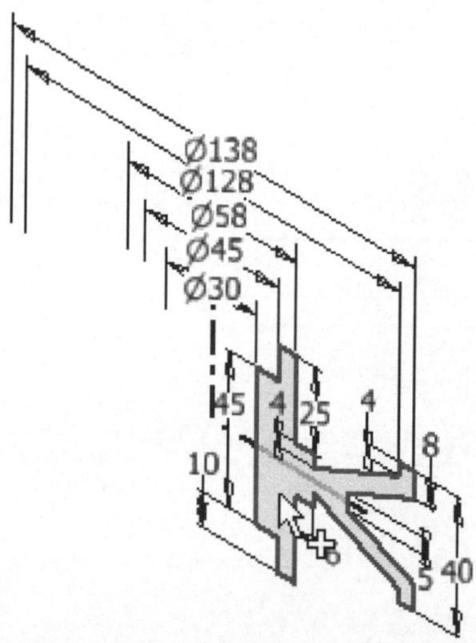

3. Click on the **Axis** selector in the **Input Geometry** rollout of the **Revolution** property panel. You are prompted to select an axis of revolution.

4. Click to select the vertical centerline of the sketch as the axis of revolution in the graphics area. A preview of the revolve feature appears in the graphics area with a default full 360 degrees angle of revolution (see Figure 5.87), since the **Full** button is activated in the **Behavior** rollout of the property panel, by default.

5. Enter **270** degrees in the **Angle A** field of the **Behavior** rollout in the property panel. The angle of revolution of the revolve feature changes to 270 degrees, as specified.

6. Click on the **Flipped** button in the **Direction** area of the **Behavior** rollout to flip the direction of revolution to the other side of the sketching plane as shown in Figure 5.88, if needed.

5.87

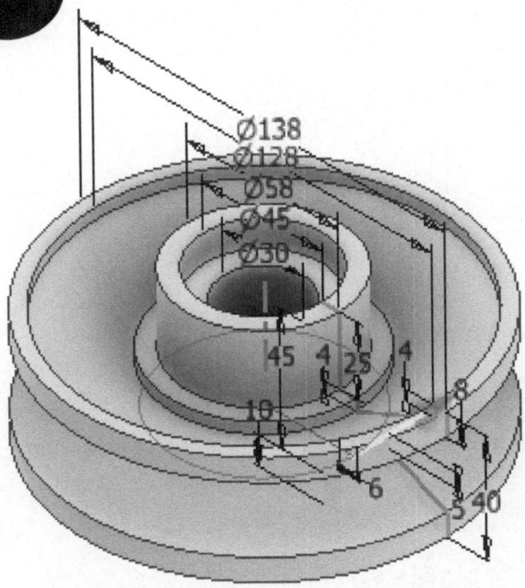

5.88

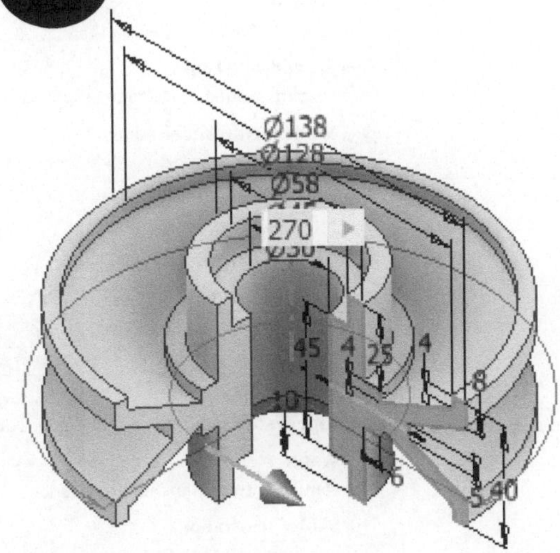

7. Click on the **OK** button in the **Revolution** property panel. The revolve feature is created, see Figure 5.89.

5.89

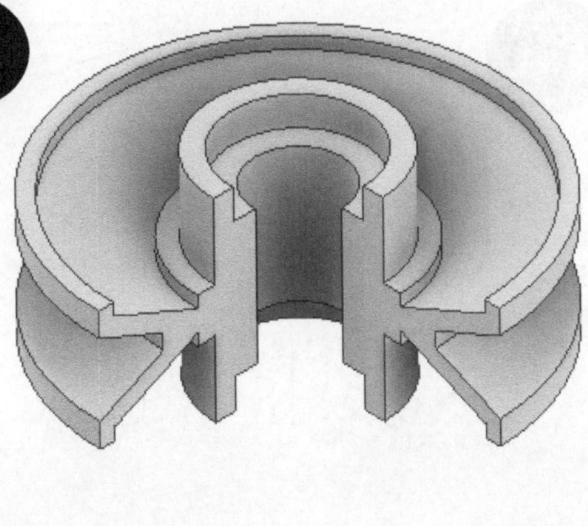

Section 5: Changing the Visual Style

As mentioned in the tutorial description, you need to change the visual style of the model to the 'wireframe with visible edges only'.

1. Click on the **View** tab in the **Ribbon** to display the tools of the **View** tab.

2. Invoke the **Visual Style** flyout in the **Appearance** panel of the **View** tab and then click on the **Wireframe with Visible Edges Only** tool, see Figure 5.90. The visual style of the model changes to a 'wireframe with visible edges only', see Figure 5.91.

5.90

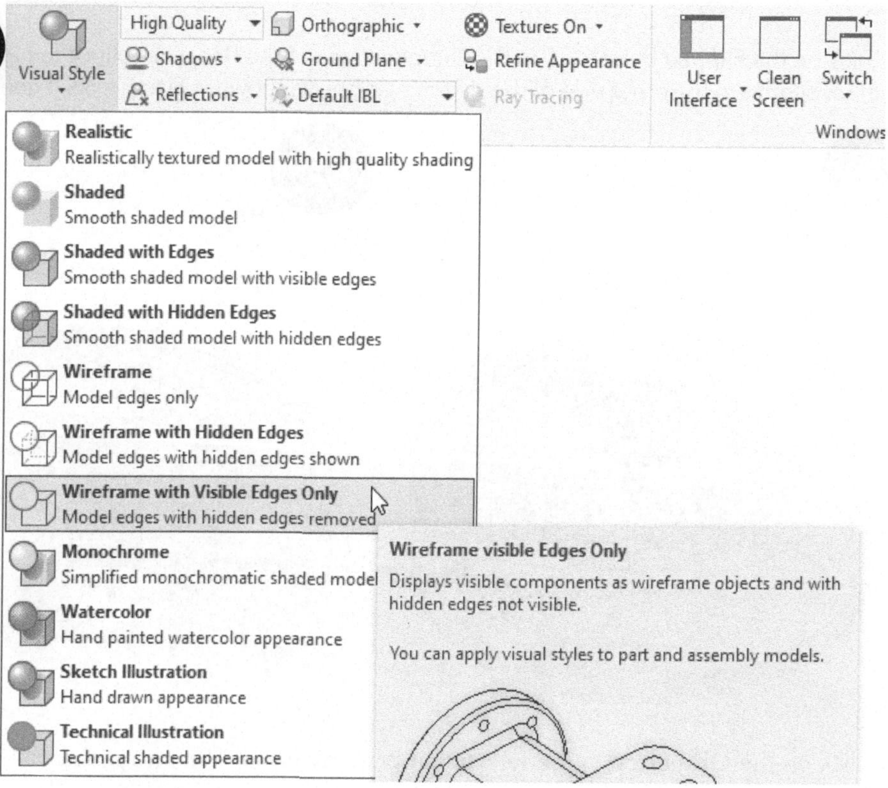

5.91

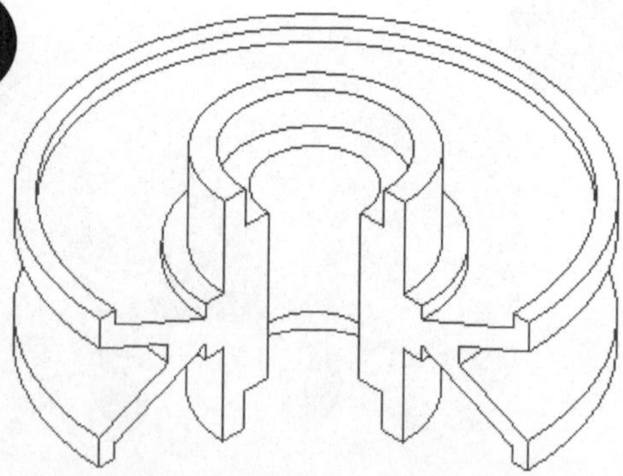

Section 6: Saving the Model

Now, you need to save the model.

1. Click on the **Save** tool in the **Quick Access Toolbar**. The model is saved with the name **Tutorial 2** in the Chapter 5 folder (*>:\Autodesk Inventor\Chapter 5*).

Tutorial 3

Open the sketch created in Tutorial 3 of Chapter 4 (see Figure 5.92), and then extrude it to a depth of 60 mm, symmetrically about the sketching plane, see Figure 5.93. All dimensions are in mm.

5.92

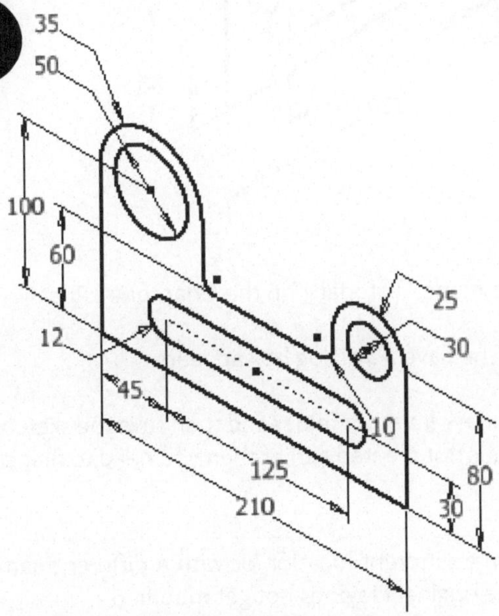

5.93

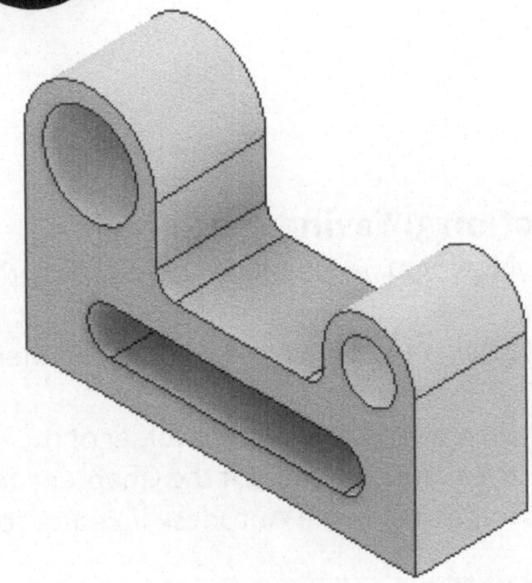

Section 1: Starting Autodesk Inventor

1. Start Autodesk Inventor by double-clicking on the Autodesk Inventor icon on your desktop. The startup user interface of Autodesk Inventor appears.

Section 2: Opening the Sketch of Tutorial 3, Chapter 4

Now, you need to open the sketch of Tutorial 3 that is created in Chapter 4.

1. Click on the **Open** tool in the startup user interface of Autodesk Inventor. The **Open** dialog box appears. You can also invoke the **Open** dialog box by pressing CTRL + O.

2. Browse to the Chapter 4 folder of the Autodesk Inventor folder in the local drive of your computer and then select the **Tutorial 3** file.

3. Click on the **Open** button in the dialog box. The sketch of Tutorial 3 created in Chapter 4 is opened in the current session of Autodesk Inventor, see Figure 5.94.

5.94

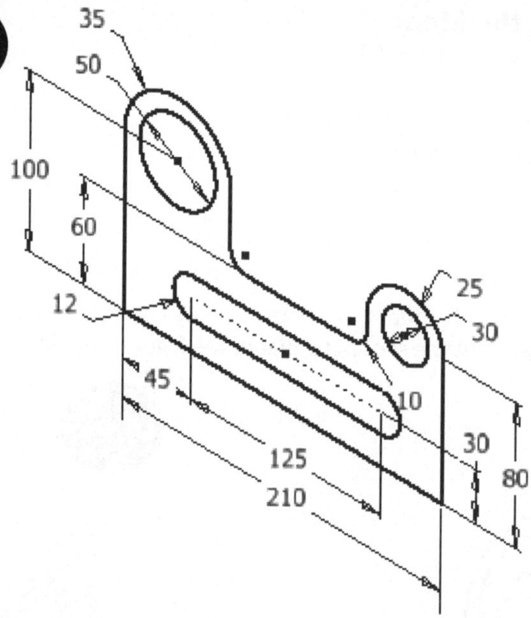

Section 3: Saving the Sketch

Now, you need to save the sketch with the name "Tutorial 3" in the Chapter 5 folder.

1. Click on **File > Save As** in the **File Menu**. The **Save As** dialog box appears.

2. Browse to the Chapter 5 folder of the Autodesk Inventor folder and then save the sketch in it with the name Tutorial 3. If the Chapter 5 folder is not created earlier then you need to first create this folder inside the Autodesk Inventor folder.

Note: It is important to save the sketch in a different location or with a different name before making any modification, so that the original file does not get modified.

Section 4: Extruding the Sketch

Now, you can extrude the sketch and convert it into a feature.

1. Click on the **Extrude** tool in the **Create** panel of the **3D Model** tab, see Figure 5.95. The **Extrusion** property panel appears and you are prompted to select a profile of the sketch to be extruded. Alternatively, you can press the **E** key to invoke the **Extrusion** property panel.

5.95

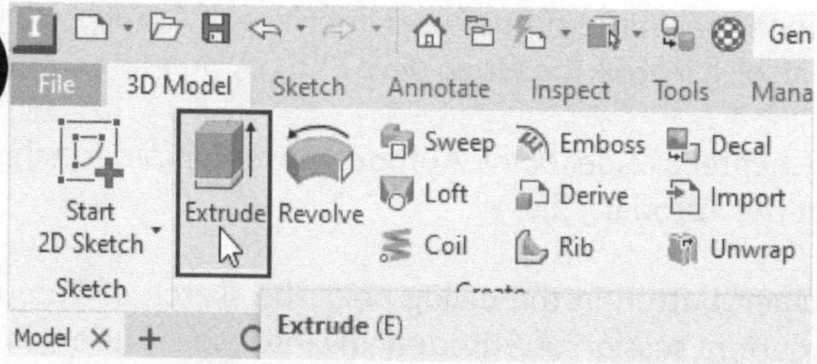

2. Move the cursor over the outer closed profile of the sketch, and then click when it gets highlighted in the graphics area, see Figure 5.96. A preview of the extrude feature appears.

5.96

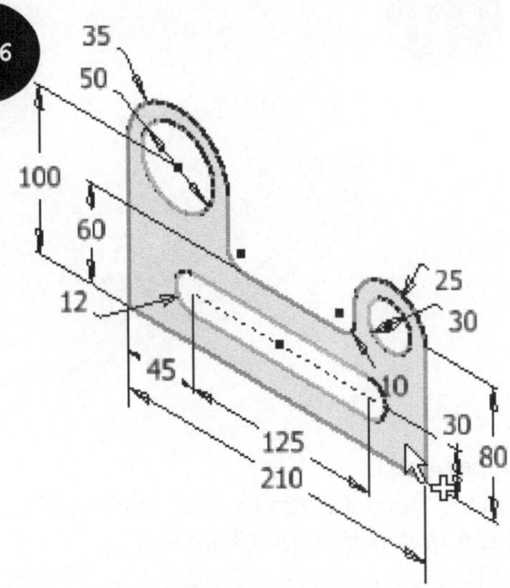

3. Enter **60** in the **Distance A** field of the **Behavior** rollout of the **Extrusion** property panel. The depth of extrusion changes to 60 mm, as specified. Note that direction of the extrusion is on one side of the sketching plane, by default.

4. Click on the **Symmetric** button in the **Direction** area of the **Behavior** rollout in the **Extrusion** property panel. The depth of extrusion gets added symmetrically on both sides of the sketching plane, see Figure 5.97.

5.97

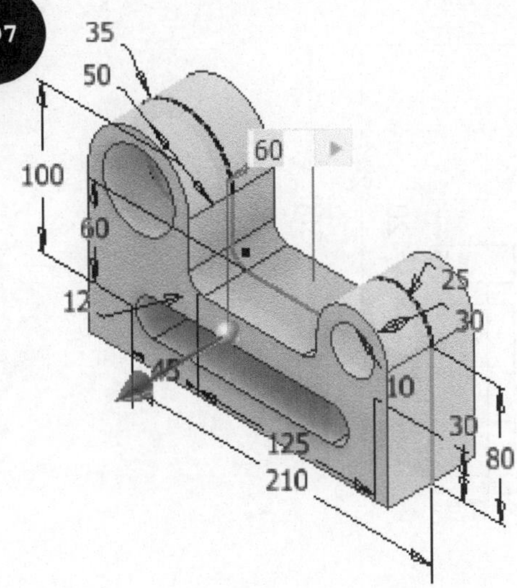

5. Click on the **OK** button in the property panel. The extrude feature is created, see Figure 5.98.

5.98

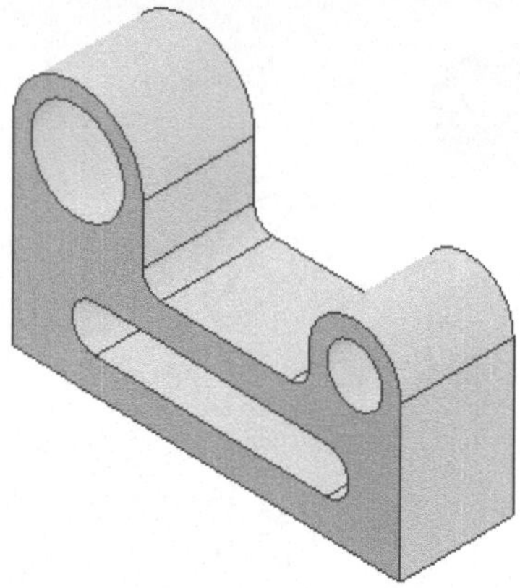

Section 5: Saving the Model

1. Click on the **Save** tool in the **Quick Access Toolbar**. The model is saved with the name **Tutorial 3** in the Chapter 5 folder (*>:\Autodesk Inventor\Chapter 5*).

Hands-on Test Drive 1

Create a revolve model, as shown in Figure 5.99. The angle of revolution is 360 degrees. All dimensions are in mm. Note that to create a revolved feature, you need to create its sketch on either side of the axis of revolution.

5.99

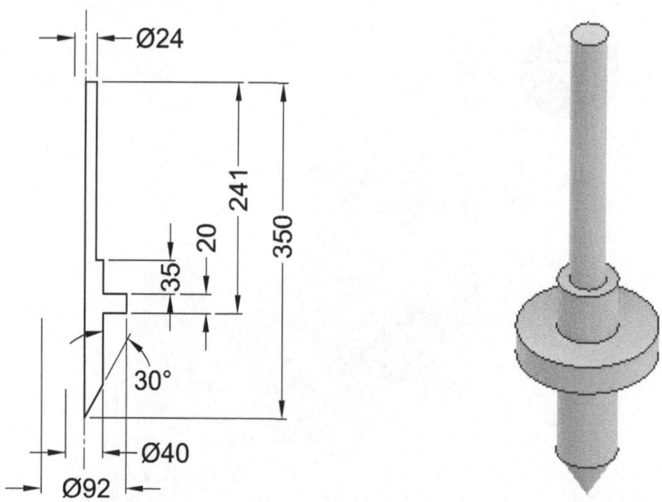

Hands-on Test Drive 2

Create an extrude model, as shown in Figure 5.100. The depth of extrusion is 2 mm. All dimensions are in mm.

5.100

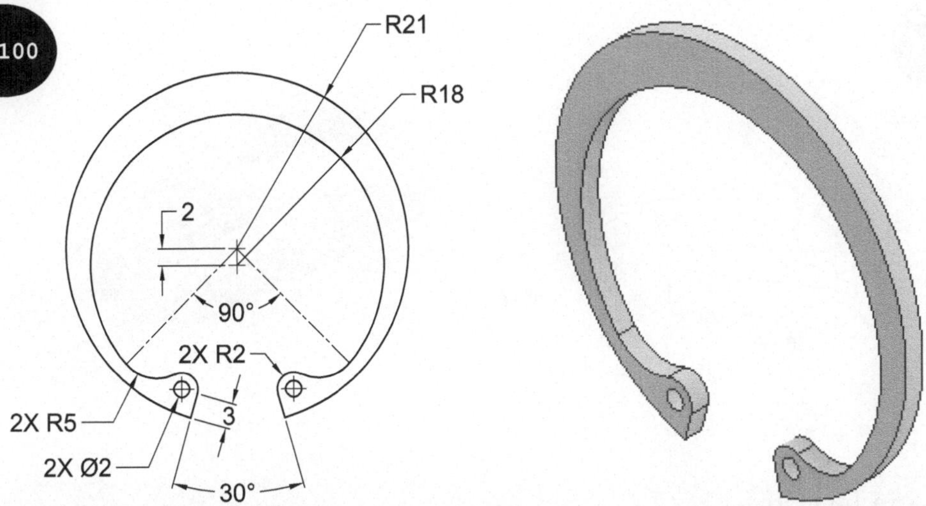

Hands-on Test Drive 3

Create a revolve model as shown in Figure 5.101. The angle of revolution is 360 degrees. All dimensions are in mm.

5.101

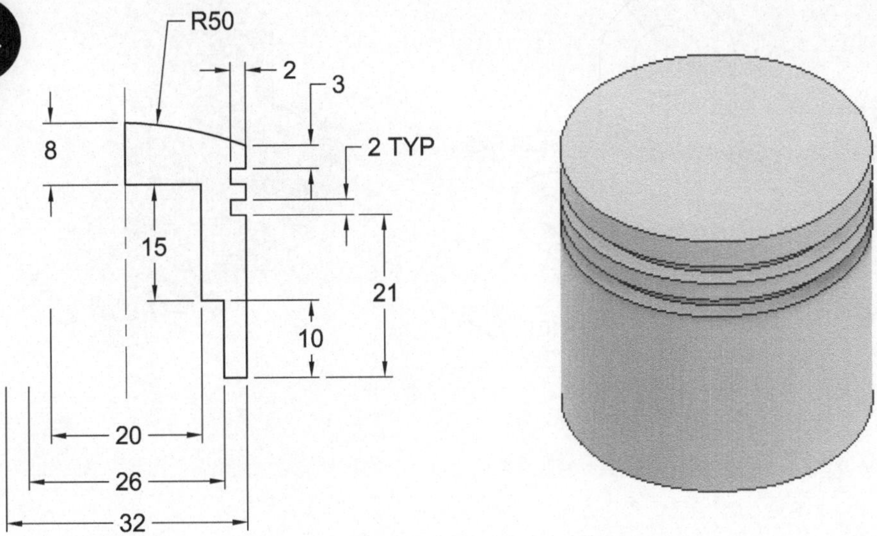

Hands-on Test Drive 4

Create an extrude model, as shown in Figure 5.102. The depth of extrusion is 10 mm. All dimensions are in mm.

5.102

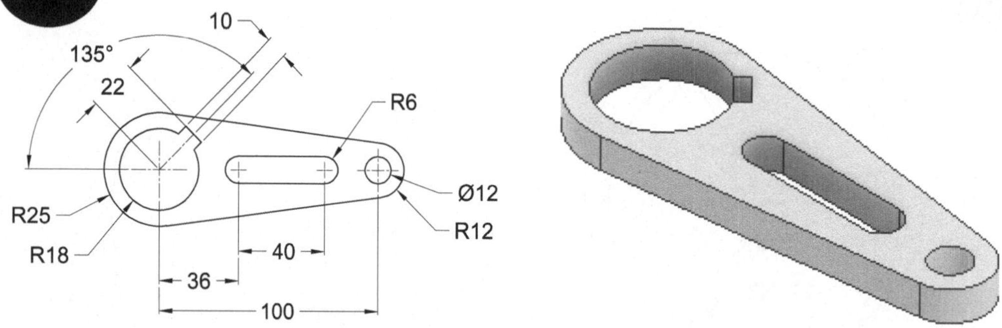

Hands-on Test Drive 5

Create an extrude model, as shown in Figure 5.103. The depth of extrusion is 20 mm. All dimensions are in mm.

5.103

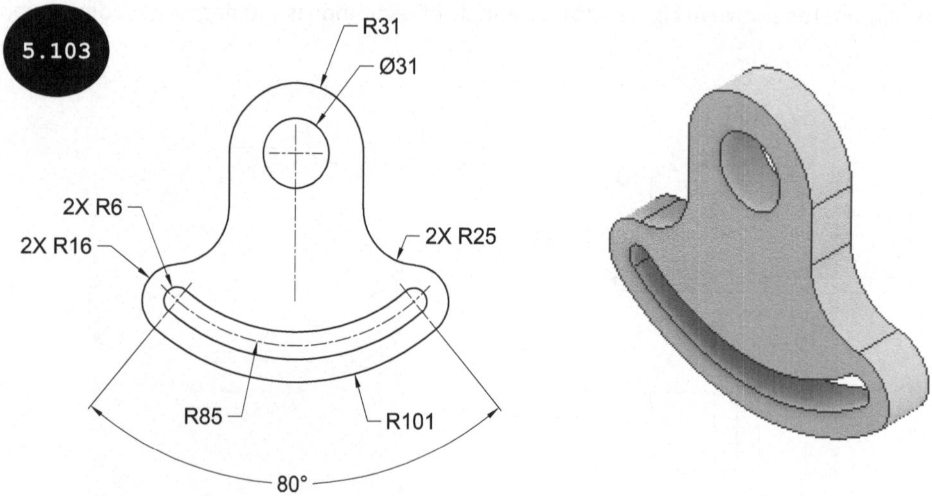

Hands-on Test Drive 6

Create an extrude model, as shown in Figure 5.104. The depth of extrusion is 3 mm. All dimensions are in mm.

5.104

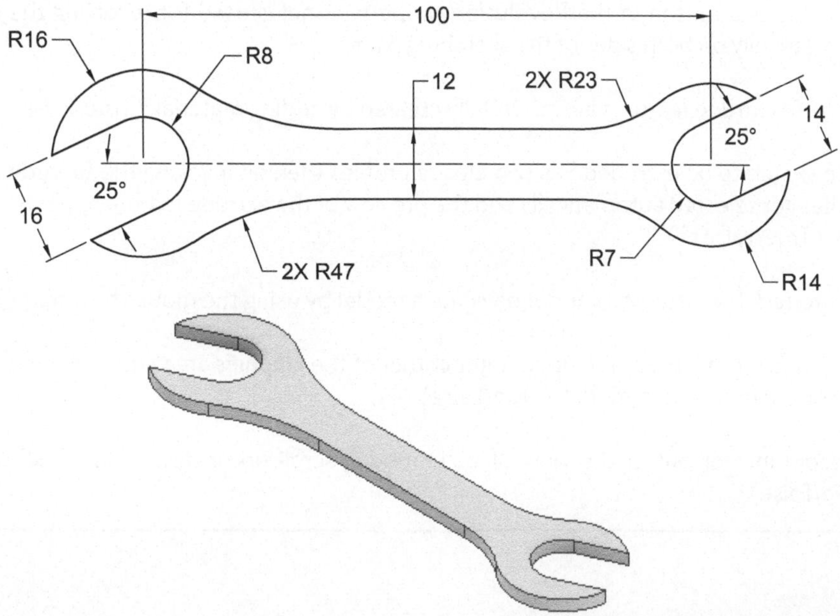

Summary

In this chapter, you have learned about creating extrude and revolve base features by using the **Extrude** and **Revolve** tools, respectively. The chapter discussed in detail, how to navigate a model by using the mouse buttons, ViewCube, and navigation tools such as **Navigation Wheel**, **Pan**, **Zoom**, and **Orbit**. It also explained the method for changing the visual style of a model.

Questions

Complete and verify the following sentences:

- The ________ tool is used for creating a feature by adding material normal to the sketching plane.
- The ________ tool is used for creating a feature by revolving a sketch profile around an axis of revolution.
- The ________ is divided into different wedges and each wedge represents a navigation tool.
- The ________ tool is used for zooming a particular portion or an area of a 3D model.

- The ______ tool is used for panning/moving a 3D model in the graphics area.
- The ______ tool is used for displaying the selected face of a 3D model normal to the viewing direction.
- The ______ button in the **Revolution** property panel is used for revolving the sketch profile symmetrically on both sides of the sketching plane.
- The base extrude features are essentially created by adding material. (True/False)
- If the sketch to be extruded has two closed profiles then on invoking the **Extrude** tool, both the profiles get selected automatically and the preview of the extrude feature appears in the graphics area. (True/False)
- In Autodesk Inventor, you cannot navigate a model by using the mouse buttons. (True/False)
- ViewCube is available at the upper right corner of the graphics area and is used for changing the view or orientation of a model. (True/False)
- To zoom into or out of the view of a 3D model, scroll up or down the wheel of the mouse. (True/False)

CHAPTER
6

Creating Work Features

In this chapter, the following topics will be discussed:

- Creating Work Planes
- Creating Work Axes
- Creating Work Points
- Creating a User Coordinate System

In this chapter, you will learn about creating work features which include work planes, work axes, and work points.

6.1

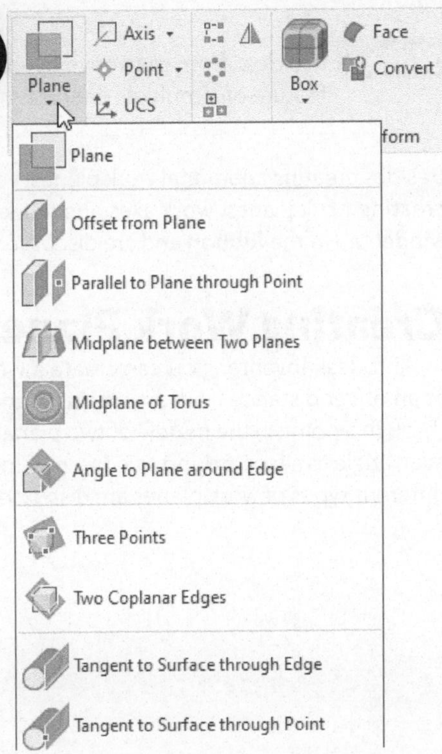

In Autodesk Inventor, three default work planes; Front (XY Plane), Top (XZ Plane), and Right (YZ Plane) are available. You can use these work planes to create the base feature of a model by extruding or revolving the sketch, as discussed in earlier chapters. However, to create a real world model having multiple features, you may need additional work planes. In other words, the three default work planes may not be enough to create all features of a real world model and you may need to create additional work planes. Autodesk Inventor allows you to create additional work planes for creating real world models, as required. You can create various types of work planes by using the tools available in the **Plane** flyout of the **Work Features** panel in the **3D Model** tab, see Figure 6.1.

Figure 6.2 shows a multiple-feature model, which is created by creating all its features one by one. This model has three features. Its base/first feature is an extrude feature created on the Right plane (YZ Plane). The second feature is a user-defined work plane created at an angle. The third feature is an extrude feature created on the user-defined work plane.

6.2

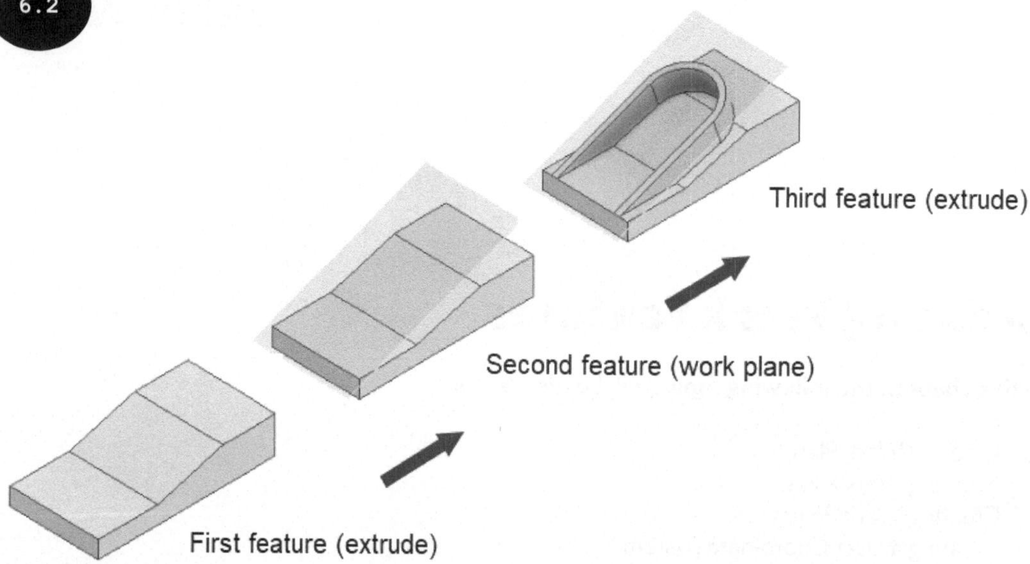

Note: It is clear from the above figure that additional work planes may be required for creating a feature of a multiple-feature model.

Besides creating additional work planes, you can also create work axes, and work points. The tools for creating work planes, work axes and work points are available in the **Work Features** panel of the **3D Model** tab in the **Ribbon** and are discussed next.

Creating Work Planes

In Autodesk Inventor, you can create a work plane passing through selected geometries of a model, at an offset distance from an existing plane or planar face, parallel to an existing plane or planar face through a point, in the middle of two planar faces or planes, through the center or midplane of a torus, at an angle to a face around an edge, passing through three points, and so on. The methods for creating different types of work planes are discussed next.

Creating a Work Plane Through Selected Geometries

The method for creating a work plane passing through selected geometries of a model is discussed below:

1. Click on the **Plane** tool in the **Work Features** panel of the **3D Model** tab, see Figure 6.3. You are prompted to define a work plane by selecting the geometries of the model.

6.3

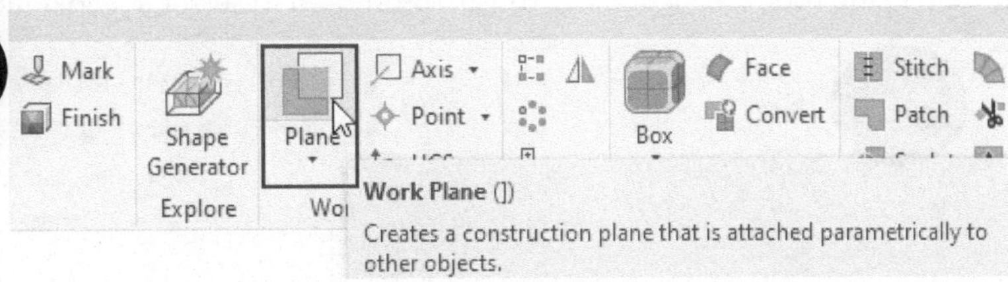

2. Select the required geometries of the model for creating a work plane. A work plane is created depending on the geometries selected. You can select vertices, edges, or faces of a model as geometries. Note that you can select maximum three geometries for creating a work plane. Figure 6.4 shows a work plane created by selecting a face and a vertex of a model (two geometries). Hence, the work plane is created parallel to the selected face and passes through the selected vertex. Figure 6.5 shows a work plane created by selecting three vertices of a model (three geometries). Hence, the work plane is created passing through three selected vertices.

6.4

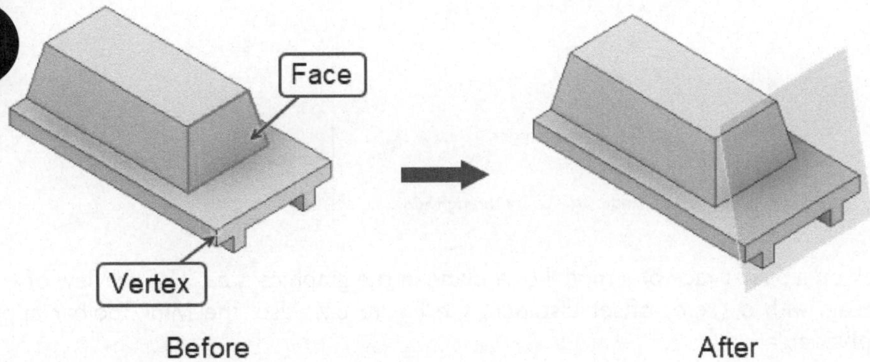

6.5

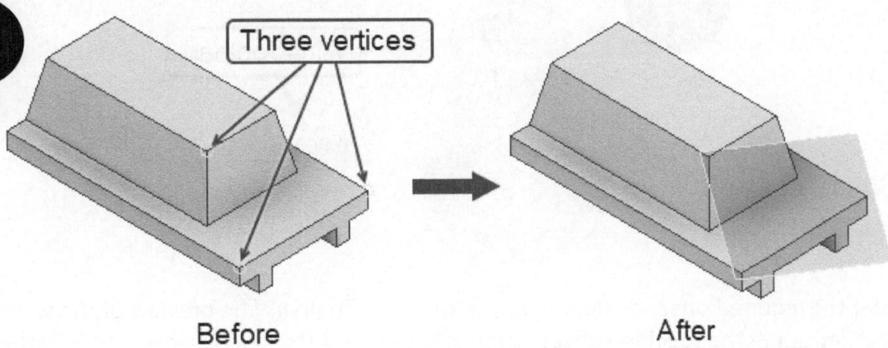

Creating a Work Plane at an Offset Distance

The method for creating a work plane at an offset distance from an existing plane or a planar face is discussed below:

1. Invoke the **Plane** flyout in the **Work Features** panel of the **3D Model** tab and then click on the **Offset from Plane** tool, see Figure 6.6. You are prompted to select a planar face.

6.6

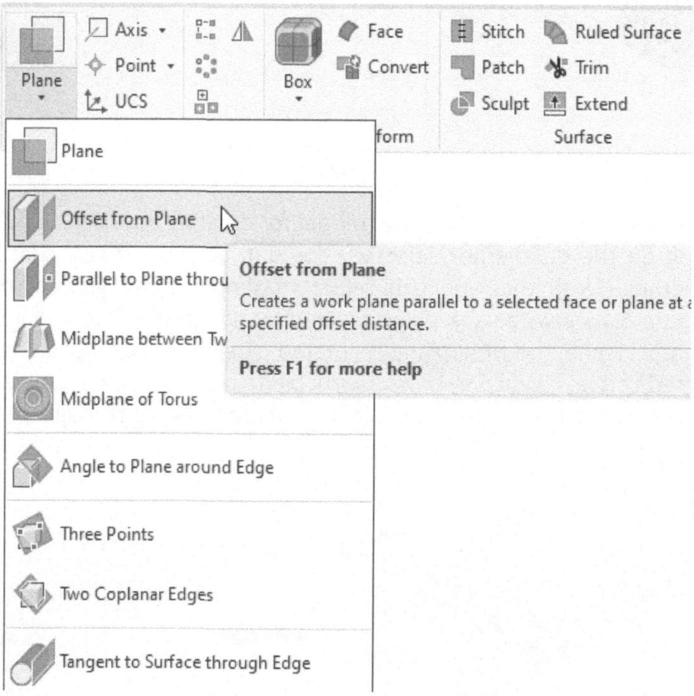

2. Click on a planar face of a model or a plane in the graphics area. The preview of a work plane appears with 0 (zero) offset distance, see Figure 6.7. Also, the Mini-Toolbar appears in the graphics area.

6.7

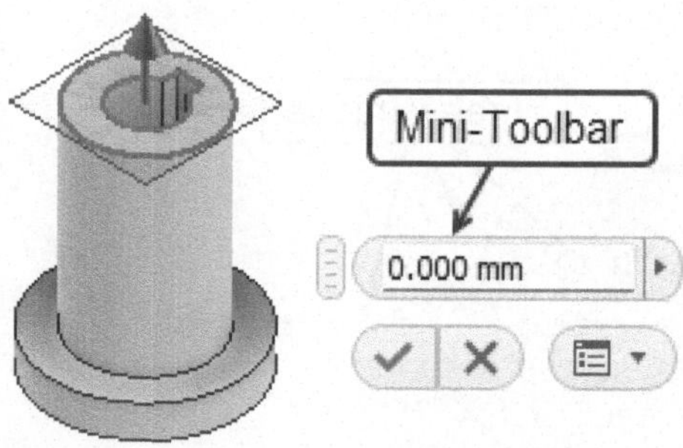

3. Enter the required offset distance value in the Mini-Toolbar. The preview of the work plane gets modified as per the specified offset distance in the graphics area. You can also drag the plane that appears in the graphics area to adjust the offset distance of the work plane, dynamically.

Note: To reverse the direction of the work plane, you need to either enter a negative offset distance value or drag the arrow to the other side of the selected planar face.

4. Click on the **OK** button (green tick-mark) in the Mini-Toolbar. A work plane is created at the specified offset distance, see Figure 6.8.

6.8

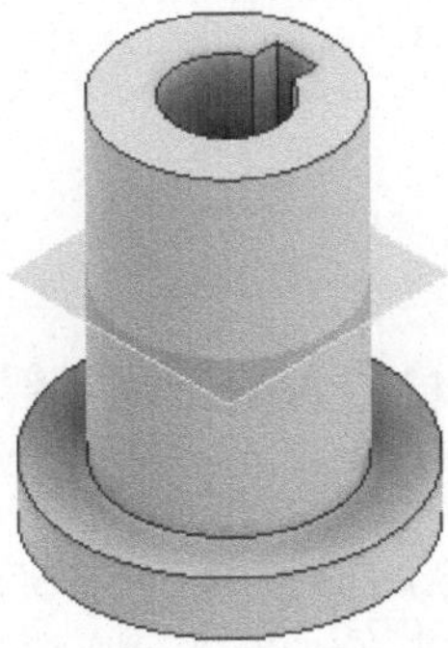

Creating a Work Plane Parallel to a Face/Plane

The method for creating a work plane parallel to a planar face or an existing plane through a point is discussed below:

1. Invoke the **Plane** flyout in the **Work Features** panel and then click on the **Parallel to Plane through Point** tool, see Figure 6.9. You are prompted to select a plane or a point.

6.9

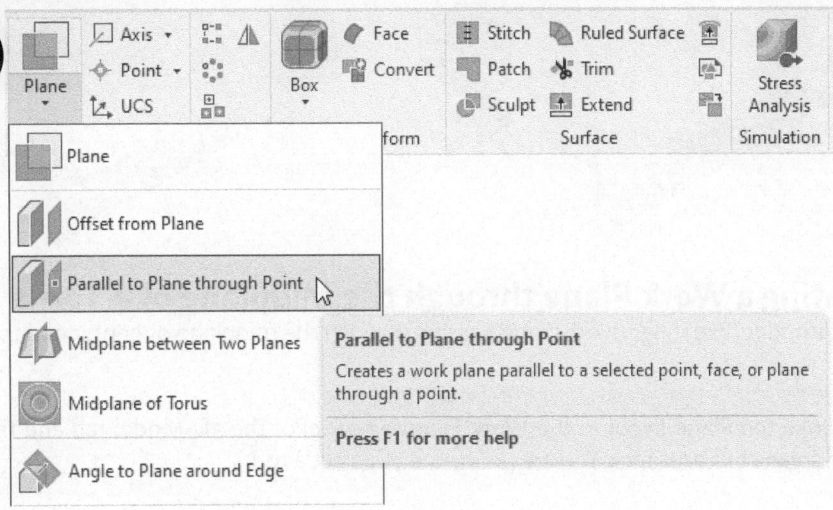

2. Select a planar face of a model or a plane and then select a vertex/point in the graphics area, see Figure 6.10. A work plane parallel to the selected planar face and passing through the selected vertex/point is created in the graphics area, see Figure 6.11.

6.10

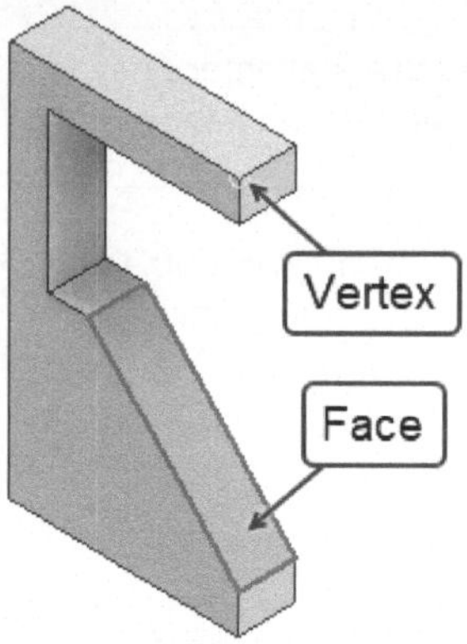

6.11

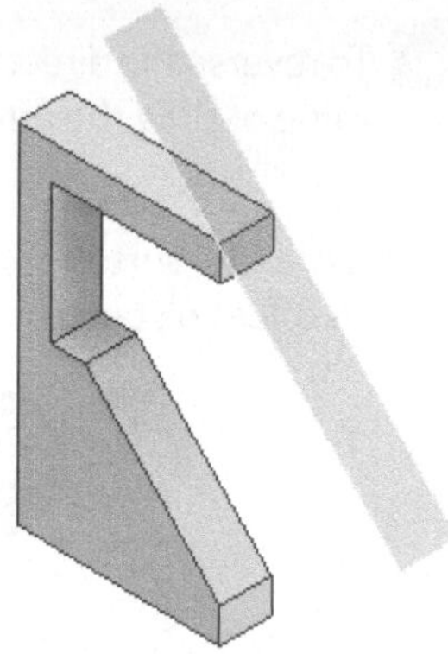

Creating a Work Plane in the Middle of Two Faces/Planes

The method for creating a work plane in the middle of two planar faces or planes is discussed below:

1. Invoke the **Plane** flyout in the **Work Features** panel of the **3D Model** tab and then click on the **Midplane between Two Planes** tool. You are prompted to select a plane.

2. Select two planes or planar faces of a model in the graphics area one by one, see Figure 6.12. A work plane in the middle of two selected faces or planes is created, see Figure 6.13.

6.12

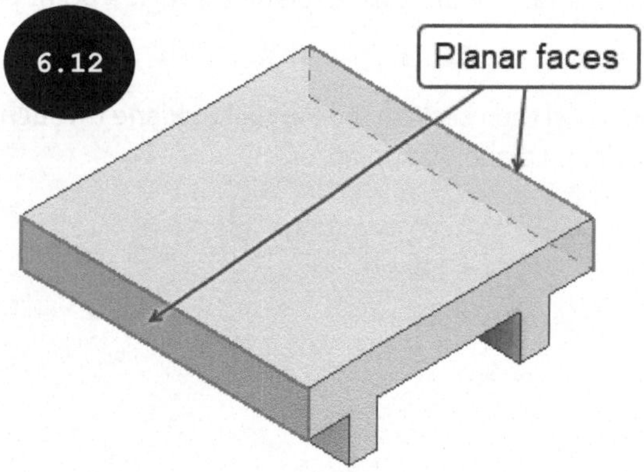

6.13

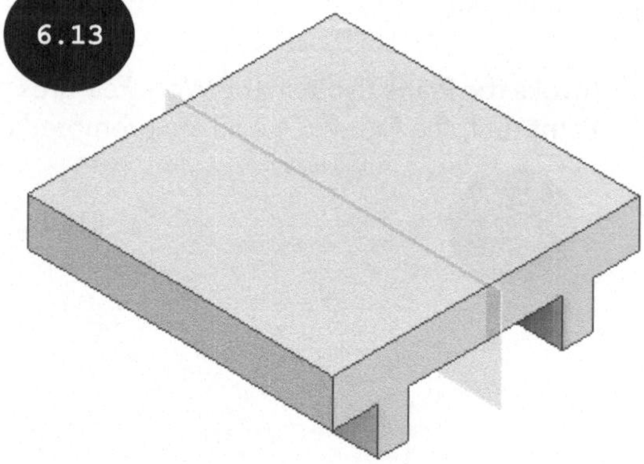

Creating a Work Plane through the Midplane of a Torus

The method for creating a work plane passing through the midplane or center of a torus is discussed below:

1. Invoke the **Plane** flyout in the **Work Features** panel of the **3D Model** tab and then click on the **Midplane of Torus** tool. You are prompted to select a torus.

2. Select a torus in the graphics area, see Figure 6.14. A work plane is created by passing through the midplane or center of the selected torus, see Figure 6.15.

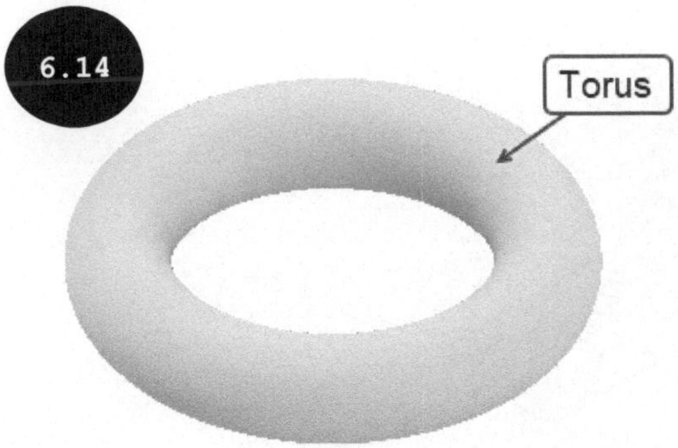

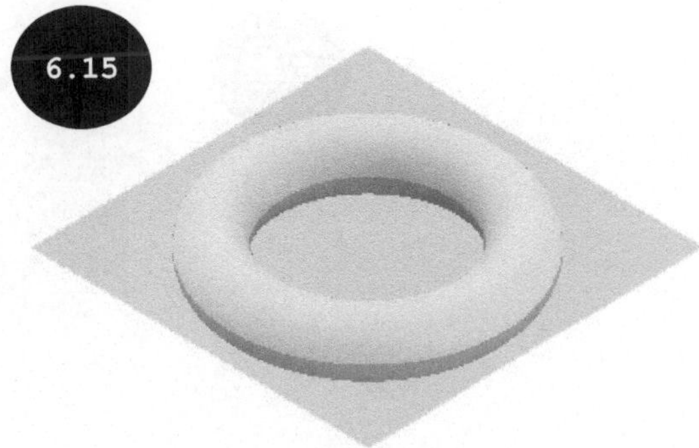

Tip: You can create a torus by revolving a circle at an angle of 360 degrees around an axis of revolution using the **Revolve** tool.

Creating a Work Plane at an Angle

The method for creating a work plane at an angle to a face around an edge of a model is discussed below:

1. Invoke the **Plane** flyout in the **Work Features** panel of the **3D Model** tab and then click on the **Angle to Plane around Edge** tool. You are prompted to select a line or a plane.

2. Select a linear edge, a sketch line, or an axis as the axis of revolution for the work plane, see Figure 6.16.

3. Select a planar face or a plane in the graphics area. The Mini-Toolbar appears, see Figure 6.16. Also, the preview of a work plane appears at an angle to the selected face around the selected edge. In this figure, an edge and a planar face of a model are selected.

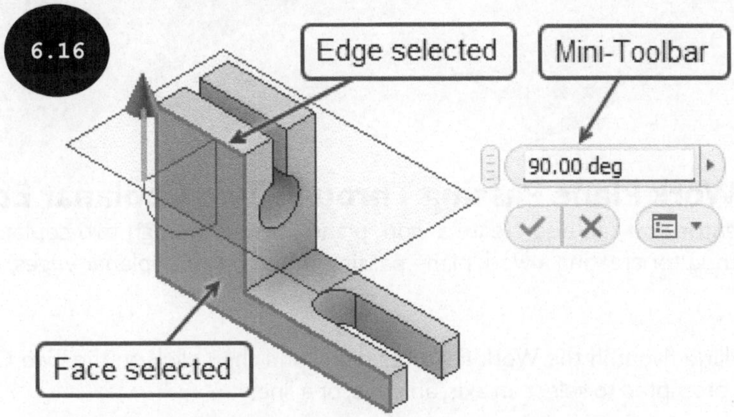

4. Enter the required angle value in the Mini-Toolbar. The preview of the plane appears as per the specified angle value.

5. Click on the **OK** button (green tick-mark) in the Mini-Toolbar. A work plane is created at the specified angle to the selected face around the selected edge, see Figure 6.17.

6.17

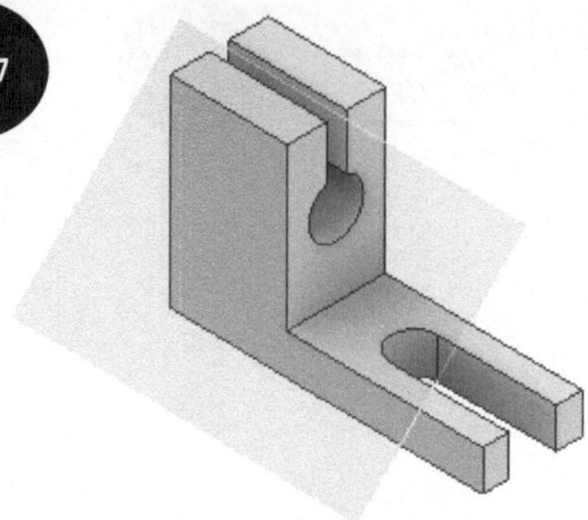

Creating a Work Plane Passing Through Three Points

The method for creating a work plane passing through three points or vertices is discussed below:

1. Invoke the **Plane** flyout in the **Work Features** panel of the **3D Model** tab and then click on the **Three Points** tool. You are prompted to select a point.

2. Click to select three points or vertices of a model one by one in the graphics area, see Figure 6.18. A work plane passing through the selected points or vertices is created, see Figure 6.19.

6.18

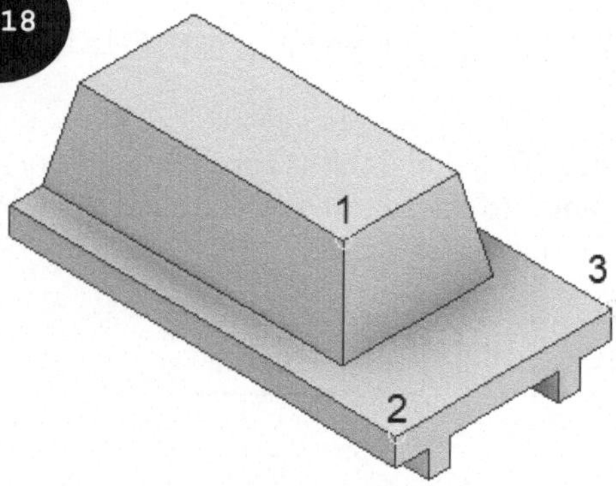

6.19

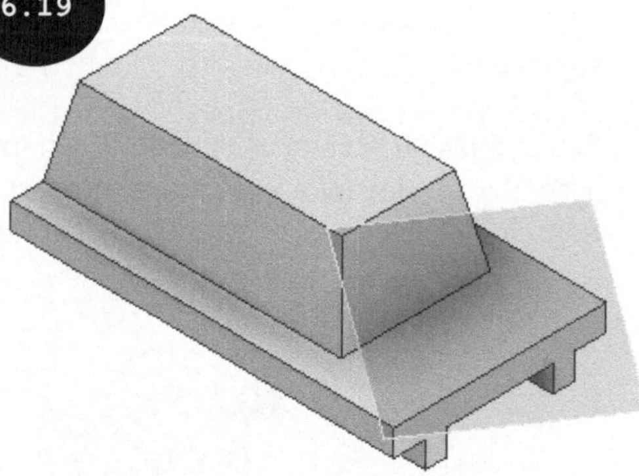

Creating a Work Plane Passing Through Two Coplanar Edges

In Autodesk Inventor, you can also create a work plane passing through two coplanar edges, axes, or lines. The method for creating a work plane passing through two coplanar edges, axes, or lines is discussed below:

1. Invoke the **Plane** flyout in the **Work Features** panel and then click on the **Two Coplanar Edges** tool. You are prompted to select an axis, an edge, or a line.

2. Click to select two coplanar edges, axes, or lines one by one in the graphics area, see Figure 6.20. In this figure, two coplanar edges of a model are selected. A work plane passing through the selected coplanar edges, axes, or lines is created.

Creating a Work Plane Tangent to a Face through an Edge

The method for creating a work plane tangent to a curved face and passing through an edge of a model is discussed below:

1. Invoke the **Plane** flyout in the **Work Features** panel and then click on the **Tangent to Surface through Edge** tool. You are prompted to select a surface or an edge.

2. Select a curved face and then a linear edge of a model, see Figure 6.21. A work plane tangent to the curved face and passing through the selected edge is created.

6.20

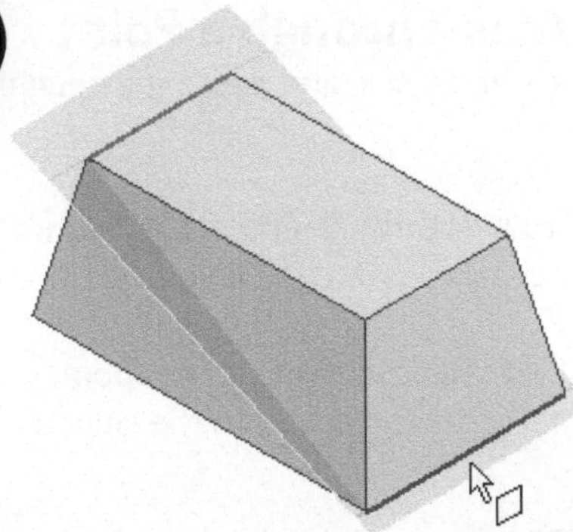

6.21

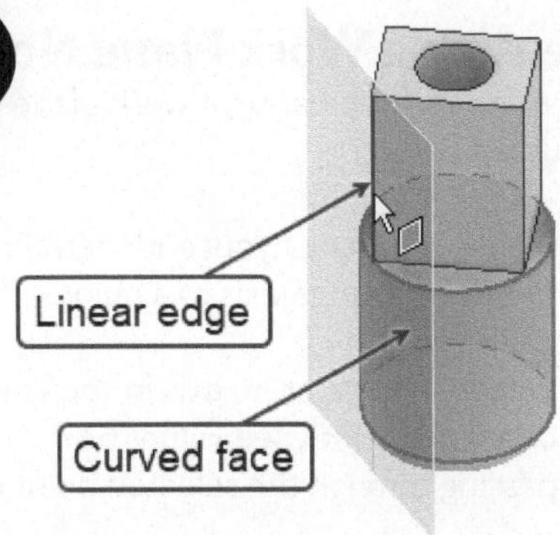

Note: The curved face and the linear edge of a model to be selected for creating a tangent work plane should be aligned with each other.

Creating a Work Plane Tangent to a Face through a Point

The method for creating a work plane tangent to a curved face and passing through a point of a model is discussed below:

1. Invoke the **Plane** flyout and then click on the **Tangent to Surface through Point** tool. You are prompted to select a surface or a point.

2. Select a curved face and a point in the graphics area one by one, see Figure 6.22. You can select an endpoint, a midpoint, or a work point. A work plane tangent to the curved face and passing through the selected point is created.

6.22

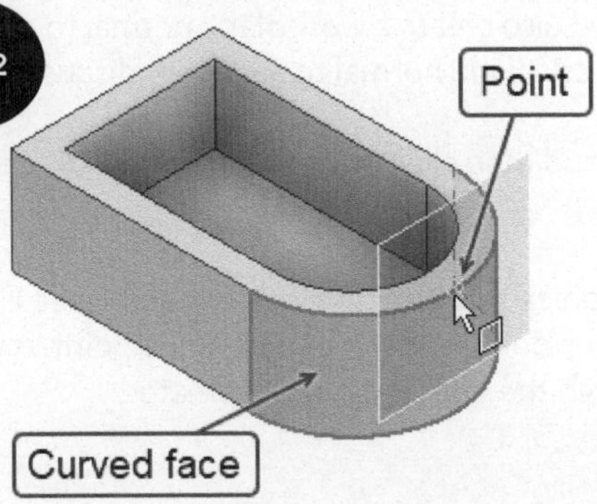

Creating a Work Plane Tangent to a Face and Parallel to a Plane

The method for creating a work plane tangent to a curved face and parallel to a plane or a planar face of a model is discussed below:

1. Invoke the **Plane** flyout and then click on the **Tangent to Surface and Parallel to Plane** tool. You are prompted to select a curved surface and a planar face.

2. Select a curved face and a planar face or a plane in the graphics area one by one, see Figure 6.23. A work plane tangent to the curved face and parallel to the selected planar face is created.

Creating a Work Plane Normal to an Axis Through a Point

The method for creating a work plane normal to an edge or an axis and passing through a point is discussed below:

1. Invoke the **Plane** flyout and then click on the **Normal to Axis through Point** tool. You are prompted to select an edge/axis or a point.

2. Select an edge or an axis in the graphics area and then select a point (an endpoint, a midpoint, or a work point), see Figure 6.24. A work plane normal (perpendicular) to the selected edge and passing through the selected point is created.

6.23

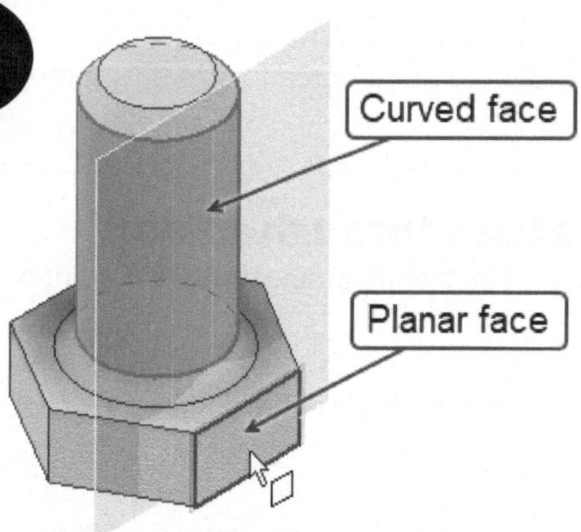

6.24

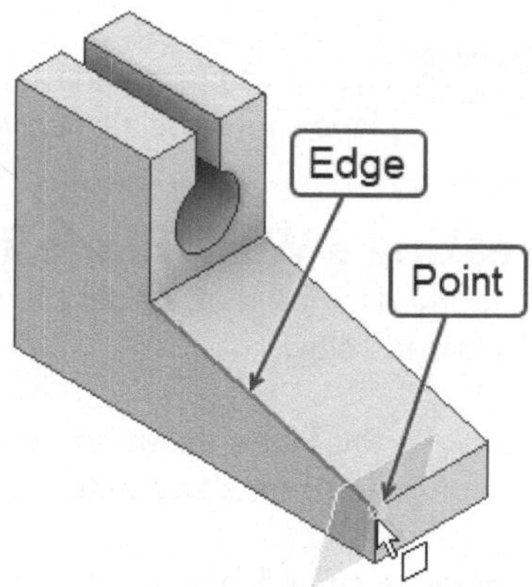

Creating a Work Plane Normal to a Curve

In Autodesk Inventor, you can also create a work plane normal to a curve and passing through a point. The method for creating a work plane normal to a curve is discussed below:

1. Invoke the **Plane** flyout and then click on the **Normal to Curve at Point** tool. You are prompted to select a curve or a point.

2. Select a curve in the graphics area and then select a point, see Figure 6.25. You can select a vertex, an edge midpoint, a sketch point, or a work point as the point. A work plane normal to the selected curve and passing through the selected point is created.

6.25

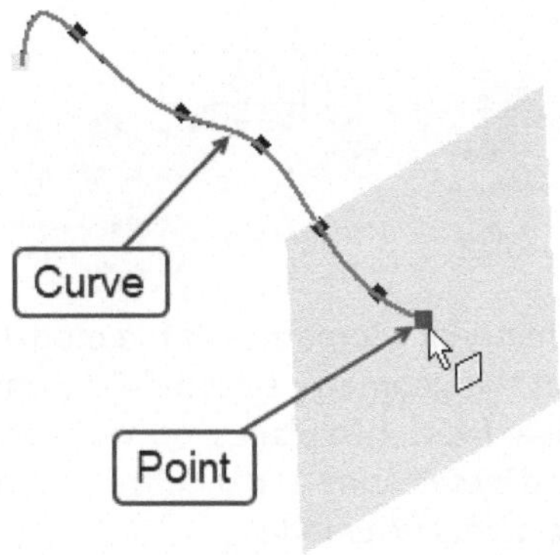

Creating Work Axes

Similar to creating a work plane, you can create a work axis. The work axis is used as the axis of revolution for creating features such as revolve and circular patterns. The tools for creating different types of work axes are available in the **Axis** flyout of the **Work Features** panel in the **3D Model** tab, see Figure 6.26. All these tools are discussed next.

6.26

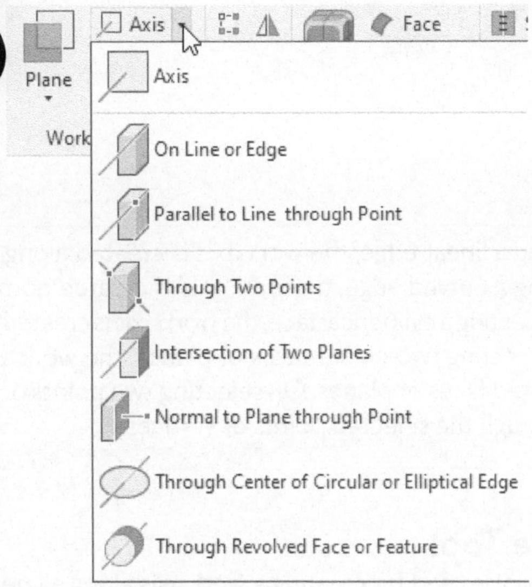

Axis Tool

The **Axis** tool is used for creating a work axis depending upon the type of geometry or geometries of a model selected. The method for creating a work axis by using the **Axis** tool is discussed below:

1. Click on the **Axis** tool in the **Work Features** panel of the **3D Model** tab, see Figure 6.27. You are prompted to select a geometry of the model.

6.27

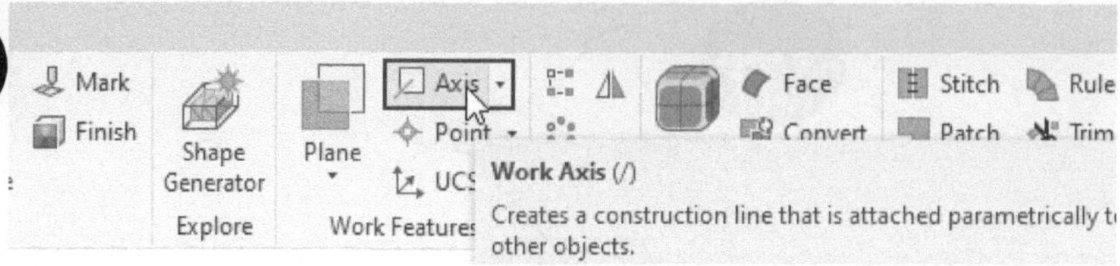

2. Select the required geometry or geometries of the model for creating a work axis. The work axis is created depending on the geometry selected. You can select an edge (linear or curved), a cylindrical face, two planar faces, two planes, or two points (vertices) as geometries. Figure 6.28 shows a work axis created by selecting a linear edge of a model and Figure 6.29 shows a work axis created by selecting two points of a model.

6.28

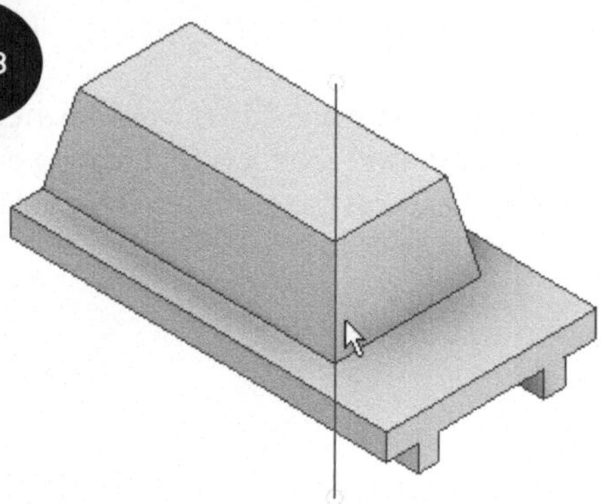

6.29

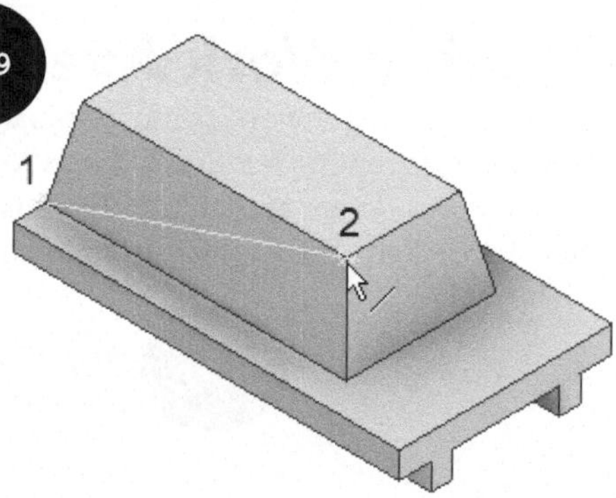

Note: On selecting a linear edge, the work axis is created along the selected edge of the model. On selecting a curved edge, the work axis is created normal to the center of the selected edge. On selecting a cylindrical face, the work axis is created along the center of the cylindrical face. On selecting two planar faces or planes, the work axis is created at the intersection of the selected faces or planes. On selecting two points or vertices, the work axis is created passing through the selected points or vertices.

On Line or Edge Tool

The **On Line or Edge** tool is used for creating a work axis along a linear edge of a model. The method for creating a work axis by using this tool is discussed below:

1. Invoke the **Axis** flyout in the **Work Features** panel and then click on the **On Line or Edge** tool, see Figure 6.30. You are prompted to select an edge or a line.

2. Click to select a linear edge or a line in the graphics area, see Figure 6.31. The work axis is created along the selected edge.

6.30

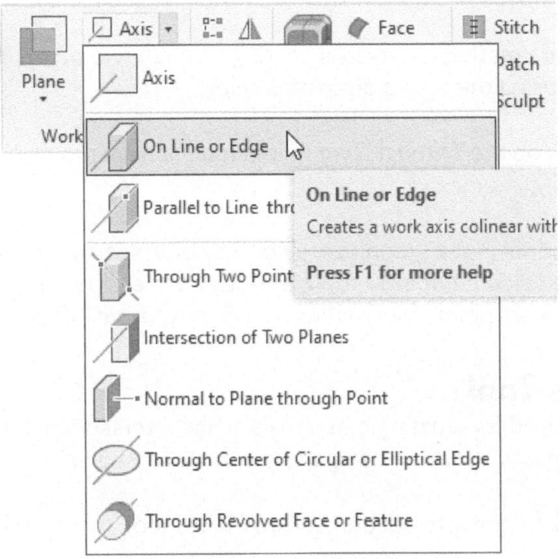

6.31

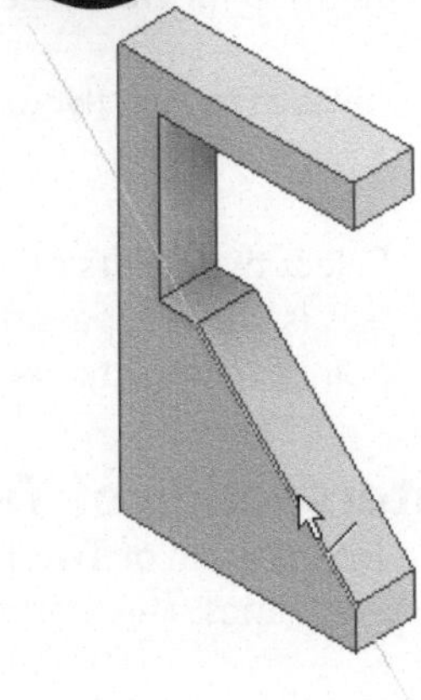

Parallel to Line through Point Tool

The **Parallel to Line through Point** tool is used for creating a work axis parallel to a linear edge and passing through a point. The method for creating a work axis by using this tool is discussed below:

1. Invoke the **Axis** flyout in the **Work Features** panel and then click on the **Parallel to Line through Point** tool. You are prompted to select an edge/axis or a point.

2. Select a linear edge and then select a point in the graphics area, see Figure 6.32. A work axis is created parallel to the selected edge and passes through the selected point.

6.32

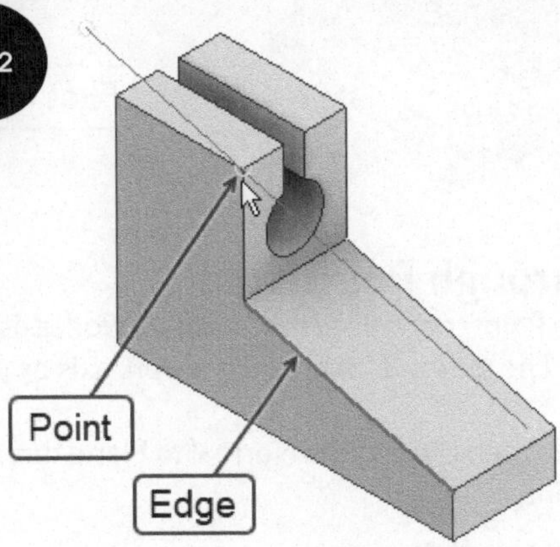

Through Two Points Tool

The **Through Two Points** tool is used for creating a work axis passing through two points or vertices. The method for creating a work axis by using this tool is discussed below:

1. Invoke the **Axis** flyout and then click on the **Through Two Points** tool. You are prompted to select a point.

2. Select two points or vertices of a model in the graphics area one by one, see Figure 6.33. A work axis is created, passing through the selected points. You can select two endpoints, intersection points, midpoints, sketch points, or work points for creating a work axis passing through them.

Intersection of Two Planes Tool

The **Intersection of Two Planes** tool is used for creating a work axis at the intersection of two planar faces or planes. The method for creating a work axis by using this tool is discussed below:

1. Invoke the **Axis** flyout and then click on the **Intersection of Two Planes** tool. You are prompted to select a plane.

2. Select two non-parallel faces of a model in the graphics area one by one, see Figure 6.34. A work axis is created at the intersection of the selected faces of the model.

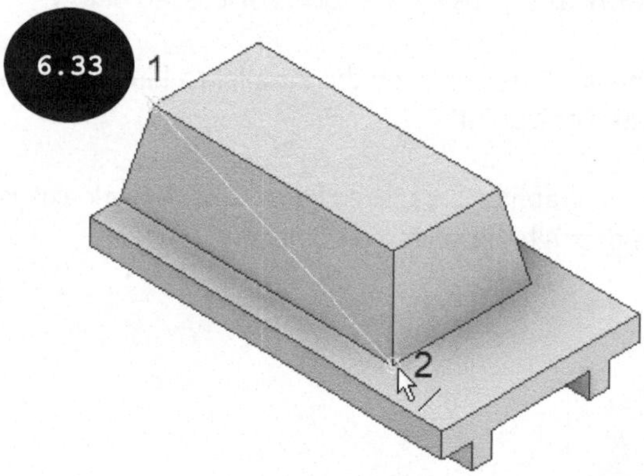

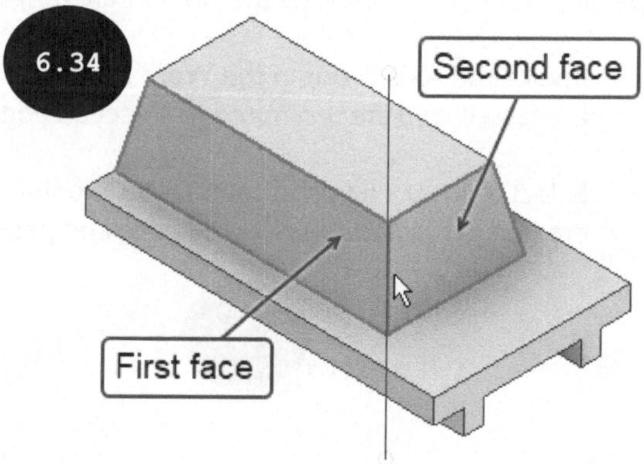

Normal to Plane through Point Tool

The **Normal to Plane through Point** tool is used for creating a work axis normal to a planar face or a plane and passing through a point. The method for creating a work axis by using this tool is discussed below:

1. Invoke the **Axis** flyout and then click on the **Normal to Plane through Point** tool. You are prompted to select a plane or a point.

2. Select a planar face of a model and then select a point or vertex in the graphics area, see Figure 6.35. A work axis is created normal to the selected face passing through the selected point in the graphics area.

6.35

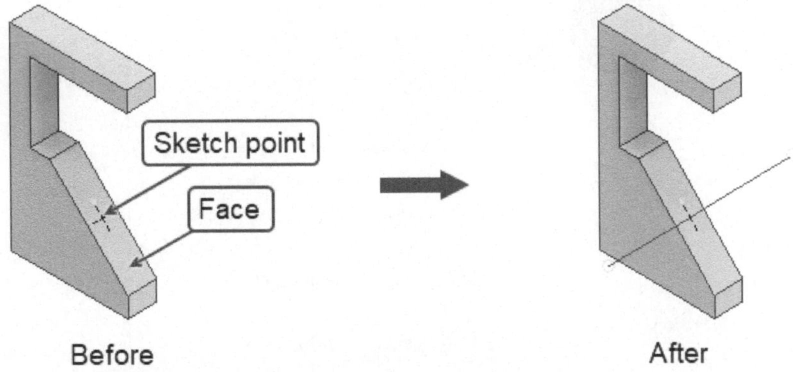

Through Center of Circular or Elliptical Edge Tool

The **Through Center of Circular or Elliptical Edge** tool is used for creating a work axis passing through the center of a circular or elliptical edge of a model. The method for creating a work axis by using this tool is discussed below:

6.36

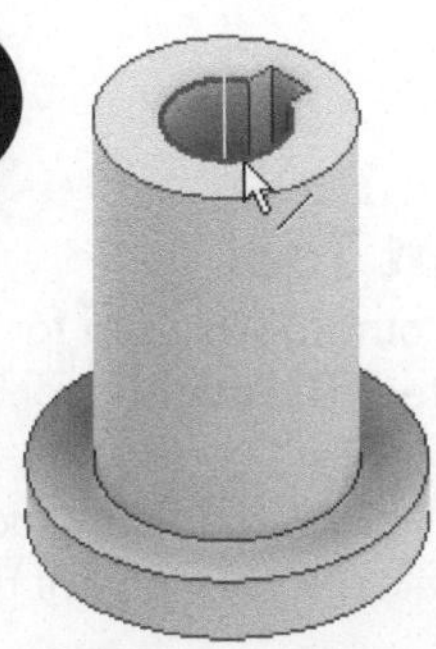

1. Invoke the **Axis** flyout and then click on the **Through Center of Circular or Elliptical Edge** tool. You are prompted to select a circular or elliptical edge.

2. Click to select a circular or elliptical edge of a model in the graphics area, see Figure 6.36. A work axis is created passing through the center of the selected circular or elliptical edge of the model.

Through Revolved Face or Feature Tool

The **Through Revolved Face or Feature** tool is used for creating a work axis passing through the center of a circular face or cylindrical feature of a model. The method for creating a work axis by using this tool is discussed below:

6.37

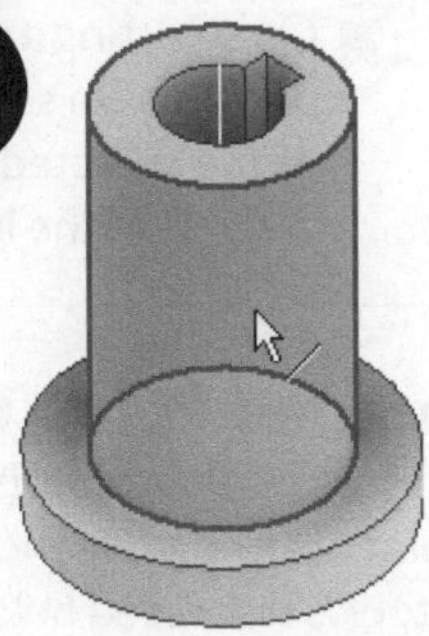

1. Invoke the **Axis** flyout and then click on the **Through Revolved Face or Feature** tool. You are prompted to select a cylindrical or a revolved surface.

2. Click to select a circular face of a model or a cylindrical feature in the graphics area, see Figure 6.37. A work axis is created by passing through the center of the selected circular face or cylindrical feature of the model.

Creating Work Points

A work point can be created anywhere in a 3D model and is used as a reference point for measuring distance, creating planes, and so on. The tools for creating different types of work points are available in the **Point** flyout of the **Work Features** panel in the **3D Model** tab, see Figure 6.38. All these tools are discussed below:

6.38

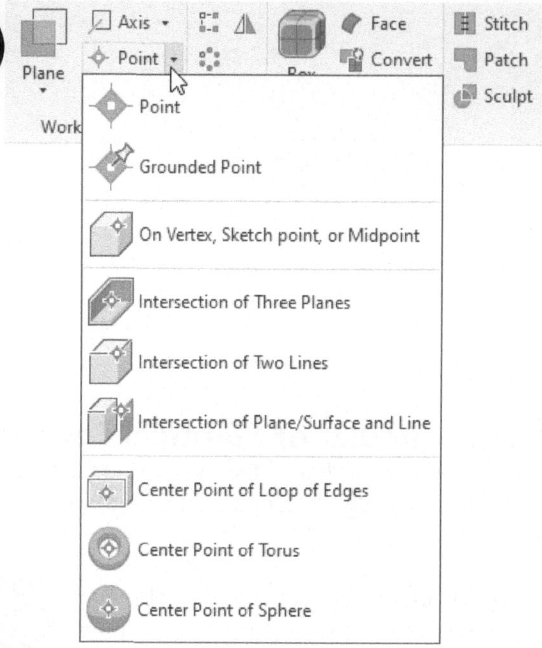

Point Tool

The **Point** tool is used for creating a work point depending upon the type of geometry of the model selected. The method for creating a work point by using the **Point** tool is discussed below:

1. Click on the **Point** tool in the **Work Features** panel of the **3D Model** tab. You are prompted to select a geometry of the model.

2. Select the required geometry of the model for creating a work point. A work point is created depending on the geometry selected. You can select a vertex, a point, two edges, or three non-parallel faces.

Note: On selecting a vertex or a point, the work point is created coincident to the selected vertex or point. On selecting two edges of the model, the work point is created at the intersection of the selected edges. On selecting three non-parallel faces or planes, the work point is created at the intersection of three selected faces or planes.

Grounded Point Tool

The **Grounded Point** tool is used for creating a grounded work point on a vertex or a point (endpoint or midpoint of an edge) in the graphics area. The method for creating a work point by using the **Grounded Point** tool is discussed below:

1. Invoke the **Point** flyout in the **Work Features** panel of the **3D Model** tab and then click on the **Grounded Point** tool. You are prompted to select a vertex or a point to define the initial position of the work point.

2. Click to select a vertex of a model or a point (endpoint or midpoint of an edge) in the graphics area. The 3D Move/Rotate handles appear in the graphics area on the selected geometry, see Figure 6.39. Also, the Mini-Toolbar appears in the graphics area with the display of the coordinates of the initial position of the work point.

6.39

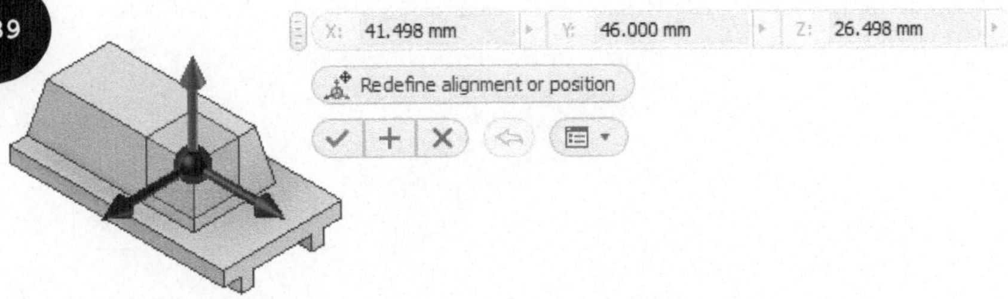

Note: You can redefine the alignment or the position of the work point by using the Mini-Toolbar. For doing so, click on the **Redefine alignment or position** button in the Mini-Toolbar and then enter the coordinates of the work point position in the respective X, Y, and Z fields of the Mini-Toolbar.

3. Drag the 3D Move/Rotate handles that appear in the graphics area to define the position of the work point.

4. After defining the position of the work point, click on the **OK** button (green tick-mark) in the Mini-Toolbar. A grounded point is created.

On Vertex, Sketch point, or Midpoint Tool

The **On Vertex, Sketch point, or Midpoint** tool is used for creating a work point on a vertex, a sketch point, or a point (endpoint or midpoint of an edge or a line). The method for creating a work point by using this tool is discussed below:

1. Invoke the **Point** flyout in the **Work Features** panel and then click on the **On Vertex, Sketch point, or Midpoint** tool. You are prompted to select a vertex, a point, or a midpoint.

2. Click to select a vertex, a sketch point, or a point (endpoint or midpoint of an edge or a line) in the graphics area. A work point is created on the selected geometry of the model.

Intersection of Three Planes Tool

The **Intersection of Three Planes** tool is used for creating a work point at the intersection of three planar faces or planes. The method for creating a work point by using this tool is discussed below:

1. Invoke the **Point** flyout in the **Work Features** panel and then click on the **Intersection of Three Planes** tool. You are prompted to select a plane.

2. Select three planes or planar faces of a model one by one in the graphics area, see Figure 6.40. A work point is created at the intersection of the selected faces.

6.40

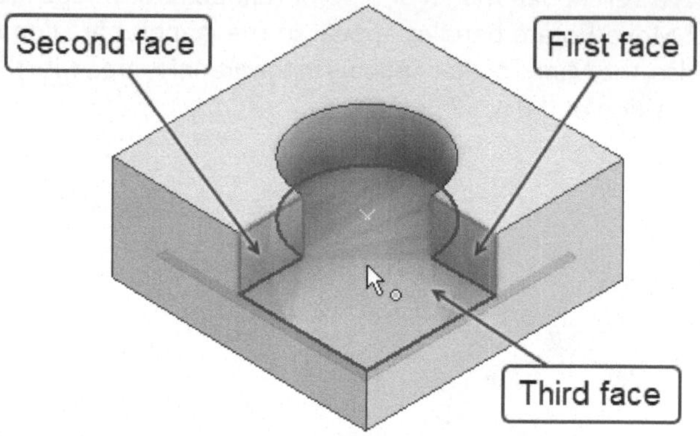

Intersection of Two Lines Tool

The **Intersection of Two Lines** tool is used for creating a work point at the intersection of two edges or lines. The method for creating a work point by using this tool is discussed below:

1. Invoke the **Point** flyout in the **Work Features** panel and then click on the **Intersection of Two Lines** tool. You are prompted to select a line.

2. Select two non-parallel linear edges, two sketch lines, or two axes one by one in the graphics area, see Figure 6.41. A work point is created at the intersection of selected edges.

6.41

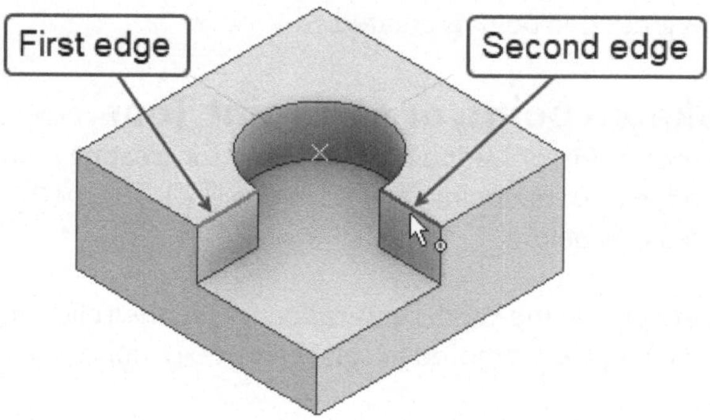

Intersection of Plane/Surface and Line Tool

The **Intersection of Plane/Surface and Line** tool is used for creating a work point at the intersection of a planar face and an edge or a line. The method for creating a work point by using this tool is discussed below:

1. Invoke the **Point** flyout in the **Work Features** panel and then click on the **Intersection of Planes/Surface and Line** tool. You are prompted to select a surface or a line.

2. Select a plane or a planar face of a model and then select an edge or a line in the graphics area one by one, see Figure 6.42. A work point is created at the intersection of the selected planar face and edge.

6.42

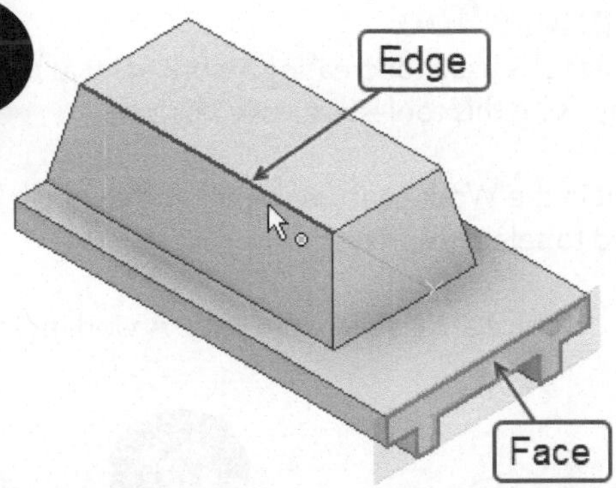

Center Point of Loop of Edges Tool

The **Center Point of Loop of Edges** tool is used for creating a work point at the center of a closed loop of model edges. The method for creating a work point by using this tool is discussed below:

1. Invoke the **Point** flyout in the **Work Features** panel and then click on the **Center Point of Loop of Edges** tool. You are prompted to select a loop of edges.

2. Ensure that the Loop Selection mode is activated. For doing so, right-click in the graphics area and then click on the **Loop Select** option in the Marking Menu that appears.

3. Move the cursor over a closed loop of model edges to be selected and then click when it gets highlighted in the graphics area, see Figure 6.43. A work point is created at the center of the selected closed loop of the model.

6.43

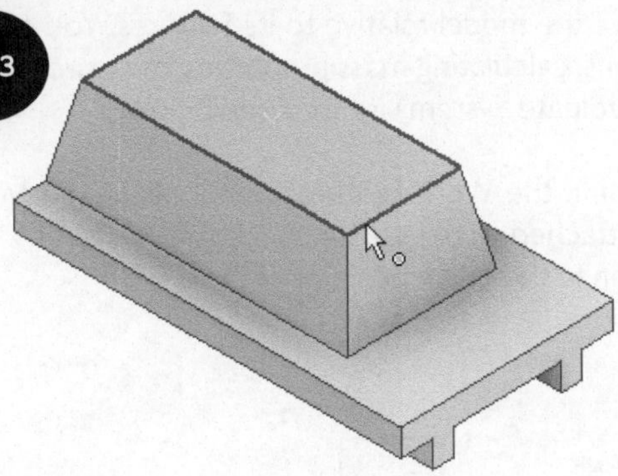

Center Point of Torus Tool

The **Center Point of Torus** tool is used for creating a work point at the center of a torus. The method for creating a work point by using this tool is discussed below:

1. Invoke the **Point** flyout in the **Work Features** panel and then click on the **Center Point of Torus** tool. You are prompted to select a torus.

2. Select a torus in the graphics area, see Figure 6.44. A work point is created at the center of the selected torus.

Center Point of Sphere Tool

The **Center Point of Sphere** tool is used for creating a work point at the center of a sphere. The method for creating a work point by using this tool is discussed below:

1. Invoke the **Point** flyout in the **Work Features** panel and then click on the **Center Point of Sphere** tool. You are prompted to select a sphere.

2. Select a sphere in the graphics area, see Figure 6.45. A work point is created at the center of the selected sphere.

6.44

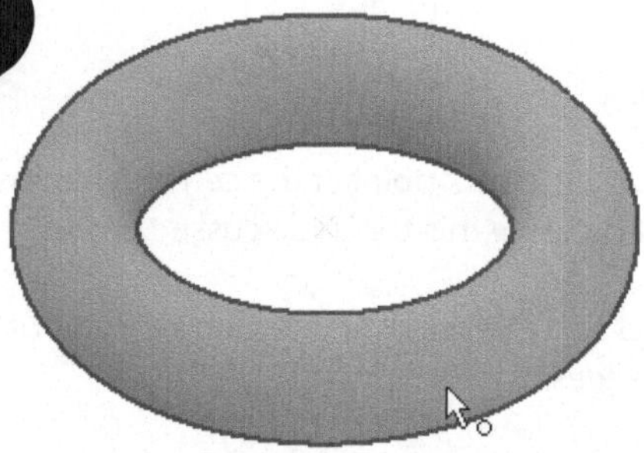

6.45

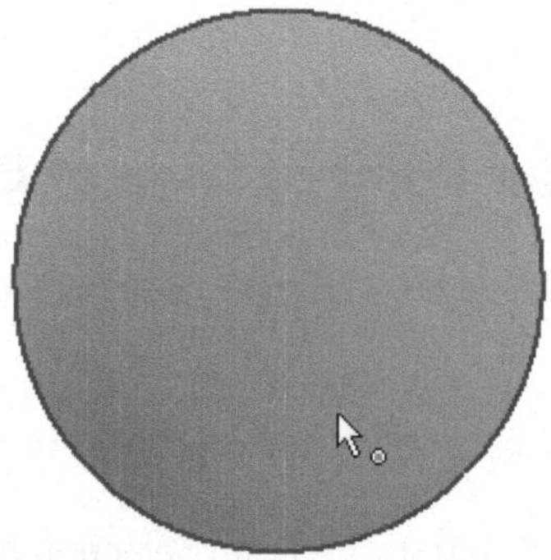

Creating a User Coordinate System

In Autodesk Inventor, you can also create a user coordinate system by using the **UCS** tool of the **Work Features** panel in the **3D Model** tab. UCS (User Coordinate System) is a collection of work features (three work planes, three axes, and a center point). It is mainly used in machining or analyzing a part for positioning the origin of the model relative to its features. You can also use the user coordinate system for applying relations, calculating mass properties, measurements, and so on. The method for creating a UCS (User Coordinate System) is discussed below:

1. Click on the **UCS** tool in the **Work Features** panel of the **3D Model** tab, see Figure 6.46. The preview of a UCS is attached to the cursor, see Figure 6.47. Also, you are prompted to specify a placement point to define the origin position of the UCS.

6.46

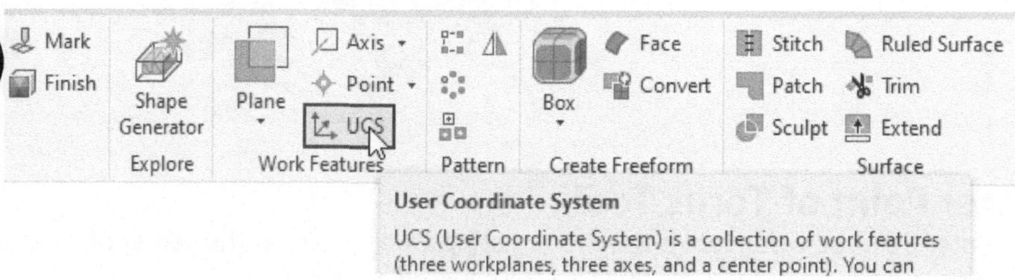

6.47

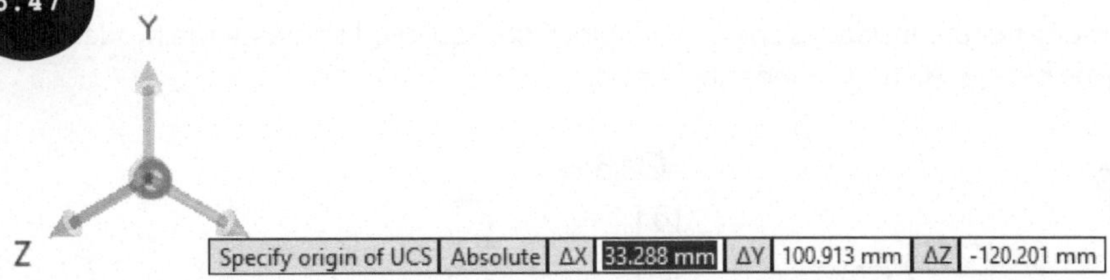

2. Click on a vertex or a work point in the graphics area to define the origin position of the UCS. The origin of the UCS is placed at the specified location, see Figure 6.48. Also, you are prompted to define the direction of the X axis of the UCS.

Tip: You can also click anywhere in the graphics area to define the position of the UCS. In addition, you can specify the coordinates in the respective fields that appear attached to the cursor to define the position of the UCS. After defining the position of the UCS anywhere in the graphics area, you can further change its position by translating or rotating the triad segments to the required position in the graphics area.

3. Select a point (midpoint or endpoint of an edge) to define the direction of the X axis of the UCS. You are prompted to define the direction of the Y axis.

4. Select a point (midpoint or endpoint of an edge) to define the direction of the Y axis. The resultant UCS is created, see Figure 6.49.

6.48

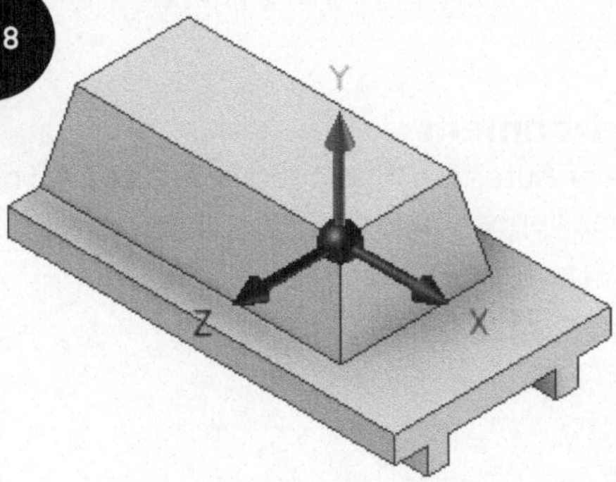

6.49

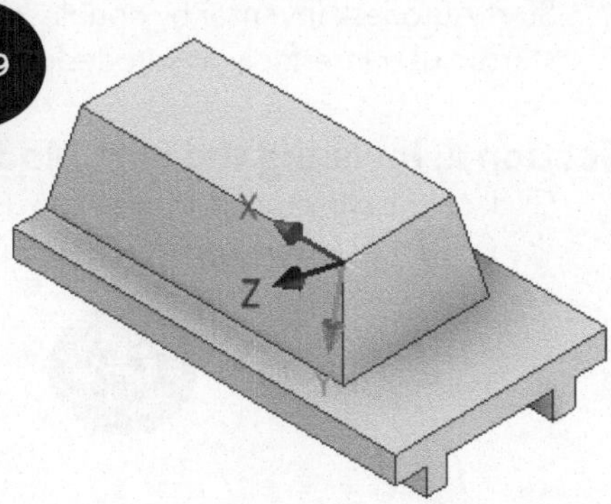

Tutorial 1

Create a multi-feature model, as shown in Figure 6.50. You need to create the model by creating all its features one by one. All dimensions are in mm.

6.50

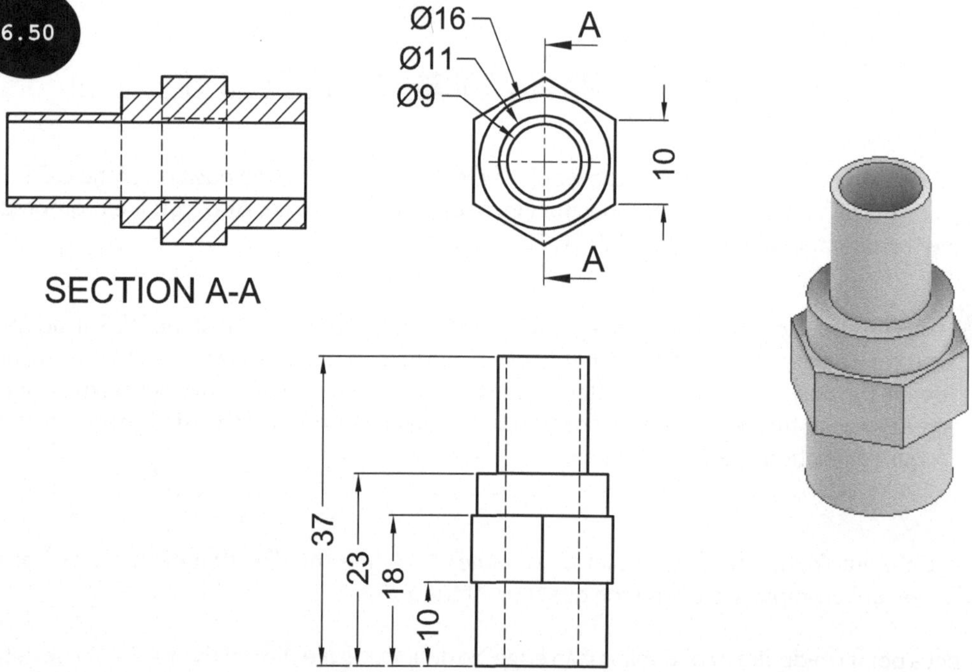

Section 1: Starting Autodesk Inventor

1. Start Autodesk Inventor by double-clicking on the Autodesk Inventor icon on your desktop. The startup user interface of Autodesk Inventor appears.

Section 2: Invoking the Part Modeling Environment

1. Click on the **New** tool in the startup user interface of Autodesk Inventor (see Figure 6.51) or press the CTRL + N keys. The **Create New File** dialog box appears, see Figure 6.52.

6.51

2. Select the Metric template folder on the left panel of the dialog box and then double-click on the **Standard (mm).ipt** template that appears on the right panel of the dialog box, refer to Figure 6.52. The Part Modeling environment is invoked.

6.52

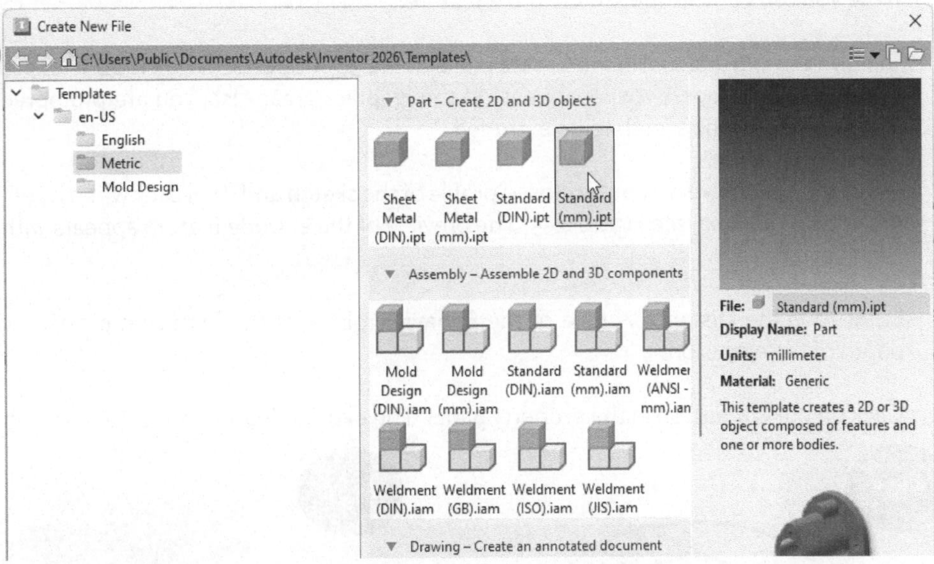

Section 3: Creating the Base Feature

Now, you need to invoke the Sketching environment to create the sketch of the base feature of the model.

1. Click on the **Start 2D Sketch** tool of the **Sketch** panel in the **3D Model** tab, see Figure 6.53. The three default planes: Front (XY Plane), Top (XZ Plane), and Right (YZ Plane), which are mutually perpendicular to each other appear in the graphics area. Also, you are prompted to select a plane for creating a sketch.

2. Select the Top plane (XZ Plane) as the sketching plane. The Sketching environment is invoked and the Top plane is oriented normal to the viewing direction.

3. Create two circles of diameters 9 mm and 16 mm as the sketch of the base feature and apply dimensions, see Figure 6.54. Ensure that the center points of both circles are at the origin.

6.53

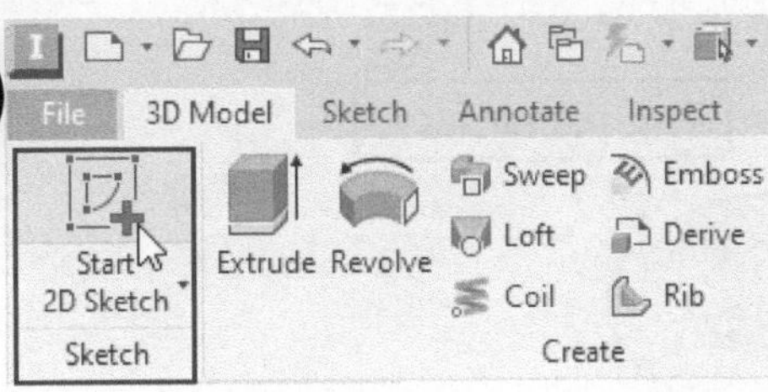

6.54

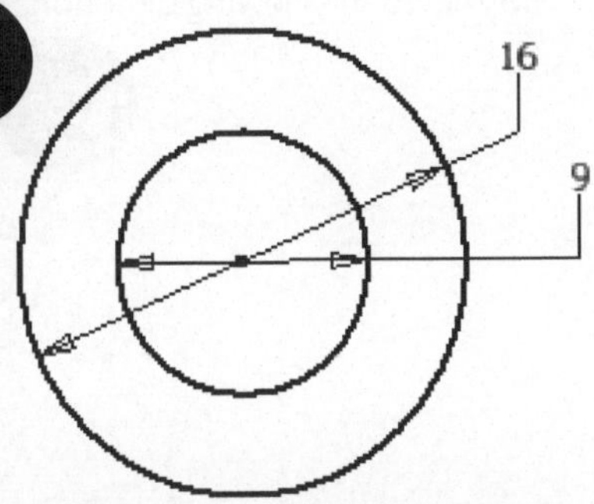

4. After creating the sketch of the base feature, exit the Sketching environment by clicking on the **Finish Sketch** tool in the **Exit** panel of the **Sketch** tab.

   Now, you can convert the sketch into a feature.

5. Click on the **Extrude** tool in the **Create** panel of the **3D Model** tab in the **Ribbon** or press the **E** key. The **Extrusion** property panel appears in the graphics area. Also, you are prompted to select a closed profile of the sketch to be extruded.

6. Move the cursor over the outer closed profile of the sketch and then click when it gets highlighted in the graphics area, see Figure 6.55. The preview of the extrude feature appears with the default depth of extrusion.

7. Enter **10** in the **Distance A** field of the **Behavior** rollout of the **Extrusion** property panel as the depth of the extrusion.

8. Click on the **OK** button in the property panel. The extrude feature is created, see Figure 6.56.

6.55

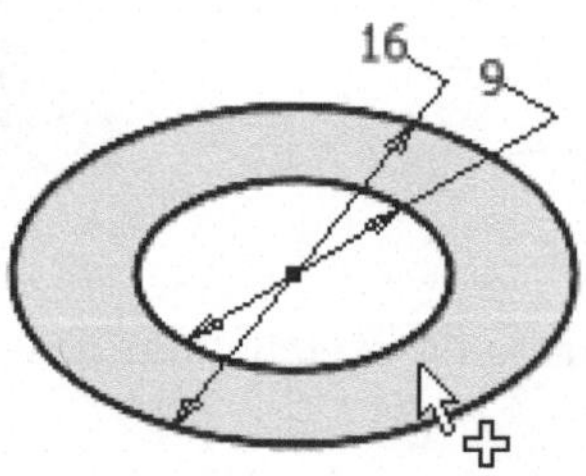

6.56

9. Click on the **Home** button in the ViewCube to change the view orientation to isometric.

Section 4: Creating the Second Feature

1. Click on the **Start 2D Sketch** tool in the **Sketch** panel in the **3D Model** tab or press the S key. You are prompted to select a plane for creating a sketch.

2. Click on the top planar face of the base feature to select it as the sketching plane, see Figure 6.57. The Sketching environment is invoked and the top planar face of the base feature gets orientated normal to the viewing direction.

6.57

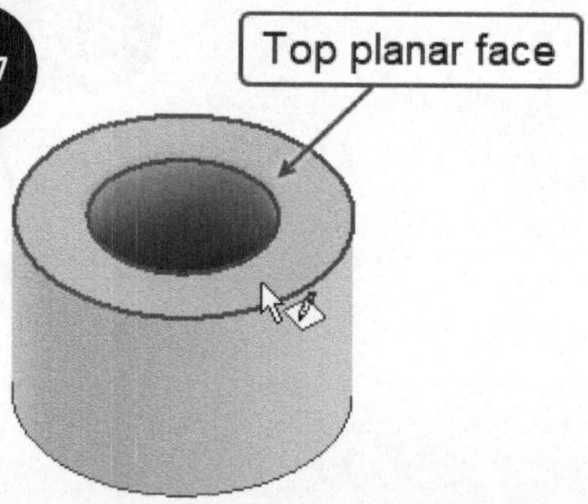

3. Create a polygon of 6 sides, measuring 10 mm each, and a circle of diameter 9 mm by using the **Polygon** and **Center Point Circle** tools as the sketch of the second feature, see Figure 6.58. Also, apply the required dimensions and constraints to make the sketch fully defined.

Tip: In addition to the required dimensions, you need to apply a vertical constraint to a vertical line of the polygon to make the sketch fully defined.

---

4. Click on the **3D Model** tab in the **Ribbon** to display the tools for creating features of a model.

5. Click on the **Extrude** tool in the **Create** panel of the **3D Model** tab or press the **E** key. The **Extrusion** property panel appears in the graphics area. Also, you are prompted to select a closed profile of the sketch to be extruded.

6. Move the cursor over the outer closed profile of the sketch and then click when it gets highlighted in the graphics area, see Figure 6.59. The preview of the extrude feature appears with the default depth of extrusion.

6.58

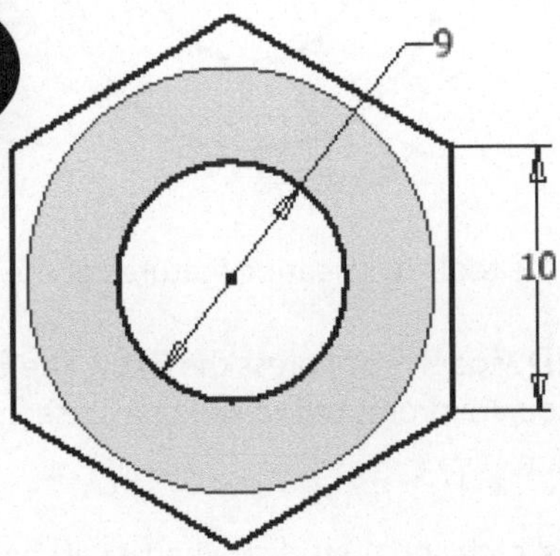

6.59

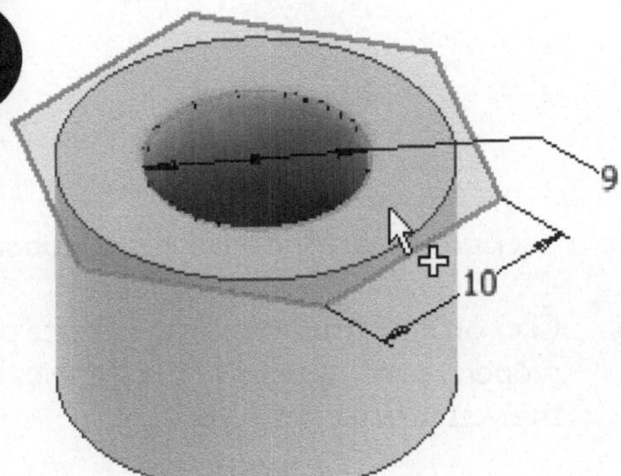

7. Enter **8** in the **Distance A** field of the **Behavior** rollout of the **Extrusion** property panel as the depth of the extrusion.

8. Click on the **OK** button in the property panel. The extrude feature is created, see Figure 6.60.

6.60

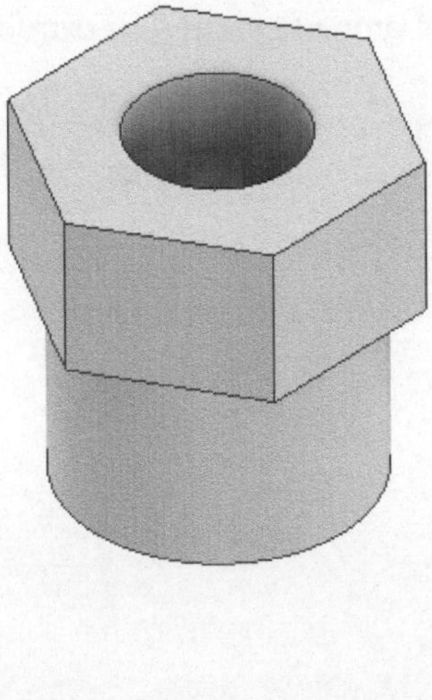

Section 5: Creating the Third Feature

1. Click on the **Start 2D Sketch** tool in the **Sketch** panel in the **3D Model** tab or press the S key. You are prompted to select a plane for creating a sketch.

2. Click on the top planar face of the second feature as the sketching plane, see Figure 6.61. The Sketching environment is invoked and the top planar face of the second feature gets orientated normal to the viewing direction.

3. Create the sketch of the third feature by creating two circles of diameter 9 mm and 16 mm and then apply dimensions, see Figure 6.62.

6.61

6.62

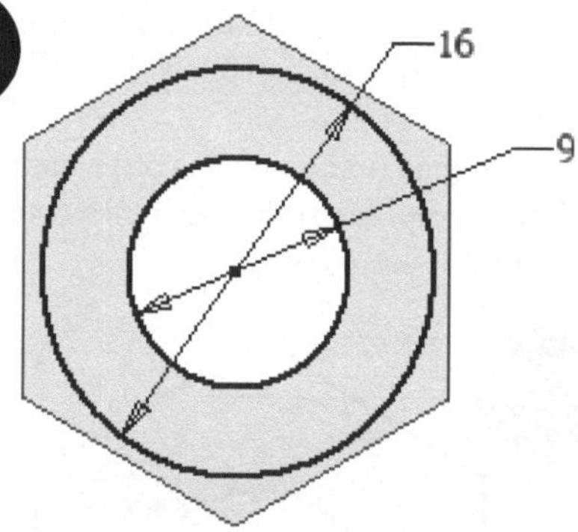

4. Click on the **3D Model** tab in the **Ribbon** to display the tools for creating features of the model.

5. Click on the **Extrude** tool in the **Create** panel of the **3D Model** tab or press the **E** key. The **Extrusion** property panel appears in the graphics area. Also, you are prompted to select a closed profile of the sketch to be extruded.

6. Move the cursor over the outer closed profile of the sketch and then click when it gets highlighted in the graphics area, see Figure 6.63. The preview of the extrude feature appears.

7. Enter **5** in the **Distance A** field of the **Behavior** rollout of the **Extrusion** property panel as the depth of the extrusion.

8. Click on the **OK** button in the property panel. The extrude feature is created, see Figure 6.64.

6.63

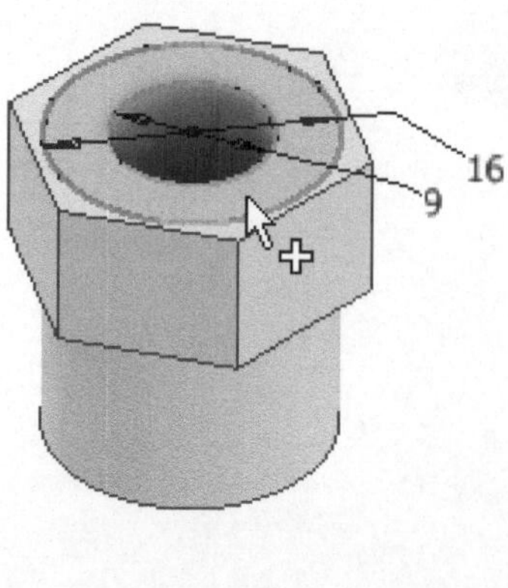

6.64

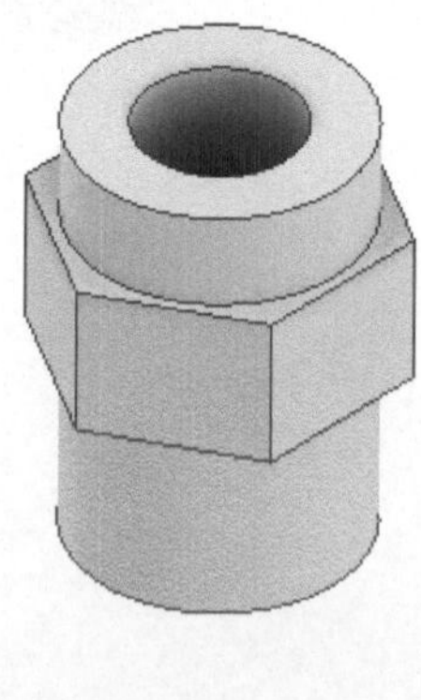

Section 6: Creating the Fourth Feature

1. Invoke the Sketching environment by selecting the top planar face of the third feature as the sketching plane, see Figure 6.65.

2. Create the sketch of the fourth feature by creating two circles of diameter 9 mm and 11 mm and then applying dimensions, see Figure 6.66.

6.65

6.66

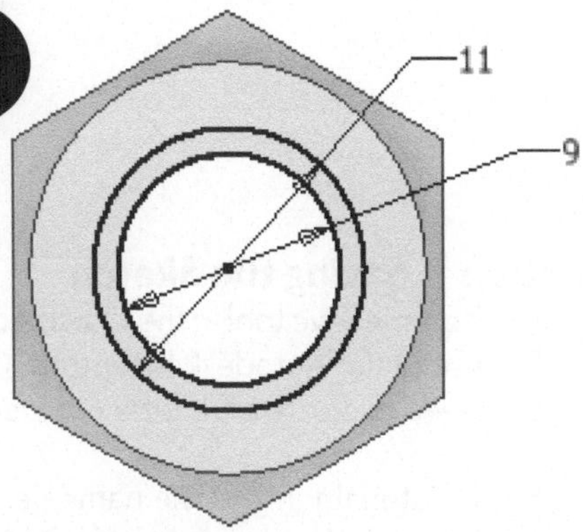

3. Click on the **3D Model** tab in the **Ribbon** to display the tools for creating features of a model.

4. Click on the **Extrude** tool in the **Create** panel of the **3D Model** tab or press the **E** key. The **Extrusion** property panel appears in the graphics area. Also, you are prompted to select a closed profile of the sketch to be extruded.

5. Move the cursor over the outer closed profile of the sketch and then click when it gets highlighted in the graphics area, see Figure 6.67. The preview of the extrude feature appears.

6.67

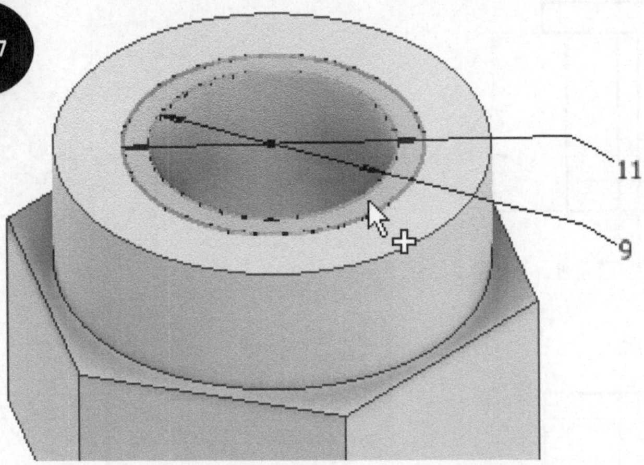

6. Enter **14** in the **Distance A** field of the **Behavior** rollout of the **Extrusion** property panel as the depth of the extrusion.

7. Click on the **OK** button in the property panel. The extrude feature is created, see Figure 6.68.

6.68

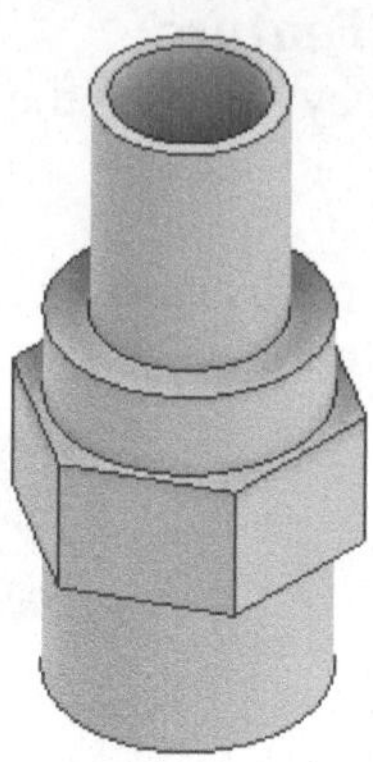

Section 7: Saving the Sketch

1. Click on the **Save** tool in the **Quick Access Toolbar** toolbar. The **Save As** dialog box appears. Next, browse to the **Autodesk Inventor > Chapter 6** folder in the local drive of your system. Note that you need to create a Chapter 6 folder inside the Autodesk Inventor folder, if not created earlier.

2. Enter **Tutorial 1** in the **File name** field of the dialog box and then click on the **Save** button. The model is saved at the specified location (>:\Autodesk Inventor\Chapter 6).

Tutorial 2

Create the model, as shown in Figure 6.69. All dimensions are in mm.

6.69

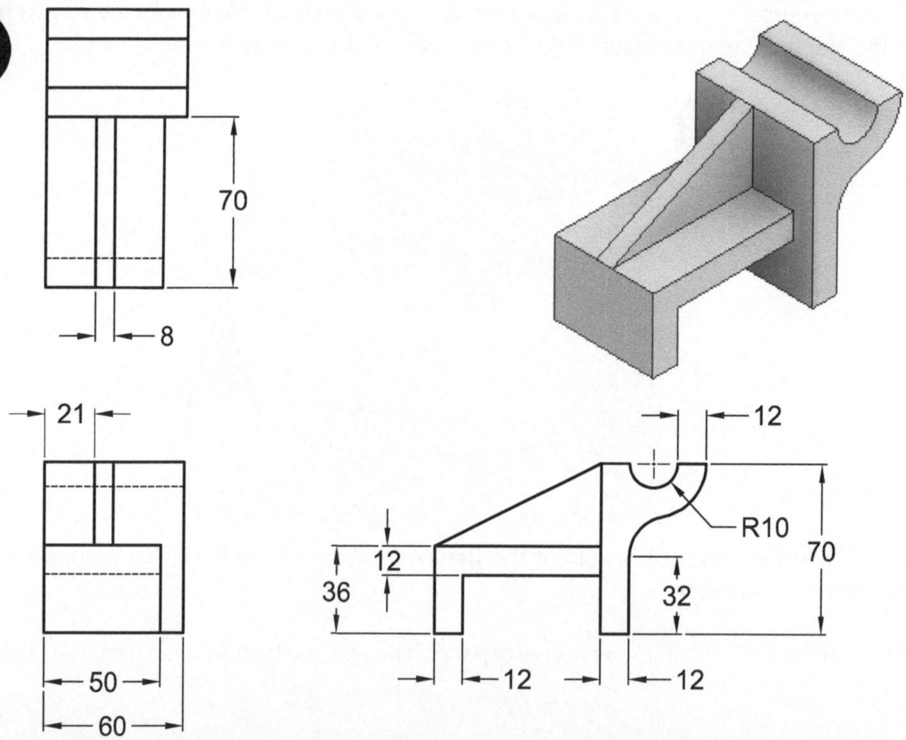

Section 1: Starting Autodesk Inventor

1. Start Autodesk Inventor by double-clicking on the Autodesk Inventor icon on your desktop. The startup user interface of Autodesk Inventor appears.

Section 2: Invoking the Part Modeling Environment

1. Click on the **New** tool in the startup user interface of Autodesk Inventor (see Figure 6.70) or press the CTRL + N key. The **Create New File** dialog box appears, see Figure 6.71.

6.70

2. Select the **Metric** template folder on the left panel of the dialog box and then double-click on the **Standard (mm).ipt** template that appears on the right panel of the dialog box, refer to Figure 6.71. The Part Modeling environment is invoked.

6.71

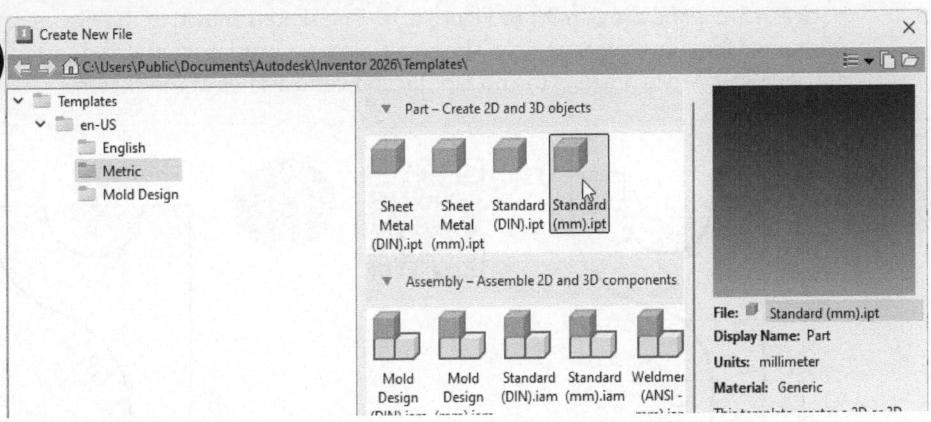

Section 3: Creating the Base Feature

Now, you need to invoke the Sketching environment to create the sketch of the base feature of the model.

1. Click on the **Start 2D Sketch** tool of the **Sketch** panel in the **3D Model** tab, see Figure 6.72. The three default planes: Front (XY Plane), Top (XZ Plane), and Right (YZ Plane), which are mutually perpendicular to each other appear in the graphics area. Also, you are prompted to select a plane for creating a sketch.

6.72

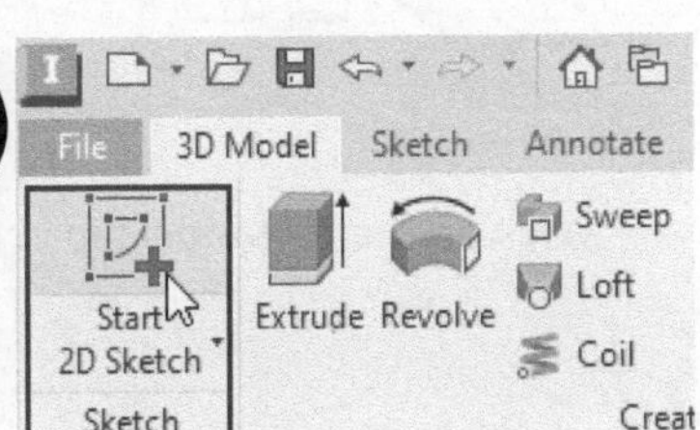

2. Select the Right plane (YZ Plane) as the sketching plane. The Sketching environment is invoked and the Right plane is oriented normal to the viewing direction.

3. Ensure that the direction of Y axis of the triad that appears at the lower left corner of the screen is upward and the direction of Z axis of the triad is toward the left, see Figure 6.73. You can change the direction of the Y and Z axes of the triad by using the rotational arrows of the ViewCube that appear on the upper right corner of the screen, see Figure 6.73. It helps to get the right orientation of the model.

6.73

Triad ViewCube

4. Create a sketch of the base feature and then apply the required constraints and dimensions to the sketch, see Figure 6.74.

Tip: To make the sketch fully defined, you need to apply a tangent constraint between line 2 and arc 3, arc 3 and arc 4 of the sketch, refer to Figure 6.75. Also, apply a concentric constraint between arc 4 and arc 6, refer to Figure 6.75. The sketch shown in the Figure 6.75 has been numbered for your reference only. The constraints such as horizontal and vertical are applied automatically while drawing the horizontal and vertical lines of the sketch.

6.74

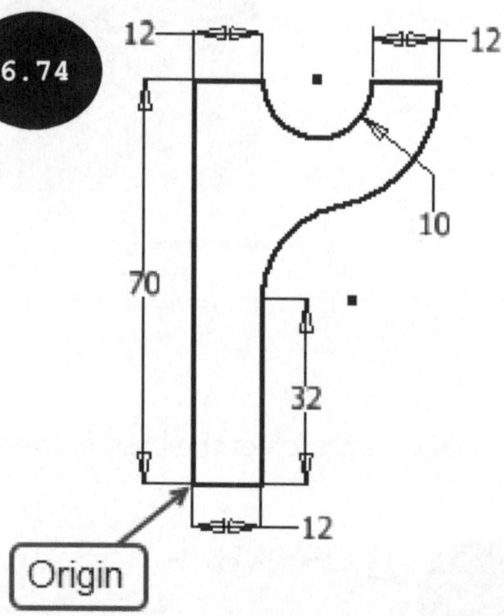

6.75

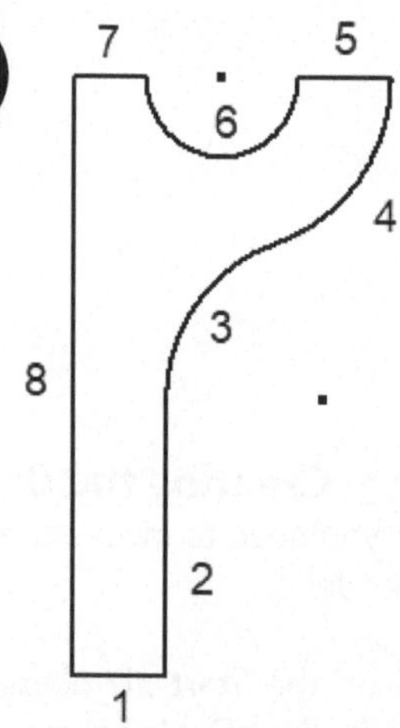

5. Click on the **3D Model** tab in the **Ribbon** to display the tools for creating features of a model.

6. Click on the **Extrude** tool in the **Create** panel of the **3D Model** tab or press the **E** key. The **Extrusion** property panel appears in the graphics area. Also, the preview of an extrude feature appears in the graphics area with a default depth of extrusion, since, the sketch contains only one closed profile.

7. Click on the **Symmetric** button in the **Direction** area of the **Behavior** rollout in the **Extrusion** property panel to extrude the sketch symmetrically on both sides of the sketching plane.

8. Enter **60** in the **Distance A** field of the **Behavior** rollout of the **Extrusion** property panel. The depth of extrusion is added symmetrically on both sides of the sketching plane, see Figure 6.76.

9. Click on the **OK** button in the property panel. The extrude feature is created, see Figure 6.77.

6.76

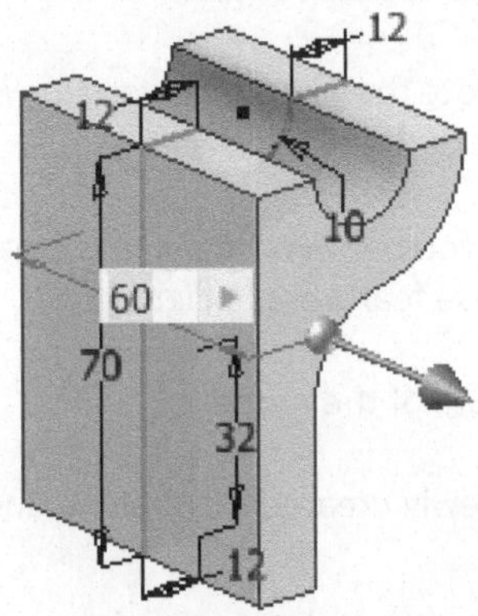

6.77

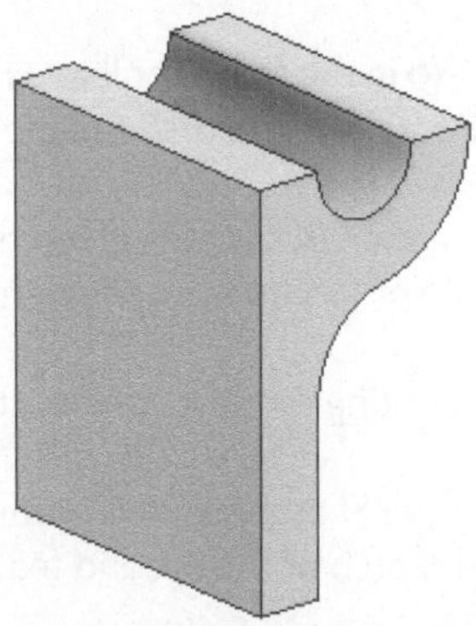

Section 4: Creating the Second Feature

To create the second feature of the model, you first need to create a work plane at an offset distance of 10 mm from the right planar face of the base feature.

1. Invoke the **Plane** flyout in the **Work Features** panel of the **3D Model** tab and then click on the **Offset from Plane** tool, see Figure 6.78. You are prompted to select a planar face or a plane.

6.78

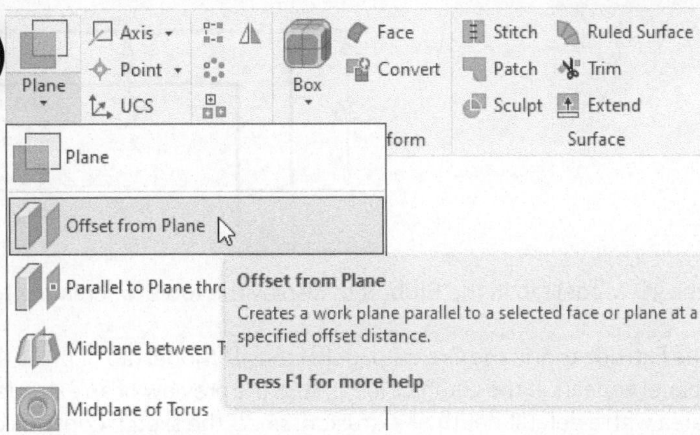

2. Select the right planar face of the base feature. The preview of an offset reference plane and the Mini-Toolbar appear in the graphics area, see Figure 6.79.

6.79

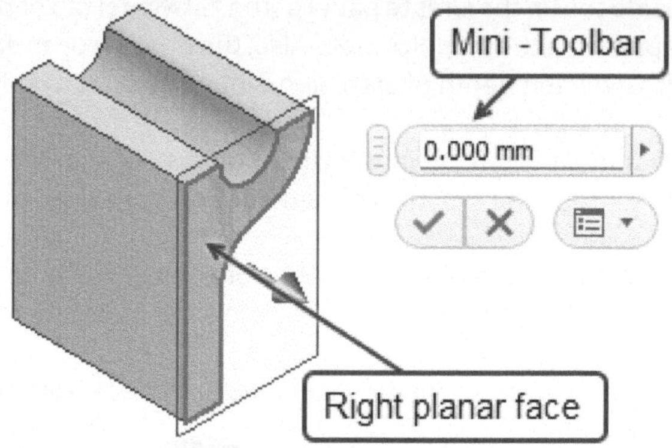

3. Enter **-10** in the Mini-Toolbar as the offset distance. Note that the negative value is entered to flip the direction of the offset plane toward the other side of the planar face.

4. Click on the **OK** button (green tick-mark) in the Mini-Toolbar. A work plane is created at an offset distance of 10 mm from the right planar face of the base feature, see Figure 6.80.

   After creating the work plane, create the second feature of the model.

5. Invoke the Sketching environment by selecting the newly created work plane and then create a closed sketch of the second feature, see Figure 6.81.

6.80

6.81

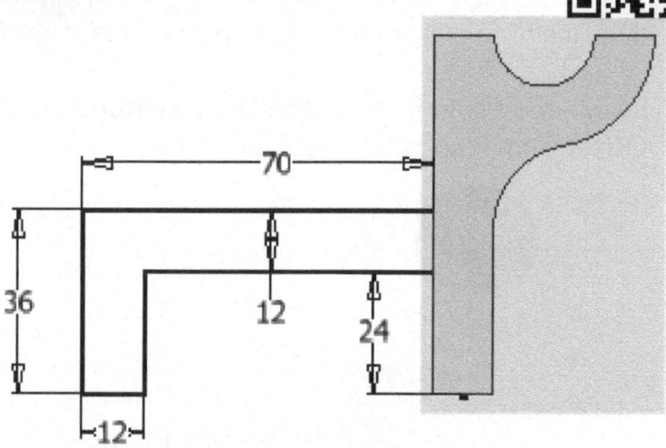

6. Click on the **3D Model** tab in the **Ribbon** to display the tools for creating features of a model.

7. Click on the **Extrude** tool in the **Create** panel of the **3D Model** tab or press the **E** key. The **Extrusion** property panel appears in the graphics area. Also, the preview of an extrude feature appears in the graphics area with a default depth of extrusion, since, the sketch contains only one closed profile.

8. Click on the **Flipped** button in the **Direction** area of the **Behavior** rollout in the **Extrusion** property panel to reverse the direction of extrusion to the back side of the sketching plane, see Figure 6.82.

9. Enter **50** in the **Distance A** field of the **Behavior** rollout of the **Extrusion** property panel.

10. Click on the **OK** button in the property panel. The extrude feature is created, see Figure 6.83.

6.82

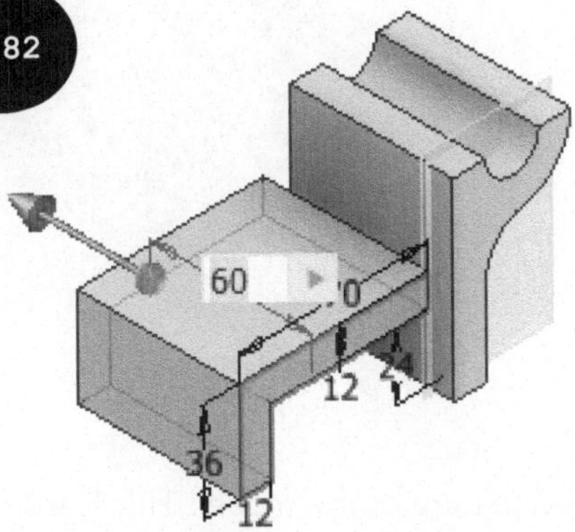

6.83

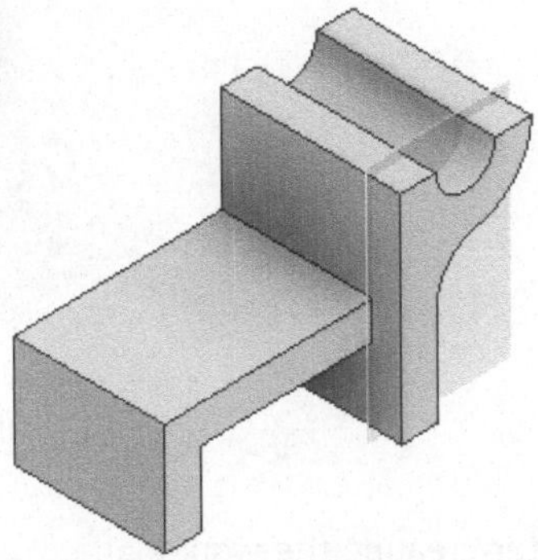

Section 5: Creating the Third Feature

To create the third feature of the model, you need to create a work plane in the middle of the second feature.

1. Invoke the **Plane** flyout in the **Work Features** panel of the **3D Model** tab and then click on the **Midplane between Two Planes** tool, see Figure 6.84. You are prompted to select a planar face or a plane.

6.84

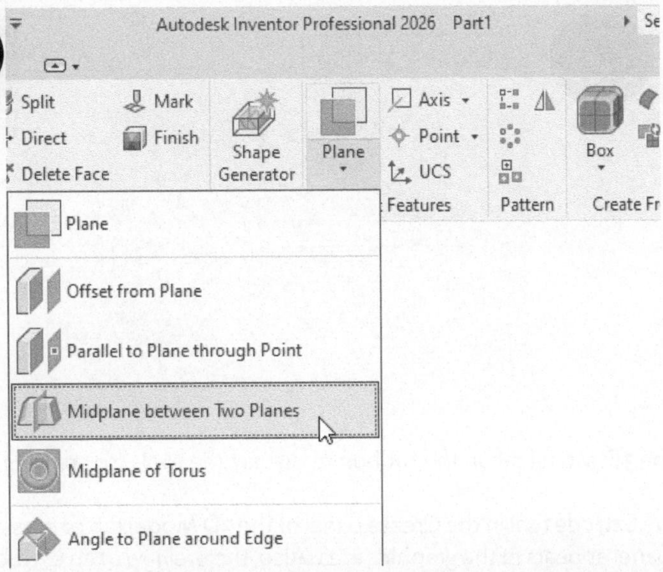

2. Select the right and left planar faces of the second feature one by one in the graphics area, see Figure 6.85. A work plane is created in the middle of the selected faces of the second feature, see Figure 6.86.

6.85

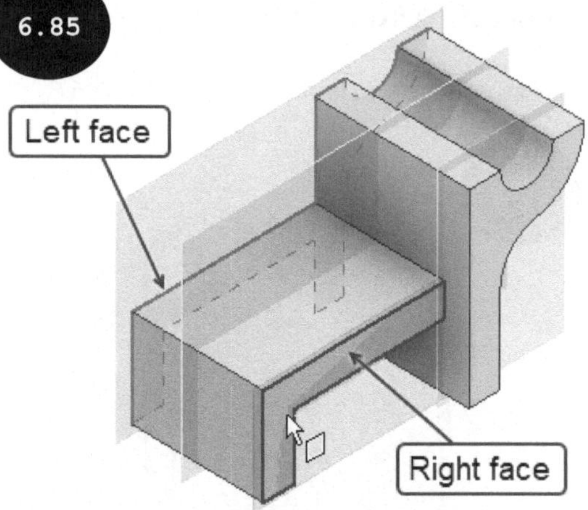

6.86

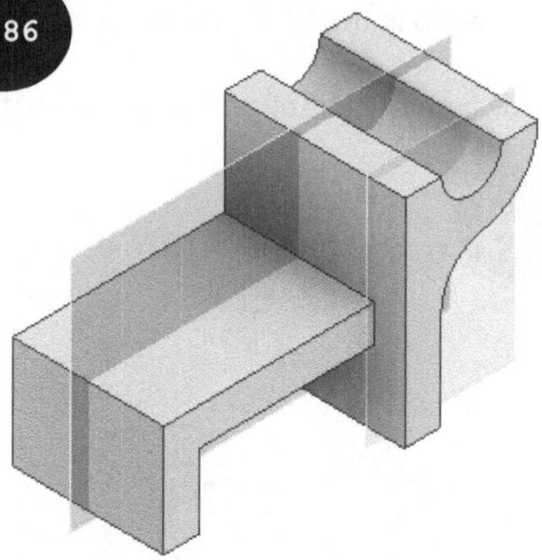

After creating the work plane, you can create the third feature of the model. This feature can be created easily by using the **Rib** tool. You will learn about the **Rib** tool in later chapters. In this tutorial, you will create this feature by using the **Extrude** tool.

3. Invoke the Sketching environment by selecting the newly created work plane that is created in the middle of the second feature.

4. Create a closed sketch of the third feature (three line entities), see Figure 6.87. The entities of the sketch shown in Figure 6.87, have been created by taking reference of the vertices of the existing features of the model.

6.87

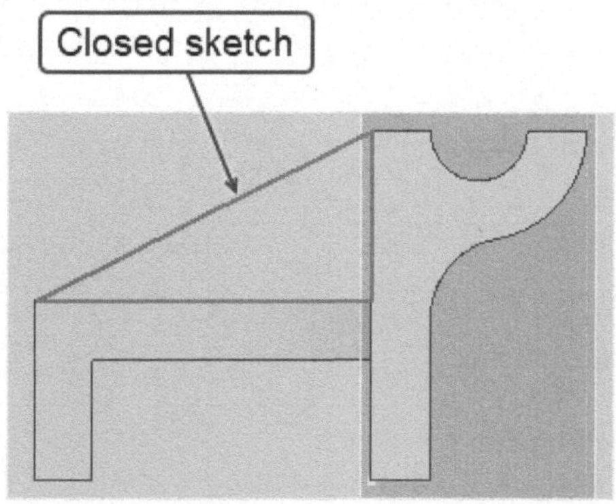

5. Click on the **3D Model** tab in the **Ribbon** to display the tools for creating features of a model.

6. Click on the **Extrude** tool in the **Create** panel of the **3D Model** tab or press the **E** key. The **Extrusion** property panel appears in the graphics area. Also, the preview of an extrude feature appears in the graphics area with a default depth of extrusion, since the sketch contains only one closed profile.

7. Click on the **Symmetric** button in the **Direction** area of the **Behavior** rollout in the **Extrusion** property panel to extrude the sketch symmetrically on both sides of the sketching plane, see Figure 6.88.

8. Enter **8** in the **Distance A** field of the **Behavior** rollout of the **Extrusion** property panel. The depth of extrusion is added symmetrically on both sides of the sketching plane.

9. Click on the **OK** button in the property panel. The extrude feature is created, see Figure 6.89.

6.88

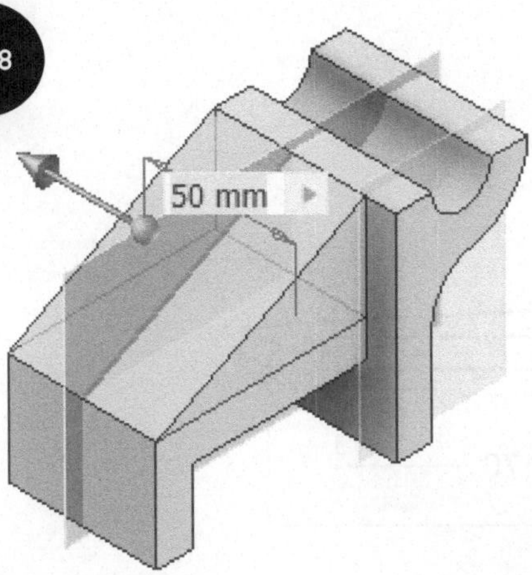

6.89

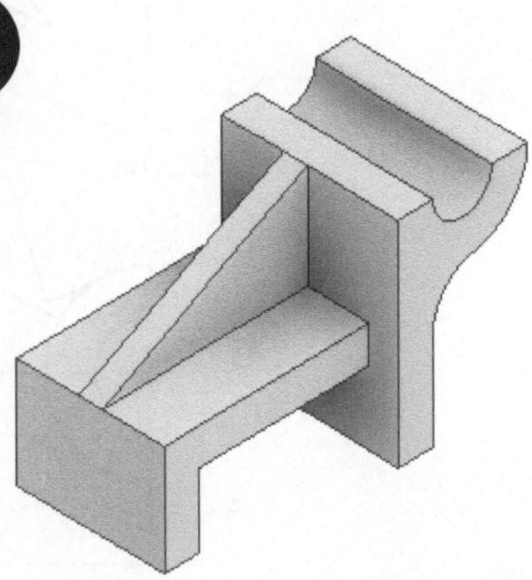

Note: In Figure 6.89, the visibility of the work planes is turned off. To turn off the visibility of a work plane in the graphics area, right-click on the work plane in the **Browser** that appears on the left side of the screen and then click on the **Visibility** option in the shortcut menu that appears. The visibility of the selected work plane gets turned off. Note that a tick-mark on the **Visibility** option in the shortcut menu indicates that the selected work plane is visible in the graphics area.

Section 6: Saving the Sketch

1. Click on the **Save** tool in the **Quick Access Toolbar** toolbar. The **Save As** dialog box appears. Next, browse to the **Autodesk Inventor > Chapter 6** folder in the local drive of your system. Note that you need to a create Chapter 6 folder inside the Autodesk Inventor folder, if not created earlier.

2. Enter **Tutorial 2** in the **File name** field of the dialog box and then click on the **Save** button. The model is saved in the specified location (>:\Autodesk Inventor\Chapter 6).

Hands-on Test Drive 1

Create a model, as shown in Figure 6.90. All dimensions are in mm.

6.90

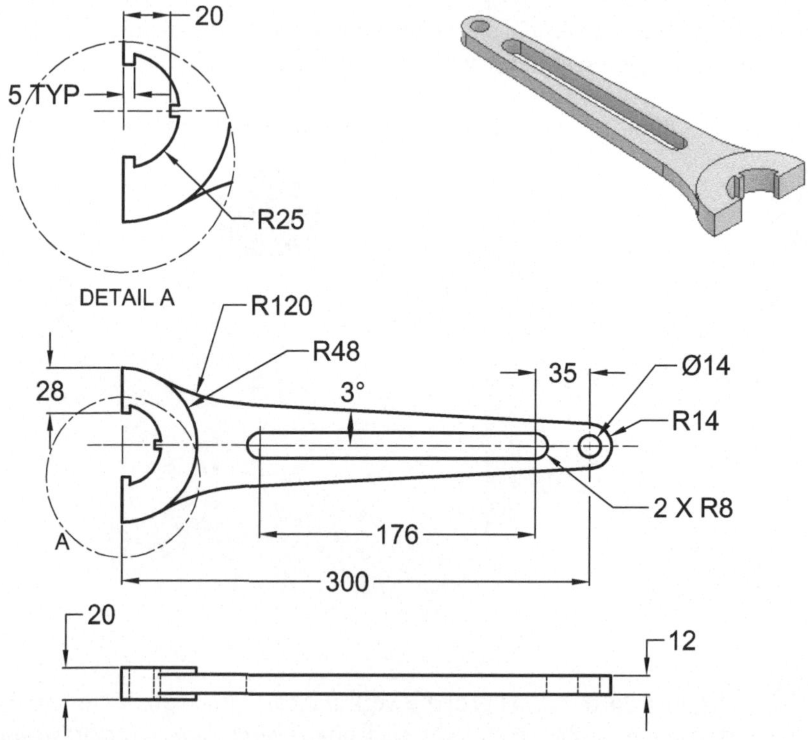

Hands-on Test Drive 2

Create a model, as shown in Figure 6.91. All dimensions are in mm.

6.91

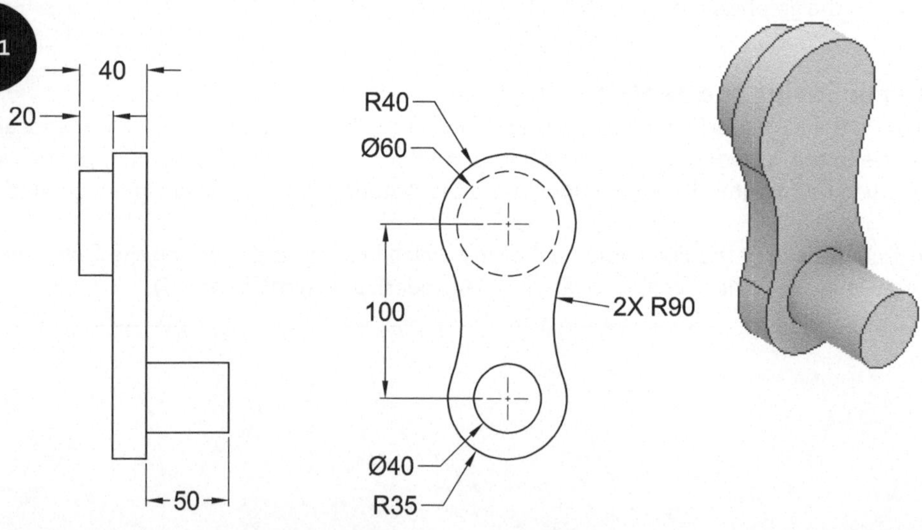

Hands-on Test Drive 3

Create a model, as shown in Figure 6.92. All dimensions are in mm.

6.92

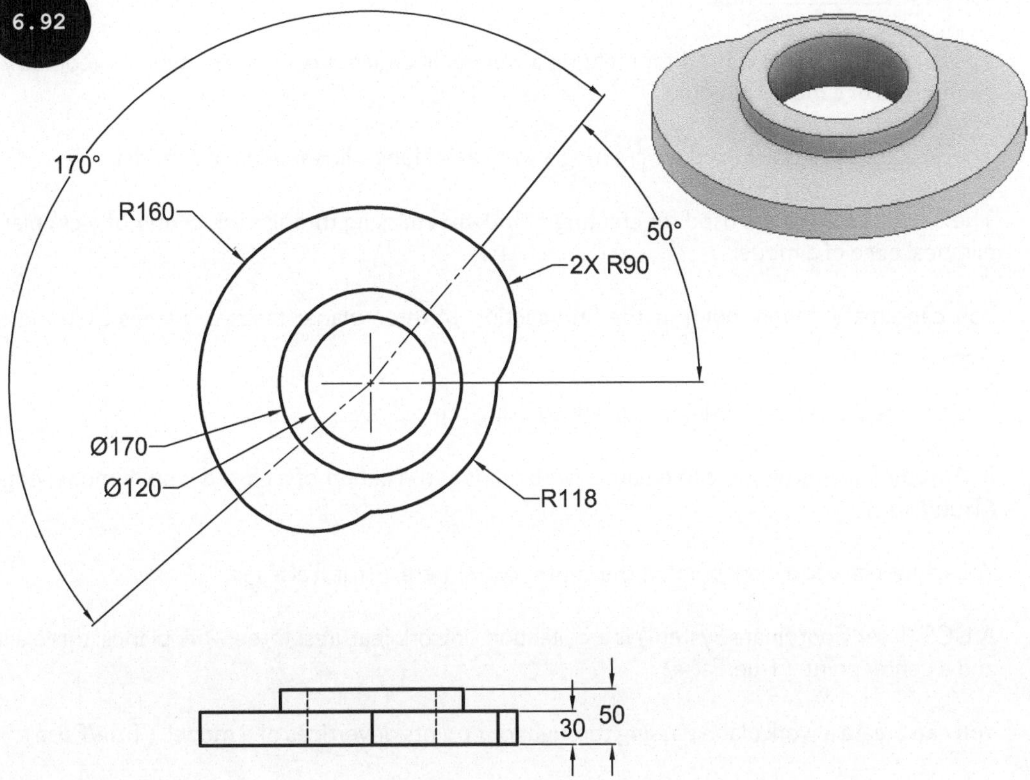

Summary

In this chapter, you have learned about the three default planes: Front, Top, and Right. These three default planes may not be enough for creating models having multiple features. Therefore, you need to create additional work planes. The chapter discussed in detail how to create additional work planes, work axes, work points, and coordinate systems.

Questions

Complete and verify the following sentences:

- The _________ tool is used for creating a work plane at an offset distance from an existing plane or a planar face.
- The _________ tool is used for creating a work plane in the middle of two planar faces or planes.

- The _________ tool is used for creating a work plane at an angle to a face around an edge of a model.
- In Autodesk Inventor, you can create a work plane normal to a curve and pass through a point by using the _________ tool.
- The _________ tool is used for creating a work axis depending upon the type of geometry or geometries of a model selected.
- The _________ tool is used for creating a work axis along a linear edge of a model.
- The _________ tool is used for creating a work axis passing through the center of a circular or elliptical edge of a model.
- You can create a work point at the intersection of three planar faces or planes by using the _________ tool.
- You can create a user coordinate system by using the _________ tool.
- In Autodesk Inventor, you can create a work point at the center of a closed loop of model edges. (True/False)
- You cannot create a work point at the center of a sphere. (True/False)
- A UCS (User Coordinate System) is a collection of work features: three work planes, three axes, and a center point. (True/False)
- You can create a work plane passing through four points or vertices of a model. (True/False)
- You cannot select a planar face of an existing feature of a model as the sketching plane. (True/False)

CHAPTER

7

Advanced Modeling - I

In this chapter, the following topics will be discussed:

- Using Advanced Options of the **Extrude** Tool
- Using Advanced Options of the **Revolve** Tool
- Working with a Sketch having Multiple Profiles
- Projecting Geometries
- Creating a Section View
- Editing a Feature and its Sketch
- Displaying Earlier State of a Model
- Re-ordering Features of a Model
- Measuring the Distance between Entities
- Assigning an Appearance
- Applying a Material
- Assigning Finishes/Manufacturing Data
- Calculating Physical Properties

In the previous chapters, you have learned how to create base features by using the **Extrude** and **Revolve** tools. In this chapter, you will learn how to use the advanced options of the **Extrude** and **Revolve** tools, which include defining start and end conditions for extrusion and creating features by removing material from a model. Besides, you will learn how to work with a sketch having multiple profiles, project geometries of a model, create section views, measure the distance between entities of a model, apply a material, calculate the physical properties of a model, and so on.

Using Advanced Options of the Extrude Tool

As discussed earlier, while extruding a sketch by using the **Extrude** tool, the **Extrusion** property panel appears, see Figure 7.1. Some of the options of this property panel have been discussed earlier while creating the base feature of a model. The remaining options are discussed below:

7.1

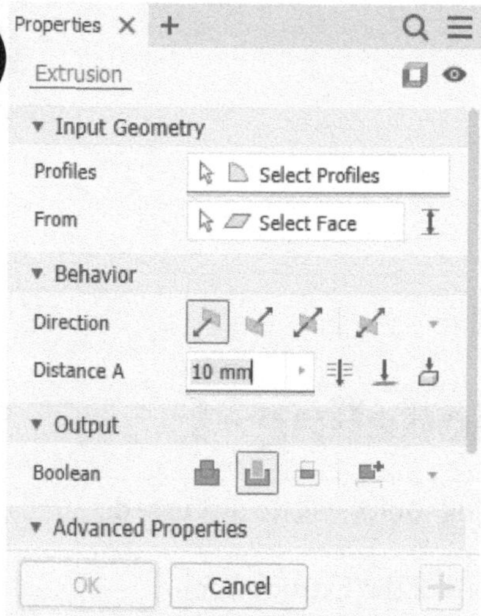

Input Geometry

The **Profiles** selector and the **From** selector of the **Input Geometry** rollout in the property panel are used for defining profiles of a sketch to be extruded and a start condition for the feature, respectively. Both these options have been discussed earlier while creating a base feature of a model. However, in this chapter, you will learn more about defining the start condition for a feature by using the **From** selector, which is discussed next.

From

When you extrude a sketch, the extrusion starts exactly from the sketching plane of the sketch, by default. However, you can select a plane or a face of an existing feature of a model to define the start condition for a feature, see Figures 7.2 and 7.3. For doing so, click on the **From** selector to activate its selection mode and then select a plane or a face of an existing feature as the start condition. The extrusion starts from the selected plane or face of the model. Figure 7.2 shows a sketch (circle) to be extruded and a face to be selected as the start condition of extrusion. Figure 7.3 shows the preview of the resultant extrude feature after selecting the face as the start condition.

7.2

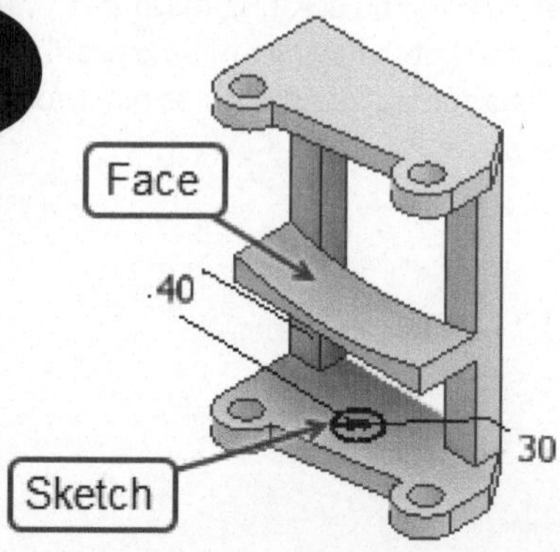

7.3

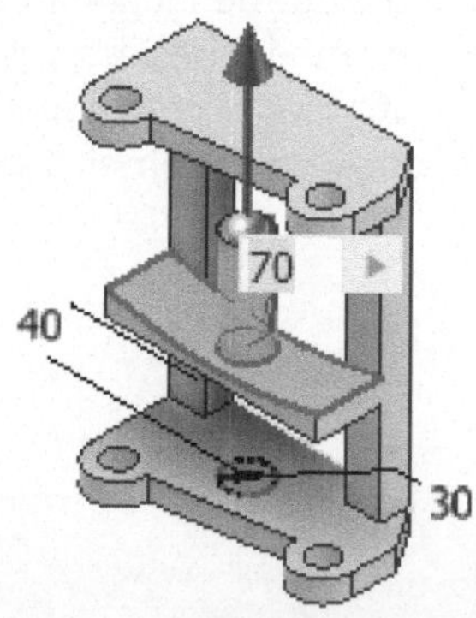

Note: On selecting a plane or a face as the start condition of an extrusion, the **Extend face to start feature** and **Alternate Solution** buttons become available next to the **From** selector in the **Input Geometry** rollout of the property panel. By default, the **Extend face to start feature** button is activated. As a result, even if the sketch profile to be extruded does not completely get projected or encapsulated onto the face that is selected as the start condition, the extrusion starts exactly from the selected face. This is because, the selected face of the model gets extended imaginarily such that it intersects the extrusion.

If you have selected a curved face as the start condition of an extrusion, then on clicking the **Alternate Solution** button, you can toggle the extrusion start condition from the nearest intersection to the farthest intersection with the selected curved face or vice-versa.

Between

The **Between** button is used for defining the start and end condition of extrusion between two selected faces, refer to Figure 7.4. For doing so, click on the **Between** button available next to the **From** selector in the **Input Geometry** rollout of the property panel. The **From** and **To** selection options become available in the **Input Geometry** and **Behavior** rollouts, respectively. By default, the **From** selection option is activated for defining the start condition of the extrusion. After selecting a face or a plane to define the start condition, the **To** selection option gets activated, automatically. Select a plane or a face to define the end condition of the extrusion in the graphics area. A preview of the extrude feature appears in between the selected start and end faces, see Figure 7.4.

7.4

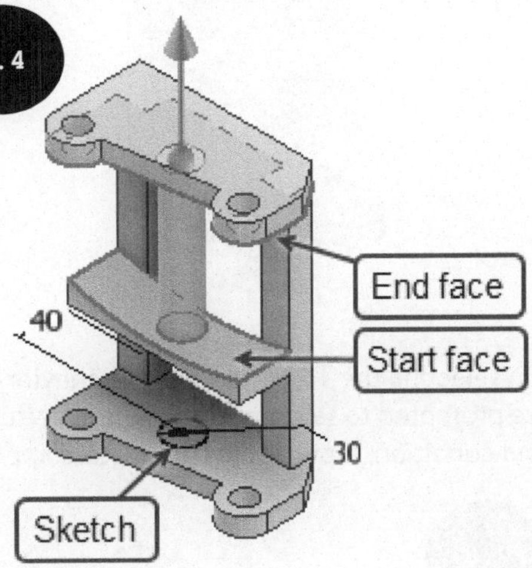

Behavior

The options in the **Behavior** rollout of the **Extrusion** property panel are used for defining the direction and the end condition of extrusion, see Figure 7.5. The options for defining the direction and the depth of extrusion in this rollout have been discussed earlier while creating base features and the remaining options are discussed below:

7.5

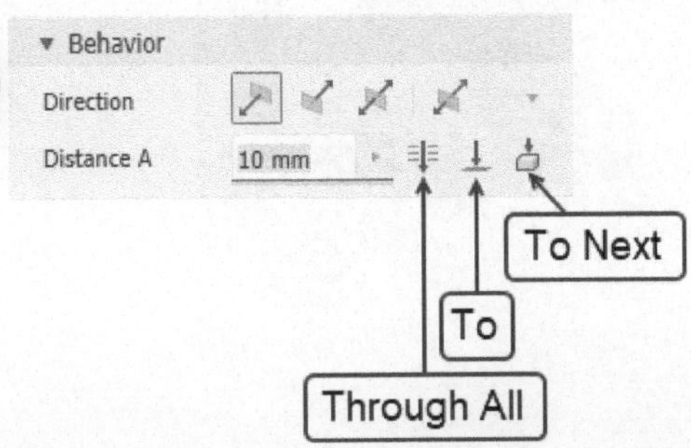

Through All

The **Through All** button of the **Behavior** rollout is used for defining the end condition or termination of the extrusion through all the faces of the model, see Figure 7.6.

To

The **To** button is used for defining the end condition or termination of the extrusion up to a face, a plane, or a point or vertex of a model, see Figures 7.7 and 7.8. In Figure 7.7, a curved face is selected as the end condition of the extrusion, whereas in Figure 7.8, a vertex is selected as the end condition.

7.6

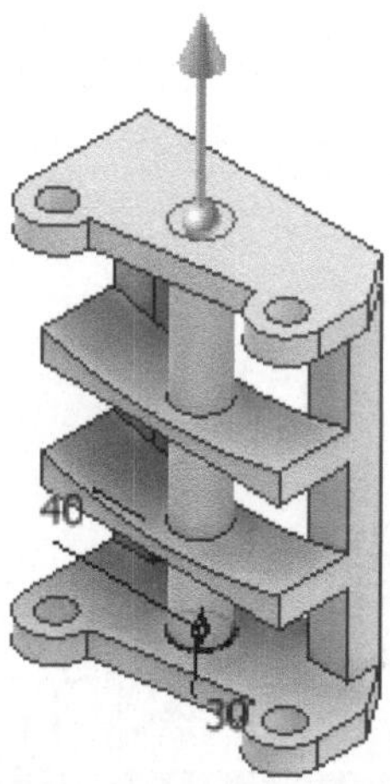

7.7

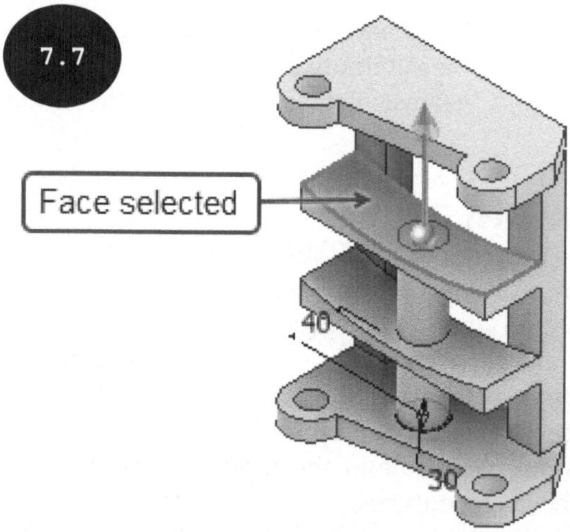

On selecting the **To** button in the **Behavior** rollout, the **To** selector appears, see Figure 7.9. Also, you are prompted to select a work plane, a vertex, or a face. Next, select a face, a plane, or a vertex as the end condition. A preview of the feature appears up to the selected face or vertex.

7.8

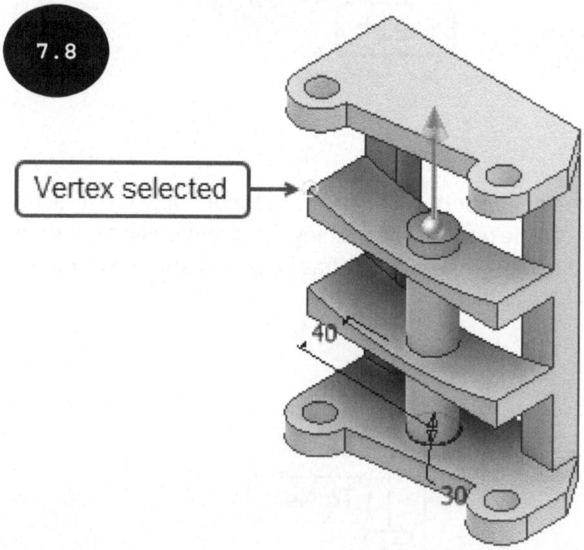

7.9

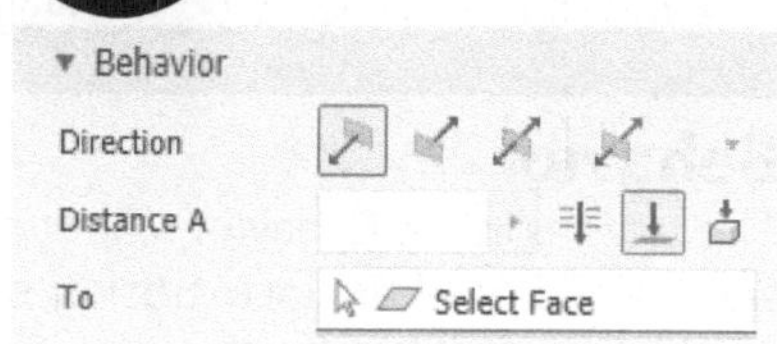

Note: On selecting a plane or a face as the end condition of an extrusion, the **Extend face to end feature** and **Alternate Solution** buttons become available next to the **To** selector in the **Behavior** rollout of the property panel. By default, the **Extend face to end feature** button is activated. As a result, even if the sketch profile to be extruded does not completely get projected or encapsulated onto the face that is selected as the end condition, the extrusion terminates on the selected face, see Figure 7.10. This is because, the selected face of the model gets extended imaginarily such that it intersects the extrusion.

If you have selected a curved face as the end condition of extrusion, then the extrusion terminates on the nearest intersection with the selected curved face by default, see Figure 7.11. However, you can toggle the extrusion end condition or termination from the nearest intersection to the farthest intersection with the selected curved face (see Figure 7.12) or vice-versa by clicking on the **Alternate Solution** button.

7.10

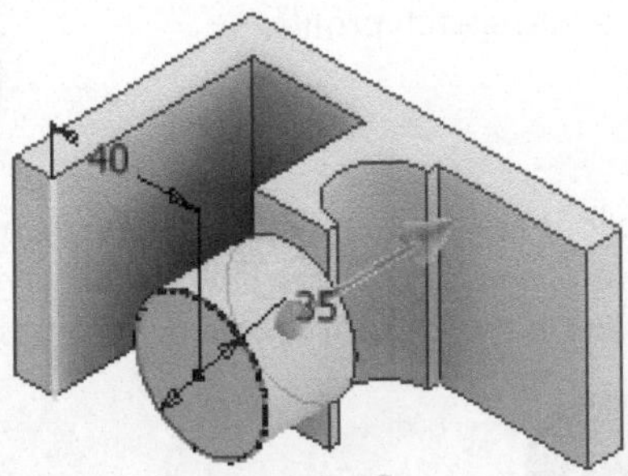

7.11

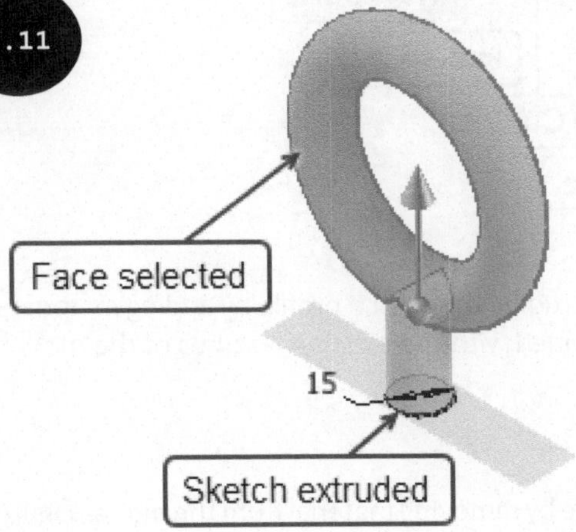

7.12

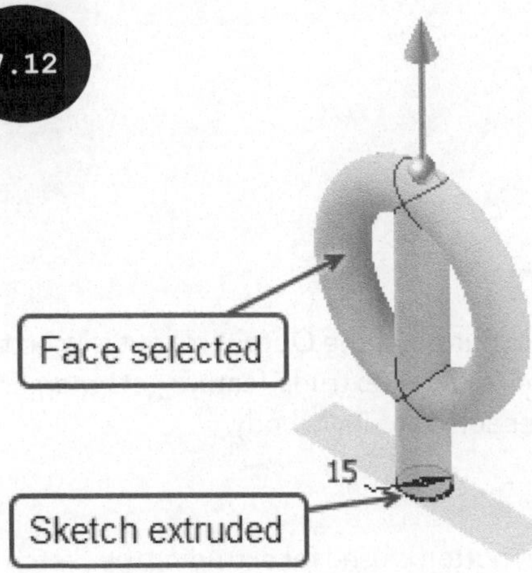

To Next

The **To Next** button of the **Behavior** rollout in the property panel is used for defining the end condition or termination of the extrusion up to the next intersection with a solid body, see Figure 7.13. On selecting the **To Next** button, the **To Next** selector appears in the rollout and the available solid body gets selected automatically. Also, a preview of the extrude feature appears such that it terminates at the next intersection with the selected solid body.

7.13

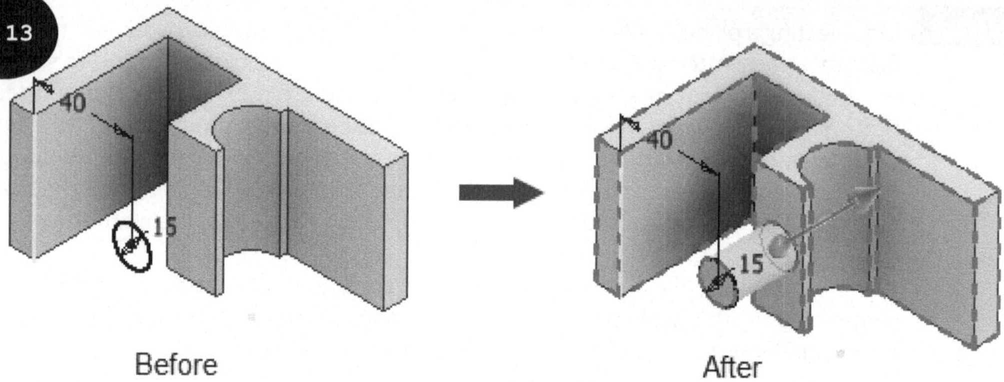

Note: The extrusion terminates on the next intersection geometry of the selected solid body that encapsulates the entire sketch profile.

Output

The options in the **Output** rollout are used for defining the type of boolean operation to be performed for creating the extrude feature, see Figure 7.14. This rollout is not available while creating the base feature of a model. The options in the **Output** rollout are discussed below:

7.14

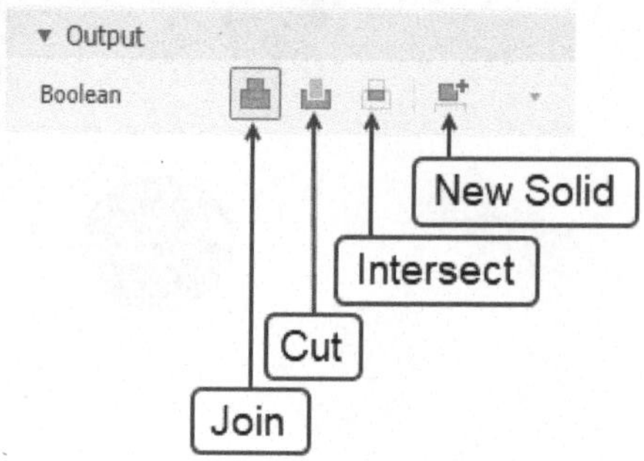

Join

The **Join** button of the **Output** rollout is used for extruding the sketch profile by adding material such that the resultant extrude feature gets merged or joined with the existing features of the model and together acts as a single body.

Cut

The **Cut** button is used for extruding the sketch profile by removing material from the model. Figure 7.15 shows a sketch profile, which is created on the top planar face of the model and Figure 7.16 shows the resultant extrude cut feature created by selecting the **Cut** button in the **Output** rollout of the property panel.

7.15

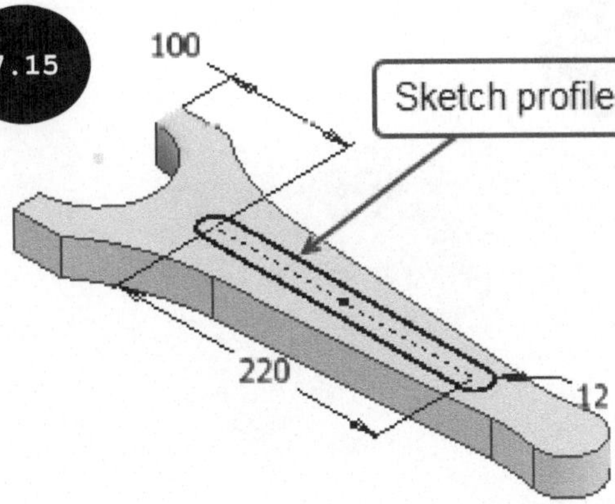

7.16

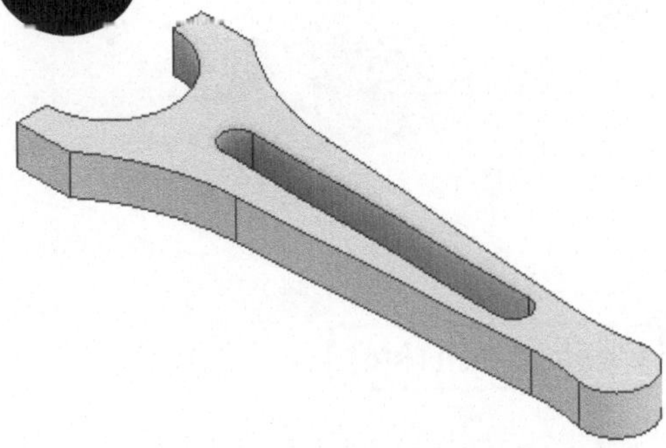

Intersect

The **Intersect** button is used for creating a feature by only keeping the intersecting/common material between the existing feature and the feature being created. Figure 7.17 shows a sketch profile, which is created on the top planar face of the model and Figure 7.18 shows the resultant intersect feature.

7.17

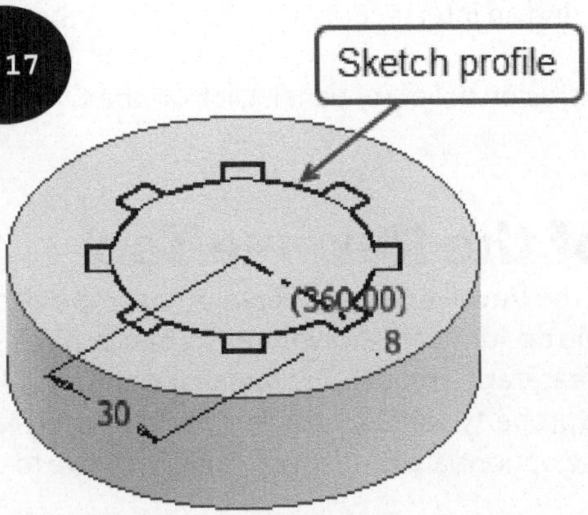

7.18

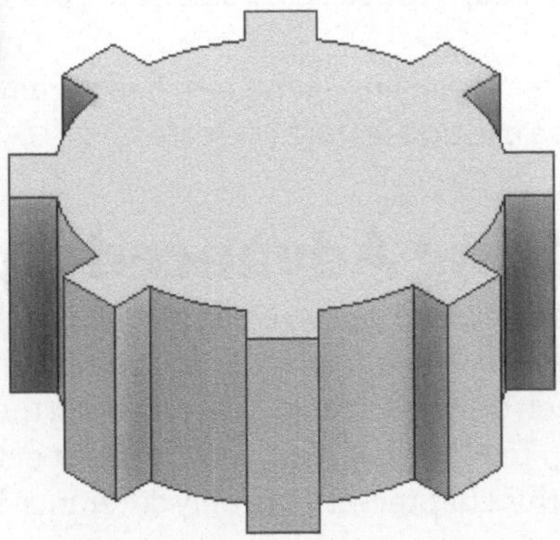

New Solid

On selecting the **New Solid** button, the feature being created does not merge with the existing features of the model and a separate solid body will be created.

Advanced Properties

Some of the options for the **Advanced Properties** rollout have been discussed earlier while creating the base feature. The **Match Shape** check box is discussed below:

Match Shape

The **Match Shape** check box of the **Advanced Properties** rollout is enabled only when you are extruding an open sketch. This check box is used for creating an extrude feature from an open sketch by extending the open ends of the sketch and matching it with the shape of the model, see Figures 7.19 and 7.20. Figure 7.19 shows an open sketch created on a work plane which is at an offset distance from the bottom face of the model and Figure 7.20 shows the preview of the resultant extrude feature.

7.19

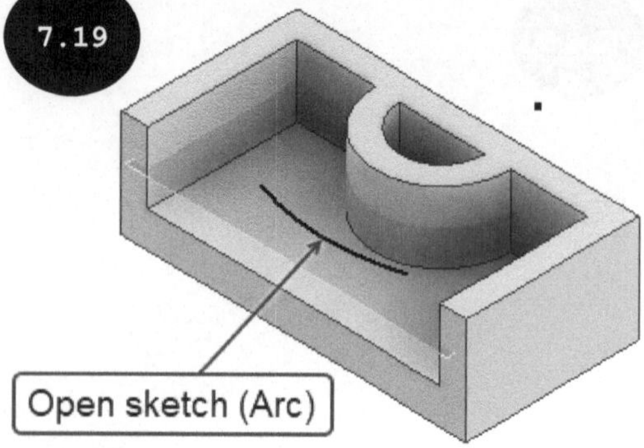

7.20

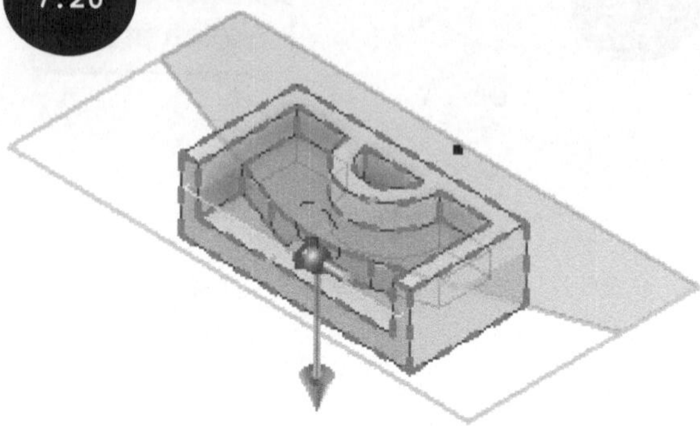

When the **Match Shape** check box is selected, the open ends of the sketch get extended in the graphics area such that they create imaginary profiles on both sides of the sketch (see Figure 7.20), and you are prompted to select either side of the sketch. Click to select a side (profile) of the sketch to be extruded up to the next intersection with the faces of the model. Note that the extrude feature will not be created, if the selected side of the extrusion does not find an intersection with the faces of the model.

After specifying all the required parameters in the **Extrusion** property panel, click on the **OK** button. The extrude feature is created.

Using Advanced Options of the Revolve Tool

As discussed earlier, while revolving a sketch by using the **Revolve** tool, the **Revolution** property panel appears in the graphics area, see Figure 7.21. Some of the options of the **Revolution** property panel have been discussed earlier while creating the base revolve feature of a model. The remaining options such as **To**, **To Next**, **Join**, **Cut**, and **Intersect** of the **Revolution** property panel are the same as discussed earlier in this chapter with the only difference being that these options are used for creating a revolve feature.

7.21

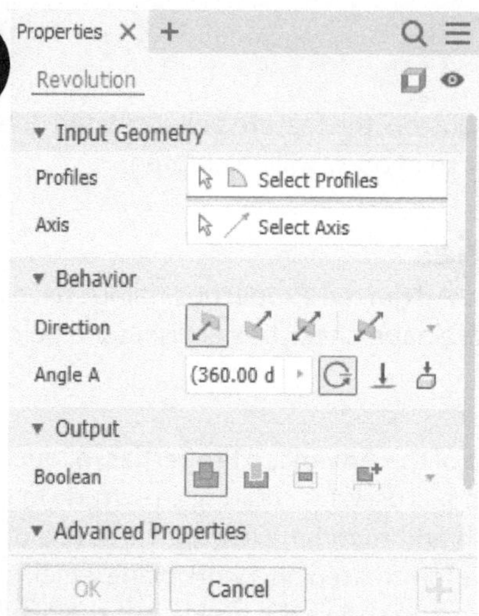

Working with a Sketch having Multiple Profiles

In Autodesk Inventor, you can create multiple features by using a single sketch that has multiple closed profiles. Figure 7.22 shows a sketch having multiple closed profiles and Figure 7.23 shows the resultant multi-feature model created by using this sketch.

7.22

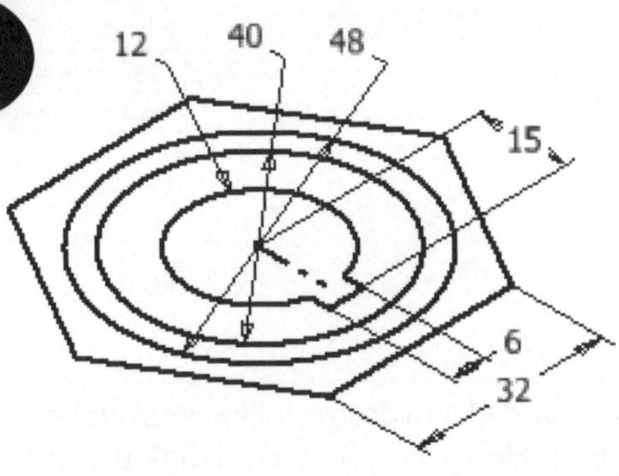

7.23

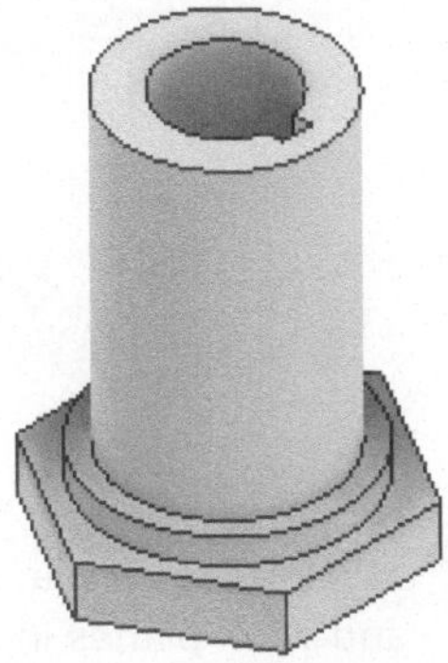

The method for creating features by extruding closed profiles of a sketch is discussed below:

1. Create a sketch that has multiple profiles by using the sketching tools, refer to Figure 7.24.

2. Invoke the **Extrusion** property panel by clicking on the **Extrude** tool in the **3D Model** tab of the **Ribbon**. Alternatively, press the **E** key to invoke the **Extrusion** property panel.

3. Move the cursor over a closed profile of the sketch to be extruded and then click when it gets highlighted in the graphics area, refer to Figure 7.25. The preview of the extrude feature appears in the graphics area with a default depth of extrusion.

7.24

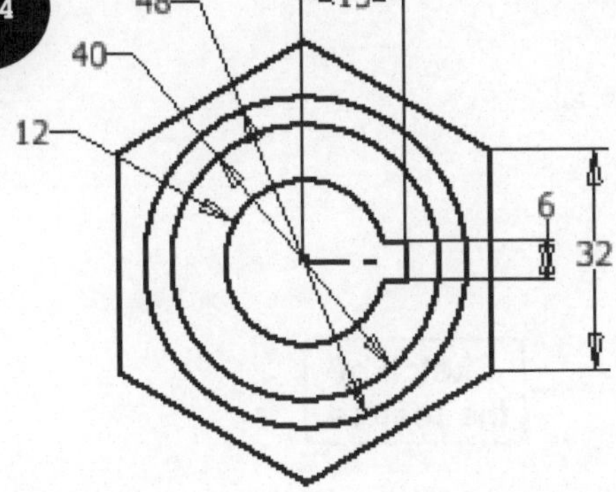

7.25

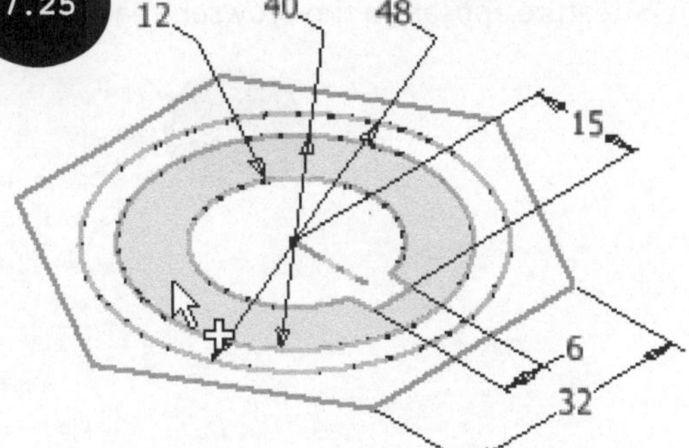

4. Specify the depth of extrusion and other parameters for creating the feature in the **Extrusion** property panel.

5. Click on the **OK** button in the property panel. An extrude feature is created with specified parameters, refer to Figure 7.26. Also, its default name is added in the **Browser**, see Figure 7.27. Besides, the sketch disappears from the graphics area. This is because the sketch is consumed by the feature. As a result, it no longer appears in the graphics area. In Figure 7.26, the depth of extrusion is specified as 75 mm.

7.26

7.27

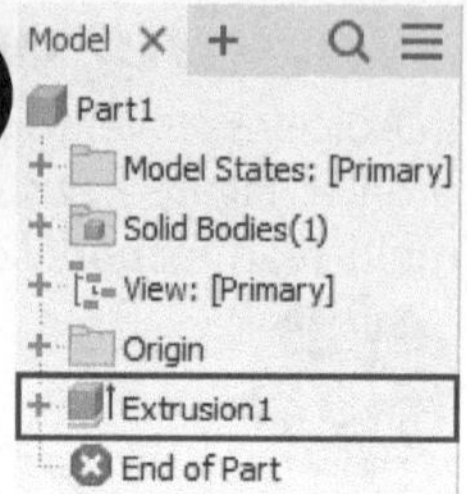

Note: The **Browser** displays all the operations performed on a design, including sketches, features, and work planes in their order of creation. However, you can change the order of the operations by dragging them in the **Browser**. Note that Autodesk Inventor maintains the parent-child relationship between the features. As a result, you cannot place a child feature at the top of its parent feature in the **Browser**.

Tip: In the **Browser**, you can rename or change the default name of a feature. For doing so, click on the name of the feature to be renamed in the **Browser** and then after a pause, click on it again. The name of the feature appears in an edit field. Now, you can enter a new name for the feature in the edit field as required, and then click anywhere in the graphics area.

6. Expand the **Extrusion** node in the **Browser** by clicking on the + sign in front of it. A sketch of the feature appears in the **Browser**, see Figure 7.28.

7.28

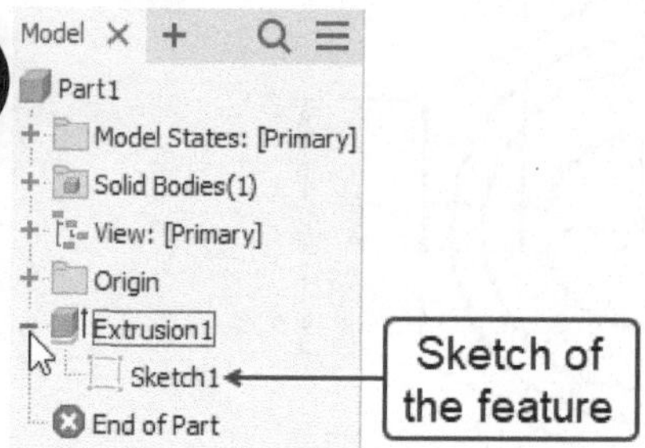

7. Click on the **Sketch** in the **Browser**. The sketch gets highlighted in the graphics area and a Mini-Toolbar appears, see Figure 7.29.

8. Click on the **Share Sketch** tool in the Mini-Toolbar, see Figure 7.29. The sketch becomes visible in the graphics area and becomes a shared sketch. Note that a shared sketch is a sketch that can be used or shared for creating other features of a model. In the **Browser**, the shared sketch appears at the top of all the features.

7.29

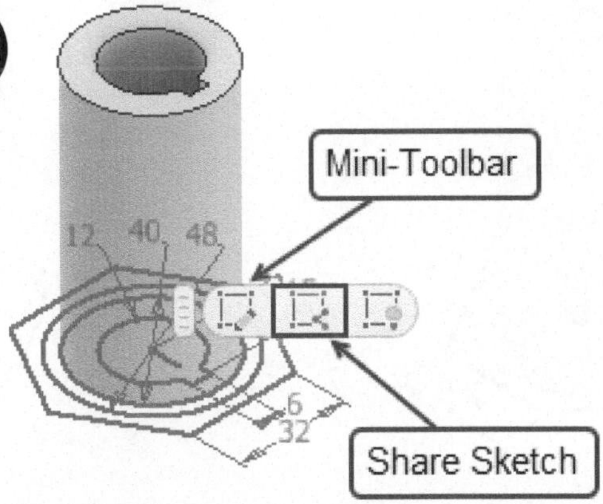

Now, you can extrude the closed profiles of a shared sketch one by one to create other features of a model.

9. Invoke the **Extrusion** property panel and then move the cursor over a closed profile of the sketch to be extruded. Next, click when it gets highlighted in the graphics area, refer to Figure 7.30. A preview of the extrude feature appears in the graphics area with a default depth of extrusion.

7.30

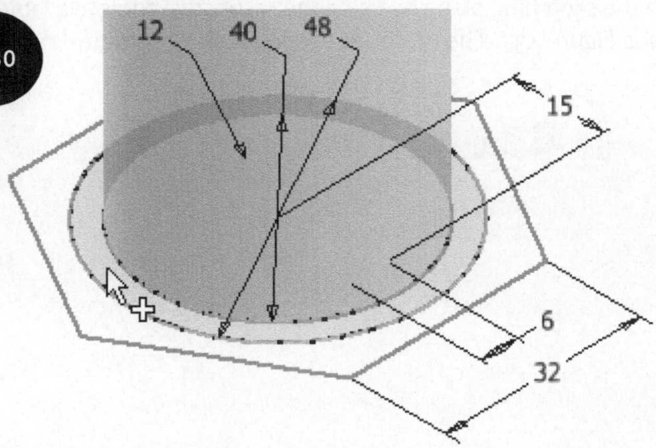

10. Specify the depth of extrusion and other parameters for creating the feature in the **Extrusion** property panel.

11. Click on the **OK** button in the property panel. An extrude feature is created with specified parameters, refer to Figure 7.31. Also, the shared sketch is still visible in the graphics area. In Figure 7.31, the depth of extrusion is specified as 15 mm.

12. Similarly, you can create the remaining features by extruding the closed profiles of the sketch one by one, refer to Figure 7.32.

7.31

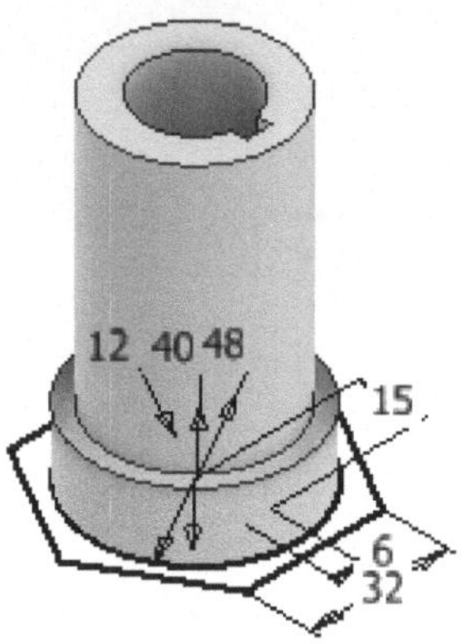

7.32

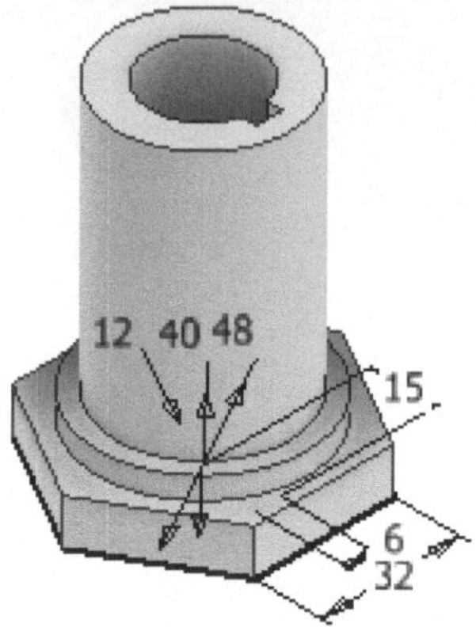

13. After creating all the features, turn off the visibility of the shared sketch. For doing so, right-click on the shared sketch in the **Browser** and then click on the **Visibility** option in the shortcut menu that appears. The visibility of the shared sketch gets turned off.

Projecting Geometries

In Autodesk Inventor, you can project geometries of existing features onto the sketching plane, edges of a model that intersect with the sketching plane, 2D sketch onto a face of a model, and geometries of a DWG file onto the sketching plane by using the respective tools available in the **Project** flyout of the **Create** panel, see Figure 7.33. The methods for projecting geometries are discussed below:

7.33

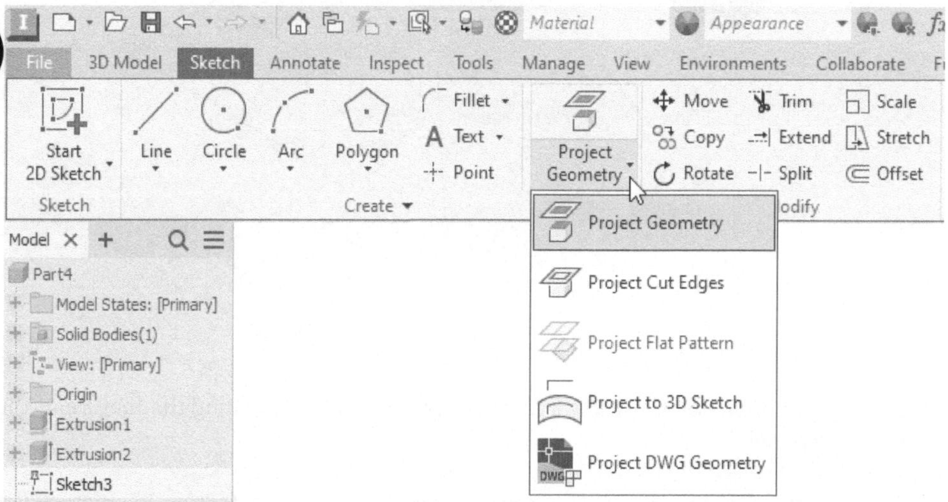

Projecting Geometries onto the Sketching Plane

While sketching in the Sketching environment, you can project geometries such as edges, loops, vertices, work features, and curves of a model onto the currently active sketching plane by using the **Project Geometry** tool. Figure 7.34 shows a model in which the edges of the existing features have been projected as sketch entities onto the active sketching plane. The method for projecting the geometries of a model onto the sketching plane is discussed below:

1. Invoke the Sketching environment by selecting a plane or a planar face of a model.

2. Invoke the **Project** flyout in the **Create** panel and then click on the **Project Geometry** tool, see Figure 7.35. You are prompted to select an edge, a vertex, a work geometry, or a sketch geometry to be projected.

7.34

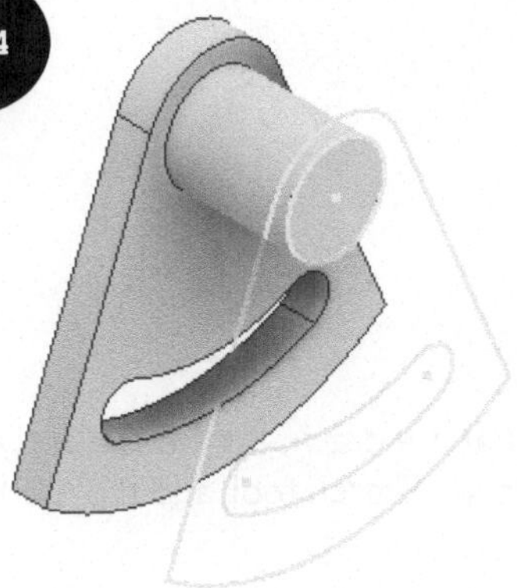

7.35

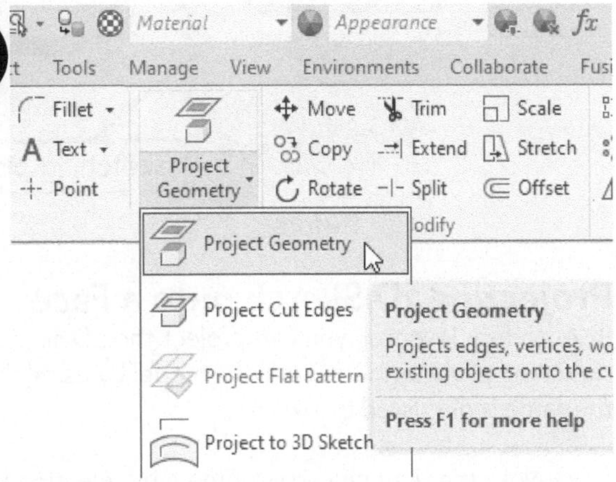

3. Click to select the geometry of a model to be projected. The selected geometry gets projected onto the sketching plane. You can select an edge, a face, a vertex, a work feature, or a sketch entity as a geometry to be projected. Note that on selecting the face of a model, all its edges get projected onto the sketching plane. You can also select multiple geometries one by one by clicking the left mouse button.

4. After projecting the geometries of the model onto the sketching plane, right-click in the drawing area and then click on the **OK** button in the Marking Menu that appears or press the ESC key to exit the tool.

Tip: You can use the projected sketch entities for creating features by using the modeling tools such as **Extrude** and **Revolve** tools.

Projecting Intersecting Edges onto the Sketching Plane

You can also project the edges of a model that intersect with the currently active sketching plane in the Sketching environment and the method for the same is discussed below:

1. Invoke the **Project** flyout in the **Create** panel and then click on the **Project Cut Edges** tool. All the edges of the model that intersect with the sketching plane get projected, see Figure 7.36.

7.36

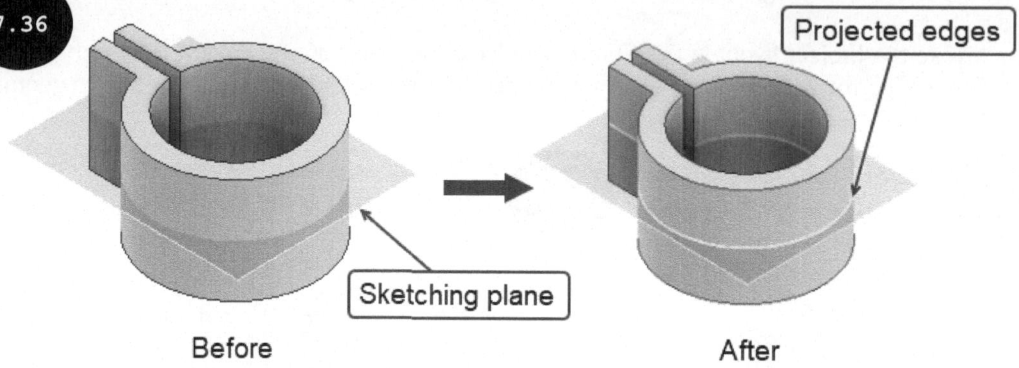

Projecting 2D Sketch onto a Face

In Autodesk Inventor, you can project the 2D sketch entities that are drawn on the currently active sketching plane onto the face of a model by using the **Project to 3D Sketch** tool, and the method for the same is discussed below:

1. Invoke the Sketching environment by selecting a plane or a planar face of a model as the sketching plane.

2. Create a sketch to be projected onto the face of the model, see Figure 7.37.

3. Invoke the **Project** flyout in the **Create** panel and then click on the **Project to 3D Sketch** tool, see Figure 7.38. The **Project to 3D Sketch** dialog box appears and you are prompted to select a face, a surface, or a work plane.

7.37

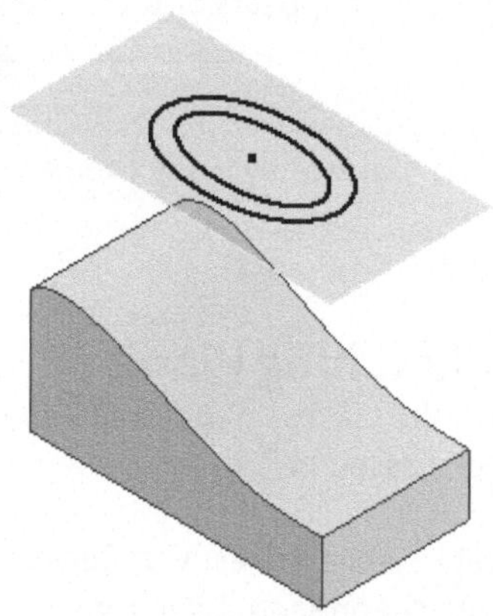

7.38

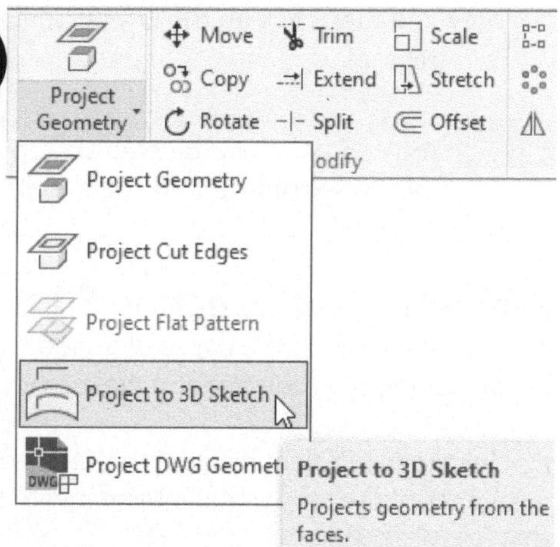

4. Click to select the face of the model in the graphics area. The preview of a projected curve appears on the selected face of the model.

5. Click on the **OK** button in the dialog box. The sketch gets projected onto the selected face of the model, see Figure 7.39.

7.39

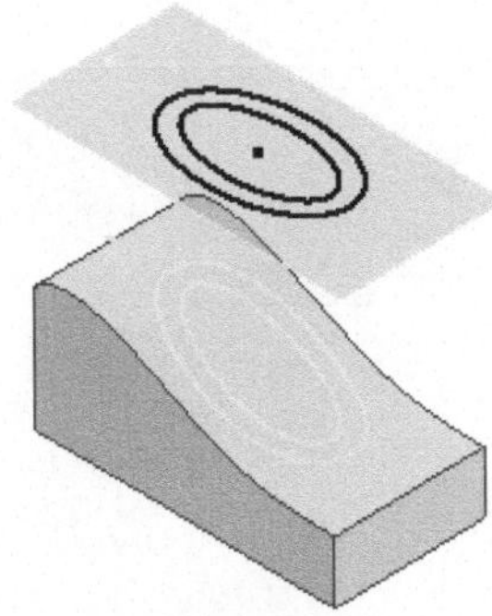

Projecting Geometries of a .DWG File

In Autodesk Inventor, you can project geometries of an existing DWG underlay drawing by using the **Project DWG Geometry** tool and the method for the same is discussed below:

1. Invoke the Sketching environment by selecting a plane or a planar face of a model as the sketching plane.

2. Invoke the **Project** flyout in the **Create** panel and then click on the **Project DWG Geometry** tool. The Mini-Toolbar appears in the drawing area, see Figure 7.40.

7.40

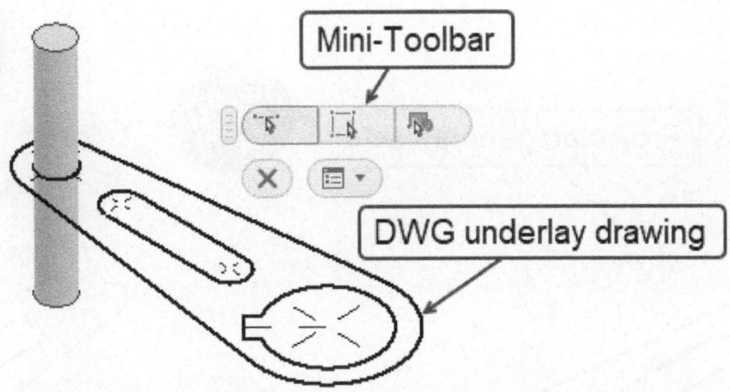

Mini-Toolbar: By default, the **Project Single Geometry** tool is activated in the Mini-Toolbar. As a result, you can select DWG line, arc, polyline or any other single geometry of an existing DWG underlay drawing that is imported into the model by clicking the left mouse button as the geometry to be projected. You can also draw a window around the DWG geometries to be projected onto the sketching plane. On activating the **Project Connected Geometry** tool, you can select DWG closed or open loops to be projected onto the sketching plane. On activating the **Project DWG Block** tool, you can select DWG blocks to be projected onto the sketching plane.

Note: A DWG underlay drawing is a *.dwg* file that is imported into a model by using the **Import** tool of the **Insert** panel in the **Manage** tab, see Figure 7.41. This tool is only enabled in the Part modeling environment. Note that a DWG underlay drawing is linked to the original DWG file such that any change made in the original DWG file also reflects in the imported DWG file after you click on the **Local Update** tool in the **Quick Access Toolbar**.

7.41

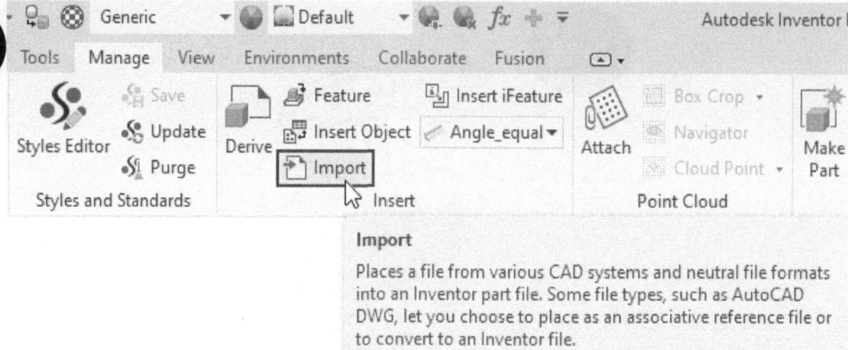

3. Select the geometries of the DWG underlay drawing to be projected. All the selected geometries get projected onto the sketching plane, see Figure 7.42. In this figure, all the DWG geometries have been projected by drawing a window around them.

4. Press the ESC key to exit the tool.

Tip: After projecting the DWG geometries, you can create a feature by using a modeling tool such as **Extrude** or **Revolve**, see Figure 7.43. As mentioned earlier, any change made in the original DWG file also reflects in the imported DWG file as well as the feature created by projecting its geometries after you click on the **Local Update** tool in the **Quick Access Toolbar**.

7.42

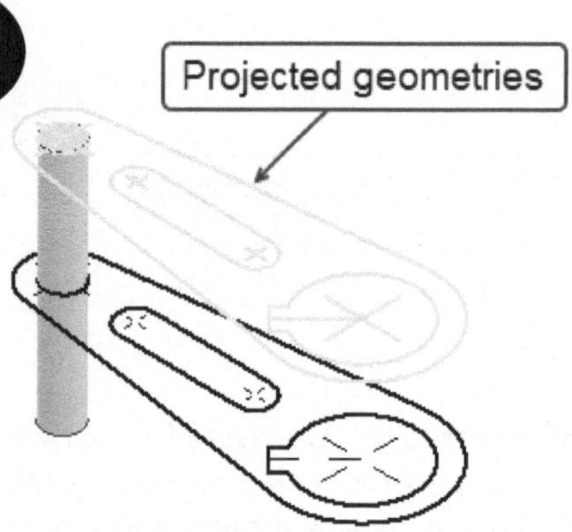

7.43

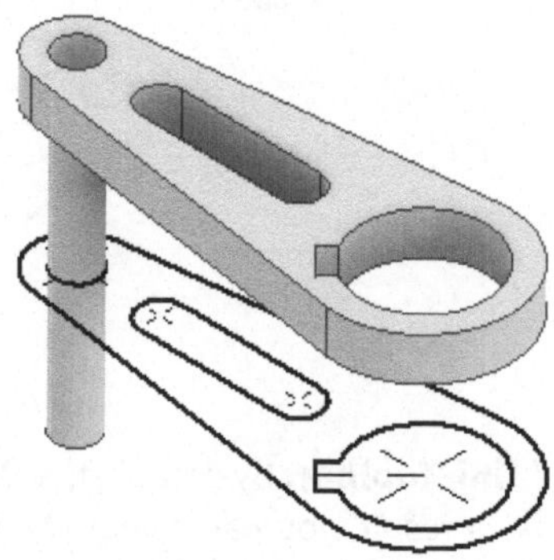

Creating a Section View

In Autodesk Inventor, you can create a quarter section view, half section view, and three quarter section view of a model in the graphics area by using the respective tools available in the **Section View** flyout of the **Visibility** panel in the **View** tab. Figure 7.44 shows a half section view of a model and Figure 7.45 shows the **Section View** flyout. Note that creating a section view does not change or modify the geometry of the model. It is only used for viewing the internal features or geometries of a model. The methods for creating different section views are discussed next.

7.44

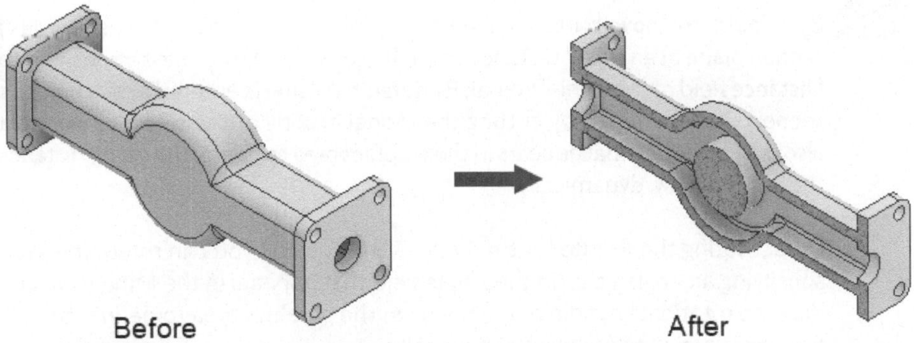

7.45

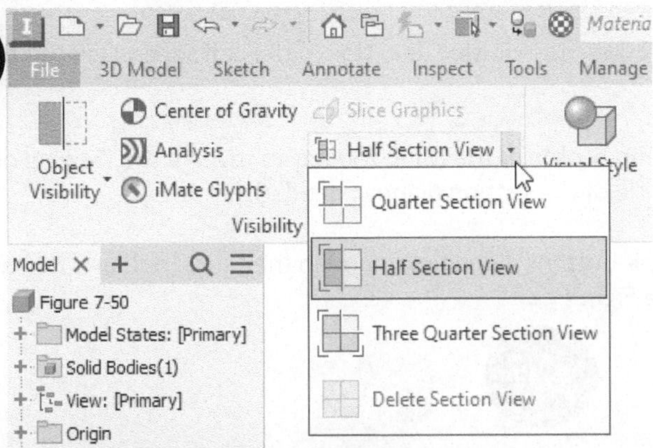

Creating a Half Section View

The method for creating a half section view is discussed below:

1. Invoke the **Section View** flyout in the **Visibility** panel in the **View** tab and then click on the **Half Section View** tool, refer to Figure 7.45. You are prompted to select a work plane or a planar face for sectioning a model.

2. Select a work plane in the **Browser** or in the graphics area. The half section view of the model appears in the graphics area such that the geometry in front of the selected work plane gets hidden. Also, the Mini-Toolbar appears, see Figure 7.46.

7.46

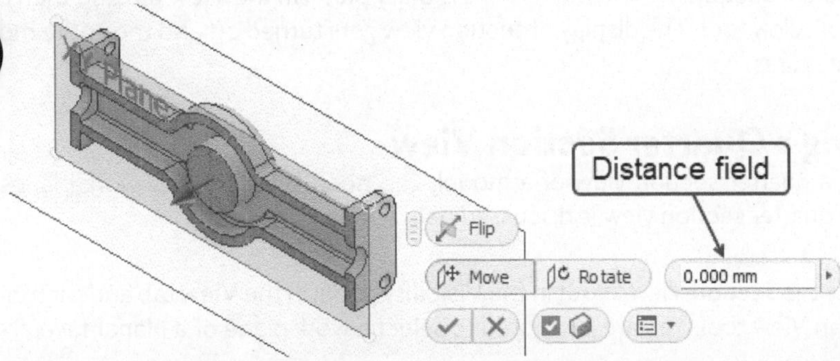

Note: By default, the **Move** button is activated in the Mini-Toolbar. As a result, you can move the section plane at an offset distance from the selected work plane by specifying a value in the **Distance** field of the Mini-Toolbar. By default, 0 value is entered in this field. As a result, the section view is created by cutting the model exactly at the selected work plane. You can also drag the arrow that appears in the graphics area to define the offset distance for creating the section view, dynamically.

On activating the **Rotate** button in the Mini-Toolbar, you can rotate the section plane by specifying an angle value in the **Angle** field that appears in the Mini-Toolbar. You can also drag the rotational handle that appears in the graphics area to define the rotational angle for creating the section view, dynamically.

You can also reverse the viewing direction of the half section view to the other side of the selected work plane.

3. Click on the **Flip** button in the Mini-Toolbar to reverse the viewing direction of the section view to the other side of the section plane, if needed.
4. Click on the **OK** button (green tick-mark) in the Mini-Toolbar. The half section view of the model is created, see Figure 7.47.

7.47

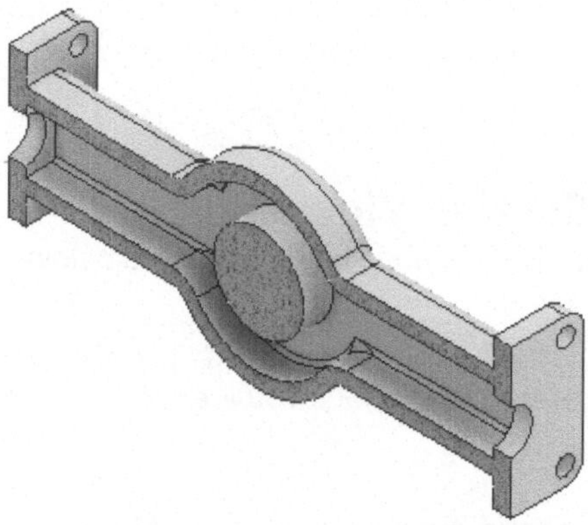

After creating the section view, you can return to the full view of the model again.

5. Invoke the **Section View** flyout in the **Visibility** panel in the **View** tab and then click on the **Delete Section View** tool. The display of section view gets turned off and the entire model appears in the graphics area.

Creating a Quarter Section View

To create a quarter section view of a model, you need to select two work planes. The method for creating a quarter section view is discussed below:

1. Invoke the **Section View** flyout in the **Visibility** panel in the **View** tab and then click on the **Quarter Section View** tool. You are prompted to select a work plane or a planar face.

2. Select a work plane in the **Browser** or in the graphics area. The half section view of the model and the Mini-Toolbar appear in the graphics area.

3. Specify an offset distance in the Mini-Toolbar for creating a section view at an offset distance for the selected work plane, if needed. You can also create a section view by rotating the section plane using the **Rotate** button, as discussed earlier.

4. Click on the **Continue** button in the Mini-Toolbar that appears, see Figure 7.48. You are prompted to select a work plane for creating a quarter section view.

7.48

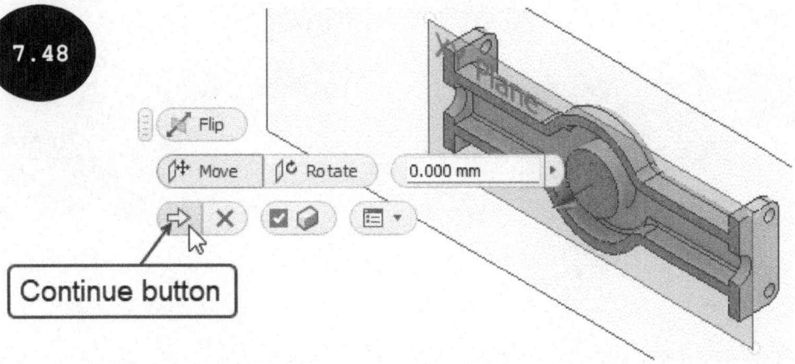

5. Select the second work plane in the **Browser** or in the graphics area. The quarter section view of the model appears in the graphics area, see Figure 7.49.

Tip: In Autodesk Inventor, you can also toggle between the quarter section view and the three-quarter section view of the model by activating the respective button in the Mini-Toolbar, see Figure 7.49.

7.49

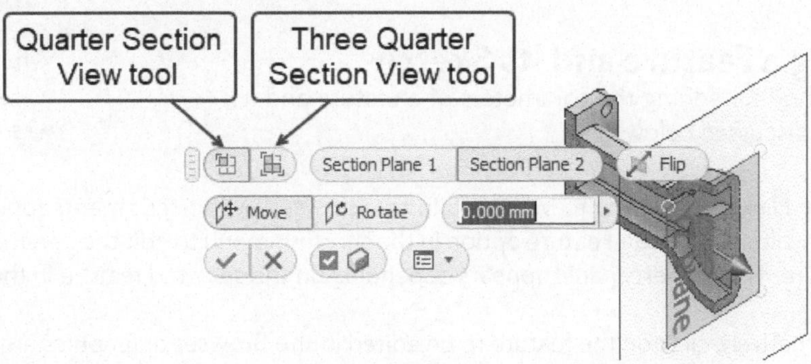

6. Click on the **OK** (green tick-mark) button in the Mini-Toolbar. The quarter section view of the model is created, see Figure 7.50.

   After creating the section view, you can return to the full view of the model again.

7. Invoke the **Section View** flyout in the **Visibility** panel in the **View** tab and then click on the **Delete Section View** tool. The display of section view gets turned off and the entire model appears in the graphics area.

Creating a Three Quarter Section View

You can create a three quarter section view of a model by using the **Three Quarter Section View** tool of the **Section View** flyout. To create a three quarter section view of a model, you need to select two work planes. The method for creating a three quarter section view is the same as discussed earlier while creating a quarter section view. Figure 7.51 shows a three quarter section view of a model.

7.50

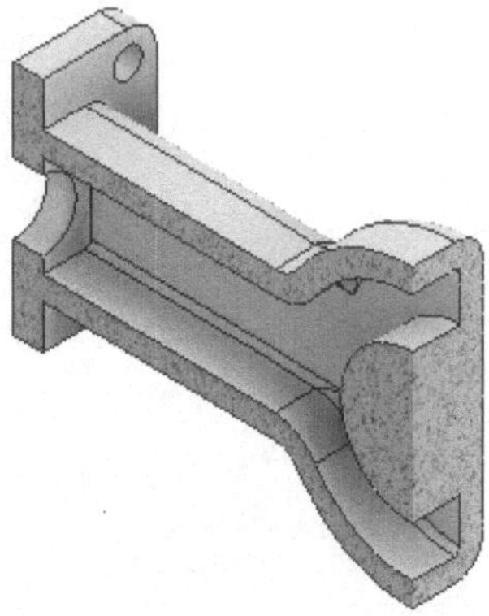

7.51

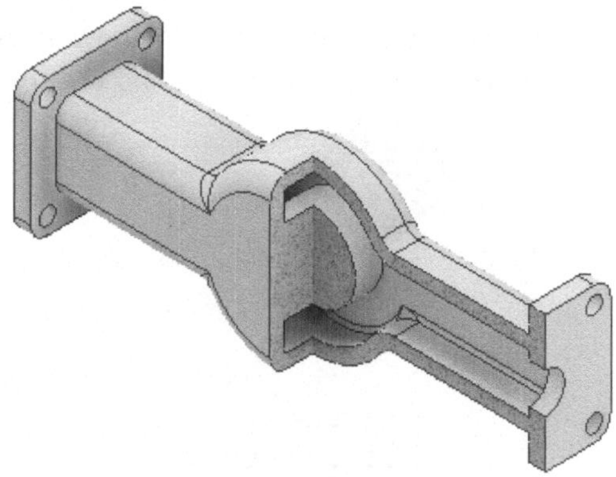

Editing a Feature and its Sketch

Autodesk Inventor allows you to edit features of a model at any point of design as per the design change or revision by using the **Browser**. As discussed earlier, the **Browser** displays a list of all features including sketches and work features created for a model, see Figure 7.52. The method for editing an individual feature and its sketch is discussed next.

7.52

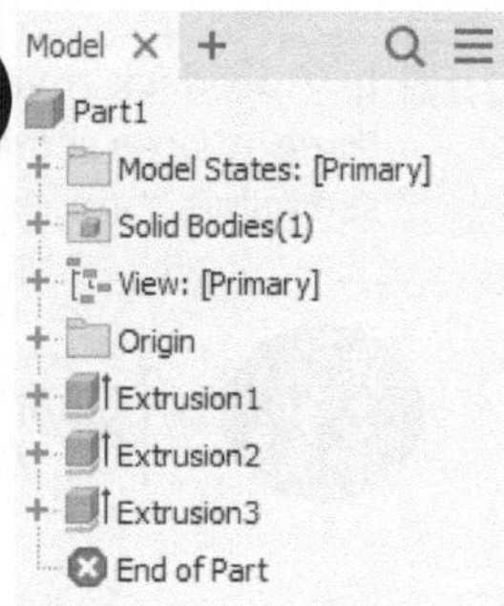

Editing a Feature and its Sketch

The method for editing the parameters of a feature and its sketch is discussed below:

1. Right-click on a feature to be edited in the **Browser**. A shortcut menu appears, see Figure 7.53. Next, click on the **Edit Feature** option in the shortcut menu to edit the parameters of the selected feature. The property panel appears depending on the selected feature in the graphics area.

   Alternatively, click on the feature to be edited in the **Browser** or graphics area. The Mini-Toolbar appears, see Figure 7.54. In this Mini-Toolbar, click on the **Edit Feature** tool. The property panel appears depending upon the selected feature.

7.53

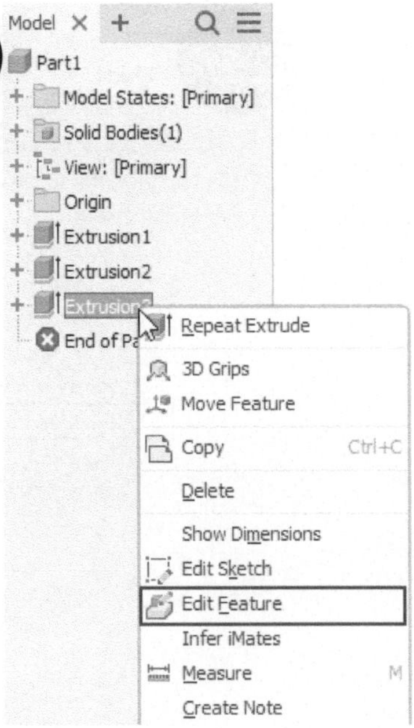

7.54

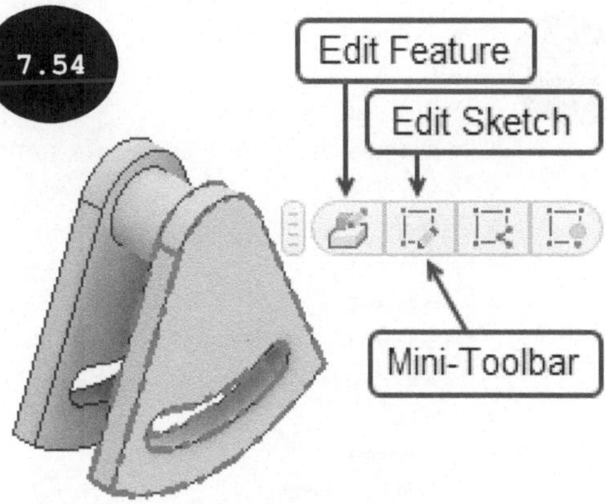

Note: To edit the sketch of the selected feature, click on the **Edit Sketch** option in the shortcut menu or Mini-Toolbar that appears, refer to Figures 7.53 and 7.54. On doing so, the sketch of the selected feature appears in the Sketching environment. Now, you can edit or modify the sketch of the feature by using the sketching tools, as required.

2. Edit the parameters of the feature as required by entering new values in the property panel.

3. After editing the feature parameters, click on the **OK** button in the property panel. Note that in case of editing the sketch of the feature, you need to exit the Sketching environment to finish the editing operation.

Tip: In Autodesk Inventor, you can also edit an individual sketch. For doing so, right-click on the sketch to be edited in the **Browser** and then click on the **Edit Sketch** option in the shortcut menu that appears. Note that to display the consumed sketch of a feature in the **Browser**, you need to expand the feature node in the **Browser** by clicking on its + sign.

Displaying Earlier State of a Model

In Autodesk Inventor, you can display the earlier state of a model by using the **End of Part** marker. By default, the **End of Part** marker displays at the end of the last feature of the model in the **Browser**, see Figure 7.55. You can drag the **End of Part** marker up in the **Browser** and place it above the features to be rolled back, see Figure 7.56. The earlier state of the model appears in the graphics area such that all the features that are below the **End of Part** marker are not displayed in the model. Also, the names of the features that are below the **End of Part** marker appear in grey in the **Browser**. You can add new features or edit existing features while the model is in the rolled-back state. You can also drag the **End of Part** marker down in the **Browser**.

7.55

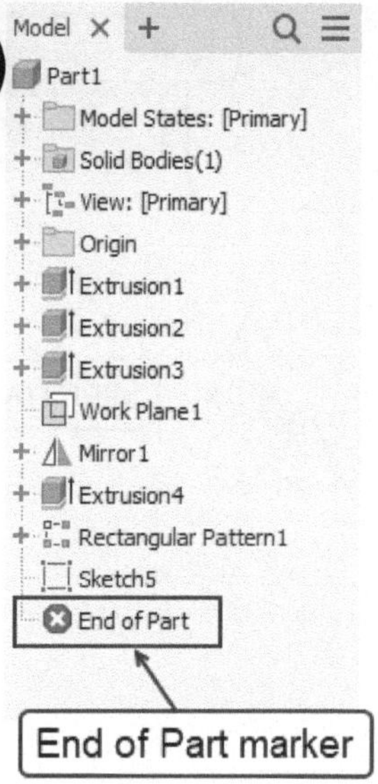

7.56

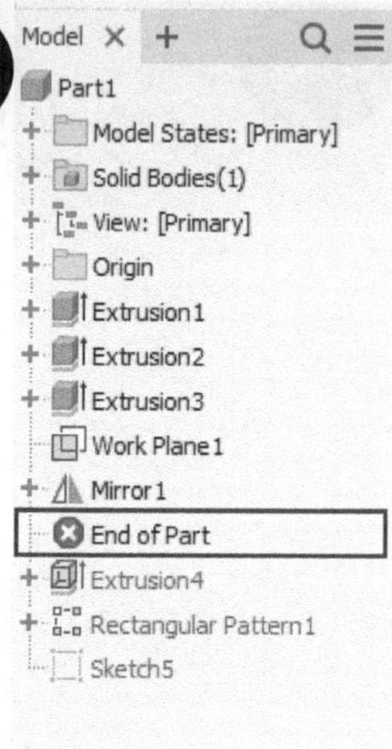

Tip: You can delete all the features of a model that are below the **End of Part** marker. For doing so, right-click on the **End of Part** marker in the **Browser** and then click on the **Delete All Features Below EOP** option in the shortcut menu that appears, see Figure 7.57. The **Move EOP to Top** option in this shortcut menu is used for moving the **End of Part** marker at the top of all features in the **Browser**. The **Move EOP to End** option is used for moving the **End of Part** marker at the end of all the features in the **Browser**.

7.57

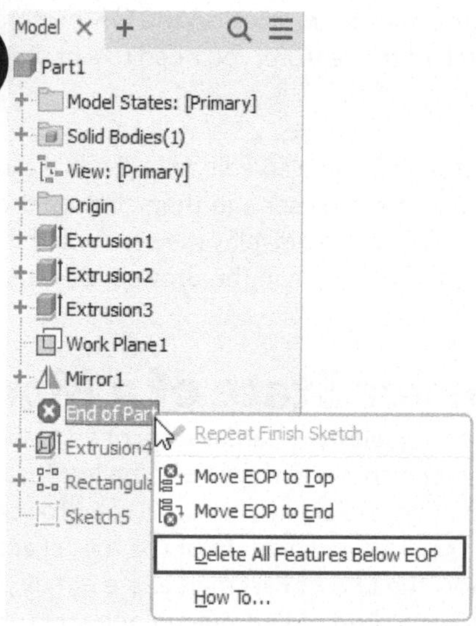

Re-ordering Features of a Model

By default, all the features of a model appear in a sequential order in the **Browser**. The first created feature appears at the top and the next created features appear one after another in **Browser**. In Autodesk Inventor, you can change the order of a feature by dragging it to a new location (above or below a feature) in the **Browser**. Note that you cannot drag and place a child feature above its parent feature in the **Browser**.

Measuring the Distance between Entities

In Autodesk Inventor, you can measure position, length, angle, loop, area, distance, radius, and diameter for selected entities or between selected entities by using the **Measure** tool in the **Measure** panel of the **Tools** tab in the **Ribbon**, see Figure 7.58. The method for measuring the size, distance, or position of an entity or between entities is discussed below:

7.58

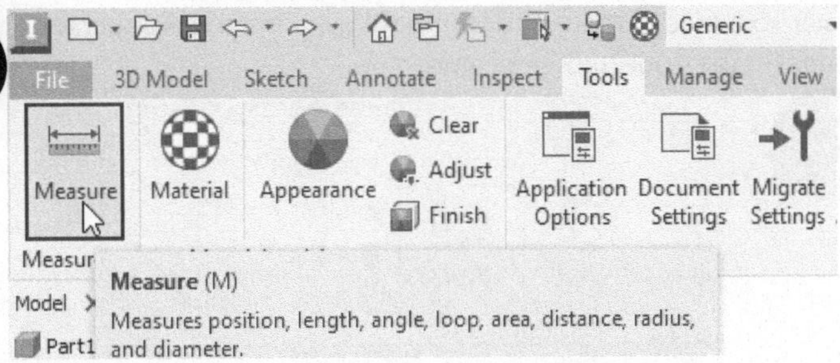

1. Click on the **Measure** tool in the **Measure** panel of the **Tools** tab or **Inspect** tab in the **Ribbon**, or press the M key. The **Measure** property panel appears, see Figure 7.59. Also, you are prompted to select the first item to measure size, distance, or position.

2. Select an entity of a model or sketch to be measured. The different measuring results of the selected entity are displayed in the **Measure** property panel, see Figure 7.60. Also, you are prompted to select the second entity (a point, a line, an edge, an axis, a plane, or a face). Figure 7.60 shows the results of selecting a cylindrical face of a model.

7.59

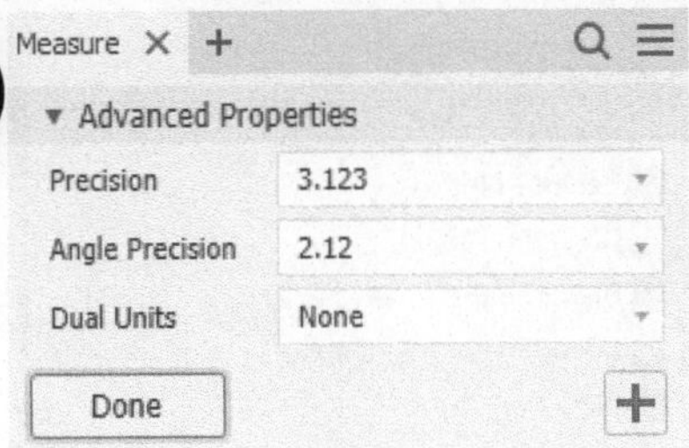

7.60

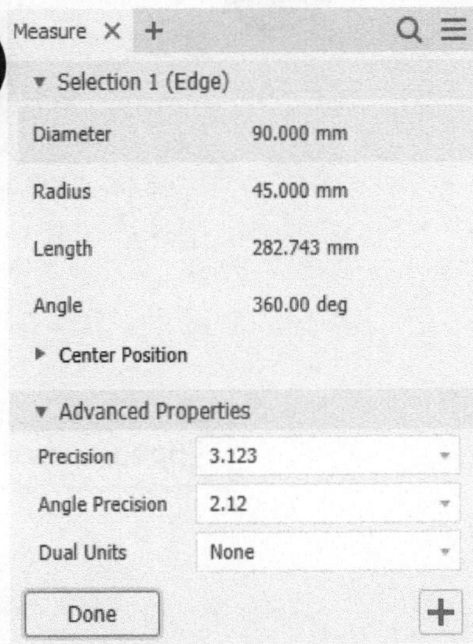

3. Click to select the second entity of the model or sketch. The different measuring results for individually selected entities and between selected entities get displayed in the **Measure** property panel as well as in the graphics area.

4. Click the left mouse button anywhere in the empty space in the graphics area to reset the **Measure** property panel.

5. Similarly, you can measure different measuring results for another set of entities.

6. Press the ESC key to exit the **Measure** property panel.

Assigning an Appearance

In Autodesk Inventor, you can change the default appearance or assign a new predefined or customized appearance/color to a face, a feature, or a model by using the **Appearance** tool of the **Material and Appearance** panel in the **Tools** tab, see Figure 7.61.

7.61

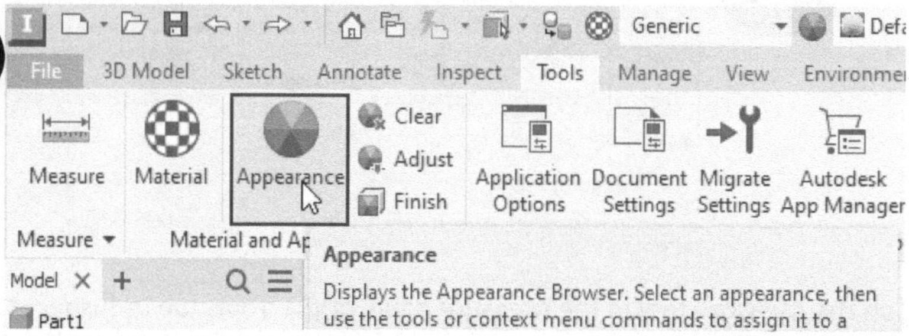

You can also assign an appearance to a face, a feature, or a model by using the **Appearance** drop-down list of the **Quick Access Toolbar**, see Figure 7.62. Moreover, you can copy and paste an appearance from one feature or face to another by using the **Adjust** tool of the **Quick Access Toolbar**, see Figure 7.62. The methods for assigning appearance are discussed next.

7.62

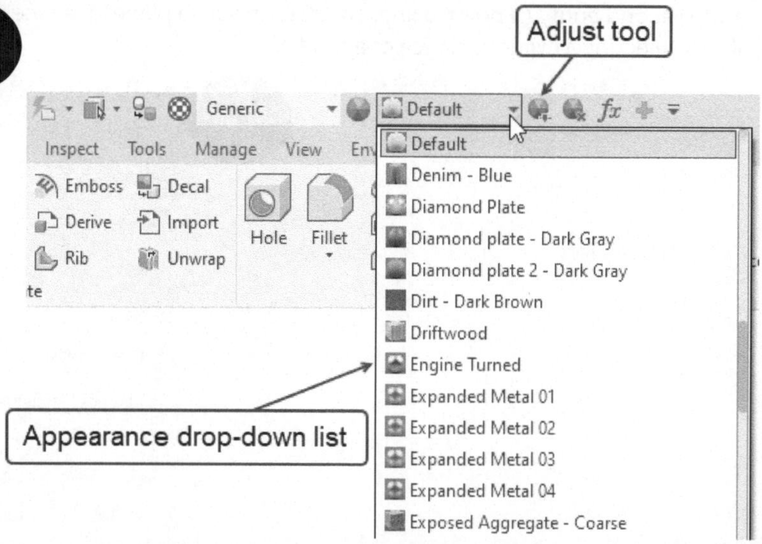

Assigning Appearance by using the Appearance Tool

To assign an appearance/color to a face, a feature, or a model by using the **Appearance** tool, click on the **Appearance** tool in the **Material and Appearance** panel of the **Tools** tab, refer to Figure 7.61. The **Appearance Browser** appears, see Figure 7.63. It is divided into two sections: **Document Appearances** and **Appearance Library**. Both are discussed below:

7.63

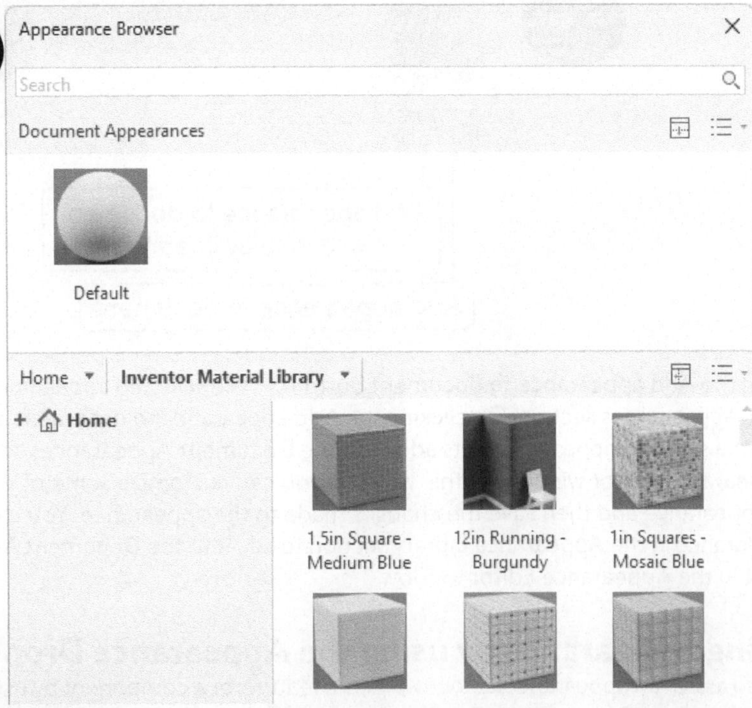

Document Appearances

The **Document Appearances** section of the **Appearance Browser** displays all the appearances that are applied to the current document. To apply an appearance available in the **Document Appearances** section, select a face, a feature, or an object (component) and then pause the cursor over the appearance in the **Document Appearances** section. A preview of the appearance appears on the selected face, feature, or object in the graphics area. Next, click on the appearance to assign it to the selection.

Appearance Library

The **Appearance Library** section displays a list of all appearances that are available in the selected appearance library. To select the required appearance library, click on the **Home** icon Home ▾ in the title bar of the **Appearance Library** section and then select the required appearance library in the list that appears.

To apply an appearance available in the **Appearance Library** section, select a face, a feature, or an object (component) and then pause the cursor over the appearance in the **Appearance Library** section. A preview of the appearance appears on the selected face, feature, or object in the graphics area. Next, right-click on the appearance to be assigned and then click on the **Assign to Selection** option in the shortcut menu that appears. The selected appearance gets assigned to the selection and also gets added in the **Document Appearances** section of the **Appearance Browser**.

You can also add an appearance of the **Appearance Library** section to the **Document Appearances** section and then apply it to a face, a feature, or an object. For doing so, move the cursor over an appearance in the **Appearance Library** section. The **Add appearance to document** button and the **Add appearance to document and display in editor** button appear, see Figure 7.64.

7.64

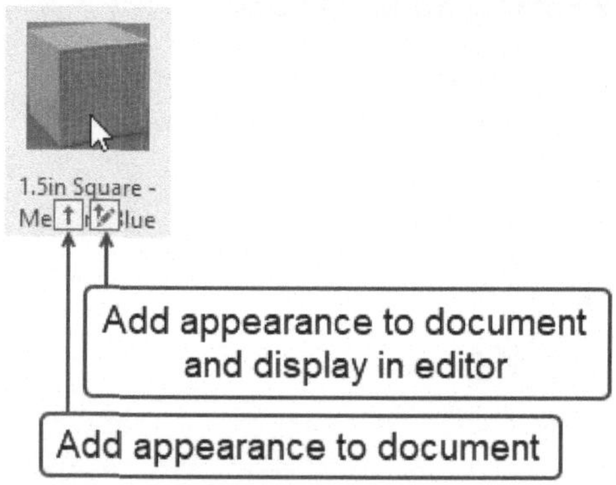

On clicking the **Add appearance to document** button, the selected appearance gets added in the **Document Appearances** section. On clicking the **Add appearance to document and display in editor** button, the selected appearance gets added to the **Document Appearances** section and is opened in the **Appearance Editor** window. In this window, you can customize some of the properties of the selected appearance and then save the changes made to the appearance. You can also double-click on an appearance in the **Appearance Library** section to add it to the **Document Appearances** section and open it in the **Appearance Editor** window.

Assigning Appearance by using the Appearance Drop-down List

You can also assign an appearance/color to a face, a feature, or a component by using the **Appearance** drop-down list of the **Quick Access Toolbar**. For doing so, select a face, a feature, or a component for assigning an appearance and then select an appearance from the **Appearance** drop-down list of the **Quick Access Toolbar**, see Figure 7.65. The appearance gets assigned to the selection. Note that if you do not make any selection for assigning the appearance, then the selected appearance gets assigned to the entire model.

7.65

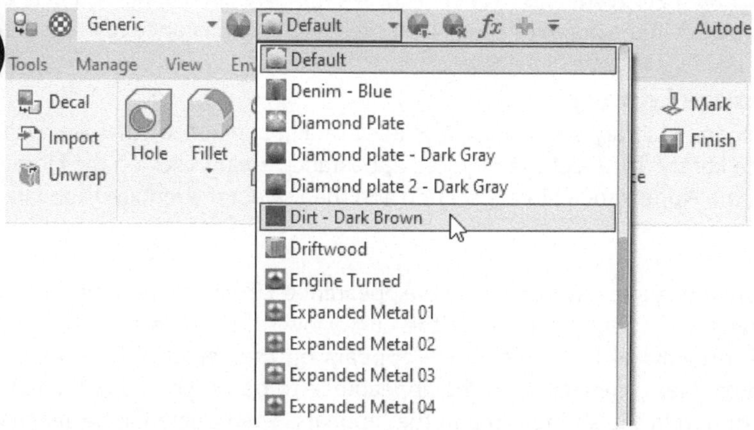

Tip: You can also click to select single or multiple faces of a model in the graphics area by pressing the CTRL key. You can click to select single or multiple features in the **Browser** by pressing the CTRL key.

Note: The availability of appearances in the **Appearance** drop-down list depends upon the material library selected at the bottom of the **Appearance** drop-down list. You can select the required appearance library to display the respective appearances in the Appearance drop-down list of the **Quick Access Toolbar**.

Copying and Pasting an Appearance by Using the Adjust Tool

In Autodesk Inventor, you can copy and paste an appearance from one feature or face to another by using the **Adjust** tool of the **Quick Access Toolbar**, see Figure 7.66.

7.66

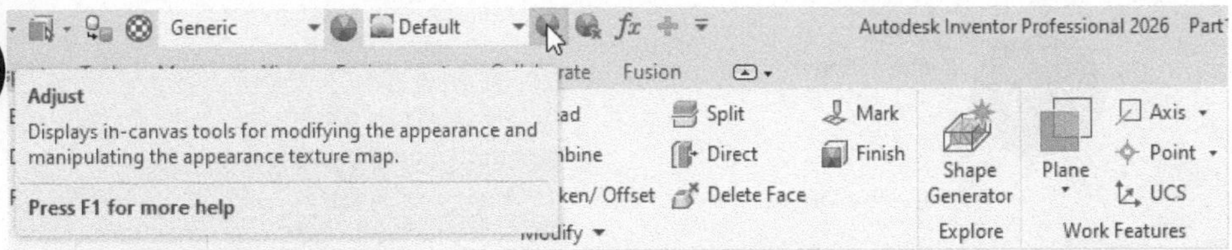

To copy and paste an appearance from one feature or face to another, click on the **Adjust** tool in the **Quick Access Toolbar**. The In-canvas interface appears in the graphics area, see Figure 7.67. Also, you are prompted to select an appearance. Click to select an appearance that is assigned to a face or a feature in the graphics area. Alternatively, you can select an appearance in the **Appearances** drop-down list of the In-canvas interface, see Figure 7.67. After selecting an appearance, you are prompted to select faces, features, bodies, or a part. Click to select faces, features, bodies, or a part in the graphics area. The selected appearance gets assigned to the selected geometries in the graphics area.

7.67

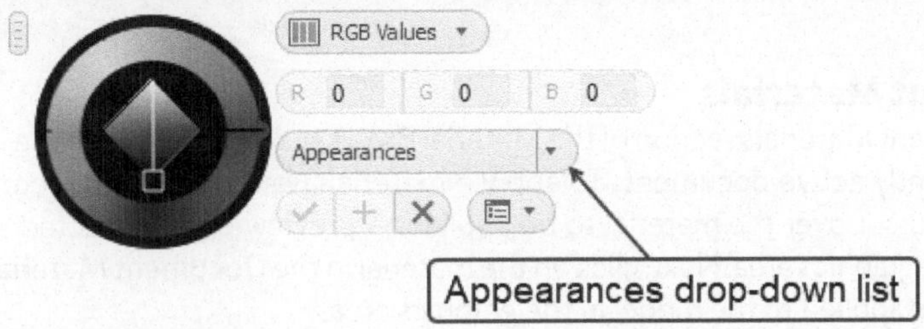

Applying a Material

In Autodesk Inventor, you can apply standard material properties such as density, elastic modulus, and tensile strength to a model. Note that assigning standard material properties to a model is important in order to calculate its mass properties as well as to perform static and dynamic analysis. Autodesk Inventor contains almost all standard materials in its material library. You can directly apply the required standard material to a model from the material library. Besides, you can also customize the material properties and apply them to a model. You can apply a material to a model by using the **Material** tool in the **Material and Appearance** panel of the **Tools** tab or the **Material** drop-down list in the **Quick Access Toolbar**. The methods for applying a material are discussed next.

Applying a Material by Using the Material Tool

To apply a material to a model, click on the **Material** tool in the **Material and Appearance** panel of the **Tools** tab, see Figure 7.68. The **Material Browser** dialog box appears in the graphics area, see Figure 7.69. It is divided into two sections: **Document Materials** and **Material Library**. Both are discussed next.

7.68

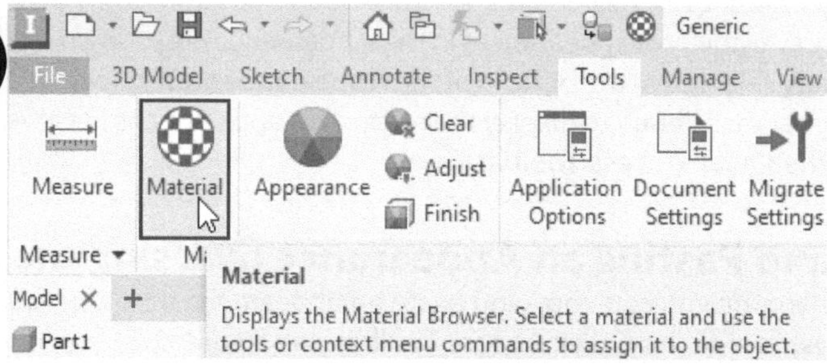

7.69

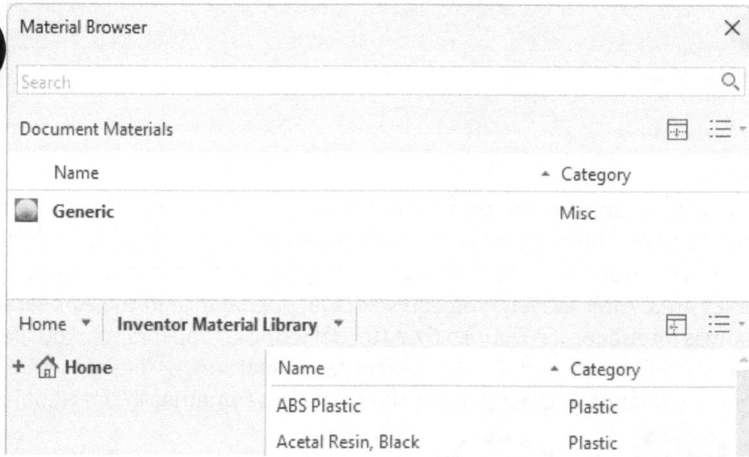

Document Materials

The **Document Materials** section of the **Material Browser** dialog box displays a list of materials available in the currently active document. To apply a material available in the **Document Materials** section, pause the cursor over the material to be applied. A preview of the selected material appears on the model in the graphics area. Next, click on the material in the **Document Materials** section. The selected material gets applied to the model in the graphics area.

Note: You can edit the material properties of a material in the **Document Materials** section. For doing so, right-click on the material to be edited and then click on the **Edit** option in the shortcut menu that appears. The material properties of the selected material appear in the **Material Editor** window. In this window, you can edit the material properties and then click on the **Apply** button to save the changes made and then close the window.

To delete a material in the **Document Materials** section, right-click on the material to be deleted and then click on the **Delete** option in the shortcut menu that appears. Note that you cannot delete the material that is currently applied to the model.

Material Library

The **Material Library** section displays a list of all materials available in the selected material library. You can switch between the Inventor Material Library and Autodesk Material Library. For doing so, click on the arrow next to the **Home** icon Home ▾ in the title bar of the **Material Library** section and then select the required material library.

To apply a material of the **Material Library** section, pause the cursor over the material. A preview of the selected material appears on the model in the graphics area. Next, right-click on the material to be applied and then click on the **Assign to Selection** option in the shortcut menu that appears. The selected material gets applied to the model and also gets added in the **Document Materials** section of the **Material Browser** dialog box.

Note that when you move the cursor over a material in the **Material Library** section, the **Adds material to document** button and **Adds material to document and displays in editor** button buttons appear, see Figure 7.70.

7.70

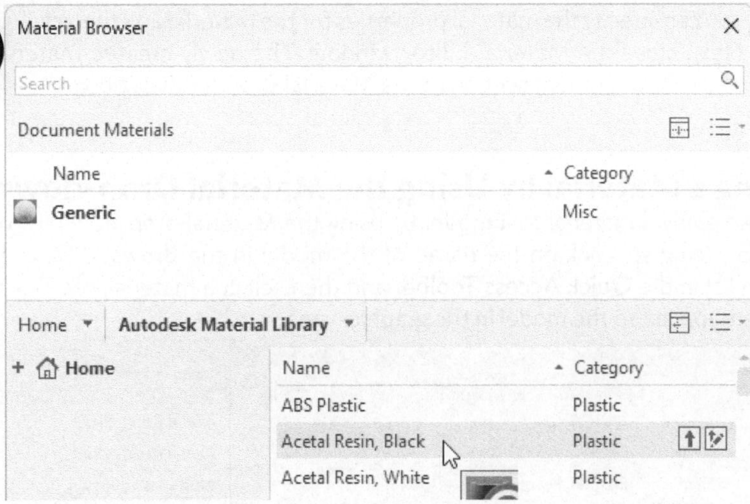

On clicking the **Adds material to document** button, the selected material gets applied to the model as well as added in the **Document Materials** section. On clicking the **Adds material to document and displays in editor** button, the selected material gets applied to the model, added to the **Document Materials** section, and opened in the **Material Editor** window. In this window, you can customize the properties of the selected material and then click on the **Apply** button to save the changes made in the material. Next, close the **Material Editor** window.

Tip: You can filter the display of materials by category in the **Material Library** section of the **Material Browser** dialog box. For doing so, click on the arrow next to the name of the active material library in the title bar of the **Material Library** section. A list of different categories appears, see Figure 7.71. In this list, you can select the required category. Only the materials of the selected category are displayed in the **Material Library** section.

7.71

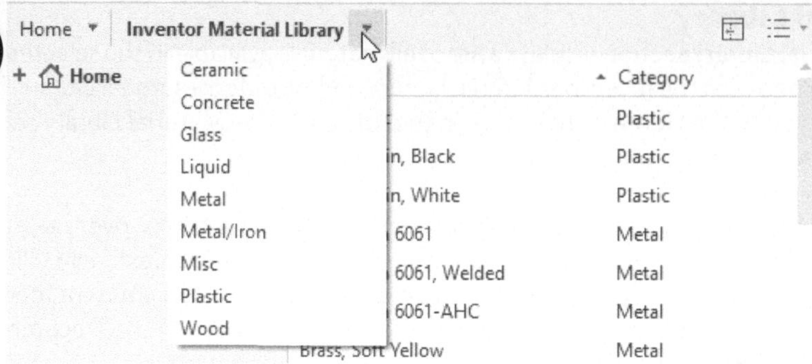

Note: You can also create a new material in the **Material Browser dialog box**. For doing so, click on the **Creates a new material in the document** button available at the lower left corner of the **Material Browser** dialog box. The **Material Editor** window appears. In this window, you can specify the material properties for the material and then click on the **Apply** button. Next, close the **Material Editor** window. The newly created material gets added in the **Material Document** section of the **Material Browser** dialog box.

Applying a Material by Using the Material Drop-down List

You can also apply a material to a model by using the **Material** drop-down list of the **Quick Access Toolbar**. For doing so, click on the name of the model in the **Browser**. Next, invoke the **Material** drop-down list in the **Quick Access Toolbar** and then select a material, see Figure 7.72. The selected material gets applied to the model in the graphics area.

7.72

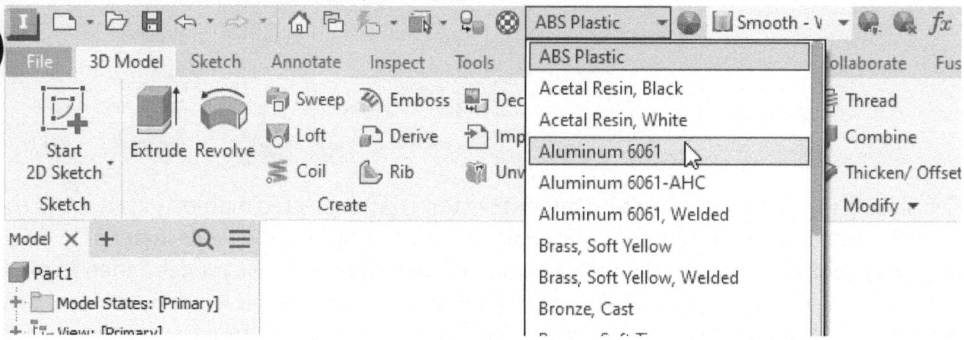

Note: The availability of materials in the **Material** drop-down list depends upon the material library selected at the bottom of the **Material** drop-down list. You can select the required material library to display the respective materials in the **Material** drop-down list of the **Quick Access Toolbar**.

Assigning Finishes/Manufacturing Data

In Inventor 2026, you can assign manufacturing data such as material coating, heat treatment, surface finish, and paint to the different faces of a model or assembly for use in later processes by using the **Finish** tool. The assigned manufacturing data can also be included in the 2D engineering drawing of the design. You will learn about creating 2D drawings in later chapters. The method for assigning manufacturing data to a final design is discussed below:

1. Click on the **Finish** tool in the **Modify** panel of the **3D Model** tab, see Figure 7.73. The **Finish** property panel appears, see Figure 7.74. Also, you are prompted to select one or more faces for assigning manufacturing data, since the **Face selection mode** button is activated in the **Selection Filter** flyout, by default, see Figure 7.74.

7.73

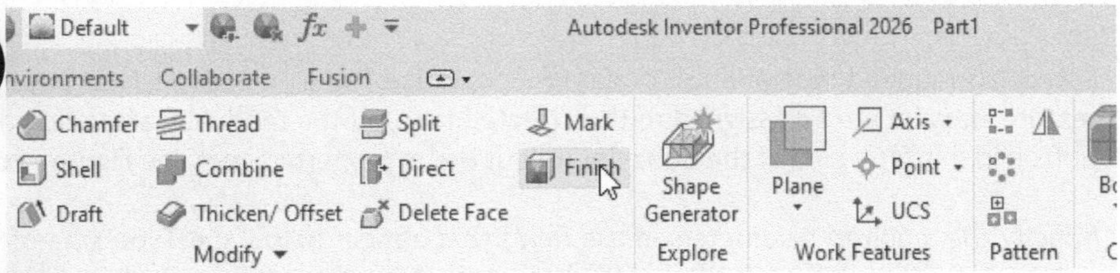

7.74

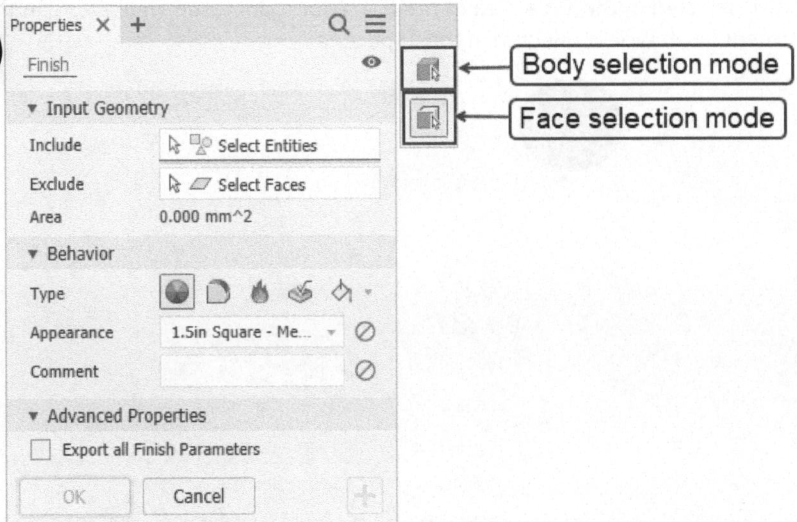

2. Select one or more faces of a model in the graphics area, see Figure 7.75. The area of the selected face or faces gets calculated and displayed in the **Area** field of the **Input Geometry** rollout.

7.75

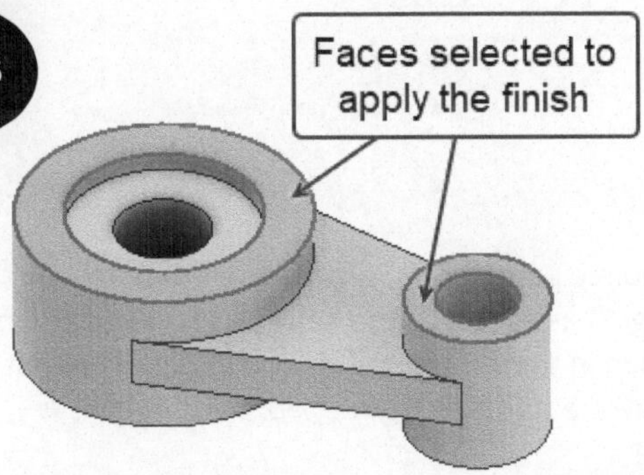

Note: You can also select one or more bodies for assigning the manufacturing data to them. To select a body, you need to activate the **Body selection mode** button in the **Selection Filter** flyout, refer to Figure 7.74.

If needed, you can also exclude one or more faces of the selected body from the assignment of manufacturing data. To do this, activate the **Exclude** selection field in the **Input Geometry** rollout, and then select the faces of the body to be excluded from the selection set.

3. Select the required type of finish or data (appearance, material coating, heat treatment, surface texture, or paint) to be assigned to the selected faces of the model by activating the respective button in the **Type** area of the **Behavior** rollout in the property panel, see Figure 7.76.

4. Specify the required parameters in the fields that appear below the **Type** area of the **Behavior** rollout. Note that the availability of fields for specifying the parameters depends upon the type of finish selected in the **Type** area of the **Behavior** rollout, see Figure 7.76. In this figure, the heat treatment finish type is selected in the **Type** area.

7.76

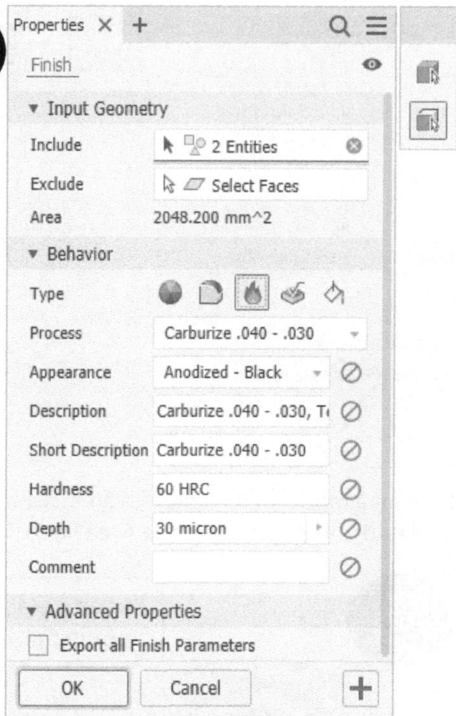

5. After defining the required parameters, click on the **OK** button in the property panel. The specified manufacturing data gets assigned to the selected faces of the model, see Figure 7.77. Also, the **Finishes** folder is added in the **Browser**. This folder displays a list of all the applied finishes in the order in which they are created, see Figure 7.78.

7.77

7.78

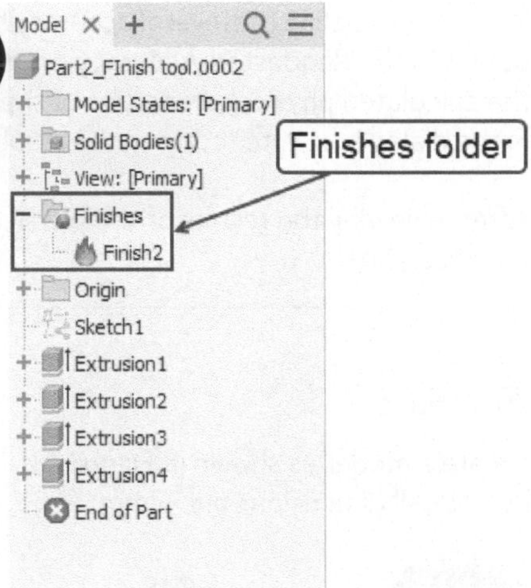

6. Similarly, you can assign finishes or manufacturing data to other faces of the design, as required.

Calculating Physical Properties

In Autodesk Inventor, after assigning a material to a model, you can calculate its physical properties such as mass, area, volume, center of gravity, and principle moments of inertia. For doing so, right-click on the name of the model in the **Browser**, see Figure 7.79. Next, select the **iProperties** option in the shortcut menu that appears. The **iProperties** dialog box appears. In the **iProperties** dialog box, click on the **Physical** tab and then click on the **Update** button. All the physical properties of the model appear in the different fields of the **Physical** tab of the dialog box, see Figure 7.80.

7.79

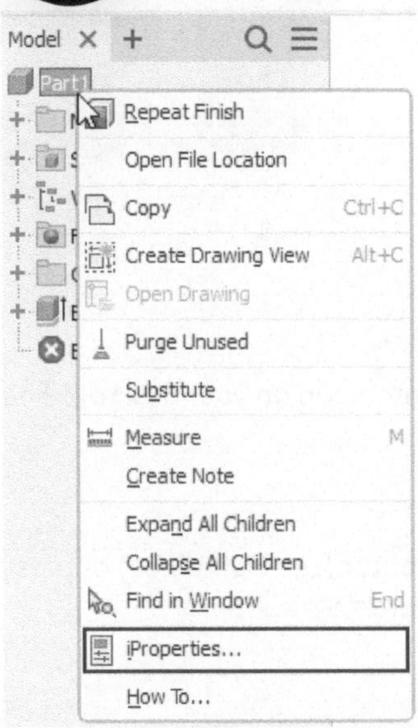

7.80

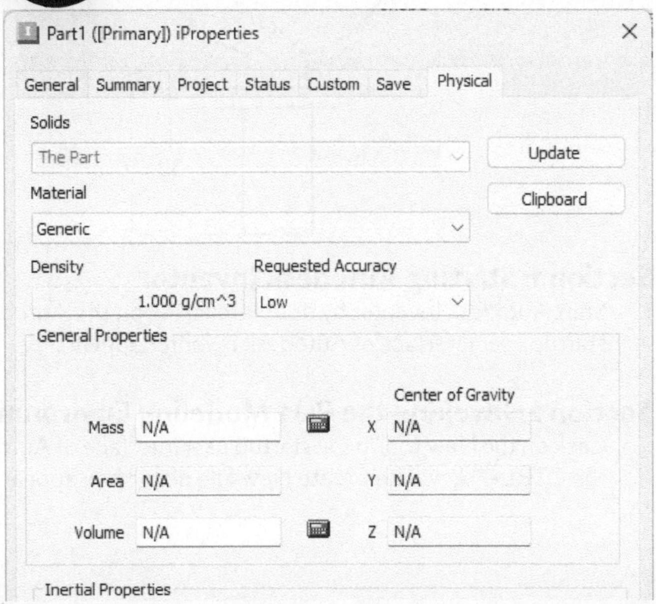

You can also define the level of accuracy for the calculated physical properties by selecting the required option in the **Requested Accuracy** drop-down list of the dialog box. You can also copy the results of the calculated physical properties of the model to the clipboard by clicking on the **Clipboard** button in the dialog box. After copying the results, you can paste them into any other document.

After reviewing the results of the physical properties of the model in the **iProperties** dialog box, exit the dialog box.

Tutorial 1

Create a model, as shown in Figure 7.81. You need to create the model by creating all its features one by one. All dimensions are in mm.

7.81

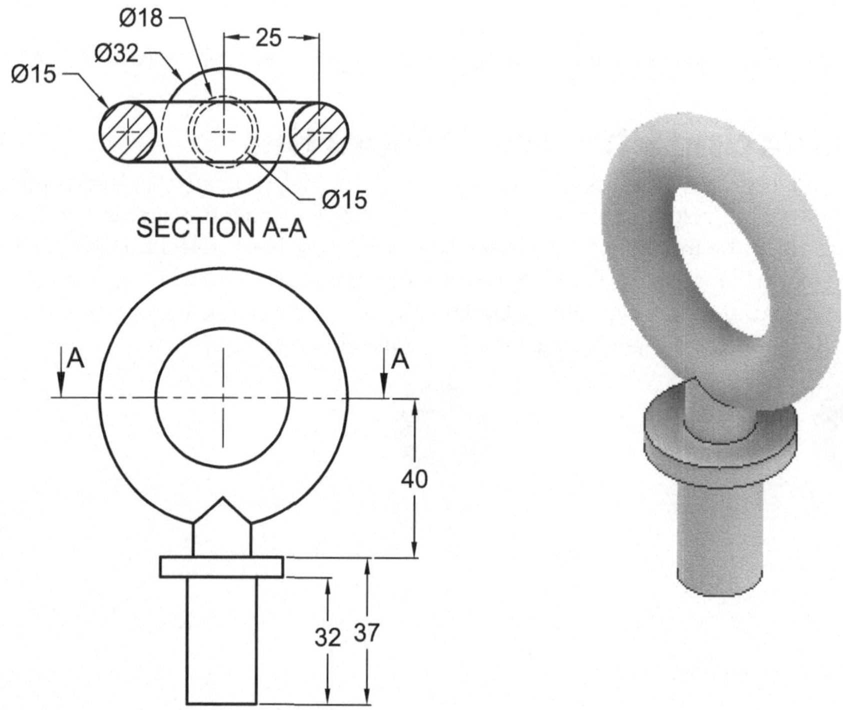

Section 1: Starting Autodesk Inventor

1. Start Autodesk Inventor by double-clicking on the Autodesk Inventor icon on your desktop. The startup user interface of Autodesk Inventor appears.

Section 2: Invoking the Part Modeling Environment

1. Click on the **New** tool in the startup user interface of Autodesk Inventor (see Figure 7.82) or press the CTRL+N key. The **Create New File** dialog box appears, see Figure 7.83.

7.82

2. Click on the **Metric** template folder on the left panel of the dialog box and then double-click on the **Standard (mm).ipt** template that appears on the right panel of the dialog box, refer to Figure 7.83. The Part Modeling environment is invoked.

7.83

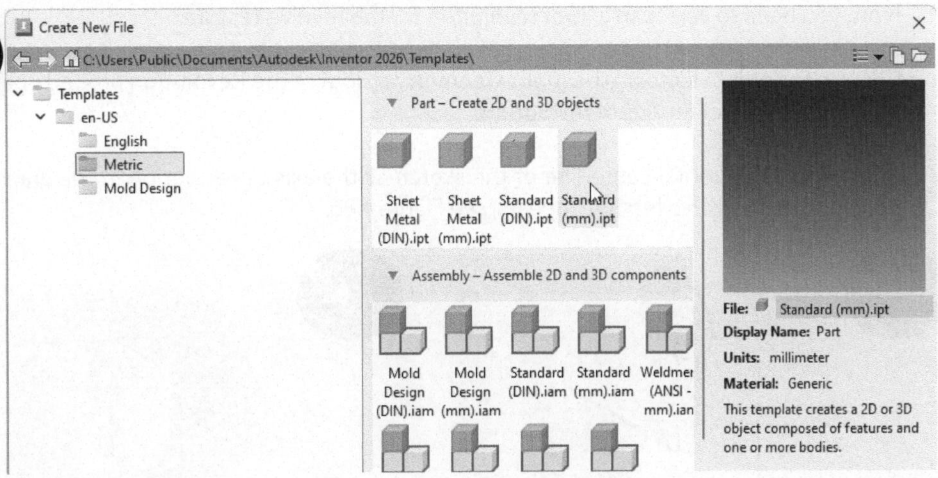

Section 3: Creating the Base Feature - Revolve Feature

1. Invoke the Sketching environment by selecting the Right plane (YZ Plane) as the sketching plane and then create the sketch of the base feature, see Figure 7.84. The base feature of the model is a revolve feature.

7.84

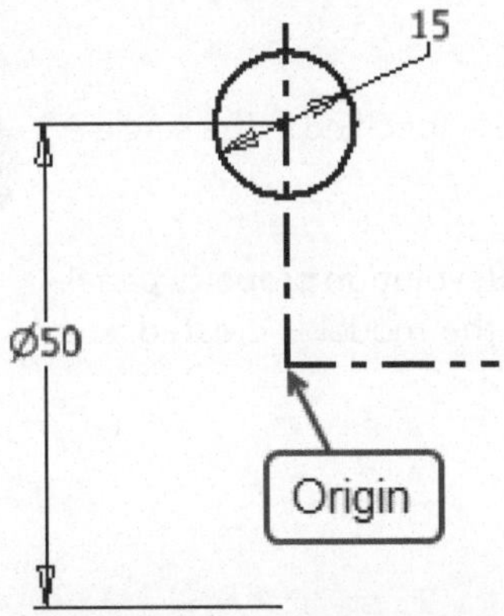

Tip: To make the sketch of the base feature fully defined as shown in Figure 7.84, you need to ensure that the center point of the circle has coincident constraint with the vertical centerline. The horizontal centerline in the figure will be used as the axis of revolution for creating the revolve feature.

2. Click on the **3D Model** tab in the **Ribbon** to display the tools for creating features of the model.

3. Click on the **Revolve** tool in the **Create** panel of the **3D Model** tab or press the **R** key. The **Revolution** property panel appears in the graphics area. Also, you are prompted to select a profile to be revolved.

4. Move the cursor over the circumference of the circle and then click when the circle profile gets highlighted in the graphics area, see Figure 7.85.

   Now, you need to select an axis of revolution for the revolve feature.

5. Click on the **Axis** selector in the **Input Geometry** rollout of the **Revolution** property panel. You are prompted to select an axis of revolution.

6. Click on the horizontal centerline of the sketch as the axis of revolution in the graphics area. A preview of the revolve feature appears, see Figure 7.86.

7.85

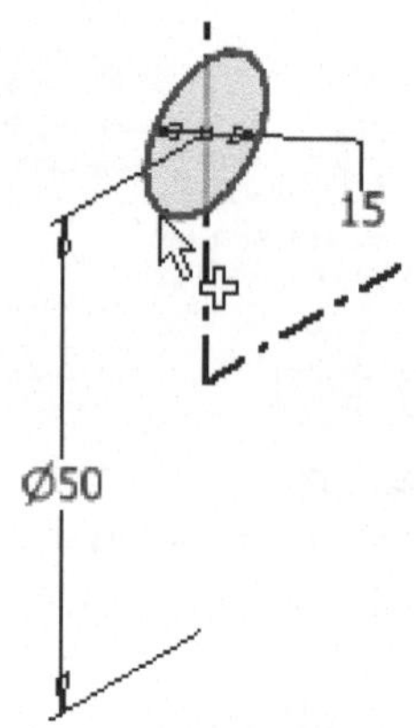

7.86

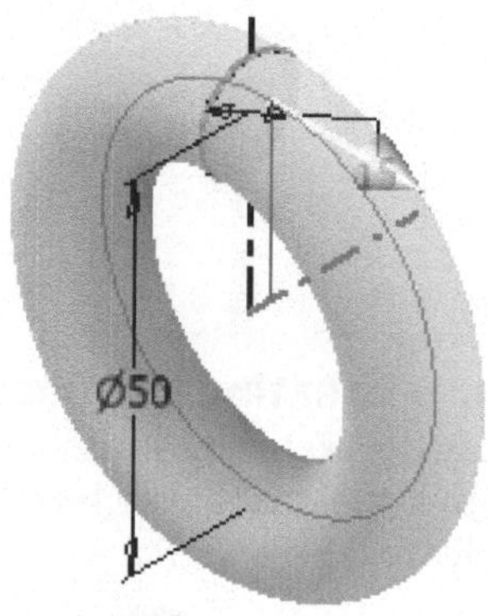

7. Ensure that a 360 degrees angle is specified in the **Angle A** field of the property panel.

8. Click on the **OK** button in the **Revolution** property panel. The base feature (revolve) of the model is created, see Figure 7.87.

7.87

Section 4: Creating the Second Feature - Extrude Feature

To create the second feature of the model, you first need to create a work plane at an offset distance of 40 mm from the Top plane.

1. Invoke the **Plane** flyout in the **Work Features** panel of the **3D Model** tab and then click on the **Offset from Plane** tool, see Figure 7.88. You are prompted to select a plane or a planar face of a model.

7.88

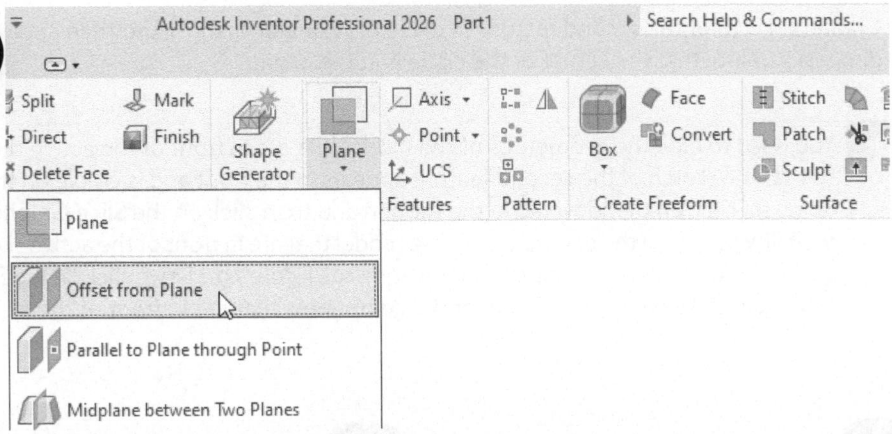

2. Expand the **Origin** node in the **Browser** and then click on the **XZ Plane**, see Figure 7.89. The preview of an offset work plane and the Mini-Toolbar appears in the graphics area, see Figure 7.90.

7.89

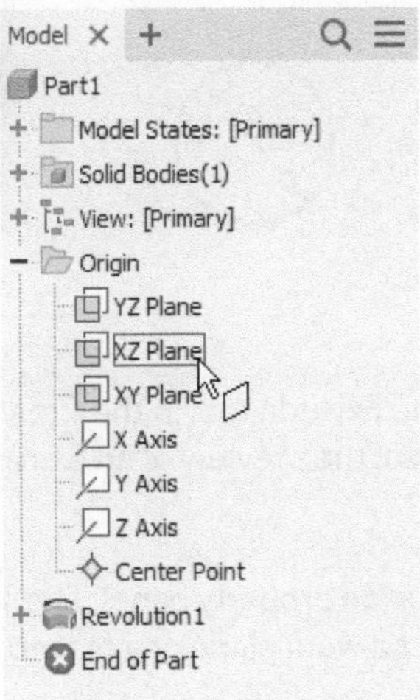

7.90

3. Enter **-40** in the Mini-Toolbar as the offset distance from the Top Plane (XZ Plane) in the downward direction.

4. Click on the **OK** button (green tick-mark) in the Mini-Toolbar. A work plane is created at an offset distance of 40 mm from the Top Plane, see Figure 7.91.

   Now, you need to create the second feature of the model by selecting the newly created plane as the sketching plane.

5. Invoke the Sketching environment by selecting the newly created plane as the sketching plane.

6. Create a sketch of the second feature (a circle of diameter 15 mm) and then apply the diameter dimension. Note that the center of the circle is at the origin.

Tip: You need to hide the geometries of the model that are in front of the active sketching plane so that the sketch of the second feature appears in the front and is visible on the screen. For doing so, click on the **View** tab in the **Ribbon** and then click on the **Slice Graphics** tool in the **Visibility** panel. All the geometries of the model that are in front of the active sketching plane get hidden and the sketch appears in the front, see Figure 7.92. Next, click on the **Slice Graphics** tool again to turn on the visibility of the geometries that are in front of the active sketching plane.

7.91

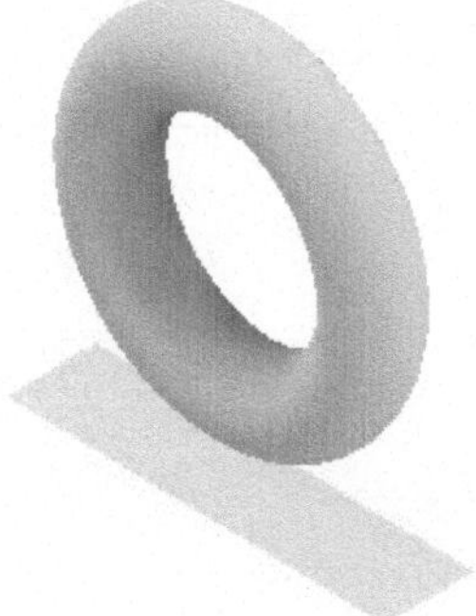

7.92

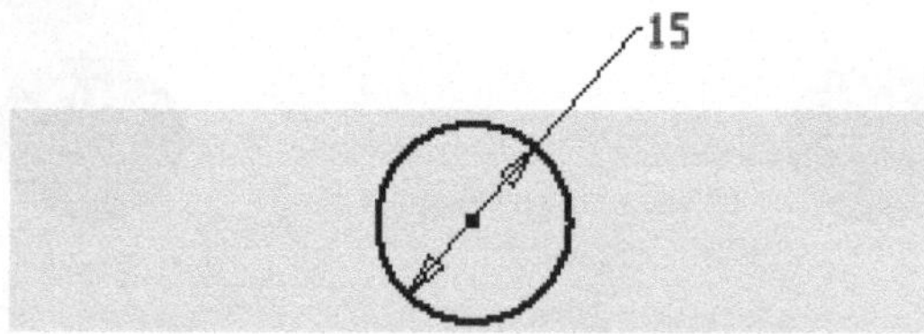

7. Click on the **3D Model** tab in the **Ribbon** and then click on the **Extrude** tool in the **Create** panel of the **3D Model** tab. The **Extrusion** property panel appears. Also, the preview of an extrude feature appears in the graphics area.

8. Click on the **To** button in the **Behavior** rollout of the **Extrusion** property panel. The **To** selector appears in the property panel and you are prompted to select a work plane or a face to terminate the extrusion.

9. Click to select the outer face of the base feature in the graphics area, see Figure 7.93. A preview of the extrude feature appears such that it gets terminated to the nearest intersection with the selected face of the base feature, see Figure 7.94.

7.93

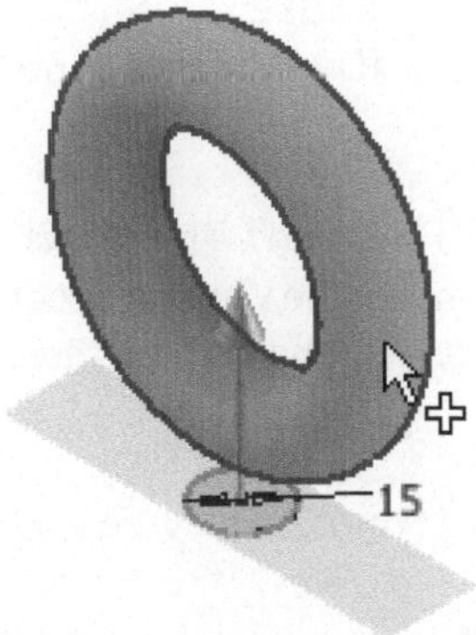

7.94

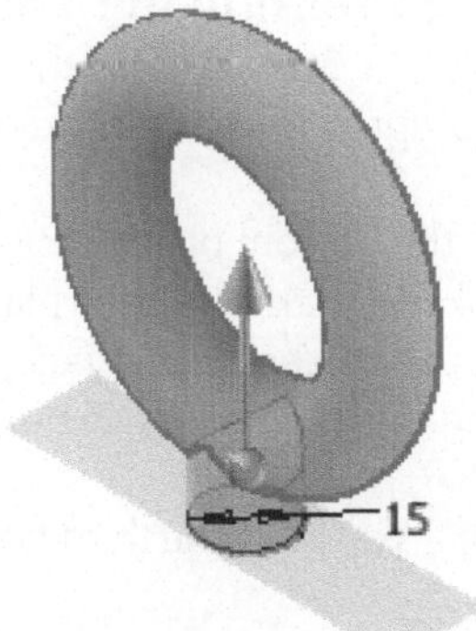

10. Ensure that the **Join** button is activated in the **Output** rollout of the property panel to merge the second feature with the first feature of the model, so that both together act as a single body.

11. Click on the **OK** button in the **Extrusion** property panel. The second feature (extrude) of the model gets created, see Figure 7.95.

Section 5: Hiding the Work Plane

1. Right-click on the work plane in the **Browser** to display a shortcut menu, see Figure 7.96.

2. Click on the **Visibility** option in the shortcut menu. The selected work plane gets hidden in the graphics area.

7.95

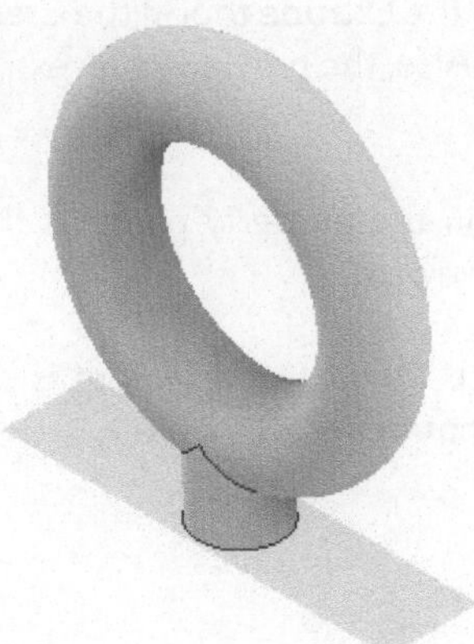

7.96

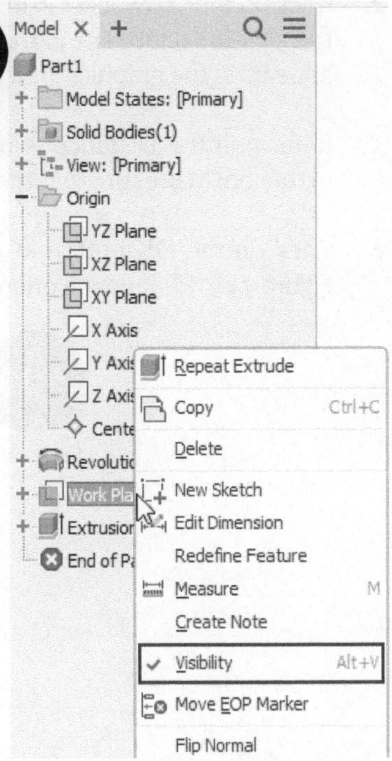

Section 6: Creating the Third Feature - Extrude Feature

1. Click on the **Start 2D Sketch** tool in the **Sketch** panel of the **3D Model** tab or press the S key. You are prompted to select a plane as the sketching plane.

2. Select the bottom planar face of the second feature, see Figure 7.97. The Sketching environment is invoked and the selected planar face gets oriented normal to the viewing direction. Note that to select the bottom planar face, you need to rotate the model in the graphics area by pressing and holding the middle mouse button with the SHIFT key.

3. Create a sketch of the third feature (a circle of diameter 32 mm), see Figure 7.98.

7.97

7.98

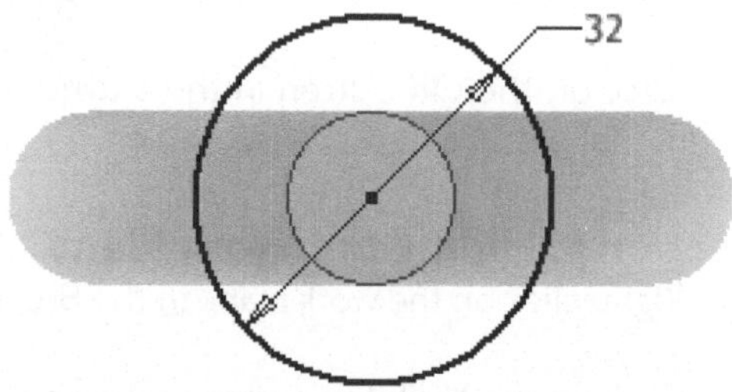

4. Click on the **3D Model** tab in the **Ribbon** and then click on the **Extrude** tool in the **Create** panel of the **3D Model** tab. The **Extrusion** property panel appears. Also, the preview of an extrude feature appears in the graphics area.

5. Enter **5** in the **Distance A** field of the **Behavior** rollout in the property panel as the depth of extrusion. Make sure that the direction of extrusion is downward.

6. Click on the **OK** button in the **Extrusion** property panel. The extrude feature is created, see Figure 7.99. Change the orientation of the model to the isometric view.

7.99

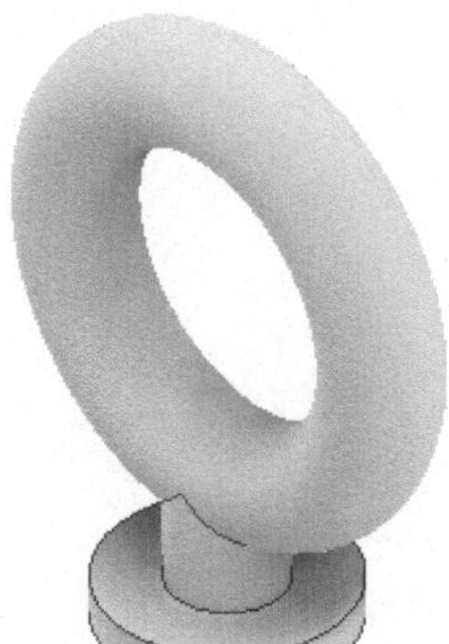

Section 7: Creating the Fourth Feature - Extrude Feature

1. Invoke the Sketching environment by selecting the bottom planar face of the third feature as the sketching plane.

2. Create the sketch of the fourth feature (a circle of diameter 18 mm), see Figure 7.100.

3. Click on the **3D Model** tab in the **Ribbon** and then click on the **Extrude** tool in the **Create** panel of the **3D Model** tab. The **Extrusion** property panel appears. Also, the preview of an extrude feature appears in the graphics area.

4. Enter **32** in the **Distance A** field of the **Behavior** rollout in the property panel as the depth of extrusion. Ensure that the direction of extrusion is downward.

5. Click on the **OK** button in the **Extrusion property panel**. The extrude feature is created, see Figure 7.101. Change the orientation of the model to the isometric view.

7.100

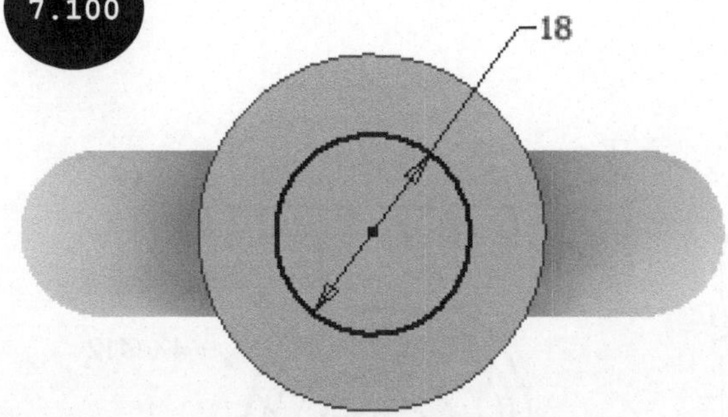

7.101

Section 8: Saving the Model

Now, you need to save the model.

1. Click on the **Save** tool in the **Quick Access Toolbar** toolbar. The **Save As** dialog box appears.

2. Browse to **Autodesk Inventor > Chapter 7** folder in the local drive of your system. Note that you need to create a Chapter 7 folder inside the Autodesk Inventor folder.

3. Enter **Tutorial 1** in the **File name** field of the dialog box and then click on the **Save** button. The model is saved in the specified location (>:\Autodesk Inventor\Chapter 7).

Tutorial 2

Create a model, as shown in Figure 7.102. After creating the model, assign the **Steel, Alloy** material and calculate its physical properties. All dimensions are in mm.

7.102

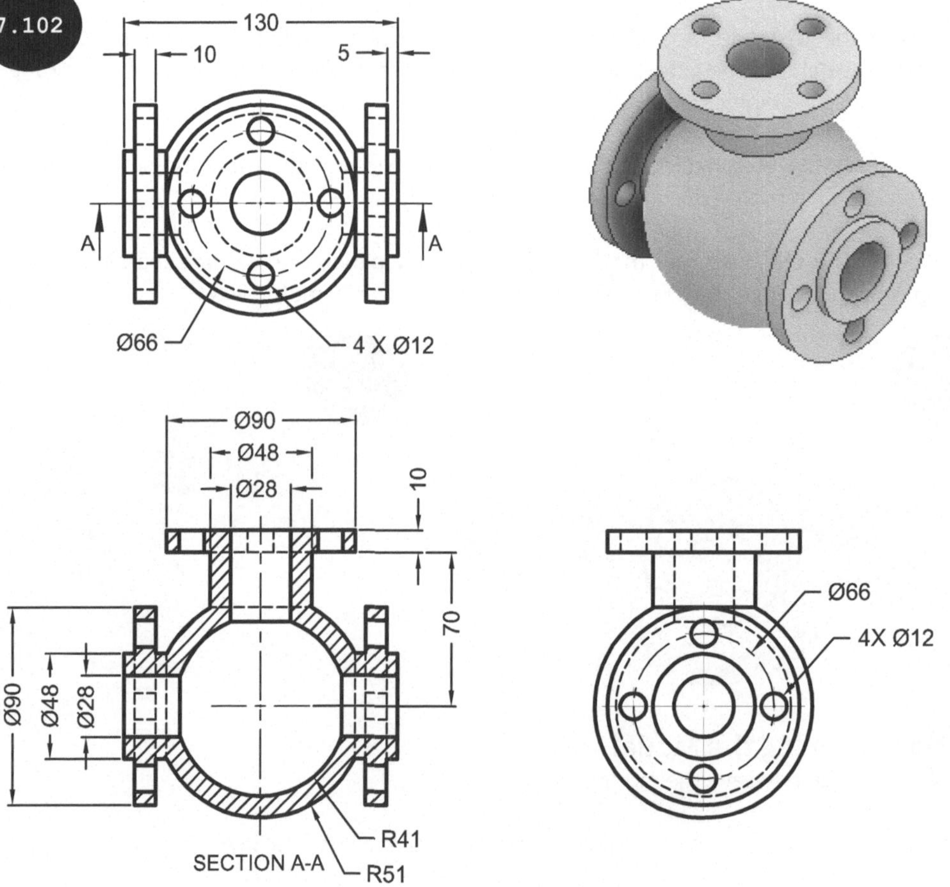

Section 1: Starting Autodesk Inventor

1. Start Autodesk Inventor by double-clicking on the Autodesk Inventor icon on your desktop. The startup user interface of Autodesk Inventor appears.

Section 2: Invoking the Part Modeling Environment

1. Click on the **New** tool in the startup user interface of Autodesk Inventor or press the CTRL+N keys. The **Create New File** dialog box appears.

2. Select the Metric template folder on the left panel of the dialog box and then double-click on the **Standard (mm).ipt** template that appears on the right panel of the dialog box. The Part Modeling environment is invoked.

Section 3: Creating the Base Feature - Revolve Feature

1. Invoke the Sketching environment by selecting the Front plane (XY Plane) as the sketching plane and then create the sketch of the base feature, see Figure 7.103. Do not exit the Sketching environment. Note that the base feature of the model is a revolve feature.

7.103

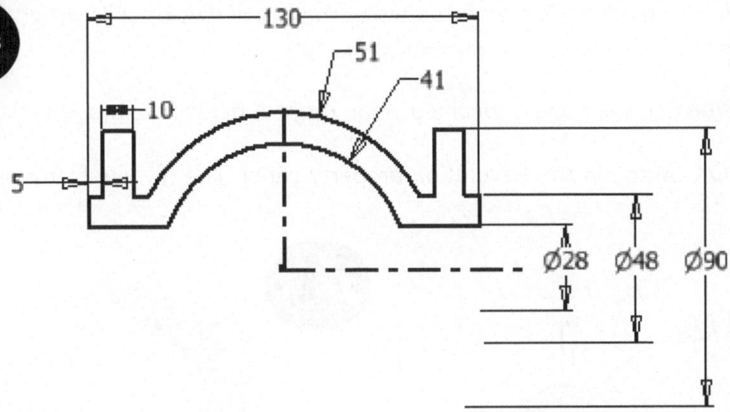

Tip: The sketch of the base feature shown in Figure 7.103 is symmetric about the vertical centerline. As a result, you need to apply symmetric constraints to the sketch entities with respect to the vertical centerline. Also, you need to apply equal constraints between the entities of equal length and collinear constraints between the aligned entities of the sketch. You can also create entities on one side of the vertical centerline and then mirror them to create entities on the other side.

2. Click on the **3D Model** tab in the **Ribbon** to display the tools for creating features of a model.

3. Click on the **Revolve** tool in the **Create** panel of the **3D Model** tab or press the **R** key. The **Revolution** property panel appears and you are prompted to select a profile to be revolved.

4. Move the cursor over an entity of the sketch in the graphics area and then click when the entire closed profile of the sketch gets highlighted, see Figure 7.104.

7.104

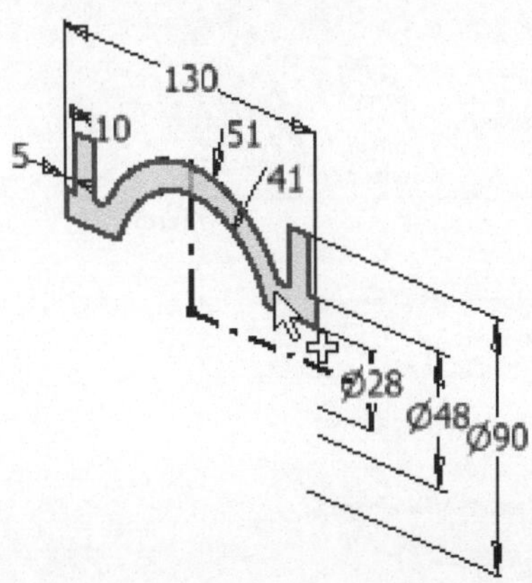

Now, you need to select an axis of revolution for the revolve feature.

5. Click on the **Axis** selector in the **Input Geometry** rollout of the **Revolution** property panel. You are prompted to select an axis of revolution.

6. Click on the horizontal centerline of the sketch as the axis of revolution in the graphics area. The preview of the revolve feature appears, see Figure 7.105.

7. Ensure that a 360 degrees angle is specified in the **Angle A** field of the property panel.

8. Click on the **OK** button in the **Revolution** property panel. The revolve feature is created, see Figure 7.106.

7.105

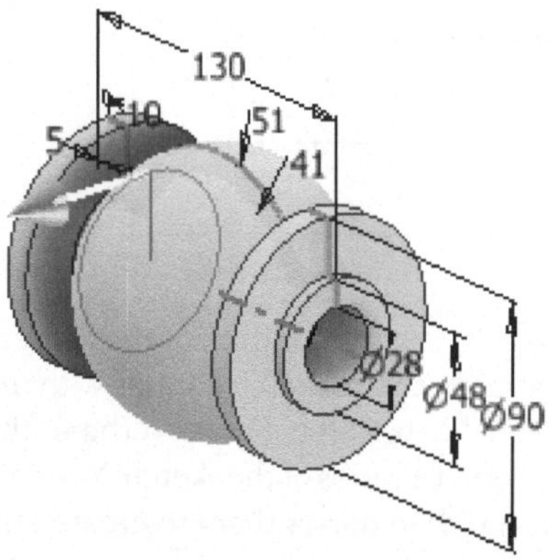

7.106

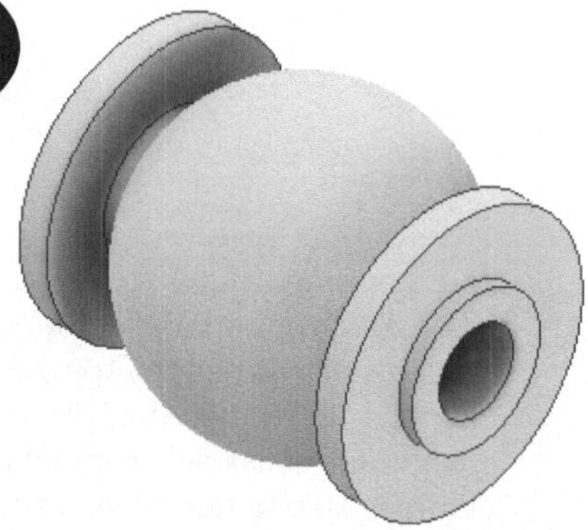

Section 4: Creating the Second Feature - Extrude Feature

To create the second feature of the model, you first need to create a work plane at an offset distance of 70 mm from the Top plane.

1. Invoke the **Plane** flyout in the **Work Features** panel of the **3D Model** tab and then click on the **Offset from Plane** tool, see Figure 7.107. You are prompted to select a plane or a planar face of a model.

7.107

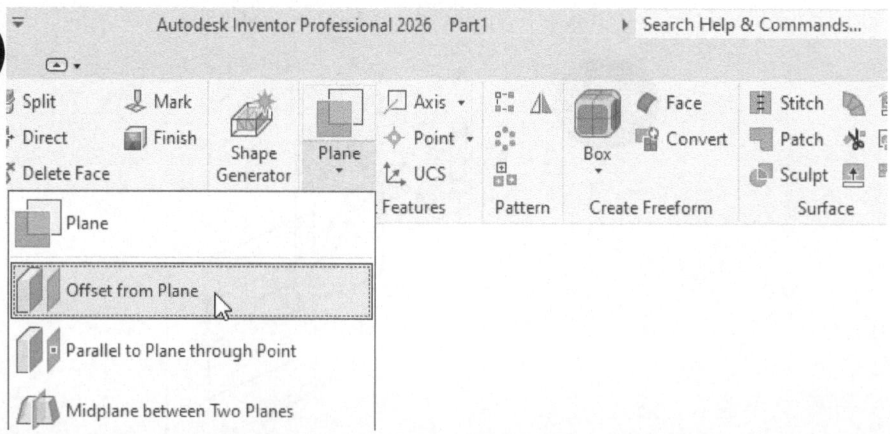

2. Expand the **Origin** node in the **Browser** and then click on the **XZ Plane**, see Figure 7.108. The preview of an offset work plane and the Mini Toolbar appear in the graphics area.

3. Enter **70** in the Mini-Toolbar as the offset distance from the Top Plane (XZ Plane) in the upward direction, see Figure 7.109.

7.108

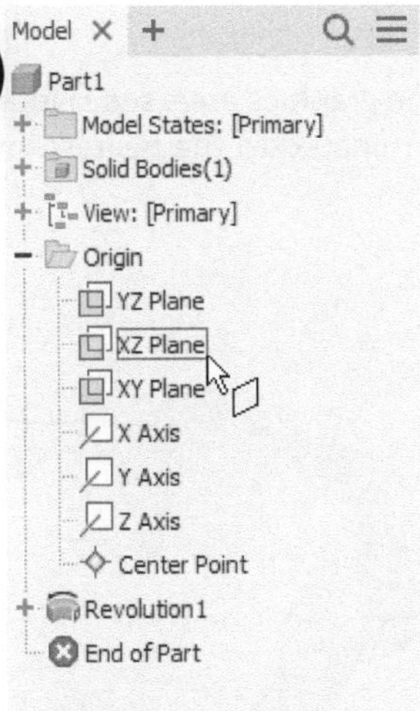

7.109

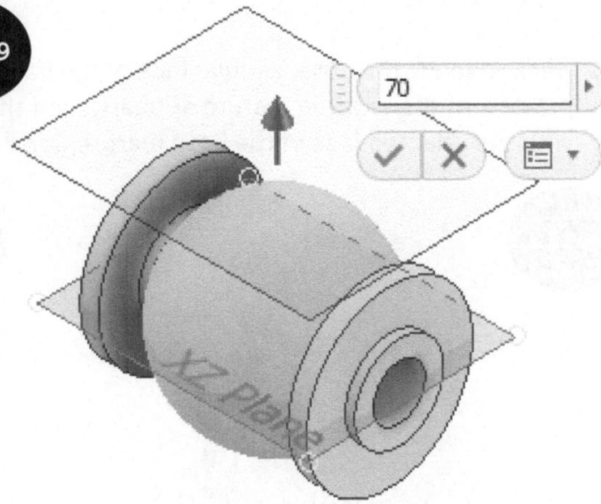

4. Click on the **OK** button (green tick-mark) in the Mini-Toolbar. A work plane is created at an offset distance of 70 mm from the Top Plane.

   Now, you need to create the second feature of the model by selecting the newly created plane as the sketching plane.

5. Invoke the Sketching environment by selecting the newly created plane as the sketching plane.

6. Create the sketch of the second feature (a circle of diameter 48 mm), see Figure 7.110.

7. Click on the **3D Model** tab in the **Ribbon** and then click on the **Extrude** tool. The **Extrusion** property panel appears. Also, the preview of an extrude feature appears, see Figure 7.111.

7.110

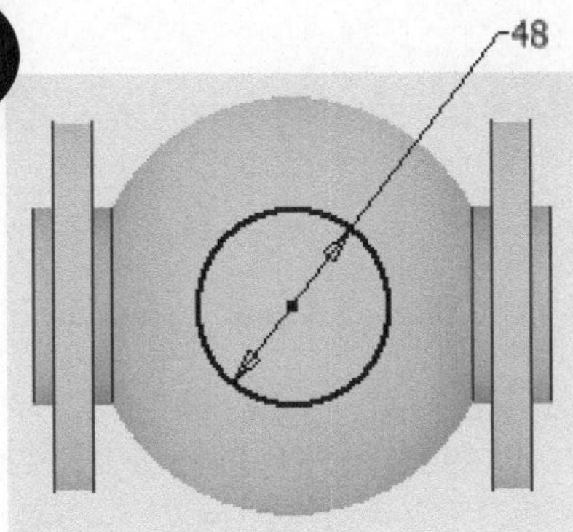

7.111

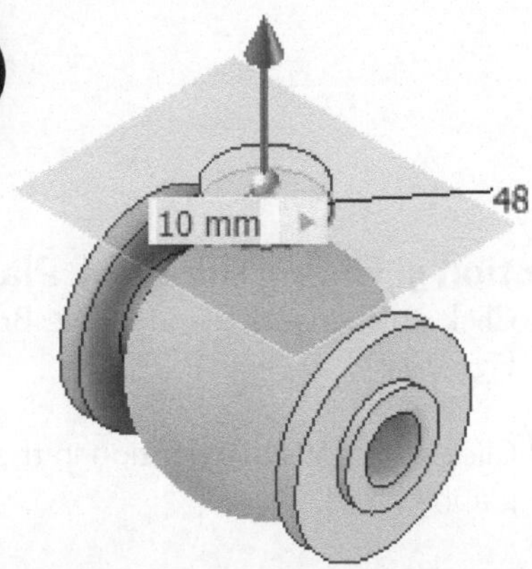

8. Click on the **Flipped** button in the **Direction** area of the **Behavior** rollout to reverse the direction of extrusion downward.

9. Click on the **To** button in the **Behavior** rollout of the **Extrusion** property panel. The **To** selector appears in the property panel and you are prompted to select a work plane or a face to terminate the extrusion.

10. Click to select the outer circular face of the base feature in the graphics area, see Figure 7.112. The preview of the extrude feature appears such that it gets terminated to the nearest intersection with the selected face of the base feature, see Figure 7.113.

7.112

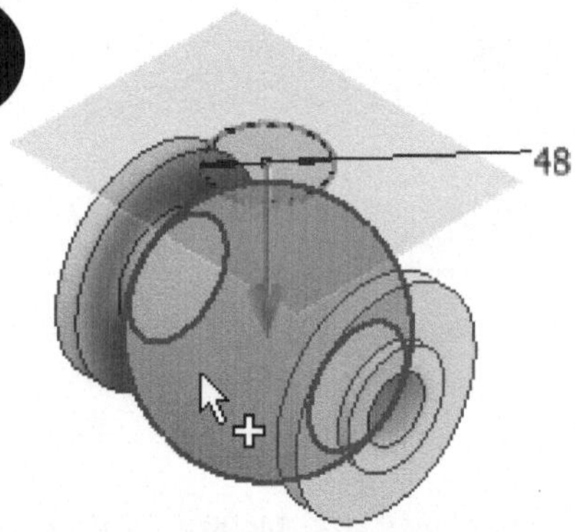

7.113

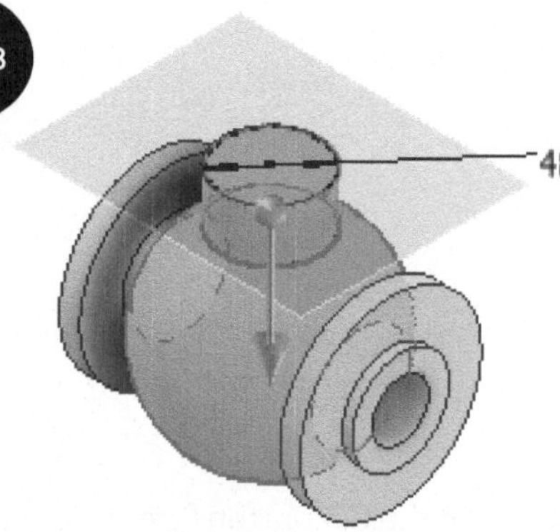

11. Ensure that the **Join** button is activated in the **Output** rollout of the property panel to merge the second feature with the first feature of the model so that both together act as a single body.

12. Click on the **OK** button in the **Extrusion** property panel. The second feature (extrude) of the model gets created, see Figure 7.114.

7.114

Section 5: Hiding the Work Plane

1. Click on the work plane in the **Browser** and then right-click to display a shortcut menu, see Figure 7.115.

2. Click on the **Visibility** option in the shortcut menu. The selected work plane gets hidden in the graphics area.

Section 6: Creating the Third Feature - Extrude Feature

1. Invoke the Sketching environment by selecting the top planar face of the second feature as the sketching plane.

2. Create a sketch of the third feature (a circle of diameter 90 mm), see Figure 7.116.

7.115

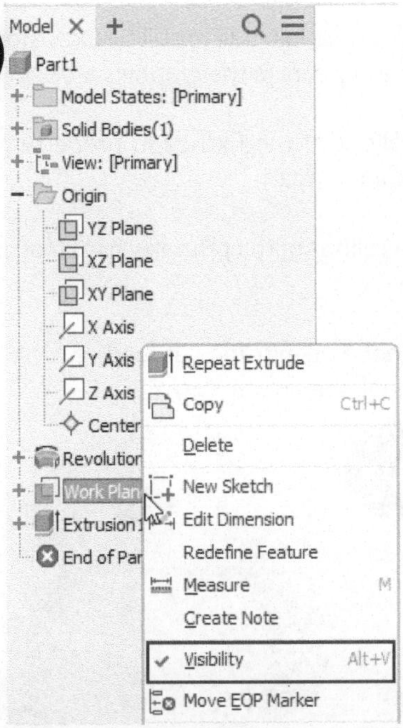

7.116

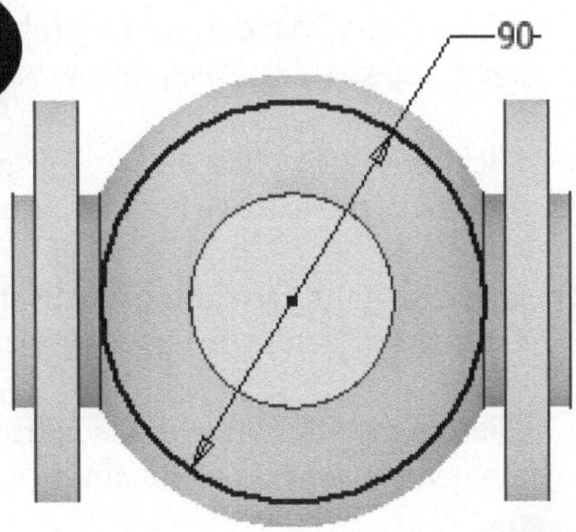

3. Click on the **3D Model** tab in the **Ribbon** and then click on the **Extrude** tool. The **Extrusion** property panel appears. Also, the preview of an extrude feature appears in the graphics area.

4. Enter 10 in the **Distance A** field of the **Behavior** rollout in the property panel as the depth of extrusion. Ensure that the direction of extrusion is upward.

5. Click on the **OK** button in the **Extrusion** property panel. The extrude feature is created, see Figure 7.117.

7.117

Section 7: Creating the Fourth Feature - Extrude Cut Feature

1. Invoke the Sketching environment by selecting the top planar face of the third feature as the sketching plane.

2. Create a sketch of the fourth feature (a circle of diameter 28 mm), see Figure 7.118.

3. Click on the **3D Model** tab in the **Ribbon** and then click on the **Extrude** tool. The **Extrusion** property panel appears. Also, the preview of an extrude feature appears in the graphics area.

4. Click on the **To Next** button in the **Behavior** rollout of the **Extrusion** property panel. The preview of the extrude cut feature appears in the graphics area.

5. Ensure that the **Cut** button is activated in the **Output** rollout of the property panel for creating an extrude cut feature by removing material.

6. Click on the **OK** button in the **Extrusion** property panel. The extrude cut feature is created up to the nearest or next point of intersection with the model, see Figure 7.119.

7.118

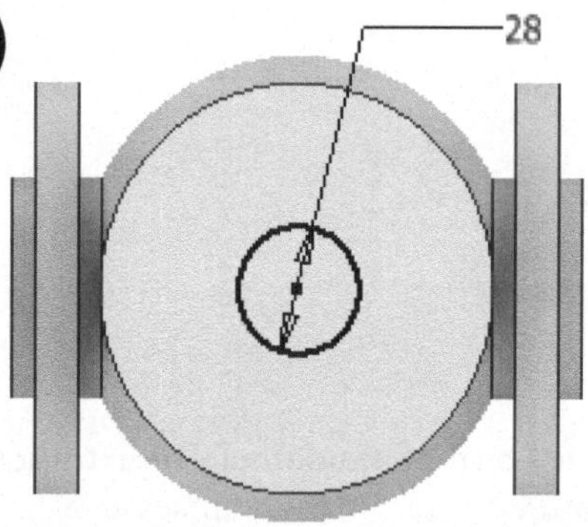

7.119

Section 8: Creating a Half Section View

Now, you can create a half section view of the model to view its internal features and better understanding of the previously created extrude cut feature.

1. Click on the **View** tab in the **Ribbon** and then select the **Half Section View** tool in the **Section** flyout of the **Visibility** panel of the **View** tab, see Figure 7.120. You are prompted to select a work plane or a face for sectioning the model.

7.120

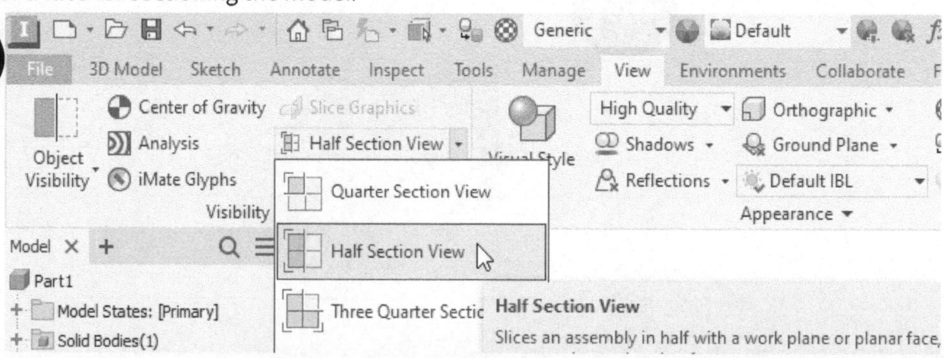

2. Expand the **Origin** node in the **Browser** and then click on the **XY Plane** (Front Plane) as the section plane. The preview of the half section view of the model appears in the graphics area with the display of the Mini-Toolbar, see Figure 7.121.

7.121

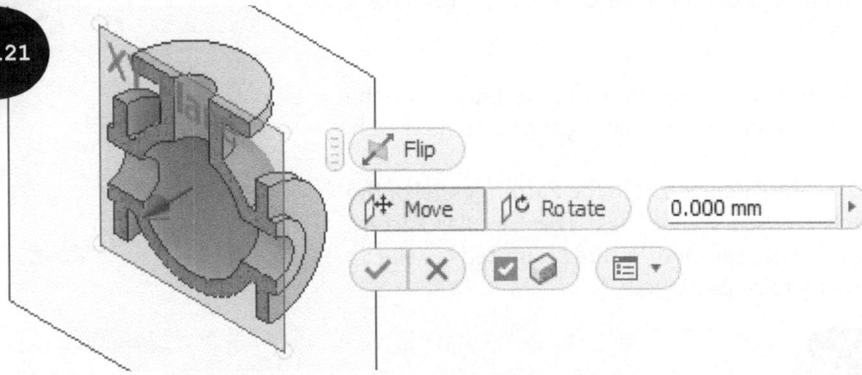

Note: By default, a 0 value is entered in the Mini-Toolbar. As a result, the section view is created exactly at the selected section plane. You can specify an offset distance in the Mini-Toolbar for creating a section view at an offset distance from the section plane.

3. Click on the **OK** button in the Mini-Toolbar. The half section view of the model gets created, see Figure 7.122.

   After reviewing the internal features of the model, you need to display the complete or full model in the graphics area.

4. Expand the **Section** flyout in the **Visibility** panel of the **View** tab and then click on the **Delete Section View** tool. The model is returned to its full view and the complete model appears in the graphics area, refer to Figure 7.123.

Section 9: Creating the Fifth Feature - Extrude Cut Feature

1. Invoke the Sketching environment by selecting the right planar face of the model as the sketching plane, see Figure 7.123.

7.122

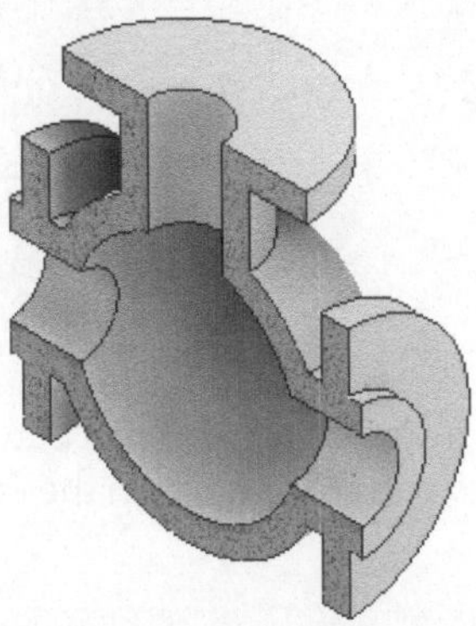

7.123

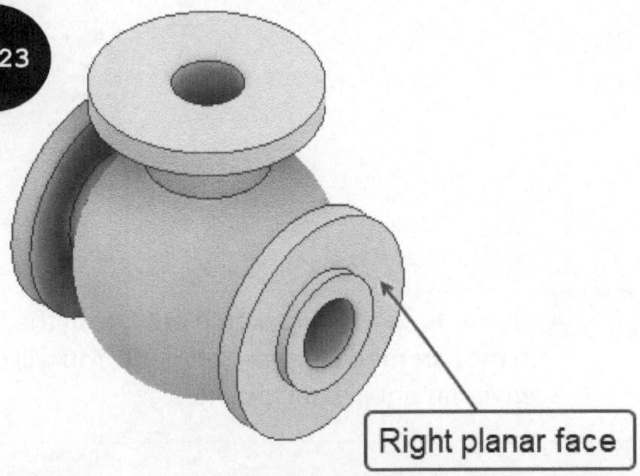

2. Create a circle of diameter 12 mm and apply the required dimensions, see Figure 7.124. Note that you need to apply a vertical constraint between the origin and the center point of the circle to make it fully defined.

   Now, you need to create a circular pattern of the circle for creating the remaining circles of the sketch.

7.124

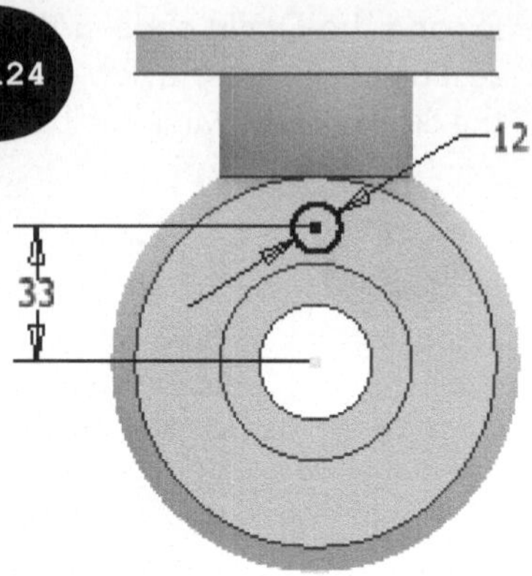

3. Click on the **Circular** tool in the **Pattern** panel of the **Sketch** tab, see Figure 7.125. The **Circular Pattern** dialog box appears and you are prompted to select a geometry to be patterned.

7.125

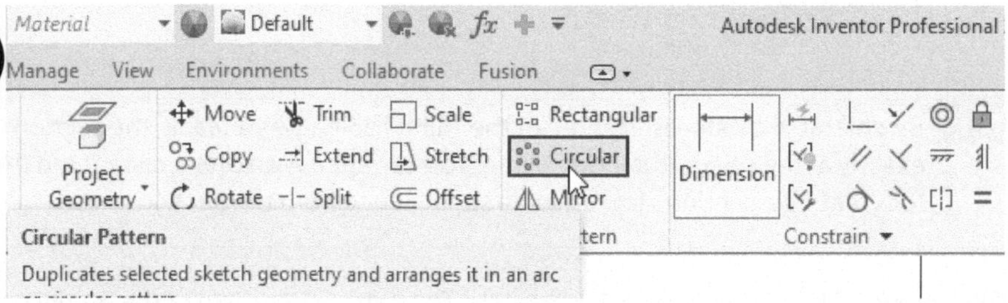

4. Select the previously created circle as the geometry to be patterned. Next, click on the **Axis** button in the dialog box and then select the origin as the axis of revolution of the pattern. A preview of the circular pattern appears in the graphics area.

5. Enter **4** in the **Count** field of the dialog box and ensure that the angle of revolution is specified as 360 degrees in the **Angle** field. Next, click on the **OK** button in the dialog box. The circular pattern is created, see Figure 7.126.

7.126

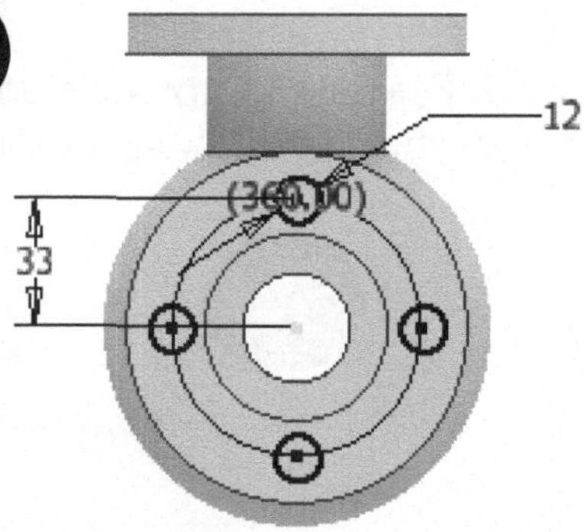

Tip: Similar to patterning sketch entities in the Sketching environment, you can pattern features in the Part modeling environment. You will learn how to pattern features in the Part modeling environment in later chapters.

Now, you can convert the sketch into an extruded cut feature.

6. Click on the **3D Model** tab in the **Ribbon** and then click on the **Extrude** tool. The **Extrusion** property panel appears. Also, you are prompted to select closed profiles of the sketch.

7. Select closed profiles of all the circles of the sketch one by one in the graphics area. The preview of the extrude feature appears in the graphics area, see Figure 7.127.

8. Click on the **To Next** button in the **Behavior** rollout of the **Extrusion** property panel. A preview of the extrude cut feature appears in the graphics area. Ensure that the **Cut** button is activated in the **Output** rollout of the property panel.

9. Click on the **OK** button in the **Extrusion** property panel. The extrude cut feature is created up to the nearest or next intersection face of the model, see Figure 7.128.

7.127

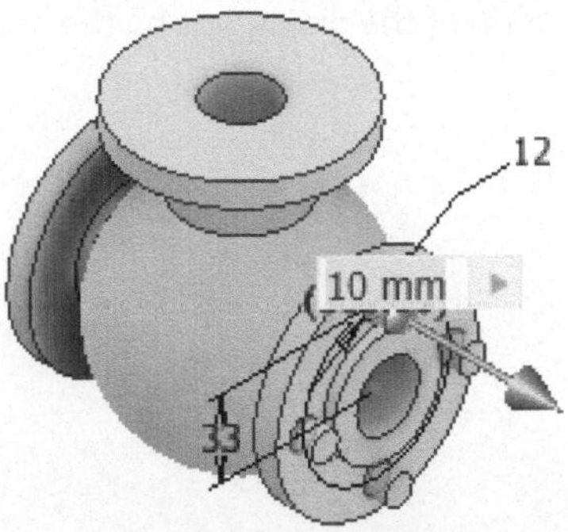

7.128

Section 10: Creating the Sixth Feature - Extrude Cut Feature

1. Similar to creating the extrude cut feature on the right planar face of the model, create the extruded cut feature on the left planar face of the model, see Figure 7.129. You can also mirror the extrude cut feature by selecting the Right plane as the mirroring plane to create the extrude cut feature on the left planar face. You will learn about mirroring features in later chapters.

Section 11: Creating the Seventh Feature - Extrude Cut Feature

1. Similar to creating the extruded cut feature on the right and left planar faces of the model, create the extrude cut feature on the top planar face of the model, see Figure 7.130.

7.129

7.130

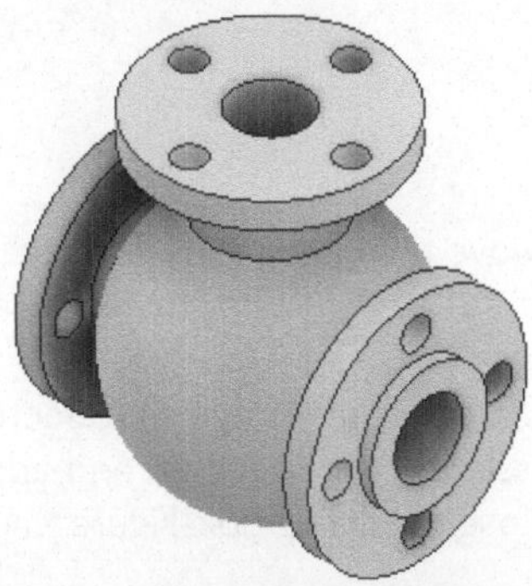

Section 12: Assigning the Material

Now, you need to assign the **Steel, Alloy** material to the model.

1. Click on the **Tools** tab in the **Ribbon** and then click on the **Material** tool in the **Material and Appearance** panel, see Figure 7.131. The **Material Browser** dialog box appears.

7.131

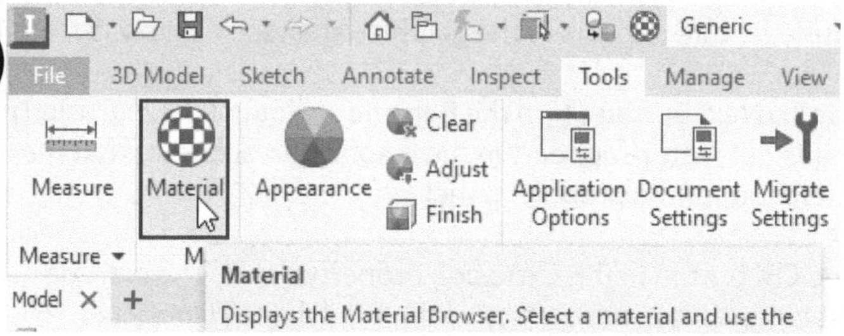

2. Filter the list of materials in the **Material Library** section of the dialog box by the **Metal** category, see Figure 7.132.

7.132

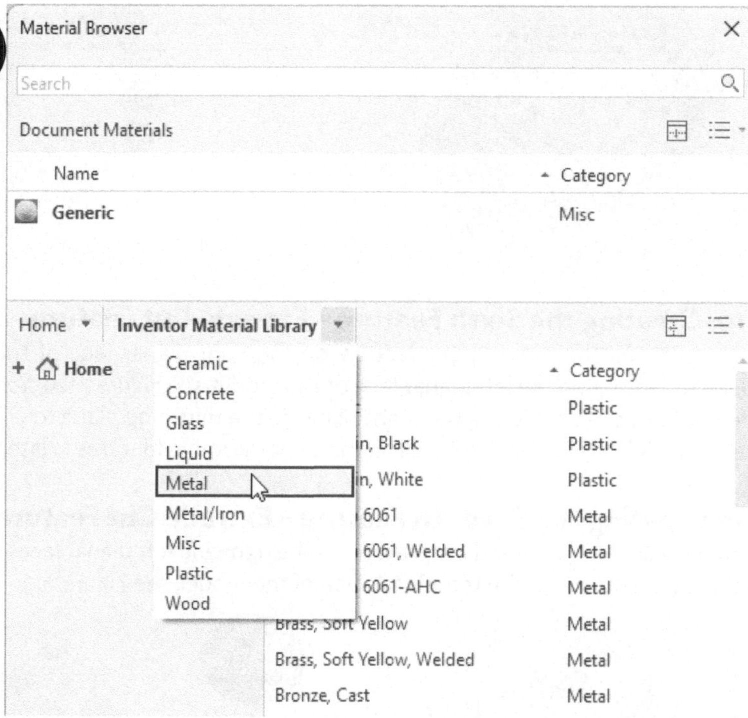

3. Move the cursor over the **Steel, Alloy** material in the **Material Library** section of the dialog box and then right-click to display a shortcut menu.

4. Click on the **Assign to Selection** option in the shortcut menu. The Steel, Alloy material gets assigned to the model and added in the **Document Materials** section of the dialog box. Next, close the dialog box. Figure 7.133 shows the model after assigning the Steel, Alloy material.

Section 13: Calculating Physical Properties

Now, you can calculate the physical properties of the model such as mass, area, and volume.

1. Right-click on the name of the model in the **Browser** and then click on the **iProperties** option in the shortcut menu that appears, see Figure 7.134. The **iProperties** dialog box appears.

7.133

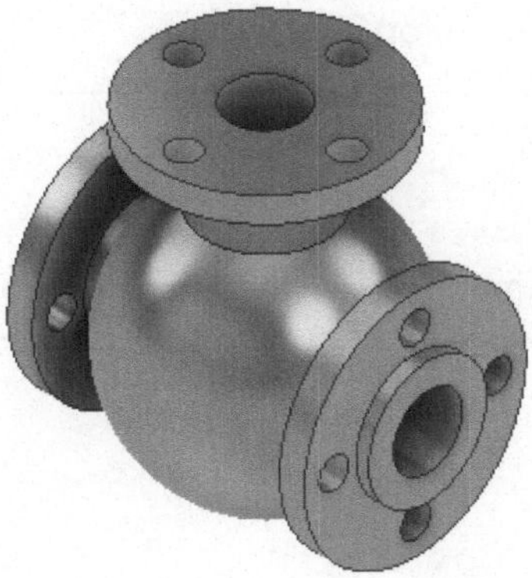

7.134

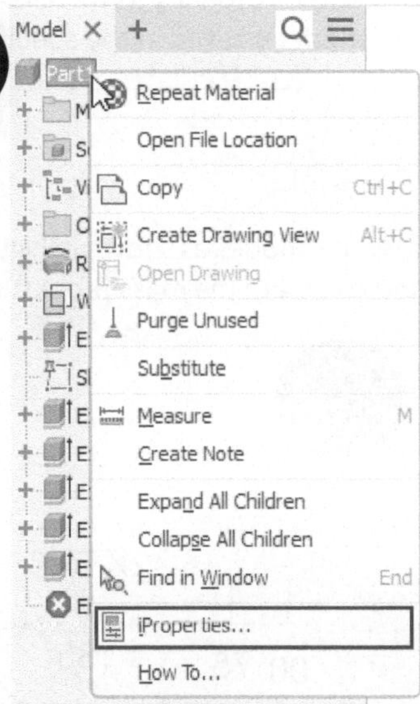

2. Click on the **Physical** tab in the **iProperties** dialog box and then click on the **Update** button. All the physical properties of the model appear in the dialog box, see Figure 7.135.

7.135

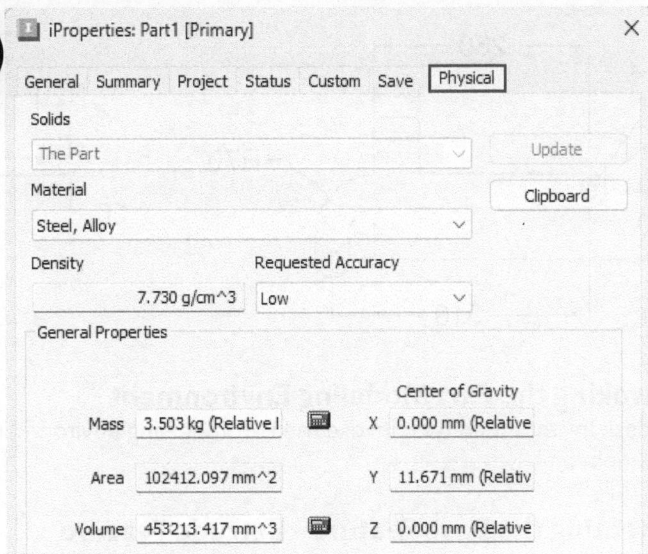

3. After reviewing the mass properties, exit the **iProperties** dialog box.

Section 14: Saving the Model

1. Click on the **Save** tool in the **Quick Access Toolbar** toolbar. The **Save As** dialog box appears. Next, browse to **Autodesk Inventor > Chapter 7** folder in the local drive of your system. Note that you need to create Chapter 7 folder, if not created earlier.

2. Enter **Tutorial 2** in the **File name** field of the dialog box and then click on the **Save** button. The model is saved in the specified location (>:\Autodesk Inventor\Chapter 7).

Tutorial 3

Create a model, as shown in Figure 7.136. After creating the model, assign the Aluminum 6061 material and calculate the mass properties of the model. All dimensions are in mm.

7.136

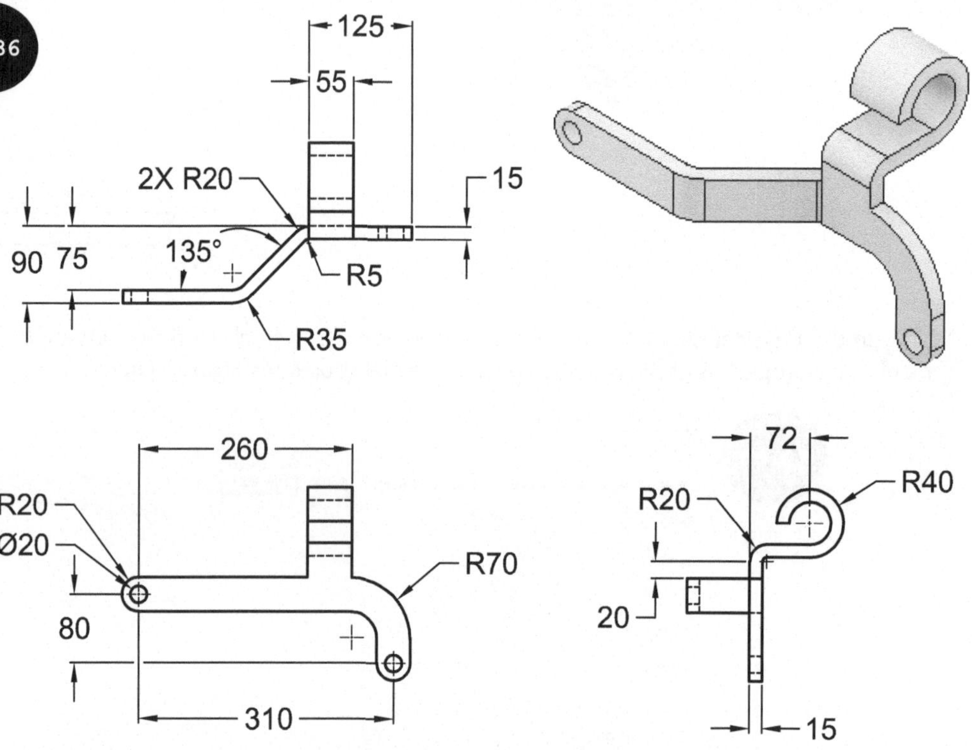

Section 1: Invoking the Part Modeling Environment

1. Start Autodesk Inventor and then invoke the Part modeling environment by using the **Standard (mm).ipt** template.

Section 2: Creating the Base Feature - Extrude Feature

1. Invoke the Sketching environment by selecting the Front Plane (XY Plane) as the sketching plane and then create the sketch of the base feature, see Figure 7.137. After creating the sketch, do not exit the Sketching environment.

7.137

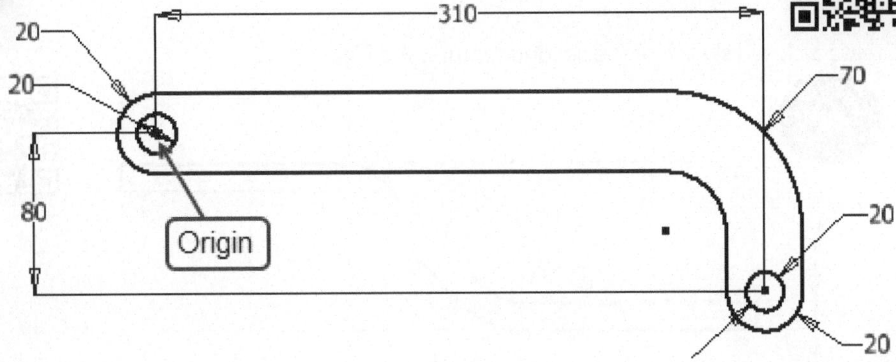

Tip: To make the sketch of the base feature fully defined as shown in Figure 7.137, you need to apply the required constraints such as tangent constraints between connecting lines and arcs, and the concentric constraint between the arcs sharing the same center point.

2. Click on the **3D Model** tab in the **Ribbon** and then click on the **Extrude** tool. The **Extrusion** property panel appears and you are prompted to select a closed profile of the sketch.

3. Select the outer closed profile of the sketch to be extruded, see Figure 7.138. A preview of the extrude feature appears in the graphics area.

4. Enter **90** in the **Distance A** field of the **Behavior** rollout in the property panel as the depth of extrusion.

5. Click on the **Symmetric** button in the **Behavior** rollout of the property panel to extrude the sketch symmetrically on both sides of the sketching plane.

6. Click on the **OK** button in the **Extrusion** property panel. The extrude feature is created, see Figure 7.139.

7.138

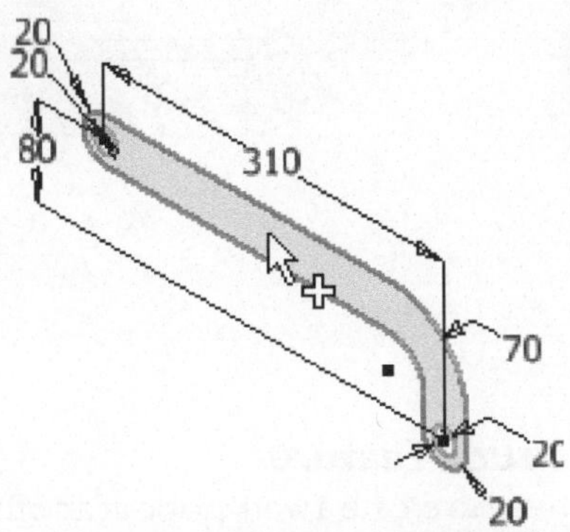

7.139

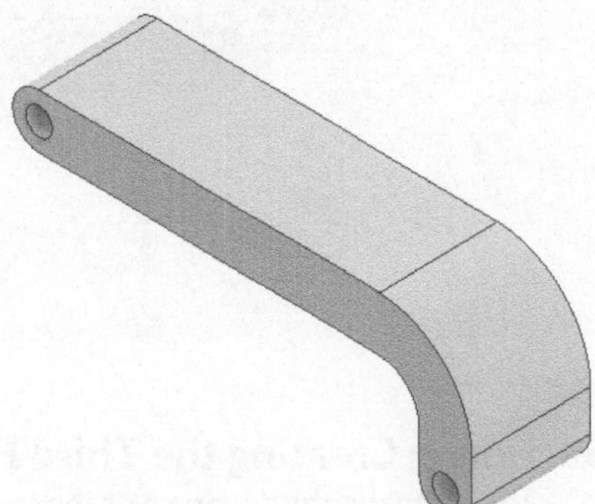

Section 3: Creating the Second Feature - Extrude Intersect Feature

1. Invoke the Sketching environment by selecting the top planar face of the base feature as the sketching plane.

2. Create a closed sketch of the second feature, see Figure 7.140.

7.140

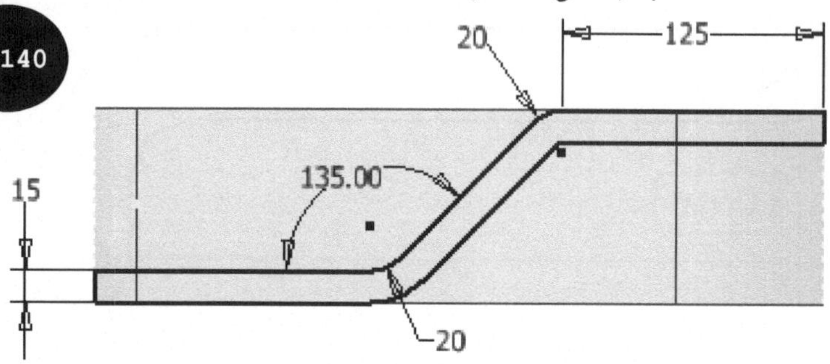

3. Click on the **3D Model** tab in the **Ribbon** and then click on the **Extrude** tool. The **Extrusion** property panel appears and the preview of an extrude feature appears in the graphics area.

4. Click on the **Flipped** button in the **Direction** area of the **Behavior** rollout to reverse the direction of extrusion downward.

5. Click on the **Through All** button in the **Behavior** rollout of the property panel for extruding the profile throughout the geometry of the model.

6. Click on the **Intersect** button in the **Output** rollout of the property panel for creating a feature by only keeping the intersecting or common material between the existing feature and the feature being created. A preview of the feature appears, see Figure 7.141.

7. Click on the **OK** button in the **Extrusion** property panel. The extrude intersect feature is created, see Figure 7.142.

7.141

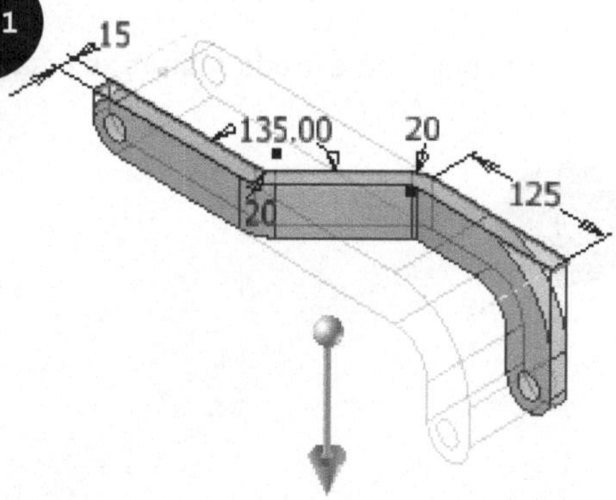

7.142

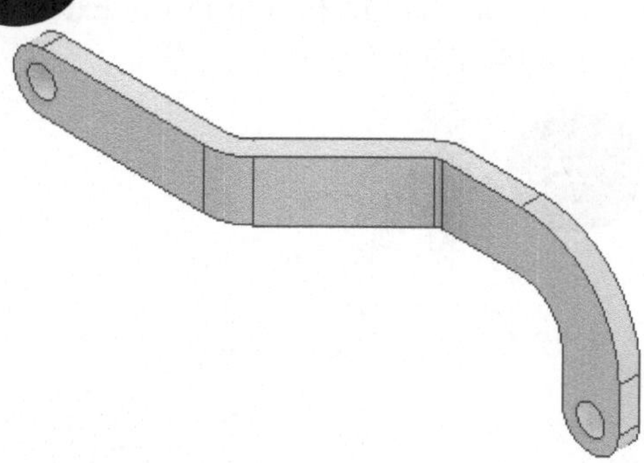

Section 4: Creating the Third Feature - Extrude Feature

To create the third feature of the model, you first need to create a work plane at an offset distance of 205 mm from the Right Plane (YZ Plane).

1. Create a work plane at an offset distance of 205 mm from the Right Plane (YZ Plane) by using the **Offset from Plane** tool, refer to Figure 7.143.

   After creating the work plane, you need to create the third feature of the model.

2. Invoke the Sketching environment by selecting the newly created work plane as the sketching plane.

3. Create a closed sketch of the third feature, see Figure 7.144.

7.143

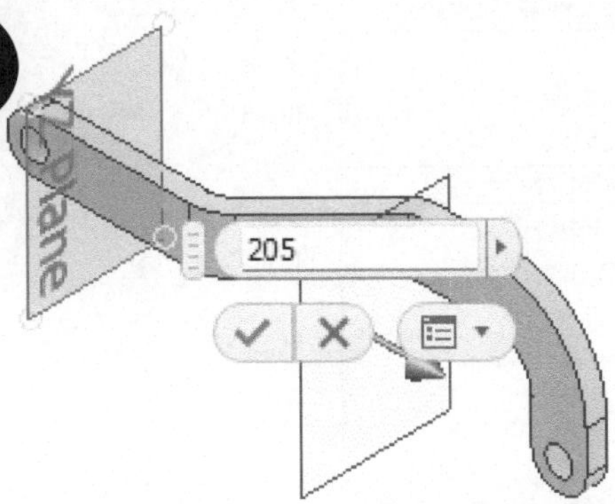

7.144

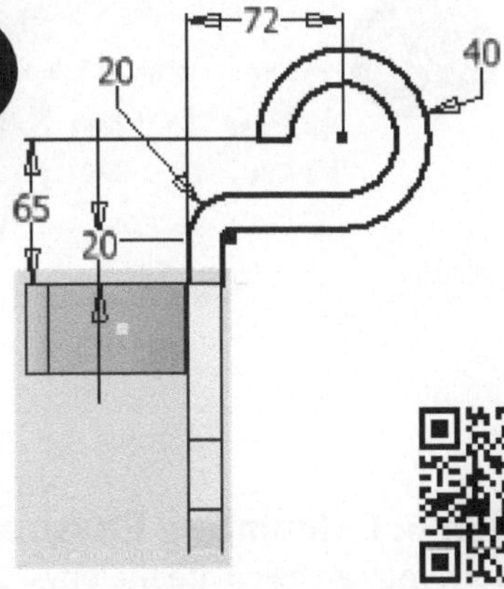

Tip: To make the sketch of the third feature fully defined as shown in Figure 7.144, you need to apply the required constraints such as tangent constraints between connecting lines and arcs, and concentric constraint between the arcs sharing the same center point.

4. Click on the **3D Model** tab in the **Ribbon** and then click on the **Extrude** tool. The **Extrusion** property panel appears and the preview of an extrude feature appears, see Figure 7.145.

5. Enter **55** in the **Distance A** field of the **Behavior** rollout in the property panel as the depth of extrusion.

6. Click on the **OK** button in the **Extrusion** property panel. The extrude feature is created, see Figure 7.146.

7.145

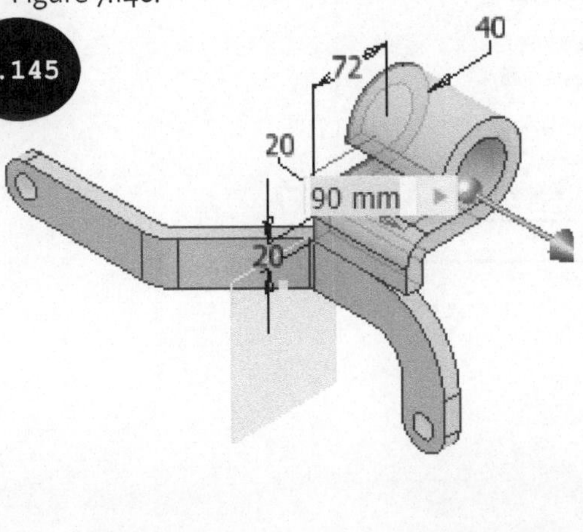

7.146

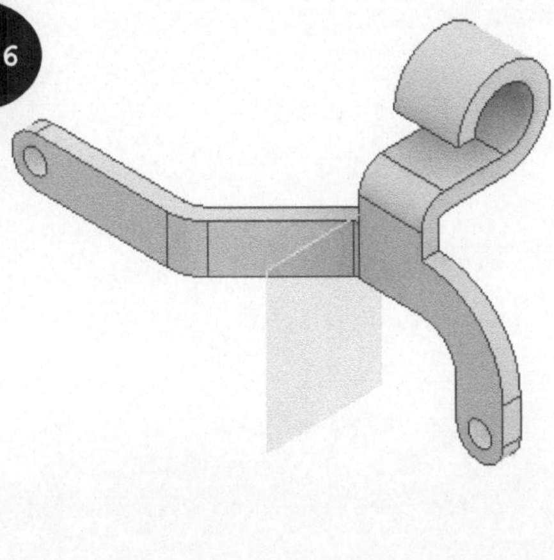

7. Hide the display of work plane in the graphics area.

Section 5: Assigning the Material

Now, you need to assign the Aluminum 6061 material to the model.

1. Click on the name of the model in the Browser and then invoke the **Material** drop-down list in the **Quick Access Toolbar**, and then select the **Aluminum 6061** material, see Figure 7.147. The selected material (Aluminum 6061) gets applied to the model.

7.147

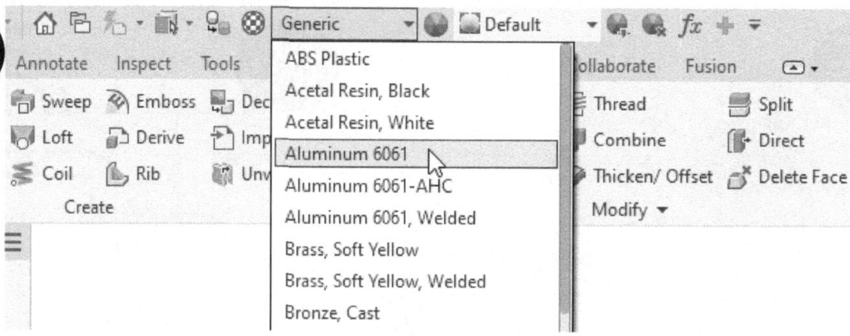

Section 6: Calculating Physical Properties

Now, you can calculate the physical properties of the model such as mass, area, and volume.

1. Right-click on the name of the model in the **Browser** and then click on the **iProperties** option in the shortcut menu that appears, see Figure 7.148. The **iProperties** dialog box appears.

7.148

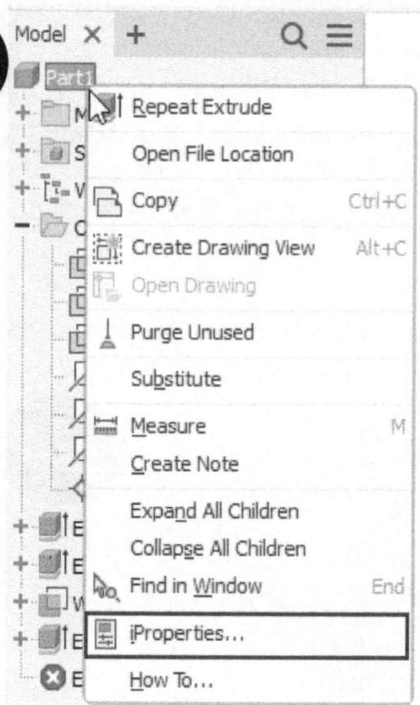

2. Click on the **Physical** tab in the **iProperties** dialog box and then click on the **Update** button. All the physical properties of the model appear in the dialog box, see Figure 7.149.

3. After reviewing the mass properties, exit the **iProperties** dialog box.

7.149

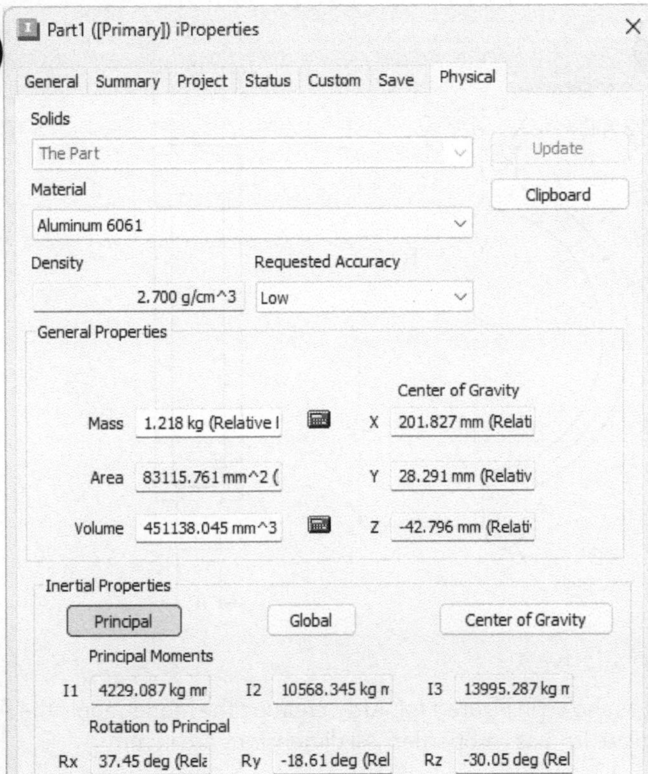

Section 7: Saving the Model

Now, you need to save the model.

1. Click on the **Save** tool in the **Quick Access Toolbar** toolbar. The **Save As** dialog box appears.

2. Browse to **Autodesk Inventor > Chapter 7** folder in the local drive of your system. Note that you need to create Chapter 7 folder inside the Autodesk Inventor folder, if not created earlier.

3. Enter **Tutorial 3** in the **File name** field of the dialog box and then click on the **Save** button. The model is saved in the specified location (>:\Autodesk Inventor\Chapter 7).

Hands-on Test Drive 1

Create a model, as shown in Figure 7.150. After creating the model, apply the Alloy Steel material to the model and calculate its mass properties. All dimensions are in mm.

7.150

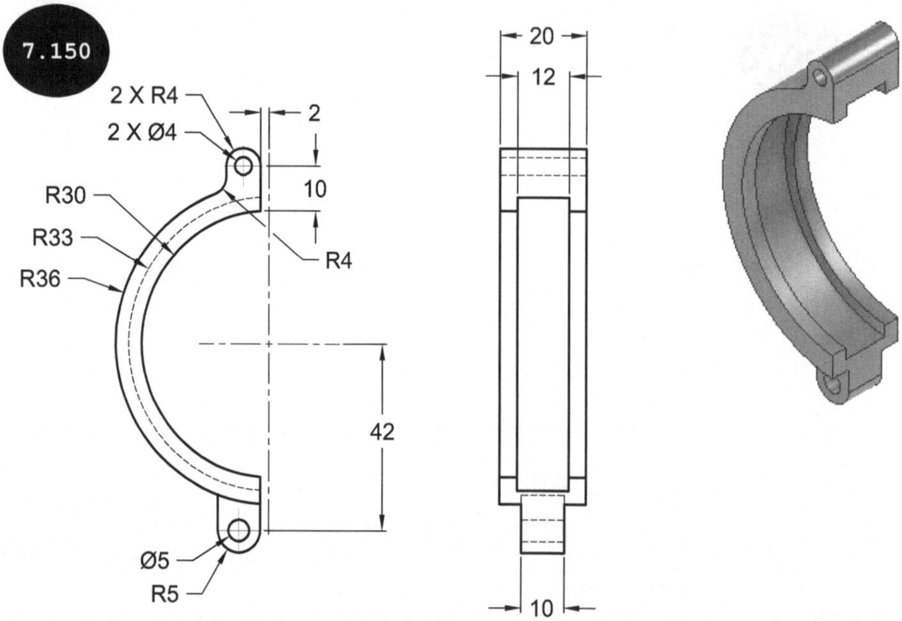

Hands-on Test Drive 2

Create a model, as shown in Figure 7.151. After creating the model, apply the Alloy Steel material to the model and calculate its mass properties. All dimensions are in mm.

7.151

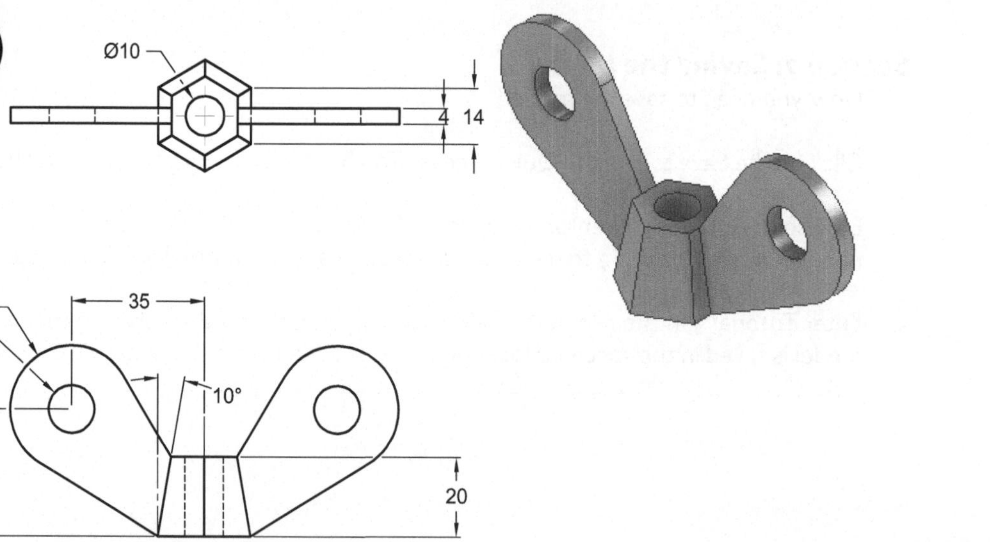

Summary

In this chapter, you have learned about using the advanced options of the **Extrude** and **Revolve** tools, which include defining the start and end conditions for extrusion, and creating features by removing material from a model. The chapter discussed in detail about working with a sketch having multiple profiles, projecting geometries of a model onto the current sketching plane, creating different section views of a model, editing a feature and its sketch, displaying earlier state of a model, reordering features of a model, and measuring the distance between entities of a model. The chapter also discussed assigning an appearance to a model, applying a material, assigning finishes/manufacturing data, and calculating physical properties of a model.

Questions

Complete and verify the following sentences:

- The _________ button of the **Extrusion** property panel is used for defining the end condition or termination of the extrusion up to the nearest intersection of the selected curved face of the model.
- The _________ button of the **Extrusion** property panel is used for defining the end condition or termination of the extrusion through all the faces of the model.
- The _________ button is used for defining the end condition or termination of extrusion up to a face, a plane, or a point or vertex of a model.
- On activating the _________ button in the **Extrusion** property panel, the resultant feature is created by removing material from the model.
- You can project the edges of existing features as sketch entities onto the current sketching plane by using the _________ tool.
- The _________ tool is used for projecting the edges of a model that intersect with the current sketching plane.
- The _________ tool is used for projecting geometries of an existing DWG underlay drawing onto the current sketching plane.
- You can assign a predefined or customized appearance or color to a face, a feature, or a model by using the _________ tool.
- The _________ tool is used for applying standard material properties such as density, elastic modulus, and tensile strength to a model.
- In Autodesk Inventor, you can copy and paste an appearance from one feature or face to another by using the _________ tool.

- A revolve cut feature is created by removing material from the model by revolving a sketch around a centerline or an axis. (True/False)
- You can edit individual features and their sketches as per your requirements. (True/False)
- In Autodesk Inventor, you cannot customize the material properties of a material. (True/False)
- A DWG underlay drawing is linked to the original DWG file such that any change made in the original DWG file also reflects in the imported DWG file. (True/False)
- In Autodesk Inventor, you cannot display the earlier state of a model. (True/False)

CHAPTER

8

Advanced Modeling - II

In this chapter, the following topics will be discussed:

- Creating a Sweep Feature
- Creating a Loft feature
- Creating a Coil feature
- Creating an Emboss Feature
- Creating a Mark Feature
- Creating a Rib Feature
- Applying an Image on the Face of a Model
- Creating a Shell Feature

In the previous chapters, you have learned about the primary modeling tools that are used for creating 3D parametric models. You have also learned about the basic workflow for creating models, which is to first create the base feature of a model and then create the remaining features of the model one after the other. In this chapter, you will explore some of the advanced tools such as **Sweep**, **Loft**, **Coil**, and **Emboss**. Also, you will learn about creating a rib feature by using the **Rib** tool, applying images on the face of a model by using the **Decal** tool, and creating a shell feature by using the **Shell** tool.

Creating a Sweep Feature

A sweep feature is created by sweeping a profile along a path. Figure 8.1 shows a profile and a path. Figure 8.2 shows the resultant sweep feature created by sweeping the profile along the path.

8.1

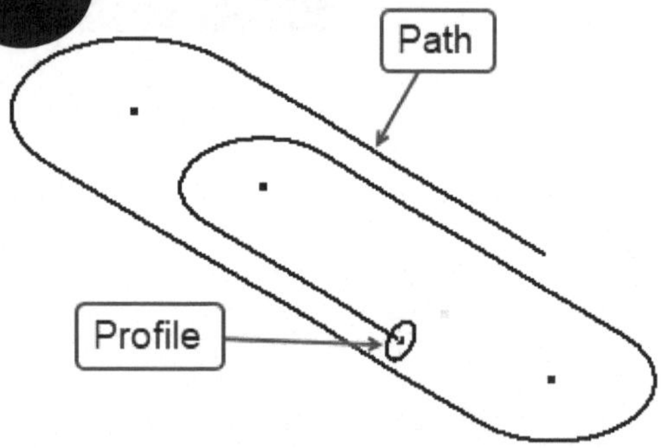

8.2

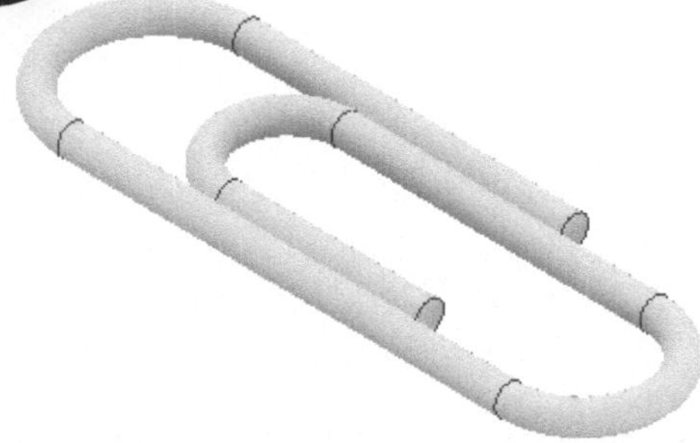

It is evident from the above figures that to create a sweep feature, you first need to create a path and a profile where it follows the path and creates a sweep feature. To create a profile, you need to identify the cross-section of the feature to be created. To create a path, you need to identify the route/path taken by the profile for creating the feature. In Autodesk Inventor, you can create a sweep feature by using the **Sweep** tool of the **Create** panel in the **3D Model** tab. Note that to create a solid sweep feature, you need to take care of the following points:

1. The profile must be a closed sketch for creating a solid sweep feature, whereas for creating a surface sweep feature, it can be a closed or open sketch.
2. The path can be an open or closed sketch, which is made up of a set of end-to-end connected sketched entities, a curve, or a set of model edges.
3. The starting point of the path must intersect the plane of the profile for best results.
4. The profile and path as well as the resultant sweep feature must not self-intersect.
5. It is recommended to create a profile on a plane that is normal to the start point of the path for best results.

After creating a path and a profile, click on the **Sweep** tool in the **Create** panel in the **3D Model** tab. The **Sweep** property panel appears, see Figure 8.3. The options in the **Sweep** property panel are used for creating different types of sweep features such as sweep feature along a path, sweep feature along a path with fixed orientation, sweep feature along a path and a guide rail, sweep feature along a path and a guide surface, and sweep feature by sweeping a toolbody along a path. The methods for creating various types of sweep features are discussed next.

8.3

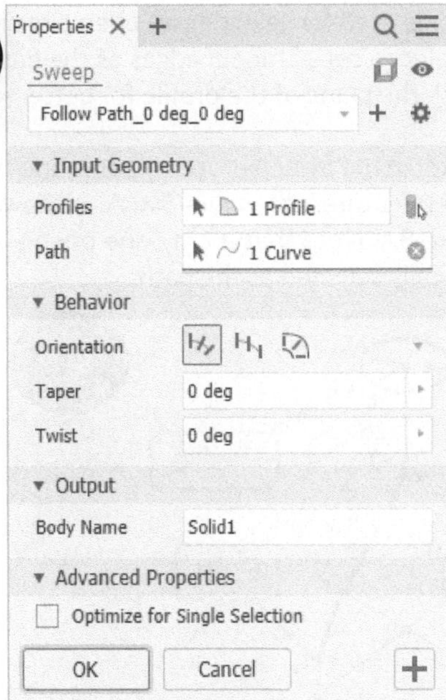

Creating a Sweep Feature Along a Path

The method for creating a sweep feature along a path is discussed below:

1. Invoke the **Sweep** property panel by clicking on the **Sweep** tool in the **Create** panel.

   Surface mode: By default, the solid mode is activated in the **Sweep** property panel. As a result, the resultant sweep feature will be created as a solid feature. You can switch to the surface mode for creating a surface sweep feature by clicking on the **Surface mode** button at the top right corner of the **Sweep** property panel. Note that to switch back to the solid mode, you need to click on the **Surface mode** button again. Its a toggle button to switch between the solid and surface modes.

2. Ensure that the **Surface mode** at the top right corner of the property panel is deactivated to create a solid sweep feature.

   Profiles: By default, the **Profiles** selector is activated in the property panel. As a result, you can select a closed profile in the graphics area to create a solid sweep feature. If the surface mode is activated, then you can select a closed or an open sketch as a profile for creating a surface sweep feature. In Autodesk Inventor, you can also select a solid body (toolbody) as a profile for creating a sweep feature by activating the **Solid Sweep** button available to the right of the **Profiles** selector in the **Sweep** property panel. You will learn about creating a sweep feature by sweeping a solid body or toolbody along a path later in this chapter.

3. Select a closed sketch as a profile for creating a solid sweep feature, see Figure 8.4. Note that if only one closed sketch is available in the graphics area then it will be automatically selected as the profile.

Path: The **Path** selector is used for selecting an open or a closed sketch as the path of the sweep feature. You can also select a set of model edges as the path. Note that the starting point of the path must intersect with the plane of the profile for better results.

4. Click on the **Path** selector in the **Sweep** property panel and then select an open or a closed sketch as the path of the sweep feature, see Figure 8.4. A preview of the sweep feature appears in the graphics area, see Figure 8.5. Note that if only one open sketch is available in the graphics area then it will be automatically selected as the path.

8.4

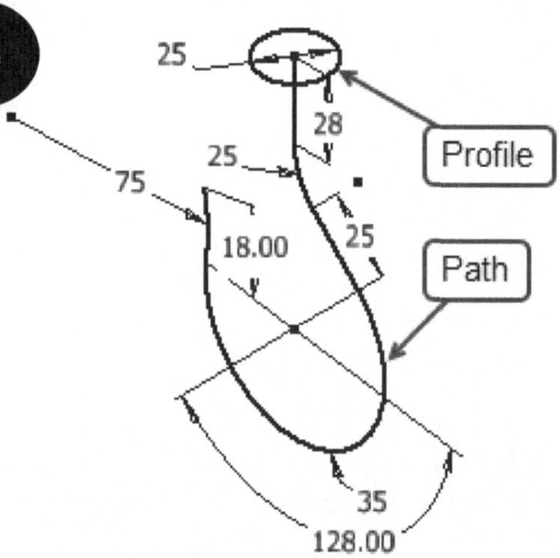

8.5

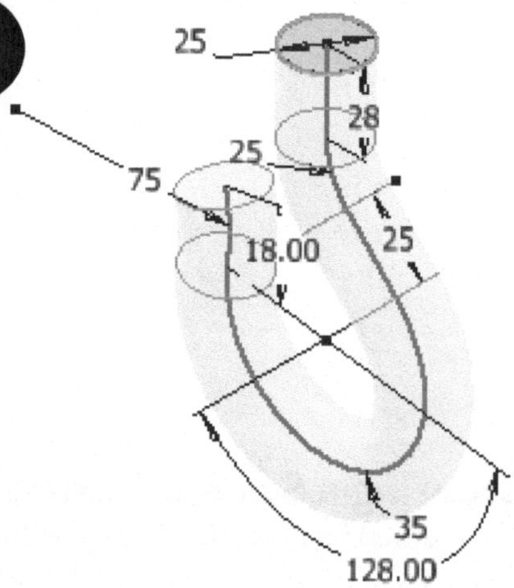

Orientation: The options in the **Orientation** area of the **Behavior** rollout in the property panel are used for defining the orientation and the type of sweep feature to be created. By default, the **Follow Path** button is activated in the **Orientation** area. As a result, the profile follows the path by maintaining the same angle of orientation from start to end. The **Fixed** button is used for creating a sweep feature along a path with a fixed orientation. This means that the profile follows a path such that it remains parallel throughout the path. The **Guide** button is used for creating a sweep feature along a path and a guide (guide rail or guide surface). You will learn about creating a sweep feature by using the **Fixed** and **Guide** buttons later in this chapter.

5. Ensure that the **Follow Path** button is activated in the **Orientation** area of the **Behavior** rollout in the **Sweep** property panel.

8.6

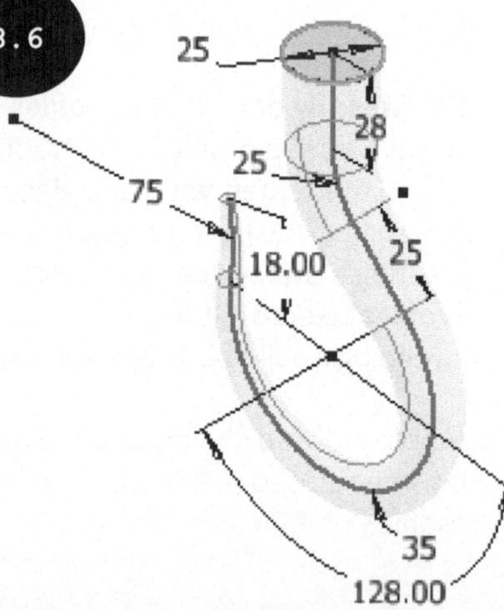

Taper: By default, the taper angle is specified as 0 degrees in the **Taper** field of the property panel. As a result, the resultant sweep feature is created without any tapering. You can enter the required taper angle in this field. Figure 8.6 shows the preview of a sweep feature having a taper angle set to -2.5 degrees. To reverse the taper direction from the outward to the inward side of the profile, you need to enter a negative taper angle value. Note that the **Taper** field is available in the **Behavior** rollout, when the **Follow Path** button is activated in the **Orientation** area.

6. Enter the required taper angle value in the **Taper** field of the **Behavior** rollout in the property panel. Note that for creating a sweep feature without any tapering, ensure that 0 degrees is entered in this field.

   Twist: By default, 0 degrees is entered in the **Twist** field of the **Behavior** rollout in the property panel. As a result, the resultant sweep feature does not have any twisting. You can enter the required twist angle in this field to twist the profile along the path. Figure 8.7 shows the preview of a sweep feature with 0 degrees twist angle and Figure 8.8 shows the preview of a sweep feature with 180 degrees twist angle. Note that the **Twist** field is available in the **Behavior** rollout of the property panel, only when the **Follow Path** button is activated in the **Orientation** area.

8.7

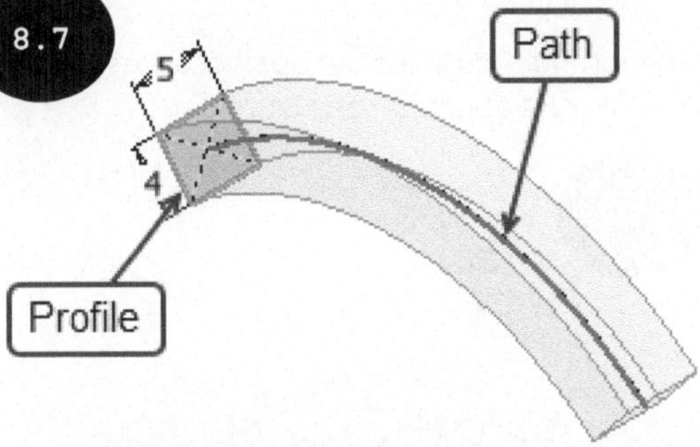

8.8

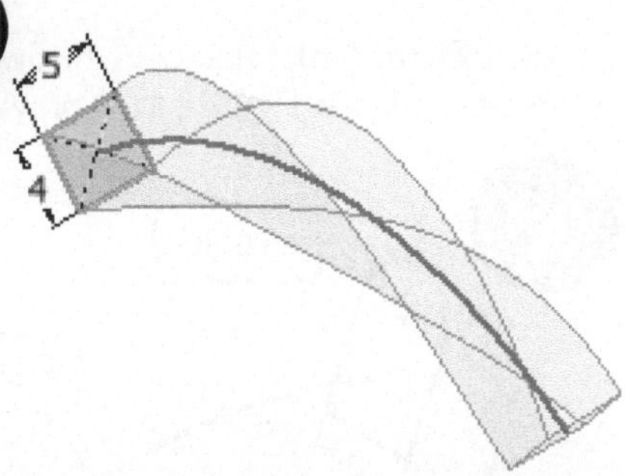

7. Enter the required twist angle in the **Twist** field of the property panel. Note that if you do not want to create any twisting in the resultant sweep feature then ensure that 0 degrees is entered in this field.

   Body Name: In the **Body Name** field of the **Output** rollout, you can specify a name for the solid body being created. By default, the name of a solid body appears as *Solid1, Solid2, ... or Solid(n)* in this field. Note that this **Body Name** field is available only while creating a base feature of a model.

   Optimize for Single Selection: When the **Optimize for Single Selection** check box is cleared in the **Advanced Properties** rollout of the property panel, you can make multiple profile selections for a sweep feature one by one in the graphics area. When the **Optimize for Single Selection** check box is selected, on selecting a single profile for the sweep feature in the **Profile** selector, the **Path** selector gets activated automatically and you are prompted to select a path for the sweep feature.

8. Select the required boolean operation (**Join**, **Cut**, or **Intersect**) in the **Output** rollout of the property panel. Note that the options for selecting the boolean operation are not available while creating the base or first feature of a model.

8.9

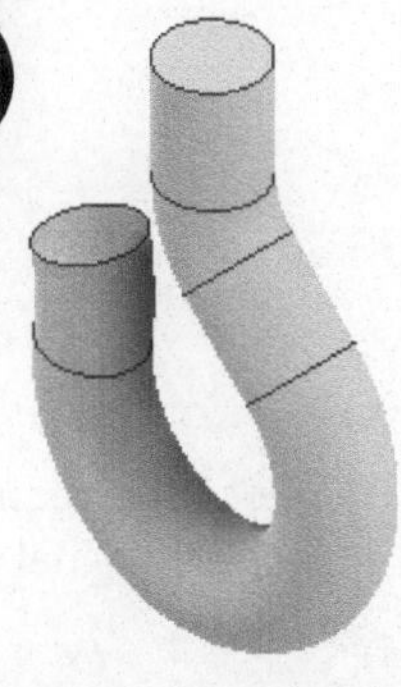

9. Click on the **OK** button in the **Sweep** property panel. The sweep feature is created by sweeping the profile along the path, see Figure 8.9. The sweep feature shown in Figure 8.9 is created by specifying 0 degrees as the taper angle in the **Taper** field of the **Sweep** property panel.

Creating a Sweep Feature Along a Path with Fixed Orientation

You can also create a sweep feature along a path with fixed orientation, such that the profile follows a path and remains parallel throughout the path. In other words, the start and end sections of the resultant sweep feature are parallel to each other. The method for creating a sweep feature along a path with fixed orientation is discussed below:

1. Invoke the **Sweep** property panel by clicking on the **Sweep** tool in the **Create** panel. Some of the options for the **Sweep** property panel have been discussed earlier.

2. Select a closed sketch as a profile, see Figure 8.10. Note that if only one closed sketch is available in the graphics area then it will be automatically selected as the profile.

3. Click on the **Path** selector in the **Sweep** property panel and then select an open or a closed sketch as the path, see Figure 8.10. A preview of the sweep feature appears, see Figure 8.11.

8.10

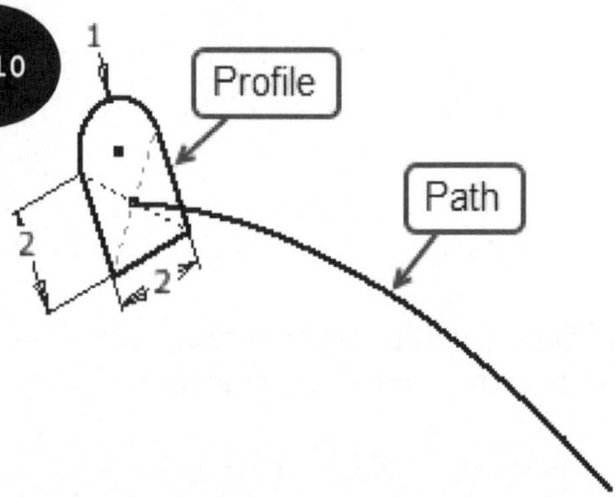

8.11

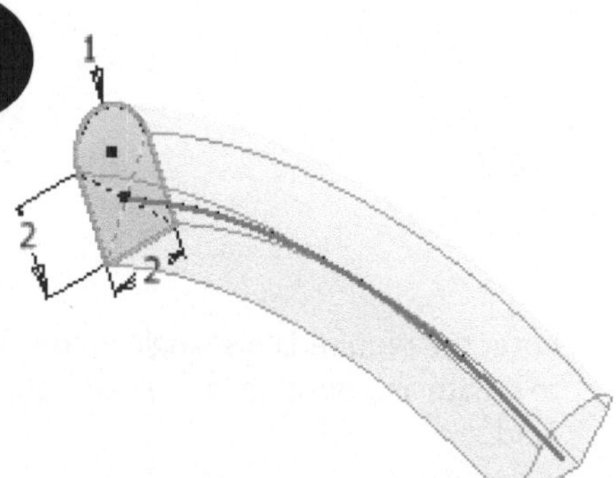

4. Click on the **Fixed** button in the **Orientation** area of the **Behavior** rollout. A preview of the sweep feature appears such that the profile follows the path and remains parallel throughout the path, see Figure 8.12. Note that the start and end sections of the resultant feature are parallel to each other.

8.12

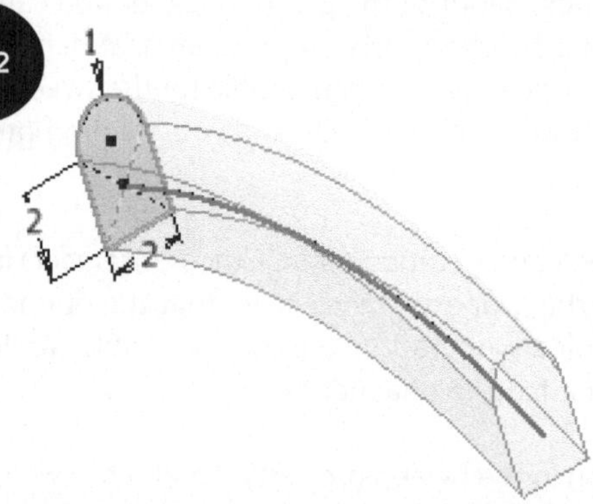

5. Select the required boolean operation (**Join**, **Cut**, or **Intersect**) in the **Output** rollout of the property panel. Note that the **Output** rollout is not available while creating the base or first feature.

6. Click on the **OK** button in the **Sweep** property panel. The sweep feature is created, see Figure 8.13. In this figure, the front view of the sweep feature is shown for a better understanding of the orientation of the resultant sweep feature.

8.13

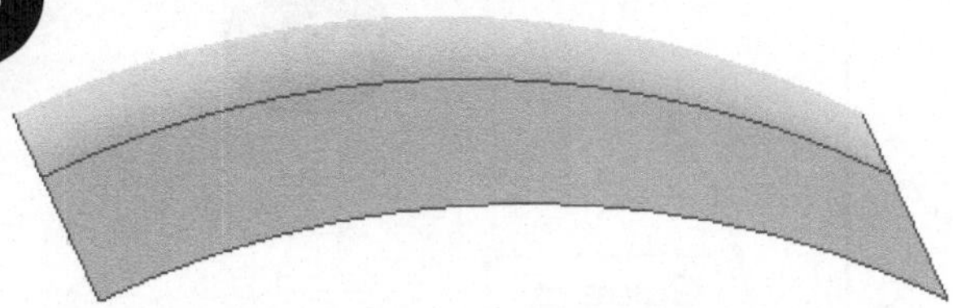

Creating a Sweep Feature Along a Path and a Guide Rail

In Autodesk Inventor, you can create a sweep feature such that the profile follows the path as well as the guide rail, see Figures 8.14 and 8.15. A guide rail is used for guiding the profile (section) of the sweep feature. The method for creating a sweep feature along a path and a guide rail is discussed below:

8.14

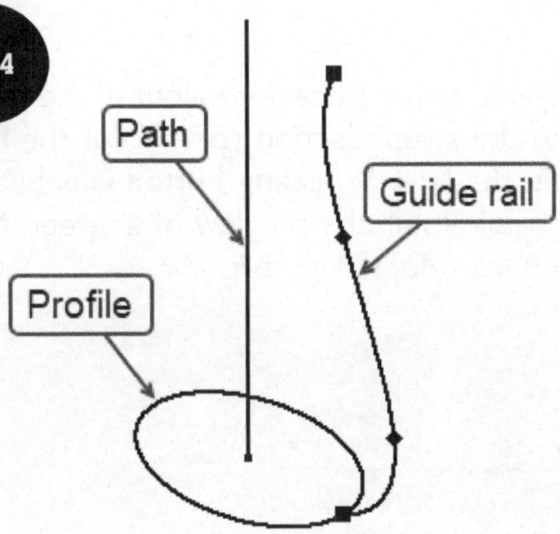

8.15

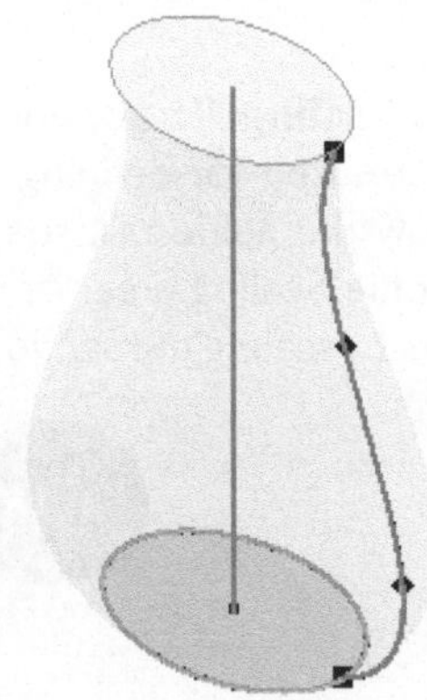

Note: In Figure 8.14, the path and the guide rail are created on the Front plane as individual sketches, and the profile is created on the Top plane. Also, the start point of the guide rail is aligned with the start point of the path.

1. Invoke the **Sweep** property panel by clicking on the **Sweep** tool in the **Create** panel. Some of the options for the **Sweep** property panel have been discussed earlier.

2. Select a closed sketch as the profile, see Figure 8.16. Note that if only one closed sketch is available in the graphics area then it will be automatically selected as the profile.

3. Click on the **Path** selector in the **Sweep** property panel and then select an open or a closed sketch as the path, see Figure 8.16. A preview of the sweep feature appears.

4. Click on the **Guide** button in the **Orientation** area of the **Behavior** rollout. The **Guide** selector appears in the **Behavior** rollout of the property panel and you are prompted to select a guide rail or a guide surface. You will learn about selecting a guide surface later in this chapter.

5. Select an open curve as a guide rail in the graphics area, see Figure 8.16. The preview of a sweep feature appears such that the profile follows the path as well as the guide rail in the graphics area, see Figure 8.17. Also, the **Profile Scaling** area appears below the **Guide** selector in the **Behavior** rollout, see Figure 8.18.

8.16

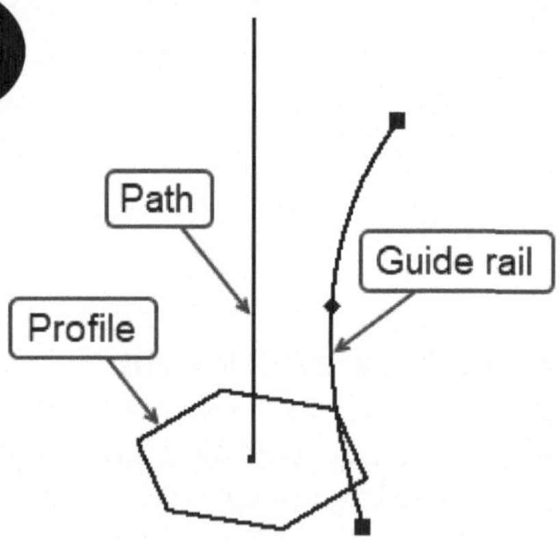

8.17

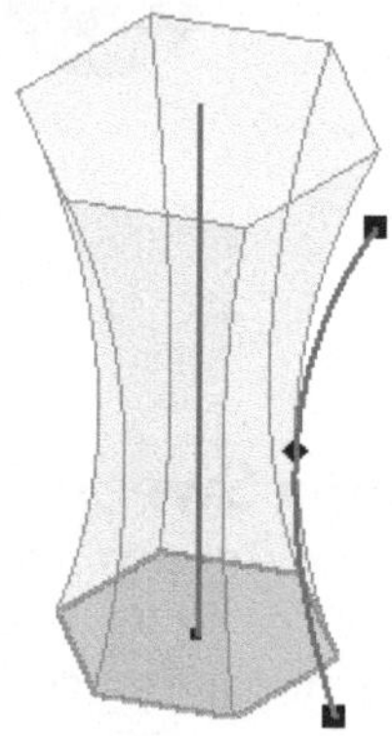

Profile Scaling: The options in the **Profile Scaling** area of the **Behavior** rollout of the property panel are used for defining the scaling method for the swept section (profile) of the feature to follow the guide rail, see Figure 8.18. By default, the **X & Y Scaling** button is activated in the **Profile Scaling** area. As a result, on selecting a guide rail, the preview of a sweep feature appears by scaling the section in both X and Y directions, refer to Figure 8.17.

8.18

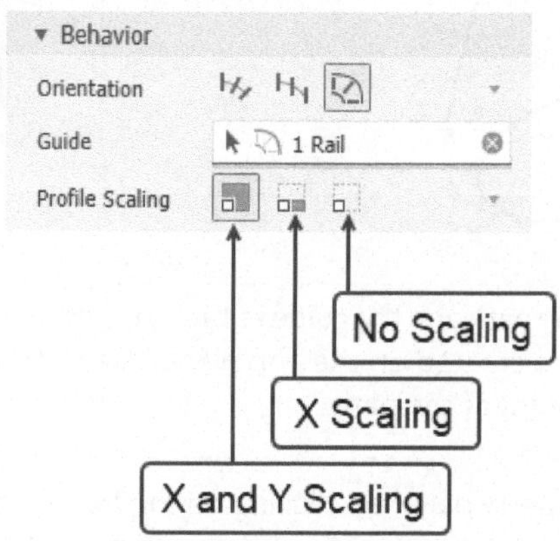

On activating the **X Scaling** button in the **Profile Scaling** area, the preview of a sweep feature appears by scaling the section only along the X direction, see Figure 8.19. On activating the **No Scaling** button, the preview of a sweep feature appears with no scaling along any direction, see Figure 8.20.

8.19

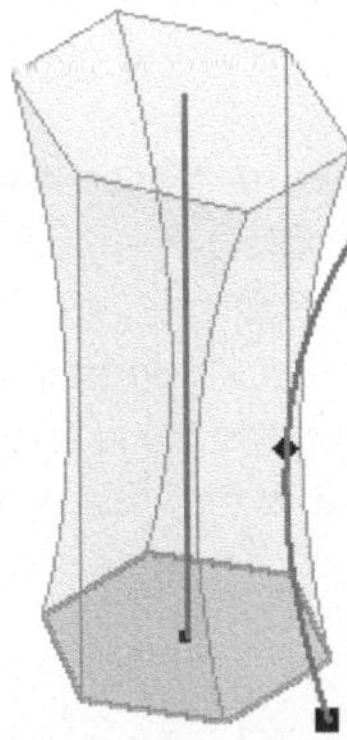

8.20

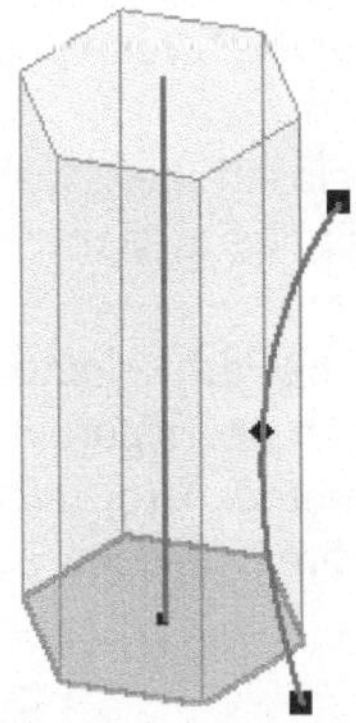

6. Select the required button (**X & Y Scaling**, **X Scaling**, or **No Scaling**) in the **Profile Scaling** area of the property panel, as discussed above.

7. Select the required boolean operation (**Join**, **Cut**, or **Intersect**) in the **Output** rollout of the property panel. Note that the **Output** rollout is not available while creating the base feature.

8. Click on the **OK** button in the **Sweep** property panel. The sweep feature is created such that the profile follows the path as well as the guide rail, see Figure 8.21. In this figure, the sweep feature is created by scaling the profile in both X and Y directions.

8.21

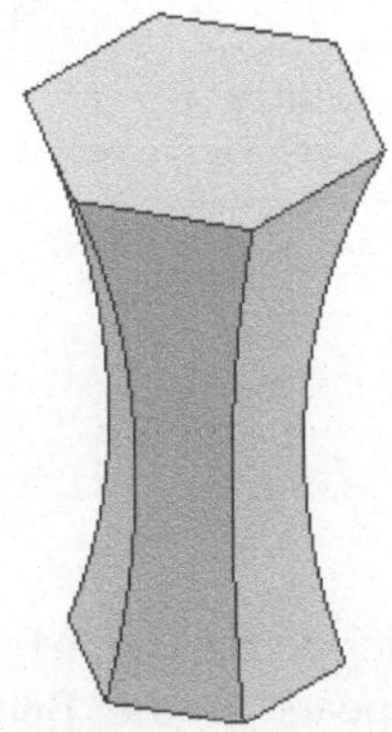

Creating a Sweep Feature Along a Path and a Guide Surface

You can create a sweep feature such that the profile follows the path and its twist is controlled by the guide surface, see Figures 8.22 and 8.23. A guide surface is used for controlling the shape and twist of the profile (section) of the sweep feature. The method for creating a sweep feature along a path and a guide surface is discussed below:

8.22

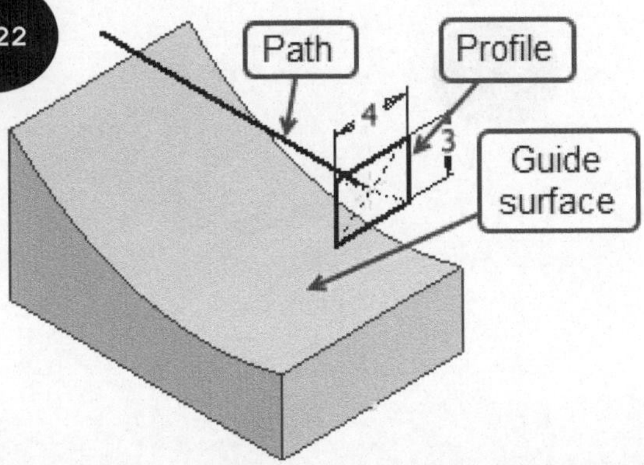

8.23

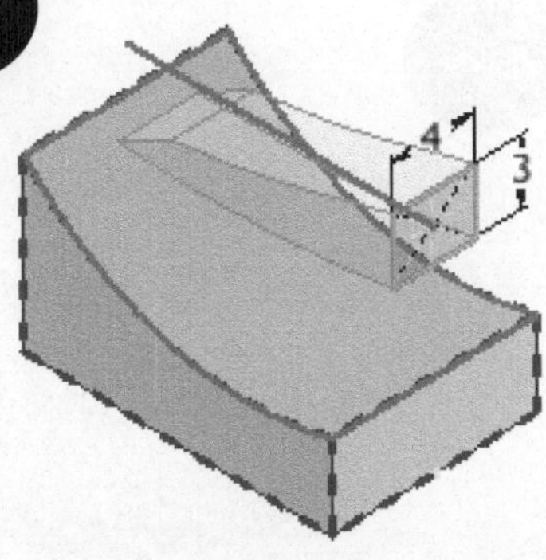

1. Invoke the **Sweep** property panel by clicking on the **Sweep** tool in the **Create** panel. Some of the options of the **Sweep** property panel have been discussed earlier.

2. Select a closed sketch as a profile, see Figure 8.24. Note that if only one closed sketch is available in the graphics area then it will be automatically selected as the profile.

3. Click on the **Path** selector in the **Sweep** property panel and then select an open or a closed sketch as the path, see Figure 8.24. In this figure, a 3D circular edge of the model is shown as the path to be selected. After selecting a profile and a path, the preview of a sweep feature appears in the graphics area, see Figure 8.25.

8.24

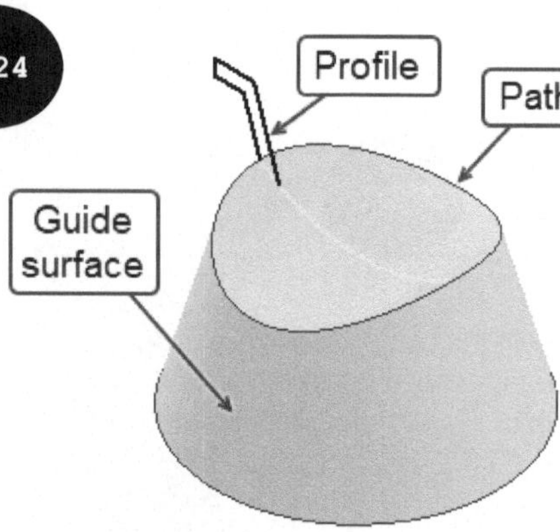

8.25

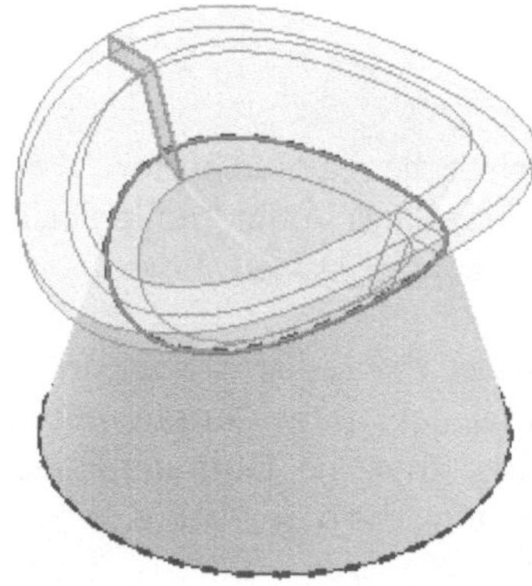

4. Click on the **Guide** button in the **Orientation** area of the **Behavior** rollout. The **Guide** selector appears in the **Behavior** rollout of the property panel and you are prompted to select a guide rail or a guide surface.

5. Select a surface in the graphics area, refer to Figure 8.24. The preview of a sweep feature appears such that the profile follows the path and its twist is controlled by the selected guide surface, see Figure 8.26. Note that if the preview of the sweep feature does not get updated in the graphics area then click on the **Follow Path** button in the **Orientation** area and then again click on the **Guide** button.

6. Click on the **OK** button in the **Sweep** property panel. The sweep feature is created, see Figure 8.27.

8.26

8.27

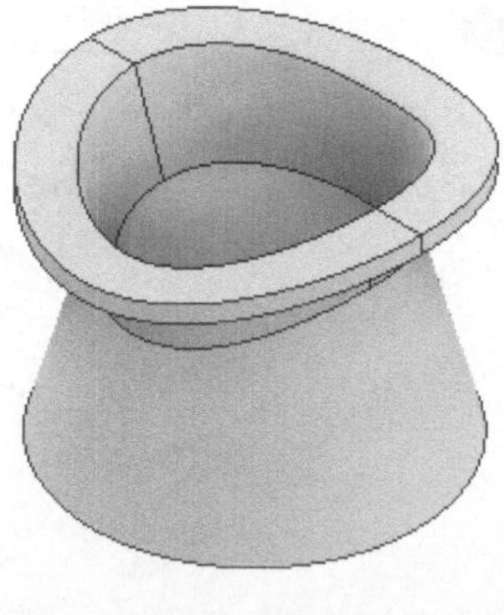

Creating a Sweep Feature by Sweeping a Toolbody Along a Path

In Autodesk Inventor, you can also create a sweep feature by sweeping a toolbody along a path, see Figures 8.28 and 8.29. Figure 8.28 shows a tool body and a helical path, and Figure 8.29 shows the resultant sweep cut feature. The method for creating a sweep feature by sweeping a toolbody along a path is discussed below:

8.28

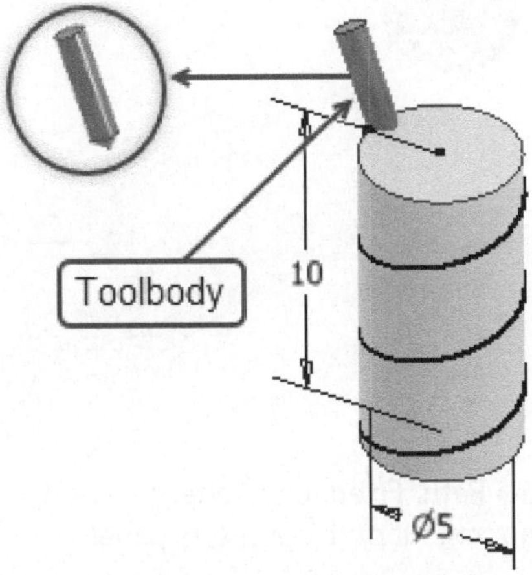

8.29

Note: In Figure 8.28, the toolbody is created as a separate solid body by selecting the **New Solid** button in the **Boolean** area of the **Output** rollout in the property panel. Also, a helical curve is used as a path. You will learn about creating helical curves later in this chapter.

1. Invoke the **Sweep** property panel by clicking on the **Sweep** tool in the **Create** panel.

2. Click on the **Solid Sweep** button available to the right of the **Profiles** selector in the **Sweep** property panel. The **Toolbody** selector appears in the **Input Geometry** rollout of the property panel, see Figure 8.30. Also, you are prompted to select a solid body as a toolbody.

8.30

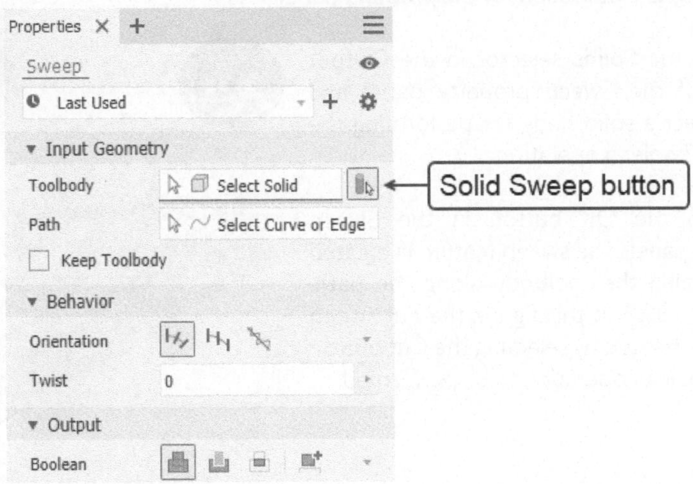

3. Select a solid body as a toolbody in the graphics area, see Figure 8.31. Note that a solid body to be selected as a toolbody should be created as a separate or independent body.

After selecting a toolbody, you are prompted to select a path for creating a sweep feature.

4. Select an open or a closed sketch as the path, see Figure 8.31. The preview of a sweep feature appears in the graphics area such that the toolbody follows the path, see Figure 8.32.

8.31

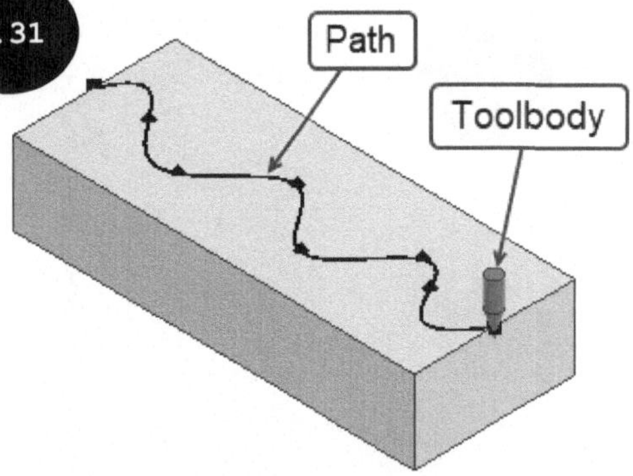

8.32

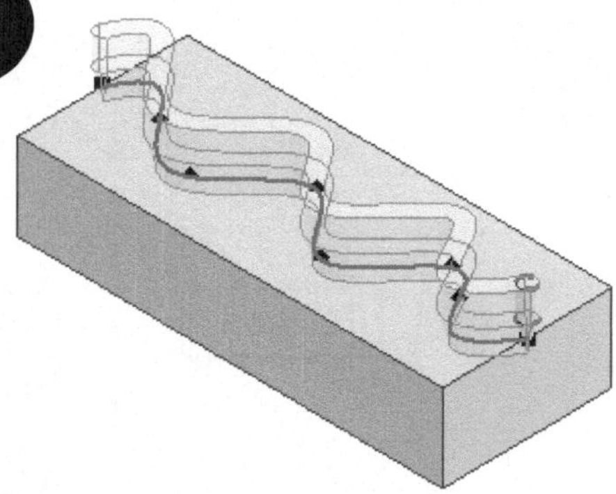

5. Select the required type of orientation (**Follow Path**, **Fixed**, or **Aligned**) to be followed by the toolbody in the **Orientation** area of the **Behavior** rollout of the property panel.

Note: On selecting the **Aligned** button in the **Orientation** area, you need to select the axial direction vector for the toolbody in the **Vector** selector that appears in the **Behavior** rollout of the property panel. You can also specify the twist angle and the twist axis for the toolbody in the **Twist** field and the **Twist Axis** selector of the **Behavior** rollout, respectively. Note that the **Twist Axis** selector appears on specifying a twist angle value other than 0 degrees in the respective field.

6. Select the required boolean operation to be performed (**Join**, **Cut**, or **Intersect**) in the **Boolean** area of the **Output** rollout of the property panel.

7. Click on the **Solids** selector in the **Output** rollout of the **Sweep** property panel and then select a solid body for performing the selected boolean operation.

8. Click on the **OK** button in the **Sweep** property panel. The sweep feature is created by sweeping the toolbody along the path, see Figure 8.33. In this figure, the cut sweep feature is created by selecting the **Cut** button as the boolean operation to be performed.

8.33

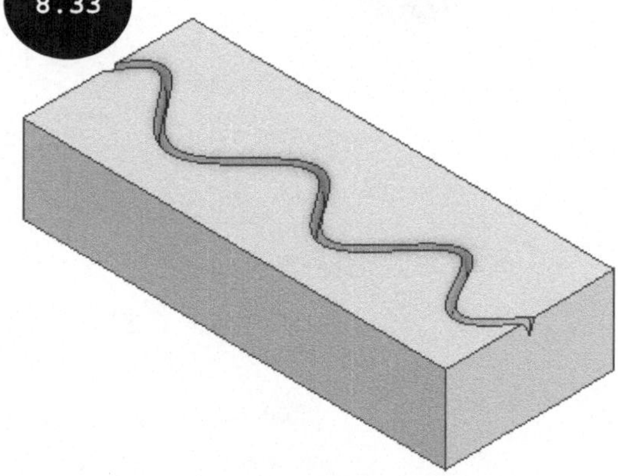

Creating a Loft feature

A loft feature is created by lofting two or more than two profiles such that the cross-sectional shape of the loft feature transits from one profile to another. Figure 8.34 shows two dissimilar profiles that are created on different planes having an offset distance between each other. Figure 8.35 shows the resultant loft feature created.

8.34

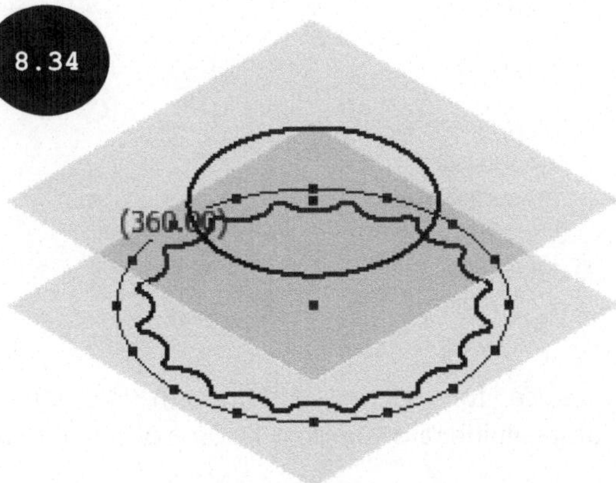

8.35

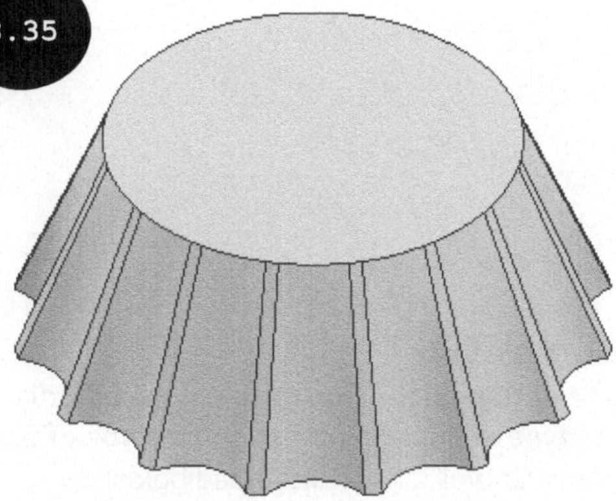

It is evident from the above figures that for creating a loft feature, you first need to create all its sections that define the shape of the loft feature. In Autodesk Inventor, you can create a loft feature by using the **Loft** tool of the **Create** panel in the **3D Model** tab. Note that for creating a loft feature, you need to take care of the following points:

1. Two or more than two profiles or sections (similar or dissimilar) must be available in the graphics area before invoking the **Loft** tool.
2. Profiles must be closed. You can select closed sketches, sketch points, faces, or vertices as profiles.
3. All profiles must be created as different sketches.
4. The profiles and the resultant lofted feature must not self intersect.

In Autodesk Inventor, you can create different types of loft features by using the **Loft** tool. The methods for creating different types of loft features are discussed next.

Creating a Loft Feature with Sections

To create a loft feature with sections, click on the **Loft** tool in the **Create** panel of the **3D Model** tab, see Figure 8.36. The **Loft** dialog box appears, see Figure 8.37. Some of the options of the **Loft** dialog box are discussed below:

8.36

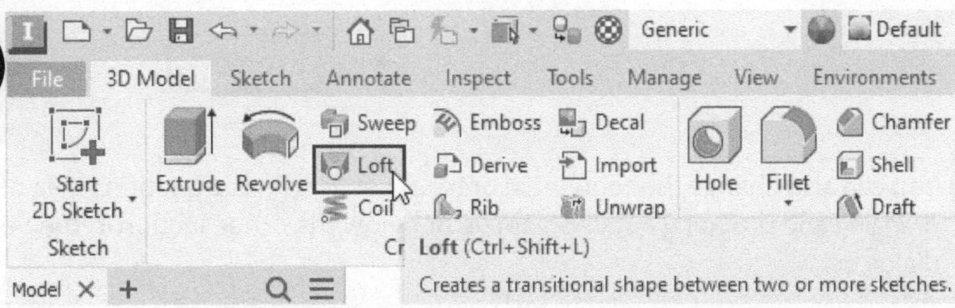

8.37

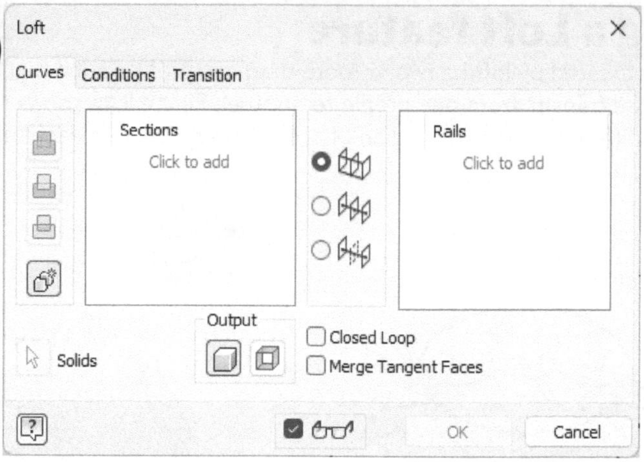

Curves Tab

The options in the **Curves** tab of the **Loft** dialog box are used for selecting sections of the loft feature, the type of boolean operation, the type of output feature, guide rails, and so on. Some of the options of the Curves tab are discussed below:

Sections Area

The **Sections** area in the **Curves** tab of the dialog box is used for selecting closed profiles for creating a loft feature. You can select two or more than two similar or dissimilar closed sketches as profiles. You can also select sketch points, faces, or vertices as profiles for creating a loft feature. After selecting the profiles, a preview of the loft feature appears in the graphics area with the display of green arrows, which indicates the transitional direction of the loft feature from one section to another, see Figure 8.38. Also, the names of the selected profiles appear in the **Sections** area of the dialog box in a sequential order.

8.38

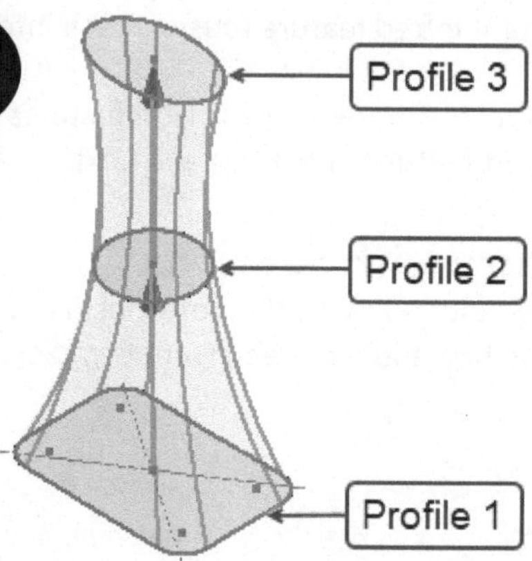

Tip: You can also change the sequential order of sections in the **Sections** area of the dialog box by dragging and dropping a section above or below the other section in the **Sections** area of the dialog box.

Operation Area

The options in the **Operation** area of the **Loft** dialog box are used for defining the type of boolean operation to be performed for creating the loft feature, see Figure 8.39. Note that the **Join**, **Cut**, and **Intersect** options of this area are not enabled while creating the base feature. All these options are same as discussed in earlier chapters.

8.39

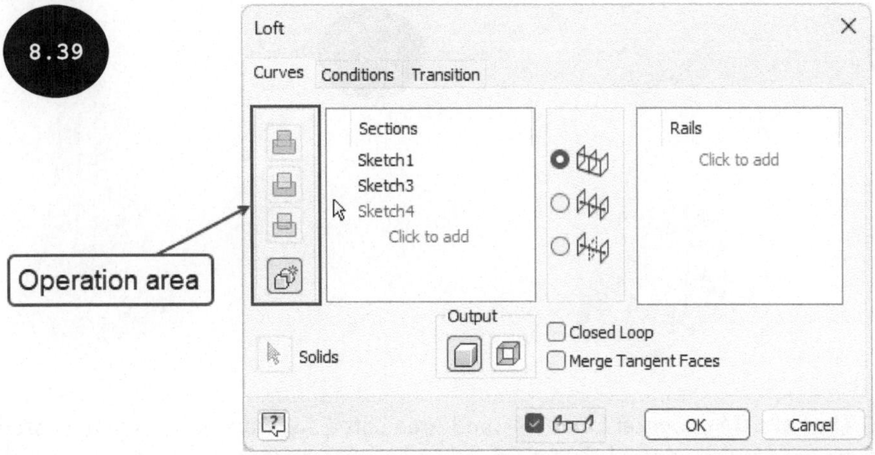

Output Area

By default, the **Solid** button is activated in the **Output** area of the **Loft** dialog box. The resultant loft feature will be created as a solid. On activating the **Surface** button, the resultant loft feature will be created as a surface.

Closed Loop

The **Closed Loop** check box is used for creating a closed loft feature by joining its start and end sections with each other. Figure 8.40 shows the preview of an open loft feature when the **Closed Loop** check box is cleared and Figure 8.41 shows the preview of a closed loft feature when the **Closed Loop** check box is selected.

8.40

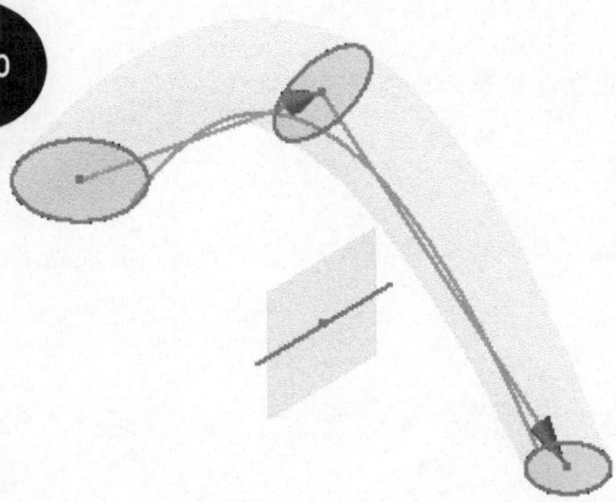

8.41

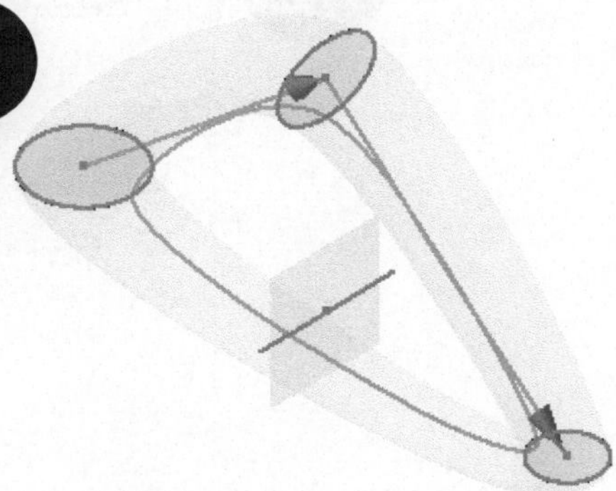

Note: To create a closed lofted feature, minimum three sections are required.

Merge Tangent Faces

On selecting the **Merge Tangent Faces** check box, the tangent faces of the sections merge with each other in the resultant loft feature. Figure 8.42 shows a loft feature that is created when the **Merge Tangent Faces** check box is selected and Figure 8.43 shows a loft feature that is created when the **Merge Tangent Faces** check box is cleared.

8.42

8.43

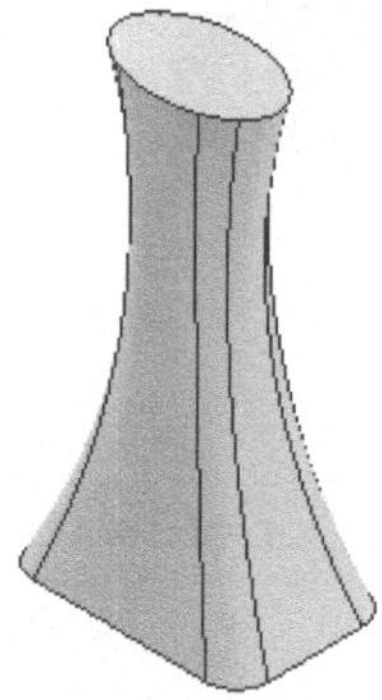

Note: The **Rails**, **Center Line**, and **Area Loft** radio buttons of the **Loft** dialog box are used for creating a loft feature with rails, centerline, and area loft respectively, and are discussed later in this chapter.

Conditions Tab

The options in the **Conditions** tab of the **Loft** dialog box are used for defining the boundary condition for the start and end sections in order to control the shape of the loft feature. For doing so, click on the arrow next to the name of a section whose boundary condition is to be defined. A drop-down list appears, see Figure 8.44. The options in this drop-down list are discussed below:

8.44

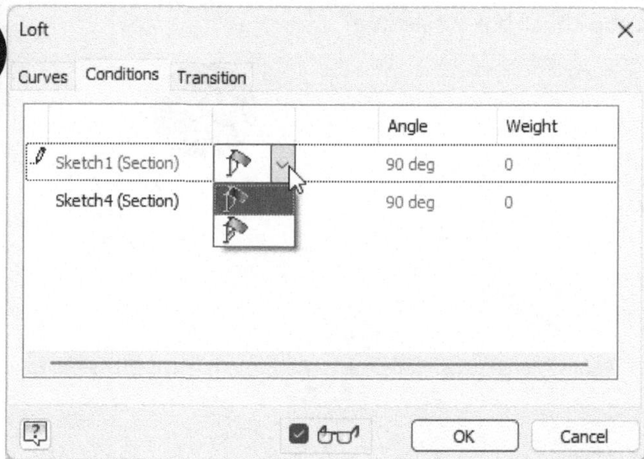

Free Condition

By default, the **Free Condition** option is selected as the boundary condition for the start and end sections of the loft feature. As a result, no boundary condition is applied and the cross-sectional shape transits from one profile to another, freely, see Figures 8.45 and 8.46. Figure 8.45 shows two sections and Figure 8.46 shows the preview of a resultant loft feature with the **Free Condition** option selected as the boundary condition for the start and end sections of the loft feature. Note that when this option is selected, the **Angle** and **Weight** fields in the dialog box are not enabled in the respective columns of the dialog box.

8.45

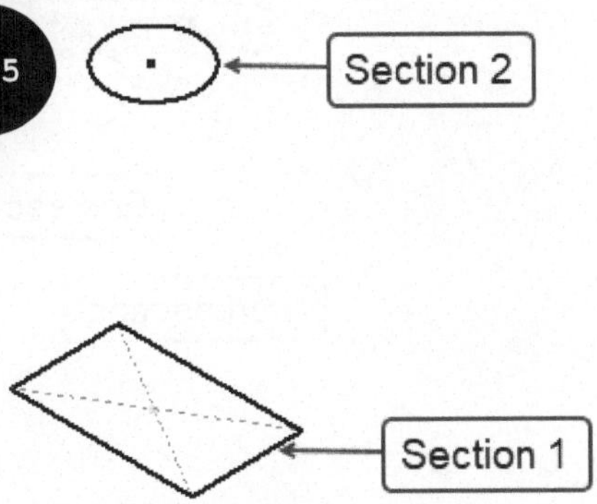

8.46

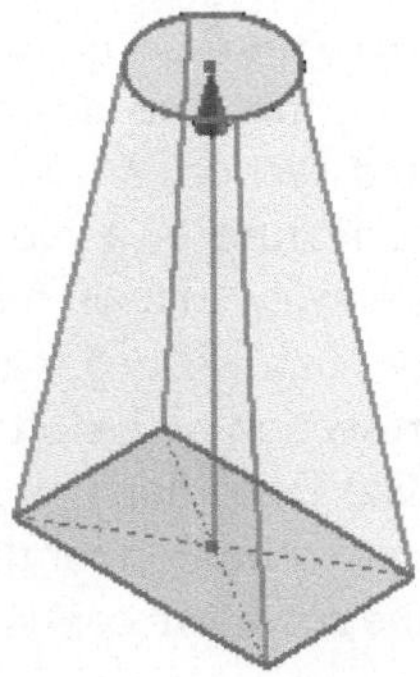

Direction Condition

On selecting the **Direction Condition** option, you can define the boundary condition for the start and end sections of the loft feature by specifying the angle and weight values in the respective fields of the **Angle** and **Weight** columns in the dialog box, see Figure 8.47. Note that the angle value specified in the **Angle** field is used for defining the angular transition between the section and the faces of the resultant loft feature. You can define the angle in the range from 0 to 180 degrees. The weight value specified in the **Weight** field is used for defining the transition tangent length for the angle. Figure 8.47 shows the preview of a loft feature with an angle of 120 degrees and weight value 1 specified at the start section.

8.47

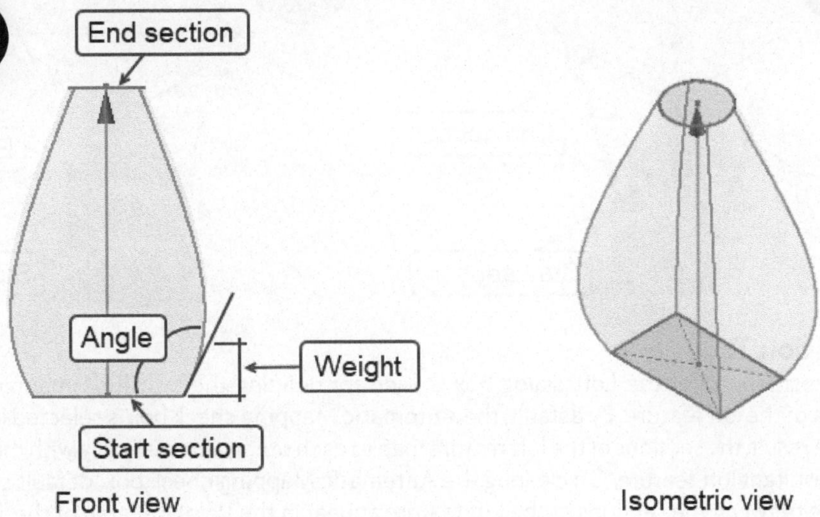

Note: The **Direction Condition** option is available only when the sections of the loft feature are 2D sections.

Smooth (G2) Condition

The **Smooth (G2) Condition** option is used for defining the curvature continuity (G2 continuity) with the adjacent faces of the selected section (planar face) of the loft feature, see Figure 8.48. Note that this option is available in the drop-down list only when the selected section is a face or a loop of an existing feature of a model. Figure 8.48 shows the preview of a loft feature where the planar face of an existing feature is selected as the start section of the loft feature and the **Smooth (G2) Condition** option is selected as the boundary condition for the start section, enabling the curvature continuity with its adjacent face.

8.48

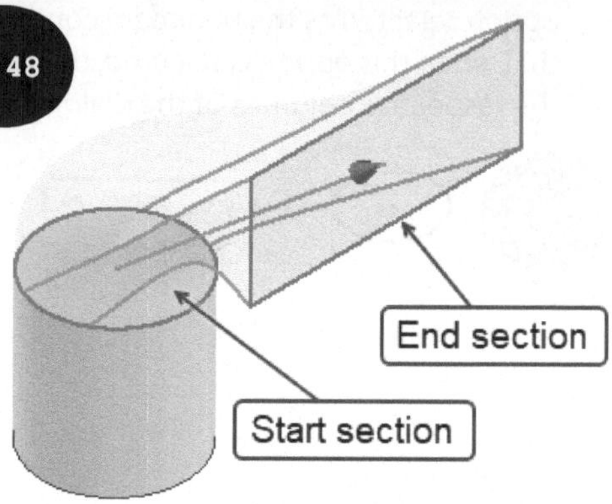

Tangent Condition

The **Tangent Condition** option is used for defining the tangent continuity (G1 continuity) with the adjacent faces of the selected section (planar face) of the loft feature, see Figures 8.49 and 8.50. In Figure 8.49, the default **Free Condition** option is selected as the boundary condition for the start section of the loft feature, whereas in Figure 8.50, the **Tangent Condition** option is selected as the boundary condition for the start section of the loft feature. Note that the **Tangent Condition** option is available in the drop-down list only when the selected section is a face or a loop of an existing feature of a model.

8.49

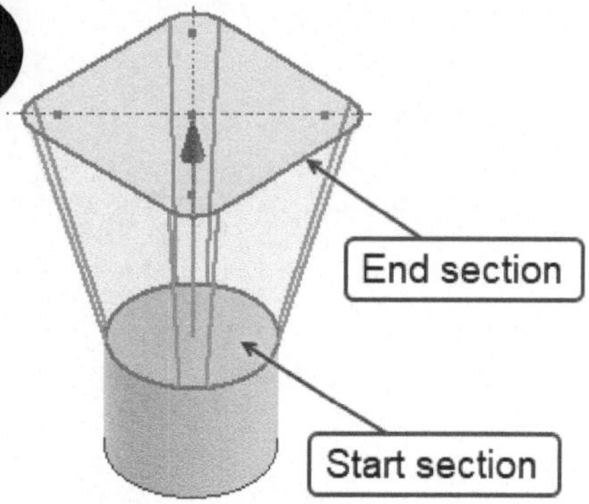

8.50

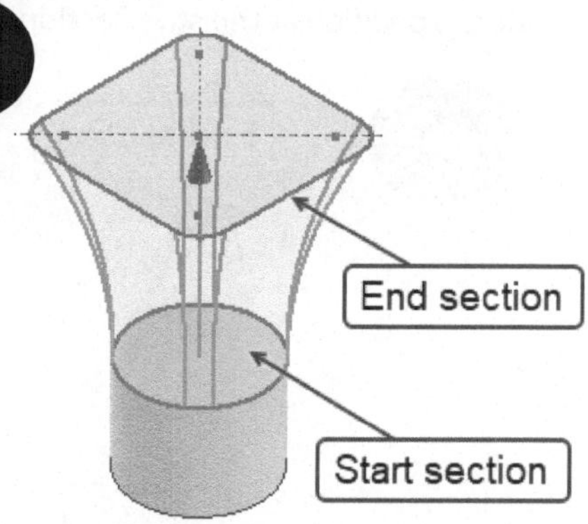

Transition Tab

The **Transition** tab of the **Loft** dialog box is used for defining the transition mapping between the sections of the loft feature. By default, the **Automatic Mapping** check box is selected in the **Transition** tab. As a result, the sections of the loft feature map to each other, automatically with minimum twisting in the resultant loft feature. On clearing the **Automatic Mapping** check box, default sets of segments available between the sections of the loft feature appear in the **Point Set** area of the **Transition** tab in the dialog box as well as in the graphics area, see Figures 8.51 and 8.52. These sets of segments are used for controlling or creating twisting in the resultant loft feature.

8.51

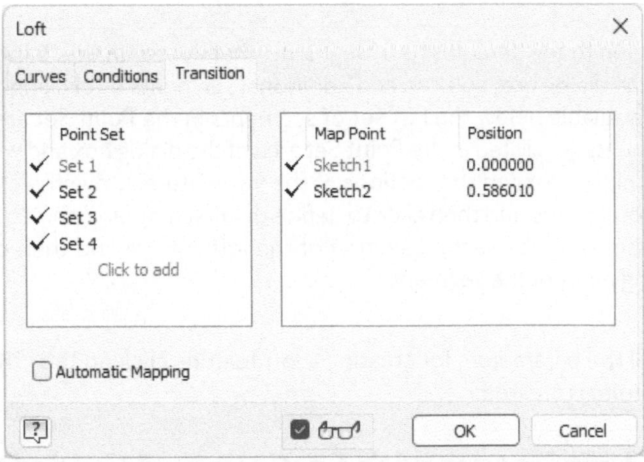

To control or create twisting in the resultant loft feature, select a set of segments in the **Point Set** area of the **Transition** tab in the dialog box. The mapping points and the current positions of the selected segments appear on the right panel of the dialog box. Also, the selected segment gets highlighted in the graphics area, see Figure 8.52. Next, move the cursor over a section of the loft feature in the graphics area near the mapping point of the segment to be changed, and then click to define its new position for creating twisting in the resultant loft feature, see Figure 8.53. Similarly, you can change the position of the mapping points of other segments of the loft feature, as required. Figure 8.54 shows the resultant twisted loft feature.

8.52

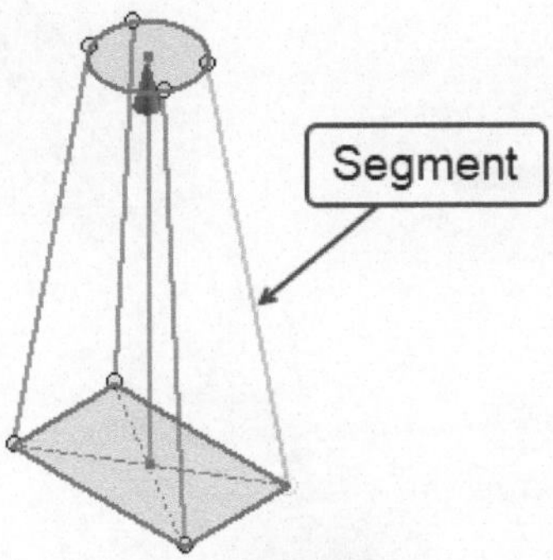

8.53

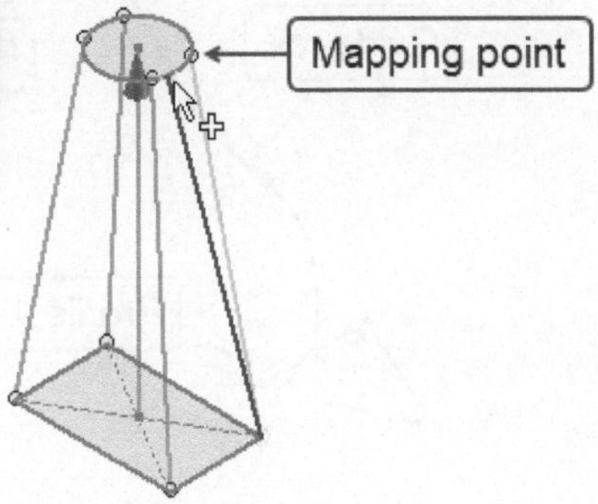

8.54

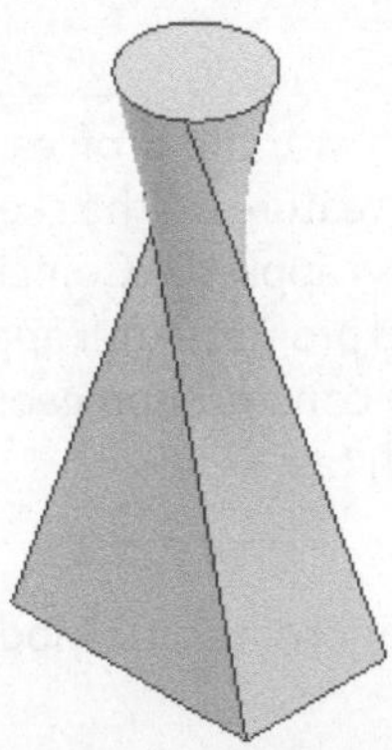

Tip: In addition to the default sets of segments that appear in the **Point Set** area of the **Transition** tab in the dialog box, you can add additional segments by clicking on the **Click to add** option that is available below the last set of segments in the **Point Set** area. On doing so, a new set of segments gets listed in the **Point Set** area of the dialog box and you are prompted to specify its mapping points on the sections of the loft feature. Move the cursor over the first section of the loft feature and then click to define the first mapping point of the segment. Next, move the cursor over the second section of the loft feature and then click to define the second mapping point of the segment.

After defining all the parameters for creating a loft feature, click on the **OK** button in the **Loft** dialog box. The loft feature is created.

Creating a Loft feature with Sections and Guide Rails

In Autodesk Inventor, you can also create a loft feature with profiles and guide rails. Guide rails are used for guiding the cross-sectional shape of the loft feature, see Figure 8.55. In this figure, two profiles and one guide rail are selected to guide the cross-sectional shape of the loft feature. You can select multiple guide rails for controlling the shape of the loft feature. Note that the guide rails must intersect with the profiles of the loft feature. The method for creating a loft feature with profiles and guide rails is discussed below:

8.55

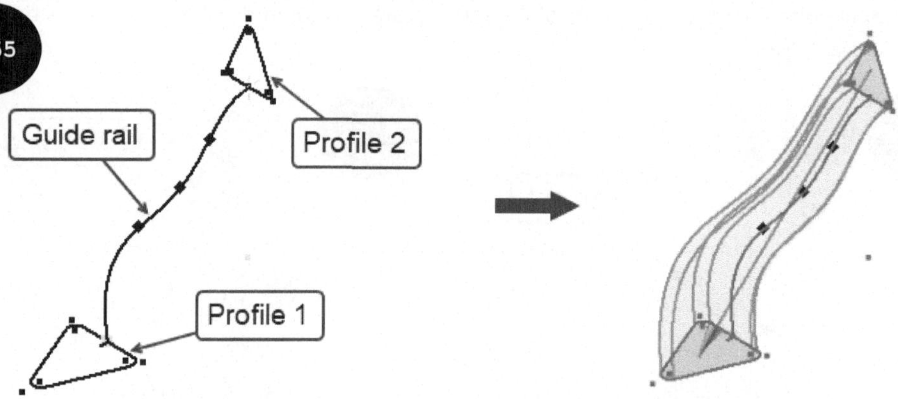

1. Create all profiles and guide rails as individual sketches for creating a loft feature in the graphics area.

Note: The guide rails must intersect with the profiles of the loft feature. For doing so, you can project the profiles of the loft feature on the sketching plane of the guide rail by using the **Project Geometry** tool and then apply the Coincident constraint between the endpoints of the guide rail and the projected profiles. After applying the constraints, you need to convert the projected geometries into construction geometries by using the **Construction** tool of the **Format** panel in the **Sketch** tab.

2. Click on the **Loft** tool in the **Create** panel of the **3D Model** tab, see Figure 8.56. The **Loft** dialog box appears.

8.56

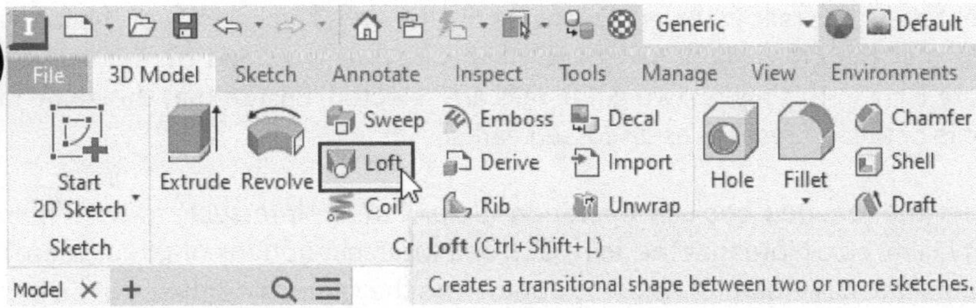

3. Select the profiles of the loft feature in the graphics area one by one. The names of the selected profiles appear in the **Sections** area of the dialog box in a sequential order. Also, a preview of the loft feature appears in the graphics area, see Figure 8.57. In this figure, two closed circles are selected as profiles of the loft feature.

8.57

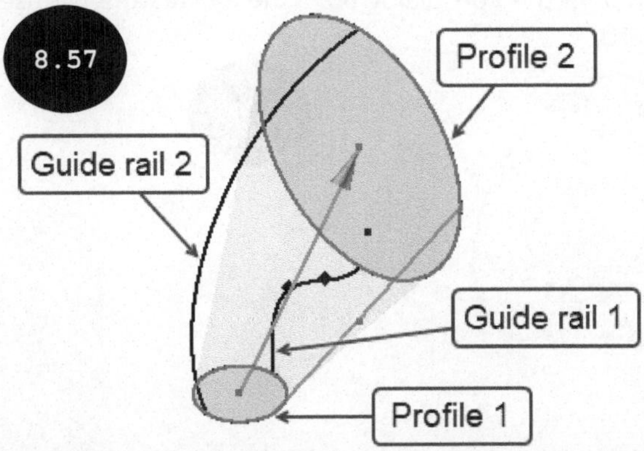

Tip: You can define the boundary condition for the start and end sections of the loft feature by using the options of the **Conditions** tab of the **Loft** dialog box, as discussed earlier.

Now, you can select the guide rails to guide the cross-sectional shape of the loft feature.

4. Ensure that the **Rails** radio button is selected in the **Loft** dialog box, see Figure 8.58.

5. Click on the **Click to add** option in the **Rails** area of the dialog box, see Figure 8.58. You are prompted to select a sketch as a guide rail for the loft feature.

8.58

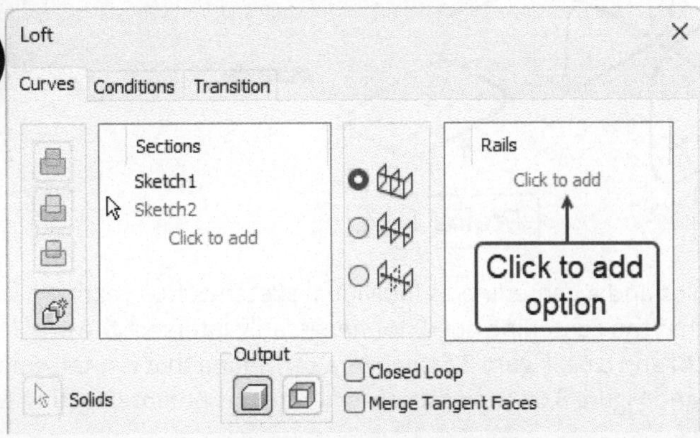

6. Select the guide rails in the graphics area one by one. The preview of the loft feature is modified such that the cross-sectional shape of the feature is guided by the selected guide rails, see Figure 8.59. In this figure, two guide rails are selected. Ensure that the guide rails intersect each profile of the loft feature, as discussed earlier.

7. Select the required boolean operation (**Join**, **Cut**, or **Intersect**) in the **Operation** area of the **Loft** dialog box. Note that the **Join**, **Cut**, and **Intersect** options of this area are not enabled while creating the base feature. All these options are the same as discussed in earlier chapters.

8. Ensure that the **Solid** button is activated in the **Output** area of the dialog box for creating a solid loft feature. The other options of the **Loft** dialog box are the same as discussed earlier.

9. Click on the **OK** button in the **Loft** dialog box. The loft feature with sections and guide rails is created, see Figure 8.60.

8.59

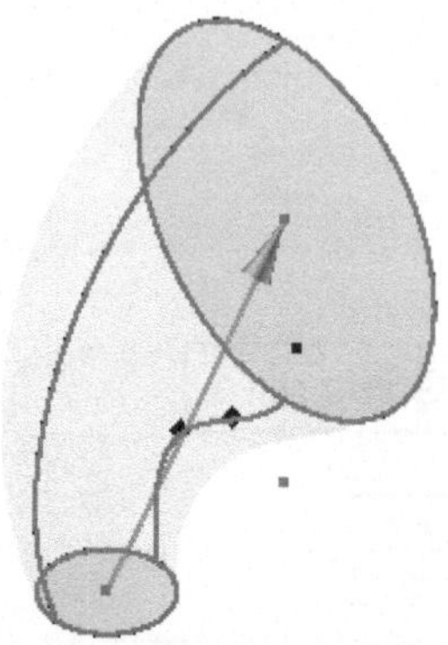

8.60

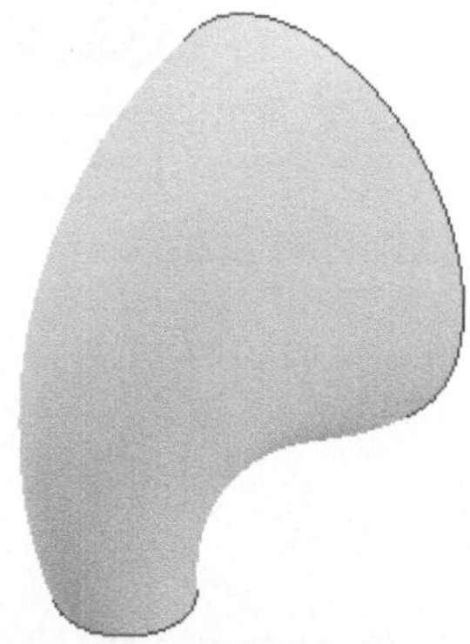

Creating a Loft feature with Sections and a Centerline

In Autodesk Inventor, you can also create a loft feature with profiles and a centerline. The centerline is used for maintaining a neutral axis of the loft feature and a consistent transition between the profiles, see Figure 8.61. Note that you can select only one centerline to create a loft feature. The method for creating a loft feature with profiles/sections and a centerline is discussed below:

8.61

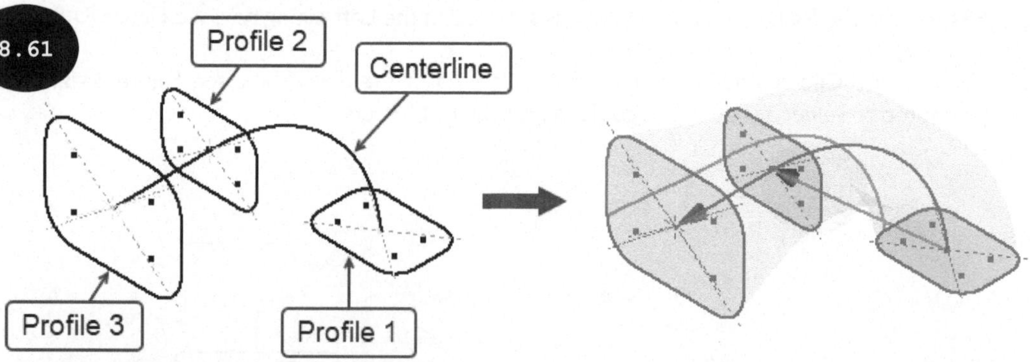

1. Create profiles and a centerline as individual sketches for creating a loft feature in the graphics area. Note that the centerline need not necessarily intersect the profiles of the loft feature, refer to Figures 8.61 and 8.62. Figure 8.61, shows a centerline that is intersecting with the profiles of the loft feature and Figure 8.62 shows a centerline that is not intersecting with the profiles of the loft feature.

2. Click on the **Loft** tool in the **Create** panel of the **3D Model** tab. The **Loft** dialog box appears.

3. Select the profiles of the loft feature in the graphics area one by one. The names of the selected profiles appear in the **Sections** area of the dialog box in a sequential order. Also, a preview of the loft feature appears in the graphics area, see Figure 8.63.

8.62

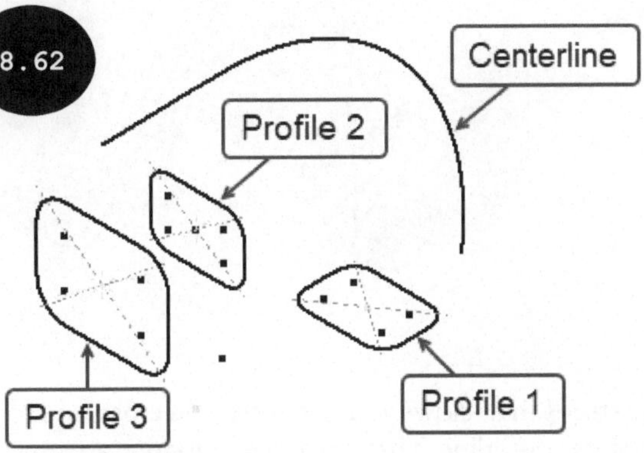

8.63

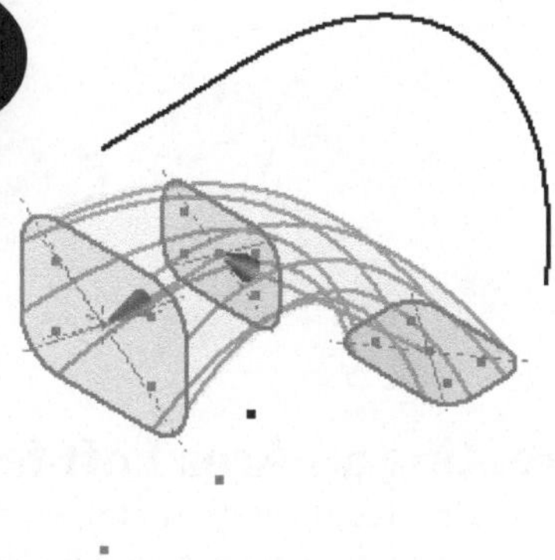

Now, you can select a centerline for creating a loft feature.

4. Select the **Center Line** radio button in the **Loft** dialog box, see Figure 8.64. The **Center Line** area appears on the right panel of the dialog box and you are prompted to select a centerline.

8.64

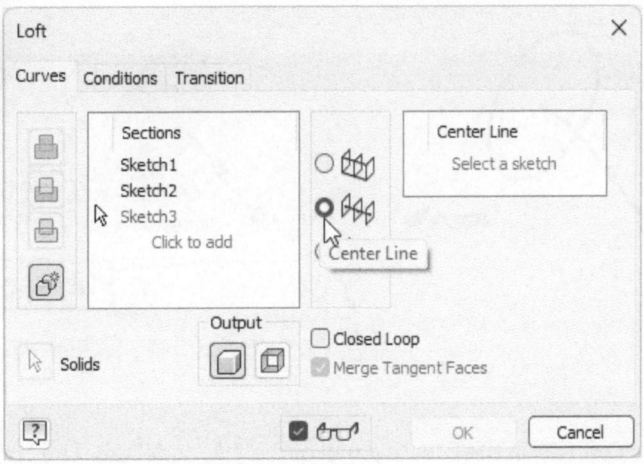

5. Select a centerline in the graphics area. A preview of the loft feature appears in the graphics area, see Figure 8.65.

6. Select the required boolean operation (**Join**, **Cut**, or **Intersect**) in the **Operation** area of the **Loft** dialog box. Note that the options in the **Operation** area are not enabled while creating the base feature.

7. Ensure that the **Solid** button is activated in the **Output** area of the dialog box for creating a solid loft feature. The other options of the **Loft** dialog box are same as discussed earlier.

8. Click on the **OK** button in the **Loft** dialog box. A loft feature with sections and a centerline is created, see Figure 8.66.

8.65

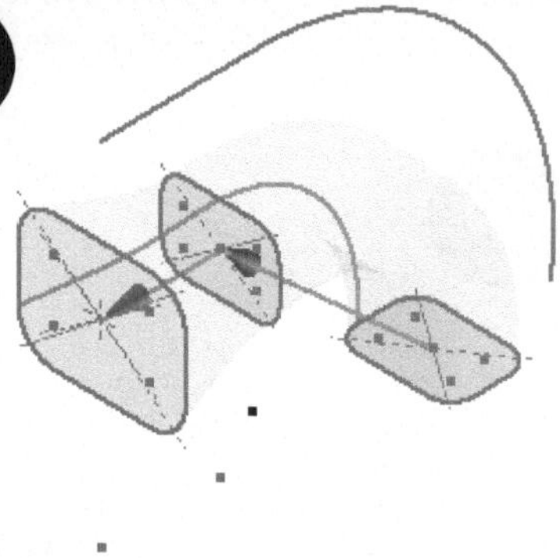

8.66

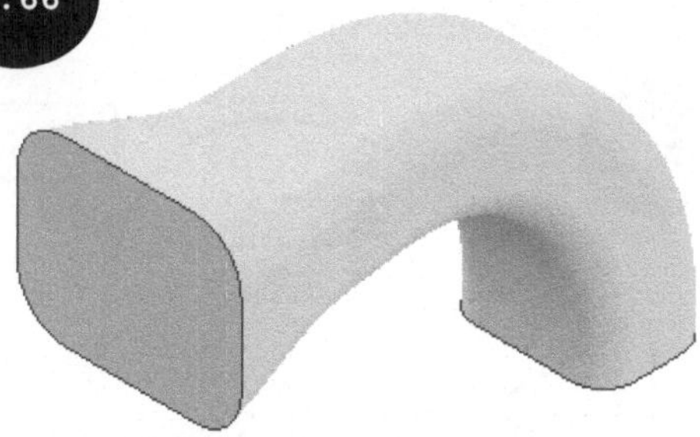

Creating an Area Loft feature

An area loft feature is one of the most powerful features that allows you to control the cross-sectional areas of the loft feature at specified locations along its centerline. The method for creating an area loft feature is same as creating a loft feature with a centerline. However, in an area loft feature, you can create additional cross-sections along the centerline of the loft feature and edit their parameters to control the shape of the feature, as required, see Figure 8.67. In this figure, a cross-section is added at the middle of the centerline of the loft feature. The method for creating an area loft feature is discussed below:

8.67

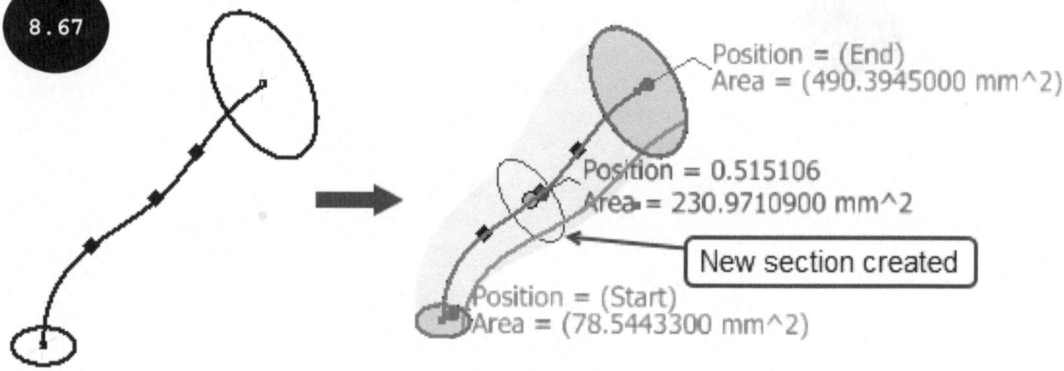

1. Click on the **Loft** tool in the **Create** panel of the **3D Model** tab. The **Loft** dialog box appears.

2. Select the profiles of the loft feature in the graphics area one by one. The preview of a loft feature appears in the graphics area.

3. Select the **Area Loft** radio button in the **Loft** dialog box. The **Center Line** area and the **Placed Sections** area appear on the right panel of the dialog box. Also, you are prompted to select a centerline.

4. Select a centerline in the graphics area. The preview of a loft feature appears with the display of section dimensions (position and area) at the start and end of the centerline of the feature, see Figure 8.68.

8.68

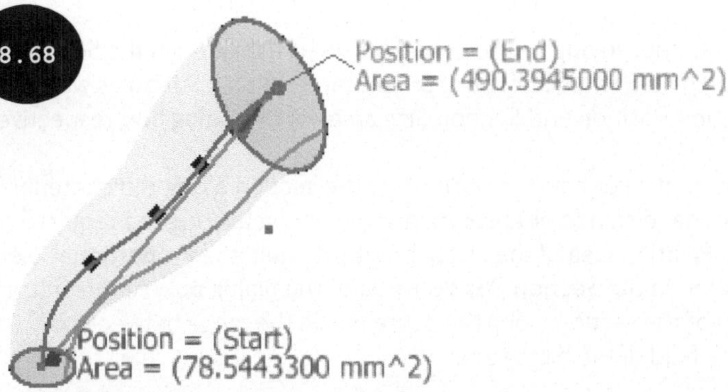

Now, you can create additional sections along the centerline of the loft feature to control the cross-sectional shape of the loft feature.

5. Move the cursor over the centerline of the loft feature in the graphics area. A yellow dot appears at the cursor tip as you move the cursor along the centerline of the loft feature.

6. Click on the centerline of the loft feature. A new section is created at the specified position on the centerline of the loft feature and displays its current position and area in the graphics area, see Figure 8.69. Also, the **Section Dimensions** dialog box appears with the display of current position and area of the newly added section, see Figure 8.70.

8.69

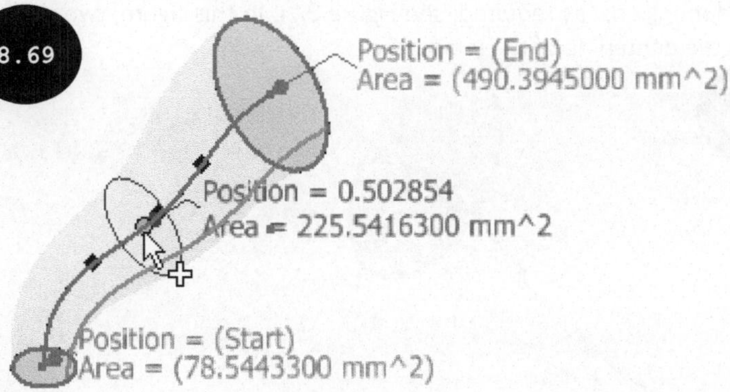

8.70

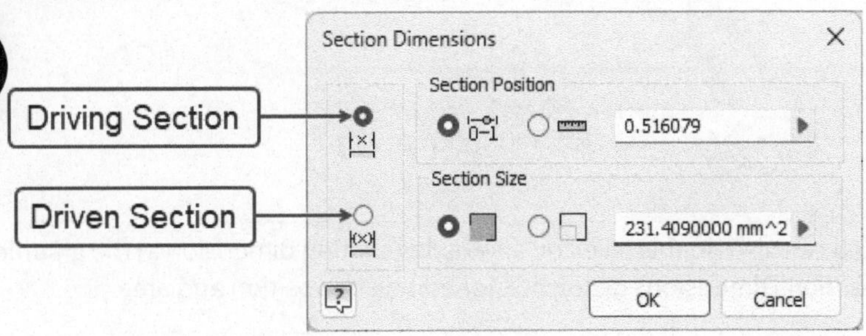

Now, you can control or edit the current position and area of the newly added section.

7. Edit the current position and area of the newly added section by using the required fields of the **Section Dimensions** dialog box, if needed.

Note: By default, the **Driving Section** radio button is activated in the **Section Dimensions** dialog box. As a result, you can control or edit the section position as well as the section area in the **Section Position** and **Section Size** areas of the dialog box, respectively.

You can control or edit the position of the section along the centerline by specifying the proportional distance or absolute distance on activating the required radio button in the **Section Position** area of the dialog box. By default, the **Proportional Distance** radio button is activated in the **Section Position** area of the dialog box. As a result, you can specify the position of the section along the centerline in the range between 0 to 1 in the **Proportional Distance** field of the dialog box.

The area of the section can be defined by specifying the area value or scale factor on activating the **Area** or **Scale Factor** radio button in the **Section Size** area of the dialog box, respectively. The **Section Size** area is enabled only when the **Driving Section** radio button is activated in the **Section Dimensions** dialog box.

8. After editing the section dimensions (position and area), click on the **OK** button in the **Section Dimensions** dialog box. The section dimensions get modified in the preview of the loft feature, as specified.

9. Similarly, you can create multiple additional sections along the centerline of the loft feature and control their dimensions, as required, see Figure 8.71. In this figure, two additional sections are created along the centerline of the loft feature.

8.71

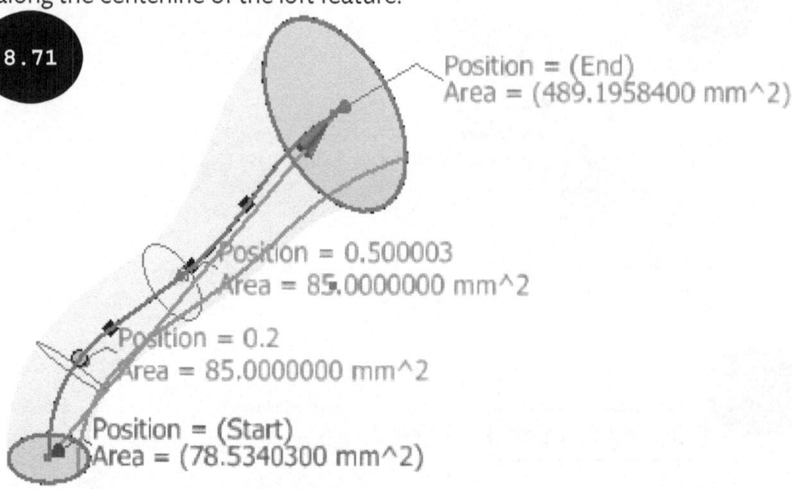

Tip: You can also double-click on an existing section dimension in the graphics area to invoke the **Section Dimensions** dialog box for editing its position and area.

10. Select the required boolean operation (**Join**, **Cut**, or **Intersect**) in the **Operation** area of the **Loft** dialog box. Note that the options in the **Operation** area are not enabled while creating the base feature. The other options of the dialog box are the same as discussed earlier.

11. Click on the **OK** button in the **Loft** dialog box. An area loft feature is created, see Figure 8.72.

8.72

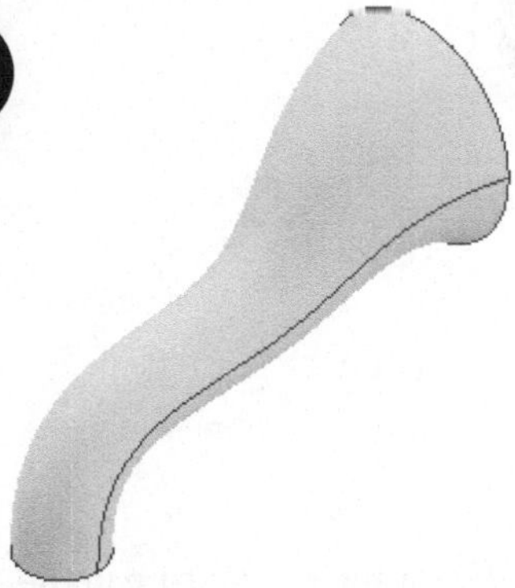

Creating a Coil Feature

A coil feature is used for creating a helical spring or a thread on a cylinder by sweeping a profile around an axis of revolution, see Figure 8.73. You can create a coil feature by using the **Coil** tool. The method for creating a coil feature is discussed below:

8.73

1. Create a profile and an axis in the graphics area for creating a coil feature, see Figure 8.74. In this figure, a vertical line is created to be selected as the axis of revolution. Note that you can select a default axis, a work axis, a line, a centerline, or a construction line as an axis of revolution.

2. Click on the **Coil** tool in the **Create** panel of the **3D Model** tab, see Figure 8.75. The **Coil** property panel appears, see Figure 8.76.

8.74

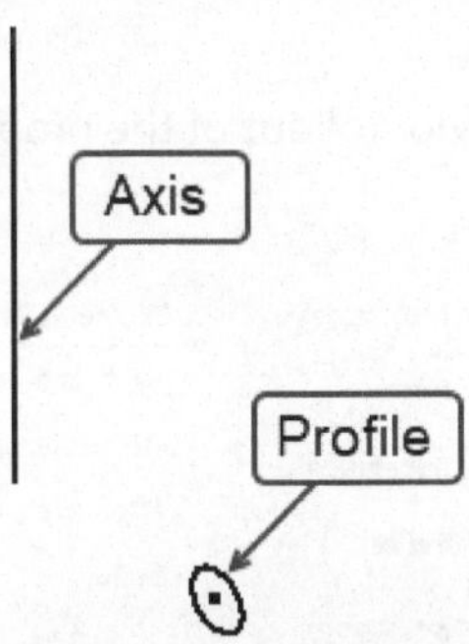

8.75

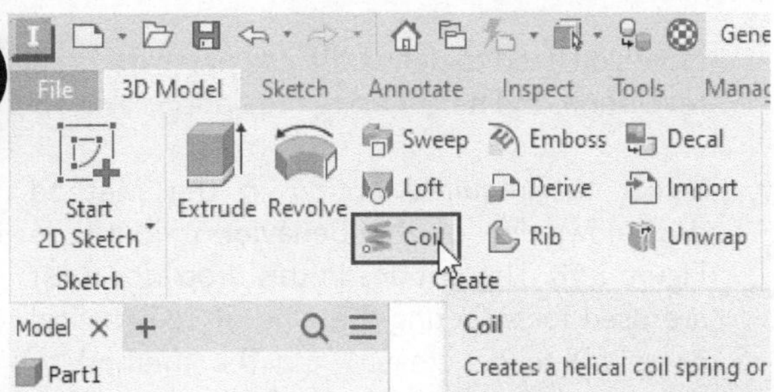

8.76

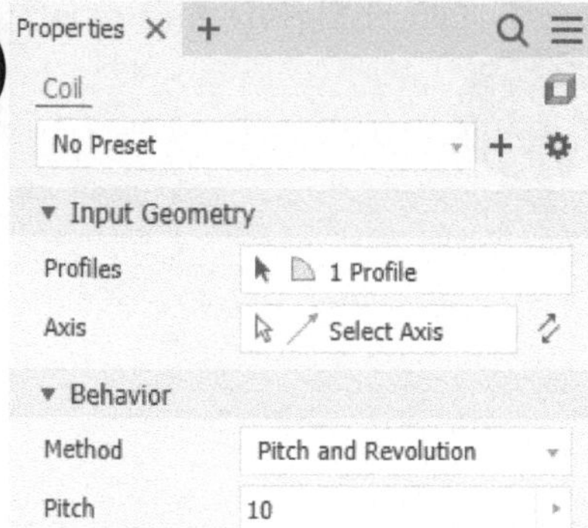

3. Select a closed sketch as the profile of the coil feature in the graphics area. Note that if only one closed sketch is available in the graphics area then it will automatically be selected as the profile of the feature and you will be prompted to select an axis of revolution.

Tip: By default, the **Profiles** selector is activated in the property panel. As a result, you can select a closed profile in the graphics area for creating a solid coil feature. If the surface mode is activated, then you can select a closed or an open sketch as a profile for creating a surface coil feature. You can switch to the surface mode by clicking on the **Surface mode** button at the top right corner of the property panel. Note that to switch back to the solid mode, you need to click on the **Surface mode** button again. Its a toggle button to switch between the solid and surface modes.

After selecting a profile of the coil feature, you need to select an axis of revolution.

4. Ensure that the **Axis** selector is activated in the **Coil** property panel.

5. Select an axis of revolution in the graphics area. The preview of a coil feature appears in the graphics area with default parameters, see Figure 8.77. You can select a default axis, a work axis, a line, a centerline, or a construction line as the axis of revolution.

8.77

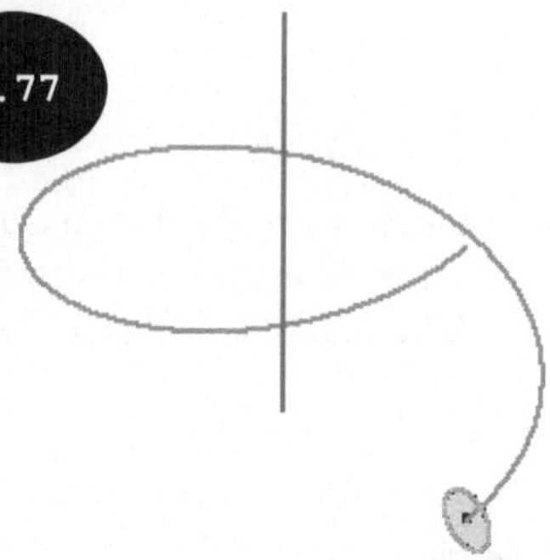

6. Click on the **Reverses pitch direction along axis** button in front of the **Axis** selector in the property panel to reverse the direction of helical coil creation, if needed.

Now, you need to define the coil parameters such as pitch, revolution, and height using the options available in the **Behavior** rollout of the property panel.

7. Select the required option in the **Method** drop-down list of the **Behavior** rollout, see Figure 8.78. The options in this drop-down list are used for selecting the type of coil (helical or spiral) to be created and the method to be adopted for creating it. The options are discussed next.

8.78

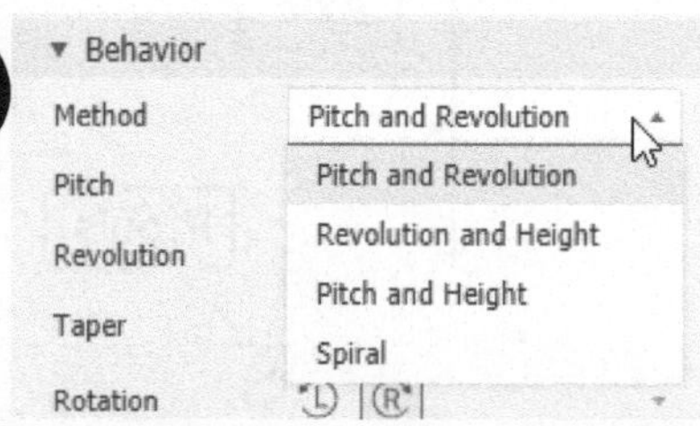

Pitch and Revolution: The **Pitch and Revolution** option is used for creating a helical coil by defining its pitch and number of revolutions. When this option is selected, the **Pitch** and **Revolution** fields get enabled in the property panel.

Revolution and Height: The **Revolution and Height** option is used for creating a helical coil by defining its number of revolutions and total height. When this option is selected, the **Revolution** and **Height** fields are enabled in the property panel.

Pitch and Height: The **Pitch and Height** option is used for creating a helical coil by defining its pitch and total height. When this option is selected, the **Pitch** and **Height** fields get enabled in the property panel.

Spiral: The **Spiral** option is used for creating a spiral coil by defining its pitch and number of revolutions. Figure 8.79 shows the preview of a spiral coil feature. When this option is selected, the **Pitch** and **Revolution** fields get enabled in the property panel.

After selecting the required option in the **Method** drop-down list of the **Behavior** rollout, you need to define the coil parameters.

8. Define the coil parameters such as pitch, height, and revolution in the respective fields of the property panel depending upon the option selected in the **Method** drop-down list, see Figure 8.80. In this figure, the **Revolution and Height** option is selected in the **Method** drop-down list of the property panel. As a result, you can specify the number of revolutions and total height of the helical coil in the respective fields of the property panel for creating the helical coil feature.

8.79

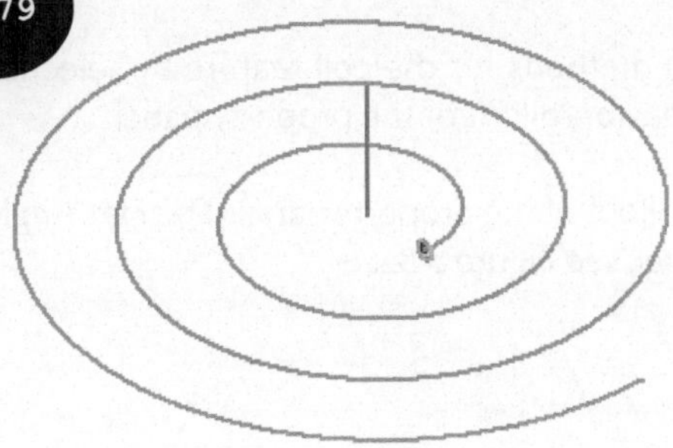

8.80

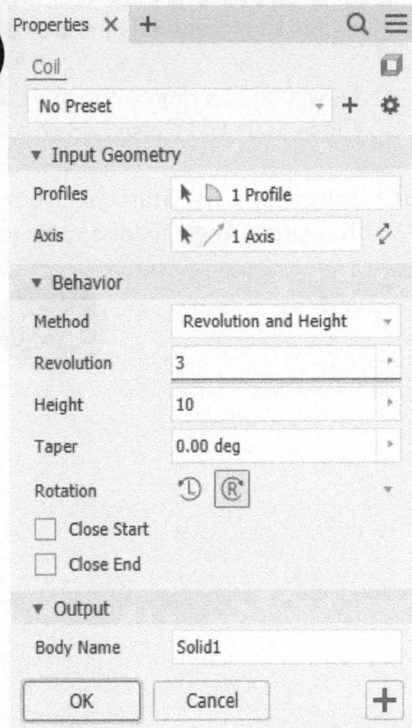

Taper: The **Taper** field in the **Behavior** rollout in the property panel is used for specifying taper angle to create a tapered helical coil feature, see Figure 8.81. Note that to reverse the direction of the taper from outward to inward, you need to enter a negative angle value in the **Taper** field of the property panel.

8.81

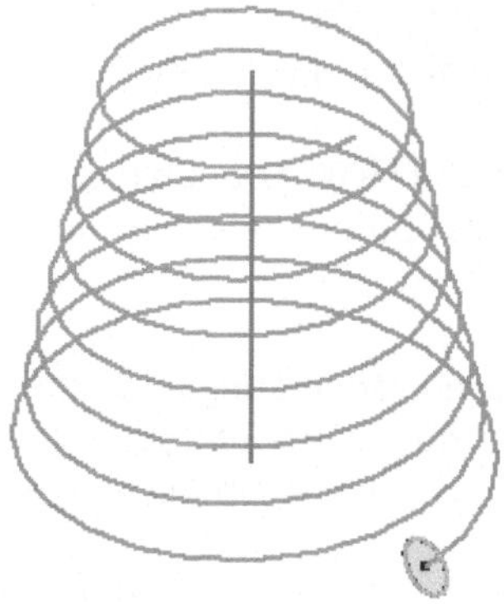

9. Enter the taper angle value in the **Taper** field of the property panel for creating a tapered helical coil feature, if needed. Note that if you do not want to create any tapering in the resultant coil feature then ensure that the taper angle value is specified as **0** in the **Taper** field.

   Now, you can define the rotational direction of the coil feature.

10. Click on the **Left Hand** or **Right Hand** button in the **Behavior** rollout of the property panel to define the rotational direction of the coil feature, as required.

    Now, you can define the start and end transition methods for the coil feature by selecting the **Close Start** and **Close End** check boxes in the **Behavior** rollout of the property panel.

11. Select the **Close Start** check box in the **Behavior** rollout of the property panel. The **Flat Angle** and **Transition Angle** fields appear in the property panel, see Figure 8.82.

8.82

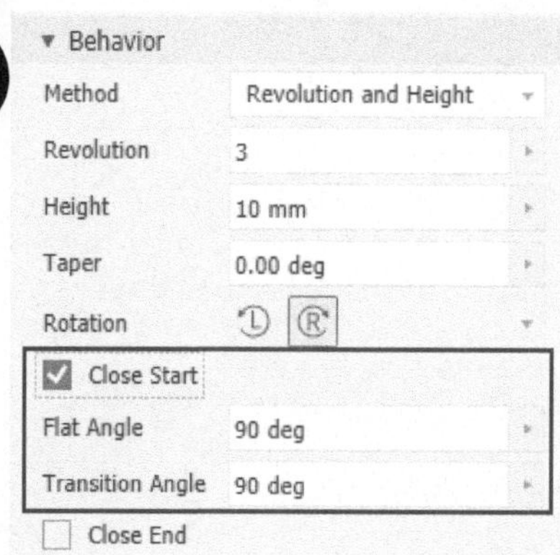

Transition Angle and Flat Angle fields: The Transition Angle field is used for defining the transition angle, in which the coil achieves the transition to become flat at the start, refer to Figure 8.83. For example, the 90 degrees transition angle achieves the transition to become flat over a quarter turn of the coil. You can define a transition angle between 0 to 360 degrees. The **Flat Angle** field is used for defining the flat angle through which the coil extends after transition with no pitch. You can define a flat angle between 0 and 360 degrees. Figure 8.83 shows a resultant coil with flat transition at the start of the coil feature, created by specifying the transition angle and flat angle as 90 degrees.

12. Define the transition angle and the flat angle values in the respective fields of the property panel for specifying the transition at the start of the coil feature.

13. Select the **Close End** check box in the **Behavior** rollout of the property panel. The **Flat Angle** and **Transition Angle** fields appear below this check box. These fields are used for defining the flat and transition angles at the end of the coil feature and are same as discussed earlier. Figure 8.84 shows a coil with flat transition at the start and end of the coil feature. Figure 8.85 shows a coil feature with no transition defined at the start and end of the coil feature.

8.83

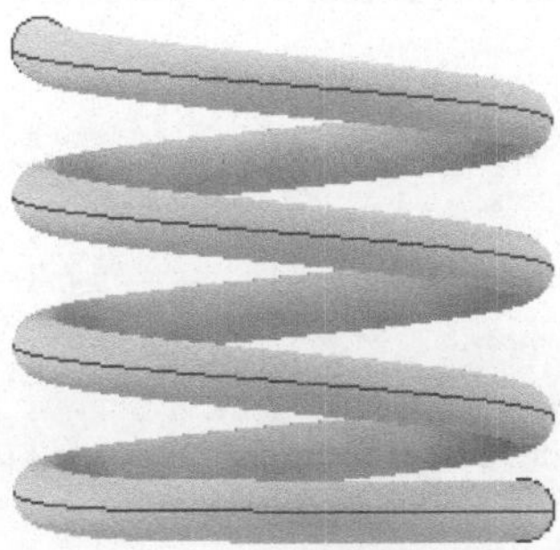

8.84

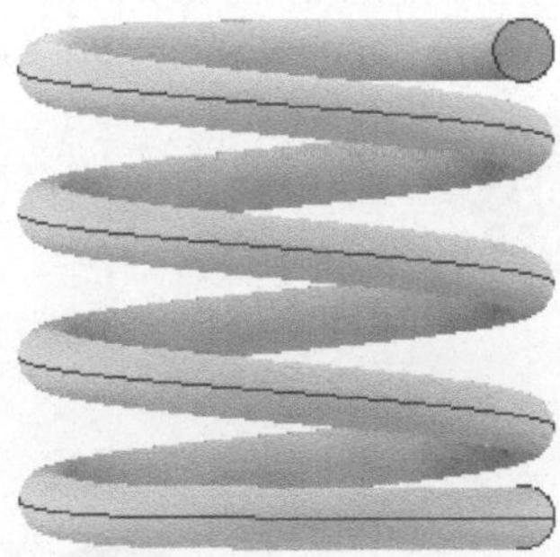

8.85

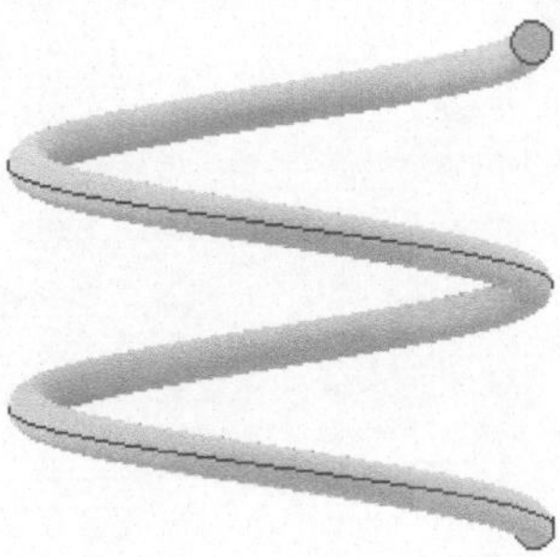

14. Click on the **OK** button in the **Coil** property panel. The coil feature is created.

Creating an Emboss Feature

An emboss feature is created by embossing or engraving a sketch or text onto a face of a model, see Figure 8.86. In this figure, text is embossed on a curved face of the model. You can create an emboss feature by using the **Emboss** tool and the method for the same is discussed below:

8.86

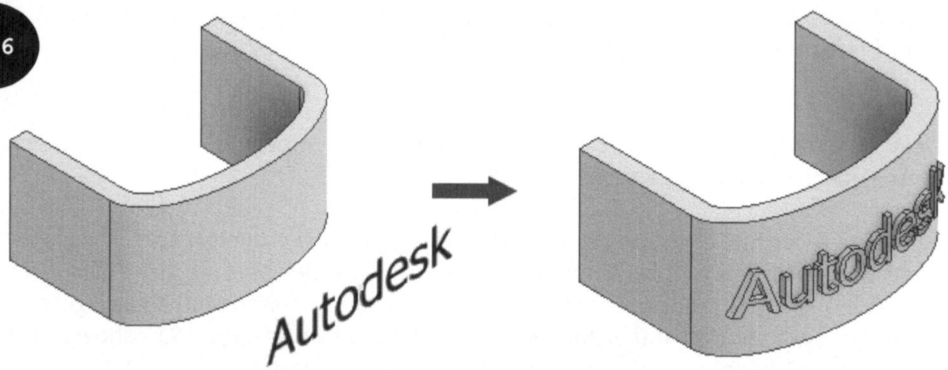

1. Click on the **Emboss** tool in the **Create** panel of the **3D Model** tab, see Figure 8.87. The **Emboss** dialog box appears, see Figure 8.88.

8.87

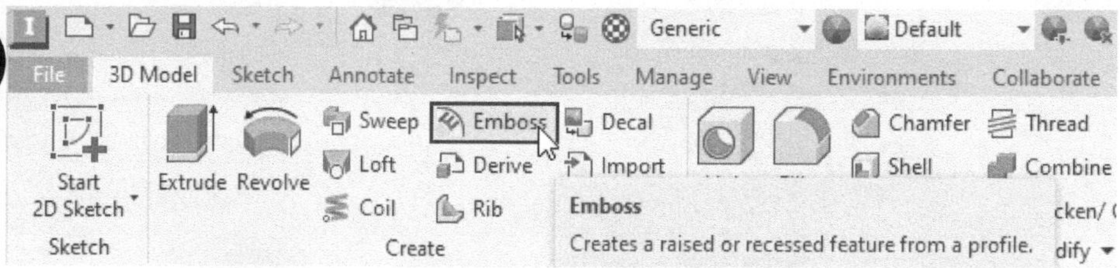

8.88

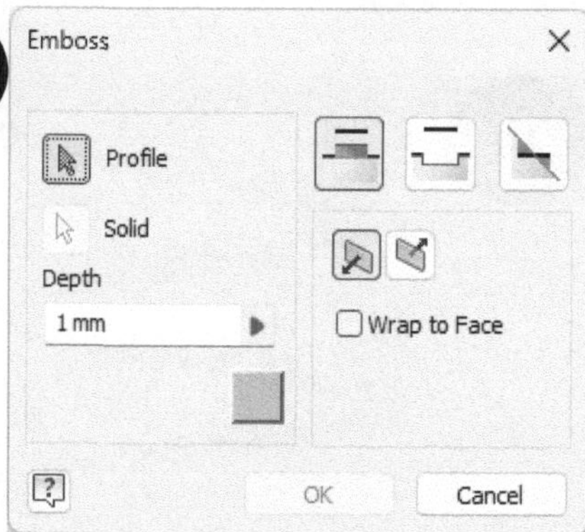

Note: If a text or a sketch is not available in the graphics area then on clicking the **Emboss** tool, the **Emboss** dialog box does not get invoked. Instead, the **Autodesk Inventor Professional Tip** window appears, informing you that no visible, unadaptive sketches are available in the graphics area for creating an emboss feature.

By default, the **Profile** button is activated in the **Emboss** dialog box. As a result, you are prompted to select a profile (sketch geometry or text) to be embossed or engraved onto a face of a model.

2. Select a profile (sketch geometry or text) in the graphics area. A green colored arrow appears in the graphics area, defining the direction of the feature to be created.

3. Ensure that the direction of the feature to be created is toward the face of an existing model. You can reverse the direction of the feature by using the direction buttons available in the dialog box, as required.

   Now, you need to define the type of feature to be created by clicking on the **Emboss From Face**, **Engrave From Face**, or **Emboss/Engrave From Plane** buttons in the dialog box.

   Emboss From Face: The **Emboss From Face** button is used for creating an embossed feature by adding material to the face of the model, see Figure 8.89. You can specify the depth of material to be added in the **Depth** field of the dialog box.

   Engrave From Face: The **Engrave From Face** button is used for creating an engraved feature by removing material from the model, see Figure 8.90. You can specify the depth of material to be removed in the **Depth** field of the dialog box.

8.89

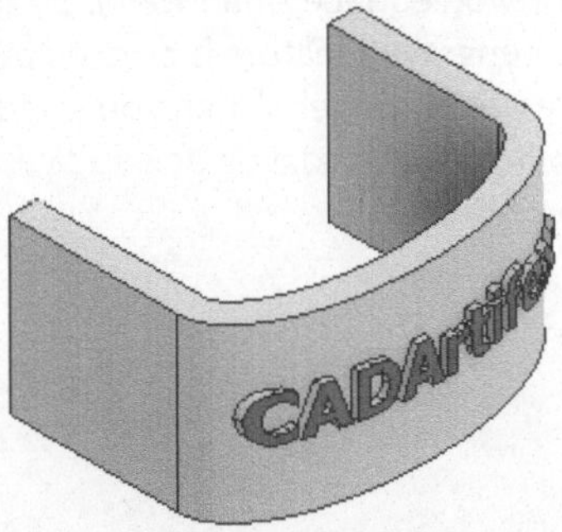

8.90

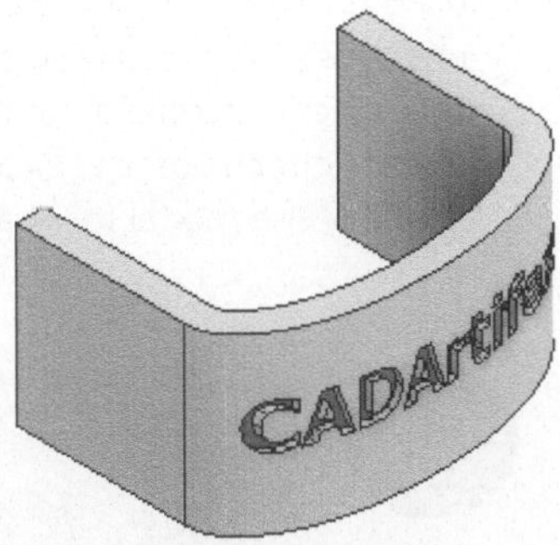

   Emboss/Engrave From Plane: The **Emboss/Engrave From Plane** button is used for creating a feature by adding and removing material on both sides of the sketching plane of the profile. If the profile intersects the model then on activating this button, the profile can be extruded on both sides of its sketching plane creating a feature by adding as well as removing material at the same time, see Figure 8.91. Note that when the **Emboss/Engrave From Plane** button is activated, the **Depth** field is no longer available in the dialog box. Instead, the **Taper** field becomes available for specifying a taper angle for the feature.

8.91

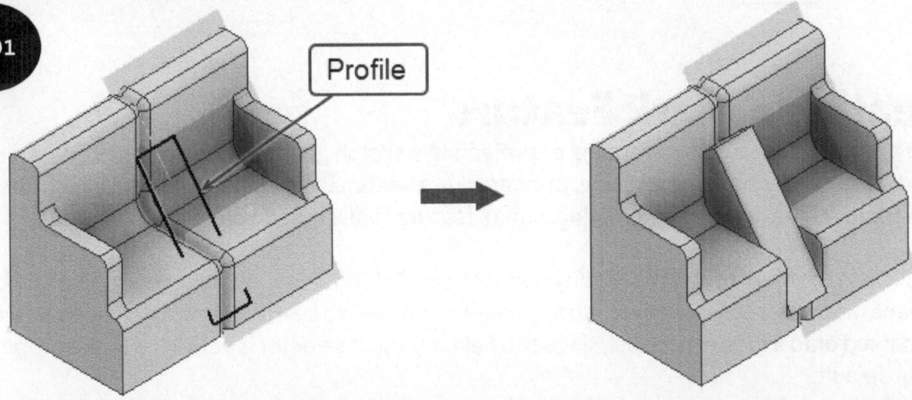

4. Click on the required button (**Emboss From Face**, **Engrave From Face**, or **Emboss/Engrave From Plane**) to create the feature, respectively.

5. Enter the depth value or the taper angle depending upon the button (**Emboss From Face**, **Engrave From Face**, or **Emboss/Engrave From Plane**) activated in the dialog box.

   Now, you can define a different color for the top face of the feature being created.

6. Click on the **Top Face Appearance** button in the dialog box. The **Appearance** dialog box appears. In this dialog box, you can select a color to be applied to the top face of the feature being created.

7. Click on the **OK** button in the dialog box. The embossed or engraved feature is created.

Note: On selecting the **Wrap to Face** check box, you can create an embossed or engraved feature by wrapping the selected profile onto a selected face of a model, see Figure 8.92. It is mainly used for wrapping the profile onto a curved or revolved face of a model. By default, this check box is cleared. As a result, the embossed or engraved feature is created by projecting the selected profile on the next intersecting face of the model. When you select the **Wrap to Face** check box, the **Face** button becomes available in the dialog box and you can select a face of the model for wrapping the selected profile.

8.92

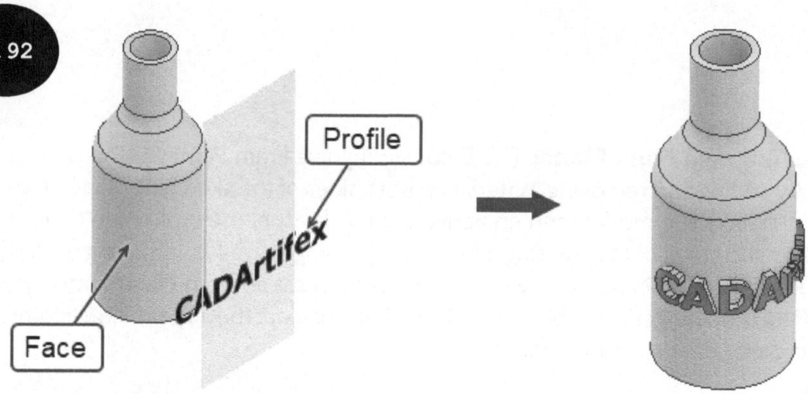

Creating a Mark Feature

A mark feature is created by wrapping or projecting a sketch geometry or text onto a face of a model. It represents a laser marking, etching, or engraving a feature. You can create a mark feature by using the **Mark** tool. The method for creating a mark feature is discussed below:

1. Click on the **Mark** tool in the **Modify** panel of the **3D Model** tab, see Figure 8.93. The **Mark** property panel appears, see Figure 8.94. Also, you are prompted to select a sketch geometry or a text to be marked onto a face of a model, since the **Select Object** selector is activated in the property panel, by default.

8.93

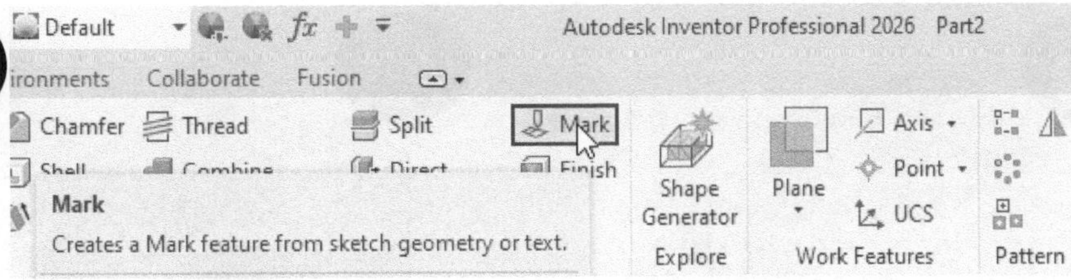

8.94

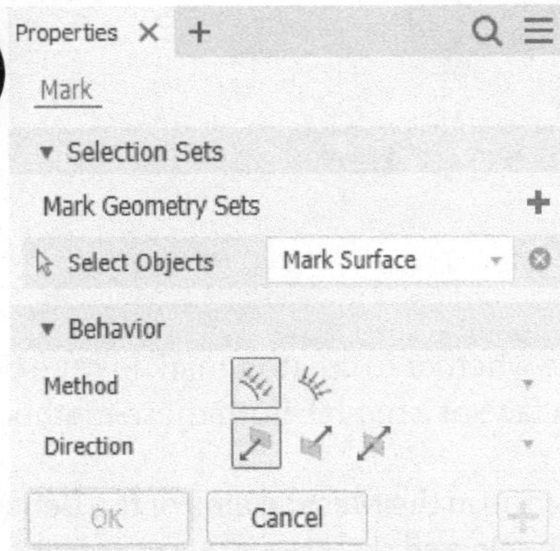

Note: If a text or a sketch is not available in the graphics area then on clicking the **Mark** tool, the **Mark** property panel does not get invoked. Instead, you are prompted to select a sketching plane for creating a sketch of the mark feature.

2. Select a sketch geometry or a text in the graphics area. The preview of a mark feature appears on a front face of a model. Note that, you can select the entities one by one by clicking the left mouse button or by drawing a window from left to right around the entities to be selected.

Tip: You can also select multiple sketches or geometries to be marked on a face of the model. For doing so, click on the **Add Mark Set** button + in the **Selection Sets** rollout of the dialog box. A new row will be added in the **Selection Sets** rollout for selecting a new sketch geometry or a text to be marked onto a face of a model.

3. Select the required option (**Mark Surface** or **Mark Through**) in the drop-down list that appears on the right of the **Select Object** field for creating a marked feature, see Figures 8.95 and 8.96. Both these options are discussed next.

   Mark Surface: The **Mark Surface** option is used for creating a mark feature by projecting or wrapping the selected sketch/text onto the front visible face of the model, see Figure 8.95.

   Mark Through: The **Mark Through** option is used for creating a mark feature by projecting or wrapping the selected sketch/text across the intersected face(s) of the model, see Figure 8.96.

8.95

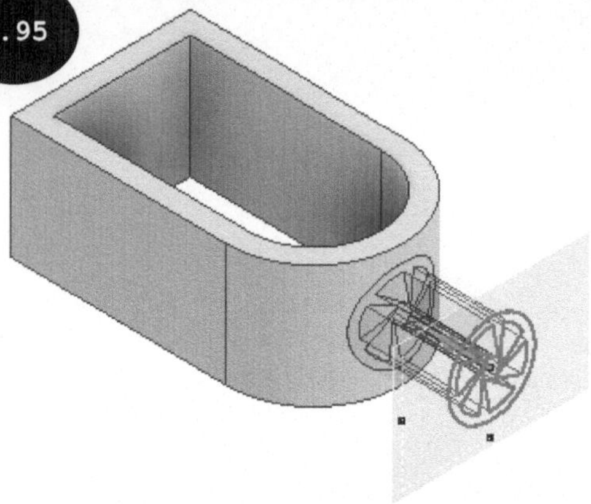

8.96

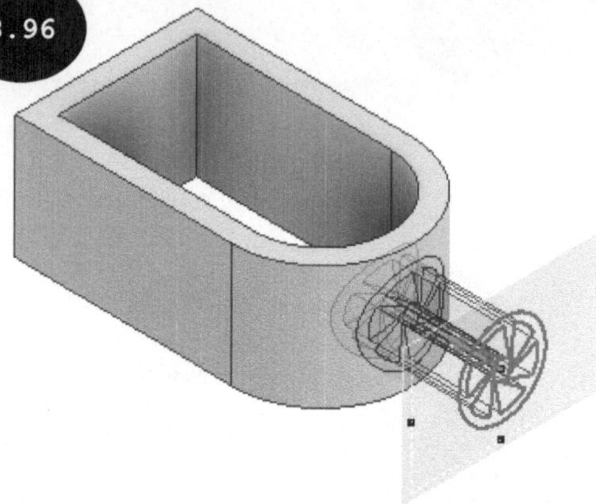

Now, you need to define whether to create a mark feature by projecting or wrapping the selected sketch geometry onto a face of a model. Both these methods are discussed next.

Project: The **Project** button in the **Method** area of the **Behavior** rollout is used for creating a mark feature by projecting the selected sketch geometry or text on the face of a model, see Figure 8.97.

Wrap: The **Wrap** button in the **Method** area of the **Behavior** rollout is used for creating a mark feature by wrapping the selected sketch geometry or text on the face of a model, see Figure 8.98. On selecting this button the **Select Face** field and **Automatic Face Chain** check box appear in the **Behavior** rollout of the dialog box. The **Select Face** field allows you to select a face of a model for wrapping the selected sketch geometry or text to create a mark feature. The **Automatic Face Chain** check box is used for wrapping the selected sketch geometry or text onto all the faces that are tangentially connected to the selected face of the model. By default, this check box is cleared. As a result, the sketch geometry or text wraps only on the selected face of the model.

8.97

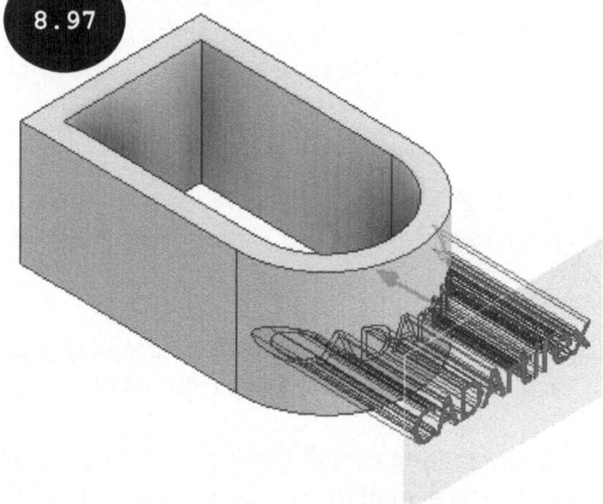

8.98

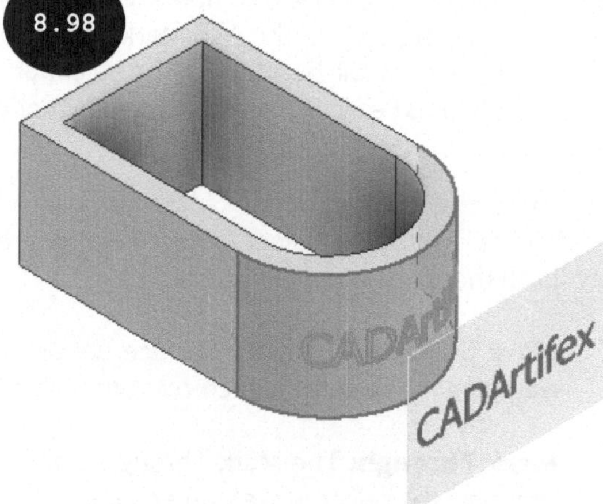

4. Click on the required button (**Project** or **Wrap**) to create the respective feature.

5. Ensure that the direction of projection is towards the face of an existing model. You can reverse the direction of the projection by using the direction buttons available in the dialog box, as required.

6. Click on the **OK** button in the dialog box. The mark feature is created.

Creating a Rib Feature

Rib features act as supporting features and are generally used for increasing the strength of a model. You can create a rib feature from an open sketch by adding thickness in a specified direction. In Autodesk Inventor, you can create a rib feature that is normal or parallel to the sketching plane by using the **Rib** tool, see Figures 8.99 and 8.100. Figure 8.99 shows a model with an open sketch and the resultant rib feature created normal to the sketching plane. Figure 8.100 shows a model with an open sketch and the resultant rib feature created parallel to the sketching plane. The methods for creating different types of rib features are discussed below:

8.99

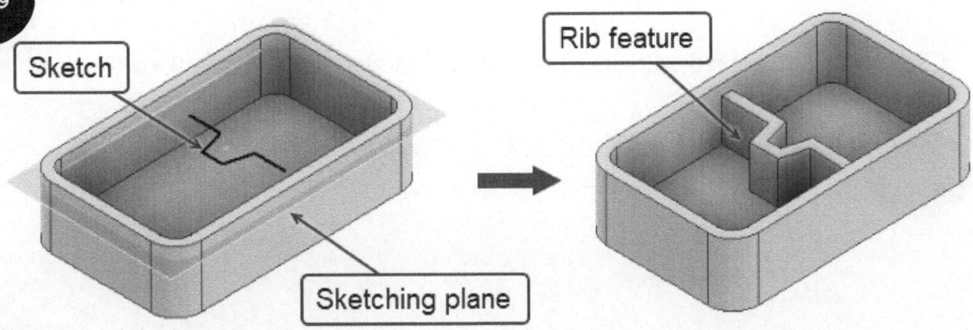

8.100

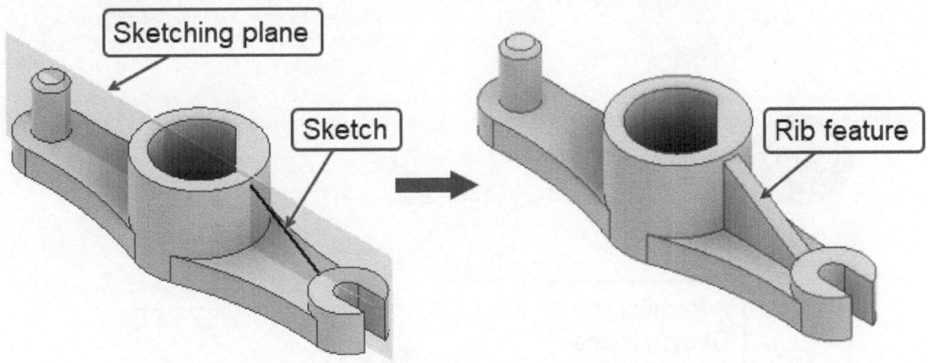

Creating a Rib Feature Normal to the Sketching Plane

The method for creating a rib feature normal to the sketching plane is discussed below:

1. Create an open or closed sketch as a profile for creating a rib feature normal to the sketching plane, see Figure 8.101. In this figure, an open sketch with multiple line entities is created. Note that the projection of both ends of the sketch entities should lie on the geometry of the model.

8.101

2. Click on the **Rib** tool in the **Create** panel of the **3D Model** tab, see Figure 8.102. The **Rib** dialog box appears, see Figure 8.103.

8.102

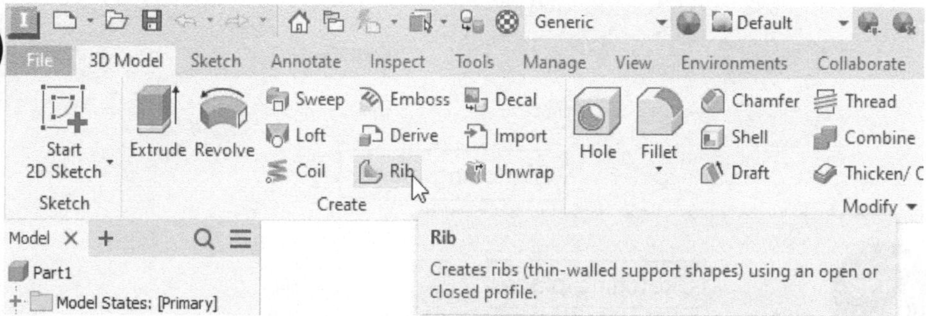

8.103

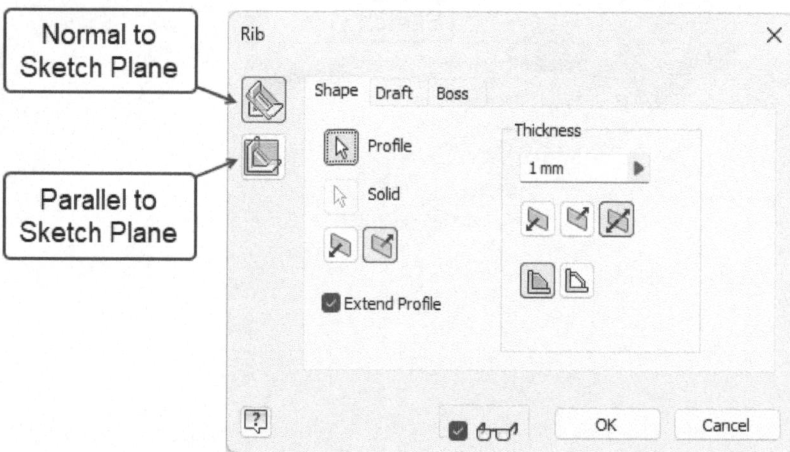

By default, the **Normal to Sketch Plane** button is activated in the **Rib** dialog box. As a result, you can create a rib feature that is normal to the sketching plane of the sketch. The **Parallel to Sketch Plane** button is used for creating a rib feature that is parallel to the sketching plane and is discussed later in this chapter.

3. Ensure that the **Normal to Sketch Plane** button is activated in the **Rib** dialog box, refer to Figure 8.103.

4. Select an entity of the sketch in the graphics area. The preview of a rib feature normal to the sketching plane appears in the graphics area, see Figure 8.104. If needed, you can continue selecting other entities of the sketch one by one, see Figure 8.105. In this figure, a total of 4 sketch entities are selected.

Note: If the preview of the rib feature does not appear in the graphics area then you may need to reverse the direction of the rib feature to the other side of the sketching plane by using the **Direction 1** or **Direction 2** button of the dialog box.

8.104

8.105

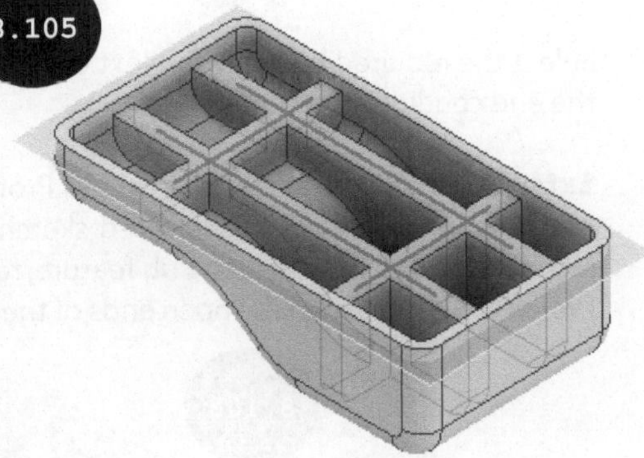

5. Enter the thickness value of the rib feature in the **Thickness** field of the dialog box.

   Now, you need to define the thickness direction of the rib feature. In Autodesk Inventor, you can create a rib feature by adding thickness to any one side of the sketch, or equally on both sides of the sketch by activating the required thickness direction button in the **Thickness** area of the dialog box.

6. Click on the required thickness direction button in the **Thickness** area of the dialog box.

   Now, you need to define the end condition of the rib feature by activating the **To Next** or **Finite** button in the **Thickness** area of the dialog box. Both these are discussed below:

   To Next: By default, the **To Next** button is activated in the **Thickness** area of the dialog box.

As a result, the rib feature is created by adding material up to the next intersecting face of the model, see Figure 8.106.

Finite: The **Finite** button in the **Thickness** area of the dialog box is used for creating a rib feature by adding material up to a specified depth, see Figure 8.107. On activating the **Finite** button, the **Extent** field appears in the dialog box. In this field, you can specify the extended depth of the rib feature.

8.106

8.107

7. Select the required button (**To Next** or **Finite**) in the **Thickness** area of the dialog box to define the end condition of the rib feature.

   Extend Profile: By default, the **Extend Profile** check box is selected in the dialog box. As a result, both the open ends of the selected sketch entities get extended up to their next intersection face of the model and create a rib feature, refer to Figures 8.106 and 8.107. If you clear the **Extend Profile** check box, then the open ends of the sketch entities will not be extended, see Figure 8.108.

8.108

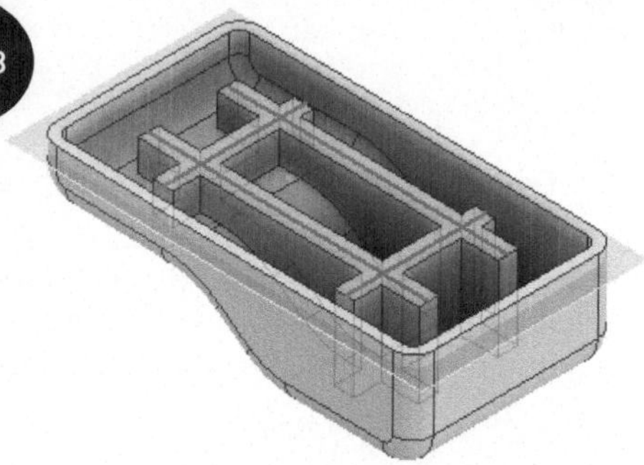

8. Ensure that the **Extend Profile** check box is selected in the dialog box for creating a rib feature by extending the open ends of the sketch profile up to their next intersection face.

   You can also create a tapered rib feature of a specified draft angle by using the options available in the **Draft** tab of the dialog box. Method for the same is described in the following point.

9. Click on the **Draft** tab in the **Rib** dialog box. The options for creating a tapered rib feature appear, see Figure 8.109. Note that the **Draft** tab is available only when the **Normal to Sketch Plane** button is activated in the **Rib** dialog box.

8.109

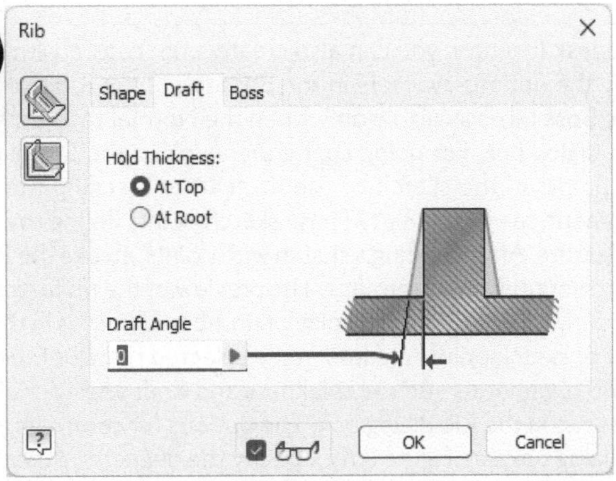

At Top: By default, the **At Top** radio button is selected in the **Draft** tab of the dialog box. As a result, the specified thickness of the rib feature remains unchanged at its top face and the thickness at the bottom face of the rib feature is controlled by the draft angle. Note that the bottom face of the rib feature is a face where the feature ends. You can specify a draft angle in the **Draft Angle** field of the dialog box.

At Root: On selecting the **At Root** radio button, the specified thickness of the rib feature remains unchanged at its bottom face and the thickness at the top face of the rib feature is controlled by the draft angle specified in the **Draft Angle** field of the dialog box.

10. Select the required radio button (**At Top** or **At Root**) in the **Draft** tab of the dialog box and then specify a draft angle in the **Draft Angle** field of the dialog box.

11. Click on the **OK** button in the **Rib** dialog box. A rib feature normal to the sketching plane is created, see Figure 8.110.

8.110

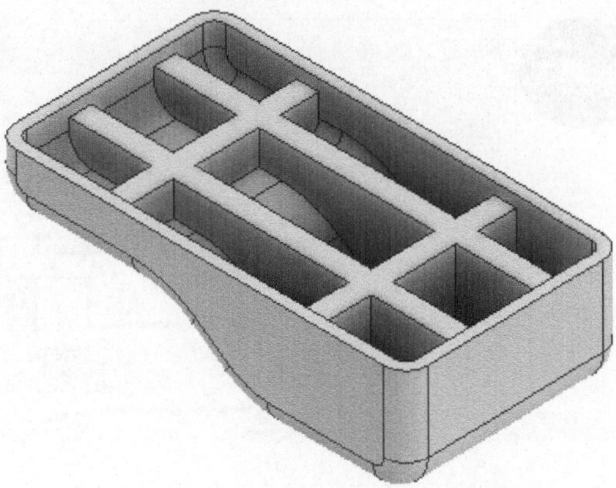

Note: In Autodesk Inventor, you can also create a rib feature with bosses at specified locations by using the options available in the **Boss** tab of the **Rib** dialog box, see Figure 8.111. Note that the **Boss** tab is available only when the **Normal to Sketch Plane** button is activated in the **Rib** dialog box. For doing so, before invoking the **Rib** dialog box, you need to create sketch points in the sketch of the rib feature by using the **Point** tool in the Sketching environment, see Figure 8.112. These sketch points define the center positions of bosses in the rib feature. After creating a sketch with points, invoke the **Rib** dialog box and then select the sketch entities as the profiles. The preview of the rib feature appears with bosses in the graphics area. Note that the display of number of bosses in the preview depends upon the number of sketch points created in the selected sketch of the rib feature. After specifying all the rib parameters such as thickness and draft angle for creating a rib feature, click on the **Boss** tab in the **Rib** dialog box. The options for controlling the boss parameters appear in the dialog box, see Figure 8.113. Specify the diameter, offset distance, and draft angle for the bosses of the rib feature in the respective fields of the dialog box and then click on the **OK** button. The rib feature with bosses is created.

8.111

8.112

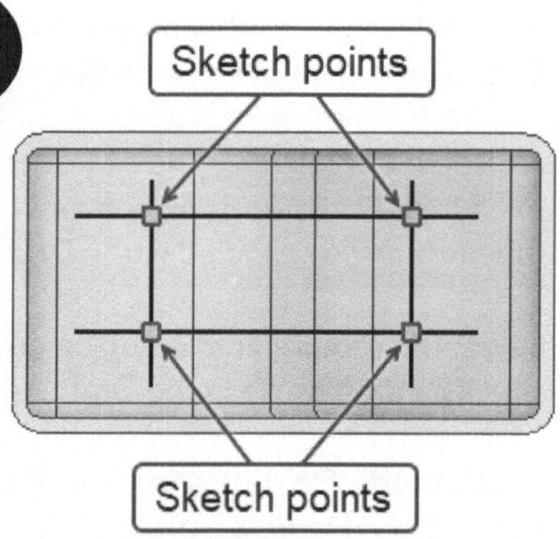

8.113

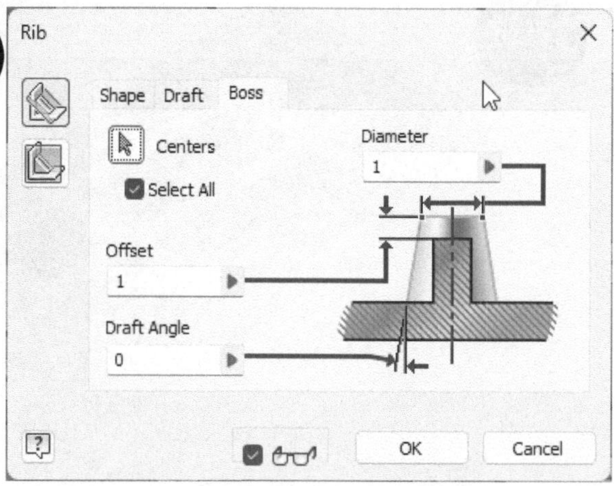

Creating a Rib Feature Parallel to the Sketching Plane

The method for creating a rib feature parallel to the sketching plane is discussed below:

1. Create an open sketch as a profile of the rib feature on a plane that intersects the model, see Figure 8.114. Note that the projection of the sketch entity should lie on the geometry of the model.

8.114

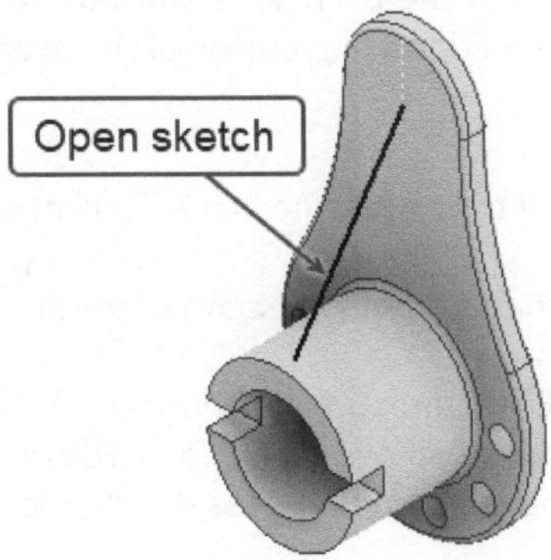

Tip: While creating an open sketch of the rib feature, if the geometries of the model get projected onto the current sketching plane as sketch entities, then it is recommended to convert the projected entities into construction entities by using the **Construction** tool of the **Format** panel in the Sketching environment.

2. Click on the **Rib** tool in the **Create** panel of the **3D Model** tab. The **Rib** dialog box appears.

3. Click on the **Parallel to Sketch Plane** button in the **Rib** dialog box to create a rib feature parallel to the sketching plane of the sketch, see Figure 8.115.

8.115

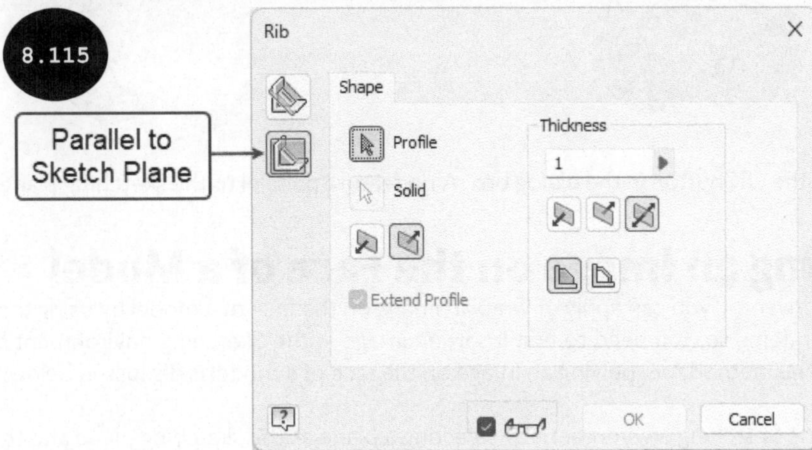

Note: If the sketch of the rib feature contains only one sketch entity then it will be automatically selected as the profile of the rib feature and the preview of the rib feature appears in the graphics area.

4. Select a sketch as a profile of the rib feature, if not selected automatically. The preview of the rib feature appears in the graphics area with default parameters, see Figure 8.116.

Note: If the preview of the rib feature does not appear in the graphics area then you may need to reverse the direction of the rib feature toward the geometry of the model by using the **Direction 1** or **Direction 2** button of the dialog box.

5. Enter the thickness value of the rib feature in the **Thickness** field of the dialog box.

   Now, you need to define the thickness direction of the rib feature.

6. Click on the required thickness direction button in the **Thickness** area of the dialog box. You can create a rib feature by adding thickness to any one side of the sketch or equally on both sides of the sketch by activating the required thickness direction button.

7. Select the required button (**To Next** or **Finite**) in the **Thickness** area of the dialog box to define the end condition of the rib feature, as discussed earlier. Figure 8.116 shows a rib feature when the **To Next** button is activated and Figure 8.117 shows a rib feature when the **Finite** button is activated.

8.116

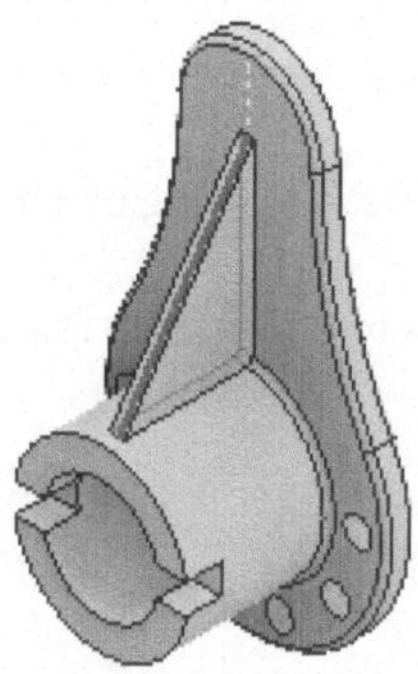

8.117

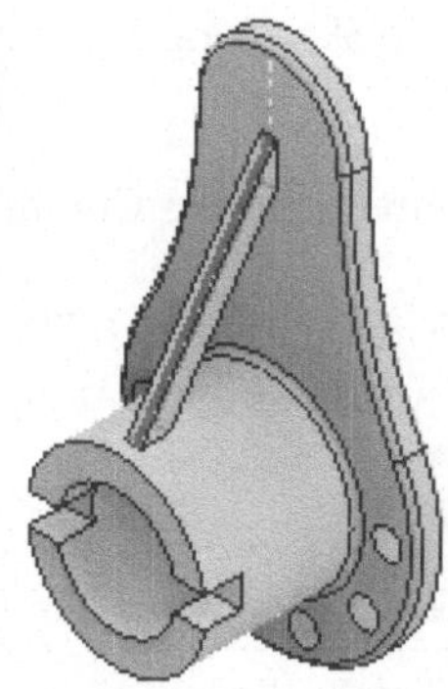

8. Click on the **OK** button in the dialog box. A rib feature parallel to the sketching plane is created.

Applying an Image on the Face of a Model

In Autodesk Inventor, you can apply or wrap an image on the face of a model by using the **Decal** tool. Note that for doing so, you need to first insert an image in the Sketching environment by using the **Image** tool. The method for applying an image on the face of a model is discussed below:

1. Invoke the Sketching environment by selecting a plane as the sketching plane and then insert an image by using the **Image** tool in the **Insert** panel of the **Sketch** tab, see Figure 8.118. Note that you can insert an image of different file formats such as *.jpg*, *.png*, *.bmp*, *.gif*, *.doc*, or *.xls* by using the **Image** tool. Figure 8.119 shows an image inserted in the Sketching environment.

8.118

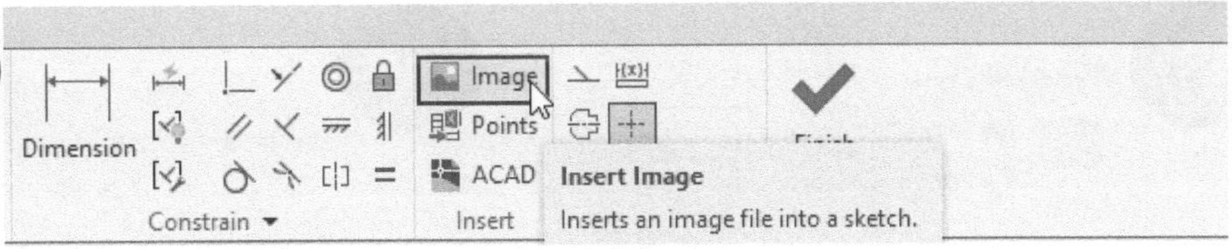

8.119

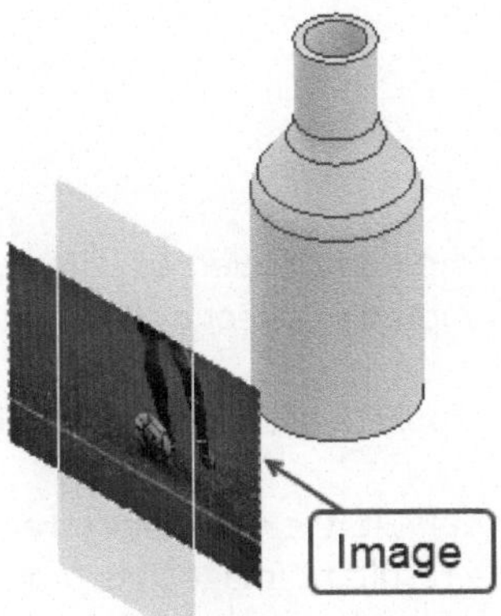

Tip: After inserting an image into the Sketching environment, you can change its orientation, position, scale, and so on by using tools such as **Rotate**, **Move**, and **Scale** available in the **Modify** panel of the **Sketch** tab. Alternatively, you can change the scale of the image by dragging its corners, and the position of the image by dragging it to the new position, dynamically in the drawing area. You can also edit the properties of the inserted image by using the **Image Properties** dialog box. For doing so, right-click on the image in the drawing area and then click on the **Properties** option in the Marking Menu that appears. The **Image Properties** dialog box appears. By using this dialog box, you can change the orientation and control the transparency of the image.

2. After inserting an image, exit the Sketching environment by clicking on the **Finish Sketch** tool in the **Exit** panel of the **Ribbon**.

   Now, you can apply the inserted image to a face of the model.

3. Click on the **Decal** tool in the **Create** panel of the **3D Model** tab, see Figure 8.120. The **Decal** property panel appears, see Figure 8.121. Also, you are prompted to select an image to be applied on a face of the model. Note that if only one image is available in the graphics area then it gets automatically selected, and you are prompted to select a face.

8.120

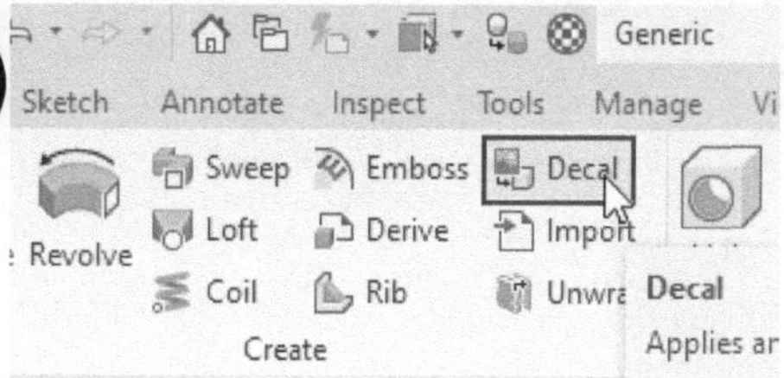

8.121

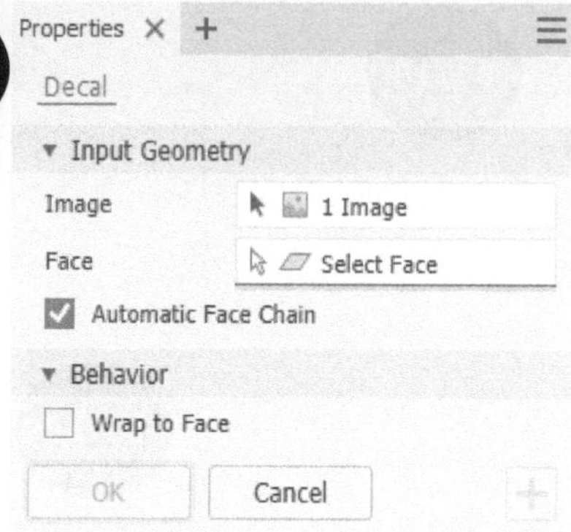

4. Select an image in the graphics area, if not selected. The **Face** selector gets activated in the **Decal** property panel and you are prompted to select a face of the model.

5. Click on a face of the model to apply the selected image, see Figure 8.122.

   Automatic Face Chain: By default, the **Automatic Face Chain** check box is selected in the property panel. As a result, the resultant image gets projected or applied to all the tangentially connected faces of the selected face. If you clear this check box, then the projection of the image gets applied only to the selected face of the model.

   Wrap to Face: On selecting the **Wrap to Face** check box in the **Behavior** rollout of the property panel, the resultant image gets wrapped onto the selected curved or revolved face of the model.

6. Select the **Wrap to Face** check box in the property panel and then click on the **OK** button. The selected image gets applied on the face of the model, see Figure 8.123.

8.122

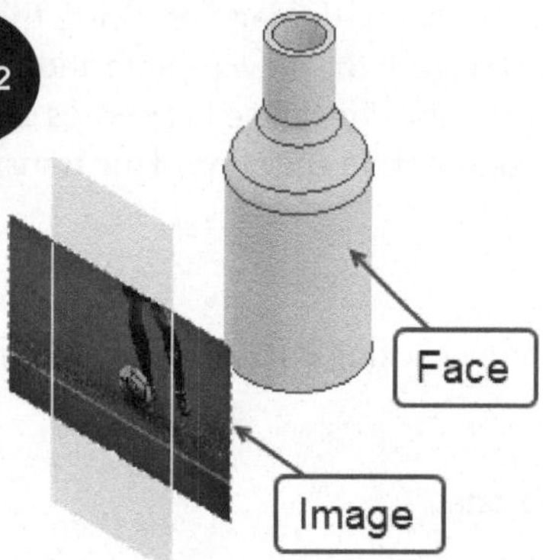

8.123

Creating a Shell Feature

A shell feature is a thin walled feature, that is created by making a model hollow from inside or by removing the faces of a model, see Figures 8.124 and 8.125. In Figure 8.124, the shell feature is created by making the model hollow, whereas in Figure 8.125, the shell feature is created by removing the top planar face of the model. The method for creating a shell feature is discussed below:

8.124

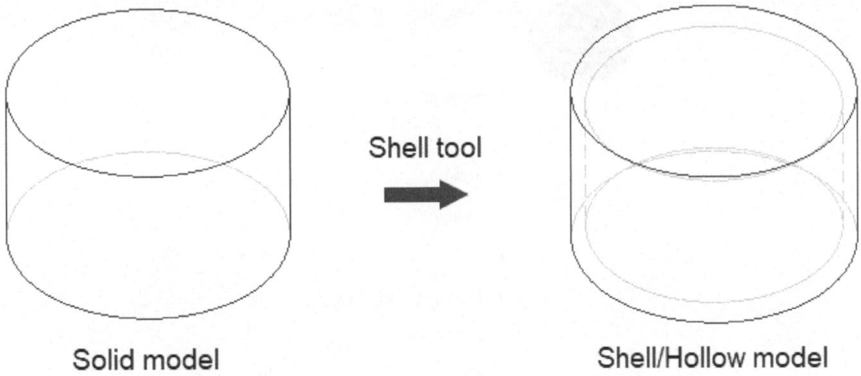

8.125

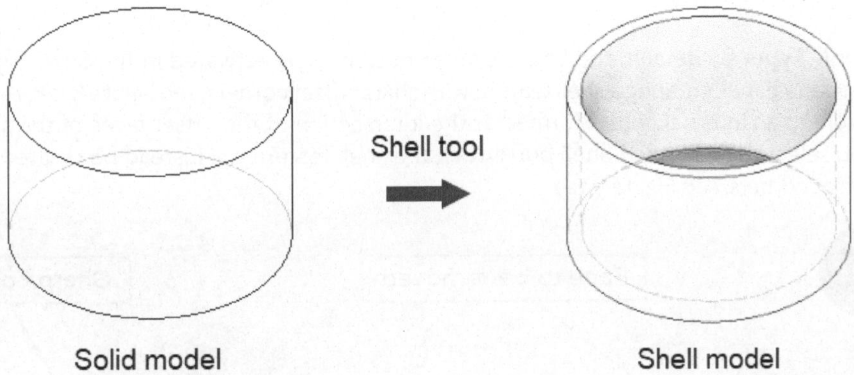

Note: In Figures 8.124 and 8.125, the visual style of the model has been changed to 'wireframe with hidden edges' so that the hidden edges of the shell model can be visualized.

1. Click on the **Shell** tool in the **Modify** panel of the **3D Model** tab, see Figure 8.126. The **Shell** property panel appears, see Figure 8.127. Also, the preview of a shell feature with default thickness appears in the graphics area. The options are discussed below next:

8.126

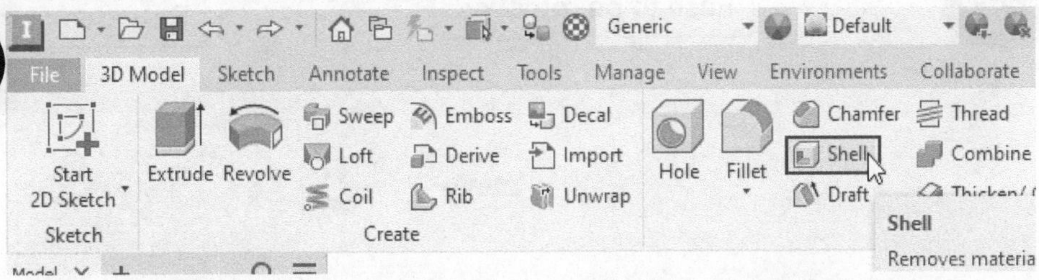

8.127

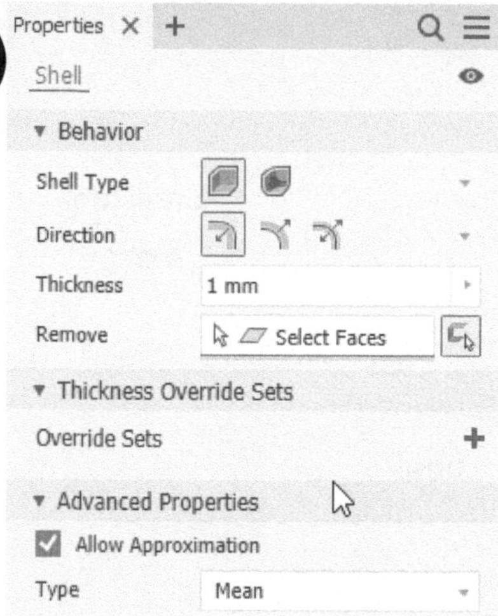

Shell Type: By default, the **Sharp Corner** button is activated in the **Shell Type** area of the property panel, creating a shell feature with sharp offset corners, see Figure 8.128. An offset corner refers to an internal corner formed at the intersection of the offset faces of the shell feature. If you select the **Rounded Shell** button, the shell feature will instead be created with rounded offset corners, see Figure 8.129.

8.128

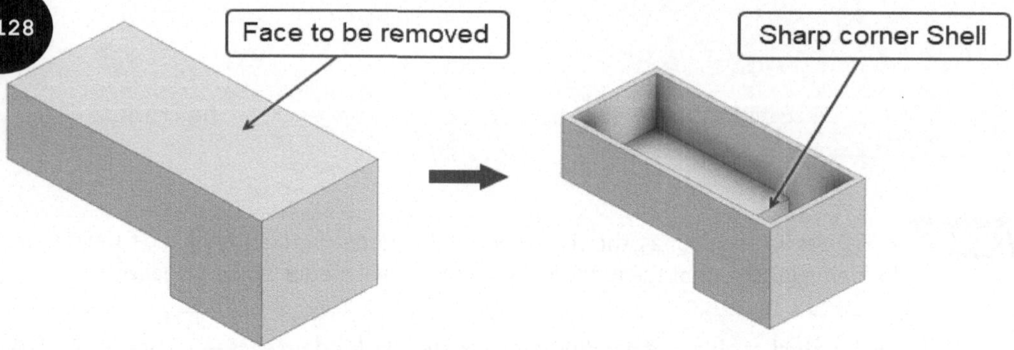

8.129

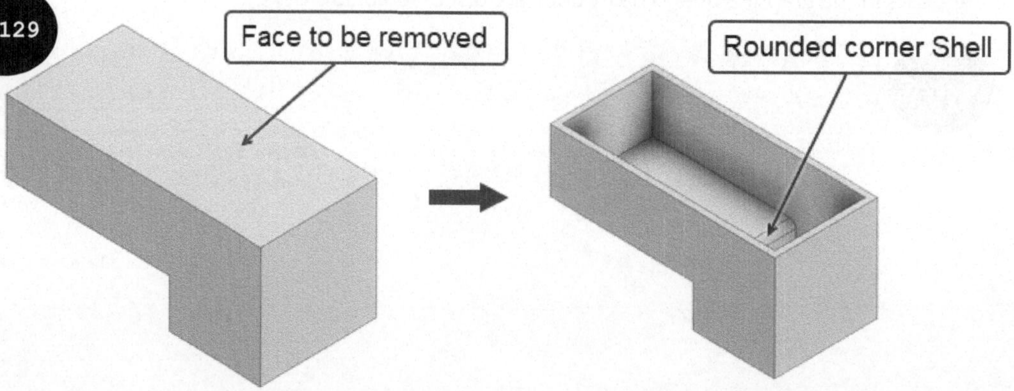

Direction: By default, the **Inside** button is activated in the **Direction** area of the property panel. As a result, the resultant shell feature is created by adding wall thickness inward to the outer geometry of the original model. You can specify wall thickness in the **Thickness** field of the property panel.

On activating the **Outside** button in the **Direction** area, the resultant shell feature is created by adding wall thickness outward to the outer geometry of the original model.

On activating the **Center** button in the **Direction** area, the resultant shell feature is created by adding wall thickness equally on both sides of the outer geometry of the original model.

Thickness: The **Thickness** field is used for specifying wall thickness for the shell feature. Note that the thickness value specified in this field is applied to all the walls of the feature, such that a shell feature is created with uniform thickness.

Remove: The **Remove** selector is used for selecting faces of the model to be removed from the resultant shell feature. Figure 8.130 shows the face of a solid model to be removed and the resultant shell model after removing the selected face of the model.

8.130

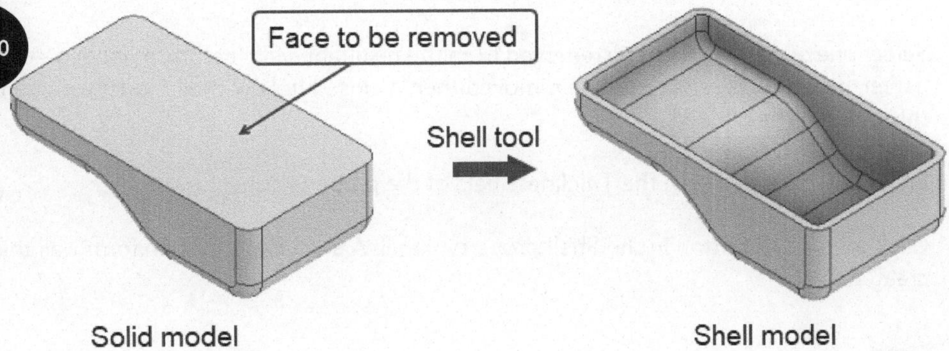

Note: If you do not select any face to be removed from the model then a closed hollow shell model with uniform wall thickness will be created.

Automatic Face Chain: By default, the **Automatic Face Chain** button is activated next to the **Remove** selector in the **Shell** property panel. As a result, when you select a face to remove, all of its tangentially connected faces will automatically be selected and removed from the resultant shell model, see Figure 8.131. If you prefer to remove only the face you specifically selected, simply disable this button.

8.131

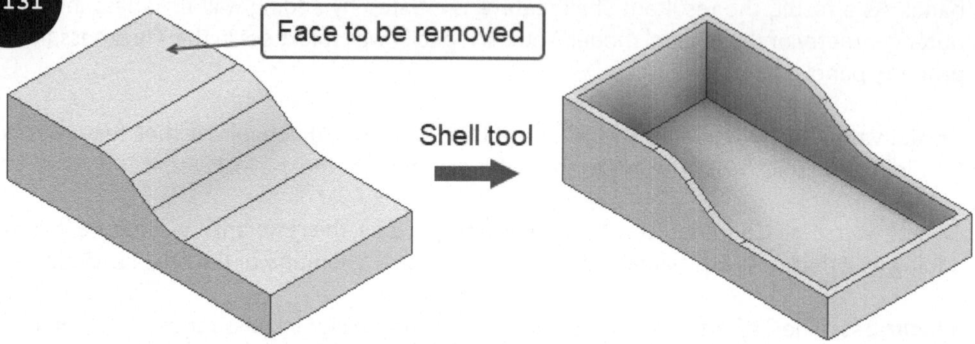

Solids: The **Solids** selector in the property panel is used for selecting a solid model to be shelled. Note that this **Solids** selector is enabled in the property panel only when two or more than two solid bodies are available in the graphics area.

2. Select the required button (**Inside, Outside**, or **Both**) in the **Shell** dialog box to define the thickness direction of the shell feature, as discussed above.

3. Select one or more faces to be removed from the resultant shell feature, if needed. As discussed earlier, if no face is selected to be removed then a closed hollow shell model with uniform wall thickness will be created.

4. Enter a thickness value in the **Thickness** field of the property panel.

5. Click on the **OK** button in the **Shell** property panel. A shell feature of uniform wall thickness is created.

Note: In Autodesk Inventor, you can also create a multi-thickness shell model by overriding the default thickness value using the **Shell** property panel. To do this, click on the **Add Shell Set** button in the **Thickness Override Sets** rollout of the property panel. The **Select Faces** selector appears and you are prompted to select a set of faces to override the default thickness value, see Figure 8.132. Select one or more faces of the model in the graphics area and then enter a different thickness value for the selected face(s) in the respective field. The thickness of the selected model face(s) gets changed, as specified. Similarly, you can define different thickness values for the other set of faces. Figure 8.133 shows a shell model with multi-thickness walls.

8.132

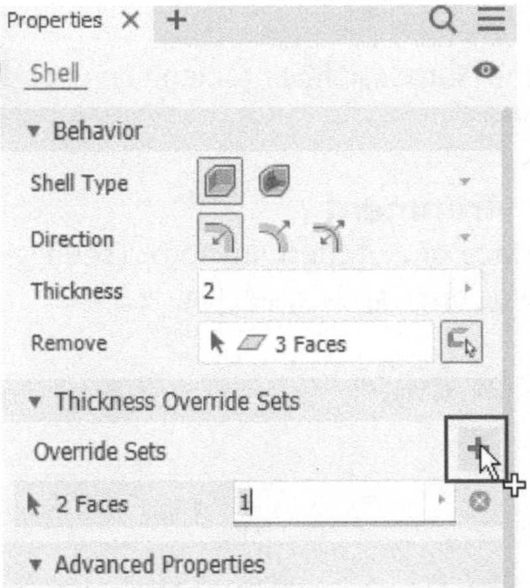

8.133

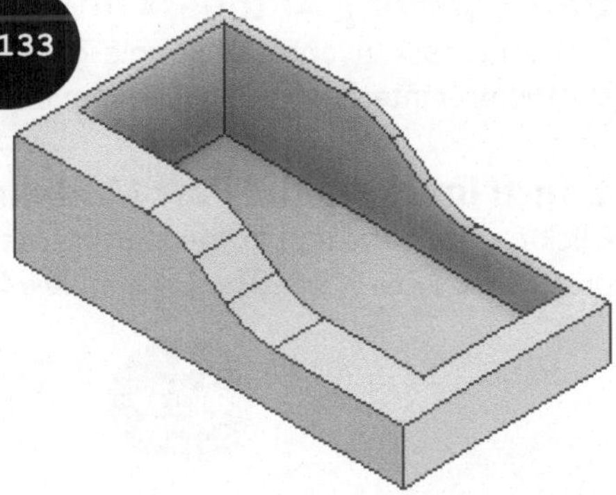

Tutorial 1

Create the model shown in Figure 8.134. All dimensions are in mm.

8.134

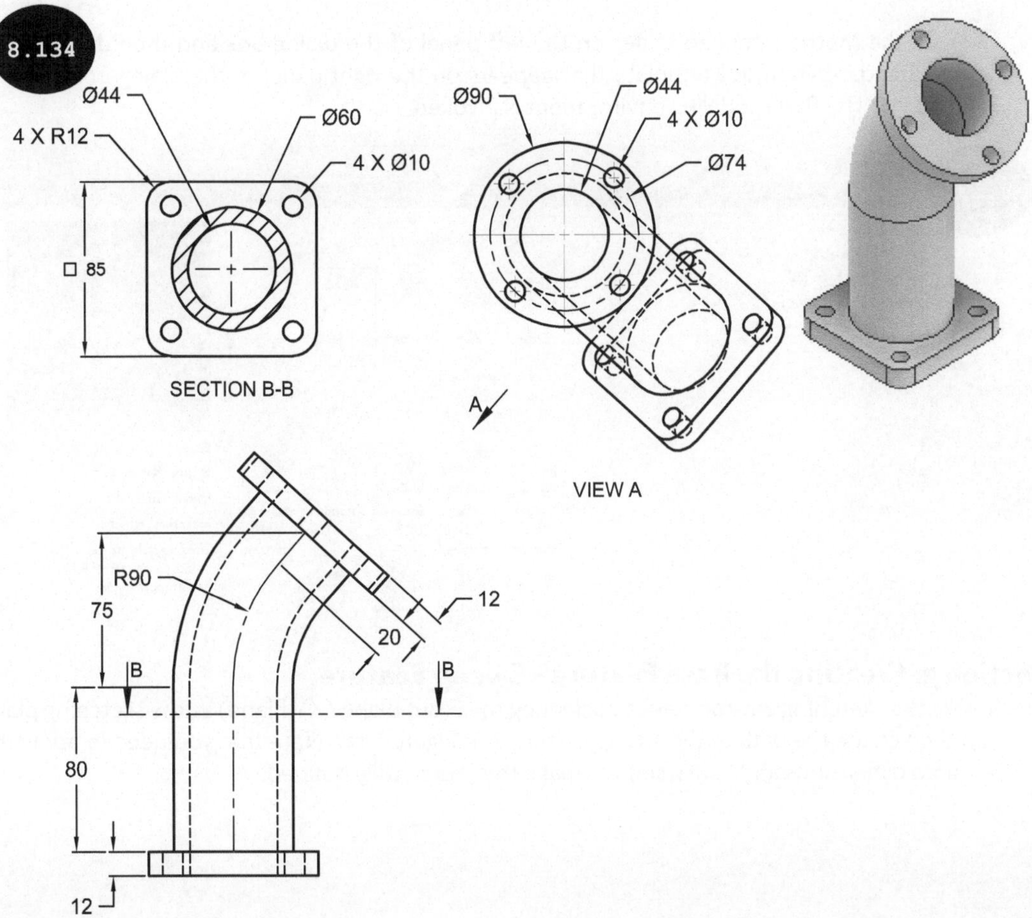

Section 1: Starting Autodesk Inventor

1. Start Autodesk Inventor by double-clicking on the Autodesk Inventor icon on your desktop. The startup user interface of Autodesk Inventor appears.

Section 2: Invoking the Part Modeling Environment

1. Click on the **New** tool in the startup user interface of Autodesk Inventor (see Figure 8.135) or press the CTRL+N key. The **Create New File** dialog box appears, see Figure 8.136.

8.135

2. Click on the **Metric** template folder on the left panel of the dialog box and then double-click on the **Standard (mm).ipt** template that appears on the right panel of the dialog box, refer to Figure 8.136. The Part Modeling environment is invoked.

8.136

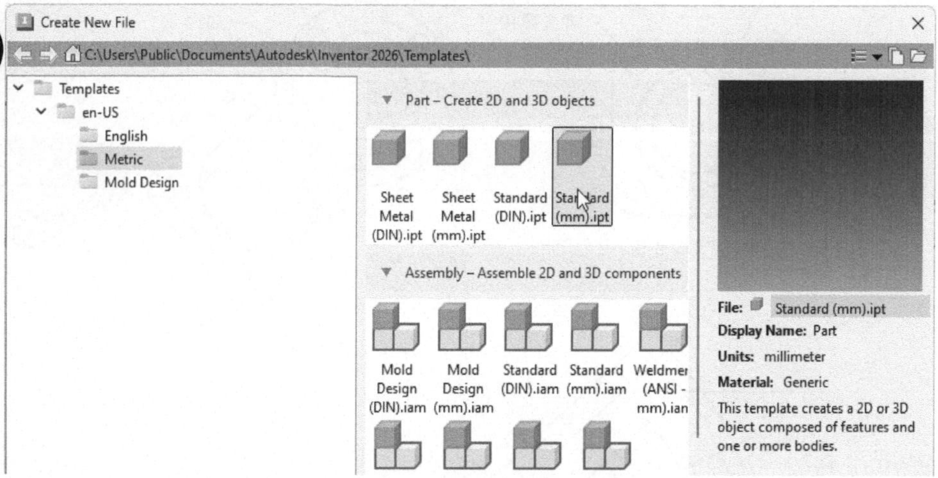

Section 3: Creating the Base Feature - Sweep Feature

1. Invoke the Sketching environment by selecting the Front plane (XY Plane) as the sketching plane and then create the path of the sweep feature, see Figure 8.137. Note that you need to apply the required dimensions and constraints to make the sketch fully defined.

8.137

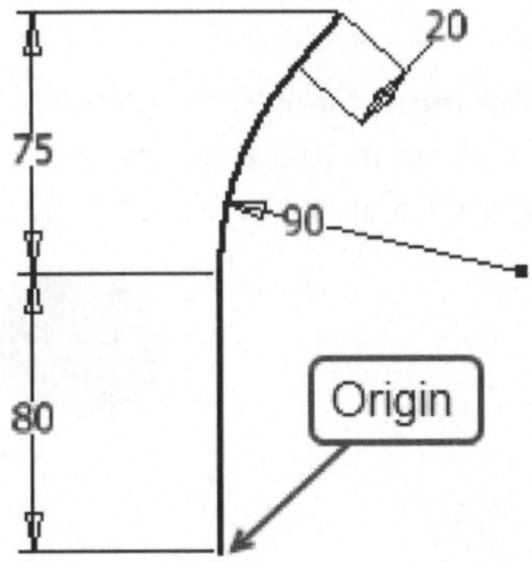

2. Exit the Sketching environment by clicking on the **Finish Sketch** tool in the **Exit** panel of the Ribbon.

   After creating the path, you need to create the profile of the sweep feature.

3. Invoke the Sketching environment by selecting the Top plane (XZ Plane) as the sketching plane and then create a sketch (two circles) as the profile of the sweep feature, see Figure 8.138. Next, exit the Sketching environment.

   After creating a path and a profile, you can create a sweep feature.

8.138

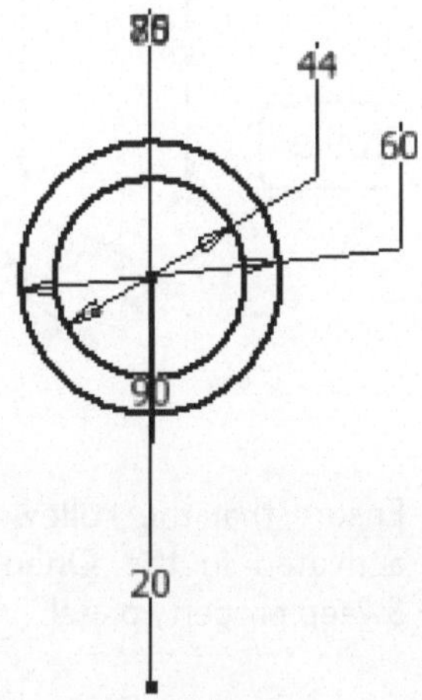

4. Click on the **Sweep** tool in the **Create** panel of the **3D Model** tab, see Figure 8.139. The **Sweep** property panel appears, see Figure 8.140. Also, you are prompted to select a profile.

8.139

8.140

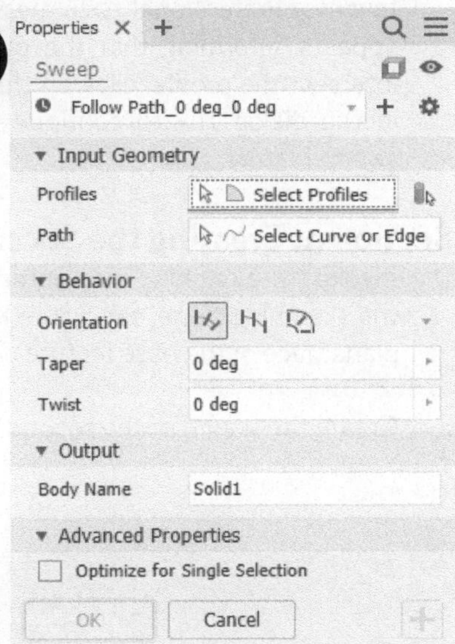

5. Select the profile (outer closed area of the sketch) of the sweep feature in the graphics area, see Figure 8.141.

6. Click on the **Path** selector in the **Input Geometry** rollout of the **Sweep** property panel and then select the path of the sweep feature in the graphics area, see Figure 8.141. The preview of the sweep feature appears in the graphics area, see Figure 8.142.

8.141

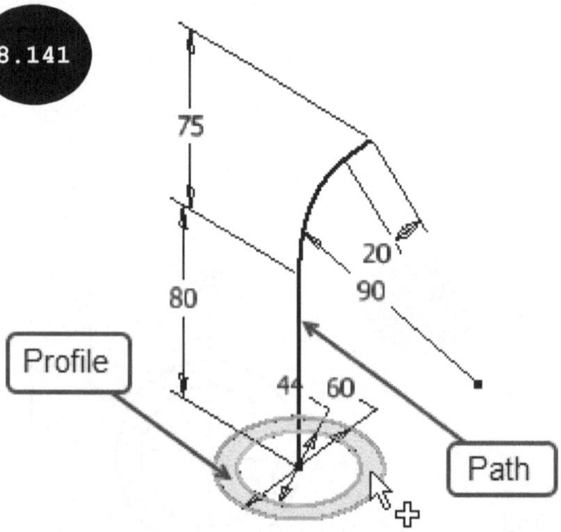

8.142

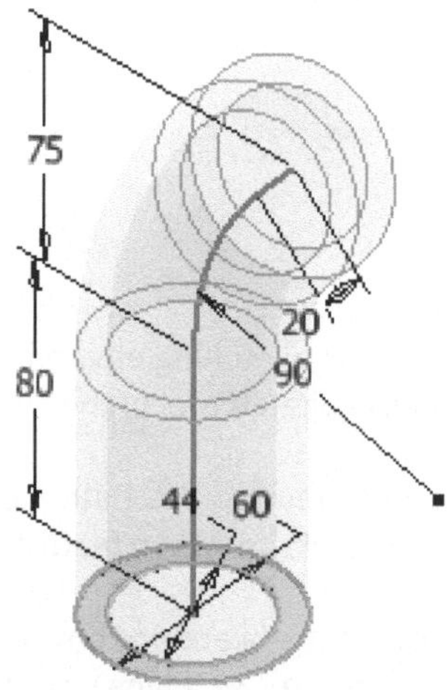

7. Ensure that the **Follow Path** button is activated in the **Orientation** area of the **Sweep** property panel.

8. Click on the **OK** button in the **Sweep** property panel. The sweep feature is created, see Figure 8.143. Note that if the **Autodesk Inventor Professional 2026** message window appears, informing that the path does not intersect the profile, click on the **Yes** button in the dialog box to continue creating the sweep feature.

8.143

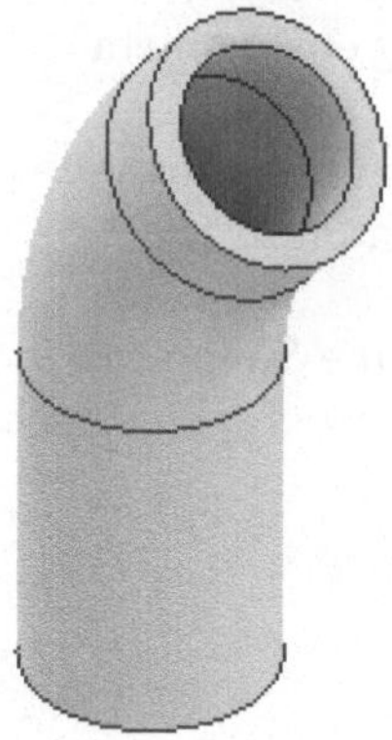

Section 4: Creating the Second Feature - Extrude Feature

1. Invoke the Sketching environment by selecting the bottom face of the base feature (sweep) as the sketching plane, see Figure 8.144. Note that you can rotate the model such that the bottom planar face of the base feature can be viewed for selecting it as the sketching plane.

2. Create the sketch of the second feature, see Figure 8.145.

8.144

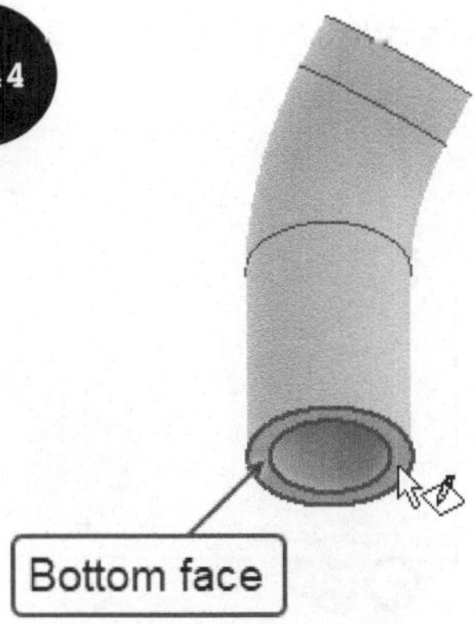

8.145

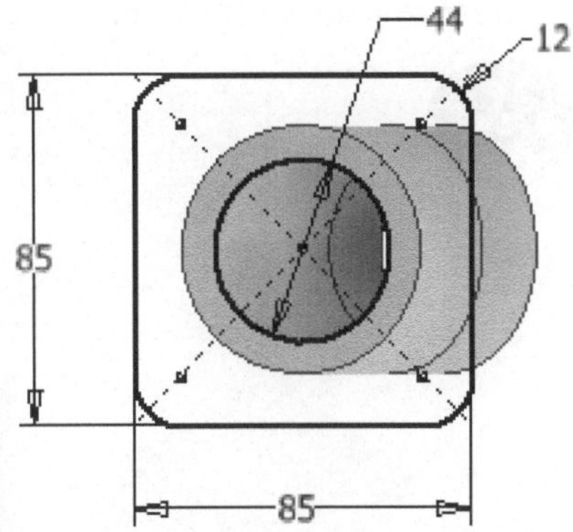

3. Click on the **3D Model** tab in the **Ribbon** and then click on the **Extrude** tool in the **Create** panel. The **Extrusion** property panel appears and you are prompted to select a closed profile. Change the orientation of the model to isometric.

4. Select outer closed area of the sketch as the profile to be extruded, see Figure 8.146. The preview of an extruded feature appears in the graphics area.

5. Ensure that the direction of extrusion is downward.

6. Enter **12** in the **Distance A** field of the **Extrusion** property panel as the depth of the extrusion.

7. Ensure that the **Join** button is activated in the **Boolean** area of the property panel.

8. Click on the **OK** button in the property panel. The second feature (extrude) is created, see Figure 8.147.

8.146

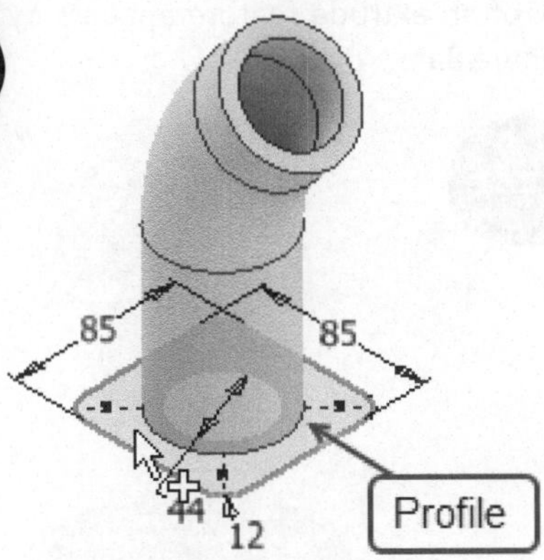

8.147

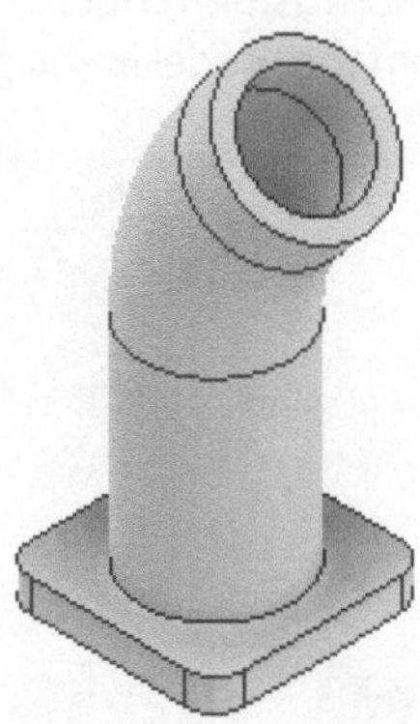

Section 5: Creating the Third Feature - Cut Feature

1. Invoke the Sketching environment by selecting the top planar face of the second feature as the sketching plane, see Figure 8.148.

2. Create the sketch (four circles of diameter 10 mm) of the third feature, see Figure 8.149.

8.148

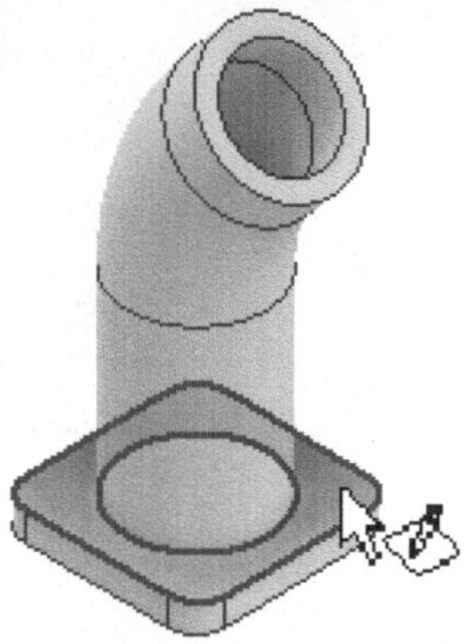

8.149

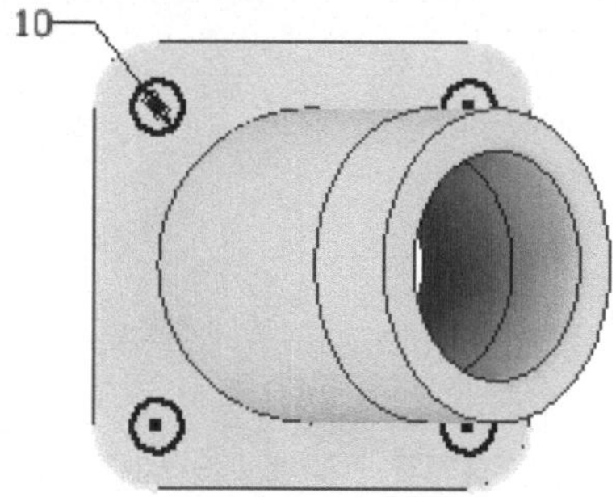

Tip: The sketch of the third feature shown in Figure 8.149 has four circles of the same diameter; therefore, an equal constraint is applied among all the circles. Also, a concentric constraint is applied between each circle and the respective semi-circular edge of the second feature. You can also create one circle and then pattern it to create the remaining circles.

3. Click on the **3D Model** tab in the **Ribbon** and then click on the **Extrude** tool in the **Create** panel. The **Extrusion** property panel appears and you are prompted to select a closed profile.

4. Select the closed areas of all the four circles one by one as profiles to be extruded in the graphics area, see Figure 8.150. The preview of an extrude feature appears by adding material in the graphics area.

5. Reverse the direction of extrusion downward by clicking on the **Flipped** button in the **Direction** area of the **Extrusion** property panel. The preview of an extrude feature appears by removing material from the model in the graphics area, see Figure 8.151.

8.150

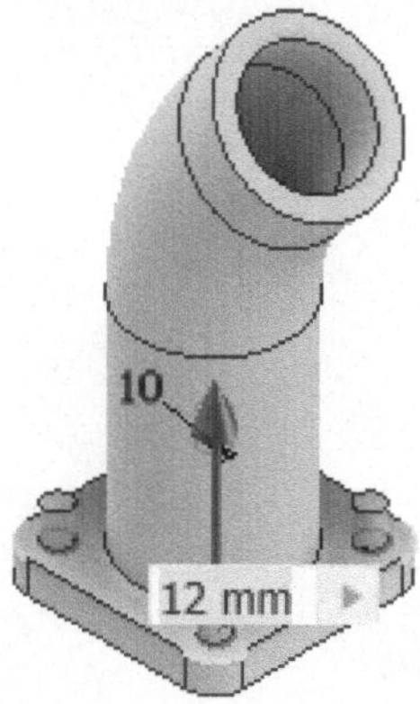

8.151

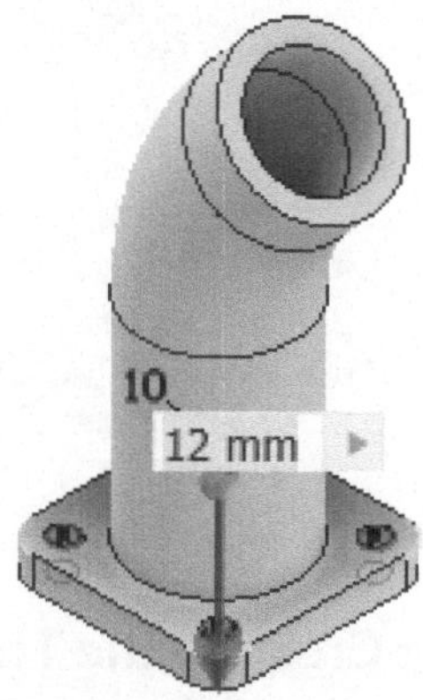

6. Click on the **To Next** button in the **Behavior** rollout of the property panel. The preview of the extrude cut feature appears in the graphics area such that it terminates at its next intersection.

7. Ensure that the **Cut** button is activated in the **Boolean** area of the property panel.

8. Click on the **OK** button in the **Extrusion** property panel. The cut feature is created by removing material from the model, see Figure 8.152.

8.152

Section 6: Creating the Fourth Feature - Extrude Feature

1. Invoke the Sketching environment by selecting the top planar face of the sweep feature (base feature) as the sketching plane, see Figure 8.153.

2. Create the sketch (two circles of diameter 90 mm and 44 mm) of the fourth feature, see Figure 8.154.

8.153

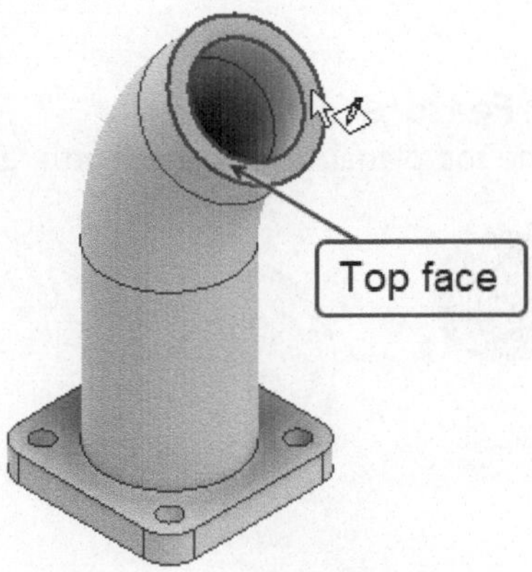

8.154

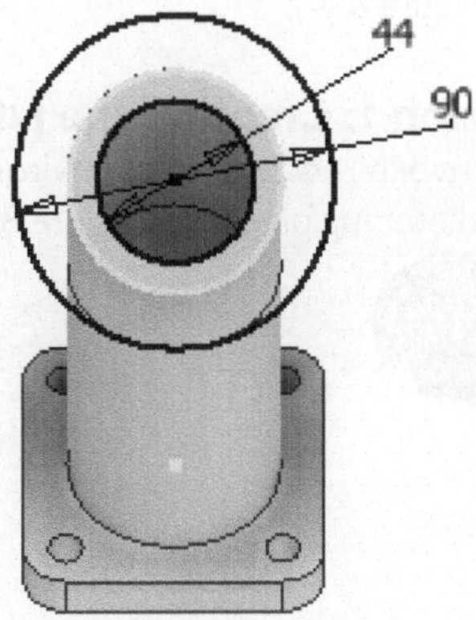

Tip: The sketch of the fourth feature shown in Figure 8.154 has two circles, which are concentric to the top circular edge of the sweep feature. You need to take the reference of the top circular edges of the sweep feature for specifying the center point of the circles.

3. Click on the **3D Model** tab in the **Ribbon** and then click on the **Extrude** tool in the **Create** panel. The **Extrusion** property panel appears and you are prompted to select a closed profile.

4. Select closed profiles of the sketch to be extruded, see Figure 8.155. Note that you may need to select two profiles of the sketch for creating the fourth feature of the model if the outer circular edge of the model gets projected as an entity while creating the sketch of the feature. The preview of an extruded feature appears, see Figure 8.156.

8.155

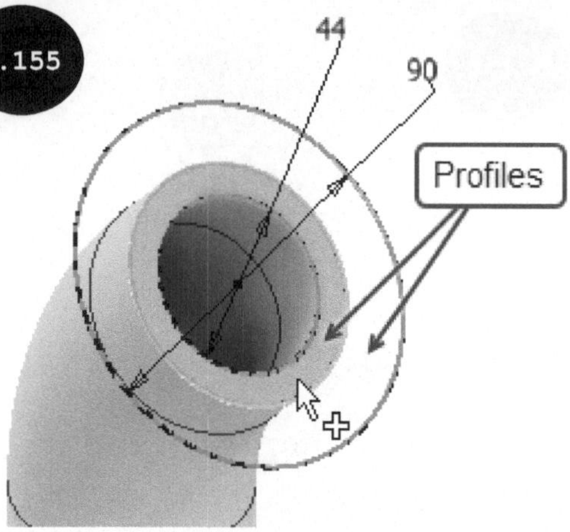

8.156

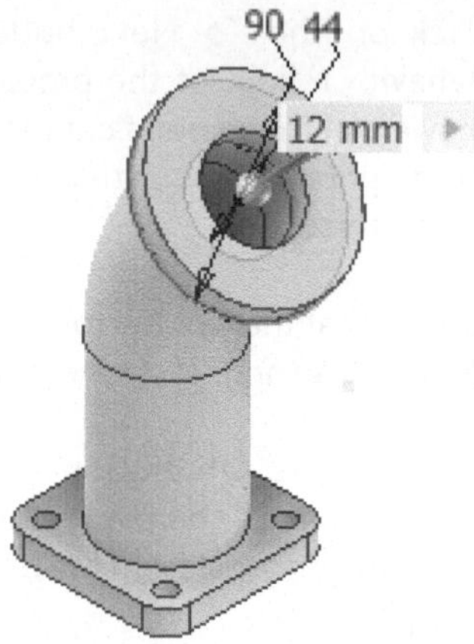

5. Ensure that the direction of extrusion is upward.

6. Enter **12** in the **Distance A** field of the **Extrusion** property panel as the depth of the extrusion.

7. Ensure that the **Join** button is activated in the **Boolean** area of the property panel.

8. Click on the **OK** button in the property panel. The fourth feature (extrude) is created, see Figure 8.157.

Section 7: Creating the Fifth Feature - Cut Feature

1. Invoke the Sketching environment by selecting the top planar face of the fourth feature as the sketching plane, see Figure 8.158.

8.157

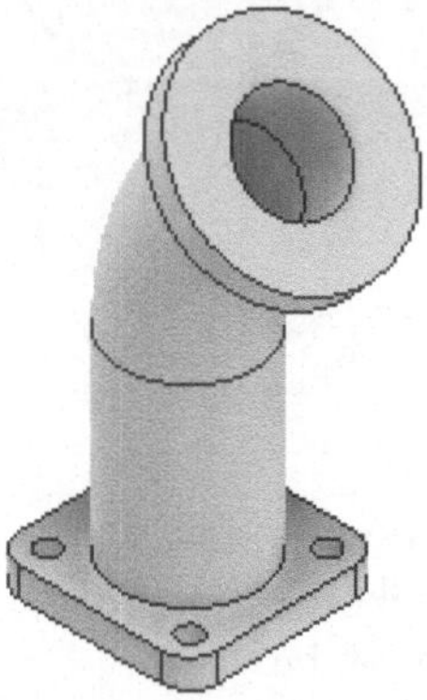

8.158

2. Create a circle of diameter 10 mm, see Figure 8.159. Next, create its circular pattern to create the remaining circles of the same diameter using the **Circular Pattern** tool, see Figure 8.160.

3. Click on the **3D Model** tab in the **Ribbon** and then click on the **Extrude** tool in the **Create** panel. The **Extrusion** property panel appears and you are prompted to select a closed profile.

4. Select the closed areas of all four circles one by one as profiles to be extruded in the graphics area. The preview of an extrude feature appears by adding material in the graphics area.

8.159

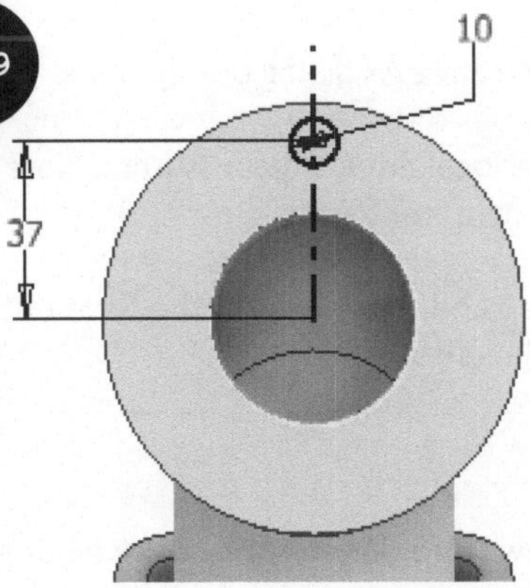

8.160

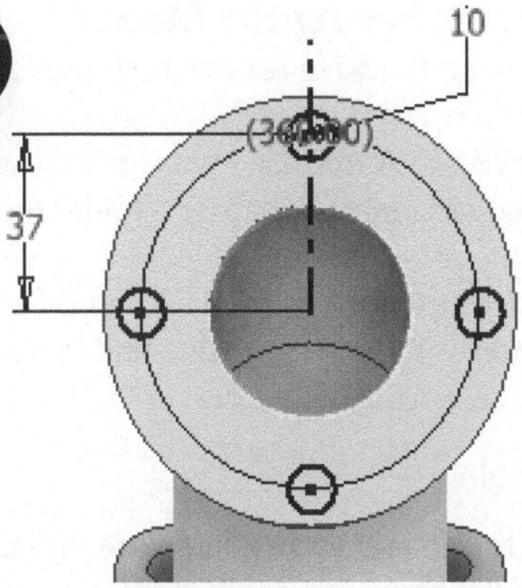

Tip: In Figure 8.159, the center point of the circle has coincident constraint with the vertical centerline. Also, the start point of the vertical centerline is coincident with the center of the circular edge of the fourth feature.

While specifying the start point of the vertical centerline as shown in Figure 8.159, move the cursor over the outer circular edge of the fourth feature. The center point of the circular edge gets highlighted. Next, move the cursor to the highlighted center point and then click to specify the start point of the vertical centerline when the cursor snaps to it.

5. Reverse the direction of extrusion downward by clicking on the **Flipped** button in the **Direction** area of the **Extrusion** property panel. The preview of an extrude feature appears by removing the material from the model (see Figure 8.161) and the **Cut** button gets activated automatically in the **Boolean** area of the property panel.

6. Click on the **To Next** button in the **Behavior** rollout of the property panel. The preview of the extrude cut feature appears in the graphics area such that it terminates at its next intersection.

7. Ensure that the **Cut** button is activated in the **Boolean** area of the property panel.

8. Click on the **OK** button in the **Extrusion** property panel. The cut feature is created by removing the material from the model, see Figure 8.162.

8.161

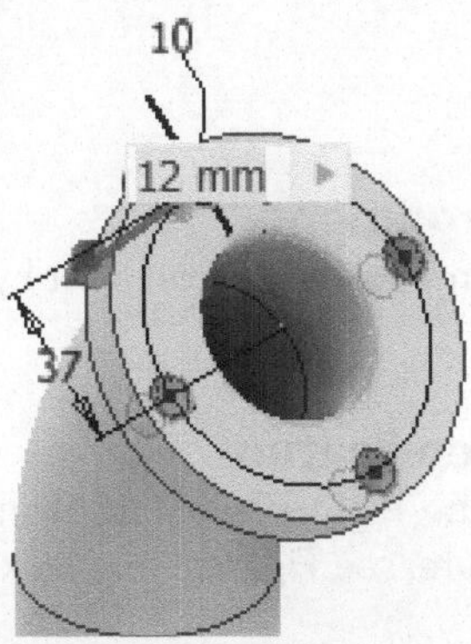

8.162

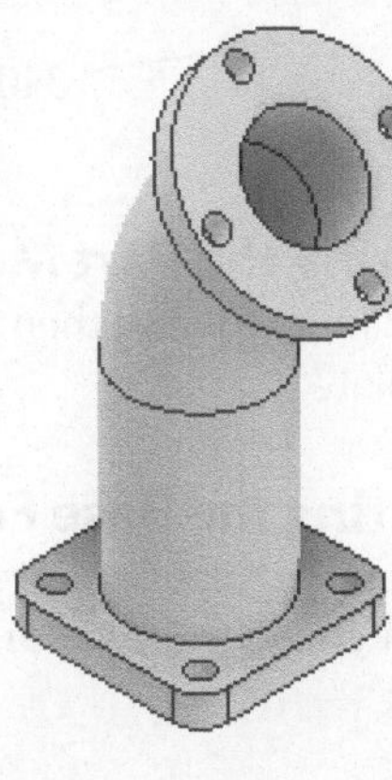

Section 8: Saving the Model

1. Click on the **Save** tool in the **Quick Access Toolbar**. The **Save As** dialog box appears.

2. Browse to **Autodesk Inventor > Chapter 8** folder in the local drive of your system. Note that you need to create a Chapter 8 folder inside the Autodesk Inventor folder.

3. Enter **Tutorial 1** in the **File name** field of the dialog box and then click on the **Save** button. The model is saved in the specified location (>:\Autodesk Inventor\Chapter 8).

Tutorial 2

Create the model shown in Figure 8.163. The different views and dimensions are given in the same figure. All dimensions are in mm.

8.163

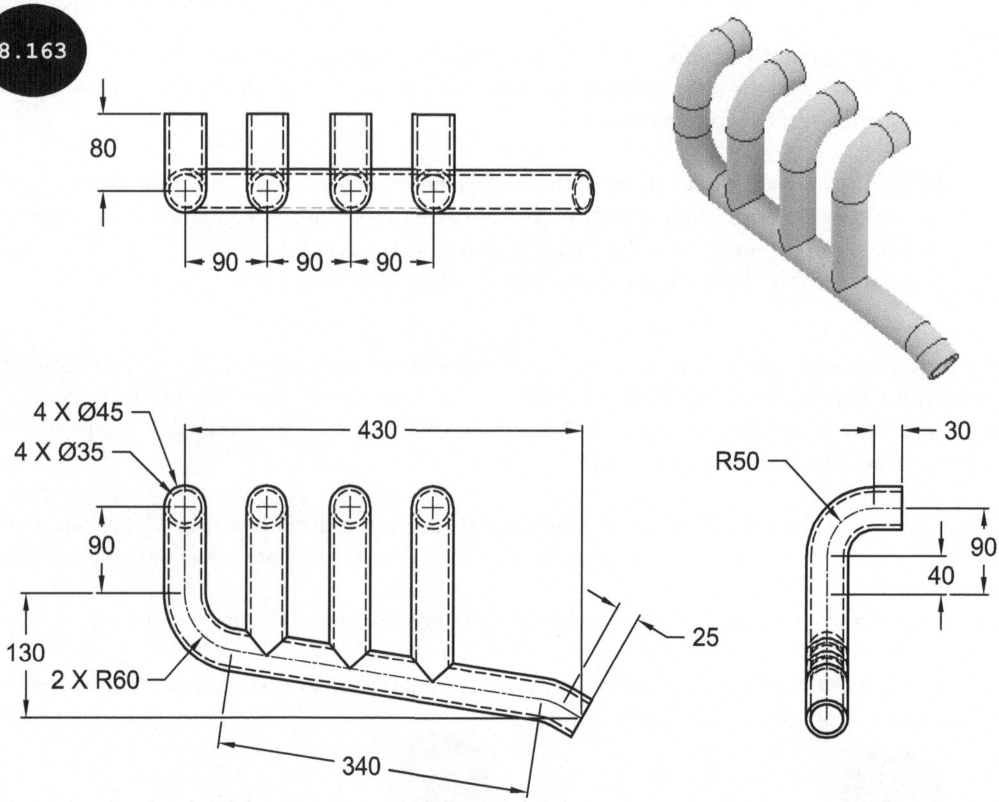

Section 1: Invoking the Part Modeling Environment

1. Start Autodesk Inventor and then invoke the Part modeling environment by using the **Standard (mm).ipt** template.

Section 2: Creating the Base Feature - Sweep Feature

1. Invoke the Sketching environment by selecting the Right plane (YZ Plane) as the sketching plane and then create the path of the sweep feature, see Figure 8.164. Next, exit the Sketching environment.

After creating the path, you need to create the profile of the sweep feature.

2. Invoke the Sketching environment by selecting the Front plane (XY Plane) as the sketching plane and then create a circle of diameter 45 mm as the profile of the sweep feature, see Figure 8.165. Next, exit the Sketching environment.

8.164

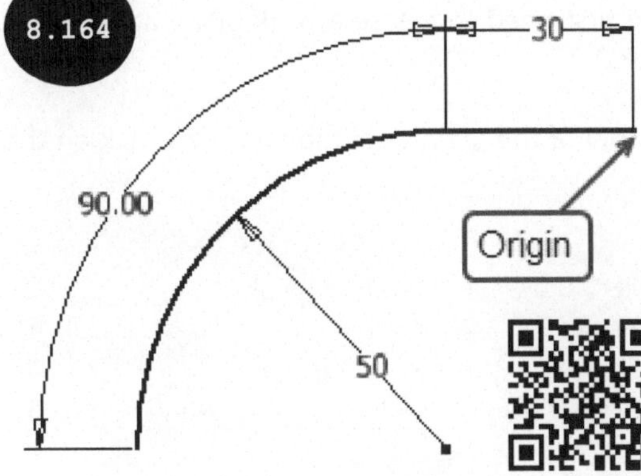

8.165

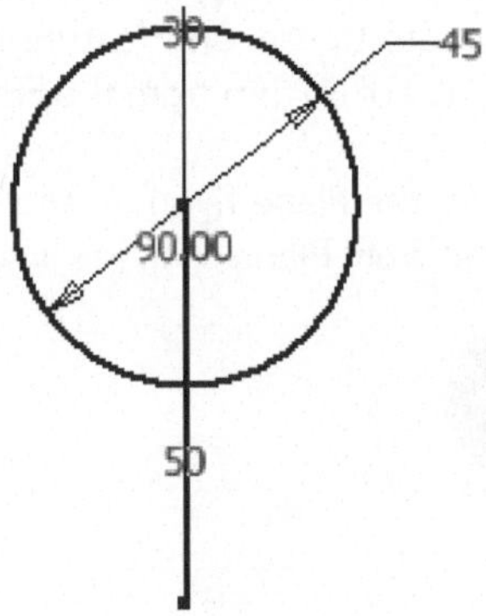

After creating a path and a profile, you can create a sweep feature.

3. Click on the **Sweep** tool in the **Create** panel, see Figure 8.166. The **Sweep** property panel appears. Also, you are prompted to select a profile. Note that if only one closed sketch is available in the graphics area, then it will be selected as the profile of the sweep feature, automatically.

8.166

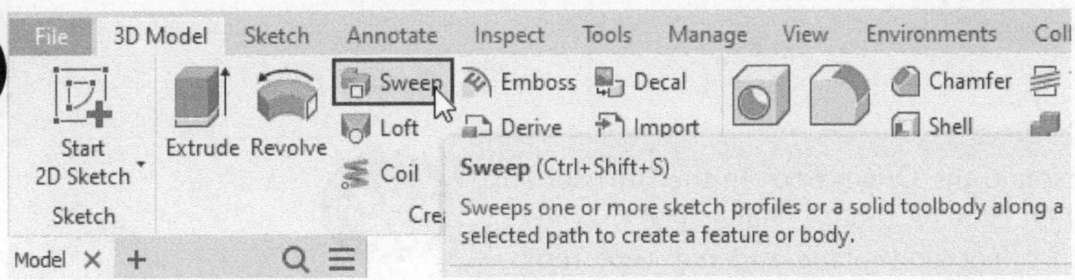

4. Select the profile (circle) of the sweep feature, if not selected by default, see Figure 8.167.

5. Click on the **Path** selector in the **Input Geometry** rollout, if not activated, by default. Next, select the path of the feature, see Figure 8.167. A preview of the sweep feature appears, see Figure 8.168.

8.167

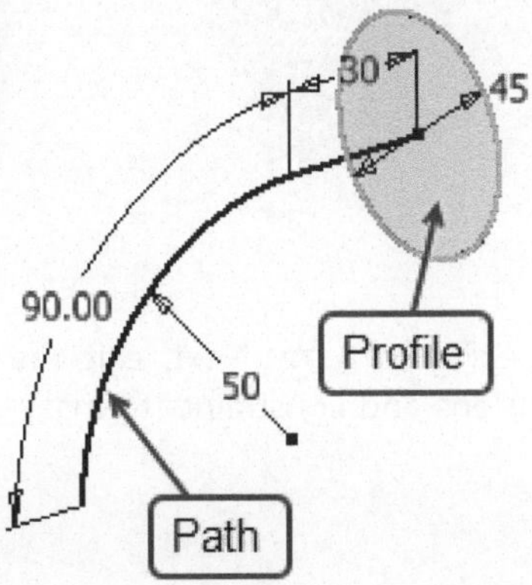

8.168

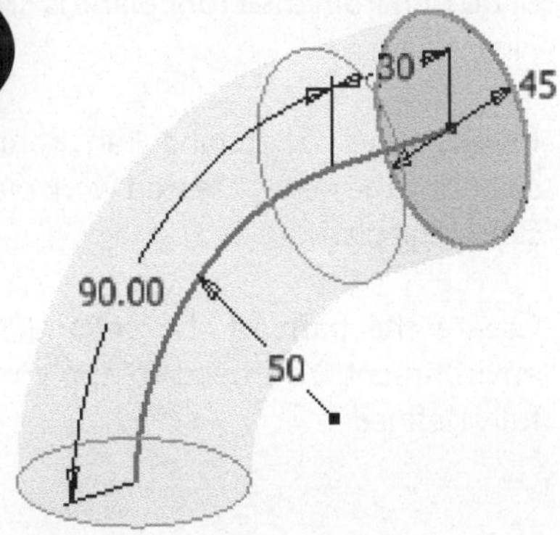

6. Ensure that the **Follow Path** button is activated in the **Orientation** area of the **Sweep** property panel.

7. Click on the **OK** button in the **Sweep** property panel. The sweep feature is created, see Figure 8.169.

Section 3: Creating the Second Feature - Sweep Feature

To create the second feature of the model, you first need to create a work plane at an offset distance of 80 mm from the Front plane (XY Plane).

1. Invoke the **Plane** flyout in the **Work Features** panel of the **3D Model** tab and then click on the **Offset from Plane** tool, see Figure 8.170.

8.169

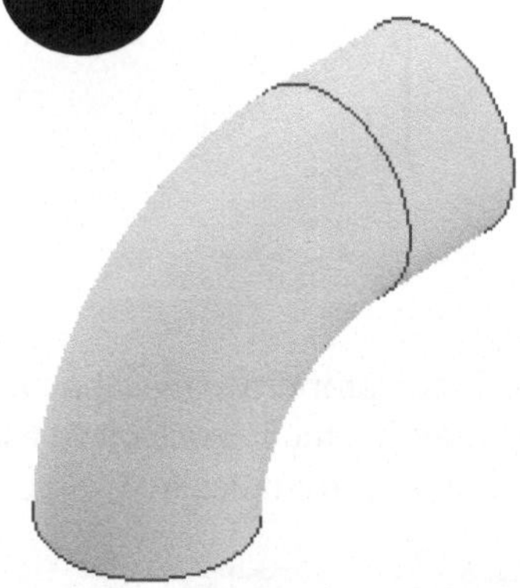

8.170

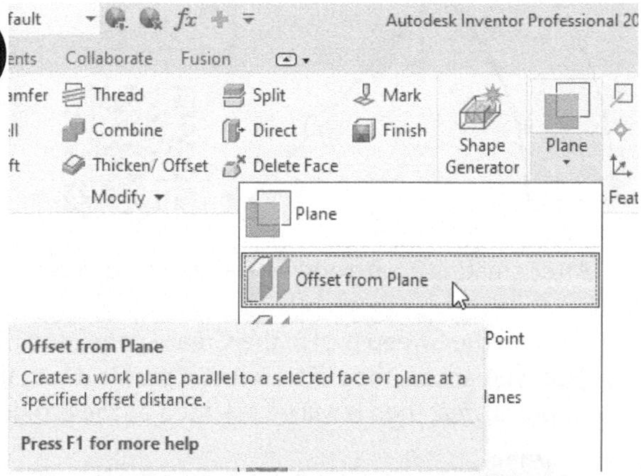

2. Expand the **Origin** node in the **Browser** and then click on the XY Plane. The preview of an offset work plane and the Mini-Toolbar appear in the graphics area.

3. Enter **80** in the Mini-Toolbar as the offset distance and then click on the green tick-mark. A work plane at an offset distance of 80 mm from the Front plane is created, see Figure 8.171.

4. Invoke the Sketching environment by selecting the newly created work plane as the sketching plane.

8.171

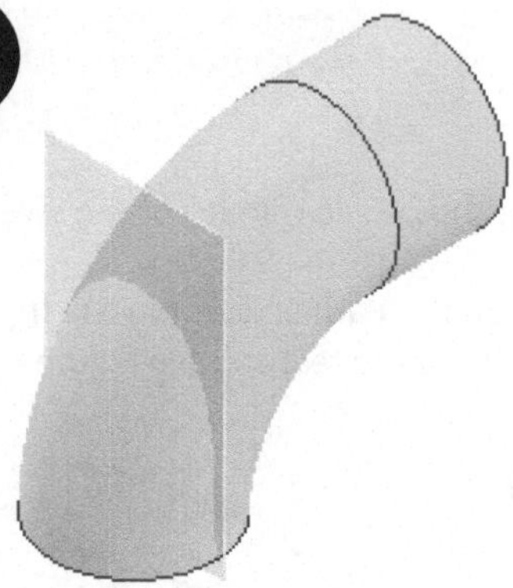

5. Create the path of the second sweep feature, see Figure 8.172. Next, exit the Sketching environment. You need to apply the required dimensions and constraints to make the sketch fully defined.

8.172

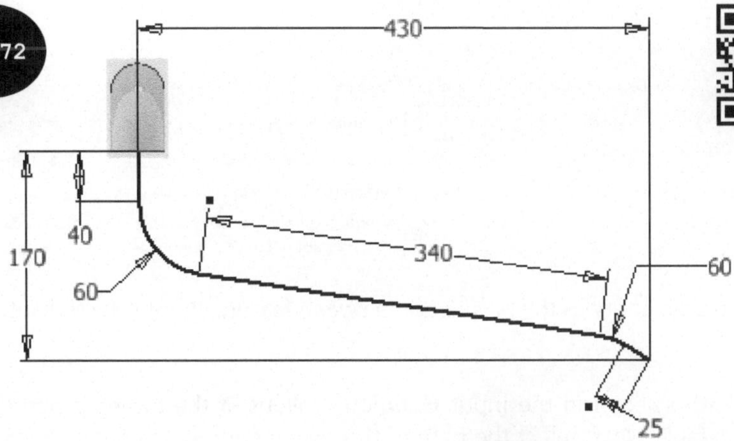

Now, you need to create the profile of the second sweep feature.

8.173

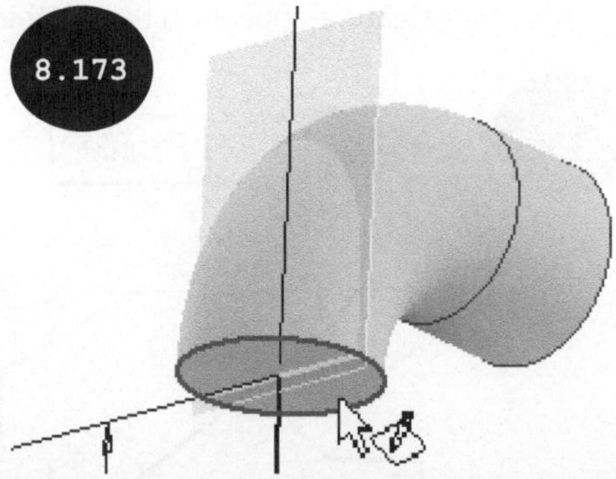

6. Invoke the Sketching environment by selecting the bottom face of the base feature (sweep) as the sketching plane, see Figure 8.173. Note that you can rotate the model such that the bottom planar face of the base feature can be viewed for selecting it as the sketching plane.

7. Project the circular edge of the bottom face of the base feature as the sketch entity onto the sketching plane by using the **Project Geometry** tool, see Figure 8.174. You can use this projected entity as the profile of the sweep feature. Next, exit the Sketching environment.

8.174

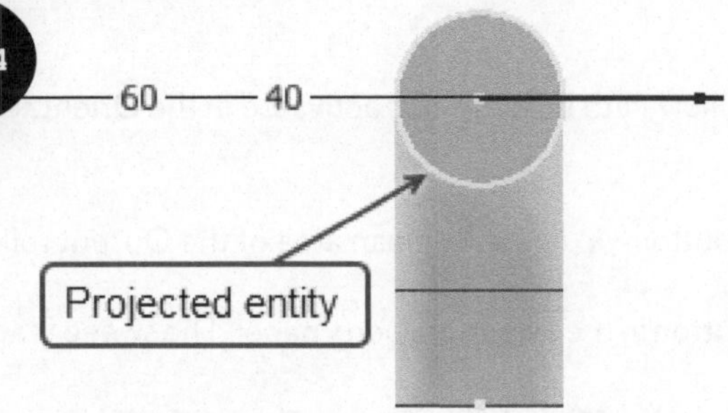

After creating a path and a profile, you can create a sweep feature.

8. Click on the **Sweep** tool in the **Create** panel of the **3D Model** tab, see Figure 8.175. The **Sweep** property panel appears. Note that if only one closed sketch is available in the graphics area, then it will be selected as the profile of the sweep feature automatically and you are prompted to select the path of the feature.

8.175

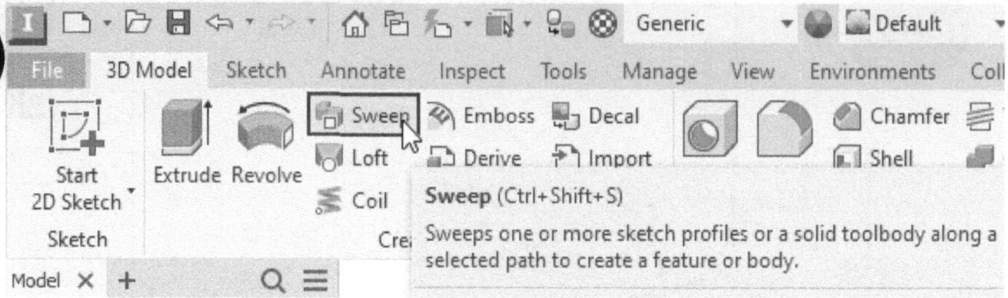

9. Select the projected entity as the profile of the sweep feature, if not selected automatically, see Figure 8.176.

10. Click on the **Path** selector in the **Input Geometry** rollout of the **Sweep** property panel, if not activated, by default. Next, select the path of the sweep feature, see Figure 8.176. A preview of the sweep feature appears in the graphics area, see Figure 8.177.

8.176

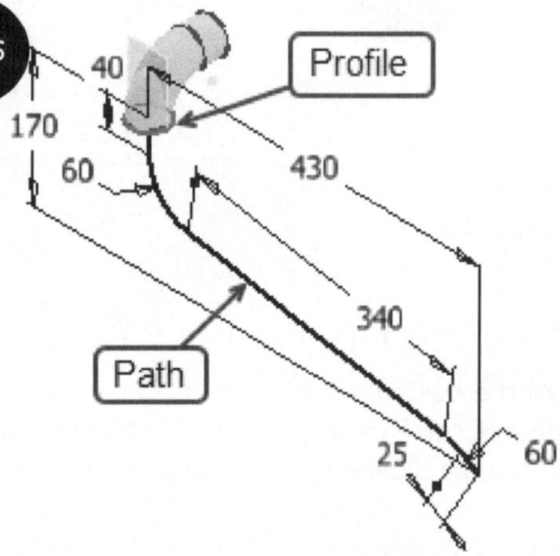

8.177

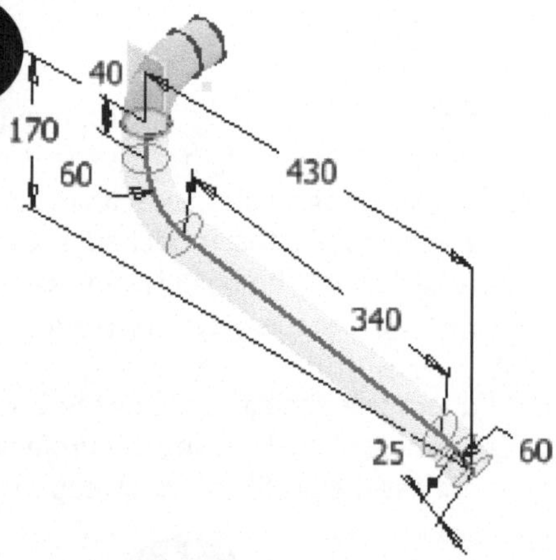

11. Ensure that the **Follow Path** button is activated in the **Orientation** area of the **Sweep** property panel.

12. Click on the **Join** button in the **Boolean** area of the **Output** rollout in the property panel.

13. Click on the **OK** button in the **Sweep** property panel. The sweep feature is created, see Figure 8.178.

Section 4: Creating the Third Feature - Extrude Feature

To create the third feature of the model, you first need to create a work plane at an offset distance of 50 mm from the Top plane (XZ Plane).

1. Create a work plane at an offset distance of 50 mm downward from the Top plane (XZ Plane) by using the **Offset from Plane** tool of the **Plane** flyout, see Figure 8.179. Note that you need to specify a negative offset value (-50) for creating the work plane facing downward.

8.178

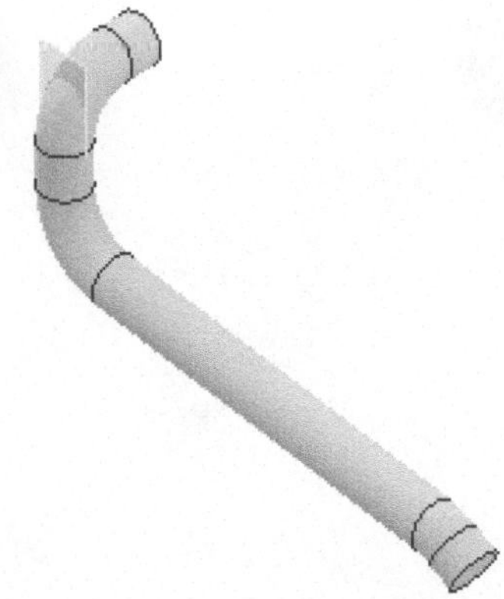

8.179

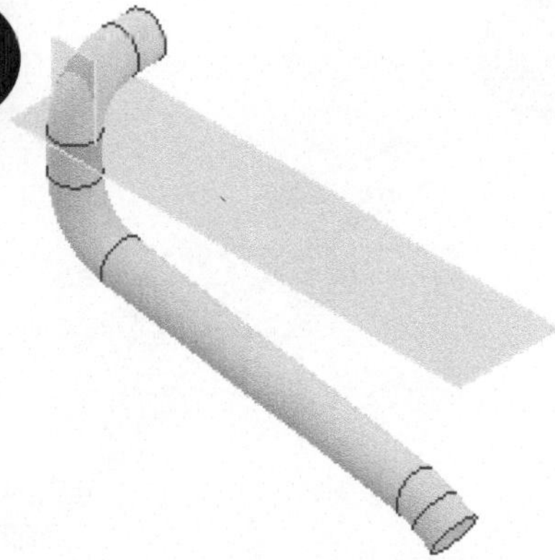

2. Invoke the Sketching environment by selecting the newly created work plane as the sketching plane.

3. Create a sketch of the third feature (three circles of the same diameter 45 mm), see Figure 8.180. You need to apply the required dimensions and constraints to make the sketch fully defined.

8.180

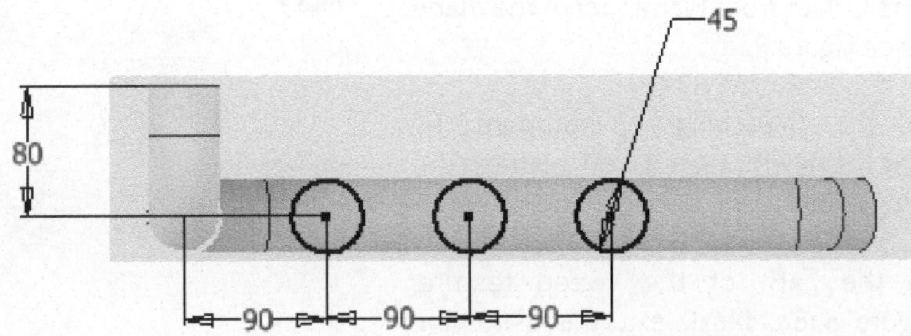

4. Click on the **3D Model** tab in the **Ribbon** and then click on the **Extrude** tool in the **Create** panel. The **Extrusion** property panel appears and you are prompted to select a closed profile.

5. Select the closed areas of all three circles one by one as profiles to be extruded in the graphics area. The preview of an extruded feature appears in the graphics area.

6. Reverse the direction of extrusion downward by clicking on the **Flipped** button in the **Direction** area of the **Extrusion** property panel.

7. Click on the **To Next** button in the **Behavior** rollout of the property panel. The preview of the extrude feature appears in the graphics area such that it terminates at its next intersection, see Figure 8.181.

8. Ensure that the **Join** button is activated in the **Boolean** area of the property panel.

9. Click on the **OK** button in the property panel. The third feature (extrude) is created, see Figure 8.182.

8.181

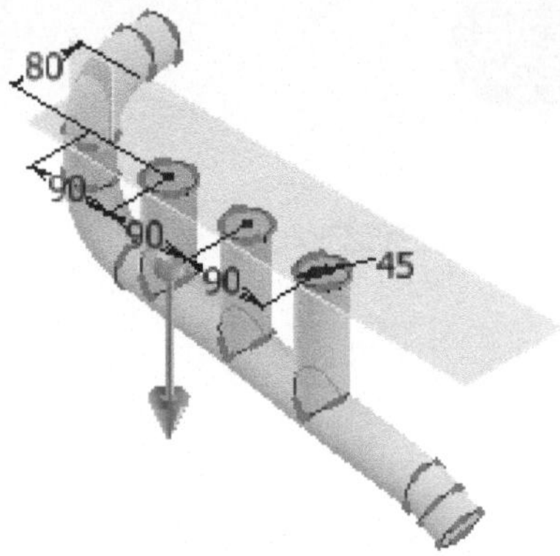

8.182

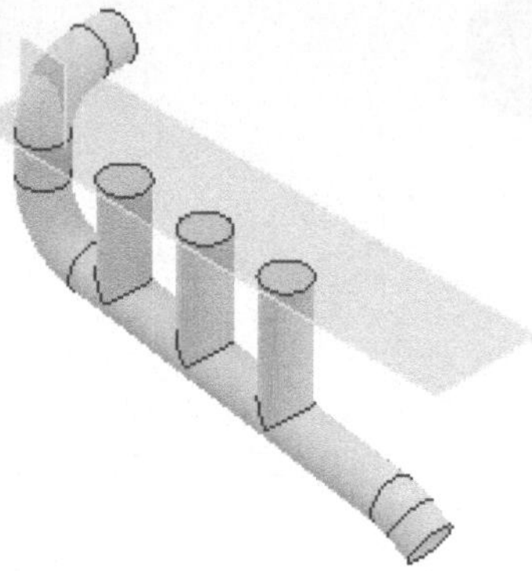

Section 5: Creating the Fourth Feature - Sweep Feature

To create the fourth feature of the model, you first need to create a work plane at an offset distance of 90 mm from the Right plane (YZ Plane).

1. Create a work plane at an offset distance of 90 mm from the Right plane (YZ Plane) by using the **Offset from Plane** tool of the **Plane** flyout, see Figure 8.183.

2. Invoke the Sketching environment by selecting the newly created work plane as the sketching plane.

3. Create the path of the sweep feature, see Figure 8.184. Next, exit the Sketching environment.

8.183

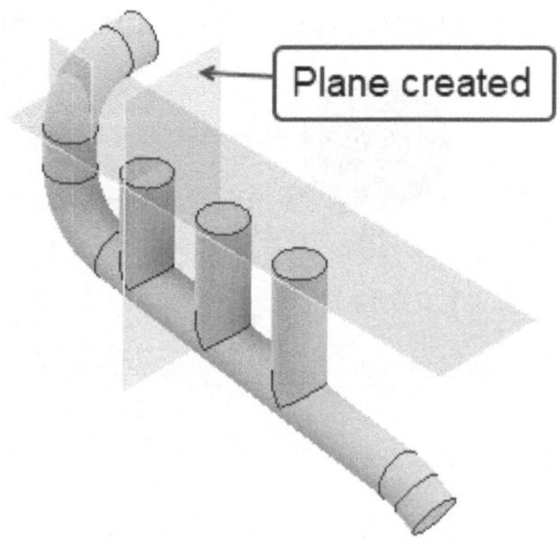

Now, you need to create the profile of the sweep feature.

4. Invoke the Sketching environment by selecting the top planar face of the third feature as the sketching plane, see Figure 8.185.

8.184

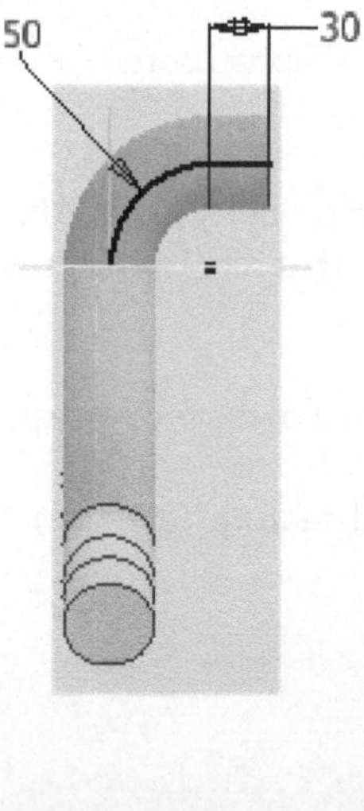

8.185

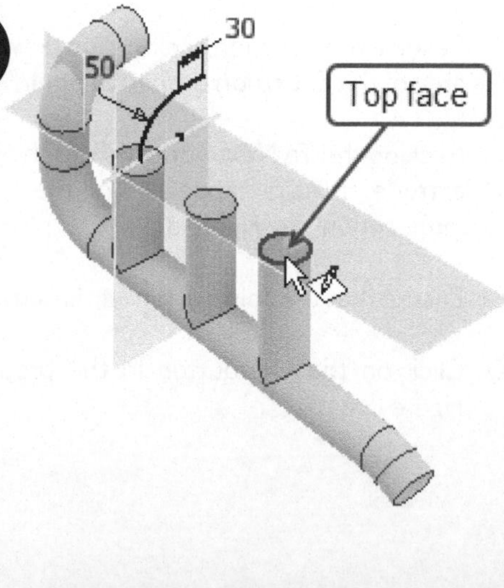

5. Project all the top circular edges of the third feature as sketch entities onto the sketching plane by using the **Project Geometry** tool, see Figure 8.186. You can use these projected entities as the profiles of the sweep feature. Next, exit the Sketching environment.

8.186

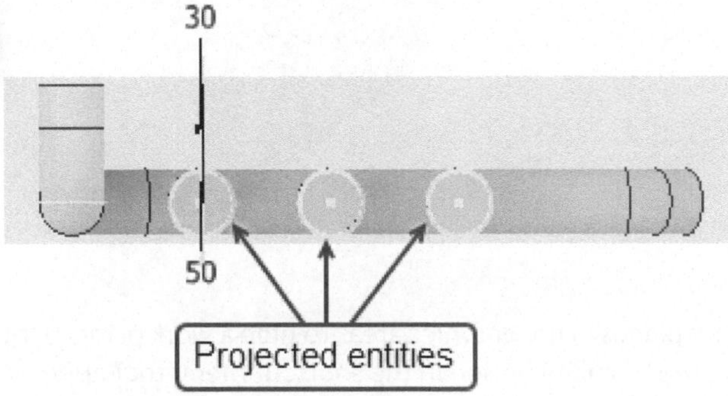

Now, you can create a sweep feature.

6. Click on the **Sweep** tool in the **Create** panel of the **3D Model** tab. The **Sweep** property panel appears.

7. Select all the projected entities of the sketch as the profiles (3 profiles), one by one in the graphics area, see Figure 8.187.

8. Click on the **Path** selector in the **Input Geometry** rollout of the **Sweep** property panel and then select the path of the sweep feature. A preview of the sweep feature appears in the graphics area, see Figure 8.188.

8.187

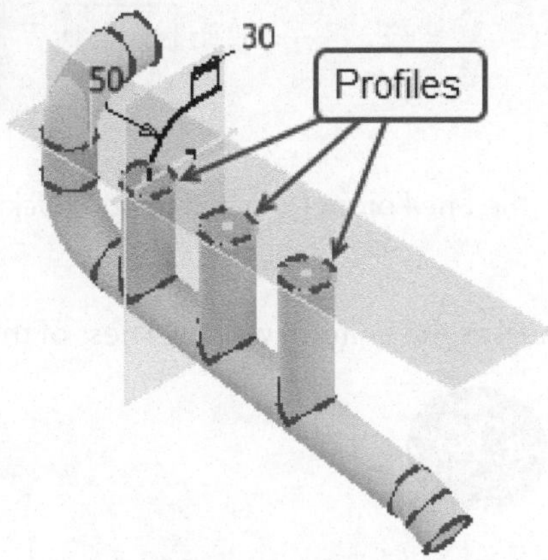

8.188

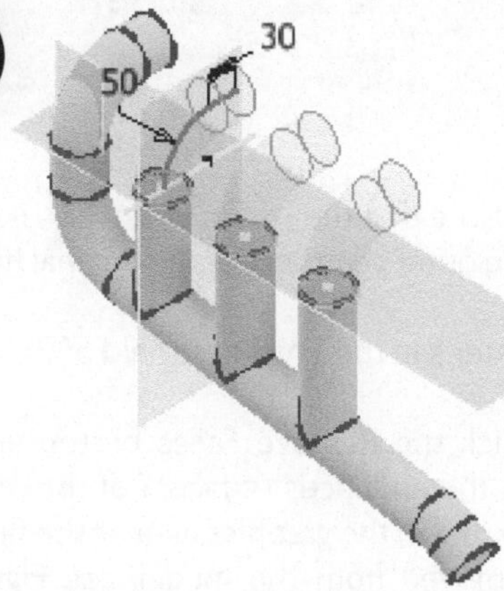

9. Ensure that the **Join** button is activated in the **Boolean** area of the **Sweep** property panel.

10. Click on the **OK** button in the **Sweep** property panel. The fourth feature (sweep) is created, see Figure 8.189.

8.189

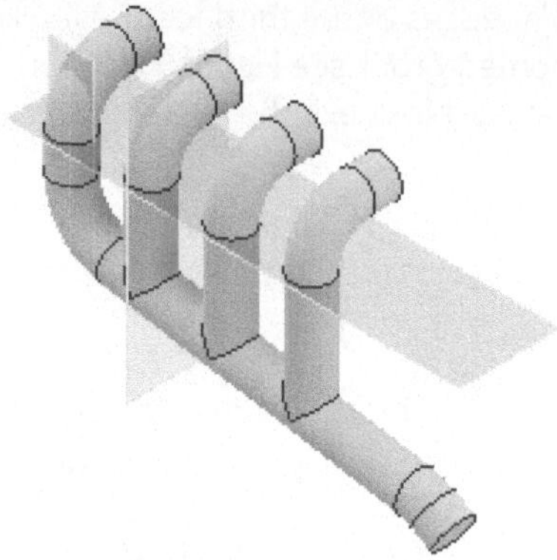

11. Hide all the work planes in the graphics area. To hide a work plane, right-click on it in the **Browser** and then select the **Visibility** option in the shortcut menu that appears.

Section 6: Creating the Fifth Feature - Shell Feature

Now, you need to create a shell feature of uniform wall thickness (5 mm) by removing the end faces of the model.

1. Click on the **Shell** tool in the **Modify** panel of the **3D Model** tab, see Figure 8.190. The **Shell** property panel appears. Also, the preview of a hollow model with default wall thickness appears in the graphics area.

8.190

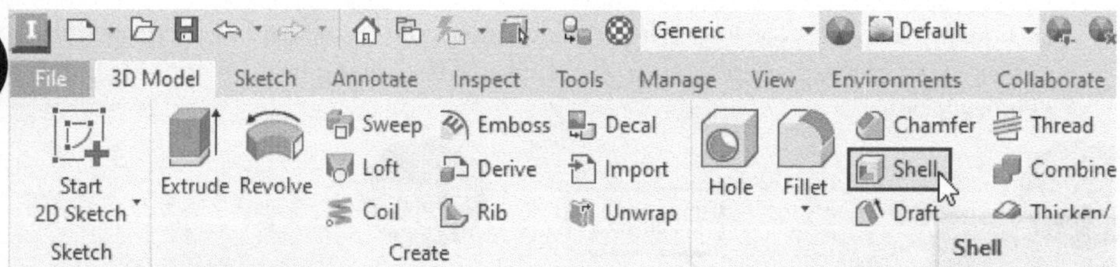

2. Ensure that the **Inside** button is activated in the **Shell** property panel to add thickness inside the outer geometry of the original model.

3. Enter **5** in the **Thickness** field of the property panel as the uniform wall thickness of the model.

4. Click the **Remove Faces** button and select all the end faces (5 faces) of the model one by one in the graphics area as the faces to be removed from the model, see Figure 8.191. You can rotate the model to select the end faces of the model.

5. Click on the **OK** button in the **Shell** property panel. A shell feature of uniform wall thickness is created. Also, the selected faces of the model get removed, see Figures 8.192 and 8.193. Both these figures show the final model in different orientations.

8.191

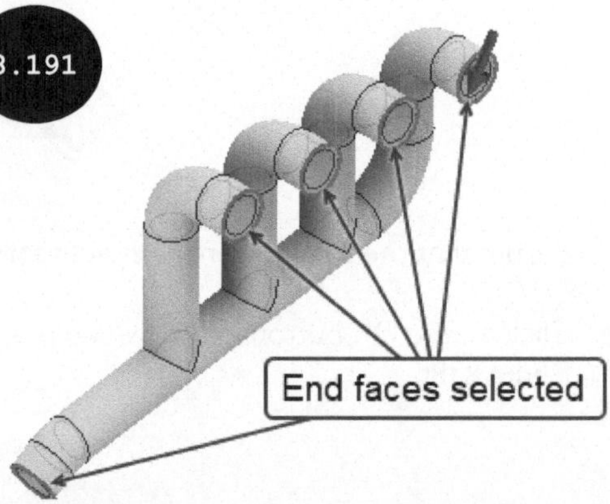

8.192

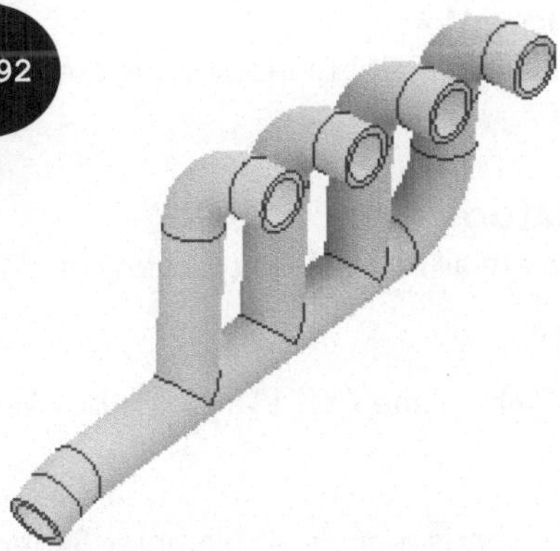

8.193

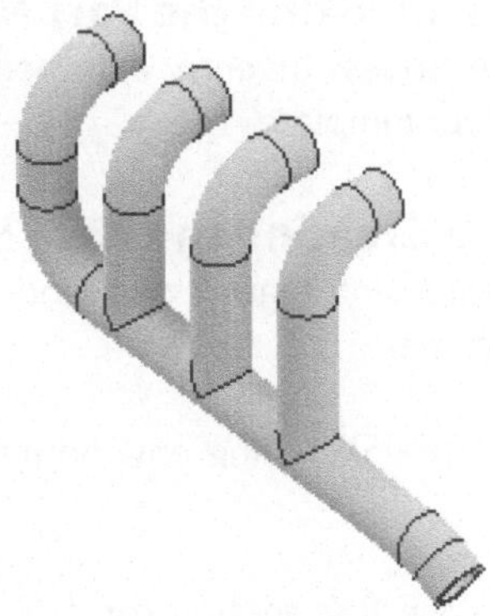

Section 7: Saving the Model

1. Click on the **Save** tool in the **Quick Access Toolbar** toolbar. The **Save As** dialog box appears.
2. Browse to **Autodesk Inventor > Chapter 8** folder in the local drive of your system. Note that you need to create a Chapter 8 folder inside the Autodesk Inventor folder, if not created earlier.
3. Enter **Tutorial 2** in the **File name** field of the dialog box and then click on the **Save** button. The model is saved in the specified location (>:\Autodesk Inventor\Chapter 8).

Tutorial 3

Create the model shown in Figure 8.194. All dimensions are in mm.

8.194

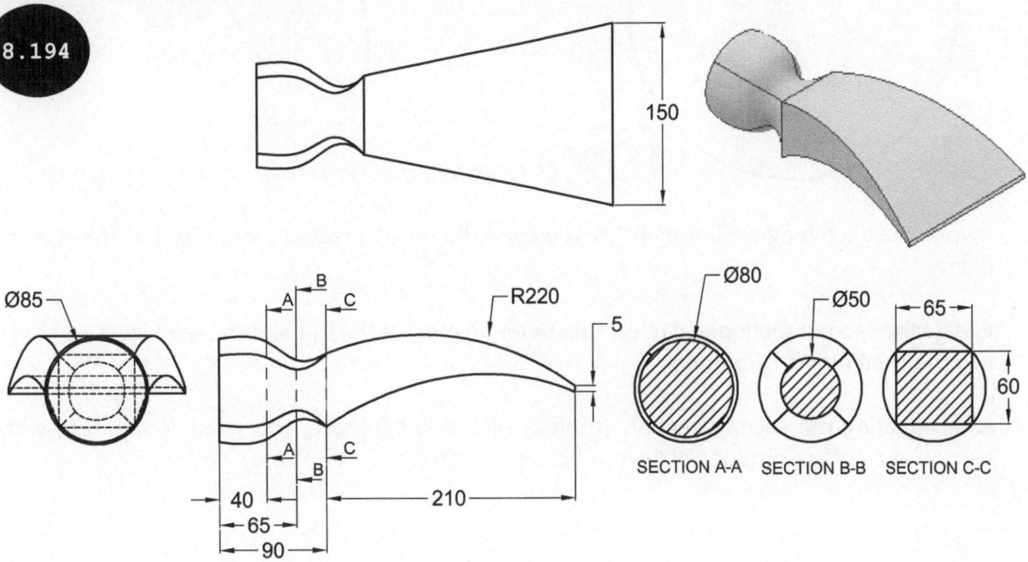

Section 1: Invoking the Part Modeling Environment

1. Start Autodesk Inventor and then invoke the Part modeling environment by using the **Standard (mm).ipt** template.

Section 2: Creating the Base Feature - Loft Feature

To create a loft feature of a model, you first need to create all its sections (profiles) on different work planes.

1. Invoke the Sketching environment by selecting the Right plane (YZ Plane) as the sketching plane.

2. Create the first section (profile) of the loft feature, which is a circle of diameter 85 mm, see Figure 8.195. Note that the center point of the circle is at the origin. Next, exit the Sketching environment.

   After creating the first section (profile) of the loft feature, you need to create the second section at an offset distance of 40 mm from the Right plane (YZ Plane).

3. Create a work plane at an offset distance of 40 mm from the Right plane (YZ Plane) by using the **Offset from Plane** tool of the **Plane** flyout, see Figure 8.196.

8.195

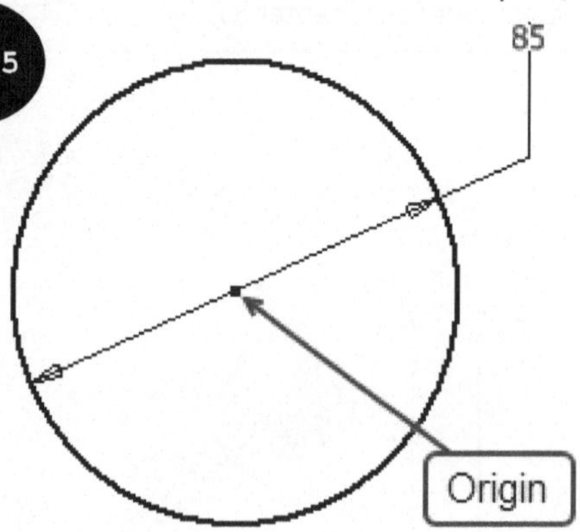

8.196

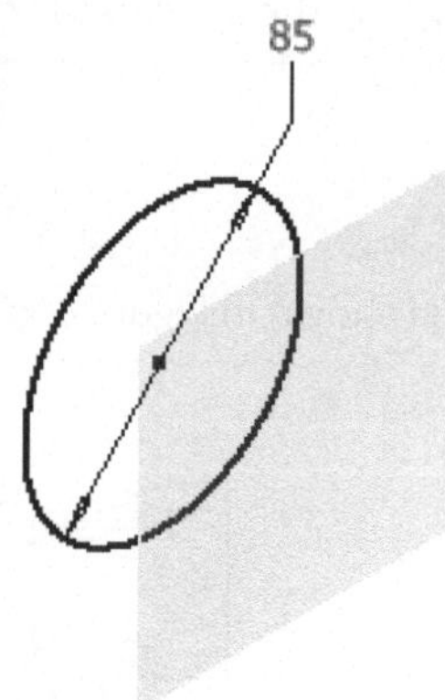

4. Invoke the Sketching environment by selecting the newly created work plane as the sketching plane.

5. Create the second section (a circle of diameter 80 mm) of the loft feature, see Figure 8.197. Next, exit the Sketching environment.

   After creating the second section (profile) of the loft feature, you need to create the third section at an offset distance of 65 mm from the Right plane (YZ Plane).

6. Create a work plane at an offset distance of 65 mm from the Right plane (YZ Plane) by using the **Offset from Plane** tool, see Figure 8.198.

8.197

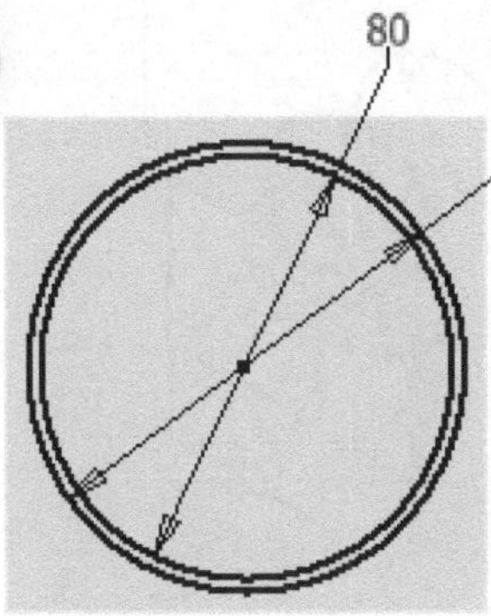

8.198

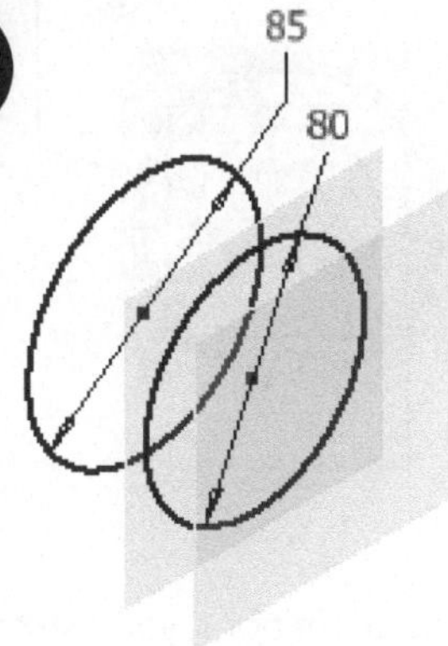

7. Invoke the Sketching environment by selecting the newly created work plane as the sketching plane.

8. Create the third section (a circle of diameter 50 mm) of the loft feature, see Figure 8.199. Next, exit the Sketching environment.

   After creating the third section (profile) of the loft feature, you need to create the fourth section at an offset distance of 90 mm from the Right plane (YZ Plane).

9. Create a work plane at an offset distance of 90 mm from the Right plane (YZ Plane) by using the **Offset from Plane** tool, see Figure 8.200.

8.199

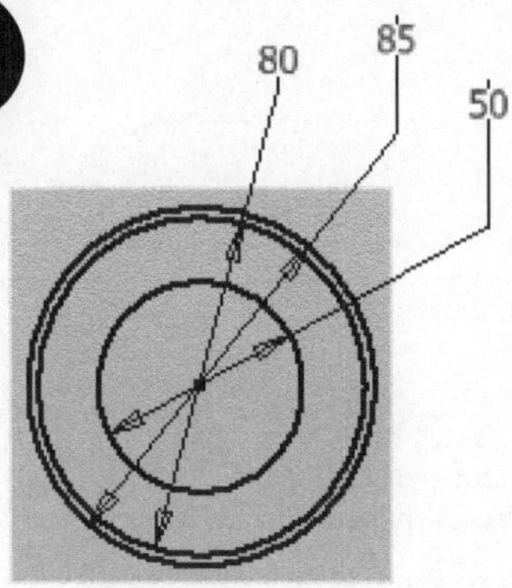

8.200

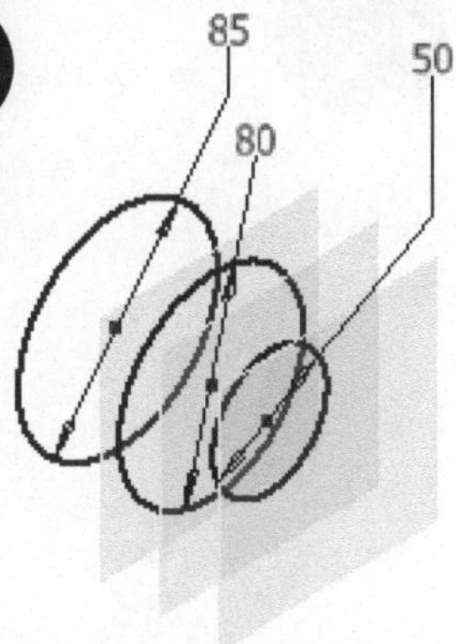

10. Invoke the Sketching environment by selecting the newly created work plane as the sketching plane.

11. Create the fourth section (rectangle of 65 X 60) of the loft feature, see Figure 8.201. Next, exit the Sketching environment, see Figure 8.202.

8.201

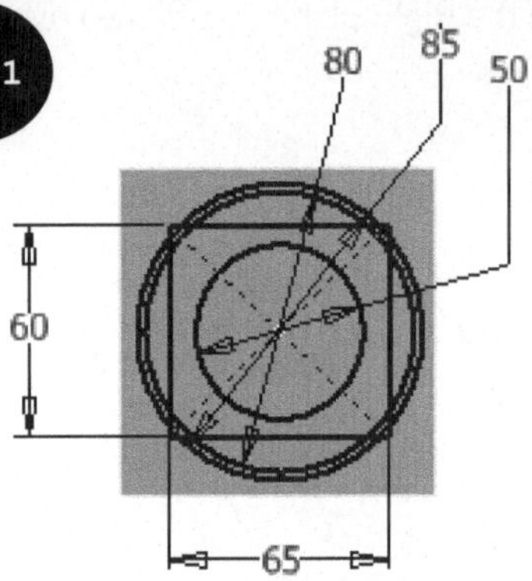

8.202

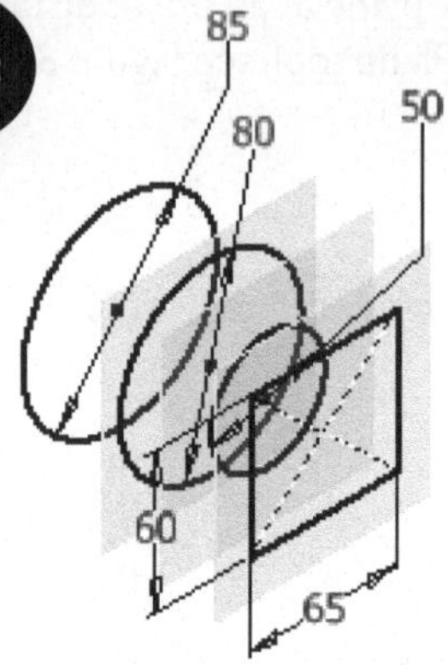

After creating all sections, you can create the loft feature.

12. Click on the **Loft** tool in the **Create** panel of the **3D Model** tab, see Figure 8.203. The **Loft** dialog box appears, see Figure 8.204.

8.203

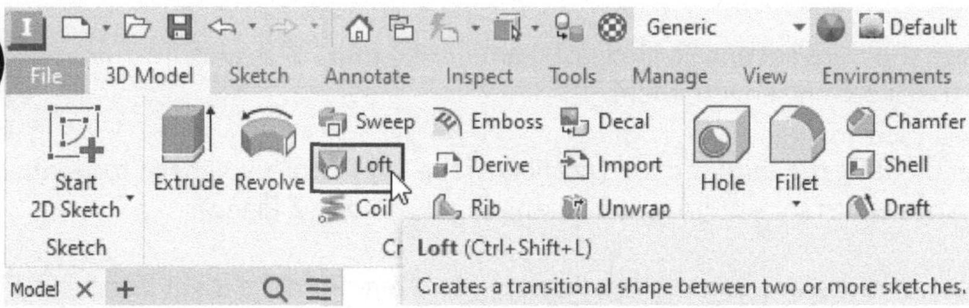

8.204

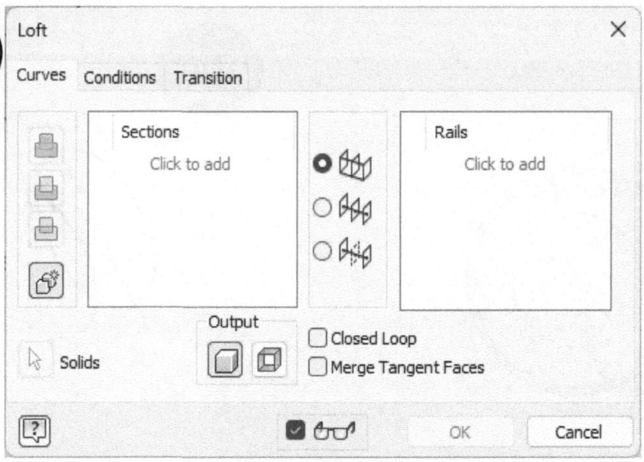

13. Select all the sections (profiles) of the loft feature in the graphics area one by one by clicking the left mouse button. The preview of a loft feature appears in the graphics area, see Figure 8.205. Note that you need to select the sections in a sequential order to avoid twisting the feature.

14. Ensure that the **Solid** button is activated in the dialog box for creating a solid feature.

15. Click on the **OK** button in the **Loft** dialog box. The loft feature is created, see Figure 8.206. In this figure, all the work planes have been hidden for clarity of image.

8.205

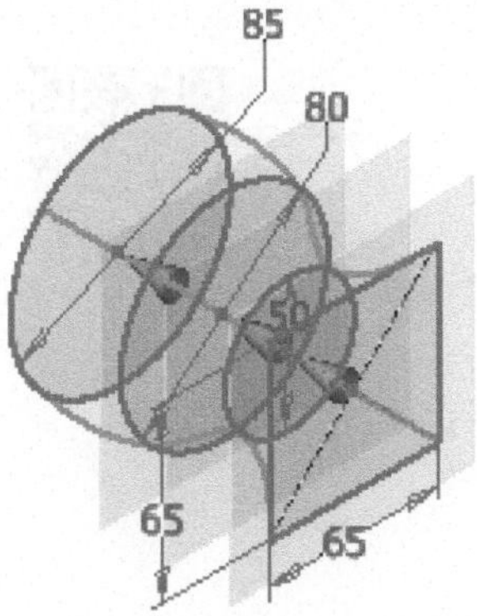

8.206

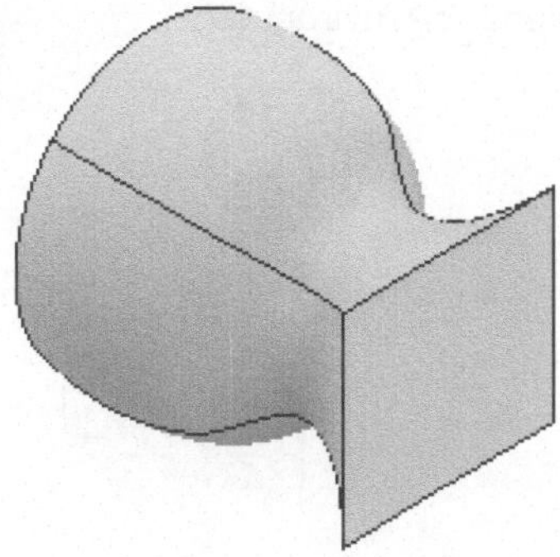

16. Hide all the work planes in the graphics area. To hide a work plane, right-click on it in the **Browser** and then select the **Visibility** option in the shortcut menu that appears.

Section 3: Creating the Second Feature - Loft Feature

Now, you need to create the second feature of the model, which is a loft feature.

1. Create a work plane at an offset distance of 210 mm from the right planar face of the base feature by using the **Offset from Plane** tool, see Figure 8.207.

2. Invoke the Sketching environment by selecting the newly created work plane as the sketching plane.

3. Create a section (rectangle of 150 X 5) of the loft feature, see Figure 8.208. Next, exit the Sketching environment.

8.207

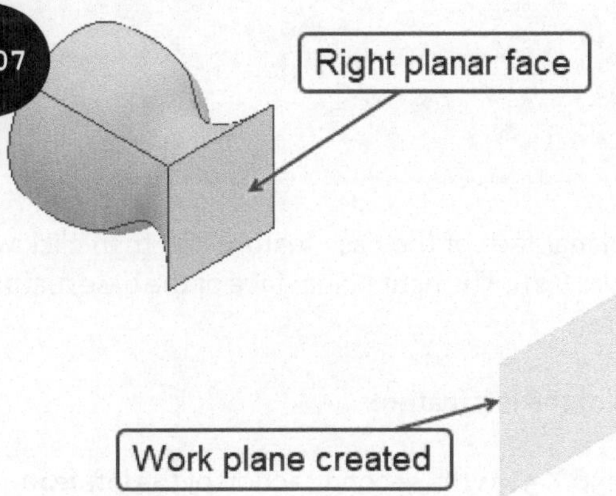

8.208

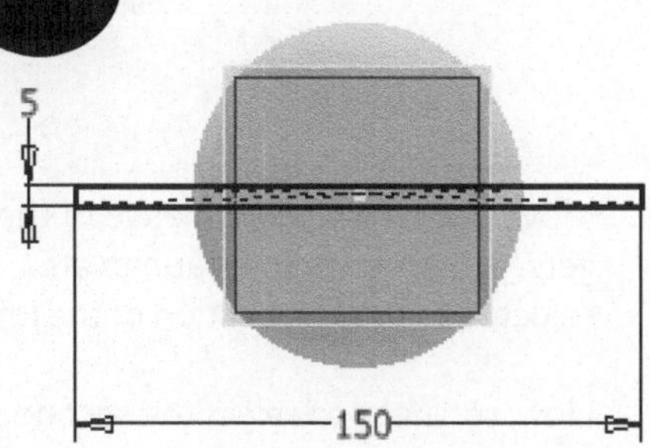

Now, you need to create a guide rail on the Front plane for creating the loft feature. A guide rail is used for guiding the cross-sectional shape of the loft feature.

4. Invoke the Sketching environment by selecting the Front plane (XY Plane) as the sketching plane.

5. Create an arc of radius 220 mm as the guide rail of the loft feature, see Figure 8.209. Next, exit the Sketching environment.

8.209

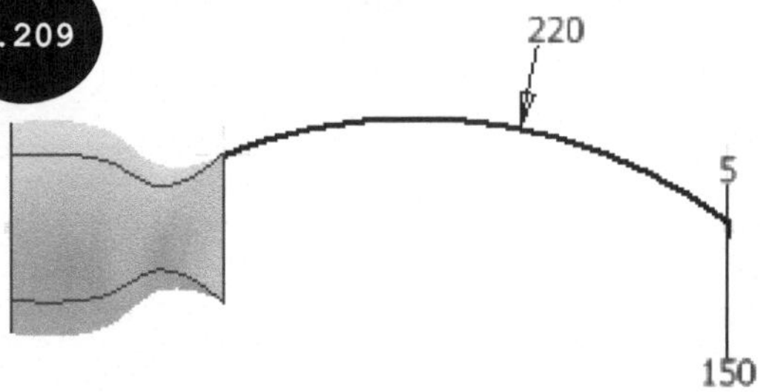

Note: The endpoints of the guide rail (arc) shown in the Figure 8.209 have coincident constraint with the top entity of the rectangular section of the loft feature and the top edge of the right planar face of the base feature. For doing so, you can project the entities onto the sketching plane of the guide rail by using the **Project Geometry** tool and then apply the coincident constraint between the endpoints of the guide rail and the projected entities.

Now, you need to create a loft feature.

6. Click on the **Loft** tool in the **Create** panel of the **3D Model** tab, see Figure 8.210. The **Loft** dialog box appears. Also, you are prompted to select sections.

8.210

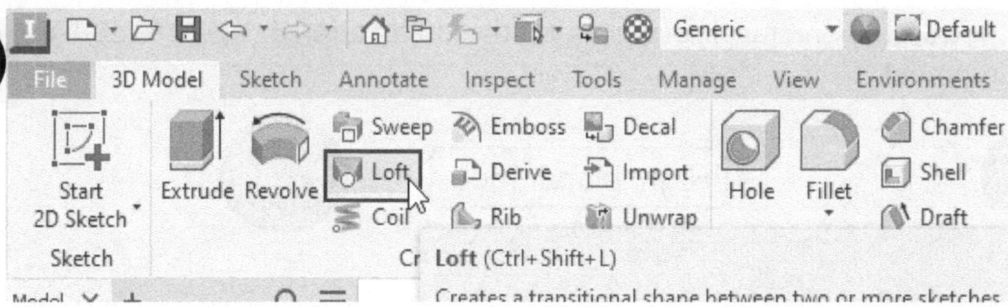

7. Move the cursor over an edge of the right planar face of the base feature and then click when it gets highlighted in the graphics area, see Figure 8.211. The right planar face of the base feature gets selected as the first section of the loft feature.

Now, you need to select the second section of the loft feature.

8. Select the rectangular section (rectangle of 150 X 5) as the second section of the loft feature. The preview of a loft feature appears in the graphics area, see Figure 8.212.

8.209

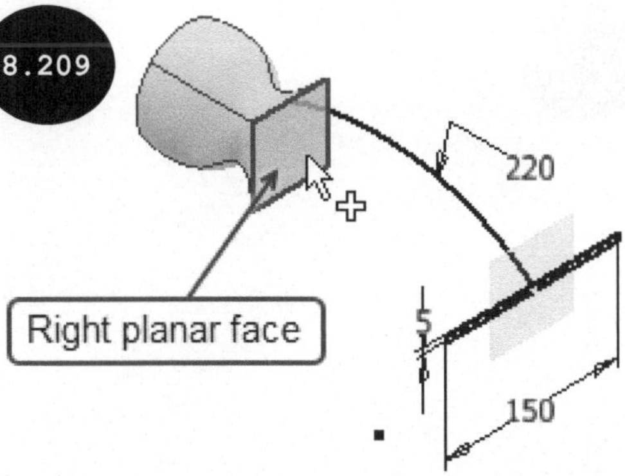

8.210

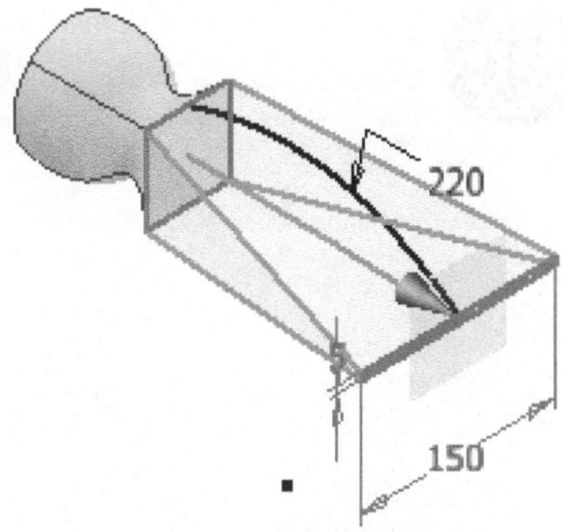

Now, you can select a guide rail for guiding the cross-sectional shape of the loft feature.

9. Ensure that the **Rails** radio button is selected in the **Loft** dialog box, see Figure 8.213.

10. Click on the **Click to add** option in the **Rails** area of the dialog box, see Figure 8.213. You are prompted to select a sketch as a guide rail for the loft feature.

8.213

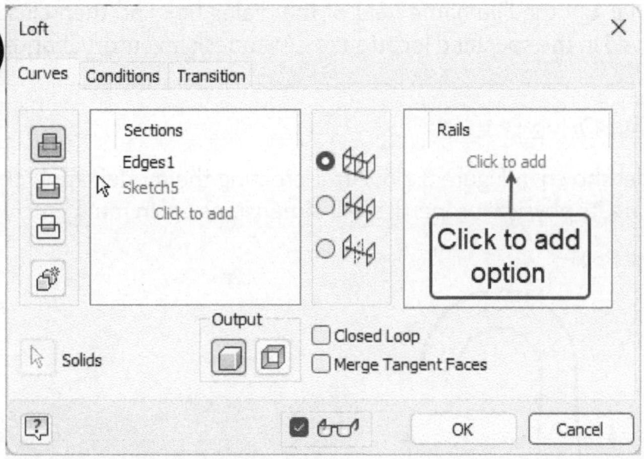

11. Select an arc of radius 220 mm as the guide rail in the graphics area. The preview of the loft feature gets modified such that its cross-sectional shape is guided by the selected guide rail, see Figure 8.214.

12. Ensure that the **Join** button is activated in the **Operation** area of the **Loft** dialog box.

13. Ensure that the **Solid** button is activated in the **Output** area of the dialog box for creating a solid loft feature.

14. Click on the **OK** button in the **Loft** dialog box. The loft feature is created, see Figure 8.215. Hide the display of the work plane in the graphics area.

8.214

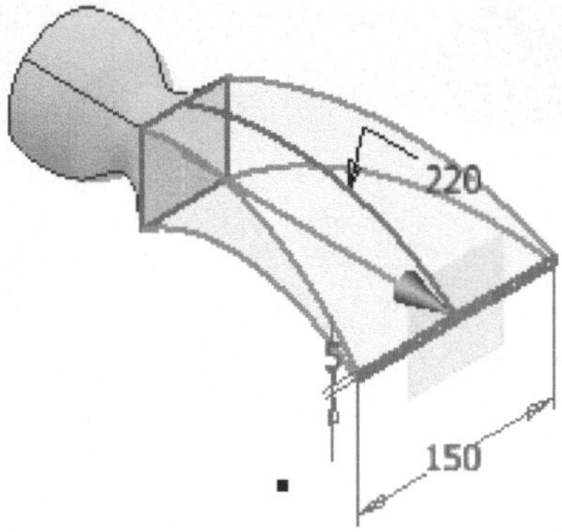

8.215

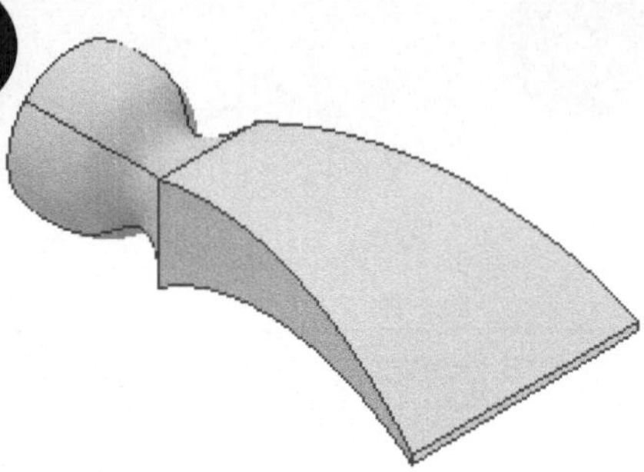

Section 4: Saving the Model

1. Click on the **Save** tool in the **Quick Access Toolbar**. The **Save As** dialog box appears.
2. Browse to **Autodesk Inventor > Chapter 8** folder in the local drive of your system. Note that you need to create a Chapter 8 folder inside the Autodesk Inventor folder, if not created earlier.
3. Enter **Tutorial 3** in the **File name** field of the dialog box and then click on the **Save** button. The model is saved in the specified location (>:\Autodesk Inventor\Chapter 8).

Hands-on Test Drive 1

Create the model shown in Figure 8.216. After creating the model, apply the Stainless Steel material and then calculate its physical properties. All dimensions are in mm.

8.216

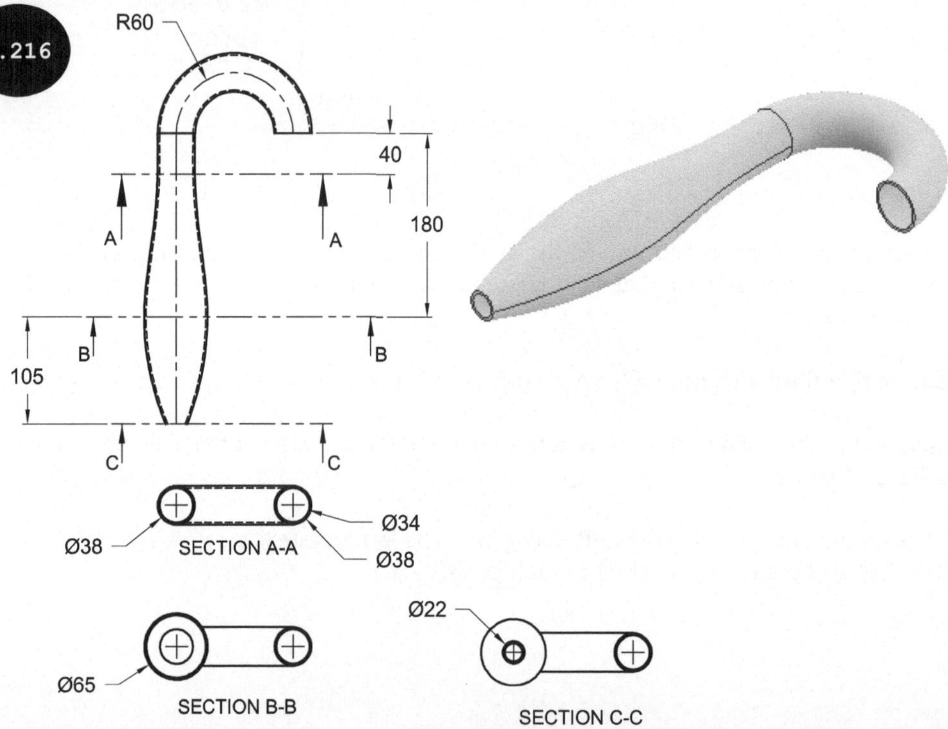

Hands-on Test Drive 2

Create the model shown in Figure 8.217 and then apply the Steel, Alloy material. Also, calculate the physical properties of the model. All dimensions are in mm.

8.217

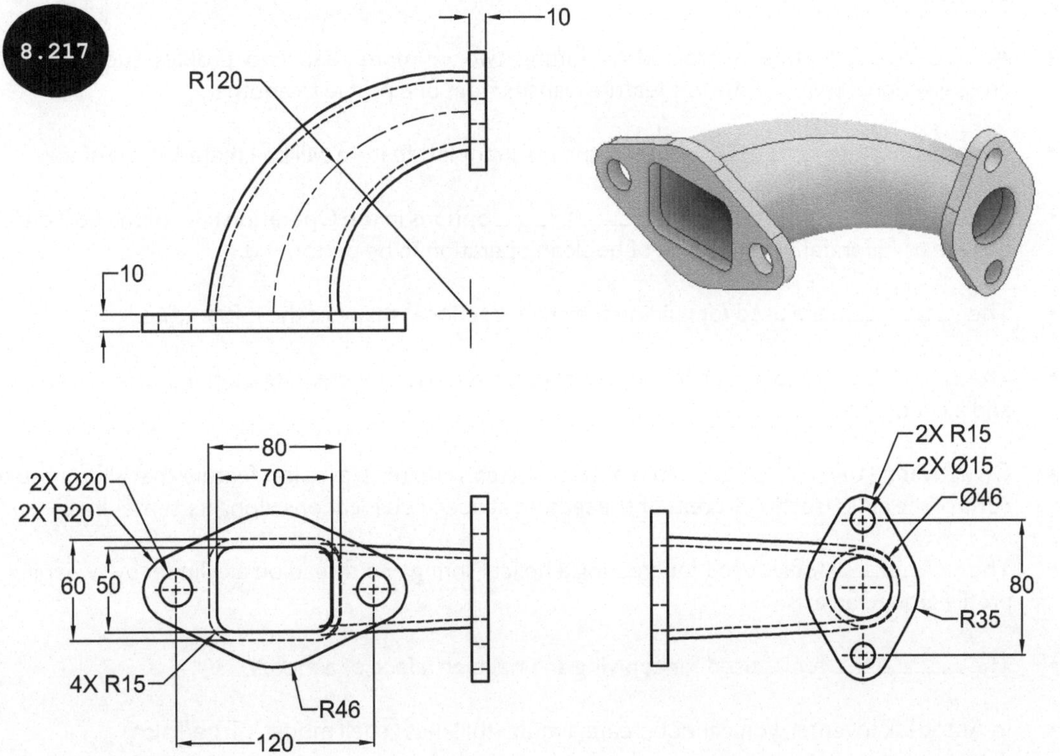

Summary

In this chapter, you have learned how to create a sweep feature, a loft feature, a coil feature, an emboss feature, a mark feature, a rib feature, and a shell feature, in addition to applying images on a face of a model.

Questions

Complete and verify the following sentences:

- The ________ tool is used for creating a sweep feature.
- While creating a sweep feature, the ________ option is selected in the **Orientation** area of the **Sweep** property panel, by default. As a result, the profile follows the path by maintaining the same angle of orientation from start to end.

- On selecting the _________ option in the **Sweep** property panel, the profile follows the path such that it remains parallel throughout the path.
- By selecting the _________ button, you can create a sweep feature by sweeping a toolbody along a path.
- A _________ feature is created by lofting two or more than two profiles such that the cross-sectional shape of the loft feature transits from one profile to another.
- On activating the _________ button, the resultant loft feature will be created as a surface.
- The _________, _________, and _________ options in the **Operation** area of the **Loft** dialog box are used for defining the type of boolean operation to be performed.
- The _________ are used for guiding the cross-sectional shape of the loft feature.
- The _________ radio button in the **Loft** dialog box is used for creating a loft feature with profiles and a centerline.
- On activating the _________ radio button, you can create an area loft feature that allows you to control the cross-sectional areas of the feature at specified locations along its centerline.
- The _________ tool is used for creating a helical spring or a thread on a cylinder by sweeping a profile around an axis.
- The _________ tool is used for applying an image on a face of a model.
- In Autodesk Inventor, you cannot create a multi-thickness shell model. (True/False)
- An emboss feature is created by embossing or engraving a sketch or text onto a face of a model. (True/False)
- You can create a rib feature from an open sketch by adding thickness in a specified direction. (True/False)
- You cannot remove one or more faces of a model while creating a shell feature. (True/False)
- The profiles or sections of a loft feature must be closed. (True/False)
- The guide rails must intersect with the profiles of the loft feature. (True/False)

CHAPTER

9

Patterning and Mirroring

In this chapter, the following topics will be discussed:

- Creating a Rectangular Pattern
- Creating a Circular Pattern
- Creating a Sketch Driven Pattern
- Suppressing Features and Pattern Occurrences
- Unsuppressing Features and Pattern Occurrences
- Mirroring a Feature or a Body

Patterning and mirroring tools are very powerful tools that help designers speed up the creation of a design, increase efficiency, and save time. For example, if a plate has 1000 holes of the same diameter, instead of creating all the holes one by one, you can create one hole and then pattern it to create the remaining holes. Similarly, if a geometry is symmetric, you can create one of its sides and then mirror it to create the other side. In Autodesk Inventor, you can create rectangular patterns, circular patterns, and sketch driven patterns of features or bodies. The methods for creating various types of patterns are discussed next.

Creating a Rectangular Pattern

You can create a rectangular pattern by creating multiple occurrences of features or bodies in one or two linear directions by using the **Rectangular Pattern** tool, see Figure 9.1. The method for creating a rectangular pattern is discussed below:

9.1

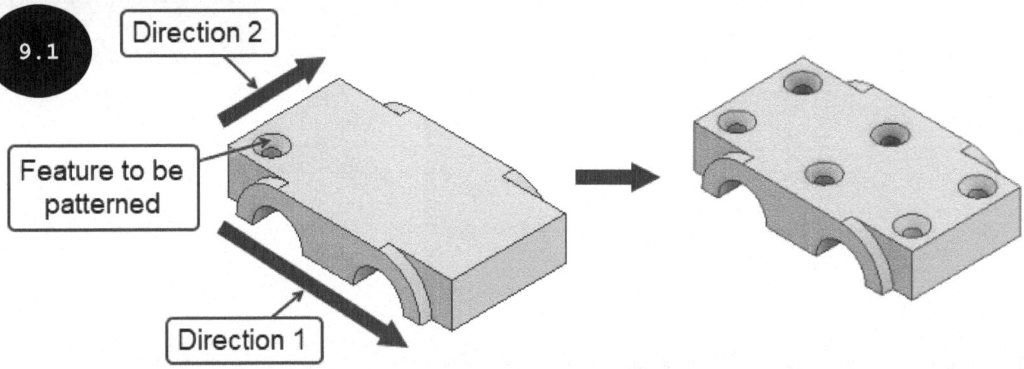

1. Click on the **Rectangular Pattern** tool in the **Pattern** panel of the **3D Model** tab, see Figure 9.2. The **Rectangular Pattern** property panel appears along with the tool palette on its right, see Figure 9.3. Also, you are prompted to select features to be patterned.

9.2

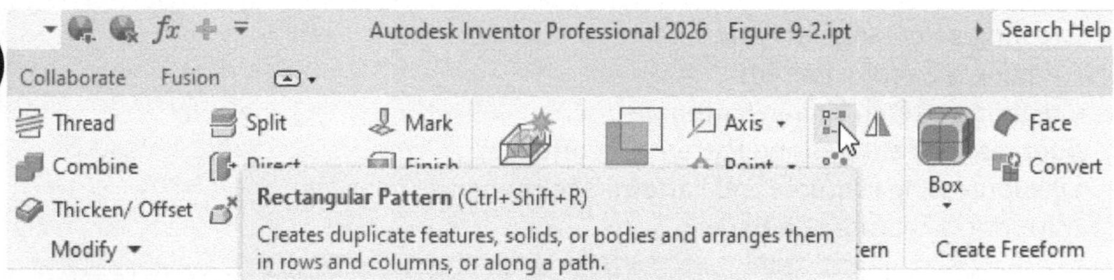

9.3

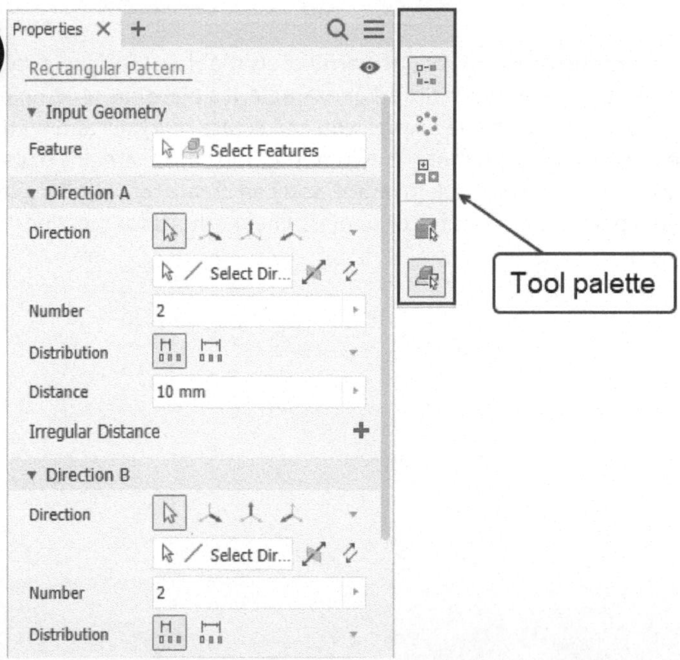

Tool Palette: The options available in the tool palette allow you to switch between different pattern types, such as **Rectangular Pattern**, **Circular Pattern**, or **Sketch Driven Pattern**. Additionally, it provides filters for selection options, including **Pattern individual feature** and **Pattern solids**, which are explained in below:

Pattern individual features : By default, the **Pattern individual features** button is activated in the **Rectangular Pattern** property panel. As a result, the **Features** selector is activated and you are prompted to select features to be patterned. You can select single or multiple features in the graphics area to be patterned rectangularly, in one or two linear directions.

Pattern solids : On activating the **Pattern solids** button in the tool palette, the **Solid** and **Work Feature** selector becomes available in the property panel, see Figure 9.4. The **Solid** selector allows you to choose a solid body to be patterned. If only one solid body is present in the graphics area, it will automatically be selected by default, and the selector field is disabled.

The **Work Features** selector is used for selecting work features such as planes, axes, and points of the selected body to be included in the pattern.

Note: While patterning a solid body in the graphics area, you can define whether the occurrences of the resultant pattern are to be joined with the parent body or new separate bodies are to be created by activating the **Join** or **New Solid** button in the **Output Geometry** rollout, respectively. By default, the **Join** button is activated in the property panel. As a result, all the pattern occurrences get merged or joined with the parent body and together act as a single body.

9.4

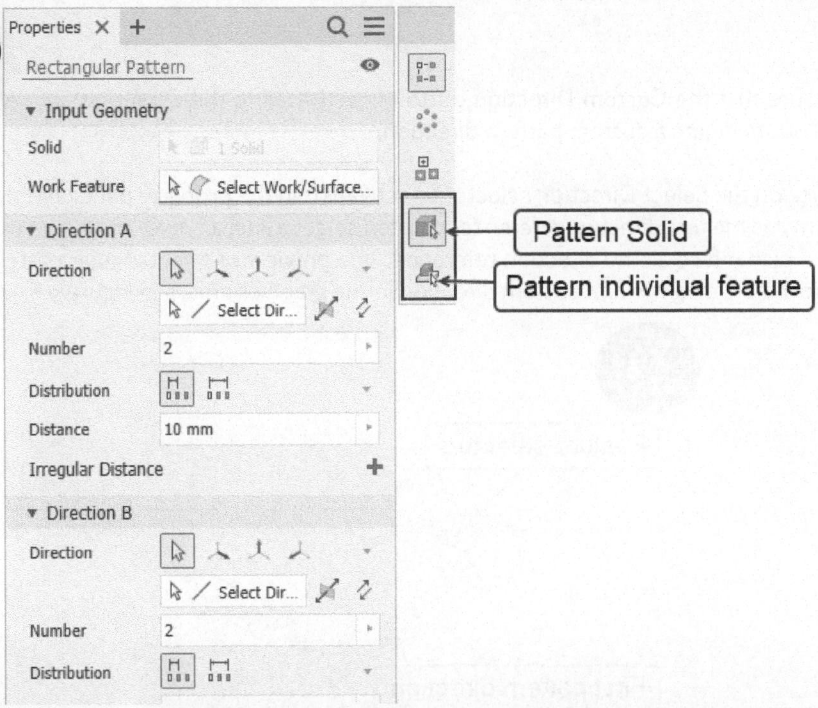

2. Ensure that the **Pattern individual features** button is activated in the tool palette to select one or more features to be patterned. Note that to pattern the entire model or bodies, you need to activate the **Pattern solids** button in the tool palette, as discussed above.

3. Select one or more features of a model to be patterned in the graphics area.

   Now, you need to define the first pattern direction.

   Direction: By deault, the **Custom Direction** button is activated in the **Direction** area of the **Direction A** rollout. As a result, the **Select Direction** selector field become avaialble in the rollout to define a custom pattern direction, see Figure 9.5.

   You can also define the pattern direction along the default X-axis, Y-axis, or Z-axis by selecting the respective button available in the **Direction** area.

9.5

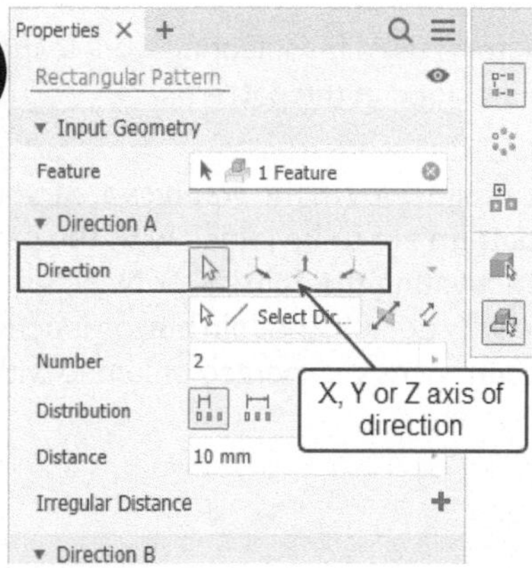

4. Ensure that the **Custom Direction** button is activated in the **Direction** area of the **Direction A** rollout to define a custom pattern direction.

5. Click on the **Select Direction** selector to activate it in the property panel and then select a linear entity as the first direction reference. You can select a line, a curve, an edge, a work plane, an axis, or a planar face as the direction reference. The preview of a rectangular pattern appears with a arrow indicating the first pattern direction in the graphics area, see Figure 9.6.

9.6

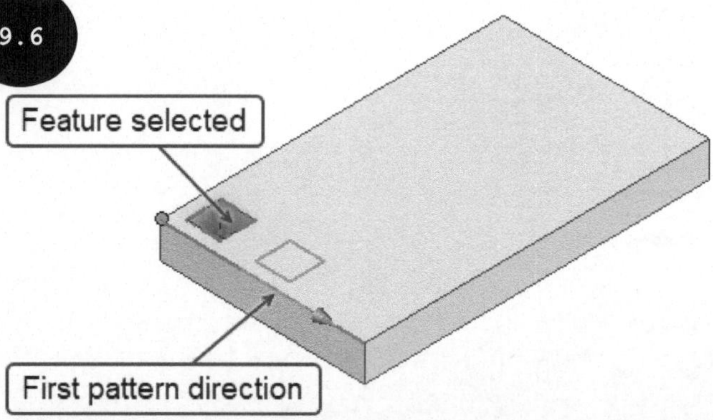

Now, you can define the required parameters such as number of instances and distance between the instances in their respective field of the rollout, see Figure 9.7. The options are discussed next.

9.7

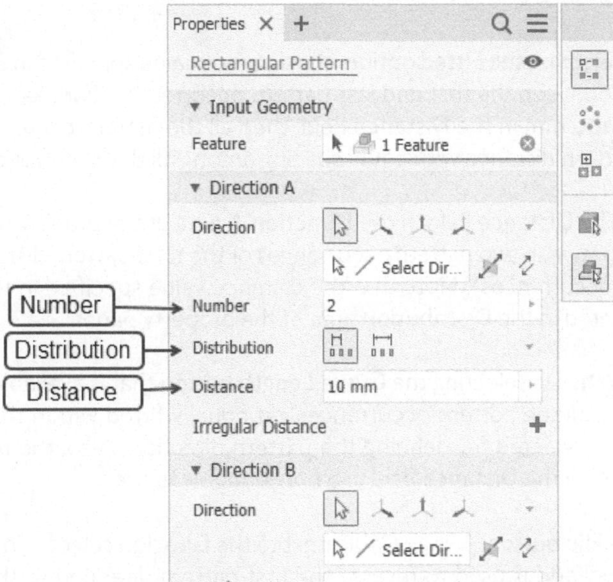

Number: The **Number** field in the **Direction A** area of the property panel is used for specifying the number of pattern occurrences to be created in the first pattern direction.

Note: The number of pattern occurrences specified in the **Number** field is counted along with the parent or original occurrence. For example, if 3 is specified in the **Number** field, then a total of 3 pattern occurrences will be created including the parent occurrence, see Figure 9.8.

9.8

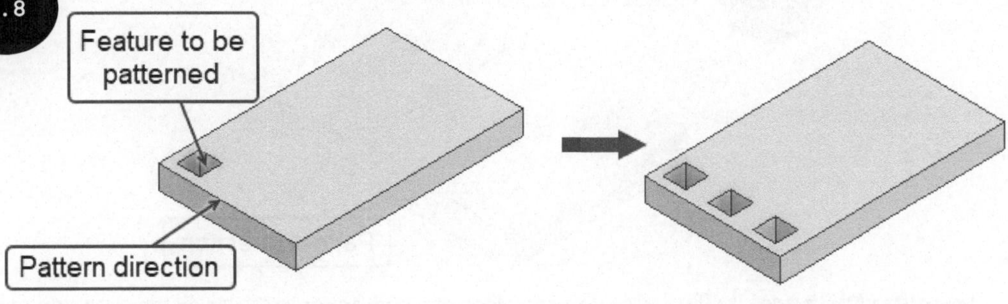

Distribution: The options in the **Distribution** area of the property panel are used for specifying the type of distance measurement between the pattern occurrences. The options are discussed below:

Incremental: By default, the **Incremental** button is selected in the **Distribution** area. As a result, the distance value specified in the **Distance** field is used as the spacing between two consecutive pattern occurrences.

Fitted: On selecting the **Fitted** option, the distance value specified in the **Distance** field is used as the spacing between the first and last pattern occurrences. For example, if the distance value is specified as 100 mm in the **Distance** field, then all the pattern occurrences will adjust within the specified pattern distance with equal spacing among all the occurrences.

Distance: The **Distance** field in the **Direction A** area of the property panel is used for specifying the spacing between two pattern occurrences or the total pattern distance (between the first and last pattern occurrences). Note that the distance value specified in this field depends upon the button activated in the **Distribution** area of the property panel.

Curve Length: On selecting the **Curve Length** button that is available next to the **Distance** field in the rollout, all the pattern occurrences get equally fitted within the total length of the entity that has been selected for defining the pattern direction. Also, the total length of the selected entity appears in the **Distance** field in a non-editable mode.

Flip : The **Flip** button is available next to the **Direcion** selector in the **Direction A** area of the property panel and is used to reverse the first pattern direction to the other side of the parent feature.

Midplane : The **Midplane** button is used for creating pattern occurrences symmetrically on both sides of the parent feature. For example, if the total number of pattern occurrences is specified as **5** in the **Number** field, then 2-2 pattern occurrences will be created symmetrically on each side of the parent feature along the pattern direction, see Figure 9.9. Note that the number of pattern occurrences specified also includes the parent feature. If you have specified an even number of pattern occurrences then the additional occurrence will be created on the side in which the pattern direction arrow points.

9.9

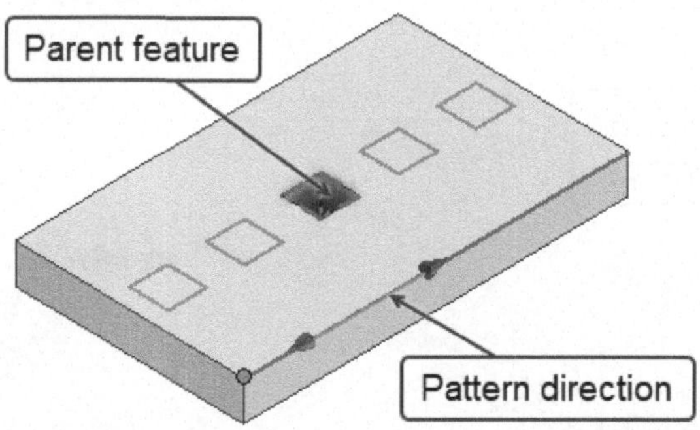

Irregular Distance + : If needed you can also set a custom or irregular distance to one or more specific pattern occurrence. To do this, activate the **Irregular Distnace** + button available below the **Distance** field in the rollout. The **Select Members** selector appears along with a distance value. Next, select a desired pattern occurrence in the graphcis area and then set the required irregular distance value in the distance field. The preview of the pattern updates accordingly.

6. Enter the number of pattern occurrences to be created along the first pattern direction in the **Number** field of the **Direction A** rollout.

7. Select the required option (**Incremental, Fitted**, or **Curve Length**) in the **Direction A** rollout of the property panel.

8. Specify the spacing between pattern occurrences in the **Distance** field depending upon the option selected in the **Distribution** area of the **Direction A** rollout.

   After specifying the number of pattern occurrences and spacing between pattern occurrences in the first pattern direction, you can define the second pattern direction in the **Direction B** rollout. The options in this rollout are same as discussed earlier with the only difference that the options in this rollout area used to define the pattern instances in second direction, see Figure 9.10.

9.10

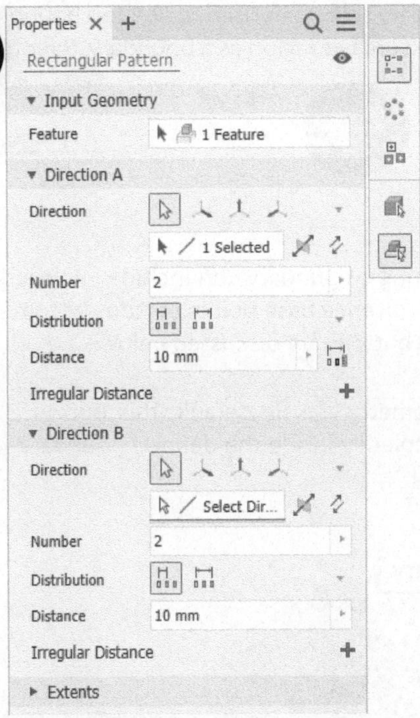

9. Click on the **Select Direction** selector in the **Direction B** rollout of the property panel and then select a linear entity as the second pattern direction. The options in the **Direction B** rollout of the property panel are used for creating multiple occurrences of the selected feature in the second pattern direction and are the same as discussed earlier.

10. Click on the **Flip** button in the **Direction** area of the **Direction B** rollout to reverse the direction of the pattern, if needed.

11. Enter the number of pattern occurrences to be created along the second pattern direction in the **Number** field of the **Direction B** rollout. Figure 9.11 shows the preview of a rectangular pattern with 3 occurrences in the first direction and 5 occurrences in the second direction.

12. Select the required option in the **Distribution** area of the **Direction B** rollout.

13. Specify the spacing between pattern occurrences in the **Distance** field depending upon the option selected in the **Distribution** area of the **Direction B** rollout.

9.11

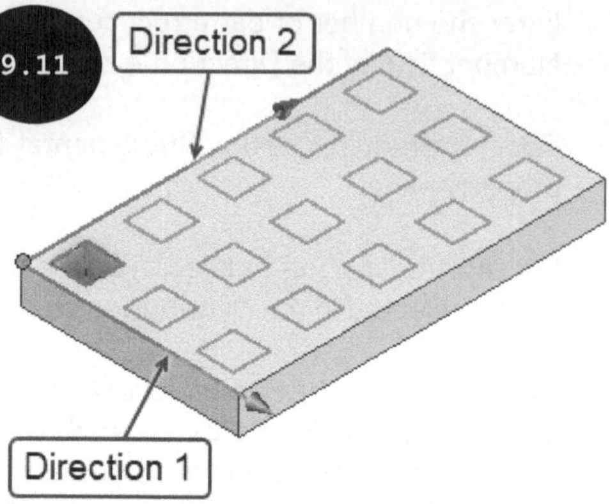

Extents: The options in the **Extents** rollout in the property panel are used to create pattern instances within a defined boundary, see Figure 9.12. The options are discussed below:

Boundary: The **Boundary** selector is used to define a boundary to be filled with pattern instances. You can select a closed area or region as a boundary, refer to Figure 9.12.

9.12

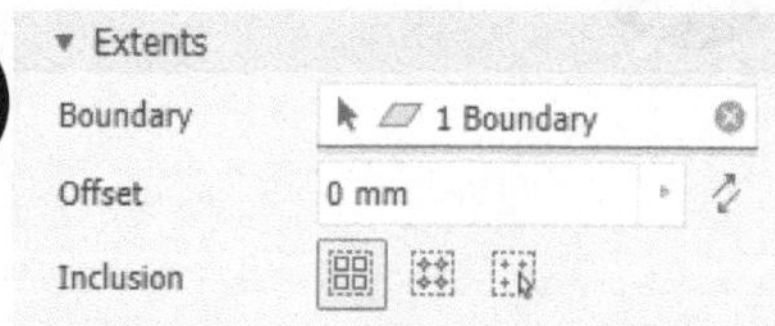

Note that upon selecting a boundary, the **Include enclosed geometry**, **Include using centroids**, and **Includes using occurrence base points** buttons become enabled in the **Inclusion** area of the **Extents** rollout. These buttons are discussed below:

Include enclosed geometry: By default, this button is activated. As a result, the pattern instances that lie completely inside the defined boundary will only be included in the resultant pattern, see Figure 9.13.

9.13

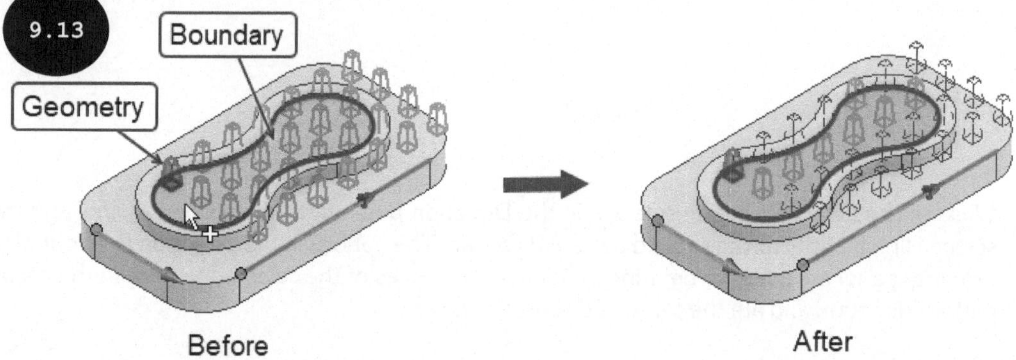

Tip: Figure 9.13 shows the preview of a pattern before and after selecting the **Include enclosed geometry** button.

Include using centroids : On activating the **Include using centroids** button, the pattern instances whose center point lies inside the defined boundary will only be included in the resultant pattern, see Figure 9.14.

9.14

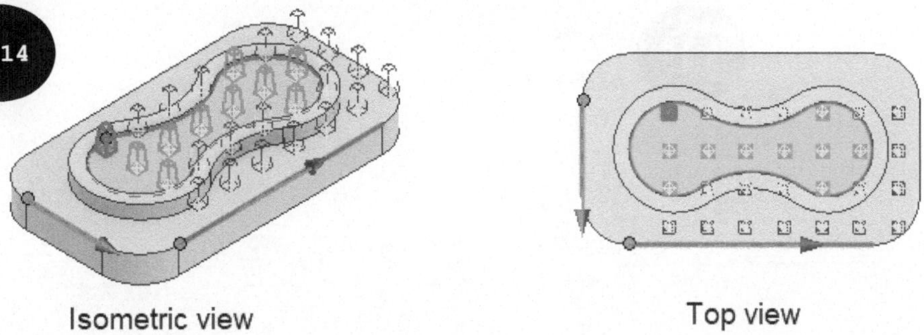

Include using occurrence base points : On activating the **Include using occurrence base points** button, the **Occurrence Base** selector gets enabled to define a base point on the parent geometry. In doing so, all the pattern instances with defined base points lying inside the boundary will be included in the resultant pattern, see Figure 9.15.

9.15

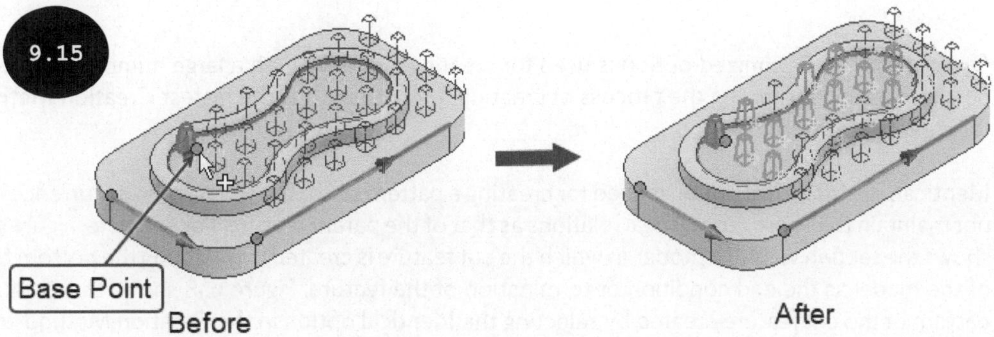

Boundary Offset : The **Boundary Offset** field is used to define an offset distance to be maintained between the outermost pattern instance and the selected boundary.

Flip Offset direction: The **Flip Offset direction** button next to the **Boundary Offset** field is used to reverse the direction of offset distance to the other side of the selected boundary.

Output Geometry: The options in the **Output Geometry** rollout in the **Rectangular Pattern** property panel are discussed below:

Creation Method: The options in the **Creation Method** drop-down list of the **Output Geometry** rollout are used for defining the computational method for creating a pattern, see Figure 9.16. The options are discussed below:

9.16

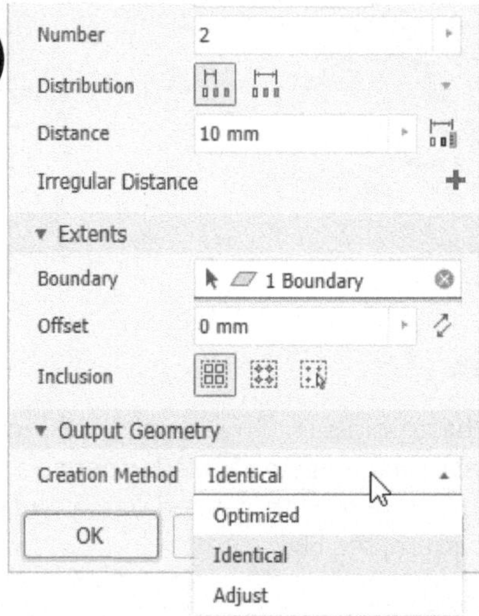

Optimized: The **Optimized** option is used for creating a pattern with a large number of pattern occurrences by optimizing the process of creating the pattern. It is the fastest **Creation Method** for creating a pattern.

Identical: The **Identical** option is used for creating a pattern such that the pattern occurrences do not maintain the same geometrical relations as that of the parent feature. For example, Figure 9.17 shows the section view of a model, in which the cut feature is created by selecting the bottom face of the model as the end condition or termination of the feature. Figure 9.18 shows the resultant pattern of the cut feature created by selecting the **Identical** option in the **Creation Method** area of the property panel.

9.17

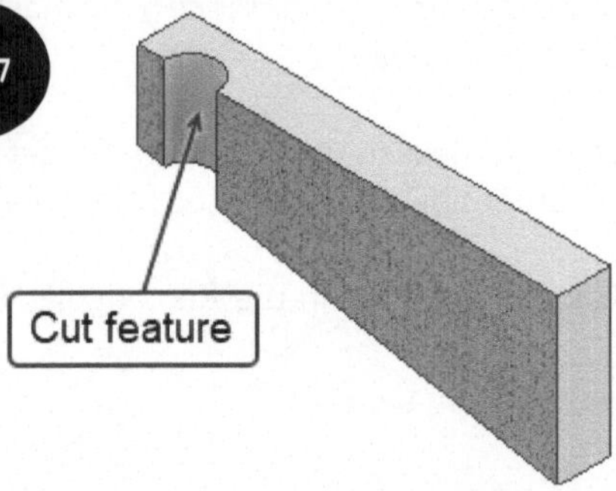

9.18

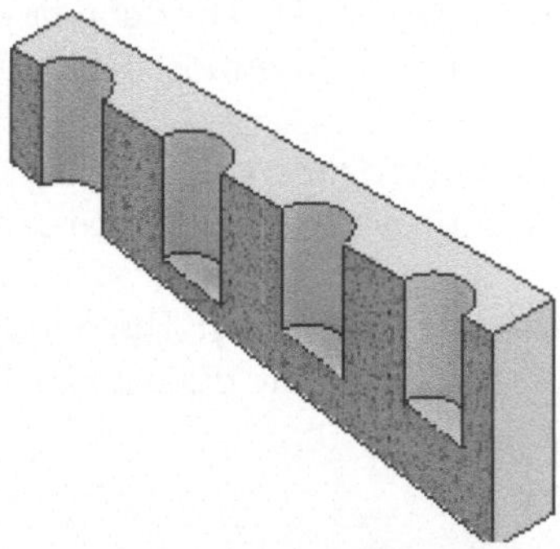

Adjust: The **Adjust** option is used for creating a pattern such that all the pattern occurrences maintain the same geometrical relation as that of the parent feature, see Figure 9.19. In this figure, the pattern occurrences maintain the geometrical relation of the parent feature which is the bottom face of the model, as the end condition.

9.19

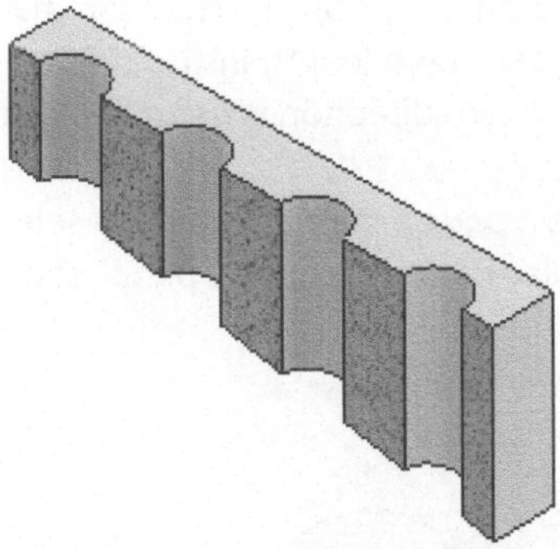

Orientation: The options the **Orientation** drop-down list of the **Output Geometry** rollout are used for defining the orientation of the pattern occurrences with respect to the parent feature. The options are discussed below:

Identical: The **Identical** option in the **Orientation** drop-down list is used for maintaining the orientation of the pattern occurrences same as the parent feature, see Figure 9.20.

9.20

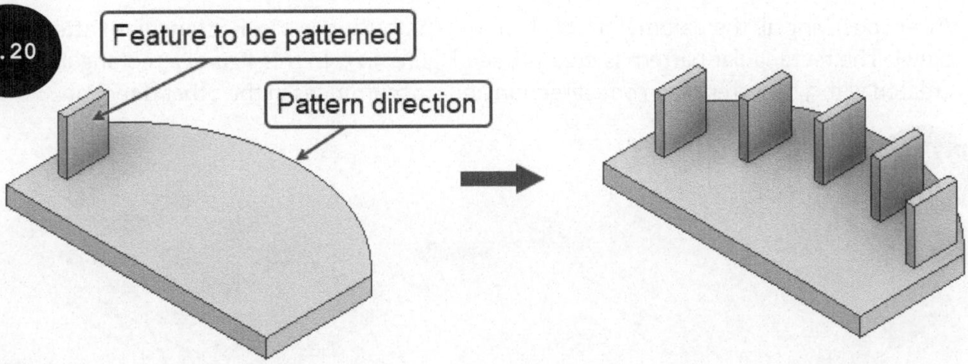

Note: In Figure 9.20, a curve is selected to define the first pattern direction. On selecting a curve as a pattern direction, the **Start Point** selector enabled in the respective rollout of the property panel. This field allows you to define the start point along the selected curve from which the pattern instances will be created.

Direction 1: The **Direction 1** option is used for maintaining the orientation of the pattern occurrences relative to the curve length in the first pattern direction, see Figure 9.21.

9.21

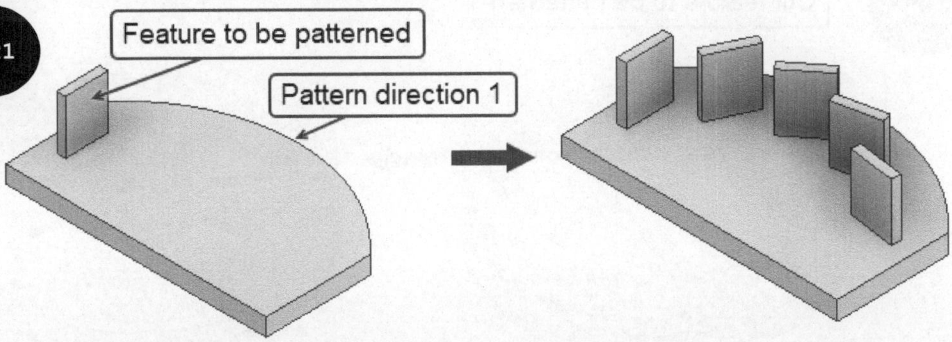

Direction 2: The **Direction 2** option is used for maintaining the orientation of the pattern occurrences relative to the curve length in the second pattern direction. This option is enabled only when the second pattern direction is defined by selecting a curve or a curved edge.

Tip: You can also create a pattern along a path, by selecting a curve as the first pattern direction using the **Rectangular Pattern** property panel, see Figure 9.22.

9.22

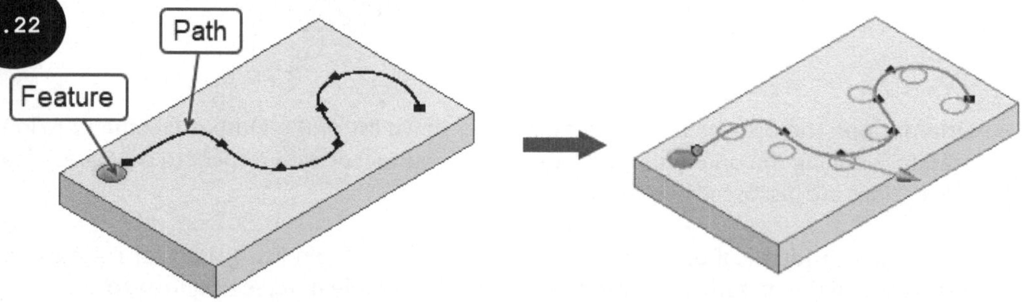

14. After specifying all the parameters, click on the **OK** button in the **Rectangular Pattern** property panel. The rectangular pattern is created, see Figure 9.23. In this figure, a rectangular pattern is created with 3 occurrences in one direction and 5 occurrences in the other direction.

9.23

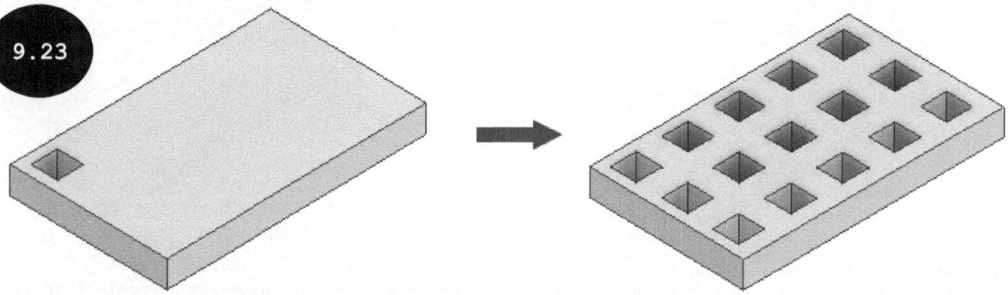

Creating a Circular Pattern

You can create a circular pattern by creating multiple occurrences of features or bodies, circularly around an axis by using the **Circular Pattern** tool, see Figure 9.24. The method for creating a circular pattern is discussed below:

9.24

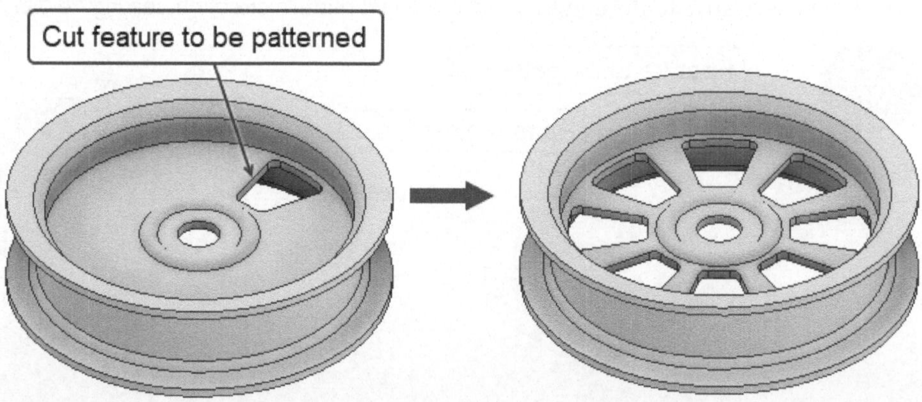

1. Click on the **Circular Pattern** tool in the **Pattern** panel of the **3D Model** tab, see Figure 9.25. The **Circular Pattern** property panel appears, see Figure 9.26. Also, you are prompted to select features to be patterned.

9.25

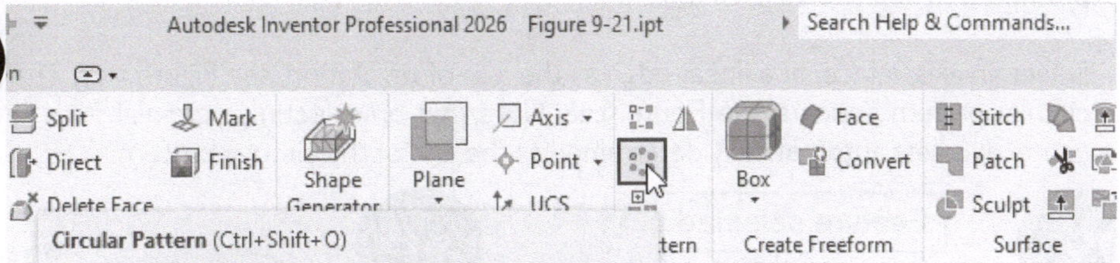

9.26

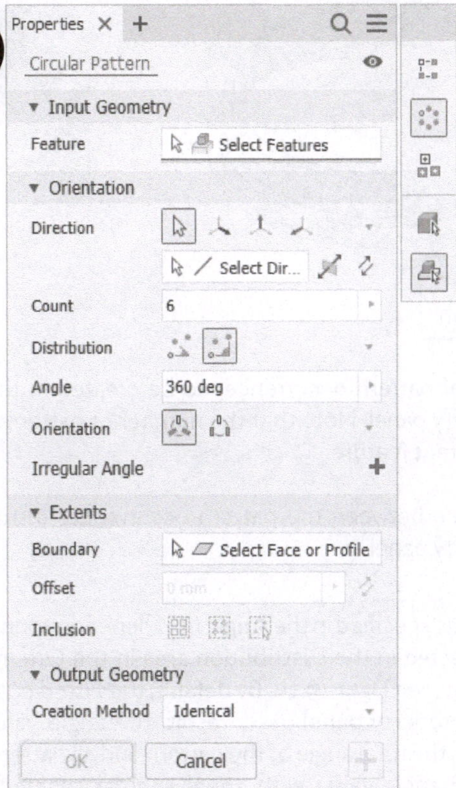

2. Select one or more features of the model to be patterned in the graphics area or in the **Browser**.

Note: By default, the **Pattern individual features** button is activated in the **Circular Pattern** property panel. As a result, you can select features of the model to be patterned. To select the entire model or bodies to be patterned, you need to activate the **Pattern solids** button in the tool palette of the property panel, as discussed earlier.

After selecting features to be patterned, you need to select an axis of revolution.

3. Click on the **Select Direction** selector below the **Direction** area of the property panel. You are prompted to define an axis of rotation.

4. Select an axis, a face, or a linear edge as the axis of revolution, see Figure 9.27. The preview of a circular pattern appears, see Figure 9.28. Note that on selecting a circular face, the respective center axis gets automatically determined as the axis of the circular pattern.

9.27

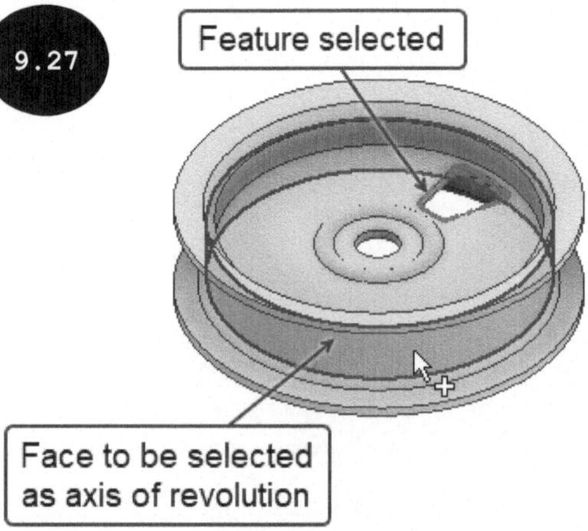

9.28

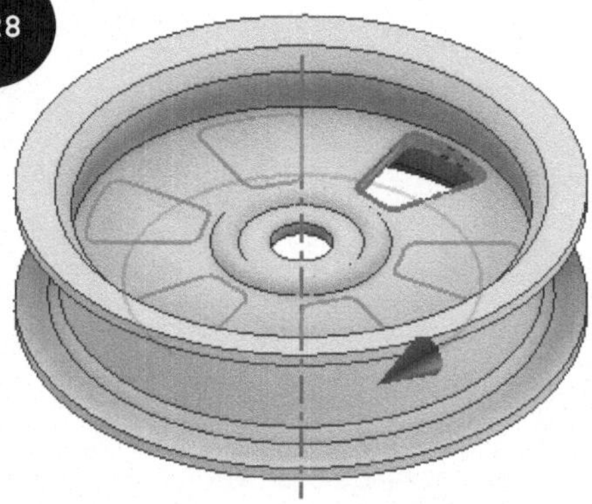

5. Enter the number of pattern occurrences to be created in the **Count** field of the **Orientation** rollout in the property panel. Note that the number of pattern occurrences specified in this field also includes the parent feature.

6. Enter the angle value between the pattern occurrences in the **Angle** field of the **Orientation** rollout in the property panel.

Note: The angle value specified in the **Angle** field depends upon whether the **Fitted** or **Incremental** button is selected in the **Distribution** area in the **Orientation** rollout of **Circular Pattern** property panel, see Figure 9.29. By default, the **Fitted** button is selected in the **Distribution** area of the property panel. As a result, the angle value specified in the **Angle** field is considered as the total angle of the pattern and all pattern occurrences are arranged within the specified angle value with equal angular spacing among them. On selecting the **Incremental** button, the angle value specified in the **Angle** field is used as the angle between two consecutive pattern occurrences. The options in the **Creation Method** area of the expanded property panel are same as discussed earlier.

9.29

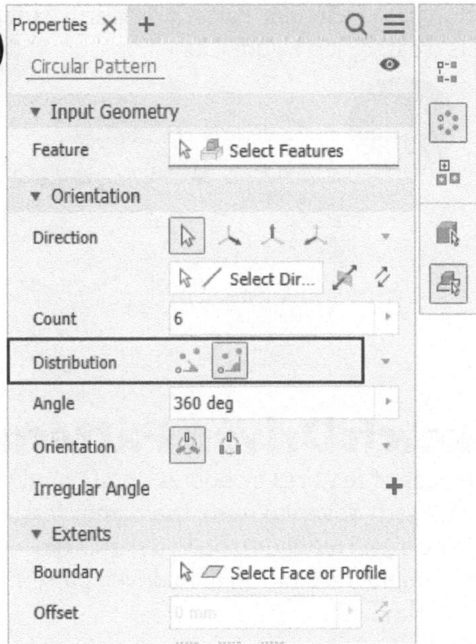

Boundary Area: The options in the **Boundary** area of the property panel are used to create pattern instances within a defined boundary. These options are the same as discussed earlier.

7. Define a type of orientation for the pattern occurrences by activating the **Rotational** or **Fixed** button in the **Orientation** area of the property panel. By default, the **Rotational** button is activated. As a result, the orientation of the pattern occurrences changes as they rotate around the axis of revolution, see Figure 9.30. On activating the **Fixed** button, the orientation of the pattern occurrences remains identical to the parent feature as they rotate around the axis of revolution, see Figure 9.31.

9.30

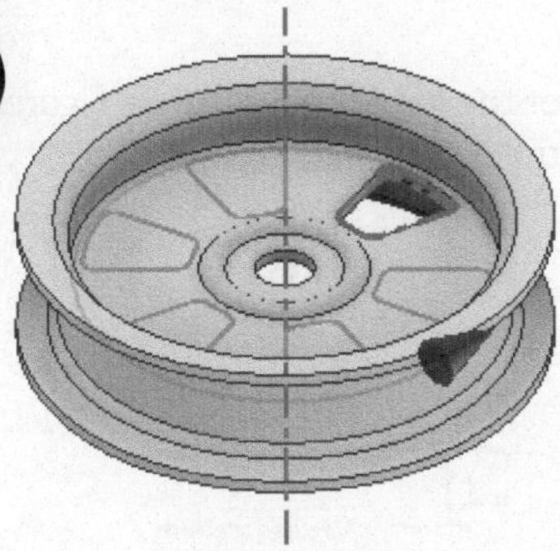

9.31

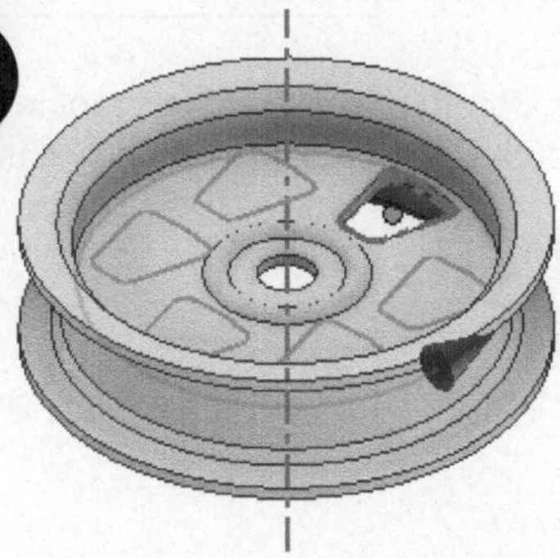

Tip: On activating the **Fixed** button in the **Orientation** area of the property panel, the center of the parent feature gets automatically selected as a base point for creating the pattern occurrences with the fixed orientation. However, you can redefine the base point by selecting a vertex or a point using the **Base Point** field in the **Base Point** area of the property panel.

8. Click on the **OK** button in the **Circular Pattern** property panel. A circular pattern with specified pattern instances gets created, see Figure 9.32.

9.32

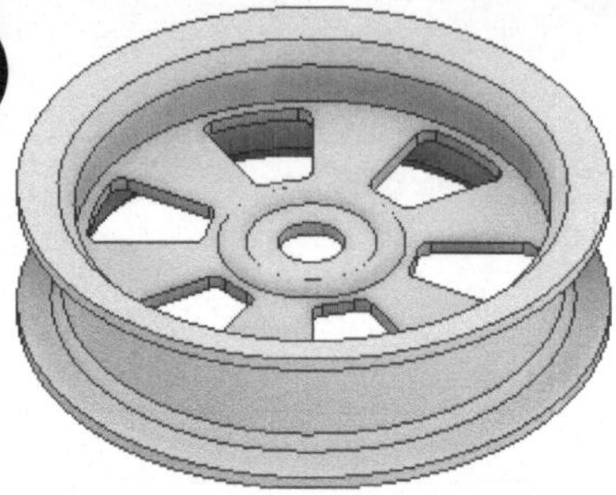

Creating a Sketch Driven Pattern

Creating multiple occurrences of features or bodies on 2D or 3D sketch points of a sketch forms a sketch driven pattern. In a sketch driven pattern, the parent feature gets propagated to each sketch point of the sketch, see Figure 9.33. This figure shows a sketch having multiple points, features (extrude and fillet) to be patterned, and the resultant sketch driven pattern. The method for creating a sketch driven pattern is discussed below:

9.33

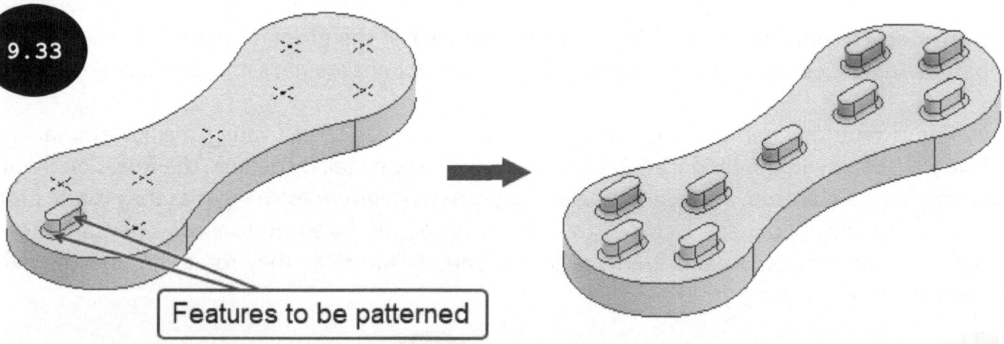

1. Click on the **Sketch Driven** tool in the **Pattern** panel of the **3D Model** tab, see Figure 9.34. The **Sketch Driven Pattern** property panel appears, see Figure 9.35.

9.34

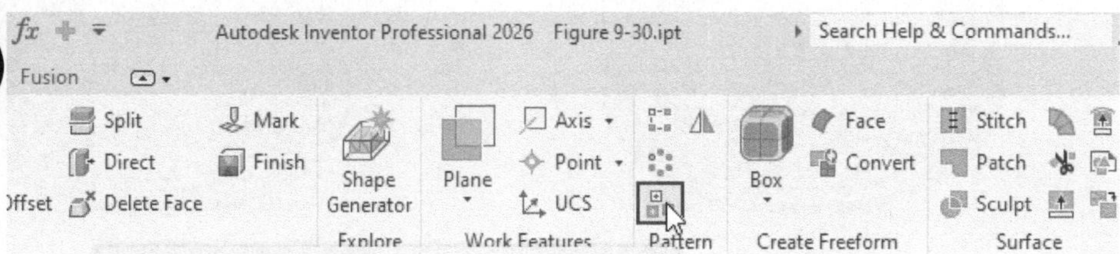

9.35

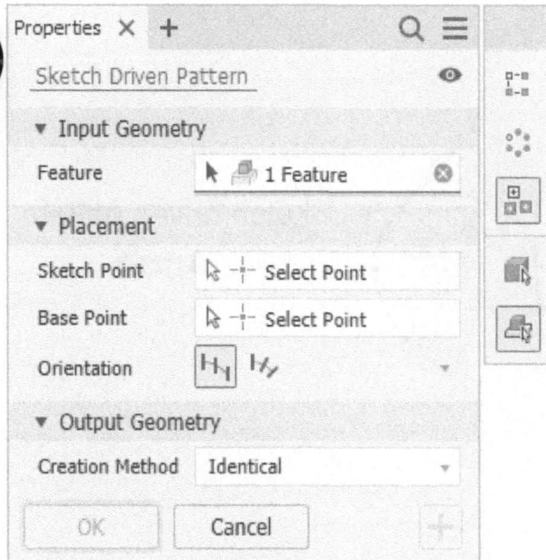

2. Select one or more features of the model to be patterned in the graphics area or in the **Browser**.

Note: By default, the **Pattern individual features** button is activated in the tool palette of the **Sketch Driven Pattern** property panel. As a result, you can select features of a model to be patterned. To select the entire model or bodies to be patterned, you need to activate the **Pattern solids** button in the tool palette, as discussed earlier.

After selecting features to be patterned, you need to select a sketch having multiple points for driving the pattern occurrences.

3. Click on the **Select Point** selector to select the **Sketch Point** area in the **Placement** rollout of the property panel. You are prompted to select a 2D or 3D sketch.

4. Select a sketch having multiple sketch points in the graphics area or in the **Browser**. The preview of a sketch driven pattern appears such that the parent feature gets propagated to each sketch point of the sketch, see Figures 9.36 and 9.37. In Figure 9.36, a 2D sketch is selected and in Figure 9.37, a 3D sketch is selected.

9.36

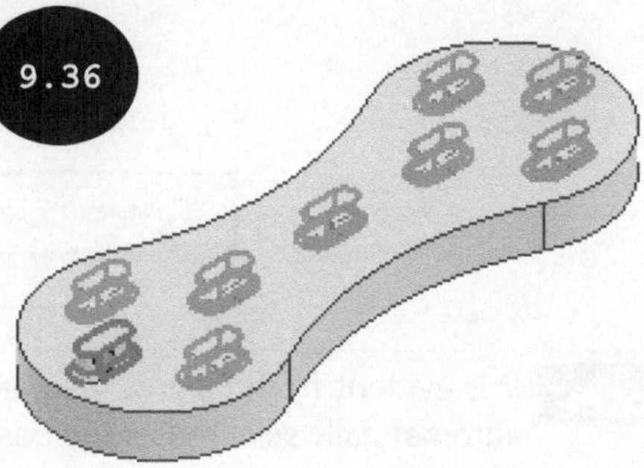

9.37

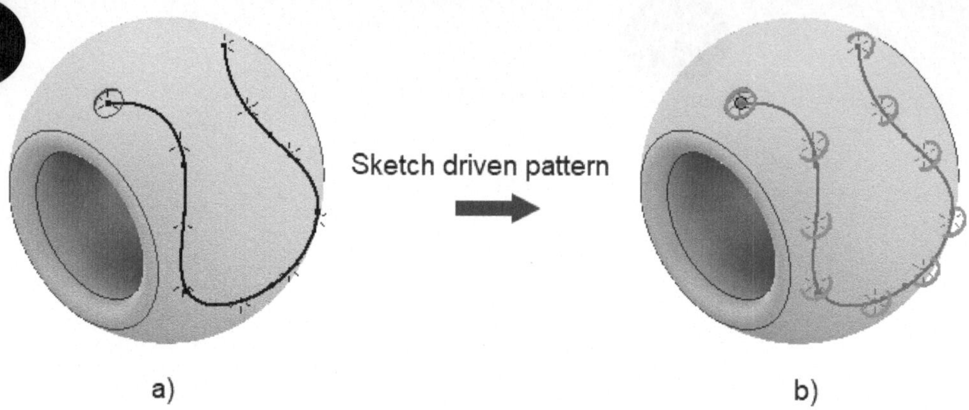

Tip: In Figure 9.37 (a), a 3D curve is created on the curved face of the model by using the **Curve On Face** tool in the 3D Sketching environment and then sketch points are created on the 3D curve at a particular distance. To invoke the 3D Sketching environment, click on the arrow at the **Start 2D Sketch** tool in the **3D Model** tab of the **Ribbon** and then click on the **Start 3D Sketch** tool in the flyout that appears, see Figure 9.38. You will learn more about creating 3D sketches in the 3D Sketching environment in later chapters.

9.38

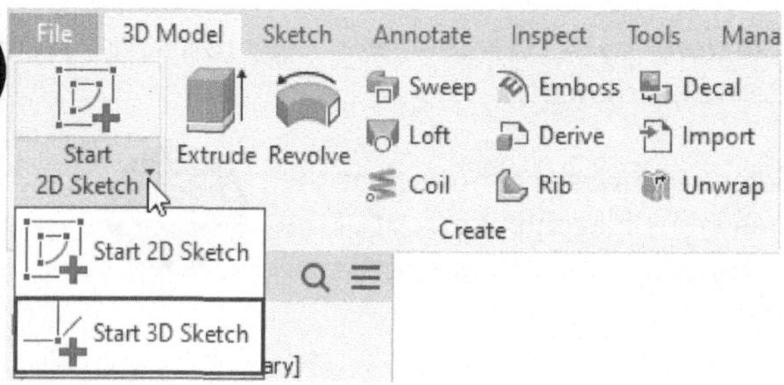

Note: It is evident from Figures 9.36 and 9.37, that the center point of the parent feature gets automatically selected as the base point of the pattern occurrences. Also, the orientation of the pattern occurrences is identical to the parent feature, by default. You can change the base point of the pattern occurrences and the orientation by using the **Base Point** field and **Referance Faces** field in the **Placement** rollout of the property panel. To change the base point, click on the **Base Point** field in the **Placement** rollout and then select a vertex or a sketch point, refer to Figure 9.39. Also, to change the orientation of the pattern occurrences, click on the **Follow Faces** button in the **Orientation** area and then select a face of the model. Figure 9.39 shows a sketch point to be selected as a base point and a curved face to be selected for defining the orientation of the pattern occurrences. Figure 9.40 shows a preview of the resultant ketch driven pattern.

9.39

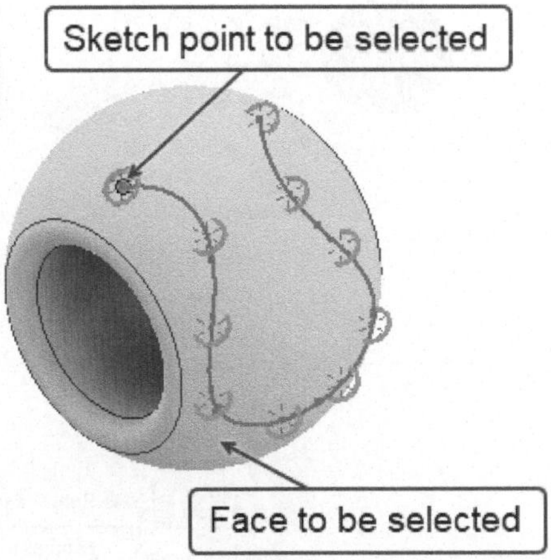

9.40

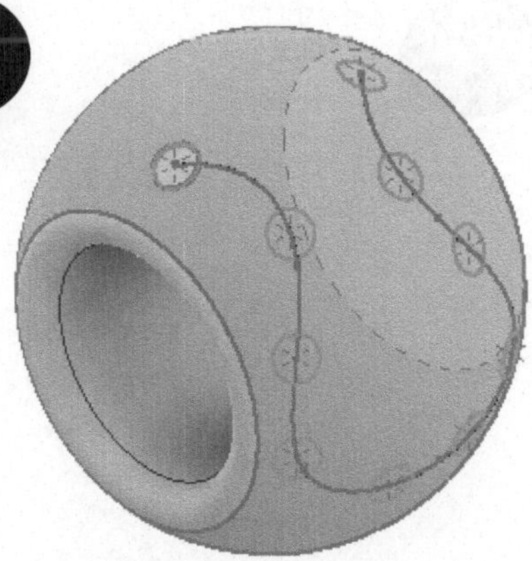

5. Click on the **OK** button in the **Sketch Driven Pattern** property panel. A sketch driven pattern gets created such that the parent feature gets propagated to each sketch point of the sketch, see Figures 9.41 and 9.42.

9.41

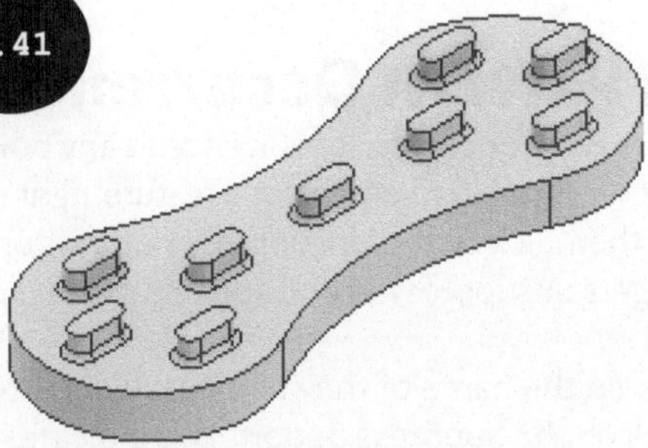

9.42

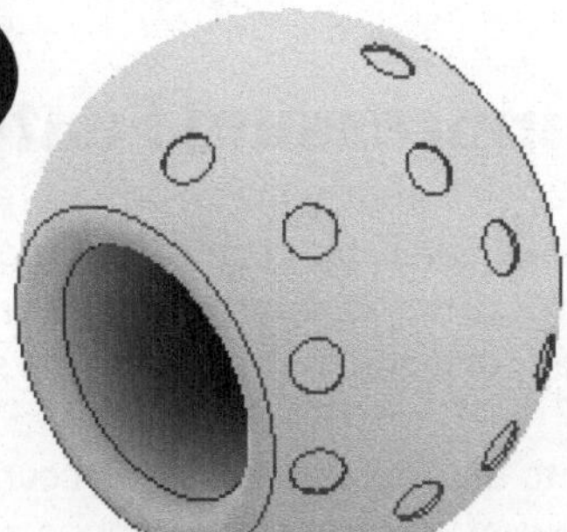

Suppressing Features and Pattern Occurrences

In Autodesk Inventor, you can suppress the features of a model as well as the individual pattern occurrences. The suppressed feature or pattern occurrence is removed from the model and does not appear in the graphics area. Also, the name of the suppressed feature or pattern occurrence appears in gray, and struck through its center in the **Browser**. Note that the suppressed feature or pattern occurrence is not deleted from the model, it is only removed such that it does not load into the RAM (Random Access Memory) while rebuilding the model. This helps you to speed up the overall performance of the system when you are working with complex models. Also, suppressing pattern occurrences allows you to remove or skip the unwanted occurrences from a pattern.

To suppress a feature of a model, right-click on the feature to be suppressed in the **Browser** and then click on the **Suppress Features** option in the shortcut menu that appears, see Figure 9.43. The selected feature gets suppressed and no longer appears in the graphics area. Similarly, to suppress a pattern occurrence, expand the node of the pattern feature in the **Browser**. Next, right-click on the pattern occurrence to be suppressed and then click on the **Suppress** option in the shortcut menu that appears, see Figure 9.44.

9.43

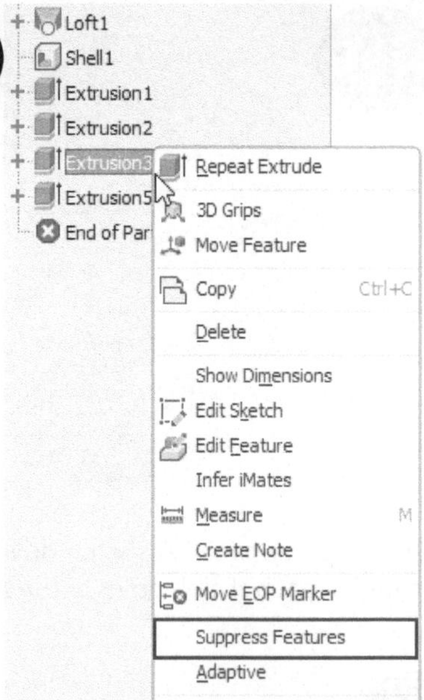

9.44

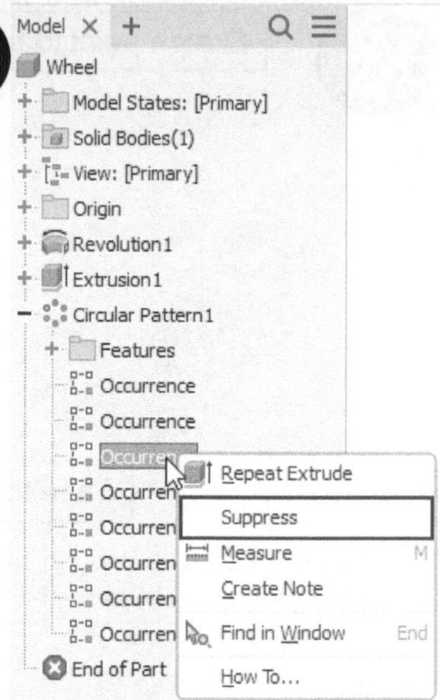

Unsuppressing Features and Pattern Occurrences

In Autodesk Inventor, you can unsuppress a suppressed feature or pattern occurrence at any point in time to make it available in the model and visible in the graphics area. To unsuppress a feature, right-click on the name of the suppressed feature in the **Browser** and then click on the **Unsuppress Features** option in the shortcut menu that appears. The selected feature gets unsuppressed and appears in the model.

Similarly, to unsuppress a pattern occurrence, right-click on the name of the suppressed occurrence in the **Browser**. A shortcut menu appears with a tick-mark on the **Suppress** option. This indicates that the selected occurrence is currently suppressed. Click on the **Suppress** option in the shortcut menu. The selected pattern occurrence gets unsuppressed and becomes a part of the pattern.

Mirroring a Feature or a Body

In Autodesk Inventor, you can mirror features or bodies about a mirroring plane by using the **Mirror** tool. You can select a plane or a planar face of a model as the mirroring plane. Figure 9.45 shows features to be mirrored, mirroring plane, and the resultant mirrored feature. The method for mirroring a feature or a body is discussed below:

9.45

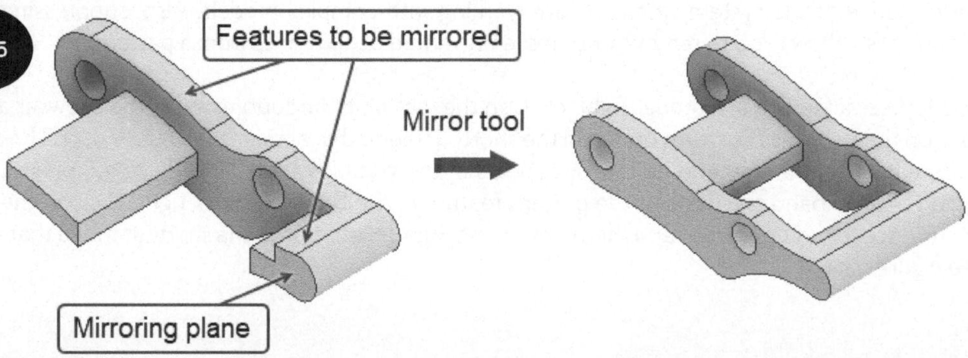

1. Click on the **Mirror** tool in the **Pattern** panel of the **3D Model** tab, see Figure 9.46. The **Mirror** dialog box appears, see Figure 9.47.

9.46

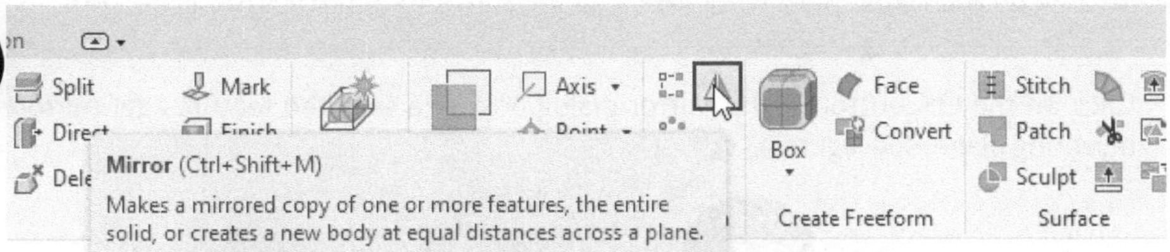

9.47

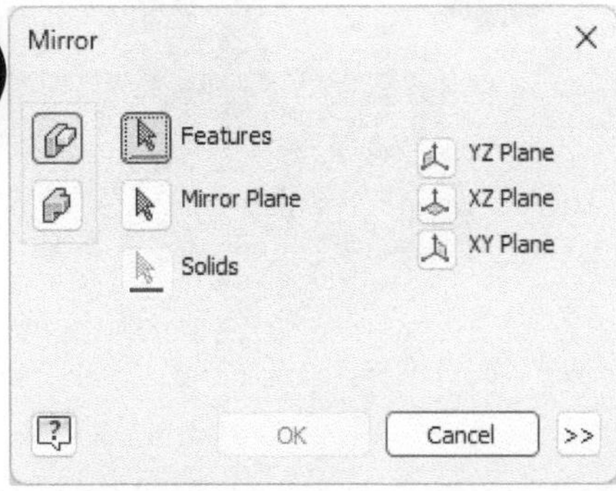

2. Select one or more features of the model to be mirrored in the graphics area or the **Browser**, see Figure 9.48.

Note: By default, the **Mirror individual features** button is activated in the **Mirror** dialog box. As a result, you can select features of the model to be mirrored. To select the entire model or bodies to be mirrored, you need to activate the **Mirror solids** button in the dialog box, as discussed earlier.

After selecting features to be mirrored, you need to select a mirroring plane.

3. Click on the **Mirror Plane** button in the **Mirror** dialog box and then select a plane or a planar face of a model as the mirroring plane, see Figure 9.48. The preview of a mirror feature appears in the graphics area, see Figure 9.49.

9.48

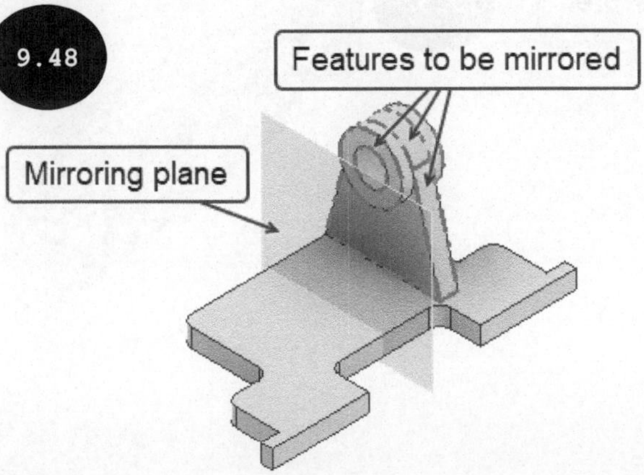

9.49

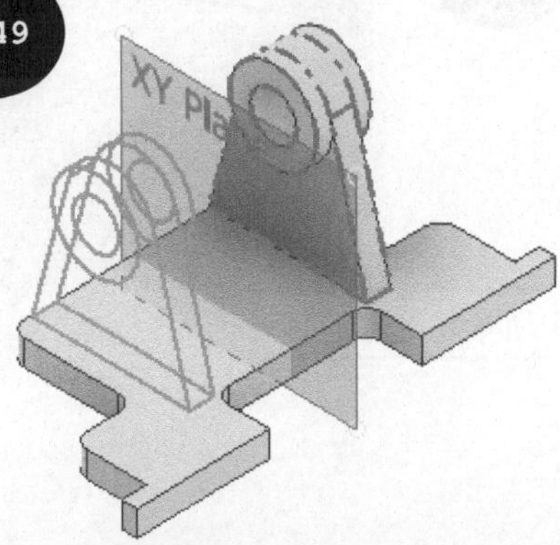

Tip: You can also select a work plane as a mirroring plane by clicking on the **Origin YZ Plane**, **Origin XZ Plane**, or **Origin XY Plane** buttons in the **Mirror** dialog box.

4. Click on the **OK** button in the **Mirror** dialog box. The selected features get mirrored about the mirroring plane, see Figure 9.50.

9.50

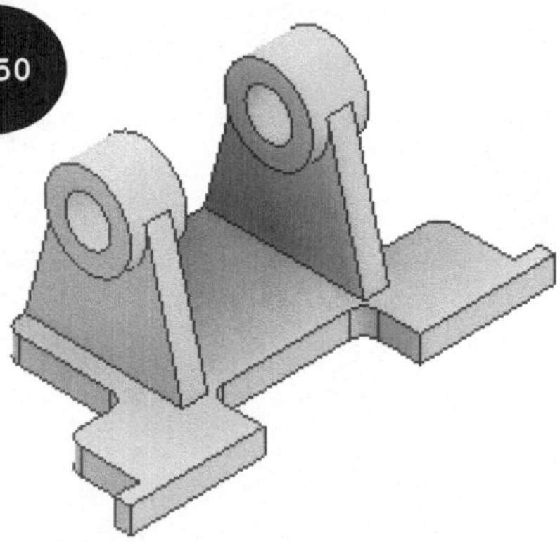

Note: The options in the expanded **Mirror** dialog box are same as discussed earlier. On selecting the **Identical** radio button, the mirrored feature does not maintain the same geometrical relations as that of the parent feature, see Figures 9.51 and 9.52. Figure 9.51 shows the section view of a model, in which the cut feature is created by selecting the bottom face of the model as the end condition or termination of the feature. Figure 9.52 shows the resultant mirror feature created by mirroring the cut feature about a mirroring plane by selecting the **Identical** radio button.

On selecting the **Adjust** radio button, the mirror feature is created such that it maintains the same geometrical relation as that of the parent feature, see Figure 9.53.

9.51

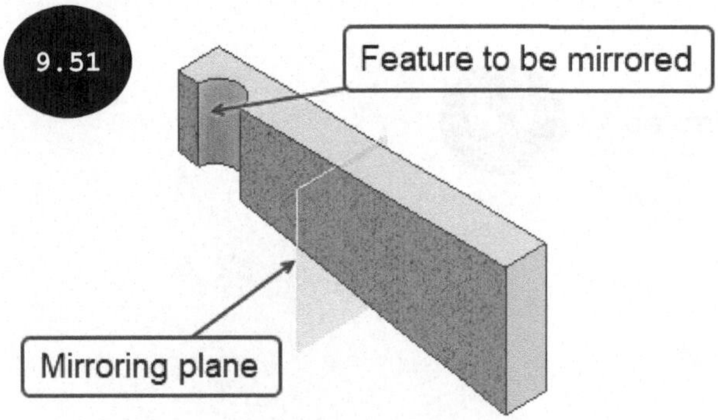

9.52

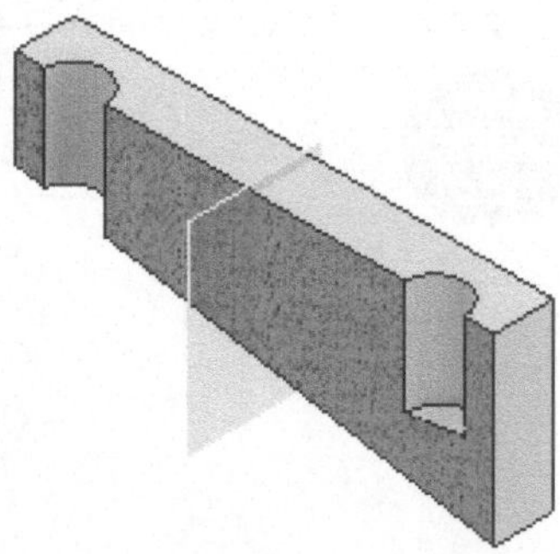

9.53

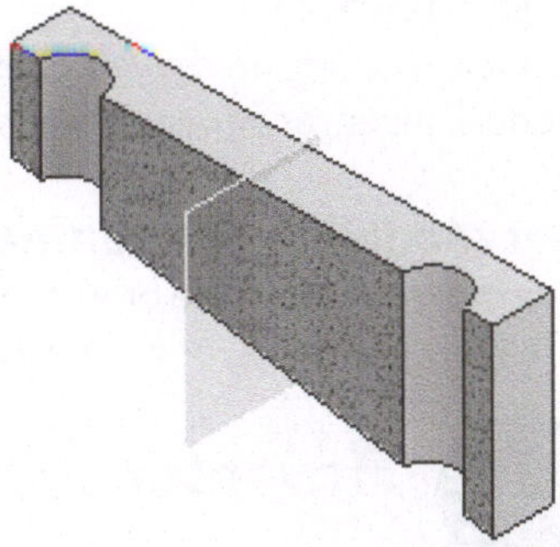

Tutorial 1

Create the model shown in Figure 9.54. All dimensions are in mm.

9.54

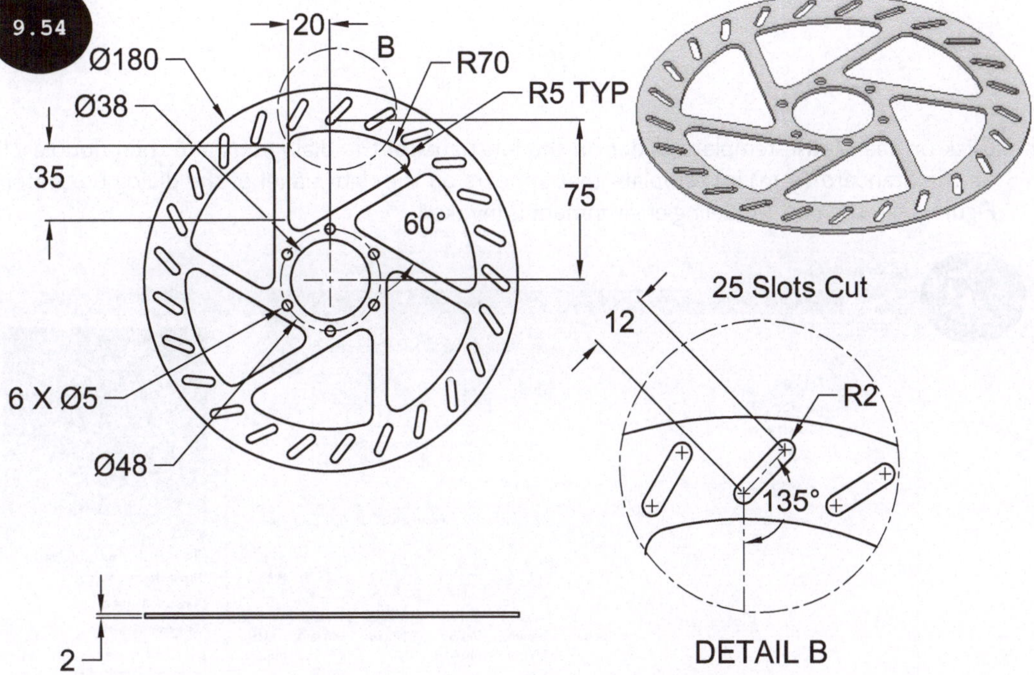

Section 1: Starting Autodesk Inventor

1. Start Autodesk Inventor by double-clicking on the Autodesk Inventor icon on your desktop. The startup user interface of Autodesk Inventor appears.

Section 2: Invoking the Part Modeling Environment

1. Click on the **New** tool in the startup user interface of Autodesk Inventor (see Figure 9.55) or press the CTRL+N keys. The **Create New File** dialog box appears, see Figure 9.56.

9.55

2. Click on the **Metric** template folder on the left panel of the dialog box and then double-click on the **Standard (mm).ipt** template that appears on the right panel of the dialog box, refer to Figure 9.56. The Part Modeling environment is invoked.

9.56

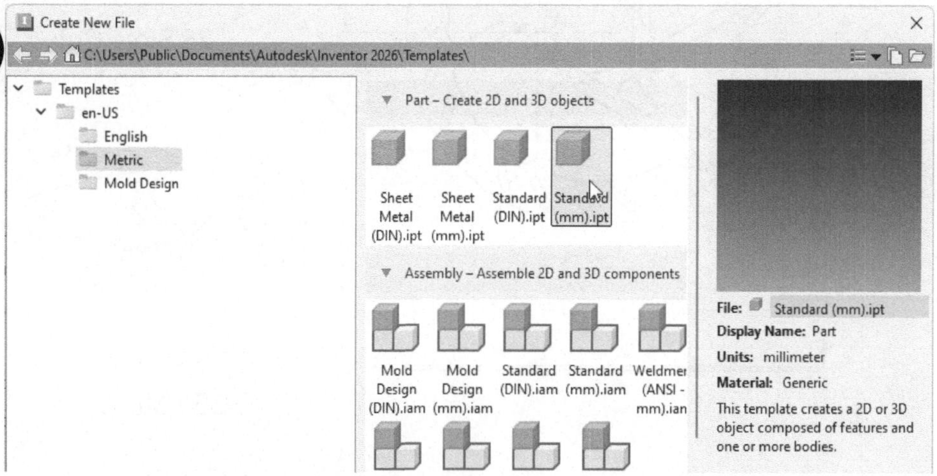

Section 3: Creating the Base Feature - Extrude Feature

1. Invoke the Sketching environment by selecting the Top plane (XZ Plane) as the sketching plane and then create a sketch of the base feature of the model, see Figure 9.57. Note that the center points of both circles are at the origin.

9.57

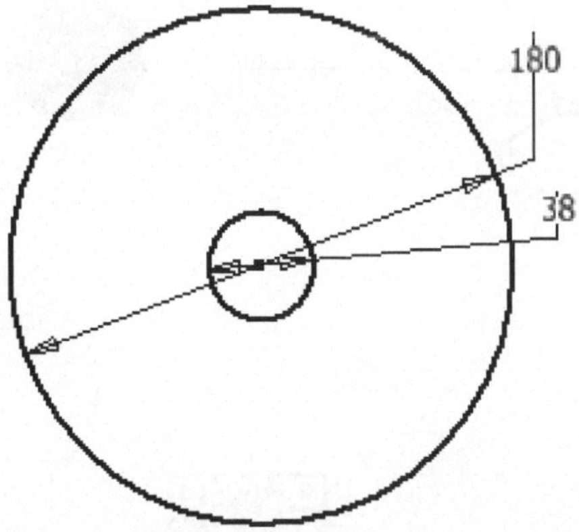

2. Click on the **3D Model** tab in the **Ribbon** and then click on the **Extrude** tool in the **Create** panel. The **Extrusion** property panel appears and you are prompted to select a closed profile.

3. Select the outer closed area of the sketch as the profile to be extruded, see Figure 9.58. The preview of an extruded feature appears in the graphics area.

4. Ensure that the direction of extrusion is upward.

5. Enter **2** in the **Distance A** field of the **Extrusion** property panel as the depth of the extrusion.

6. Click on the **OK** button in the property panel. The base feature (extrude) is created, see Figure 9.59.

9.58

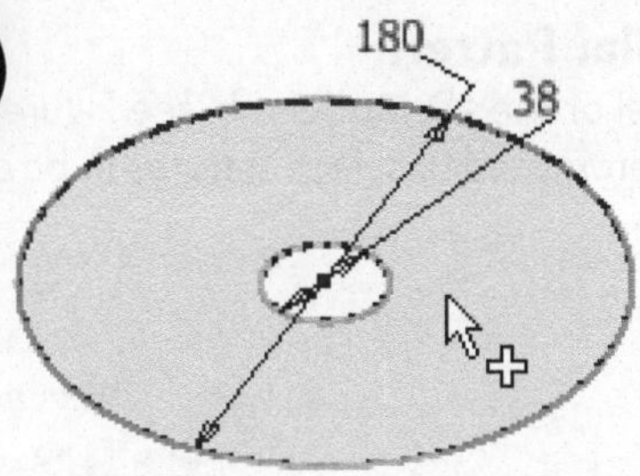

9.59

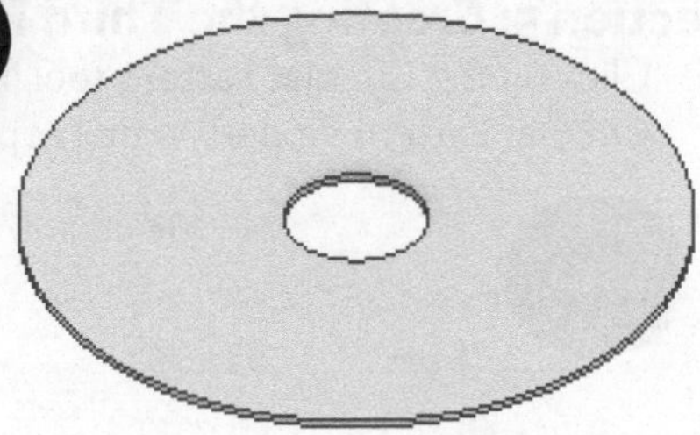

Section 4: Creating the Second Feature - Cut Feature

1. Invoke the Sketching environment by selecting the top planar face of the base feature as the sketching plane.

2. Create the sketch of the second feature, see Figure 9.60.

3. Click on the **3D Model** tab in the **Ribbon** and then click on the **Extrude** tool in the **Create** panel. The **Extrusion** property panel appears. As the sketch has only one closed profile, a preview of the extrude feature appears in the graphics area, see Figure 9.61.

9.60

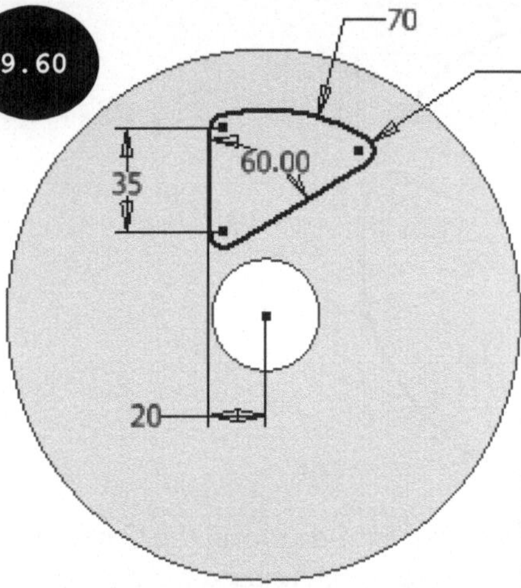

9.61

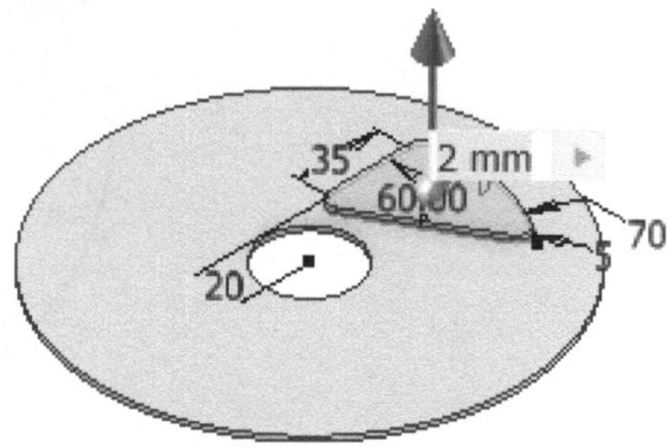

4. Click on the **Through All** button in the **Behavior** rollout of the property panel. The direction of extrusion gets changed to downward and the **Cut** button gets activated automatically in the **Boolean** area of the property panel. Also, a preview of the cut feature appears in the graphics area.

5. Click on the **OK** button in the property panel. The second feature (cut) is created, see Figure 9.62.

9.62

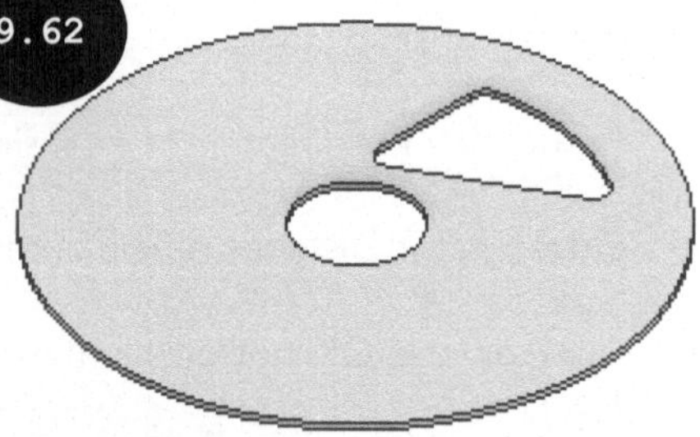

Section 5: Creating the Third Feature - Circular Pattern

1. Click on the **Circular Pattern** tool in the **Pattern** panel of the **3D Model** tab, see Figure 9.63. The **Circular Pattern** property panel appears and you are prompted to select features to be patterned.

9.63

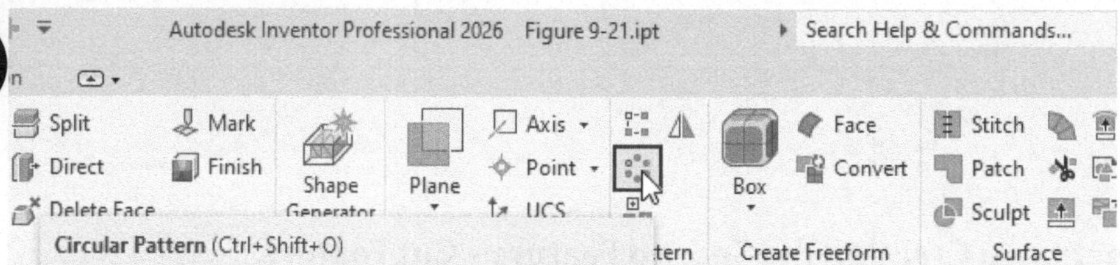

2. Select the second feature (cut feature) of the model in the graphics area or the **Browser** as the feature to be patterned.

   Now, you need to define the axis of revolution.

3. Click on the **Select Direction** selector below the **Direction** area of the property panel and then click on the outer circular face of the base feature to define the axis of revolution, see Figure 9.64. A preview of the circular pattern appears in the graphics area, see Figure 9.65.

9.64

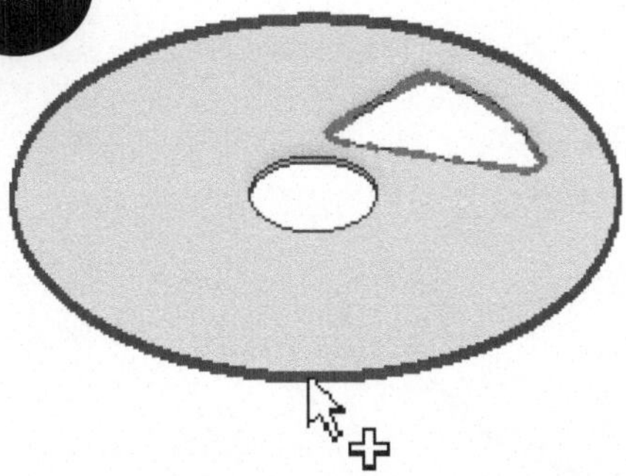

9.65

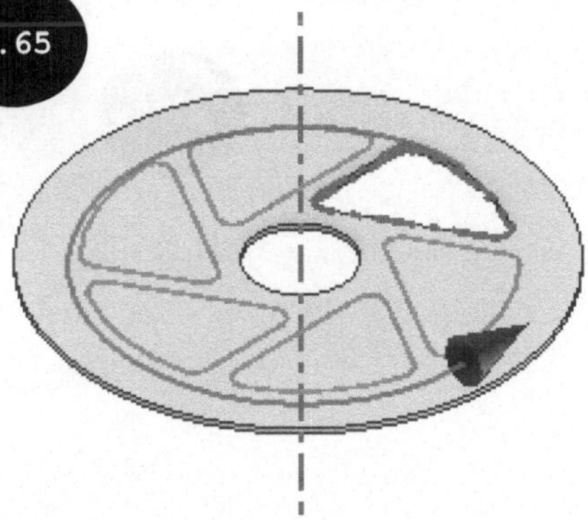

4. Enter **6** in the **Count** field in the **Orientation** rollout of the property panel.

5. Ensure that a **360** degrees angle value is specified in the **Angle** field of the **Orientation** rollout in the property panel.

6. Ensure that the **Fitted** button is selected in the **Distribution** area of the **Circular Pattern** property panel, see Figure 9.66.

9.66

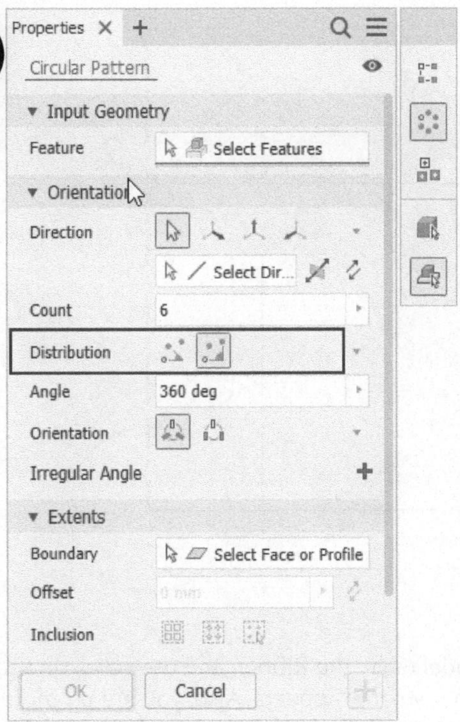

7. Click on the **OK** button in the property panel. The circular pattern is created, see Figure 9.67.

9.67

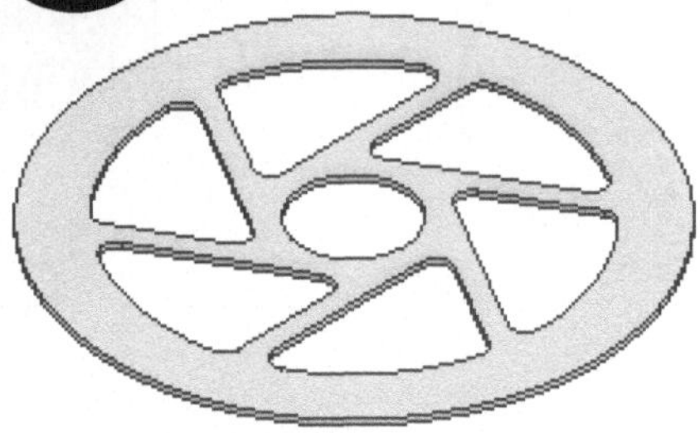

Section 6: Creating the Fourth Feature - Cut Feature

1. Invoke the Sketching environment by selecting the top planar face of the base feature as the sketching plane.

2. Create the sketch of the fourth feature of the model, see Figure 9.68.

9.68

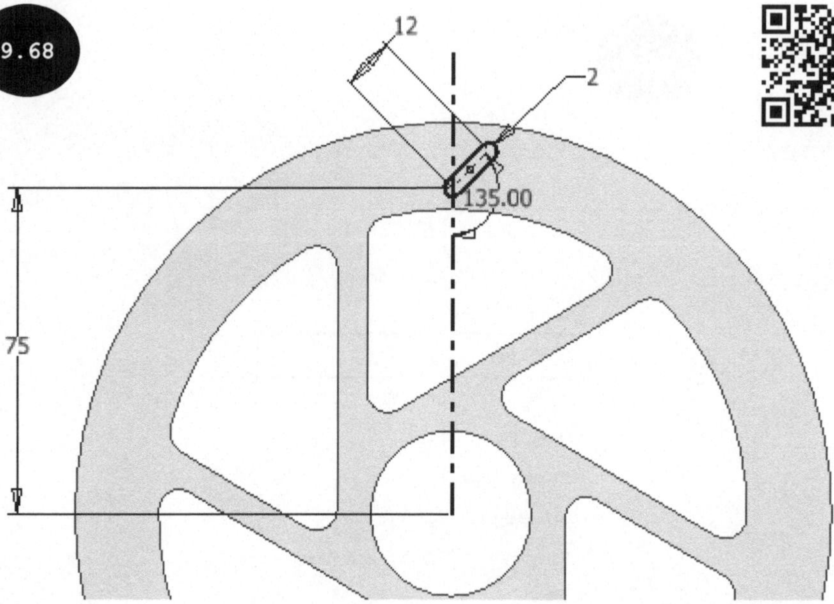

3. Click on the **3D Model** tab in the **Ribbon** and then click on the **Extrude** tool in the **Create** panel. The **Extrusion** property panel appears. Also, you are prompted to select a closed profile of the sketch.

4. Move the cursor over an entity of the sketch and then click when the complete closed profile of the sketch gets highlighted in the graphics area, see Figure 9.69.

9.69

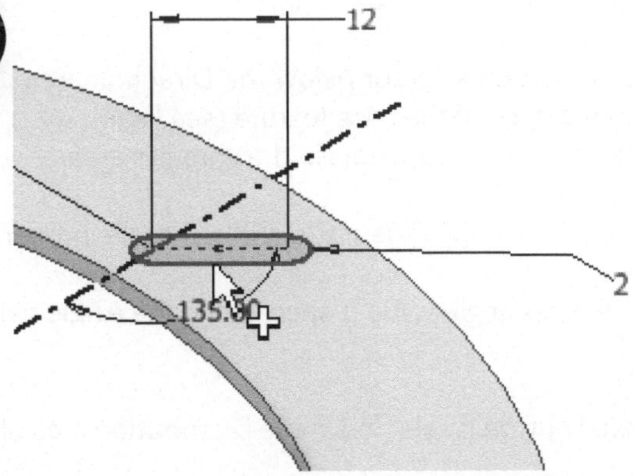

5. Click on the **Through All** button in the **Behavior** rollout of the property panel. The direction of extrusion gets changed to downward and the **Cut** button gets activated automatically in the **Boolean** area of the property panel. Also, a preview of the cut feature appears in the graphics area.

6. Click on the **OK** button in the property panel. The cut feature gets created, see Figure 9.70.

9.70

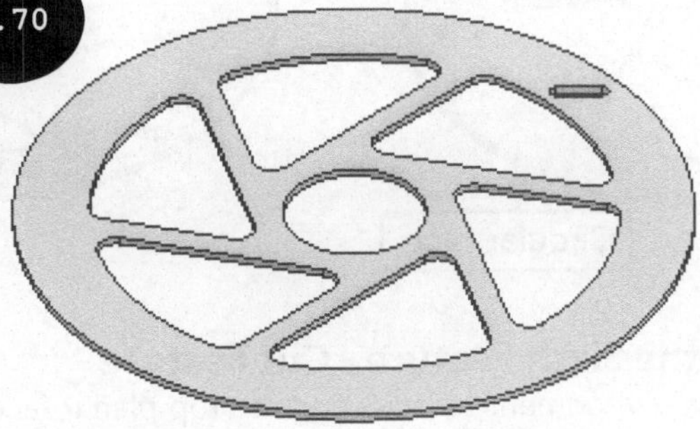

Section 7: Creating the Fifth Feature - Circular Pattern

1. Click on the **Circular Pattern** tool in the **Pattern** panel of the **3D Model** tab, see Figure 9.71. The **Circular Pattern** property panel appears and you are prompted to select features to be patterned.

9.71

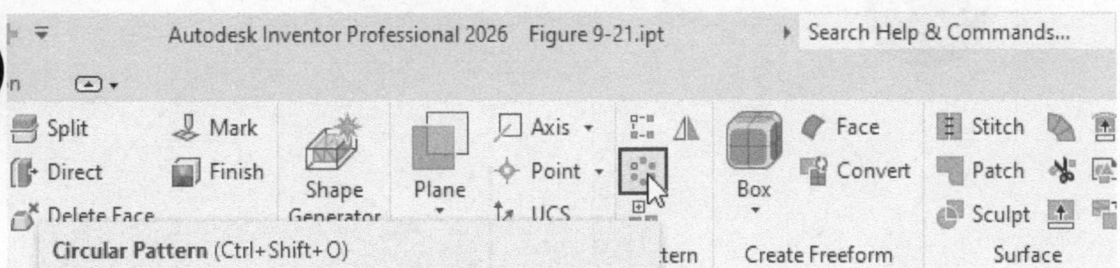

2. Select the fourth feature (previously created cut feature) of the model in the graphics area or the **Browser** as the feature to be patterned.

Now, you need to define the axis of revolution.

3. Click on the **Select Direction** selector below the **Direction** area of the property panel and then select the outer circular face of the base feature (see Figure 9.72) to define an axis of revolution. A preview of the circular pattern appears in the graphics area.

4. Enter **25** in the **Count** field in the **Orientation** rollout of the property panel.

5. Ensure that a **360** degrees angle value is specified in the **Angle** field of the **Orientation** rollout in the property panel.

6. Ensure that the **Fitted** button is selected in the **Distribution** area of the expanded property panel.

7. Click on the **OK** button in the property panel. The circular pattern is created, see Figure 9.73.

9.72

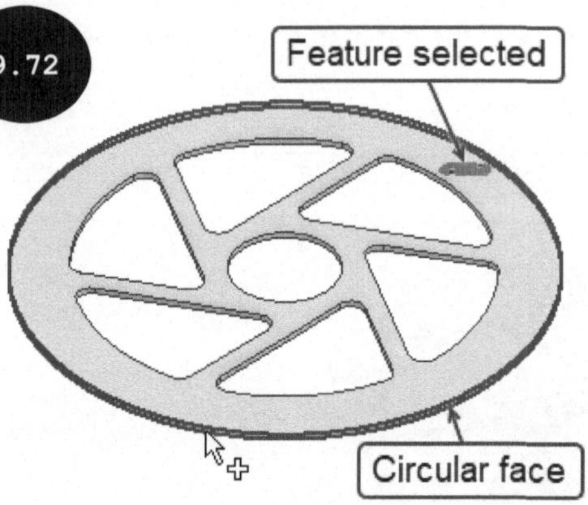

9.73

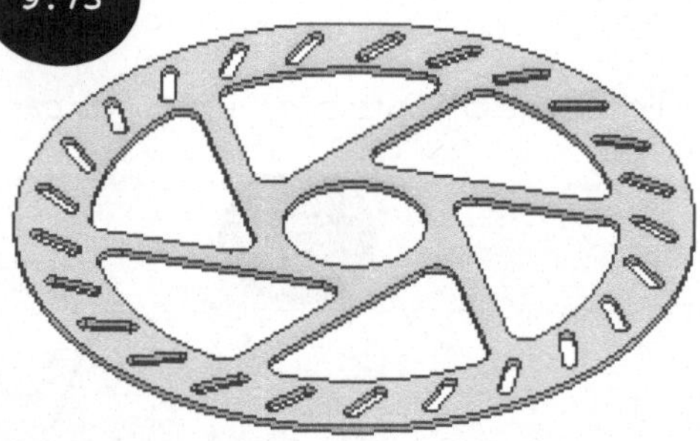

Section 8: Creating the Sixth Feature - Cut Feature

1. Invoke the Sketching environment by selecting the top planar face of the base feature as the sketching plane.

2. Create the sketch of the sixth feature (circle of diameter 5 mm), see Figure 9.74.

9.74

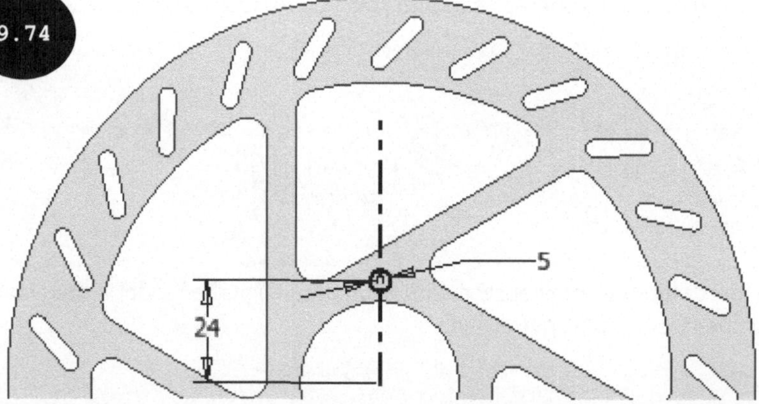

3. Click on the **3D Model** tab in the **Ribbon** and then click on the **Extrude** tool in the **Create** panel. The **Extrusion** property panel appears and you are prompted to select a closed profile.

4. Select the closed profile of the circle. A preview of the extrude feature appears.

5. Click on the **Through All** button in the **Behavior** rollout of the property panel. The direction of extrusion gets changed to downward and the **Cut** button gets activated automatically in the **Boolean** area of the property panel. Also, a preview of the cut feature appears.

6. Click on the **OK** button in the property panel. The cut feature gets created, see Figure 9.75.

9.75

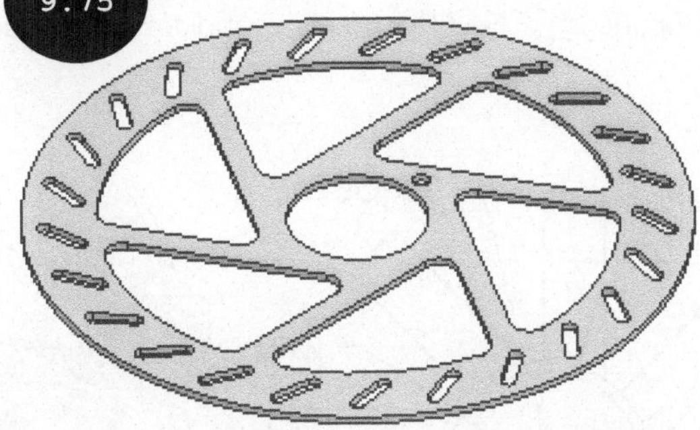

Section 9: Creating the Seventh Feature - Circular Pattern

1. Click on the **Circular Pattern** tool in the **Pattern** panel of the **3D Model** tab. The **Circular Pattern** property panel appears and you are prompted to select features to be patterned.

2. Select the sixth feature (previously created cut feature) of the model in the graphics area or the **Browser** as the feature to be patterned.

   Now, you need to define the axis of revolution.

3. Click on the **Select Direction** selector below the **Direction** area of the property panel and then select the outer circular face of the base feature to define the axis of revolution. A preview of the circular pattern appears in the graphics area.

4. Enter **6** in the **Count** field in the **Orientation** rollout of the property panel.

5. Ensure that a **360** degrees angle value is specified in the **Angle** field of the **Orientation** rollout in the property panel.

6. Click on the **OK** button in the property panel. The circular pattern is created, see Figure 9.76.

9.76

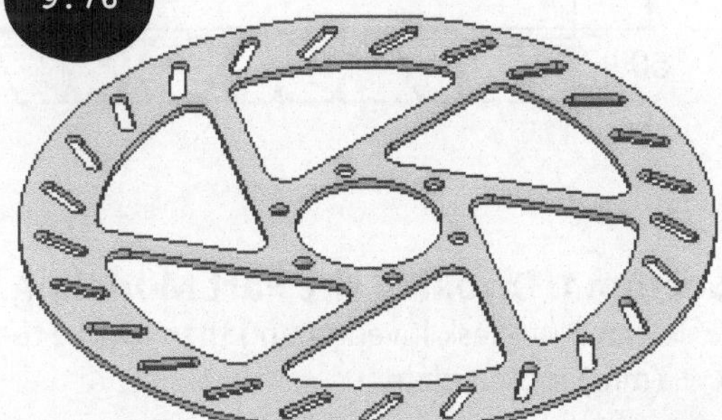

Section 10: Saving the Model

1. Click on the **Save** tool in the **Quick Access Toolbar** toolbar. The **Save As** property panel appears.

2. Browse to **Autodesk Inventor > Chapter 9** folder in the local drive of your system. Note that you need to create a Chapter 9 folder inside the Autodesk Inventor folder.

3. Enter **Tutorial 1** in the **File name** field of the property panel and then click on the **Save** button. The model is saved in the specified location (>:\Autodesk Inventor\Chapter 9).

Tutorial 2

Create the model shown in Figure 9.77. The different views and dimensions are given in the same figure. All dimensions are in mm.

9.77

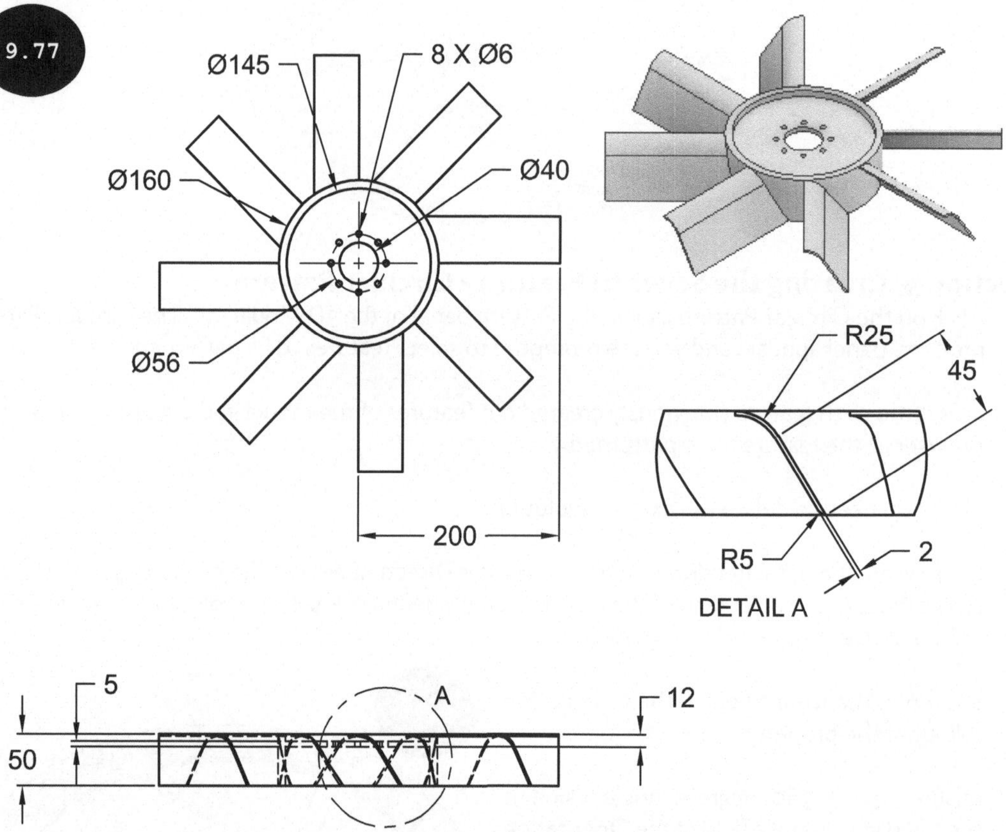

Section 1: Invoking the Part Modeling Environment

1. Start Autodesk Inventor and then invoke the Part modeling environment by using the **Standard (mm).ipt** template.

Section 2: Creating the Base Feature - Extrude Feature

1. Invoke the Sketching environment by selecting the Top plane (XZ Plane) as the sketching plane.

2. Create the sketch of the base feature of the model, see Figure 9.78. Note that the center points of both the circles are at the origin.

3. Click on the **3D Model** tab in the **Ribbon** and then click on the **Extrude** tool in the **Create** panel. The **Extrusion** property panel appears and you are prompted to select a closed profile.

4. Select the outer closed area of the sketch as the profile to be extruded, see Figure 9.79. A preview of the extrude feature appears in the graphics area.

9.78

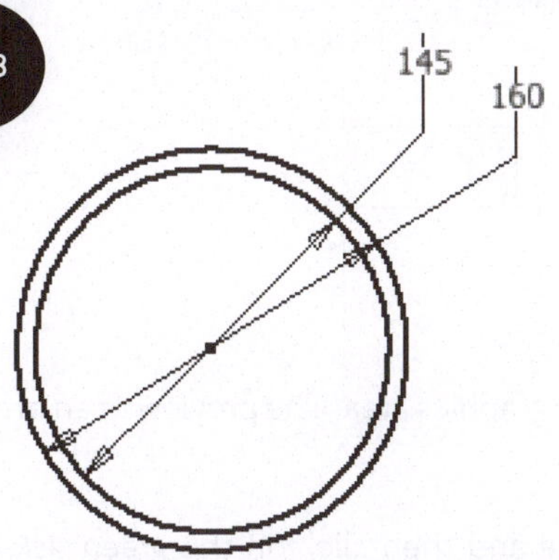

9.79

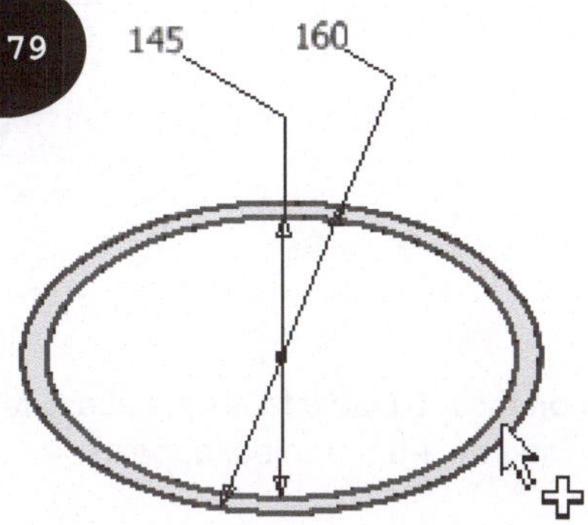

5. Enter **50** in the **Distance A** field of the **Extrusion** property panel as the depth of the extrusion.

6. Click on the **Symmetric** button in the **Direction** area of the **Behavior** rollout in the property panel. A preview of the extrude feature appears such that the material is added symmetrically on both sides of the sketching plane, see Figure 9.80.

7. Click on the **OK** button in the **Extrusion** property panel. The extrude feature gets created, see Figure 9.81.

9.80

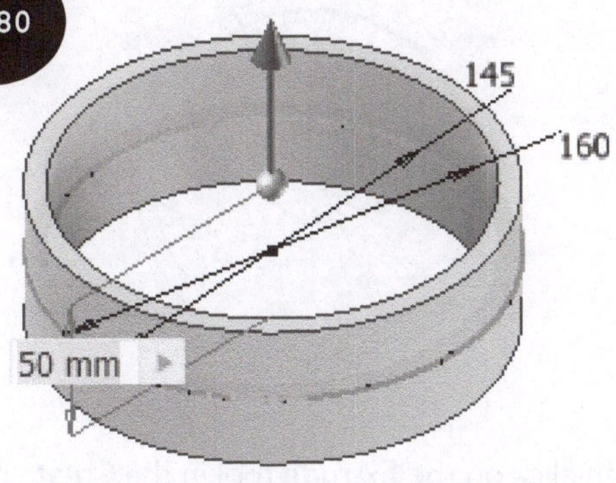

9.81

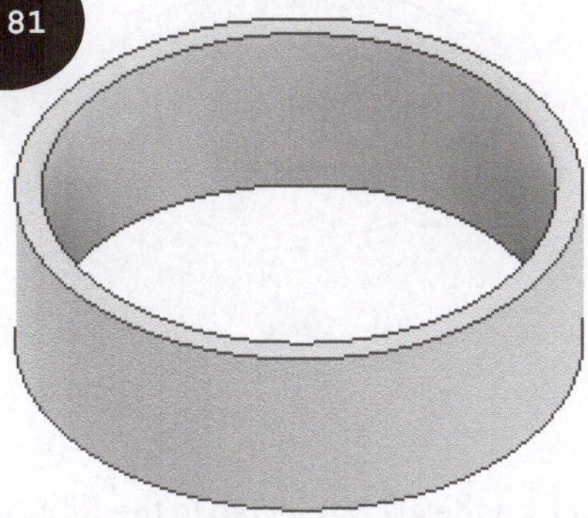

Section 3: Creating the Second Feature - Extrude Feature

To create the second feature of the model, you first need to create a work plane at an offset distance of 12 mm from the top planar face of the model.

1. Invoke the **Plane** flyout in the **Work Features** panel of the **3D Model** tab and then click on the **Offset from Plane** tool, see Figure 9.82.

9.82

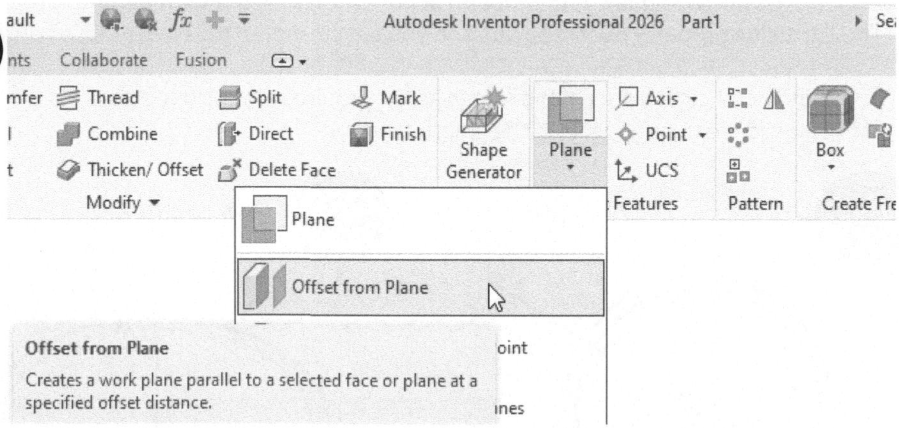

2. Click on the top planar face of the base feature in the graphics area. The preview of an offset work plane and the Mini-Toolbar appears.

3. Enter **-12** in the Mini-Toolbar as the offset distance and then click on the green tick-mark. A work plane at an offset distance of 12 mm from the top planar face of the model is created, see Figure 9.83. Note that the negative offset value is entered to reverse the direction of the offset plane to downward.

4. Invoke the Sketching environment by selecting the newly created work plane as the sketching plane and then create a sketch (two circles of diameter 145 mm and 40 mm) of the second feature, see Figure 9.84.

9.83

9.84

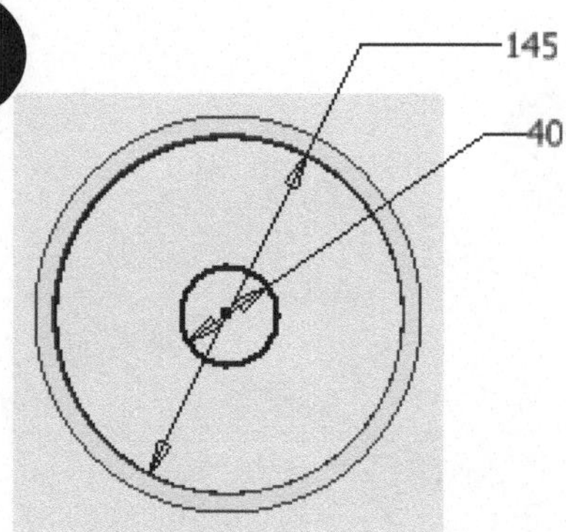

5. Click on the **3D Model** tab in the **Ribbon** and then click on the **Extrude** tool in the **Create** panel. The **Extrusion** property panel appears and you are prompted to select a closed profile.

6. Select the outer closed area of the sketch as a profile to be extruded, see Figure 9.85. The preview of an extruded feature appears in the graphics area.

7. Ensure that the direction of extrusion is upward.

8. Enter **5** in the **Distance A** field of the **Extrusion** property panel as the depth of extrusion.

9. Click on the **OK** button in the property panel. The extrude feature is created, see Figure 9.86. In this figure, the work plane has been hidden.

9.85

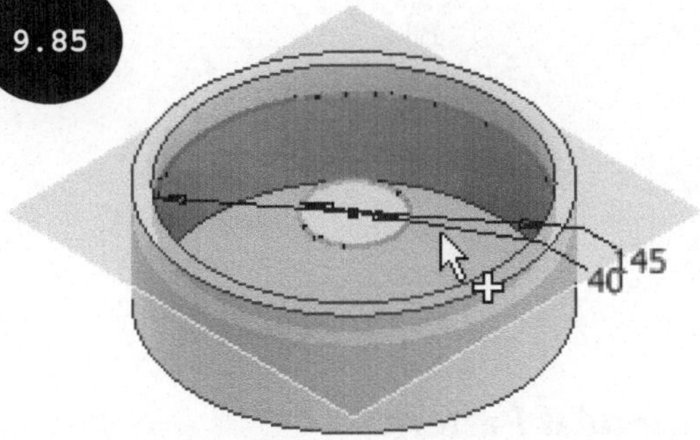

9.86

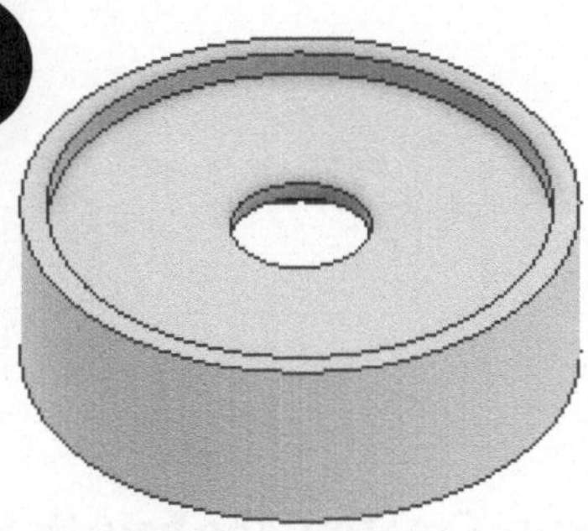

10. Hide the work plane of the model in the graphics area.

Section 4: Creating the Third Feature - Cut Feature

1. Invoke the Sketching environment by selecting the top planar face of the second feature (previously created extrude feature) as the sketching plane.

2. Create a circle of diameter 6 mm as the sketch of the third feature, see Figure 9.87.

9.87

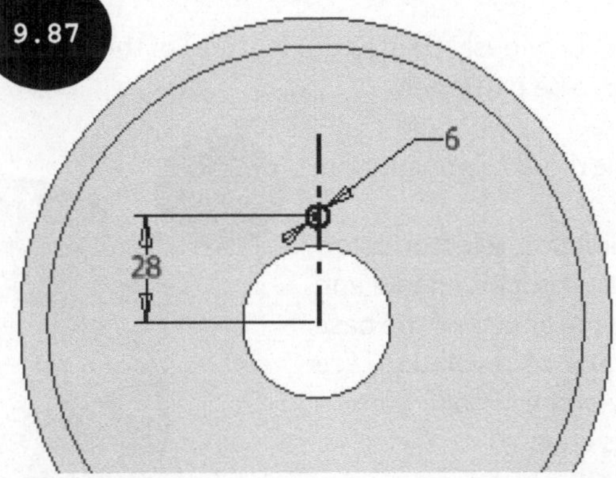

3. Click on the **3D Model** tab in the **Ribbon** and then click on the **Extrude** tool in the **Create** panel. The **Extrusion** property panel appears and you are prompted to select a closed profile.

4. Select the closed area of the sketch as a profile. A preview of the extrude feature appears in the graphics area.

5. Click on the **Through All** button in the **Behavior** rollout of the property panel and then select the **Cut** button in the **Boolean** area of the property panel, if not selected automatically. The direction of extrusion gets changed to downward. Also, the preview of a cut feature appears in the graphics area.

6. Click on the **OK** button in the property panel. The cut feature gets created, see Figure 9.88.

9.88

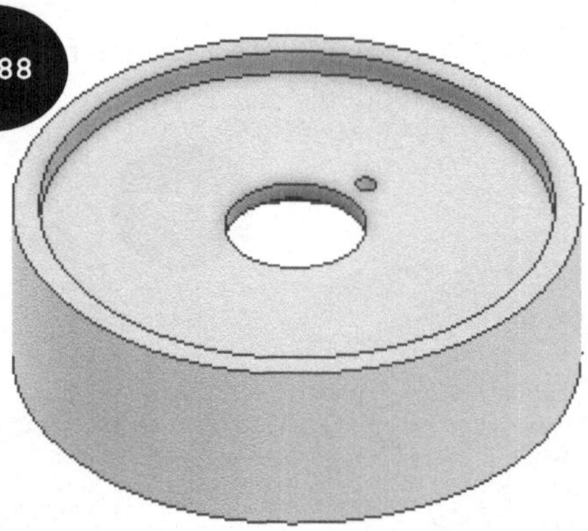

Section 5: Creating the Fourth Feature - Circular Pattern

1. Click on the **Circular Pattern** tool in the **Pattern** panel of the **3D Model** tab, see Figure 9.89. The **Circular Pattern** property panel appears and you are prompted to select features to be patterned.

9.89

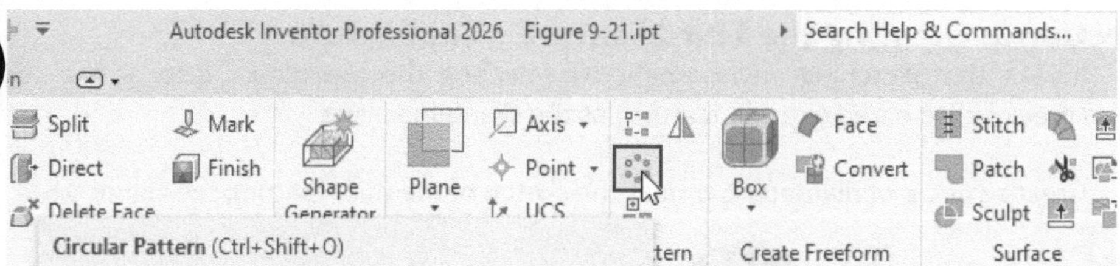

2. Select the third feature (previously created cut feature) of the model in the graphics area or in the **Browser** as the feature to be patterned.

   Now, you need to define the axis of revolution.

9.90

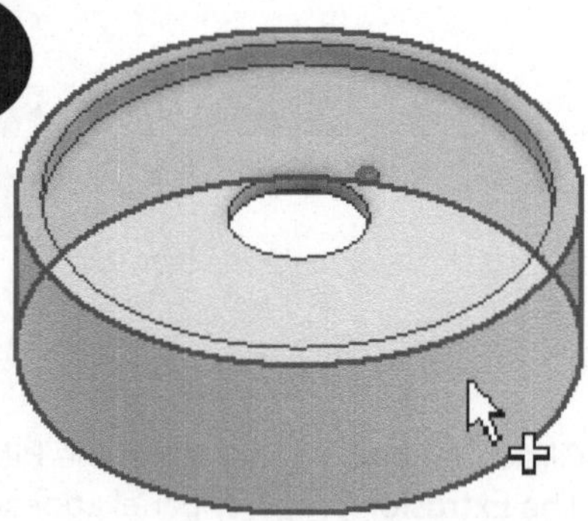

3. Click on the **Select Direction** selector below the **Direction** area of the property panel and then select the outer circular face of the base feature to define an axis of revolution, see Figure 9.90. A preview of the circular pattern appears in the graphics area.

4. Enter **8** in the **Count** field in the **Orientation** rollout of the property panel.

5. Ensure that a **360** degrees angle value is specified in the **Angle** field of the **Orientation** rollout in the property panel.

6. Ensure that the **Fitted** button is selected in the **Distribution** area of the expanded property panel.

7. Click on the **OK** button in the property panel. The circular pattern is created, see Figure 9.91.

9.91

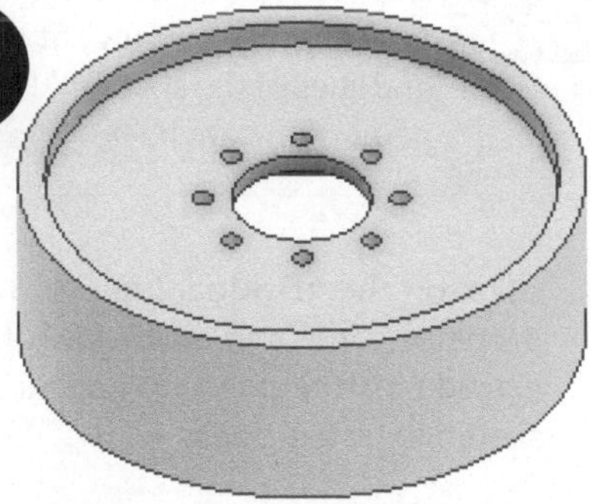

Section 6: Creating the Fifth Feature - Extrude Feature

The fifth feature of the model is an extrude feature and its sketch is to be created on a work plane, which is at an offset distance of 200 mm from the Right plane (YZ Plane).

1. Create a work plane at an offset distance of 200 mm from the Right plane (YZ Plane) by using the **Offset from Plane** tool of the **Plane** flyout, see Figure 9.92.

9.92

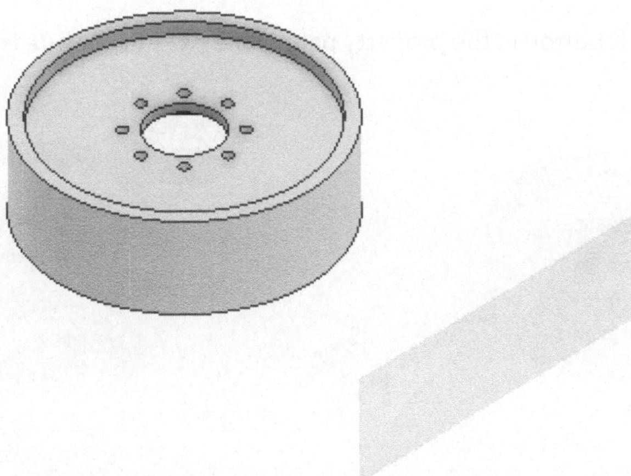

2. Invoke the Sketching environment by selecting the newly created work plane as the sketching plane. Now, create the sketch of the extrude feature, see Figure 9.93.

9.93

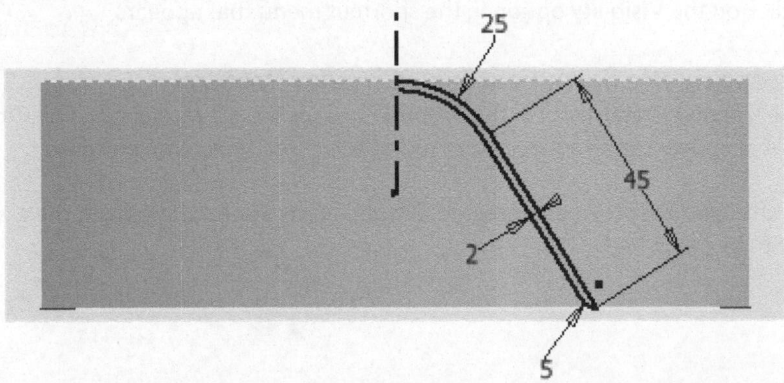

Note: In Figure 9.93, a tangent relation has been applied between the connecting tangent arcs and lines of the sketch. Also, the both inclined lines are parallel to each other and the center point of the arc having a radius of 25 mm is coincident with the origin.

3. Click on the **3D Model** tab in the **Ribbon** and then click on the **Extrude** tool. The **Extrusion** property panel and a preview of the extrude feature appear. Note that if the preview of the extrude feature does not appear in the graphics area, then you need to select the profile of the sketch to be extruded.

4. Click on the **Flipped** button in the **Direction** area of the property panel to reverse the direction of extrusion toward the model.

5. Click on the **To Next** button in the **Behavior** rollout of the property panel. A preview of the extrude feature appears such that it terminates at its next intersection, see Figure 9.94.

6. Ensure that the **Join** button is activated in the **Boolean** area of the property panel.

7. Click on the **OK** button in the property panel. The extrude feature is created, see Figure 9.95.

9.94

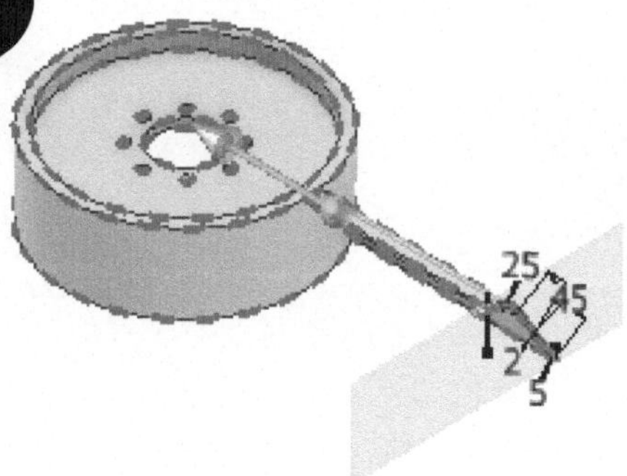

9.95

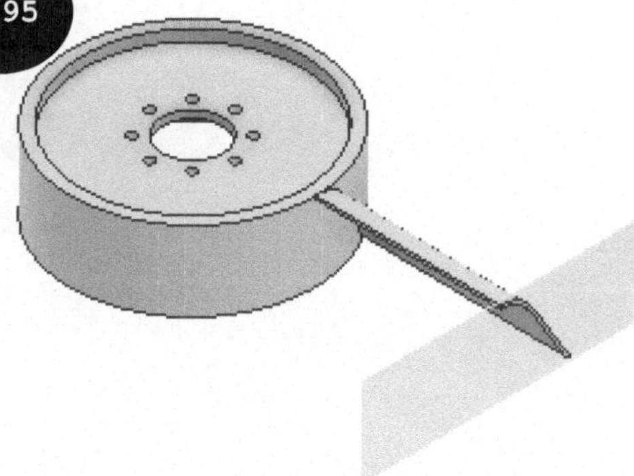

8. Hide the work plane in the graphics area. For doing so, right-click on the work plane in the **Browser** and then click on the **Visibility** option in the shortcut menu that appears.

Section 7: Creating the Sixth Feature - Circular Pattern

1. Click on the **Circular Pattern** tool in the **Pattern** panel of the **3D Model** tab. The **Circular Pattern** property panel appears and you are prompted to select features to be patterned.

2. Select the fifth feature (previously created extrude feature) of the model in the graphics area as the feature to be patterned.

Now, you need to define the axis of revolution.

3. Click on the **Select Direction** selector below the **Direction** area of the property panel and then select the outer circular face of the base feature to define the axis of revolution, see Figure 9.96. A preview of the circular pattern appears in the graphics area, see Figure 9.97.

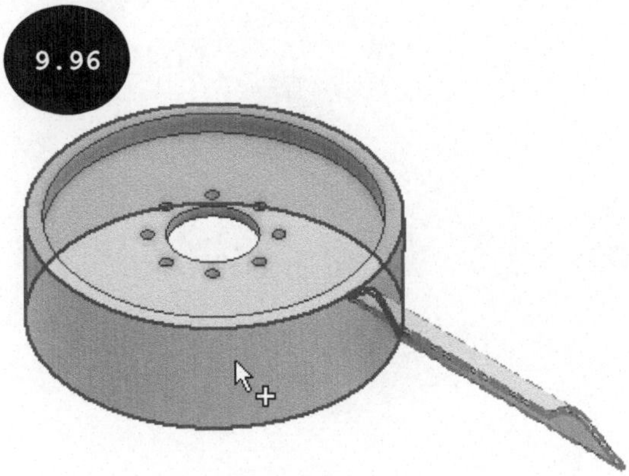

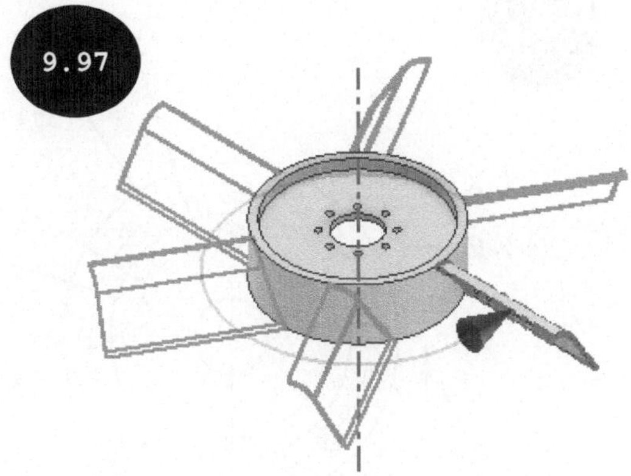

4. Enter **8** in the **Count** field in the **Orientation** rollout of the property panel.

5. Ensure that a **360** degrees angle value is specified in the **Angle** field of the **Orientation** rollout in the property panel.

6. Click on the **OK** button in the property panel. The circular pattern is created, see Figure 9.98.

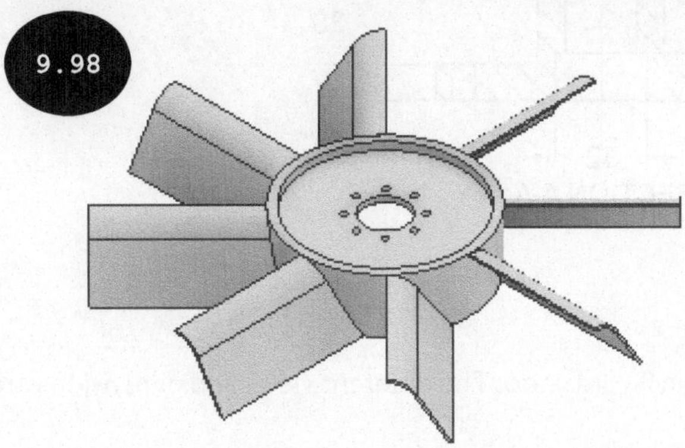

Section 8: Saving the Model

1. Click on the **Save** tool in the **Quick Access Toolbar** toolbar. The **Save As** dialog box appears.

2. Browse to **Autodesk Inventor > Chapter 9** folder in the local drive of your system. Note that you need to create Chapter 9 folder inside the Autodesk Inventor folder, if not created earlier.

3. Enter **Tutorial 2** in the **File name** field of the property panel and then click on the **Save** button. The model is saved in the specified location (>:\Autodesk Inventor\Chapter 9).

Hands-on Test Drive 1

Create the model shown in Figure 9.99. The different views and dimensions are given in the same figure for your reference. All dimensions are in mm.

9.99

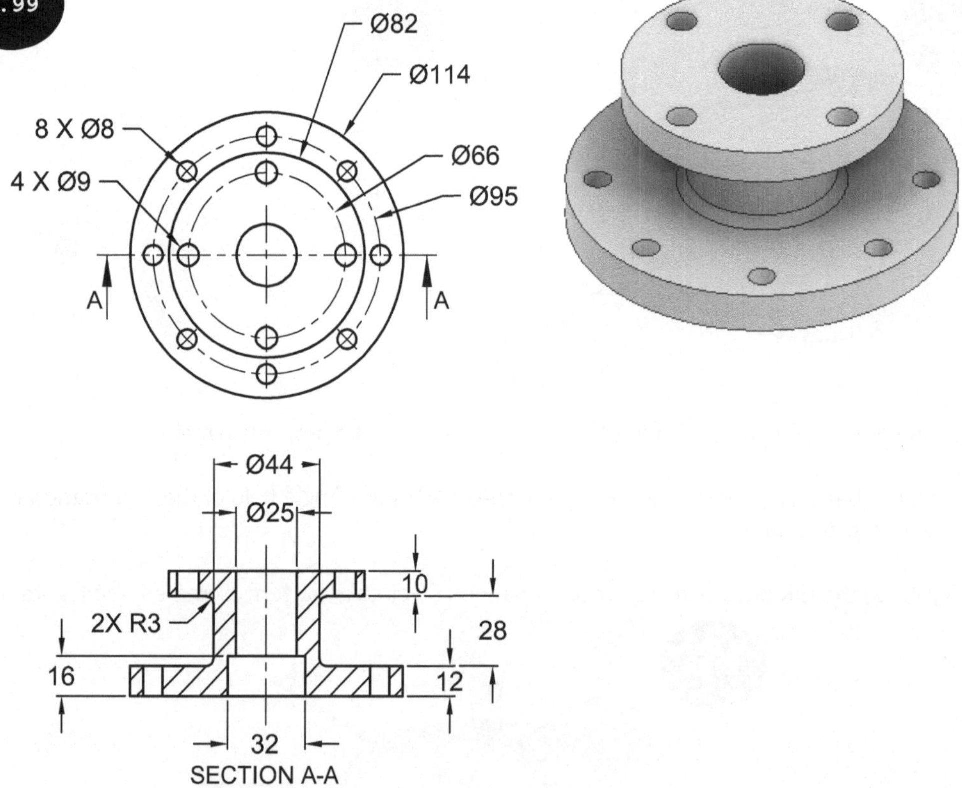

Hands-on Test Drive 2

Create the model shown in Figure 9.100. The different views and dimensions are given in Figure 9.101. All dimensions are in mm.

9.100

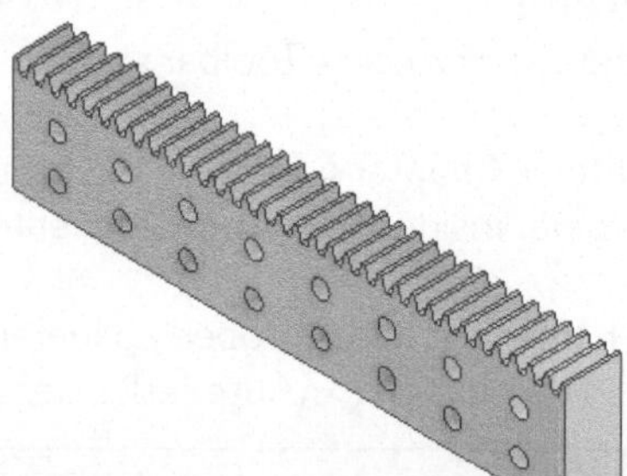

9.101

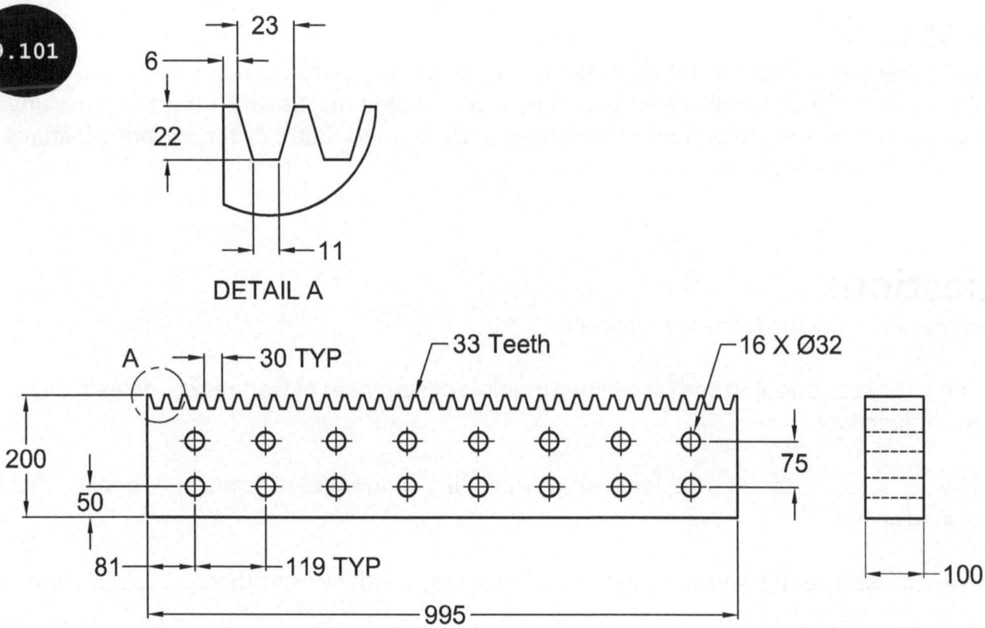

Hands-on Test Drive 3

Create the model shown in Figure 9.102. All dimensions are in mm.

9.102

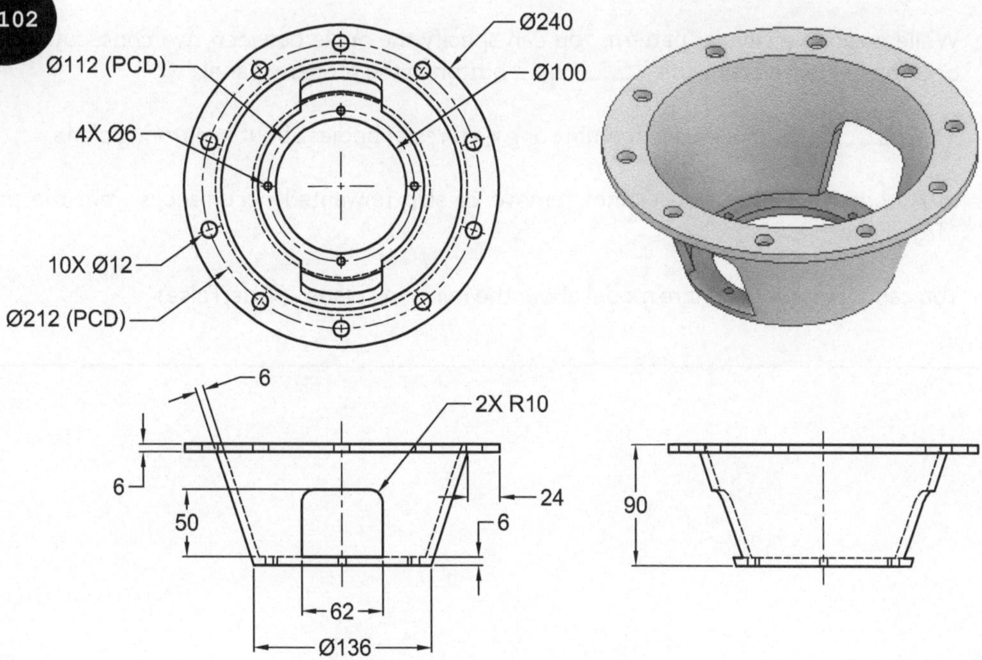

Summary

In this chapter, you have learned about creating various types of patterns such as rectangular patterns, circular patterns, and sketch driven patterns, with detailed discussions about suppressing and unsuppressing features and pattern occurrences, in addition to methods for mirroring features and bodies about a mirroring plane.

Questions

Complete and verify the following sentences:

- The _________ tool is used for creating multiple occurrences of features or bodies in one or two linear directions.
- The _________ tool is used for creating multiple occurrences of features or bodies, circularly around an axis.
- In Autodesk Inventor, you can create a pattern along a path by using the _________ tool.
- On selecting the _________ button in the **Rectangular Pattern** property panel, all pattern occurrences maintain the same geometrical relations as that of the parent feature.
- The _________ pattern is created such that the parent feature gets propagated to each sketch point (2D or 3D) of the sketch.
- While creating a circular pattern, you can specify the angle between two consecutive pattern occurrences by selecting the _________ button in the property panel.
- The _________ tool is used for mirroring features or bodies about a mirroring plane.
- In Autodesk Inventor, you cannot remove or skip unwanted occurrences from the pattern. (True/False)
- You cannot mirror the entire model about the mirroring plane. (True/False)

CHAPTER

10

Advanced Modeling - III

In this chapter, the following topics will be discussed:

- Creating Holes
- Creating Threads
- Creating Fillets
- Creating Chamfers
- Splitting a Face and a Solid Body
- Creating 3D Sketches and Curves

In this chapter, you will learn how to create simple, clearance, tapped, and taper tapped holes as per the standard specifications by using the **Hole** tool. Besides, you will learn about creating threads, fillets, and chamfers. You will also learn how to create a face draft, split the faces of a model, create 3D sketches, and so on.

Creating Holes

The **Hole** tool is used for creating various types of holes as per the standard specifications. You can create simple, clearance, tapped, and taper tapped holes with different seat types such as counterbore, spotface, and countersink, see Figures 10.1 through 10.4. Figure 10.1 shows a simple hole, Figure 10.2 shows a simple hole with a counterbore seat, Figure 10.3 shows a simple hole with a spotface seat, and Figure 10.4 shows a simple hole with a countersink seat. The method for creating a hole is discussed below:

10.1

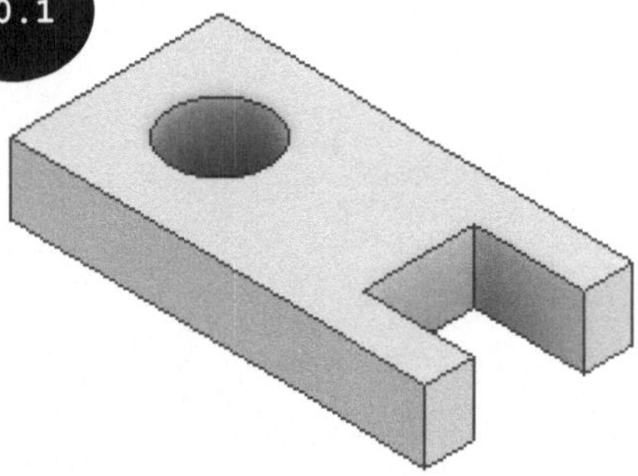

10.2

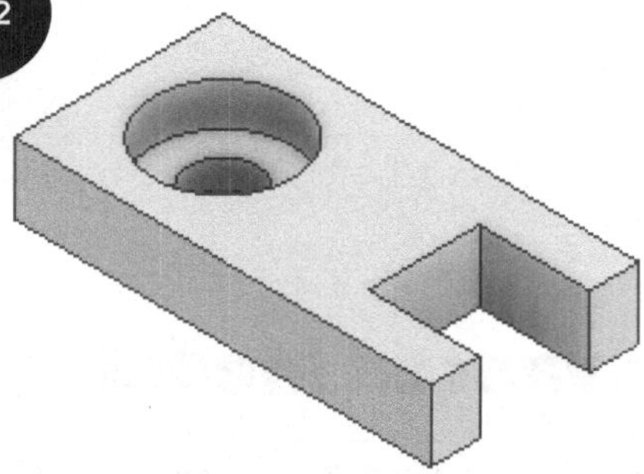

10.3

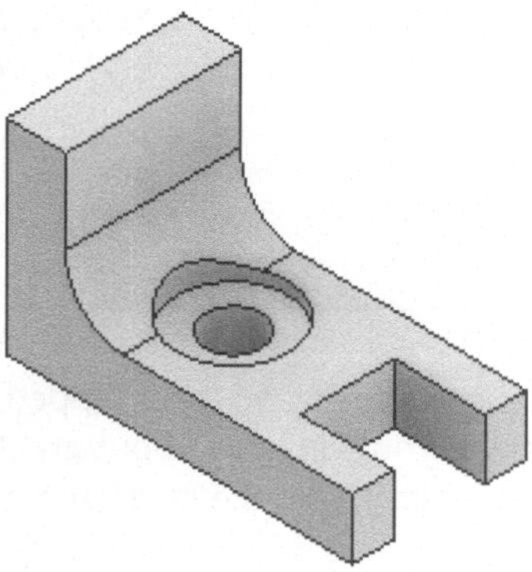

10.4

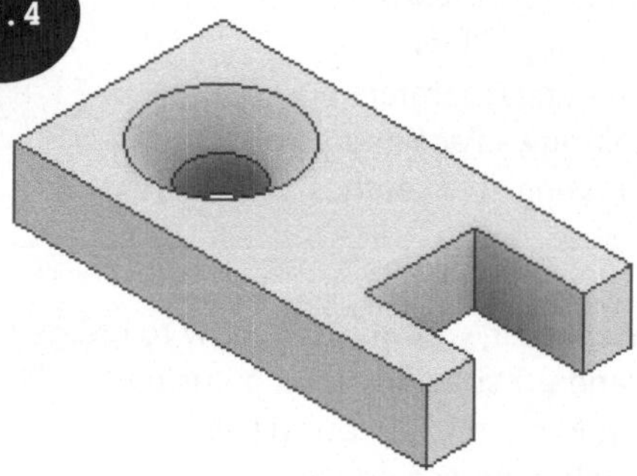

1. Click on the **Hole** tool in the **Modify** panel of the **3D Model** tab, see Figure 10.5. The **Hole** property panel appears, see Figure 10.6. Also, you are prompted to specify a point for defining the position of the hole center.

10.5

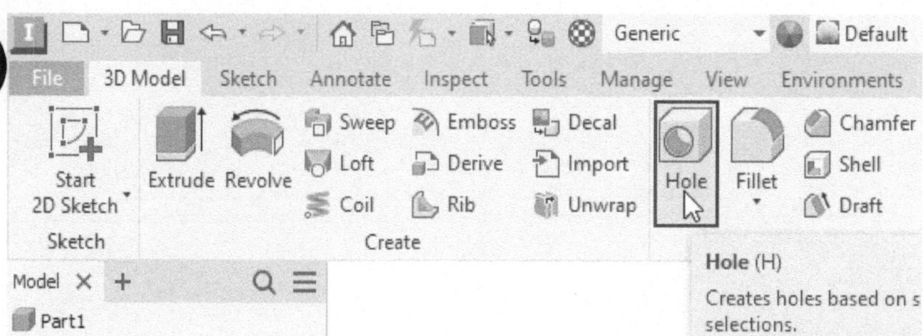

10.6

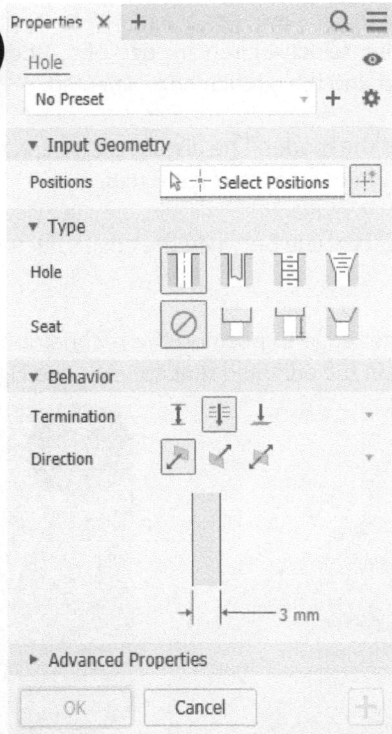

Positions: By default, the **Positions** selector is activated in the **Input Geometry** rollout of the **Hole** property panel. As a result, you are prompted to define the position of the hole center. You can click on the face of a model to define the position of the hole center arbitrarily. Alternatively, you can select a sketch point or a work point to define the position of the hole center. You need to expand the **Input Geometry** rollout by clicking on its title bar, if not expanded by default.

Note: On specifying the position of the hole center arbitrarily on a face of a model, you need to select linear edges of a model for applying dimensions or a circular edge of a model for applying concentric constraint to position the hole, as required.

2. Click anywhere on the face of a model to define the position of the hole center. The preview of a hole appears on the face with default parameters, see Figure 10.7.

10.7

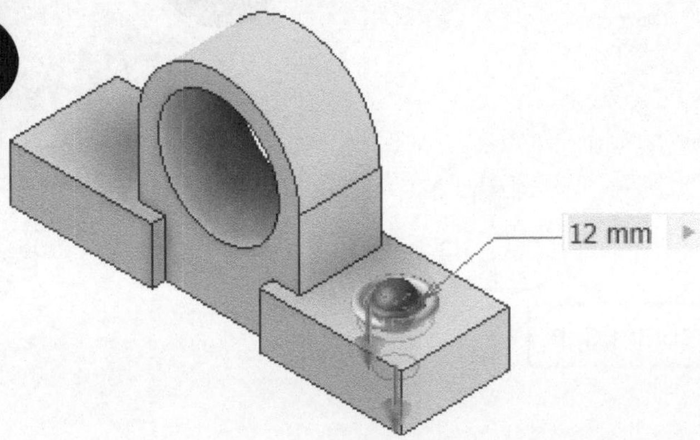

Now, you need to select the linear edges of a model for applying dimensions to position the hole, as required. You can also select a circular edge of a model for applying concentric constraint between the hole center and the circular edge selected.

3. Click on a linear edge of the model. The distance between the edge and the hole center appears in an edit field in the graphics area, see Figure 10.8.

4. Enter the required distance value between the edge selected and the hole center in the edit field that appears.

5. Similarly, click on another edge to position the second direction of the hole and then enter the required distance value in the edit field that appears, see Figure 10.9.

10.8

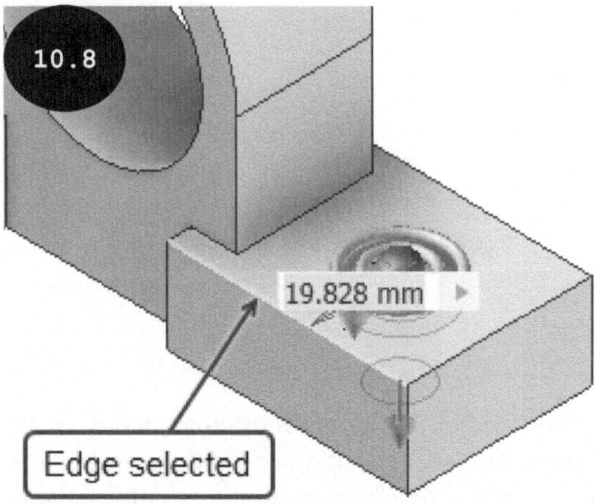

10.9

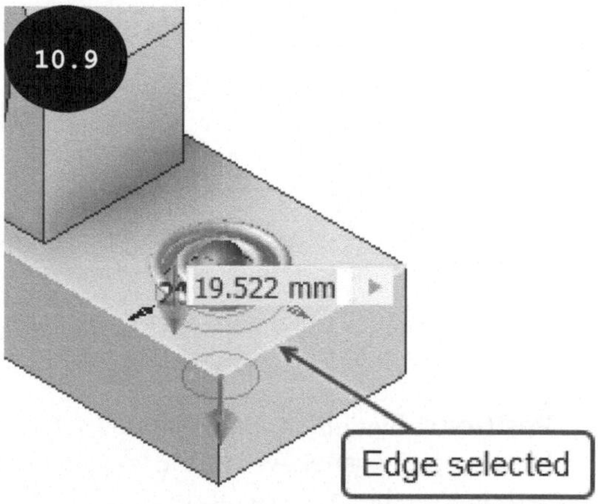

Note: Instead of selecting linear edges for positioning the hole by applying dimensions, if you select a circular edge, the concentric constraint gets applied and the center points of the selected circular edge and the hole become concentric to each other, see Figures 10.10 and 10.11.

10.10

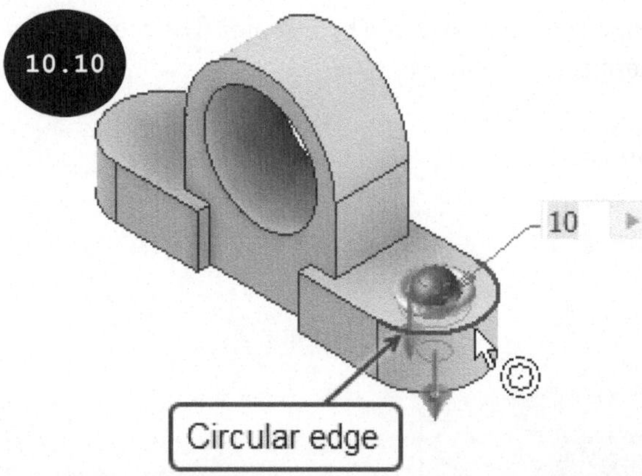

10.11

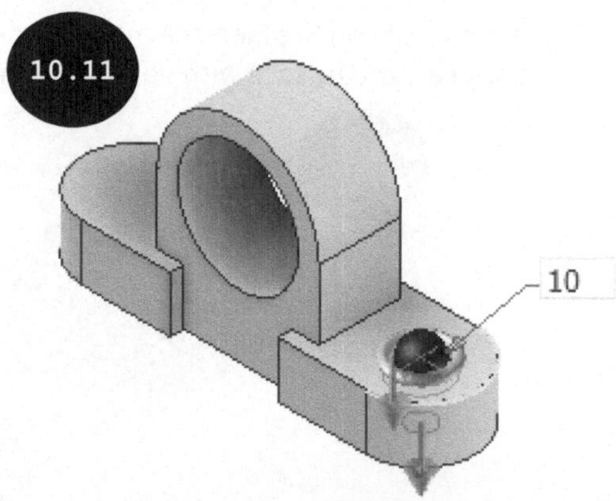

After defining the position of the hole, you need to select the type of hole (simple, clearance, tapped, or taper tapped) to be created in the **Hole** area of the **Type** rollout in the property panel, see Figure 10.12. The options are discussed below:

10.12

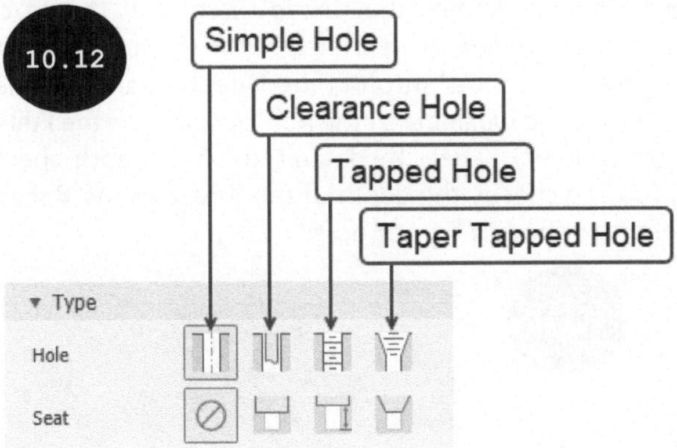

Simple Hole : The **Simple Hole** button is used for creating a simple hole without a thread.

Clearance Hole : The **Clearance Hole** button is used for creating a standard untapped hole for accommodating a standard fastener. On activating this button, the **Fastener** rollout appears in the property panel, see Figure 10.13. In this rollout, you can select the fastener standard, fastener type, size, and fit type for the fastener to be accommodated in the hole. Figure 10.14 shows a clearance hole.

10.13

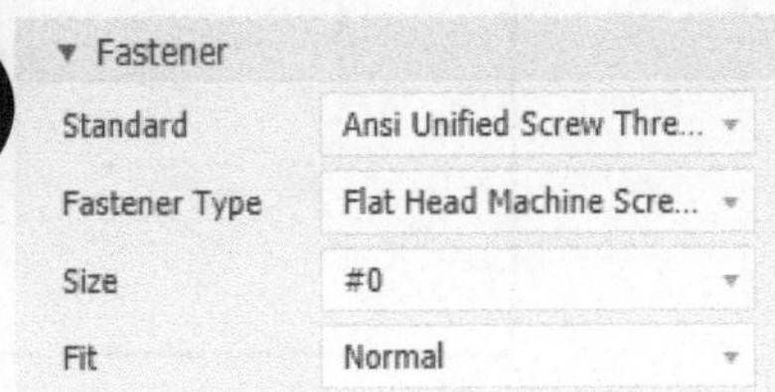

10.14

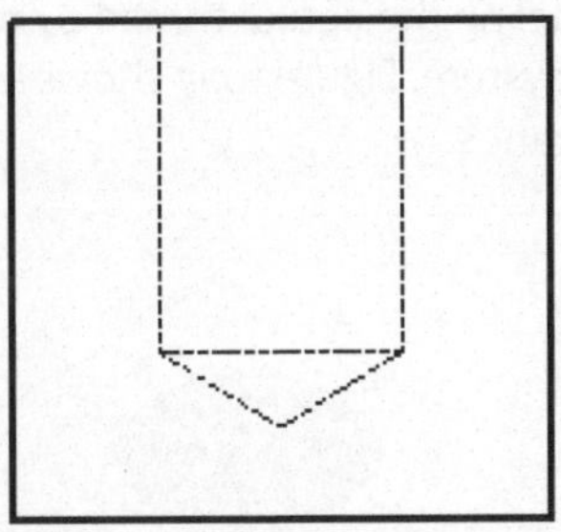

Tip: The availability of options in the **Fastener Type** drop-down list of the **Fastener** rollout in the property panel depends upon the fastener standard selected in the **Standard** drop-down list of the rollout.

Tapped Hole : The **Tapped Hole** button is used for creating a hole with a thread. On activating the **Tapped Hole** button, the **Threads** rollout appears in the **Hole** property panel, see Figure 10.15. In this rollout, you can select the standard thread type, nominal size of the selected thread type, designation that defines the thread pitch, and thread class in the respective drop-down lists. You can also define the direction of the thread (left-hand thread or right-hand thread) by activating the respective button in the **Direction** area of this rollout. Also, you can specify the thread length to the full depth of the hole by selecting the **Full Depth** check box in the **Threads** rollout of the property panel. By default, the **Full Depth** check box is cleared in this rollout. As a result, you can specify the depth of the thread in the **Behavior** rollout of the **Hole** property panel. Figure 10.16 shows a tapped hole.

10.15

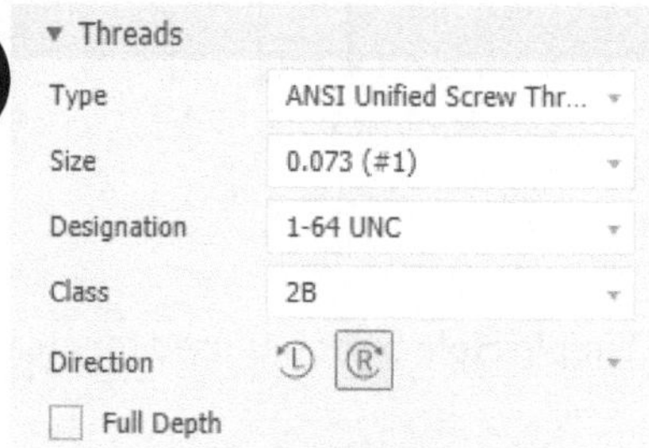

10.16

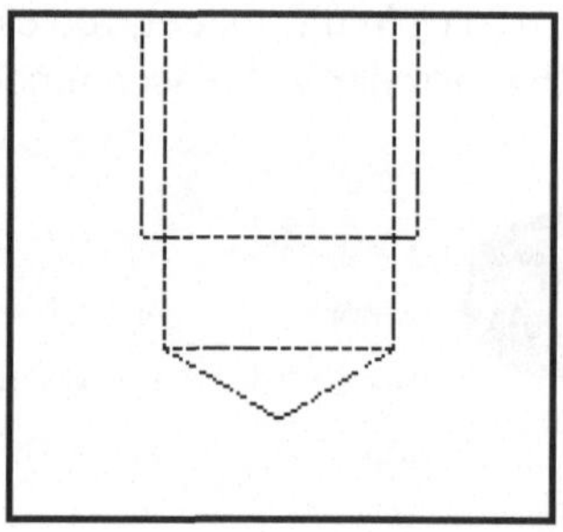

Note: In Autodesk Inventor, the thread in a hole is represented using a cosmetic appearance or texture rather than modeling the actual thread by removing material in order to maximize the performance of the system. Figure 10.17 shows a tapped hole with a thread represented using a cosmetic appearance.

10.17

Taper Tapped Hole : The **Taper Tapped Hole** button is used for creating a hole with a taper thread. On activating the **Taper Tapped Hole** button, the options in the **Threads** rollout appear as shown in Figure 10.18. Note that the **Taper Tapped Hole** button is not enabled, if the **Counterbore** button is activated as the seat type in the **Seat** area of the **Type** rollout. In the **Threads** rollout, you can select the taper thread type, thread size, and thread direction (left-hand thread or right-hand thread). Note that on selecting the thread type and the size, Autodesk Inventor automatically calculates the thread diameter, taper angle, and thread depth. Figure 10.19 shows a tapped hole.

10.18

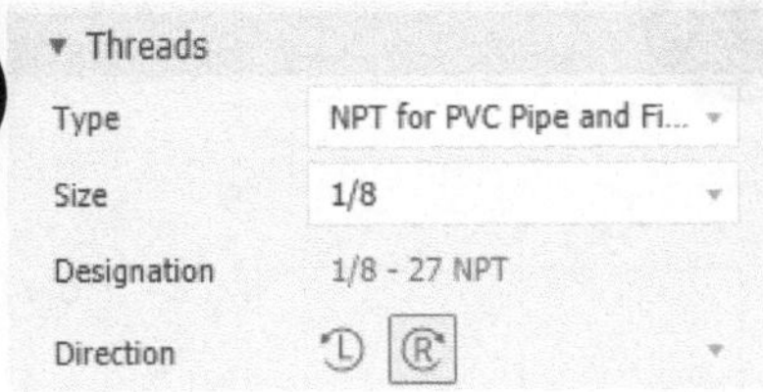

10.19

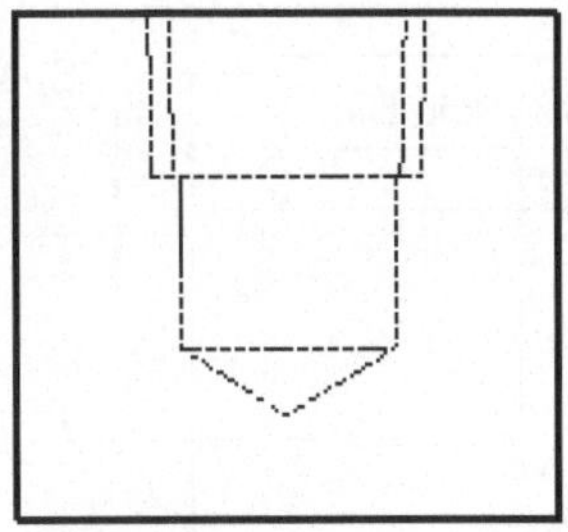

6. Select the required type of hole (**Simple Hole**, **Clearance Hole**, **Tapped Hole**, or **Taper Tapped Hole**) to be created in the **Hole** area of the **Type** rollout in the property panel.

   Now, you need to select a seat type (**None**, **Counterbore**, **Spotface**, or **Countersink**) for the hole in the **Seat** area of the Type rollout. The options are discussed below:

   None : The **None** button is used for creating a simple drilled hole with a specified drill hole diameter to the full depth of the hole, see Figure 10.20.

   Counterbore : The **Counterbore** button is used for creating a counterbore hole or stepped hole with a specified drill hole diameter, counterbore diameter, and counterbore depth, see Figure 10.21. Note that the **Counterbore** button is not enabled if the **Taper Tapped Hole** button is activated in the **Hole** area of the **Type** rollout in the property panel.

10.20

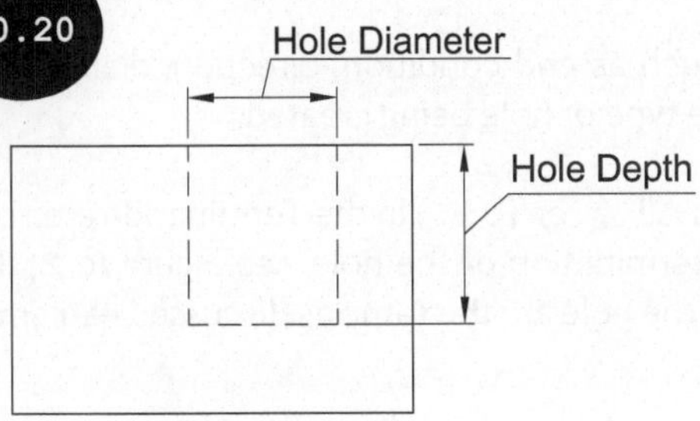

Simple Drilled Hole

10.21

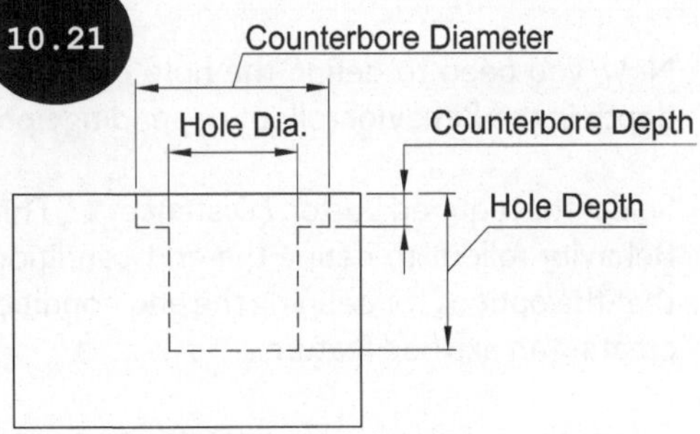

Counterbore Hole

Spotface : The **Spotface** button is used for creating a spotface hole. It is the same as a counterbore hole with the only difference being that it has a very shallow counterbore that provides a flat or high surface finish at the top of the hole for the washer to sit flat on the surface, see Figure 10.22.

Countersink : The **Countersink** button is used for creating a countersink hole with a specified drill hole diameter, countersink diameter, and countersink angle, see Figure 10.23.

10.22

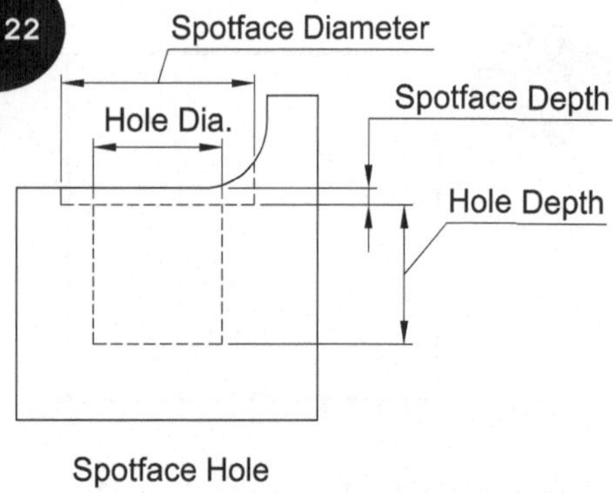

10.23

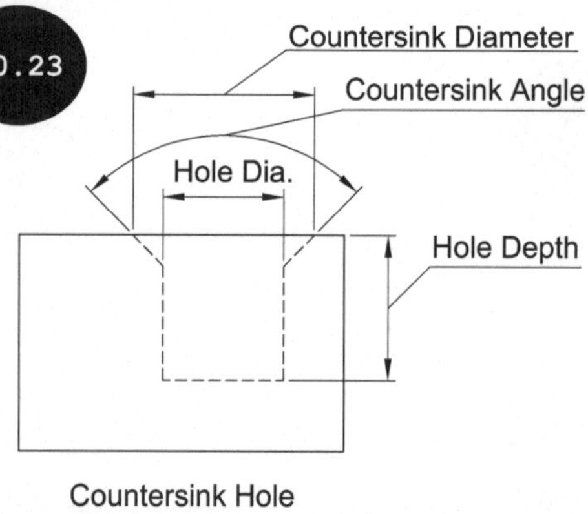

7. Select the required button (**None**, **Counterbore**, **Spotface**, or **Countersink**) in the **Seat** area of the **Type** rollout in the property panel for creating the hole.

Note: If you are creating a clearance hole, then you need to select the fastener standard, fastener type, size, and fit type for the fastener to be accommodated in the hole by using the **Fastener** rollout of the property panel. The **Fastener** rollout is available only when the **Clearance Hole** button is activated in the **Hole** area of the **Type** rollout in the property panel.

Also, if you are creating a tapped hole or a taper tapped hole, then you need to define the thread parameters in the **Threads** rollout of the property panel, as discussed earlier. The **Threads** rollout is available only when the **Tapped Hole** or **Taper Tapped Hole** button is activated in the **Hole** area of the **Type** rollout.

Now, you need to define the hole parameters such as end condition, direction, diameter, and depth in the **Behavior** rollout depending upon the type of hole being created.

8. Select the required button (**Distance** , **Through All** , or **To**) in the **Termination** area of the **Behavior** rollout to define the end condition or termination of the hole, see Figure 10.24. Note that the options for defining the end condition of the hole are the same as discussed earlier while creating an extrude feature.

9. Select the required button (**Default** or **Flipped**) in the **Direction** area of the **Behavior** rollout to reverse or flip the direction of the hole, see Figure 10.24.

10. Select the required button (**Flat** , **Angle** , **Flat W** , **Angle V** , or **Angle Y**) in the **Drill Point** area to define the respective drill point. All these buttons are discussed next. Note that

these buttons are not available when the **Through All** button is activated in the **Termination** area of the **Behavior** rollout.

Flat : The **Flat** button creates a flat drill point for the hole, refer to Figure 10.24.

Angle : The **Angle** button creates an angled drill point for the hole, refer to Figure 10.25.

10.24

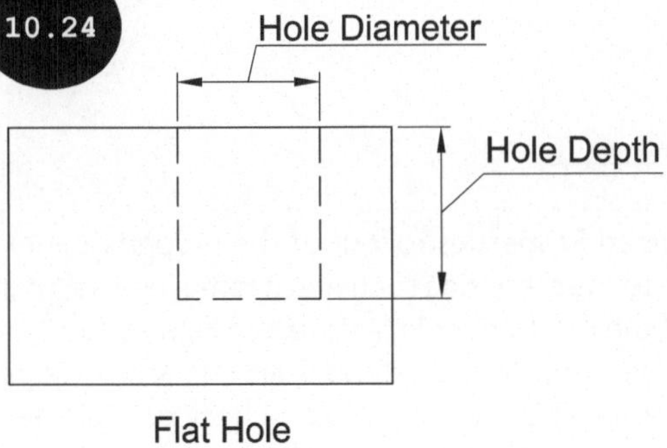

10.25

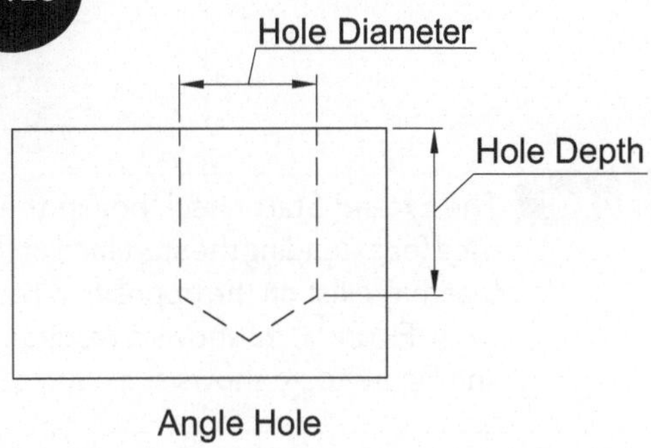

Flat W : The **Flat** W button creates a flat drill point using a drilling tool that follows the ISO standard and adds a "W" drill point "<DPOINT>" tag to the 2D and 3D Hole Note annotations. You will learn about adding Hole Note annotations to a 2D drawing in Chapter 14.

Angle V : The **Angle** V button creates an angled drill point and adds a "V" drill point "<DPOINT>" tag to the 2D and 3D Hole Note annotations. You will learn about adding Hole Note annotations to a 2D drawing in Chapter 14.

Angle Y : The **Angle Y** button creates an angled drill point as part of the hole depth parameter, refer to Figure 10.26.

10.26

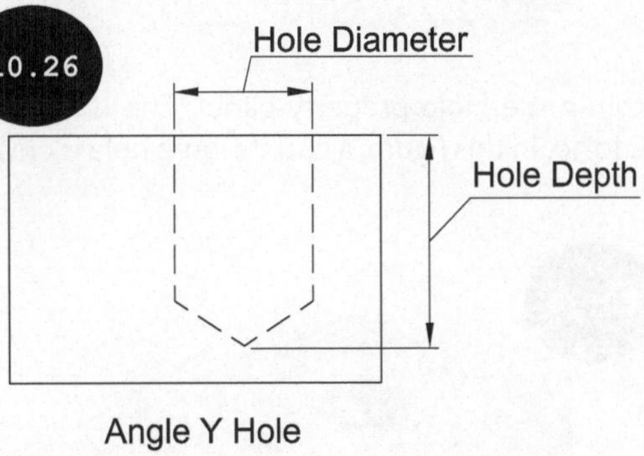

11. Edit the default hole parameters such as diameter and depth values in the respective fields of the hole illustration in the **Behavior** rollout, see Figure 10.27. Note that the availability of fields in the hole illustration depends on the type of hole and the seat type selected in the **Type** rollout of the property panel.

10.27

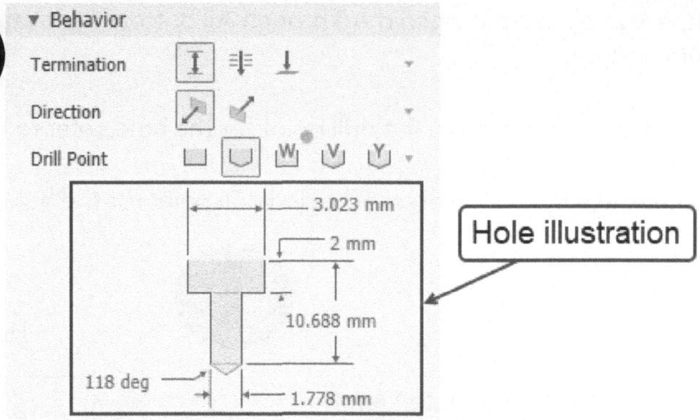

Note: The **Extend Start** check box in the **Advanced Properties** rollout of the property panel is used for extending the start face of the hole to the other side such that it removes a fragment that may exist on the opposite direction of the resultant hole feature, see Figures 10.28 and 10.29. Figure 10.28 shows a resultant hole feature with the **Extend Start** check box cleared and Figure 10.29 shows a resultant hole feature with the **Extend Start** check box selected.

10.28

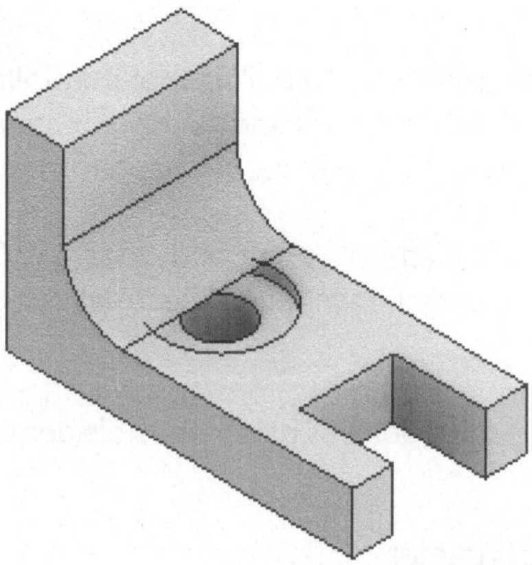

10.29

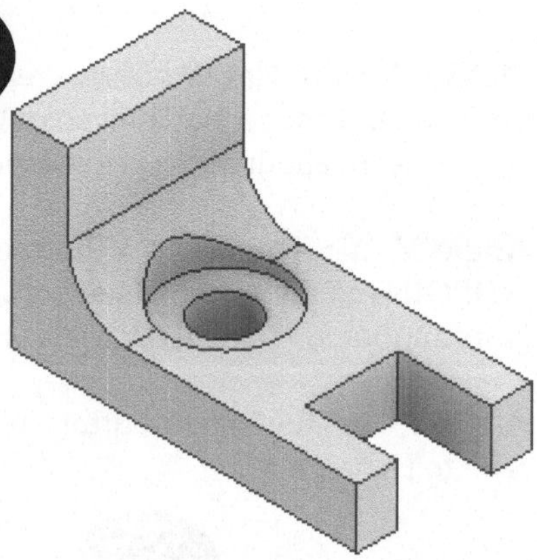

12. Click on the **OK** button in the **Hole** property panel. The hole is created as per the specified parameters, see Figure 10.30. In this figure, a counterbore hole is created on the top planar face of the model.

10.30

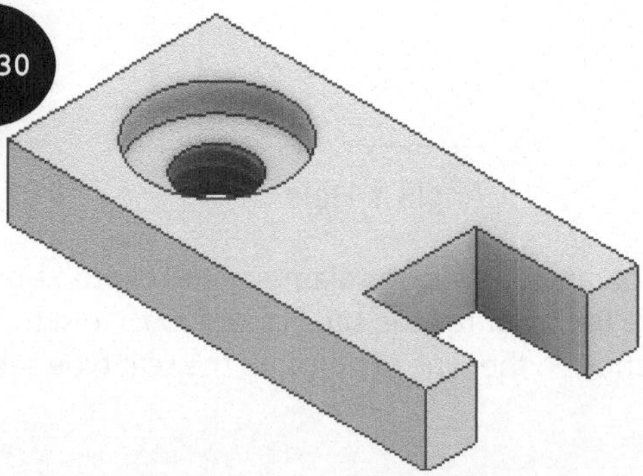

Creating Threads

In Autodesk Inventor, you can create cosmetic threads on features such as holes, shafts, studs, and bolts. A cosmetic thread represents the real thread on a feature by using a cosmetic appearance or texture. It is recommended to add cosmetic threads to holes, fasteners, or cylindrical features of a model to reduce the complexity of the model and to improve the overall performance of the system. Figure 10.31 shows a cosmetic thread created on a cylindrical feature and Figure 10.32 shows cosmetic threads created on a hole/cut feature. The method for creating a thread is discussed below:

10.31

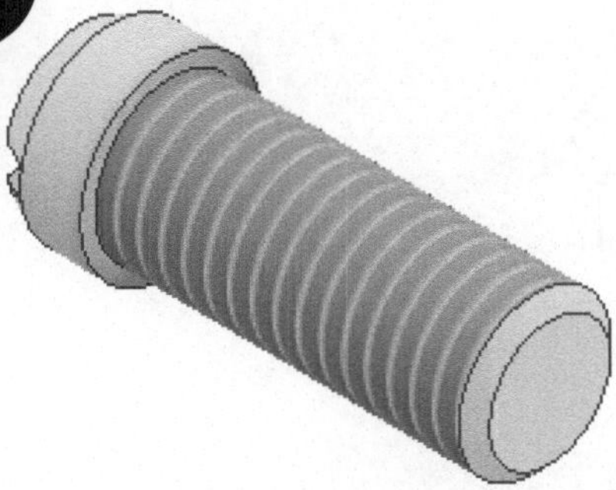

10.32

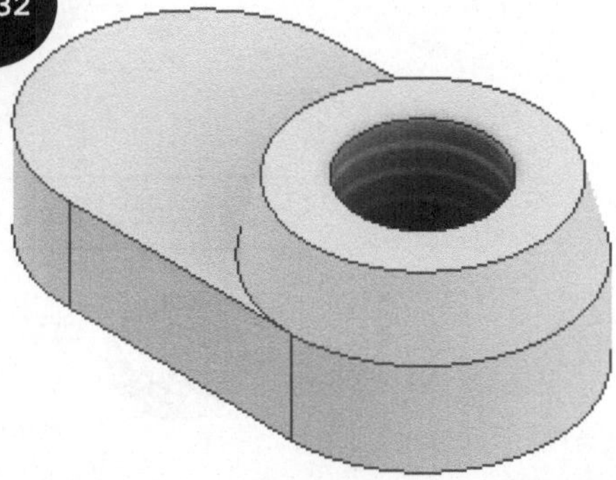

1. Click on the **Thread** tool in the **Modify** panel of the **3D Model** tab, see Figure 10.33. The **Thread** property panel appears, see Figure 10.34. Also, you are prompted to select a cylindrical or conical face of a model for creating a thread, since the **Face** selector is activated in the **Input Geometry** rollout of the **Thread** property panel, by default.

10.33

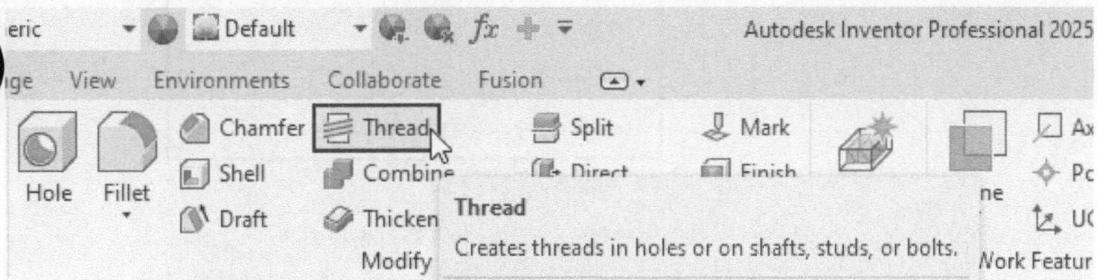

10.34

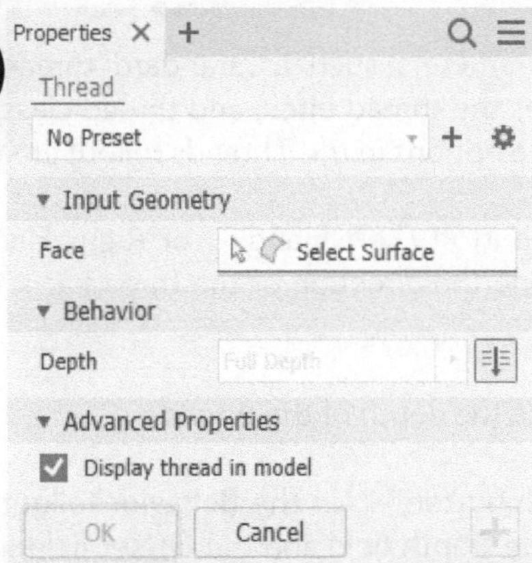

2. Click on a cylindrical or conical face of a model to create a thread. The preview of a thread appears on the selected face, see Figure 10.35. Also, the **Threads** rollout appears in the property panel with default parameters, see Figure 10.36.

10.35

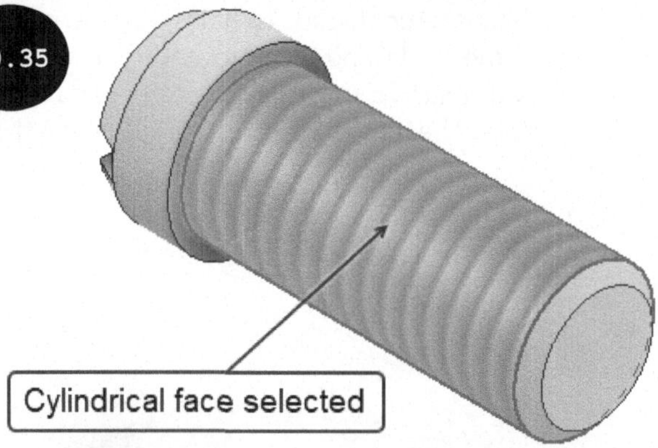

10.36

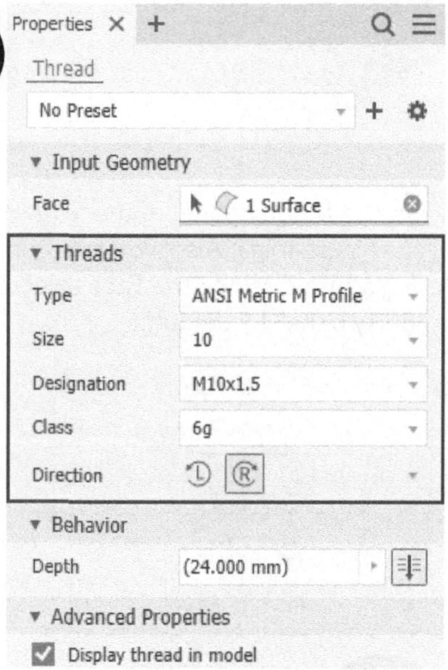

3. Specify the thread parameters such as standard thread type, nominal size of the thread, designation that defines the thread pitch, and thread class in the respective drop-down lists of the **Threads** rollout. The options in the **Threads** rollout are the same as discussed earlier.

4. Click on the required button (**Left Hand** or **Right Hand**) in the **Direction** area of the **Threads** rollout to define the direction of the thread as left-hand thread or right-hand thread, respectively.

   Now, you need to define the depth of the thread.

5. Click on the **Full Depth** button in the **Behavior** rollout of the property panel to define the depth of the thread. The **Depth** field and the **Offset** field are enabled in the **Behavior** rollout of the property panel, see Figure 10.37.

10.37

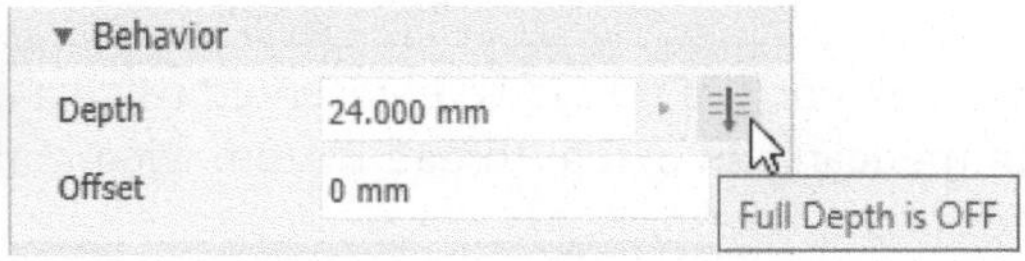

Note: By default, the **Full Depth** button is activated in the **Behavior** rollout of the property panel. As a result, the full depth mode is turned on and the depth of the thread is defined throughout the length of the selected face, by default. This is a toggle button and you can click on this button to turn off the full depth mode in order to specify the required depth of the thread in the **Depth** field of the rollout.

6. Enter the depth of the thread in the **Depth** field of the **Behavior** rollout measuring from the start face of the thread, see Figure 10.38.

   Offset: The Offset field in the **Behavior** rollout of the property panel is used for creating a thread at an offset distance from its start face, see Figure 10.39. By default, the offset distance is specified as 0 in this field. As a result, the thread starts exactly from the start face of the thread.

10.38

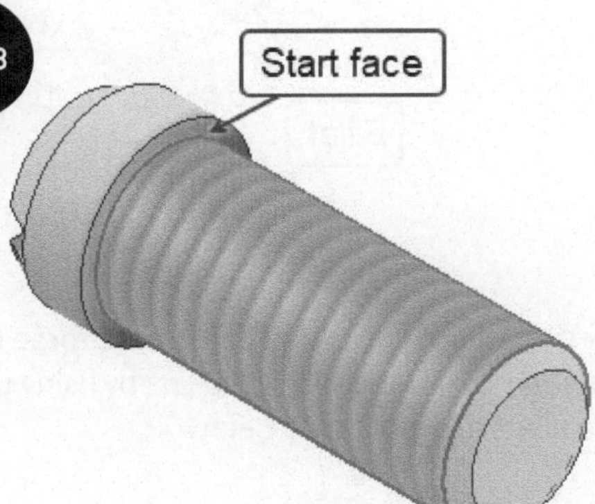

10.39

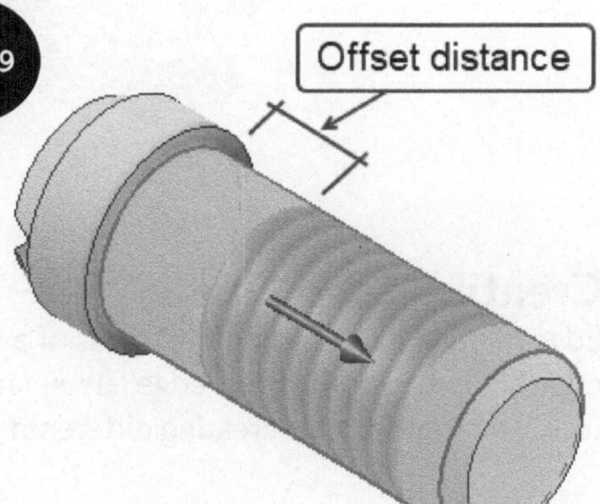

   Display thread in model: By default, the **Display thread in model** check box is selected in the **Advanced Properties** rollout of the **Thread** property panel. As a result, the display of thread appearance or texture becomes visible in the resultant model.

7. Click on the **OK** button in the **Thread** property panel. The thread is created on the selected face of the model, see Figure 10.40.

10.40

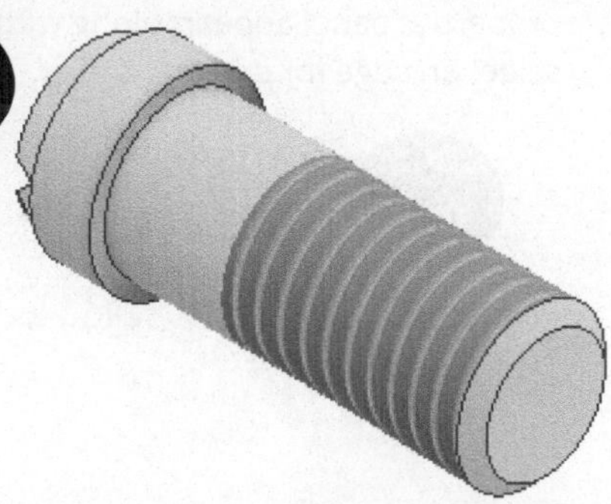

Note: In Autodesk Inventor, the thread is represented using a cosmetic appearance or texture rather than modeling an actual thread by removing material in order to maximize the performance of the system.

Creating Fillets

A fillet is a curved face with a constant radius or variable radii and is used for removing sharp edges of a model that may cause injury while handling the model. Figure 10.41 shows a model before and after creating a constant radius fillet on an edge. In Autodesk Inventor, you can create edge fillets, face fillets, and full round fillets. The various types of fillets are discussed below:

10.41

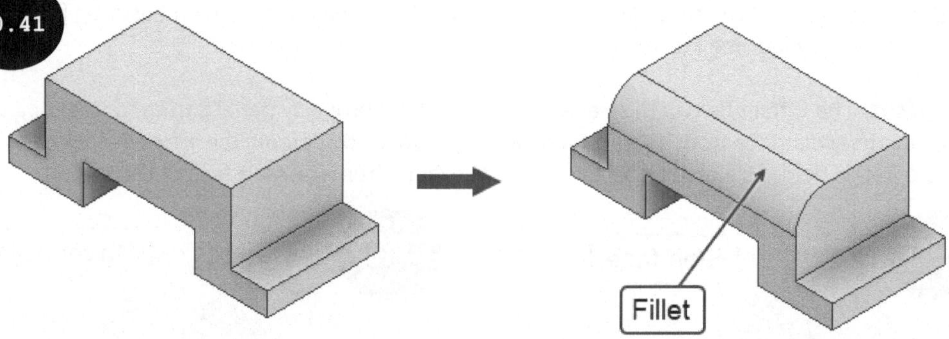

Creating Edge Fillets

Edge fillets are created on the edges of a model. In Autodesk Inventor, you can create three types of edge fillets: constant radius edge fillets, variable radius edge fillets, and setback fillets by using the **Fillet** tool. The methods for creating different types of edge fillets are discussed below:

Creating Constant Radius Edge Fillets

A constant radius edge fillet is a fillet that has a constant radius throughout the selected edge of the model. The method for creating constant radius edge fillets is discussed below:

1. Click on the **Fillet** tool in the **Modify** panel of the **3D Model** tab, see Figure 10.42. The **Fillet** properties panel appears along with the **Tool Palette**, see Figure 10.43. Also, you are prompted to select an edge for creating a fillet.

10.42

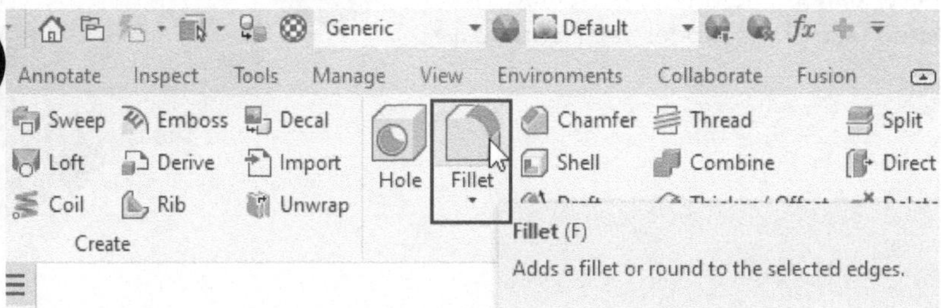

10.43

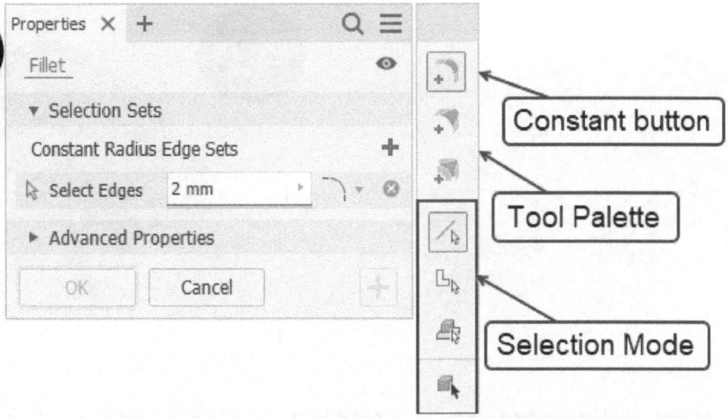

Constant : By default, the **Constant** button is activated in the **Tool Palette** of the **Fillet** property panel, refer to Figure 10.43. As a result, you can create constant radius edge fillets by using the options available in the property panel.

Select Edges: By default, the **Select Edges** selector is activated in the **Fillet** property panel. As a result, you are prompted to select one or more edges to be filleted. Upon selecting the edges, the interface displays the number of edges chosen for creating fillets of the same radius.

2. Ensure that the **Constant** button is activated in the **Tool Palette** of the **Fillet** property panel for creating a constant radius edge fillet and then select an edge for creating a fillet. The preview of a constant radius fillet appears on the selected edge with a default radius value, see Figure 10.44. Note that you can select a set of multiple edges one after the other for creating fillets of the same radius value. All the fillets that are created as a single set act as a single feature.

10.44

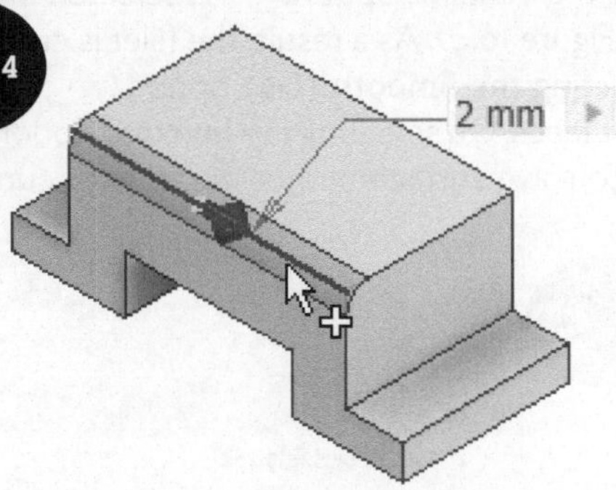

Note: By default, the **Edge** button is selected in the **Selection Mode** area of the **Tool Palette** in the **Fillet** property panel. As a result, you can select individual edges of a model for creating fillets. On selecting the **Loop** button in the **Selection Mode** area, you can select a loop of edges for creating fillets, see Figure 10.45. On selecting the **Feature** button , you can select individual features of a model for creating fillets on all the edges of the selected features, see Figure 10.46. On selecting the **Solid** button , you can select a solid body for creating fillets.

10.45

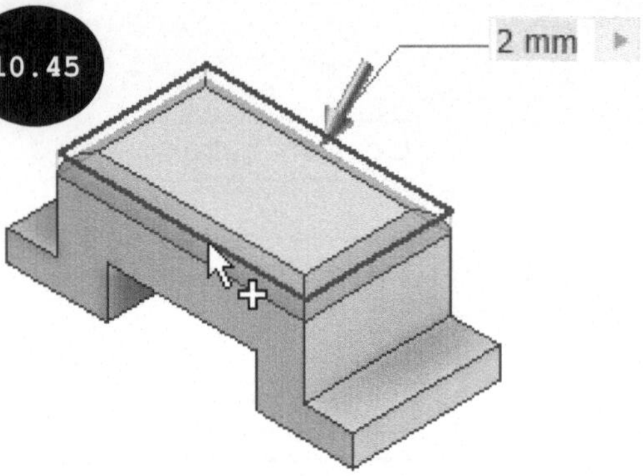

10.46

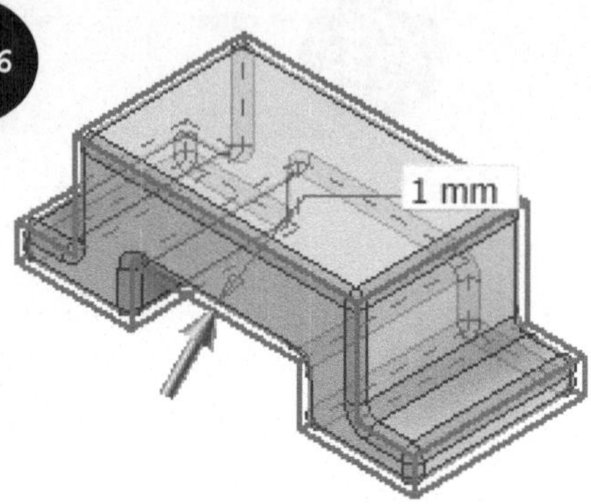

Add constant radius edge set: The Add constant radius edge set button in the property panel is used for creating multiple sets of fillets having different radii. To do so, click on the **Add constant radius edge set** button; a new row gets added in the property panel. Next, select an edge or multiple edges as the second set of fillets.

Tip: The number of edges that appear in the **Select Edges** selector acts as a single set of edges, that are selected for creating fillets of the same radius.

Fillet Radius: The **Fillet Radius** field displays the current or the default radius value of the fillet. You can click on the **Fillet Radius** field of the first row to specify a new radius value for the fillet, as required. You can define different radii for each set of fillets that are represented by different rows in the dialog box.

Continuity: By default, the **Tangent** option is selected in the **Continuity** drop-down list in the property panel, see Figure 10.47. As a result, the fillet is created with tangent continuity to its adjacent faces. On selecting the **Smooth (G2)** option, the fillet is created with curvature continuity to its adjacent faces. On selecting the **Inverted** option, the fillet gets inverted from a convex surface to a concave surface or vice versa, with curvature continuity to its adjacent faces.

10.47

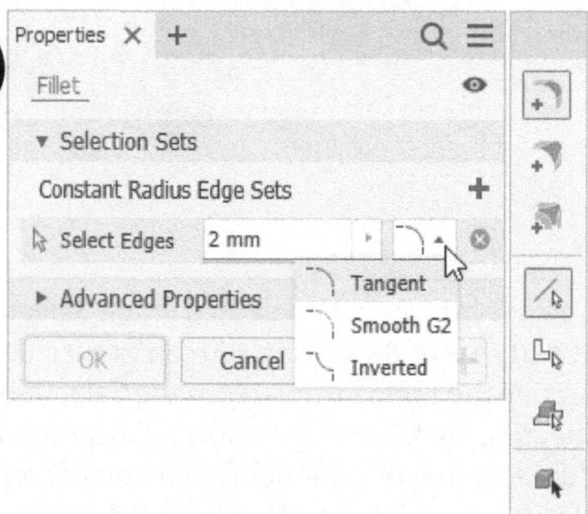

3. Specify the radius value in the **Fillet Radius** field of the property panel. The radius of the fillets gets modified in the graphics area, as specified.

4. Select the required option (**Tangent**, **Smooth (G2)**, or **Inverted**) in the **Continuity** drop-down list of the **Selection Sets** rollout of the property panel.

   You can expand the **Advanced** rollout in the **Fillet** property panel to display additional options for creating a fillet, see Figure 10.48. The options in the expanded property panel are discussed below:

10.48

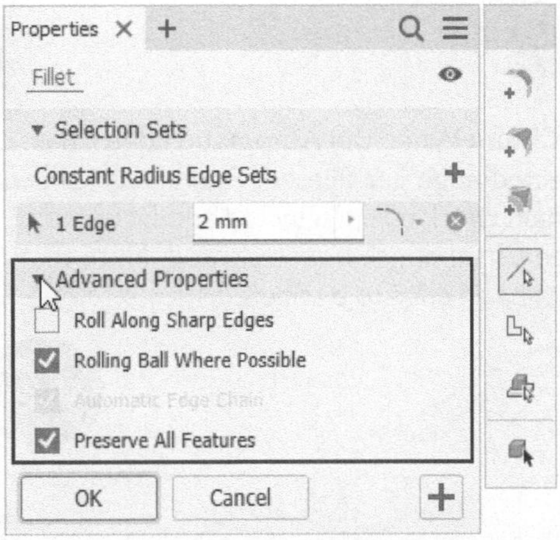

Roll Along Sharp Edges : On selecting the **Roll Along Sharp Edges** check box, the specified radius of the fillet varies to preserve the edges of the adjacent faces of the fillet. Figure 10.49 shows the preview of a fillet when the **Roll Along Sharp Edges** check box is selected, and Figure 10.50 shows the preview of a fillet when the **Roll Along Sharp Edges** check box is cleared.

10.49

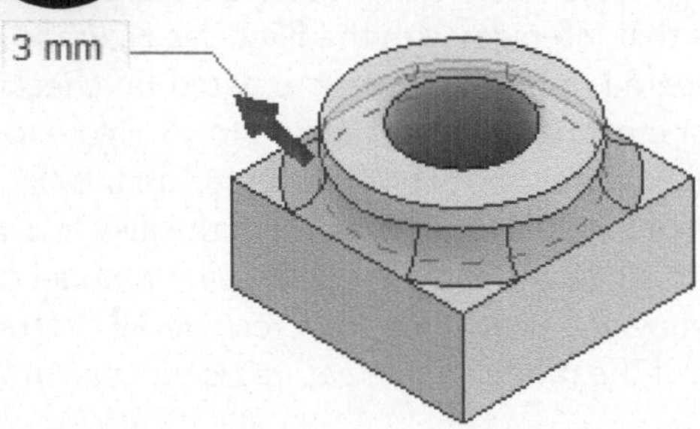

10.50

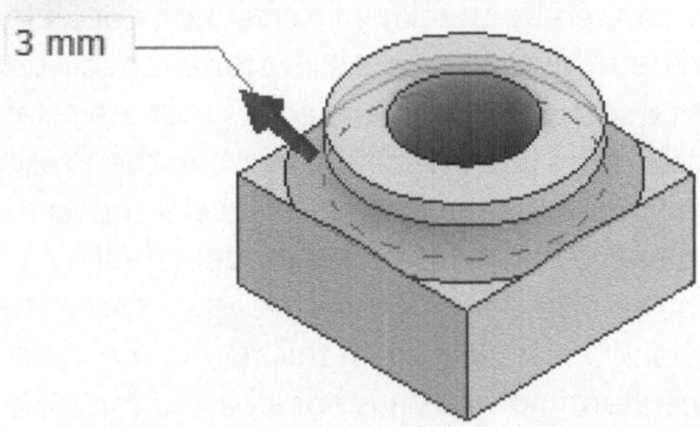

Rolling Ball Where Possible: On selecting the **Rolling Ball Where Possible** check box, the edge fillet is created such that a ball has been rolled along all the selected edges and their intersecting corners. Figure 10.51 shows an edge fillet when the **Rolling Ball Where Possible** check box is selected, and Figure 10.52 shows an edge fillet when the **Rolling Ball Where Possible** check box is cleared. Note that when the **Rolling Ball Where Possible** check box is cleared, a continuous tangent transition is created at the sharp corners of the fillet, see Figure 10.52.

10.51

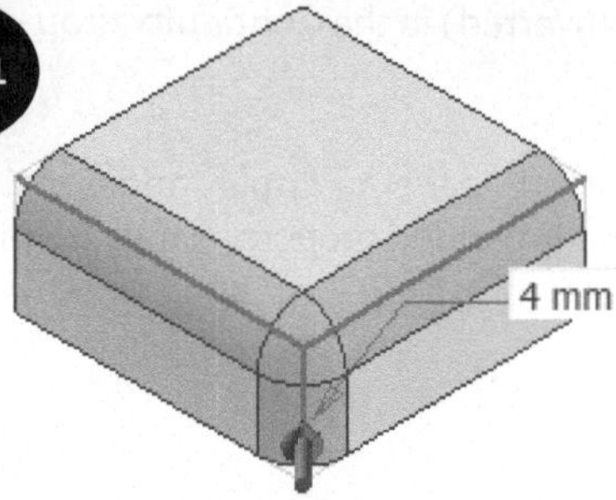

10.52

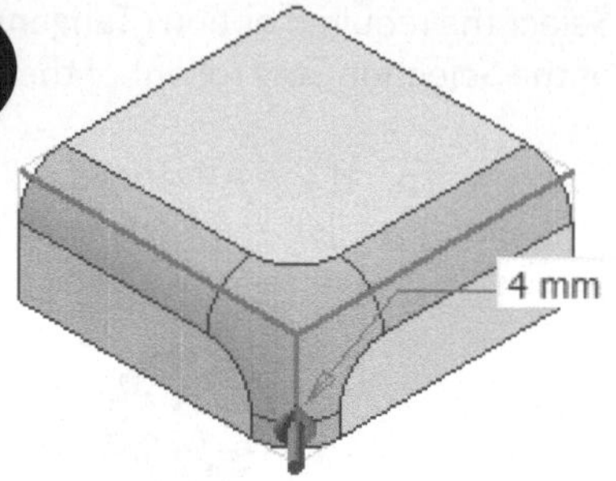

Automatic Edge Chain: When the **Automatic Edge Chain** check box is selected, all the edges tangent to the selected edge get filleted. Figure 10.53 shows the preview of a fillet when the **Automatic Edge Chain** check box is selected and Figure 10.54 shows the preview of a fillet when the **Automatic Edge Chain** check box is cleared. Note that this check box can be selected or cleared before selecting an edge to be filleted.

10.53

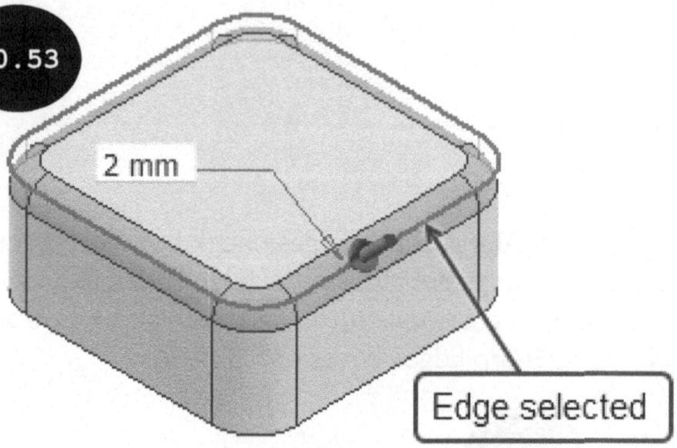

10.54

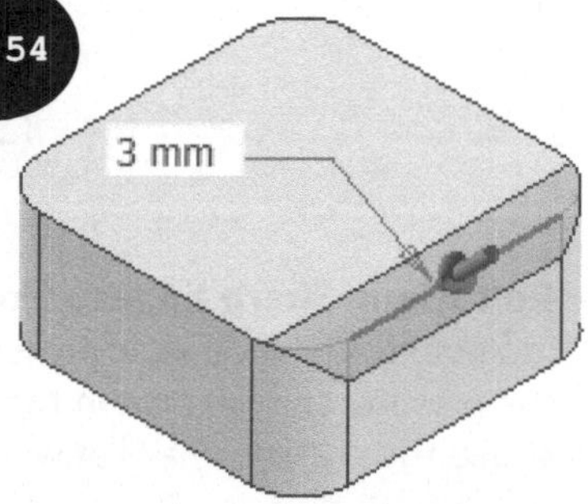

Preserve All Features: When the **Preserve All Features** check box is selected, a fillet feature is created by checking intersections of all features that intersect with the fillet, see Figure 10.55. When the **Preserve All Features** check box is cleared, a fillet feature is created by checking intersections of only the edges that are selected for creating a fillet, see Figure 10.56. Figure 10.55 shows the preview of a fillet when the **Preserve All Features** check box is selected. In this figure, the outer edge of the model is selected as the edge of the fillet and the radius of the fillet is larger than the thickness of the model (shell). As a result, a gap is created in the resultant model due to the fillet operation. Figure 10.56 shows the preview of a fillet when the **Preserve All Features** check box is cleared. In this figure, the inside edge of the model (shell feature) is retained in the resultant model as it is not a part of the fillet.

10.55

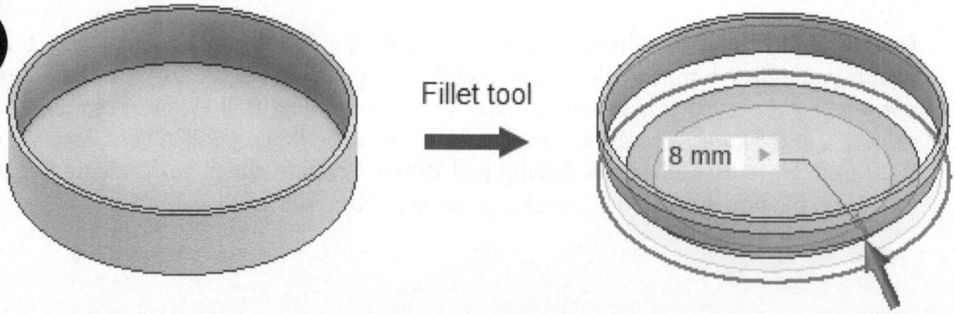

10.56

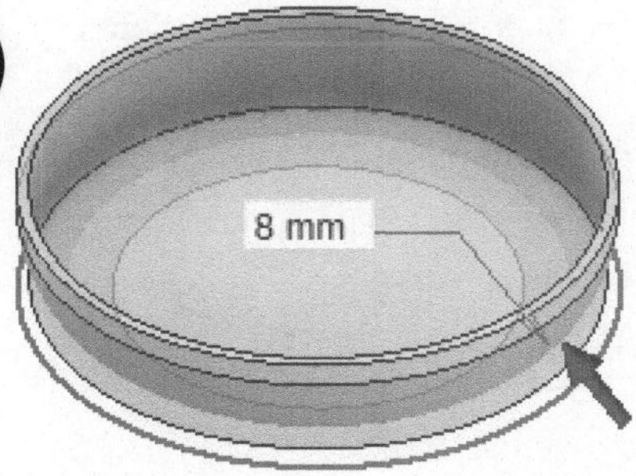

5. Click on the **Apply and create new fillet feature** button on the lower right corner of the property panel. A fillet of specified radius value is created and the **Fillet** property panel is still displayed in the graphics area. As a result, you can continue creating other fillet features.

6. Similarly, you can create other fillet features by using the Fillet property panel.

7. Click on the **OK** button in the **Fillet** property panel to create the fillets and exit the property panel.

Creating Variable Radius Edge Fillets

A variable radius edge fillet is a fillet that has variable radii along an edge, see Figure 10.57. You can create a variable radius edge fillet by using the options available in the **Fillet** property panel. The method for creating variable radii edge fillets is discussed below:

10.57

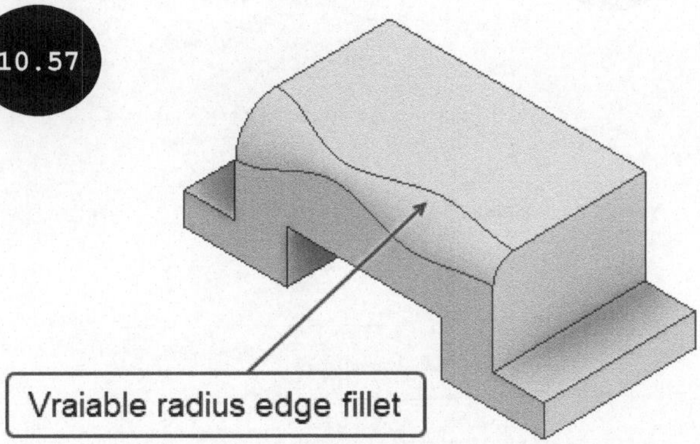

1. Click on the **Fillet** tool in the **Modify** panel of the **3D Model** tab or press the F key, see Figure 10.58. The **Fillet** property panel appears along with the **Tool Palette**.

10.58

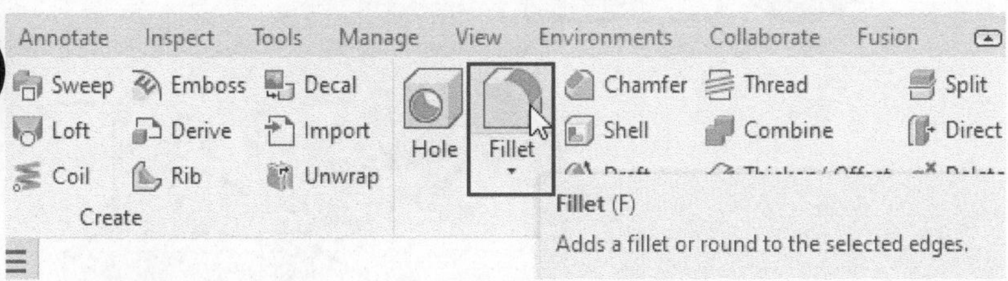

2. Click on the **Variable** button in the **Tool Palette** of the **Fillet** property panel. The options for creating variable radius fillets appear, see Figure 10.59.

10.59

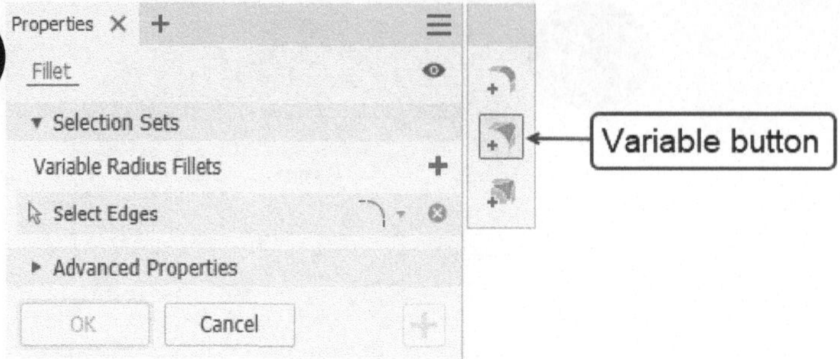

3. Select an edge for creating a variable radius fillet. The preview of a fillet appears on the selected edge with a default radius value at the start and end points of the selected edge. Also, the default radius value and the current position ratio of the start and end points of the selected edge appear in the **Variable Fillet Behavior** rollout of the property panel, refer to Figure 10.60. Note that this rollout appears after selecting an edge.

4. Specify different radius values on both the ends (start and end) of the selected edge in the respective fields of the **Variable Fillet Behavior** rollout, see Figure 10.60. In this figure, the radius value at the start point of the edge is specified as 2 mm and the radius value at the end point of the edge is specified as 5 mm. Figure 10.61 shows the preview of a resultant variable fillet.

10.60

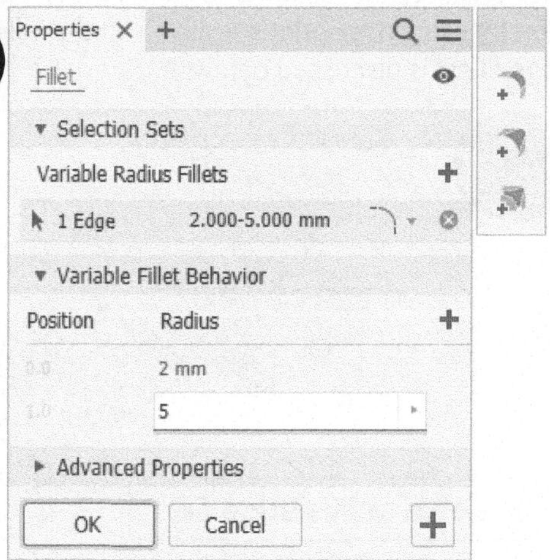

10.61

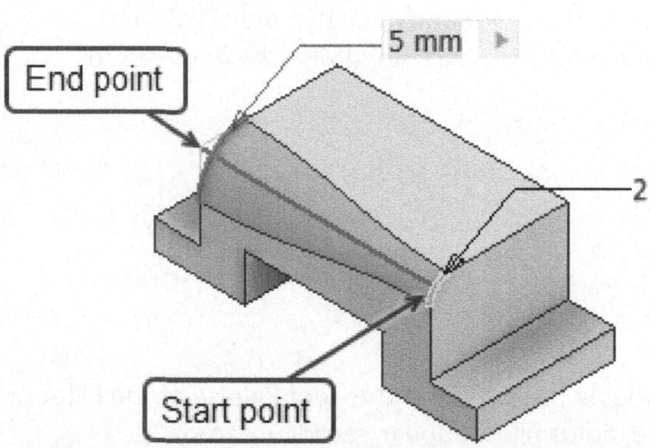

Tip: You can also specify radius values on both the ends of the selected edge in the **Radius** fields that appear in the graphics area. Note that the **Radius** field appears only on the active point (end or start) of the edge. You can click on the field in the property panel or in the graphics area to make it active for specifying its radius value.

In addition to defining variable radii on both ends of the selected edge, you can add multiple control points along the edge and specify a different radius value for each control point.

5. Move the cursor over the selected edge of the model in the graphics area, a yellow dot appears, see Figure 10.62. Next, click the left mouse button on the edge. A new control point gets added at the specified location on the edge and becomes an active point with the display of a **Radius** field in the graphics area, see Figure 10.63. Also, a new row gets added with default radius and position ratio in the **Variable Fillet Behavior** rollout of the property panel.

10.62

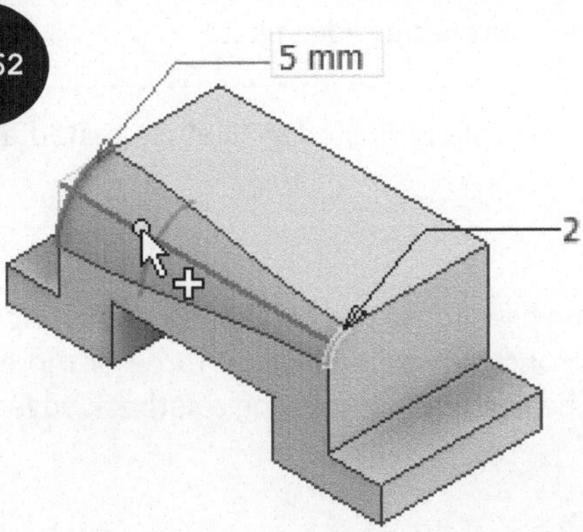

10.63

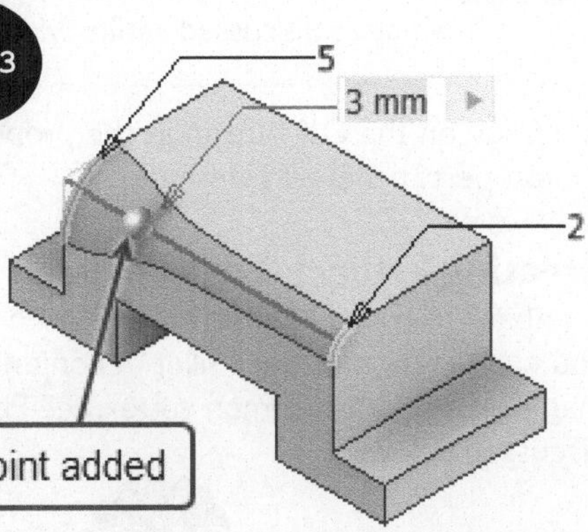

6. Specify a different radius value for the newly added control point in the respective **Radius** field. You can also specify the position of the control point on the selected edge by entering a position ratio in the range between 0 to 1 in the respective **Position** field of the property panel. Note that the position ratio is calculated in terms of the total length of the selected edge.

7. Similarly, you can add multiple control points by clicking the left mouse button on the selected edge and defining a different radius value for each control point.

   Smooth Radius Transition: By default, the **Smooth Radius Transition** check box is selected in the **Advanced Properties** rollout of the property panel. As a result, the resultant variable fillet is created such that a smooth transition is carried out from one radius value to the other, see Figure 10.64. When the **Smooth Radius Transition** check box is cleared, the resultant variable fillet is created such that a linear or straight transition is carried out from one radius value to the other, see Figure 10.65.

10.64

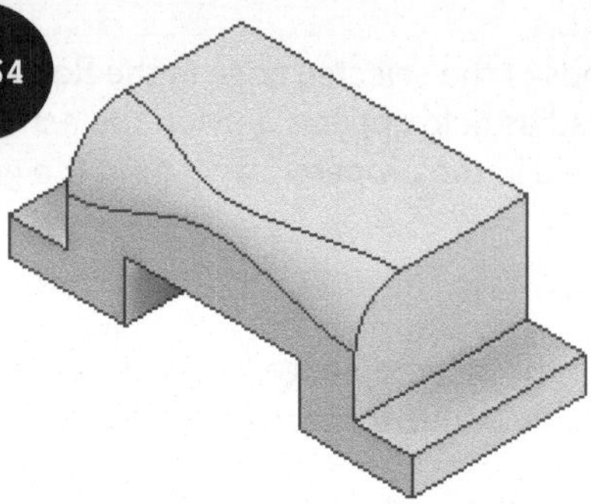

10.65

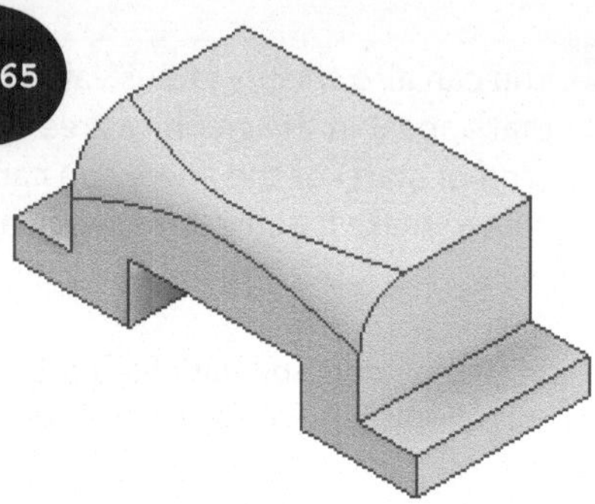

8. Ensure that the **Smooth Radius Transition** check box is selected in the **Advanced Properties** rollout of the property panel for a smooth transition between one radius value to the other.

Note: The remaining options in the **Advanced Properties** rollout of the **Fillet** property panel are same as discussed earlier while creating a constant radius edge fillet.

9. Click on the **OK** button in the property panel. A variable radius edge fillet is created and the property panel gets closed.

Creating Setback Edge Fillets

A setback fillet is a fillet that has a smooth transition from fillet edges to a common intersecting vertex. You can create a setback fillet in conjunction with a constant radius fillet on three or more edges that intersect at a common vertex, see Figure 10.66. The method for creating a setback edge fillet is discussed below:

10.66

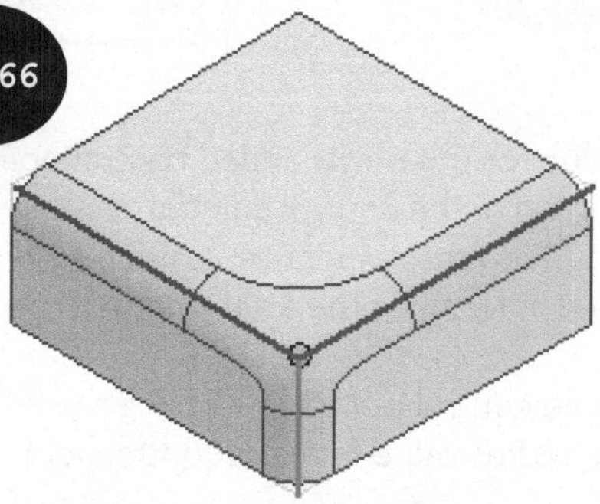

1. Click on the **Fillet** tool in the **Modify** panel of the **3D Model** tab. The **Fillet** property panel appears.

2. Select three or more edges one by one, that intersect at a common vertex. The preview of a constant radius fillet appears in the graphics area, see Figure 10.67.

3. Specify the radius value in the **Radius** field of the property panel.

   Now, you need to define a setback vertex for creating a setback edge fillet.

4. Click on the **Setback** button in the **Tool Palette** of the **Fillet** property panel and then select a vertex where the selected edges intersect each other, see Figure 10.68. The setback vertex gets

selected and its name appears in the **Corner Setbacks** area of the property panel. Also, the default setback distance of each selected edge appears in the **Corner Setback Behavior** rollout of the property panel, see Figure 10.69. Note that the setback distance of each selected edge is calculated from the selected vertex.

10.67

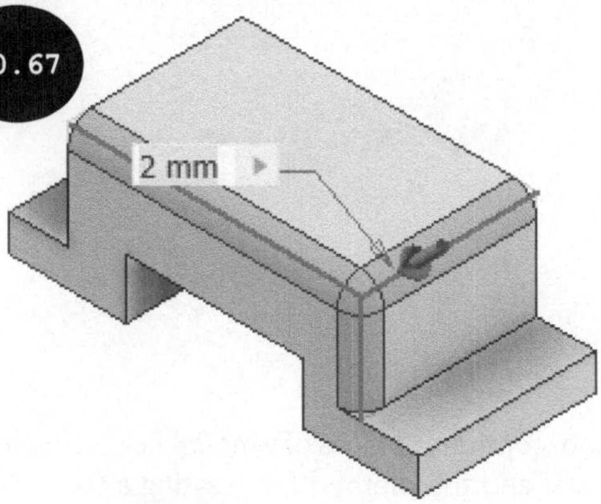

10.68

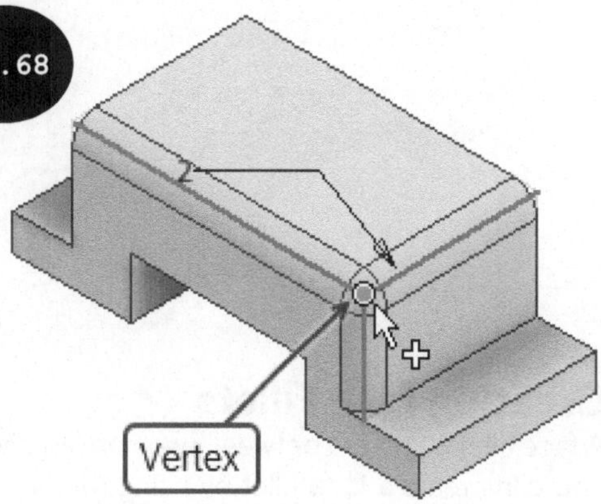

10.69

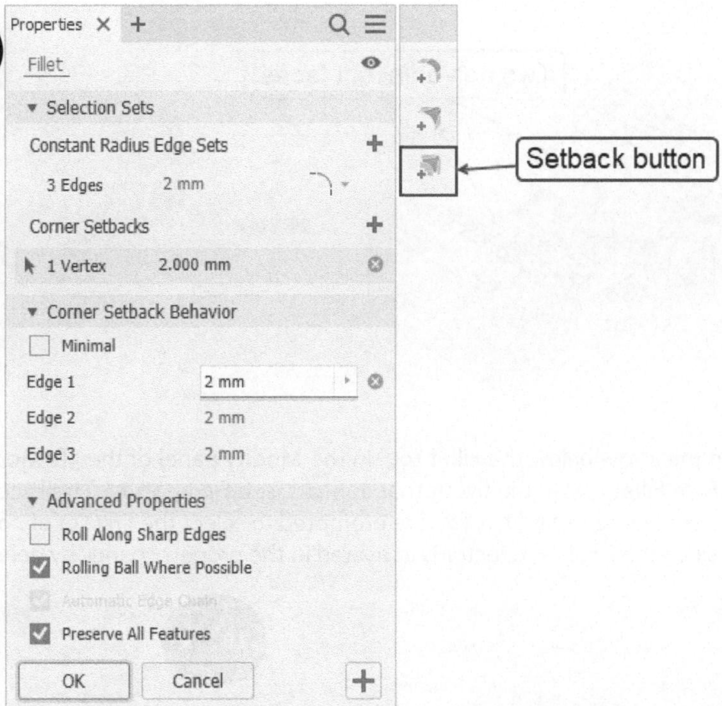

5. Enter the required setback distance for each individual edge of the fillet from the setback vertex in the respective field of the **Corner Setback Behavior** rollout of the property panel. Figure 10.70 shows the preview of a setback fillet with different setback distances assigned.

6. Click on the **OK** button in the dialog box. A setback fillet gets created and the dialog box gets closed. Figure 10.71 shows the resultant setback fillet.

10.70

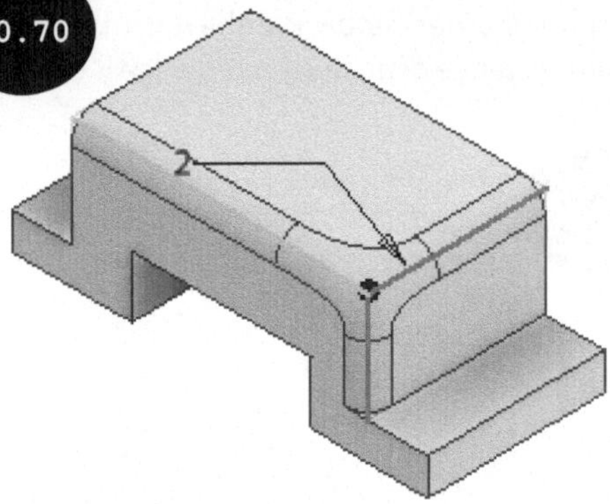

10.71

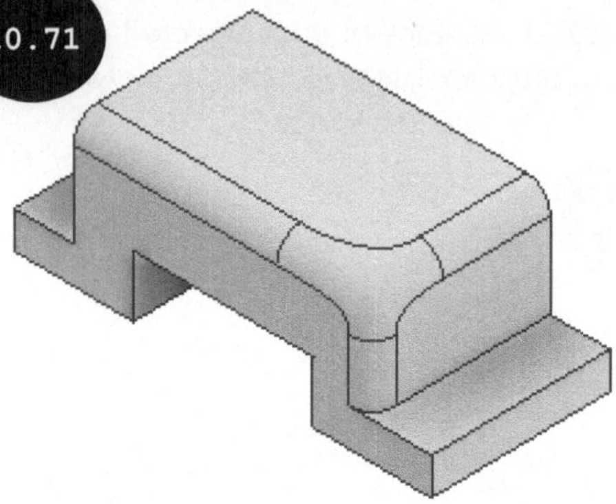

Creating Face Fillets

A face fillet is created between two non-adjacent or non-continuous faces of a model, see Figure 10.72. You can create a face fillet by using the **Face Fillet** tool and the method for creating a face fillet is discussed below:

10.72

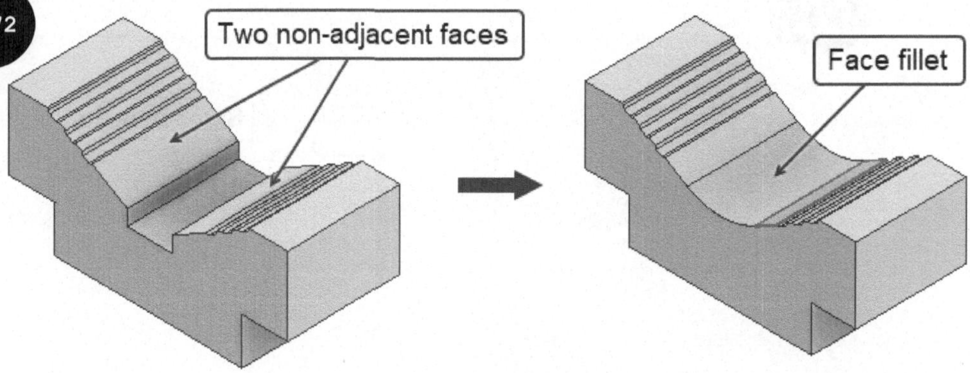

1. Click on the arrow below the **Fillet** tool in the **Modify** panel of the **3D Model** tab and then click on the **Face Fillet** tool in the flyout that appears, see Figure 10.73. The **Face Fillet** property panel appears, see Figure 10.74. Also, you are prompted to select the first set of non-adjacent faces of a model, since the **Faces A** selector is activated in the property panel, by default.

10.73

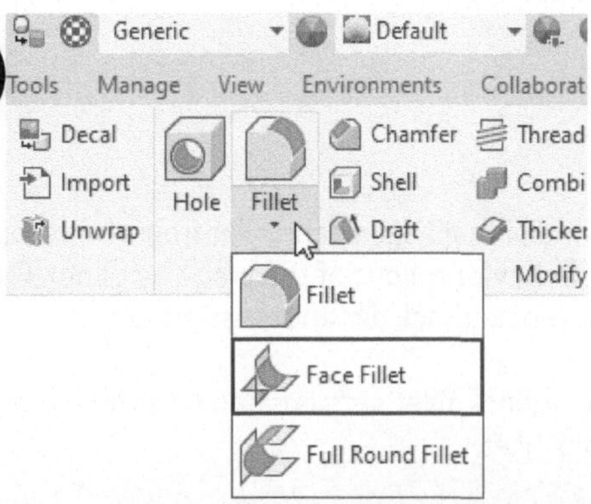

10.74

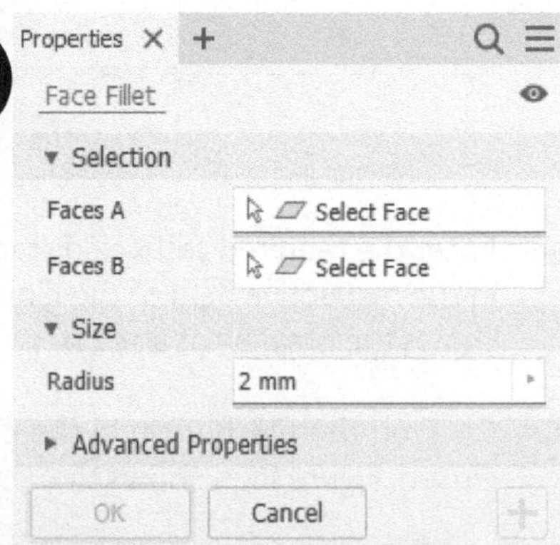

2. Select the first non-adjacent face of the model, see Figure 10.75. The **Faces B** selector gets activated in the dialog box and you are prompted to select the second set of non-adjacent faces.

Note: To select more than one face in each (first and second) set of the non-adjacent faces, you need to clear the **Optimize for Single Selection** check box in the **Advanced Properties** rollout of the property panel.

3. Select the second non-adjacent face of the model, see Figure 10.75. The preview of a face fillet appears in the dialog box.

4. Enter the radius value for the face fillet in the **Radius** field of the dialog box. In case the preview of the face fillet does not appear on the specified radius value then you need to adjust the radius value of the fillet.

5. Click on the **OK** button in the property panel. The face fillet is created between the selected faces of the model, see Figure 10.76.

10.75

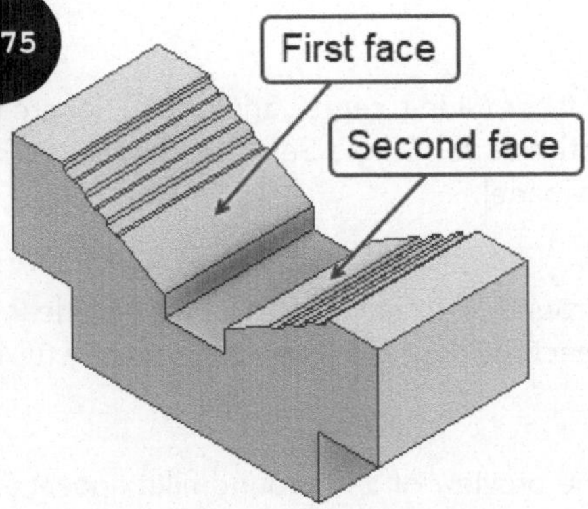

10.76

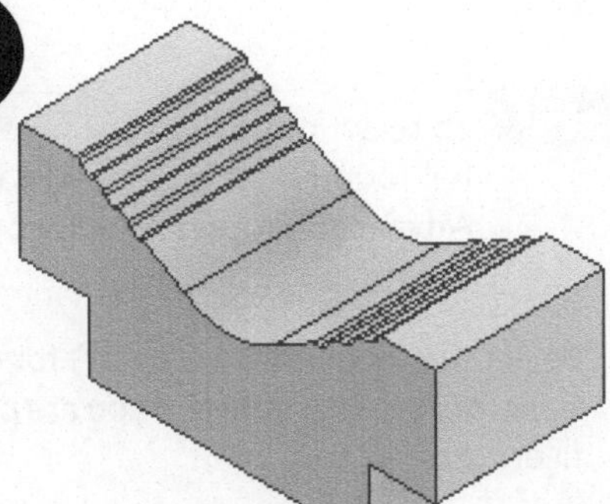

Creating Full Round Fillets

A full round fillet is created tangent to three adjacent faces of a model, see Figure 10.77. You can create a full round fillet by using the **Full Round Fillet** tool, the method for which is discussed below:

10.77

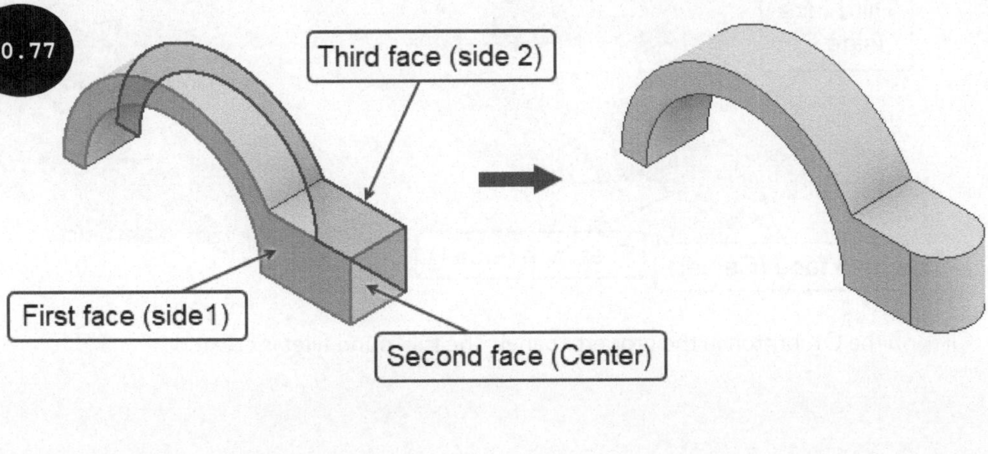

1. Click on the arrow below the **Fillet** tool in the **Modify** panel of the **3D Model** tab and then click on the **Full Round Fillet** tool in the flyout that appears. The **Full Round Fillet** property panel appears, see Figure 10.78. Also, you are prompted to select the first set of faces for creating a full round fillet, since the **Side A** Faces selector is activated in the property panel, by default.

10.78

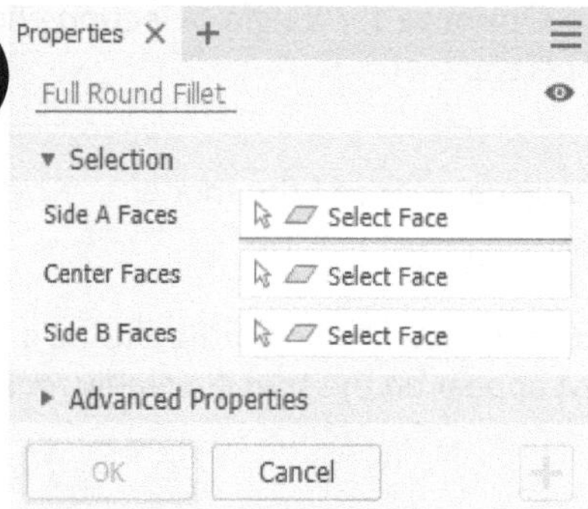

2. Select the first face (side 1) of the model, see Figure 10.79. The **Center Faces** selector gets activated in the dialog box and you are prompted to select a center face for creating a full round face.

Note: To select more than one face in each set of faces (side 1, center, and side 2), for creating a full round fillet, you need to clear the **Optimize for Single Selection** check box in the **Advanced Properties** rollout of the property panel.

3. Select the second face (center) for creating a full round fillet, see Figure 10.79. The **Side B Faces** selector gets activated and you are prompted to select the third face (side 2) to create a full round fillet.

4. Select the third face (side 2), see Figure 10.79. The preview of a full round fillet appears in the graphics area, see Figure 10.80.

10.79

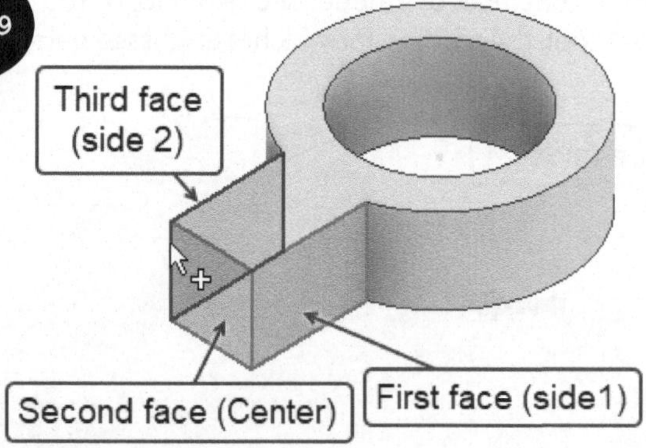

10.80

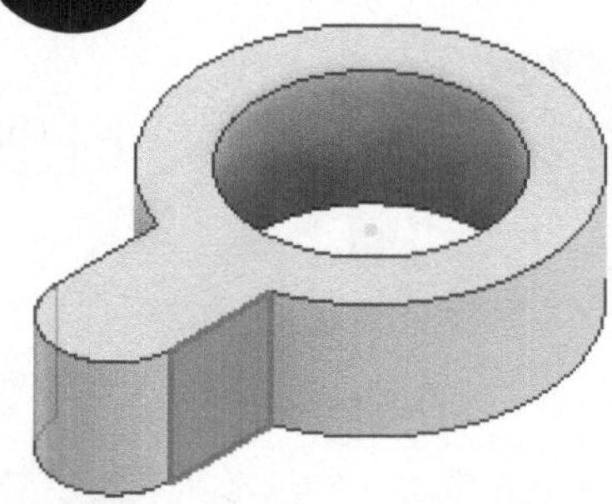

5. Click on the **OK** button in the property panel. The full round fillet is created.

Creating Chamfers

A chamfer is a bevel face that is non-perpendicular to its adjacent faces, see Figure 10.81. In Autodesk Inventor, you can create a chamfer by specifying a distance, distance, and angle, or two distances by using the **Chamfer** tool. The method for creating a chamfer is discussed below:

10.81

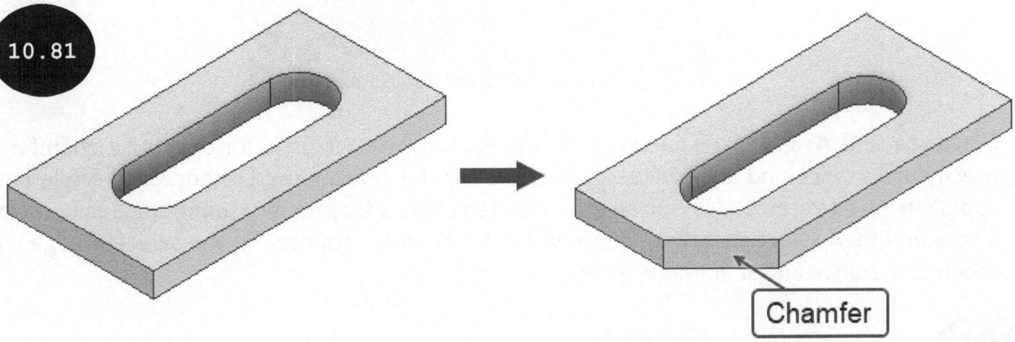

1. Click on the **Chamfer** tool in the **Modify** panel of the **3D Model** tab, see Figure 10.82. The **Chamfer** dialog box appears, see Figure 10.83.

10.82

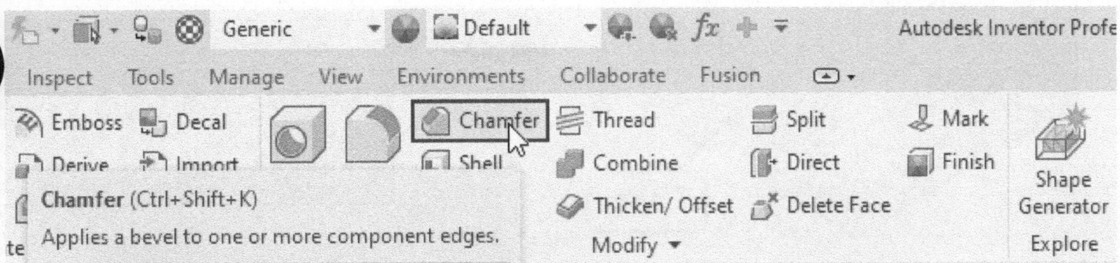

10.83

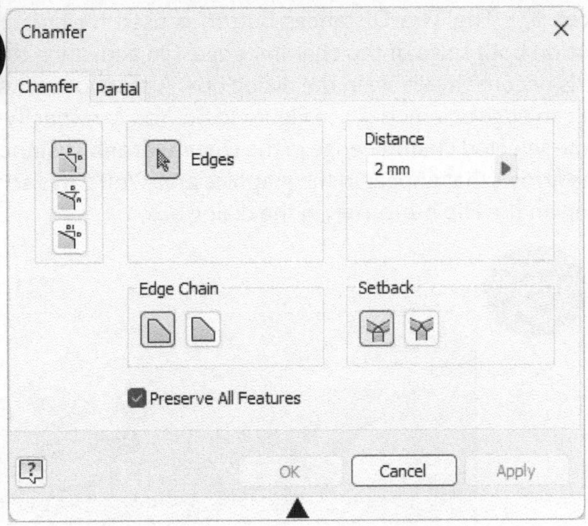

Distance: By default, the **Distance** button is activated in the **Chamfer** tab of the dialog box. As a result, you can create a chamfer with equal distance on both sides of the chamfer edge, see Figure 10.84. You can either specify the distance value in the **Distance** field of the dialog box or by dragging the arrow that appears in the graphics area after you select an edge of a model.

10.84

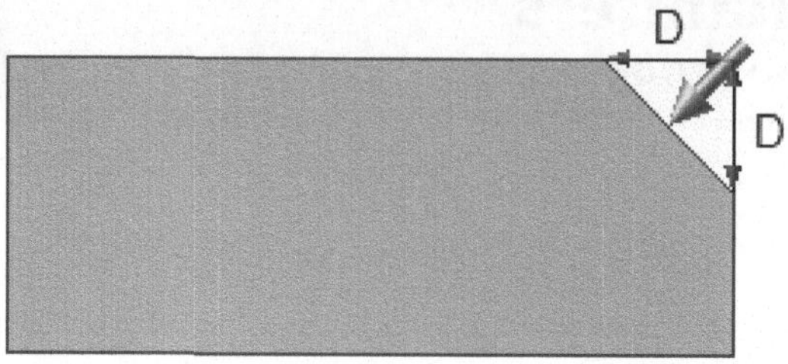

Distance and Angle: The **Distance and Angle** button is used for creating a chamfer by specifying distance and angle values. On activating this button, the **Distance** and **Angle** fields appear in the dialog box. Also, you are prompted to select a face for measuring angle value. Select a face and then select an edge. The preview of a chamfer appears on the selected edge with specified distance and angle values, see Figure 10.85.

10.85

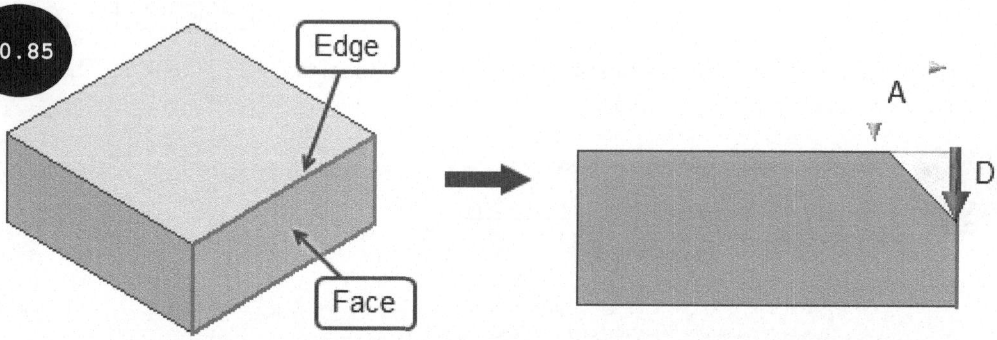

Two Distances: The **Two Distances** button is used for creating a chamfer with different distance values on both sides of the chamfer edge. On activating this button, the **Distance1** and **Distance2** fields become available in the dialog box. Also, two arrows appear in the graphics area after you select an edge of a model, see Figure 10.86. You can specify different distance values on both sides of the selected chamfer edge in the **Distance1** and **Distance2** fields of the dialog box or by dragging the arrows that appear in the graphics area. You can also flip the sides of the chamfer edge by clicking on the **Flip** button in the dialog box.

10.86

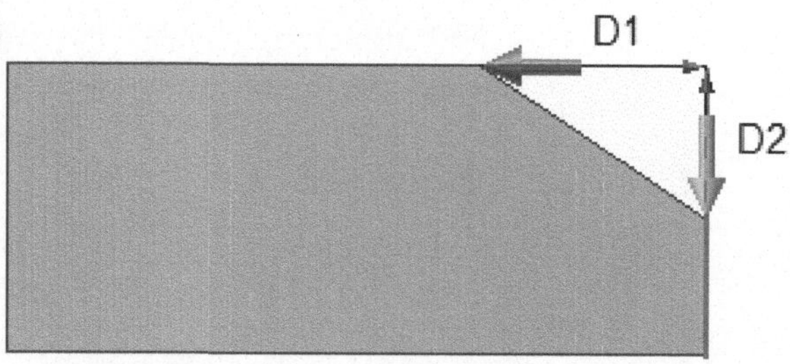

2. Click on the required button (**Distance, Distance and Angle**, or **Two Distances**) in the **Chamfer** dialog box to create a chamfer.

3. Select an edge of a model. The preview of a chamfer appears on the selected edge in the graphics area. Note that if the **Distance and Angle** button is activated then you first need to select a face of a model for measuring the angle value and then an edge for creating a chamfer.

4. Specify a distance value, distance and angle values, or two distance values in the respective fields depending upon the button activated (**Distance**, **Distance and Angle**, or **Two Distances**) in the dialog box for creating a chamfer.

Note: By default, the **All tangentially connected edges** button is activated in the **Edge Chain** area of the **Chamfer** dialog box. As a result, all the tangent edges of the selected edge get chamfered. Figure 10.87 shows the preview of a chamfer when the **All tangentially connected edges** button is activated, and Figure 10.88 shows the preview of a chamfer when the **Single edge** button is activated in the **Edge Chain** area of the dialog box.

10.87

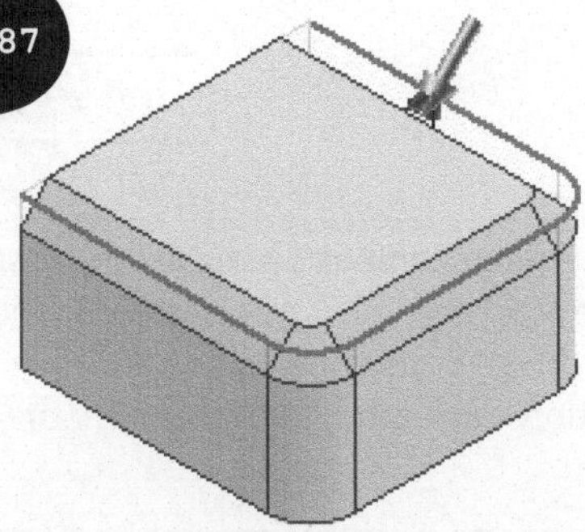

10.88

Setback or No Setback: By default, the **Setback** button is activated in the **Setback** area of the dialog box. As a result, the chamfer is created with a setback at the intersection of three or more than three chamfer edges, see Figure 10.89. On selecting the **No Setback** button, the chamfer is created with a corner point at the intersection of three or more than three chamfer edges, see Figure 10.90.

10.89

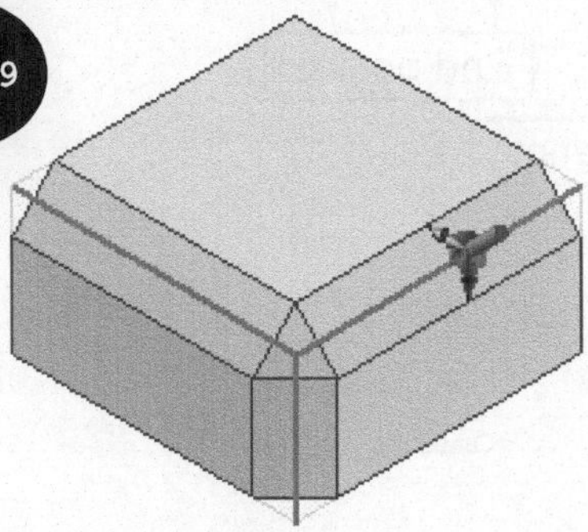

10.90

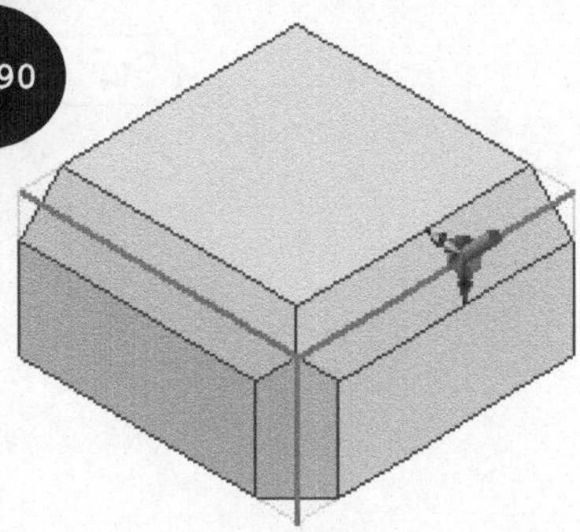

Partial tab: The options in the **Partial** tab of the **Chamfer** dialog box are used for creating a partial chamfer by specifying its start and end positions (vertices) along the chamfer edge. To do so, select an edge of a model for creating a partial chamfer and then click on the **Partial** tab in the dialog box. A point appears on the selected edge indicating the default start vertex of the partial chamfer, see Figure 10.91. You are prompted to specify a point along the chamfer edge for defining the end vertex (position) of the chamfer. Move the cursor along the chamfer edge and then click to specify the end vertex of the chamfer. The partial chamfer is created up to the specified end vertex along the edge, see Figure 10.92. The current position of the start and end vertices, and the length of the partial chamfer appear in the respective fields of the **To Start**, **To End**, and **Chamfer** columns, see Figure 10.93. You can specify the required start position, end position, and the length of the partial chamfer in the respective fields of the dialog box.

10.91

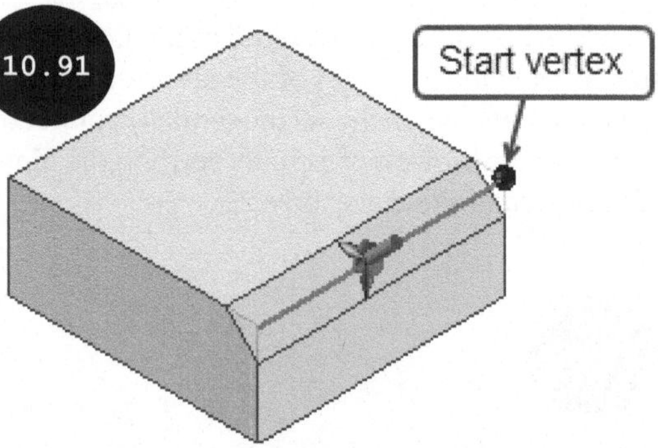

10.92

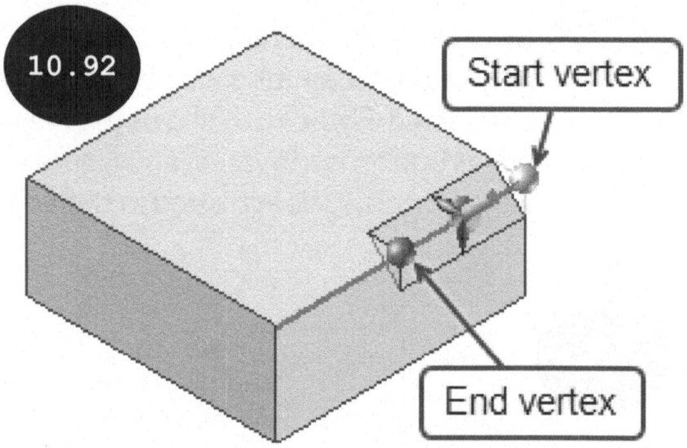

Note: When the **To Start** option is selected in the **Set Driven Dimension** drop-down list of the **Partial** tab in the dialog box, the field under the **To Start** column is not enabled in the dialog box and the start position of the partial chamfer is driven by its end position and the chamfer length. Similarly, when the **To End** or **Chamfer** option is selected, the field under the **To End** or **Chamfer** column is not enabled.

10.93

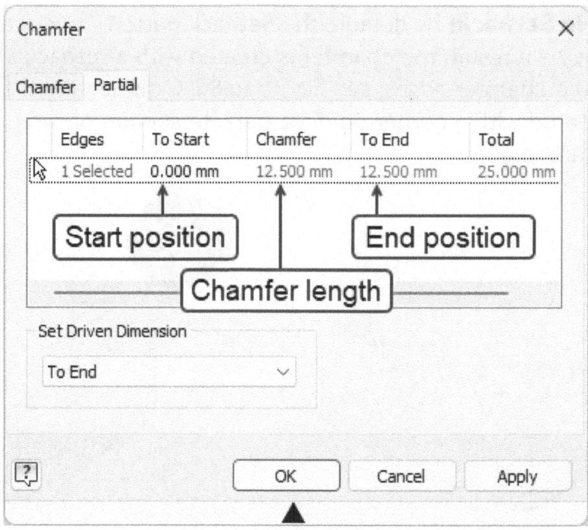

Tip: You can also drag the start vertex and the end vertex handles that appear in the graphics area for defining the start and end positions of the partial chamfer, respectively.

5. After defining all parameters for creating a chamfer, click on the **Apply** button and then the **Cancel** button. The chamfer is created.

Splitting a Face and a Solid Body

In Autodesk Inventor, you can split the face of a model or a solid body by using the **Split** tool. The methods for splitting a face or a body are discussed next.

Splitting the Face of a Model

1. Click on the **Split** tool in the **Modify** panel of the **3D Model** tab, see Figure 10.94. The **Split** property panel appears, see Figure 10.95.

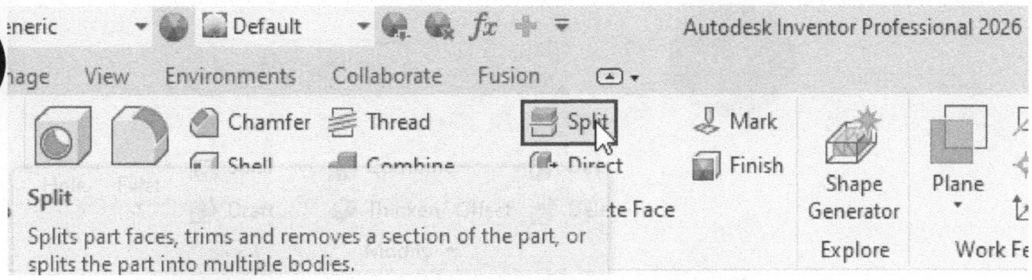

10.94

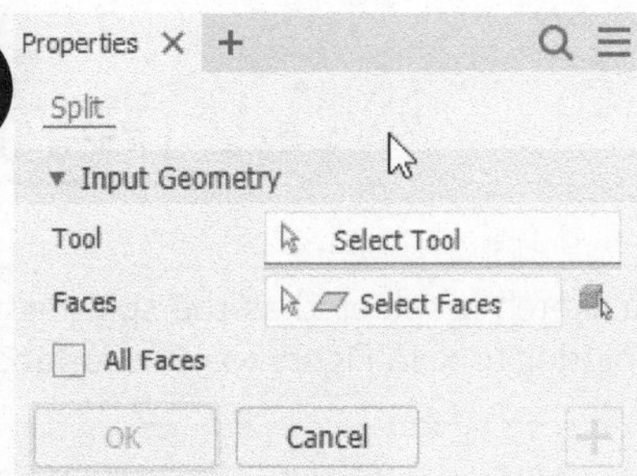

10.95

Tool: By default, the **Tool** selector is activated in the property panel and is used for selecting a splitting tool to split one or more faces of a model. You can select a sketch, a work plane, or a surface as a splitting tool.

2. Select a sketch, a work plane, or a surface as a splitting tool, see Figures 10.96 through 10.98. After selecting a splitting tool, the **Faces** selector gets activated in the property panel and you are prompted to select the faces of the model.

Tip: If the **Solid selection** button is activated in the property panel then the **Solid** selector appears for selecting a solid body to be split. You will learn about splitting a solid body later in this chapter.

3. Select one or more faces of a model to be split, see Figures 10.96 through 10.98.

10.96

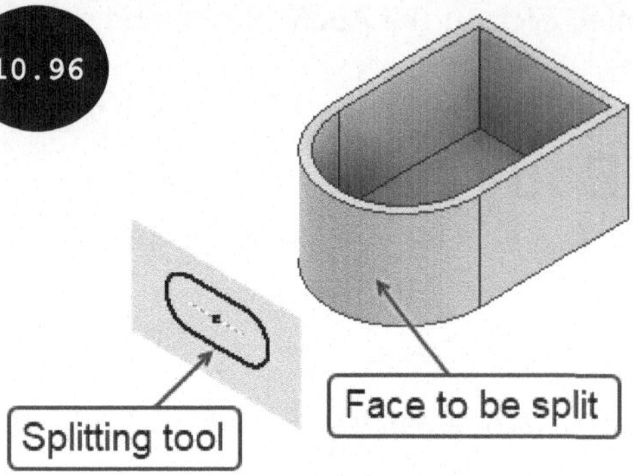

10.97

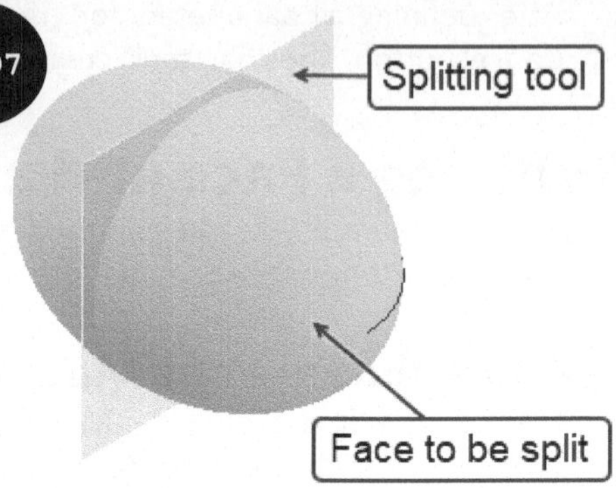

10.98

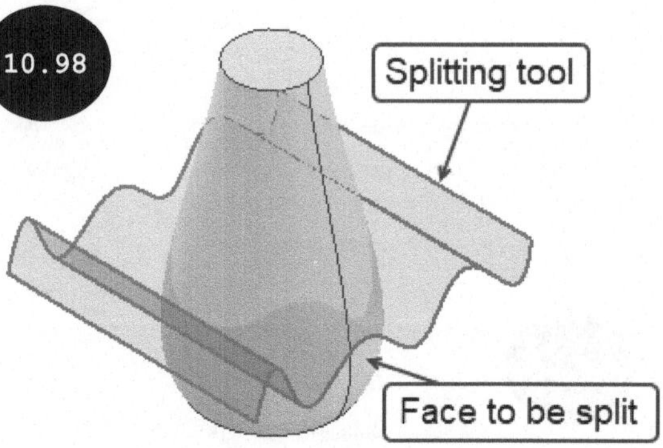

Note: In Figure 10.96, a sketch is selected as the splitting tool. In Figure 10.97, a work plane is selected as the splitting tool. In Figure 10.98, a surface is selected as the splitting tool.

All Faces: By default, the **All Faces** check box is cleared in the property panel. As a result, only the selected face(s) of the model gets split. On selecting the **All Faces** check box, all faces of the model that intersect the selected splitting tool get split.

4. Ensure that the **All Faces** check box is cleared in the property panel for splitting only the selected face(s) of the model.

5. Click on the **OK** button in the property panel. The selected face(s) of the model gets split, see Figures 10.99 through 10.101.

10.99

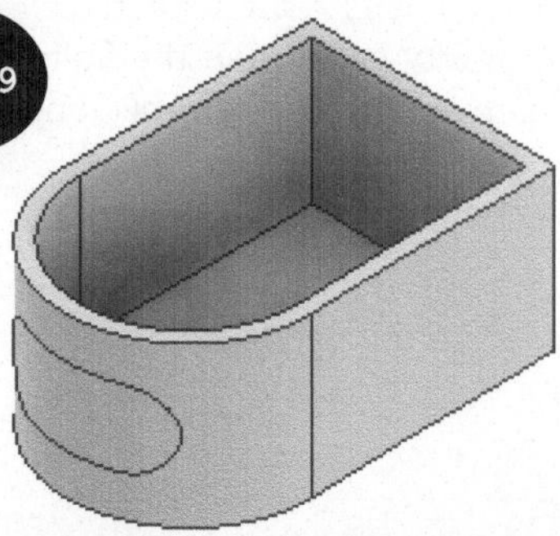

10.100

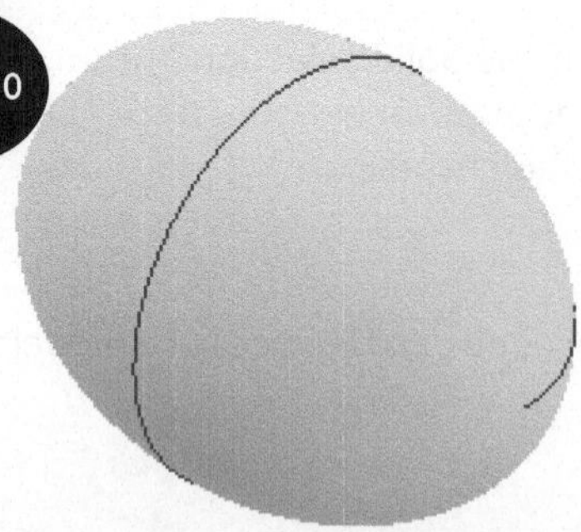

10.101

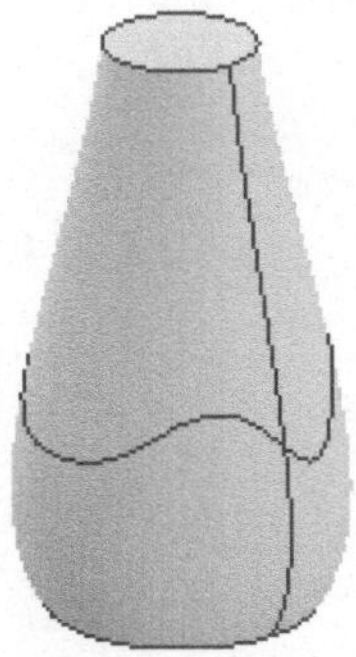

Splitting a Solid Body

In Autodesk Inventor, you can split a solid body into two bodies or remove one of its sides using the **Split** tool. The method for the same is discussed below:

1. Click on the **Split** tool in the **Modify** panel of the **3D Model** tab. The **Split** property panel appears.

2. Select a sketch, a work plane, or a surface as a splitting tool, see Figures 10.102 and 10.103. The name of the selection appears in the **Tools** selector of the property panel. In both these figures, a work plane is selected as the splitting tool.

10.102

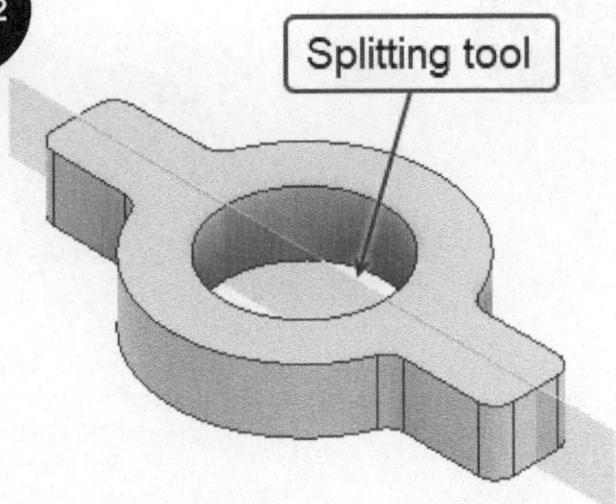

10.103

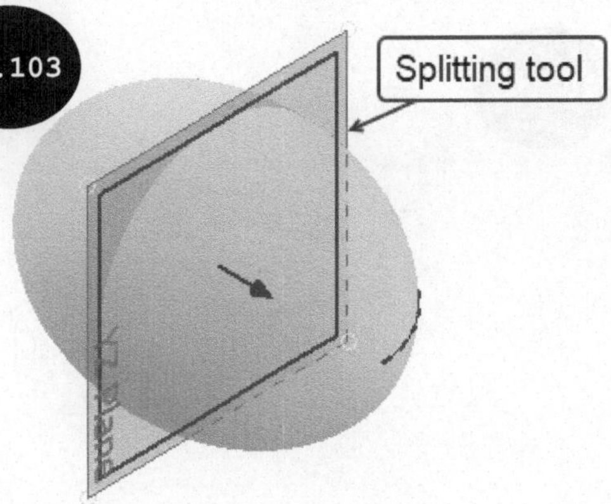

Solid selection : The **Solid selection** button in the **Split** property panel is used for selecting a solid body to be split.

3. Click on the **Solid selection** button in the property panel to activate it. The **Solid** selector appears and the entire solid body gets selected as the body to be split, see Figure 10.104. Also, the **Behavior** rollout appears in the property panel. Note that if two or more solid bodies are available in the graphics area then you need to select a solid body to be split.

10.104

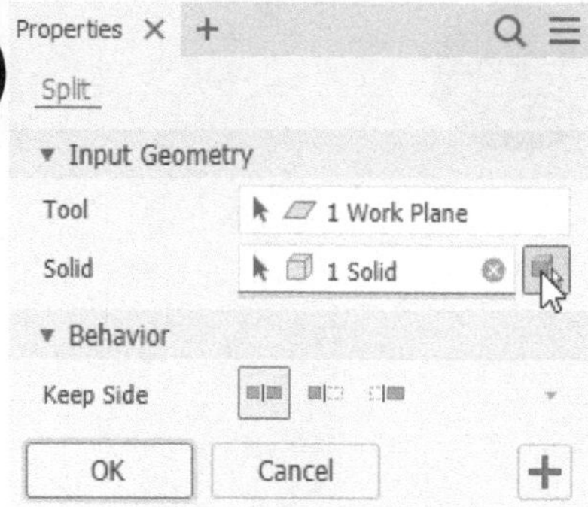

4. Click on the required button (**Split the solid and keep both sides**, **Split the solid and keep the default side**, or **Split the solid and keep the opposite side**) in the **Behavior** rollout of the property panel for keeping both sides of the body or defining the side of the body to be retained. On selecting the **Split the solid and keep the default side** or **Split the solid and keep the opposite side** button, an arrow appears in the graphics area pointing toward the side of the body to be removed.

5. Click on the **OK** button in the property panel. The body gets split into two bodies or one of its sides gets removed depending upon the button selected in the **Behavior** rollout, see Figures 10.105 and 10.106.

10.105

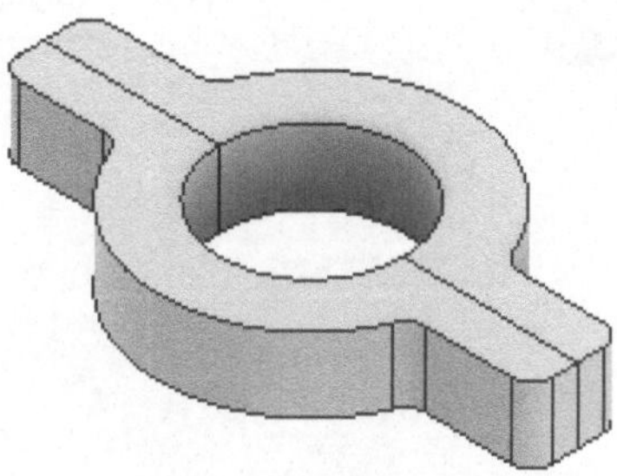

10.106

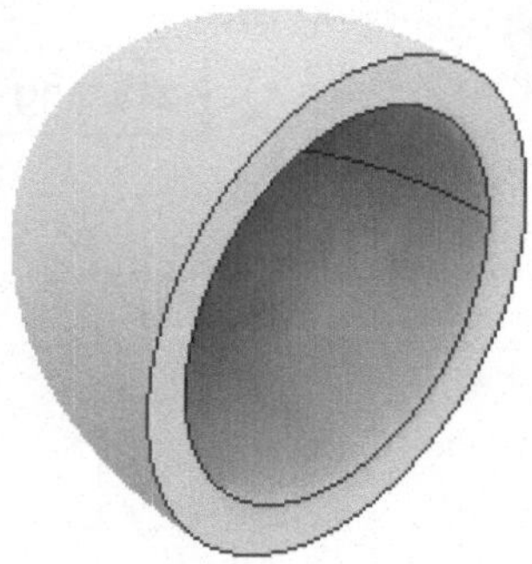

Tip: The **Solid Bodies** folder in the **Browser** displays the number of bodies available in the graphics area.

Creating 3D Sketches and Curves

In Autodesk Inventor, in addition to creating 2D sketches, you can also create 3D sketches and curves in the 3D Sketching environment, for which you need to invoke the 3D Sketching environment of Autodesk Inventor. To do so, click on the arrow at the bottom of the **Start 2D Sketch** tool in the **Sketch** panel of the **3D Model** tab, see Figure 10.107. Next, click on the **Start 3D Sketch** tool in the flyout that appears, see Figure 10.107. The 3D Sketching environment is invoked and the **3D Sketch** tab appears in the **Ribbon**, see Figure 10.108. Now, you can create 3D sketches by using the tools available in the **3D Sketch** tab of the **Ribbon**. Some of the tools of the **3D Sketch** tab are discussed below:

10.107

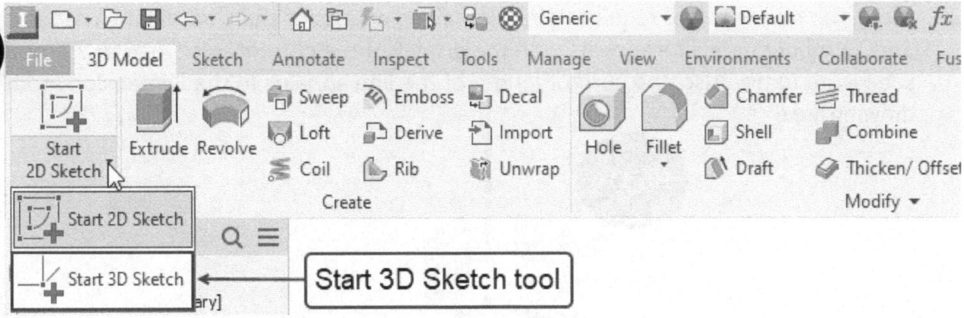

10.108

Creating a 3D Sketch by Using the Line Tool

The method for creating a 3D sketch by using the **Line** tool of the **3D Sketch** tab is discussed below:

1. Click on the **Line** tool in the **Draw** panel of the **3D Sketch** tab or press the **L** key. The Coordinate Triad appears at the origin of the drawing area and you are prompted to specify the start point of the line, see Figure 10.109. Also, the coordinates of the current location of the cursor appear in the Pointer Input boxes. Change the view orientation to isometric.

10.109

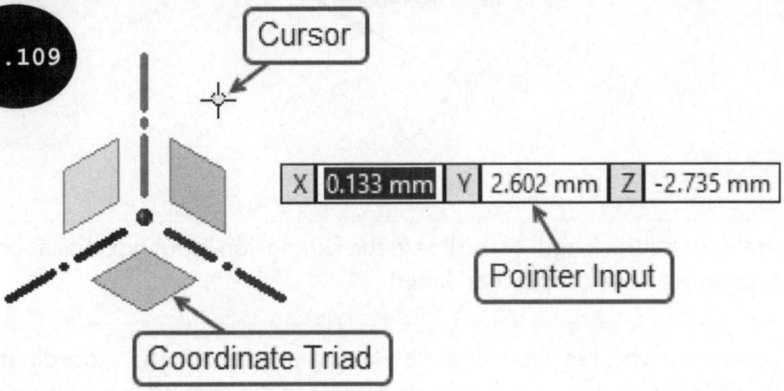

2. Click to specify the start point of the line in the graphics area. Alternatively, you can enter the coordinates of the start point in the Pointer Input boxes.

   After specifying the start point, you need to specify the endpoint of the line. You can turn on the Ortho mode for creating horizontal or vertical straight lines.

3. Ensure that the **Ortho Mode** button is activated in the Status Bar for creating horizontal or vertical straight lines. To create lines at an angle, you can turn off the ortho mode by clicking on the **Ortho Mode** button in the Status Bar. It is a toggle button.

4. Move the cursor to the required direction along an axis of the Coordinate Triad in the drawing area. A rubber band line appears with the display of the current axis (X, Y, or Z) near the cursor, see Figure 10.110. Also, the current length of the line appears in the Dimension Input box in the drawing area.

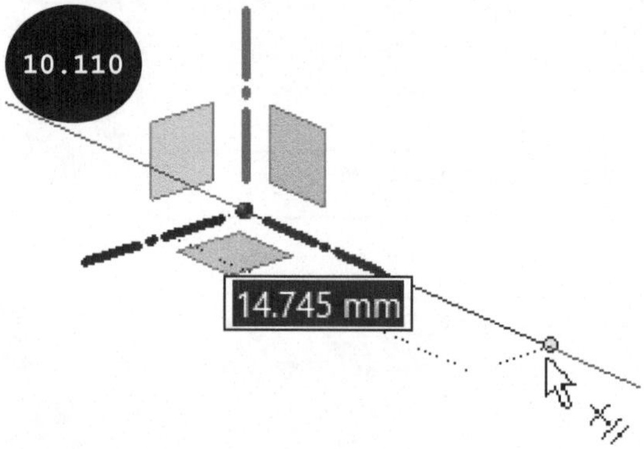

5. Click to specify the endpoint of the first line segment. A line is created and the Coordinate Triad is moved to the last specified point in the drawing area, see Figure 10.111. Also, you are prompted to specify the end point of the second line segment.

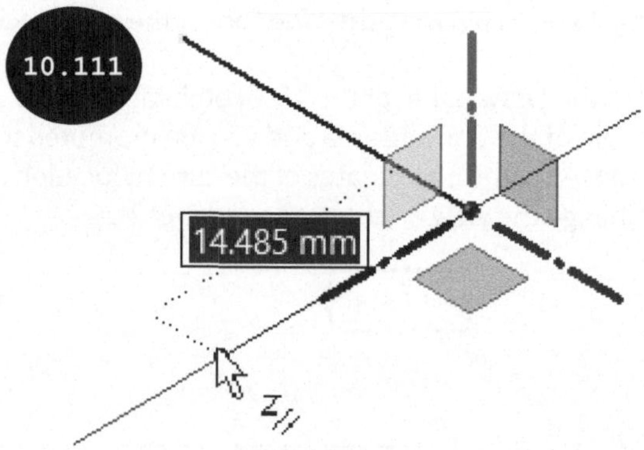

Tip: You can also enter the length of the line in the Dimension Input box that appears in the drawing area for creating a line of specified length.

6. Move the cursor to the required direction along an axis of the Coordinate Triad (refer to Figure 10.111) and then click to specify the end point of the second line segment. The second line segment gets created and you are prompted to specify the end point of the third line.

Tip: You can also click on a plane of the Coordinate Triad in the drawing area for specifying the end point of a line segment on that selected plane.

7. Similarly, you can continue to create contiguous straight line segments one after the other by specifying points in the drawing area, refer to Figure 10.112.

8. After creating all the line segments, right-click in the drawing area and then click on the **OK** button in the Marking Menu that appears to end the creation of line segments and exit the **Line** tool. Figure 10.113 shows a 3D sketch created by using the **Line** tool for your reference.

10.112

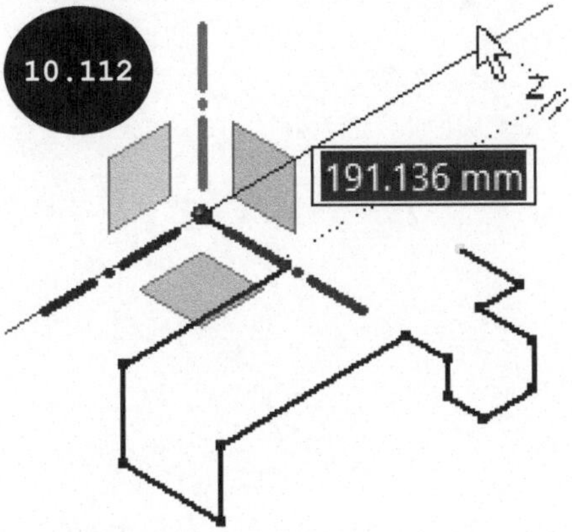

10.113

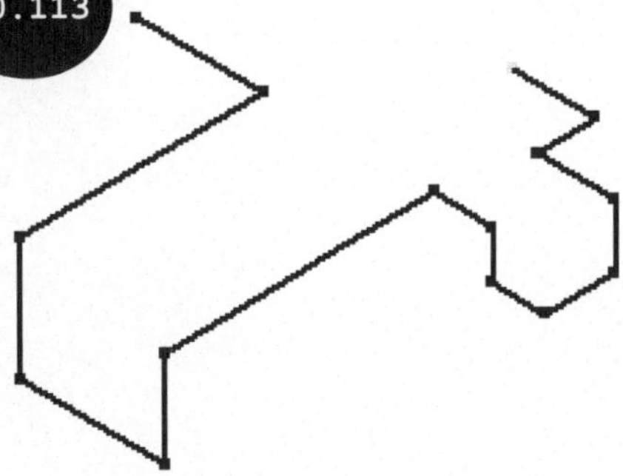

Tip: After creating a 3D sketch, you can apply dimensions and constraints. The method for applying dimensions and constraints to a 3D sketch in the 3D Sketching environment is same as applying dimensions and constraints to a 2D sketch.

Note: In Autodesk Inventor, you can also add tangent bends automatically at the corners of 3D line segments, see Figure 10.114. For doing so, after involving the **Line** tool in the 3D Sketching environment, right-click in the drawing area and then click on the **Auto-Bend** option in the Marking Menu that appears, see Figure 10.115. Now, on creating a chain of straight line segments one after the other, tangent bends get added automatically at the corners of the line segments with a default radius value. To change the default radius value of the tangent bends, click on the **Document Settings** tool in the **Tools** tab of the **Ribbon** and then click on the **Sketch** tab in the **Document Settings** dialog box that appears. Next, enter the required bend radius in the **Auto-Bend Radius** field of the dialog box.

10.114

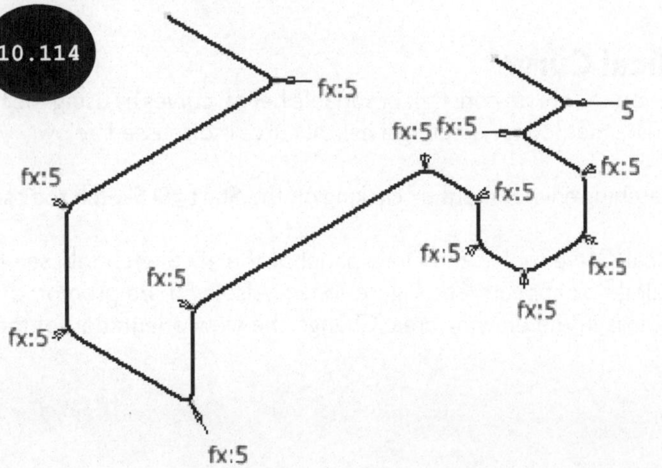

10.115

9. After creating a 3D sketch by using the **Line** tool, click on the **Finish Sketch** tool in the **Exit** panel to exit the 3D Sketching environment.

   Figure 10.116 shows a 3D sketch and Figure 10.117 shows a sweep feature created by sweeping a circular profile along the 3D sketch (3D sketch is selected as the path). Note that to create a sweep feature, you also need to create a profile that will be swept along the path.

10.116

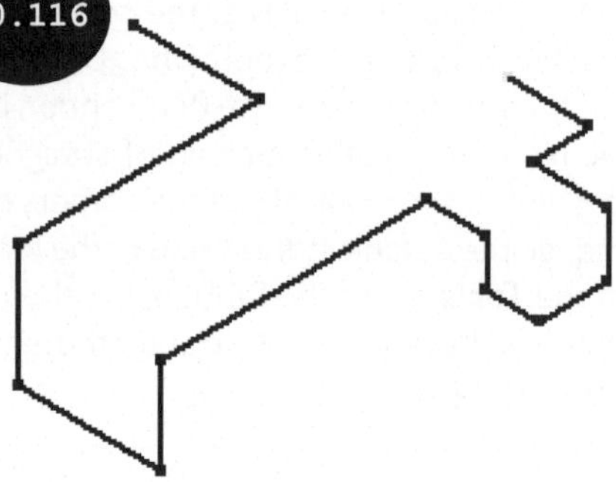

10.117

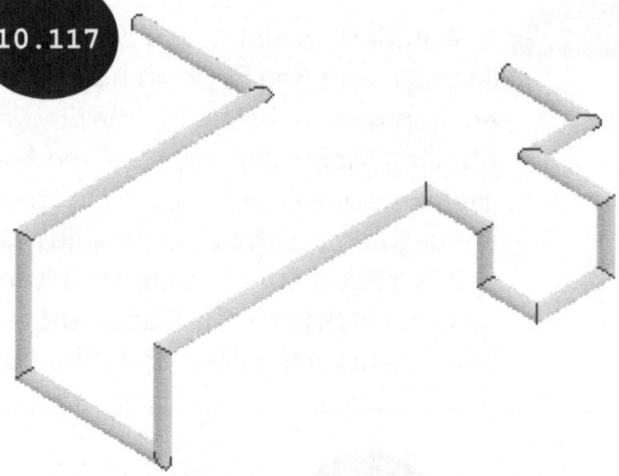

Creating a Helical Curve

In Autodesk Inventor, you can create constant or variable helical curves by using the **Helical Curve** tool of the **3D Sketch** tab. The method for creating a helical curve is discussed below:

1. Invoke the 3D Sketching environment by clicking on the **Start 3D Sketch** tool, see Figure 10.118.

2. Click on the **Helical Curve** tool in the **Draw** panel of the **3D Sketch** tab, see Figure 10.119. The **Helical Curve** dialog box appears, see Figure 10.120. Also, you are prompted to specify a start point of the helix axis in the drawing area. Change the view orientation of the drawing area to isometric.

10.118

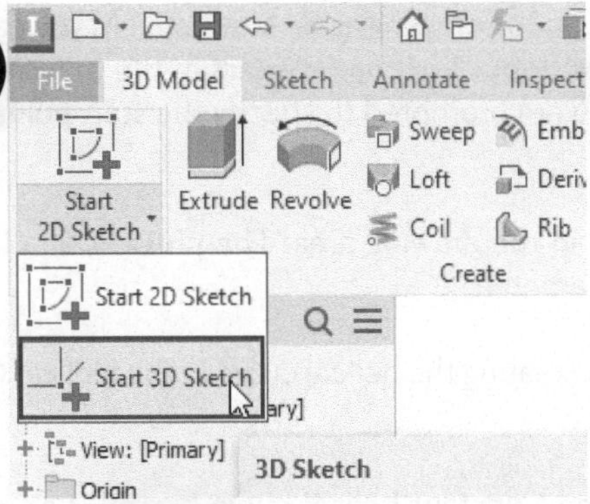

10.119

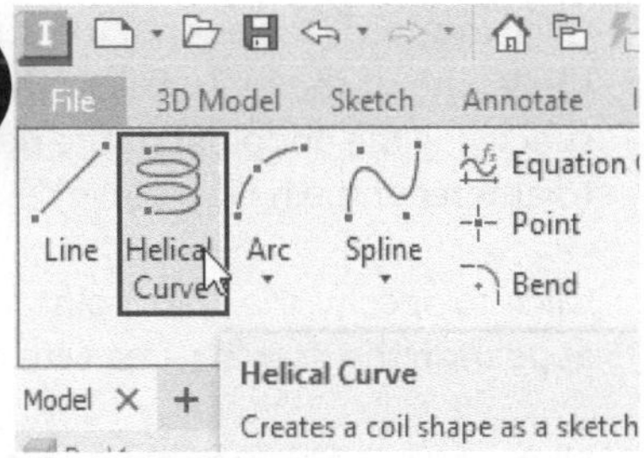

10.120

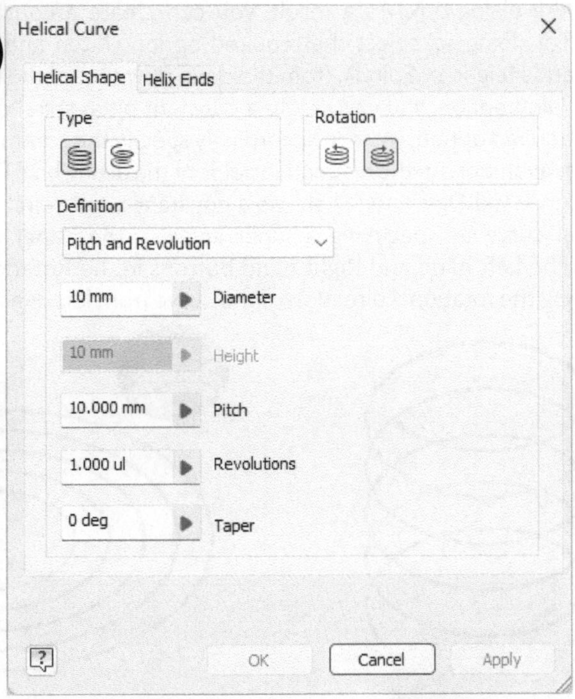

3. Click to specify the start point of the helix axis in the drawing area. You are prompted to specify the endpoint of the helix axis.

4. Move the cursor to the required direction along an axis of the Coordinate Triad in the drawing area. The preview of a helical curve appears with default parameters, see Figure 10.121.

10.121

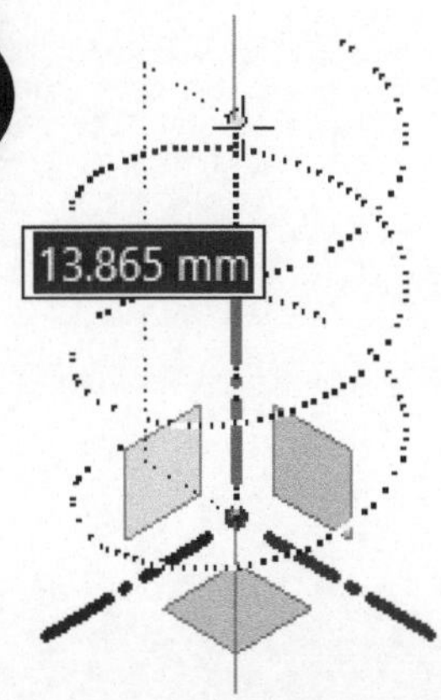

5. Click to specify the endpoint of the helix axis in the drawing area. Alternatively, you can also enter the length of the helix axis in the Dimension Input box that appears in the drawing area. After specifying the endpoint of the helix axis, you are prompted to specify the start point of the helix (diameter of the helical curve).

6. Click to specify the start point of the helix in the drawing area. The preview of a helical curve appears in the drawing area with default parameters.

   Now, you need to define the parameters for creating the helical curve in the **Helical Curve** dialog box. The options are discussed below:

   Constant helical curve : By default, the **Constant helical curve** button is activated in the **Type** area of the dialog box. As a result, you can create a constant pitch helical curve, see Figure 10.122. For doing so, select the required option (**Pitch and Revolution**, **Revolution and Height**, **Pitch and Height**, or **Spiral**), from the drop-down list of the **Definition** area. Note that on selecting the **Spiral** option, you can create a constant pitch spiral curve, see Figure 10.123. After selecting the required option, you can accordingly specify the parameters such as diameter, pitch, and number of revolutions in the respective fields of the dialog box. Figure 10.122 shows a constant pitch helical curve and Figure 10.123 shows a constant pitch spiral curve. You can also create a tapered helical curve by specifying a taper angle in the **Taper** field of the dialog box, see Figure 10.124. The **Left hand** and **Right hand** buttons in the **Rotation** area of the dialog box are used for defining the rotational direction of the curve from left hand to right hand or vice-versa.

10.122

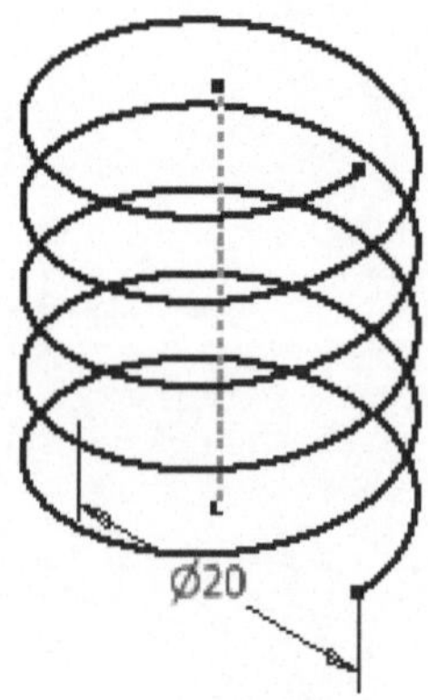

10.123

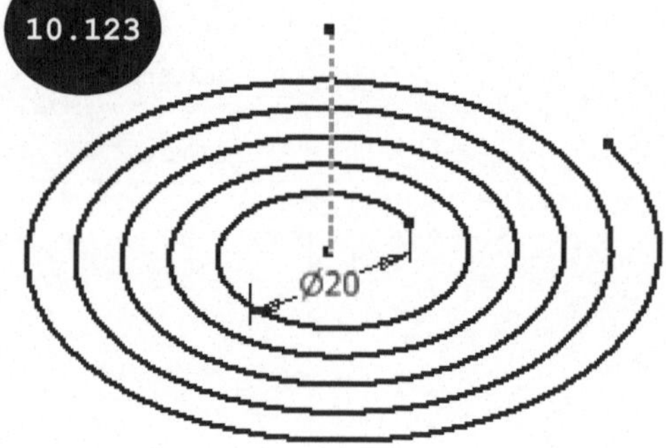

10.124

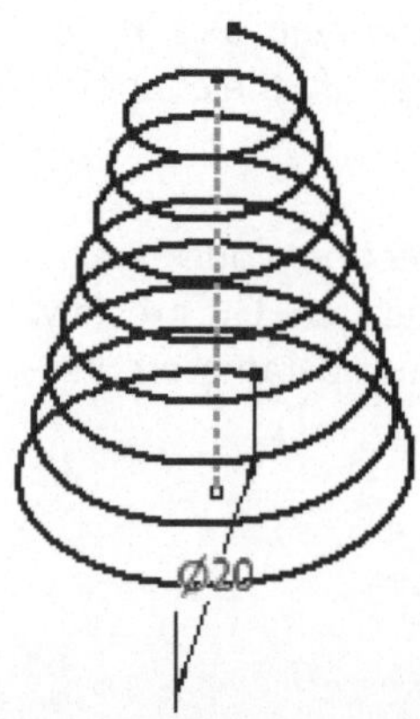

Variable helical curve : The **Variable helical curve** button in the **Type** area of the dialog box is used for creating a variable helical curve with variable pitch and variable diameter. Click on the **Variable helical curve** button in the **Type** area of the dialog box. The **Definition** area appears with a table in the dialog box, refer to Figure 10.125. Select the required option (**Pitch and Revolution**, **Revolution and Height**, or **Pitch and Height**), in the drop-down list of the **Definition** area. Next, enter the variable parameters such as pitch, revolution, and diameter in the respective fields of the table depending upon the option selected in the drop-down list. Note that by default only two rows are available in the table. The first row defines the start parameters of the helical curve, and the second row defines the parameters of the helical curve at a specified height. You can add multiple rows in the table by clicking on the **Click to add** option and defining the variable pitch and diameter for each row, refer to Figure 10.125. Figure 10.126 shows a variable helical curve with variable pitch and diameter.

10.125

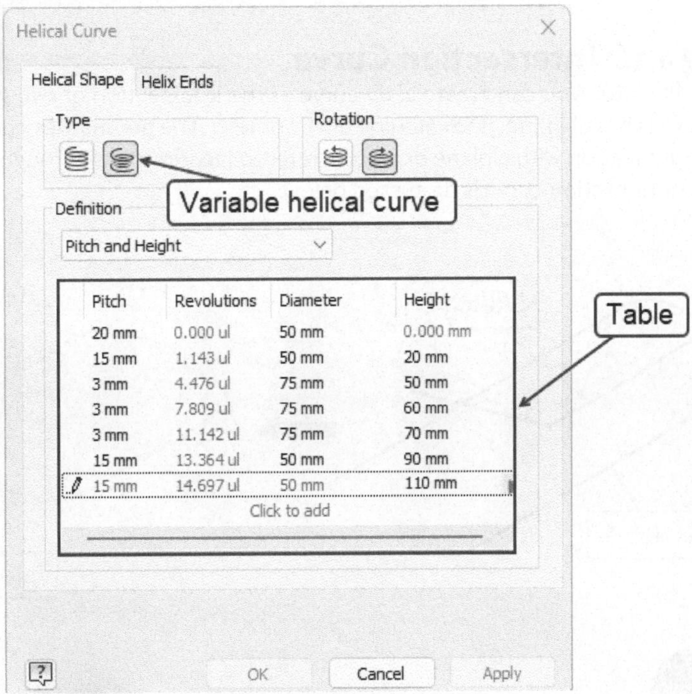

10.126

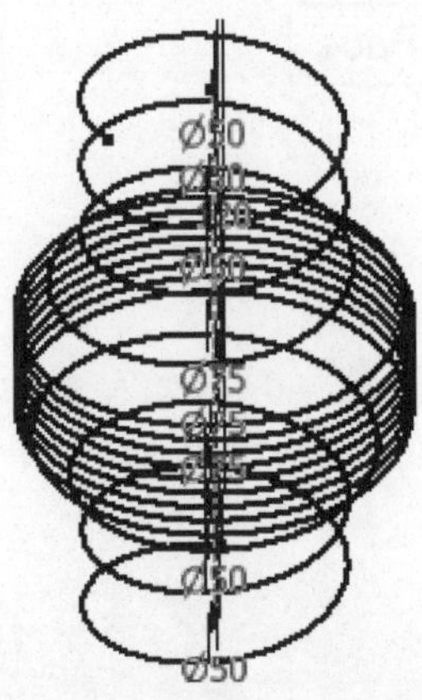

Note: The options in the **Helix Ends** tab of the **Helical Curve** dialog box are used for defining the start and end transition methods for creating the helical curve, and are same as those discussed earlier while creating a coil feature in Chapter 8.

7. Click on the required button (**Constant helical curve** or **Variable helical curve**) in the **Type** area of the dialog box to create a constant pitch helical curve or variable helical curve, respectively.

8. Specify the required parameters for creating a helical curve, as discussed above.

9. Click on the **Apply** button and then the **Cancel** button in the dialog box. A helical curve is created, as per the specified parameters.

Creating a 3D Intersection Curve

In Autodesk Inventor, you can create a 3D curve at the intersection of two geometries by using the **Intersection Curve** tool in the 3D Sketching environment. The geometries can be sketches, surfaces, faces, or in combination with a plane or a body, refer to Figures 10.127 through 10.129. The method for creating a 3D intersection curve is discussed below:

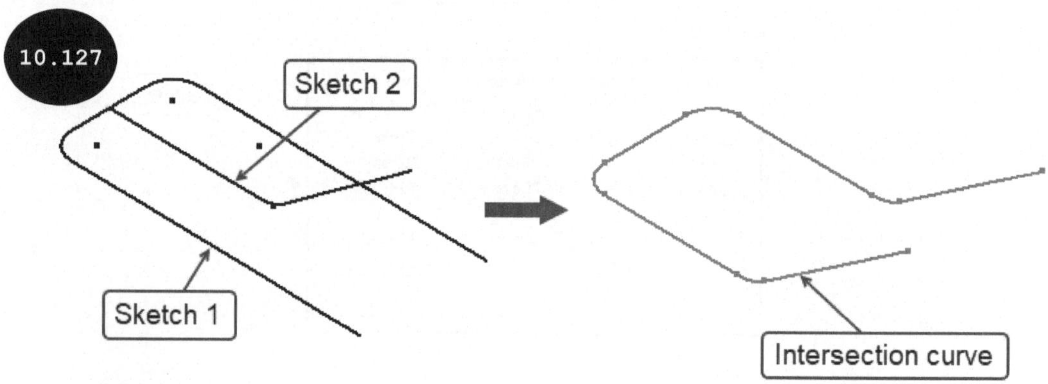

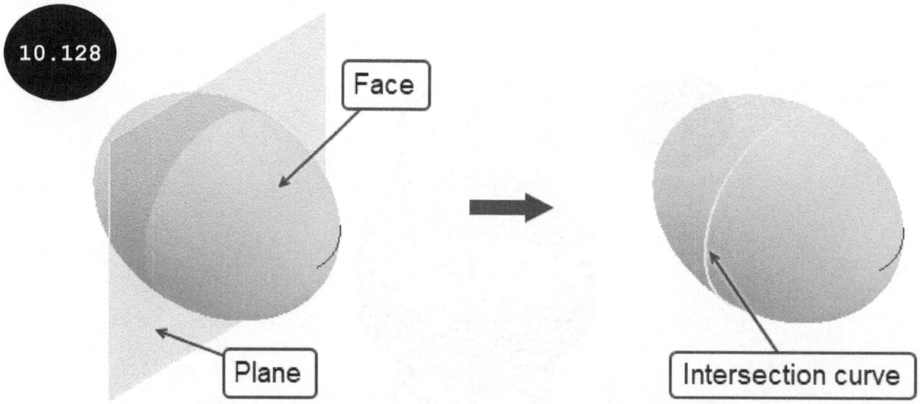

10.129

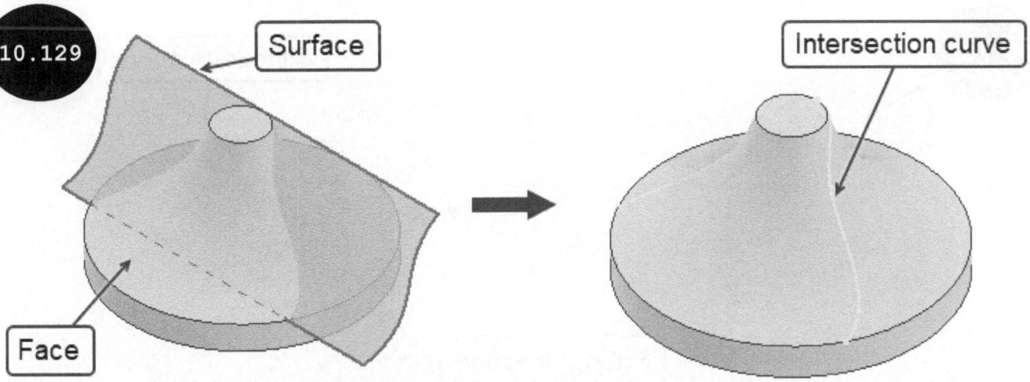

1. Invoke the 3D Sketching environment and then click on the **Intersection Curve** tool in the **Draw** panel of the **3D Sketch** tab, see Figure 10.130. The **3D Intersection Curve** dialog box appears, see Figure 10.131. Also, you are prompted to select an intersecting geometry.

10.130

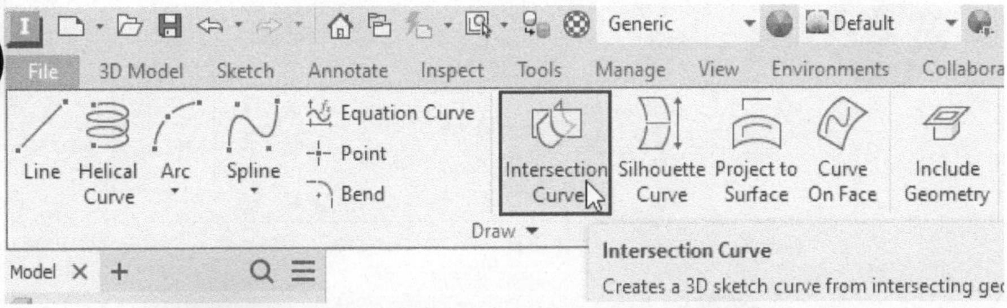

10.131

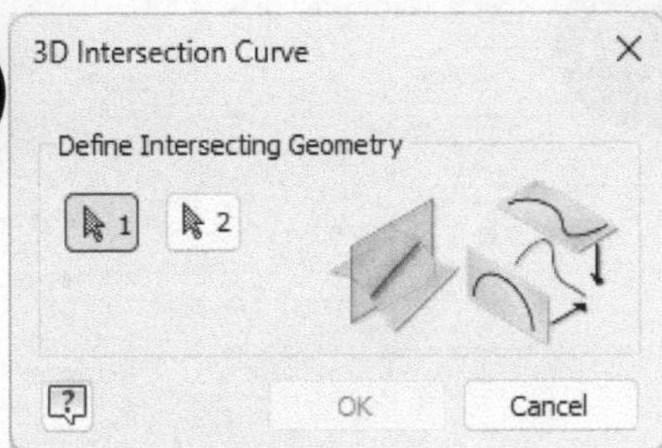

2. Click to select two intersecting geometries in the graphics area one by one, refer to Figures 10.127 through 10.129.

3. After selecting the geometries, click on the **OK** button in the dialog box. A 3D intersecting curve is created at the intersection of the selected geometries.

Creating a Silhouette Curve

In Autodesk Inventor, you can create a silhouette curve on the outer boundary of a model relative to a particular pulling direction, see Figure 10.132. A silhouette curve is often used for determining a natural parting line of a plastic part. The method for creating a silhouette curve is discussed below:

10.132

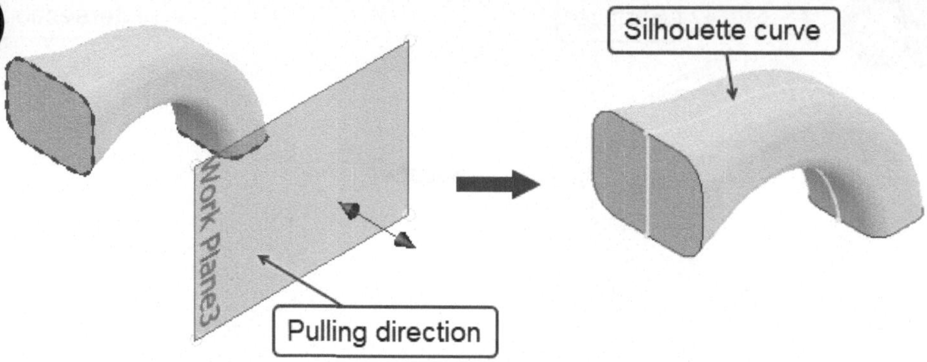

1. Click on the **Silhouette Curve** tool in the **Draw** panel of the **3D Sketch** tab, see Figure 10.133. The **Create Silhouette Curve** dialog box appears, see Figure 10.134.

10.133

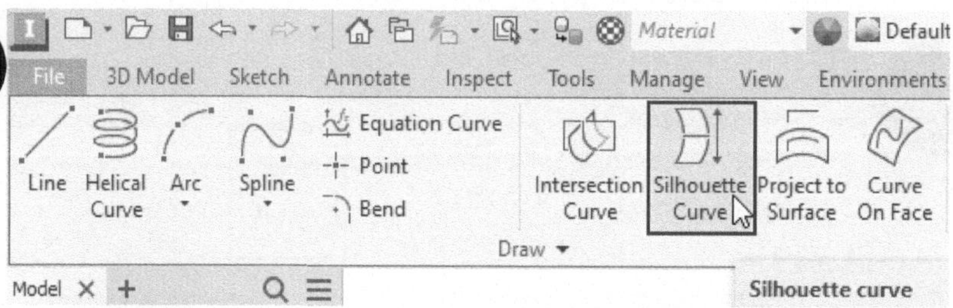

10.134

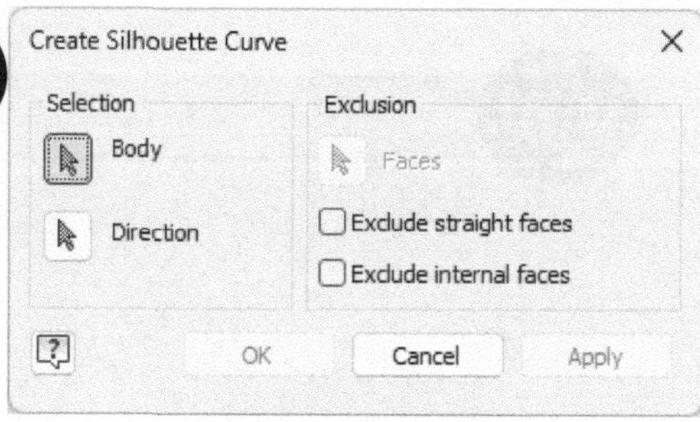

2. Click to select a pulling direction for creating a silhouette curve. You can select a work plane, a planar face, an edge, or an axis to specify the pull direction.

3. Click on the **Apply** button and then **Cancel** button. A silhouette curve is created on the outer boundary of the model relative to the selected pulling direction.

Note: By default, a silhouette curve includes both inner and outer boundaries of a model. However, you can exclude straight faces and internal faces of a model by selecting the **Exclude straight faces** and **Exclude internal faces** check boxes of the **Create Silhouette Curve** dialog box, respectively. Also, you can select one or more faces of a model to be excluded by using the **Faces** button of the dialog box.

Creating a 3D Projected Curve

In Autodesk Inventor, you can create a 3D projected curve by projecting sketch entities or edges onto an existing face of a model by using the **Project to Surface** tool, see Figure 10.135. The method for creating a 3D projected curve is discussed below:

10.135

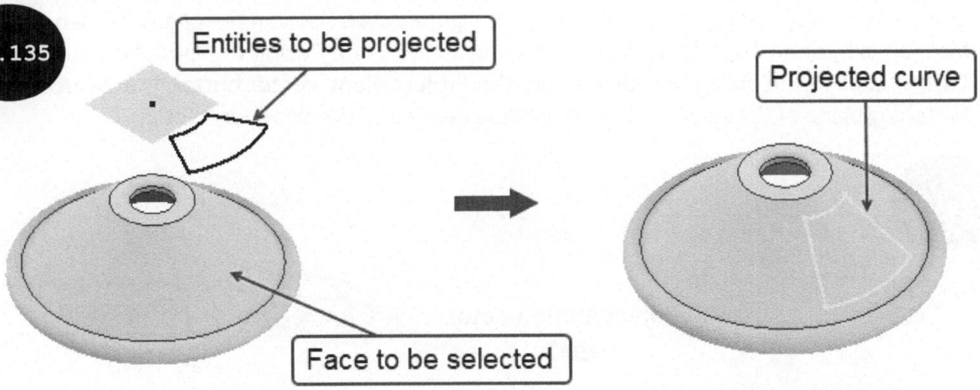

1. Invoke the 3D Sketching environment and then click on the **Project to Surface** tool in the **Draw** panel of the **3D Sketch** tab, see Figure 10.136. The **Project Curve to Surface** dialog box appears, see Figure 10.137. Also, you are prompted to select one or more faces to project on, since the **Faces** button is activated in the dialog box, by default.

10.136

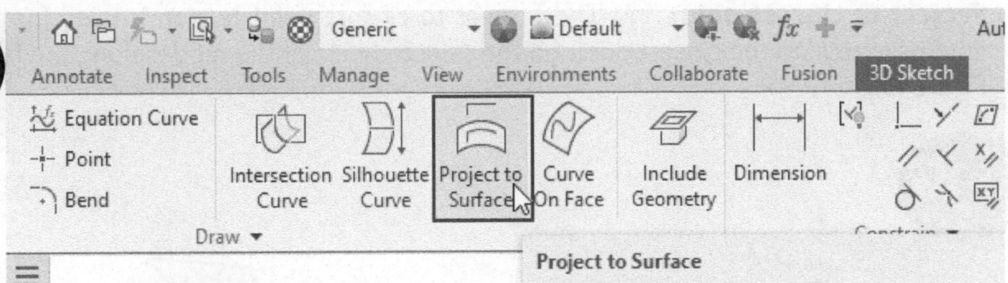

10.137

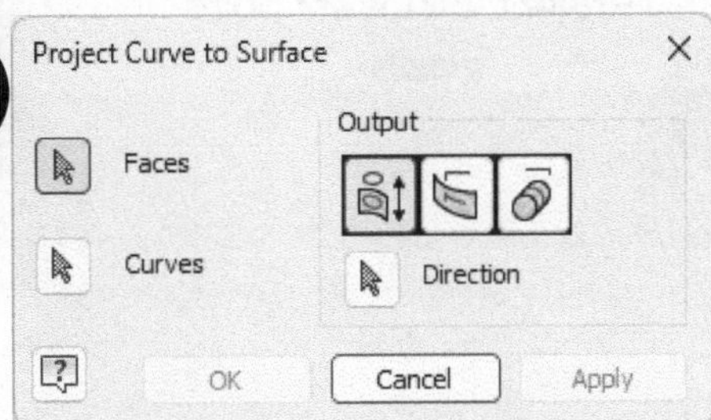

2. Select a face of a model onto which you want to project entities.

3. Click on the **Curves** button in the dialog box. You are prompted to select sketch entities, edges, vertices, or workpoints to be projected.

4. Select sketch entities, edges, vertices, or workpoints one by one in the graphics area.

Now, you need to define the type of projection for creating a projected curve by selecting the required button (**Project along vector**, **Project to closest point**, or **Wrap to surface**) in the **Output** area of the dialog box. Different options in the **Output** area of the dialog box are discussed below:

Project along vector : The **Project along vector** button is used for projecting the selected entities along a specified direction vector, see Figure 10.138. You can select a work plane, a planar face, an axis, or an edge for defining the direction vector by using the **Direction** button of the **Output** area in the dialog box. By default, the **Project along vector** button is activated and the sketching plane of the selected sketch entity is defined as the direction vector.

10.138

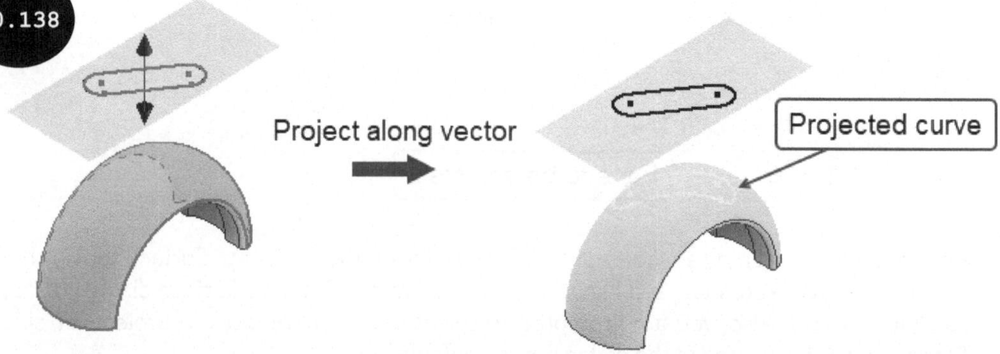

Project to closest point : The **Project to closest point** button is used for projecting the entities normal to the closest point on the selected face of the model along the face vector, see Figure 10.139.

10.139

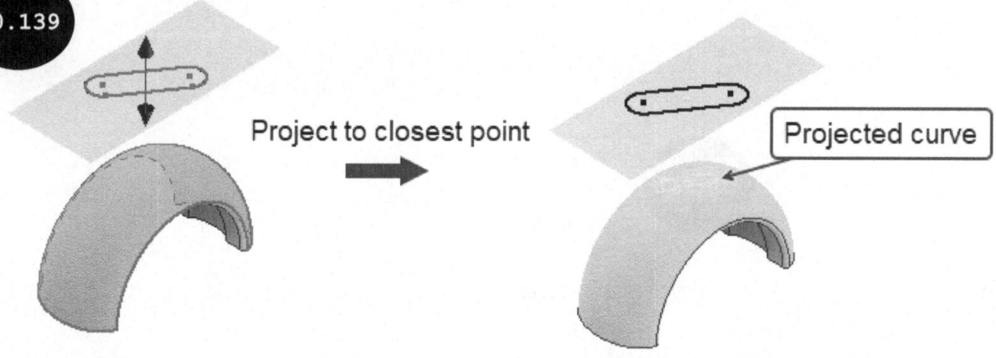

Wrap to surface : The **Wrap to surface** button is used for creating a projected curve by wrapping 2D sketch entities onto one or more faces of a model, see Figure 10.140. Note that the sketch entities to be projected must be created on a plane that is tangent to one of the selected faces of the model. You cannot wrap 3D sketch entities, points, or edges.

10.140

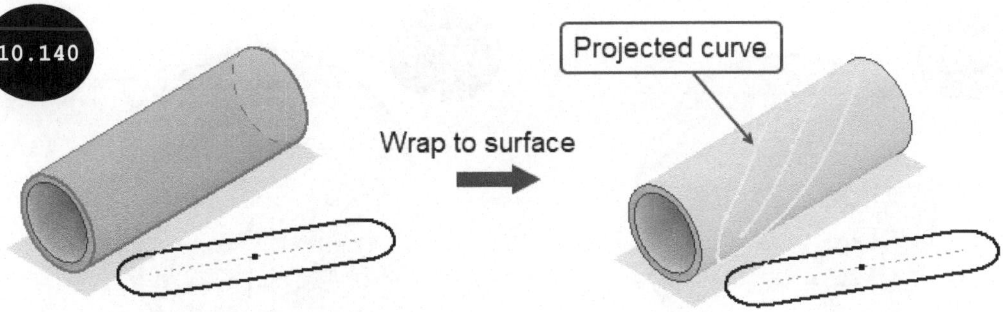

5. Select the required button (**Project along vector**, **Project to closest point**, or **Wrap to surface**) in the **Output** area of the dialog box.

6. Click on the **Apply** button and then the **Cancel** button in the dialog box. A 3D projected curve is created on the selected face of the model.

Creating a 3D Curve on a Face

In Autodesk Inventor, you can create an associative 3D curve directly on the face of a model by using the **Curve on Face** tool. The method for the same is discussed below:

1. Click on the **Curve on Face** tool in the **Draw** panel of the **3D Sketch** tab, see Figure 10.141. You are prompted to specify the first point on a face.

10.141

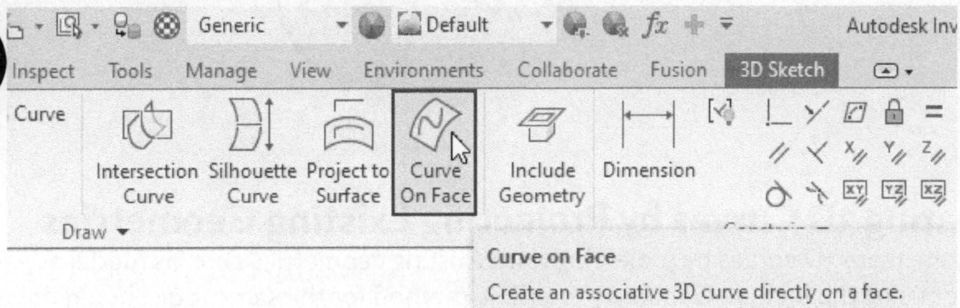

2. Move the cursor over a face (curved or planar) of a model and then click to specify the first point of a 3D curve when the face gets highlighted and the cursor snaps to it, see Figure 10.142. The first point of the curve gets specified on the face and you are prompted to specify the second point of the curve.

3. Click to specify the second point of the curve on the face of the model. You are prompted to specify the next point of the curve.

4. Similarly, you can continue specifying multiple points one after the other for creating a curve, see Figure 10.143.

10.142

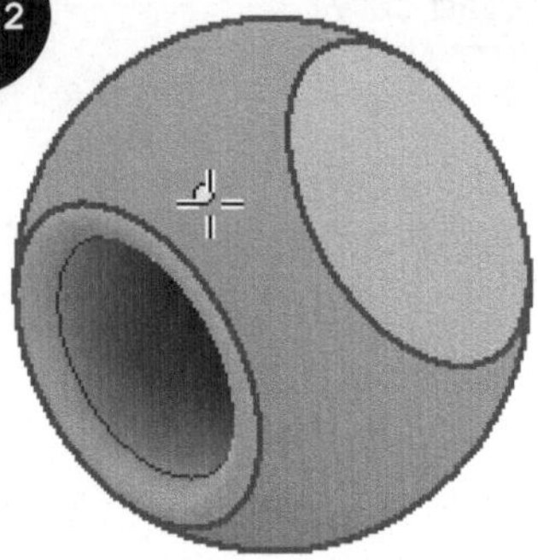

10.143

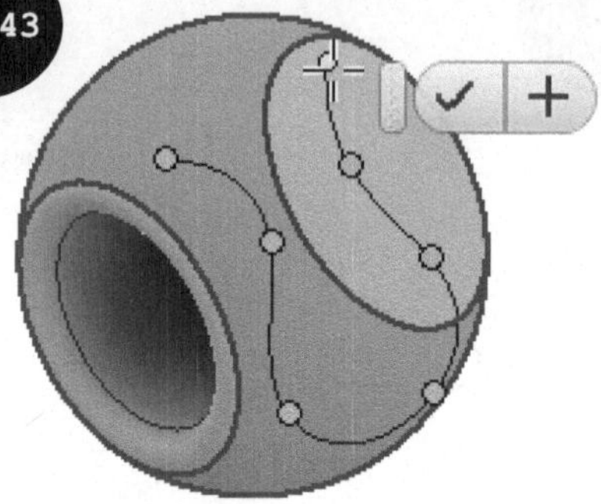

5. After specifying all the points of the curve, click on the **OK** button (green tick-mark) in the Mini-Toolbar that appears in the graphics area. A 3D curve is created on the face of the model, see Figure 10.144.

10.144

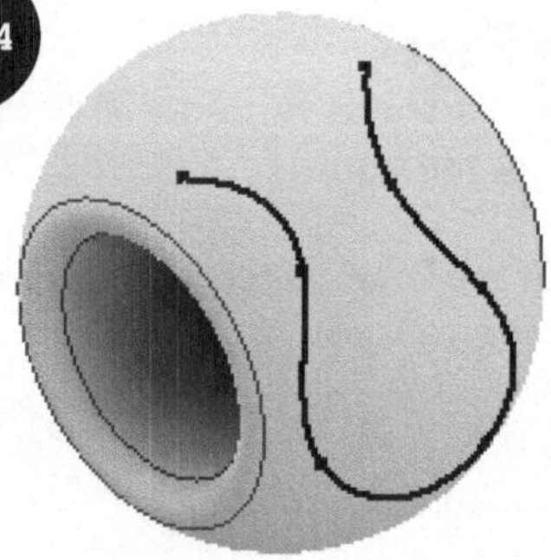

Creating 3D Curves by Projecting Existing Geometries

You can create 3D curves by projecting onto existing geometries such as model edges and 2D sketch entities using the **Include Geometry** tool. The method for the same is discussed below:

1. Click on the **Include Geometry** tool in the **Draw** panel of the **3D Sketch** tab, see Figure 10.145. You are prompted to select an edge or sketch geometry for creating a curve.

10.145

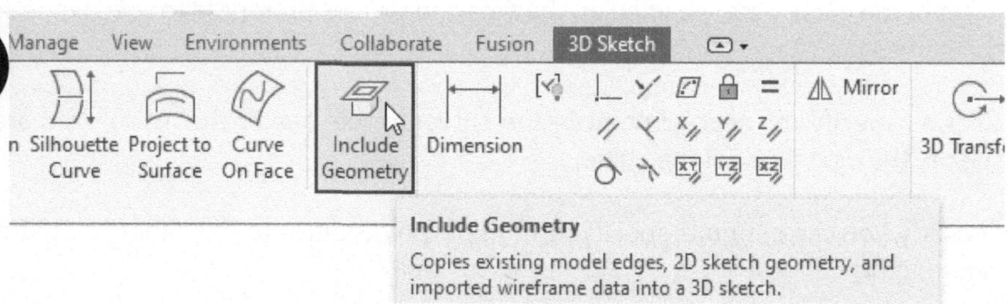

2. Move the cursor over an edge of a model or a sketch entity and then click when it gets highlighted, see Figure 10.146. A 3D curve is created on the selected edge, see Figure 10.147. Similarly, you can select other edges or sketch entities to be included in the curve.

10.146

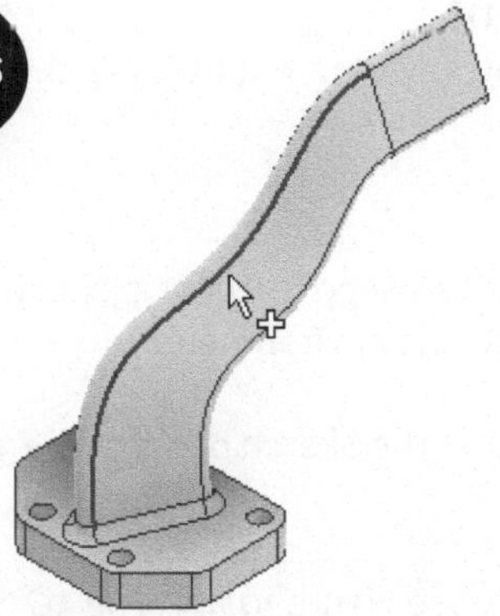

10.147

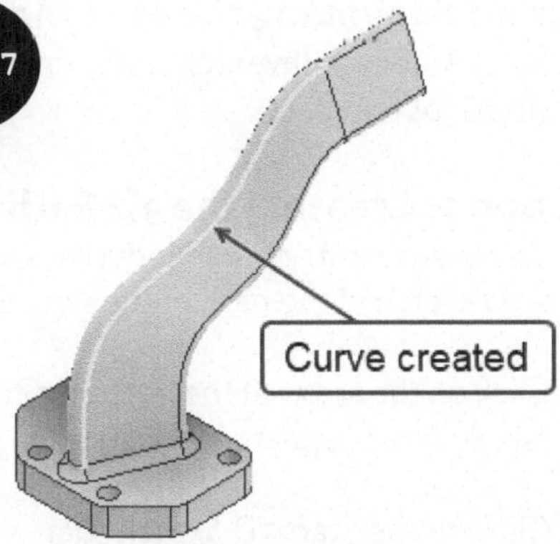

3. Right-click in the graphics area and then click on the **OK** button in the Marking Menu that appears to exit the tool.

After creating a 3D Sketch or a curve, exit the 3D Sketching environment by clicking on the **Finish Sketch** tool in the **Exit** panel in the **Ribbon**.

Tutorial 1

Create the model, as shown in Figure 10.148. All dimensions are in mm.

10.148

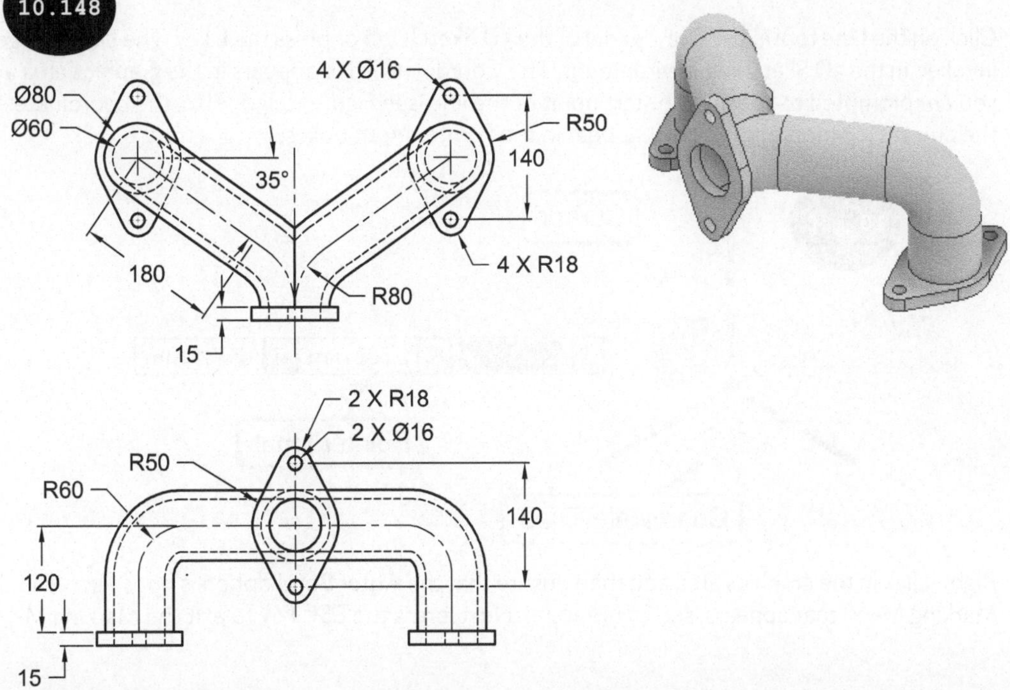

Section 1: Invoking the Part Modeling Environment

1. Start Autodesk Inventor and then invoke the Part modeling environment by using the **Standard (mm).ipt** template.

Section 2: Creating the 3D Path - Sweep Feature

The base feature of the model is a sweep feature. To create this sweep feature, you need to create a 3D sketch of the path of the sweep feature in the 3D Sketching environment.

1. Click on the arrow at the bottom of the **Start 2D Sketch** tool in the **Sketch** panel of the **3D Model** tab. A flyout appears, see Figure 10.149.

2. Click on the **Start 3D Sketch** tool in the flyout that appears, see Figure 10.149. The 3D Sketching environment is invoked and the **3D Sketch** tab appears in the **Ribbon**.

10.149

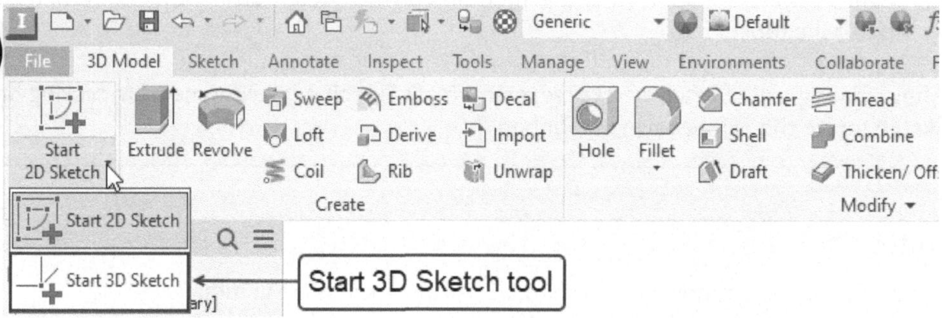

3. Change the view orientation to isometric by clicking on the **Home** icon of the ViewCube.

4. Click on the **Line** tool in the **Draw** panel of the **3D Sketch** tab or press the **L** key. The **Line** tool gets invoked in the 3D Sketching environment. The Coordinate Triad appears in the graphics area and you are prompted to specify the start point of the line, see Figure 10.150. Also, the coordinates of the current location of the cursor appear in the Pointer Input boxes.

10.150

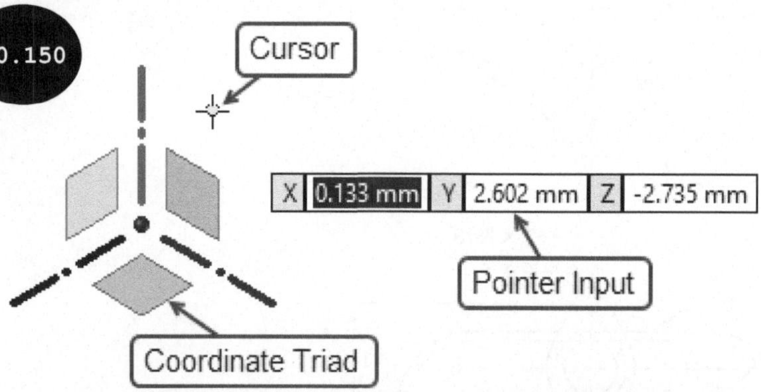

5. Right-click in the graphics area and then ensure that the **Auto-Bend** option is not selected in the Marking Menu that appears, see Figure 10.151. Next, press the ESC key to exit the Marking Menu.

10.151

Tip: When the **Auto-Bend** option is not selected, the continuous chain of 3D line segments is created with sharp corners, whereas when the **Auto-Bend** option is selected, the line segments are created with tangent bends at the corners, automatically.

6. Ensure that the **Ortho Mode** and the **Dynamic Dimension** buttons are activated in the Status Bar for creating straight horizontal or vertical line segments and specifying dimension values in the graphics area, respectively.

7. Move the cursor toward the origin and then click to specify the start point of the line when the coordinates 0, 0, 0 appear in the Pointer Input boxes.

8. Move the cursor vertically upward along the Y-axis and then enter **120** in the Dimension Input box as the length of the line, see Figure 10.152. Next, press ENTER. A vertical line of length 120 mm gets created and you are prompted to specify the end point of the next line in the graphics area.

10.152

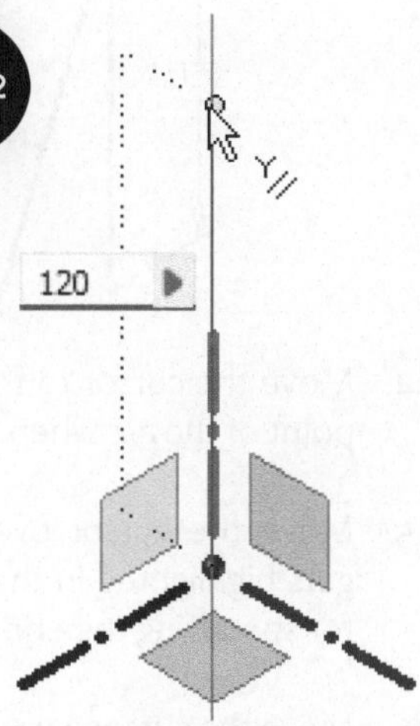

9. Move the cursor over the top plane of the Coordinate Triad that now appears at the last specified point in the graphics area and then click on it when it gets highlighted, see Figure 10.153. The top plane gets selected as the plane for specifying the end point of the second line segment. Also, the Ortho mode gets turned off, automatically.

10. Move the cursor at an angle on the top plane of the Coordinate Triad, refer to Figure 10.154.

11. Enter **180** mm as the length and **35** degrees as the angle of the line segment in the Dimension Input boxes, respectively. Note that you need to press the TAB key to switch between the Dimension Input boxes for specifying the length and angle values. The second line segment gets created and the **Line** tool is still activated, see Figure 10.154.

10.153

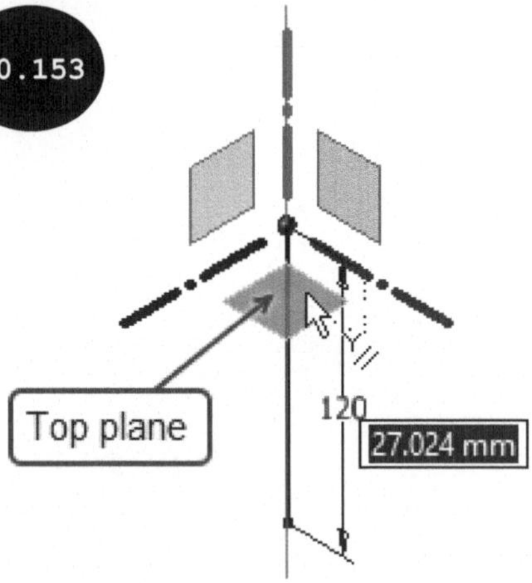

10.154

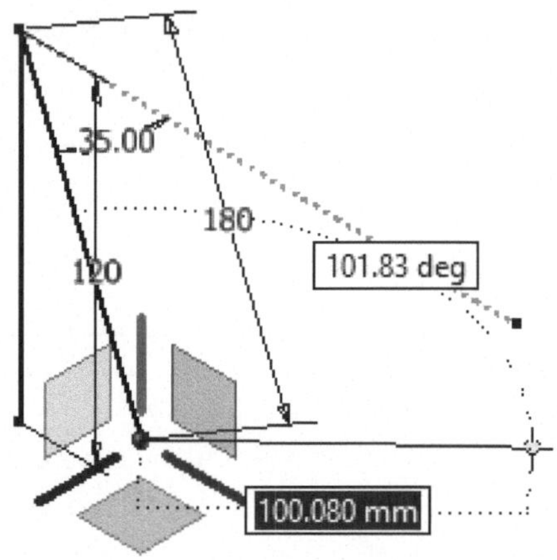

12. Right-click in the graphics area and then click on the **OK** button in the Marking Menu that appears to exit the **Line** tool. Figure 10.155 shows the sketch after creating the line segments.

Now, you need to create an arc in the sketch.

13. Click on the **Three Point Arc** tool in the **Draw** panel of the **3D Sketch** tab, see Figure 10.156. You are prompted to specify a start point for the arc.

10.155

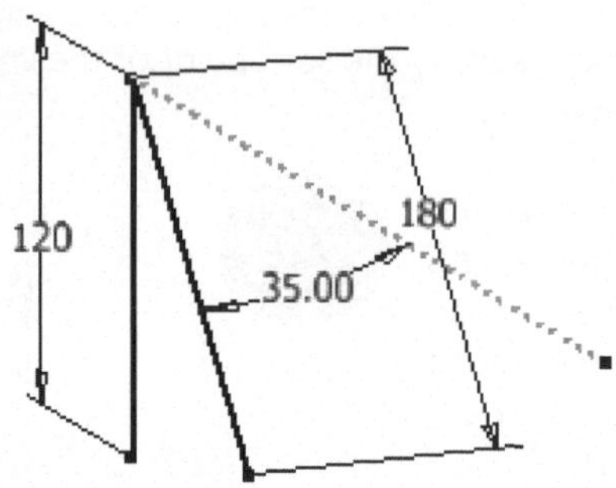

10.156

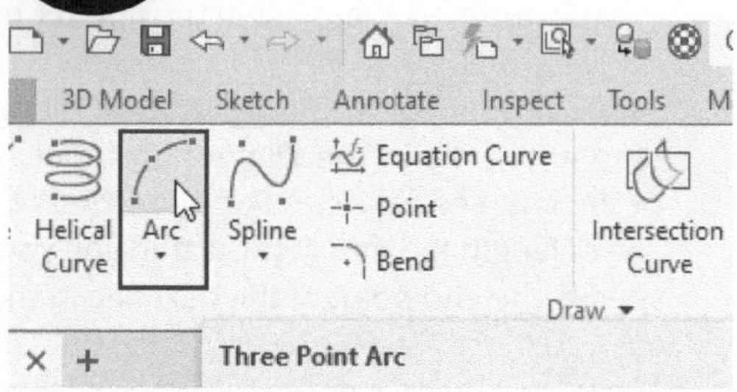

14. Move the cursor to the endpoint of the second line segment and then click to specify the start point of the arc when the cursor snaps to it. You are prompted to specify the endpoint of the arc.

15. Move the cursor over the top plane of the Coordinate Triad and then click on it when it gets highlighted in the graphics area, see Figure 10.157. The top plane gets selected as the plane for specifying the endpoint of the arc.

16. Move the cursor away from the start point at an angle (see Figure 10.158), and then click to specify the endpoint of the arc, arbitrarily. You are prompted to specify a point to define the radius of the arc.

10.157

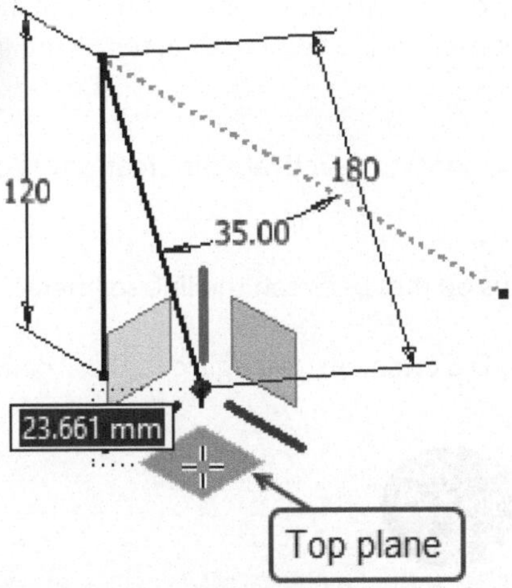

10.158

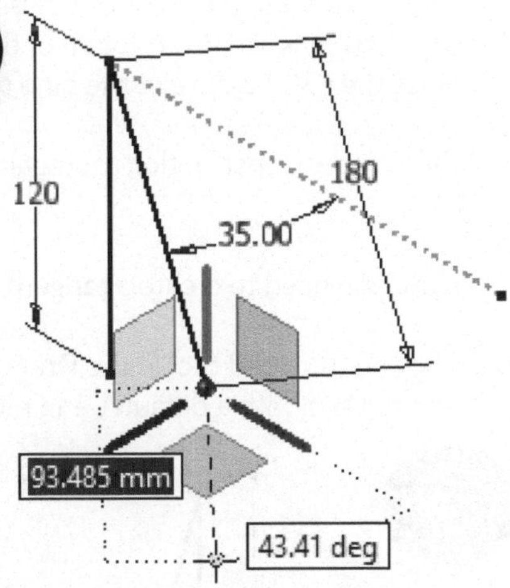

17. Enter **80** as the radius of the arc in the Dimension Input box and then press ENTER. An arc of radius 80 mm is created, see Figure 10.159. Next, press the ESC key to exit the tool.

10.159

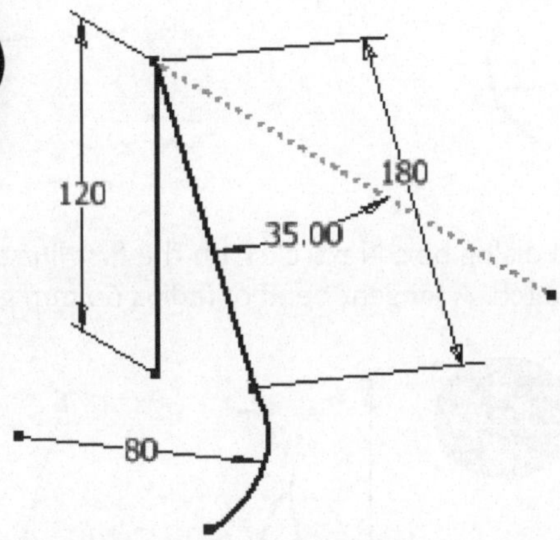

Now, you need to create a construction line connecting the center point and the endpoint of the previously drawn arc. This construction line will be used for aligning the center point and the endpoint of the arc, horizontally.

18. Click on the **Line** tool in the **Draw** panel of the **3D Sketch** tab or press the **L** key. The **Line** tool gets activated and you are prompted to specify the start point of a line.

19. Click on the **Construction** tool in the **Format** panel of the **3D Sketch** tab for creating a construction line, see Figure 10.160.

10.160

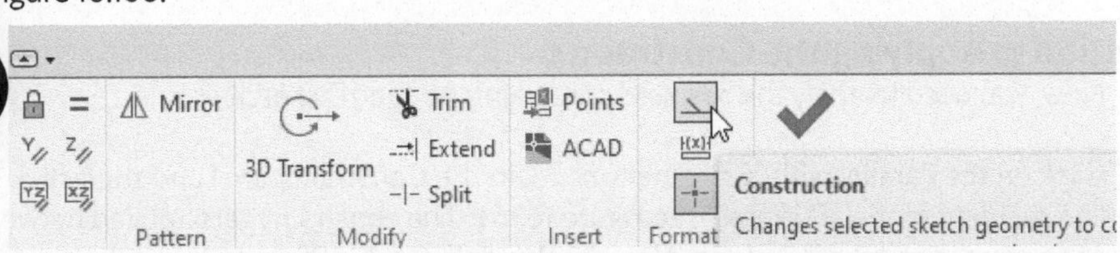

20. Click on the center point of the previously drawn arc as the start point of the construction line and then click on the endpoint of the arc. A construction line gets created, see Figure 10.161. Next, press the ESC key to exit the **Line** tool.

21. Click on the **Construction** tool again in the **Format** panel to deactivate the creation of construction lines.

    Now, you need to create a tangent bend of radius 60 mm between the line segments.

22. Click on the **Bend** tool in the **Draw** panel of the **3D Sketch** tab, see Figure 10.162. The **Bend** dialog box appears with a default bend radius value.

10.161

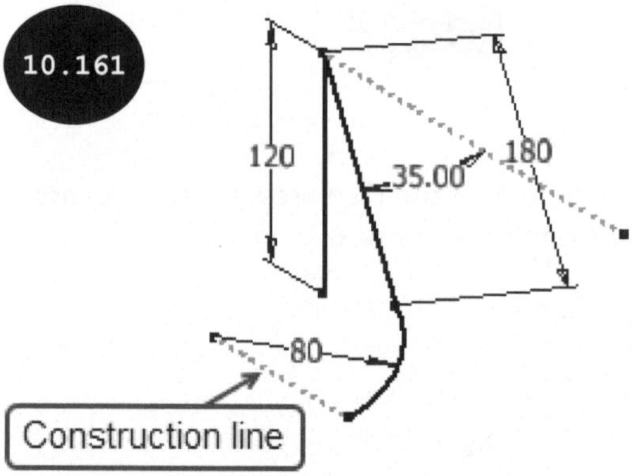

10.162

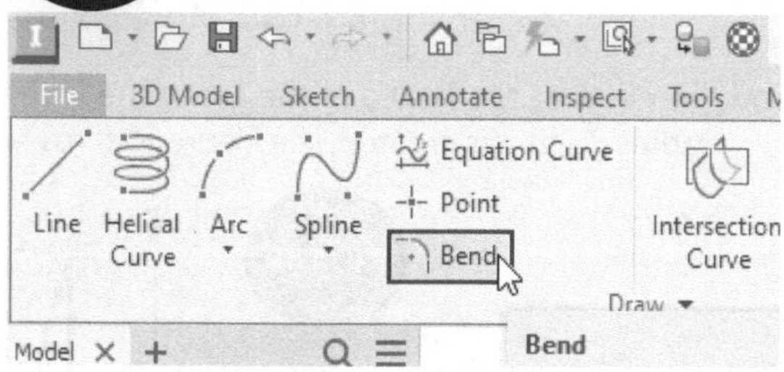

23. Enter **60** in the **Bend** dialog box. Next, click on the first line segment and then the second line segment of the 3D sketch. A tangent bend of radius 60 mm gets created between the lines, see Figure 10.163.

10.163

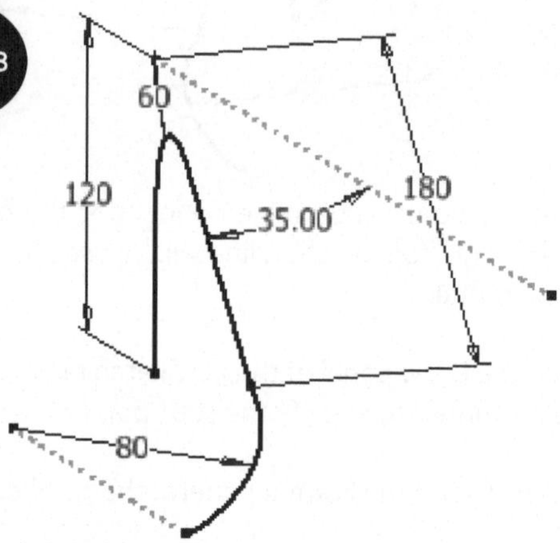

Section 3: Applying the Constraints

Now, you need to apply the required constraints to the 3D sketch entities.

1. Click on the **Parallel with XZ Plane** tool in the **Constrain** panel and then click on the second line segment of the 3D sketch, see Figure 10.164. The constraint gets applied between the second line segment and the XZ plane. Also, the **Parallel with XZ Plane** tool is still activated.

2. Click on the arc segment of the 3D sketch, see Figure 10.165. The Parallel with XZ constraint gets applied between the arc and the XZ plane. Next, press the ESC key to exit the tool.

10.164

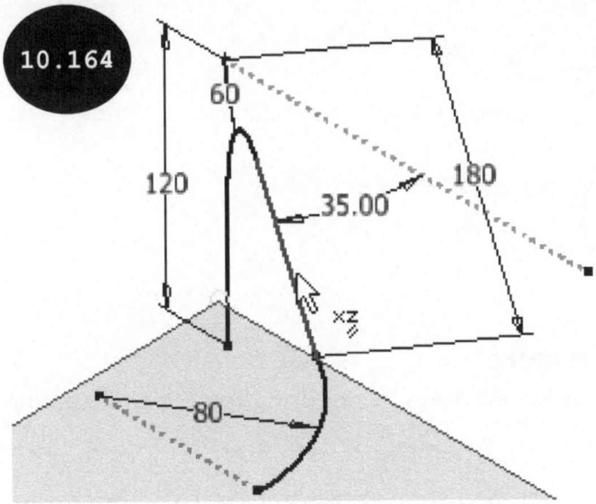

10.165

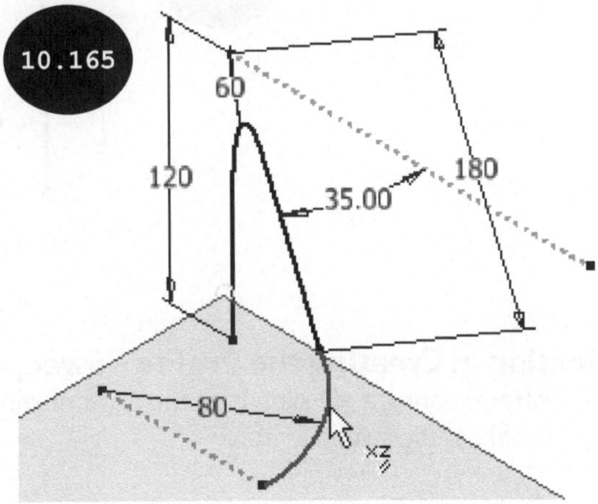

3. Click on the **Fix** tool in the **Constrain** panel and then click on the start point (P1) of the first line segment, see Figure 10.166. The fix constraint gets applied.

4. Click on the **Parallel with X Axis** tool in the **Constrain** panel and then click on the construction line, see Figure 10.167. The construction line becomes parallel to the X axis. Next, press the ESC key to exit the tool.

10.166

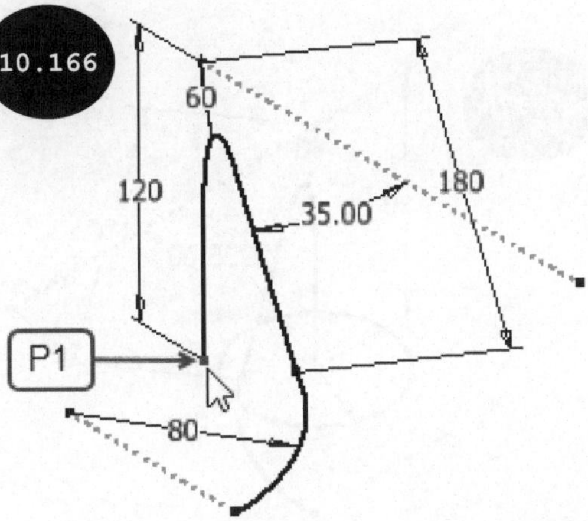

10.167

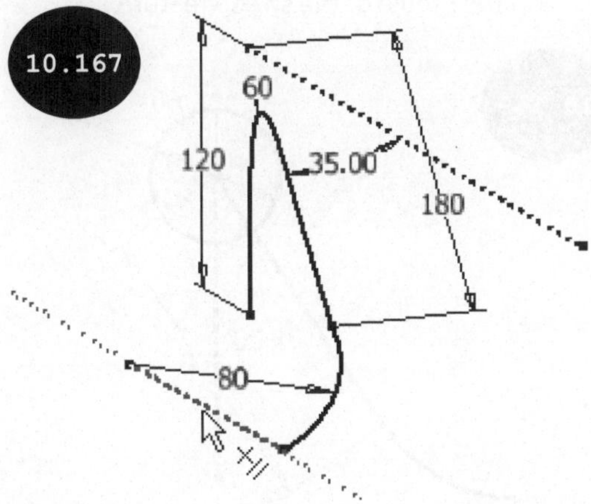

5. Similarly, apply the tangent constraint between the line and the arc of the 3D sketch by using the **Tangent** tool of the **Constrain** panel. Figure 10.168 shows the final 3D sketch (path) after applying all constraints.

6. Click on the **Finish Sketch** tool in the **Exit** panel to exit the 3D Sketching environment.

10.168

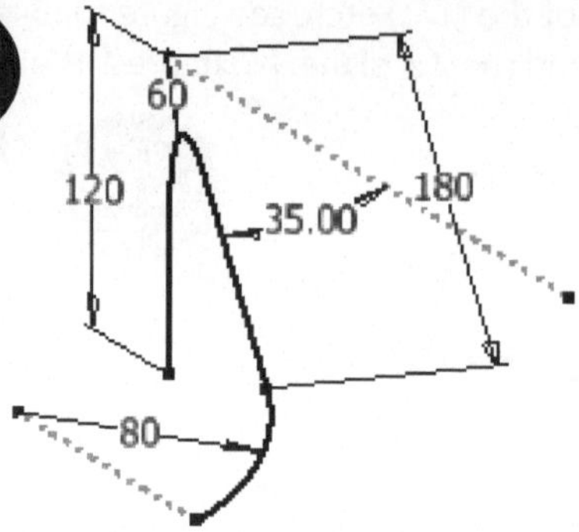

Section 4: Creating the Profile - Sweep Feature

After creating a 3D sketch as the path of the sweep feature, you need to create a circle as the profile of the sweep feature.

1. Click on the **Start 2D Sketch** tool and then select the Top plane (XZ Plane) as the sketching plane for creating the profile of the sweep feature. The Sketching environment gets invoked.

2. Create a circle of diameter 80 mm as the profile of the sweep feature, see Figure 10.169. Note that the center point of the circle is at the origin.

3. Exit the Sketching environment. Figure 10.170 shows the isometric view after creating the path and the profile of the sweep feature.

10.169

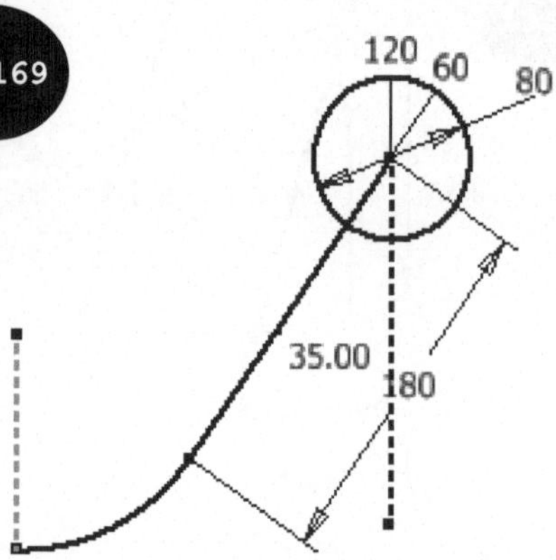

10.170

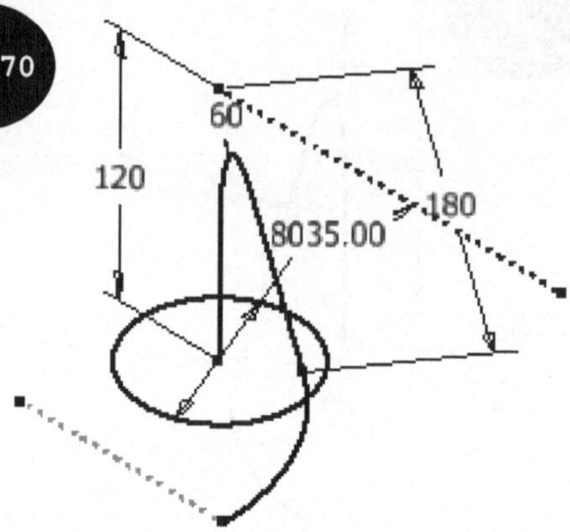

Section 5: Creating the Base Feature - Sweep Feature

After creating the path and the profile of the sweep feature, you need to create the sweep feature.

1. Click on the **Sweep** tool in the **Create** panel of the **3D Model** tab. The **Sweep** property panel appears and the profile of the sweep feature gets selected automatically. Also, you are prompted to select a path of the sweep feature.

2. Select the 3D sketch as the path of the sweep feature in the graphics area. The preview of a sweep feature appears, see Figure 10.171.

10.171

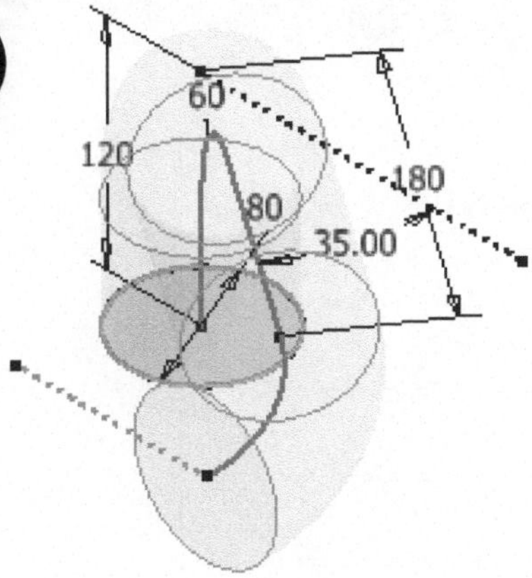

3. Click on the **OK** button in the **Sweep** property panel. The sweep feature gets created, see Figure 10.172.

10.172

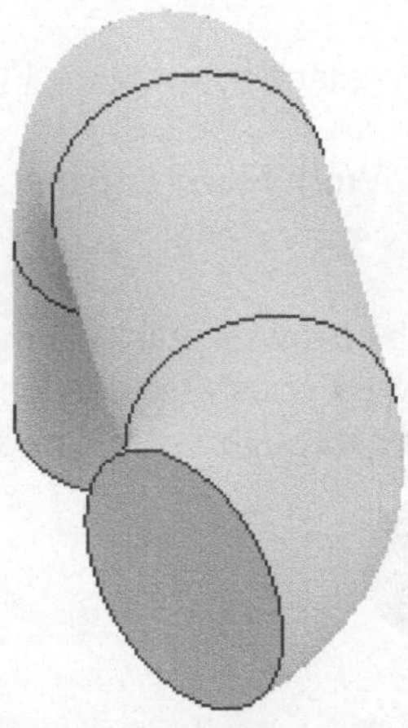

Section 6: Creating the Second Feature - Mirror Feature

The second feature of the model can be created by mirroring the first feature about a work plane, which passes through the center of the end circular face of the first feature, and is parallel to the Right plane. To create this work plane, you need to first create a work point at the center of the end circular face of the first feature.

1. Invoke the **Point** flyout in the **Work Features** panel of the **3D Model** tab and then click on the **Center Point of Loop of Edges** tool, see Figure 10.173. You are prompted to select a loop of edges.

2. Move the cursor over the edge of the end circular face of the first feature (sweep) and then click when the edge gets highlighted and the preview of a point appears at its center, see Figure 10.174. A work point gets created at the center of the selected circular edge of the sweep feature.

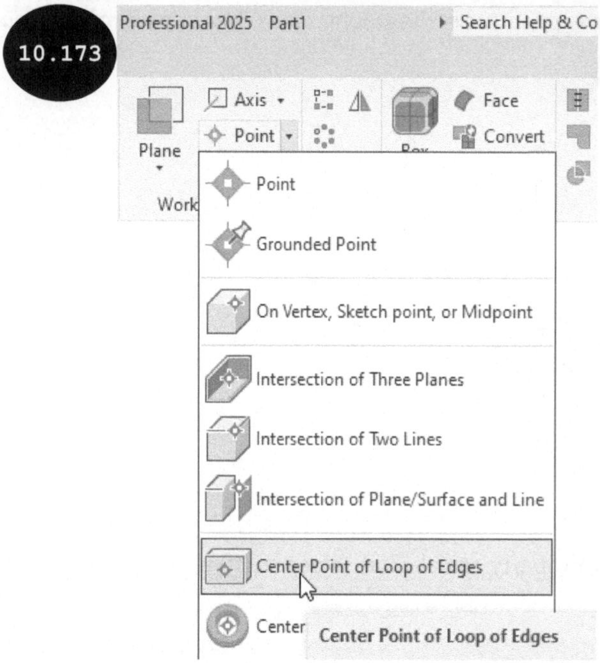

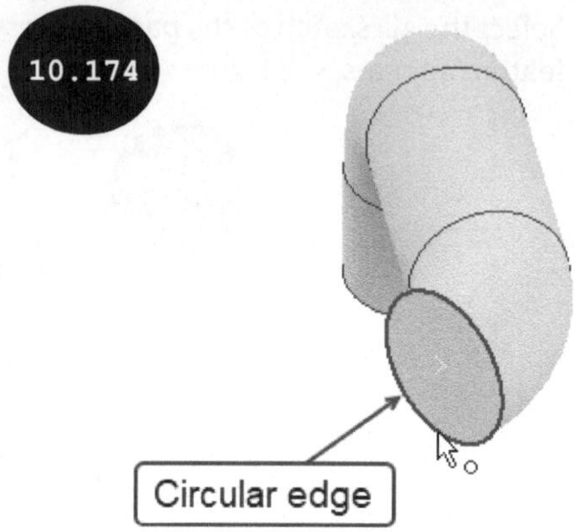

Now, you need to create a work plane by using the **Plane** tool.

3. Click on the **Plane** tool in the **Work Features** panel of the **3D Model** tab. You are prompted to select geometries for creating a work plane.

4. Expand the **Origin** folder in the **Browser**, click on the **YZ Plane** as the first reference, and then select the previously created work point as the second reference. A work plane parallel to the YZ Plane (Right plane) and passing through the selected work point is created, see Figure 10.175.

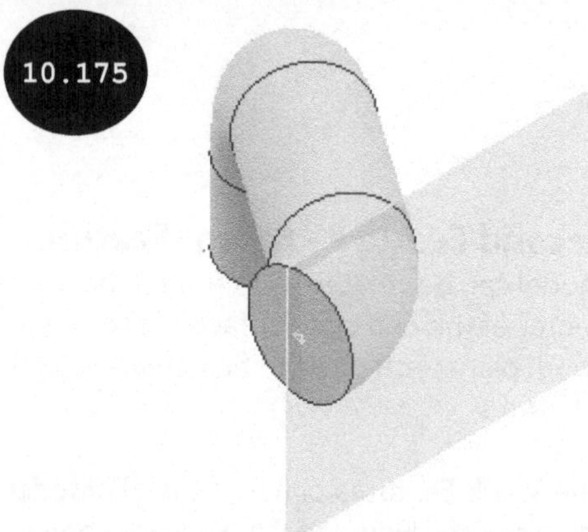

After creating the work plane, you need to mirror the first feature (sweep) about it.

5. Click on the **Mirror** tool in the **Pattern** panel of the **3D Model** tab. The **Mirror** dialog box appears and you are prompted to select a feature to be mirrored.

6. Select the base feature (sweep) in the graphics area as the feature to be mirrored.

7. Click on the **Mirror Plane** button in the **Mirror** dialog box and then select the previously created work plane as the mirroring plane.

8. Click on the **OK** button in the dialog box. The mirror feature gets created, see Figure 10.176. Next, hide the display of the work plane and work point in the graphics area.

10.176

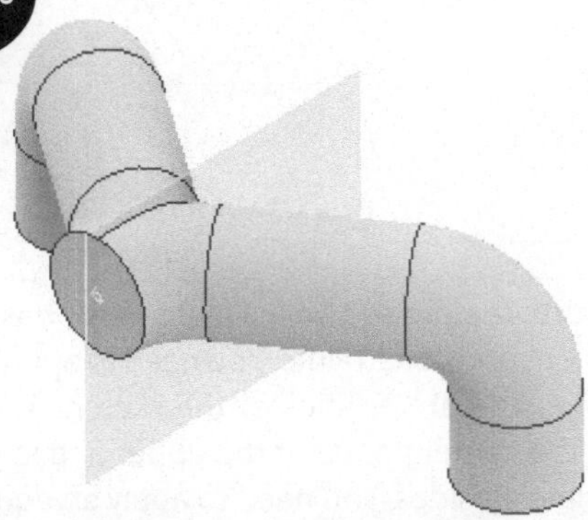

Section 7: Creating the Third Feature - Shell Feature

1. Click on the **Shell** tool in the **Modify** panel of the **3D Model** tab. The **Shell** dialog box appears.

2. Enter **10** in the **Thickness** field of the dialog box as the thickness of the shell feature.

3. Select the three end faces of the model as the faces to be removed, see Figure 10.177.

4. Click on the **OK** button in the dialog box. The shell feature gets created, see Figure 10.178.

10.177

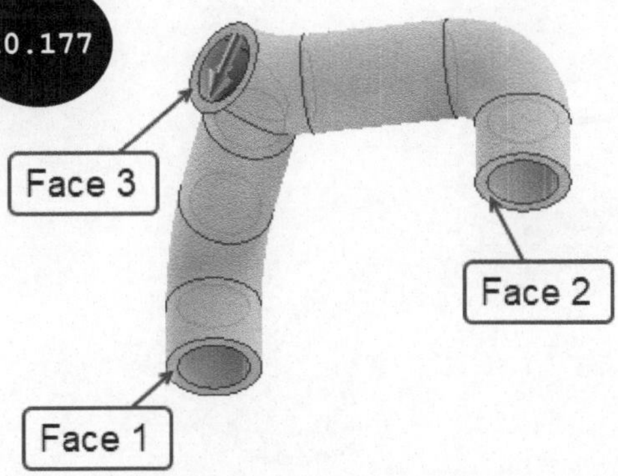

10.178

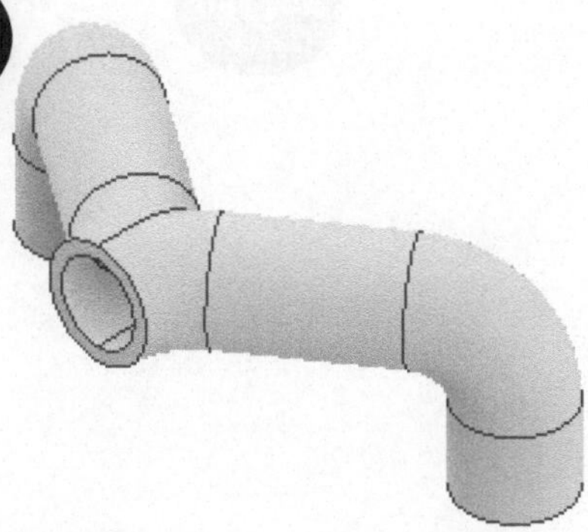

Section 8: Creating the Fourth Feature - Extrude Feature

1. Invoke the Sketching environment by selecting the Top plane (XZ Plane) as the sketching plane.

2. Create the sketch of the fourth feature (extrude feature), see Figure 10.179.

10.179

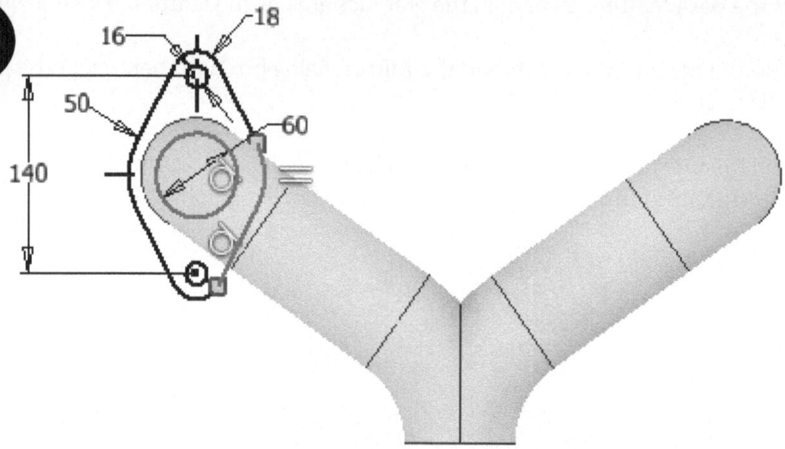

Tip: The sketch of the fourth feature shown in Figure 10.179 has been fully constrained by applying the required dimensions and constraints. You need to apply tangent constraints between each set of connected lines and arc entities of the sketch. You also need to apply a symmetric constraint between the center points of the upper and lower arcs of the sketch with respect to horizontal centerline. Besides, you need to apply an equal relation between the upper and lower arcs and circles of the sketch.

3. Click on the **3D Model** tab and then click on the **Extrude** tool in the **Create** panel. The **Extrusion** property panel appears and you are prompted to select a profile to be extruded.

4. Move the cursor over the outer closed profile of the sketch and click when it gets highlighted in the graphics area, see Figure 10.180. The preview of an extrude feature appears.

10.180

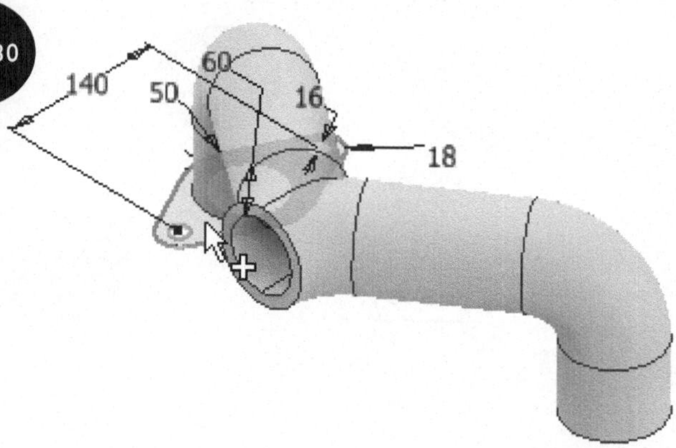

5. Click on the **Flipped** button in the **Direction** area of the property panel to reverse the direction of extrusion downward.

6. Enter **15** in the **Distance A** field of the property panel as the depth of the extrusion.

7. Ensure that the **Join** button is activated in the **Boolean** area of the property panel.

8. Click on the **OK** button in the **Extrusion** property panel. The extrude feature gets created, see Figure 10.181.

10.181

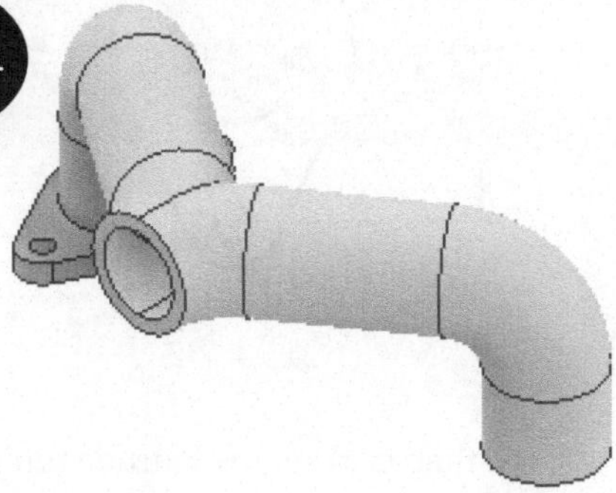

Section 9: Creating the Fifth Feature - Mirror Feature

1. Click on the **Mirror** tool in the **Pattern** panel of the **3D Model** tab. The **Mirror** dialog box appears and you are prompted to select a feature to be mirrored.

2. Select the fourth feature (previously created extrude feature) as the feature to be mirrored in the graphics area.

3. Click on the **Mirror Plane** button in the **Mirror** dialog box. You are prompted to select a mirroring plane.

4. Select the **Work Plane1** in the **Browser** as the mirroring plane. The preview of a mirror feature appears in the graphics area, see Figure 10.182.

5. Click on the **OK** button in the dialog box. The mirror feature gets created, see Figure 10.183.

10.182

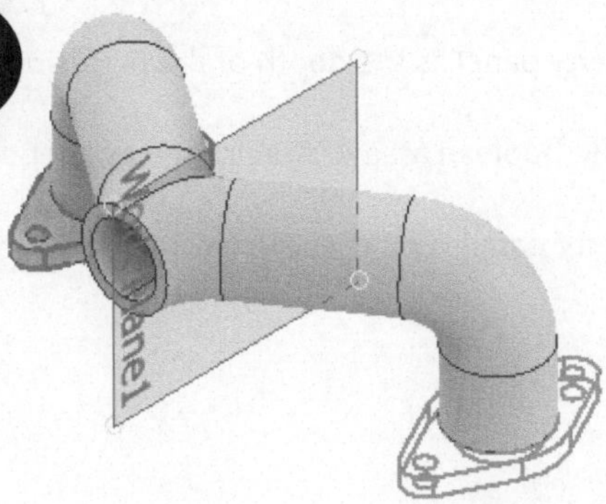

10.183

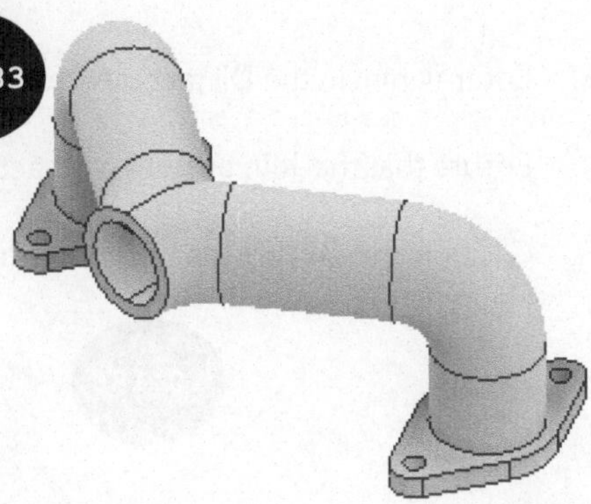

Section 10: Creating the Sixth Feature - Extrude Feature

1. Invoke the Sketching environment by selecting the front planar face of the model as the sketching plane and then create the sketch of the sixth feature (extrude feature), see Figure 10.184.

10.184

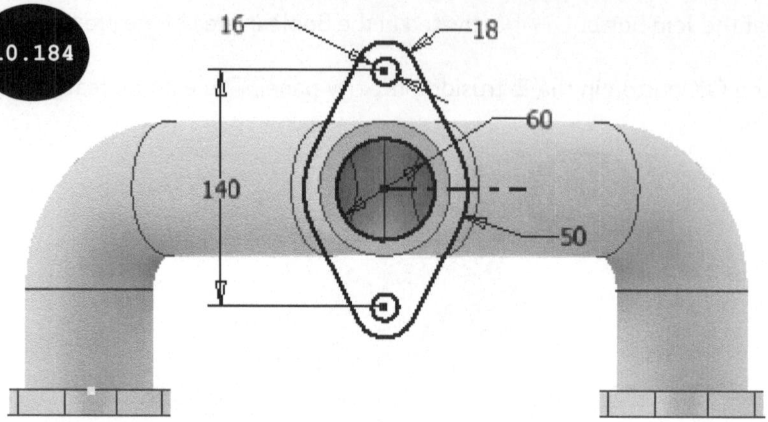

2. Click on the **3D Model** tab and then click on the **Extrude** tool in the **Create** panel. The **Extrusion** property panel appears and you are prompted to select a profile to be extruded.

3. Move the cursor over the outer closed profile of the sketch and click when it gets highlighted in the graphics area, see Figure 10.185. The preview of an extrude feature appears.

10.185

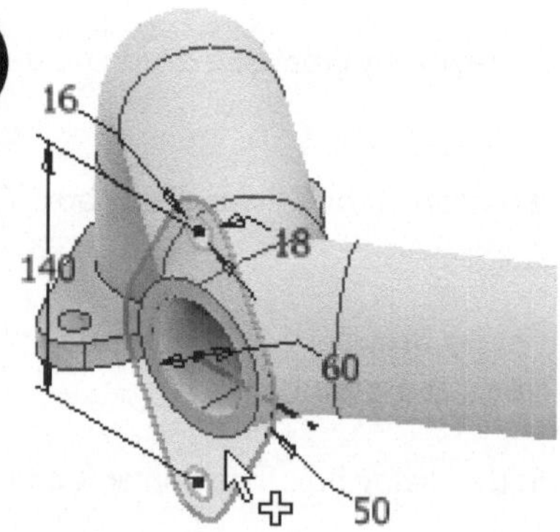

4. Enter **15** mm in the **Distance A** field of the property panel as the depth of the extrusion.

5. Ensure that the **Join** button is activated in the **Boolean** area of the property panel.

6. Click on the **OK** button in the **Extrusion** property panel. The extrude feature gets created, see Figure 10.186.

10.186

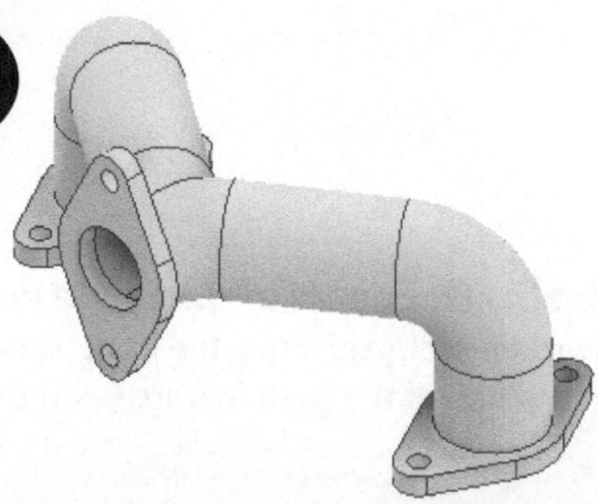

Section 11: Saving the Model

1. Click on the **Save** tool in the **Quick Access Toolbar** toolbar. The **Save As** dialog box appears.

2. Browse to **Autodesk Inventor > Chapter 10** folder in the local drive of your system. Note that you need to create a Chapter 10 folder inside the Autodesk Inventor folder.

3. Enter **Tutorial 1** in the **File name** field of the dialog box and then click on the **Save** button. The model is saved in the specified location (>:\Autodesk Inventor\Chapter 10).

Tutorial 2

Create the model shown in Figure 10.187. All dimensions are in mm.

10.187

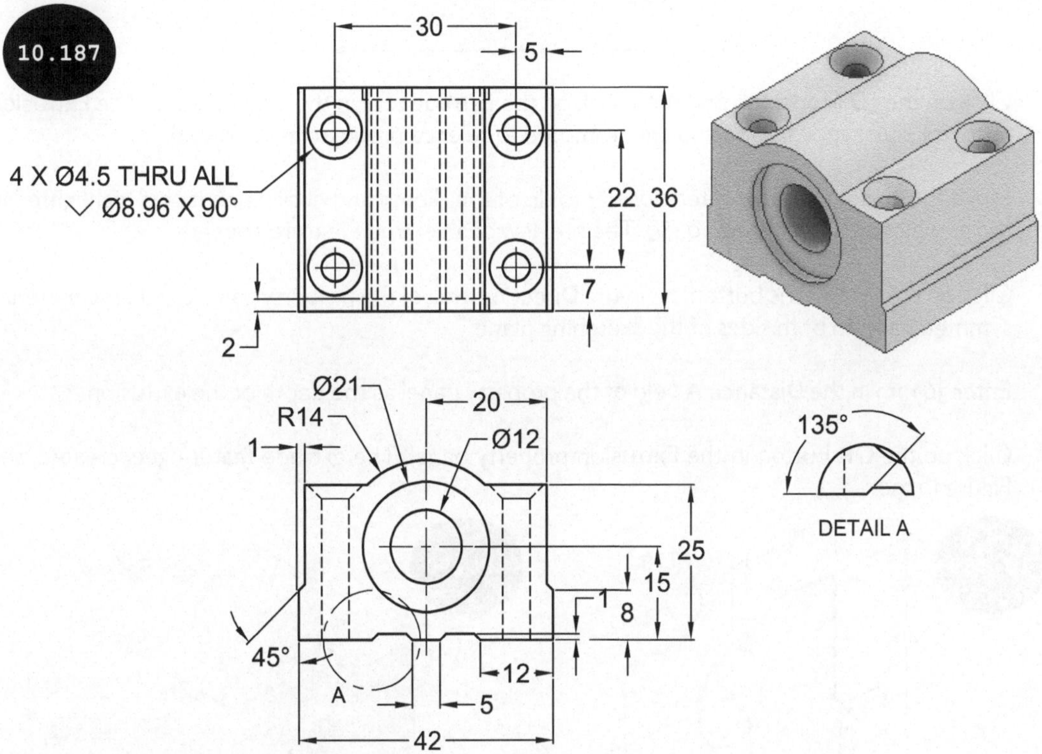

Section 1: Invoking the Part Modeling Environment

1. Start Autodesk Inventor and then invoke the Part modeling environment by using the **Standard (mm).ipt** template.

Section 2: Creating the Base Feature - Extrude Feature

1. Invoke the Sketching environment by selecting the Front plane (XY Plane) as the sketching plane.

2. Create the sketch of the base feature by using the sketching tool, see Figure 10.188. Note that you need to apply the required dimensions and constraints to make the sketch fully constrained.

10.188

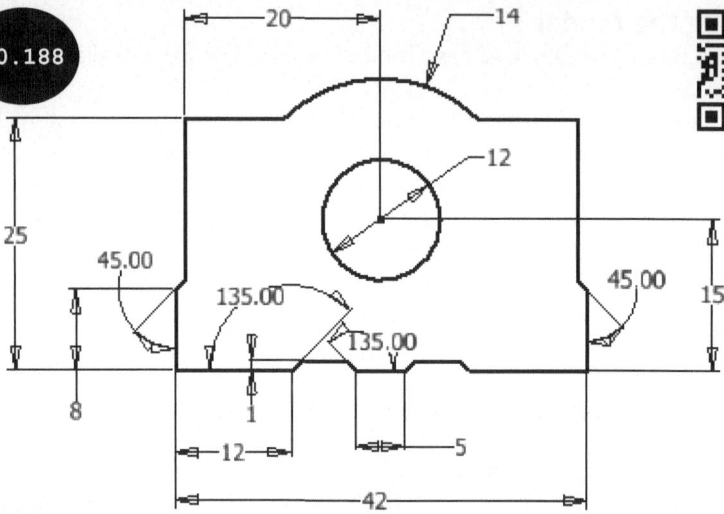

3. Click on the **3D Model** tab and then click on the **Extrude** tool in the **Create** panel. The **Extrusion** property panel appears and you are prompted to select a profile to be extruded.

4. Move the cursor over the outer closed profile of the sketch and click when it gets highlighted in the graphics area, see Figure 10.189. The preview of an extrude feature appears.

5. Click on the **Symmetric** button in the **Direction** area of the property panel to add the material, symmetrically on both sides of the sketching plane.

6. Enter **36** mm in the **Distance A** field of the property panel as the depth of the extrusion.

7. Click on the **OK** button in the **Extrusion** property panel. The extrude feature gets created, see Figure 10.190.

10.189

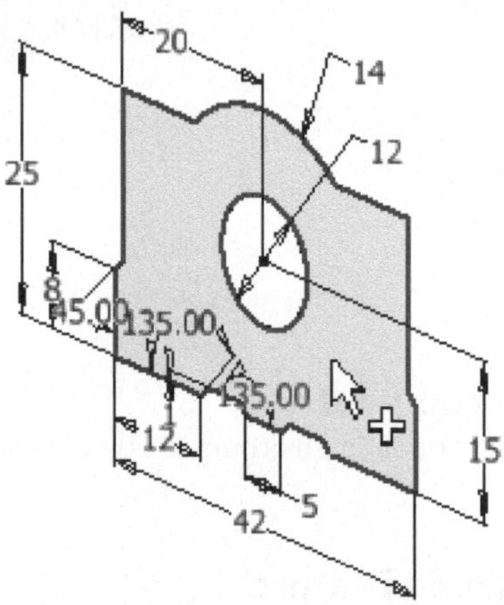

10.190

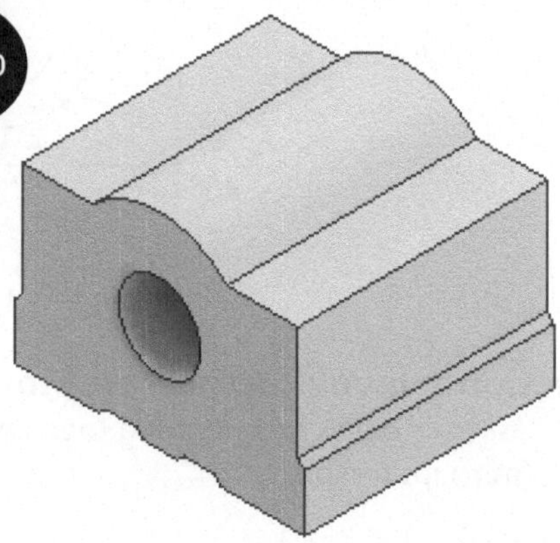

Section 3: Creating the Second Feature - Cut Feature

1. Invoke the Sketching environment by selecting the front planar face of the model as the sketching plane, see Figure 10.191.

2. Create a circle of diameter 21 mm as the sketch of the second feature, see Figure 10.192.

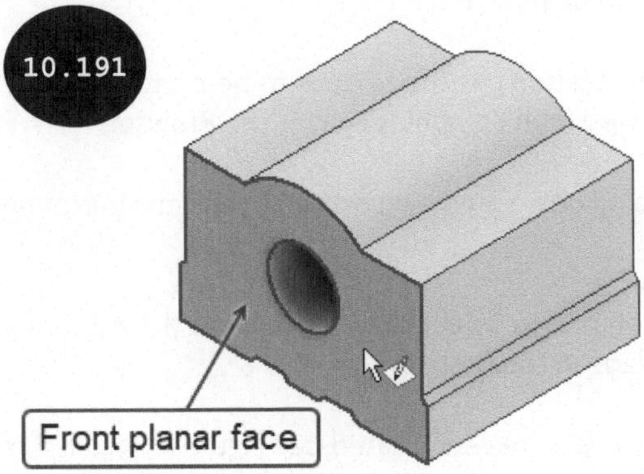

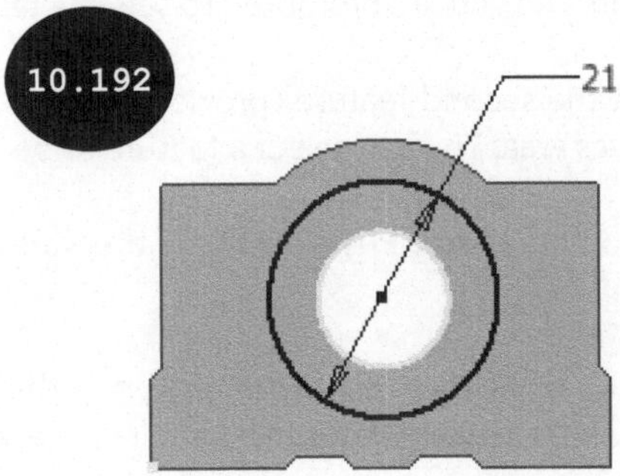

3. Click on the **3D Model** tab and then click on the **Extrude** tool in the **Create** panel. The **Extrusion** property panel appears with a preview of an extrude feature. Note that you need to select the closed profile of the sketch in the graphics area to be extruded, if not selected, by default.

4. Click on the **Flipped** button in the **Direction** area of the property panel to reverse the direction of extrusion backward.

5. Enter **2** mm in the **Distance A** field of the property panel as the depth of the extrusion for removing the material.

6. Ensure that the **Cut** button is activated in the **Boolean** area of the property panel for creating a cut feature by removing the material.

7. Click on the **OK** button in the **Extrusion** property panel. The cut feature gets created, see Figure 10.193.

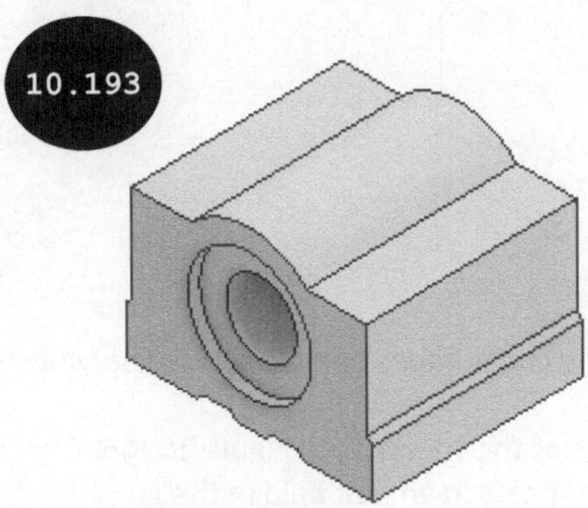

Section 4: Creating the Third Feature - Mirror Feature

The third feature of the model can be created by mirroring the second feature about the Front plane (XY Plane).

1. Click on the **Mirror** tool in the **Pattern** panel of the **3D Model** tab. The **Mirror** dialog box appears and you are prompted to select a feature to be mirrored.

2. Select the second feature (previously created cut feature) as the feature to be mirrored in the graphics area. You can select a feature to be mirrored in the graphics area or the **Browser**.

3. Click on the **Mirror Plane** button in the **Mirror** dialog box. You are prompted to select a mirroring plane.

4. Click on the **Origin XY Plane** button in the dialog box to select the XY Plane as the mirroring plane. Alternatively, you can also select the XY Plane in the Browser.

5. Click on the **OK** button in the dialog box. The mirror feature gets created, see Figure 10.194. In this figure, the visual style of the model has been changed to a "wireframe with hidden edges" visual style for viewing the hidden edges of the model.

Section 5: Creating the Fourth Feature - Hole Feature

Now, you need to create a hole feature by using the **Hole** tool.

1. Click on the **Hole** tool in the **Modify** panel of the **3D Model** tab. The **Hole** property panel appears and you are prompted to define the center of the hole.

2. Move the cursor over the top planar face of the model and then click anywhere on the face when it gets highlighted, see Figure 10.195. The preview of a hole appears on the face with default parameters.

10.194

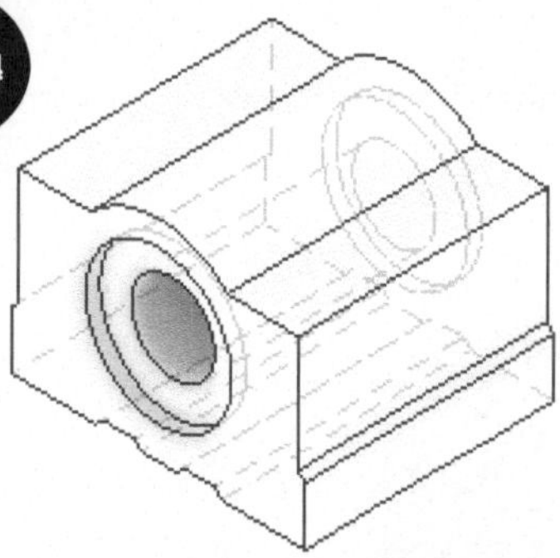

10.195

Now, you need to select the linear edges of a model for applying dimensions to position the hole.

3. Click on the top side edge of the model, see Figure 10.196. The distance between the selected edge and the hole center appears in an edit field in the graphics area, see Figure 10.197.

10.196

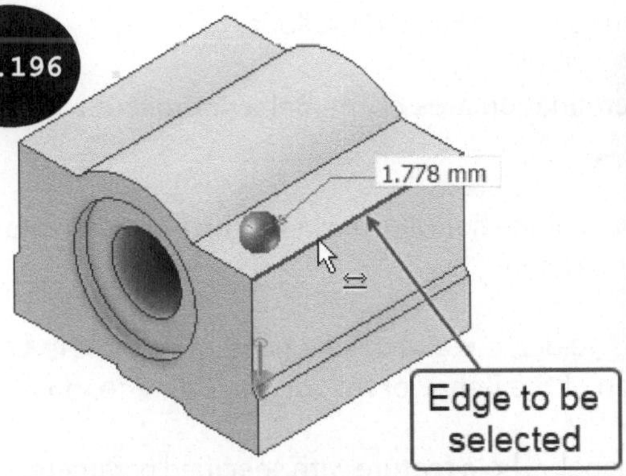

10.197

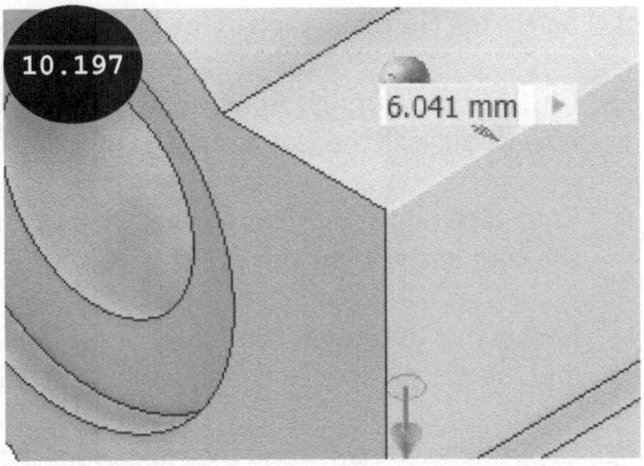

4. Enter **5** mm in the edit field that appears in the graphics area. The dimension between the top side edge and the center of the hole gets applied.

5. Click on the top front edge of the model and then enter **7** mm in the edit field that appears in the graphics area, see Figure 10.198. The dimension between the top front edge and the center of the hole gets applied.

10.198

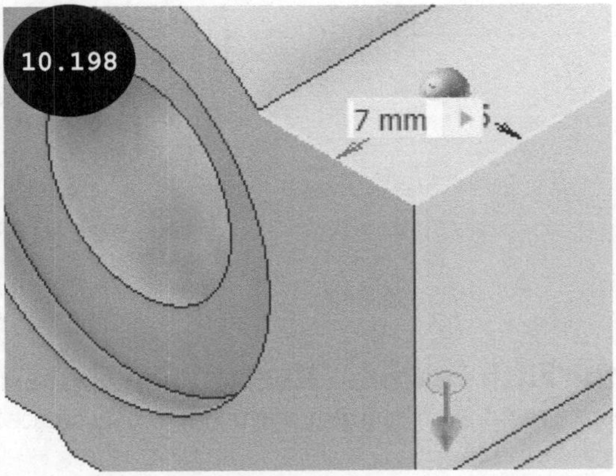

Now, you need to define the hole parameters in the Hole property panel.

6. Click on the **Clearance Hole** button in the **Hole** area of the **Type** rollout in the property panel to create a standard untapped hole.

7. Click on the **Countersink** button in the **Seat** area of the **Type** rollout to create a countersink hole.

8. Select the **Ansi Metric M Profile** option in the **Standard** drop-down list of the **Fastener** rollout in the property panel.

9. Select the **Flat Head Machine Screw** option in the **Fastener Type** drop-down list of the **Fastener** rollout in the property panel.

10. Select the **M4** option in the **Size** drop-down list of the **Fastener** rollout as the size of the hole.

11. Select the **Normal** option in the **Fit** drop-down list of the **Fastener** rollout.

12. Click on the **Through All** button in the **Termination** area of the **Behavior** rollout to create a hole through all the features of the model.

13. Enter **8.96 mm** in the **Countersink Diameter** field of the hole illustration in the **Behavior** rollout as the countersink diameter of the hole, see Figure 10.199.

14. Ensure that the countersink angle of the hole is 90 degrees and the diameter of the hole is 4.5 mm and the same is specified in the hole illustration of the **Behavior** rollout, see Figure 10.199.

15. Click on the **OK** button in the **Hole** property panel. A hole feature with specified parameters gets created, see Figure 10.200.

10.199

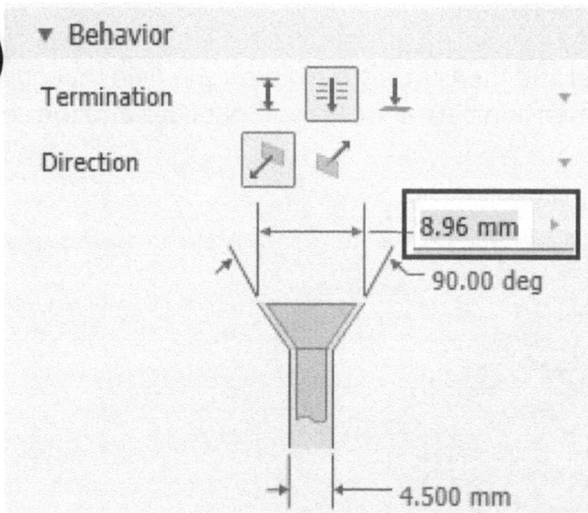

10.200

Section 6: Creating the Fifth Feature - Rectangular Pattern

Now, you need to create a rectangular pattern of the previously created hole feature for creating the remaining holes in the model.

1. Click on the **Rectangular Pattern** tool in the **Pattern** panel of the **3D Model** tab. The **Rectangular Pattern** dialog box appears and you are prompted to select features to be patterned.

2. Select the hole feature as the feature to be patterned in the graphics area or the **Browser**.

   Now, you need to define the first and second pattern directions.

3. Click on the **Direction A** button in the **Direction A** area of the dialog box and then select the top front linear edge of the model as the first pattern direction, see Figure 10.201. The **Column Count** and **Column Spacing** fields get enabled in the **Direction A** area of the dialog box. Also, an arrow appears in the graphics area, which is pointing towards the first pattern direction.

4. Enter **2** in the **Column Count** field in the **Direction 1** area as the number of pattern occurrences to be created in the first pattern direction.

5. Enter **30** mm in the **Column Spacing** field in the **Direction A** area as the spacing between two pattern occurrences. The preview of a rectangular pattern appears in the graphics area, see Figure 10.202. Ensure that the direction of the pattern is the same as shown in Figure 10.202.

6. Ensure that the **Spacing** option is selected in the **Distance Type** drop-down list in the **Direction 1** area of the dialog box.

10.201

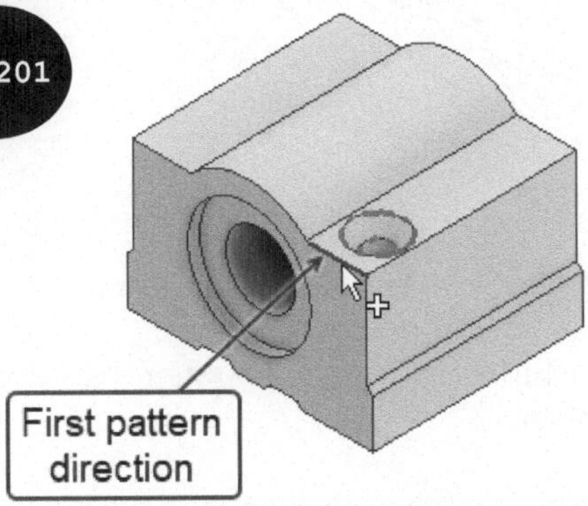

10.202

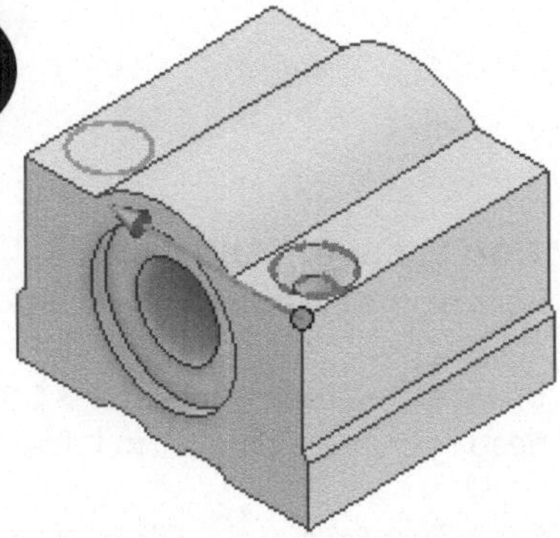

7. Click on the **Direction B** button in the **Direction B** area of the dialog box and then select the top side linear edge of the model as the second pattern direction, see Figure 10.203. The **Column Count** and **Column Spacing** fields get enabled in the **Direction B** area of the dialog box. Also, an arrow appears in the graphics area, which is pointing towards the second pattern direction.

8. Click on the **Flip** button in the **Direction B** area of the dialog box to reverse the pattern direction similar to the one shown in Figure 10.203.

9. Enter **2** in the **Column Count** field in the **Direction 2** area as the number of pattern occurrences to be created in the second pattern direction.

10. Enter **22** mm in the **Column Spacing** field in the **Direction 2** area as the spacing between two pattern occurrences. The preview of a rectangular pattern appears in the graphics area, see Figure 10.203.

10.203

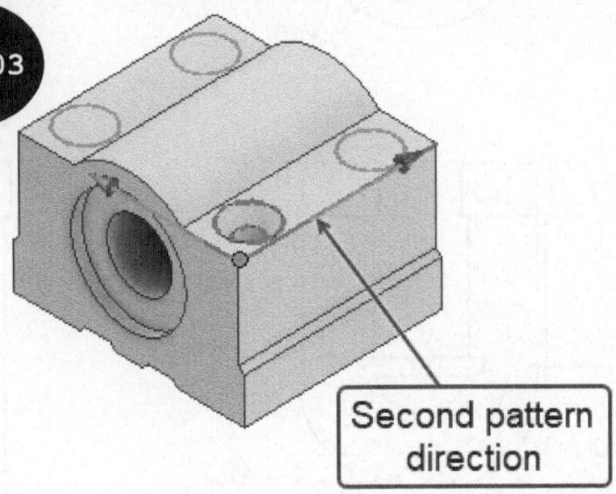

11. Ensure that the **Spacing** option is selected in the **Distance Type** drop-down list in the **Direction 2** area of the dialog box.

12. Click on the **OK** button in the dialog box. The rectangular pattern is created, see Figure 10.204.

10.204

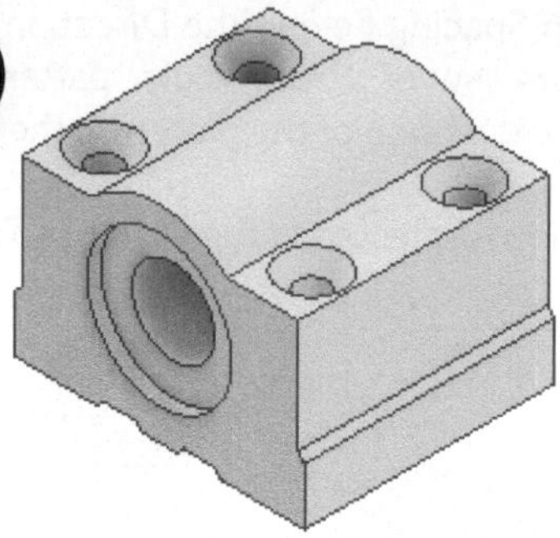

Section 7: Saving the Model

1. Click on the **Save** tool in the **Quick Access Toolbar**. The **Save As** dialog box appears.

2. Browse to **Autodesk Inventor > Chapter 10** folder in the local drive of your system. Note that you need to create a Chapter 10 folder, if not created earlier.

3. Enter **Tutorial 2** in the **File name** field of the dialog box and then click on the **Save** button. The model is saved in the specified location (>:\Autodesk Inventor\Chapter 10).

Hands-on Test Drive 1

Create the model shown in Figure 10.205. All dimensions are in mm.

10.205

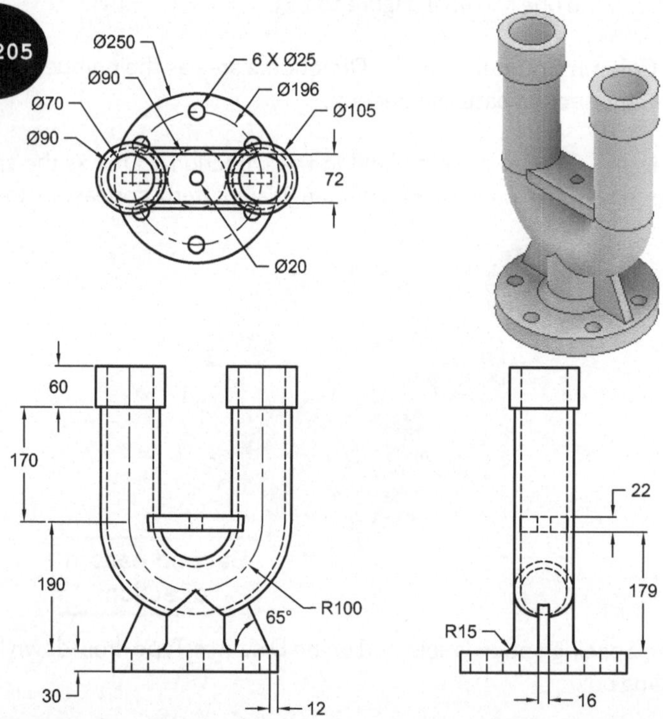

Hands-on Test Drive 2

Create the model shown in Figure 10.206. All dimensions are in mm.

10.206

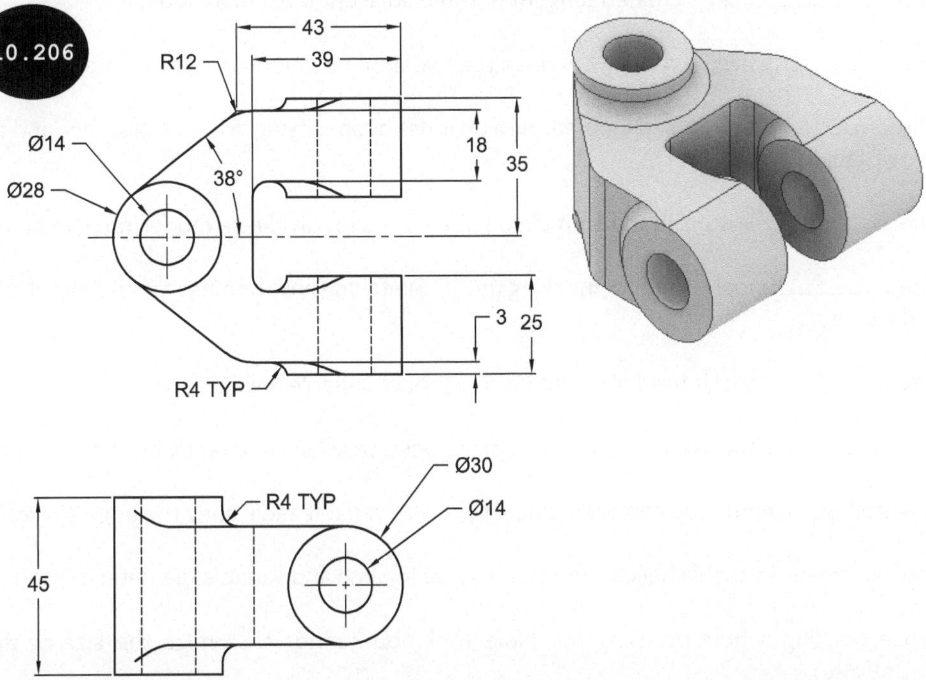

Summary

This chapter discussed how to create standard or customized holes such as clearance, tapped, and taper tapped by using the **Hole** tool. It explored methods for creating cosmetic threads, edge fillets, face fillets, full round fillets, and chamfers. Detailed methods are given for splitting the faces of a model, removing one side of a model, dividing a model into two bodies, and creating 3D sketches. The chapter also focussed on creating constant or variable helical curves, creating a 3D curve at the intersection of two geometries, creating a 3D silhouette curve on the outer boundary of a model, creating a 3D projected curve by projecting sketch entities or edges onto an existing face of a model, and creating a 3D curve directly on a face of a model in the 3D Sketching environment.

Questions

Complete and verify the following sentences:

- The _________ tool is used for creating standard holes such as clearance, tapped, and taper tapped.
- The _________ tool is used for adding cosmetic threads to features such as holes, shafts, studs, and bolts.

- In Autodesk Inventor, you can create three types of edge fillets: _________, _________, and _________.
- The _________ fillet is created tangent to three adjacent faces of a model.
- The _________ fillet is created between the two non-continuous faces of a model.
- The _________ tool is used for creating a chamfer by specifying distance, distance and angle, or two distances.
- The _________ button in the **Split** dialog box is used for dividing a model into two bodies.
- The _________ tool is used for invoking the 3D Sketching environment for creating 3D sketches and curves.
- The _________ tool is used for creating constant or variable helical curves.
- The _________ tool is used for creating an associative 3D curve directly on the face of a model.
- In Autodesk Inventor, you cannot create a fillet with variable radii along the edge. (True/False)
- You can create a variable helical curve with variable pitch and variable diameter. (True/False)
- While creating a hole by using the **Hole** tool, you cannot customize the size of the hole. (True/False)

CHAPTER
11

Working with Assemblies - I

In this chapter, the following topics will be discussed:

- Working with Bottom-up Assembly Approach
- Working with Top-down Assembly Approach
- Creating an Assembly using Bottom-up Approach
- Inserting Components in the Assembly Environment
- Working with Degrees of Freedom
- Applying Constraints
- Applying Joints
- Editing Constraints and Joints
- Deleting Constraints and Joints
- Moving and Rotating Individual Components

In the earlier chapters, you have learned about the basic and advanced techniques of creating real world mechanical components. In this chapter, you will learn about different techniques for creating mechanical assemblies. You will also learn about applying joints and constraints. An assembly is made up of two or more than two components joined together by applying joints and constraints, refer to Figure 11.1.

11.1

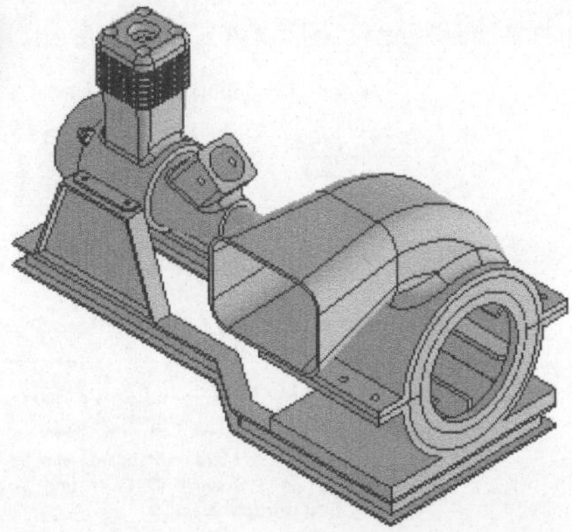

In Autodesk Inventor, you can create an assembly by using two approaches: Bottom-up Assembly Approach and Top-down Assembly Approach. Moreover, you can use a combination of both these approaches for creating an assembly. Both approaches are discussed below.

Working with Bottom-up Assembly Approach

The Bottom-up Assembly Approach is the most widely used approach for assembling components. In this approach, first all the components of an assembly are created one by one in the Part modeling environment and then saved in a common location. Later, all the components are inserted one by one in the Assembly environment and then assembled by applying the required joints and constraints.

Tip: Autodesk Inventor has a bidirectional association between all its environments. As a result, if any change or modification is made to a component in the Part modeling environment, the same change automatically reflects in the Assembly environment as well as in the Drawing environment, and vice-versa.

Working with Top-down Assembly Approach

In the Top-down Assembly Approach, all the components of an assembly are created within the Assembly environment. It helps in creating a concept-based design, in which new components of an assembly are created by taking reference from the existing components. You will learn about creating an assembly by using the Top-down assembly approach in Chapter 12.

Creating an Assembly using Bottom-up Approach

After creating all components of an assembly in the Part modeling environment and saving them in a common location, you need to invoke the Assembly environment of Autodesk Inventor for assembling them. To invoke the Assembly environment, click on the **New** tool in the **Quick Access Toolbar**. The **Create New File** dialog box appears, see Figure 11.2. In this dialog box, select the **Metric** template folder on the left panel and then double-click on the **Standard (mm).iam** template that appears in the **Assembly** rollout on the right panel of the dialog box, refer to Figure 11.2. The Assembly environment gets invoked with a Metric template, see Figure 11.3 (*.iam* is the file extension of an assembly file). Note that to invoke the Assembly environment with an English template, you need to select the **English** folder and then double-click on the **Standard (in).iam** template that appears in the dialog box.

11.2

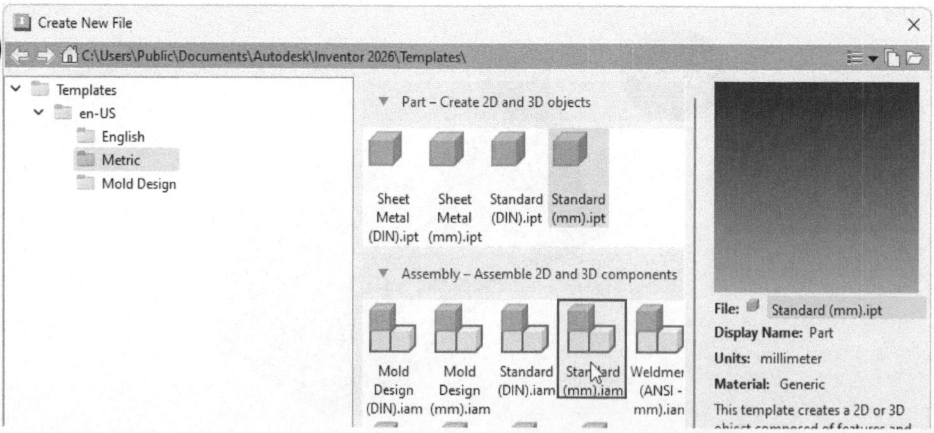

11.3

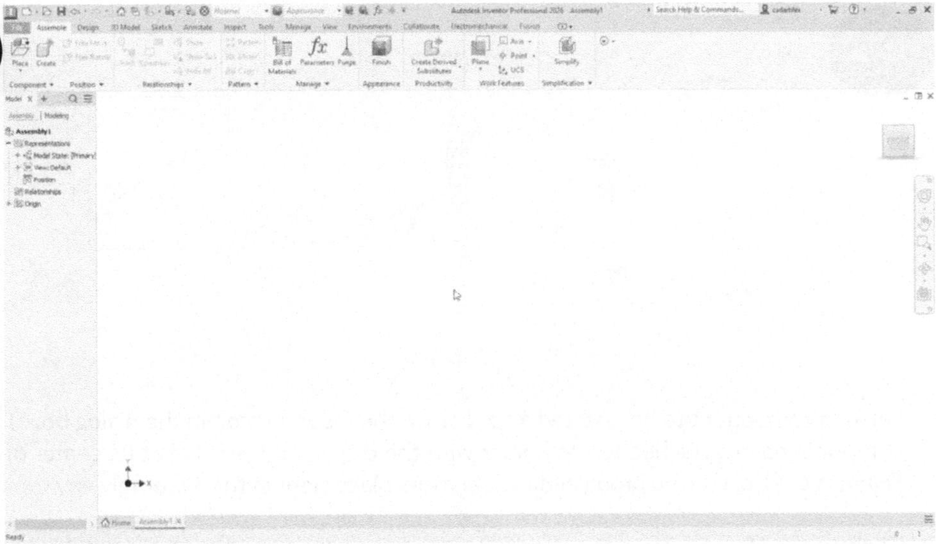

After invoking the Assembly environment, you can insert the components and assemble them by applying the required joints and constraints. The method for inserting components in the Assembly environment is discussed below.

Inserting Components in the Assembly Environment

In Autodesk Inventor, you can insert a component in the Assembly environment by using the **Place** tool, the method for which is given below:

1. Click on the **Place** tool in the **Component** panel of the **Assemble** tab, see Figure 11.4. The **Place Component** dialog box appears, see Figure 11.5. Alternatively, press the **P** key to invoke the **Place Component** dialog box.

11.4

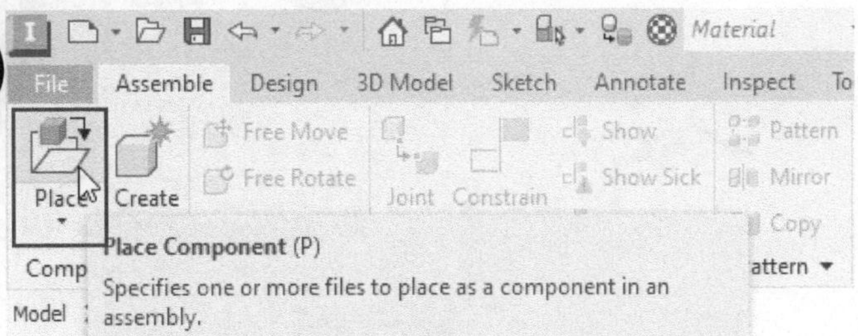

2. Browse to the location where all components of the assembly are saved.

3. Select the required file type in the **Files of type** drop-down list of the **Place Component** dialog box. By default, the **Component Files (*.ipt, *.iam)** file type is selected in this drop-down list. As a result, the native Inventor part and assembly files are displayed in the **Place Component** dialog box.

11.5

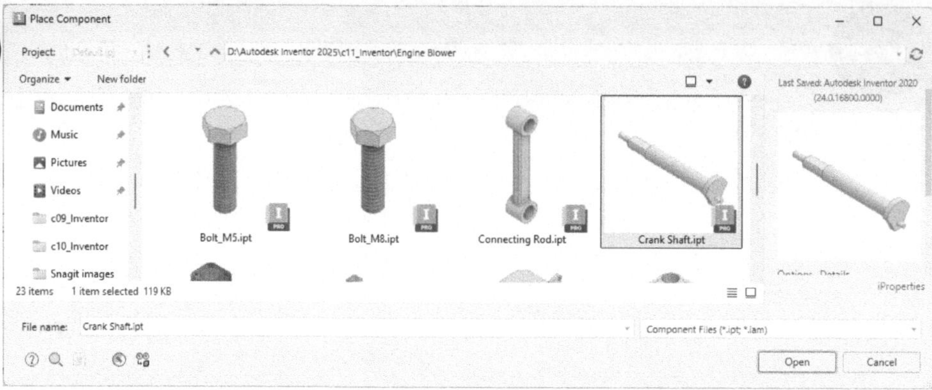

4. Select a component to be inserted and click on the **Open** button in the dialog box. The selected component gets attached to the cursor with the display of the Triad at its center of gravity, see Figure 11.6. Also, you are prompted to specify its placement in the Assembly environment.

5. Click on the **Home** icon in the ViewCube to change the view orientation of the component to isometric.

   Now, before defining the placement of a component in the Assembly environment, you can change its orientation, if needed.

6. Right-click in the graphics area and then click on the required option (**Rotate X 90**, **Rotate Y 90**, or **Rotate Z 90**) in the Marking Menu that appears, see Figure 11.7. The component gets rotated 90 degrees about the respective axis. By using these options, you can change the orientation of the component in 90 degrees increments about the X, Y, or Z axes, as desired.

11.6

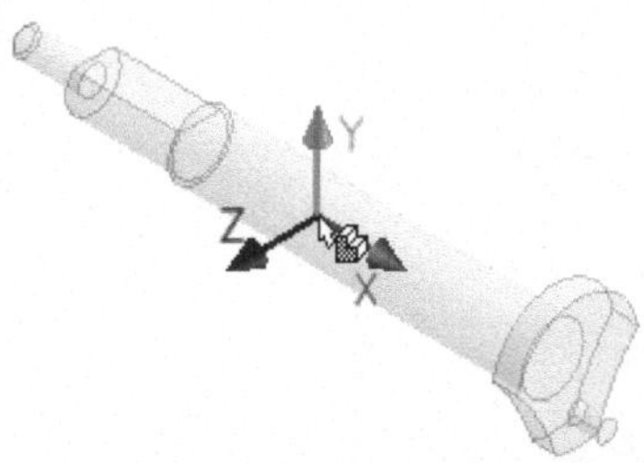

11.7

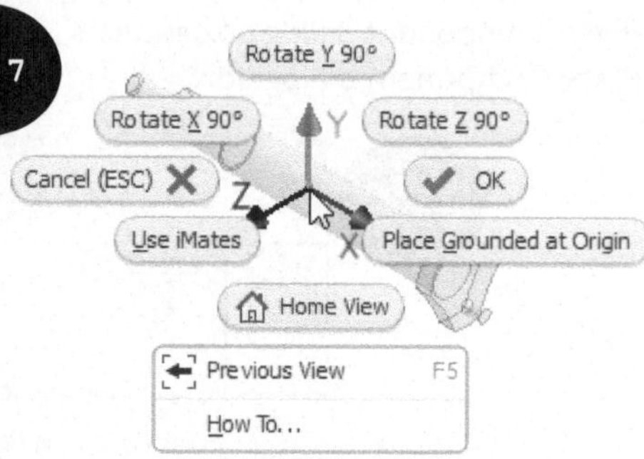

After the desired orientation of the component has been achieved, you can place the component in the Assembly environment.

Tip: It is recommended to make the first component of an assembly grounded or fixed at the origin. A grounded component does not allow any translational or rotational movement and all its degrees of freedom are fixed. You will learn more about a grounded component later in this chapter.

7. Right-click in the graphics area and then click on the **Place Grounded at Origin** tool in the Marking Menu that appears, see Figure 11.8. The component gets placed in the Assembly environment such that the origin of the component and the origin of the assembly file get coincident with each other. Also, the component becomes a grounded component and cannot move or rotate in any direction. Notice that the component is still attached to the cursor. This indicates that you can place multiple occurrences of a component one by one by clicking the left mouse button in the graphics area.

11.8

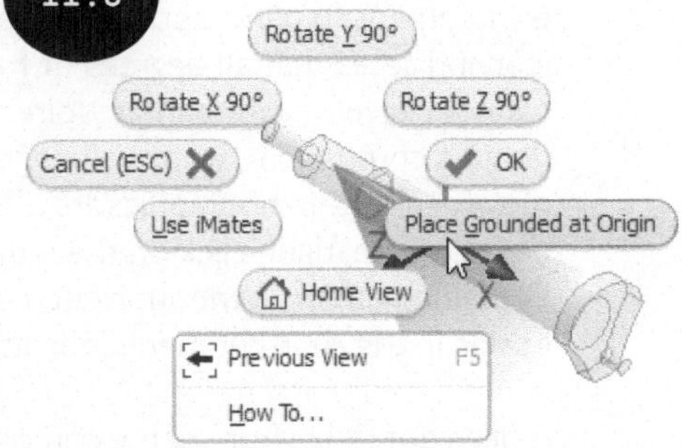

Note: In Autodesk Inventor, you can also specify a setting such that the first component of an assembly becomes a grounded component, by default. For doing so, click on the **Tools** tab in the **Ribbon** and then click on the **Application Options** tool in the **Options** panel. The **Application Options** dialog box appears. In this dialog box, click on the **Assembly** tab and then select the **Place and ground first component at origin** check box, see Figure 11.9. Next, click on the **Apply** button and then the **Close** button in the dialog box.

11.9

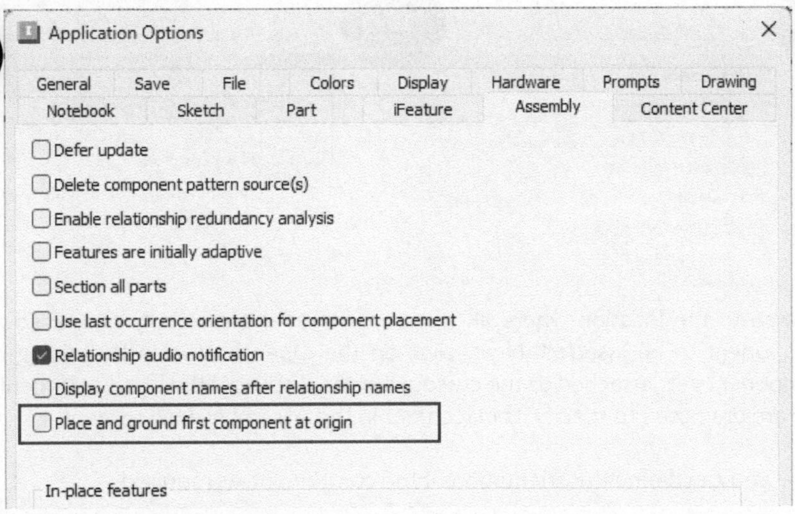

8. After inserting the first component, right-click in the graphics area and then click on the **OK** button in the Marking Menu that appears. Figure 11.10 shows the Browser with the name of the first inserted component as a grounded component.

Tip: As the first component has been inserted as a grounded component in the Assembly environment, its name appears in the Browser with a pushpin icon, see Figure 11.10. The pushpin icon indicates that all degrees of freedom of the component are fixed and the component cannot move or rotate in any direction. You can also change a grounded component to a floating component, whose all degrees of freedom are free. A floating component is free to move or rotate in the graphics area. To change a grounded component to a floating component or vice-versa, right-click on the name of a component in the Browser and then click on the **Grounded** option in the shortcut menu that appears. Note that a tick-mark on the **Grounded** option in the shortcut menu indicates that the current state of the component is grounded.

A filled dot [•] in front of the component name in the **Browser** indicates that the component is fully constrained, while an empty dot [○] indicates that the component is not fully constrained.

Now, you can insert the second component of the assembly in the graphics area by using the **Place** tool.

9. Click on the **Place** tool in the **Component** panel of the **Assemble** tab, see Figure 11.11. The **Place Component** dialog box appears. Alternatively, press the **P** key to invoke the **Place Component** dialog box.

11.10

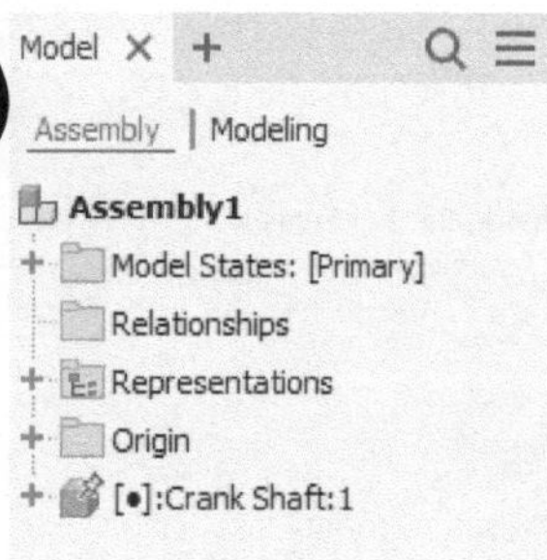

11.11

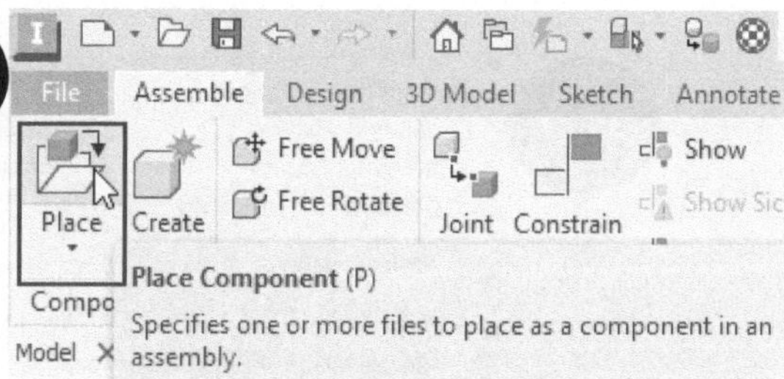

10. Browse to the location where all components of the assembly are saved and then select a component to be inserted. Next, click on the **Open** button in the dialog box. The selected component gets attached to the cursor with the display of the Triad at its center of gravity. Also, you are prompted to specify its placement in the Assembly environment.

Now, you can define the orientation of the component, as required.

11. Right-click in the graphics area and then click on the required option (**Rotate X 90**, **Rotate Y 90**, or **Rotate Z 90**) in the Marking Menu that appears. The component gets rotated 90 degrees about the respective axis. By using these options, you can change the orientation of the component in 90 degrees increments about the X, Y, or Z axes, as desired.

After the desired orientation of the component has been achieved, you can place the component in the Assembly environment.

12. Click the left mouse button anywhere in the graphics area to define the placement for the attached component. The component gets placed in the defined location. Also, the name of the inserted component is added in the Browser. Notice that the component is still attached to the cursor. This indicates that you can place multiple occurrences of a component one by one by clicking the left mouse button in the graphics area.

Tip: While defining the placement for a component in the graphics area, ensure that the component does not intersect with any existing component of the assembly.

13. Press the ESC key to exit the tool after inserting the component.

Note: By default, the component you insert into the Assembly environment is a floating component, whose all degrees of freedom are free and can move or rotate anywhere in the graphics area. You need to assemble the floating component with the existing components of the assembly by applying the required joints or constraints. You will learn about applying joints or constraints later in this chapter.

14. You can similarly insert the remaining components of an assembly in the Assembly environment one by one by using the **Place** tool.

Tip: After inserting the second component, it is recommended that you first assemble it with the first component (grounded) by applying required constraints or joints and then insert the third or next component in the Assembly environment.

Before you learn about applying constraints and joints between assembly components, it is important to first understand the concept of degrees of freedom, which is discussed below.

Working with Degrees of Freedom

In Autodesk Inventor, every component you insert into the Assembly environment is a floating component, by default. A floating or free component within the Assembly environment has six degrees of freedom: three translational and three rotational. This means that a floating component in the Assembly environment can move as well as rotate along the X, Y, and Z axes. As discussed earlier, you need to make the first component of an assembly a grounded or fixed component so that it does not undergo any translational or rotational movement. All degrees of freedom of a grounded component are fixed. However, the second or further components you insert into the Assembly environment need to be assembled by applying the required constraints and joints. The constraints and joints are used for fixing the required degrees of freedom and defining the relationship between the components of the assembly. For example, the function of a shaft in an assembly is to rotate about its axis, therefore, you need to apply constraints or joints such that the rotational degree of freedom of the shaft remains free.

Note: To check the degrees of freedom of a component, you can move or rotate the component along or about its free degrees of freedom by dragging the component in the graphics area. You will learn about moving or rotating individual components of an assembly later in this chapter.

Applying Constraints

In Autodesk Inventor, you can assemble components by applying different types of constraints: assembly constraints, motion constraints, transitional constraints, and constraint set constraints. All these types of constraints can be applied by using the **Constrain** tool. For doing so, click on the **Constrain** tool in the **Relationships** panel of the **Assemble** tab, see Figure 11.12. The **Place Constraint** dialog box appears, see Figure 11.13. By default, the **Assembly** tab is activated in this dialog box. As a result, the options for applying assembly constraints are displayed in the dialog box. The different types of constraints are discussed next.

11.12

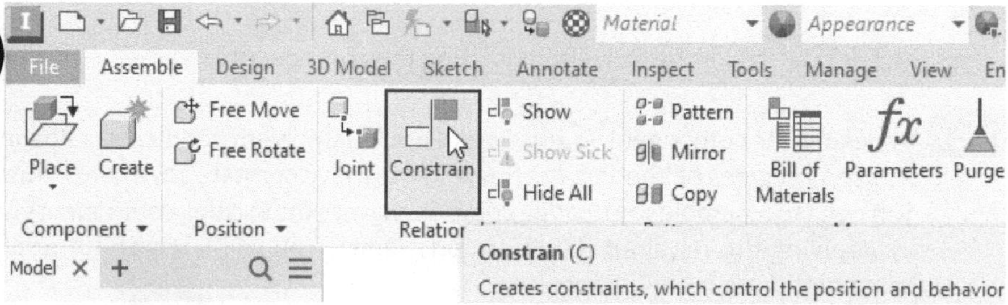

11.13

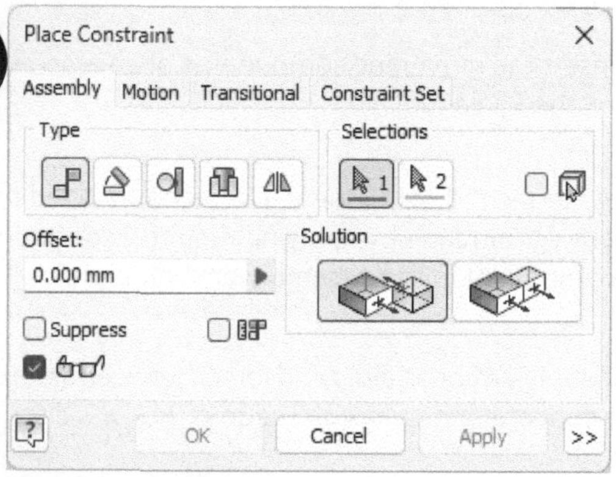

Applying Assembly Constraints

Assembly constraints are used for positioning components of an assembly by restricting or reducing some degrees of freedom of the components. You can apply assembly constraints such as mate, angle, tangent, and insert by activating the required button in the **Type** area of the **Assembly** tab in the dialog box. The different types of assembly constraints are discussed next.

Applying a Mate Constraint

Mate constraint is used for making the selected geometries of two different components coincident with each other, see Figure 11.14. You can select planar faces, edges, or axes of two different components as geometries for applying the mate constraint. The method for applying a mate constraint is discussed below:

11.14

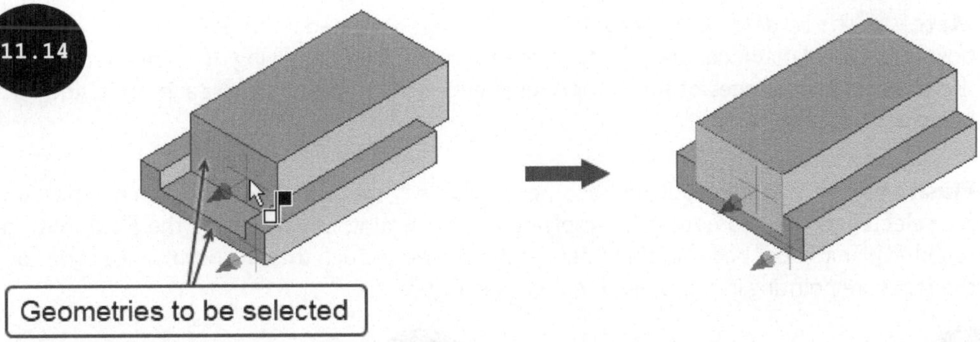

1. Click on the **Constrain** tool in the **Relationships** panel or press the C key. The **Place Constraint** dialog box appears. Also, you are prompted to select a geometry of the first component for applying the mate, since the **First Selection** button is activated in the **Selections** area of the **Assembly** tab in the dialog box.

2. Ensure that the **Mate** button is activated in the **Type** area of the dialog box for applying the mate constraint.

3. Click on a planar face, an edge, or an axis of a component as the first geometry for applying the mate, see Figure 11.15. The geometry gets selected and the **Second Selection** button gets activated automatically in the **Selections** area of the dialog box. As a result, you are prompted to select a geometry of another component.

4. Click on a planar face, an edge, or an axis of another component as the second geometry, see Figure 11.15. The mate constraint gets applied between the selected geometries of the components depending upon the solution (**Mate**, **Flush**, **Opposed**, **Aligned**, or **Undirected**) selected in the **Solutions** area of the dialog box, see Figures 11.16 and 11.17. Note that the availability of options in the **Solution** area depends upon the type of geometries selected for applying the constraint.

11.15

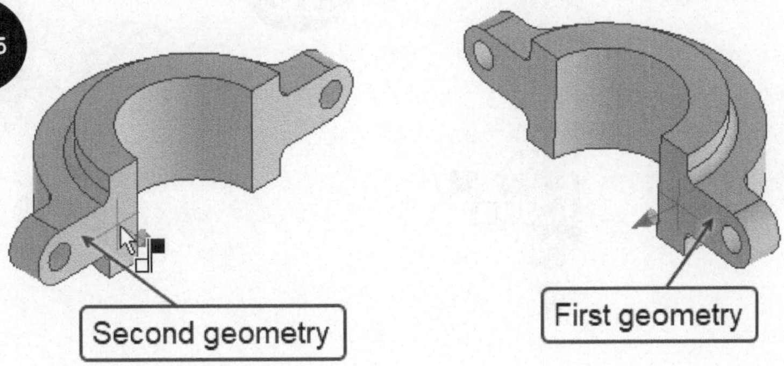

Tip: When the **Pick part first** check box is selected in the dialog box, Autodesk Inventor allows you to first select the geometry of the moveable component to be assembled, followed by the geometry of the assembly component to apply the constraint.

Mate : By default, the **Mate** button becomes activated in the **Solution** area of the dialog box when two planar faces are selected as the geometries for applying the constraint. As a result, the selected planar faces of the components get positioned normal to each other and become coincident, see Figure 11.16.

Flush : The **Flush** button becomes available in the **Solution** area when two planar faces are selected as the geometries for applying the constraint. On activating the **Flush** button, the selected planar faces become coincident with each other such that the normal directions of both the faces are pointing in the same direction, see Figure 11.17.

11.16

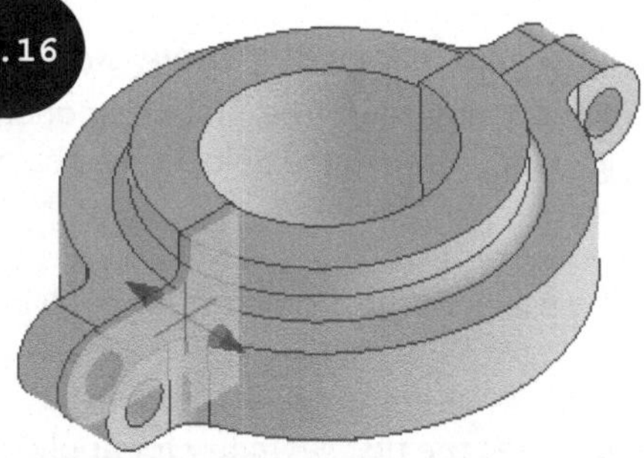

11.17

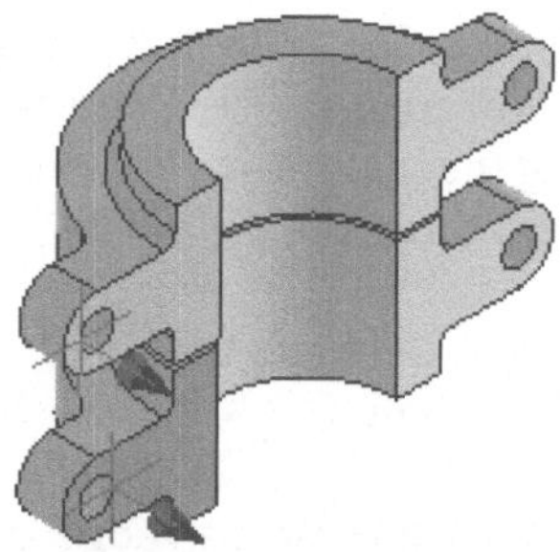

Opposed : The **Opposed** button becomes available in the **Solution** area when two linear edges, cylindrical faces, or axes are selected as the geometries for applying constraint. Note that on selecting a cylindrical/circular face, its axes get selected automatically for applying the constraint, refer to Figure 11.18. When the **Opposed** button is activated, the selected axes/edges get coincident with each other, such that the directions of the axes are opposite to each other, see Figure 11.19.

11.18

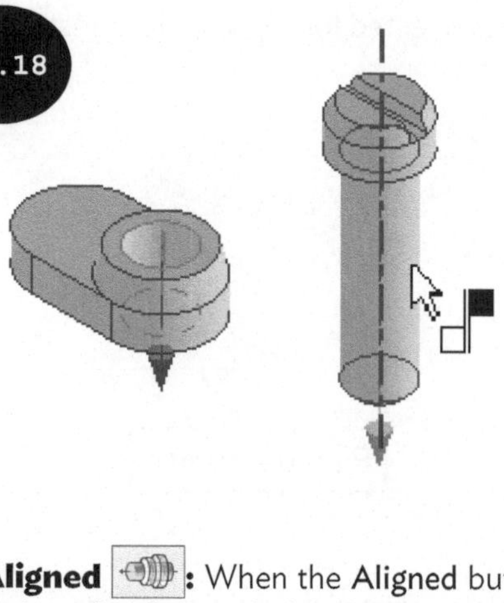

11.19

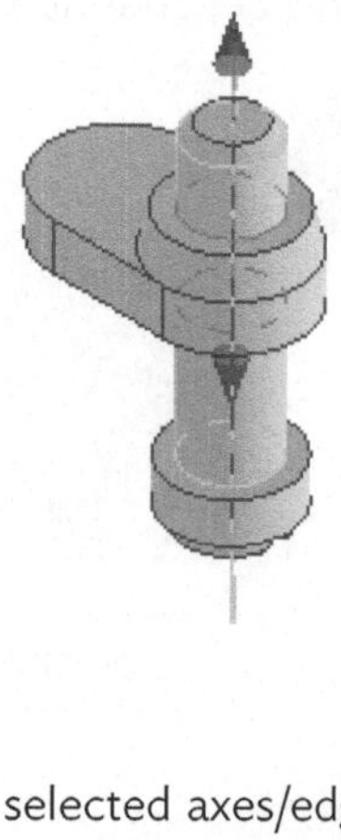

Aligned : When the **Aligned** button is activated, the selected axes/edges get coincident with each other, such that the axes are aligned in the same direction, see Figure 11.20. This button becomes available in the **Solution** area when two linear edges or axes are selected as the geometries for applying the constraint.

11.20

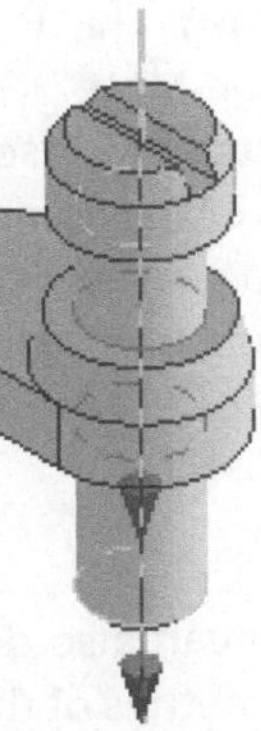

Undirected 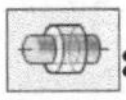**:** When the **Undirected** button is activated, the selected axes/edges get coincident with each other, undirected. This button is available only when two linear edges or axes are selected as the geometries for applying the constraint.

5. Click on the **Mate, Flush, Opposed, Aligned**, or **Undirected** button in the **Solution** area of the dialog box, as required.

   Offset: By default, a 0 value is entered in the **Offset** field of the dialog box. As a result, both the selected geometries are in contact with each other. You can also define an offset distance between the selected geometries of the components by entering an offset distance in this field. Figure 11.21 shows an offset distance specified between two selected planar faces of the components.

11.21

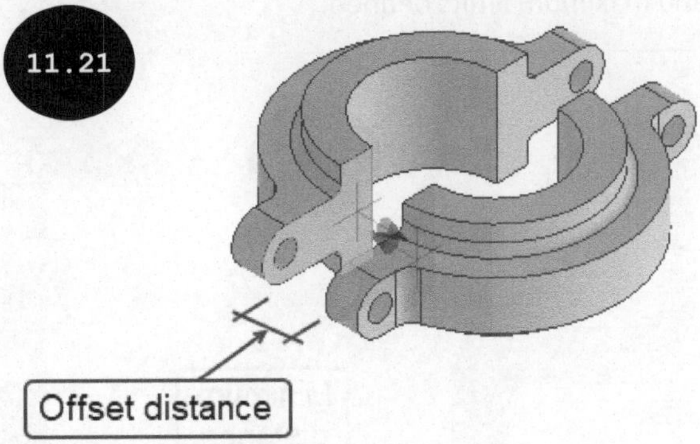

6. Enter an offset distance between the selected geometries of the components in the **Offset** field of the dialog box, if needed.

   Suppress: When the **Suppress** check box is selected, the constraint between the selected geometries of the model will be applied in its suppressed state. A suppressed constraint does not restrict any degree of freedom of the components. By default, this check box is cleared.

   Show Preview: By default, the **Show Preview** check box is selected in the dialog box. As a result, on selecting the geometries of two different components, the preview or effect of the applied constraint appears in the graphics area. Note that if the solution of the applied constraint is not adaptive, then the preview will not be displayed in the graphics area.

Predict Offset and Orientation: The Predict Offset and Orientation check box is available in the dialog box when the **Mate** or **Angle** button is activated in the **Type** area of the dialog box. On selecting the **Predict Offset and Orientation** check box, the mate gets applied between the selected geometries of the components such that the current offset distance or the angle value between the selected geometries gets predicted automatically and specified in the **Offset** or **Angle** fields of the dialog box, respectively. The **Offset** field appears when the **Mate** button is activated, while the **Angle** field appears when the **Angle** button is activated in the dialog box.

Note: In Autodesk Inventor, you can also define the maximum and minimum distance limits between two selected geometries of the components such that the components can only move or translate within the specified distance limit, see Figures 11.22 to 11.24. For doing so, expand the **Place Constraint** dialog box by clicking on the double arrow at the lower right corner of the dialog box. Figure 11.25 shows the expanded **Place Constraint** dialog box. In the **Name** field of the expanded dialog box, you can specify a name for the maximum and minimum limit constraint to be applied. Next, select the **Maximum** check box and then specify the maximum distance limit in the **Maximum** field that is enabled below the check box. After specifying the maximum distance limit, select the **Minimum** check box and then specify the minimum distance limit in the **Minimum** field that is enabled below the check box. The **Use Offset As Resting Position** check box of the expanded dialog box is used for defining the rest position of the moveable component in the **Offset** field of the dialog box. The rest position of the component is the position where the component will come into rest after a movement. You can define the rest position of the component anywhere between the minimum and maximum limits defined.

11.22

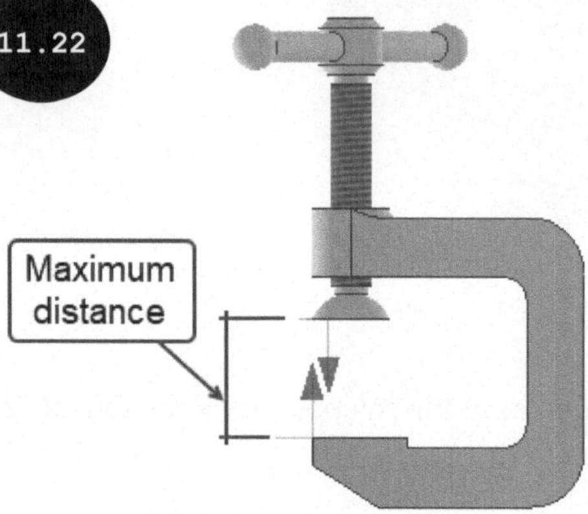

11.23

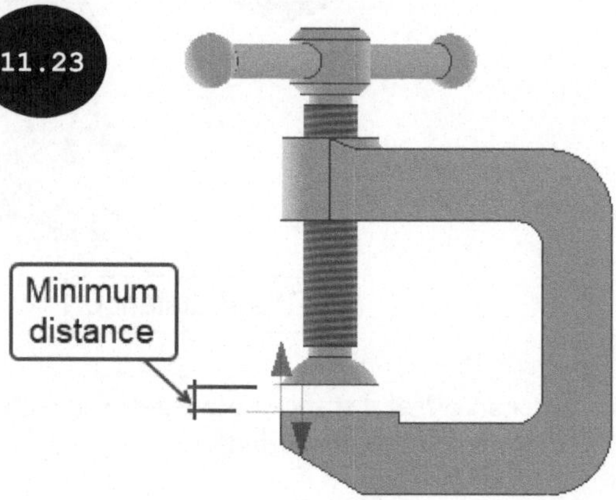

11.24

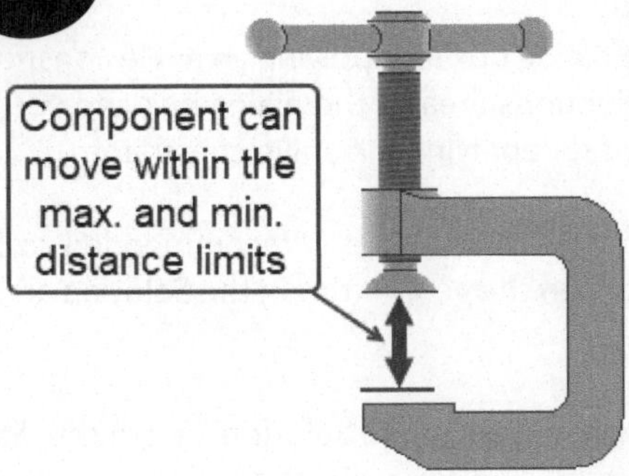

11.25

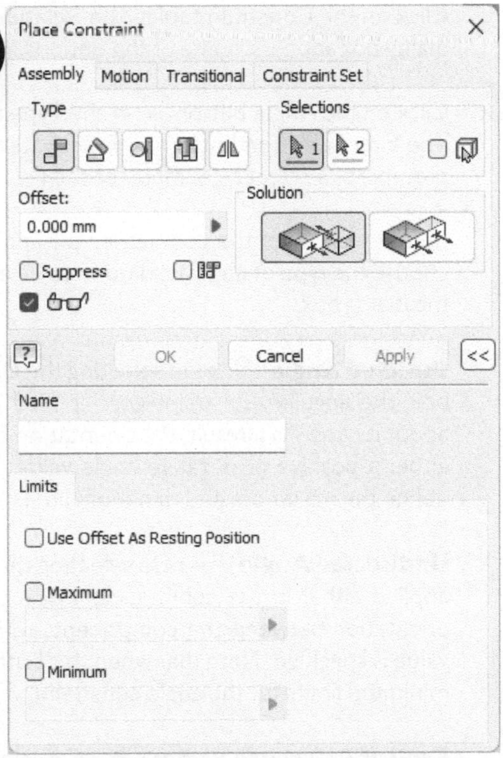

7. Click on the **Apply** button in the dialog box. The mate constraint gets applied between the selected components and the **Place Constraint** dialog box is still available. You can continue applying the remaining constraints between the components of the assembly using the dialog box and then click on the **Cancel** button to close it.

Applying an Angle Constraint

Angle constraint is used for restricting geometries of two different components at a specified angular distance, see Figure 11.26. You can select two linear edges or planar faces of two different components as geometries for applying the angle constraint. The method for applying an angle constraint is discussed below:

11.26

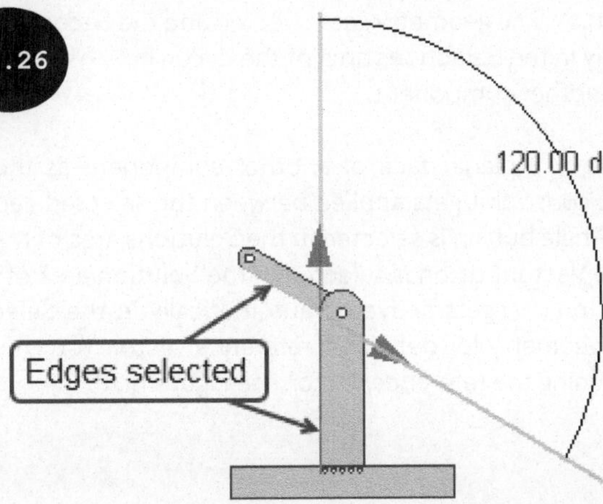

1. Click on the **Constrain** tool in the **Relationships** panel or press the **C** key. The **Place Constraint** dialog box appears. Some of the options in this dialog box have already been discussed earlier.

2. Click on the **Angle** button in the **Type** area of the dialog box for applying an angle constraint. The **First Selection** button is activated in the **Selections** area of the dialog box and you are prompted to select a geometry of the first component for applying the angle constraint.

   Before you select the geometries for applying the angle constraint, it is recommended to first choose the type of angular solution to be applied between the geometries in the **Solution** area of the dialog box.

   Directed Angle : On selecting the **Directed Angle** button in the **Solution** area of the dialog box, the angular constraint gets applied in the counter-clockwise direction (right-hand rule) about its axis. As a result, the orientation between the components can be flipped by specifying either a positive or negative angle value. Note that when this button is activated, you cannot define the maximum and minimum limits for the angle constraint.

   Undirected Angle : On selecting the **Undirected Angle** button, the angular constraint gets applied either in the counter-clockwise or clockwise direction about its axis. As a result, the orientation between the components remains the same whether a positive or negative angle value is specified. Note that when this button is activated, you can also define the maximum and minimum limits for the angle constraint.

   Explicit Reference Vector : On selecting the **Explicit Reference Vector** button, in addition to the selection of two geometries for applying angular constraint, you also need to select a reference vector for defining the axis of rotation. When this button is activated, the **Reference Vector** button gets enabled in the **Selections** area of the dialog box for defining the axis of rotation. You can also define the maximum and minimum limits for the angle constraint when this button is activated.

3. Click on the required button (**Directed Angle**, **Undirected Angle**, or **Explicit Reference Vector**) in the **Solution** area of the dialog box to apply the angle constraint.

4. Click on a linear edge or a planar face of a component as the first geometry for applying the angle constraint, see Figure 11.27. The geometry gets selected and the **Second Selection** button gets activated automatically in the **Selections** area of the dialog box. As a result, you are prompted to select a geometry of another component.

5. Click on a linear edge or a planar face of another component as the second geometry, see Figure 11.27. The angle constraint gets applied between the selected geometries, if the **Directed Angle** or **Undirected Angle** button is selected in the **Solutions** area of the dialog box. Note that if the **Explicit Reference Vector** button is selected in the **Solution** area of the dialog box, then the **Reference Vector** button gets activated automatically in the **Selections** area and you are prompted to select a geometry for defining a reference vector. You can select a planar face, an edge, or an axis for defining the reference vector, see Figure 11.28.

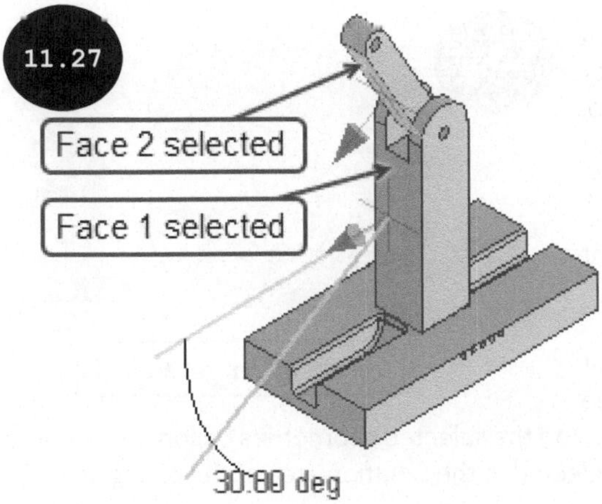

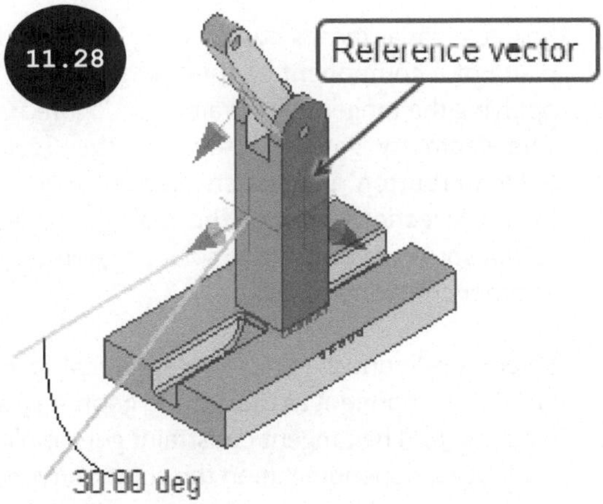

6. Enter an angle value between the selected geometries of the components in the **Angle** field of the dialog box.

Note: You can also define the maximum and minimum angle limits between the selected geometries of the components such that the components can rotate within the specified angle limit. For doing so, expand the **Place Constraint** dialog box. Next, specify the maximum and minimum angle values in the **Maximum** and **Minimum** fields of the expanded dialog box. Note that you cannot define the maximum and minimum angle limits, if the **Directed Angle** button is selected in the **Solution** area of the dialog box.

7. Click on the **OK** button in the dialog box. The angle constraint gets applied between the selected geometries of the components.

Applying a Tangent Constraint

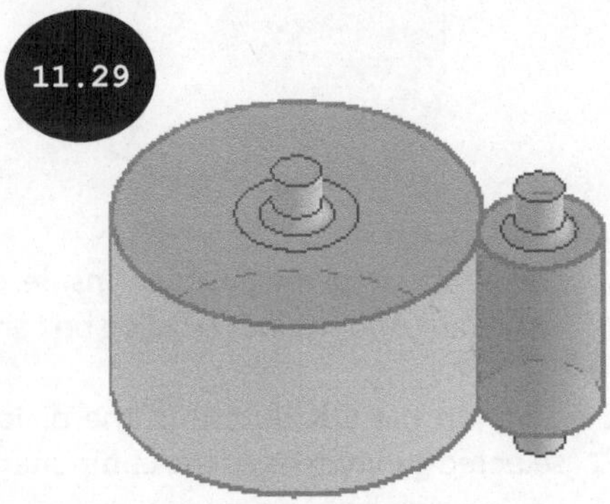

Tangent constraint is used for making the selected geometries of two different components tangent to each other, see Figure 11.29. You can select a planar face, a curved face, an edge, or a plane as the first geometry and a cylindrical, conical, or spherical face as the second geometry for applying the tangent constraint. The method for applying a tangent constraint is discussed below:

1. Click on the **Constrain** tool in the **Relationships** panel or press the **C** key. The **Place Constraint** dialog box appears. Some of the options in this dialog box have already been discussed earlier.

2. Click on the **Tangent** button in the **Type** area of the dialog box for applying a tangent constraint. The **First Selection** button is activated in the **Selections** area of the dialog box and you are prompted to select a geometry of the first component.

3. Select a planar face, a curved face, an edge, or a plane of a component as the first geometry for applying the tangent constraint, see Figure 11.30. The geometry gets selected and the **Second Selection** button gets activated automatically in the **Selections** area of the dialog box. As a result, you are prompted to select a geometry of another component.

11.30

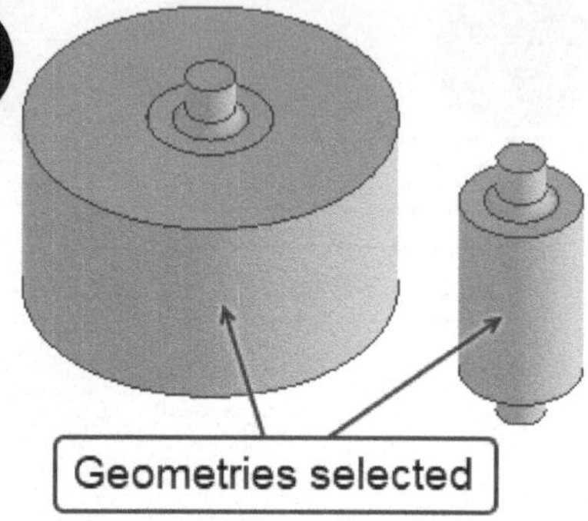

4. Select a cylindrical, conical, or spherical face of another component as the second geometry, see Figure 11.30. The tangent constraint gets applied and the selected geometries become tangent to each other depending upon the solution type selected in the **Solution** area of the dialog box.

 Inside : On selecting the **Inside** button in the **Solution** area of the dialog box, the **selected** geometries become tangent to each other such that the moveable component is placed inside the other component, see Figure 11.31.

 Outside : On selecting the **Outside** button, the **selected** geometries become tangent to each other such that the moveable component is placed outside the other component, see Figure 11.32.

11.31

11.32

5. Select the required button (**Inside** or **Outside**) in the **Solution** area of the dialog box. The remaining options in the dialog box are the same as discussed earlier.

6. Click on the **OK** button in the dialog box. The tangent constraint gets applied between the selected geometries of the components.

Applying an Insert Constraint

Insert constraint is used for inserting a bolt (cylindrical geometry of a component) into the hole of another component such that the axis of the bolt (cylindrical geometry) aligns with the axis of the hole and the bottom planar face of the bolt head is coincident with the planar face of the hole component, see Figure 11.33. The method for applying an insert constraint is discussed below:

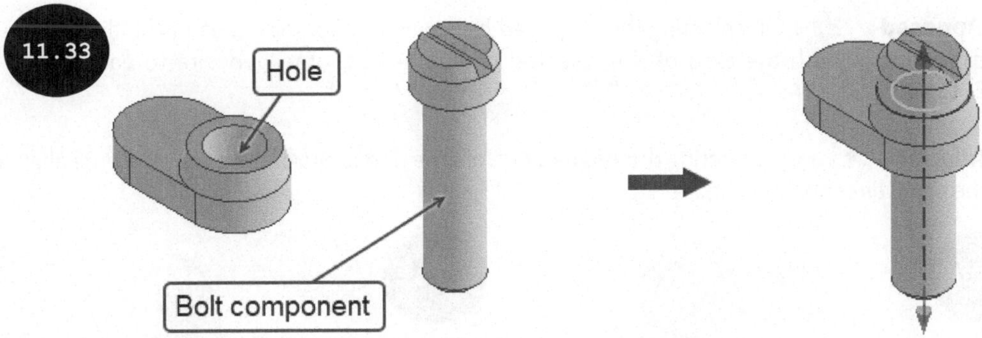

1. Click on the **Constrain** tool in the **Relationships** panel or press the **C** key. The **Place Constraint** dialog box appears.

2. Click on the **Insert** button in the **Type** area of the dialog box for applying the constraint. The **First Selection** button is activated in the **Selections** area of the dialog box and you are prompted to select a geometry of the first component.

3. Move the cursor over a cylindrical or conical geometry of a component to be inserted. The axis and an edge (which is closer to the cursor) of the geometry appear in the graphics area, see Figure 11.34.

4. Click the left mouse button when the axis and an edge of the cylindrical or conical geometry appear in the graphics area. You are prompted to select a geometry of the second component.

5. Move the cursor over a circular cut geometry (hole) of the second component. The axis and an edge (which is closer to the cursor) of the geometry appear in the graphics area, see Figure 11.35.

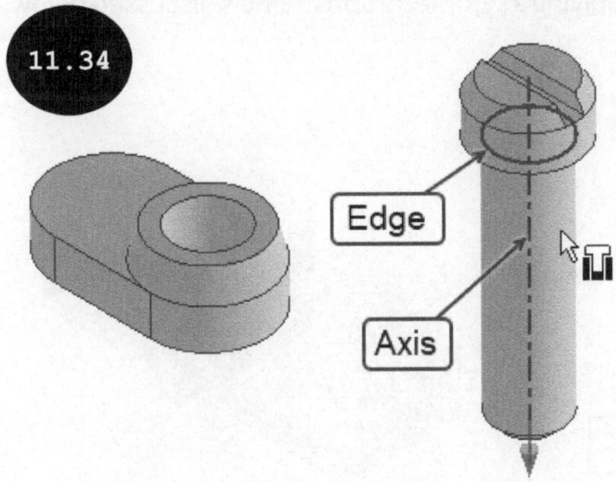

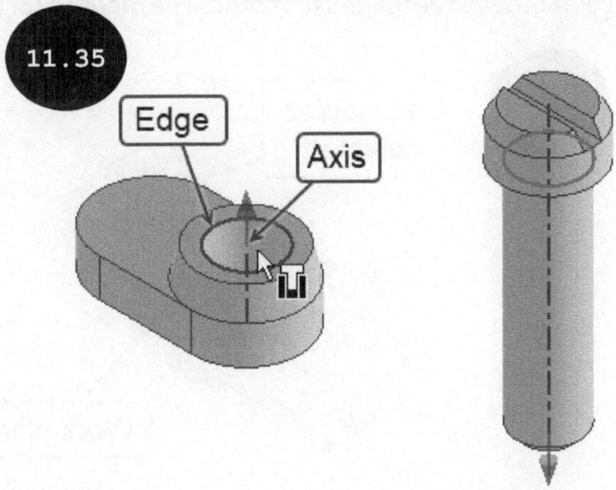

6. Click the left mouse button when the axis and the edge of the circular cut geometry (hole) appear in the graphics area. The insert constraint gets applied such that the axes of both the geometries get aligned to each other and the edges get coincident with each other, see Figure 11.36.

   Now, you need to select a solution type in the **Solution** area of the dialog box.

Opposed **:** On selecting the **Opposed** button in the **Solution** area of the dialog box, the directions of both the axes of the selected geometries become opposite to each other, see Figure 11.36.

Aligned **:** On selecting the **Aligned** button, the directions of both axes become aligned in the same direction, see Figure 11.37.

11.36

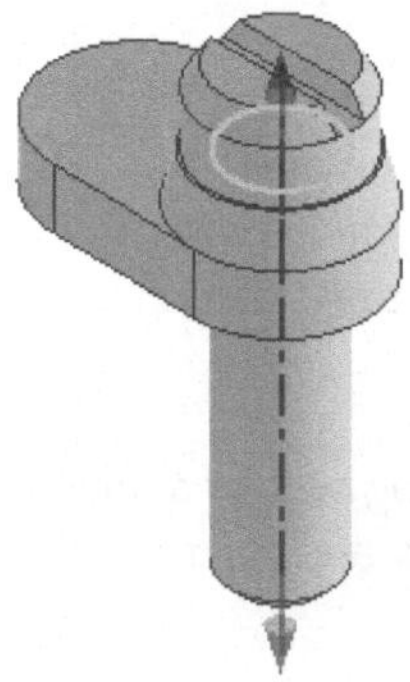

11.37

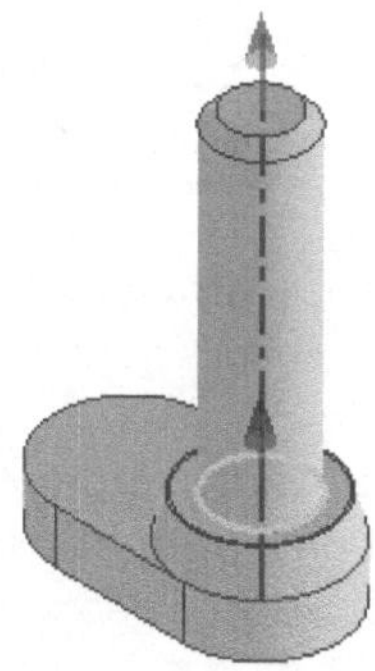

7. Select the required button (**Opposed** or **Aligned**) in the **Solution** area of the dialog box. The remaining options in the dialog box are the same as discussed earlier.

8. Click on the **OK** button in the dialog box. The insert constraint gets applied between the selected geometries of the components.

Applying a Symmetry Constraint

Symmetry constraint is used for making two geometries of different components symmetric about a work plane or a planar face, see Figure 11.38. You can select faces, edges, axes, or work points as geometries to be made symmetric. The method for applying a symmetry constraint is discussed below:

11.38

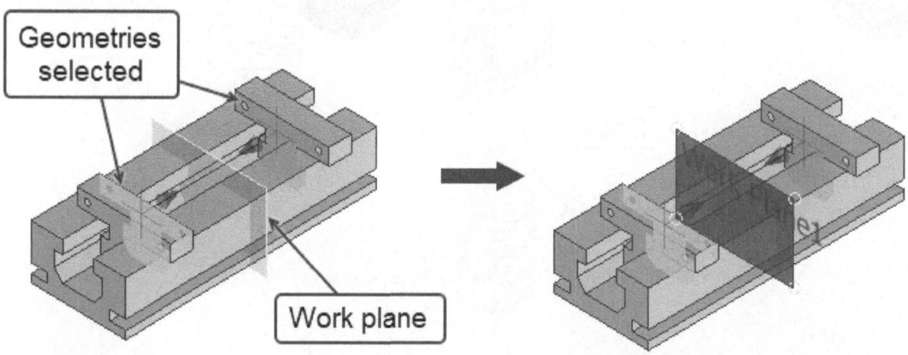

1. Click on the **Constrain** tool in the **Relationships** panel or press the **C** key. The **Place Constraint** dialog box appears.

2. Click on the **Symmetry** button in the **Type** area of the dialog box for applying a symmetry constraint. You are prompted to select a geometry of the first component.

3. Select a face, an edge, or an axis of a component as the first geometry. The geometry gets selected and you are prompted to select a geometry of the second component.

4. Select a face, an edge, or an axis of another component as the second geometry. You are prompted to select a symmetric plane.

5. Select a work plane or a planar face as the symmetric plane in the graphics area. The selected geometries become symmetric about the selected symmetric plane depending upon the button (**Opposed** or **Aligned**) activated in the **Solution** area of the dialog box, refer to Figures 11.39 and 11.40.

   Opposed : On selecting the **Opposed** button in the **Solution** area of the dialog box, the selected geometries (faces or edges) of the components become symmetric about the symmetric plane such that the normal direction of both the faces are pointing opposite to each other, see Figure 11.39.

   Aligned : On selecting the **Aligned** button, the selected geometries become symmetric about the symmetric plane such that the normal direction of both the faces is pointing in the same direction, see Figure 11.40.

11.39

11.40

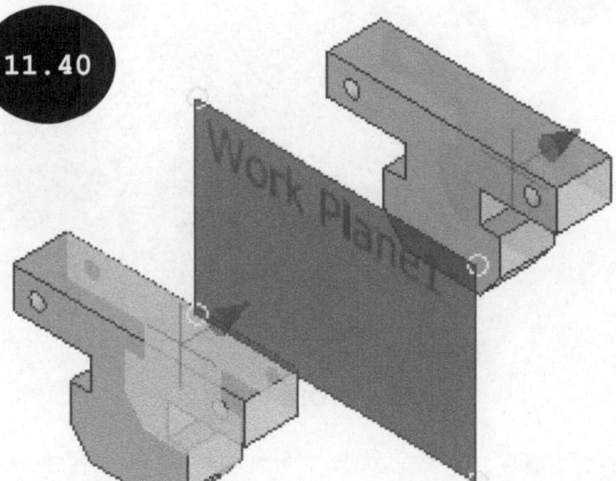

6. Select the required button (**Opposed** or **Aligned**) in the **Solution** area of the dialog box. The remaining options in the dialog box are the same as discussed earlier.

7. Click on the **OK** button in the dialog box. The symmetry constraint gets applied between the selected geometries of the components.

Applying Motion Constraints

Motion constraints are used for creating a mechanism or specifying relative motion between components of an assembly. In Autodesk Inventor, you can apply two types of motion constraints: Rotation and Rotation-Translation. Both these constraints can be applied by using the options available in the **Motion** tab of the **Place Constraint** dialog box, see Figure 11.41. The different motion constraints are discussed next.

11.41

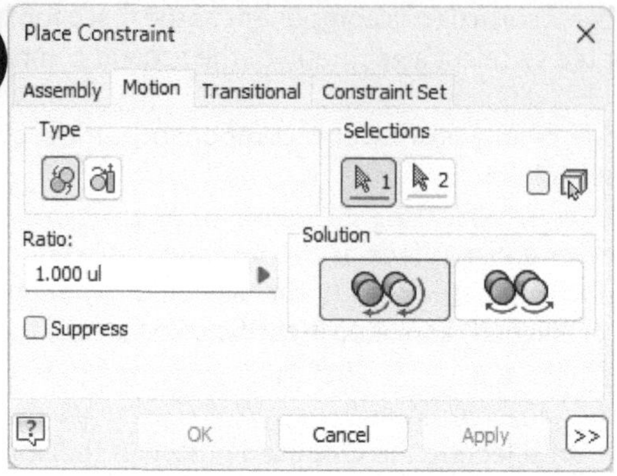

Applying a Rotation Constraint

Rotation constraint is used for creating a mechanism (gear, bearing, or pulley) between components such that the components can rotate relative to each other, refer to Figure 11.42. The method for applying a Rotation constraint is discussed below:

11.42

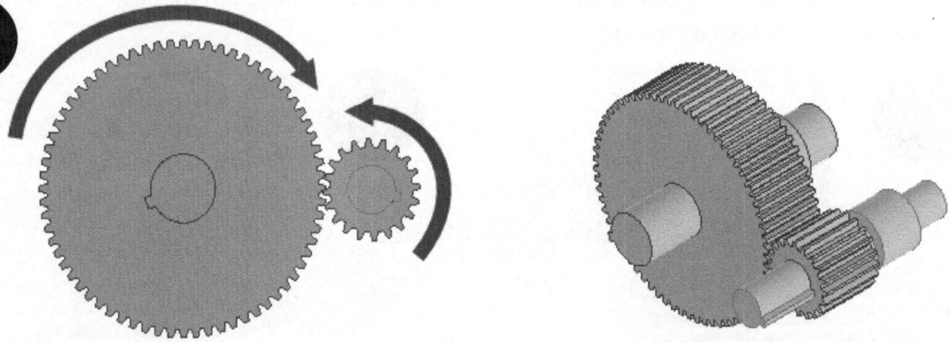

Note: To create a mechanism between components of an assembly, it is necessary to have the required degrees of freedom of components such that the components can only be translated or rotated in the desired directions. For example, to create a gear mechanism between two components (gears), you need to first constraint the components by applying the assembly constraints such that they can only rotate about their axes.

1. Click on the **Constrain** tool in the **Relationships** panel or press the **C** key. The **Place Constraint** dialog box appears.

2. Click on the **Motion** tab in the **Place Constraint** dialog box. The options for applying motion constraints appear in the dialog box.

3. Ensure that the **Rotation** button is activated in the dialog box. The **First Selection** button is activated in the **Selections** area of the dialog box and you are prompted to select a geometry of the first component.

4. Select a cylindrical or a planar face of a component as the first geometry, see Figures 11.43 and 11.44. The **Second Selection** button gets activated in the **Selections** area of the dialog box and you are prompted to select a geometry of the second component.

Note: You can select a planar face of a component as a geometry that is normal to the axis of rotation of the component.

5. Select a cylindrical or a planar face of another component as the second geometry, refer to Figures 11.43 and 11.44.

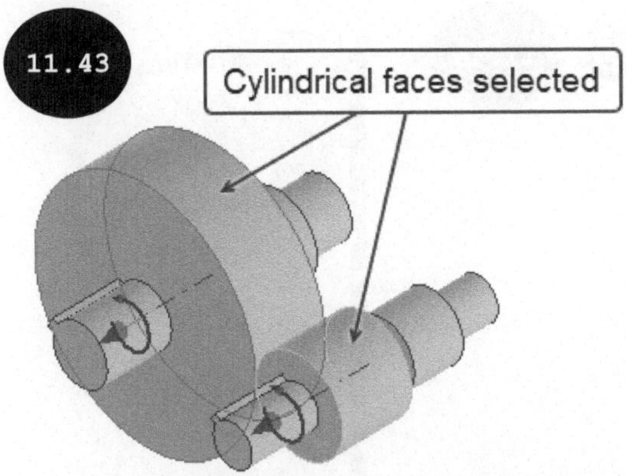

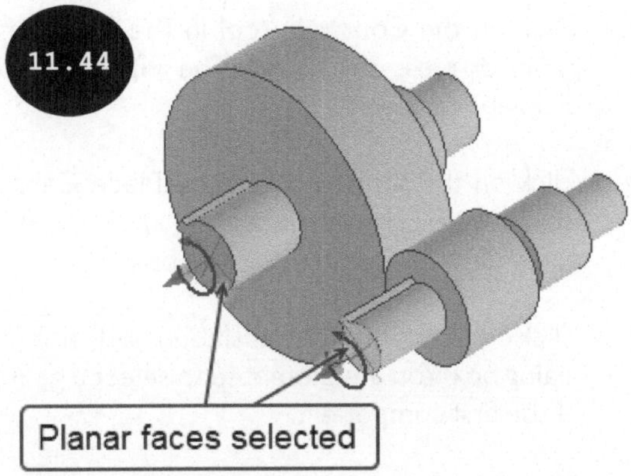

6. Specify a rotation ratio in the **Ratio** field of the dialog box. A rotation ratio defines how much the second selected component rotates relative to the rotation of the first selected component. For example, if the value **2** (2:1) is specified in the **Ratio** field, then the second component rotates twice for every rotation of the first component. Similarly, if the value **0.5** (1:2) is specified in the **Ratio** field, then the second component rotates once for every two rotations of the first component.

Note: If you select cylindrical faces of two components for applying a rotation constraint, then the rotation ratio gets automatically calculated based on the relative size of the cylindrical faces selected. If you select the planar faces, then you need to specify the rotation ratio manually in the **Ratio** field of the dialog box.

Now, you need to select a solution type in the **Solution** area of the dialog box.

Forward : On selecting the **Forward** button in the **Solution** area of the dialog box, the selected components rotate in the same direction relative to each other.

Reverse : On selecting the **Reverse** button, the selected components rotate in a direction opposite to each other.

7. Select the required button (**Forward** or **Reverse**) in the **Solution** area of the dialog box.

8. Click on the **OK** button in the dialog box. The Rotation constraint gets applied between the selected components.

Tip: To review the relative motion between the components after applying a rotation constraint, select a component and then drag it about its free degree of freedom.

Applying a Rotation-Translation Constraint

Rotation-Translation constraint is used for translating the linear motion of one component to the rotational motion of another component and vice versa. This constraint creates a rack and pinion mechanism, see Figure 11.45. The method for applying a Rotation-Translation constraint is discussed below:

11.45

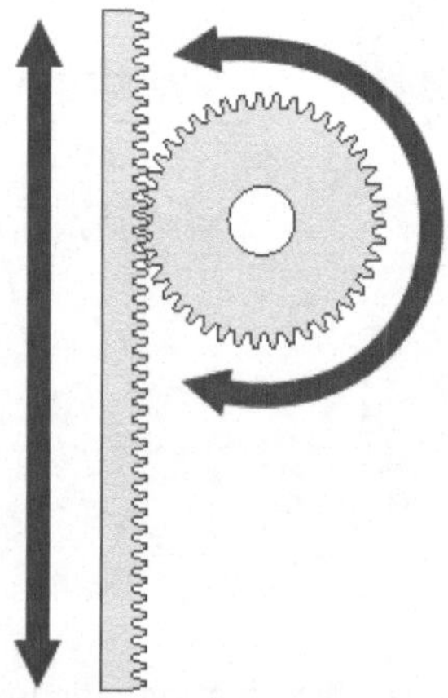

1. Click on the **Constrain** tool in the **Relationships** panel or press the **C** key. The **Place Constraint** dialog box appears.

2. Click on the **Motion** tab in the **Place Constraint** dialog box. The options for applying motion constraints appear in the dialog box.

3. Click on the **Rotation-Translation** button in the dialog box. You are prompted to select a geometry of the first component.

4. Select a circular face of the pinion/gear component as the first geometry, see Figure 11.46. The axis of rotation of the pinion component appears in the graphics area and you are prompted to select a geometry of the second component. Note that you can also select a planar face of the pinion component that is normal to its axis of rotation.

5. Select a linear edge of the rack component as the second geometry, which defines the direction of movement of the rack component, see Figure 11.46.

11.46

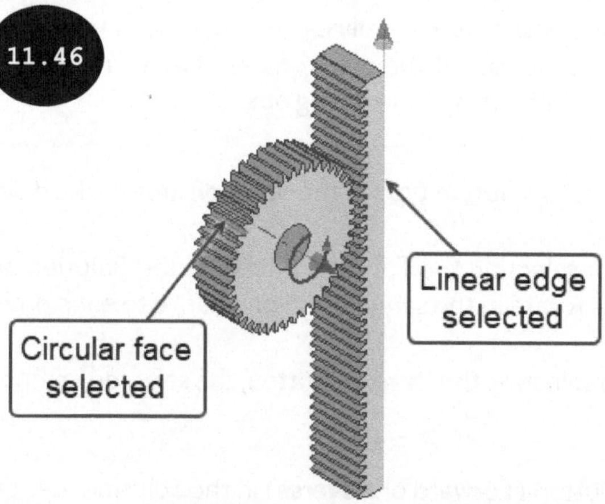

6. Enter the required distance value in the **Distance** field of the dialog box. The distance value specified in this field defines how much the second selected component (rack) translates or

moves relative to the one complete rotation of the first component (pinion). For example, if 300 mm is specified in the **Distance** field, then the second component (rack) translates or moves to a distance of 300 mm for every complete rotation of the first component (pinion).

Note: On selecting a circular face of the pinion/gear component as the first geometry, the default distance value gets computed automatically.

Now, you need to select a solution type (**Forward** or **Reverse**) in the **Solution** area.

Forward : On selecting the **Forward** button in the **Solution** area of the dialog box, the second component (rack) translates or moves in the forward direction relative to every forward rotation of the first component (pinion).

Reverse : On selecting the **Reverse** button, the second component (rack) translates or moves in the reverse direction relative to every forward rotation of the first component (pinion).

7. Select the required button (**Forward** or **Reverse**) in the **Solution** area of the dialog box.

8. Click on the **OK** button in the dialog box. The Rotation-Translation constraint gets applied between the selected components.

Tip: To review the relative motion between the components after applying the constraint, select a component and then drag it about its free degree of freedom.

Applying Transitional Constraints

Transitional constraint is used for creating a relationship between a cylindrical face of a component and a contiguous set of faces on another component such that a cam and follower or pin and slot mechanism gets created, see Figures 11.47 and 11.48. It maintains contact between the faces of the components as you slide a component along its free degree of freedom. In Autodesk Inventor, you can apply a transitional constraint by using the options available in the **Transitional** tab of the **Place Constraint** dialog box, see Figure 11.49. The method for applying a transitional constraint is discussed below:

11.47

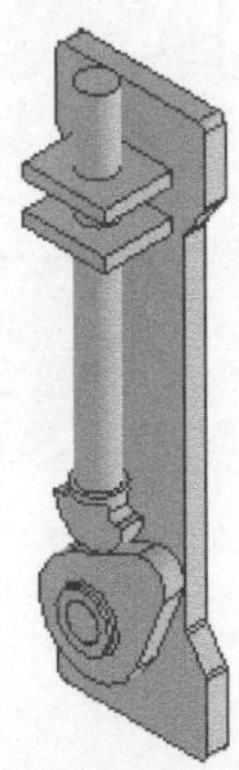

11.48

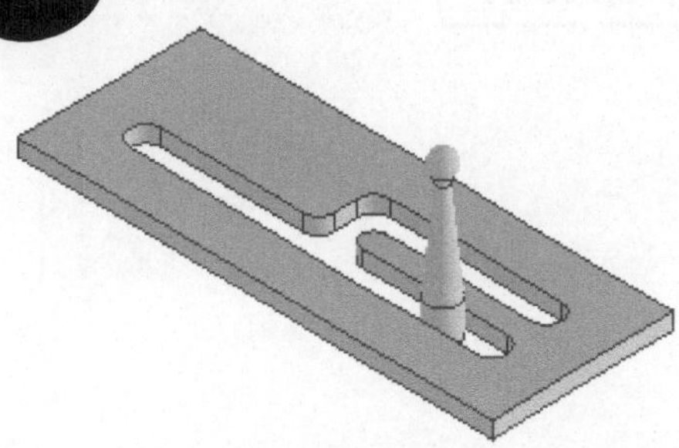

11.49

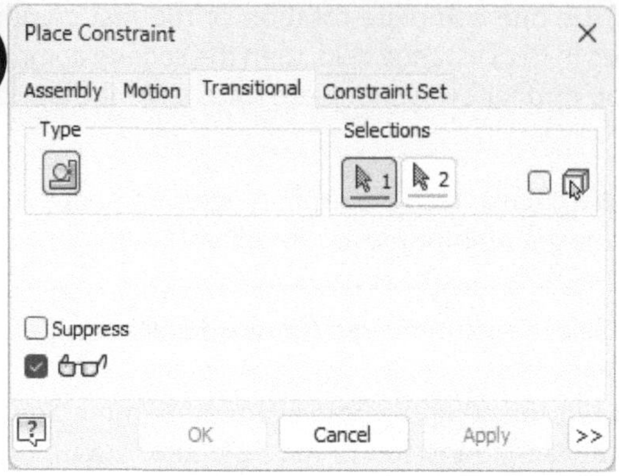

1. Click on the **Constrain** tool in the **Relationships** panel or press the **C** key. The **Place Constraint** dialog box appears.

2. Click on the **Transitional** tab in the **Place Constraint** dialog box. The **Transitional** button is activated in the **Type** area and the **Moving Face** button is activated in the **Selections** area of the dialog box. As a result, you are prompted to select a moving face of a component.

3. Click on face of a component that moves over a contiguous set of tangent faces of another component, for example, a face of a follower component that moves over the cam profile (see Figure 11.50). The face gets selected and the **Transitional Face** button gets activated in the **Selections** area of the dialog box. As a result, you are prompted to select a transitional face of another component.

4. Click on a face of another component, which is tangent to a series of other faces and forms a closed loop, refer to Figure 11.51. The selected faces of the components are placed in perfect contact with each other, see Figure 11.52.

11.50

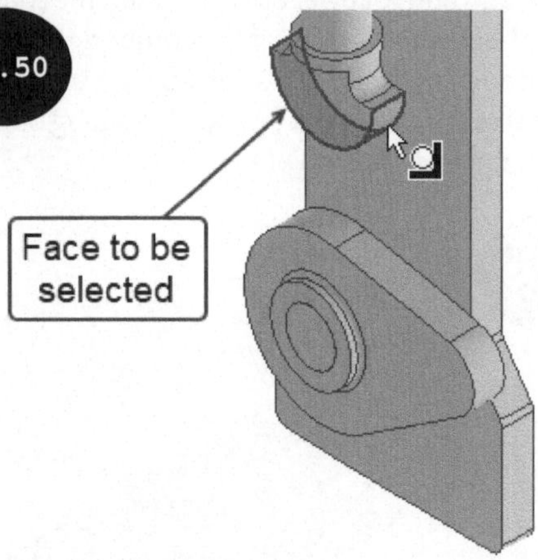

11.51

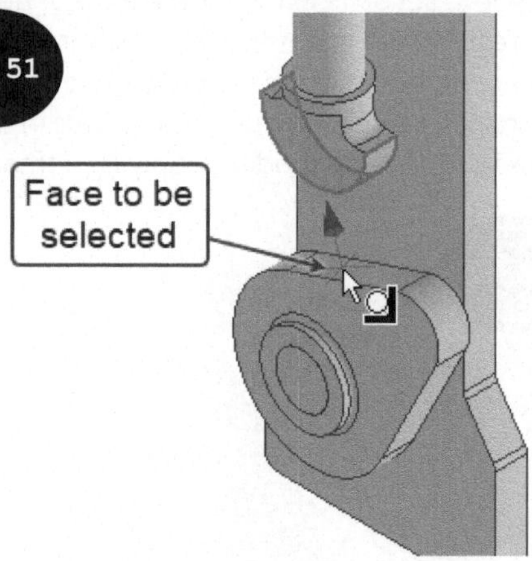

11.52

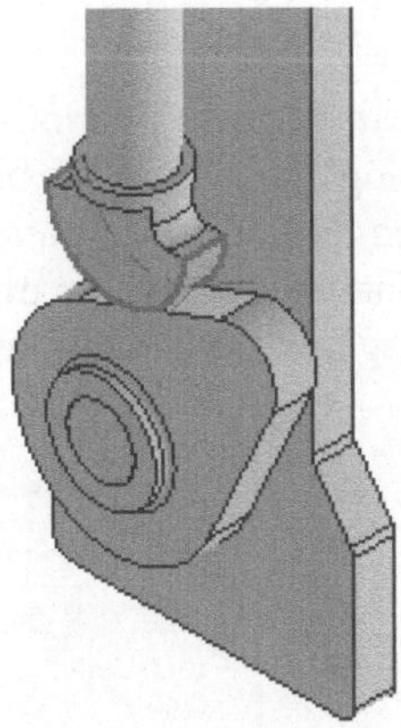

5. Click on the **Apply** button in the dialog box. The transitional constraint gets applied between the selected components such that on rotating the cam component, the follower component moves up and down with respect to the cam profile.

6. Click on the **Cancel** button to exit the dialog box.

Applying Constraint Set Constraints

In Autodesk Inventor, you can apply a UCS to UCS constraint set for constraining two UCSs together by using the options in the **Constraint Set** tab of the **Place Constraint** dialog box. The method for applying a UCS to UCS constraint set is discussed below:

1. Click on the **Constrain** tool in the **Relationships** panel or press the **C** key. The **Place Constraint** dialog box appears.

2. Click on the **Constraint Set** tab in the **Place Constraint** dialog box. The **UCS to UCS** button is activated in the **Type** area and the **First UCS** button is activated in the **Selections** area of the dialog box. As a result, you are prompted to select the first UCS of a component.

Tip: In Autodesk Inventor, you can create a UCS in a part file and in an assembly file by using the **UCS** tool. The method for creating a UCS in a part file is discussed in Chapter 6.

3. Click on a UCS of a component in the graphics area. The UCS gets selected and the **Second UCS** button gets activated in the **Selections** area of the dialog box. As a result, you are prompted to select the second UCS of another component.

4. Click on a UCS of another component in the graphics area. The selected UCSs of both the components get constrained together by applying three mate constraints between the corresponding pairs of YZ, XZ, and XY planes.

5. Click on the **Apply** button and then the **Cancel** button in the dialog box.

Applying Joints

In addition to applying constraints, you can also apply various types of joints such as rigid, rotational, slider, cylindrical, planar, and ball for defining the relationship between the components of an assembly. For doing so, click on the **Joint** tool in the **Relationships** panel of the **Assemble** tab, see Figure 11.53. The **Place Joint** dialog box appears, see Figure 11.54. Alternatively, press the **J** key to invoke the **Place Joint** dialog box. The options in this dialog box are used for applying various types of joints between the components and are discussed next.

11.53

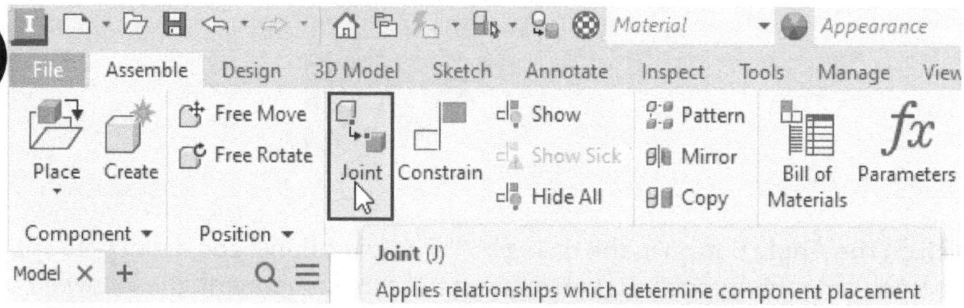

11.54

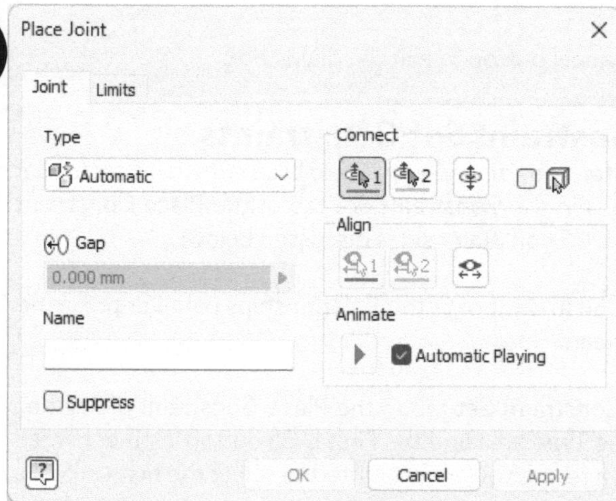

Applying a Rigid Joint

The rigid joint is used for locking or fixing components together by removing all degrees of freedom and does not allow any relative motion between the components, refer to Figure 11.55. The rigid joint is mainly applied between the components that are welded or bolted together with no allowable motion between them. The method for applying a rigid joint is discussed below:

11.55

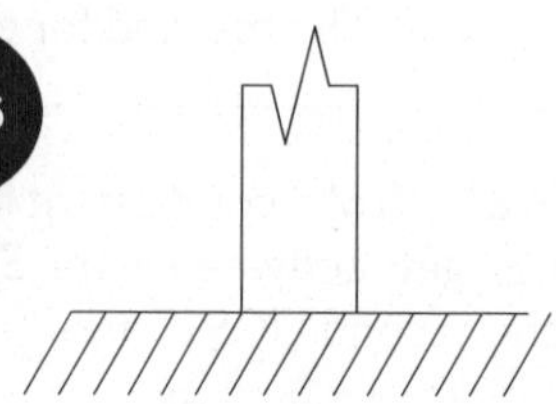

Rigid Joint
(No translational or rotational movements)

1. Click on the **Joint** tool in the **Relationships** panel of the **Assemble** tab. The **Place Joint** dialog box appears. Also, you are prompted to specify the position of the joint origin on the first component, since the **First origin** button is activated in the **Connect** area of the dialog box, by default.

Tip: In Autodesk Inventor, to apply a joint between two components, you need to specify the position of the joint origin on each component one by one.

2. Move the cursor over a face, an edge, or a vertex of the first component (moveable). The geometry gets highlighted and its snap points appear, see Figure 11.56. Also, the joint origin appears snapped to a point that is near to the cursor, refer to Figure 11.56. In this figure, the joint origin is snapped to the center snap point of the face. You can define the position of the joint origin at any of the snap points that appear.

11.56

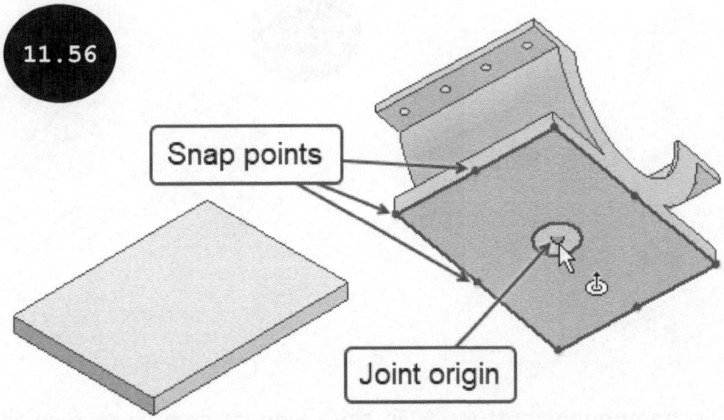

3. Click on the required snap point. The position of the joint origin is defined on the first component and its symbol appears at its specified position, see Figure 11.57. Also, the **Second origin** button gets activated in the **Connect** area of the dialog box and you are prompted to define the joint origin on the second component.

Note: The first component becomes transparent in the graphics area as soon as you define the position of the joint origin on it.

4. Move the cursor over a face, an edge, or a vertex of the second component. The geometry gets highlighted and its snap points appear, see Figure 11.58.

11.57

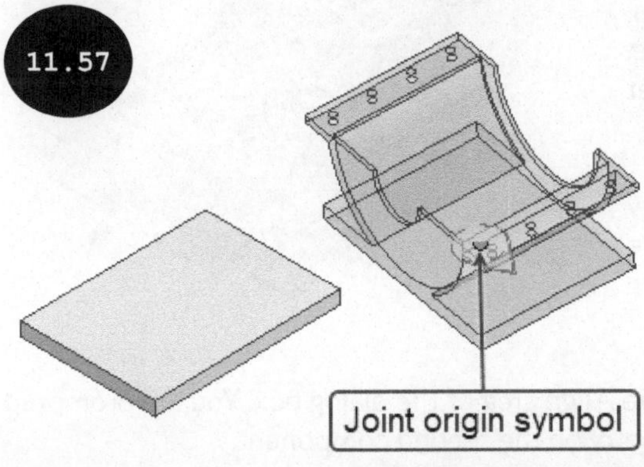

11.58

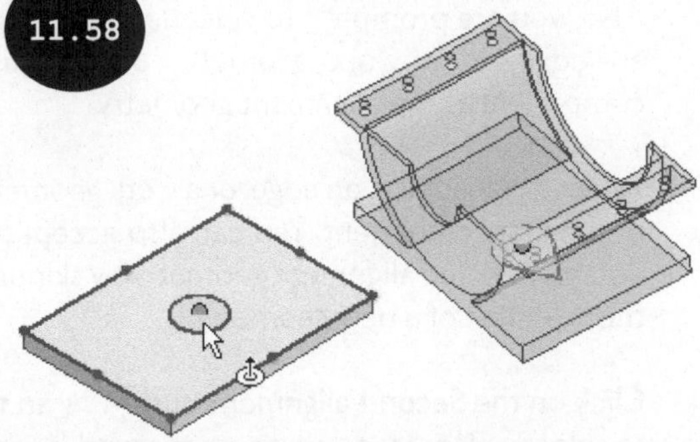

5. Specify the position of the joint origin, on the required snap point available on the face of the second component, by clicking the left mouse button. The first component moves toward the second component and the joint origins of both the components get coincident with each other in the graphics area, see Figure 11.59. Also, a joint type gets selected in the **Type** drop-down list in the dialog box based on the selected geometries of the components and the corresponding motion between the components gets animated for a few seconds in the graphics area.

   Flip component : The **Flip component** button in the **Connect** area of the dialog box is used for reversing the direction of the component, see Figure 11.60.

11.59

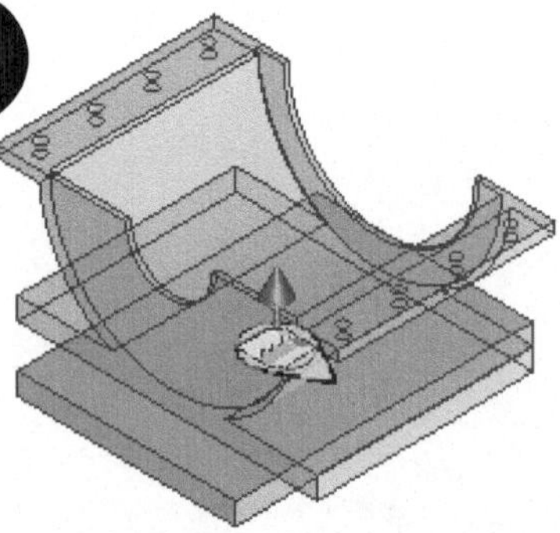

11.60

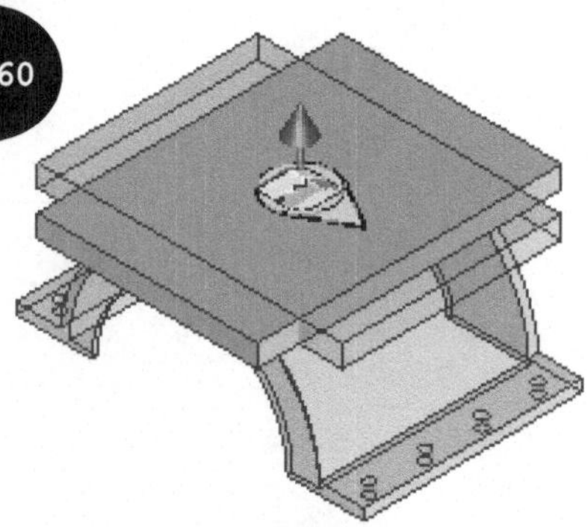

6. Click on the **Flip component** button in the **Connect** area to reverse the direction of the component, if needed.

Note: The alignment between the components shown in Figure 11.59 may be different in your case. You can define the correct alignment between the components by using the options in the **Align** area of the dialog box.

Now, you can define the alignment between the components, if needed.

7. Click on the **First alignment** button in the **Align** area of the dialog box. The default selected alignment geometry of the first component gets highlighted in the graphics area, see Figure 11.61. Also, you are prompted to select a planar face, an edge, or a work geometry on the first component as the alignment geometry.

11.61

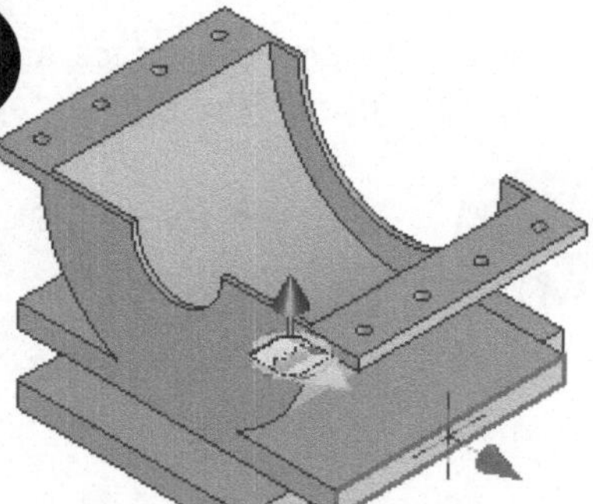

8. Select a planar face, an edge, or a work geometry of the first component. You can also accept the default selected alignment geometry by skipping the selection of a new geometry.

9. Click on the **Second alignment** button in the **Align** area of the dialog box. You are prompted to select a planar face, an edge, or a work geometry on the second component.

10. Select a planar face, an edge, or a work geometry of the second component, see Figure 11.62. The selected faces of both components get aligned with each other, see Figure 11.63.

11.62

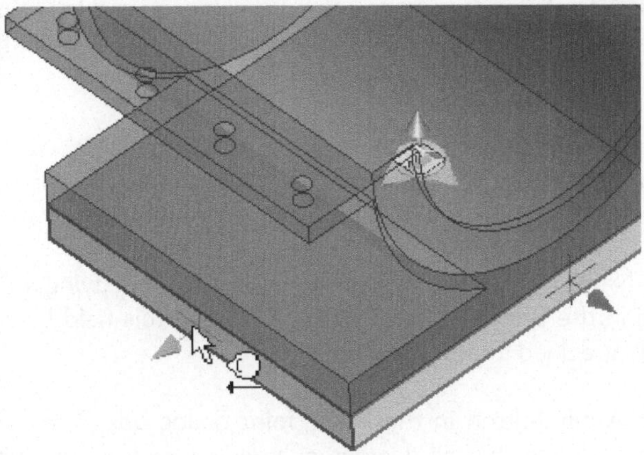

Note: If the default alignment between the components is correct, then you can skip the above steps from 7 to 10.

Invert alignment : The **Invert alignment** button in the **Align** area of the dialog box is used for reversing the alignment between the components.

11. Click on the **Invert alignment** button in the **Align** area to reverse the direction of alignment between the components, if needed, see Figure 11.64.

11.63

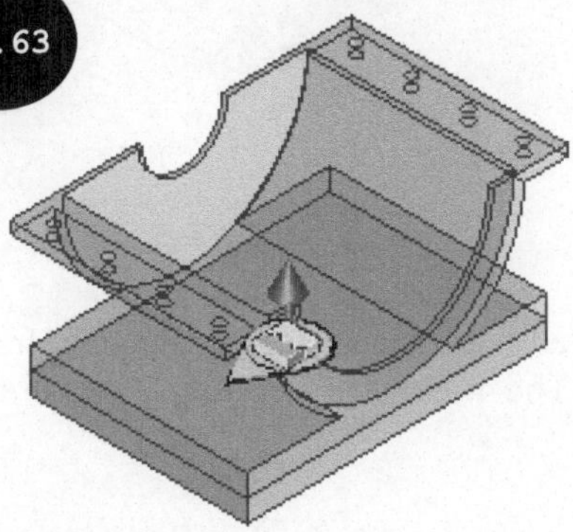

11.64

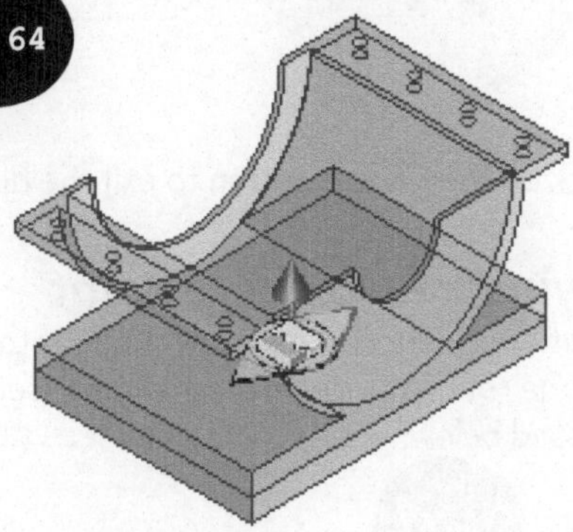

Type: The **Type** drop-down list in the dialog box is used for defining the type of joint between the components. You can define a rigid, rotational, slider, cylindrical, planar, or ball joint between the components by selecting the respective option in this drop-down list.

12. Select the **Rigid** option in the **Type** drop-down list of the dialog box to apply a rigid connection between the components, if not selected by default.

Gap: The **Gap** field is used for specifying an offset distance between the joint origins of the connected components.

13. Enter an offset distance between the connected components, if needed (see Figure 11.65).

    Animate ▶: The **Animate** button in the dialog box is used for animating the allowable motion between the components after applying the joint. It helps to identify the degrees of freedom of the components based on the joint applied.

    Automatic Playing: By default, the **Automatic Playing** check box is selected in the dialog box. As a result, on specifying the position of the joint origins on the components, the motion between the components gets animated for a few seconds in the graphics area, automatically.

    Name: The **Name** field in the dialog box is used for specifying a unique name for the joint to be displayed in the **Browser**. Note that if you leave this field blank then a default name gets automatically specified for the joint.

14. Click on the **Apply** button in the **Place Joint** dialog box. The rigid joint is applied between the components such that all degrees of freedom of the components are removed and the components are locked together, see Figure 11.66.

11.65

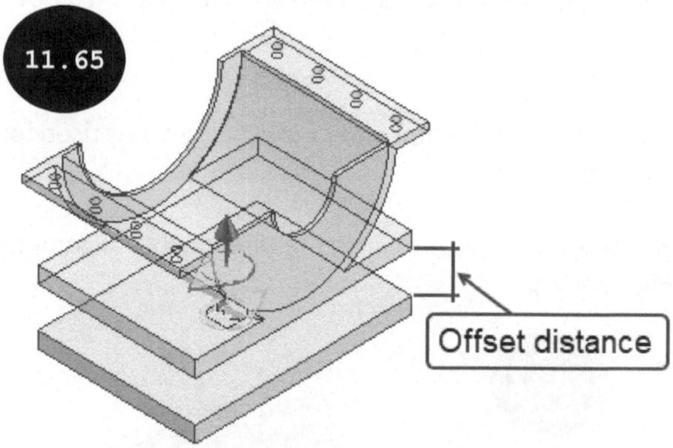

11.66

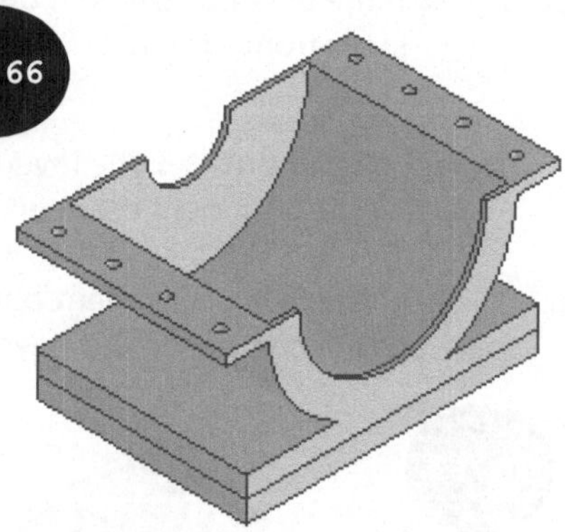

15. Click on the **Cancel** button to exit the dialog box.

Applying a Rotational Joint

The rotational joint allows the component to rotate about an axis by removing all degrees of freedom except one rotational degree of freedom, see Figure 11.67. The method for applying a rotational joint is discussed below:

11.67

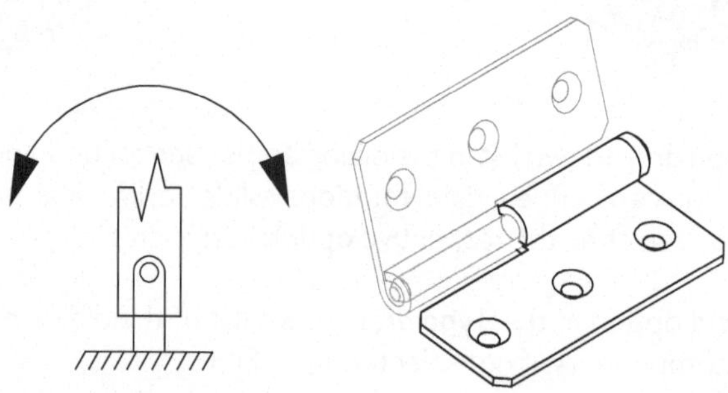

Rotational Joint
(No translational movement, only one rotational movement is allowed)

1. Click on the **Joint** tool in the **Relationships** panel of the **Assemble** tab. The **Place Joint** dialog box appears. Also, you are prompted to specify the position of the joint origin on the first component, since the **First origin** button is activated in the **Connect** area of the dialog box, by default. Note that most of the options in the **Place Joint** dialog box are discussed earlier.

2. Move the cursor over a face or an edge of the first component (moveable component). The face/edge gets highlighted and its snap points as well as the joint origin appear, see Figure 11.68. In this figure, the cursor has been moved on a circular edge of the component. As a result, only one snap point appears at the center of the edge and the joint origin is snapped to it, by default.

11.68

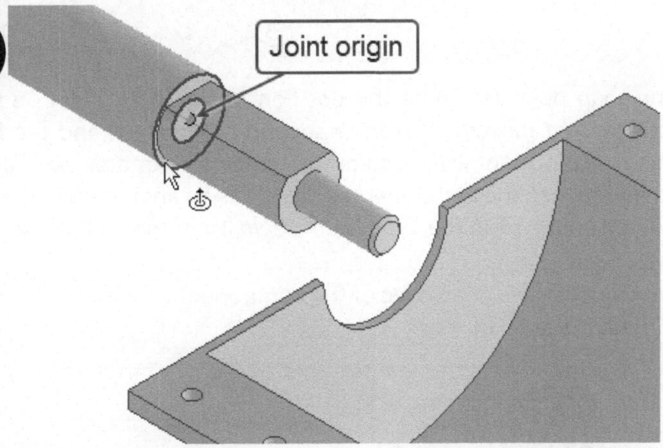

3. Click on the snap point to define the position of the joint origin on the first component (moveable). Note that to lock a face or an edge to select its snap point easily, you need to press and hold the CTRL key. The joint origin is defined on the first component, see Figure 11.69. Also, the **Second origin** button gets activated in the **Connect** area of the dialog box. As a result, you are prompted to define the joint origin on the second component.

11.69

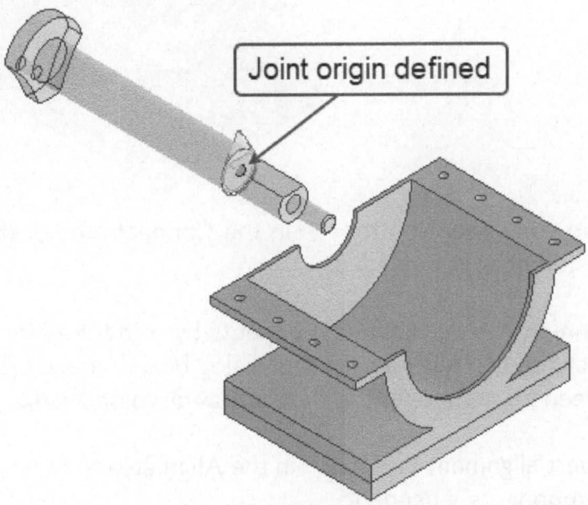

4. Move the cursor over a face or an edge of the second component. The face/edge gets highlighted and its snap points and the joint origin appear, see Figure 11.70.

11.70

5. Click on the snap point to define the position of the joint origin on the second component. The first component moves toward the second component and the joint origins of both the components get coincident with each other in the graphics area, see Figure 11.71. Also, a preview of the motion between the components appears as an animation in the graphics area as per the default selected joint type in the **Type** drop-down list of the dialog box.

Note: You can lock a face or an edge of the component to select its snap point easily by pressing and holding the CTRL key.

11.71

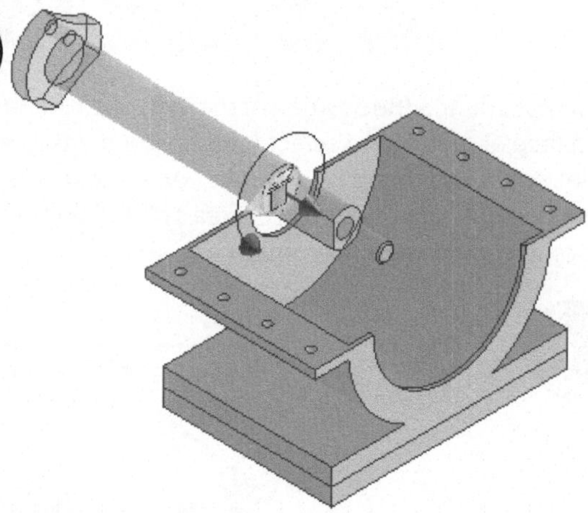

6. Click on the **Flip component** button in the **Connect** area of the dialog box to reverse the direction of the component, if needed.

7. Define the alignment between the components by using the **First alignment** and the **Second alignment** buttons of the **Align** area in the dialog box, if needed. The method for defining the alignment between the components is the same as discussed earlier while applying the rigid joint.

8. Click on the **Invert alignment** button in the **Align** area to reverse the direction of alignment between the components, if needed.

9. Ensure that the **Rotational** option is selected in the **Type** drop-down list of the dialog box to rotate the component around an axis.

Note: On applying the rotational joint, the component rotates 360 degrees around the axis of rotation, by default. However, you can also limit the rotational angle of the component by defining the start and end rotational angles. For doing so, click on the **Limits** tab in the **Place Joint** dialog box. The options for defining the joint limit appear, see Figure 11.72. Select the **Start** check box in the **Angular** area of the dialog box and then specify the required start angle of rotation for the component in the **Start** field that gets enabled below the check box. Next, specify the end angle of rotation in the **End** field of the **Angular** area. The **Current** field of the **Angular** area displays the current angular position of the component. You can also enter the required angle in this field to define the current angular position of the component. In Figure 11.73, the start angle is defined as 0 degree and end angle is defined as 180 degrees in the respective fields. As a result, the component rotates within the specified start and end rotational angle limits.

10. Click on the **OK** button in the **Place Joint** dialog box. The rotational joint is applied between the components such that all degrees of freedom of the components are removed except the rotational degree of freedom and the component can revolve around the axis of rotation.

11.72

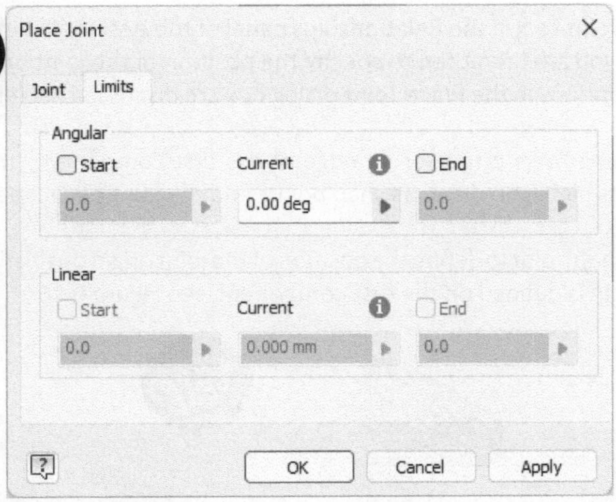

11.73

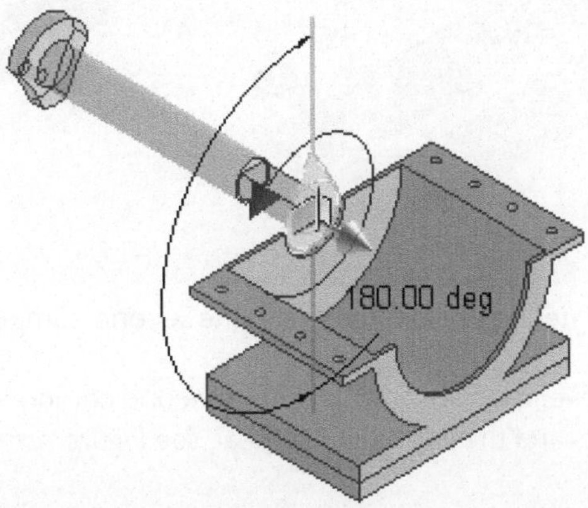

Tip: To review the movement of a component after applying a joint, select the component and then drag it along or about its free degree of freedom.

Applying a Slider Joint

The slider joint is used for translating or sliding the component along a single axis by removing all degrees of freedom except one translational degree of freedom, see Figure 11.74. The method for applying a slider joint is discussed below:

11.74

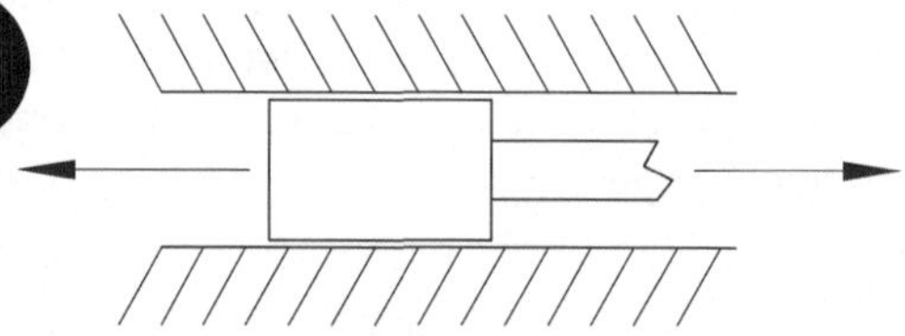

Slider Joint
(Translate freely along one direction)

1. Click on the **Joint** tool in the **Relationships** panel of the **Assemble** tab. The **Place Joint** dialog box appears and you are prompted to specify the position of the joint origin on the first component. Most of the options in the **Place Joint** dialog box are discussed earlier.

2. Move the cursor over a face or an edge of the first component (moveable component). The face/edge gets highlighted and its snap points and the joint origin appear, see Figure 11.75.

3. Click on the snap point to define the position of the joint origin on the first component (moveable). The joint origin is defined on the first component, see Figure 11.76.

11.75

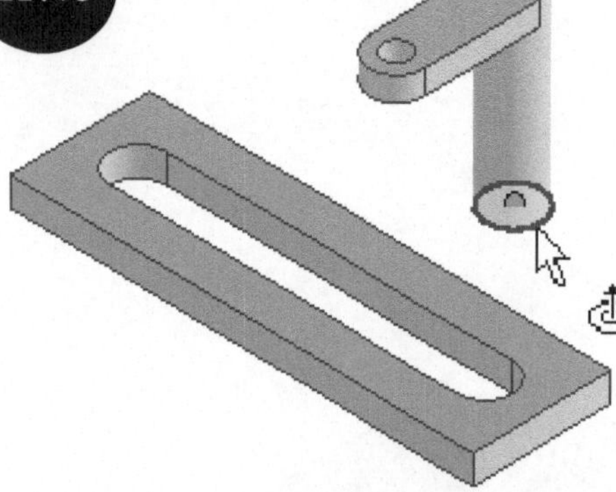

11.76

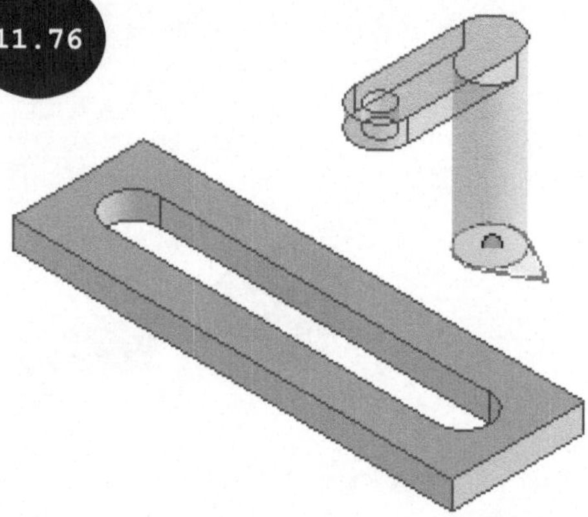

Now, you need to define the joint origin on the second component.

4. Move the cursor over a face or an edge of the second component. The face/edge gets highlighted and its snap points and the joint origin appear, see Figure 11.77.

5. Click on the snap point to define the position of the joint origin on the second component. The first component moves toward the second component and the joint origins of both the components get coincident with each other in the graphics area, see Figure 11.78. Also, the default joint type gets selected in the **Type** drop-down list in the dialog box based on the selected geometries of the components and the corresponding motion between the components gets animated for a few seconds in the graphics area.

11.77

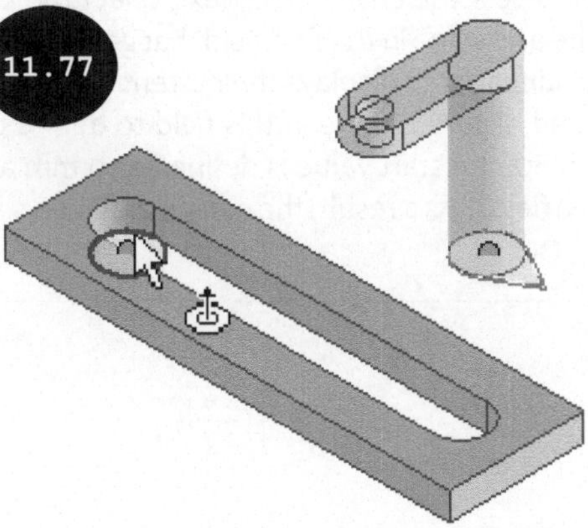

11.78

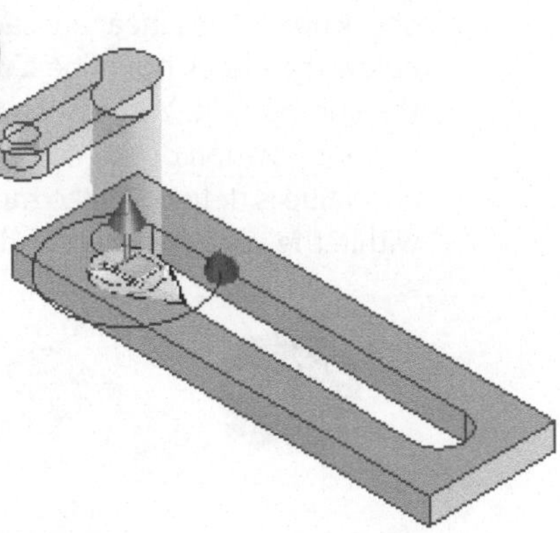

6. Select the **Slider** option in the **Type** drop-down list of the dialog box for sliding the component along a single axis. An arrow appears in the graphics area pointing toward the sliding direction of the moveable component, see Figure 11.79.

11.79

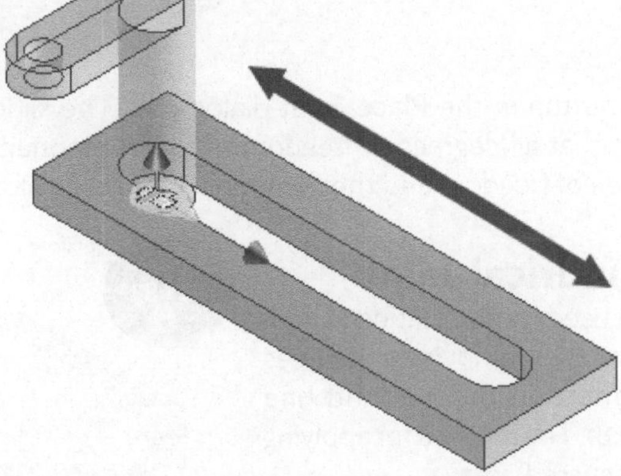

7. Define the alignment between the components to specify the required sliding direction of the moveable component by using the **First alignment** and the **Second alignment** buttons of the **Align** area in the dialog box, if needed. The method for defining the alignment between the components is the same as discussed earlier.

Note: On applying the slider joint, the component can translate or slide freely along its sliding direction, by default. However, you can also limit the translation of the component by defining the start and end translation value. For doing so, click on the **Limits** tab in the **Place Joint** dialog box. The options for defining the joint limit appear. Next, select the **Start** check box in the **Linear** area of the dialog box and then specify the required start value of the component in the **Start** field that gets enabled below the check box. Next, select the **End** check box in the **Linear** area and then specify the end value in the **End** field that gets enabled below the check box. The **Current** field of the **Linear** area displays the current position of the component. You can also enter the required distance value in this field to define the current position of the component. In Figure 11.80, the start value is defined as 0 mm and end value is defined as 150 mm in the respective fields. As a result, the component can slide within the specified start and end distance limits.

11.80

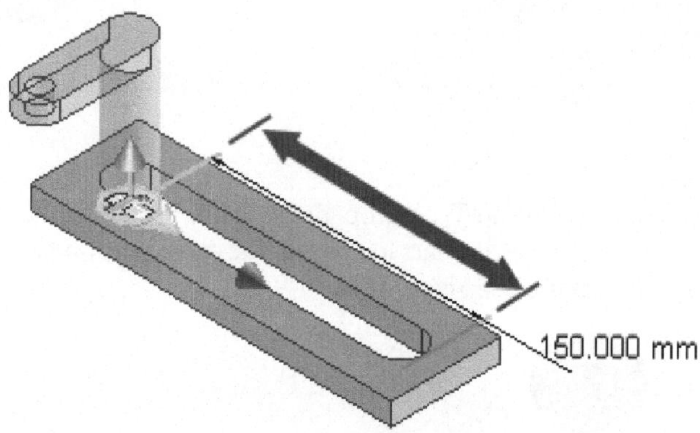

8. Click on the **OK** button in the **Place Joint** dialog box. The slider joint is applied between the components such that all degrees of freedom of the components are removed except a single translational degree of freedom and the component can slide along the specified direction.

Applying a Cylindrical Joint

The cylindrical joint is used for translating as well as rotating the component by removing all degrees of freedom except one translational and one rotational, see Figure 11.81. The method for applying a cylindrical joint is discussed next.

11.81

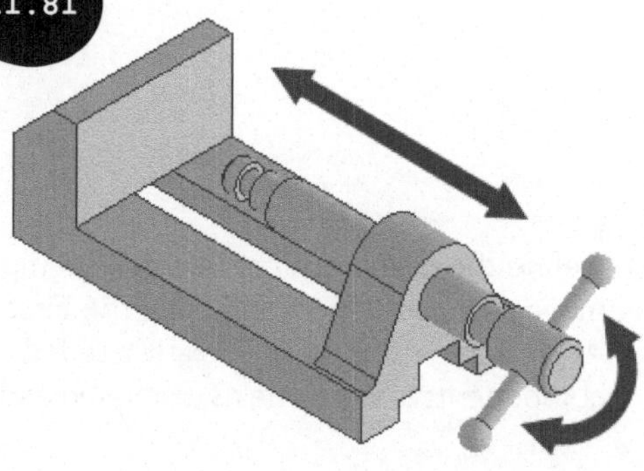

1. Click on the **Joint** tool in the **Relationships** panel of the **Assemble** tab. The **Place Joint** dialog box appears and you are prompted to specify the position of the joint origin on the first component. Most of the options in the **Place Joint** dialog box are discussed earlier.

2. Move the cursor over a face or an edge of the first component (moveable component). The face/edge gets highlighted and its snap points and the joint origin appear, see Figure 11.82.

3. Click on the snap point to define the position of the joint origin on the first component (moveable). The joint origin is defined on the first component and you are prompted to specify the joint origin on the second component.

4. Move the cursor over a face or an edge of the second component. The face/edge gets highlighted and its snap points and the joint origin appear, see Figure 11.83.

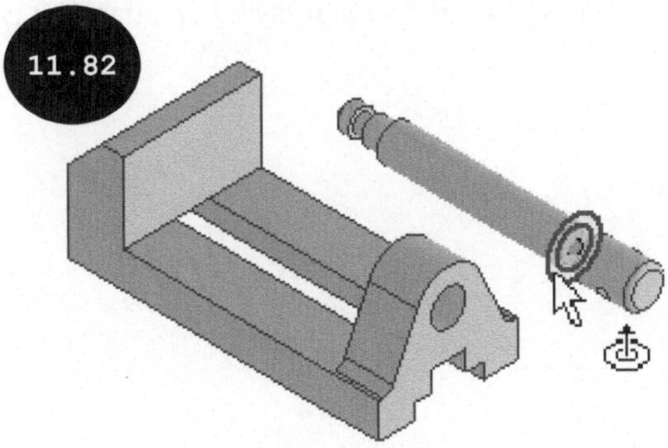
11.82

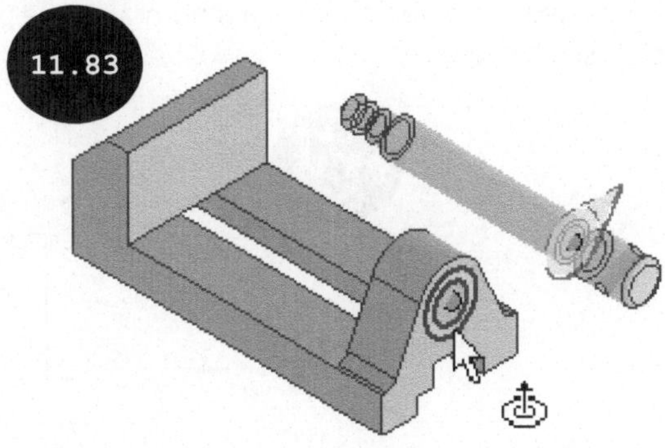
11.83

5. Click on the snap point to define the position of the joint origin on the second component. The first component moves toward the second component and the joint origins of both the components get coincident with each other in the graphics area, see Figure 11.84. Also, the default joint type gets selected in the **Type** drop-down list in the dialog box based on the selected geometries of the components and the corresponding motion between the components gets animated for a few seconds in the graphics area.

6. Select the **Cylindrical** option in the **Type** drop-down list of the dialog box for translating as well as rotating the component by removing all degrees of freedom except one translational and one rotational. The rotational and translational arrows appear in the graphics area, see Figure 11.85.

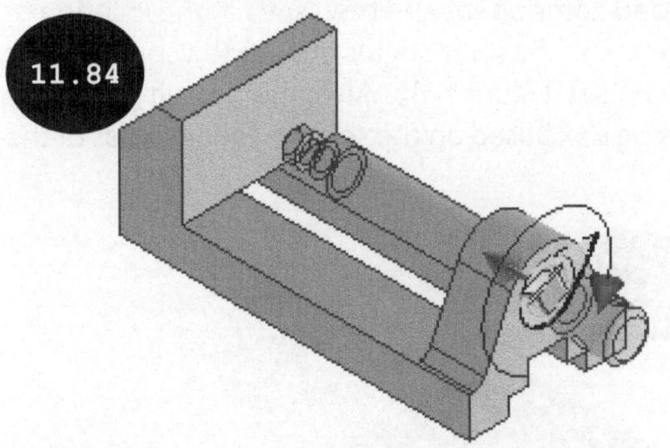
11.84

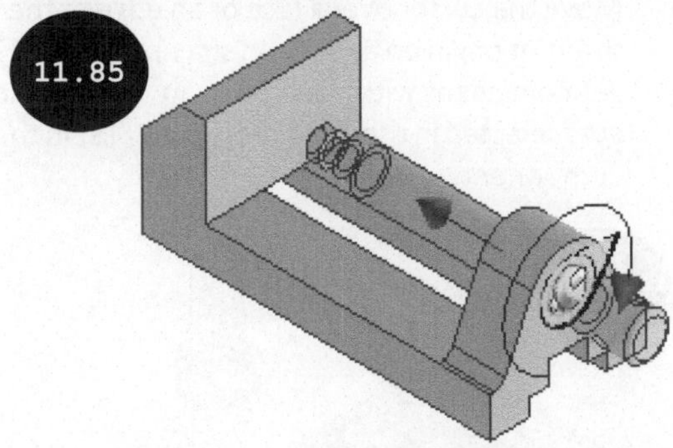
11.85

Note: You can also define the rotational and translational limits for the component by using the options in the **Angular** area and the **Linear** area of the **Limits** tab in the dialog box. The method for defining the start and end limits is same as discussed earlier.

7. Click on the **OK** button in the **Place Joint** dialog box. The cylindrical joint is applied between the components such that all degrees of freedom are removed except one translational and one rotational degree of freedom.

Applying a Planar Joint

The planar joint is used for translating the component along two axes in addition to rotating about a single axis, see Figure 11.86. In this joint, you can restrain the component to a planar face of another component such that its movement in the direction normal to the planar face gets restricted and the movement within the plane of the face is allowed. The planar joint also allows a rotational movement along an axis normal to the planar face. For example, an object can move on the planar face of a table top as well as rotate about an axis normal to the planar face. The method for applying a planar joint is discussed below:

11.86

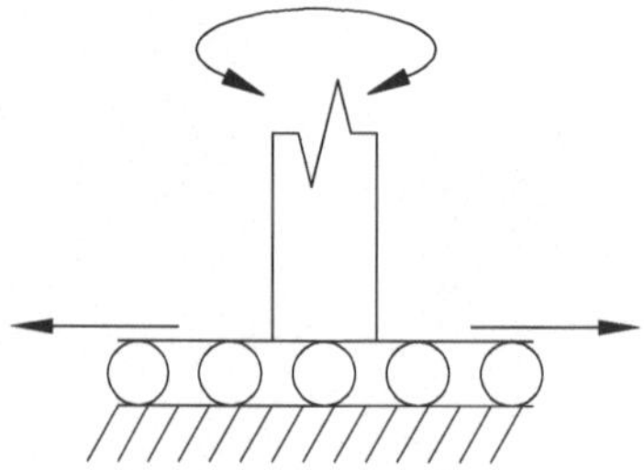

Planar Joint
(Moves freely within the plane of face with no movement in the direction normal to the planar face. Also, allows a rotational movement about an axis)

1. Invoke the **Place Joint** dialog box and then move the cursor over a face or an edge of the first component (moveable component) and then specify the location of the joint origin on a required snap point, see Figure 11.87. Note that you can lock a face or an edge to select its snap point easily by pressing and holding the CTRL key.

2. Move the cursor over a face or an edge of the second component and then specify the location of the joint origin on a required snap point, see Figure 11.88. The joint origins of both the components get coincident with each other in the graphics area, see Figure 11.89. Also, the default joint type gets selected in the **Type** drop-down list in the dialog box based on the selected geometries of the components.

11.87

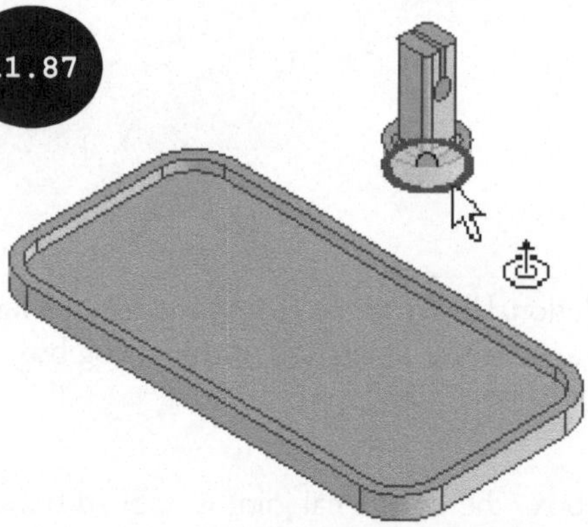

11.88

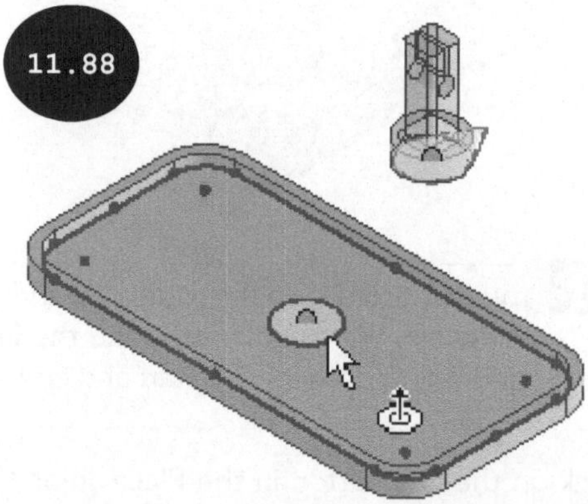

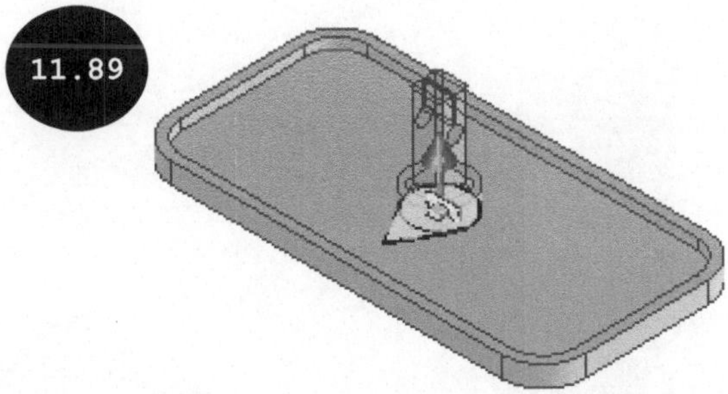

3. Select the **Planar** option in the **Type** drop-down list of the dialog box for translating the component along two axes and rotating about a single axis. The remaining options in the dialog box are discussed earlier.

4. Click on the **OK** button in the **Place Joint** dialog box. The planar joint is applied between the components such that the component can translate along two axes (plane of face) as well as rotate about an axis normal to the planar face.

Applying a Ball Joint

The ball joint is used for rotating the component about all the three rotational axes, see Figure 11.90. In this joint, all translational degrees of freedom of the component get restricted and the component can rotate about the three axes with respect to a point, which is defined by a joint origin. The method for applying a ball joint is discussed below:

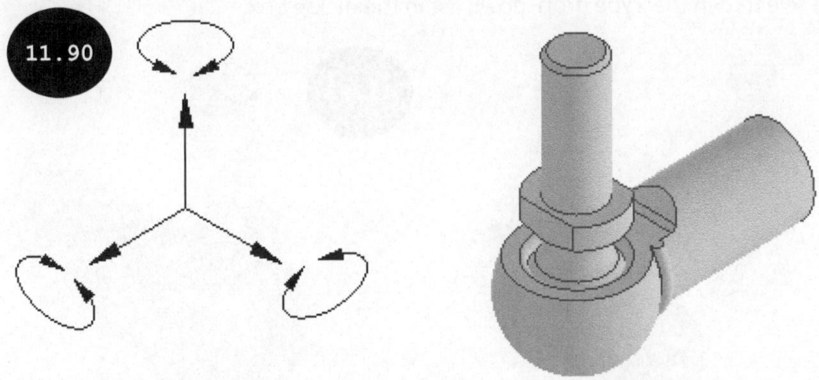

1. Invoke the **Place Joint** dialog box, move the cursor over the spherical face of the first component (moveable component), and then click to specify the location of the joint origin at its center snap point, see Figure 11.91. The joint origin is defined on the first component and you are prompted to specify the joint origin on the second component.

11.91

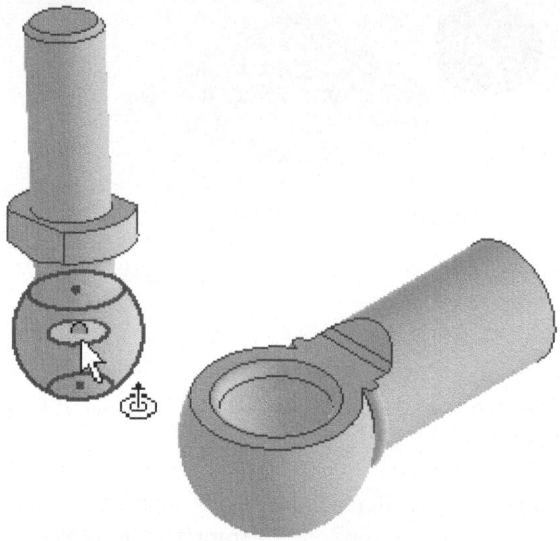

Note: You can lock a face or an edge of the component to select its snap point easily by pressing and holding the CTRL key.

2. Move the cursor over the spherical face of the second component and then click to specify the location of the joint origin at its center snap point that appears, see Figure 11.92. The joint origins of both the components get coincident with each other in the graphics area, see Figure 11.93. Also, the motion between the components gets animated in the graphics area depending upon the joint type selected in the **Type** drop-down list in the dialog box.

11.92

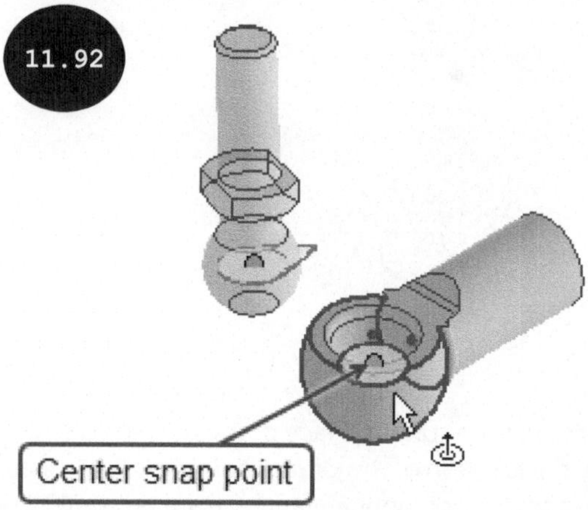

11.93

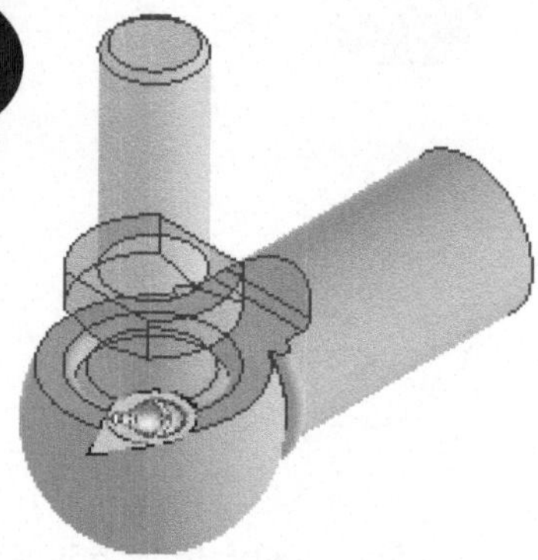

3. Ensure that the **Ball** option is selected in the **Type** drop-down list of the dialog box to allow the component to rotate about three axes. The remaining options in the dialog box are same as discussed earlier.

4. Click on the **OK** button in the **Place Joint** dialog box. The ball joint is applied between the components such that the component can rotate about three axes and all its translational movements are restricted.

Editing Constraints and Joints

In Autodesk Inventor, you can edit existing constraints and joints that are applied between the components of an assembly. All the constraints and joints that are applied to a component are listed under its node in the **Browser**. To edit a constraint or a joint of a component, expand its node in the **Browser** by clicking on the +sign. A list of all constraints and joints that are applied to the component appears, see Figure 11.94. Next, right-click on a constraint or a joint in the expanded node and then click on the **Edit** option in the shortcut menu that appears, see Figure 11.95. The **Edit Constraint** or **Edit Joint** dialog box appears for editing the selected constraint or joint, respectively. Now, you can edit the selected constraint or joint by using the options in the dialog box. Note that in the **Edit Constraint** dialog box, you can suppress or unsuppress the selected constraint by selecting or clearing the **Suppress** check box, respectively. Once the editing has been done, click on the **OK** button to accept the changes and exit the dialog box.

11.94

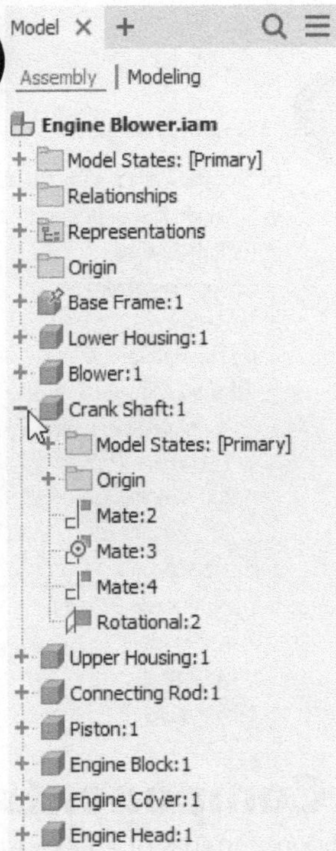

11.95

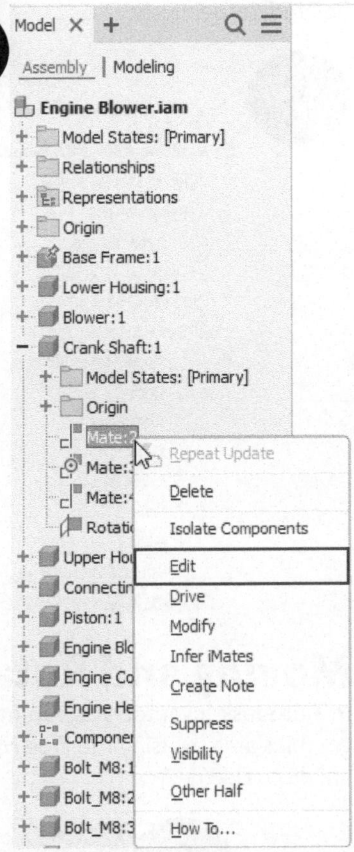

Note: On clicking a constraint or a joint in the **Browser**, an edit field appears with the display of its current offset or angle value, respectively, see Figure 11.96. In this edit field, you can enter a new offset or angle value, as required.

11.96

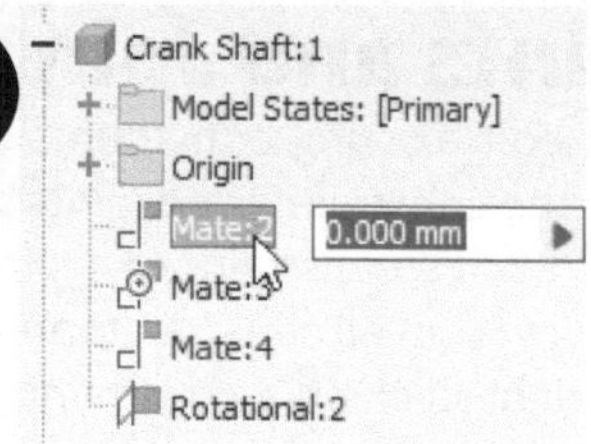

Deleting Constraints and Joints

To delete an already applied constraint or joint of a component, expand the node of the component in the **Browser** by clicking on its +sign. A list of all constraints and joints that are applied to the component appear, see Figure 11.97. Next, right-click on a constraint or a joint to be deleted and then click on the **Delete** option in the shortcut menu that appears, see Figure 11.98. The selected constraint or joint gets deleted, respectively.

11.97

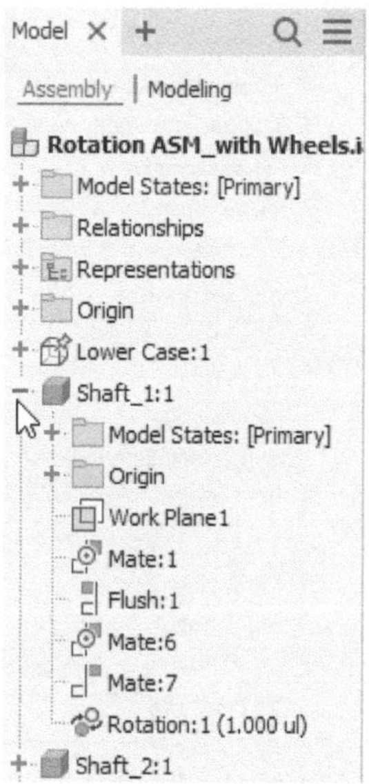

11.98

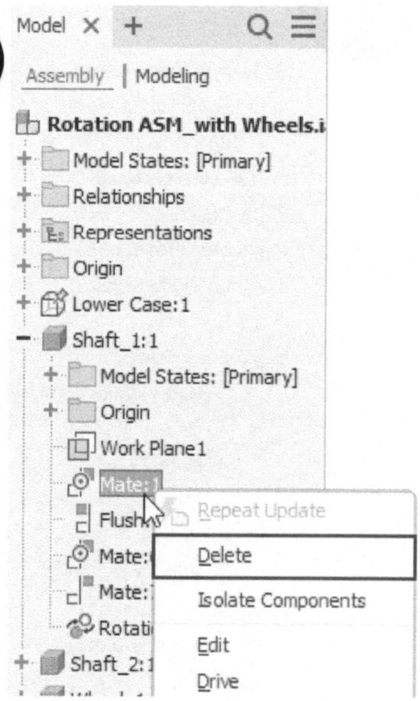

Moving and Rotating Individual Components

In Autodesk Inventor, you can freely move and rotate individual components of an assembly in the graphics area by using the **Free Move** and **Free Rotate** tools, respectively, see Figure 11.99. Both tools are discussed next.

11.99

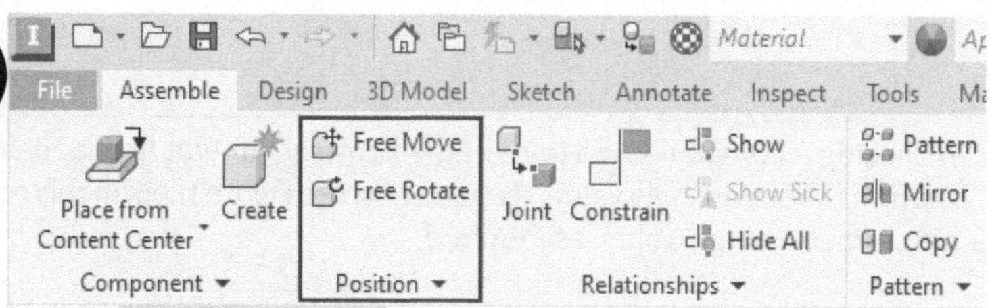

Moving a Component by using the Free Move Tool

You can move an individual component of an assembly in any direction by temporarily suppressing all the existing relationships (constraints or joints) until you update the assembly. For doing so, click on the **Free Move** tool in the **Position** panel of the **Assemble** tab, refer to Figure 11.99. Next, drag the component to a new location anywhere in the graphics area, as required. The relationship of the component with the other components of the assembly is displayed as an elastic band in the graphics area, see Figure 11.100. Also, the glyphs of the applied constraints or joints of the component appear in the graphics area. You can similarly move the other components of the assembly by dragging them one by one in the graphics area.

11.100

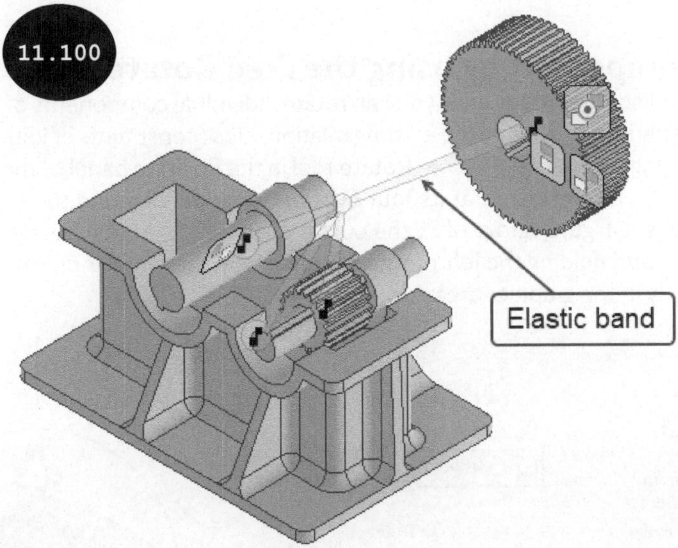

Note: To move the components back to their original positions in the assembly, click on the **Local Update** tool in the **Quick Access Toolbar**, see Figure 11.101.

11.101

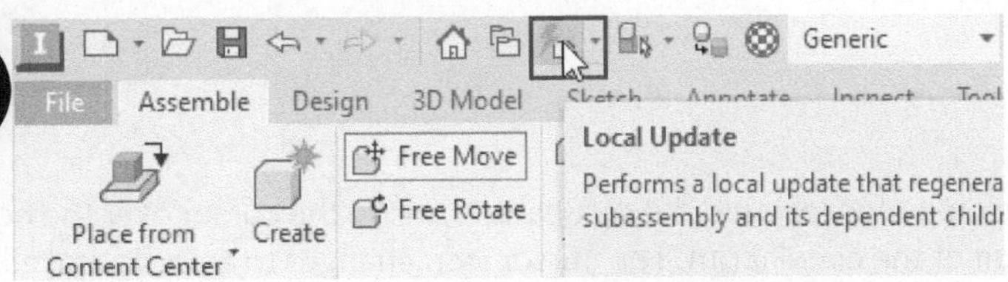

Tip: You can suppress or delete existing constraints or joints of the component that appear in the graphics area. For doing so, move the cursor over a constraint or a joint glyph to be suppressed or deleted and then right-click to display the Marking Menu, see Figure 11.102. Next, click on the **Suppress** or **Delete** option in the Marking Menu, respectively.

11.102

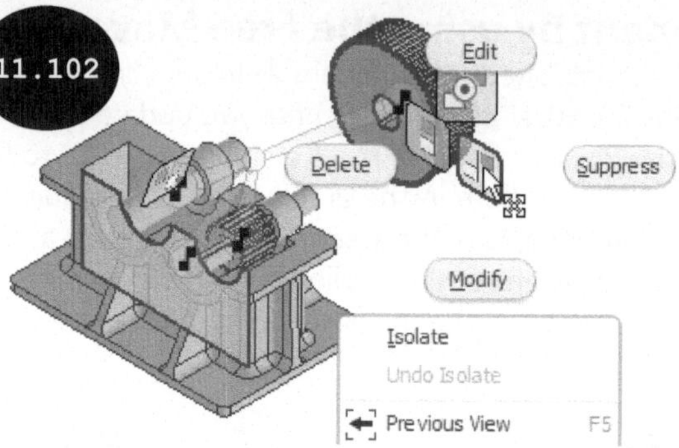

Rotating a Component by using the Free Rotate Tool

Similar to moving individual components, you can rotate individual components of an assembly about any axis by temporarily suppressing all the existing relationships (constraints or joints) until you update the assembly. For doing so, click on the **Free Rotate** tool in the **Position** panel of the **Assemble** tab, see Figure 11.103. A circular rim with lines at its four quadrants appears around the selected component in the graphics area, see Figure 11.104. Also, the cursor changes to a rotational cursor. Next, drag the cursor after pressing and holding the left mouse button inside the circular rim that appears to rotate the component freely in the graphics area.

11.103

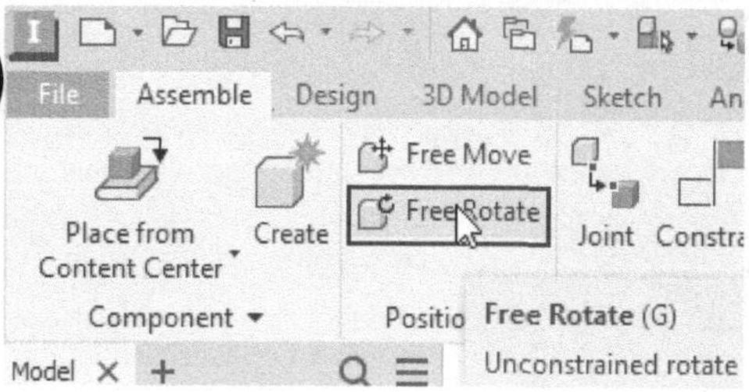

11.104

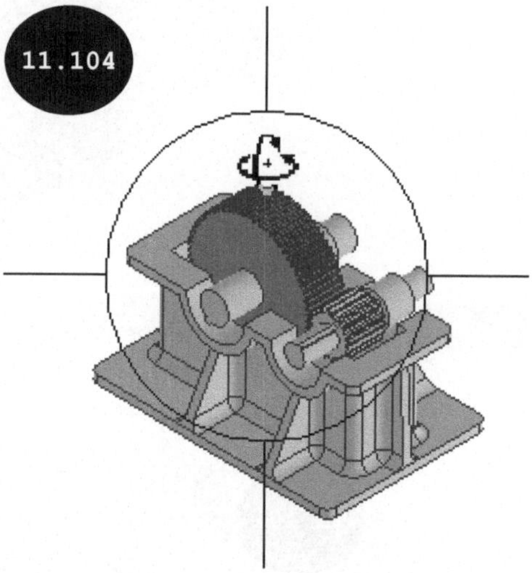

To rotate the component around the vertical axis, move the cursor over the horizontal line at the right or left quadrant of the circular rim. The cursor icon changes to a horizontal elliptical arrow. Next, drag the cursor by pressing the left mouse button to rotate the model along the vertical axis. Similarly, you can rotate the component around the horizontal axis by dragging the cursor after positioning it over a vertical line at the top or bottom quadrant of the circular rim.

Note: After rotating the component, click on the **Local Update** tool in the **Quick Access Toolbar** for restoring the component back to the original position that is defined by the applied relationships (constraints or joints).

Tutorial 1

Create the assembly shown in Figure 11.105. Different views and dimensions of individual components of the assembly are shown in Figures 11.106 through 11.110. All dimensions are in mm. You can also download all the components of the assembly by logging on to our website (www.cadartifex.com).

11.105

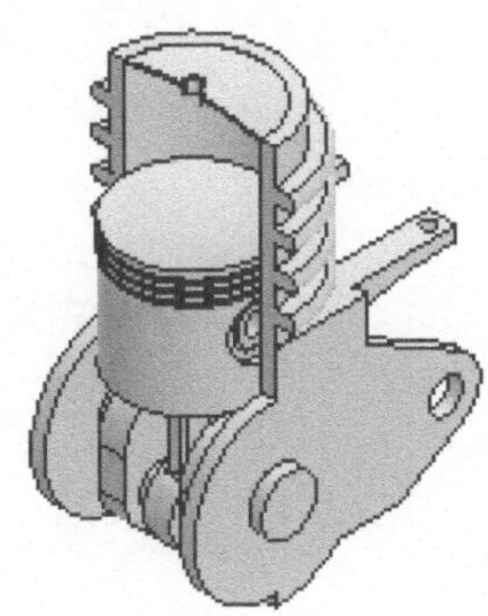

11.106

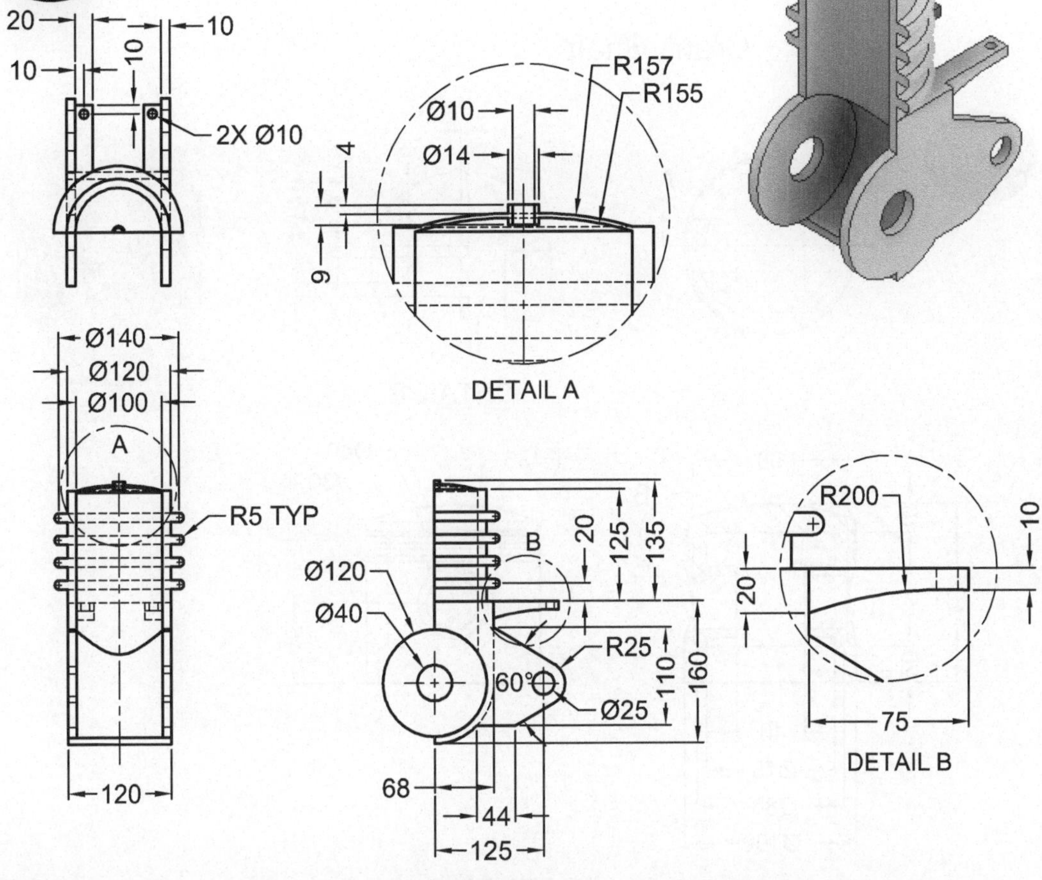

Crank Case

11.107

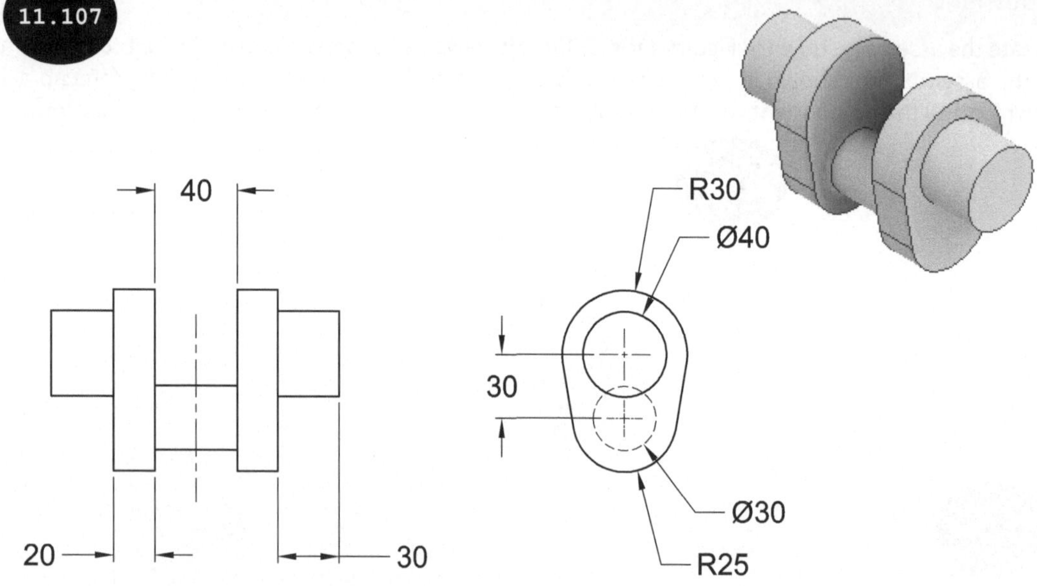

Crank Shaft

11.108

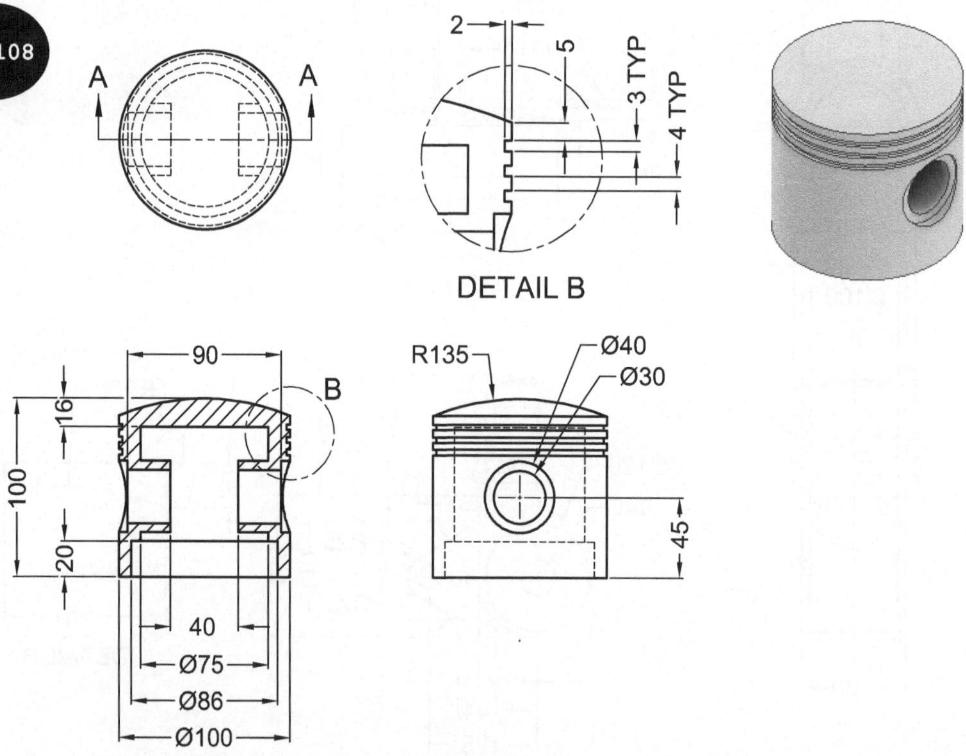

SECTION A-A

Piston

11.109

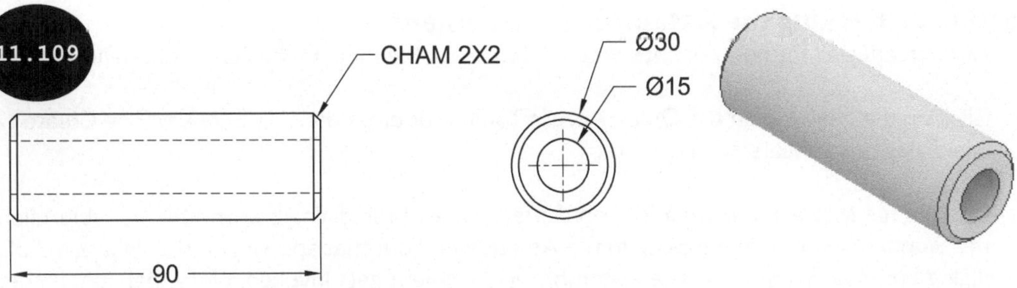

Piston Pin

11.110

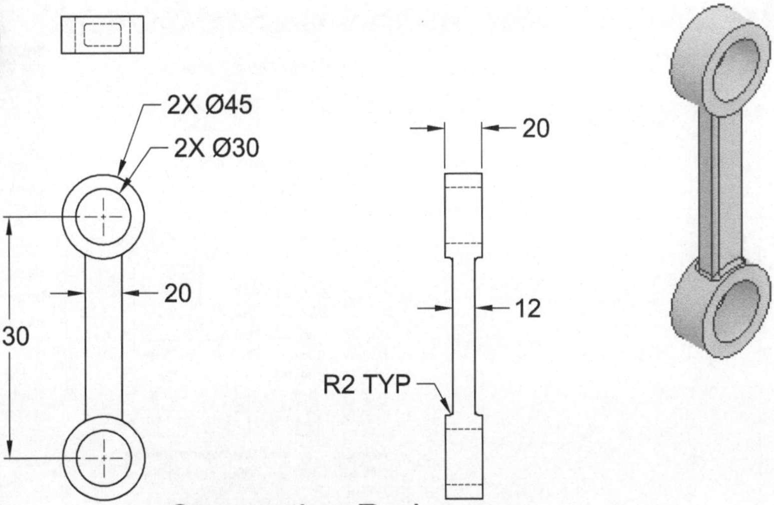

Connecting Rod

Section 1: Starting Autodesk Inventor and Creating Components

In this section, you will create all the components of the assembly in the Part modeling environment one by one.

1. Start Autodesk Inventor and create all components of the assembly one by one in the Part modeling environment. Refer to Figures 11.106 through 11.110 for the dimensions of each component. After creating the components, save them in the Tutorial 1 folder of the Chapter 11 folder. You need to create these folders in the Autodesk Inventor folder.

Note: You can also download all the components of the assembly by logging in to your account on CADArtifex website (*cadartifex.com/login*). If you are a new user, you need to first register yourself on the CADArtifex website (*cadartifex.com/register*) to access the online resources.

Section 2: Invoking the Assembly Environment

After creating all the components, you need to assemble them in the Assembly environment.

1. Click on the **New** tool in the **Quick Access Toolbar** or press the CTRL+N key. The **Create New File** dialog box appears, see Figure 11.111.

2. Click on the **Metric** template folder on the left panel of the dialog box and then double-click on the **Standard (mm).iam** template in the **Assembly** rollout that appears on the right panel of the dialog box, see Figure 11.111. The Assembly environment gets invoked. Note that *.iam* is the file extension of an assembly file.

11.111

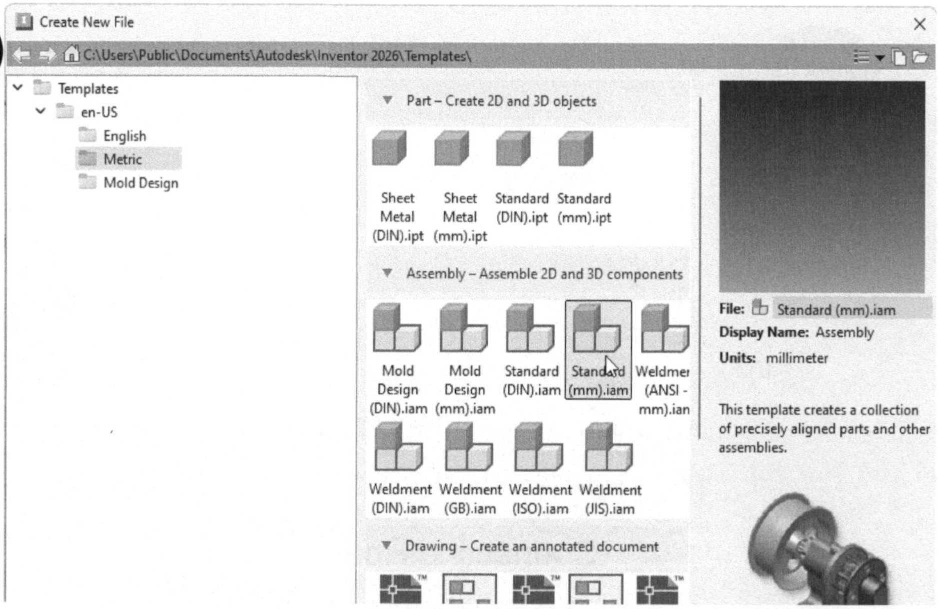

Section 3: Inserting the First Component

Now, you need to insert the first component of the assembly into the Assembly environment.

1. Click on the **Place** tool in the **Component** panel of the **Assemble** tab, see Figure 11.112. The **Place Component** dialog box appears, see Figure 11.113. Alternatively, press the **P** key to invoke the **Place Component** dialog box.

11.112

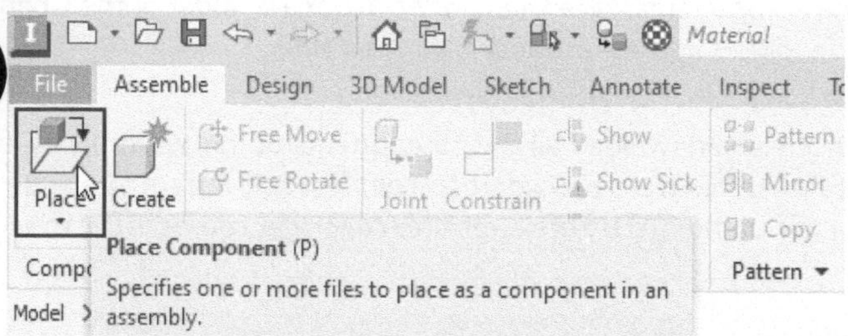

2. Browse to the location where all the components of the assembly are saved (*\Autodesk Inventor\Chapter 11\Tutorial 1*) in the **Place Component** dialog box.

11.113

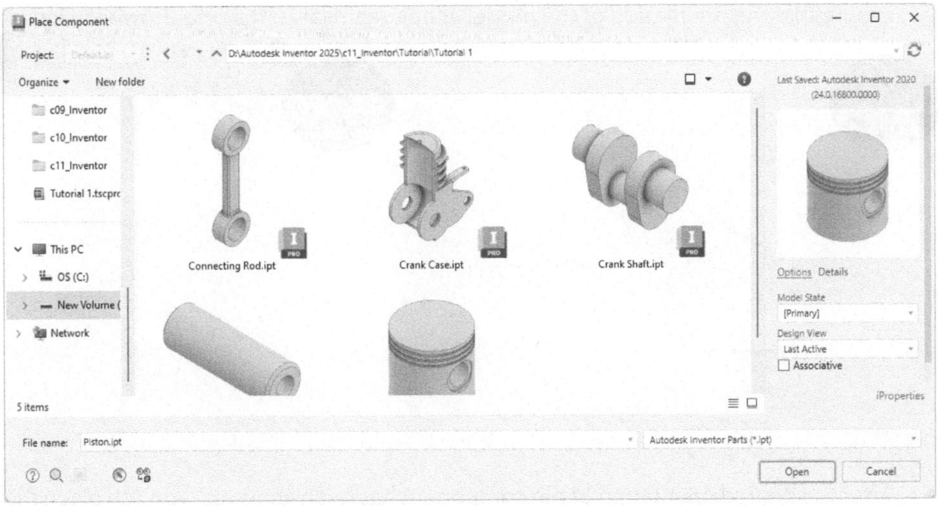

3. Select the **Crank Case** component and then click on the **Open** button in the dialog box. The selected component is attached to the cursor, see Figure 11.114.

4. Click on the **Home** icon of the ViewCube to change the view orientation to isometric, refer to Figure 11.114.

11.114

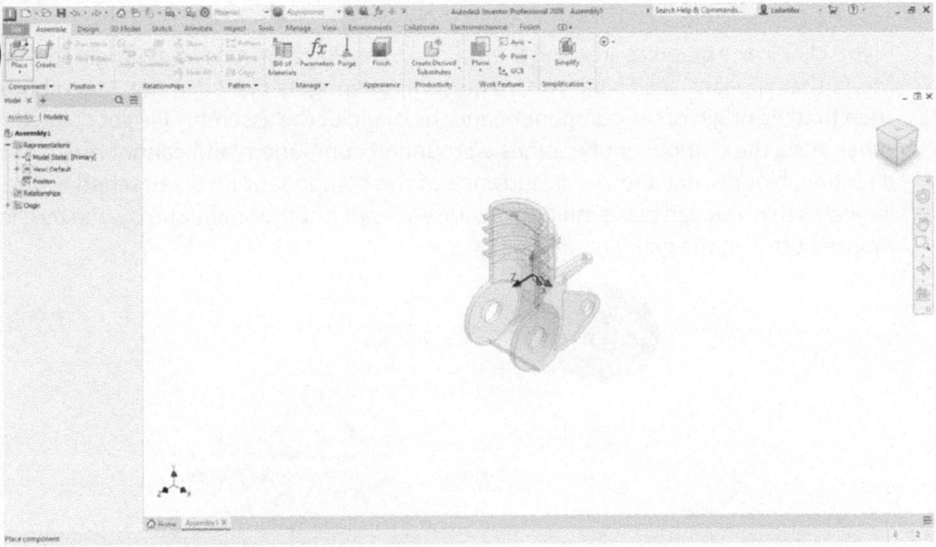

Now, you need to define the placement of the component in the Assembly environment.

Note: Before defining the placement of the component in the Assembly environment, you can change its orientation, if needed. For doing so, right-click in the graphics area and then click on the required option (**Rotate X 90, Rotate Y 90, or Rotate Z 90**) in the **Marking Menu** that appears for rotating the model about the respective axis, see Figure 11.115.

5. Ensure that the orientation of the model appears similar to the one shown in Figure 11.116.

11.115

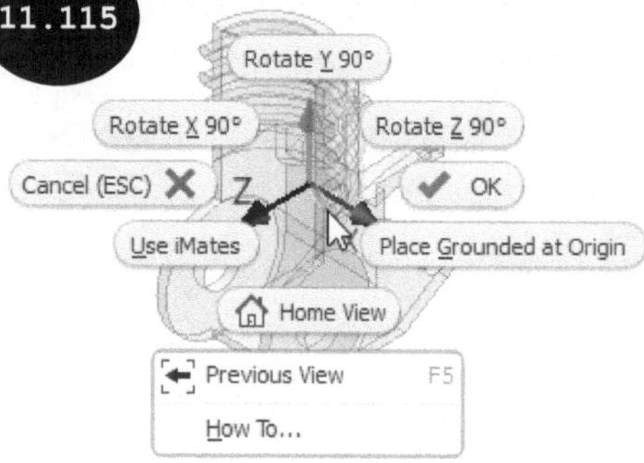

11.116

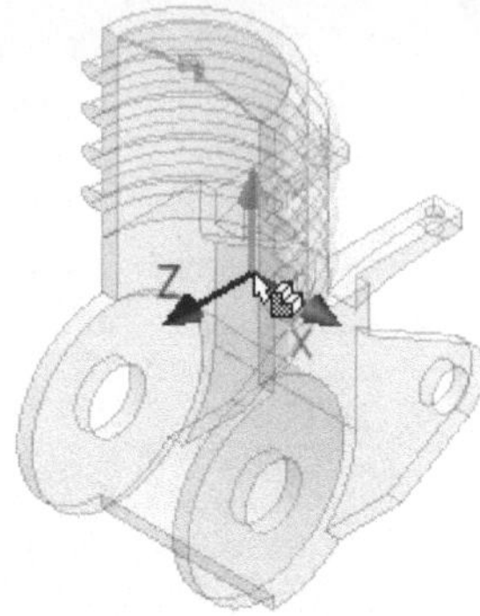

After the desired orientation of the component has been achieved, you can place the component in the Assembly environment.

Tip: You need to make the first component of an assembly grounded or fixed at the origin. A grounded component does not allow any translational or rotational movement and all its degrees of freedom are fixed.

6. Right-click in the graphics area and then click on the **Place Grounded at Origin** tool in the Marking Menu that appears, see Figure 11.117. The component gets placed in the Assembly environment such that the origin of the component and the origin of the assembly file get coincident with each other. Also, the component becomes a grounded component and cannot move or rotate in any direction. Notice that another occurrence of the component is still attached to the cursor. This indicates that you can place multiple occurrences of a component one by one by clicking the left mouse button in the graphics area.

11.117

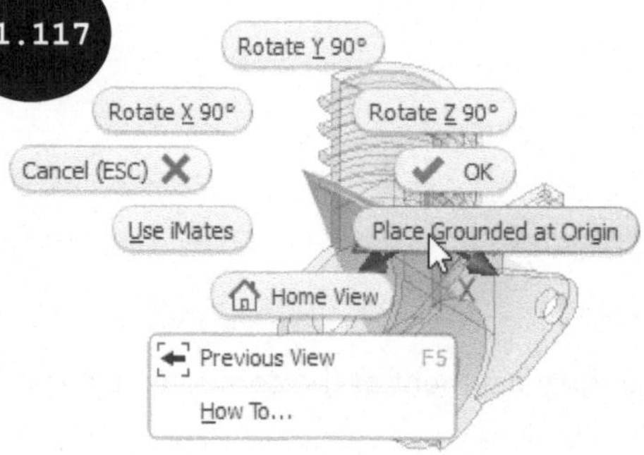

7. Press the ESC key to exit the continuous placement of components. Alternatively, right-click in the graphics area and then click on the **OK** button in the Marking Menu that appears.

8. Change the visual style of the model to "Shaded with Edges" visual style by clicking on the **View > Visual Style > Shaded with Edges** in the **Ribbon**, if needed.

Tip: As the first component has been inserted as a grounded component in the Assembly environment, its name appears in the **Browser** with a pushpin icon and a filled dot [•], see Figure 11.118. The pushpin icon indicates that all degrees of freedom of the component are fixed and the component cannot move or rotate in any direction, while the filled dot indicates that the component is fully constrained.

11.118

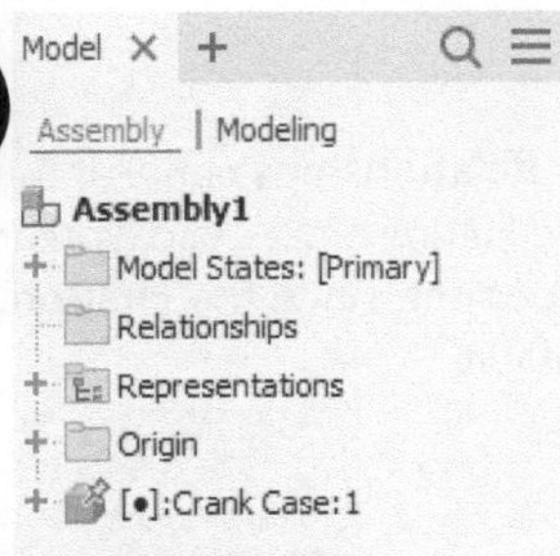

Section 4: Inserting the Second Component

Now, you can insert the second component of the assembly in the graphics area.

1. Click on the **Place** tool in the **Component** panel of the **Assemble** tab or press the P key. The **Place Component** dialog box appears.

2. In the **Place Component** dialog box, browse to the location where all the components of the assembly are saved (*\Autodesk Inventor\Chapter 11\Tutorial 1*).

3. Select the **Crank Shaft** component and then click on the **Open** button in the dialog box. The selected component is attached to the cursor, see Figure 11.119. Also, you are prompted to specify its placement in the Assembly environment.

4. Click anywhere in the graphics area to specify the placement point for the second component. The **Crank Shaft** component is placed in the specified location, refer to Figure 11.120. Ensure that you specify the placement point such that the inserted component does not intersect with the first component of the assembly.

11.119

11.120

5. Press the ESC key to exit the tool after inserting the **Crank Shaft** component.

Note: By default, the component you insert in the Assembly environment is a floating component, whose all degrees of freedom are free and it can move or rotate anywhere in the graphics area. You need to apply the required constraints or joints to fix the required degrees of freedom of the component with respect to the first component of the assembly.

Section 5: Applying the Rotational Joint

Now, you need to assemble the second component with the first component of the assembly by applying the rotational joint.

1. Click on the **Joint** tool in the **Relationships** panel of the **Assemble** tab, see Figure 11.121. The **Place Joint** dialog box appears, see Figure 11.122. Also, you are prompted to specify the position of the joint origin on the first component, since the **First origin** button is activated in the **Connect** area of the dialog box, by default.

11.121

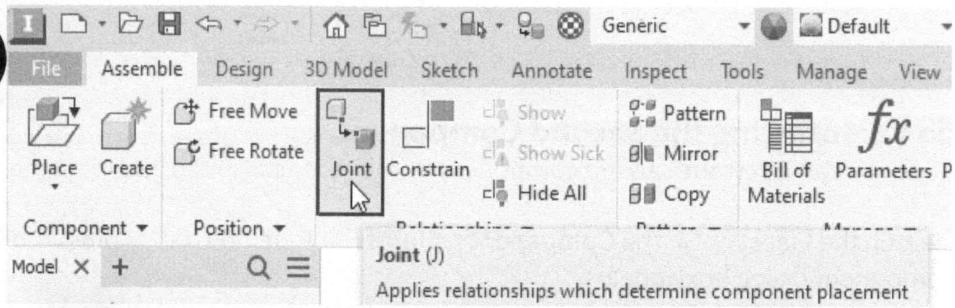

11.122

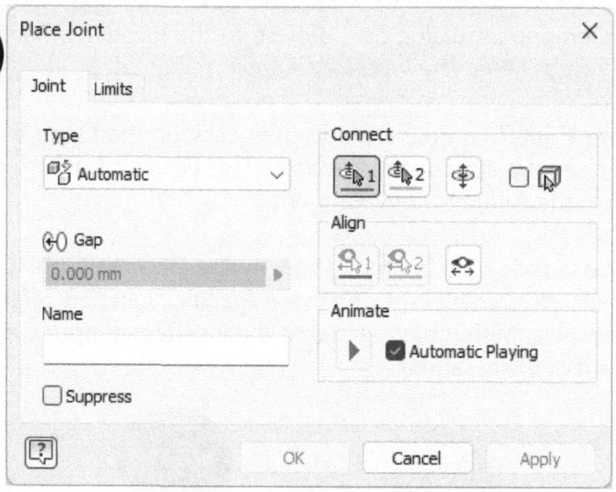

2. Move the cursor over the right circular edge of the second component (**Crank Shaft**), see Figure 11.123. The edge gets highlighted and the joint origin snaps to the snap point that appears at the center of the edge.

3. Click the left mouse button when the joint origin snaps to the center of the circular edge, refer to Figure 11.123. The position of the joint origin is defined at the center of the circular edge. Also, the second component becomes transparent in the graphics area and you are prompted to define the position of the joint origin on the first component (**Crank Case**).

4. Move the cursor over the circular edge of the first component (**Crank Case**), see Figure 11.124. The edge gets highlighted and the joint origin snaps to the center of the edge.

11.123

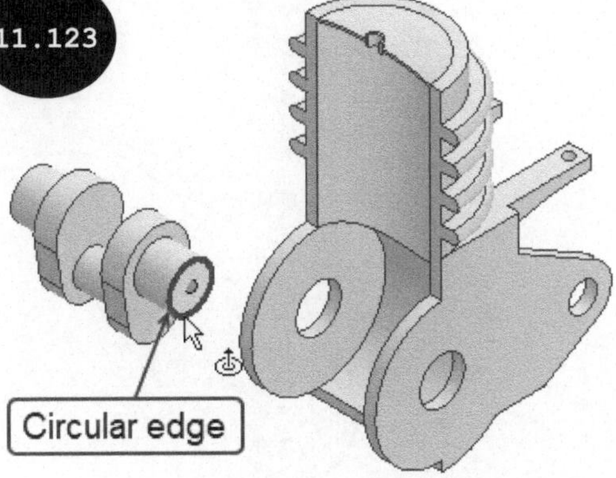

11.124

5. Click the left mouse button when the joint origin snaps to the center of the edge, refer to Figure 11.124. The position of the joint origin is defined and the second component moves toward the first component such that the defined joint origins of both components get coincident with each other in the graphics area, see Figure 11.125. Also, the component animates in the graphics area based on the default joint type selected in the **Type** drop-down list of the dialog box.

11.125

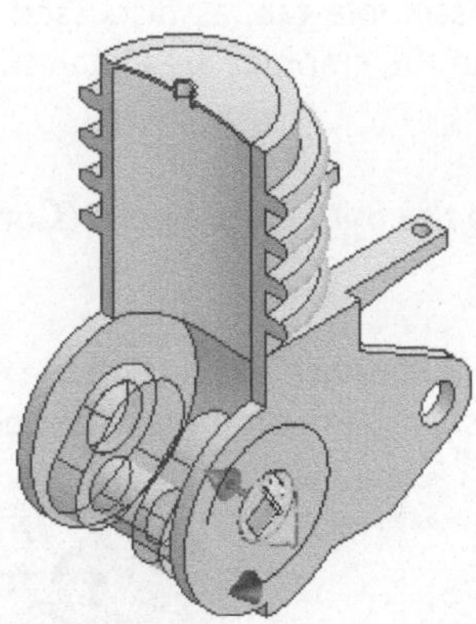

6. Ensure that the **Rotational** option is selected in the **Type** drop-down list of the dialog box as the joint to be applied between the components.

7. Enter **-10** in the **Gap** field of the **Place Joint** dialog box as an offset distance between the joint origins of the connected components, refer to Figure 11.126.

8. Click on the **OK** button in the dialog box. The rotational joint is applied such that all degrees of freedom of the second component (**Crank Shaft**) become fixed except one rotational degree of freedom. As a result, the second **Crank Shaft** component can rotate about its axis. Figure 11.127 shows the assembly after assembling the **Crank Shaft** component.

11.126

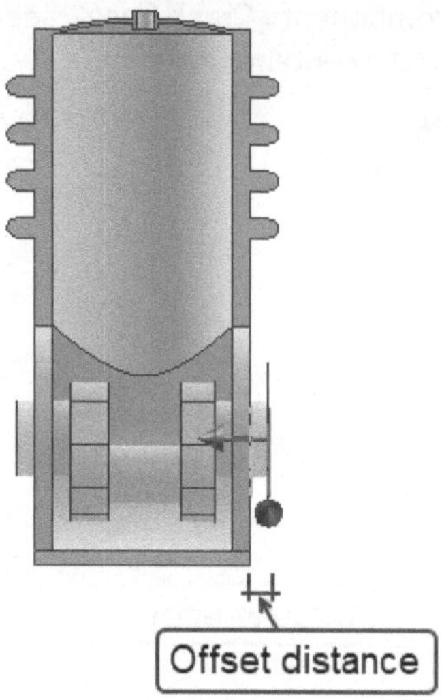

11.127

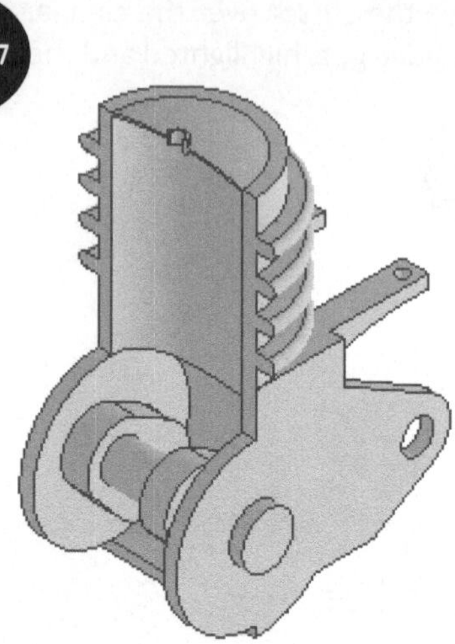

Section 6: Inserting and Assembling the Third Component

Now, you need to insert and assemble the **Connecting Rod** component of the assembly.

1. Insert the third component (**Connecting Rod**) of the assembly by using the **Place** tool of the **Component** panel in the **Assemble** tab, as discussed earlier, see Figure 11.128. Note that you need to define its position in the graphics area such that it does not intersect with the existing components of the assembly.

   Now, you need to assemble the third component (**Connecting Rod**) by applying the rotational joint.

2. Click on the **Joint** tool in the **Relationships** panel of the **Assemble** tab, see Figure 11.129. The **Place Joint** dialog box appears. Also, you are prompted to specify the position of the joint origin on the first component.

11.128

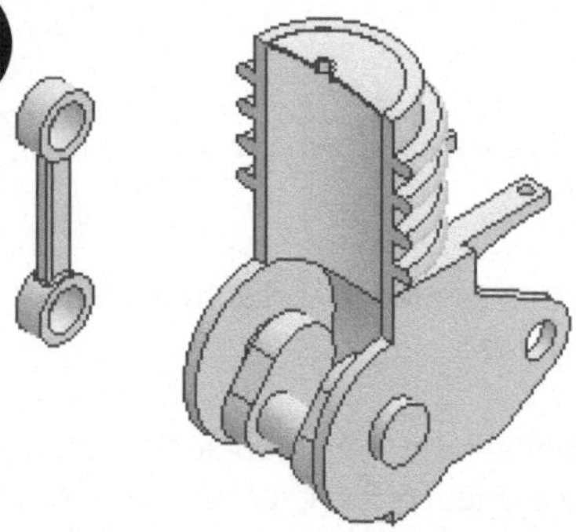

11.129

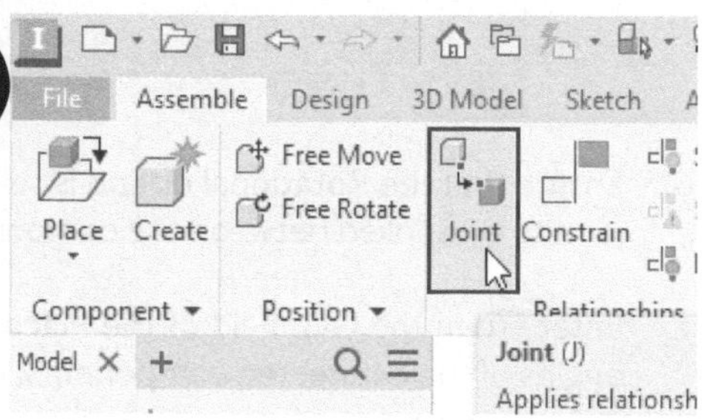

3. Move the cursor over the inner circular face of the third component (**Connecting Rod**), see Figure 11.130. The face gets highlighted and its snap points (three) appear.

4. Press and hold the CTRL key to lock the highlighted face so that you can easily select the required (middle) snap point of the face to define the position of the joint origin.

5. Move the cursor over the middle snap point of the face and then click the left mouse button when the joint origin snaps to it, see Figure 11.130. The position of the joint origin on the third component is defined and you are prompted to define the position of the joint origin on the other component. Release the CTRL key.

6. Move the cursor over the circular face of the second component (**Crank Shaft**), refer to Figure 11.131. The face gets highlighted and its snap points appear.

7. Press the CTRL key and then click on the left mouse button when the joint origin snaps to the middle snap point of the highlighted face of the second component (**Crank Shaft**), see Figure 11.131. The position of the joint origin is defined and the third component moves toward the second component such that the defined joint origins of both the components get coincident with each other in the graphics area, see Figure 11.132. Also, the component animates in the graphics area based on the default joint type selected in the **Type** drop-down list of the dialog box.

11.130

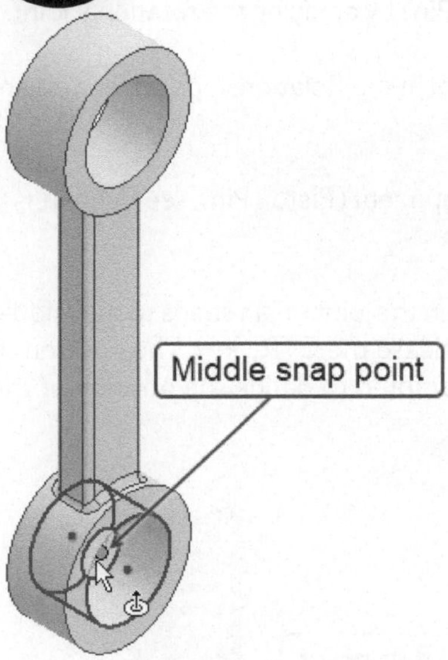

11.131

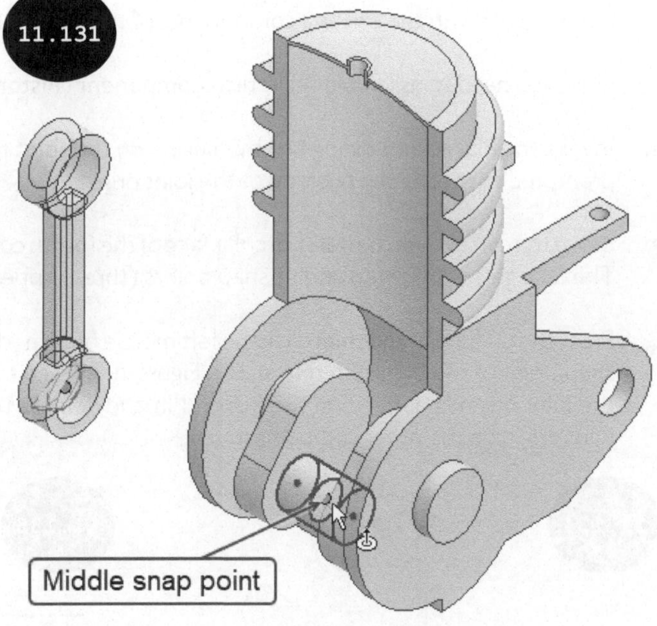

8. Select the **Rotational** option in the **Type** drop-down list of the dialog box as the joint to be applied.

9. Click on the **OK** button in the dialog box. The rotational joint is applied such that all degrees of freedom of the third component (**Connecting Rod**) become fixed except one rotational degree of freedom. As a result, the **Connecting Rod** can rotate about its axis. Figure 11.133 shows the assembly after assembling the **Connecting Rod**.

11.132

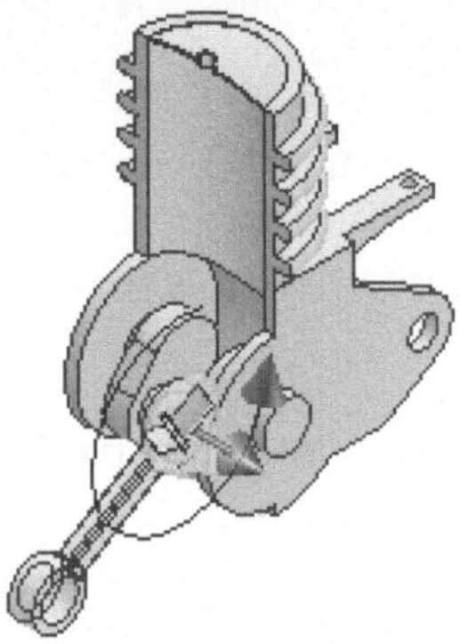

11.133

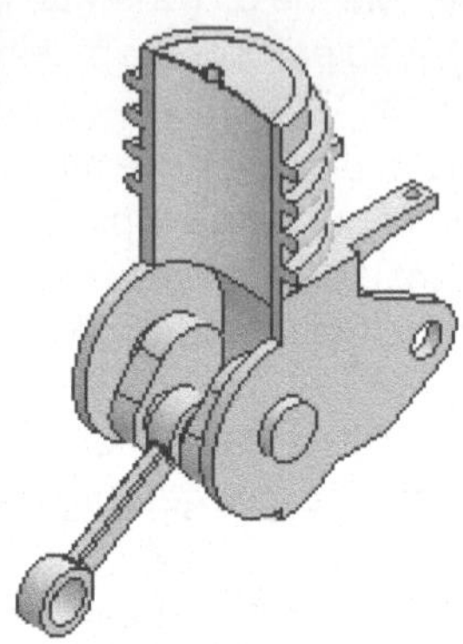

Section 7: Inserting and Assembling the Fourth Component

Now, you need to insert and assemble the **Piston Pin** of the assembly.

1. Insert the fourth component (**Piston Pin**) in the Assembly environment by using the **Place** tool, see Figure 11.134. Note that you need to define its position in the graphics area such that it does not intersect with the existing components of the assembly.

   Now, you need to assemble the fourth component (**Piston Pin**) by applying the rotational joint.

2. Invoke the **Place Joint** dialog box by clicking on the **Joint** tool in the **Relationships** panel. You are prompted to specify the position of the joint origin.

3. Move the cursor over the outer circular face of the fourth component (**Piston Pin**), see Figure 11.135. The face gets highlighted and its snap points (three) appear.

4. Press the CTRL key and then click the left mouse button when the joint origin snaps to the middle snap point of the highlighted face, see Figure 11.135. Next, release the CTRL key. The position of the joint origin is defined on the **Piston Pin** and you are prompted to define the position of the joint origin on the other component.

11.134

11.135

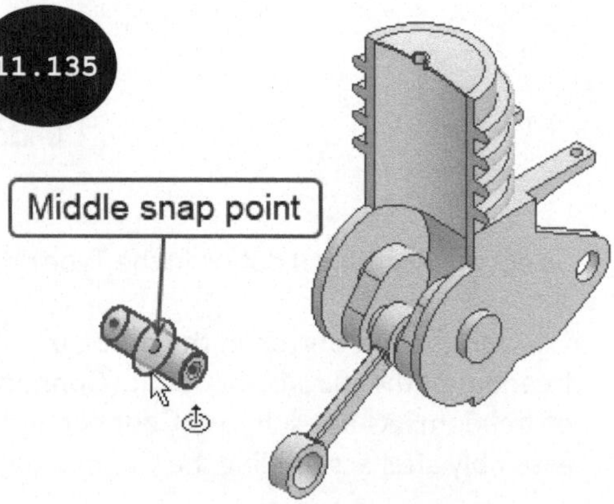

5. Move the cursor over the inner circular face of the third component (**Connecting Rod**), see Figure 11.136. The face gets highlighted and its snap points (three) appear.

6. Move the cursor over the middle snap point of the face and then click the left mouse button when the joint origin snaps to it, see Figure 11.136. The position of the joint origin is defined and the fourth component (**Piston Pin**) moves toward the third component (**Connecting Rod**) such that the defined joint origins of both the components get coincident to each other in the graphics area, see Figure 11.137. Also, the component animates in the graphics area based on the default joint type selected in the **Type** drop-down list of the dialog box.

7. Select the **Rotational** option in the **Type** drop-down list of the dialog box as the joint to be applied between the components.

8. Click on the **OK** button in the dialog box. The rotational joint is applied such that all degrees of freedom of the fourth component (**Piston Pin**) become fixed except one rotational degree of freedom. Figure 11.138 shows the assembly after assembling the **Piston Pin**.

Section 8: Inserting and Assembling the Fifth Component

Now, you need to insert and assemble the **Piston** of the assembly.

1. Insert the fifth component (**Piston**) in the Assembly environment by using the **Place** tool, see Figure 11.139. Note that you need to define its position in the graphics area such that it does not intersect with the existing components of the assembly.

Now, you need to assemble the fifth component (**Piston**).

2. Invoke the **Place Joint** dialog box by clicking on the **Joint** tool in the **Relationships** panel. You are prompted to specify the position of the joint origin.

3. Move the cursor over the inner circular edge of the fifth component (**Piston**), see Figure 11.140. The edge gets highlighted and the joint origin snaps to the center of the edge.

4. Click the left mouse button when the joint origin snaps to the center of the circular edge, see Figure 11.140. The position of the joint origin is defined on the **Piston** component and you are prompted to define the position of the joint origin on the other component.

11.139

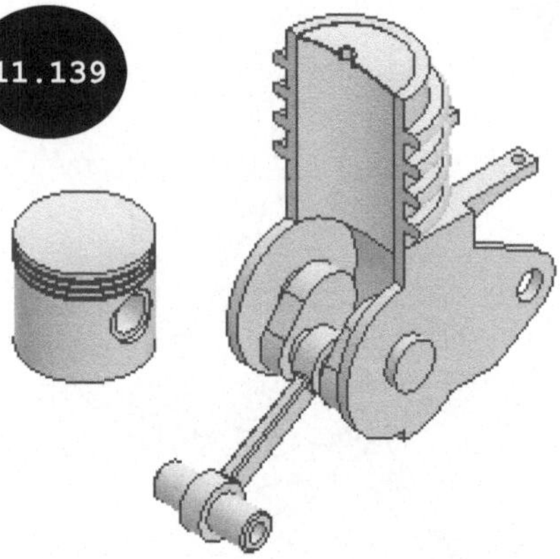

11.140

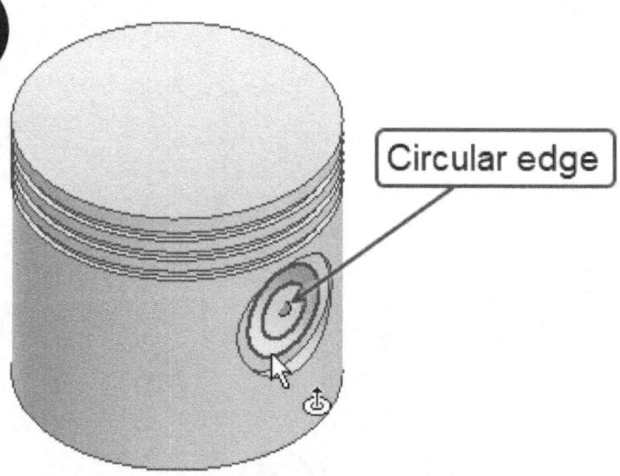

5. Move the cursor over the outer circular edge of the fourth component (**Piston Pin**), see Figure 11.141. The edge gets highlighted and the joint origin snaps to the center of the edge.

6. Click the left mouse button when the joint origin snaps to the center of the circular edge, refer to Figure 11.141. The defined joint origins of both components coincide with each other in the graphics area, see Figure 11.142. Also, the component animates in the graphics area based on the default joint type selected in the **Type** drop-down list of the dialog box.

11.141

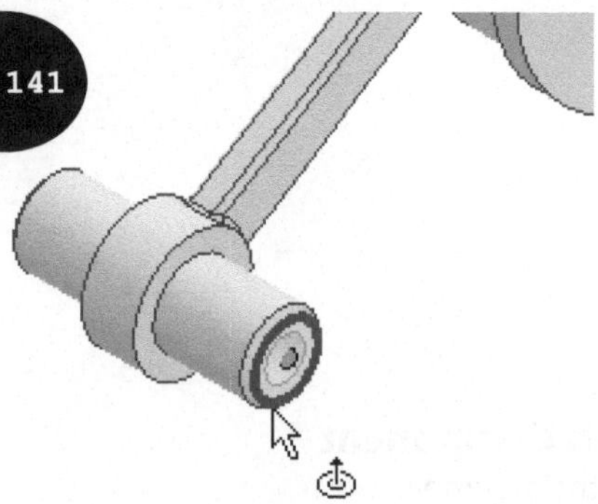

11.142

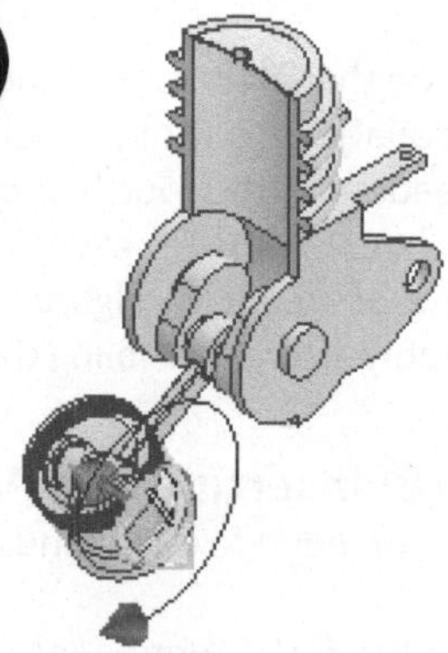

7. Ensure that the **Rotational** option is selected in the **Type** drop-down list of the dialog box.

8. Click on the **OK** button in the dialog box. The rotational joint is applied such that all degrees of freedom of the fifth component (**Piston**) become fixed except one rotational degree of freedom.

   Now, you need to apply the mate constraint.

9. Click on the **Constrain** tool in the **Relationships** panel of the **Assemble** tab, see Figure 11.143. The **Place Constraint** dialog box appears.

11.143

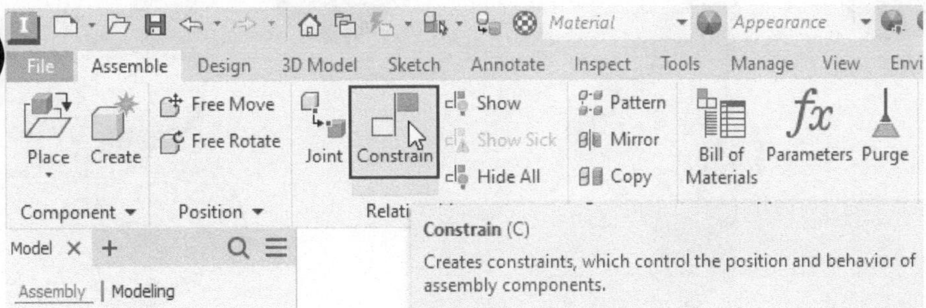

10. Ensure that the **Mate** button is activated in the **Type** area of the dialog box.

11. Move the cursor over the outer circular face of the fifth component (**Piston**) and then click when the axis of the component appears in the graphics area, see Figure 11.144.

12. Move the cursor over the inner circular face of the first component (**Crank Case**) and then click when the axis of the component appears in the graphics area, see Figure 11.145. The mate constraint gets applied between the selected geometries of the components depending upon the solution type selected in the **Solution** area of the dialog box.

11.144

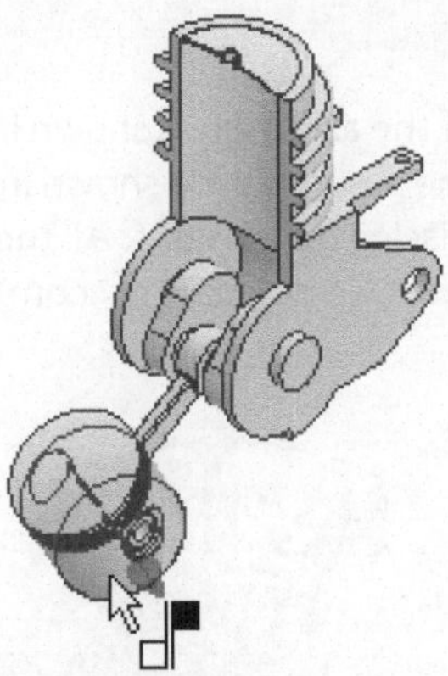

11.145

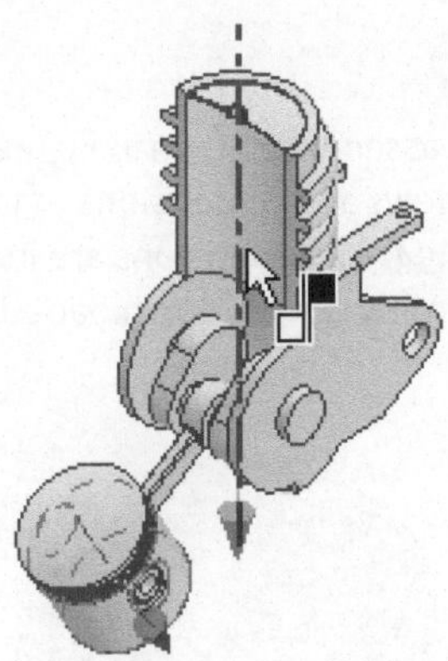

13. Ensure that the **Aligned** button is selected in the **Solution** area of the dialog box. The orientation of the **Piston** component appears similar to the one shown in the Figure 11.146.

Note: If the orientation of the **Piston** component does not appear similar to the one shown in the figure then you need to click on the **Opposed** button in the **Solution** area of the dialog box.

14. Click on the **OK** button in the dialog box. The mate constraint is applied between the selected geometries of the components, refer to Figure 11.146.

15. Drag the Piston component upwards so that it appears similar to the one shown in Figure 11.147. This figure shows the final assembly.

11.146

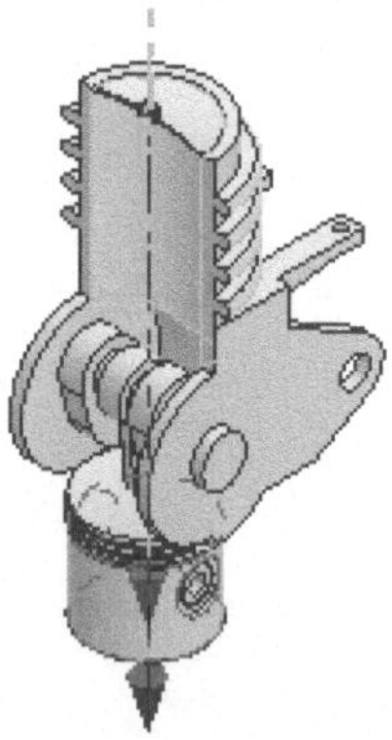

11.147

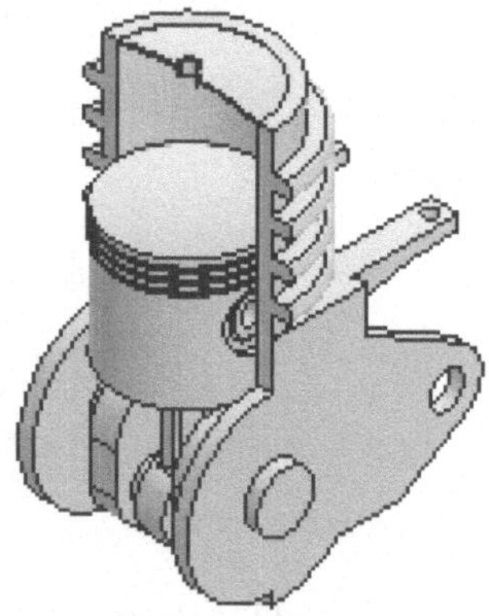

Section 9: Saving the Model

1. Click on the **Save** tool in the **Quick Access Toolbar** toolbar. The **Save As** dialog box appears.

2. Browse to **Autodesk Inventor > Chapter 11 > Tutorial 1** folder in the local drive of your system.

3. Enter **Tutorial 1** in the **File name** field of the dialog box and then click on the **Save** button. The model is saved in the specified location (>:\Autodesk Inventor\Chapter 11\Tutorial 1).

Tutorial 2

Create the assembly shown in Figure 11.148. The section view of the assembly is shown in Figure 11.149. Different views and dimensions of individual components of the assembly are shown in Figures 11.150 through 11.154. All dimensions are in mm. You can assign the missing dimensions. All the components of the assembly can be downloaded by logging on to our website (www.cadartifex.com).

11.148

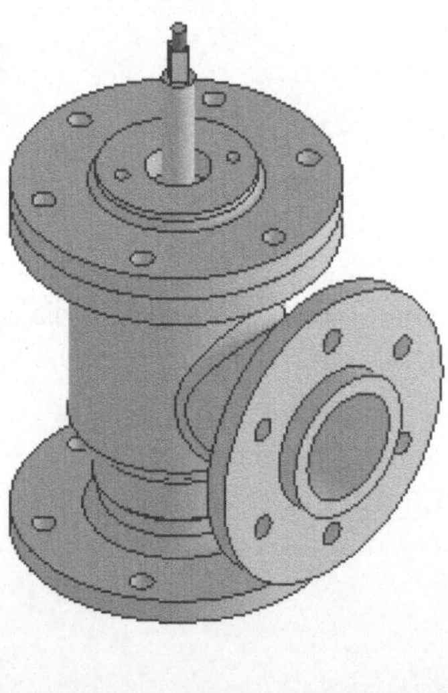

11.149

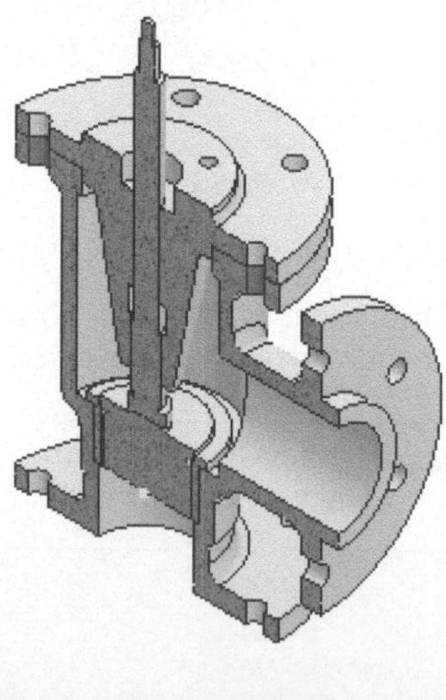

11.150

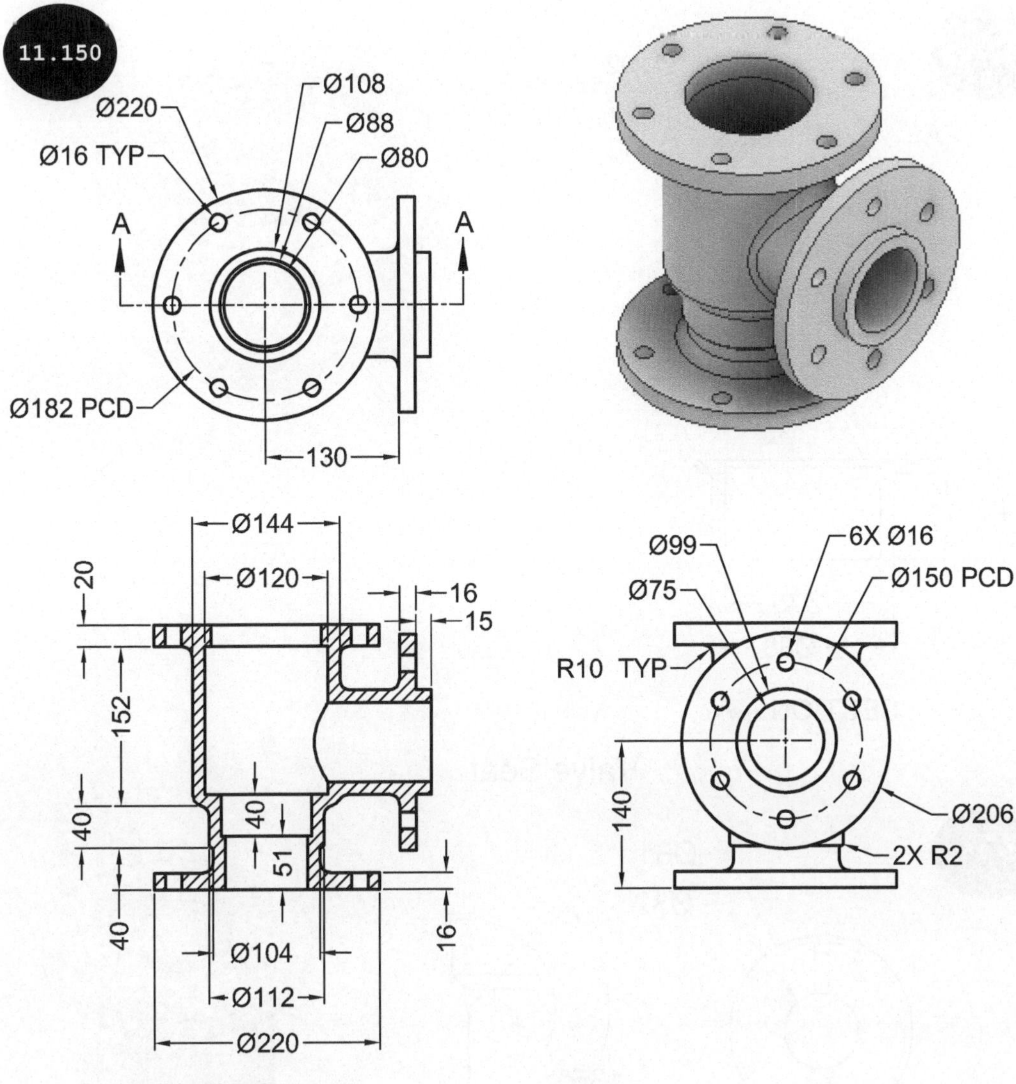
Ø220
Ø16 TYP
Ø108
Ø88
Ø80
A
A
Ø182 PCD
130
Ø144
Ø120
20
16
15
152
40
40
51
40
16
Ø104
Ø112
Ø220
SECTION A-A
Ø99
6X Ø16
Ø75
Ø150 PCD
R10 TYP
140
Ø206
2X R2

Body

11.151

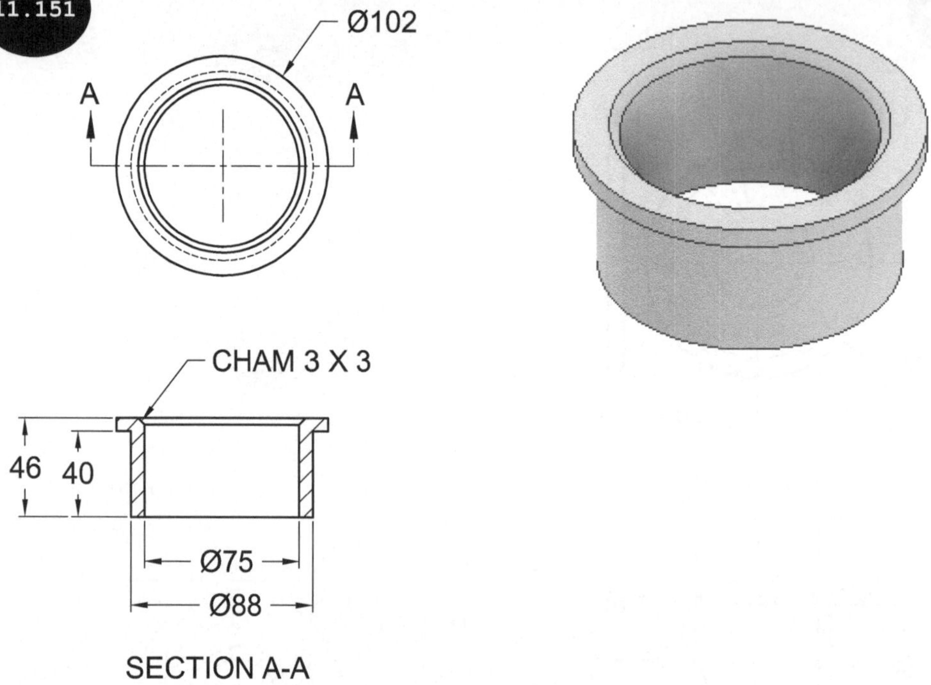

Valve Seat

11.152

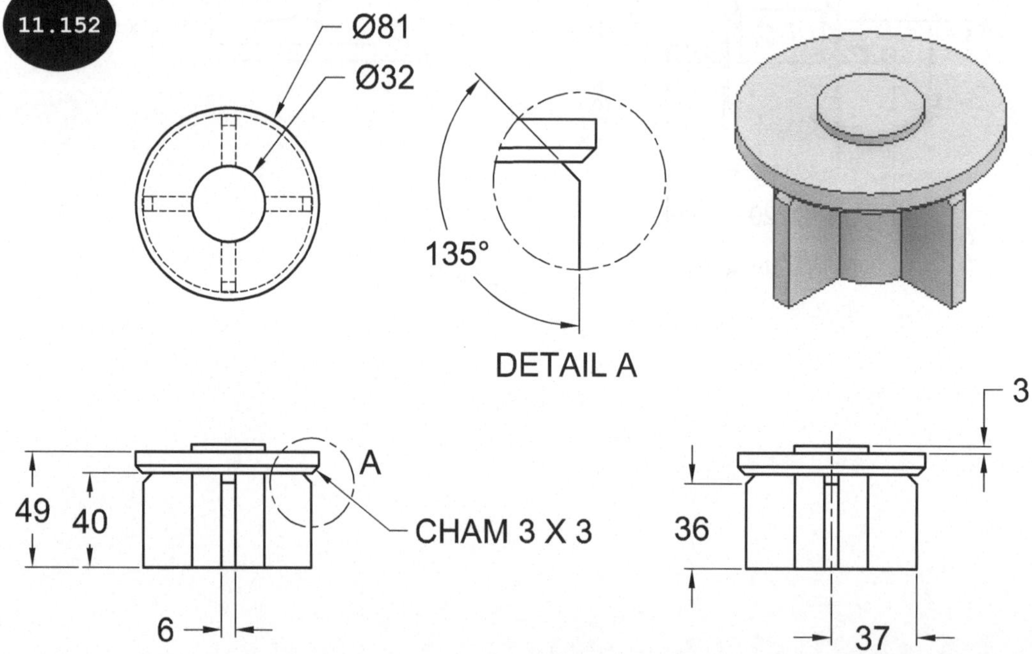

Valve

11.153

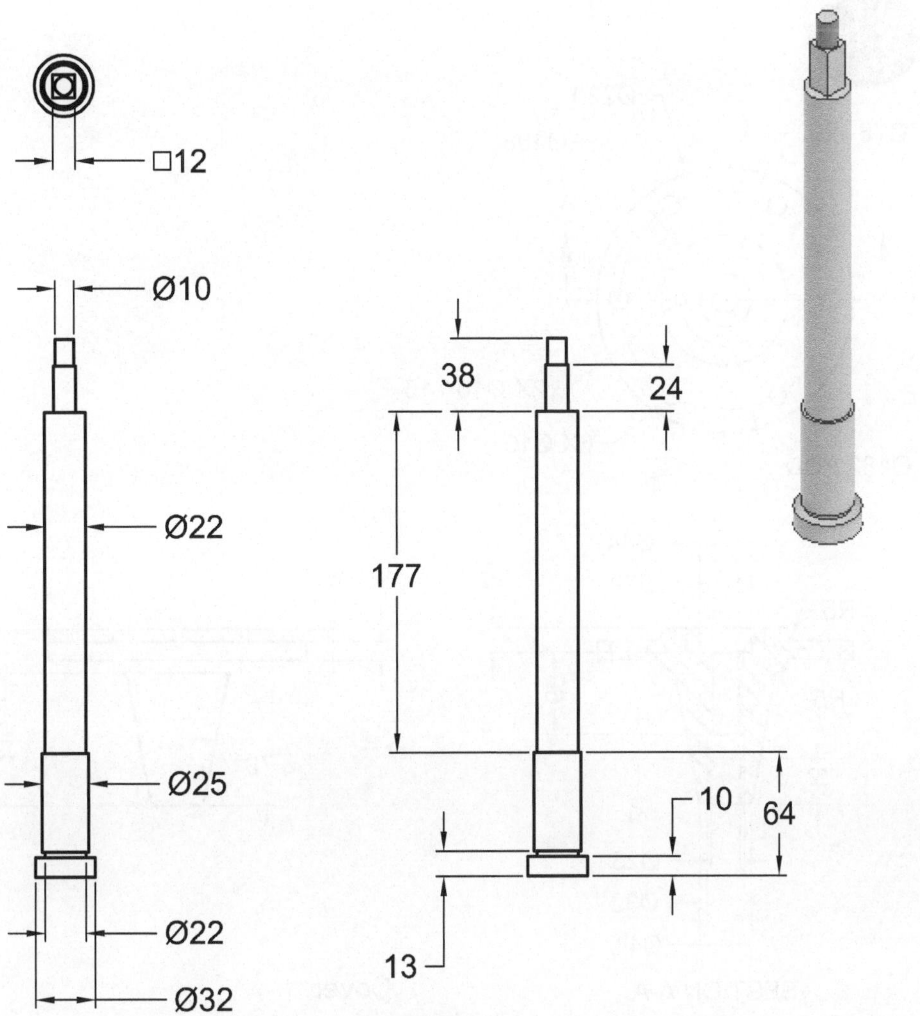

Spindle

11.154

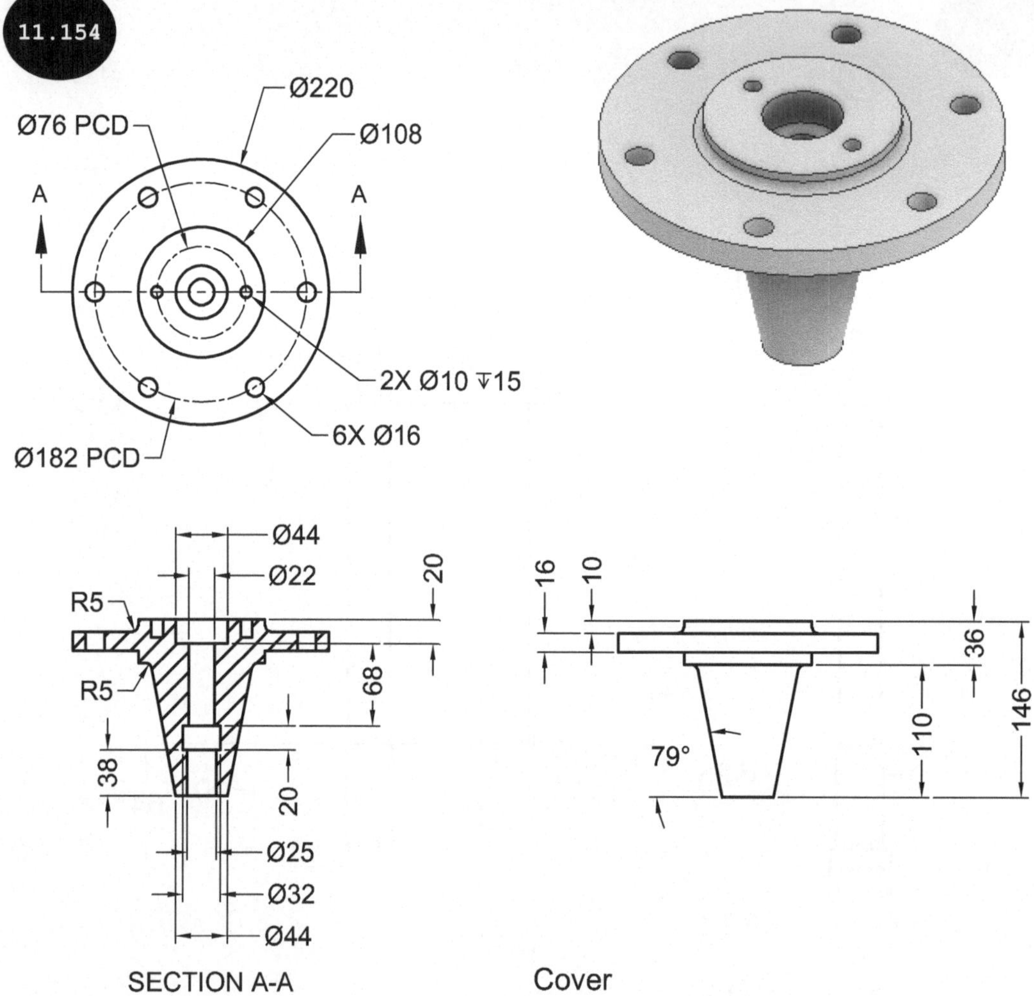

Section 1: Starting Autodesk Inventor and Creating Components

In this section, you will create all the components of the assembly in the Part modeling environment one by one.

1. Start Autodesk Inventor and create all components of the assembly one by one in the Part modeling environment. Refer to Figures 11.150 through 11.154 for the dimensions of each component. After creating components, save them in the Tutorial 2 folder of the Chapter 11 folder. You need to create these folders in the Autodesk Inventor folder.

Note: You can also download all the components of the assembly by logging in to your account on CADArtifex website (*cadartifex.com/login*). If you are a new user, you need to first register yourself on the CADArtifex website (*cadartifex.com/register*) to access the online resources.

Section 2: Invoking the Assembly Environment

After creating all the components, you need to assemble them in the Assembly environment.

1. Click on the **New** tool in the **Quick Access Toolbar** or press the CTRL+N key, see Figure 11.155. The **Create New File** dialog box appears, see Figure 11.156.

11.155

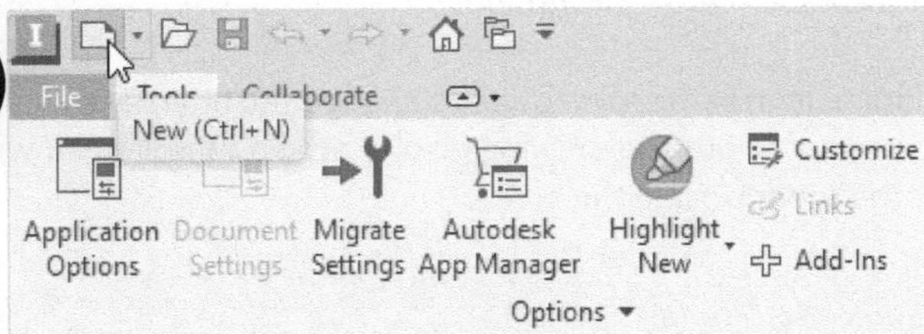

2. Click on the **Metric** template folder on the left panel of the dialog box and then double-click on the **Standard (mm).iam** template in the **Assembly** rollout that appears on the right panel of the dialog box, see Figure 11.156. The Assembly environment gets invoked. Note that *.iam* is the file extension of an assembly file.

11.156

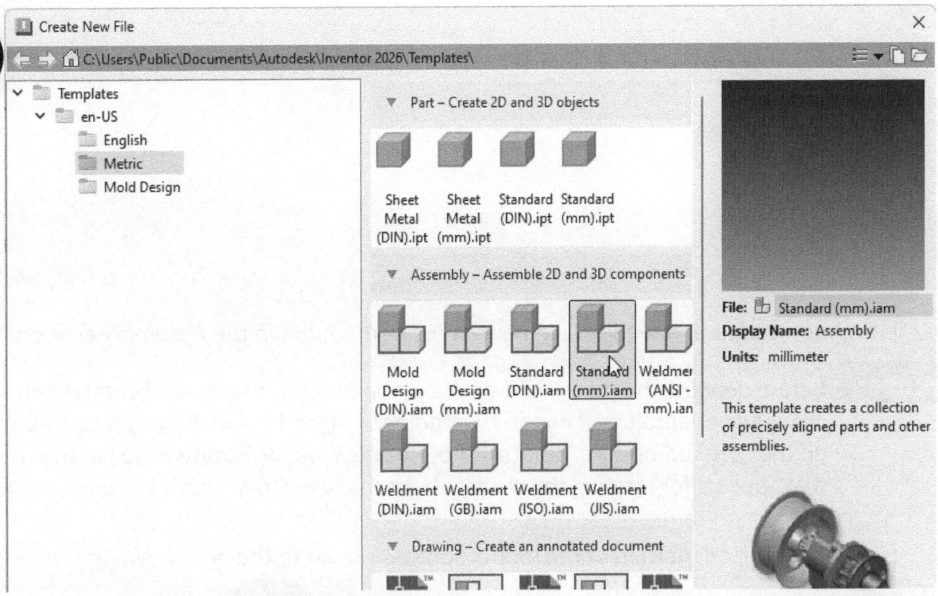

Section 3: Inserting the First Component

1. Press the P Key or click on the **Place** tool in the **Component** panel of the **Assemble** tab, see Figure 11.157. The **Place Component** dialog box appears.

11.157

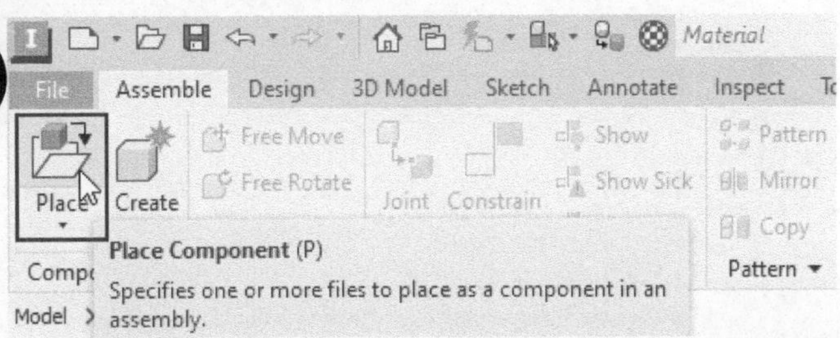

2. Browse to the location where all the components of the assembly are saved (*\Autodesk Inventor\Chapter 11\Tutorial 2*) in the **Place Component** dialog box.

3. Select the **Body** component and then click on the **Open** button in the dialog box. The selected component is attached to the cursor, refer to Figure 11.158. Also, you are prompted to specify its placement in the Assembly environment.

4. Click on the Home icon in the ViewCube to change the orientation of the model to isometric. You may also need to zoom out the drawing display area by scrolling down the middle mouse button in order to fit the model inside the screen.

11.158

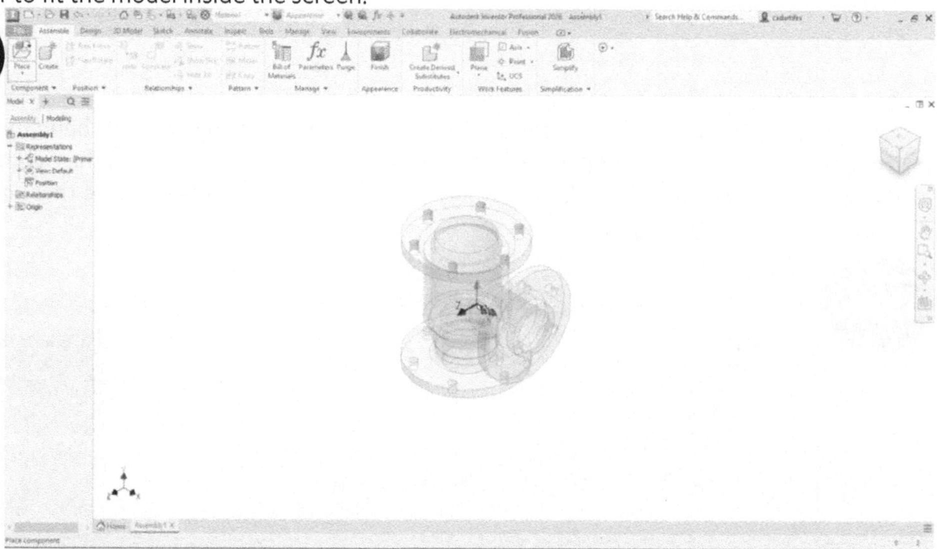

Now, you need to define the placement of the component in the Assembly environment.

Note: Before defining the placement of the component in the Assembly environment, you can change its orientation, if needed. For doing so, right-click in the graphics area and then click on the required option (**Rotate X 90**, **Rotate Y 90**, or **Rotate Z 90**) in the Marking Menu that appears for rotating the model about the respective axis, see Figure 11.159.

5. Ensure that the orientation of the model appears similar to the one shown in Figure 11.160.

11.159

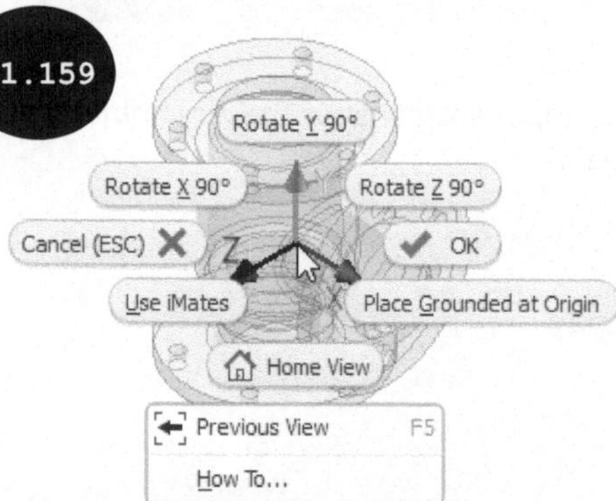

11.160

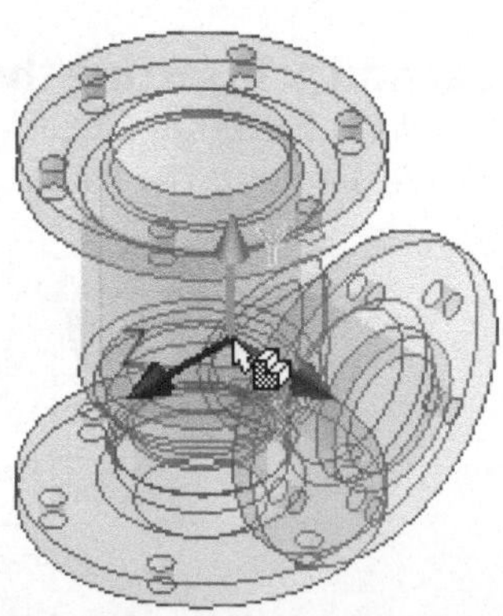

After the desired orientation of the component has been achieved, you can place the first component in the Assembly environment as a grounded component.

6. Right-click in the graphics area and then click on the **Place Grounded at Origin** tool in the Marking Menu that appears, see Figure 11.161. The component gets placed in the Assembly environment such that the origin of the component and the origin of the assembly file get coincident to each other. Also, the component becomes a grounded component and cannot move or rotate in any direction. Notice that another occurrence of the component is still attached with the cursor. This indicates that you can place multiple occurrences of a component one by one by clicking the left mouse button in the graphics area.

11.161

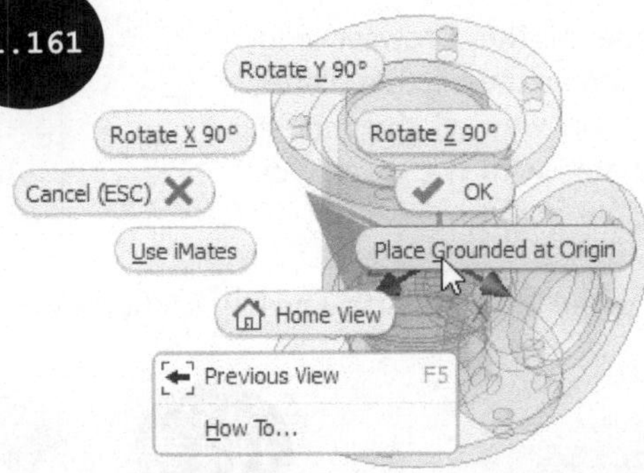

7. Press the ESC key to exit the continuous placement of components. Alternatively, right-click in the graphics area and then click on the **OK** button in the Marking Menu that appears.

8. Change the visual style of the model to "Shaded with Edges" visual style by clicking on the **View > Visual Style > Shaded with Edges** in the **Ribbon**, see Figure 11.162.

11.162

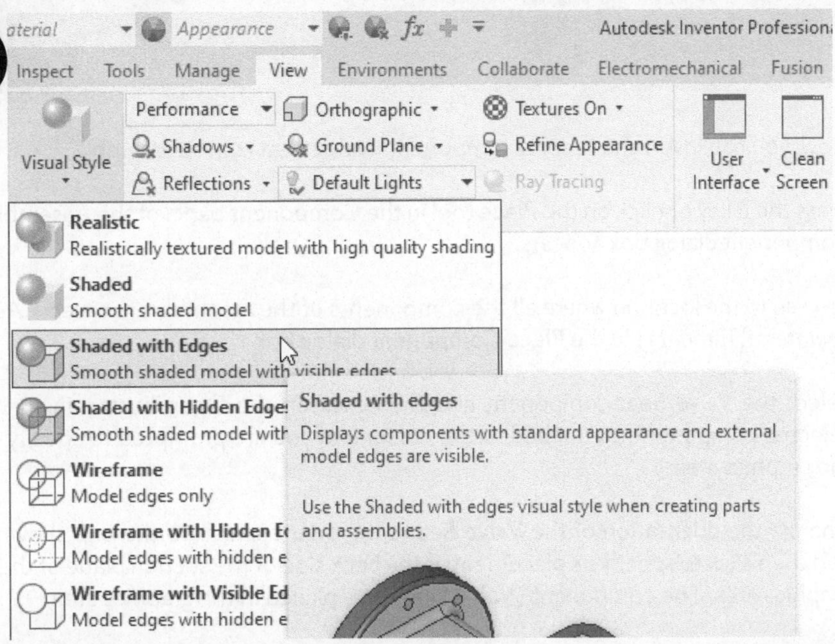

Section 4: Inserting the Second Component

Now, you can insert the second component (**Valve Seat**) of the assembly in the graphics area. As the **Valve Seat** component is an internal component of the assembly, you need to first create a half section view of the assembly for assembling it inside the first component of the assembly.

1. Click on the **View** tab in the **Ribbon** and then select the **Half Section View** tool in the **Section** flyout of the **Visibility** panel, see Figure 11.163. You are prompted to select a work plane or a face for sectioning the model.

11.163

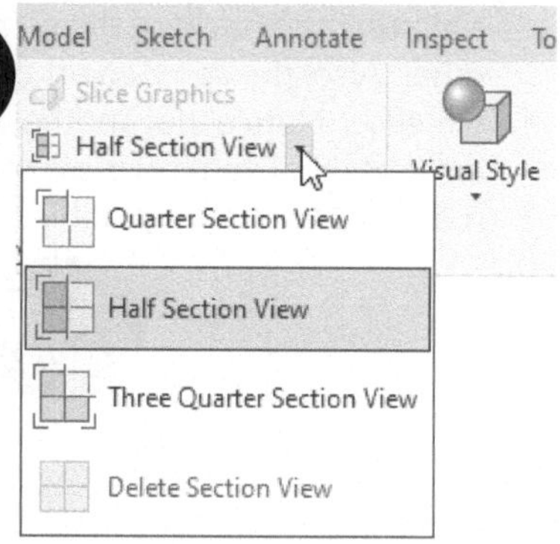

2. Expand the **Origin** node in the **Browser** and then click on the **XY Plane** as the section plane. A preview of a half section view of the model appears in the graphics area with the display of the Mini-Toolbar, see Figure 11.164.

3. Click on the **OK** button in the Mini-Toolbar. The half section view of the model gets created, see Figure 11.165.

11.164

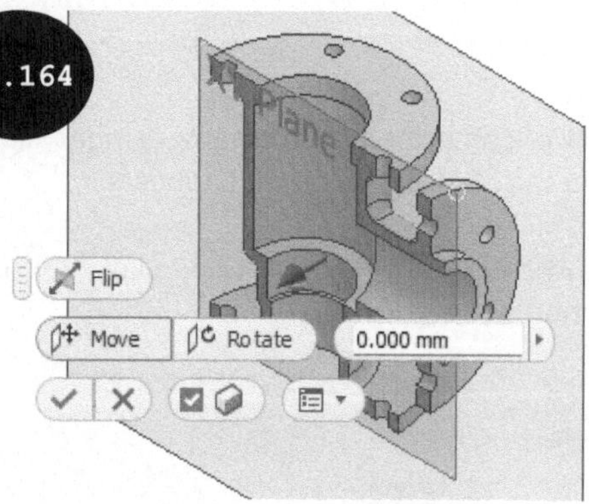

11.165

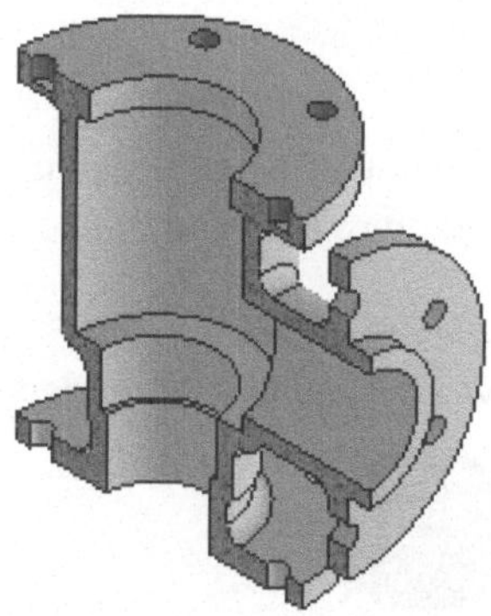

Now, you can insert the second component (**Valve Seat**) of the assembly.

4. Press the **P** key or click on the **Place** tool in the **Component** panel of the **Assemble** tab. The **Place Component** dialog box appears.

5. Browse to the location where all the components of the assembly are saved (*\Autodesk Inventor\Chapter 11\Tutorial 1*) in the **Place Component** dialog box.

6. Select the **Valve Seat** component and then click on the **Open** button in the dialog box. The selected component is attached to the cursor and you are prompted to specify its placement in the graphics area.

7. Change the orientation of the **Valve Seat** component similar to the one shown in Figure 11.166 and then click to specify its placement at the back side of the section plane of the assembly in the graphics area. The component (Valve Seat) gets placed in the graphics area.

11.166

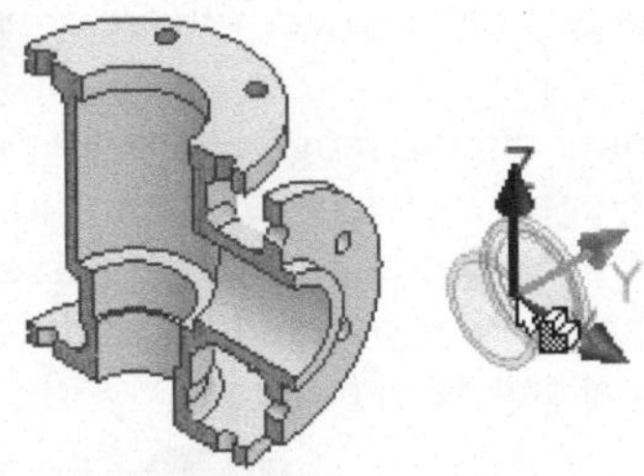

Note: If you specify the placement of the component on the front side of the assembly section plane then the placed component will also be sectioned by the section plane and it will not be visible or will be partially visible in the graphics area.

8. Press the ESC key to exit the continuous placement of components.

Section 5: Assembling the Second Component

Now, you need to assemble the second component of the assembly by applying constraints.

1. Click on the **Constrain** tool in the **Relationships** panel of the **Assemble** tab, see Figure 11.167. The **Place Constraint** dialog box appears, see Figure 11.168.

11.167

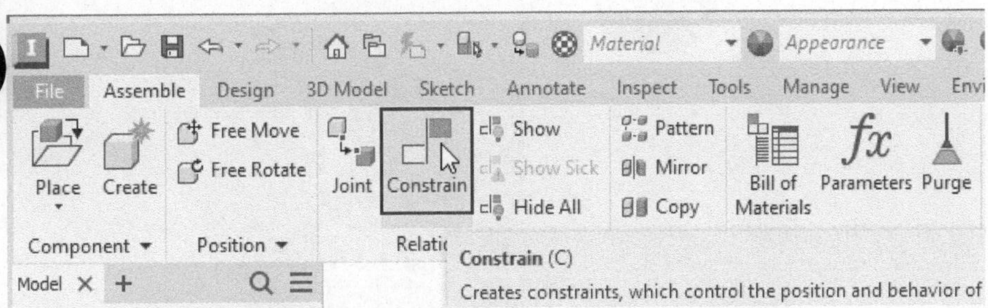

2. Click on the **Insert** button in the **Type** area of the dialog box, see Figure 11.168. You are prompted to select a geometry for applying a constraint.

11.168

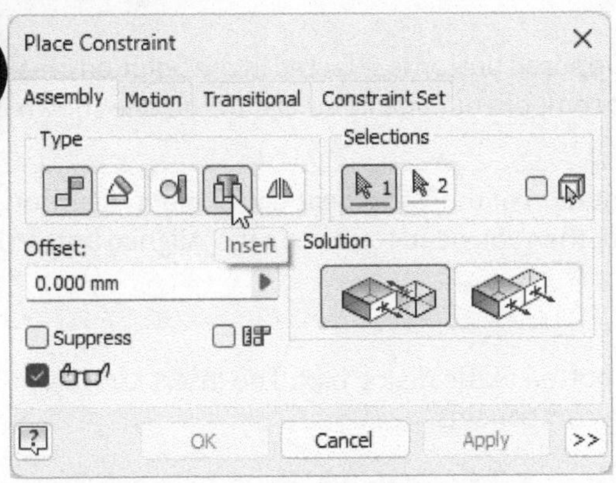

3. Move the cursor over the circular edge of the second component (**Valve Seat**), (see Figure 11.169), and then click when the edge gets highlighted. You are prompted to select another geometry.

4. Move the cursor over the inner circular edge of the first component (**Body**), see Figure 11.170 and then click when the edge gets highlighted. The insert constraint gets applied between the selected geometries and the second component gets assembled with the first component, see Figure 11.171. Note that all the degrees of freedom of the second component (Valve Seat) get restricted except the rotational degree of freedom.

11.169

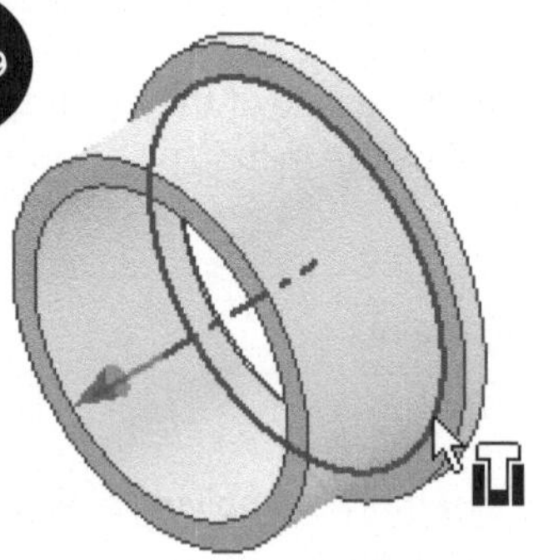

11.170

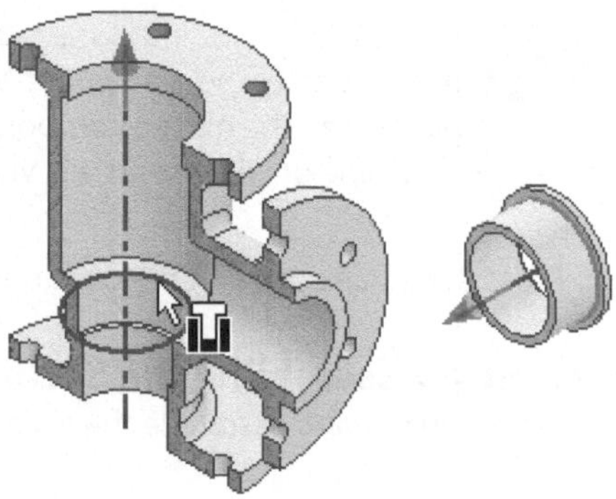

11.171

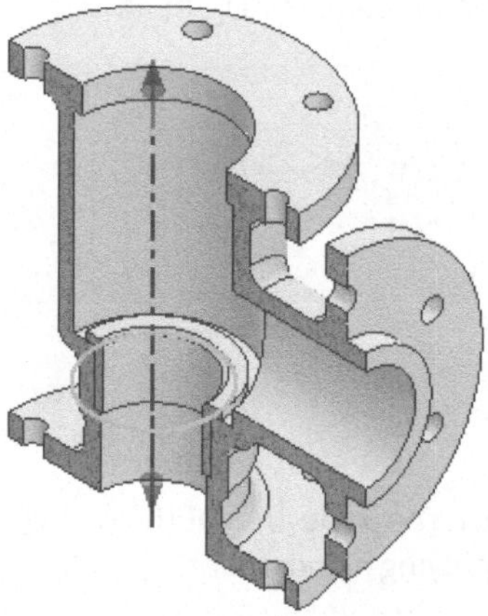

5. Ensure that the **Opposed** button is selected in the **Solution** area of the dialog box. The orientation of the **Valve Seat** component appears similar to the one shown in Figure 11.171.

Note: If the orientation of the **Valve Seat** component does not appear similar to the one shown in the figure then you need to click on the **Aligned** button in the **Solution** area of the dialog box.

6. Click on the **OK** button in the dialog box. The insert constraint is applied between the selected geometries of the components.

Section 6: Inserting and Assembling the Third Component

1. Insert the third component (**Valve**) of the assembly in the graphics area by using the **Place** tool, see Figure 11.172.

11.172

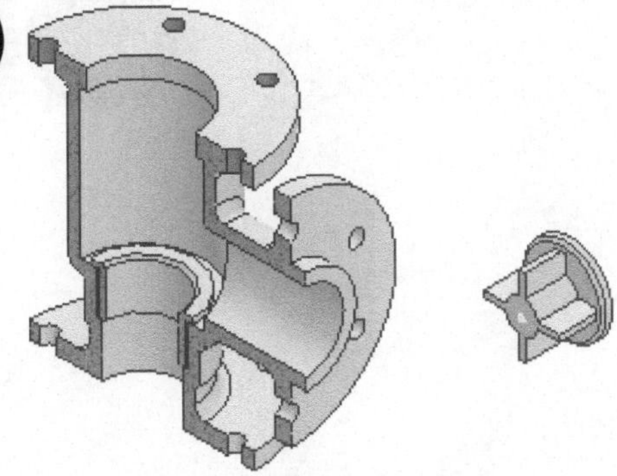

Note: You need to specify the placement of the third component on the back side of the section plane of the assembly. If you specify the placement of the component on the front side of the section plane then the placed component will also be sectioned by the section plane and it will not be visible or will be partially visible in the graphics area.

Now, you need to assemble the third component (**Valve**) by applying the required constraints.

2. Invoke the **Place Constraint** dialog box by clicking on the **Constraint** tool or pressing the **C** key.
3. Click on the **Insert** button in the **Type** area of the dialog box. You are prompted to select a geometry for applying the constraint.
4. Move the cursor over the circular edge of the third component (**Valve**), see Figure 11.173 and then click when the edge gets highlighted. You are prompted to select another geometry.

11.173

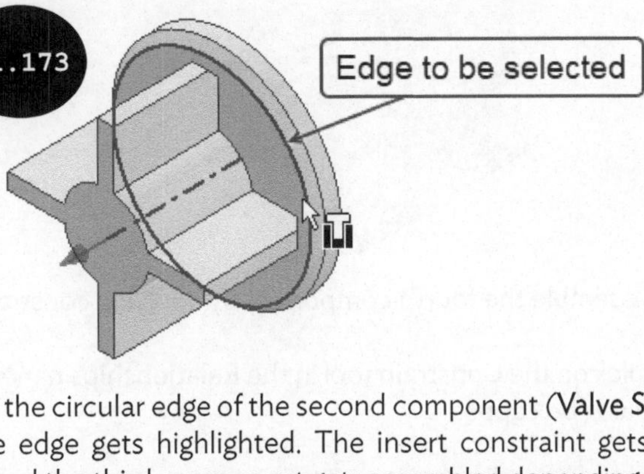

5. Move the cursor over the circular edge of the second component (**Valve Seat**) (see Figure 11.174). Next, click when the edge gets highlighted. The insert constraint gets applied between the selected geometries and the third component gets assembled depending upon the solution type selected in the **Solution** area of the dialog box. Note that all the degrees of freedom of the third component (**Valve**) get restricted except the rotational degree of freedom.

6. Ensure that the **Opposed** button is selected in the **Solution** area of the dialog box. Note that if the orientation of the **Valve** component does not appear similar to the one shown in the Figure 11.175, then you need to click on the **Aligned** button in the **Solution** area.

11.174

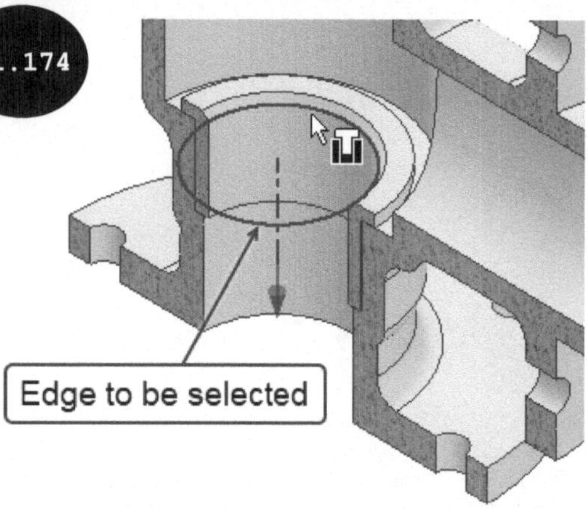

11.175

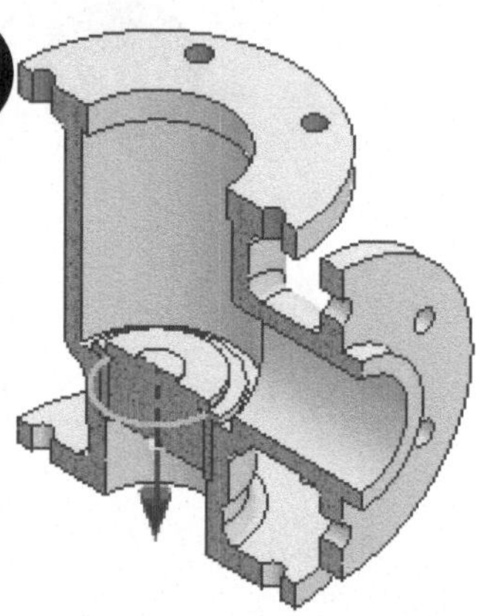

7. Click on the **OK** button in the dialog box. The insert constraint is applied between the selected geometries of the components.

Section 7: Inserting and Assembling the Fourth Component

1. Insert the fourth component (**Spindle**) of the assembly in the graphics area by using the **Place** tool, see Figure 11.176. Ensure that the orientation of the component is defined similarly to the one shown in Figure 11.176 before specifying its placement in the graphics area. Also, you need to specify the placement of the fourth component on the back side of the section plane of the assembly.

11.176

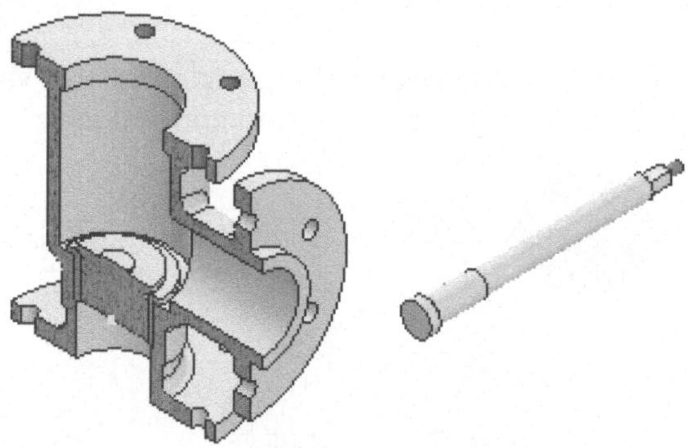

Now, you need to assemble the fourth component by applying constraints.

2. Press the **C** key or click on the **Constrain** tool in the **Relationships** panel of the **Assemble** tab. The **Place Constraint** dialog box appears.

3. Ensure that the **Mate** button is activated in the **Type** area of the dialog box.

4. Select the bottom planar face of the fourth component (**Spindle**) as the first geometry and then the top planar face of the third component (**Valve**) as the second geometry, see Figure 11.177. The mate constraint gets applied between the selected geometries of the components, refer to Figure 11.178.

11.177

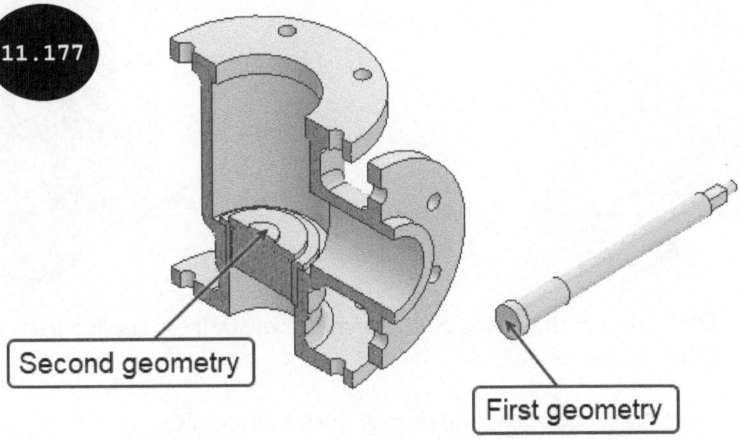

5. Ensure that the **Mate** button is selected in the **Solution** area of the dialog box. The orientation of the **Spindle** component appears similar to the one shown in Figure 11.178. Note that if the orientation of the **Spindle** component does not appear similar to the one shown in the figure then you need to click on the **Flush** button in the **Solution** area.

11.178

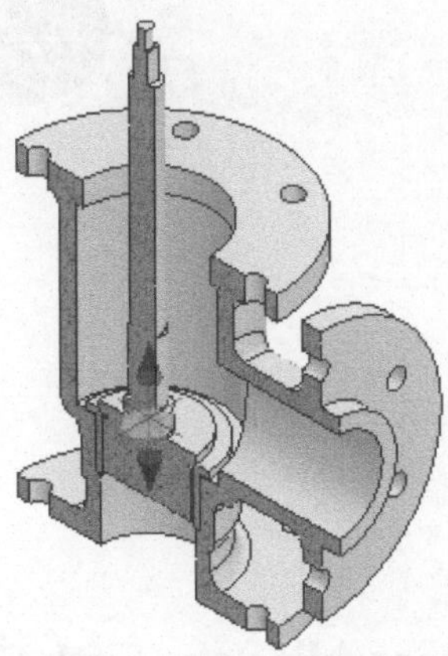

6. Click on the **Apply** button. The mate constraint gets applied and the **Place Constraint** dialog box is still available in the graphics area for applying constraints.

7. Select the circular face of the fourth component (**Spindle**) as the first geometry and then the circular face of the first component (**Body**) as the second geometry, see Figure 11.179. The mate constraint gets applied such that the axes of both the geometries become coincident with each other, see Figure 11.180.

11.179

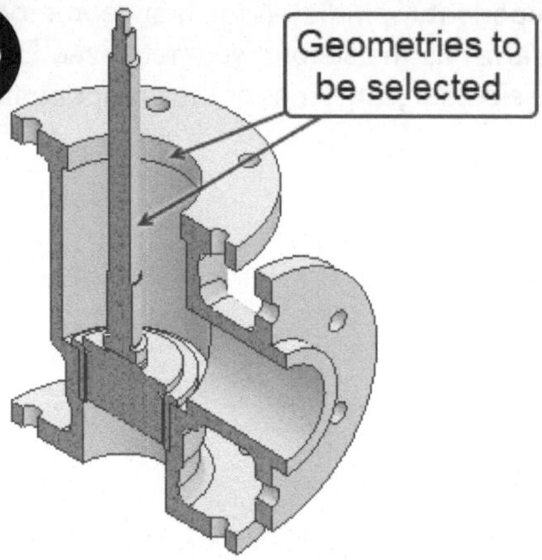

11.180

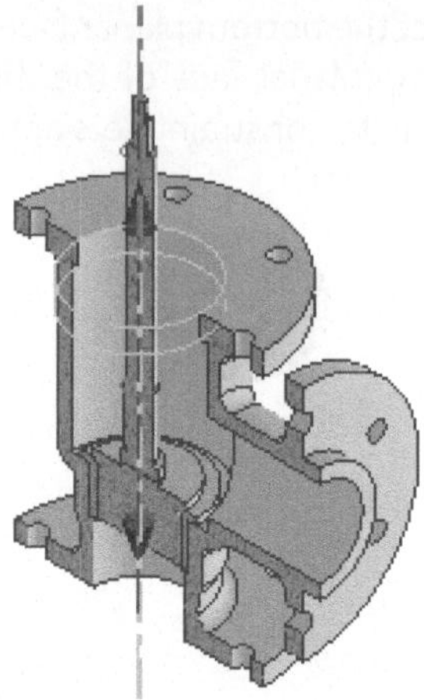

8. Click on the **OK** button in the dialog box. The mate constraint is applied between the selected geometries of the components.

   Now, you can end the section view and display the full assembly.

9. Click on the **View** tab in the **Ribbon** and then click on the **Delete Section View** tool in the **Section** flyout, see Figure 11.181. The section view ends and the assembly appears in the graphics area as shown in Figure 11.182.

11.181

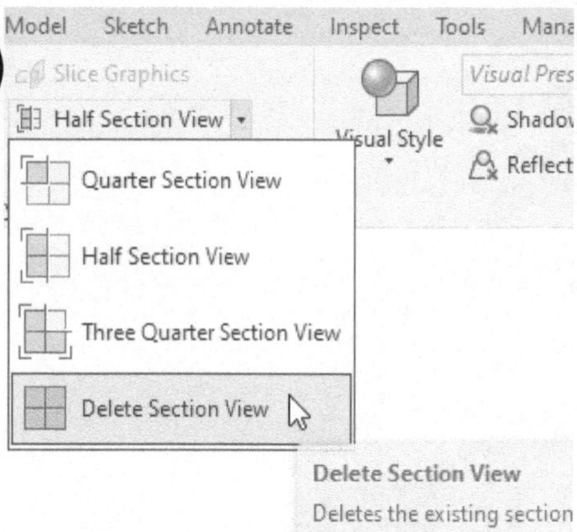

11.182

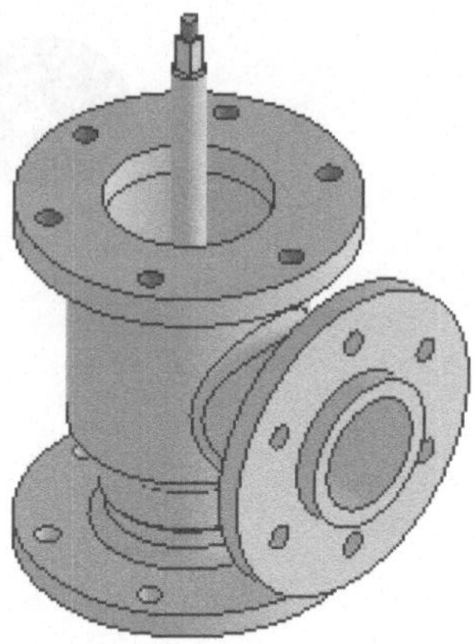

Section 8: Inserting and Assembling the Fifth Component

1. Insert the fifth component (**Cover**) of the assembly in the graphics area by using the **Place** tool, see Figure 11.183. Note that before defining the placement of the **Cover** component in the graphics area, you need to change its orientation such that its bottom planar face can be visible for applying a mate, see Figure 11.183.

11.183

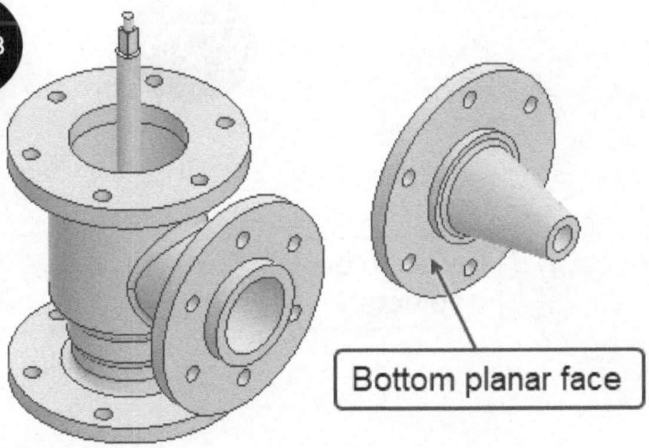

Now, you need to assemble the fifth component by applying constraints.

2. Press the **C** key or click on the **Constrain** tool in the **Relationships** panel of the **Assemble** tab. The **Place Constraint** dialog box appears.

3. Ensure that the **Mate** button is activated in the **Type** area of the dialog box.

4. Select the bottom planar face of the fifth component (**Cover**) and then the top planar face of the first component (**Body**) as the geometries, see Figure 11.184. The mate constraint gets applied such that both the geometries become coincident with each other, see Figure 11.185.

11.184

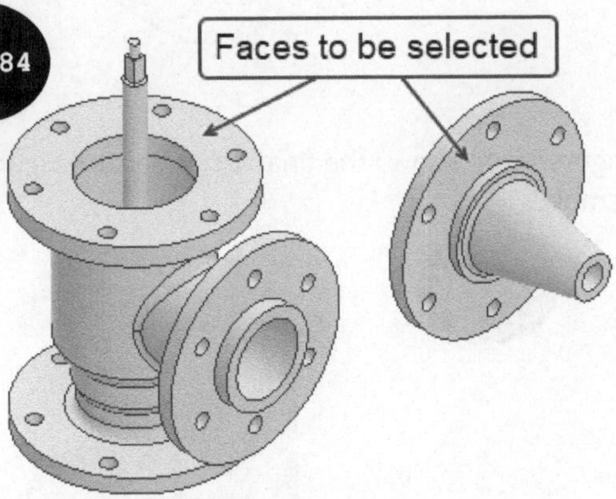

11.185

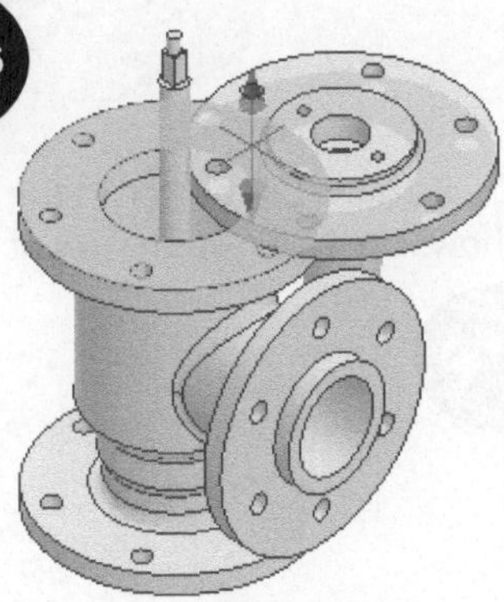

5. Click on the **Apply** button in the dialog box. The mate constraint gets applied and the dialog box is still available in the graphics area for applying constraints.

6. Select the circular face of a hole of the fifth component (**Cover**) and the circular face of a hole of the first component (**Body**) as the geometries, see Figure 11.186. The mate constraint gets applied such that the axes of both the geometries become coincident to each other, see Figure 11.187.

11.186

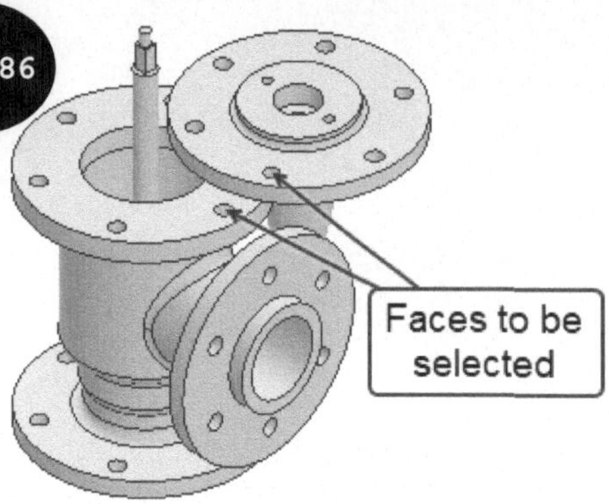

11.187

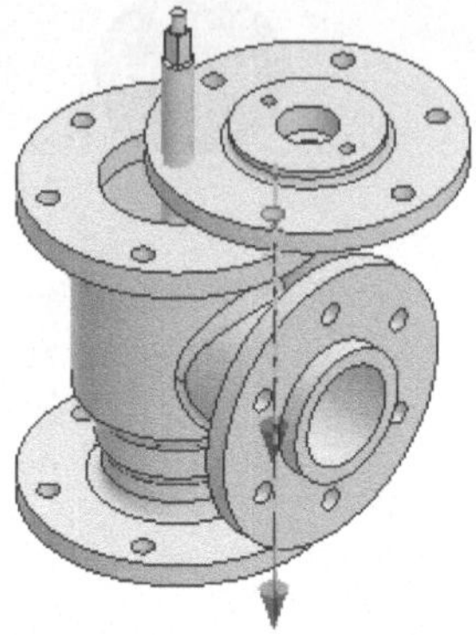

7. Click on the **Apply** button in the dialog box and then apply the mate constraint between another set of holes of the **Cover** and **Body** components, see Figures 11.188 and 11.189.

11.188

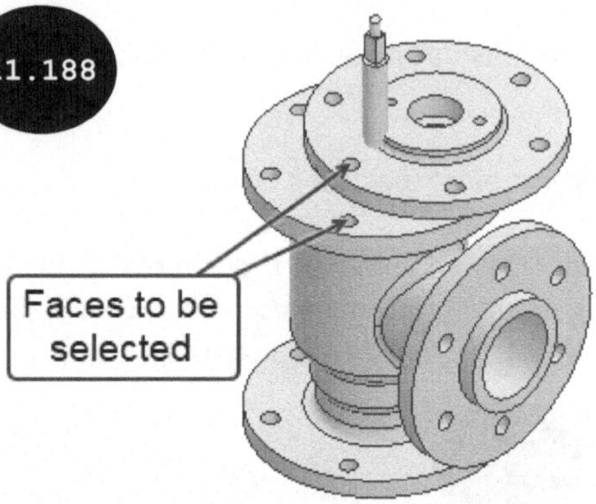

11.189

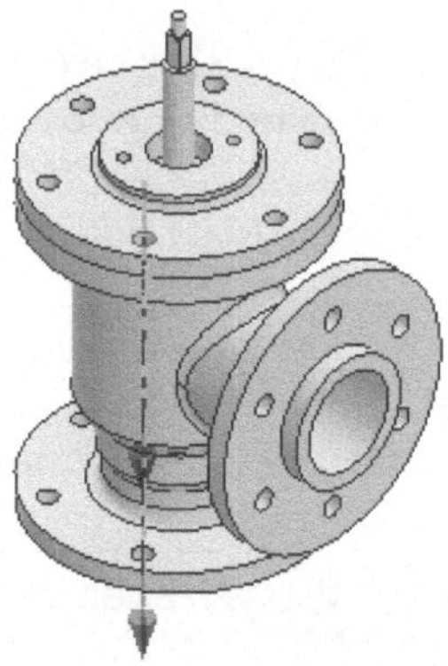

8. Click on the **OK** button in the dialog box. Figure 11.190 shows the final assembly and Figure 11.191 shows the half section view of the final assembly.

11.190

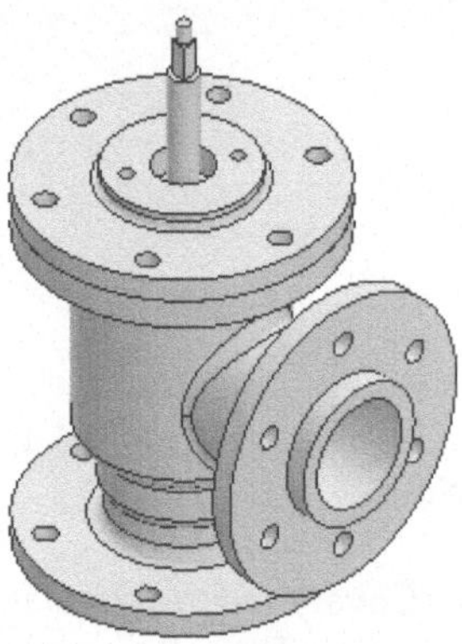

11.191

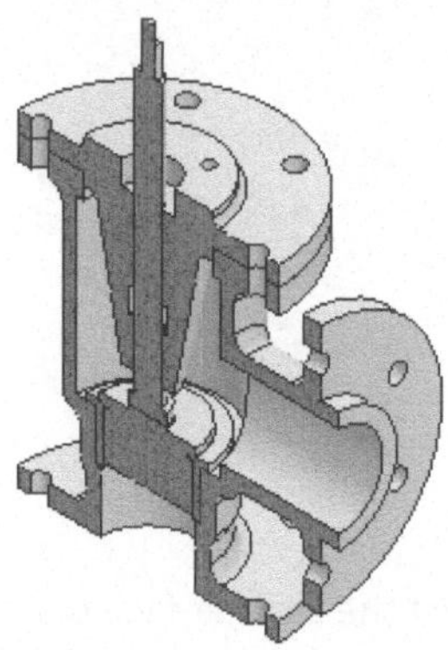

Section 9: Saving the Model

1. Click on the **Save** tool in the **Quick Access Toolbar** toolbar. The **Save As** dialog box appears.

2. Browse to **Autodesk Inventor** > **Chapter 11** > **Tutorial 2** folder in the local drive of your system.

3. Enter **Tutorial 2** in the **File name** field of the dialog box and then click on the **Save** button. The model is saved in the specified location (>:\Autodesk Inventor\Chapter 11\Tutorial 2).

Hands-on Test Drive 1

Create an assembly, as shown in Figure 11.192. The exploded view of the assembly is shown in Figure 11.193 for your reference only. Different views and dimensions of individual components of the assembly are shown in Figures 11.194 through 11.201. You can also download all components of the assembly by logging on to CADArtifex website (www.cadartifex.com). All dimensions are in mm.

11.192

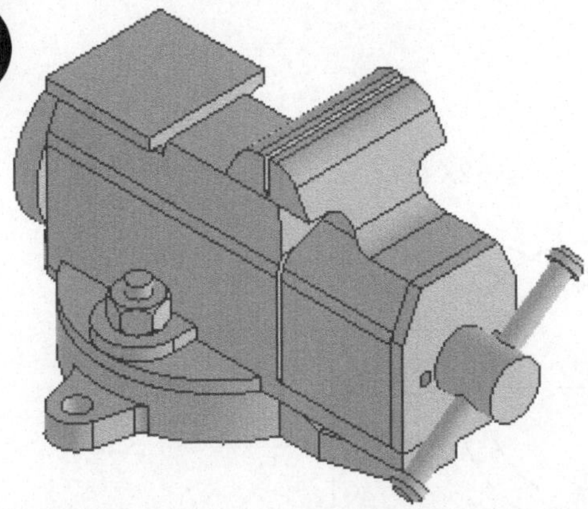

11.193

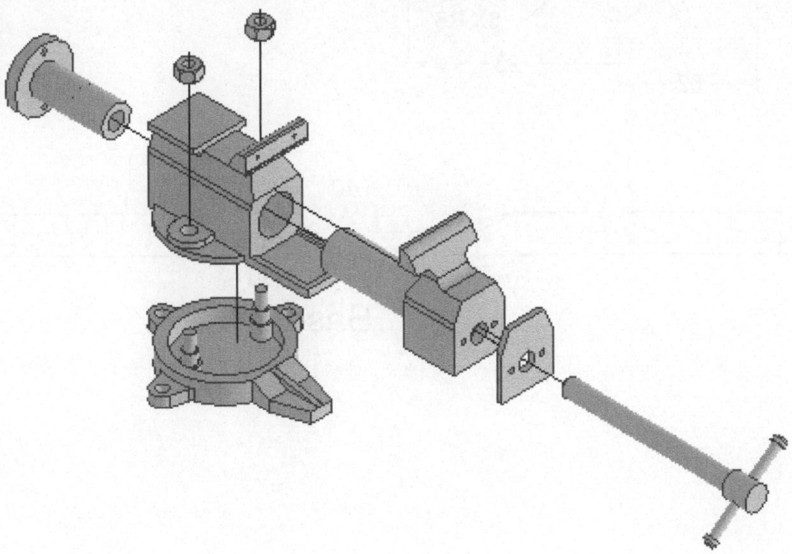

11.194

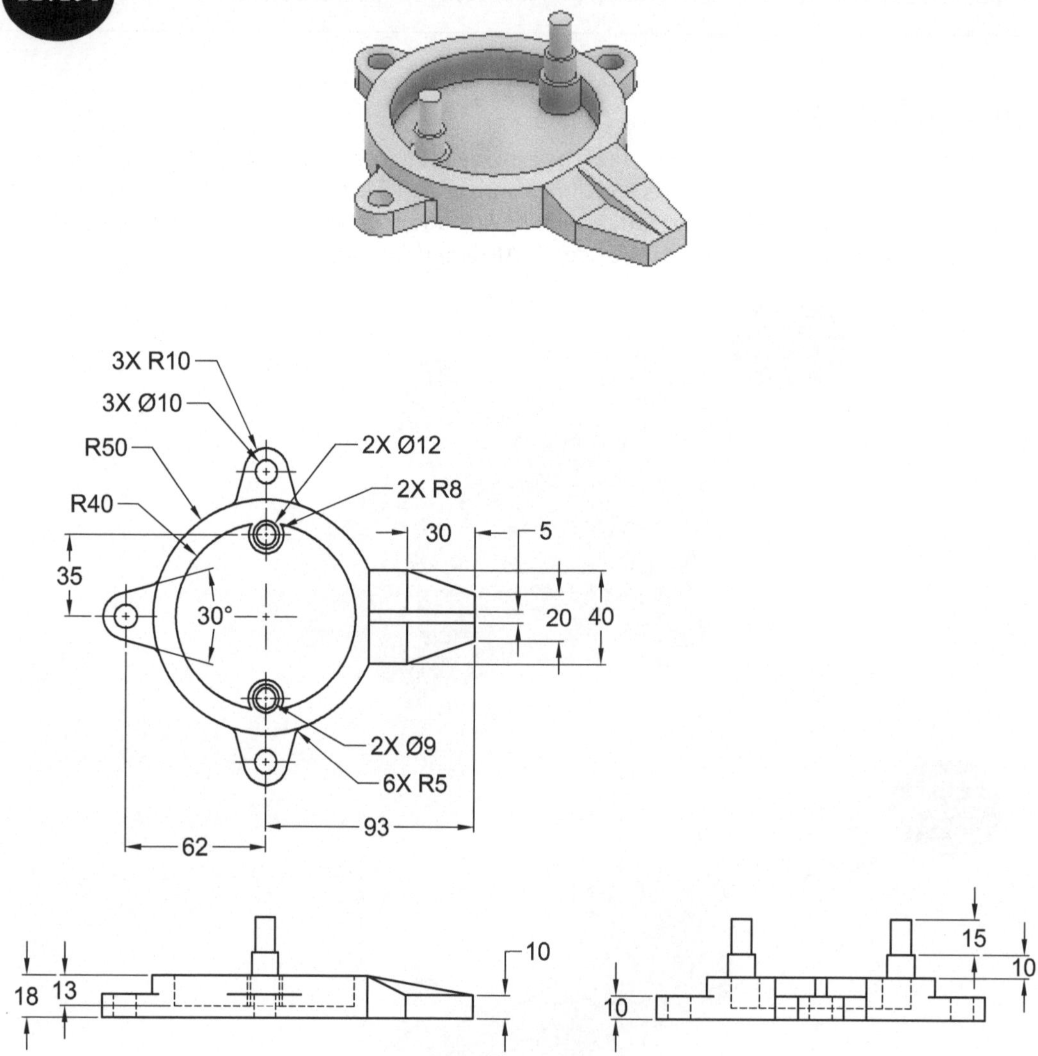
3X R10
3X Ø10
R50
2X Ø12
2X R8
R40
30
5
35
30°
20
40
2X Ø9
6X R5
93
62
10
18
13
15
10
10

Base

11.195

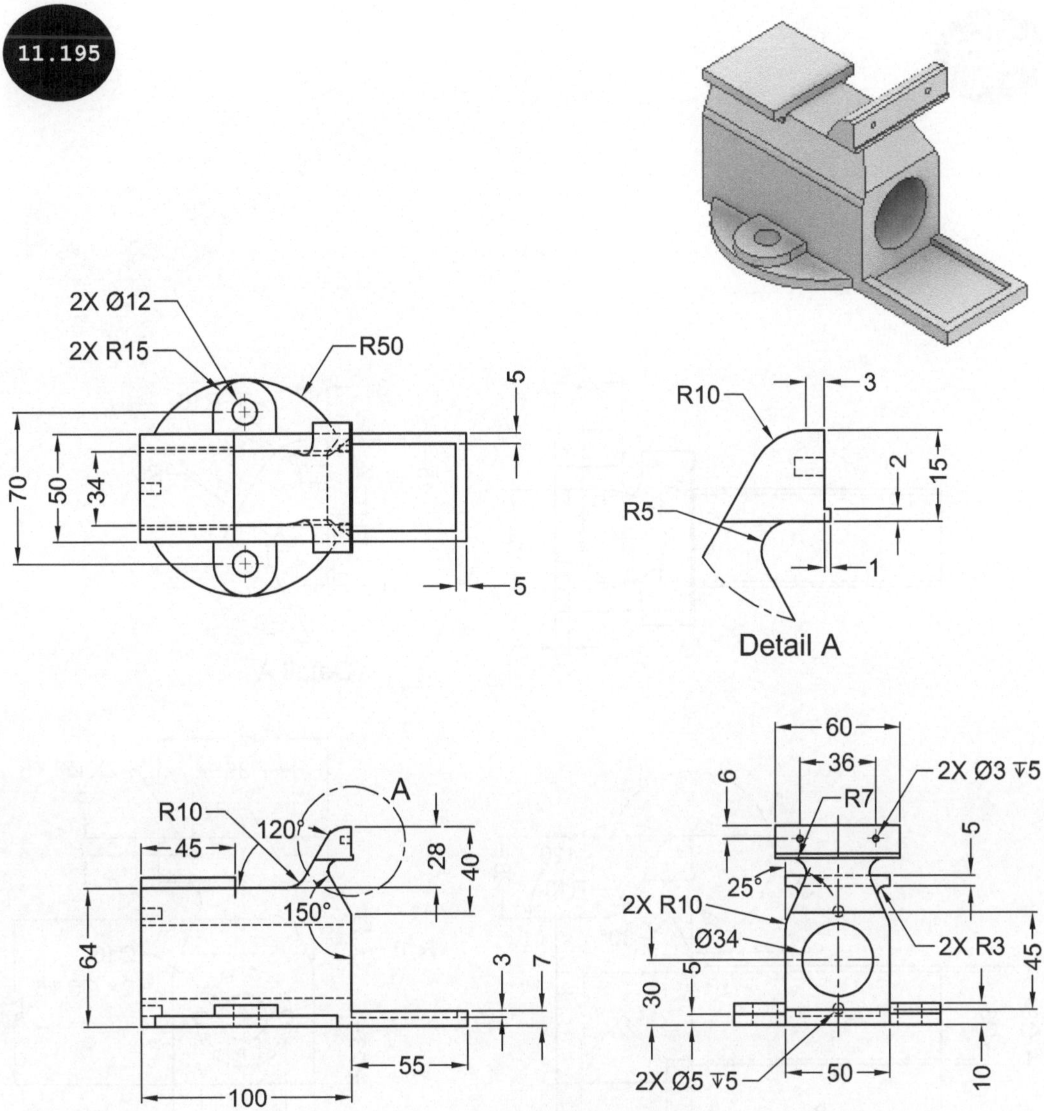

Fixed Jaw

11.196

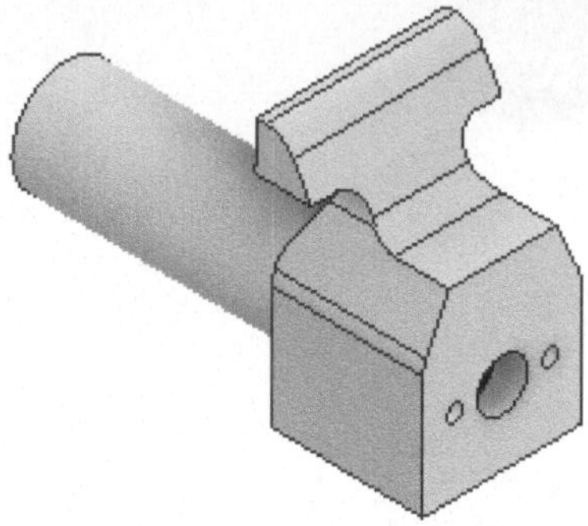

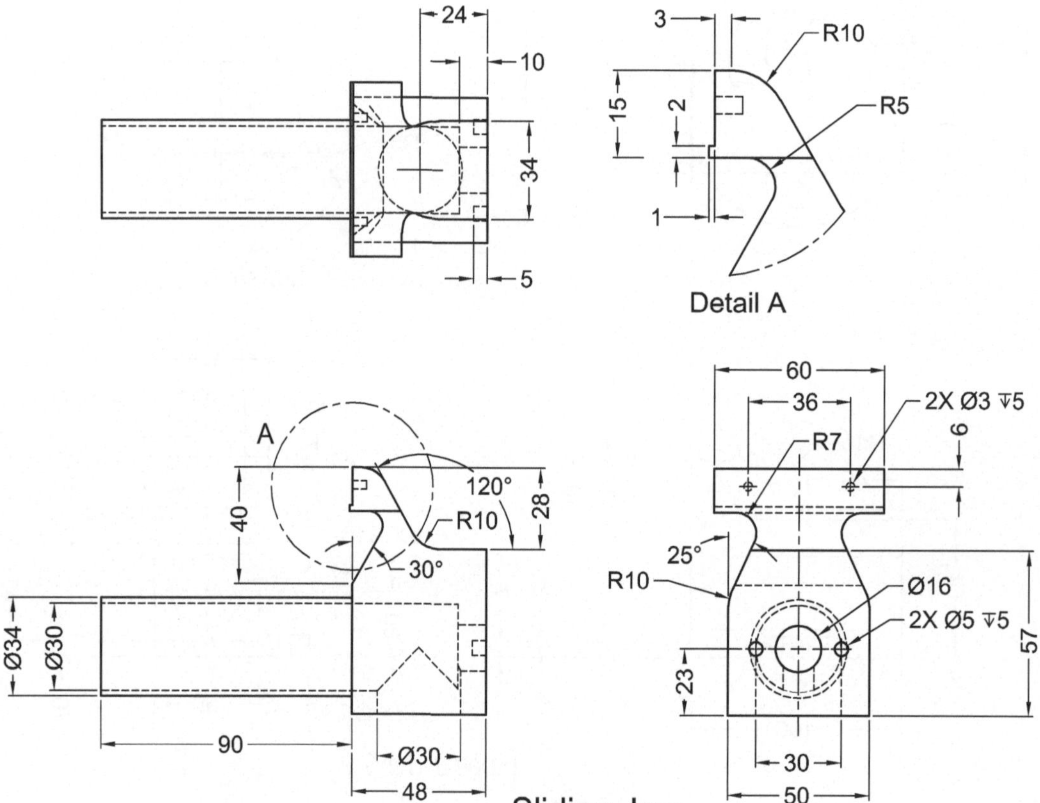

Sliding Jaw

11.197

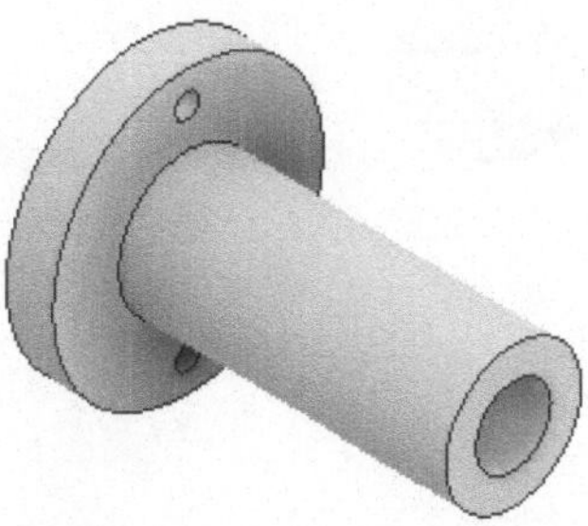

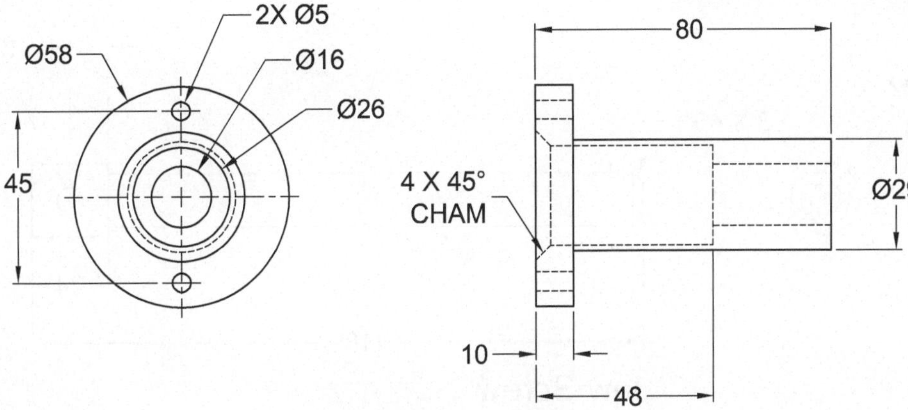

Vice Nut

11.198

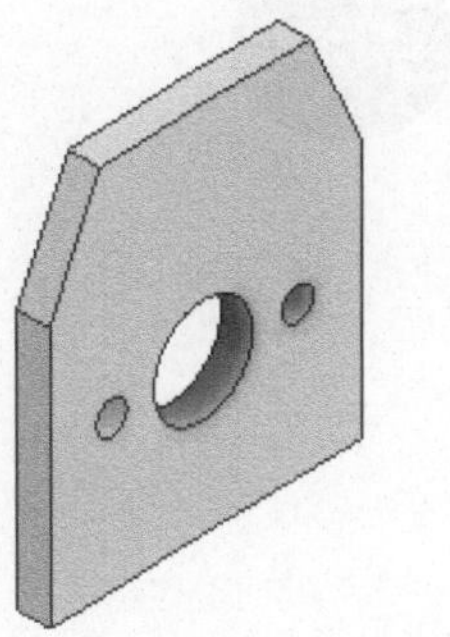

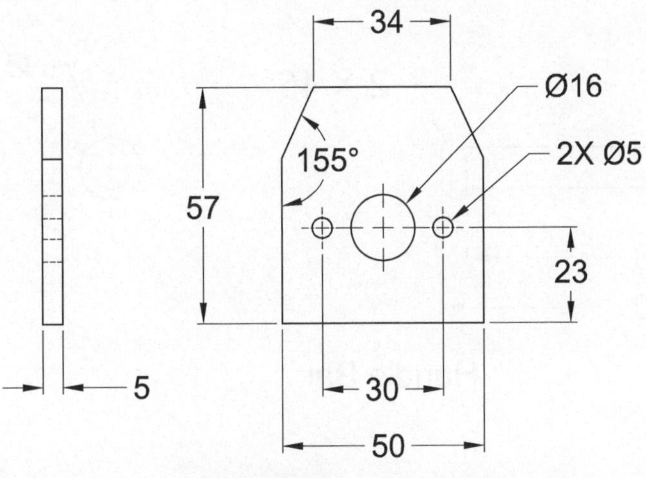

Jaw Plate

11.199

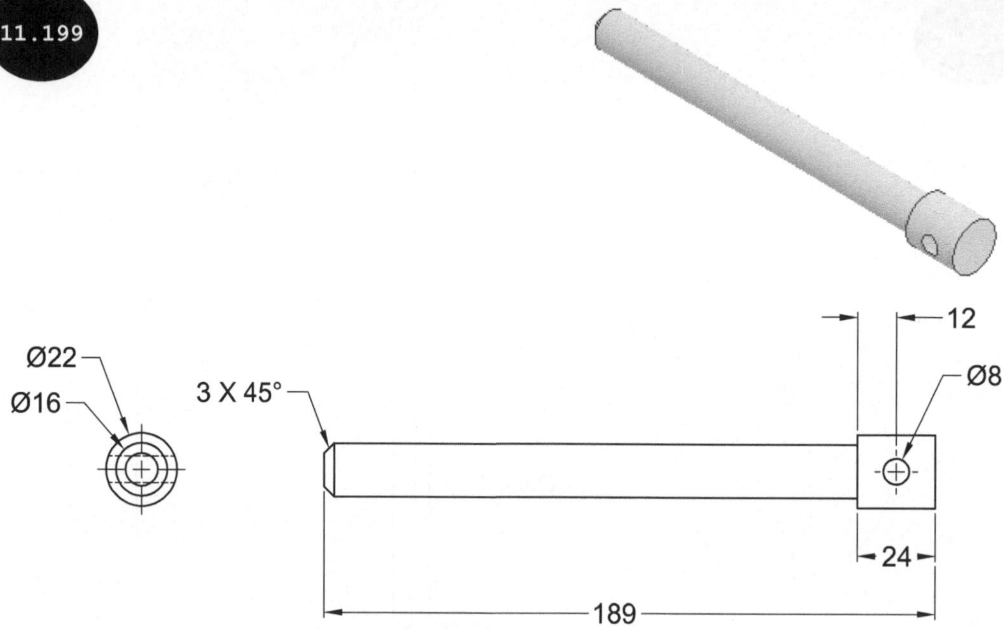

Jaw Screw

11.200

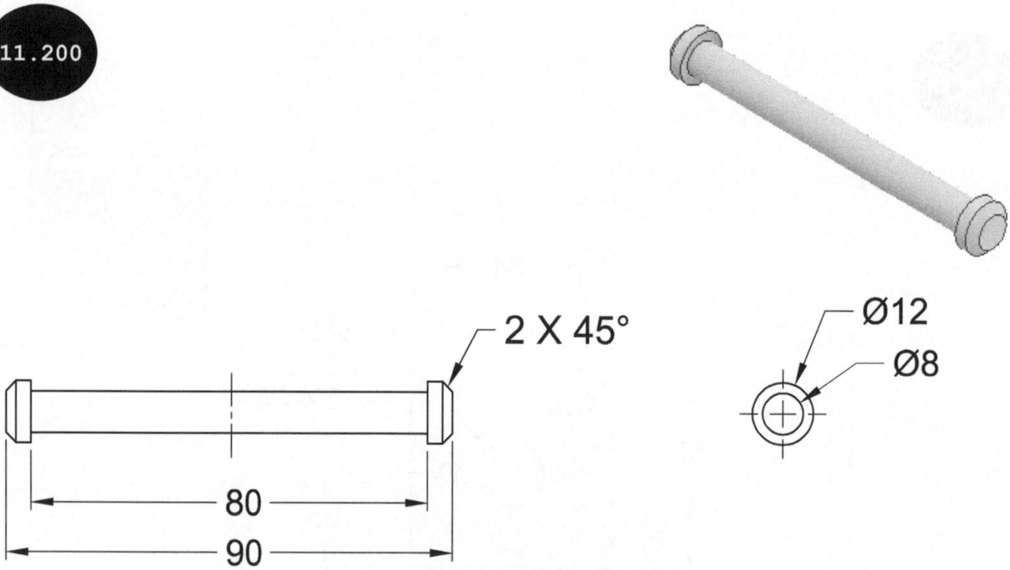

Handle Bar

11.201

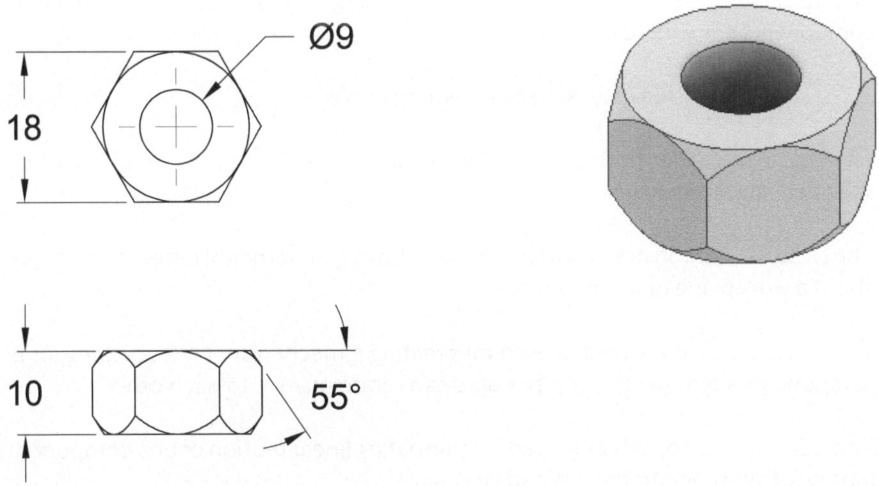

Nut

Summary

In this chapter, you have learned about creating assemblies by using the bottom-up assembly approach. In this approach, you first create all components in the Part modeling environment one by one and then assemble by applying required constraints and joints in the Assembly environment. The chapter discussed in detail about various types of constraints and joints. It also discussed methods for editing and deleting constraints and joints, in addition to moving and rotating individual components of an assembly.

Questions

Complete and verify the following sentences:

- In Autodesk Inventor, you can create assemblies by using the _________ and _________ approaches.
- Autodesk Inventor has a _________ association between all its environments. As a result, if any change or modification is made to a component in the Part modeling environment, the same change automatically reflects in the Assembly environment as well as in the Drawing environment, and vice-versa.
- The _________ tool is used for inserting a component into the Assembly environment.
- In Autodesk Inventor, you can assemble the components of an assembly by applying the required _________ and _________ .
- A free component within the Assembly environment has _________ degrees of freedom.

- The _________ constraint is used for making the selected geometries of two different components coincident with each other.
- _________ is the file extension of an assembly file.
- The _________ constraint is used for restricting geometries of two different components at a specified angular distance.
- The _________ constraint is used for making two geometries of different components symmetric about a work plane or a planar face.
- The _________ constraint is used for creating a mechanism (gear, bearing, or pulley) between components such that the components can rotate relative to each other.
- The _________ constraint is used for translating linear motion of one component into rotational motion of another component and vice versa.
- The _________ joint allows the component to rotate about an axis by removing all degrees of freedom except one rotational degree of freedom.
- The _________ joint is used for translating as well as rotating the component by removing all degrees of freedom except one translational and one rotational.
- The _________ joint is used for rotating the component about all the three rotational axes.
- You can only move the individual components of an assembly along its free degrees of freedom. (True/False)
- A grounded component does not allow any translational or rotational movement and all its degrees of freedom are fixed. (True/False)
- In Autodesk Inventor, you can define the maximum and minimum distance limits between two selected geometries of the components such that the components can move or translate within the specified distance limit. (True/False)
- You cannot change the orientation of a component before defining its placement in the Assembly environment. (True/False)

CHAPTER

12

Working with Assemblies - II

In this chapter, the following topics will be discussed:

- Creating an Assembly by using the Top-down Approach
- Editing Assembly Components
- Patterning Assembly Components
- Mirroring Components of an Assembly
- Copying Components of an Assembly
- Creating Bill of Material (BOM) of an Assembly

In the previous chapter, you have learned about creating assemblies by using the Bottom-up Assembly Approach. You have also learned about various types of constraints, joints, and their application to assemble components with respect to each other. In this chapter, you will learn about creating assemblies by using the Top-down Assembly Approach, editing assembly components, patterning, mirroring, copying, and creating a Bill of Material (BOM) for an assembly.

Creating an Assembly by using the Top-down Approach

In the Top-down Assembly Approach, all components of an assembly are created within the Assembly environment itself by using the **Create** tool. It works by taking reference from the existing components. By using this approach, you can create a concept-based design, where new components of an assembly can be created by taking reference from the existing components. The method for creating an assembly by using the Top-down Assembly Approach is discussed below:

1. Invoke the Assembly environment by double-clicking on the **Standard (mm).iam** template in the **Create New File** dialog box that appears on clicking the **New** tool in the **Quick Access Toolbar**, see Figure 12.1.

12.1

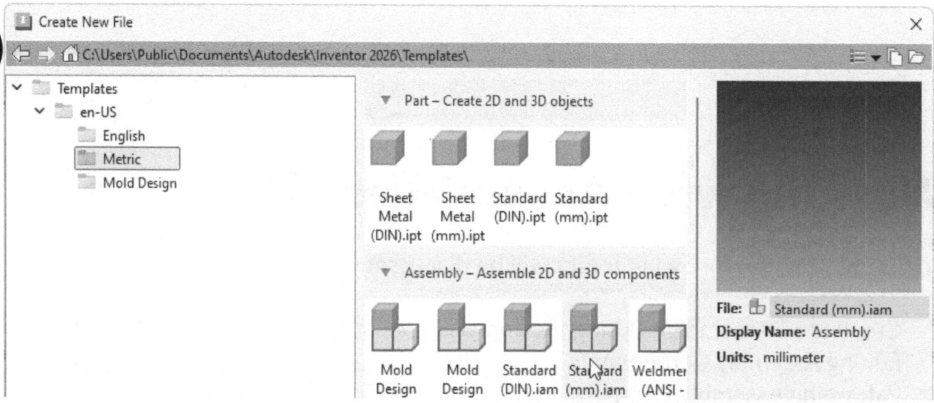

2. Click on the **Create** tool in the **Component** panel of the **Assemble** tab in the **Ribbon**, see Figure 12.2. The **Create In-Place Component** dialog box appears, see Figure 12.3. Alternatively, press the **N** key to invoke the **Create In-Place Component** dialog box. The options in this dialog box are discussed next.

12.2

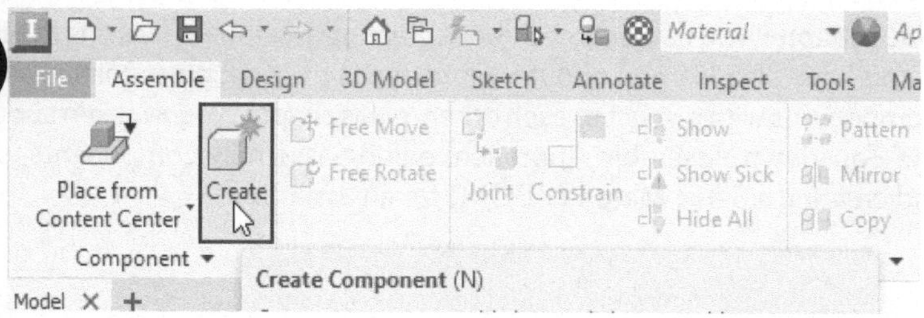

12.3

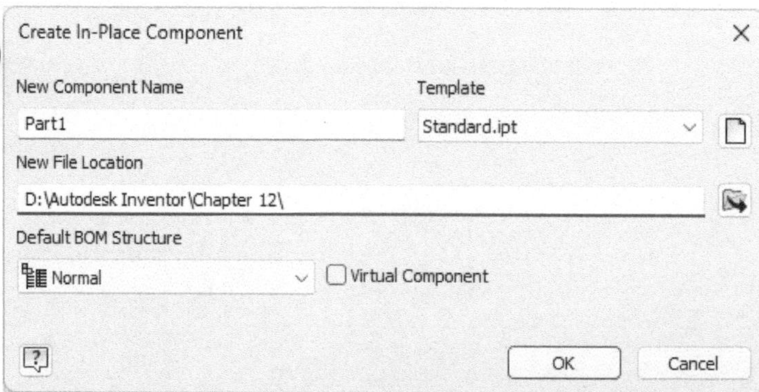

New Component Name: The **New Component Name** field in the dialog box is used for specifying a name for the component to be created.

Template: The **Template** drop-down list displays a list of four default templates for creating the new file. You can select the **Standard.ipt**, **Standard.iam**, **Sheet Metal.ipt**, or **Weldment.iam** template from this drop-down list for creating a new file. Note that depending upon the template selected, the new file will be created within the Assembly environment. For example, on selecting the **Standard.ipt** template, a solid part file gets created, whereas on selecting the **Standard.iam** template, an assembly file gets created within the Assembly environment. You can also click on the **Browse Templates** button available next to the **Template** drop-down list and then select the required template from the **Open Template** dialog box that appears. The **Open Template** dialog box displays all the available templates.

New File Location: The **New File Location** field is used for specifying the location for saving the new file. You can also click on the **Browse to New File Location** button available next to this field and then browse to the required location for saving the new file using the **Save As** dialog box that appears. Note that all the components of an assembly should be saved within the same directory of the assembly file.

Default BOM Structure: The **Default BOM Structure** drop-down list is used for specifying the default BOM structure for the new file.

Virtual Component: On selecting the **Virtual Component** check box, you can create a virtual component within the Assembly environment. A virtual component is a component that does not require any modeling of geometry and template files.

Constrain sketch plane to selected face or plane: By default, the **Constrain sketch plane to selected face or plane** check box is selected in the dialog box. As a result, a mate constraint gets applied between the selected sketching plane and the component face, by default. Note that this check box is not available in the dialog box while creating the first component in the Assembly environment.

3. Specify a name for the component to be created or accept the default name in the **New Component Name** field of the **Create In-Place Component** dialog box.

4. Click on the **Browse Templates** button available next to the **Template** drop-down list and then click on the **Metric** tab in the **Open Template** dialog box that appears. All the metric templates appear in the dialog box.

5. Select the **Standard (mm).ipt** template in the **Metric** tab of the dialog box for creating a solid component in the metric template within the Assembly environment, see Figure 12.4. Next, click on the **OK** button in the dialog box. Note that to create a new component in the English template, you need to select the **Standard (in).ipt** template in the **English** tab of the dialog box.

12.4

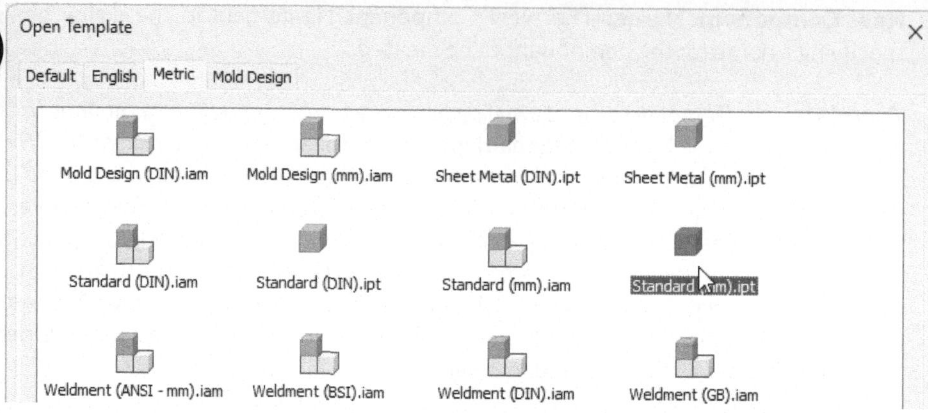

After selecting the required template, you need to specify a location for saving the new file.

6. Click on the **Browse to New File Location** button available next to the **New File Location** field in the dialog box. The **Save As** dialog box appears.

7. Browse to the location where the component is to be saved in the local drive of your system and then click on the **Save** button in the **Save As** dialog box.

8. Click on the **OK** button in the **Create In-Place Component** dialog box. You are prompted to select a sketch plane for the component.

9. Expand the **Origin** node of the assembly in the **Browser** and then click on a plane (**YZ Plane**, **XZ Plane**, or **XY Plane**) as the XY Plane (sketch plane) of the component to define its position. The part modeling environment gets invoked within the Assembly environment and an empty component is added to the **Browser**, see Figure 12.5. Also, the origin of the component is defined as the origin of the assembly. Note that the newly added component becomes an active component of the assembly for creating its features.

12.5

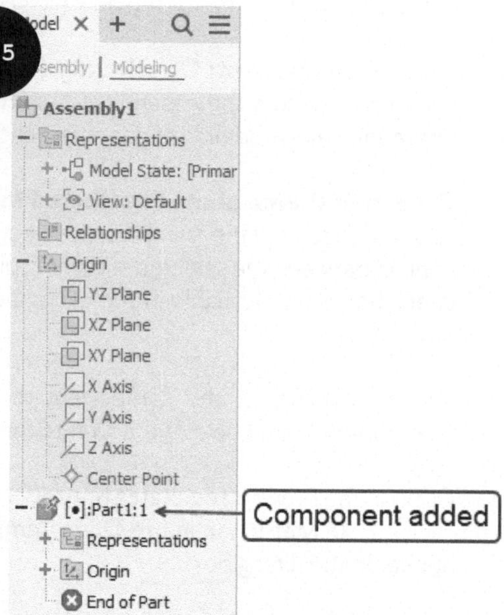

Note: Instead of selecting a plane, you can also click anywhere in the graphics area to define the position of the component. By doing so, the part modeling environment gets invoked and an empty component gets added such that its origin is defined at the specified point in the graphics area.

Now, you can add features to the newly added empty component.

10. Click on the **Start 2D Sketch** tool in the **Sketch** panel (see Figure 12.6) or press the S key. The three default planes of the component appear in the graphics area. Also, you are prompted to select a plane for creating a sketch of the base feature.

12.6

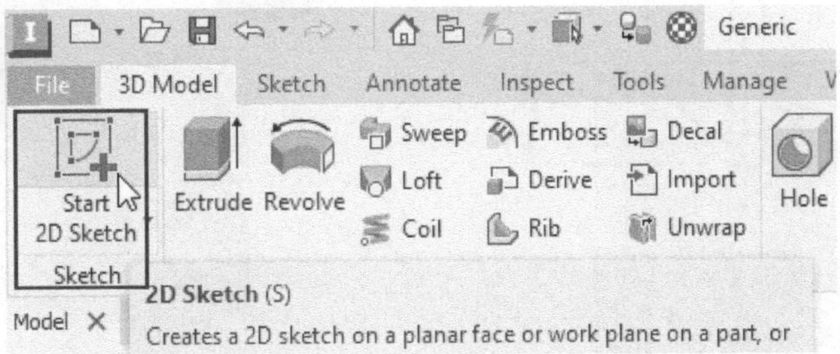

11. Click on the required plane in the graphics area. The Sketching environment gets invoked for creating the base feature of the component.

12. Draw the sketch of the base feature by using the sketching tools, refer to Figure 12.7.

After creating the sketch, you need to convert it into a solid feature by using solid modeling tools.

13. Click on the **3D Model** tab in the **Ribbon** and then convert the sketch into a solid feature by using solid modeling tools such as **Extrude**, **Revolve**, or **Sweep**, refer to Figure 12.8. In this figure, the sketch is extruded to a depth of 100 mm, symmetrical about the sketching plane by using the **Extrude** tool.

12.7

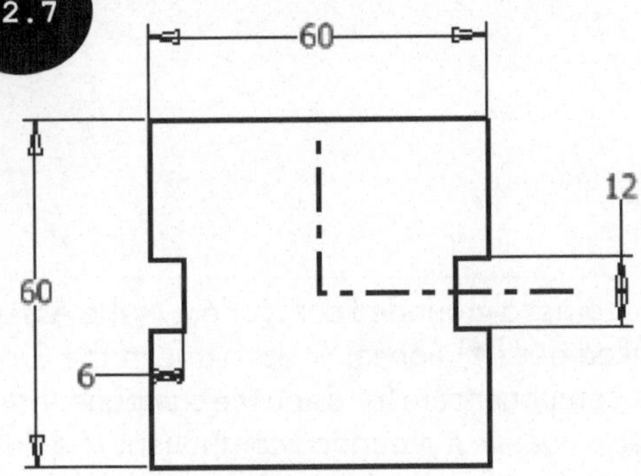

12.8

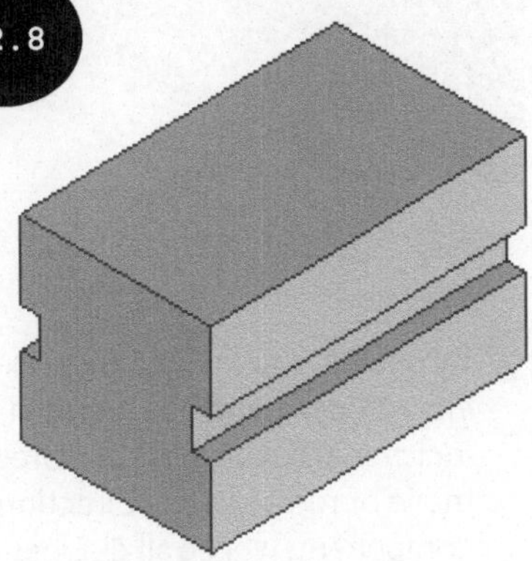

Now, you need to create the second feature of the component.

14. Invoke the Sketching environment again by selecting a planar face or a plane as the sketching plane for creating the second feature of the component.

15. Create a sketch of the second feature, refer to Figure 12.9. In this figure, the sketch is created on the front planar face of the base feature.

16. Click on the **3D Model** tab and then convert the sketch into a feature by using a solid modeling tool such as **Extrude**, **Revolve**, or **Sweep**, refer to Figure 12.10. In Figure 12.10, the extruded cut feature is created by extruding the sketch through the entire depth of the base feature.

12.9

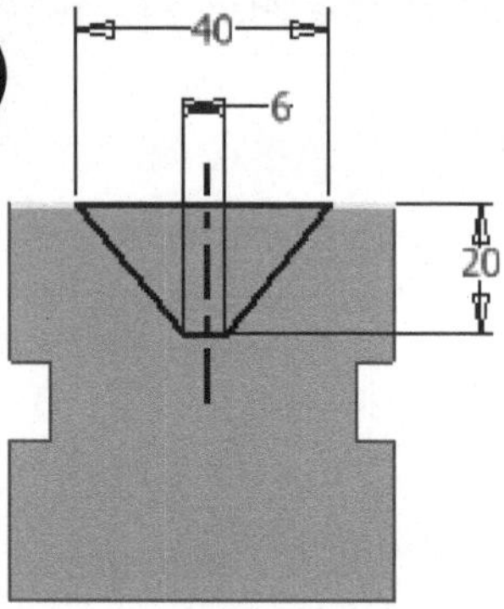

12.10

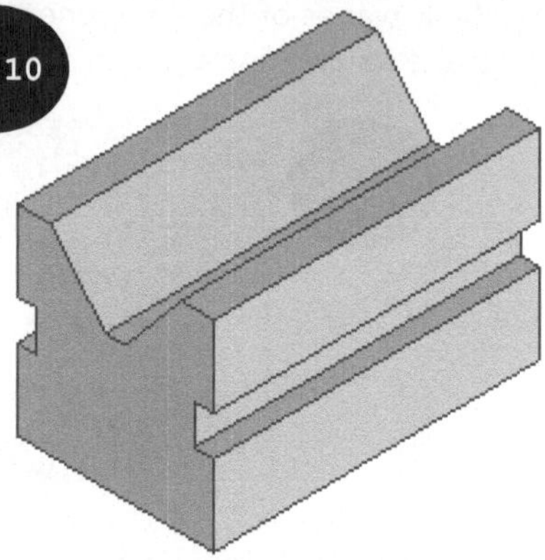

17. Similarly, you can create the remaining features of the component one by one, refer to Figure 12.11. In this figure, a mirror feature is created.

18. After creating all the features of the component, click on the **Return** tool in the **Return** panel of the **Ribbon**, see Figure 12.12. The first component is created and the Assembly environment is invoked.

12.11

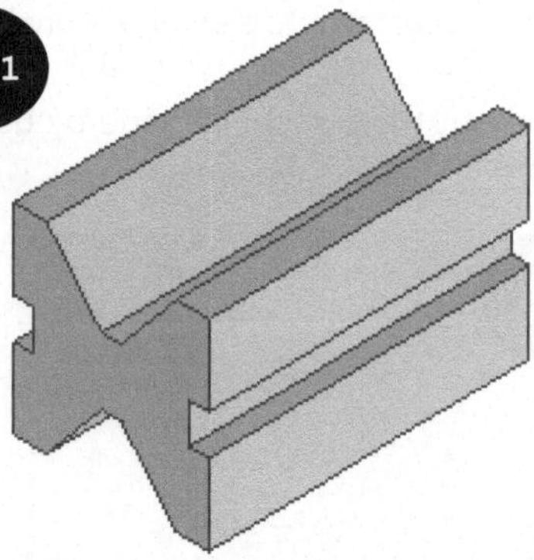

12.12

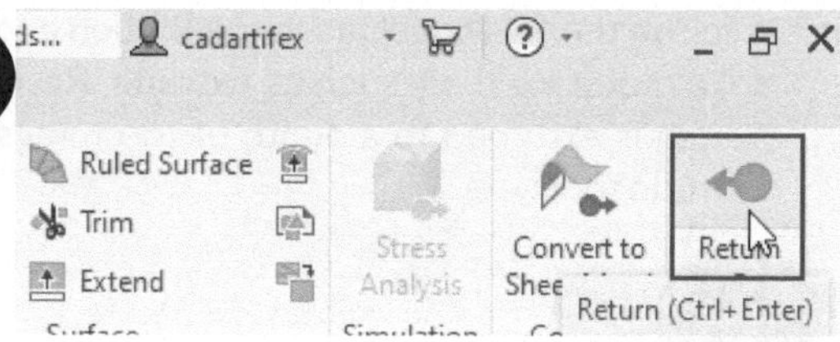

Note: By default, the first created component becomes a grounded component in the Assembly environment and the pushpin icon and filled dot [•] appear on its name in the **Browser** indicating that all degrees of freedom of the component are fixed and the component cannot move or rotate in any direction. You can also change a grounded component to a floating component, whose all degrees of freedom are free. For doing so, right-click on the name of a component in the **Browser** and then click on the **Grounded** option in the shortcut menu that appears. Note that a tick-mark on the **Grounded** option in the shortcut menu indicates that the current state of the component is grounded.

After creating the first component, you can create the second component of the assembly.

19. Press the N key or click on the **Create** tool in the **Component** panel of the **Assemble** tab. The **Create In-Place Component** dialog box appears, see Figure 12.13.

12.13

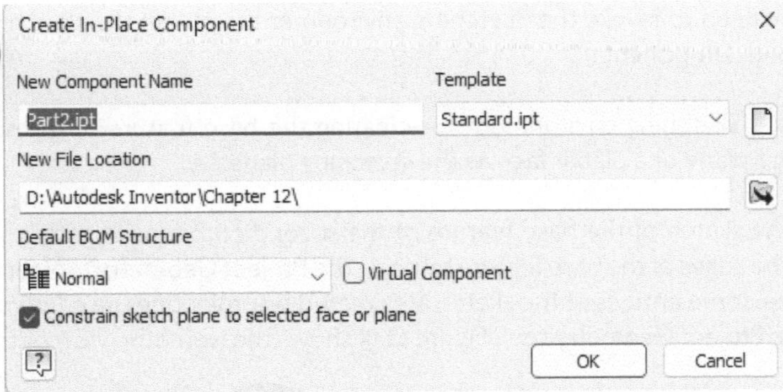

20. Specify a name for the second component or accept the default name in the **New Component Name** field of the **Create In-Place Component** dialog box.

21. Click on the **Browse Templates** button available next to the **Template** drop-down list and then click on the **Metric** tab in the **Open Template** dialog box that appears. All the metric templates appear in the dialog box.

22. Select the **Standard (mm).ipt** template in the **Metric** tab of the dialog box for creating a solid component in the metric template and then click on the **OK** button in the dialog box. Note that to create a new component in the English template, you need to select the **Standard (in).ipt** template in the **English** tab of the dialog box.

    After selecting the required template, you need to specify the location for saving the new file.

23. Ensure that the location for saving the second component is the same as the first component in the **New File Location** field of the dialog box.

Tip: All the components of an assembly as well as the assembly file should be saved within the same directory.

24. Ensure that the **Constrain sketch plane to selected face or plane** check box is selected in the dialog box for applying the mate constraint between the sketch plane and the component being created.

25. Click on the **OK** button in the **Create In-Place Component** dialog box. You are prompted to select a sketch plane for the component.

26. Select a plane or a planar face as the sketch plane to define the position of the component. The Part modeling environment gets invoked within the Assembly environment for creating the features of the second component. Also, the first component becomes transparent so that you can easily create the second component and take reference from the first component while creating it.

Now, you need to invoke the Sketching environment to create the sketch of the base feature of the second component.

27. Invoke the Sketching environment for creating the base feature of the second component by selecting a plane or a planar face as the sketching plane.

28. Create the sketch of the base feature of the second component, refer to Figure 12.14. You can project the edges of the base feature by using the **Project Geometry** tool for creating the sketch. In this figure, some entities of the sketch are created by projecting the edges of the first component using the **Project Geometry** tool. Figure 12.15 shows the isometric view of the model.

12.14

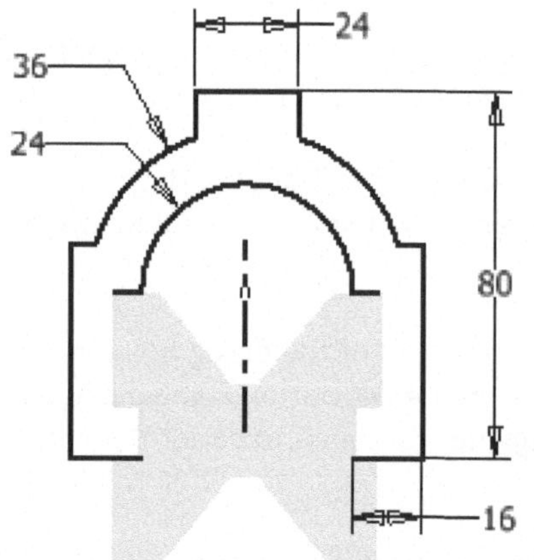

12.15

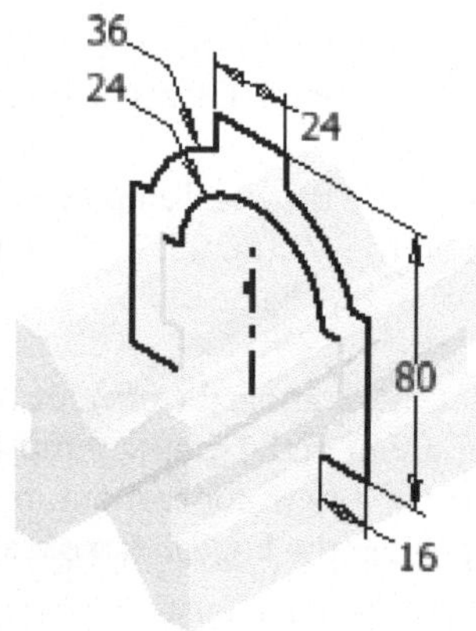

29. Convert the sketch into a feature by using a solid modeling tool such as **Extrude**, **Revolve**, or **Sweep** of the **3D Model** tab, refer to Figure 12.16. In this figure, the sketch is extruded to a depth of 20 mm, symmetrical about the sketching plane by using the **Extrude** tool.
Now, you need to create the second feature of the component.

12.16

30. Invoke the Sketching environment again by selecting a planar face or a plane as the sketching plane for creating the second feature of the component.

31. Create the sketch of the second feature, refer to Figure 12.17. In this figure, the sketch (a circle of diameter 12 mm) is created on the top planar face of the base feature.

32. Click on the **3D Model** tab and then convert the sketch into a feature by using solid modeling tools such as **Extrude**, **Revolve**, or **Sweep**, refer to Figure 12.18. In Figure 12.18, the extruded cut feature is created by extruding the sketch through the entire depth of the base feature.

12.17

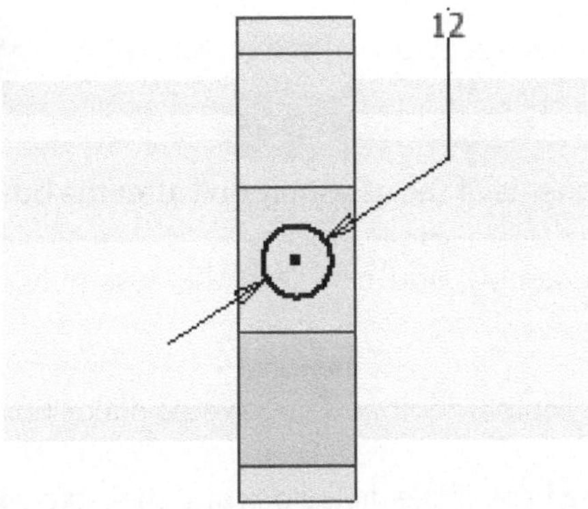

12.18

33. Similarly, you can create the remaining features of the component one by one.

34. After creating all the features of the second component, click on the **Return** tool in the **Return** panel of the **Ribbon**, see Figure 12.19. The second component is created and the Assembly environment is invoked. Also, a mate constraint is applied between the component and the sketching plane. In the Assembly environment, all the components of the assembly appear shaded, refer to Figure 12.20.

12.19

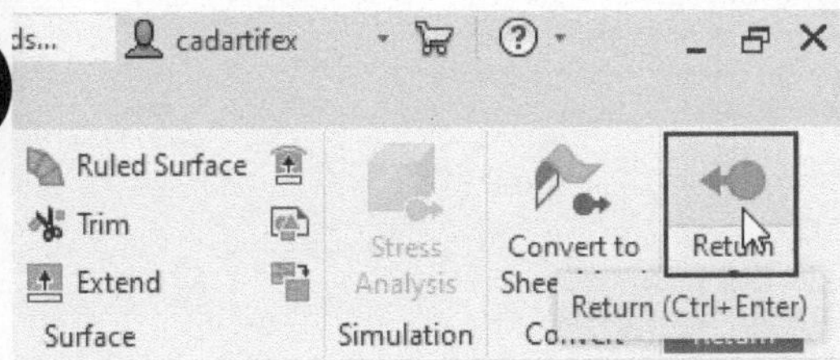

12.20

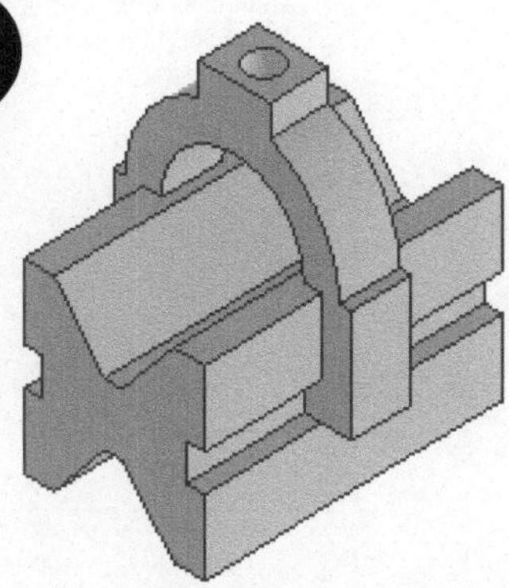

Note: By default, the component becomes an adaptive component if it is created by taking reference (projecting edges) from an existing component of the assembly. An adaptive component is driven by its associative component. Also, all of its degrees of freedom are fixed. The sign on a part in the **Browser** indicates that it is an adaptive component. To convert an adaptive component to a non-adaptive component, right-click on it in the **Browser** and then click on the **Adaptive** option in the shortcut menu that appears.

After creating the second component, you can apply the required constraints or joints to assemble the second component with the first component of the assembly, if the component is non-adaptive.

35. Apply the required constraints or joints to assemble the second component with the first component by using the **Constrain** or **Joint** tool, if needed.

Note: The method for applying constraints and joints between the components of an assembly is the same as discussed in the previous chapter.

36. Similarly, you can create the remaining components of the assembly one after the other.

    After creating all the components of the assembly, you can save the assembly file and its components.

37. Click on the **Save** button in the **Quick Access Toolbar** toolbar. The **Save As** dialog box appears.

38. Enter a name for the assembly in the **File name** field of the dialog box and then click on the **Save** button. The **Save** dialog box appears, see Figure 12.21.

12.21

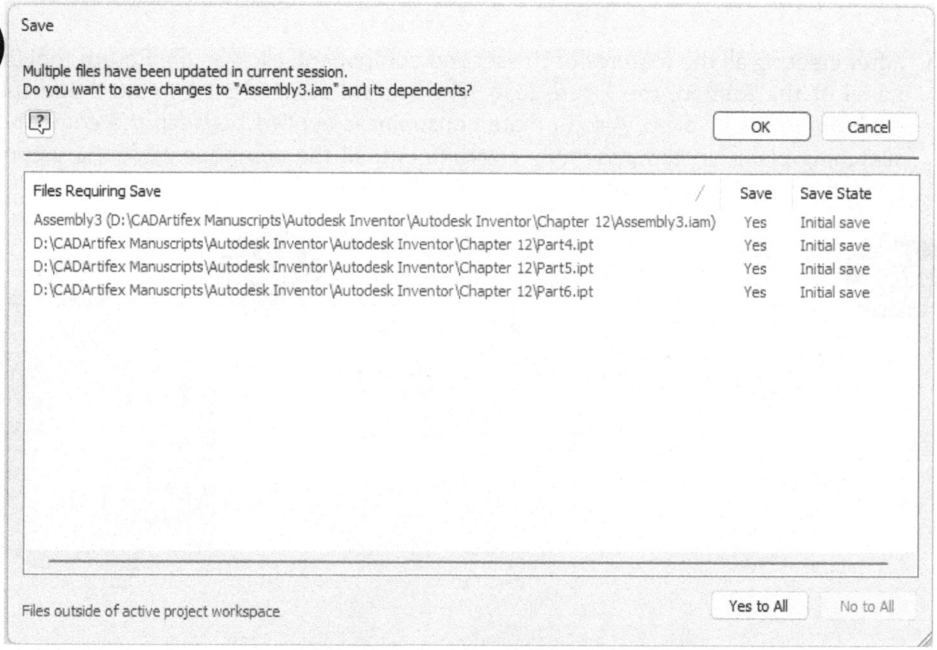

39. Click on the **Yes to All** button and the **OK** button in the dialog box. The assembly file and all its components get saved in the specified location.

Editing Assembly Components

In the process of creating an assembly, you may need to edit its components depending on the changes in the design, revisions, or so on. Autodesk Inventor allows you to edit each component of an assembly within the Assembly environment as well as in the Part modeling environment. Different methods for editing assembly components are discussed next.

Editing Assembly Components within the Assembly Environment

1. In the Assembly environment, right-click on the component to be edited in the graphics area or the **Browser** and then click on the **Edit** tool in the Marking Menu or in the shortcut menu that appears, respectively, see Figures 12.22 and 12.23. The Part modeling environment for editing the selected component appears within the Assembly environment. Also, other components of the assembly become transparent in the graphics area.

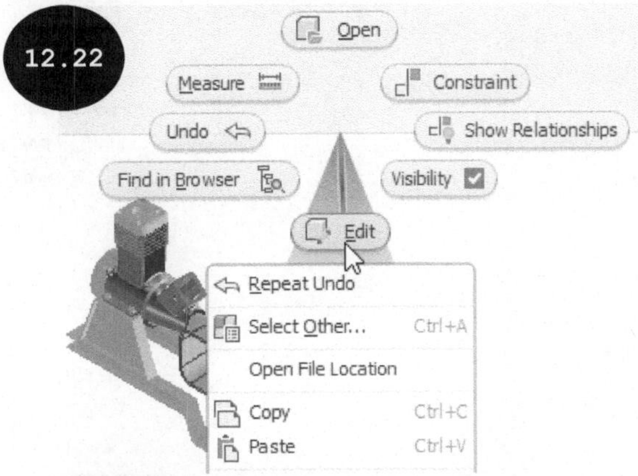

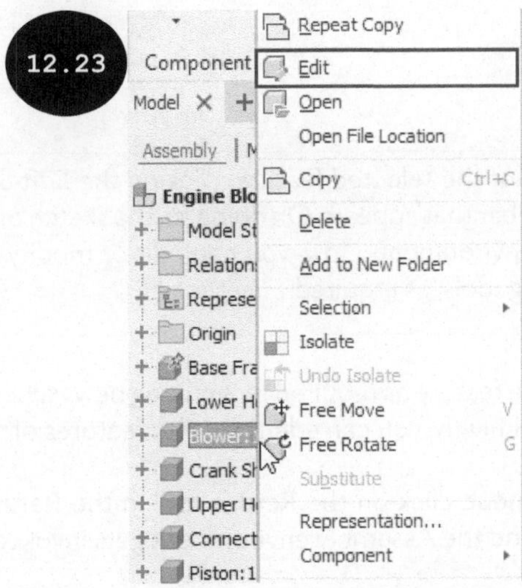

2. Expand the node of the component being edited in the **Browser** to display all its features, if not expanded automatically, see Figure 12.24.

3. Right-click on a feature of the component to be edited in the **Browser** and then click on the **Edit Feature** option in the shortcut menu that appears, see Figure 12.25. The property panel appears depending upon the selected feature in the graphics area for editing the parameters of the selected feature. Alternatively, click on the feature to be edited in the graphics area and then click on the **Edit Feature** tool in the Mini-Toolbar that appears for editing the feature.

12.24

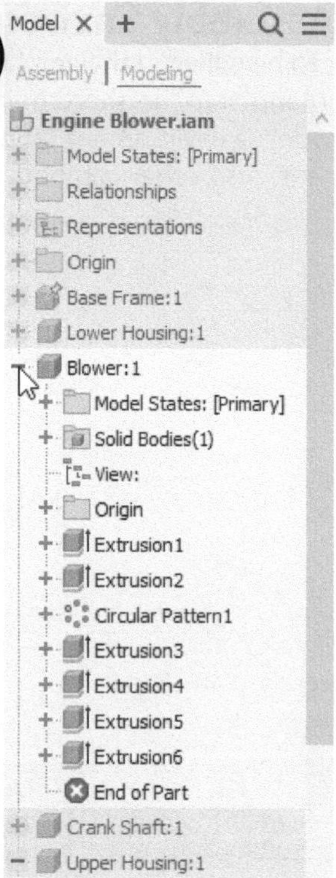

12.25

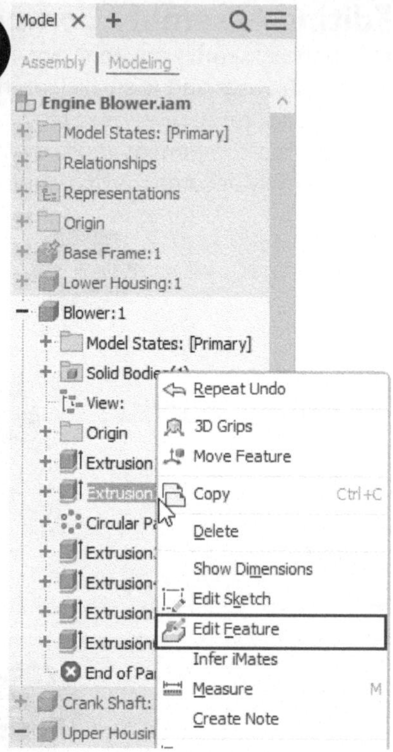

Note: To edit the sketch of the selected feature, click on the **Edit Sketch** option in the shortcut menu or Mini-Toolbar that appears. On doing so, the sketch of the selected feature appears in the Sketching environment. Now, you can edit or modify the sketch of the feature by using the sketching tools, as required.

4. Edit the parameters of the feature as required by entering new values in the property panel. Next, exit the property panel. Similarly, you can edit the other features of the component one by one.

5. After editing the component, click on the **Return** tool in the **Return** panel of the **Ribbon**. The component gets edited and the Assembly environment gets invoked.

Editing Assembly Components in the Part Modeling Environment

In addition to editing the components of an assembly in the Assembly environment, you can open a component of an assembly in the Part modeling environment and then perform the editing operations. The method for editing assembly components in the Part modeling environment is discussed below:

1. In the Assembly environment, right-click on the component to be edited in the graphics area or in the **Browser** and then click on the **Open** tool in the Marking Menu or in the shortcut menu that appears, respectively, see Figures 12.26 and 12.27. The selected component gets opened in the Part modeling environment.

12.26

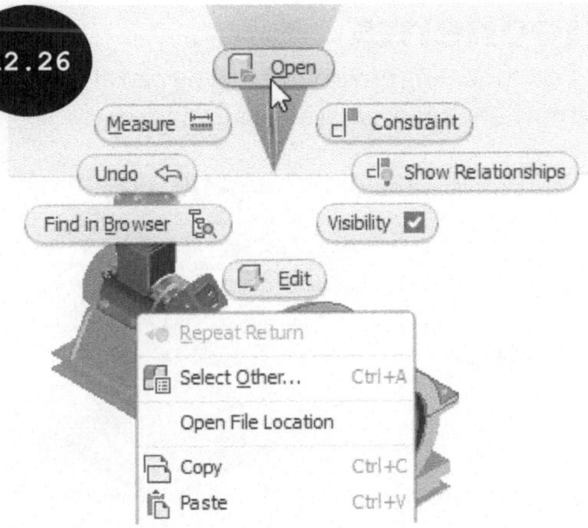

12.27

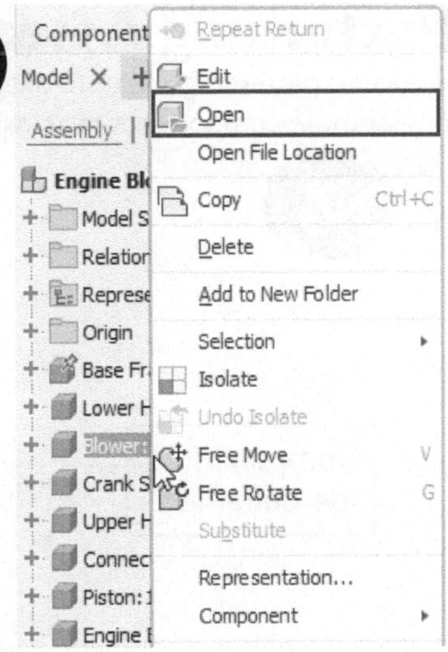

Now, you can edit the component in the Part modeling environment.

2. Edit the required features and sketches of the component in the Part modeling environment. The method for editing a component in the Part modeling environment has already been discussed earlier.

3. After editing the component, save the changes and then switch to the assembly by clicking on its tab at the lower left corner in the graphics area, see Figure 12.28. The Assembly environment gets invoked and the assembly appears in the graphics area.

12.28

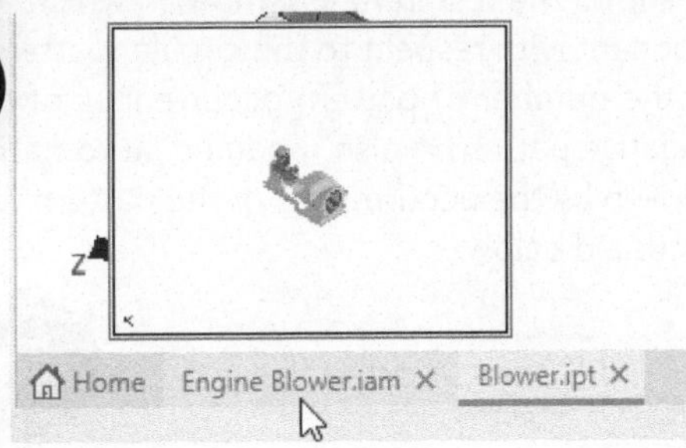

Now, you need to update the assembly.

4. Click on the **Local Update** tool in the **Quick Access Toolbar**, see Figure 12.29. The assembly gets updated and all the modifications made in the component are also reflected in the Assembly environment.

12.29

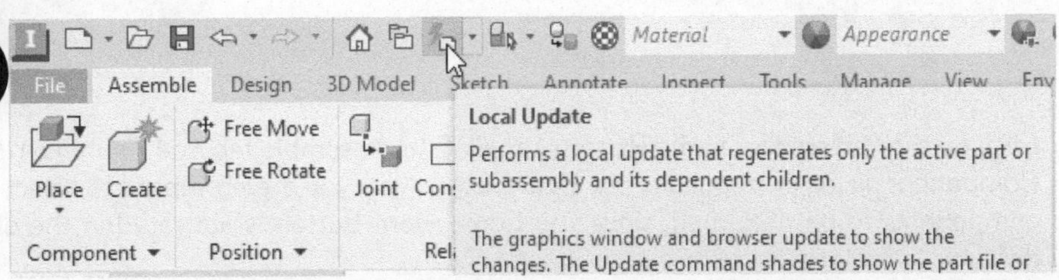

Patterning Assembly Components

Similar to patterning a feature of a component in the Part modeling environment, you can also pattern one or more components of an assembly in the Assembly environment, see Figure 12.30.

12.30

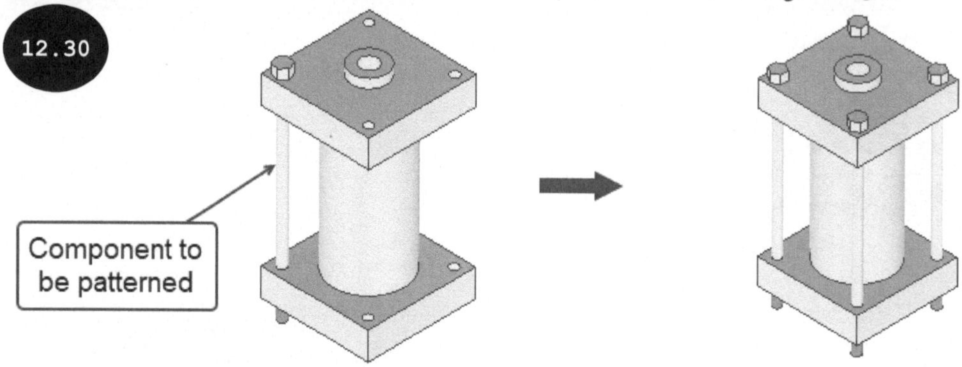

In the Assembly environment, you can create three types of patterns: associative pattern, rectangular pattern, and circular pattern by using the **Pattern** tool in the **Pattern** panel of the **Assemble** tab. The various types of patterns are discussed next.

Creating an Associative Pattern

An associative pattern is created by patterning a component of an assembly with respect to a pattern feature of another component. In this type of pattern, the component to be patterned is driven by a pattern feature of another component. Consider the case of an assembly shown in Figure 12.31, in which the bolt component is to be patterned with respect to the circular pattern feature of the flange component. Figure 12.32 shows the resultant assembly, in which an associative pattern is created by patterning the bolt component with respect to the circular pattern feature of the flange component. Note that on modifying the number of pattern occurrences of the pattern feature, the number of occurrences of the associative pattern is also modified, automatically, since the occurrences of the associative pattern are driven by the occurrences of the pattern feature. The method for creating an associative pattern is discussed below:

12.31

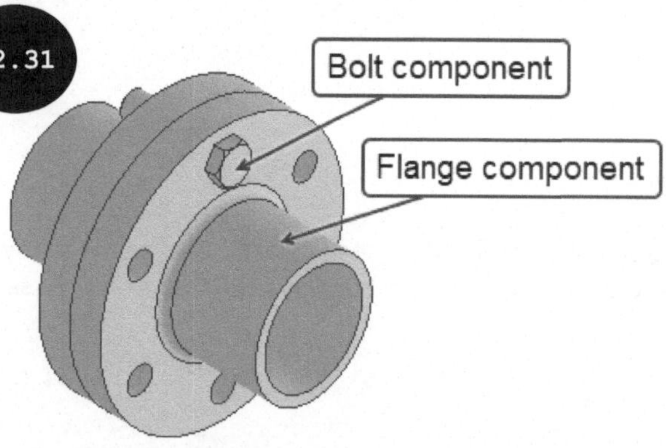

12.32

1. Click on the **Pattern** tool in the **Pattern** panel of the **Assemble** tab, see Figure 12.33. The **Pattern Component** dialog box appears, see Figure 12.34. Also, you are prompted to select one or more components to be patterned, since the **Component** button is activated in the dialog box, by default.

12.33

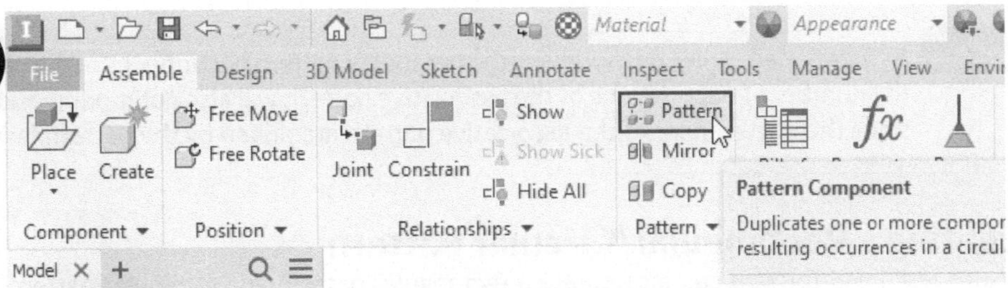

12.34

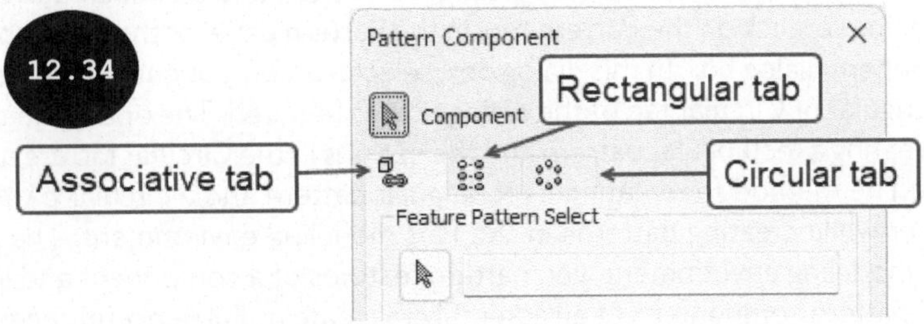

2. Ensure that the **Associative** tab is activated in the **Pattern Component** dialog box for creating an associative pattern, refer to Figure 12.34.

3. Select a component to be patterned in the graphics area or in the **Browser**, refer to Figure 12.35. You can also select multiple components to pattern.

4. After selecting a component to be patterned, click on the **Associated Feature Pattern** tool in the **Associative** tab of the dialog box. You are prompted to select a pattern feature of another component as the driving feature.

5. Move the cursor over an occurrence of a pattern feature of a component and then select it as the driving feature when all pattern occurrences are highlighted in the graphics area, refer to Figure 12.35. The pattern feature gets selected and the preview of an associative pattern appears in the graphics area, see Figure 12.36.

12.35

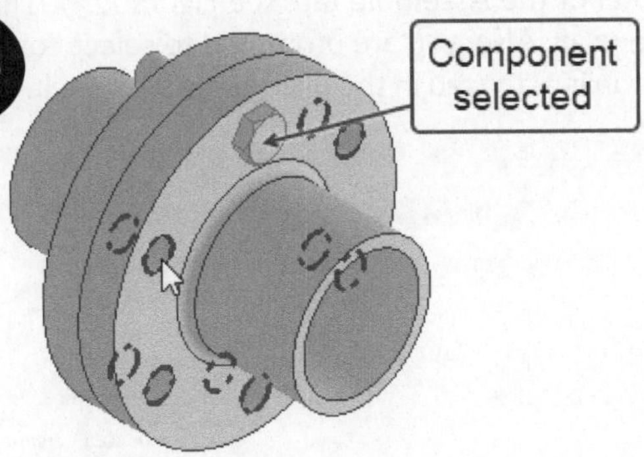

12.36

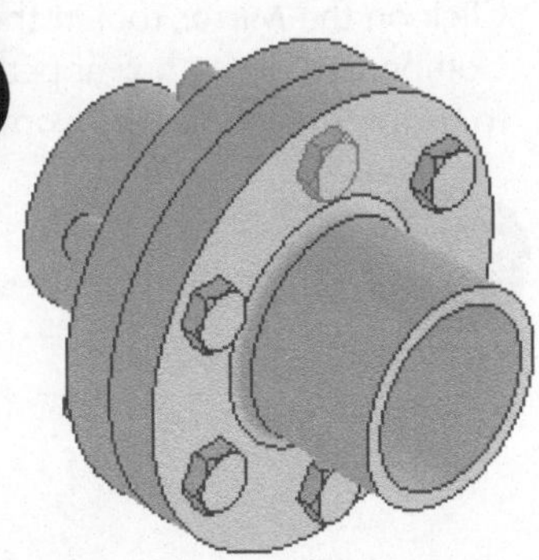

6. Click on the **OK** button in the dialog box. The associative pattern gets created.

Note: As mentioned earlier, on modifying the number of pattern occurrences of the pattern feature, the number of occurrences of the associative pattern will also get modified, automatically, since the occurrences of the associative pattern are driven by the pattern feature.

Creating a Rectangular/Circular Pattern

In Autodesk Inventor, you can also create a rectangular pattern and a circular pattern by using the **Pattern** tool. For doing so, click on the **Pattern** tool in the **Pattern** panel of the **Assemble** tab to invoke the **Pattern Component** dialog box. In this dialog box, select the component to be patterned and then click on the **Rectangular** or **Circular** tab of the dialog box, as required. The options in the **Rectangular** tab are used for creating a rectangular pattern and the options in the **Circular** tab are used for creating a circular pattern. The method for creating a rectangular pattern and a circular pattern is the same as discussed earlier while creating patterns in the Part modeling environment. The only difference is that in the Part modeling environment, you pattern features of a component and in the Assembly environment, you pattern components of an assembly to create multiple occurrences.

Note: In Autodesk Inventor, you can also define the pattern direction along the default X-axis, Y-axis, or Z-axis by selecting the respective option from the drop-down list that appears by clicking the arrow on the right of the direction buttons of the **Rectangular** and **Circular** tabs of the dialog box. You can also select a circular face of a component to define the pattern direction.

Mirroring Components of an Assembly

Similar to mirroring features in the Part modeling environment, you can also mirror components in the Assembly environment by using the **Mirror** tool. The method for mirroring components of an assembly is discussed below:

1. Click on the **Mirror** tool in the **Pattern** panel of the **Assemble** tab, see Figure 12.37. The **Mirror Component** dialog box appears, see Figure 12.38. Also, you are prompted to select components to be mirrored, since the **Components** button is activated in the dialog box, by default.

12.37

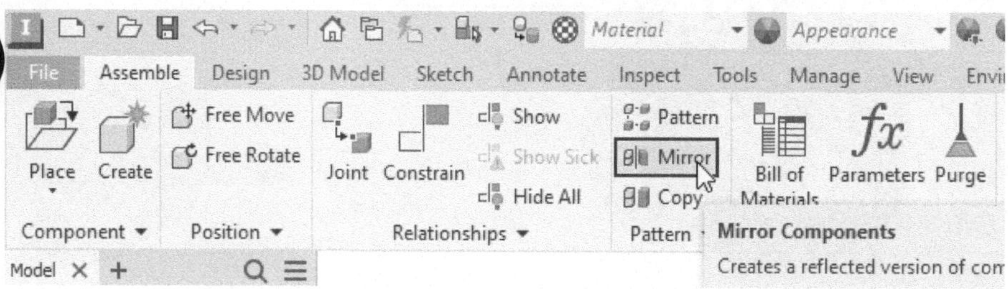

12.38

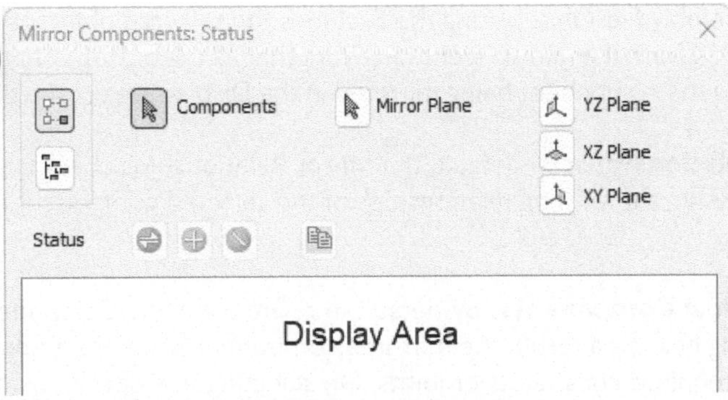

2. Select a component to be mirrored in the graphics area or in the **Browser**, see Figure 12.39. The name of the selected component of the assembly appears in the **Display** area of the dialog box. You can also select multiple components one by one by clicking the left mouse button.

3. After selecting the components to be mirrored, click on the **Mirror Plane** button in the dialog box. You are prompted to select a mirroring plane.

4. Select a plane or a planar face as the mirroring plane in the graphics area, see Figure 12.39. The preview of the mirror component appears in the graphics area, see Figure 12.40. You can also click on the **YZ Plane**, **XZ Plane**, or **XY Plane** button in the dialog box as the mirroring plane.

12.39

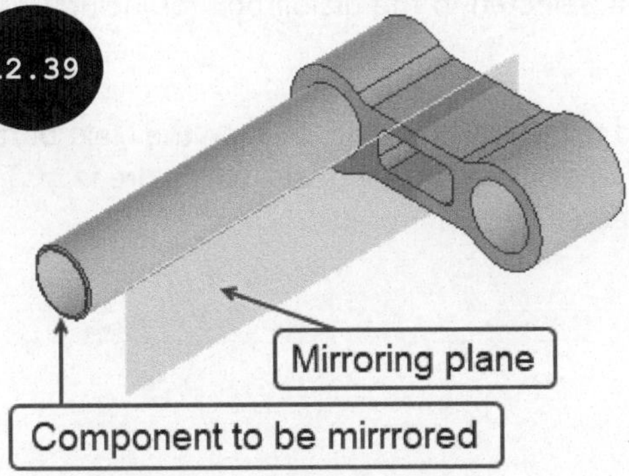

12.40

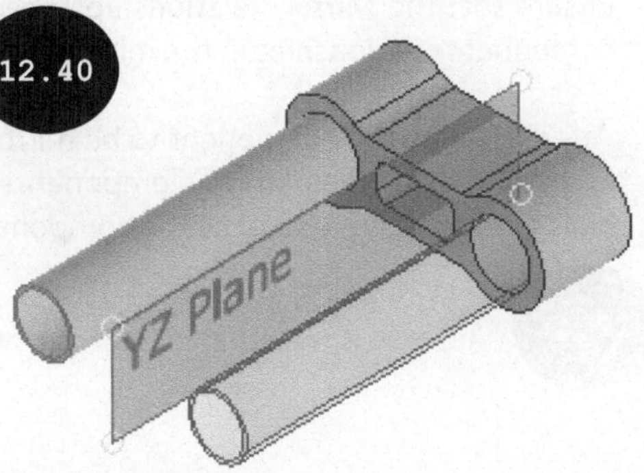

Create mirror pattern : The **Create mirror pattern** button is used to generate mirrored copies of the selected components. This operation replicates the geometry and position of the original components but does not preserve any associativity between the source and the mirrored components.

Create flat structure : Activating the **Create flat structure** option enables the **Mirror Relationships** and **Ground New Components** check boxes located below the **Display** area in the dialog box. Selecting the **Mirror Relationships** check box maintains the associativity between the source and the mirrored components. While selecting the **Ground New Components** check box fixes the mirrored components in place, grounding them in their new positions.

Status: On selecting the **Mirrors the selected objects** button in the **Status** area of the dialog box, a mirrored component is created and saved as a new file. On selecting the **Reuses the selected objects** button , a mirrored component is created as a component instance in the current assembly file. On selecting the **Excludes the selected objects** button, the component gets excluded from the mirror operation. Note that all the buttons of the **Status** area are enabled on selecting the component being mirrored in the **Display** area of the dialog box.

Mirror Relationships: By default, the **Mirror Relationships** check box is selected in the dialog box. As a result, the existing relationships of the selected component are included in the mirror operation.

Ground New Components: By default, the **Ground New Components** check box is cleared in the dialog box. As a result, the mirrored component becomes a floating component and you can apply required constraints or joints. On selecting this check box, the mirrored component becomes a grounded component.

More >>: The **More** button (double arrow) at the lower right corner of the dialog box is used for expanding the dialog box and displaying the additional options. By default, the **Reuse Standard Content and Factory Parts** check box is selected in the expanded dialog box. As a result, the default status for a library component and a factory part is reused to add component instance instead of saving a new file. The **Mirrored**, **Reused**, and **Standard Content** check boxes in the **Preview Components** area of the expanded dialog box are used for specifying the respective preview that will appear in the graphics area i.e. mirrored, reused, or content library component.

5. Ensure that the **Mirror Relationships** check box is selected in the dialog box for including the component relationships in the mirror operation.

6. After selecting the component to be mirrored and the mirroring plane, click on the **Next** button in the dialog box. The **Mirror Components: File Names** dialog box appears, see Figure 12.41. This dialog box displays a list of all the components selected to be mirrored.

12.41

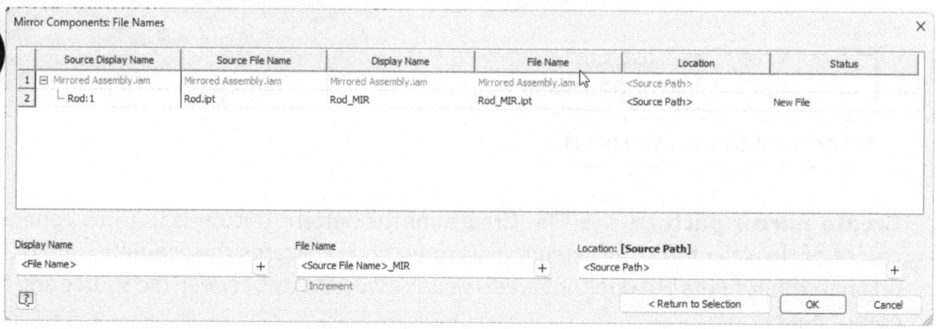

Source Display Name: The **Source Display Name** column of the dialog box displays the original name of the components selected to be mirrored.

Source File Name: The **Source File Name** column of the dialog box displays the original file name of the components selected to be mirrored.

Display Name: The **Display Name** column displays the new name of the mirrored components that will appear in the **Browser**. You can click on the field of this column and then specify the name of the mirrored component, as required in the edit field that appears.

File Name: The **File Name** column displays the new file name of the mirrored components with which the components will be saved as new files.

Location: The **Location** column displays the location of the mirrored components in which the components will be saved. By default, the **Source Path** option is displayed in the fields of this column. As a result, the mirrored components will be saved in the same location where the original or parent components are saved. You can also change the default location of a mirrored component. For doing so, right-click on the **Source Path** option of a mirrored component and then click on the **User Path** option in the shortcut menu that appears. The **Browse For Folder** dialog box appears. Browse to the required location in the **Browse For Folder** dialog box and click on the **OK** button. The new path or location appears in the field of the **Location** column.

Status: The **Status** column displays the status of the mirrored components. By default, the **New File** status appears in the fields of this column. As a result, the mirrored components are saved as new files. If the file name of the mirrored component is specified as the same as the original name, then the status of the mirrored component appears as **Reuse Existing**.

Create New Assembly: The **Create New Assembly** check box is cleared by default. As a result, the mirrored component is created in the same assembly. On selecting this check box, the mirrored component is created as a new assembly file. Note that this check box becomes available when mirroring an assembly with the **Create flat structure** option enabled.

7. Ensure that the **Create New Assembly** check box is cleared.

8. After specifying the required settings in the dialog box, click on the **OK** button. The mirrored component gets created, see Figure 12.42.

12.42

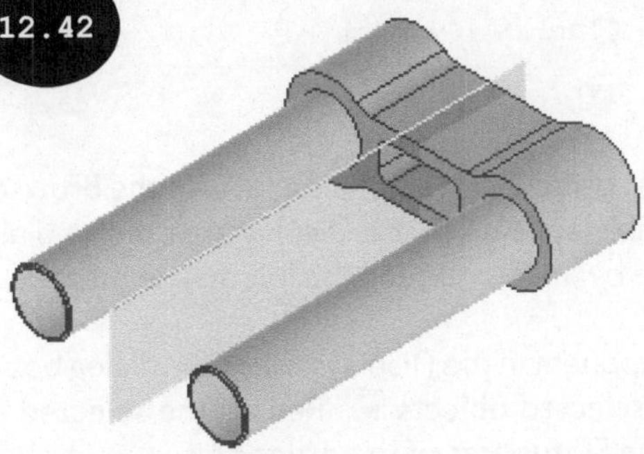

Copying Components of an Assembly

In Autodesk Inventor, you can copy a component of an assembly to create its multiple instances in the Assembly environment. The method for copying a component of an assembly is discussed below:

1. Click on the **Copy** tool in the **Pattern** panel in the **Assemble** tab, see Figure 12.43. The **Copy Components** dialog box appears, see Figure 12.44.

12.43

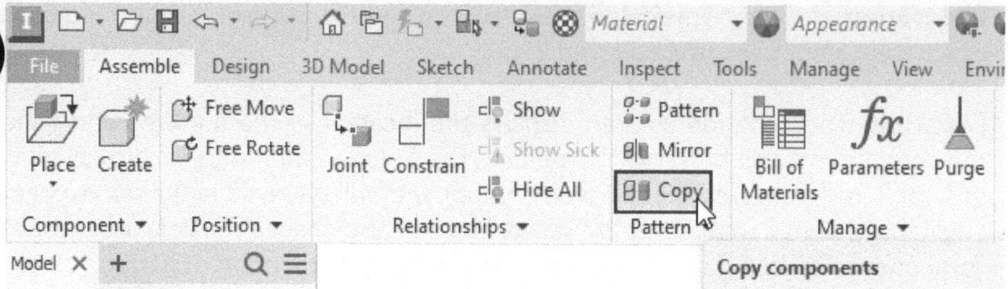

12.44

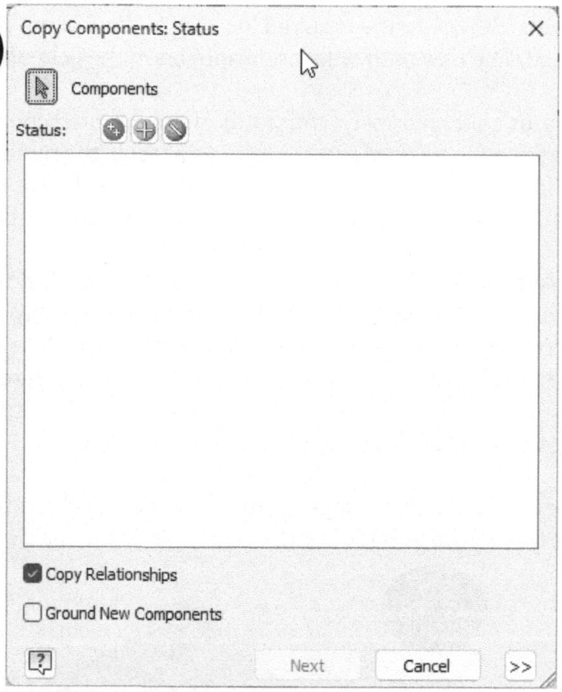

2. Select a component to be copied in the graphics area or in the **Browser**. The name of the selected component of the assembly appears in the **Display** area of the dialog box. You can also select multiple components one by one by clicking the left mouse button.

3. Click on the selected component in the **Display** area of the dialog box and then select the required status type (**Copies the selected objects** , **Reuses the selected objects** , or **Excludes the selected objects**) in the **Status** area of the dialog box.

   Status: On selecting the **Copies the selected objects** button in the **Status** area of the dialog box, a copied component is created and saved as a new file. On selecting the **Reuses the selected objects** button , a copied component is created as a component instance in the current assembly file. On selecting the **Excludes the selected objects** button , the component gets excluded from the copy operation. Note that all the buttons of the **Status** area are enabled on selecting the component being copied in the **Display** area of the dialog box.

4. After selecting the component to be copied and the status type, click on the **Next** button in the dialog box. The **Copy Components: File Names** dialog box appears, see Figure 12.45. The options in this dialog box are the same as discussed earlier.

12.45

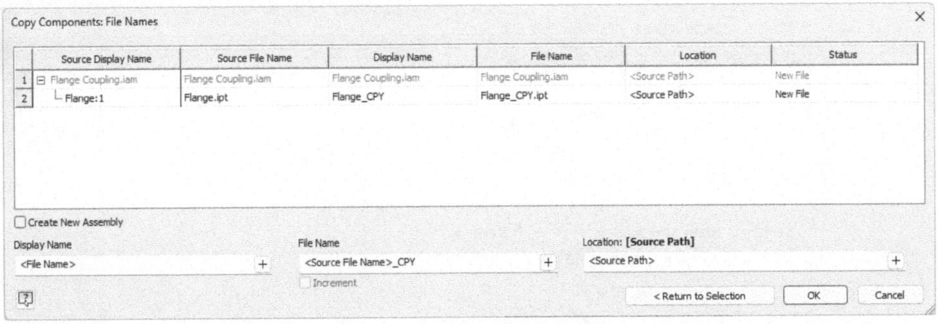

5. After specifying the required settings in the dialog box, click on the **OK** button. An instance of the selected component gets attached to the cursor and you are prompted to specify its placement in the graphics area.

6. Click to specify the placement of the attached component in the graphics area. The copy of the selected component gets placed in the graphics area. Now, you can apply the required joints or constraints to assemble the newly added components of the assembly.

Tip: You can also drag a component from the **Browser** and add its instance in the graphics area.

Creating Bill of Material (BOM) of an Assembly

A Bill of Material (BOM) is one of the most important features of any drawing. It contains information related to the part number, BOM structure, material, quantity, and so on. In addition to creating a Bill of Material (BOM) in a drawing, Autodesk Inventor also allows you to create BOM in the Assembly environment. You will learn about creating a Bill of Material (BOM) in a drawing later in Chapter 14. To create BOM in the Assembly environment, click on the **Bill of Materials** tool in the **Manage** panel of the **Assemble** tab, see Figure 12.46. The **Bill of Materials** dialog box appears with the BOM of the currently displayed assembly in the graphics area, see Figure 12.47.

12.46

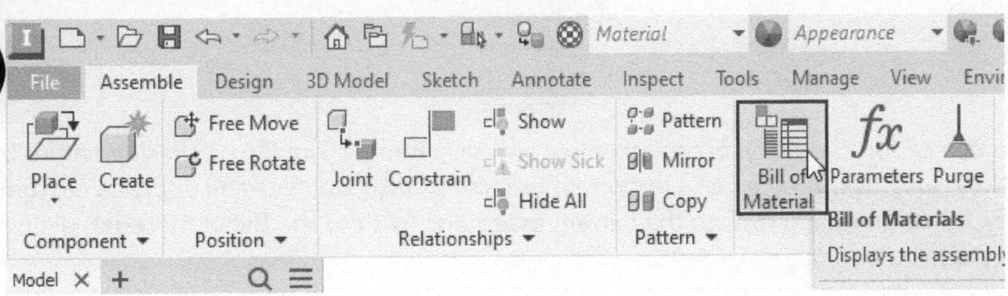

12.47

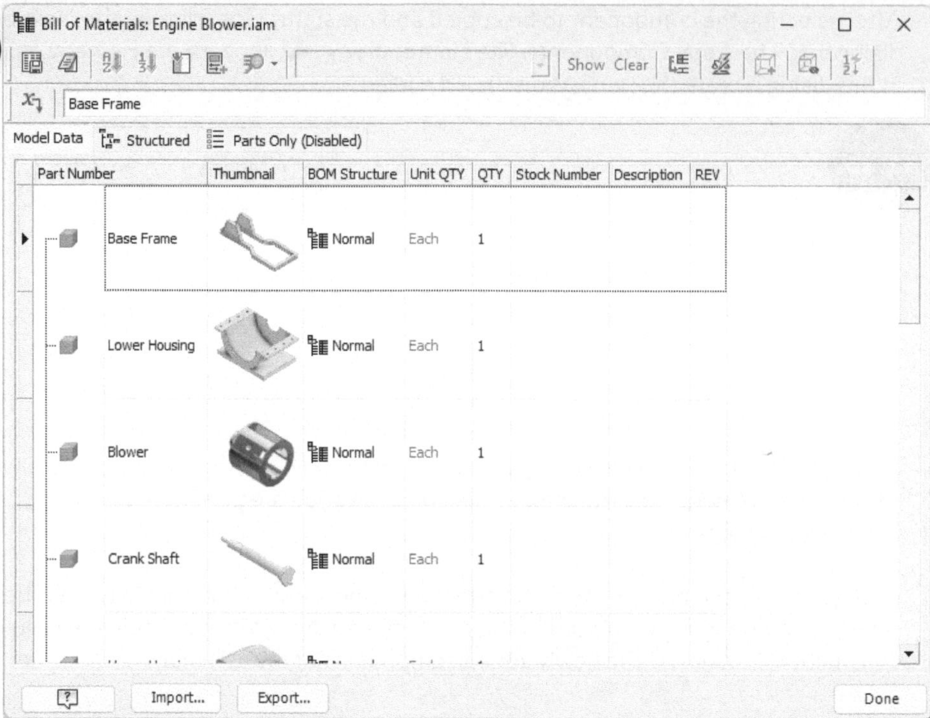

You can customize the **Bill of Materials** dialog box to add columns, as required. For doing so, click on the **Choose Columns** button in the dialog box. The **Customization** window appears with the display of various BOM categories (columns) such as **Appearance**, **Author**, **Base Unit**, **Material**, and so on, see Figure 12.48. Double-click on the required category to be added in the **Bill of Materials** dialog box as a column and then close the **Customization** window.

12.48

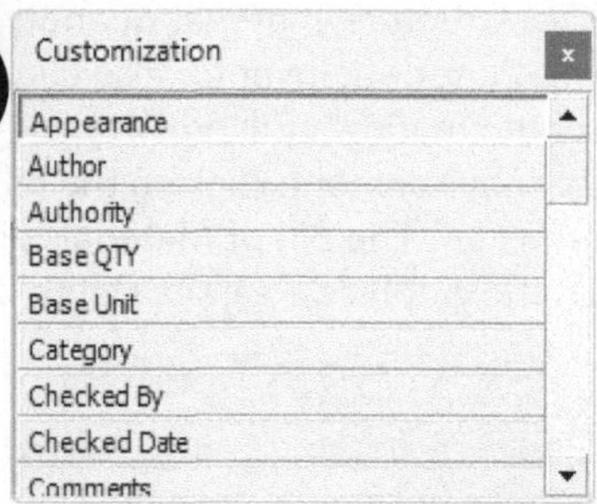

You can export the BOM of the assembly and save it in an *.xml* file by clicking on the **Export** button in the dialog box. You can also import an existing BOM (*.xml* file) and apply its customized settings of BOM columns and rows to the current assembly. To close the **Bill of Materials** dialog box, click on the **Done** button.

Tutorial 1

Create an assembly, as shown in Figure 12.49 by using the Top-down Assembly approach. Different views and dimensions of each assembly component are shown in Figures 12.50 through 12.53. All dimensions are in mm.

12.49

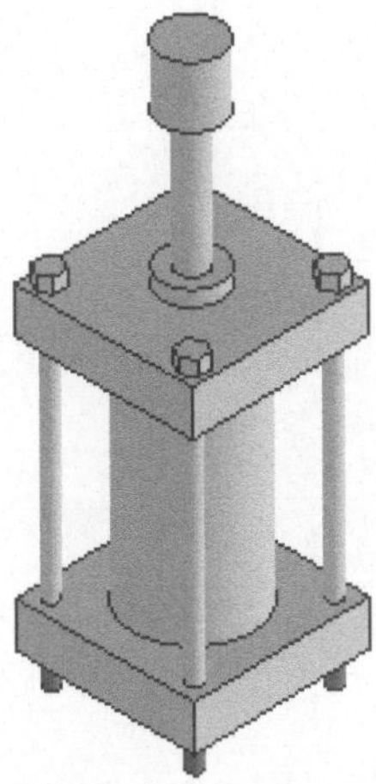

12.50

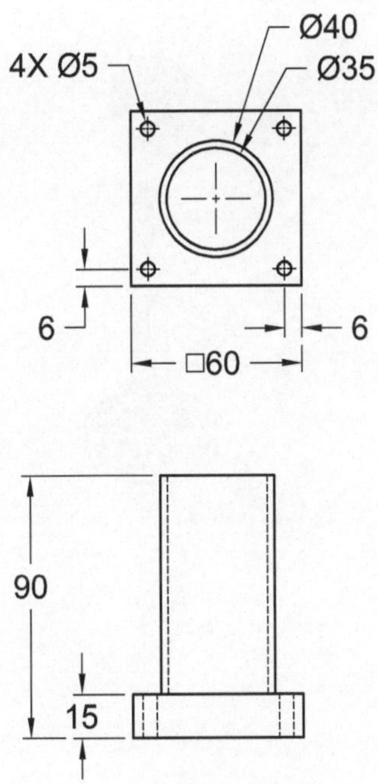

Cylinder

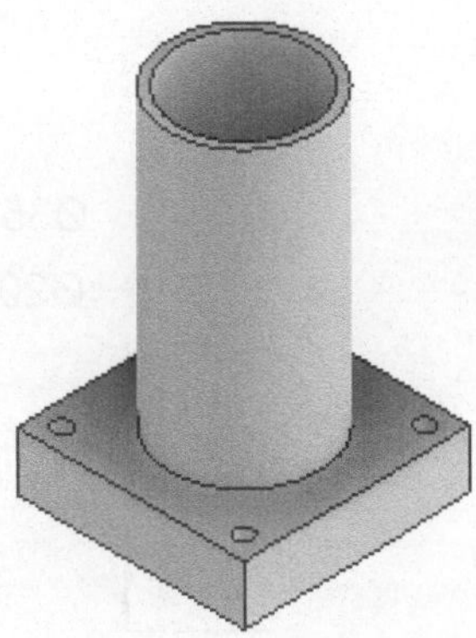

12.51

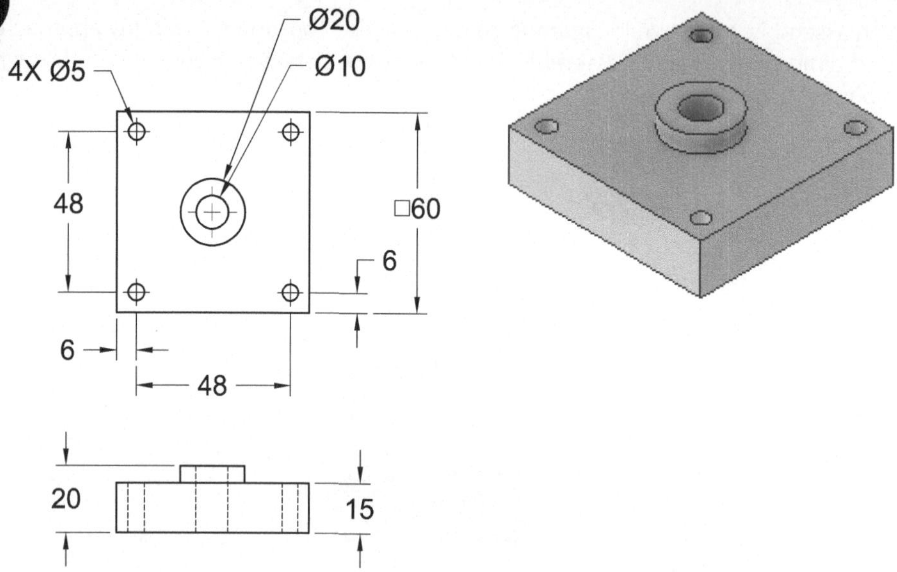

Top Plate

12.52

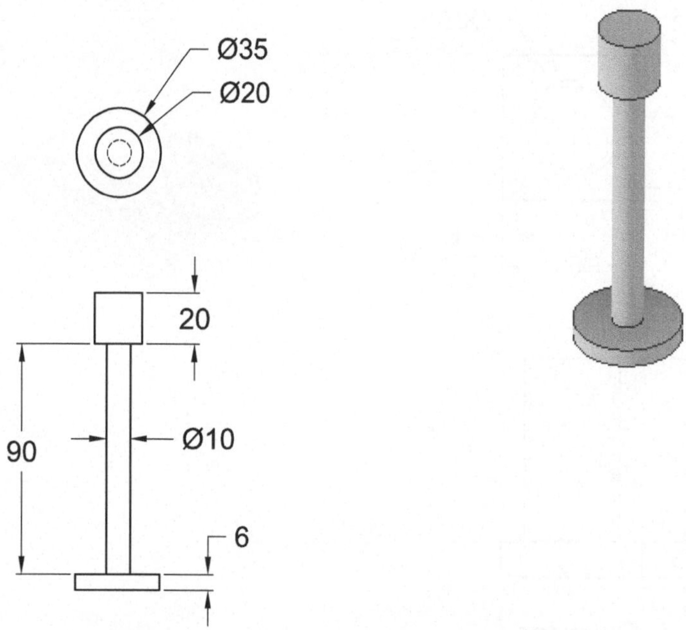

Piston

12.53

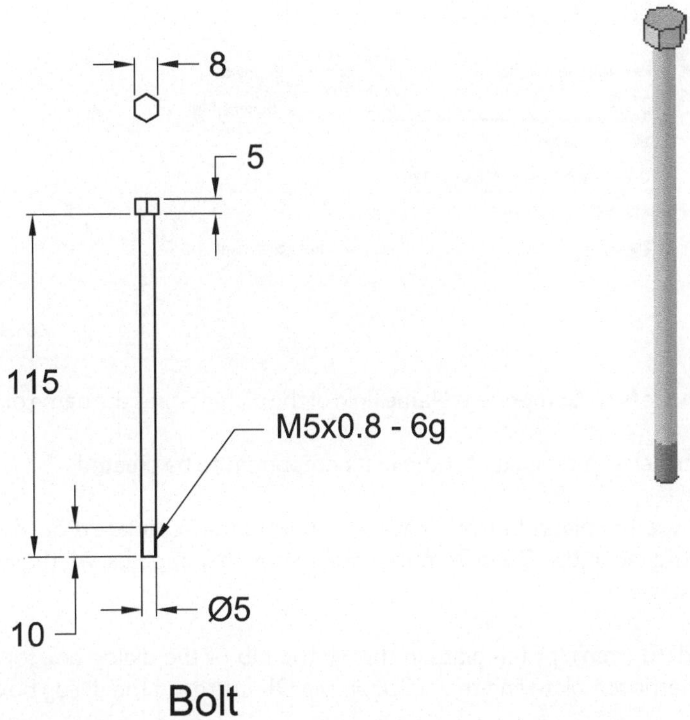

Section 1: Invoking the Assembly Environment

1. Start Autodesk Inventor and then invoke the Assembly modeling environment by using the Standard (mm).iam template.

Section 2: Creating the First Component

After invoking the Assembly environment, you can create the first component of the assembly within the Assembly environment.

1. Click on the **Create** tool in the **Component** panel of the **Assemble** tab, see Figure 12.54. The **Create In-Place Component** dialog box appears, see Figure 12.55.

12.54

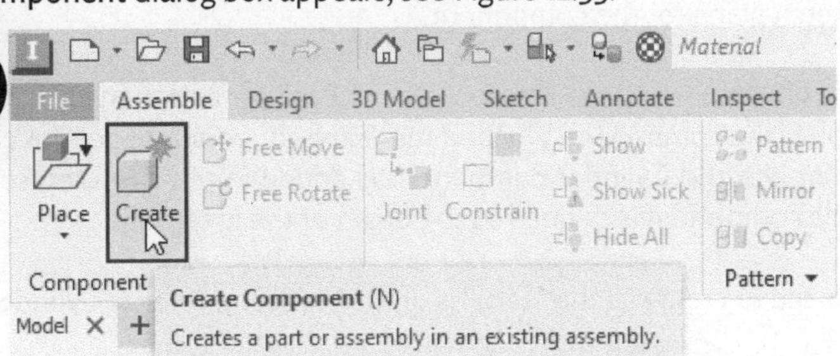

12.55

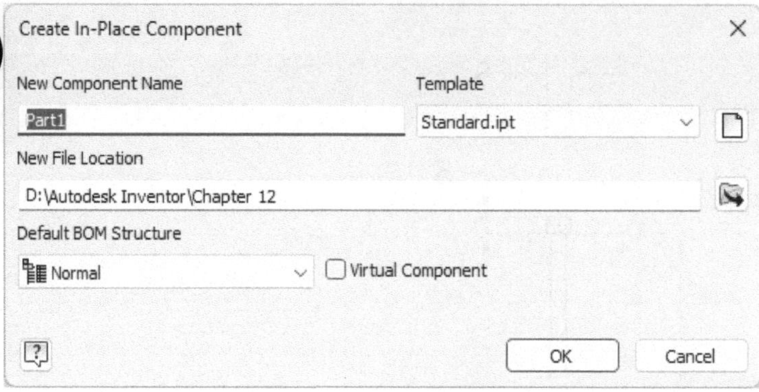

2. Enter **Cylinder** in the **New Component Name** field of the dialog box as the name of the component.

   Now, you need to select a template for the first component to be created.

3. Click on the **Browse Templates** button available next to the **Template** drop-down list and then click on the **Metric** tab in the **Open Template** dialog box that appears. All the metric templates appear in the dialog box.

4. Select the **Standard (mm).ipt** template in the **Metric** tab of the dialog box for creating a solid component in metric template and then click on the **OK** button in the dialog box.

   After selecting the template, you need to specify the location for saving the component.

5. Click on the **Browse to New File Location** button available next to the **New File Location** field in the dialog box. The **Save As** dialog box appears.

6. Browse to **Autodesk Inventor > Chapter 12 > Tutorial 1** folder in the local drive of your system. Note that you need to create these folders inside the Autodesk Inventor folder.

7. Click on the **Save** button in the **Save As** dialog box. The location for saving the component is specified (*>:\Autodesk Inventor\Chapter 12\Tutorial 1*).

8. Click on the **OK** button in the **Create In-Place Component** dialog box. You are prompted to select a sketch plane for the component.

9. Expand the **Origin** node of the assembly in the **Browser** and then click on the **XY Plane** to define the position of the component. The part modeling environment gets invoked within the Assembly environment and the **Cylinder** component is added in the **Browser**, see Figure 12.56. Also, the origin of the component is defined as the origin of the assembly.

   Now, you need to create all the features of the first component (**Cylinder**) one by one.

10. Click on the **Start 2D Sketch** tool in the **Sketch** panel, (see Figure 12.57) or press the **S** key. The three default planes of the component appear in the graphics area. Also, you are prompted to select a plane for creating the sketch of the base feature of the first component.

12.56

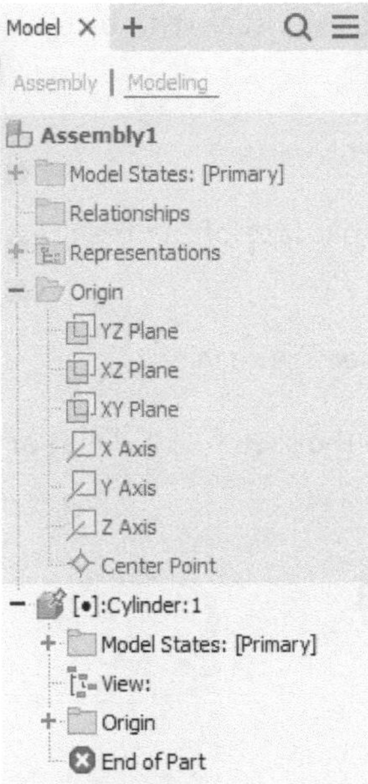

12.57

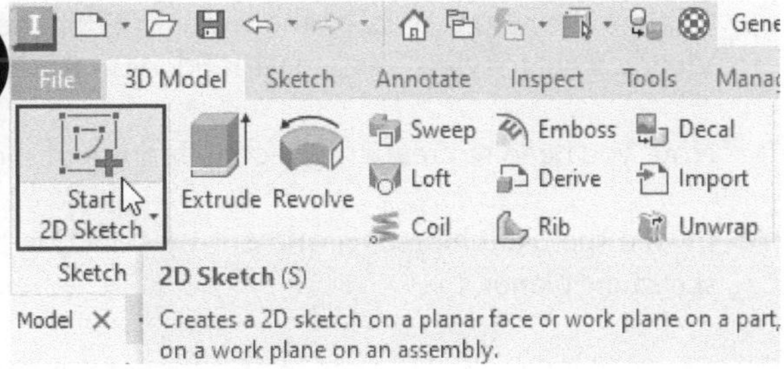

11. Click on the **Home** icon in the ViewCube to change the orientation of the component to isometric, if needed.

12. Click on the **XZ Plane** as the sketching plane for creating the base feature of the component. The Sketching environment gets invoked.

13. Draw the sketch of the base feature by using the sketching tools, see Figure 12.58.

    After creating the sketch, you need to convert it into a solid feature.

14. Click on the **3D Model** tab in the **Ribbon** and then extrude the sketch to a depth of 15 mm by using the **Extrude** tool, see Figure 12.59.

12.58

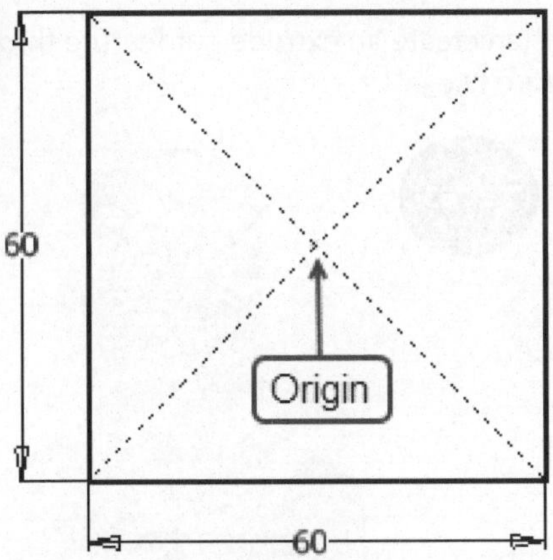

12.59

15. Change the visual style of the model to "Shaded with Edges" visual style by clicking on the **View > Visual Style > Shaded with Edges** in the **Ribbon**.

    Now, you need to create the second feature of the component.

16. Invoke the Sketching environment by selecting the top planar face of the base feature as the sketching plane.

17. Create the sketch of the second feature of the component, see Figure 12.60.

18. Click on the **3D Model** tab in the **Ribbon** and then extrude the sketch to a depth of 75 mm by using the **Extrude** tool, see Figure 12.61.

12.60

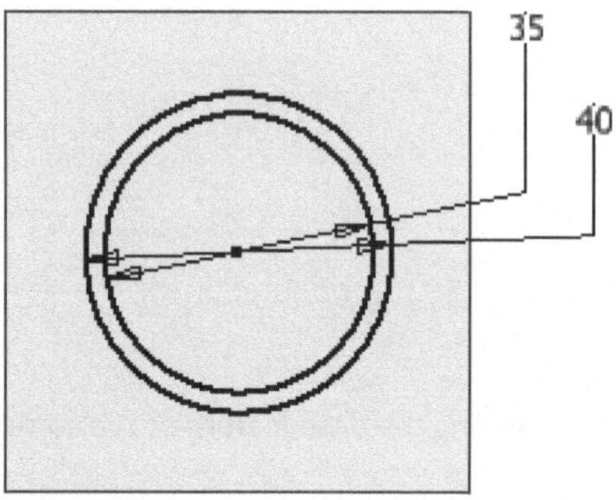

12.61

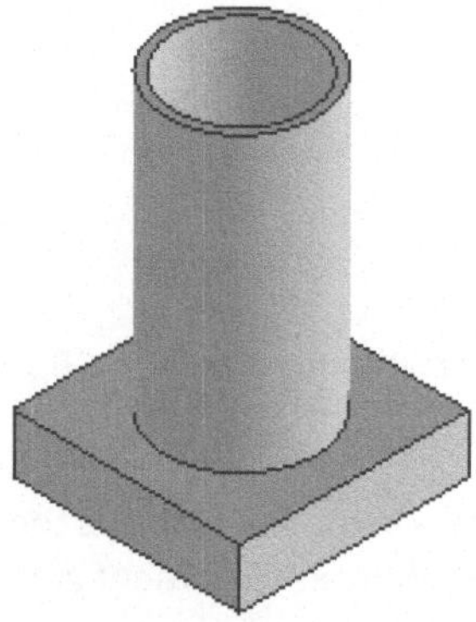

Now, you need to create the third feature of the component.

19. Invoke the Sketching environment by selecting the top planar face of the base feature as the sketching plane.

20. Create a sketch (a circle of diameter 5 mm) of the third feature of the component, see Figure 12.62.

21. Click on the **3D Model** tab in the **Ribbon** and then create an extrude cut feature through all the base features by using the **Extrude** tool, see Figure 12.63.

12.62

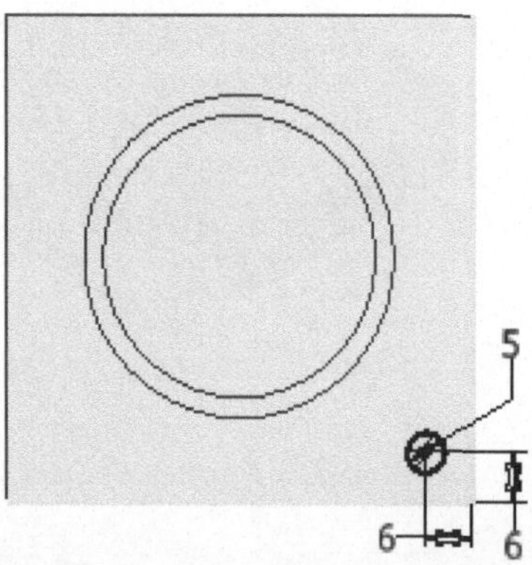

12.63

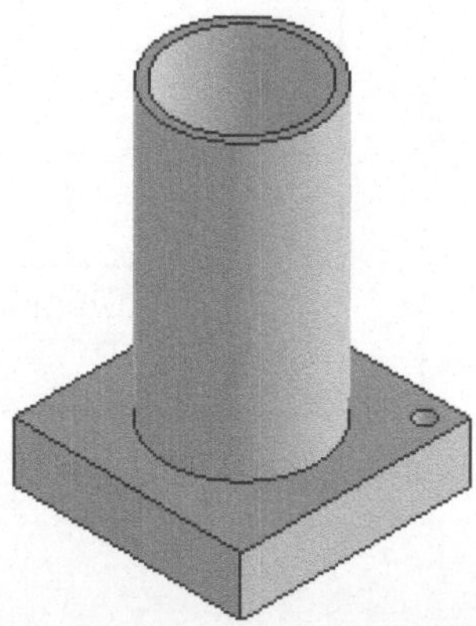

Now, you need to create the fourth feature of the component which is a rectangular pattern.

22. Create a rectangular pattern of the previously created extrude cut feature and create its remaining instances by using the **Rectangular Pattern** tool, see Figure 12.64. The distance between the pattern instances is 48 mm in both the pattern directions.

23. After creating the first component (**Cylinder**), click on the **Return** tool in the **Return** panel of the **Ribbon**, see Figure 12.65. The first component is created and switched to the Assembly environment.

12.64

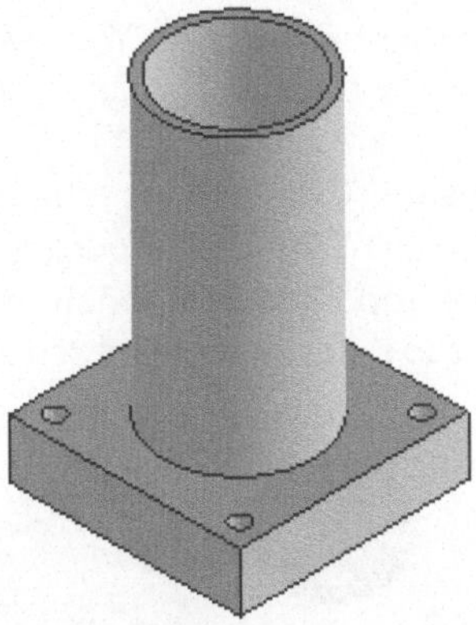

12.65

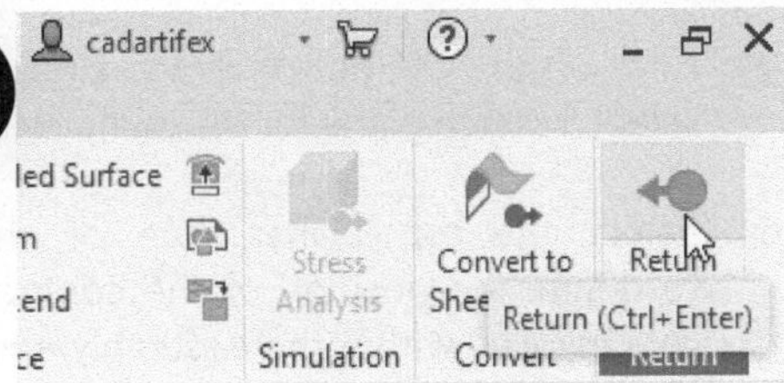

Note: By default, the first created component becomes a grounded component in the Assembly environment and the pushpin icon and filled dot [•] appear on its name in the **Browser**, indicating that all degrees of freedom of the component are fixed and the component cannot move or rotate in any direction.

Section 3: Creating the Second Component

After creating the first component, you need to create the second component (**Top Plate**) of the assembly.

1. Click on the **Create** tool in the **Component** panel of the **Assemble** tab or press the N key. The **Create In-Place Component** dialog box appears, see Figure 12.66.

12.66

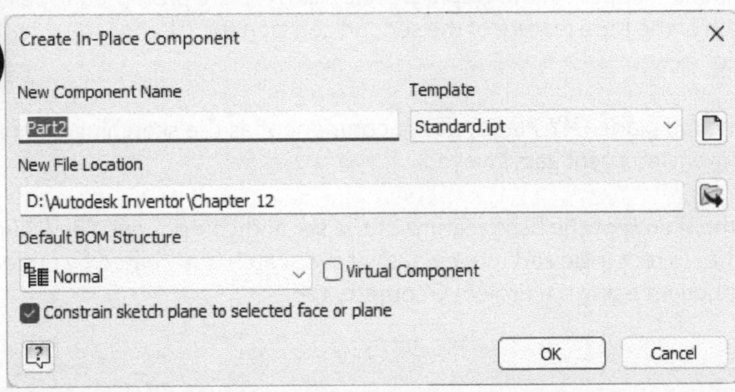

2. Enter **Top Plate** in the **New Component Name** field of the dialog box as the name of the component.

3. Click on the **Browse Templates** button available next to the **Template** drop-down list and then select the **Standard (mm).ipt** template in the **Metric** tab of the dialog box. Next, click on the **OK** button in the dialog box. The **Standard (mm).ipt** template gets selected.

4. Ensure that the location for saving the component is specified in the Tutorial 1 folder of Chapter 12 (>:*Autodesk Inventor**Chapter 12**Tutorial 1*) in the **New File Location** field of the dialog box.

5. Click on the **OK** button in the **Create In-Place Component** dialog box. You are prompted to select a sketch plane for the component.

6. Select the top planar face of the first component (**Cylinder**) as the sketch plane to define the position of the component, see Figure 12.67. The part modeling environment gets invoked within the Assembly environment and the **Top Plate** component is added in the **Browser**. Also, the first component becomes transparent so that you can easily create the second component, refer to Figure 12.68.

12.67

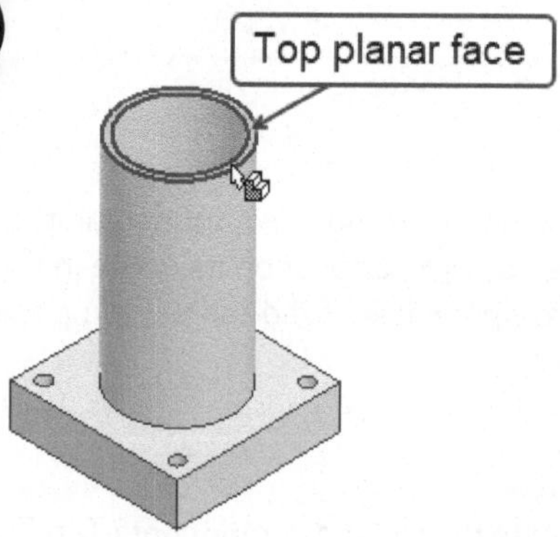

12.68

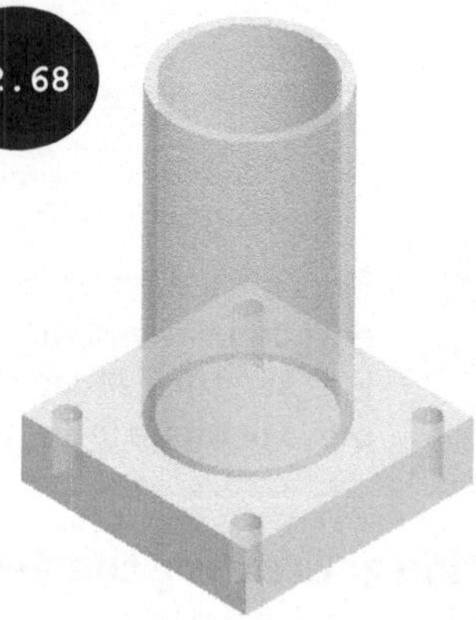

Now, you need to create the features of the second component (**Top Plate**).

7. Click on the **Start 2D Sketch** tool in the **Sketch** panel or press the S key. The three default planes of the component appear in the graphics area. Also, you are prompted to select a plane for creating the sketch of the base feature of the second component. Change the orientation of the model to isometric.

8. Select the top plane (**XY Plane**) of the component as the sketching plane, see Figure 12.69. The Sketching environment gets invoked.

9. Create the sketch of the base feature of the second component, see Figure 12.70. In this figure, the entities (a rectangle and four circles) of the sketch are created by projecting the edges of the first component using the **Project Geometry** tool.

12.69

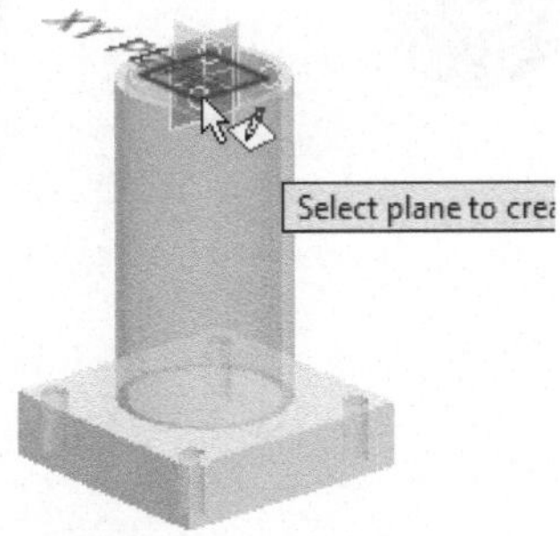

12.70

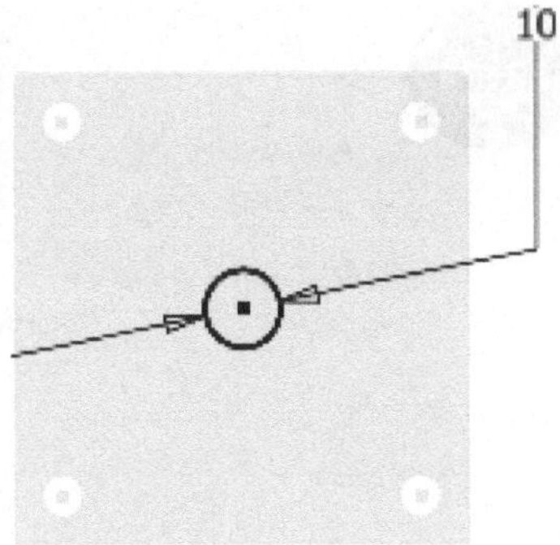

10. After creating the sketch, click on the **3D Model** tab of the **Ribbon** and then extrude the sketch to a depth of 15 mm by using the **Extrude** tool, see Figure 12.71.

    Now, you need to create the second feature of the component.

11. Invoke the Sketching environment by selecting the top planar face of the base feature as the sketching plane.

12. Create the sketch (two circles) of the second feature of the component, see Figure 12.72. In this figure, the inner circle of the sketch is created by projecting the inner circular edge of the base feature.

12.71

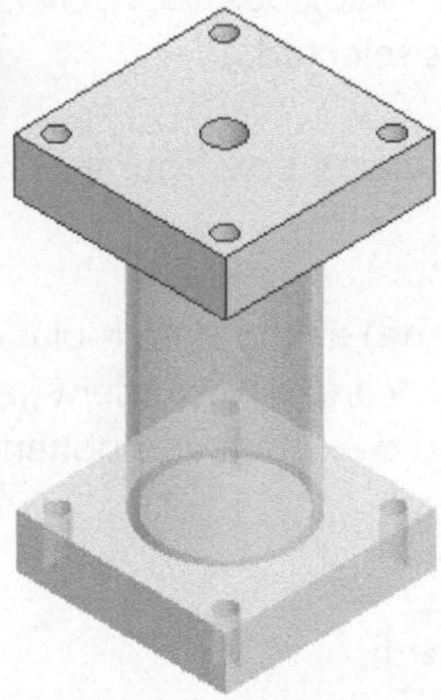

12.72

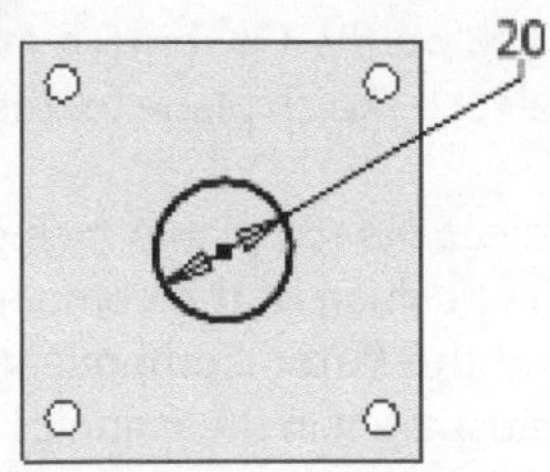

13. Click on the **3D Model** tab in the **Ribbon** and then extrude the sketch to a depth of 5 mm by using the **Extrude** tool, see Figure 12.73.

14. After creating the second component (**Top Plate**), click on the **Return** tool in the **Return** panel of the **Ribbon**, see Figure 12.74. The second component is created and switched to the Assembly environment, see Figure 12.75.

12.73

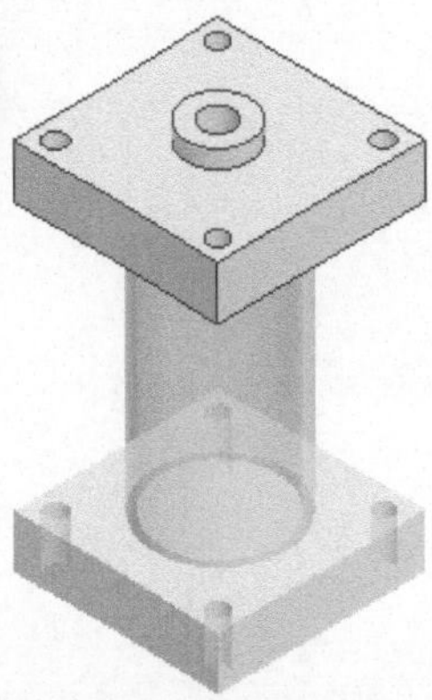

12.74

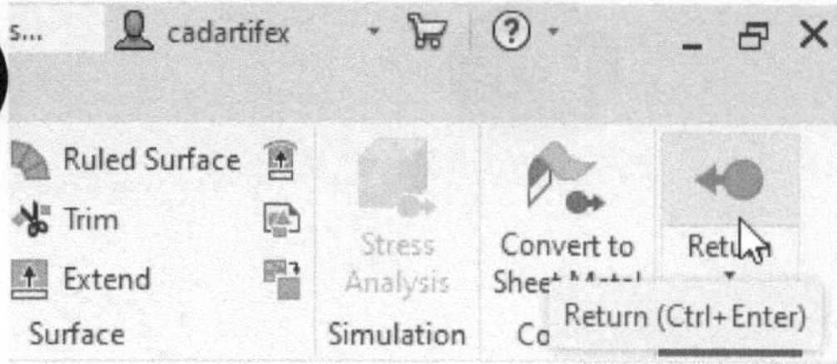

12.75

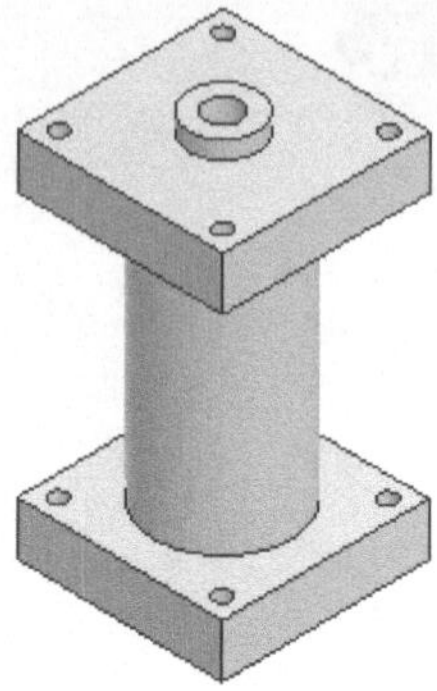

Section 4: Creating the Third Component

Now, you need to create the third component (**Piston**) of the assembly.

1. Click on the **Create** tool in the **Component** panel of the **Assemble** tab or press the N key. The **Create In-Place Component** dialog box appears.

2. Enter **Piston** in the **New Component Name** field of the dialog box as the name of the component.

3. Click on the **Browse Templates** button available next to the **Template** drop-down list and then select the **Standard (mm).ipt** template in the **Metric** tab of the dialog box. Next, click on the **OK** button in the dialog box. The **Standard (mm).ipt** template gets selected.

4. Click on the **OK** button in the **Create In-Place Component** dialog box. You are prompted to select a sketch plane for the component.

5. Select the top planar face of the second component (**Top Plane**) as the sketch plane to define the position of the component, see Figure 12.76. The part modeling environment gets invoked and the **Piston** component gets added in the **Browser**. Also, the existing components become transparent in the graphics area.

12.76

Now, you need to create the features of the third component (**Piston**).

6. Click on the **Start 2D Sketch** tool in the **Sketch** panel or press the **S** key. The three default planes of the component appear in the graphics area. Also, you are prompted to select a plane for creating the sketch of the base feature of the third component. Change the orientation of the model to isometric.

7. Select the top plane (**XY Plane**) of the component as the sketching plane, see Figure 12.77. The Sketching environment gets invoked.

8. Create a circle by projecting the inner circular edge of the second component using the **Project Geometry** tool, see Figure 12.78.

12.77

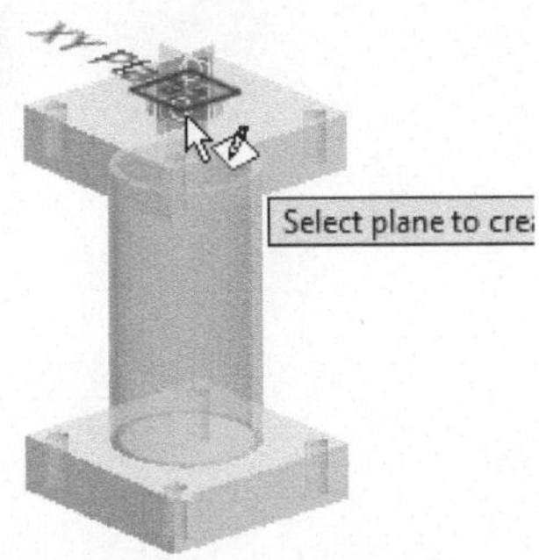

12.78

9. After creating the sketch (circle), click on the **3D Model** tab of the **Ribbon** and then extrude it to a depth of 90 mm symmetrically, on both sides of the sketching plane by using the **Extrude** tool, see Figure 12.79.

12.79

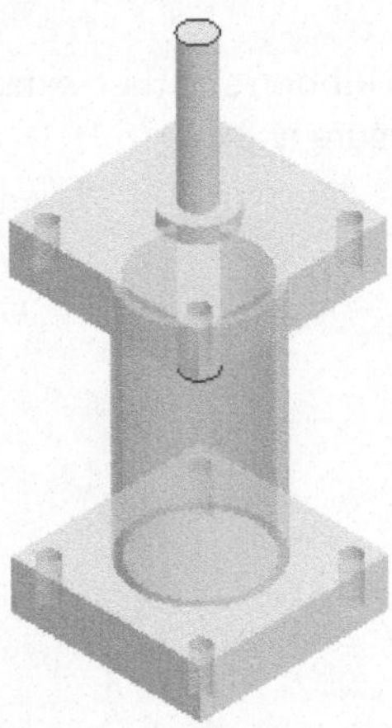

Now, you need to create the second feature of the third component.

10. Invoke the Sketching environment by selecting the bottom planar face of the base feature as the sketching plane.

11. Create a sketch of the second feature of the component, see Figure 12.80.

12. Click on the **3D Model** tab in the **Ribbon** and then extrude the sketch to a depth of 6 mm downward by using the **Extrude** tool, see Figure 12.81.

12.80

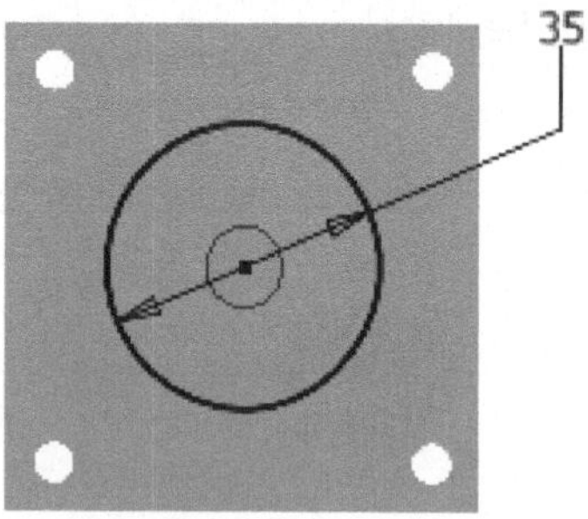

12.81

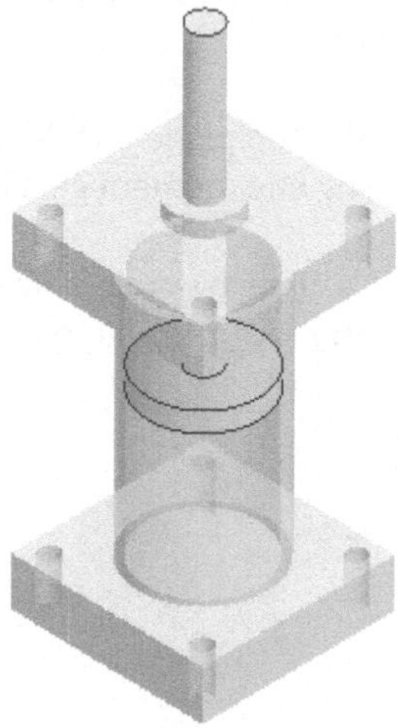

Now, you need to create the third feature of the component.

13. Invoke the Sketching environment by selecting the top planar face of the base feature as the sketching plane.

14. Create a sketch (a circle of diameter 20 mm) of the third feature of the component, see Figure 12.82.

15. Click on the **3D Model** tab in the **Ribbon** and then extrude the sketch to a depth of 20 mm upward by using the **Extrude** tool, see Figure 12.83.

12.82

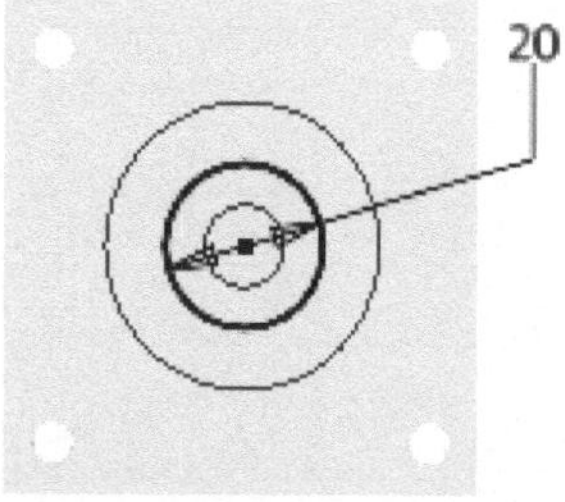

12.83

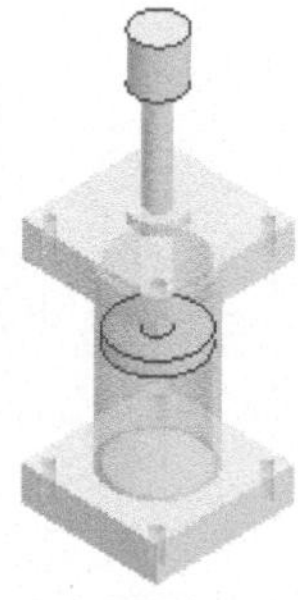

16. After creating the third component (**Piston**), click on the **Return** tool in the **Return** panel of the **Ribbon**, see Figure 12.84. The third component is created and switched to the Assembly environment, see Figure 12.85.

12.84

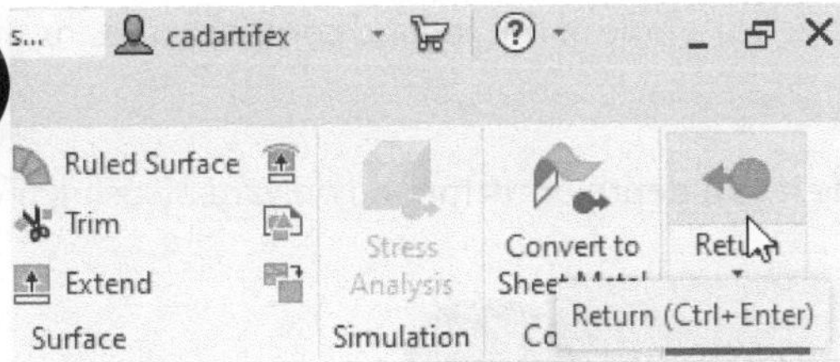

12.85

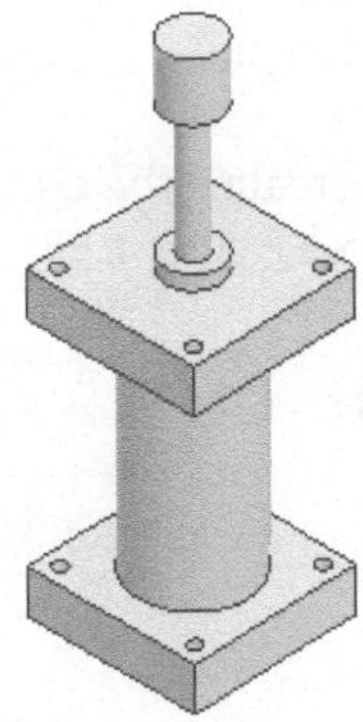

Section 5: Creating the Fourth Component

Now, you need to create the fourth component (**Bolt**) of the assembly.

1. Click on the **Create** tool in the **Component** panel of the **Assemble** tab or press the **N** key. The **Create In-Place Component** dialog box appears.

2. Enter **Bolt** in the **New Component Name** field of the dialog box.

3. Click on the **Browse Templates** button available next to the **Template** drop-down list and then select the **Standard (mm).ipt** template in the **Metric** tab of the dialog box. Next, click on the **OK** button in the dialog box. The **Standard (mm).ipt** template gets selected.

4. Click on the **OK** button in the **Create In-Place Component** dialog box. You are prompted to select a sketch plane for the component.

5. Select the top planar face of the second component (**Top Plane**) as the sketch plane to define the position of the component, see Figure 12.86. The part modeling environment gets invoked and the **Bolt** component gets added in the **Browser**. Also, the existing components become transparent in the graphics area.

   12.86

   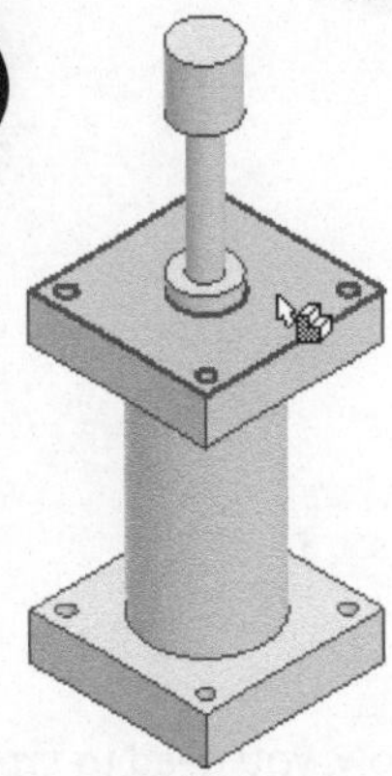

   Now, you need to create the features of the fourth component (**Bolt**).

6. Click on the **Start 2D Sketch** tool in the **Sketch** panel or press the **S** key. The three default planes of the component appear in the graphics area. Also, you are prompted to select a plane for creating the sketch of the base feature of the third component. Change the orientation of the model to isometric.

7. Select the top plane (**XY Plane**) of the component as the sketching plane. The Sketching environment gets invoked.

8. Create a circle by projecting the circular edge of a hole of the second component using the **Project Geometry** tool, see Figure 12.87.

9. After creating the sketch (circle), extrude it to a depth of 115 mm downward by using the **Extrude** tool, see Figure 12.88.

12.87

12.88

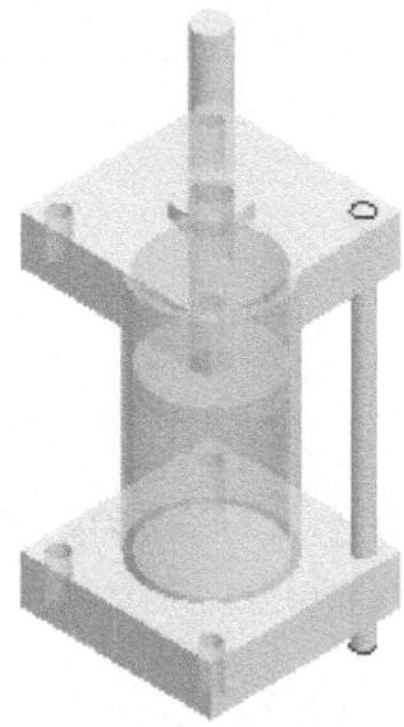

Now, you need to create the second feature of the component.

10. Invoke the Sketching environment by selecting the top planar face of the base feature as the sketching plane.

11. Create the sketch (polygon of six sides) of the second feature of the component (see Figure 12.89), and then extrude it to a depth of 5 mm by using the **Extrude** tool, see Figure 12.90.

12.89

12.90

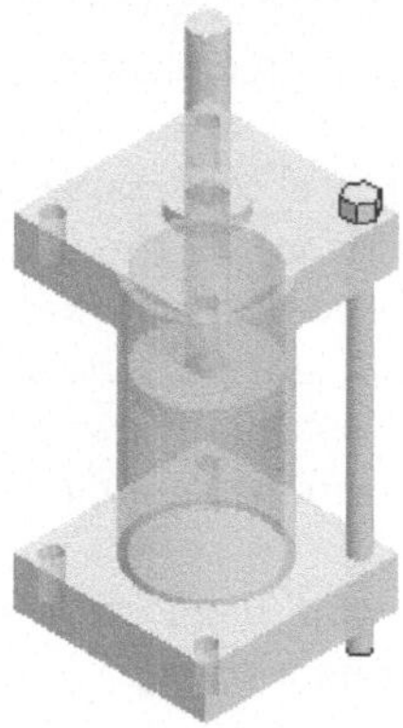

Now, you need to create a thread on the component as the third feature.

12. Create the **ANSI Metric M Profile** thread of size 5, designation M5x0.8, and class 6g from the bottom side of the fourth component (Bolt) up to a depth of 10 mm by using the **Thread** tool of the **Modify** panel, see Figure 12.91.

12.91

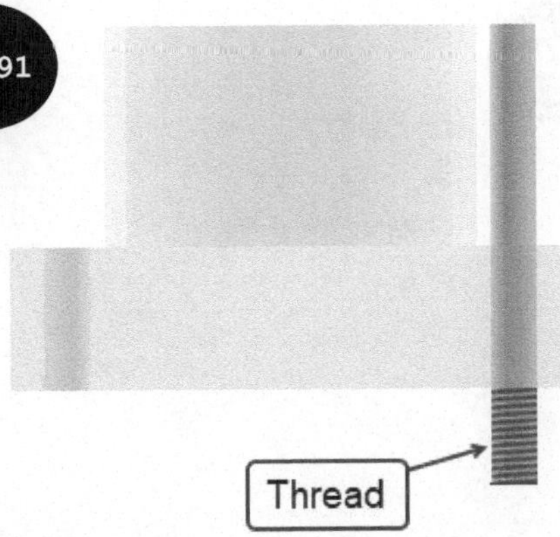

13. After creating the fourth component (**Bolt**), click on the **Return** tool in the **Return** panel of the **Ribbon**, see Figure 12.92. The fourth component is created and switched to the Assembly environment, see Figure 12.93.

12.92

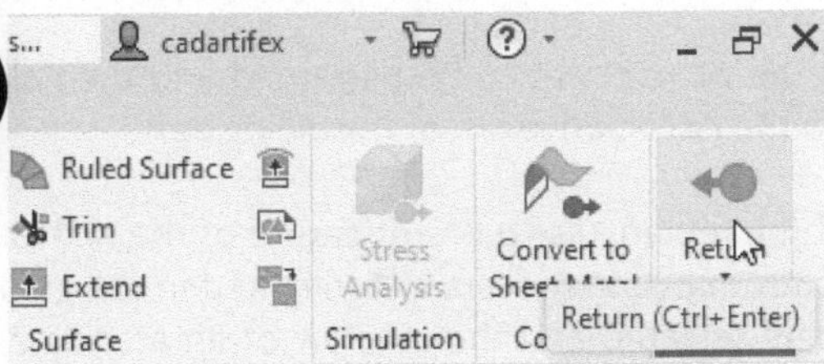

12.93

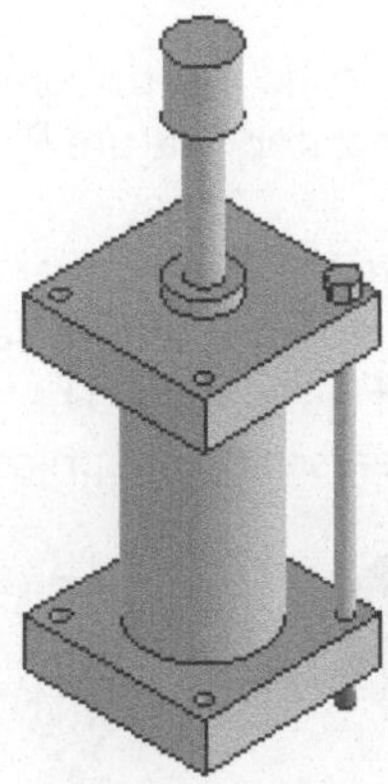

Section 6: Creating the Rectangular Pattern

Now, you need to create a rectangular pattern for creating the remaining instances of the fourth component of the assembly.

1. Click on the **Pattern** tool in the **Pattern** group of the **Assemble** tab, see Figure 12.94. The **Pattern Component** dialog box appears, see Figure 12.95. Also, you are prompted to select components to be patterned.

12.94

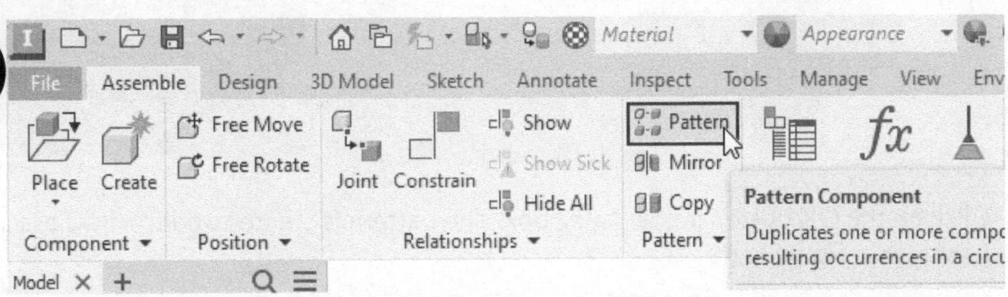

12.95

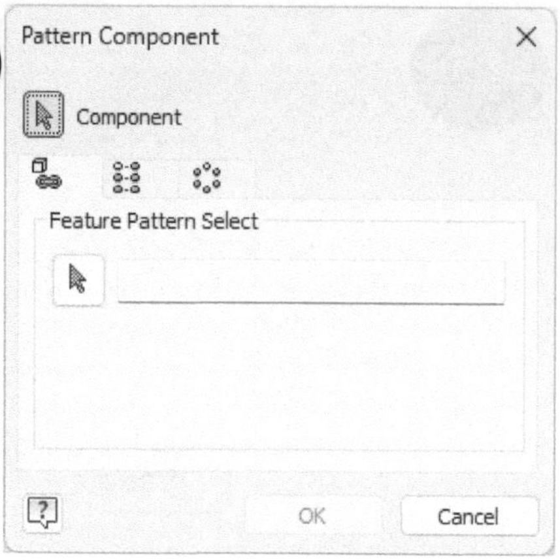

2. Ensure that the **Associative** tab is activated in the dialog box for creating an associative pattern.

3. Select the fourth component (**Bolt**) as the component to be patterned and then click on the **Associated Feature Pattern** button in the **Associative** tab of the dialog box.

4. Move the cursor over an occurrence of the rectangular pattern feature of the first component (**Cylinder**) and then select it when all pattern occurrences are highlighted in the graphics area, see Figure 12.96. The pattern feature gets selected and the preview of an associative pattern appears in the graphics area, see Figure 12.97.

12.96

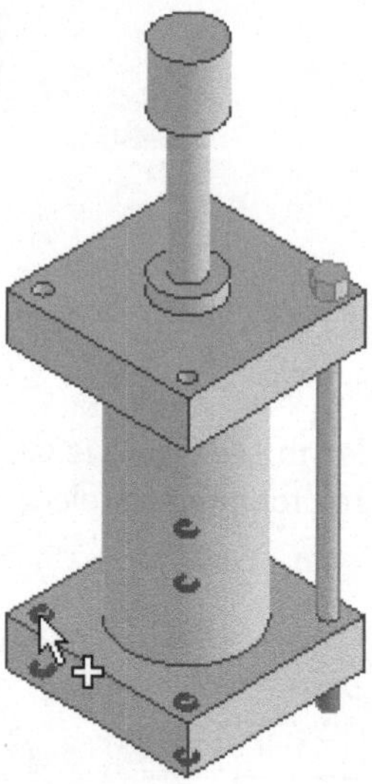

12.97

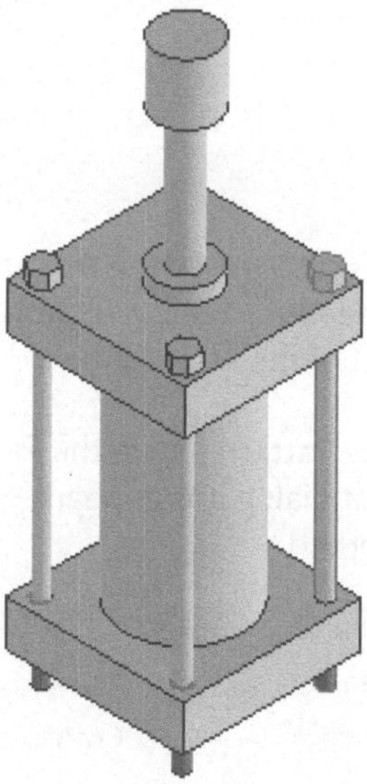

5. Click on the **OK** button in the dialog box. The pattern is created and the final assembly appears as shown in Figure 12.98.

12.98

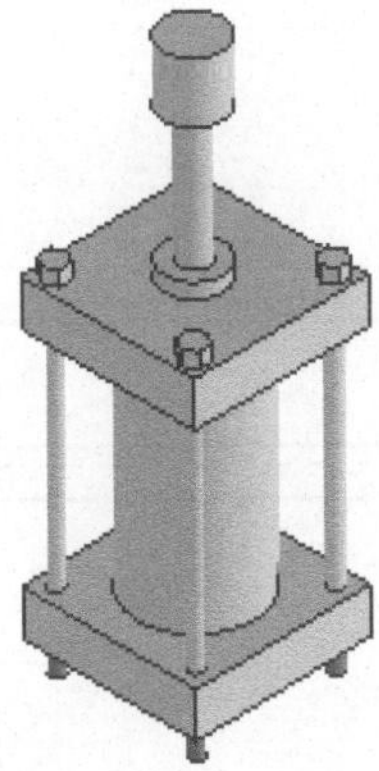

Section 7: Saving the Assembly

Now, you need to save the assembly.

1. Click on the **Save** button in the **Quick Access Toolbar** toolbar. The **Save As** dialog box appears.
2. Enter a name for the assembly in the **File name** field of the dialog box and then click on the **Save** button. The **Save** dialog box appears.
3. Click on the **Yes to All** button and the **OK** button in the dialog box. The assembly file and all its components get saved in the specified location.

Hands-on Test Drive 1

Create an assembly, as shown in Figure 12.99 by using the Top-down approach. Different views and dimensions of the individual components of the assembly are shown in Figures 12.100 through 12.103. All dimensions are in mm.

12.99

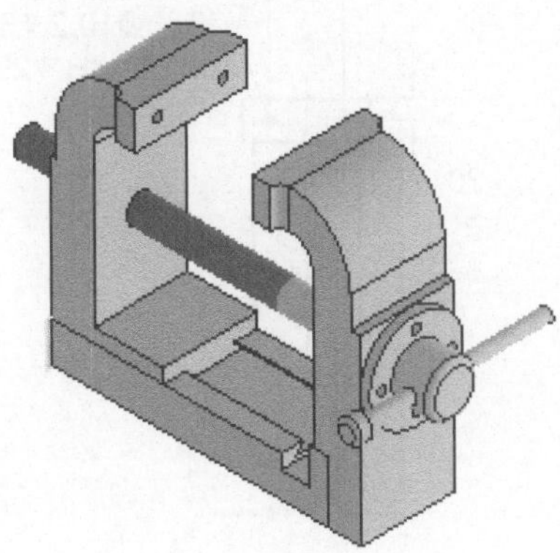

12.100

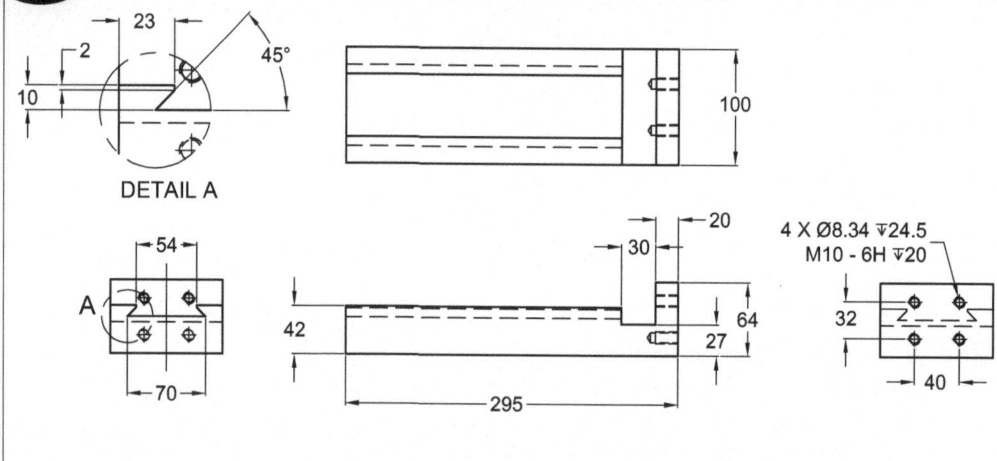

Base

12.101

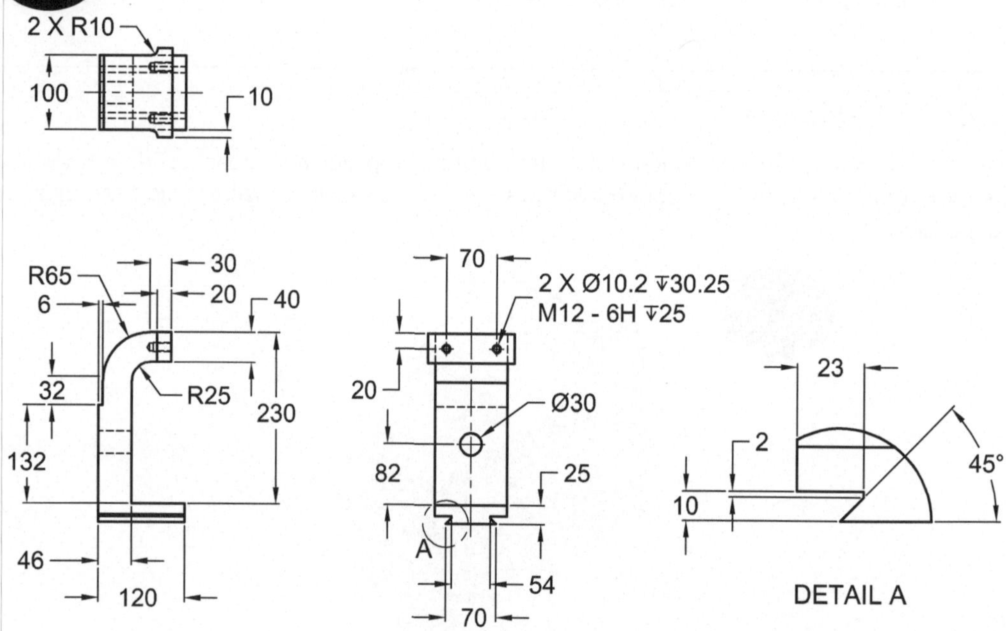

Moving Jaw

12.102

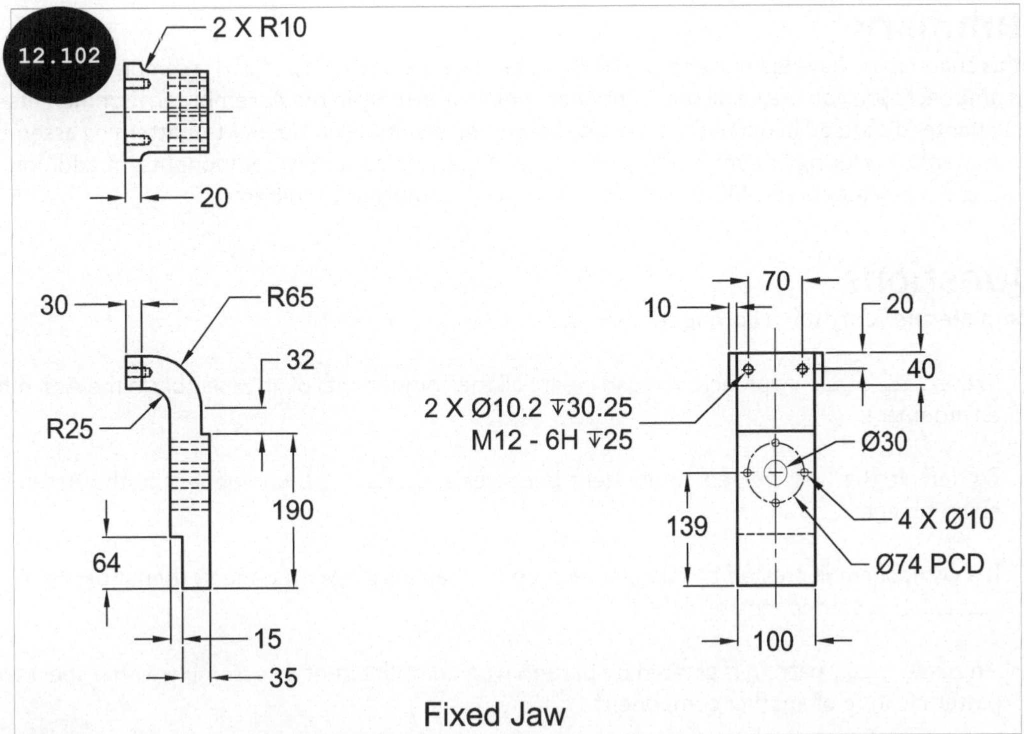
2 X R10
20
30
R65
32
R25
190
64
15
35
70
10
20
40
2 X Ø10.2 ↧30.25
M12 - 6H ↧25
Ø30
4 X Ø10
139
Ø74 PCD
100
Fixed Jaw

12.103

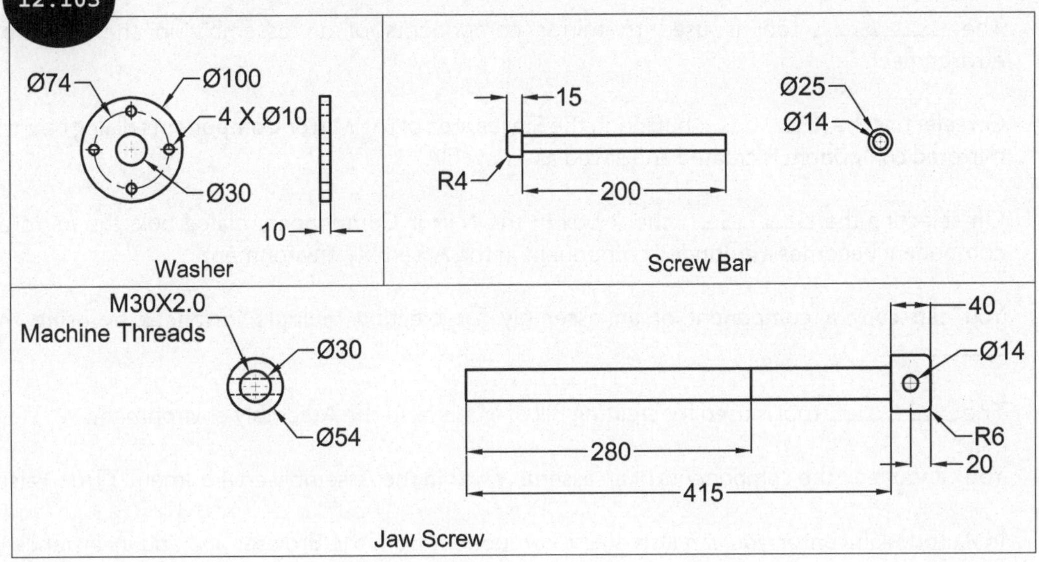
Ø74
Ø100
4 X Ø10
Ø30
10
Washer
15
Ø25
Ø14
R4
200
Screw Bar
M30X2.0
Machine Threads
Ø30
Ø54
40
Ø14
R6
20
280
415
Jaw Screw

Summary

In this chapter, you have learned about creating assemblies using the Top-down assembly approach. In this approach, you can create all the components of an assembly in the Assembly environment itself. The chapter discussed in detail the methods for editing assembly components, patterning assembly components, mirroring assembly components, and copying assembly components, in addition to creating Bill of Material (BOM) of an assembly in the Assembly environment.

Questions

Complete and verify the following sentences:

- In the _________ approach, you can create all the components of an assembly in the Assembly environment.
- By default, the first created component becomes a _________ component in the Assembly environment.
- If a component is created by taking reference from an existing component, then it becomes an _________ component, by default.
- An _________ pattern is created by patterning a component of an assembly with respect to a pattern feature of another component.
- In the Assembly environment, you can create three types of patterns: _________, _________, and _________ by using the **Pattern** tool.
- The _________ tool is used to mirror components of an assembly in the Assembly environment.
- On selecting the _________ button in the **Status** area of the **Mirror Components** dialog box, the mirrored component is created and saved as a new file.
- On selecting the _________ check box in the **Mirror Components** dialog box, the mirrored component becomes a grounded component in the Assembly environment.
- You can copy a component of an assembly for creating multiple instances by using the _________.
- The _________ tool is used for creating Bill of Material in the Assembly environment.
- You cannot edit the components of an assembly within the Assembly environment. (True/False)
- In Autodesk Inventor, you can also drag a component from the **Browser** and add its instance in the graphics area. (True/False)

CHAPTER

13

Creating Animation and Exploded Views

In this chapter, the following topics will be discussed:

- Invoking the Presentation Environment
- Capturing Actions on the Timeline
- Capturing Tweaks on the Timeline
- Editing Time and Properties of a Tweak
- Deleting a Tweak
- Creating a Snapshot View
- Editing a Snapshot View
- Renaming a Snapshot View
- Deleting a Snapshot View
- Publishing a Snapshot View to a Raster Image
- Creating an Exploded View in a Drawing File
- Creating a New Storyboard
- Creating a New Scene
- Playing Animation of a Storyboard
- Publishing Animation to a Video File

In Autodesk Inventor, you can create an animation and exploded views of an assembly. The exploded views of an assembly serve as a great marketing tool and can be used in assembly instructions, technical documentation, operation manuals, and replacement part drawings for product catalogs. In Autodesk Inventor, you can create an animation and exploded views of an assembly in the Presentation environment. The method for invoking the Presentation environment is discussed next.

Invoking the Presentation Environment

1. Start Autodesk Inventor and then click on the **New** tool in the startup user interface of Autodesk Inventor, see Figure 13.1. The **Create New File** dialog box appears, see Figure 13.2. Alternatively, click on the **New** tool in the **Quick Access Toolbar** or press the CTRL + **N** key to invoke the **Create New File** dialog box.

13.1

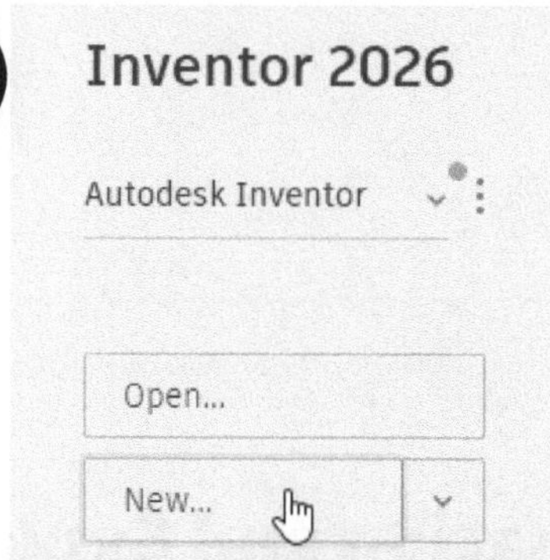

Tip: In the **Create New File** dialog box, you can select a default Metric or English template for invoking the Presentation environment.

2. Expand the **Templates** node in the **Create New File** dialog box and then select the **Metric** folder. All the default Metric templates appear on the right panel of the dialog box, refer to Figure 13.2. Note that, to display all the default English templates, you need to select the **English** folder in the **Templates** node of the dialog box.

13.2

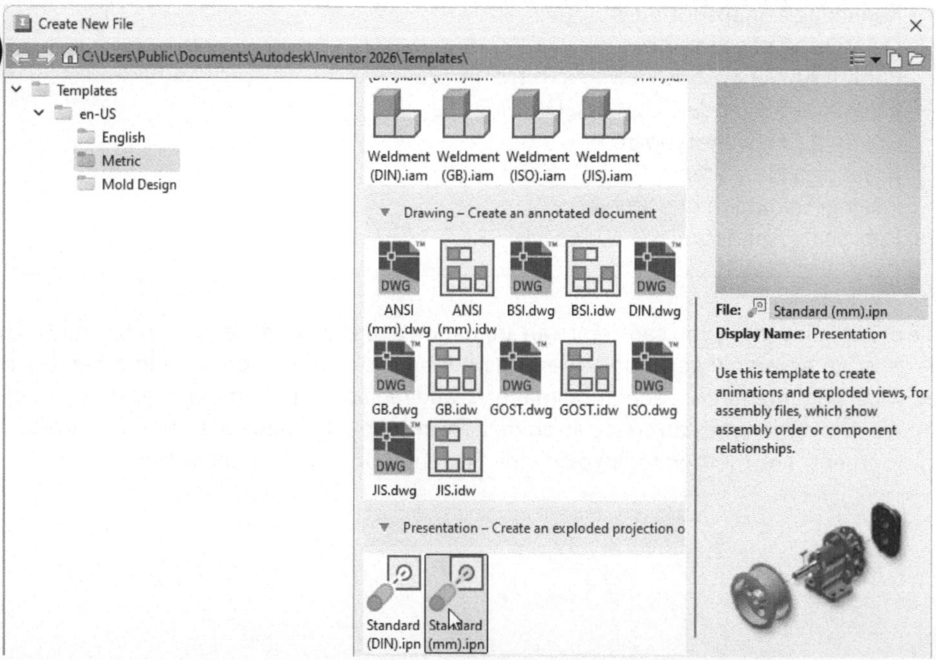

3. Scroll down in the dialog box and then double-click on the **Standard (mm).ipn** template, refer to Figure 13.2. Note that *.ipn* is the file extension of the Inventor presentation file. The Presentation environment is invoked and the **Insert** dialog box appears. Also, you are prompted to select an assembly file for creating its animation and exploded views.

4. Browse to the location where the assembly file is saved and then select it for creating its animation and exploded views.

5. Click on the **Open** button in the **Insert** dialog box. The selected assembly gets opened in the Presentation environment and **Scene1** is added in the **Browser**. The startup user interface of the Presentation environment appears as shown in Figure 13.3.

13.3

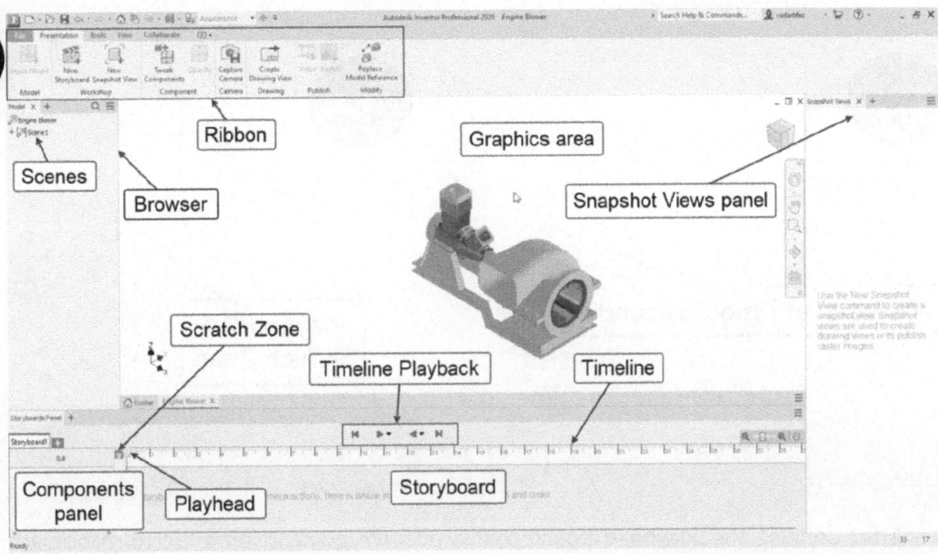

6. After invoking the Presentation environment, you can create an animation and an exploded view of the assembly. For doing so, you need to capture actions and tweaks along the **Timeline** in a storyboard, see Figure 13.4. Note that operations such as changes in camera (zoom or orbit) position and component visibility performed at a given point in time on an assembly are captured as actions on the **Timeline**. On the other hand, all transforming operations such as move and rotate performed at a given point in time on individual components of an assembly are captured as tweaks on the **Timeline**. The methods for capturing actions and tweaks on the **Timeline** of a storyboard are discussed next.

13.4

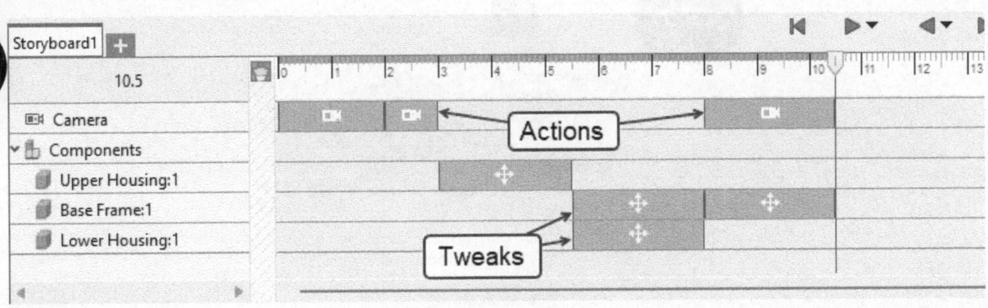

Capturing Actions on the Timeline

As discussed earlier, operations such as changes in camera (zoom or orbit) position and component visibility performed at a given point in time of an assembly, are captured as actions on the **Timeline**. The methods for capturing actions on the **Timeline** are discussed below:

1. Define the position of the **Playhead** on the **Timeline** at a positive point in time by dragging it to capture an action such as camera position or component visibility, see Figure 13.5.

Note: If the position of the **Playhead** is defined on the **Scratch Zone** (Time 0), then the action will not be captured on the **Timeline**, see Figure 13.6. However, the camera position at time 0 can be updated.

13.5

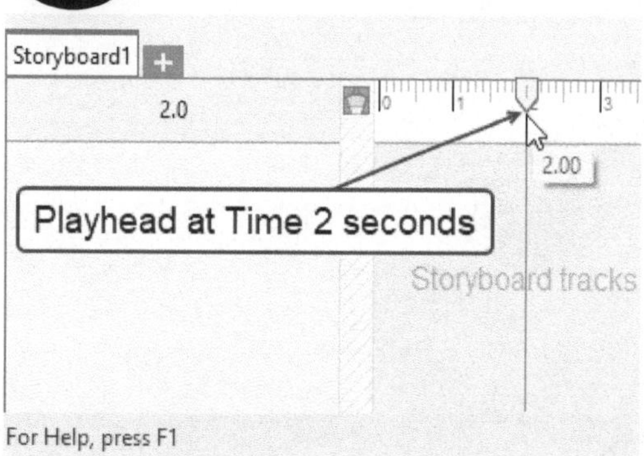

13.6

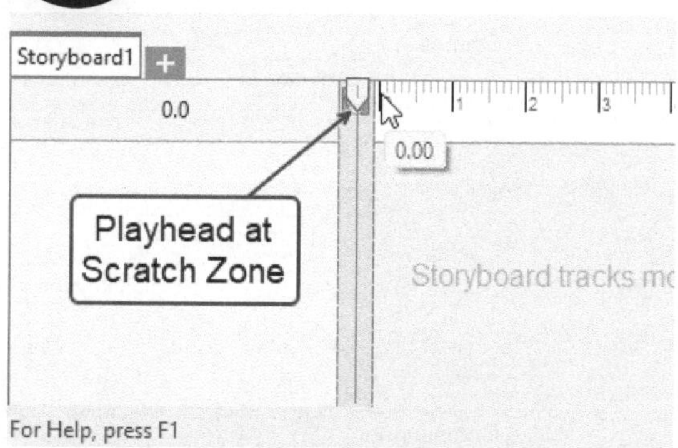

2. After defining the **Playhead** position at a positive point in time, perform operations such as changes in camera (zoom or orbit) position or component visibility/opacity of the assembly.

Tip: You can perform the navigation operations such as zoom and orbit for changing the camera position by using the mouse buttons or the navigating tools. To change the component visibility (show or hide) or opacity, right-click on a component in the graphics area and then click on the **Visibility** or **Opacity** in the **Marking Menu** that appears, respectively, see Figure 13.7.

13.7

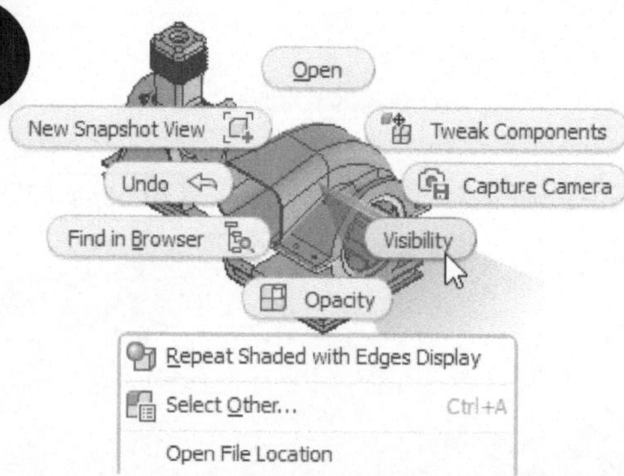

3. Click on the **Capture Camera** tool in the **Camera** panel of the **Presentation** tab, see Figure 13.8. The performed operation is captured as an action on the **Timeline** at the defined point in time, see Figure 13.9.

13.8

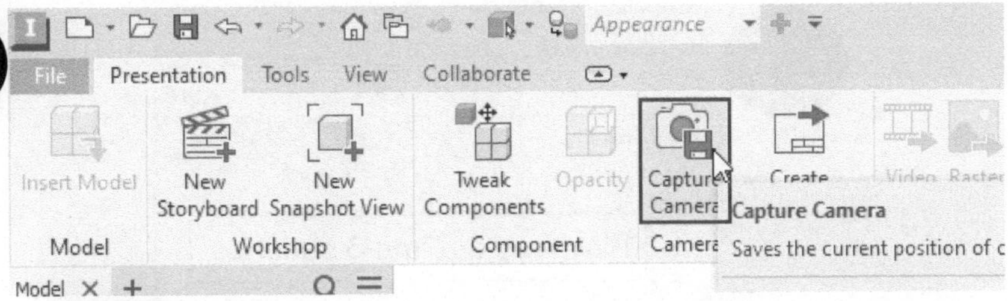

13.9

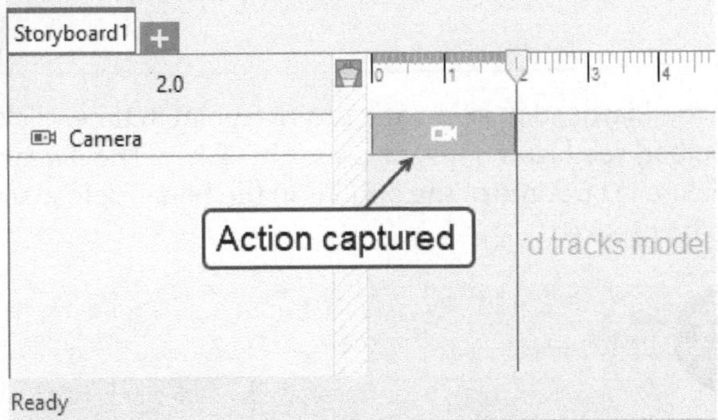

4. Similarly, you can capture multiple actions on the **Timeline** at different points in time.

   Now, you can play the animation to review the captured actions.

5. Click on the **Play Current Storyboard** button in the **Timeline Playback** present at the top center of the **Timeline**, see Figure 13.10.

13.10

Note: After capturing an action, if you further perform any navigating operation without changing the **Playhead** position on the **Timeline**, then on clicking on the **Capture Camera** tool, the existing view gets overridden by the newly performed navigating operation.

Capturing Tweaks on the Timeline

All transforming operations such as move and rotate, performed at a given point in time on individual components of an assembly are captured as tweaks on the **Timeline**. In Autodesk Inventor, you can perform transforming operations by using the **Tweak Components** tool. The method for performing the transforming operations and capturing tweaks is discussed below:

1. Define the position of the **Playhead** on the **Timeline** at a positive point in time by dragging it to specify the start position of a tweak, see Figure 13.11. In this figure, the **Playhead** is positioned on the **Timeline** at a time of 3 seconds.

13.11

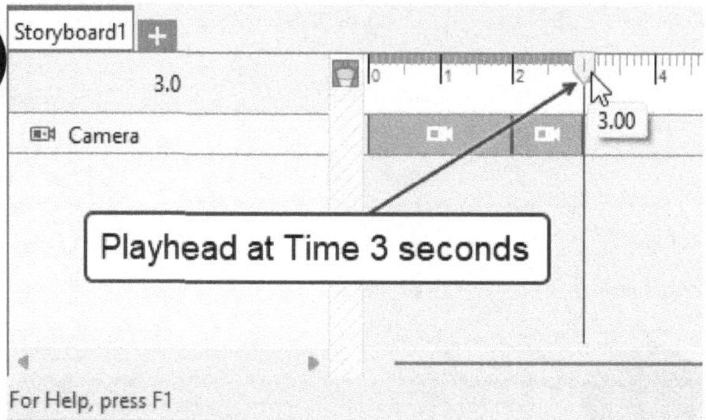

2. After defining the **Playhead** position at a positive point in time, click on the **Tweak Components** tool in the **Toolbar**, see Figure 13.12, or press the **T** key. The **Tweak Components** Mini-Toolbar appears, see Figure 13.13. Some of the options in the Mini-Toolbar are enabled only on selecting a component to be tweaked.

13.12

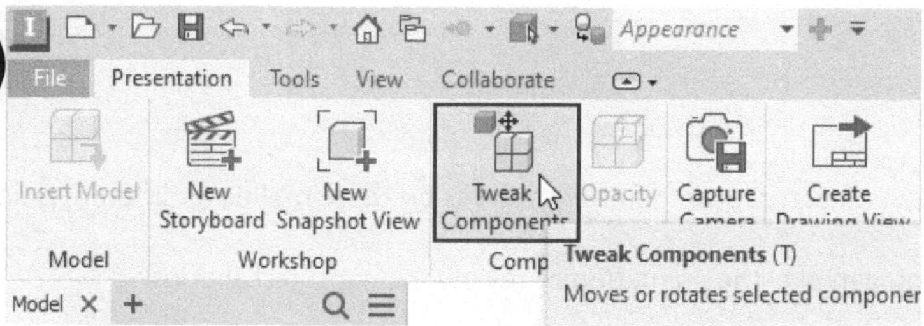

13.13

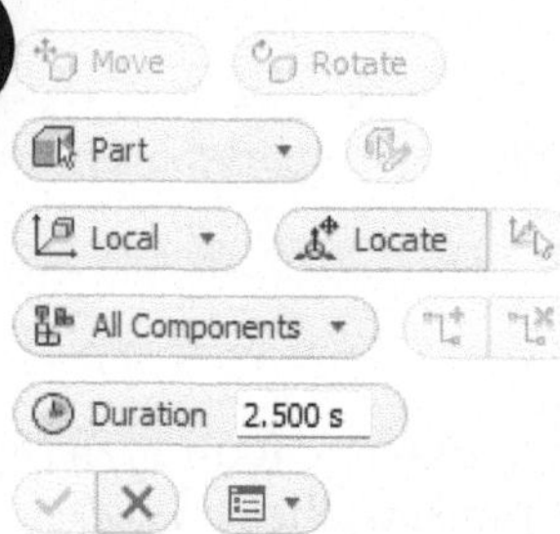

3. Select a component in the graphics area. A Triad appears in the graphics area, see Figure 13.14. Also, all options in the Mini-Toolbar are enabled in the graphics area, see Figure 13.15. Note that you can also select multiple components to be tweaked by pressing the CTRL key.

13.14

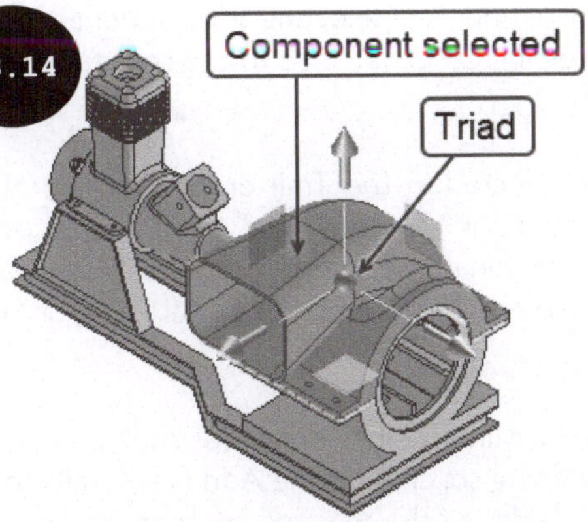

13.15

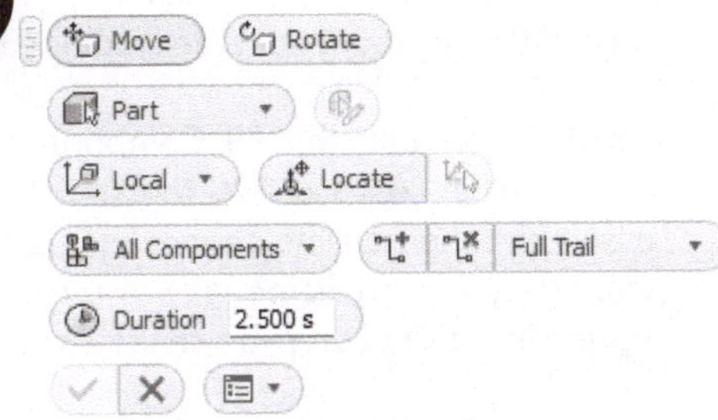

Move: By default, the **Move** tool is activated in the **Tweak Components** Mini-Toolbar, see Figure 13.15. As a result, you can move the selected component in the graphics area by dragging the Triad handles (arrow, plane, or origin point).

Rotate: On activating the **Rotate** tool in the Mini-Toolbar, you can rotate the selected component in the graphics area by dragging the Triad handles.

Selection Filter: By default, the **Part** option is selected in the **Selection Filter** drop-down list of the Mini-Toolbar. As a result, you can select individual parts of a sub-assembly as well as of the main assembly in the graphics area or in the **Browser**. On selecting the **Component** option , you can select components of the assembly. Note that a sub-assembly of an assembly is treated as a component.

Add/Remove Components **:** The **Add/Remove Components** tool in the Mini-Toolbar is used for adding or removing components from the current selection set. Note that this tool is enabled only after moving or rotating the selected component in the graphics area by using the Triad handles. When this tool is enabled, click on it in the Mini-Toolbar (see Figure 13.16) and then select the components to be added to the current selection set. To remove a component from the current selection set, ensure that the **Add/Remove Components** tool is activated. Next, press the CTRL key and then select the component to be removed from the current selection set.

13.16

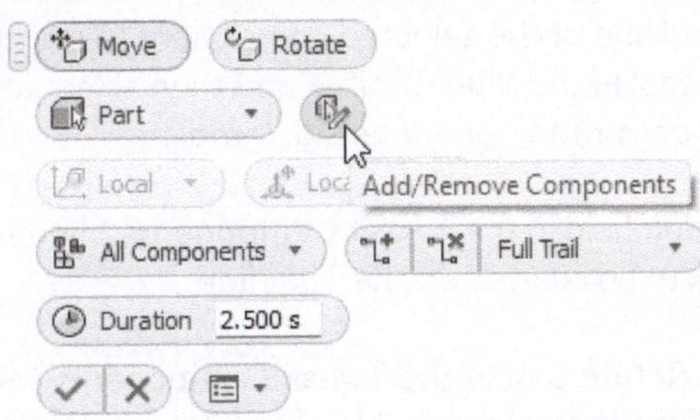

UCS: By default, the **Local** option is selected in the **UCS** drop-down list of the Mini-Toolbar. As a result, on selecting a component, the Triad appears in the graphics area using the component local UCS. On selecting the **World** option, the Triad appears in the graphics area using the world UCS. You can also define a different alignment direction for the component local UCS by activating the **Locate** tool in the Mini-Toolbar and then selecting an alignment edge or a face of a component. The handles/arrows of the local UCS get aligned to the selected edge or face of the component in the graphics area.

Trail: By default, the **All Components** option is selected in the **Trail** drop-down list of the Mini-Toolbar. As a result, the trail lines are created for all the moved components of the assembly. The trail line defines the path and the direction in which the component is moved or exploded, refer to Figure 13.17. You can select the **No trail**, **All Components**, **All Parts**, or **Single** option in the **Trail** drop-down list, as required.

Add New Trails : The **Add New Trails** tool in the Mini-Toolbar is used for adding a new trail line for the selected component being moved. For doing so, click on the **Add New Trails** tool in the Mini-Toolbar and then move the cursor over an edge of the selected component, and then click when the cursor snaps to the required snap point, see Figure 13.18. A new trail line gets added to the selected component to define its movement.

13.17

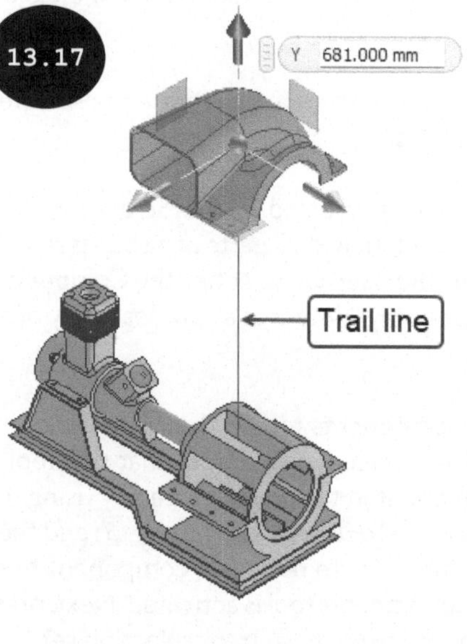

13.18

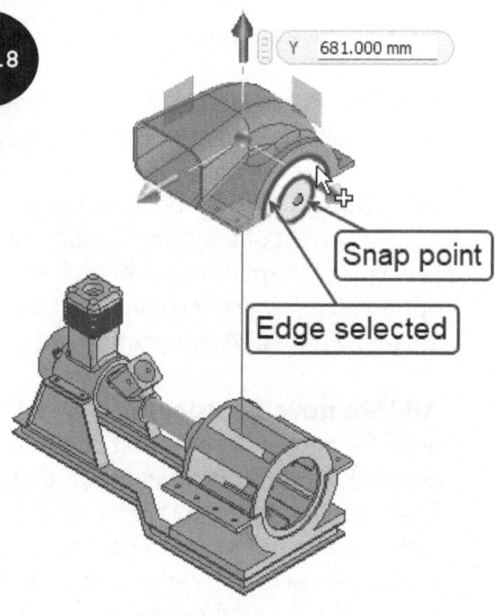

Delete Existing Trails : The **Delete Existing Trails** tool in the Mini-Toolbar is used for deleting an existing trail line of the selected component being moved. For doing so, click on the **Delete Existing Trails** tool in the Mini-Toolbar and then select an existing trail line to be deleted. The selected trail line of the component gets deleted.

Duration: The **Duration** field in the **Tweak Components** Mini-Toolbar is used for specifying the duration for the tweak to be created on the **Timeline**.

4. Click on the **Move** or **Rotate** tool in the **Tweak Components** Mini-Toolbar to create a Move or Rotate tweak on the **Timeline**, respectively.
5. Drag the Triad handle to translate the selected component or components in the graphics area.
6. Enter the duration of the tweak to be created in the **Duration** field of the Mini-Toolbar.

7. Click on the **OK** button in the **Tweak Components** Mini-Toolbar. A tweak of specified duration gets captured on the **Timeline**, see Figure 13.19. In this figure, a Move tweak of 2.5 seconds duration is captured on the **Timeline**.

13.19

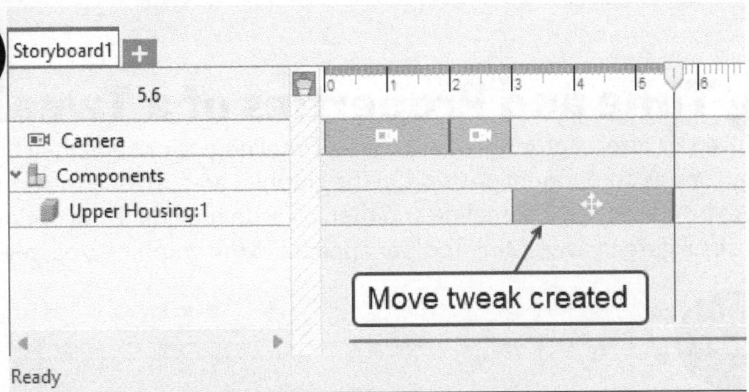

8. Similarly, you can capture multiple tweaks on the **Timeline** at different points in time by performing transforming operations on other components of the assembly one by one by using the **Tweak Components** tool, refer to Figure 13.20.

13.20

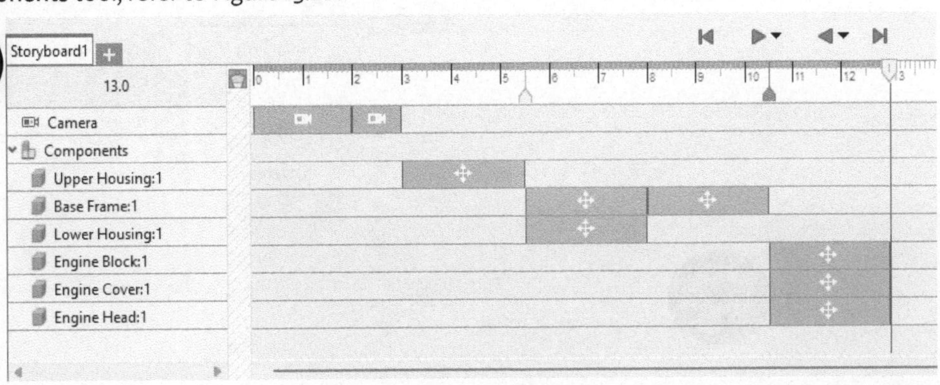

Note: The tweaks get saved on the **Timeline** of the storyboard as well as in the **Tweaks** folder of the active scene in the **Browser**, see Figure 13.21. In a presentation file (*.ipn*), you can create multiple scenes and for each scene, you can create animation and exploded views for the respective assembly. You will learn about creating multiple scenes in a presentation file later in this chapter.

13.21

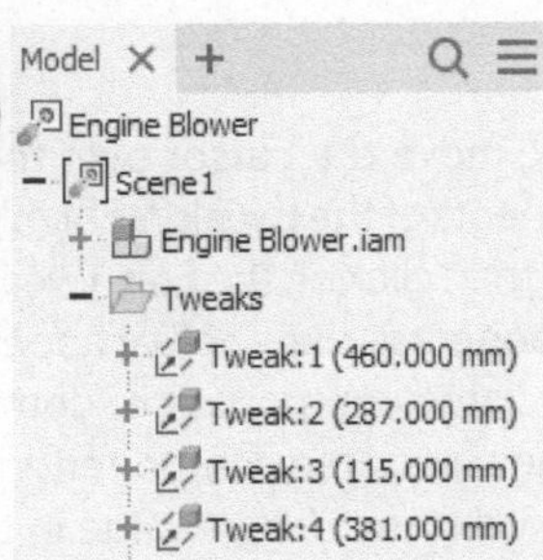

Now, you can play the animation to review the captured tweaks.

9. Click on the **Play Current Storyboard** button in the **Timeline Playback** at the top center of the **Timeline**.

Editing Time and Properties of a Tweak

In Autodesk Inventor, after capturing tweaks on the **Timeline**, you can edit their time (start time and end) and properties such as component position, in the graphics area. To edit the time of a tweak, right-click on the tweak to be edited in the **Timeline** and then click on the **Edit Time** option in the shortcut menu that appears, see Figure 13.22. A Mini-Toolbar appears in the graphics area, see Figure 13.23.

13.22

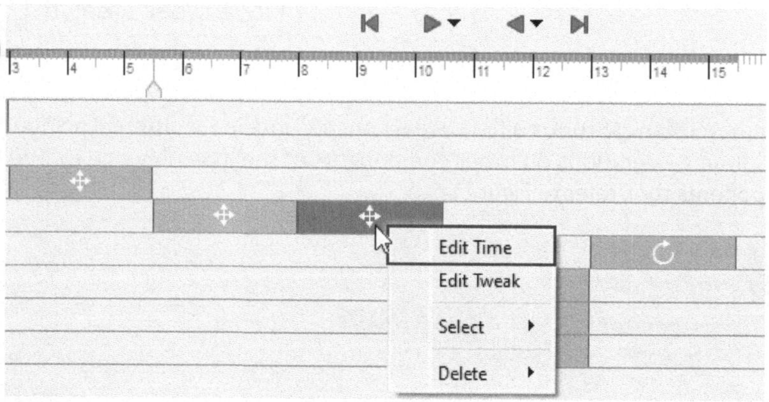

13.23

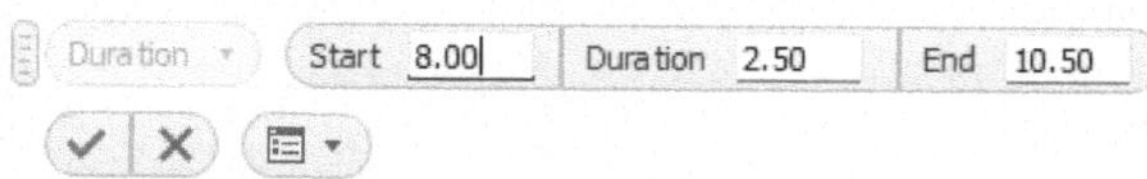

In the Mini-Toolbar, you can specify a new start time, end time, or duration for the selected tweak in the respective fields, as required. After editing the tweak time, click on the **OK** button in the Mini-Toolbar. The tweak time gets updated on the **Timeline**.

Note: Similar to editing the start and end time of a tweak, you can also edit the time of an action on the **Timeline**.

To edit the properties of a tweak, move the cursor over the tweak to be edited in the **Timeline**. The associated component or components of the tweak get highlighted in the graphics area. Next, right-click on the tweak on the **Timeline** and then click on the **Edit Tweak** option in the shortcut menu that appears, see Figure 13.24. The **Tweak Components** Mini-Toolbar appears in the graphics area. Also, the respective triad handle appears on the associated component or components of the tweak in the graphics area. You can change the position of the associated components in the graphics area by dragging the handle. Alternatively, you can enter a new distance/angle value in the **Distance** or **Angle** field that appears in the graphics area. After changing the position of the associated components of the tweak, click on the **OK** button in the **Tweak Components** Mini-Toolbar.

13.24

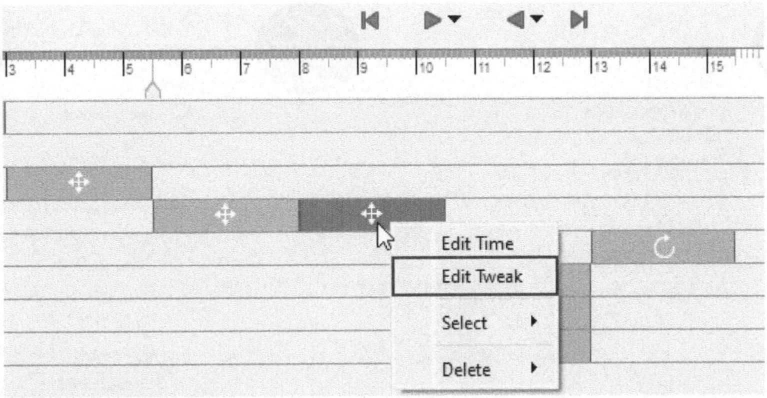

Deleting a Tweak

To delete a tweak, move the cursor over the tweak to be deleted on the **Timeline**. The associated component of the tweak gets highlighted in the graphics area. Next, right-click on the tweak on the **Timeline** and then click on the **Delete > Current** in the shortcut menu that appears, see Figure 13.25. The selected tweak gets deleted such that the associated component is removed from the tweak. On clicking the **Delete > Group** in the shortcut menu, the whole group gets deleted. Note that the **Group** option becomes available when multiple components are tweaked together or individually in the graphics area.

13.25

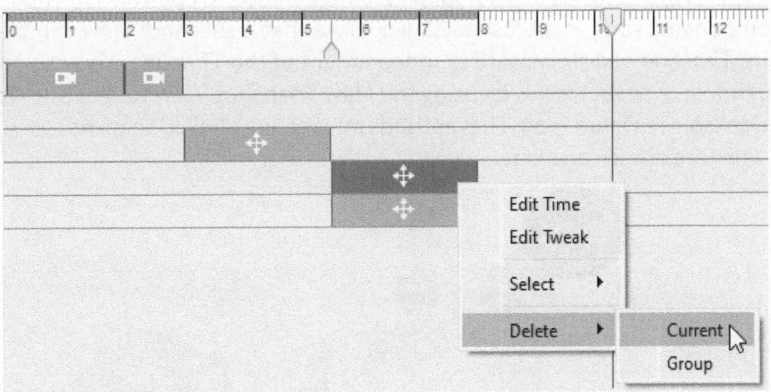

Note: You can also select a tweak to be deleted in the **Tweaks** folder of the **Browser** and then right-click to display a shortcut menu. Next, click on the **Delete** option, see Figure 13.26. The selected tweak gets deleted. To remove an individual component from a tweak, expand the tweak node in the **Tweaks** folder of the **Browser** and then right-click on the component to be removed, see Figure 13.27. Next, click on the **Delete Tweak > Current** in the shortcut menu that appears. The selected component gets removed from the tweak.

13.26

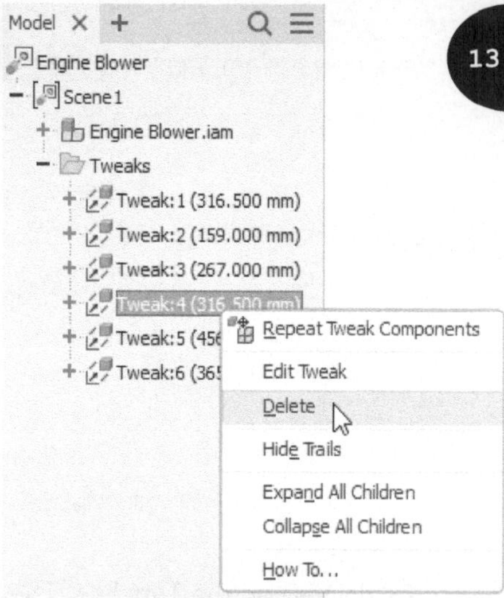

13.27

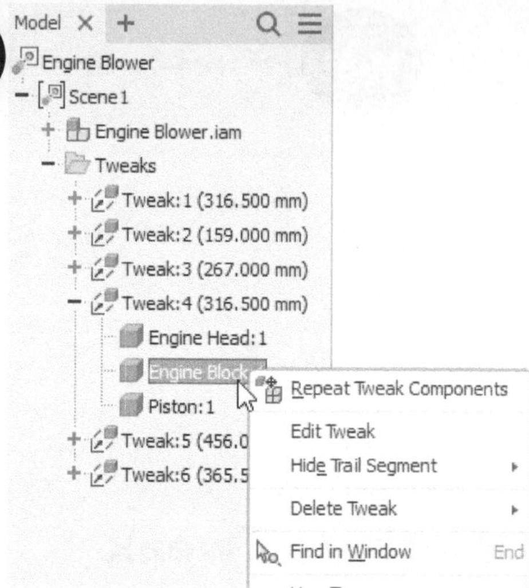

Creating a Snapshot View

Snapshot views store current position, visibility, and opacity of an assembly. You can use snapshot views to publish raster image files (*.jpg*, *.png*, *.tiff*, *.bmp*, and *.gif*) for presentation document or create exploded views in an Inventor drawing file. Note that to create an exploded view of an assembly in a drawing file, you must create a snapshot view of the exploded assembly in the Presentation environment, see Figure 13.28. This figure shows an exploded assembly created by performing multiple tweaks using the **Tweak Components** tool, as discussed earlier. Note that a snapshot view can be linked to a specific time on the **Timeline** of a storyboard or independent of the **Timeline**. You can create both the linked and independent snapshot views by using the **New Snapshot View** tool of the **Workshop** panel in the **Presentation** tab, see Figure 13.29. The methods for creating a linked snapshot view and an independent snapshot view are discussed next.

13.28

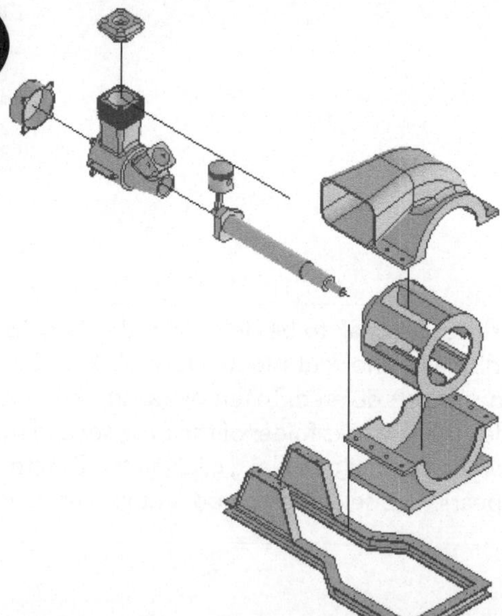

13.29

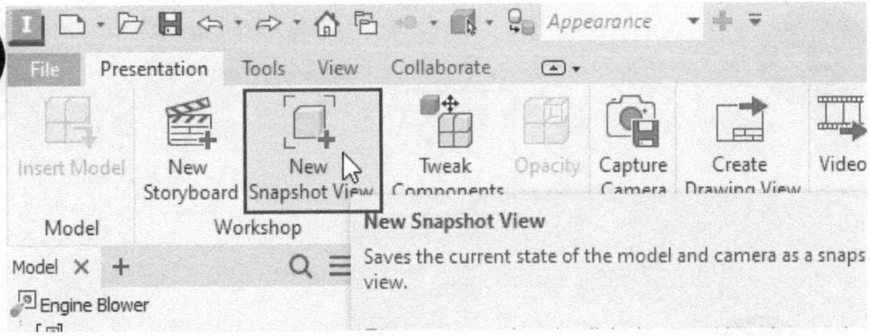

Creating a Linked Snapshot View

A linked snapshot view is associated with a specific time on the **Timeline** of a storyboard. The method for creating a linked snapshot view is discussed below:

1. Capture all actions and tweaks on the **Timeline** of a storyboard to create an exploded view and an animation of the assembly by using the **Capture Camera** and **Tweak Components** tools, respectively, as discussed earlier, refer to Figure 13.30.

13.30

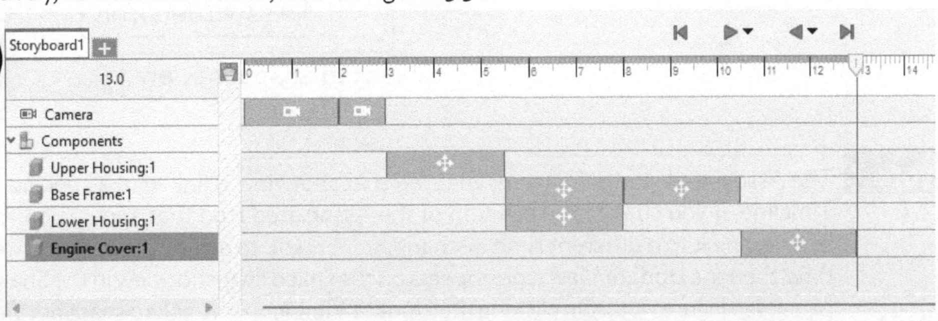

2. After capturing all actions and tweaks on the **Timeline** of a storyboard, define the position of the **Playhead** at a specific time on the **Timeline**, see Figure 13.31. The assembly appears in the graphics area as per the captured actions and tweaks at the current **Playhead** position.

13.31

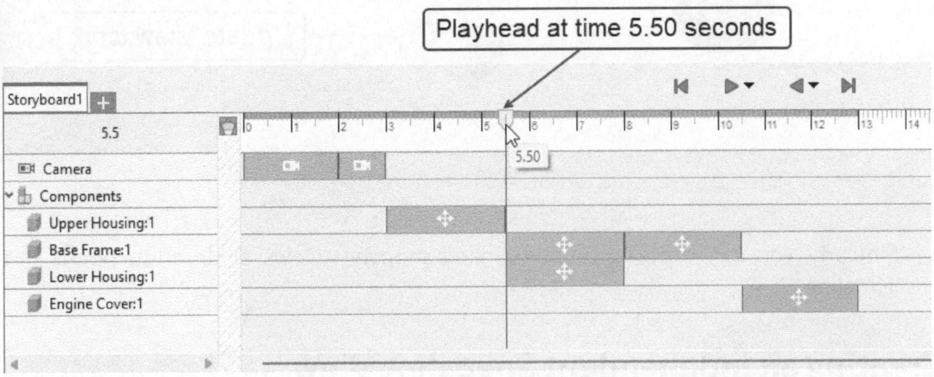

3. Click on the **New Snapshot View** tool in the **Workshop** panel of the **Presentation** tab, see Figure 13.32. A linked snapshot view that is associated with a specific time on the **Timeline** gets captured and saved in the **Snapshot Views** panel available to the right of the graphics area, see Figure 13.33. Also, the **Associated** icon appears on the linked snapshot view in the **Snapshot Views** panel as well as in the **Timeline** at the specified time.

13.32

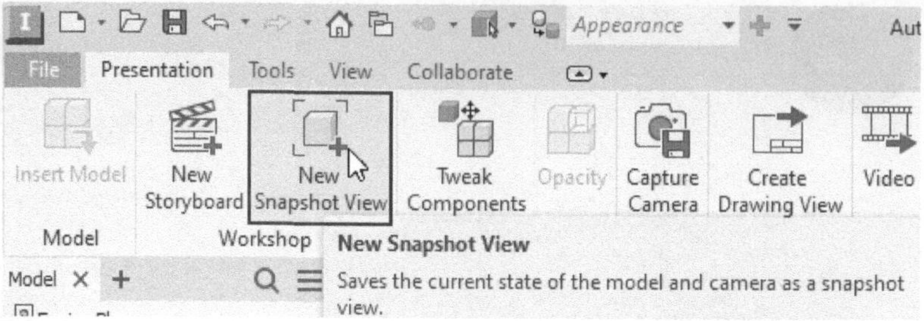

13.33

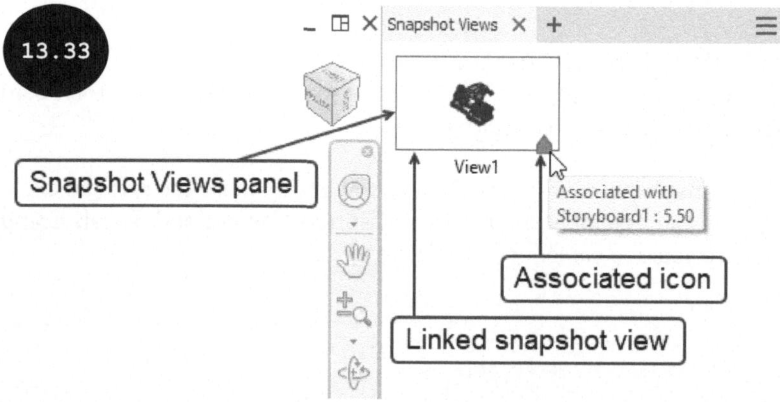

Note: The **Associated** icon indicates that the snapshot view is linked to a specific time on the **Timeline**. If you change the position of the **Associated** icon that appears on the **Timeline** by dragging it to a different time or changes are made to any of the actions/tweaks at that time, then the **Update View** icon appears on the linked snapshot view in the **Snapshot Views** panel, see Figure 13.34. On clicking the **Update View** icon, the linked snapshot view also gets updated accordingly in the **Snapshot Views** panel.

13.34

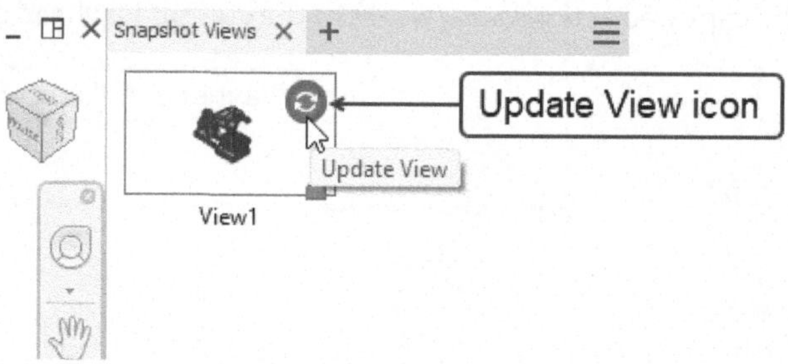

4. Similarly, you can capture multiple linked snapshot views at different points in time on the **Timeline**.

Creating an Independent Snapshot View

An independent snapshot view is a standalone view that stores the current position, visibility, and opacity of the assembly. It does not have any connection or association with the actions and tweaks on the **Timeline** or other snapshot views. The method for creating an independent snapshot view is discussed below:

1. Define the position of the **Playhead** on the **Timeline** at the **Scratch Zone** (Time 0) by dragging it (see Figure 13.35), if not defined already.

13.35

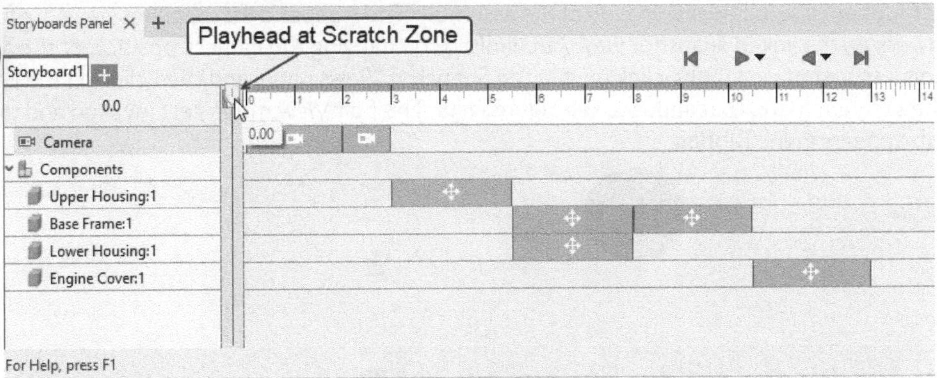

2. Set the camera position, components visibility and opacity in the graphics area, as required.

3. Click on the **New Snapshot View** tool in the **Workshop** panel of the **Presentation** tab, see Figure 13.36. An independent snapshot view gets captured and saved in the **Snapshot Views** panel available to the right of the graphics area, see Figure 13.37. Note that the **Associated** icon does not appear on the independent snapshot view in the **Snapshot Views** panel.

13.36

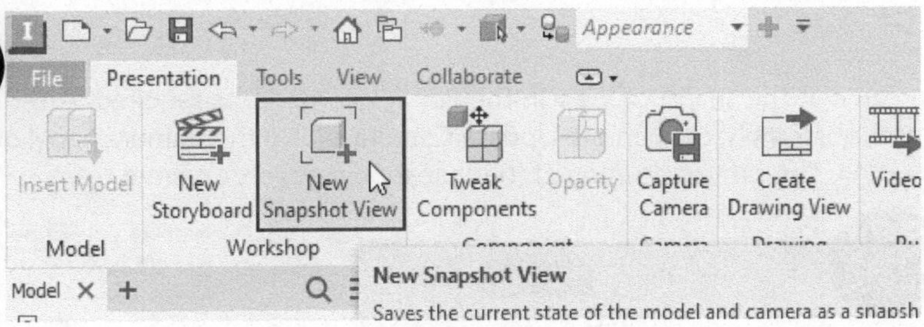

13.37

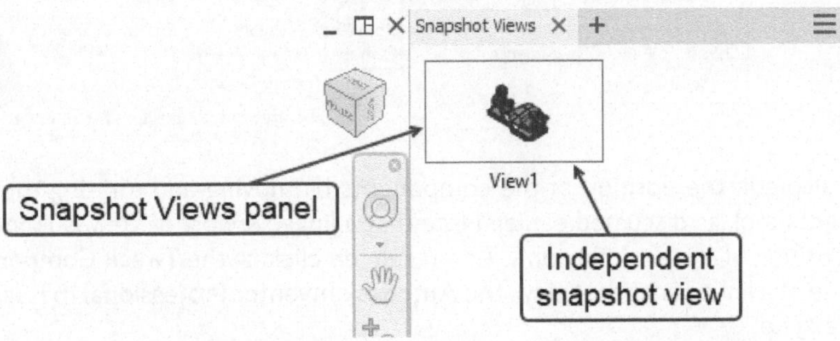

4. You can similarly capture multiple independent snapshot views of the assembly at different camera positions by using the **New Snapshot View** tool.

Editing a Snapshot View

After creating a snapshot view, you may need to edit it to change the camera position, position of components, visibility, and opacity of the assembly. The independent snapshot views are fully editable. However, the linked snapshot views are limited to changing the camera position of the assembly. To edit a snapshot view, right-click on it in the **Snapshot Views** panel and then click on the **Edit** option in the shortcut menu that appears, see Figure 13.38. The Edit View mode gets invoked and the **Edit View** tab appears in the **Ribbon**.

13.38

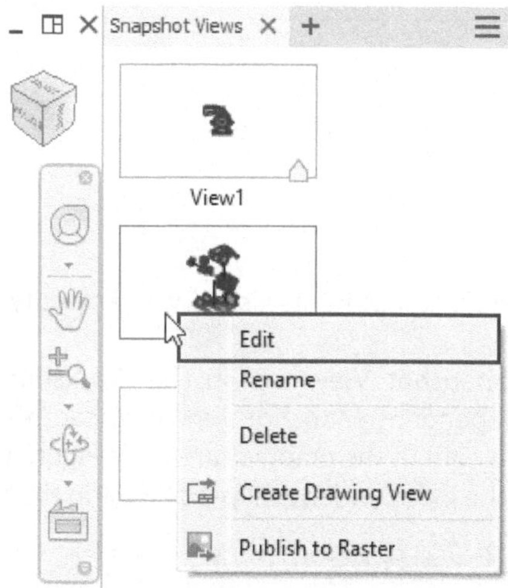

Now, you can edit the snapshot view in the Edit View mode, as required. After editing the camera position of the assembly, click on the **Update Camera** tool in the **Camera** panel of the **Edit View** tab, see Figure 13.39. The camera position of the snapshot view gets updated.

13.39

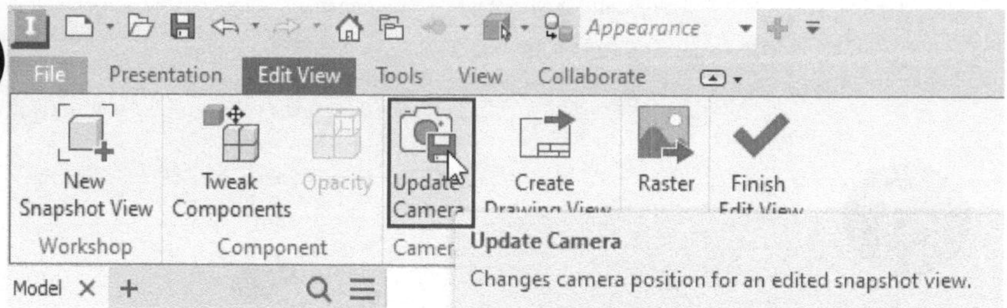

You can also edit the position of the components by moving and rotating them using the **Tweak Components** tool, as discussed earlier. Note that a linked snapshot view is limited for changing the camera position of the assembly only. As a result, on clicking the **Tweak Component** tool in the Edit View mode of a linked snapshot view, the **Autodesk Inventor Professional** message window appears, see Figure 13.40.

13.40

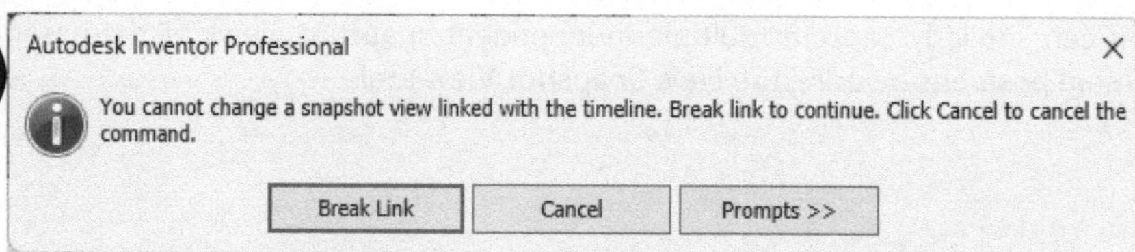

The **Break Link** button of the **Autodesk Inventor Professional** message window is used for breaking the link with the **Timeline** and continuing with the editing operation. The **Cancel** button is used for canceling the editing operation.

After editing the snapshot view in the Edit View mode, click on the **Finish Edit View** tool in the **Exit** panel of the **Ribbon**.

Renaming a Snapshot View

In Autodesk Inventor, on creating a snapshot view (independent or linked), it gets listed with a default name in the **Snapshot Views** panel. You can change the default name of a snapshot view. For doing so, right-click on a snapshot view in the **Snapshot Views** panel and then click on the **Rename** option in the shortcut menu that appears, see Figure 13.41. The name of the selected snapshot view appears in an edit field. Next, enter a new name for the snapshot view in the edit field and then click anywhere in the graphics area. The name of the snapshot view gets changed, as specified.

13.41

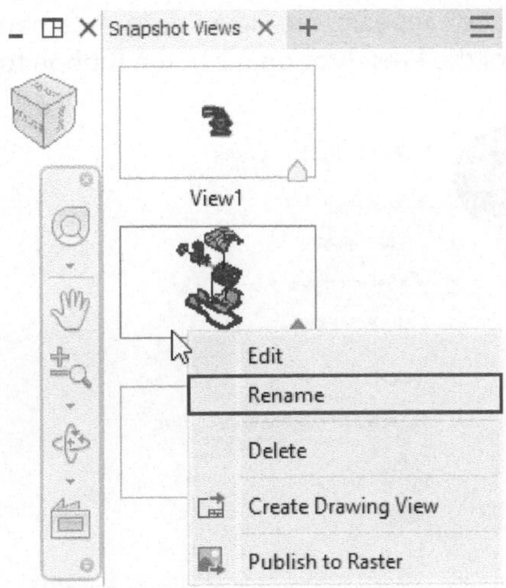

Deleting a Snapshot View

To delete a snapshot view, right-click on a snapshot view (independent or linked) to be deleted in the **Snapshot Views** panel and then click on the **Delete** option in the shortcut menu that appears. The selected snapshot view gets deleted and is no longer listed in the **Snapshot Views** panel.

Publishing a Snapshot View to a Raster Image

In Autodesk Inventor, you can publish a snapshot view (independent or linked) to a raster image for presentation, technical documentation, operation manual, or replacement part drawing for the product catalog. The method for publishing a snapshot view to a raster image is discussed below:

1. Right-click on a snapshot view (independent or linked) in the **Snapshot Views** panel available to the right of the graphics area, see Figure 13.42. A shortcut menu appears.

13.42

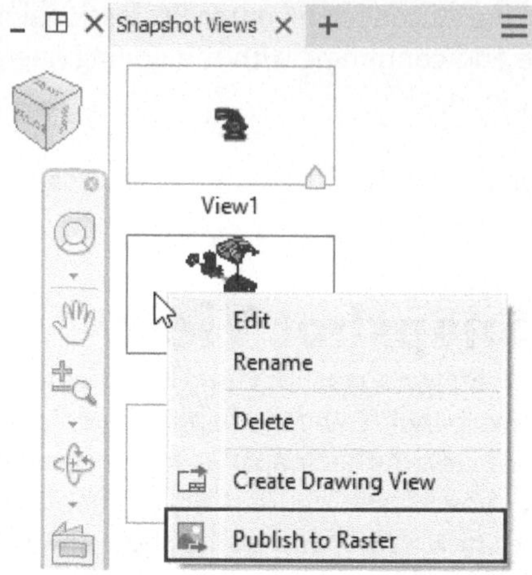

2. Click on the **Publish to Raster** option in the shortcut menu, refer to Figure 13.42. The **Publish to Raster Images** dialog box appears, see Figure 13.43. Alternatively, you can click on the **Raster** tool in the **Publish** panel of the **Presentation** tab in the **Ribbon** to invoke the **Publish to Raster Images** dialog box.

13.43

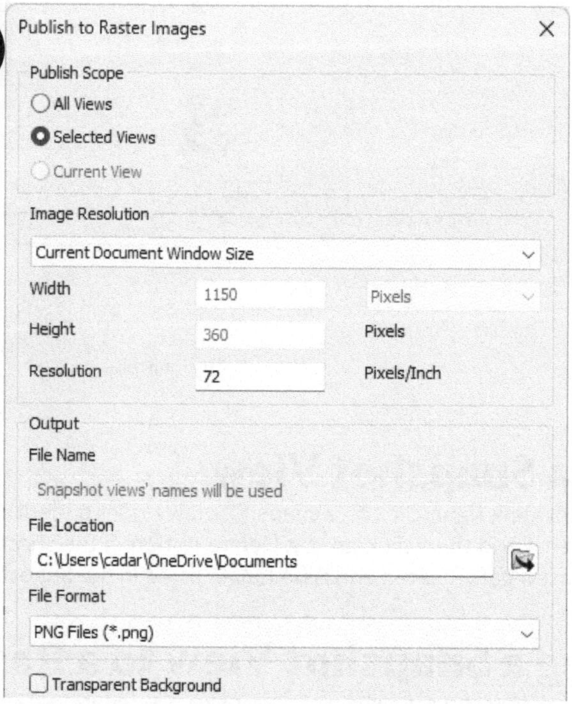

Publish Scope: The **All Views** radio button of the **Publish Scope** area in the dialog box is used for publishing all snapshot views of the currently active scene. The **Selected Views** radio button is used for publishing only the selected snapshot view. The **Current view** radio button is used for publishing the snapshot view in the Edit View mode. As a result, this radio button is enabled only in the Edit View mode.

Image Resolution: The options in the **Image Resolution** area are used for defining the image resolution, as required.

File Name: The **File Name** field is used for specifying the name of the image file to be published. Note that this field is enabled only in the Edit View mode.

File Location: The **File Location** field is used for specifying the location to save the file. You can also use the **Browse** button next to the **File Location** field to specify the location to save the image file.

File Format: The **File Format** drop-down list is used for selecting the file format to be published.

3. Ensure that the **Selected Views** radio button is selected in the **Publish Scope** area of the dialog box to publish the selected snapshot view. Note that to publish all the snapshot views, you need to select the **All Views** radio button.

4. Specify the image resolution in the **Image Resolution** area of the dialog box.

5. Specify the location to save the image file in the **File Location** field of the dialog box.

6. Select the required file format (**.bmp, *.gif, *.jpg, *.png,* or **.tiff*) to be published in the **File Format** drop-down list of the dialog box.

7. Click on the **OK** button in the **Publish to Raster Images** dialog box. The image file is published and saved in the specified location.

Creating an Exploded View in a Drawing File

You can create an exploded view in a drawing file based on a snapshot view created in the Presentation environment. The method for creating an exploded view in a drawing file is discussed below:

1. Click on the **Create Drawing View** tool in the **Drawing** panel in the **Presentation** tab, see Figure 13.44. The **Create New File** dialog box appears.

13.44

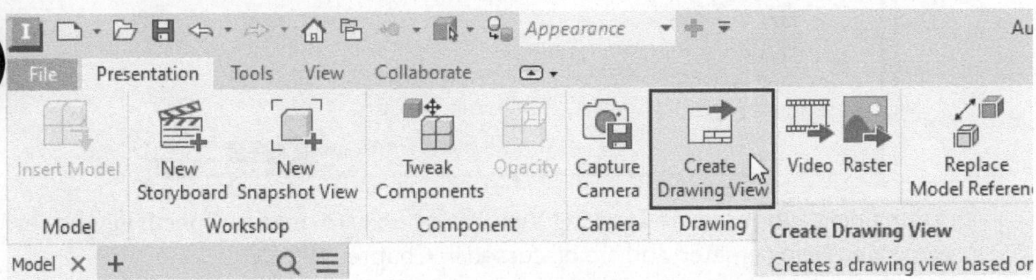

Create New File: The **Create New File** dialog box is used for selecting a template for invoking the Drawing environment. Note that the metric template files are available in the **Metric** tab of the dialog box and all the English template files are available in the **English** tab of the dialog box. You will learn in detail about invoking the Drawing environment and creating drawings in Chapter 14.

2. Double-click on the required template in the **Create New File** dialog box. Note that *.idw* is the file extension of the Inventor drawing file. The Drawing environment gets invoked and the **Drawing View** dialog box appears, see Figure 13.45. Also, the preview of a drawing view appears on the drawing sheet.

13.45

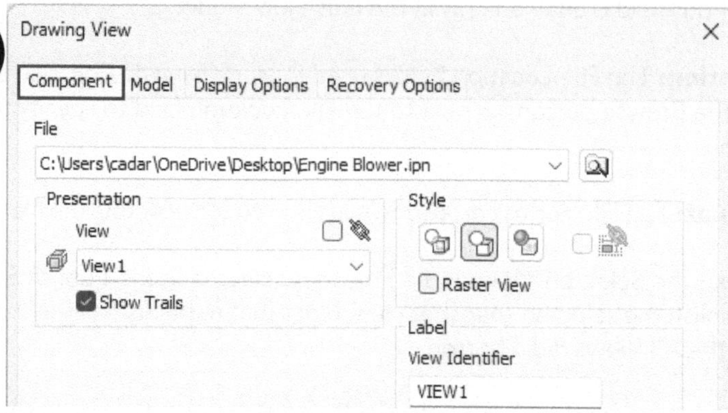

Presentation: The **View** drop-down list in the **Presentation** area of the dialog box displays a list of all the snapshot views created in the Presentation environment.

3. Select the required snapshot view in the **View** drop-down list of the **Presentation** area of the dialog box. A preview of the selected snapshot view appears on the drawing sheet, see Figure 13.46.

13.46

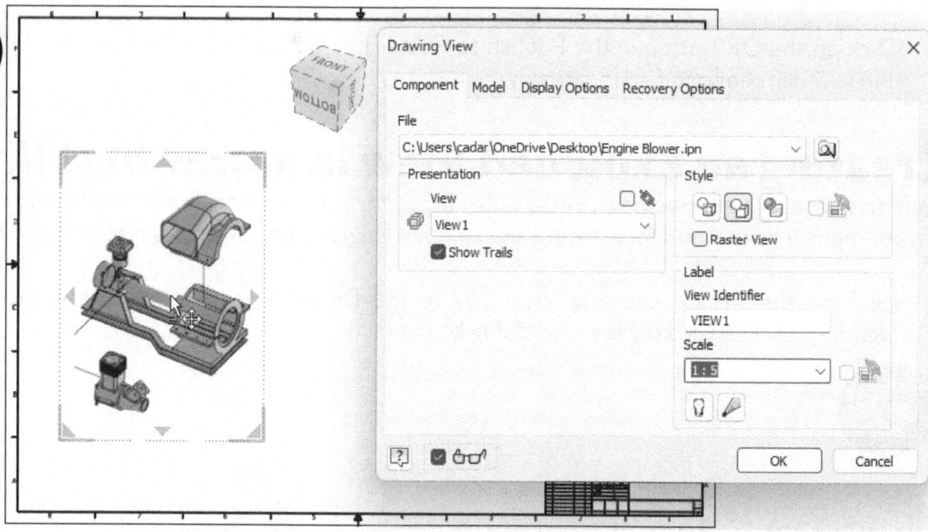

The remaining options in the **Drawing View** dialog box are used for specifying the settings of the drawing view being created and are discussed in Chapter 14.

4. Accept the remaining default selected options in the dialog box and then click on the **OK** button. The exploded view is created in the drawing sheet based on the selected snapshot view.

Note: The drawing view created in a drawing file is linked to the snapshot view and gets updated on updating the snapshot view in the Presentation environment.

Now, you can switch back to the Presentation environment.

5. Click on the Presentation file tab (*.ipn*) at the lower left corner of the drawing sheet, see Figure 13.47. The Presentation environment gets invoked.

13.47

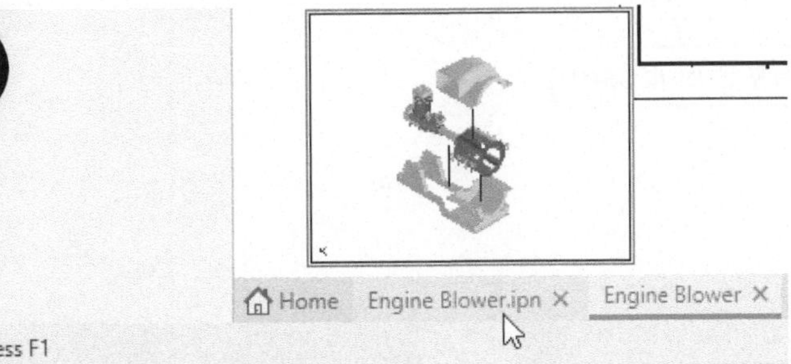

Creating a New Storyboard

In Autodesk Inventor, on invoking the Presentation environment, an empty storyboard gets created with a default name (**Storyboard1**) automatically, at the bottom of the screen. In addition to the default storyboard, you can create a new storyboard to the presentation file and add the required actions and tweaks to it. The method for creating a new storyboard is discussed below:

1. Click on the **New Storyboard** tool in the **Workshop** panel of the **Presentation** tab, see Figure 13.48. The **New Storyboard** dialog box appears, see Figure 13.49.

13.48

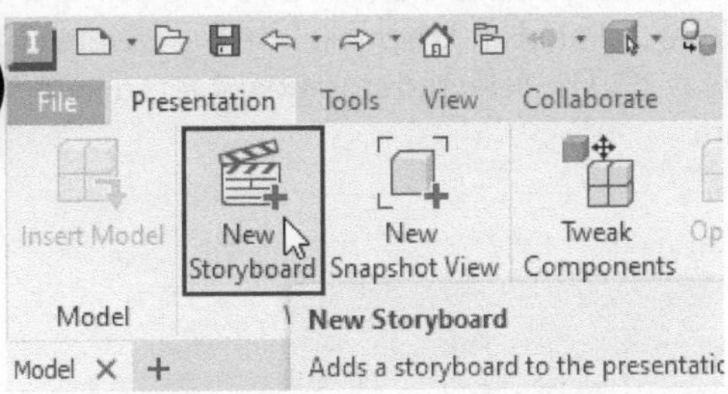

13.49

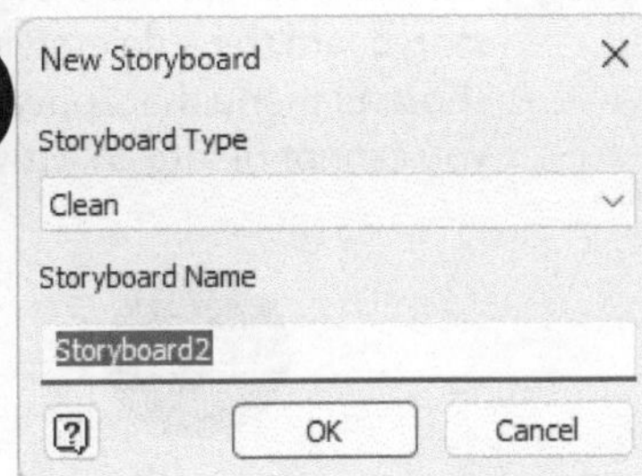

Storyboard Type: The **Clean** option in the **Storyboard Type** drop-down list of the dialog box is used for creating a new empty storyboard with no actions inherited and no change in the position of the components from the way they were inserted into the Presentation environment. The **Start from end of previous** option is used for creating a new empty storyboard with no action and the position of the components is the same as it was at the end of the previous storyboard.

Storyboard Name: You can specify a name for the new storyboard in the **Storyboard Name** field of the dialog box. By default, the name appears as ***Storyboard2***, ***Storyboard3***, ***Storyboard4***, and so on.

2. Select the required option in the **Storyboard Type** drop-down list of the **New Storyboard** dialog box and then click on the **OK** button. A new empty storyboard is created with the specified name at the end of the existing storyboard in the **Storyboards Panel**, see Figure 13.50. Also, the newly added storyboard becomes the active storyboard. Alternatively, you can create a new storyboard by clicking on the Plus sign next to the existing storyboard tab, see Figure 13.51.

13.50

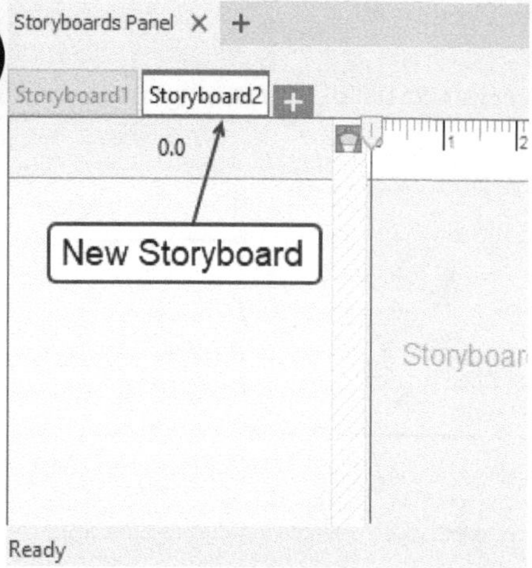

13.51

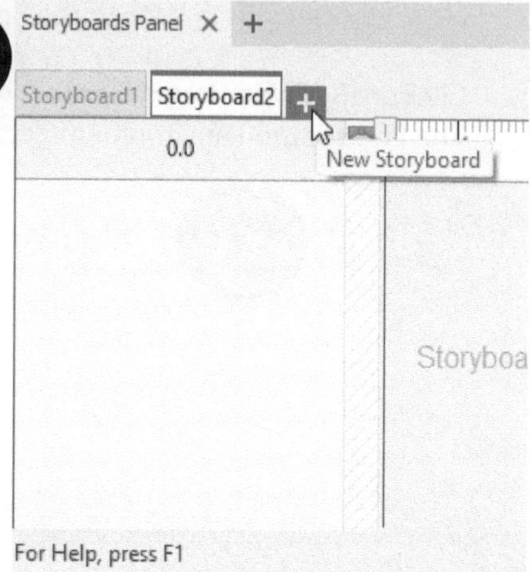

3. After creating a storyboard, you can perform the required actions and tweaks for creating an animation of the assembly file.

Note: You can create multiple storyboards in a presentation file and switch between them at any point of time by clicking on the required storyboard tab in the **Storyboards Panel**.

Tip: You can also delete a storyboard in the **Storyboards Panel**. For doing so, right-click on a storyboard to be deleted in the **Storyboards Panel** and then click on the **Delete** option in the shortcut menu that appears, see Figure 13.52. The selected storyboard gets deleted. Note that you cannot delete an active storyboard.

13.52

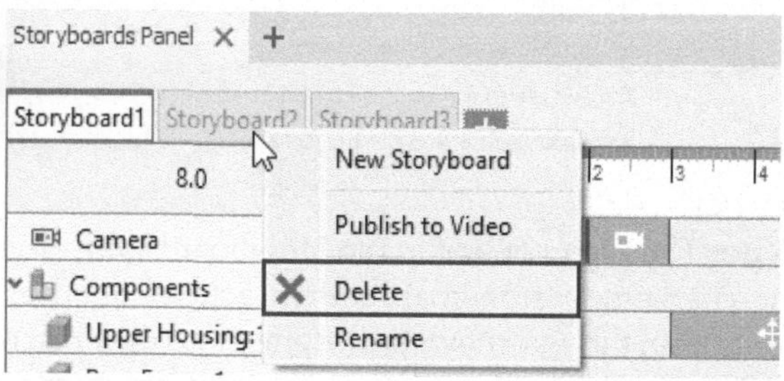

Creating a New Scene

In Autodesk Inventor, on inserting an assembly model into the Presentation environment, the first scene (**Scene1**) gets created and added to the **Browser**, see Figure 13.53. Also, the inserted assembly becomes the source model for the scene and you can create its animation by capturing required actions and tweaks on the **Timeline** of its active storyboard. In Autodesk Inventor, you can create multiple scenes to work with different source models (assemblies) in a single presentation file. The method for creating a new scene is discussed below:

1. Right-click on the name of the presentation file in the **Browser**, see Figure 13.54. A shortcut menu appears.

2. Click on the **Create Scene** option in the shortcut menu, see Figure 13.54. The **Insert** dialog box appears.

13.53

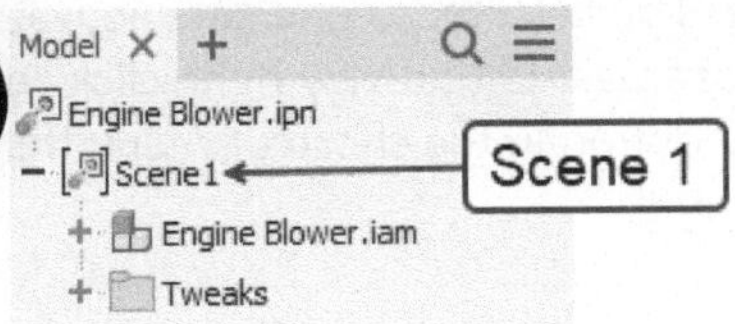

13.54

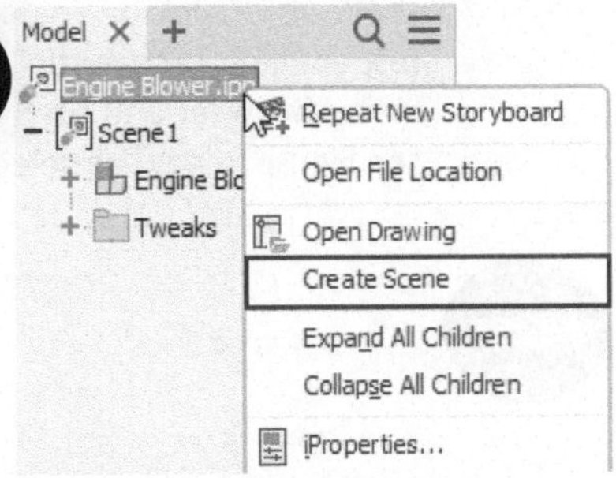

3. Browse to the required location where the assembly to be inserted is saved and then select it in the **Insert** dialog box.

4. After selecting the assembly, click on the **Options** button in the right panel of the **Insert** dialog box, see Figure 13.55.

13.55

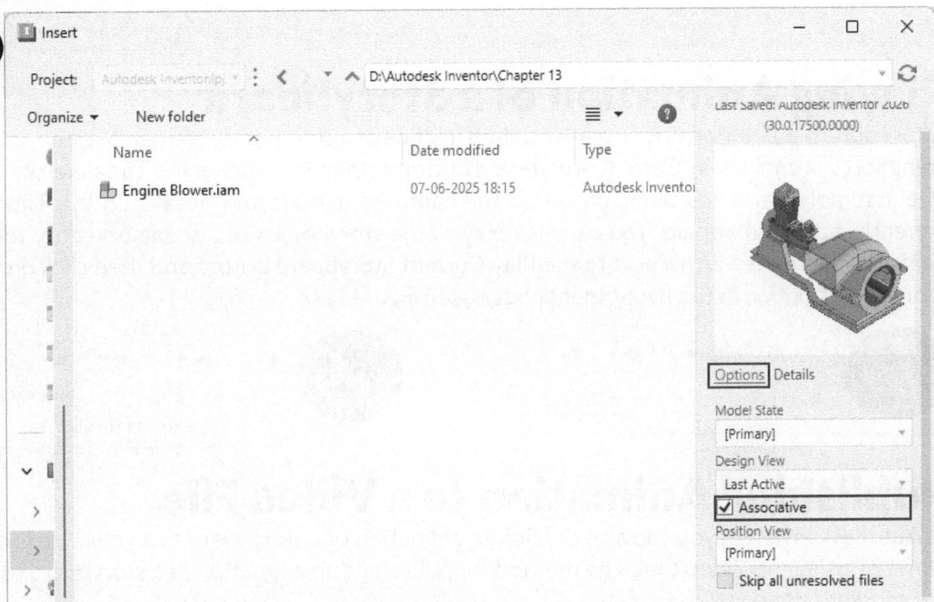

5. Ensure that the **Associative** check box is selected in the dialog box for keeping the link with the source assembly file in the Presentation environment.

6. Click on the **Open** button in the **Insert** dialog box. The selected assembly gets inserted into the graphics area and a new scene is added to the **Browser**, see Figure 13.56. Now, you can create an animation for the inserted assembly by capturing the required actions and tweaks, as discussed earlier.

Note: You can also switch between the scenes of a presentation file at any point of time. For doing so, double-click on the scene in the **Browser**. The selected scene gets activated and its respective source model appears in the graphics area. Alternatively, right-click on the scene in the **Browser** and then click on the **Activate** option in the shortcut menu that appears, see Figure 13.57. The selected scene gets activated.

13.56

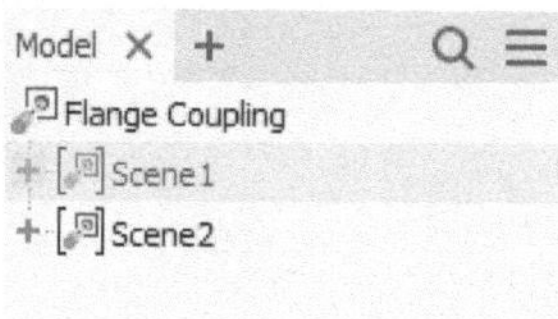

13.57

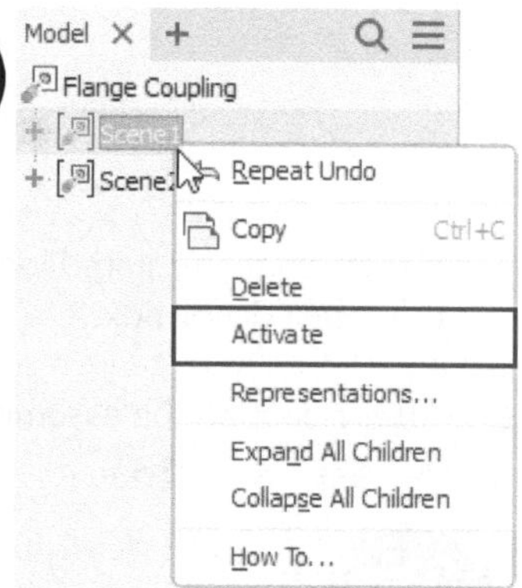

Playing Animation of a Storyboard

After capturing all actions and tweaks on the **Timeline** of a storyboard, you can play the animation. For doing so, click on the **Play Current Storyboard** button at the top center of the **Timeline**, see Figure 13.58. The assembly starts animating based on the captured actions and tweaks on the **Timeline** of the currently active storyboard. You can also play all the storyboards of a scene one after the other. For doing so, click on the arrow next to the **Play Current Storyboard** button and then click on the **Play All Storyboards** option in the flyout that appears, see Figure 13.59.

13.58

13.59

Publishing Animation to a Video File

In Autodesk Inventor, you can also publish an animation of a storyboard to a video file format (*.avi* or *.wmv*) by using the **Video** tool. The method for publishing an animation of a storyboard to a video file is discussed below:

1. Click on the **Video** tool in the **Publish** panel of the **Presentation** tab, see Figure 13.60. The **Publish to Video** dialog box appears, see Figure 13.61.

13.60

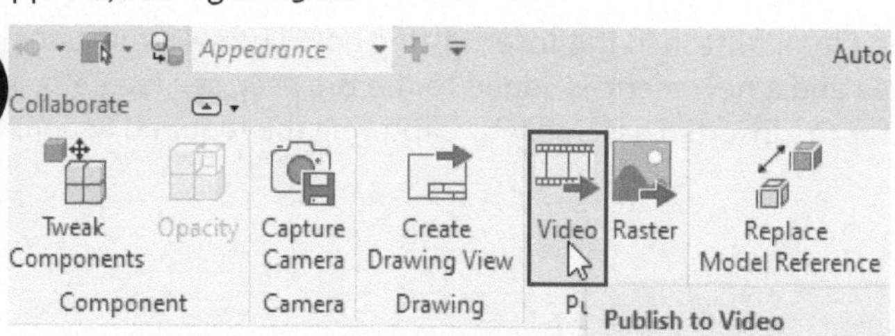

13.61

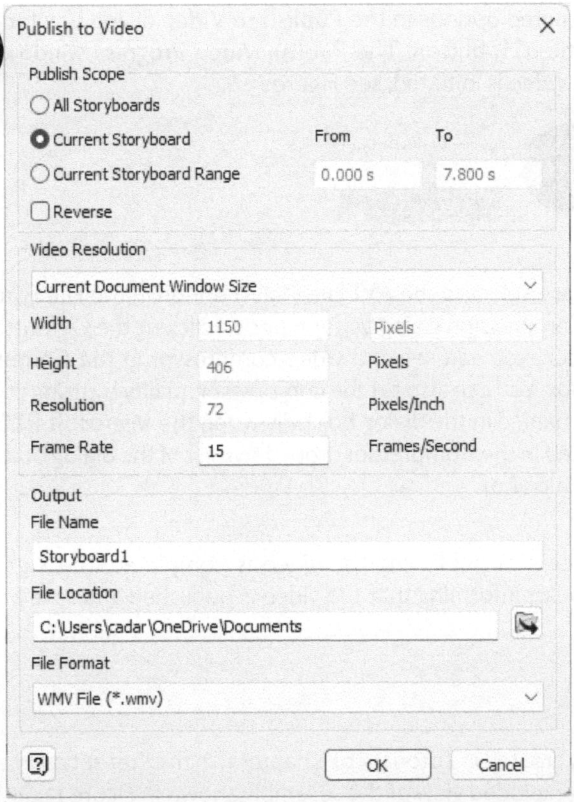

Publish Scope: The **All Storyboards** radio button of the **Publish Scope** area in the dialog box is used for publishing all storyboards of the currently active scene for creating video files of each storyboard. The **Current Storyboard** radio button is used for publishing only the currently active storyboard for creating its video file. The **Current Storyboard Range** radio button is used for publishing the currently active storyboard view to a specific time range by specifying **From** and **To** time in the respective fields that are enabled in the dialog box.

Reverse: The **Reverse** check box in the dialog box is used for publishing the video in a reverse order (from end to start).

Video Resolution: The options in the **Video Resolution** area are used for defining the video resolution for the video to be published, as required.

File Name: The **File Name** field is used for specifying the name of the video file to be published.

File Location: The **File Location** field is used for specifying the location to save the video file. You can also use the **Browse** button next to the **File Location** field to specify the location to save the video file.

File Format: The **File Format** drop-down list is used for selecting the file format for the video to be published. You can publish video as a *.avi* or *.wmv* video file by selecting the required option [**WMV File (*.wmv)** or **AVI File (*.avi)**] from this drop-down list.

2. Specify the required options in the **Publish to Video** dialog box for publishing the video file and then click on the **OK** button. The **Publish Video Progress** window appears and the process of publishing the video is initiated, see Figure 13.62.

13.62

Note: If you have selected the **AVI File (*.avi)** option in the **File Format** drop-down list, then the **Video Compression** dialog box appears on clicking the **OK** button. In the **Video Compression** dialog box, you can select a video compressor in the **Compressor** drop-down list of the dialog box. You can also set the compressor quality by using the **Compression Quality** slider that is enabled in the dialog box only when the **Microsoft RLE** or **Microsoft Video 1** option is selected in the **Compressor** drop-down list of the dialog box. Next, click on the **OK** button in the dialog box.

3. Once the process of publishing the video is completed, the **Autodesk Inventor Professional** dialog box appears informing that the video is published and saved at the specified location.

Tutorial 1

Open the assembly created in Tutorial 2 of Chapter 11 in the Presentation environment, see Figure 13.63, and then create an exploded view of the assembly shown in Figure 13.64. You need to perform various tweaks on the components to create the exploded view. After creating an exploded view, play the animation, create a snapshot view that is linked to the end of the **Timeline**, and an independent snapshot view. Also, you need to publish the animation as a video file (*.wmv*).

13.63

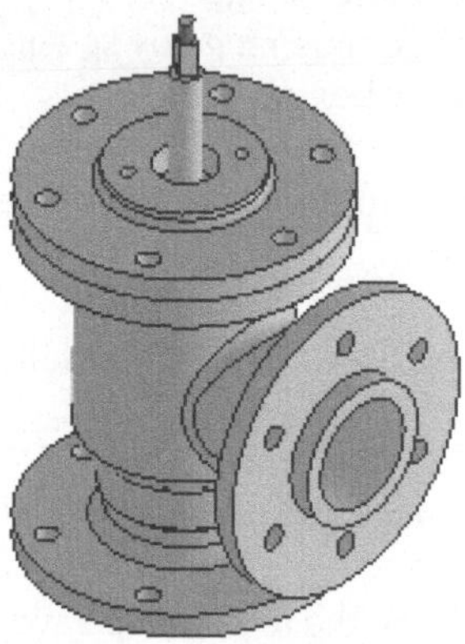

13.64

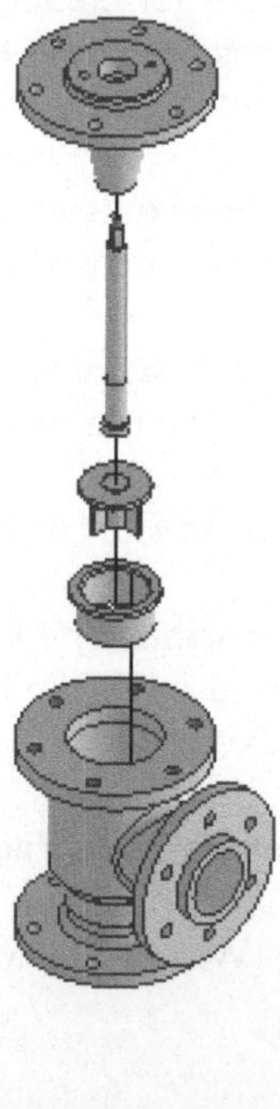

Section 1: Invoking the Presentation Environment

1. Start Autodesk Inventor and then invoke the **Create New File** dialog box by clicking on the **New** tool in the **Quick Access Toolbar**.

2. Expand the **Templates** node in the **Create New File** dialog box and then select the **Metric** folder. All the default Metric templates appear on the right panel of the dialog box, refer to Figure 13.65.

13.65

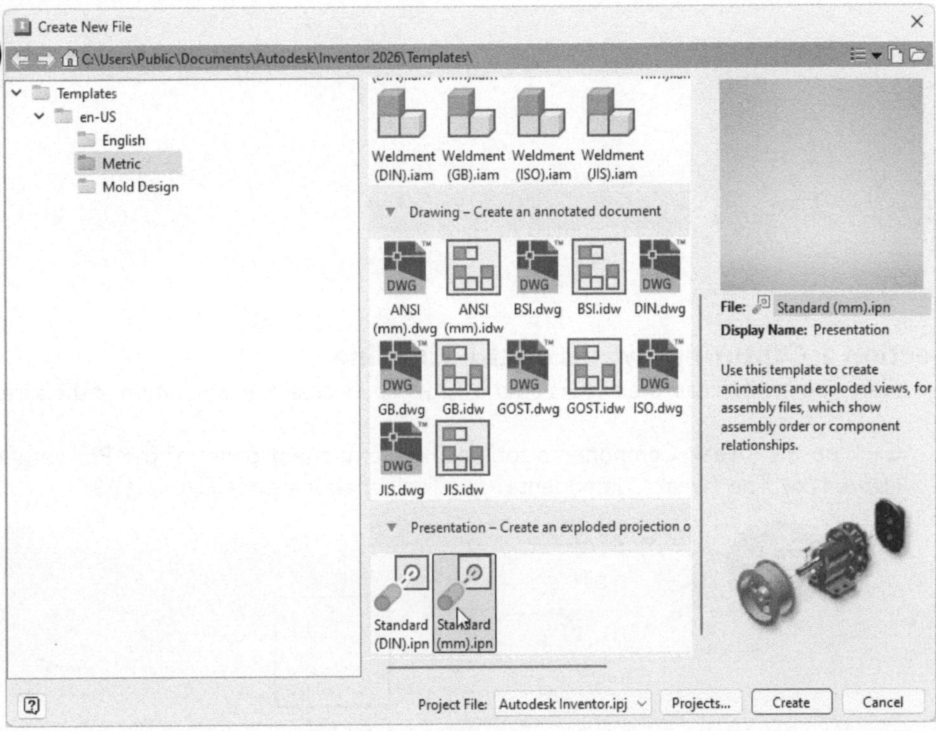

3. Scroll down to the dialog box and then double-click on the **Standard (mm).ipn** template, refer to Figure 13.66. Note that *.ipn* is the file extension of the Inventor presentation file. The Presentation environment is invoked and the **Insert** dialog box appears.

4. Browse to the Tutorial 2 folder of Chapter 11 in the Autodesk Inventor folder and then select it for creating its animation.

5. Click on the **Open** button in the **Insert** dialog box. The selected assembly gets opened in the Presentation environment and **Scene1** is added to the **Browser**, see Figure 13.66.

13.66

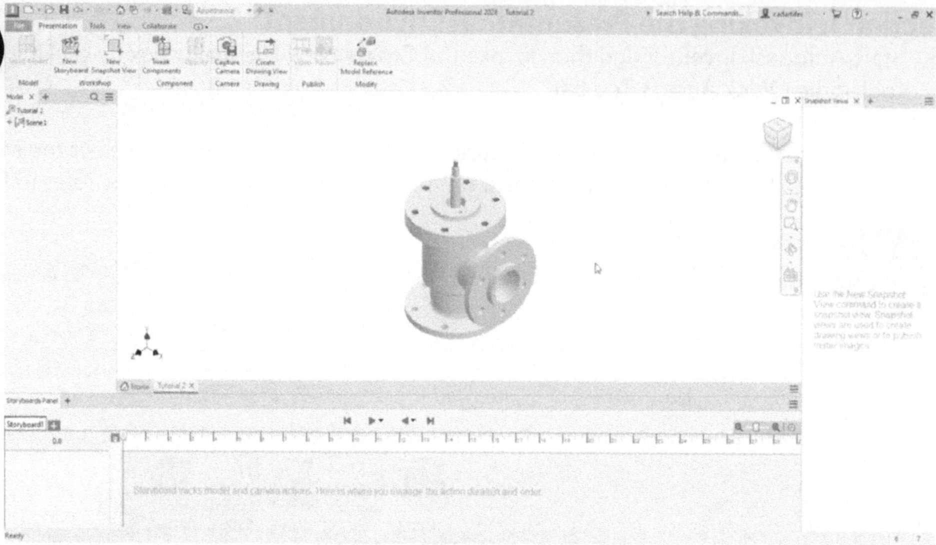

Section 2: Capturing Tweaks on the Timeline

Now, you need to capture tweaks on the Timeline to create an animation of the assembly.

1. Click on the **Tweak Components** tool in the **Component** panel of the **Presentation** tab, see Figure 13.67. The **Tweak Components** Mini-Toolbar appears, see Figure 13.68.

13.67

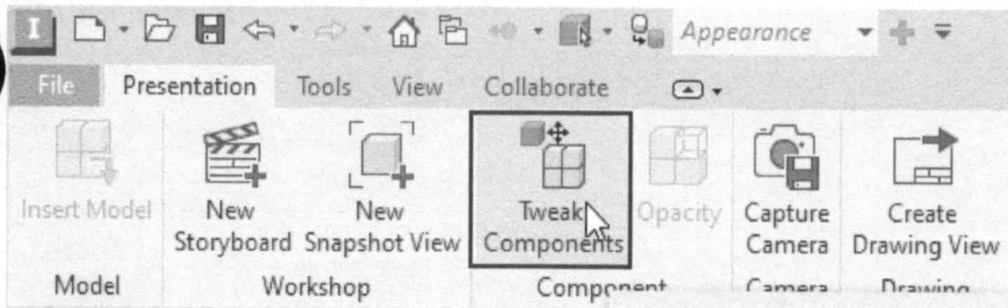

13.68

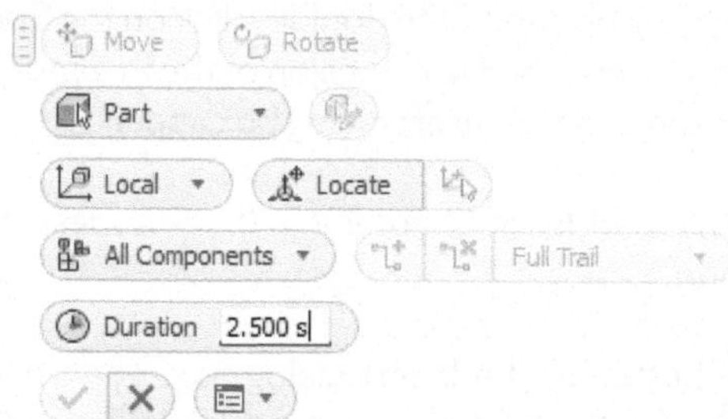

2. Select the **Body** component in the graphics area. A Triad appears, see Figure 13.69.

3. Ensure that the **Move** button is activated in the **Tweak Components** Mini-Toolbar to move the component and create a Move tweak on the **Timeline**.

4. Drag the Y axis of the Triad downward by pressing and holding the left mouse button, see Figure 13.70. The **Y Distance** field appears in the graphics area.

13.69

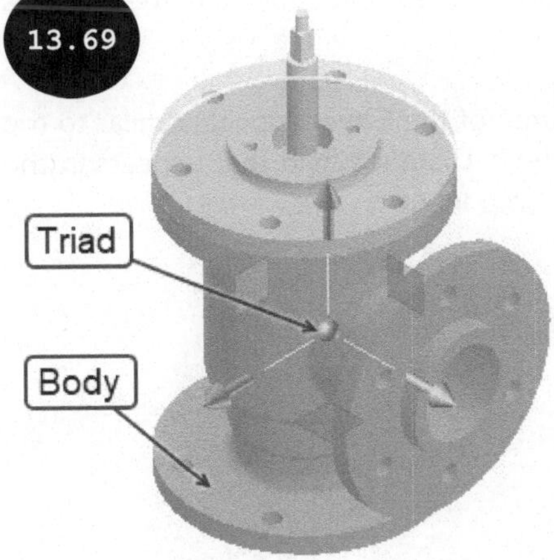

13.70

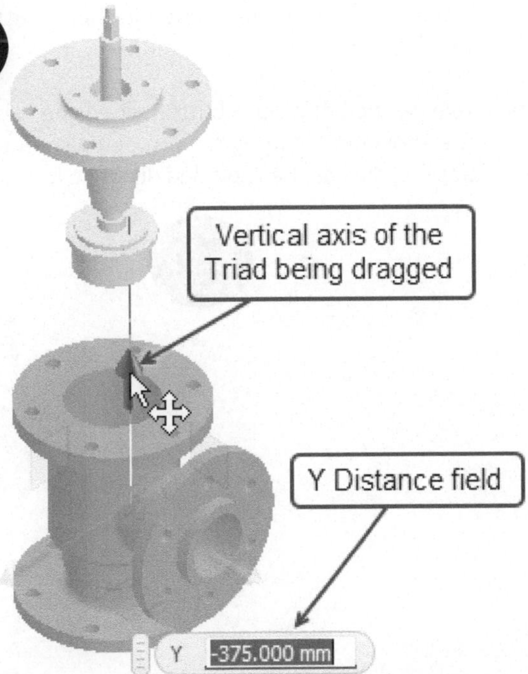

5. Release the left mouse button when the exploded location of the **Body** component appears similar to the one shown in Figure 13.70. You can also enter **-350** in the **Y Distance** field that appears in the graphics area as the exploded distance value for the selected component.

6. Enter **3** seconds in the **Duration** field of the **Tweak Components** Mini-Toolbar and then click on the **OK** button. The selected component gets exploded in the graphics area and a Move tweak of duration 3 seconds gets captured on the **Timeline**, see Figure 13.71.

13.71

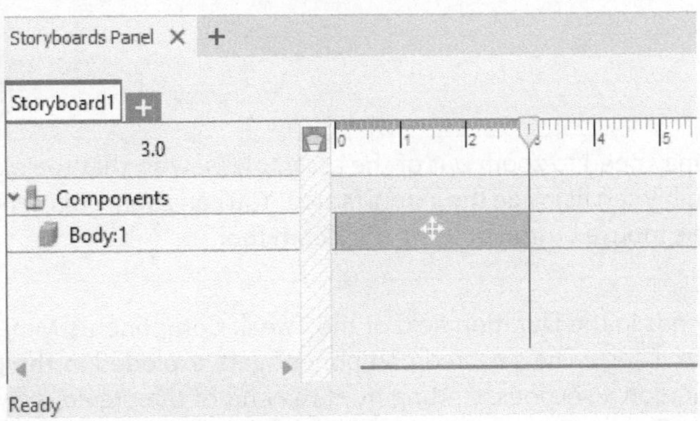

Now, you need to explode the **Cover** of the assembly.

7. Click on the **Tweak Components** tool in the **Component** panel of the **Presentation** tab or press the **T** key. The **Tweak Components** Mini-Toolbar appears.

8. Select the **Cover** component and then drag the Y axis of the Triad that appears in the graphics area, see Figure 13.72.

9. Release the left mouse button when the exploded location of the **Cover** appears similar to the one shown in Figure 13.72. You can also enter **500** in the **Y Distance** field that appears in the graphics area as the exploded distance for the selected component.

13.72

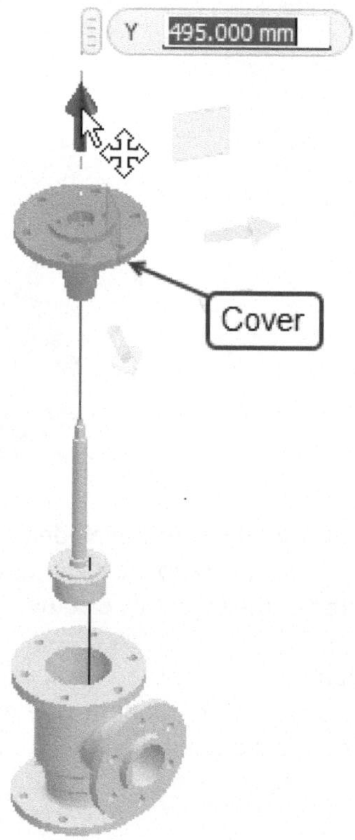

Note: You may need to zoom out of the assembly view so that the exploded component of the assembly can fit inside the graphics area. You can zoom out of the assembly by scrolling the middle mouse button or using the **Zoom** tool.

10. Enter **3** seconds in the **Duration** field of the **Tweak Components** Mini-Toolbar and then click on the **OK** button. The selected component gets exploded in the graphics area and a Move tweak of duration 3 seconds, starting from the end of the previous tweak, gets captured on the **Timeline**, see Figure 13.73.

13.73

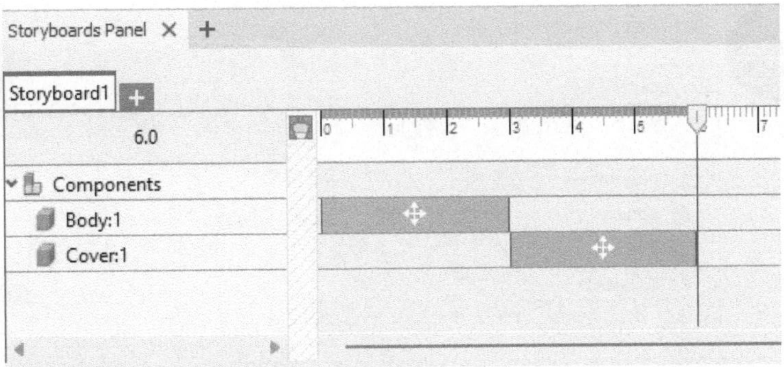

Now, you need to explode the **Spindle** of the assembly.

11. Press the **T** key or click on the **Tweak Components** tool in the **Component** panel of the **Presentation** tab. The **Tweak Components** Mini-Toolbar appears.

12. Select the **Spindle** component and then drag the Y axis of the Triad that appears in the graphics area, see Figure 13.74.

13. Release the left mouse button when the exploded location of the **Spindle** appears similar to the one shown in Figure 13.74. You can also enter **200** in the **Y Distance** field that appears in the graphics area as the exploded distance for the selected component.

13.74

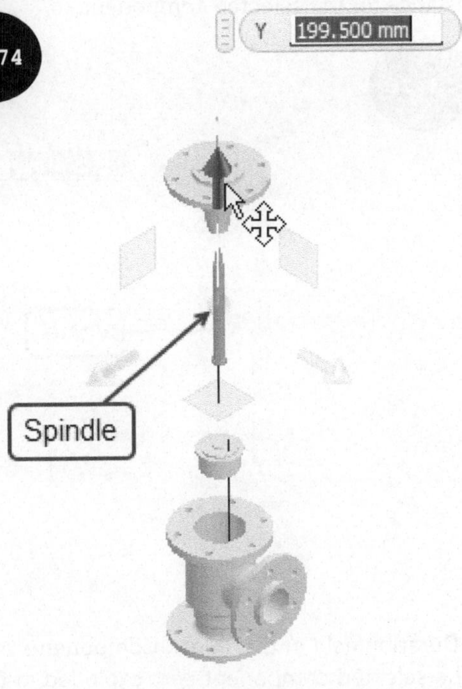

14. Enter **2** seconds in the **Duration** field of the **Tweak Components** Mini-Toolbar and then click on the **OK** button . The selected component gets exploded in the graphics area and a Move tweak of duration 2 seconds, starting from the end of the previous tweak, gets captured on the **Timeline**, see Figure 13.75.

13.75

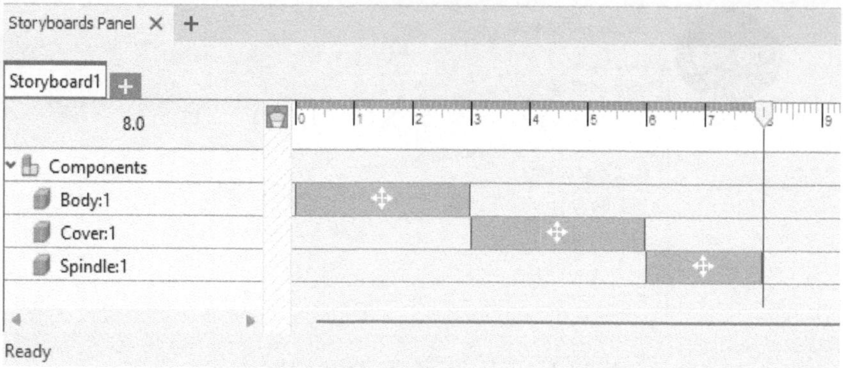

Now, you need to explode the **Valve** of the assembly.

15. Press the **T** key or click on the **Tweak Components** tool in the **Component** panel of the **Presentation** tab. The **Tweak Components** Mini-Toolbar appears.

16. Select the **Valve** component and then drag the Y axis of the Triad that appears in the graphics area, see Figure 13.76.

17. Release the left mouse button when the exploded location of the **Valve** appears similar to the one shown in Figure 13.76. You can also enter **130** in the **Y Distance** field that appears in the graphics area as the exploded distance for the selected component.

13.76

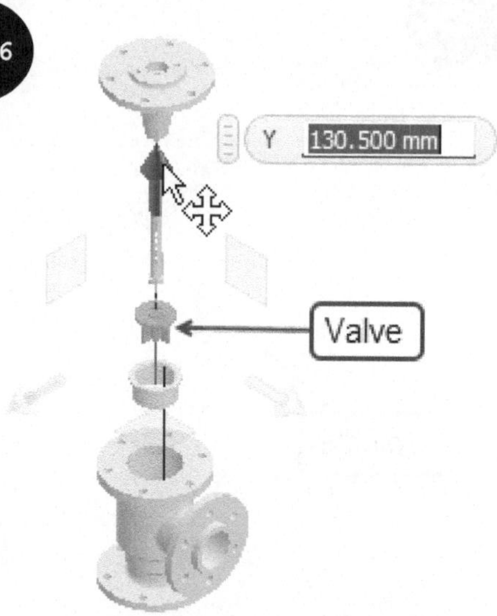

18. Enter **3** seconds in the **Duration** field of the **Tweak Components** Mini-Toolbar and then click on the **OK** button. The selected component gets exploded in the graphics area and a Move tweak of duration 3 seconds, starting from the end of the previous tweak, gets captured on the **Timeline**, see Figure 13.77. Figure 13.78 shows the final assembly.

13.77

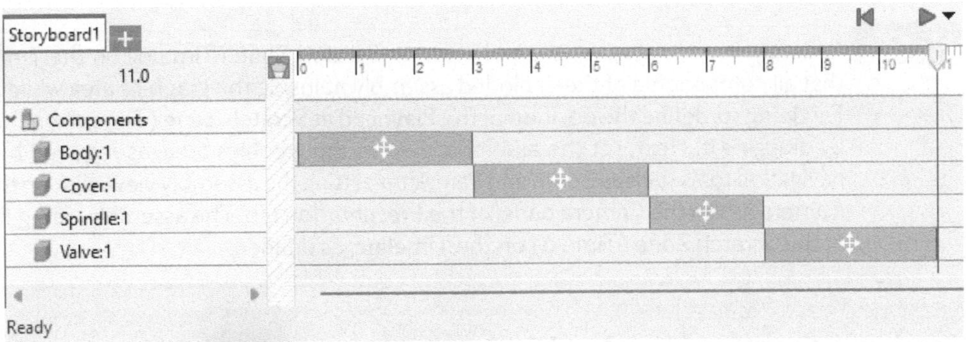

13.78

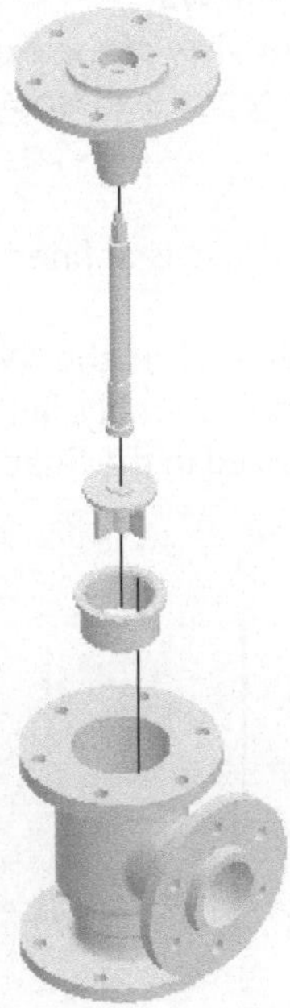

Section 3: Playing the Animation

1. Click on the **Play Current Storyboard** button at the top center of the **Timeline**, see Figure 13.79. The assembly view changes to its default position set at the **Scratch Zone** (Time 0) on the **Timeline** and starts animating based on the tweaks captured on the **Timeline**.

13.79

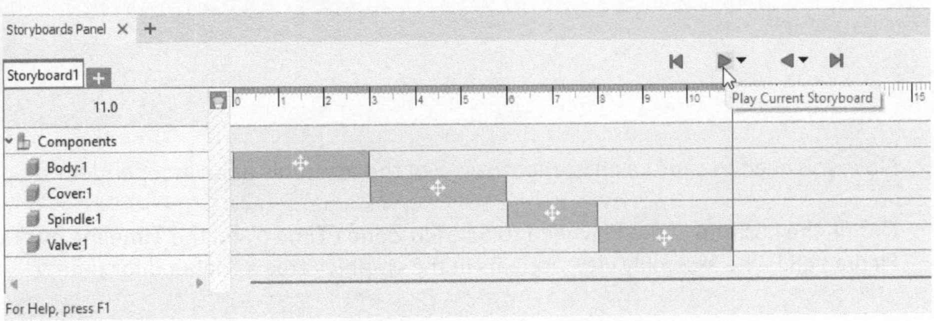

Note: You may need to set the assembly view at **Scratch Zone** (Time 0) on the **Timeline** such that all components of the exploded assembly fit inside the graphics area while animating. For doing so, define the position of the **Playhead** at **Scratch Zone** (Time 0) on the **Timeline** by dragging it. Next, set the assembly view in the graphics area, as required by using the navigation tools such as **Zoom** and **Pan**. After setting the assembly view, click on the **Capture Camera** tool in the **Camera** panel of the **Presentation** tab. The assembly view gets updated at the **Scratch Zone** (Time 0) on the **Timeline**, as defined.

Section 4: Creating Snapshot Views

Now, you need to create a snapshot view of the exploded assembly at the end (time 11 seconds) of the **Timeline**. Also, you need to capture an isometric view of the assembly as an independent snapshot view.

1. Ensure that the position of the **Playhead** is defined at time 11 seconds (end) on the **Timeline**.

2. Click on the **New Snapshot View** tool in the Workshop panel of the Presentation tab, see Figure 13.80. A snapshot view of the assembly, linked to the time 11 seconds on the **Timeline**, is captured and its thumbnail is displayed in the **Snapshot Views** panel, see Figure 13.81.

13.80

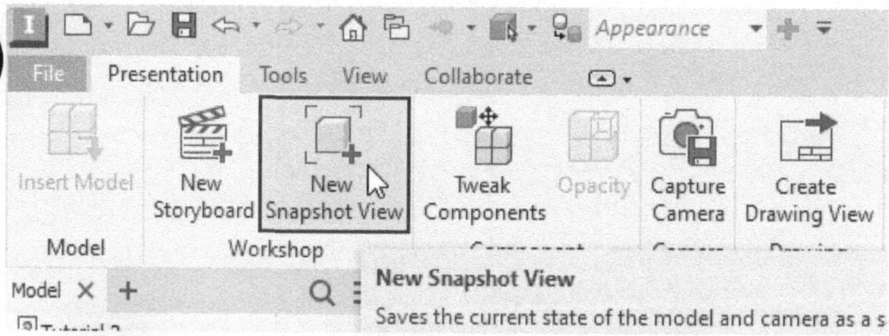

13.81

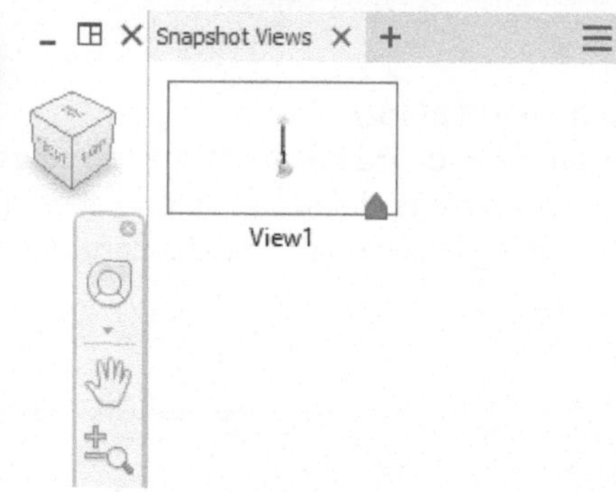

Now, you need to capture an isometric view of the assembly as an independent snapshot view.

3. Define the position of the **Playhead** to **Scratch Zone** (Time 0) on the **Timeline** by dragging it, see Figure 13.82. The assembly view appears in the graphics area as defined for time 0.

13.82

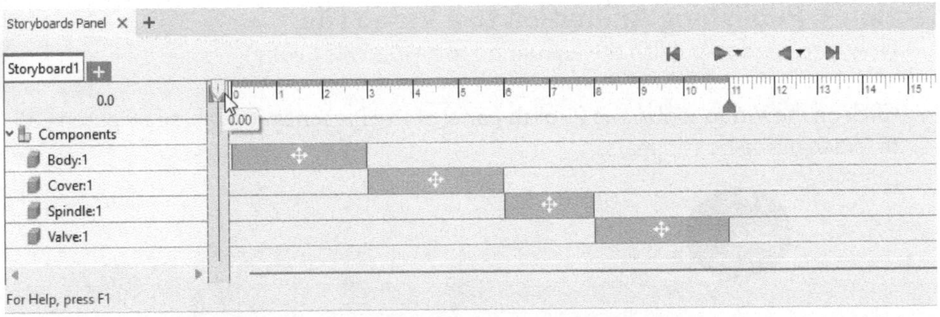

4. Ensure that the assembly appears in the graphics area similar to the one shown in Figure 13.83. If needed, you can set the assembly view, as required by using the navigation tools.

13.83

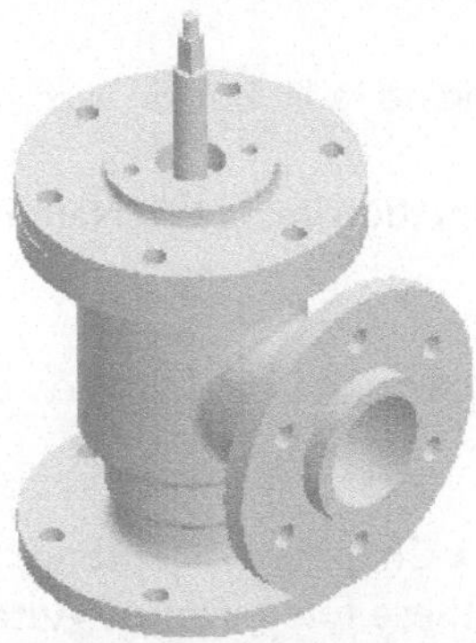

5. Click on the **New Snapshot View** tool in the **Workshop** panel of the **Presentation** tab, see Figure 13.84. An independent snapshot view of the assembly is captured and its thumbnail is displayed in the **Snapshot Views** panel, see Figure 13.85.

13.84

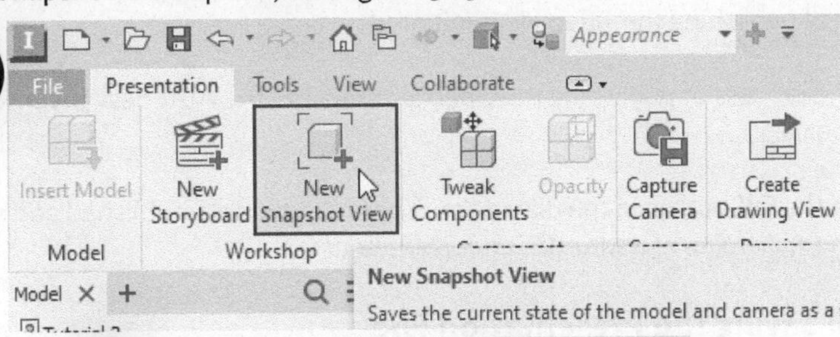

13.85

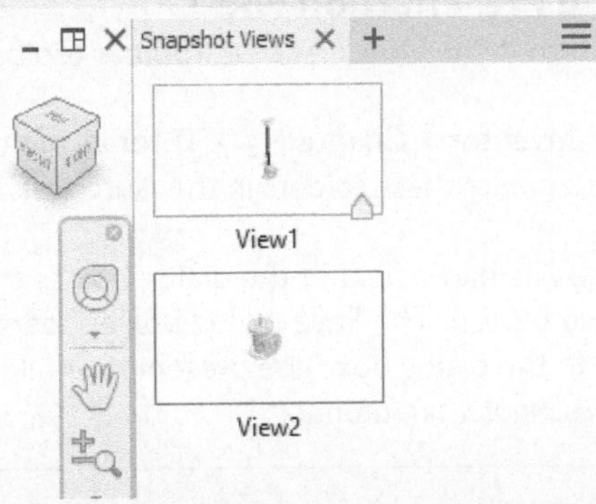

Section 5: Publishing Animation to a Video File

Now, you need to publish the animation to a video file (*.wmv*).

1. Click on the **Video** tool in the **Publish** panel of the **Presentation** tab, see Figure 13.86. The **Publish to Video** dialog box appears.

13.86

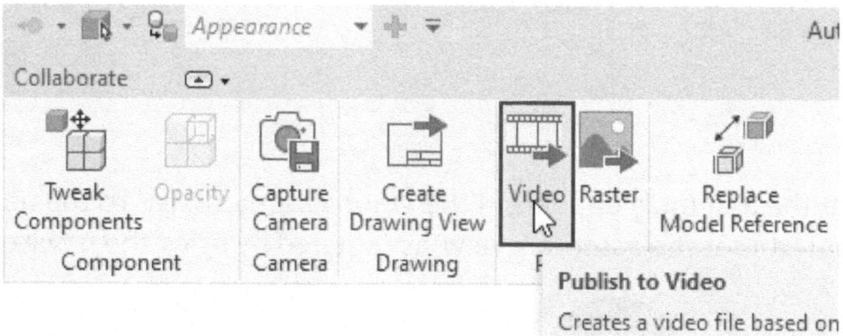

2. Ensure that the **Current Storyboard** radio button is selected in the dialog box.

3. Enter **Tutorial 1 Stop Valve Animation** in the **File Name** field of the dialog box as the name of the video file to be published.

4. Click on the **Browse** button next to the **File Location** field in the dialog box. The **Select Folder** dialog box appears.

5. Browse to **Autodesk Inventor** > **Chapter 13** > **Tutorial 1** folder in the local drive of your system. Note that you need to create these folders in the **Autodesk Inventor** folder. Next, click on the **Select Folder** button in the dialog box.

6. Ensure that the **WMV File (*.wmv)** option is selected in the **File Format** drop-down list of the dialog box and click on the **OK** button. The **Publish Video Progress** window appears and the process of publishing the video file is initiated.

7. Once the process of publishing the video is complete, the **Autodesk Inventor Professional** dialog box appears.

8. Click on the **OK** button in the dialog box. The video file gets published and saved in the specified location (*>:\Autodesk Inventor\Chapter 13\Tutorial 1*).

Section 6: Saving the Presentation File

1. Click on the **Save** button in the **Quick Access Toolbar** toolbar. The **Save As** dialog box appears.

2. Browse to **Autodesk Inventor** > **Chapter 13** > **Tutorial 1** folder in the local drive of your system. Note that you need to create these folders in the Autodesk Inventor folder.

3. Enter **Tutorial 1** in the **File name** field of the dialog box as the name of the presentation file and then click on the **Save** button. The **Save** dialog box appears. Click on the **Yes to All** button and then the **OK** button in the dialog box. The presentation file gets saved in the specified location (*>:\Autodesk Inventor\Chapter 13\Tutorial 1*).

Hands-on Test Drive 1

Open the assembly created in Hands-on Test Drive 1 of Chapter 11 in the Presentation environment (see Figure 13.87) and then create an exploded view of the assembly as shown in Figure 13.88. After creating the exploded view, play the animation and then publish it as a video file in a local drive of your system.

13.87

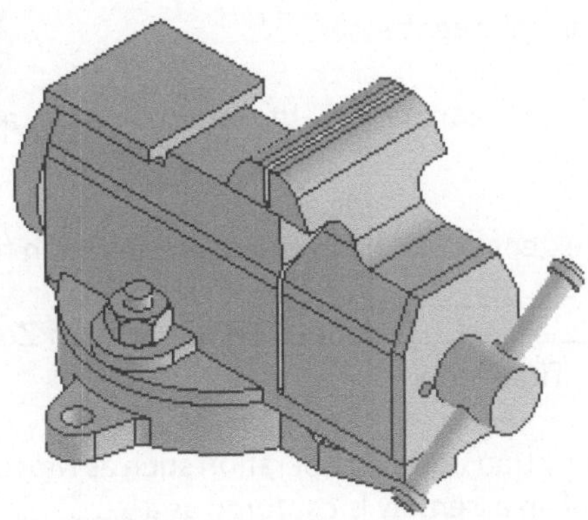

13.88

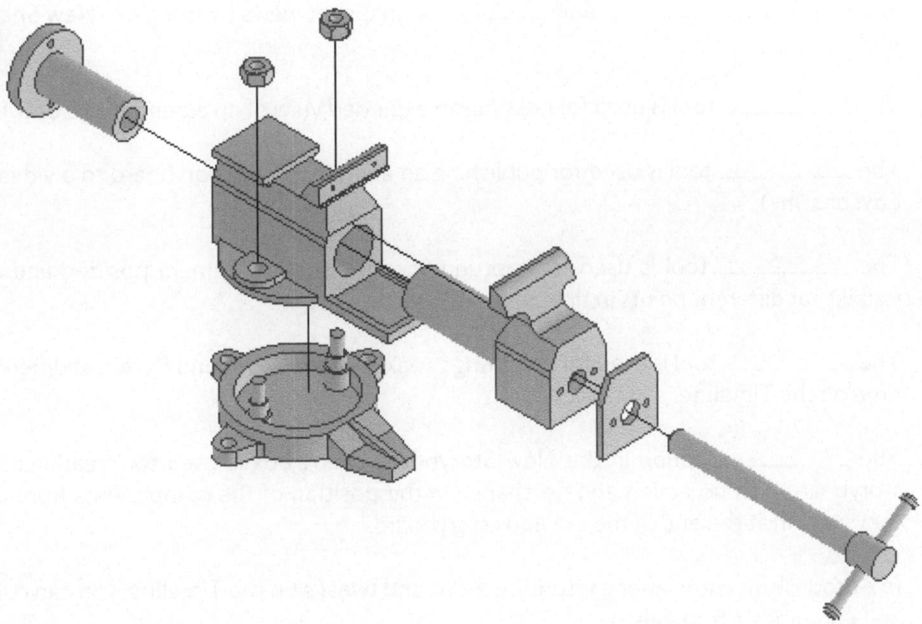

Summary

In this chapter, you have learned about creating animation of an assembly in the Presentation environment. In Autodesk Inventor, to animate an assembly, you need to capture various actions and tweaks on the **Timeline** of a storyboard. The chapter discussed in detail about capturing actions and tweaks on the **Timeline**, editing and deleting a tweak, creating linked and independent snapshot views, editing a snapshot view, renaming a snapshot view, deleting a snapshot view, and publishing a snapshot view to a raster image. It also explained methods for creating an exploded view in a drawing file, creating a new storyboard and a new scene, playing animation and publishing it to a video file.

Questions

Complete and verify the following sentences:

- In Autodesk Inventor, you can create the animation of an assembly in the _________ environment.
- _________ is the file extension of the Inventor presentation file.
- If the position of the _________ is defined on the **Scratch Zone** (Time 0), then the action will not be captured on the **Timeline**.
- In Autodesk Inventor, any transforming operation such as Move or Rotate performed at a point in time on a component of an assembly is captured as a _________ on the **Timeline**.
- You can create _________ and _________ snapshot views by using the **New Snapshot View** tool.
- The _________ tool is used for creating an exploded view of an assembly in a drawing file.
- The _________ tool is used for publishing an animation of a storyboard to a video file format (*.avi* or *.wmv*).
- The _________ tool is used for capturing actions such as camera position and component visibility at different points in time on the **Timeline**.
- The _________ tool is used for capturing tweaks such as Move and Rotate at different points in time on the **Timeline**.
- The _________ option in the **New Storyboard** dialog box is used for creating a new empty storyboard with no action and no change in the position of the components from the position they were in at the end of the previous storyboard.
- In Autodesk Inventor, after capturing actions and tweaks on the **Timeline**, you can edit their start and end times. (True/False)
- You cannot delete actions and tweaks of a storyboard. (True/False)
- You can create multiple storyboards in a presentation file and switch between them at any point of time. (True/False)

CHAPTER

14

Working with Drawings

In this chapter, the following topics will be discussed:

- Invoking the Drawing Environment
- Editing the Sheet Size
- Editing/Creating the Title Block
- Editing the Drafting Standard
- Creating the Base View of a Model
- Creating Projected Views
- Working with Angle of Projection
- Defining the Angle of Projection
- Creating Other Drawing Views
- Deleting a Drawing View
- Applying Dimensions
- Adding a Text/Note
- Adding a Surface Finish Symbol
- Adding a Weld Symbol
- Adding a Hole and Thread Note
- Adding the Parts List / Bill of Materials (BOM)
- Editing the Parts List / Bill of Materials (BOM)
- Adding Balloons

After creating parts and assemblies in SOLIDWORKS, the next step is to generate 2D drawings. These technical drawings are essential for clearly and effectively communicating all necessary information about the end product to be manufactured. A 2D drawing is not only a drawing but also a language used by engineers to communicate ideas and information about products. By using 2D drawings, a designer can communicate information about the components to be manufactured to the engineers on the shop floor. Underscoring the importance of 2D drawings, the role of designers becomes very important in generating accurate and error-free drawings for production. Inaccurate or missing information about a component in drawings can lead to faulty production. Keeping this in mind, Autodesk Inventor provides you with an environment that allows you to generate error-free 2D drawings. This environment is known as the Drawing environment. The method for invoking the Drawing environment is discussed next.

Invoking the Drawing Environment

To invoke the Drawing environment, click on the **New** tool in the **Quick Access Toolbar** or press **CTRL+N** keys. The **Create New File** dialog box appears, see Figure 14.1. In this dialog box, you can select a default Metric or English template for invoking the Drawing environment. To invoke the Drawing environment with a default Metric template, expand the **Templates** node in the **Create New File** dialog box and then select the **Metric** folder. All the default Metric templates appear on the right panel of the dialog box, refer to Figure 14.1. Next, double-click on the required drawing template in the **Drawing** rollout of the dialog box. Autodesk Inventor has various drawing templates with predefined drafting standards such as ANSI, ISO, BSI, DIN, and JIS for invoking Drawing environment and generating drawing views of a model. Note that *.idw* and *.dwg* are the file extensions of a drawing file. Figure 14.2 shows the Drawing environment invoked by using the **ANSI(mm).idw** drawing template.

14.1

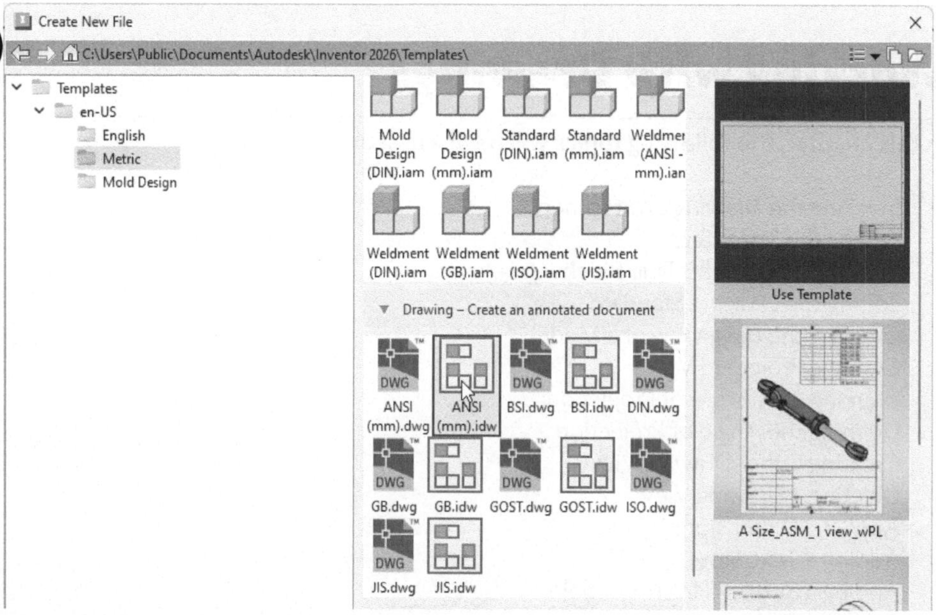

14.2

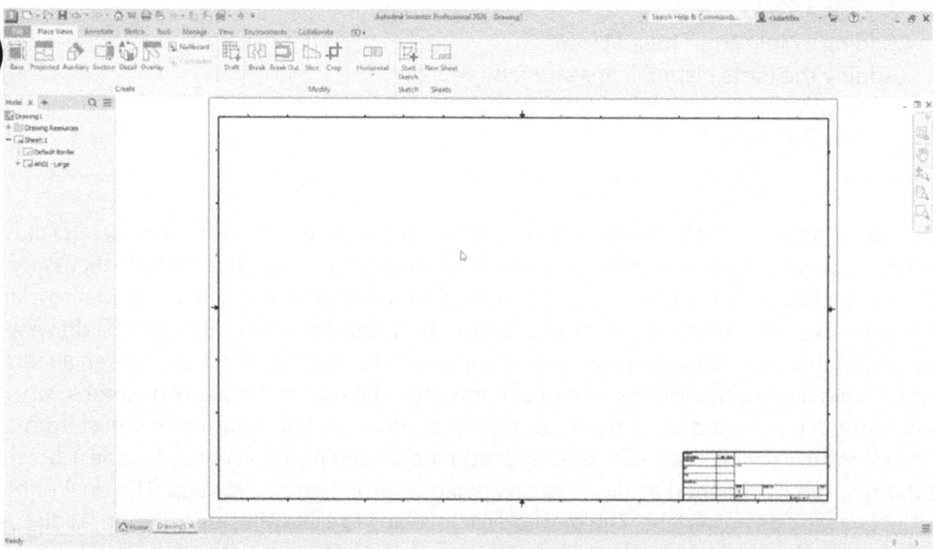

By default, the Drawing environment is invoked with a drawing sheet having sheet size, title block, style, and other properties based on the drafting standard of the selected template. In the drawing sheet, you can generate different drawing views of a model and dimension them as per the drafting standard. You will learn about generating and dimensioning drawing views of a model later in this chapter. The methods for editing sheet size, title block, and drafting standards are discussed next.

Editing the Sheet Size

To edit the default size of a drawing sheet, right-click on the name of the sheet to be edited in the **Browser**, see Figure 14.3. A shortcut menu appears. In this shortcut menu, click on the **Edit Sheet** option. The **Edit Sheet** dialog box appears, refer to Figure 14.4. The options in this dialog box are discussed below:

Name

The **Name** field in the **Format** area of the dialog box displays the default name of the sheet. You can edit or specify a new name for the selected sheet in this field.

Size

The **Size** drop-down list of the **Format** area displays a list of standard sheet sizes, see Figure 14.4. You can select a standard sheet size in this drop-down list for creating drawing views. You can also specify a custom sheet size by entering the required width and height values. For doing so, select the **Custom Size (inches)** or **Custom Size (mm)** option in the **Size** drop-down list. The **Height** and **Width** fields are enabled in the dialog box. In these fields, you can enter the required width and height values of the sheet.

14.3

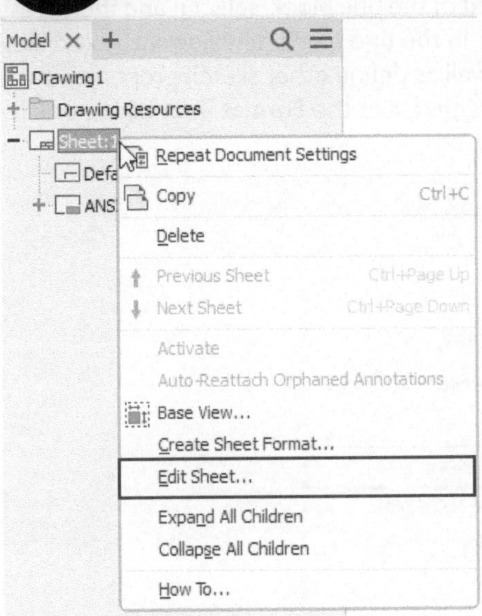

14.4

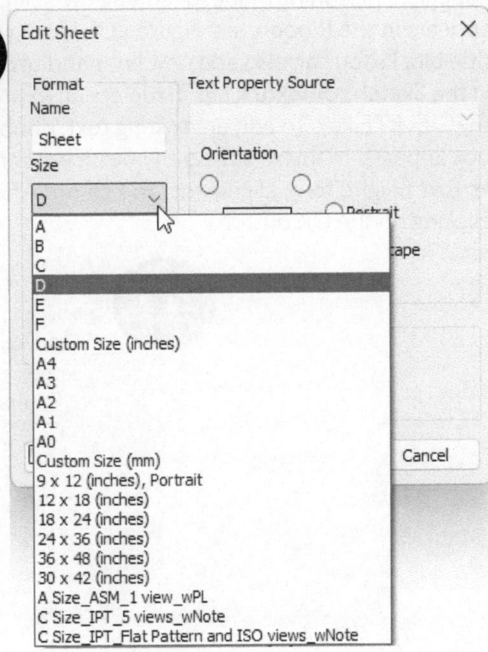

Revision

The **Revision** field is used for specifying the revision number of the sheet.

Orientation

The **Orientation** area of the dialog box is used for defining the orientation (portrait or landscape) of the selected sheet by selecting the required **Portrait** or **Landscape** radio button, respectively. In this area, you can also define the location of the title block on the sheet by selecting the required radio button. By default, the title block is located at the lower right corner of the sheet, since the lower right radio button is selected in the **Orientation** area of the dialog box.

Options

On selecting the **Exclude from count** check box, the selected sheet gets excluded from the count of sheets. On selecting the **Exclude from printing** check box, the selected sheet gets excluded while printing the drawing.

After specifying the required sheet size and other settings in the **Edit Sheet** dialog box, click on the **OK** button. The sheet size of the selected sheet gets changed, as specified.

Editing/Creating the Title Block

As discussed earlier, a drawing sheet contains a title block, which has drawing information such as project name, drawn by, checked by, approved by, date, sheet number, revision number, sheet size, and so on. You can edit or create the title block of a sheet as per the standard format of your company. To edit the title block of a sheet, expand the sheet node in the **Browser** and then right-click on the name of the title block, see Figure 14.5. Next, click on the **Edit Definition** option in the shortcut menu that appears. The editing mode for editing the selected title block is invoked and the **Sketch** contextual tab appears in the **Ribbon**, see Figure 14.6. Now, you can edit or modify the existing text and lines of the title block. You can also add new lines and text in the title block by using the sketching tools available in the **Sketch** contextual tab. To delete an existing line or text of the title block, select it and then press the DELETE key. To edit an existing text, double-click on it in the title block. The **Format Text** dialog box appears. In this dialog box, you can enter new text as well as define other sketch properties such as text height, font, alignment, and so on. After editing the text, exit the **Format Text** dialog box by clicking on the **OK** button.

14.5

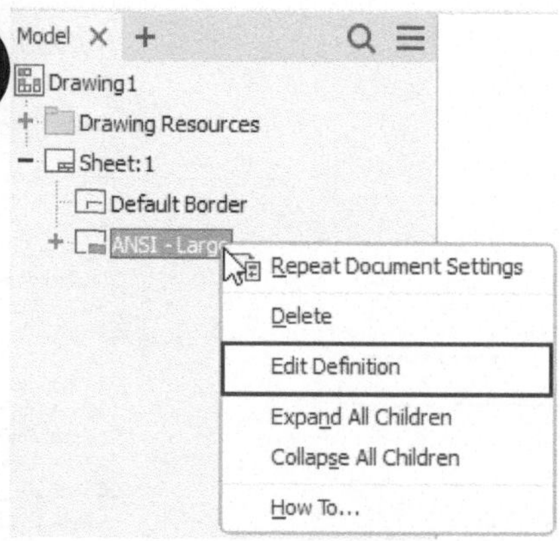

You can also insert your company logo into the title block. For doing so, click on the **Image** tool in the **Insert** panel of the **Sketch** contextual tab. Next, draw a rectangle by dragging the cursor to define the location for inserting the logo into the title block. The **Open** dialog box appears. In this dialog box, browse to the location where the image file (*.bmp, .gif, .jpg, .png, .tif*) to be inserted is saved and then select it. Next, click on the **Open** button in the dialog box. The selected image gets inserted and placed inside the defined rectangle in the title block of the sheet. Next, press the ESC key. Once you have edited the title block of the sheet, click on the **Finish Sketch** tool in the **Exit** panel of the **Sketch** contextual tab. The **Save Edits** dialog box appears. Click on the **Yes** button in this dialog box to save the changes made in the title block of the sheet and switch back to the drawing sheet.

14.6

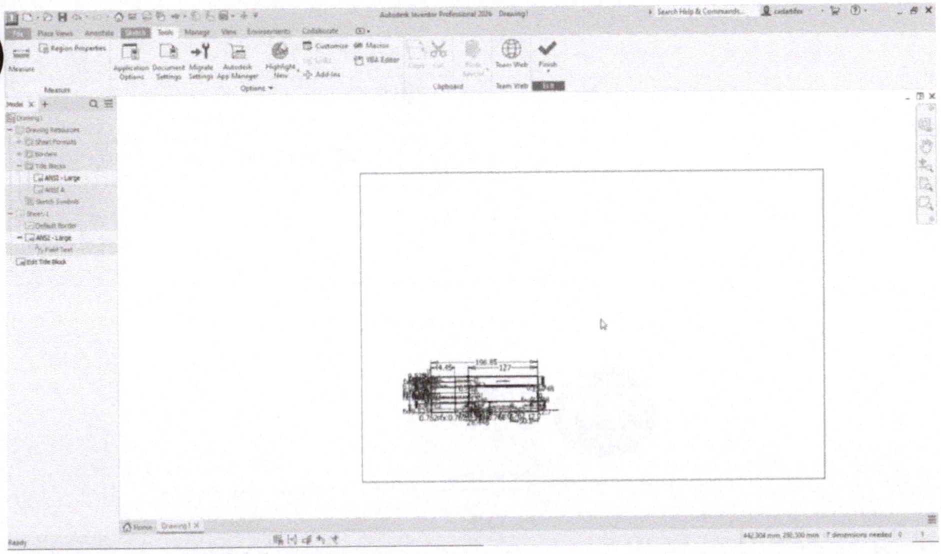

In Autodesk Inventor, you can also create a new title block and then insert it into a drawing sheet. For doing so, expand the **Drawing Resources** folder in the **Browser** and then right-click on the **Title Blocks** sub-folder in the **Drawing Resources** folder, see Figure 14.7. A shortcut menu appears. In this shortcut menu, click on the **Define New Title Block** option. The **Sketch** contextual tab appears in the **Ribbon**. Now, you can create a title block as per your company standard by using the sketching tools of the **Sketch** contextual tab, refer to Figure 14.8. After creating the title block, click on the **Finish Sketch** tool in the **Exit** panel of the **Sketch** contextual tab. The **Title Block** dialog box appears. Enter the name of the title block in this dialog box, see Figure 14.9, and then click on the **Save** button. The newly created title block gets saved and is added under the **Title Blocks** sub-folder of the **Drawing Resources** folder in the **Browser**, see Figure 14.10.

14.7

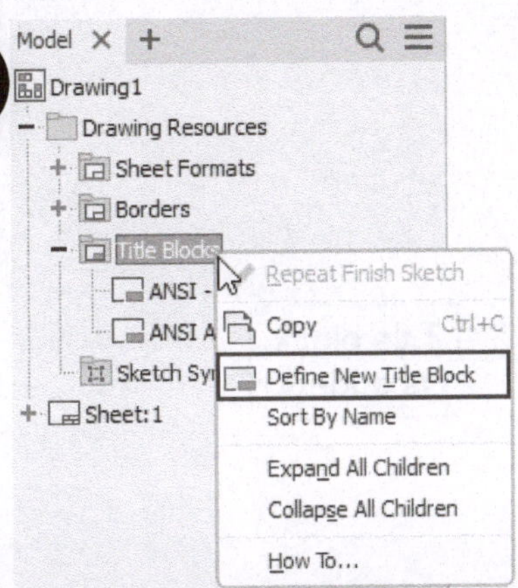

14.8

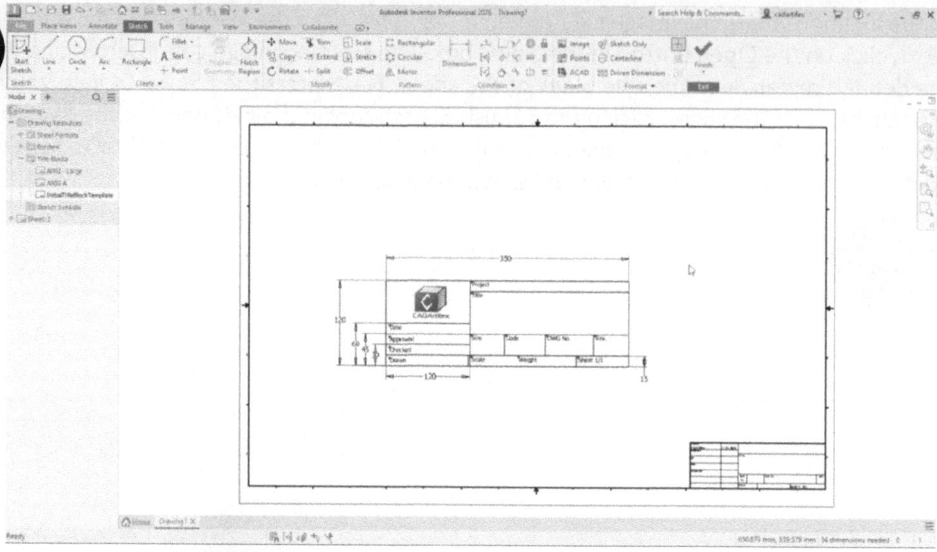

14.9

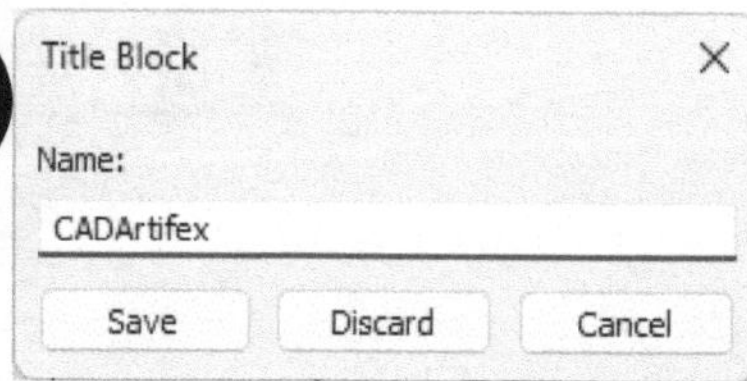

After the title block is added in the Title Blocks sub-folder, you can insert it into a drawing sheet. For doing so, you first need to delete the existing title block of the drawing sheet. Right-click on the existing title block of the drawing sheet in the sheet node of the **Browser** and then click on the **Delete** option in the shortcut menu that appears, see Figure 14.11. The selected title block of the sheet gets deleted. Now, you can insert a new title block in the drawing sheet. For doing so, right-click on the title block to be inserted in the **Title Blocks** sub-folder of the **Browser** and then click on the **Insert** option in the shortcut menu that appears. The selected title block gets added to the active drawing sheet, see Figure 14.12.

14.10

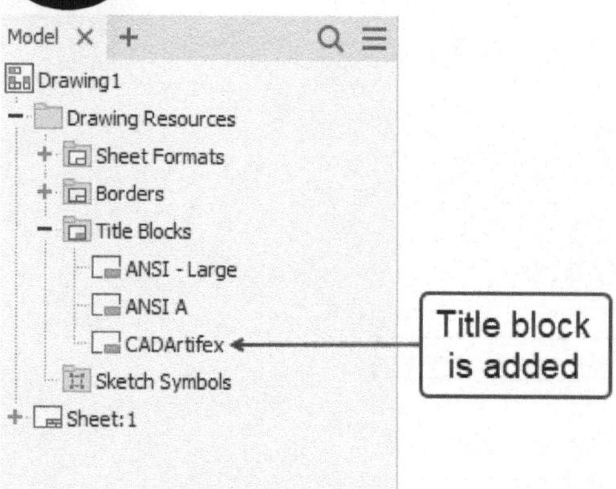

14.11

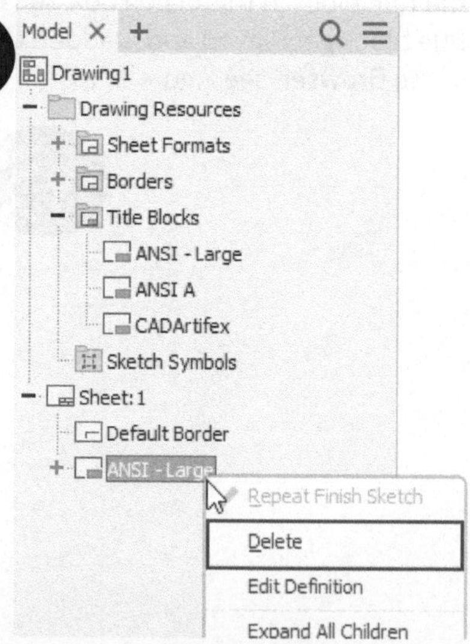

14.12

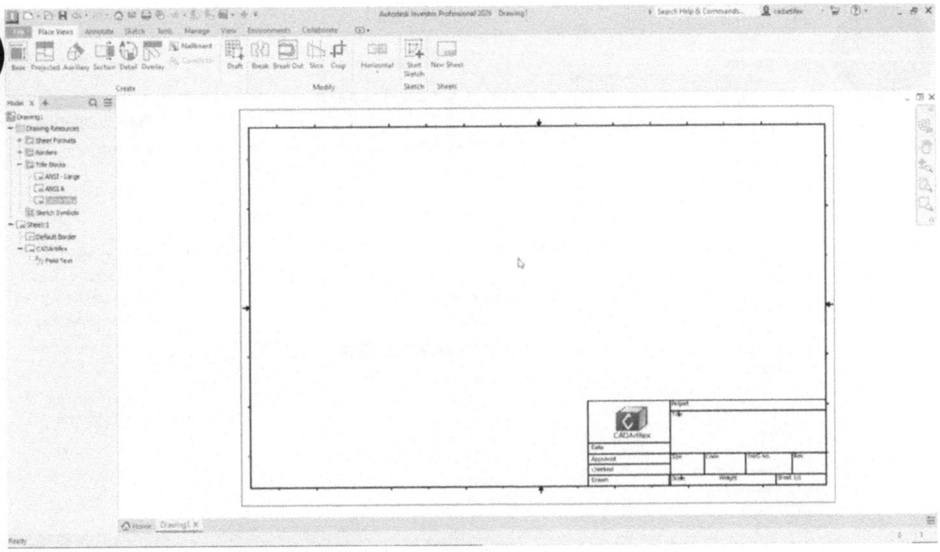

Editing the Drafting Standard

A drafting standard controls the appearance, style, and settings of dimensions, balloons, center marks, hatching, leader, part list, surface texture, text, annotations, and so on. In Autodesk Inventor, you can choose a drafting standard to be followed for creating an engineering drawing by selecting the required template while invoking the drawing file. Typically, engineering drawings are created in accordance with a drafting standard such as ANSI, ISO, BSI, DIN, or JIS. However, in order to meet a particular manufacturing requirement, you may need to customize the drafting standard of a drawing. For doing so, click on the **Manage** tab in the **Ribbon** and then click on the **Style Editor** tool in the **Styles and Standards** panel, see Figure 14.13. The **Style and Standard Editor** dialog box appears, see Figure 14.14. The drafting standards that are used in the current drawing file are listed under the **Standard** node in the left panel of the dialog box. Note that the display of drafting standards in the **Standard** node depends upon the option (**Active Standard**, **Local Styles**, or **All Styles**) selected in the **Filter** drop-down list available at the upper right corner of the dialog box, see Figure 14.14. On selecting the **Active Standard** option, only the active drafting standard of the current drawing file is listed in the **Standard** node of the dialog box. On selecting the **Local Styles** option, the drafting standards that are used in the current drawing file are listed in the **Standard** node of the dialog box. On selecting the **All Styles** option, all the available drafting standards are listed in the **Standard** node of the dialog box.

14.13

14.14

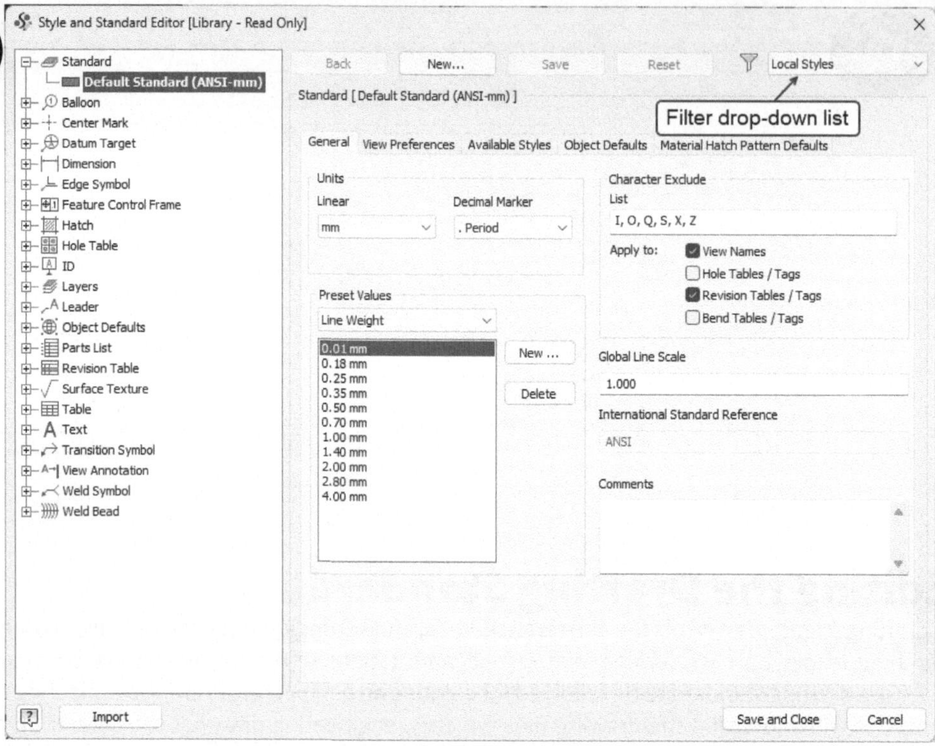

Tip: You can also create a new drafting standard for the drawing file in the **Style and Standard Editor** dialog box. For doing so, right-click on a drafting standard in the **Standard** node of the dialog box and then click on the **New Style** option in the shortcut menu that appears, see Figure 14.15. The **New Local Style** dialog box appears, see Figure 14.16. In this dialog box, specify a name for the new drafting standard in the **Name** field. Next, select the required drafting standard in the **Based On** drop-down list for creating a new drafting standard based on the selected one. Next, click on the **OK** button. A new drafting standard gets created and is listed under the **Standard** node of the **Style and Standard Editor** dialog box. To activate a drafting standard to be used in the current drawing file, double-click on it in the **Standard** node of the dialog box. The selected drafting standard becomes the active drafting standard for the current drawing file.

14.15

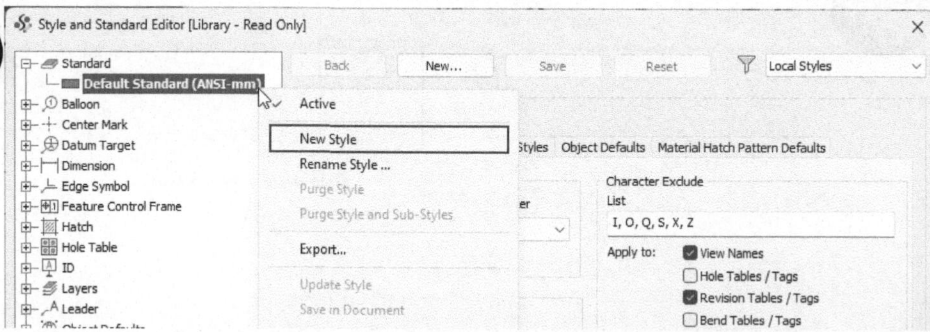

14.16

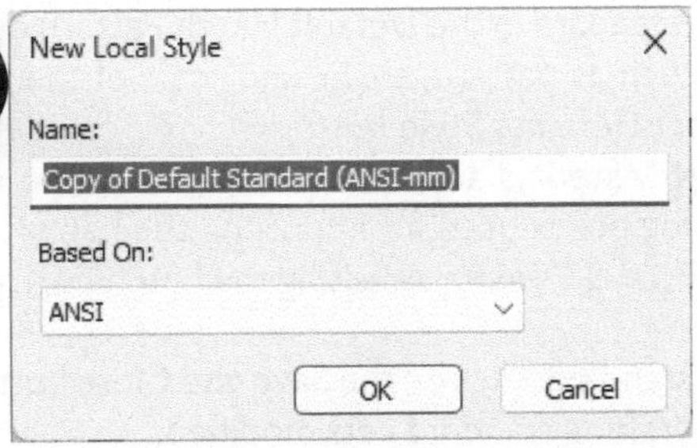

To edit a drafting standard, select it in the **Standard** node of the **Style and Standard Editor** dialog box. The various attributes of the selected drafting standard appear on the right panel of the dialog box in different tabs, refer to Figure 14.14. The options in these tabs are discussed next.

General Tab

By default, the **General** tab is activated in the dialog box and the options in this tab are used for editing the general attributes such as unit, decimal marker, line weight, text height, scale, and section hatch angle of the selected drafting standard.

View Preferences Tab

The options in the **View Preferences** tab are used for defining attributes such as default view type, label prefix, thread edge display, and the angle of projection. You will learn more about angle of projection later in this chapter.

Available Styles Tab

The options in the **Available Styles** tab are used for defining the default styles to be used for each attribute such as balloon, center mark, dimension, and so on. For example, to define the default styles for the balloon, select the **Balloon** option in the **Style Type** area of the dialog box and then select the required check boxes of the balloon styles in the **Choose Balloon Styles to Use in Standard** area of the dialog box. You can define one or more than one default style for an attribute.

Objects Defaults Tab

The options in the **Objects Defaults** tab of the dialog box are used for defining the default object style and layer for each object that is listed in the **Object Type** column of the dialog box. For doing so, ensure that the required drafting standard is selected in the **Active Object Defaults** drop-down list of the dialog box. All the objects of the selected drafting standard appear in the **Object Type** column in the dialog box. Next, click on the **Edit Object Defaults Style** button next to the **Active Object Defaults** drop-down list. Now, you can edit the object style and layer for each object type in the **Object Style** and **Layer** columns of the dialog box. If the **Autodesk Inventor Professional** dialog box appears on clicking the **Edit Object Defaults Style** button then click on the **Yes** button to continue with the editing process. After editing the object style of the objects, click on the drafting standard in the **Standard** node of the dialog box and then click on the **Yes** button in the **Autodesk Inventor Professional** dialog box to save the changes made.

Material Hatch Pattern Defaults Tab

The options in the **Material Hatch Pattern Defaults** tab of the dialog box are used for defining the default hatch pattern standard and hatching material for the selected drafting standard. You can select the default hatch pattern standard in the **Default Hatch Pattern** drop-down list of the dialog box. You can also edit properties such as pattern, angle, and scale of the selected hatch pattern standard by clicking on the **Edit Object Defaults Style** button. You can define the hatching material by using the options in the **Import Materials** area of the dialog box. The **From File** button in the **Import Materials** area of the dialog box is used for importing the hatching material from a part file and the **From Style Library** button is used for selecting the hatching material from the Autodesk library.

After editing the drafting standard, click on the **Save and Close** button in the **Style and Standard Editor** dialog box. The selected drafting standard gets modified.

Creating the Base View of a Model

The base view is an independent view of a model. It is also known as the first or the parent view for generating the orthogonal and isometric projected views of the model. You can create the base view by using the **Base** tool in the **Create** panel of the **Place Views** tab, see Figure 14.17. The method for creating the base view of a model is discussed below:

14.17

1. Click on the **Base** tool in the **Create** panel of the **Place Views** tab, see Figure 14.17. The **Drawing View** dialog box appears, see Figure 14.18.

14.18

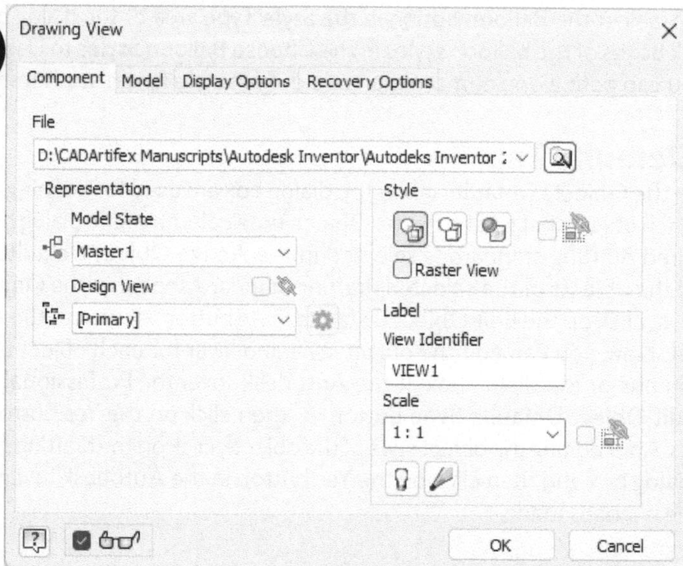

2. Click on the **Browse** button next to the **File** drop-down list of the **Component** tab in the dialog box to select an existing part or assembly file for creating its base view. The **Open** dialog box appears.

Note: If a component or an assembly is already opened in the current session of Autodesk Inventor, it gets automatically selected as the model for creating its base view in the **File** drop-down list of the dialog box. Also, a preview of the base view of the selected model appears in the drawing sheet. Note that if multiple models (parts or assemblies) are opened in the current session of Autodesk Inventor, then a list of all opened models appears in the **File** drop-down list of the **Component** tab, see Figure 14.19. You can select a model (part or assembly) in the **File** drop-down list to create its base view.

14.19

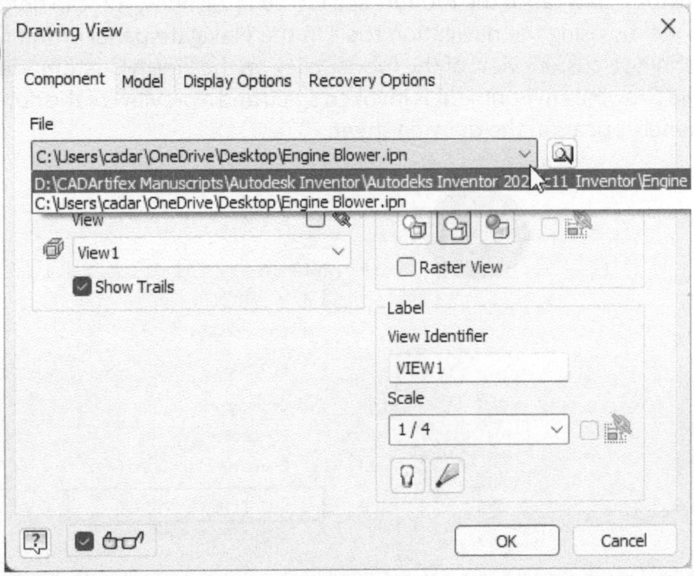

3. Browse to the location where the model, whose base view is to be created, has been saved and then select it. Next, click on the **Open** button in the dialog box. The component gets selected and its location appears in the **File** drop-down list of the dialog box. Also, the preview of the base view of the selected component appears in the drawing sheet with the display of ViewCube, see Figure 14.20.

14.20

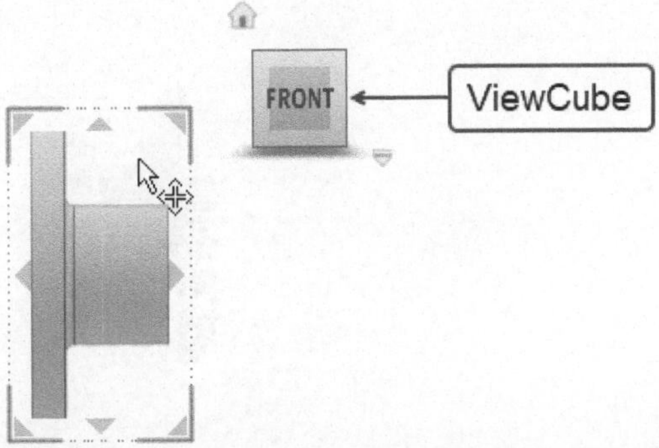

Now, you can define the orientation, display style, scale, and other properties of the base view to be created in the dialog box.

ViewCube: By using the ViewCube, you can switch between standard and isometric views of the model.

4. Set the orientation of the base view to a standard (Front, Top, Right, Left, Back, or Bottom) or an isometric view by using the ViewCube that appears in the drawing sheet.

Note: You can also create a custom view of the model in the drawing sheet. For doing so, right-click on the ViewCube and then click on the **Custom View Orientation** tool in the shortcut menu that appears, see Figure 14.21. The Navigation environment appears with the display of the **Custom View** tab in the **Ribbon**, see Figure 14.22. Now, you can define a custom view of the model by using the navigation tools in the **Navigate** panel of the **Custom View** tab. After defining a custom view of the model, click on the **Finish Custom View** tool in the **Exit** panel. The Drawing environment is invoked again and a preview of the defined custom view of the model appears in the drawing sheet.

14.21

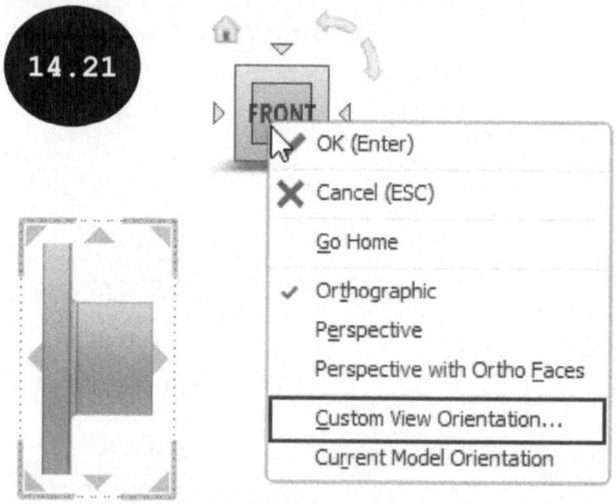

14.22

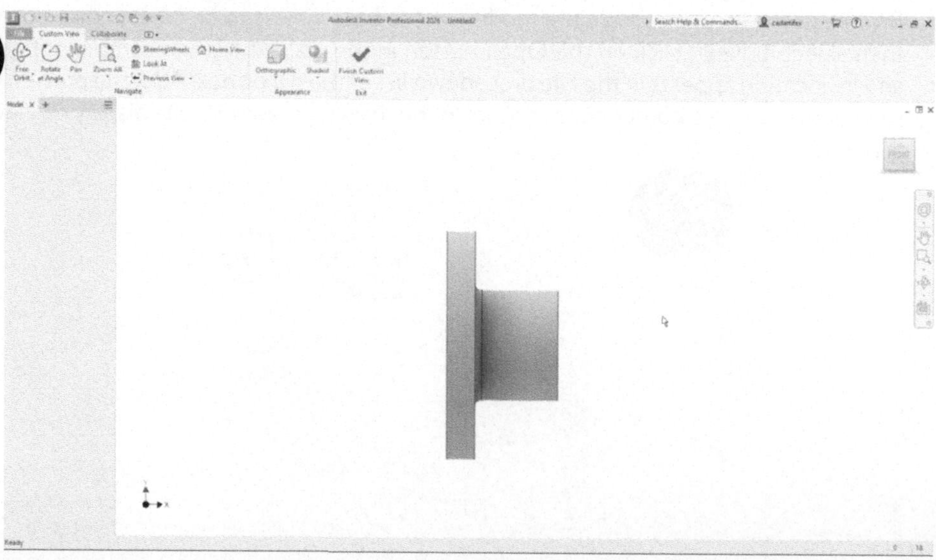

The options in the **Component** tab of the **Drawing View** dialog box are discussed below:

Style: The buttons in the **Style** area of the **Component** tab are used for defining the display style for the drawing view. On selecting the **Hidden Line** button, the visible edges appear as continuous lines and the hidden edges appear as dotted lines in the drawing view, see Figure 14.23. On selecting the **Hidden Line Removed** button, only the visible edges of the model appear in the drawing view as continuous lines, see Figure 14.24. On selecting the **Shaded** button, the drawing view is displayed in the shaded mode, with and without hidden edges of the model, see Figures 14.25 and 14.26. Note that the display of shaded mode with or without hidden edges of the model depends upon whether the **Hidden Line** or **Hidden Line Removed** button is activated along with the **Shaded** button in the **Style** area of the dialog box.

14.23

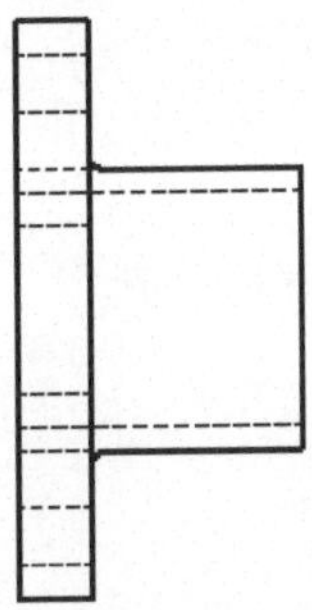

Hidden Line button selected

14.24

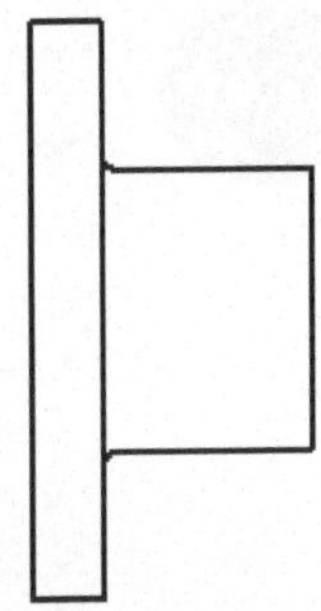

Hidden Line Removed button selected

14.25

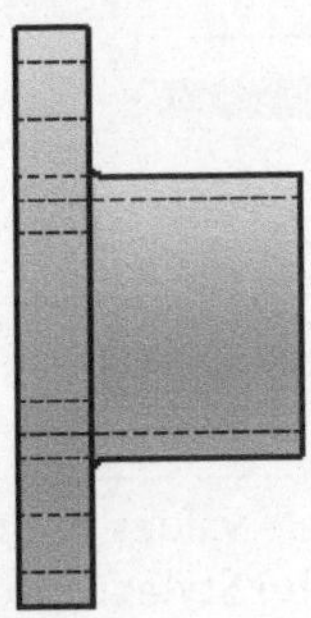

Shaded mode with hidden edges

14.26

Shaded mode without hidden edges

Raster View: On selecting the **Raster View** check box, the raster view of the model gets generated in the drawing sheet. A raster view is a pixel-based view that gets generated faster than a drawing view and is used for large assemblies.

Note: A raster view is generated inside a green box in the drawing view. Also, a diagonal red line appears on the raster view icon in the **Browser**.

Toggle Label Visibility: The **Toggle Label Visibility** button is used for turning on or off the visibility of the label on the drawing view in the drawing sheet.

Edit View Label: The **Edit View Label** button is used for editing the label text of the view in the **Format Text** dialog box that appears on clicking this button.

Label: The **Label** field is used for specifying a new label text for the drawing view.

Scale: The **Scale** field is used for specifying the scale of the drawing view. You can also click on the arrow to the right of this field to invoke a list of pre-defined scale values, see Figure 14.27. In this list, you can select a pre-defined scale value, as required.

14.27

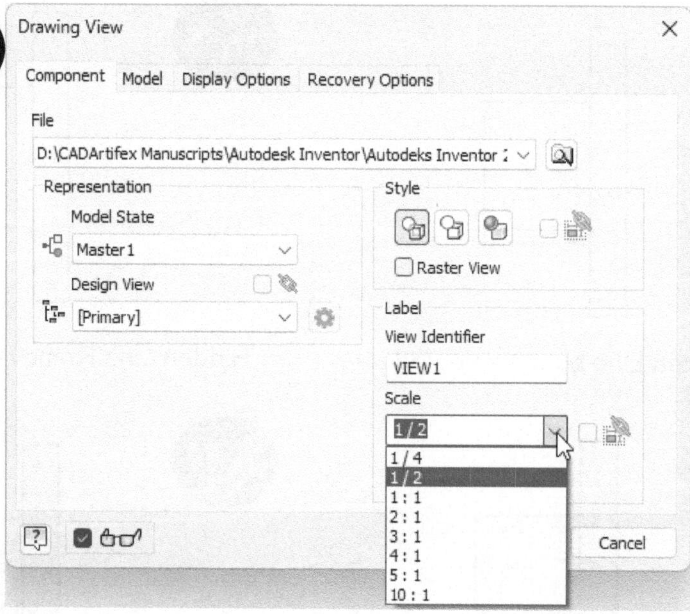

Tip: You can also customize to add or remove pre-defined scale values in the list. For doing so, click on the **Manage** tab in the **Ribbon** and then click on the **Styles Editor** tool in the **Styles and Standards** panel. The **Style and Standard Editor** dialog box appears. In this dialog box, ensure that the active drafting standard is selected in the **Standard** node of the dialog box. Next, select the **Scale** option in the **Preset Values** drop-down list of the **General** tab that appears on the right panel of the dialog box. A list of pre-defined scale values appear in the field below the **Preset Values** drop-down list. Once the list of pre-defined scale values appears, you can add new pre-defined scale values by using the **New** button and remove existing pre-defined scale values by using the **Delete** button.

Enable/Disable feature preview : By default, the **Enable/Disable feature preview** check box is selected in the **Component** tab of the dialog box. As a result, a preview of the drawing view of the model appears in a rectangular box in the sheet. On clearing this check box, the preview gets disabled and an empty rectangular box appears in the drawing sheet.

Design View: The **Design View** drop-down list in the **Representation** area of the dialog box is used for selecting a view representation of the selected assembly file for creating the drawing view. It is used when the selected file is an assembly that contains different design view representations. On selecting a view representation other than **Primary** in this drop-down list, the **Associative** check box gets enabled above the drop-down list in the dialog box. On selecting this check box, the drawing view gets updated when changes are made in the associative view representation of the assembly in the Assembly environment.

Tip: In the Assembly environment, you can create multiple design view representations of an assembly by turning on or off the visibility of its components. For doing so, open an assembly in the Assembly environment and then, expand the **Representations** folder in the **Browser** and then right-click on the **View** node, see Figure 14.28. Next, click on the **New** option in the shortcut menu that appears. A new design representation with default name "View1" gets created and becomes an active representation of the assembly in the **View** node. After creating a view representation, you can turn off the visibility of components that are not required to be present in the current view representation. Next, right-click on the newly created view representation in the **View** node of the **Browser** and then click on the **Lock** option in the shortcut menu that appears, see Figure 14.29. The newly created view representation gets saved and locked. To make any further changes in a locked view, you need to unlock it by right-clicking on it in the **Browser** and then click on the **Lock** option again in the shortcut menu that appears.

14.28

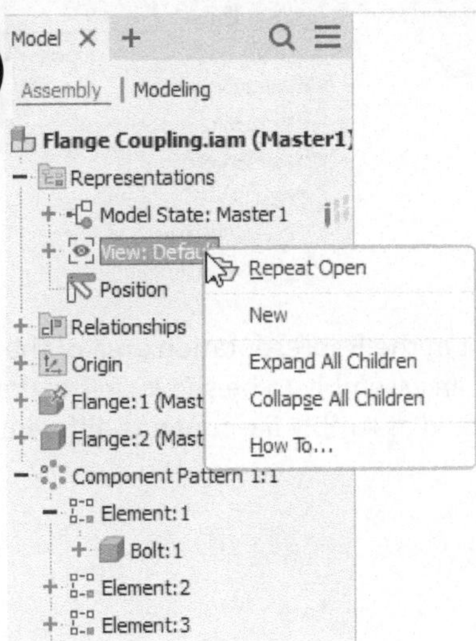

14.29

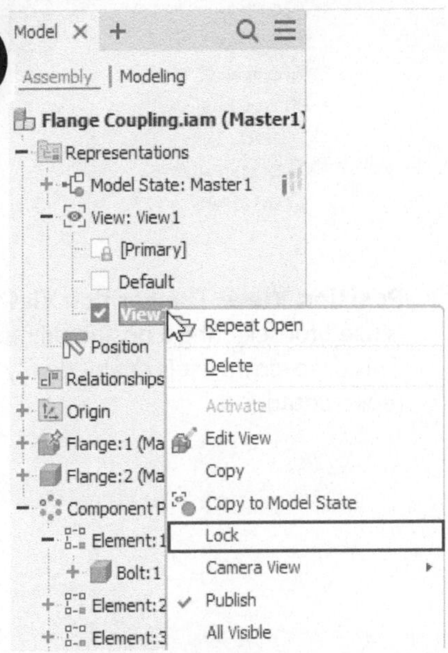

Model State: The Model State drop-down list in the **Representation** area of the dialog box is used for selecting a model state representation of the selected part or assembly file for creating the drawing view. It is used when the selected file contains multiple model state representations. By default, the active model state of the part or assembly file is selected in the **Model State** drop-down list. If the inserted part or assembly has only one model state, then the **Primary** model state, which is the default model state, is selected in this drop-down list, by default.

Tip: You can create multiple model state representations of a part or an assembly by adding, suppressing, or modifying features or components. For doing so, open a part or an assembly and then right-click on the **Model States** folder in the **Browser**, see Figure 14.30. Next, click on the **New** option in the shortcut menu. A new model state representation with default name "**Model State1**" gets created and becomes an active state. Alternatively, expand the **Model States** folder in the **Browser** and then right-click on the **Primary** node, see Figure 14.31. Next, click on the **Copy** option in the shortcut menu. A new model state representation with default name "**Primary1**" gets created. Double click on the **Primary1** node to activate it. After creating a model state, you can add, suppress, or modify features or components for the current model state, as required. You can also assign a new name to each model state by clicking on its name and entering a new name in the edit field that appears. Next, save the file. Similarly, you can create multiple model state representations of a part or an assembly.

14.30

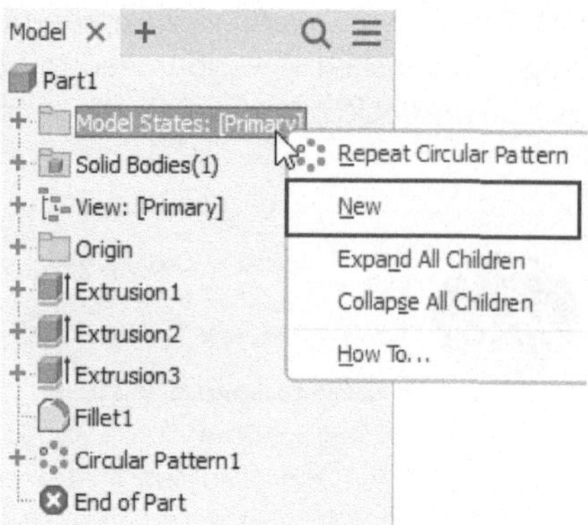

14.31

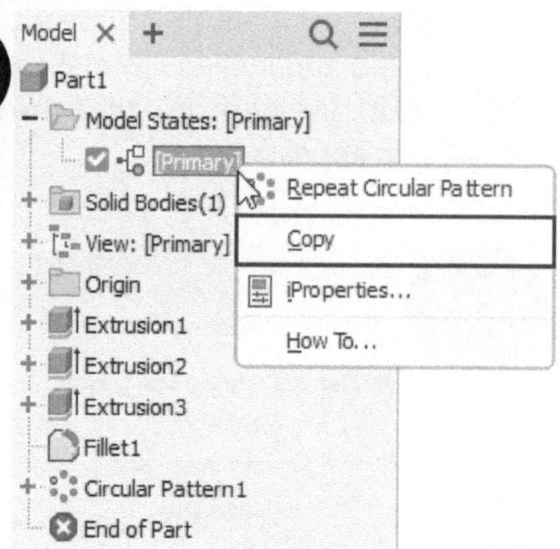

Position View: The **Position View** drop-down list in the **Representation** area of the dialog box is used for selecting a positional representation of an assembly to be shown in the drawing view. This drop-down list is enabled only when the selected assembly file contains different positional representations.

Tip: In the Assembly environment, you can create different positional representations for an assembly by changing the position of the components or overriding its constraint values. For example, two components of an assembly are in perfect contact with each other in one positional representation and at an offset distance in another positional representation, see Figures 14.32 and 14.33. To create different positional representations, open an assembly in the Assembly environment and then, expand the **Representations** folder in the **Browser** and then right-click on the **Position** node, see Figure 14.34. Next, click on the **New** tool in the shortcut menu that appears. A new positional representation with a default name "**Position1**" gets created and becomes an active representation of the assembly in the **Position** node of the **Browser**. You can rename the newly created representation by clicking on its name and entering a new name in the edit field that appears. After creating a positional representation, drag the component of the assembly to the new location along or about its free degree of freedom, refer to Figures 14.35 and 14.36. Alternatively, you can also override a constraint of the assembly to change its component position. For doing so, right-click on a constraint to be overridden in the **Browser** and then click on the **Override** option in the shortcut menu that appears, see Figure 14.37. The **Override Object** dialog box appears. In this dialog box, select the **Value** check box and then enter a new override value for the selected constraint in the **Value** field that is enabled in the dialog box. Next, click on the **OK** button. The new position of the component is defined in the newly created positional representation. Similarly, you can create multiple positional representations one after another by changing the position of the components or overriding their constraint values. You can switch between the positional representations by double-clicking on their names in the **Browser**. To save the assembly after creating positional representations, you need to activate the **Primary** positional representation by double-clicking on it in the **Position** node of the **Browser**.

14.32

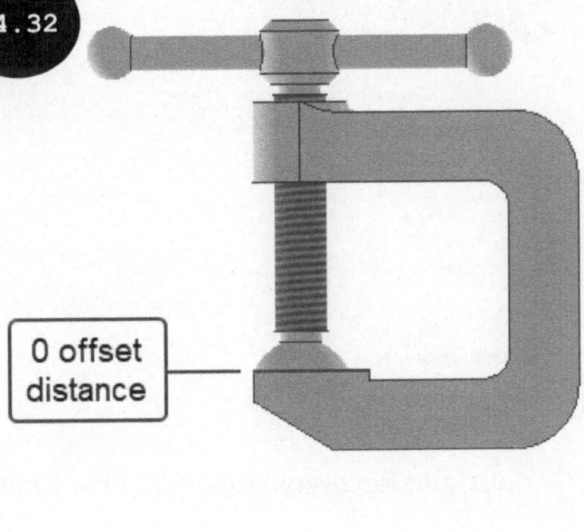

14.33

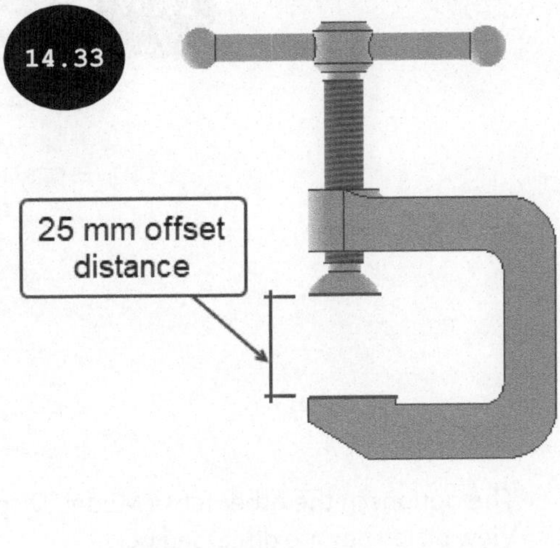

14.34

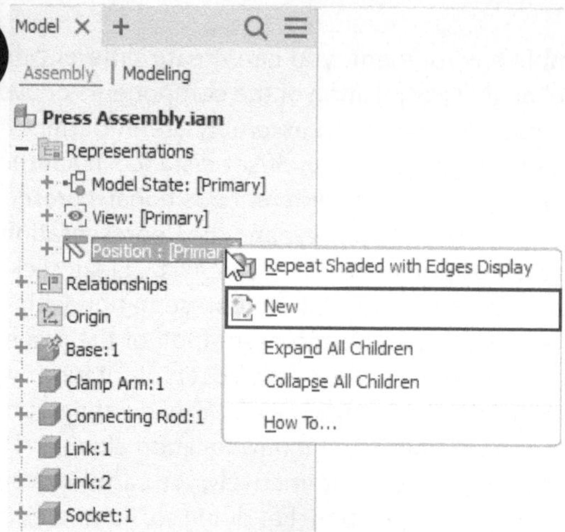

14.35

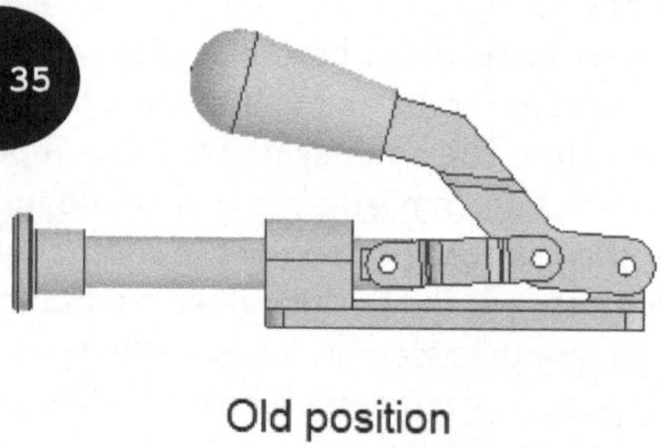

14.36

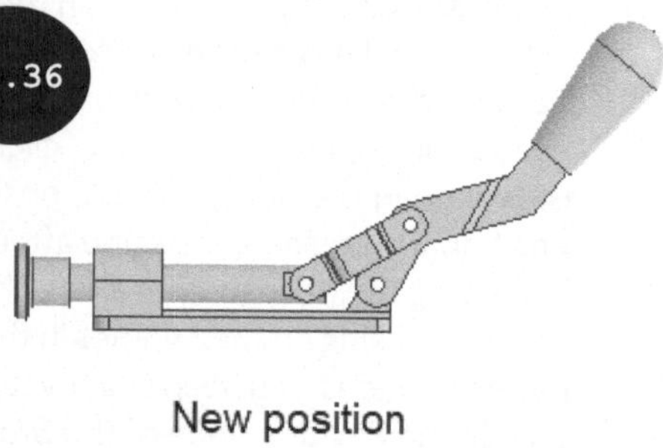

14.37

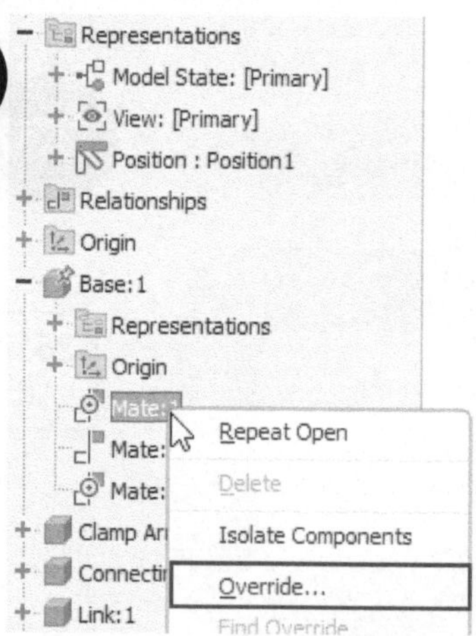

The options in the other tabs (**Model**, **Display Options**, and **Recovery Options**) of the **Drawing View** dialog box are discussed next.

Model Tab: The availability of options in the **Model** tab of the dialog box depends upon the selected file type for creating the drawing view. Figure 14.38 shows the dialog box when the selected file type is an assembly. The options in the **Model** tab are discussed below:

Member Drop-down list: The **Member** drop-down list in the **Model** tab of the dialog box is used for selecting the required configuration/member of the selected iPart or iAssembly to represent in the drawing view. Note that this drop-down list is enabled only when the selected file is an iPart or an iAssembly.

14.38

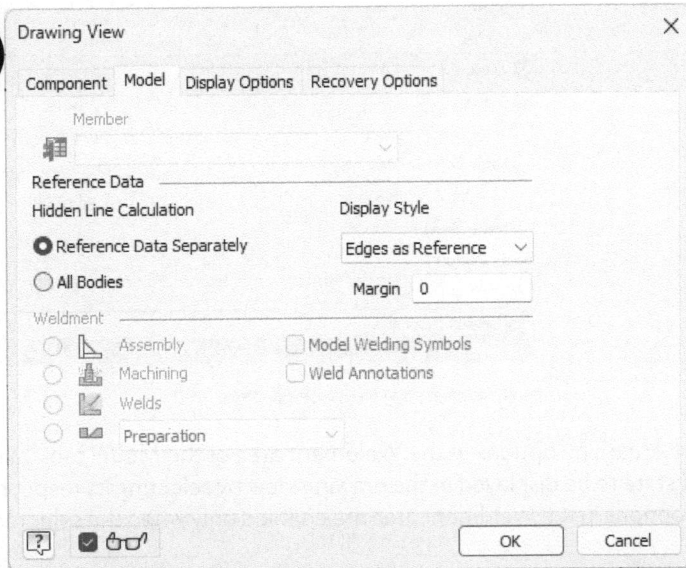

Reference Data Area: The **Display Style** drop-down list in the **Reference Data** area of the dialog box is used for selecting an option (**Edges as Reference**, **Edges as Part**, or **Off**) to define the display style for the reference components/data of the assembly. Note that on selecting the **Off** option in this drop-down list, the visibility of the reference components/data of the assembly gets turned off in the drawing view. You can also define an option for calculating the hidden lines of the reference components of the assembly in the drawing view by selecting the required radio button (**Reference Data Separately** or **All Bodies**) in the **Hidden Line Calculation** area of the dialog box. By default, the **Reference Data Separately** radio button is selected. As a result, the hidden lines are calculated for reference components/data, separately, whereas on selecting the **All Bodies** radio button, the hidden lines are calculated for all bodies of the assembly. Note that the options in the **Reference Data** area of the **Model** tab are available only when the selected file is an assembly.

Tip: In the Assembly environment, you can define some of the components of an assembly as reference components/data. For doing so, open an assembly in the Assembly environment and then right-click on one or more components to be defined as a reference component in the **Browser** or in the graphics area. Next, click on the **iProperties** option in the shortcut menu that appears. The **iProperties** dialog box appears with the name of the selected component, see Figure 14.39. Next, click on the **Occurrence** tab in the dialog box and then select the **Reference** option in the **BOM Structure** drop-down list of the dialog box, see Figure 14.39. Next, click on the **OK** button in the dialog box. The selected component becomes a reference component of the assembly.

14.39

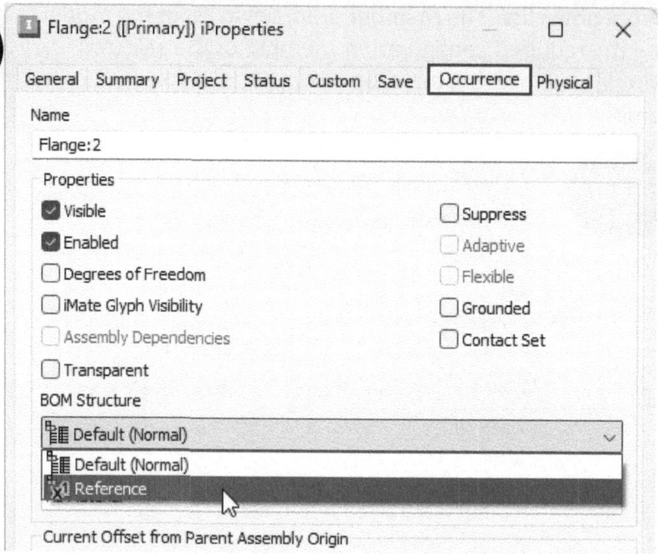

Weldment Area: The options in the **Weldment** area of the **Model** tab are used for specifying the weldment state to be displayed in the drawing view by selecting its respective radio button in this area. The options in the **Weldment** area are enabled only when the selected file is a weldment file.

Display Options Tab: The options in the **Display Options** tab of the **Drawing View** dialog box are used for controlling the display of various elements such as thread feature, tangent edges, interference edges, and so on in the drawing view, see Figure 14.40. Some of the options in the **Display Options** tab are discussed below:

14.40

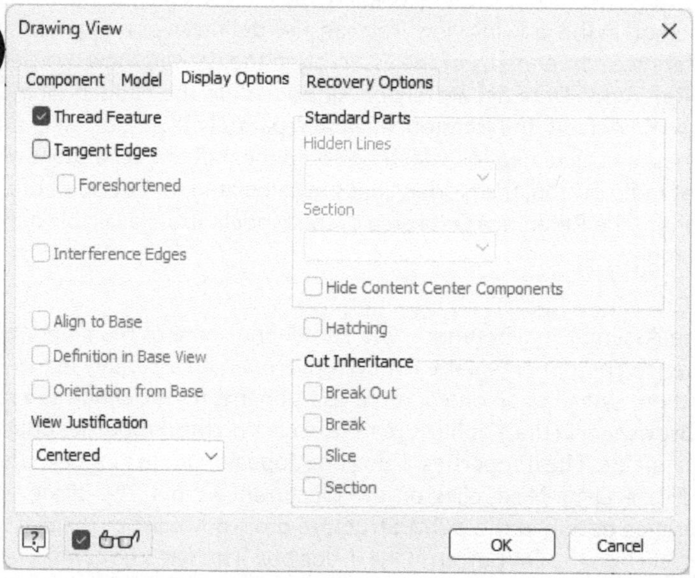

Thread Feature: On selecting the **Thread Feature** check box in the **Display Options** tab, the visibility of the thread features of the selected model gets turned on in the drawing view.

Tangent Edges: On selecting the **Tangent Edges** check box, the tangent edges of the selected model are displayed in the drawing view, see Figure 14.41. Also, the **Foreshortened** check box gets enabled in the dialog box. On selecting this check box, the length of the tangent edges are shortened in the drawing view to easily distinguish them from visible edges. If the **Tangent Edge** check box is cleared, the tangent edges of the model get hidden in the drawing view, see Figure 14.42.

14.41

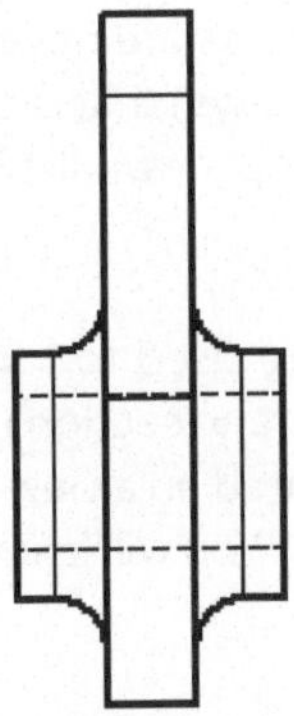

14.42

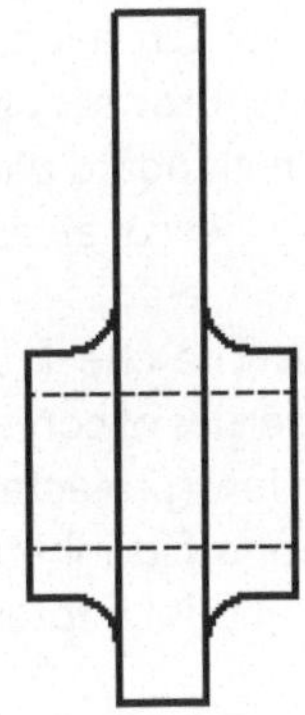

Interference Edges: On selecting the **Interference Edges** check box, the interference edges of the assembly that are created due to press-fit interference conditions such as pins in undersized holes, threaded fasteners in undersized holes, and so on are visible in the drawing view. Figure 14.43 shows a drawing view with the **Interference Edges** check box selected and Figure 14.44 shows a drawing view with the **Interference Edges** check box cleared. This check box is enabled while creating the base view of an assembly or a multi-body part.

14.43

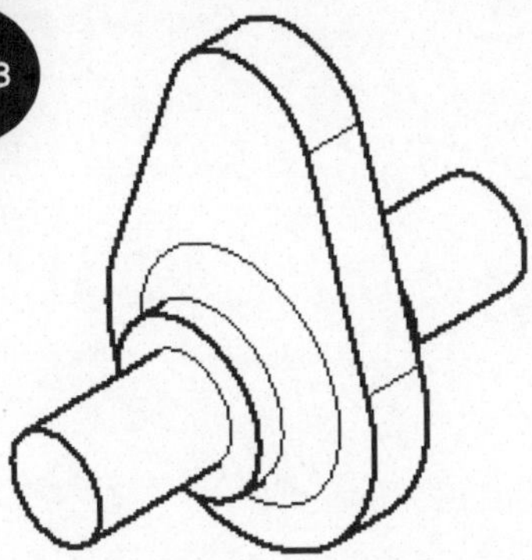

14.44

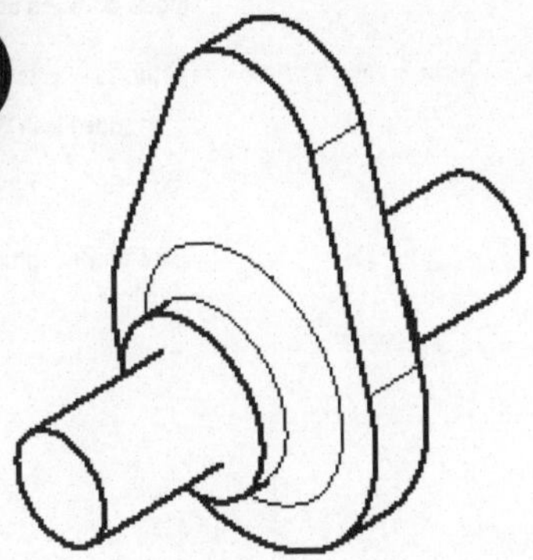

Align to Base: On selecting the **Align to Base** check box, the alignment between the projected view and its base view is maintained. If you clear this check box, the alignment between the projected view and its base view gets broken. This check box is enabled in the dialog box when you edit a projected view by double-clicking on it.

Standard Parts: The options in the **Hidden Lines** drop-down list of the **Standard Parts** area are used for controlling the display of hidden lines of the standard parts such as fasteners or parts inserted from the Content Library in the drawing view. On selecting the **Never** option in this drop-down list, the display of hidden lines of the standard parts is turned off or removed in the drawing view. On selecting the **Obey Browser** option, the default display settings that are configured in the **Browser** for each standard part are used in the drawing view. This drop-down list is enabled while creating the base view of an assembly or a multi-body part.

The options in the **Section** drop-down list of the **Standard Parts** area are used to specify whether or not the standard parts of the assembly are to be sectioned in the section view. On selecting the **Always** option in this drop-down list, the standard parts of the assembly are always sectioned in the section view. On selecting the **Never** option, the standard parts are never sectioned. On selecting the **Obey Browser** option, the default setting (**Never** or **Always**) that is configured in the **Browser** for each standard part is used in the section view. This drop-down list is enabled while creating the base view of an assembly or a multi-body part.

Cut Inheritance: The check boxes in the **Cut Inheritance** area are used to turn on or off the inheritance properties of corresponding cuts (break out, break, slice, and section) from the parent view to its child view (projected). For example, if a break view is created on a view of a model then you can turn on or off its inheritance properties in its projected view. You will learn about creating break view later in this chapter.

Recovery Options Tab: The options in the **Recovery Options** tab of the dialog box are used to specify whether or not to include surface bodies, mesh bodies, work features, and model dimensions in the drawing view by selecting or clearing the respective check boxes in the dialog box, see Figure 14.45.

14.45

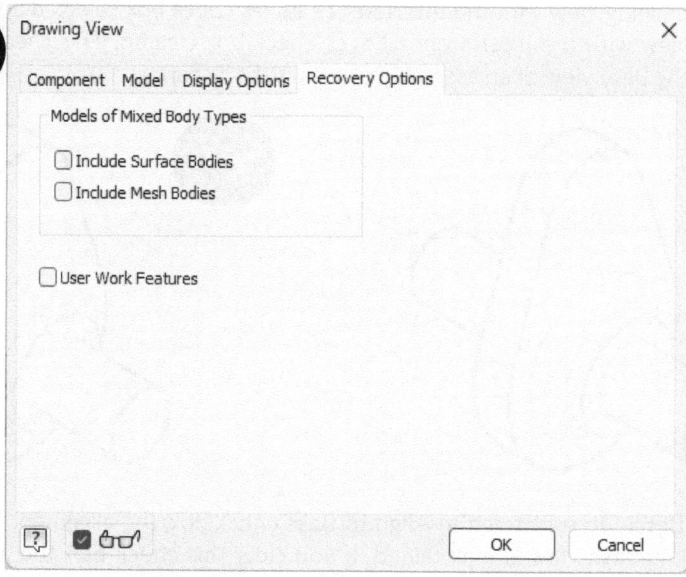

5. Specify the display style, scale, and other properties for the base view of the model in the **Drawing View** dialog box.

   After specifying the required settings for creating the base view in the dialog box, you can define its placement on the drawing sheet by dragging it to the required position. Also, you can create projection views.

6. Move the cursor over the preview of the base view inside the rectangular box in the drawing sheet. The cursor changes to Move cursor, see Figure 14.46.

7. Drag the base view to the required location on the sheet by pressing and holding the left mouse button.

8. After defining the position of the drawing view, release the left mouse button.

Note: On moving the cursor to a distance from the base view, a dotted rectangular box representing the respective projected view appears attached to the cursor, see Figure 14.47. You can click to define the position of the projected view on the drawing sheet. Alternatively, you can click on the arrows at the corner or middle segments of the base view rectangular box for creating the respective projected views on the drawing sheet, see Figure 14.48. You will learn more about creating projected views later in this chapter.

14.46

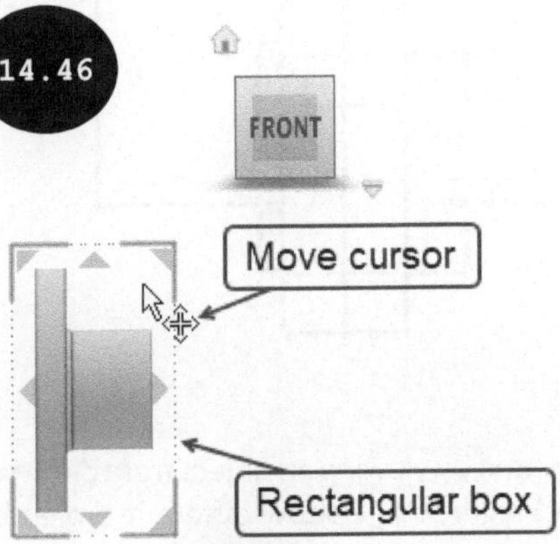

14.47

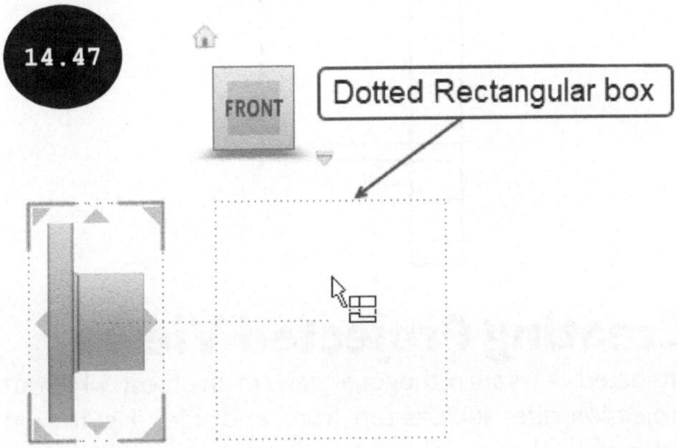

14.48

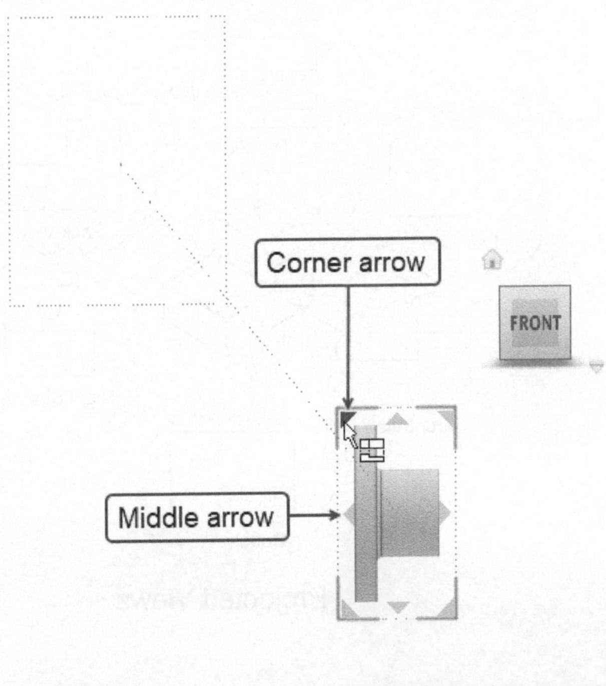

9. After specifying the required settings for creating the base view in the dialog box, click on the **OK** button in the **Drawing View** dialog box. The base view is created in the drawing area. Figure 14.49 shows the base view of a component and Figure 14.50 shows the base view of an assembly.

Note: You can also edit or modify the settings such as display style and scale factor for a drawing view that has been already placed in the drawing sheet. To modify the settings of a drawing view, double-click on the drawing view to be edited in the drawing sheet. The **Drawing View** dialog box appears. By using the options of this dialog box, you can edit the settings of the selected drawing view. The options of this dialog box are same as those discussed earlier.

14.49

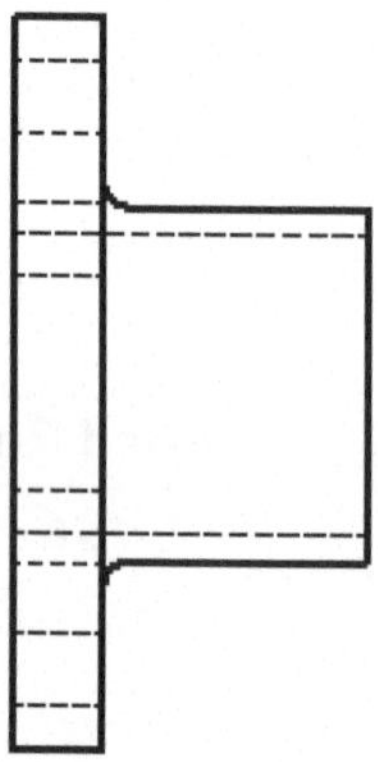

14.50

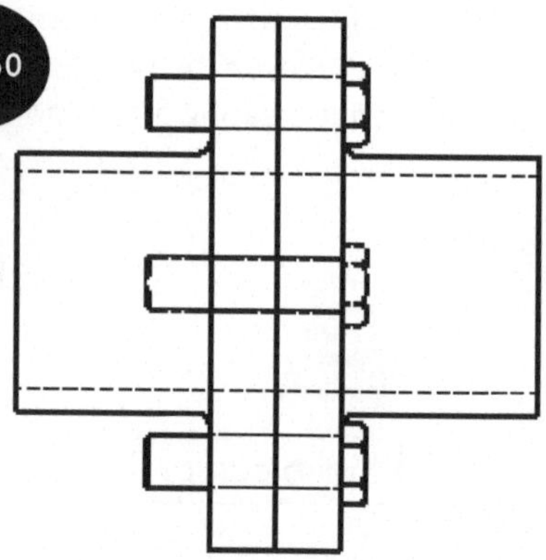

Creating Projected Views

Projected views are orthogonal views of an object, which are created by viewing an object from different projection sides such as top, front, and sides. Figure 14.51 and Figure 14.52 show different projected views of an object.

14.51

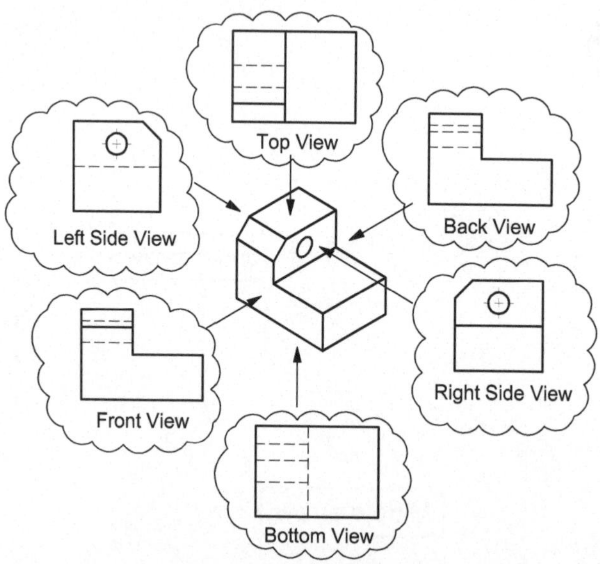

Projected Views

14.52

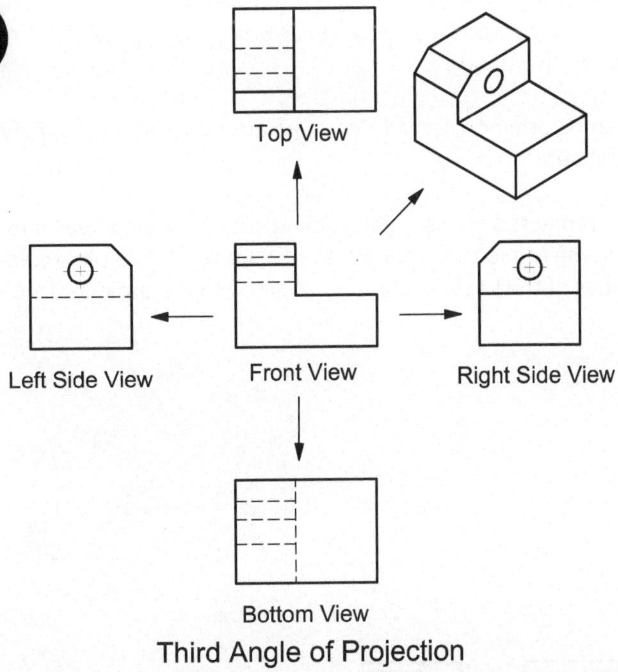

As discussed earlier, you can create projected views of a model while creating its base view. In addition, you can also create projected views by using the **Projected** tool of the **Create** panel, see Figure 14.53. The method for creating projected views by using the **Projected** tool is discussed below:

1. Click on the **Projected** tool in the **Create** panel of the **Place Views** tab, see Figure 14.53. You are prompted to select a drawing view to create its projected views.

14.53

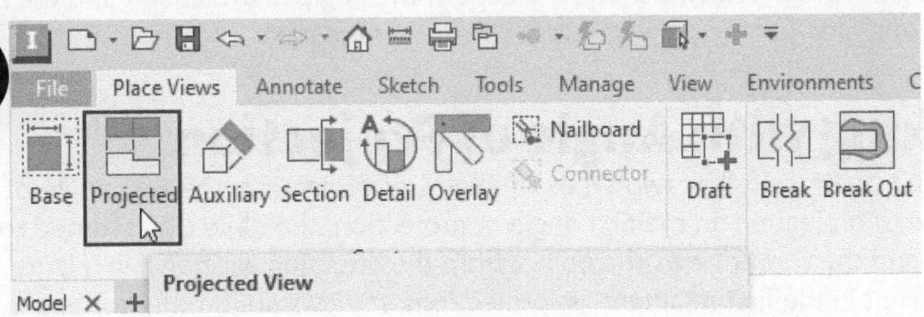

2. Select a drawing view as the base view whose projected views are to be created.

3. Move the cursor to the required location in the drawing sheet. A preview of the projected view appears attached to the cursor depending upon the direction of movement.

Note: The creation of projected views; orthogonal or isometric; depends upon the movement of the cursor. When the cursor is moved at a right angle (horizontally or vertically) to the base view, an orthogonal view gets created, whereas when it is moved at an angle to the base view, an isometric view gets created.

4. Click to specify the placement point for the projected view in the drawing sheet. The projected view is created and is represented by a rectangular box. Also, a preview of the other projected view appears attached to the cursor.

5. You can continue creating other projected views one after the other by specifying the placement points in the drawing sheet.

6. After creating all the projected views, right-click on the drawing sheet and then click on the **Create** tool in the Marking Menu that appears, see Figure 14.54. The projected views are created. Note that the properties of the base view are propagated to the projected views.

14.54

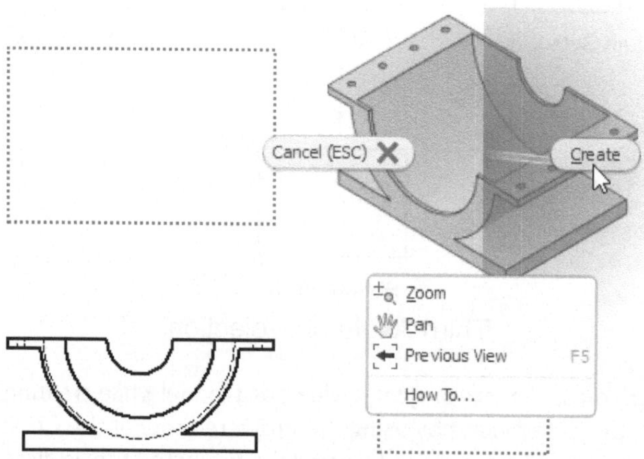

In Autodesk Inventor, the creation of orthogonal projected views depends upon the angle of projection defined for the drawing sheet. You can define the first angle of projection or the third angle of projection for creating the projected views. The concept of the angle of projection and the method for defining the angle of projection for a drawing sheet are discussed next.

Working with Angle of Projection

Engineering drawings follow two types of angles of projection: the first angle of projection and the third angle of projection. In the first angle of projection, the object is assumed to be kept in the first quadrant and the viewer views the object from the direction as shown in Figure 14.55. As the object has been kept in the first quadrant, its projections of views are on the respective planes as shown in Figure 14.55. Now on unfolding the planes of projections, the front view appears on the upper side and the top view appears on the bottom side. Also, the right side view appears on the left and the left side view appears on the right side of the front view, see Figure 14.56. In the third angle of projection, the object is assumed to be kept in the third quadrant, see Figure 14.55. In this case, the projection of the front view appears on the bottom and the projection of the top view appears on the top side of the drawing. Also, the right side view appears on the right and the left side view appears on the left of the front view, see Figure 14.57.

14.55

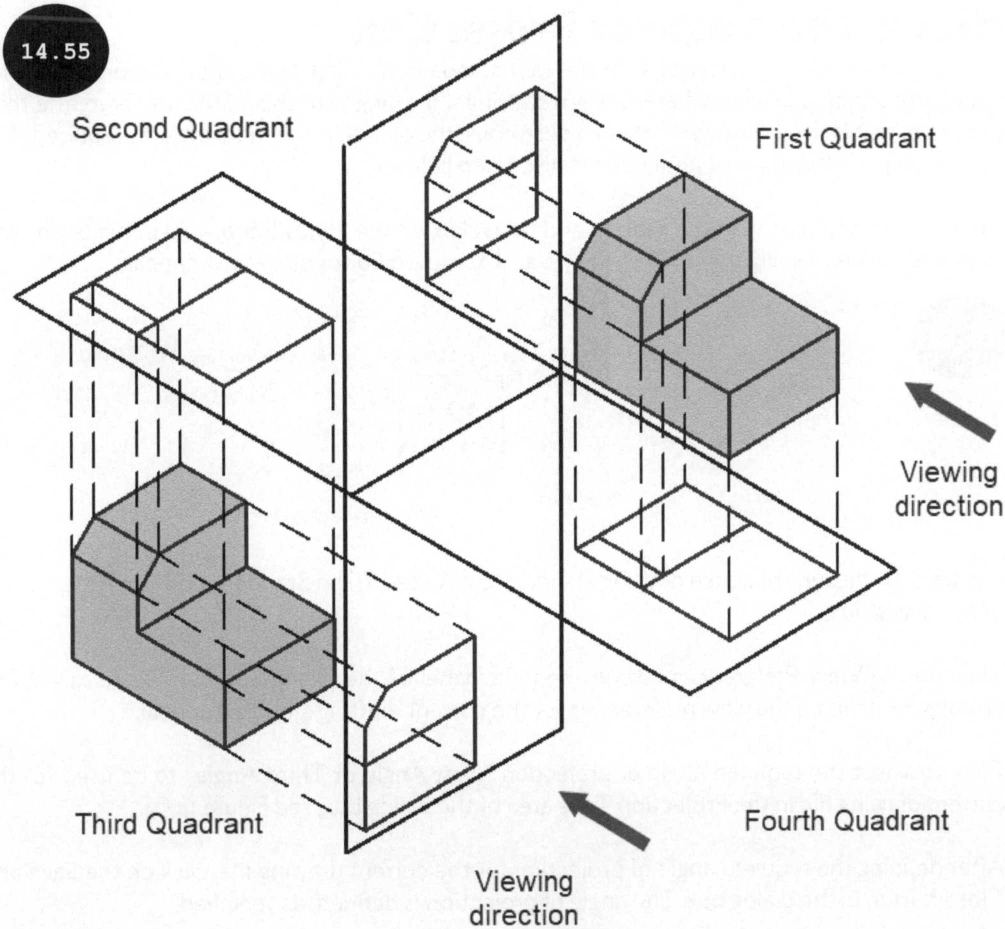

14.56

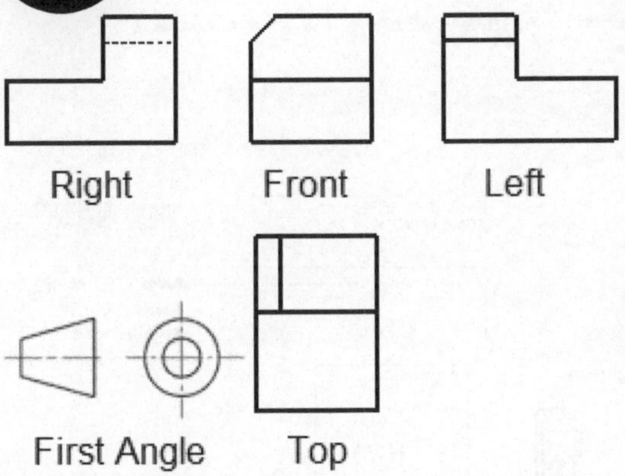

14.57

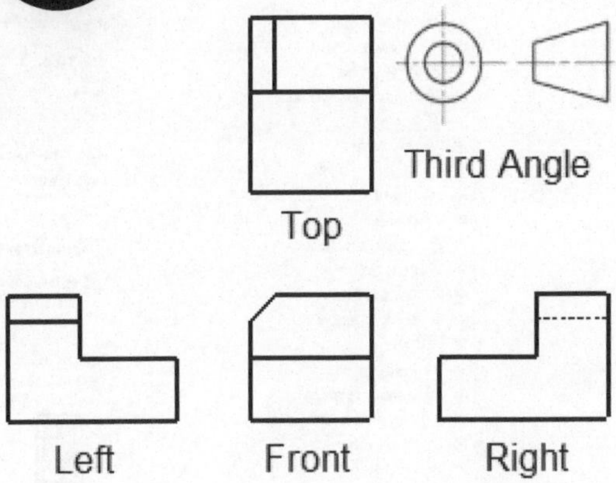

Defining the Angle of Projection

By default, when you start a drawing with the ISO standard, the first angle of projection is used for generating the projected views, whereas when starting a drawing with the ASME standard, the third angle of projection is used. However, you can customize the default projection angle, as required. The method for defining the angle of projection is discussed below:

1. Click on the **Manage** tab in the **Ribbon** and then click on the **Styles Editor** tool in the **Styles and Standards** panel, see Figure 14.58. The **Style and Standard Editor** dialog box appears.

14.58

2. Ensure that the current active drafting standard is selected in the **Standard** node in the left panel of the dialog box.

3. Click on the **View Preferences** tab on the right panel of the dialog box, see Figure 14.59. The options for defining the view preferences for the current drafting standard appear.

4. Click to select the required angle of projection (**First Angle** or **Third Angle**) to be used for the current drawing file in the **Projection Type** area of the dialog box, see Figure 14.59.

5. After defining the required angle of projection for the current drawing file, click on the **Save and Close** button in the dialog box. The angle of projection is defined, as specified.

14.59

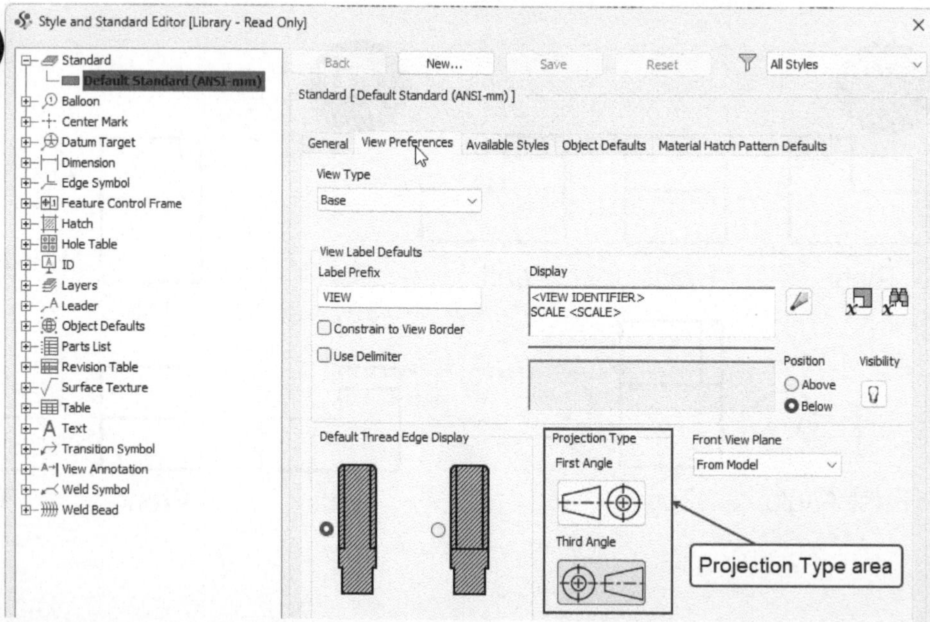

Creating Other Drawing Views

In Autodesk Inventor, in addition to creating base view and projected views of an object, you can also create the following types of drawing views:

- Auxiliary View
- Section View
- Detail View
- Overlay View
- Break View
- Break Out View
- Slice View
- Crop View

Creating an Auxiliary View

An auxiliary view is created by projecting the edges of an object normal to a specified edge of an existing view, see Figure 14.60. You can create an auxiliary view by using the **Auxiliary** tool. The method for creating an auxiliary view is discussed below:

14.60

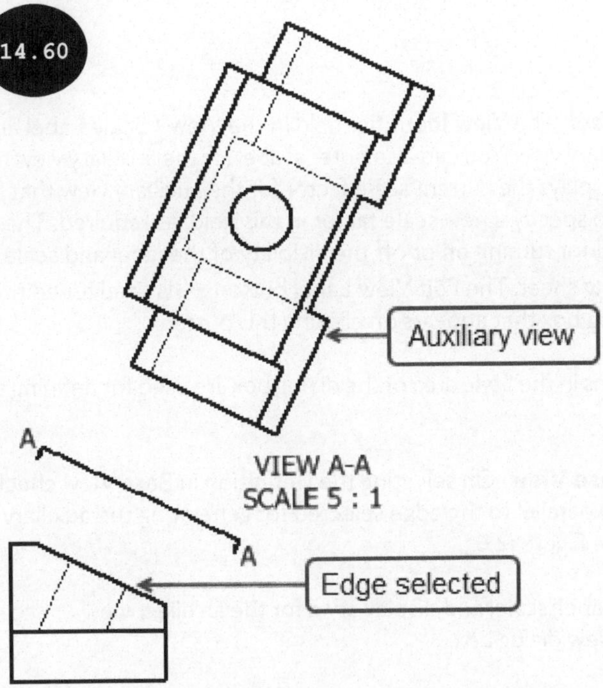

1. Click on the **Auxiliary** tool in the **Create** panel of the **Place Views** tab, see Figure 14.61. You are prompted to select an existing view for creating its auxiliary view.

14.61

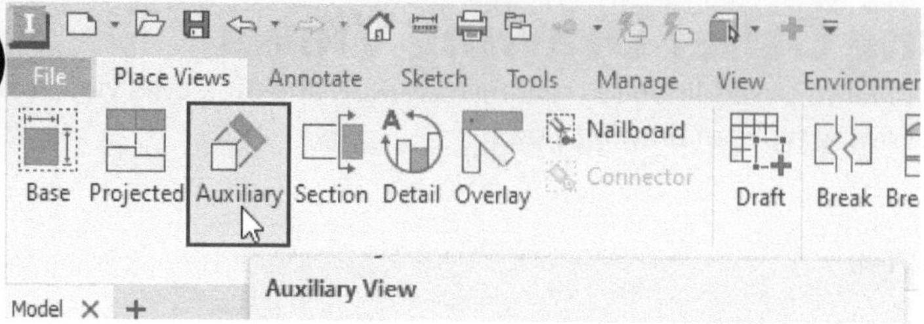

2. Select an existing drawing view in the drawing sheet. The **Auxiliary View** dialog box appears, see Figure 14.62. Also, you are prompted to select a linear edge of the selected view to define the view orientation of the auxiliary view to be created.

14.62

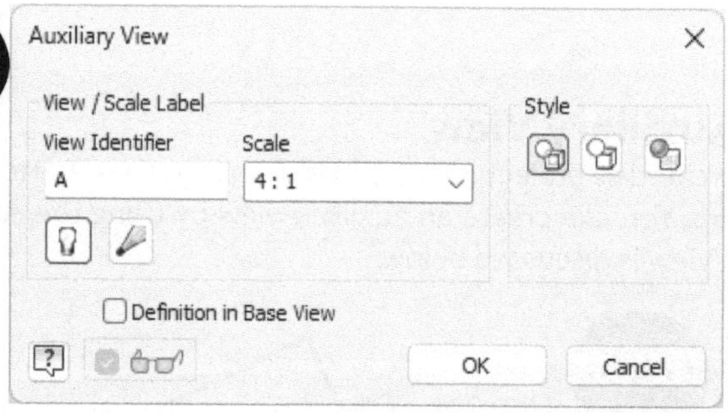

View / Scale Label: The **View Identifier** field in the **View / Scale Label** area displays the default label for the auxiliary view. You can also enter a label for the auxiliary view in this field, as required. The **Scale** field displays the current scale factor for the auxiliary view that inherits from its parent view. You can also specify a new scale factor in this field, as required. The **Toggle Label Visibility** button is used for turning on or off the visibility of the label and scale factor on the auxiliary view in the drawing sheet. The **Edit View Label** button is used for editing view label text in the **Format Text** dialog box that appears on clicking this button.

Style: The buttons in the **Style** area of the dialog box are used for defining the display style for the auxiliary view.

Definition in Base View: On selecting the **Definition in Base View** check box in the dialog box, the definition line parallel to the edge selected for generating the auxiliary view is created on the drawing sheet, see Figure 14.63.

3. Specify the view label, scale, and display style for the auxiliary view or accept the default settings in the **Auxiliary View** dialog box.

4. Select a linear edge of the selected view for defining the view orientation of the auxiliary view. The preview of an auxiliary view normal to the selected edge appears attached to the cursor.

5. Click to specify the placement point for the auxiliary view in the drawing sheet. The auxiliary view gets created onto the drawing sheet (see Figure 14.63) and the dialog box gets closed.

14.63

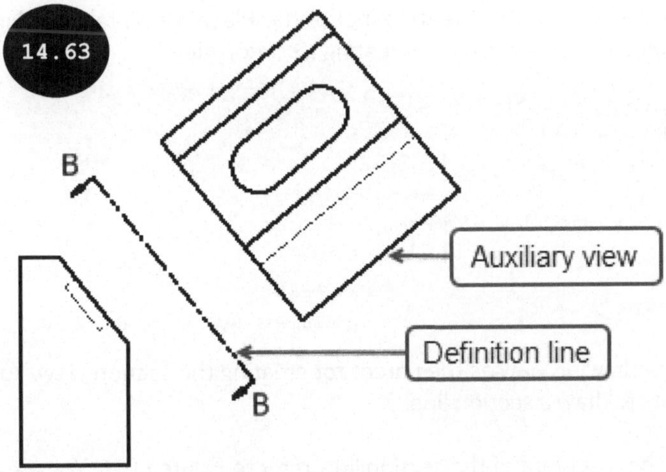

Tip: You can also realign an existing auxiliary view by selecting a new linear edge for defining its view orientation. For doing so, right-click on an existing auxiliary view and then click on the **Realign Auxiliary Views** option in the shortcut menu. Next, select a new linear edge of the parent view for defining the view orientation of the selected auxiliary view. The preview of an auxiliary view appears attached to the cursor. Next, click to specify the placement point for the auxiliary view on the drawing sheet.

Creating a Section View

A section view is created by cutting an object by using an imaginary cutting plane or a section line and then viewing the object from a direction that is normal to the cutting plane. Figure 14.64 shows a section view created by cutting an object using a cutting plane. A section view is used to illustrate internal features of the object clearly. It also reduces the number of hidden-detail lines, facilitates the dimensioning of internal features, shows cross-section, and so on. The method for creating a section view is discussed below:

14.64

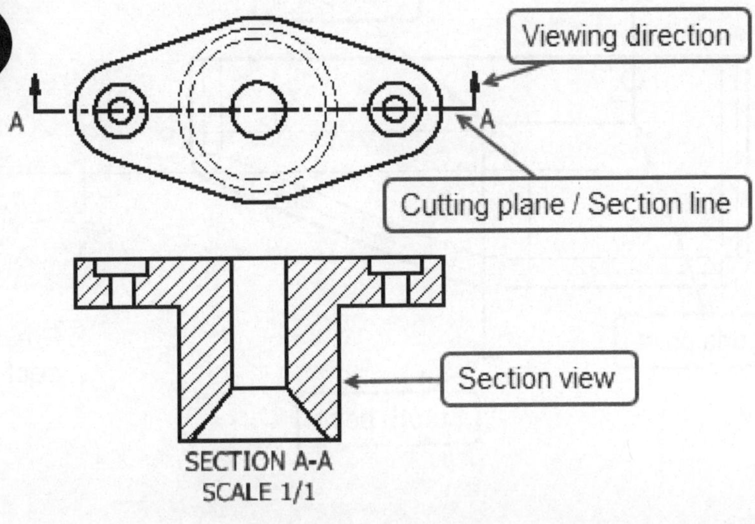

1. Click on the **Section** tool in the **Create** panel of the **Place Views** tab, see Figure 14.65. You are prompted to select an existing view for creating a section view.

14.65

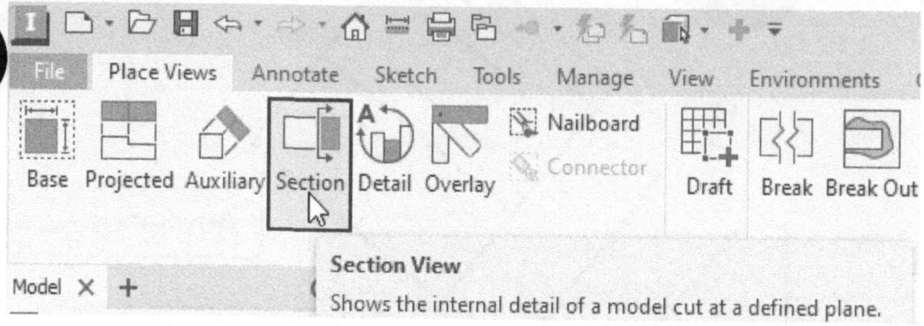

2. Select an existing drawing view as the parent for creating the section view. You are prompted to specify endpoints to draw a section line.

3. Click to specify the first point of the section line, refer to Figure 14.66. You are again prompted to specify endpoints to draw a section line.

4. Click in the drawing view to specify the second point of the section line, refer to Figure 14.66. You are again prompted to specify endpoints to draw a section line.

5. Similarly, you can specify multiple points for creating a section line, refer to Figure 14.66. In this figure, four points are defined for creating the section line.

6. After specifying all points for creating the section line, right-click on the drawing sheet and then click on the **Continue** tool in the Marking Menu that appears. The preview of a section view appears attached to the cursor, refer to Figure 14.66. Also, the **Section View** dialog box appears, see Figure 14.67. Some of the options in the **Section View** dialog box are the same as discussed earlier and the remaining options are discussed below:

14.66

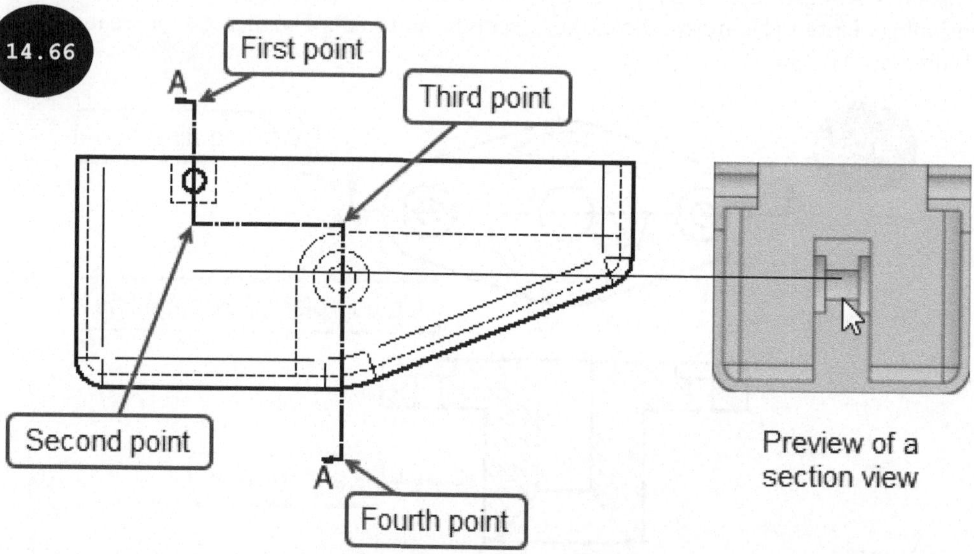

14.67

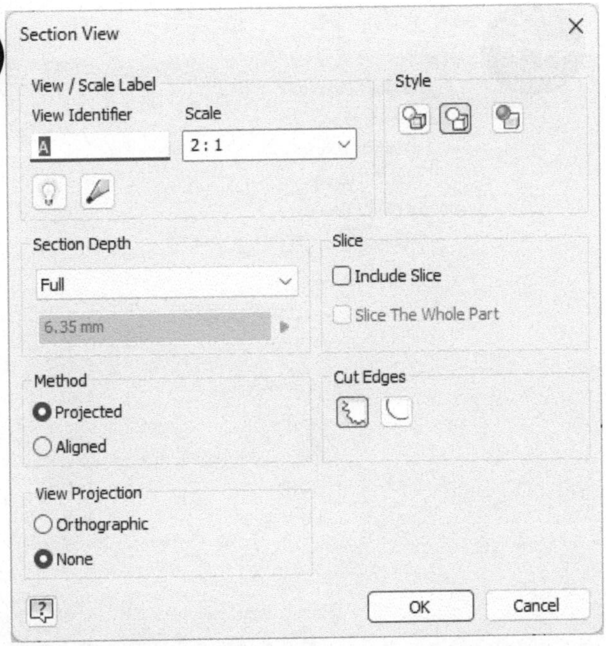

Section Depth: By default, the **Full** option is selected in the **Section Depth** drop-down list of the dialog box. As a result, the section view is created such that all geometries of the object beyond the section line are visible in the resultant section view. On selecting the **Distance** option, the **Distance** field gets enabled in the **Section Depth** area. In this field, you can specify a distance of viewing in the object beyond the section line.

Slice: On selecting the **Include Slice** check box in the **Slice** area of the dialog box, the sliced section view or the section view gets created depending upon the default section participation setting that is configured for the component in the **Browser**. On selecting the **Slice The Whole Part** check box, the sliced section view gets created for the whole part. Note that instead of the **Slice The Whole Part** check box, the **Slice All Parts** check box appears in the dialog box while sectioning an assembly and is used for creating sliced section view for all parts of the assembly that are passing through the defined section line.

Tip: To configure the default section participation setting for a component, expand its view node in the **Browser** and then right-click on the component. Next, move the cursor over the **Section Participation** option in the shortcut menu that appears, see Figure 14.68. A cascading menu appears. In this cascading menu, you can select the required option (**Section**, **Slice**, or **None**) as the default section participation setting for the selected component.

14.68

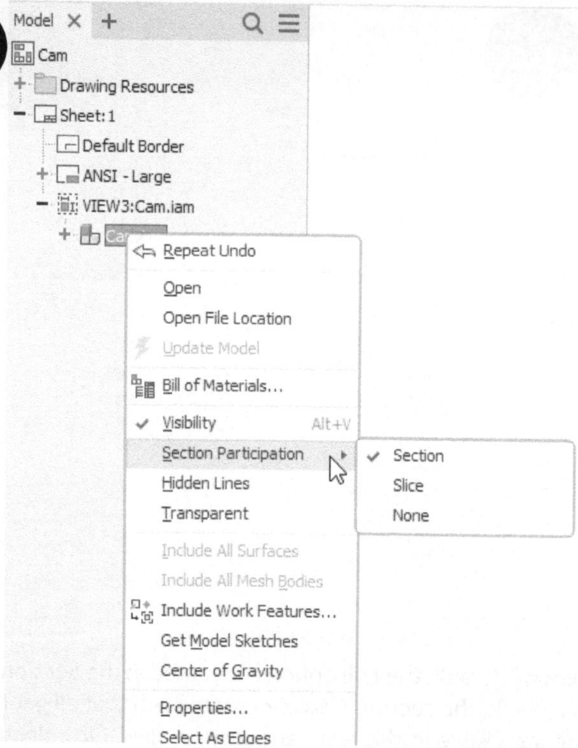

Cut Edges: The **Set Cut Edges as Jagged** button is used for displaying the cutting edge of the object as jagged, see Figure 14.69. The **Set Cut Edges as Smooth** button is used for displaying the cutting edge of the object as smooth, see Figure 14.70.

14.69

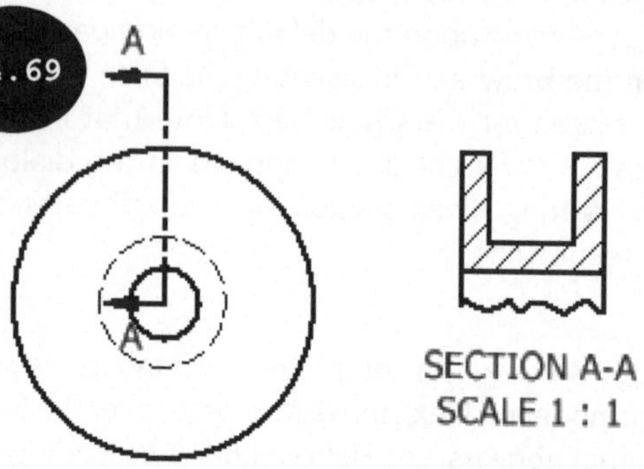

14.70

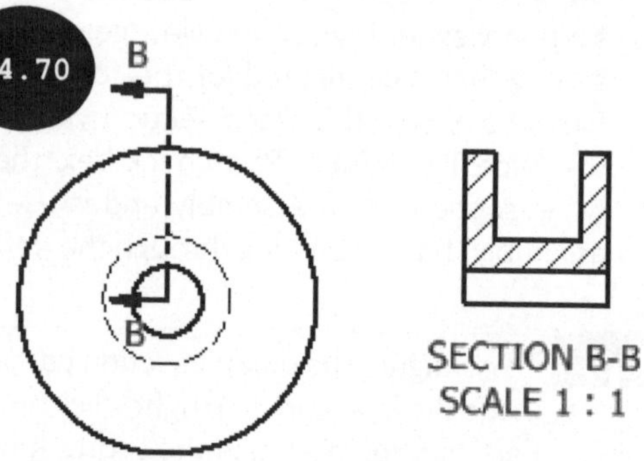

Method: On selecting the **Projected** radio button in the **Method** area, the resultant section view is created by projecting edges of the object normal to one of the line segments of the section line, see Figure 14.71. On selecting the **Aligned** radio button, an aligned section view is created by cutting an object using the section line and then straightening the cross-section by revolving it around the center point of the section line, refer to Figure 14.72. Note that the **Aligned** radio button is enabled only when the section line is comprised of two or more segments.

14.71

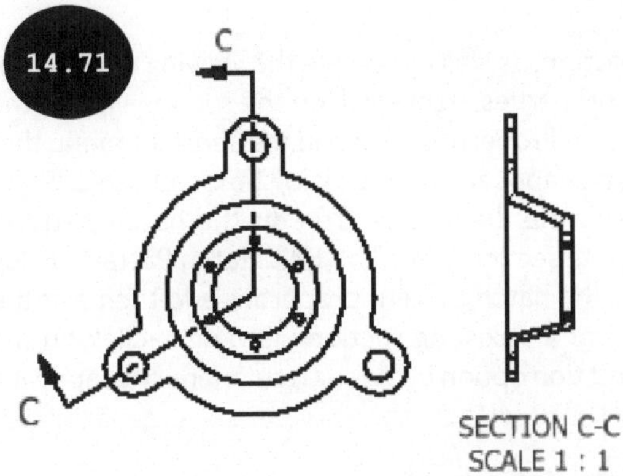

14.72

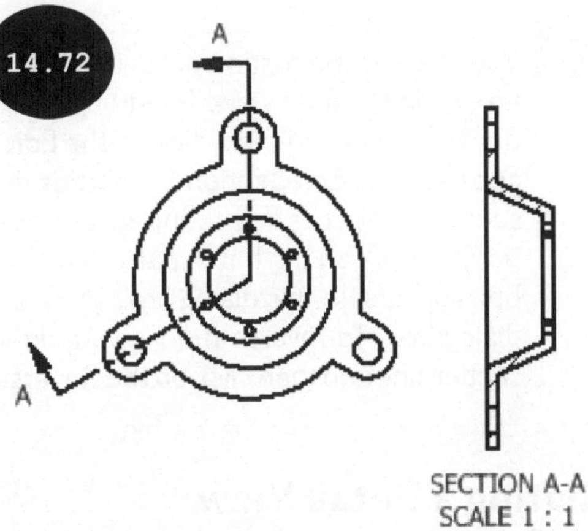

View Projection: By default, the **Orthographic** radio button is selected in the **View Projection** area of the dialog box. As a result, the alignment of the section view is restricted in a direction normal to the section line. On selecting the **None** radio button, you can override the view alignment and the section view can be placed anywhere in the drawing area.

7. Specify the view label, scale, display style, and other properties of the section view in the **Section View** dialog box.

8. After defining all the properties of the section view, click on the **OK** button in the dialog box. The section view gets created, see Figure 14.73.

14.73

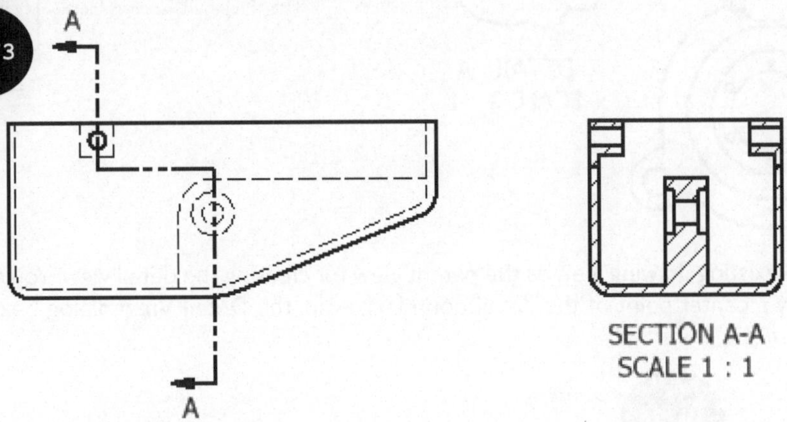

Note: After creating a section view of an assembly, you can exclude some of the components like fasteners from the section cut. For doing so, after creating the section view, expand its node in the **Browser** and then expand the assembly node. Next, right-click on the component to be excluded and then select **Section Participation > None** option in the shortcut menu that appears.

Tip: You can edit the section properties, hatch pattern, as well as reverse the viewing direction of an existing section view. To edit the section properties, right-click on the section view in the drawing sheet and then click on the **Edit Section Properties** option in the shortcut menu that appears. The **Edit Section Properties** dialog box appears. In this dialog box, you can edit the section properties as required and then exit the dialog box. To edit the hatch pattern, double-click on the hatch pattern of an existing section view. The **Edit Hatch Pattern** dialog box appears. In this dialog box, you can edit the hatch pattern properties and then exit the dialog box. To reverse the viewing direction of an existing section view, right-click on the section line and then click on the **Reverse Direction** option in the shortcut menu that appears.

Creating a Detail View

A detail view is used for showing a portion of an existing drawing view in an enlarged scale, see Figure 14.74. You can define the portion of an existing drawing view to be enlarged by creating a circular or rectangular shaped fence around it. You can create a detailed view of a portion of an existing view by using the **Detail** tool. The method for creating a detailed view is discussed below:

1. Click on the **Detail** tool in the **Create** panel of the **Place Views** tab, see Figure 14.75. You are prompted to select a view.

14.74

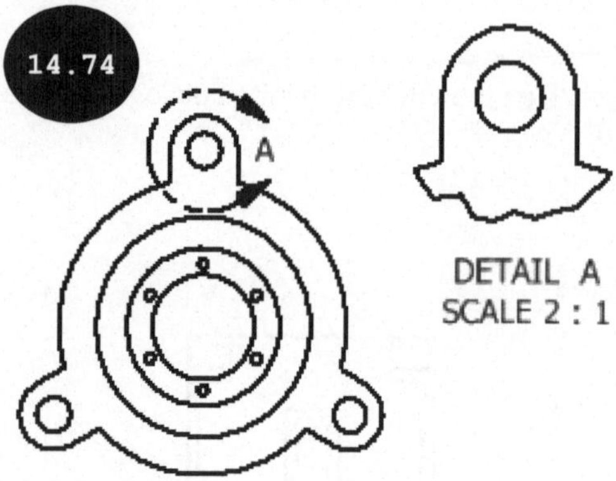

14.75

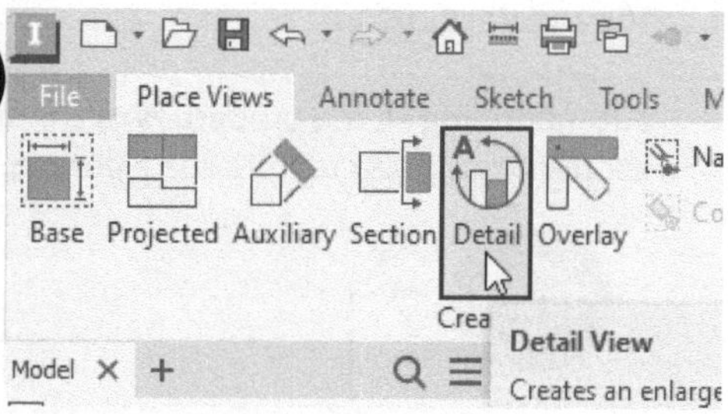

2. Select an existing drawing view as the parent view for creating the detail view. You are prompted to specify a center point of the detail boundary. Also, the **Detail View** dialog box appears, see Figure 14.76.

14.76

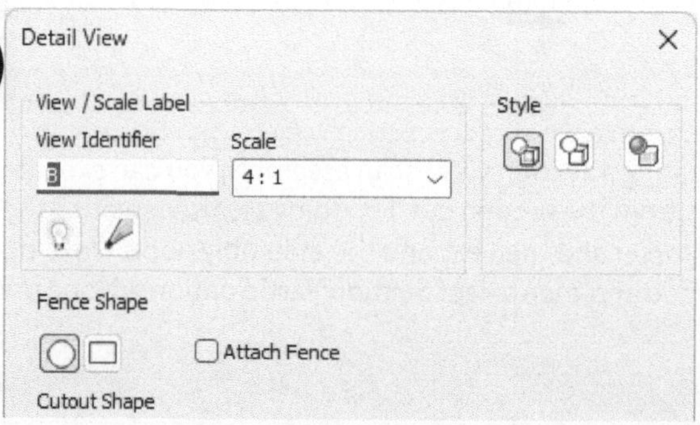

Some of the options in the **Detail View** dialog box are same as discussed earlier and the remaining options are discussed below:

Fence Shape: By default, the **Circular** button is activated in the **Fence Shape** area of the dialog box. As a result, you can draw a circle by specifying its center point and a point on the circumference for defining a portion of the selected view to be enlarged. On selecting the **Rectangular** button, you can draw a rectangle by specifying its center point and a corner point for defining a portion of the selected view to be enlarged.

Cutout Shape: The **Set Cut Edges as Jagged** button in the **Cutout Shape** area is used for displaying the cutting edges as jagged in the resultant detail view, see Figure 14.77.

14.77

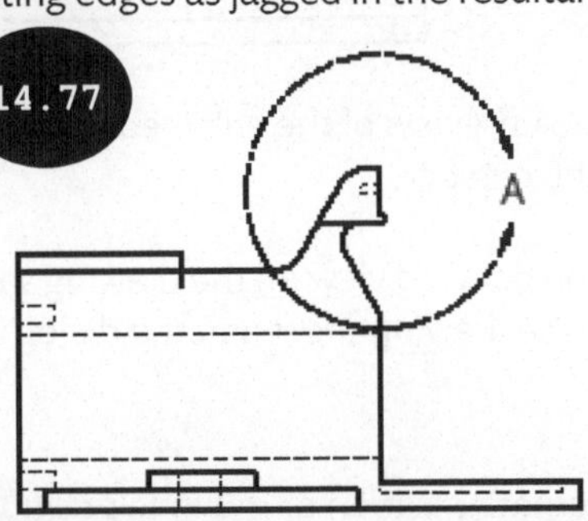

The **Set Cut Edges as Smooth** button in the **Cutout Shape** area is used for displaying the cutting edges as smooth in the resultant detail view, see Figure 14.78.

14.78

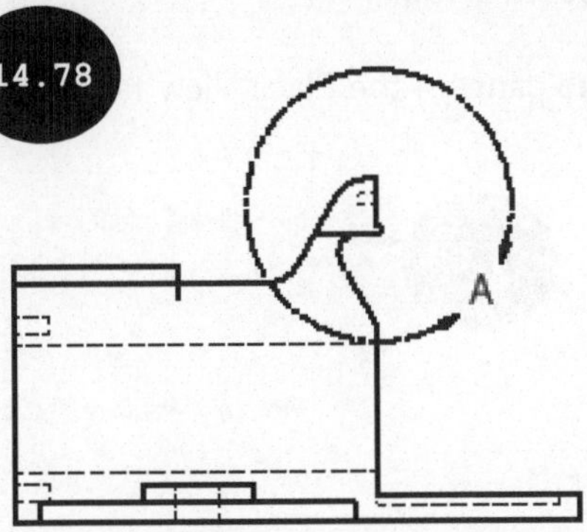

The **Display Full Detail Boundary** check box is enabled in the dialog box only when the **Set Cut Edges as Smooth** button is selected in the **Cutout Shape** area. On selecting this check box, the resultant detail view is created with full boundary around it. The **Display Connection Line** check box is enabled when the **Display Full Detail Boundary** check box is selected and is used for adding a connection line between the detail view and the detail boundary in the parent view.

3. Specify the view label, scale, display style, and other properties of the detail view in the **Detail View** dialog box.

4. Click to specify the center point of the fence (circular or rectangular) depending upon the button activated in the **Fence Shape** area of the dialog box, refer to Figures 14.79 and 14.80. You are prompted to define the endpoint of the fence by clicking the left mouse button.

14.79

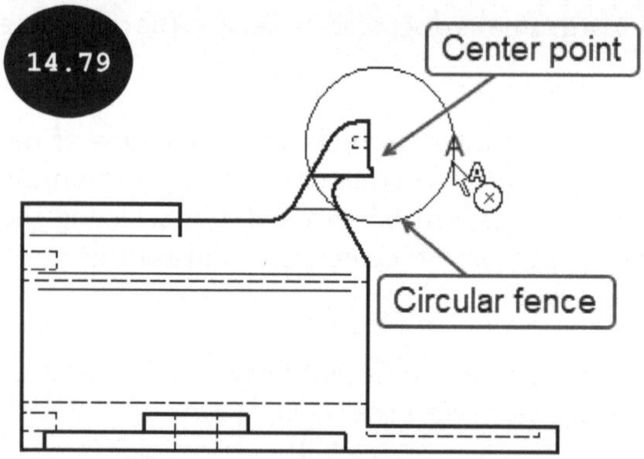

14.80

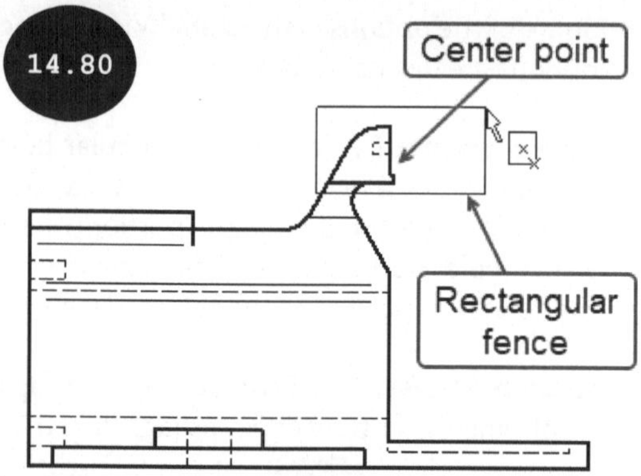

5. Click to define the endpoint of the fence. A preview of the enlarged view of the portion enclosed within the defined fence is attached to the cursor.

6. Click to define the placement point for the detailed view on the drawing sheet. The detailed view gets created at the specified location on the drawing sheet and the dialog box gets closed.

Creating an Overlay View

An overlay view is created by showing an alternate position or multiple positions of an assembly in a drawing view by using the **Overlay** tool, see Figure 14.81. Note that to create an overlay view, you need to first create multiple positional representations for the assembly in the Assembly environment. The method for creating an overlay view is discussed below:

1. Click on the **Overlay** tool in the **Create** panel of the **Place View** tab, see Figure 14.82. You are prompted to select a view.

14.81

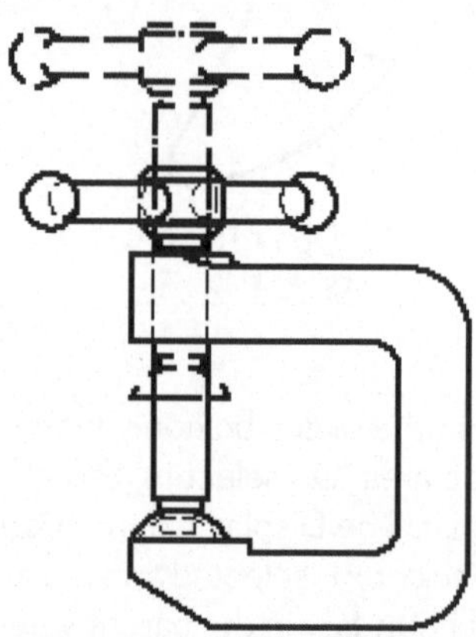

14.82

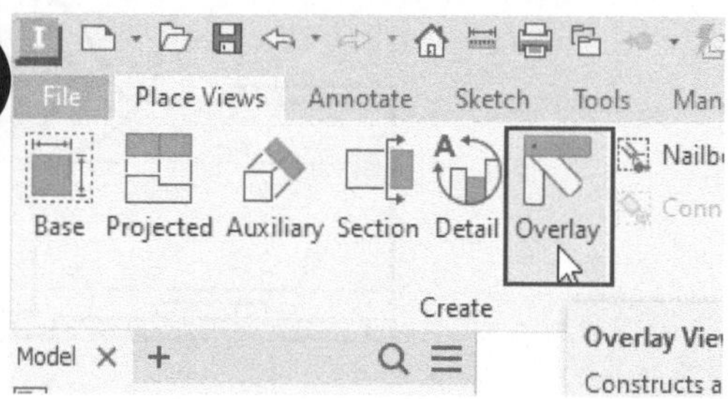

2. Select an existing drawing view to show an alternate position of the assembly. The **Overlay View** dialog box appears, see Figure 14.83. Some of the options in this dialog box are the same as discussed earlier and the remaining options are discussed below:

14.83

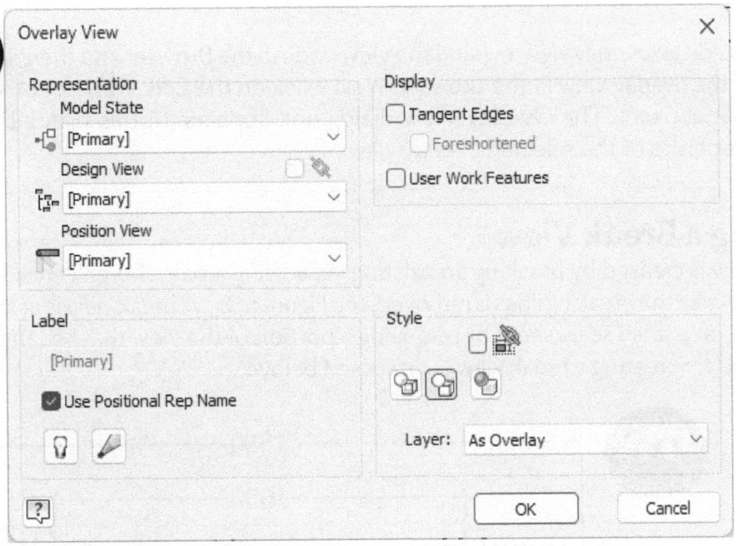

Position View: The **Position View** drop-down list in the **Representation** area of the dialog box displays a list of all the positional representations of the assembly that are created in the Assembly environment. You can select the required positional representation of the assembly to be shown in the selected drawing view as an overlay or an alternate position of the assembly. The method for creating multiple positional representations for an assembly has been discussed earlier in this chapter.

Style: The options in the **Style** area of the dialog box are used for specifying the display style (**Hidden Line**, **Hidden Line Removed**, or **Shaded**) for the overlay view (alternate position of the components), as discussed earlier. On selecting the **Style from Base** check box in this area, the overlay view follows the same line style as the parent view. The options in the **Layer** drop-down list in the **Style** area of the dialog box are used for defining the line style for the overlay view. By default, the **As Overlay** option is selected in this drop-down list. As a result, the line style for the overlay view is specified as dashed lines. On selecting the **As Part** option, the line style for the overlay view is specified as the standard line style of the part.

3. Select the required positional representation in the **Position View** drop-down list of the **Overlay View** dialog box.

4. Specify the view label, display style, and other properties in the **Overlay View** dialog box.

5. Click on the **OK** button in the dialog box. The overlay view is created and the alternative position of the assembly components appears in dashed lines, see Figure 14.84.

14.84

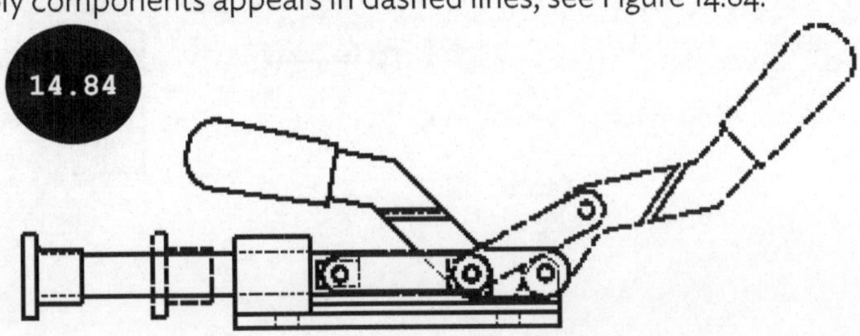

Tip: To edit an overlay view, expand the view node in the **Browser** and then right-click on the name of the overlay view in the **Browser**. Next, click on the **Edit View** option in the shortcut menu that appears. The **Overlay View** dialog box appears. In this dialog box, you can edit the properties of the selected overlay view.

Creating a Break View

A break view is created by breaking an existing view using a pair of break lines such that the portion existing between the breaking lines is removed, see Figure 14.85. A break view is used for displaying a large scaled view on a small scale sheet by removing a portion of the view that has the same cross-section. The method for creating a break view is discussed below:

14.85

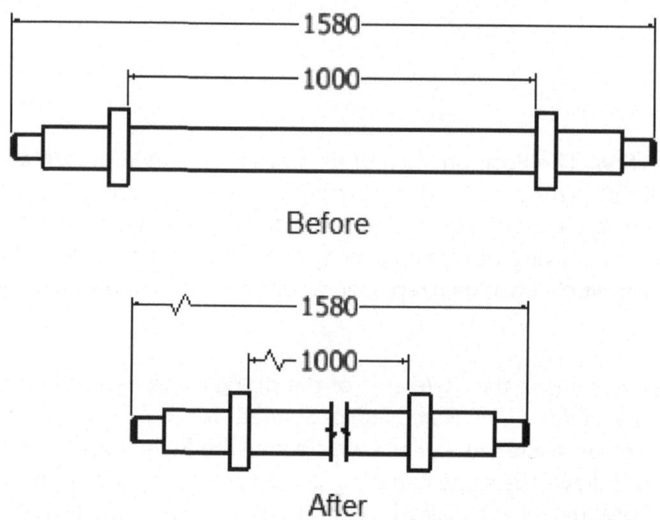

Note: The dimensions applied to a break view represents its actual dimensions, refer to Figure 14.85. It is evident from this figure that even on breaking the view, the dimension value associated with it remains the same. You will learn more about applying dimensions later in this chapter.

1. Click on the **Break** tool in the **Modify** panel of the **Place Views** tab, see Figure 14.86. You are prompted to select a view.

14.86

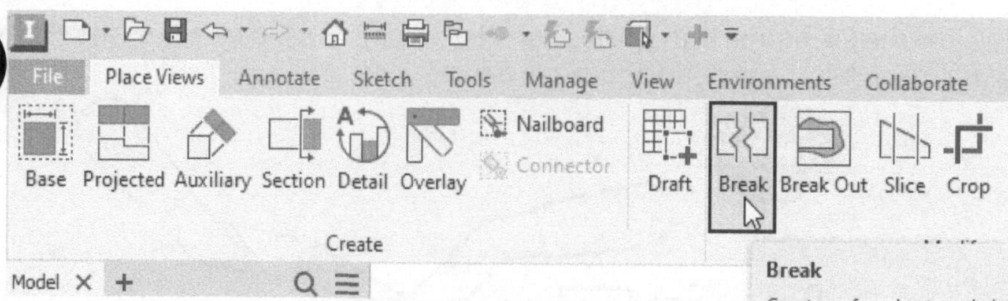

2. Select an existing drawing view for creating a break view. The **Break** dialog box appears.

   Style: In the **Style** area of the dialog box, you can choose between the rectangular style and the structural style to be used for the break lines by activating the respective button. The preview of the selected style (rectangular or structural) appears in the **Preview** field of the **Display** area of the dialog box.

   Orientation: The **Horizontal Orientation** button in the **Orientation** area is used for setting the break view orientation to horizontal, see Figure 14.87. The **Vertical Orientation** button is used for setting the break view orientation to vertical, see Figure 14.88. Note that depending upon the orientation of the selected view, the respective button in this area gets selected, automatically.

14.87

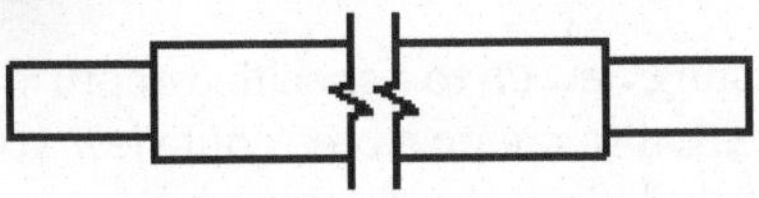

14.88

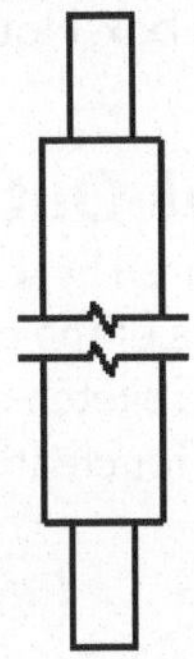

   Slider Bar: The Slider bar below the **Preview** field in the **Display** area is used for changing the size (min to max) of the break symbol in the break view.

   Gap: The **Gap** field is used for specifying the gap between the break lines.

   Symbols: The **Symbols** field is used for specifying the number of break symbols in the break lines of the break view, see Figure 14.89. This figure displays a break view with two break symbols. You can specify up to three break symbols in the break lines. Note that this field is enabled when the **Structural style** button is activated in the **Style** area of the dialog box.

14.89

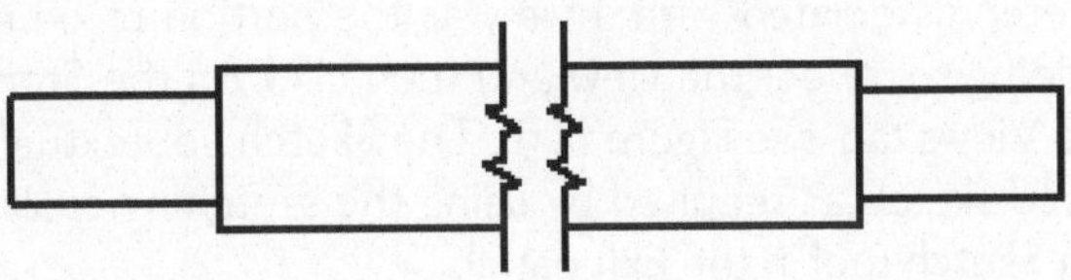

3. Specify the required break style (rectangular or structural) by selecting the respective button in the **Style** area of the dialog box.

4. Specify the break view orientation (horizontal or vertical), the gap between the break lines, and other properties in the **Break** dialog box.

Now, you need to specify the placement points for the break lines on the selected view.

5. Specify the placement point for the first break line by clicking the left mouse button on the selected view. The first break line gets specified on the view and you are prompted to specify the placement point for the second break line that appears attached to the cursor.

6. Specify the placement point for the second break line in the view. The break view gets created such that the portion inside the break lines of the view gets removed.

Tip: To edit the break view properties, right-click on the break line of the break view and then click on the **Edit Break** option in the shortcut menu that appears. The **Break** dialog box appears. By using this dialog box, you can edit the break view properties. After editing the properties, exit the dialog box. Note that you cannot change the break view orientation.

Creating a Break Out View

A break out view is created by removing the portion of an existing view up to a specified depth in order to view the inner details of the object, see Figure 14.90. Note that to create a break out view, you first need to create a closed sketch associated with the view which defines the portion of the view to be removed. The method for creating a break out view is discussed below:

14.90

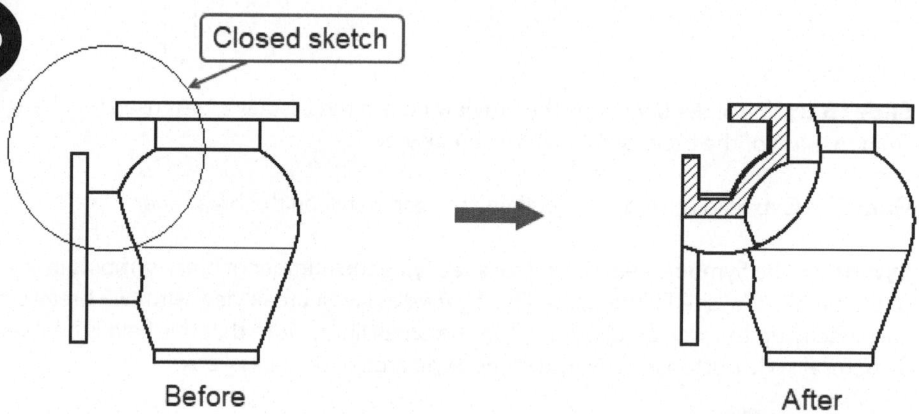

1. Draw a closed sketch associated with a view as the portion to be removed by using the **Start Sketch** tool. For doing so, select the view and then click on the **Start Sketch** tool in the **Sketch** panel of the **Place Views** tab, see Figure 14.91. The **Sketch** contextual tab appears in the **Ribbon**. Next, draw a closed sketch as required by using the sketching tools. After creating the sketch, click on the **Finish Sketch** tool in the **Exit** panel.

14.91

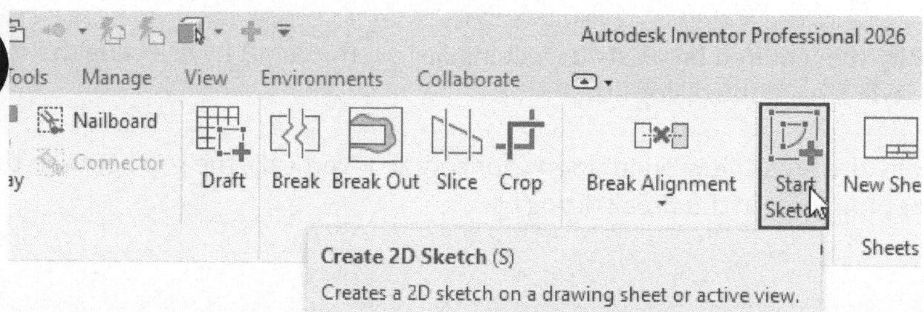

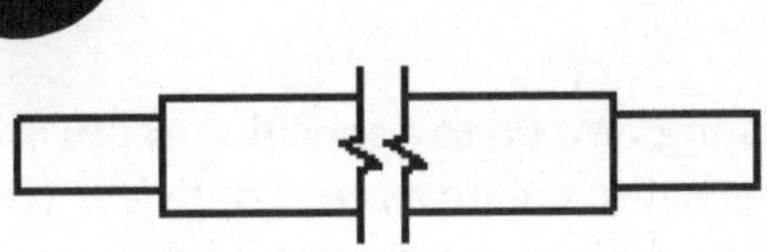

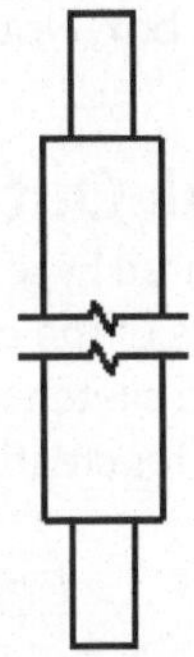

Now, you can create a break out view.

2. Click on the **Break Out** tool in the **Modify** panel of the **Place Views** tab. You are prompted to select a view.

3. Select the view having an associated closed sketch for creating the break out view. The **Break Out** dialog box appears, see Figure 14.92. Note that if you select a view that does not have any associated sketch, the Sketching environment will be invoked to create a closed sketch. After creating the sketch, exit the Sketching environment to return to the display of the **Break Out** dialog box.

14.92

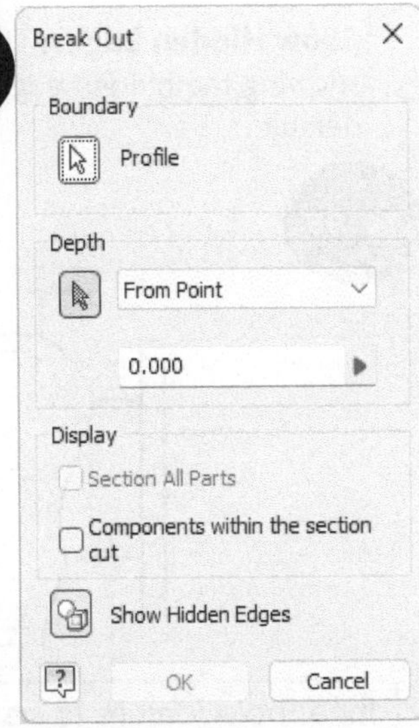

Profile: The **Profile** button in the **Boundary** area is used for selecting a closed sketch for creating the break out view. Note that if only one closed sketch is associated with the selected view then it will be selected automatically.

Depth: In the drop-down list of the **Depth** area, you can select a method for defining the depth of the break out view. By default, the **From Point** option is selected in the drop-down list. As a result, you can select a start point either in the selected view or in its child views and then specify the depth value in the **From Point** field up to which the material is to be removed from the specified start point, refer to Figures 14.93 and 14.94.

14.93

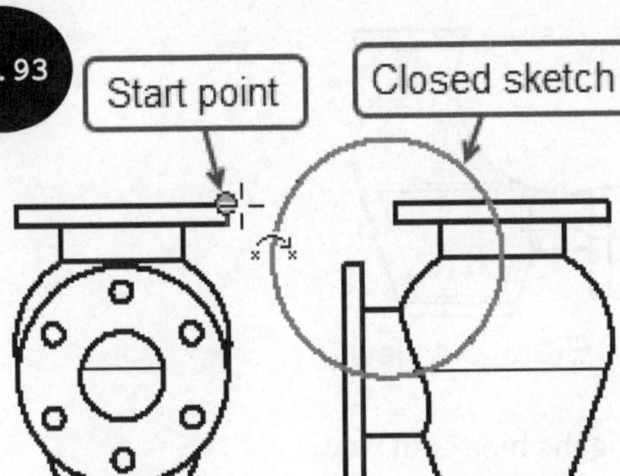

14.94

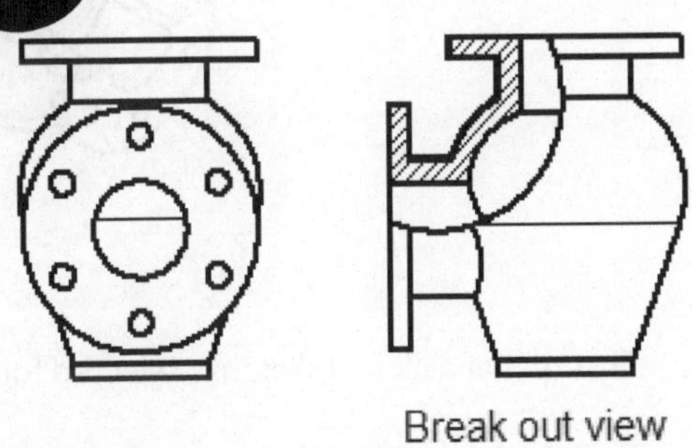

The **To Sketch** option is used for specifying the depth of the break out view by selecting an open sketch. Note that the open sketch to be used for defining the depth should be associated with a different view of the drawing. The **To Hole** option is used for specifying the depth of the break out view by selecting a hole feature of the view up to which the material is to be removed, see Figures 14.95 and 14.96. The **Through Part** option is used for specifying the depth of the break out view through a selected part, see Figure 14.97. On selecting this option, you need to select a part in the selected view by clicking the left mouse button.

Show Hidden Edges: The **Show Hidden Edges** button in the **Display** area is used for temporarily showing the hidden edges of the selected view in which the hidden edges are not visible, by default.

14.95

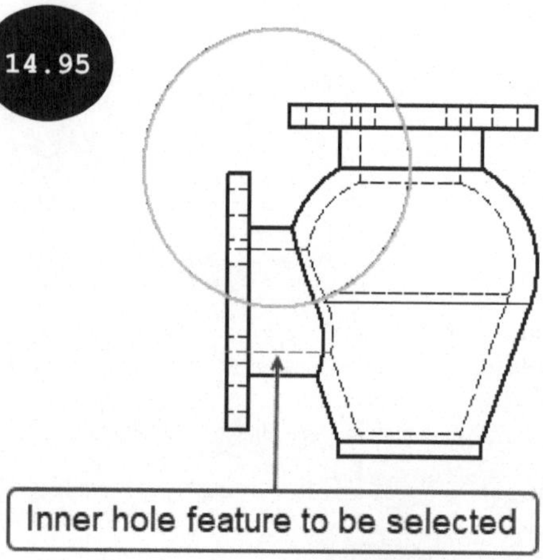

14.96

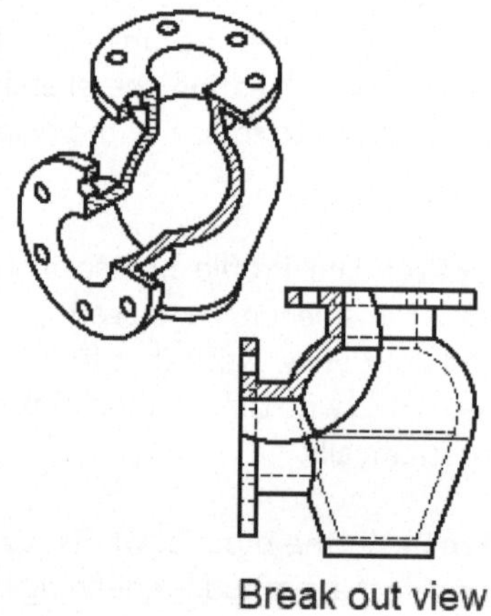

14.97

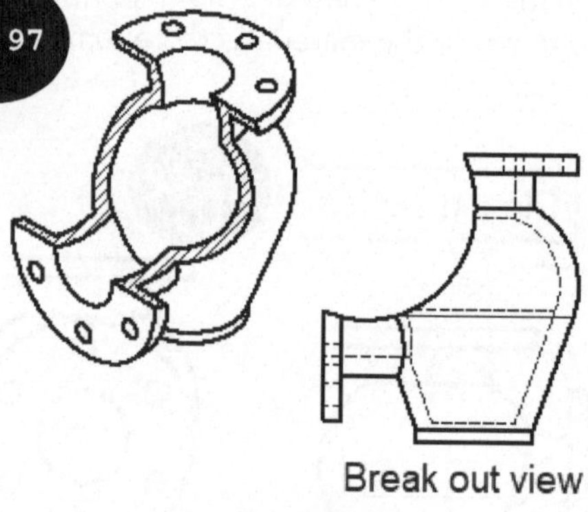

4. Ensure that a closed sketch is selected for creating the break out view.

5. Specify the depth of the break out view by using the required option of the drop-down list in the **Depth** area, as discussed above.

6. After specifying the depth of the break out view, click on the **OK** button in the **Break Out** dialog box. The break out view gets created.

Tip: To edit a break out view, expand the view node in the **Browser** and then right-click on the break out view to be edited in the **Browser**. Next, click on the **Edit Break Out** option in the shortcut menu that appears. The **Break Out** dialog box appears. By using this dialog box, you can edit the break out view properties and then close the dialog box.

Creating a Slice View

A slice view is used for showing a cross-sectional slice (zero-depth section) of an object at a particular location on an existing drawing view, see Figure 14.98. Note that to show a cross-sectional slice on a drawing view, you first need to create an open sketch associated with a source view which defines the cut profile location, see Figure 14.98. The method for creating a slice view is discussed below:

14.98

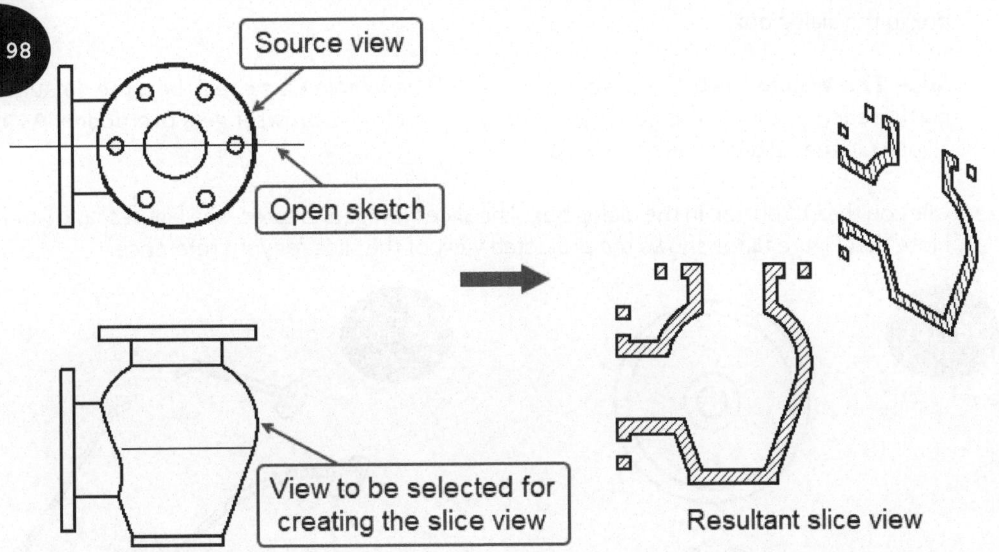

1. Draw an open sketch associated with a source view by using the **Start Sketch** tool of the **Sketch** panel, see Figure 14.99. In this figure, two line segments are created as an open sketch.

14.99

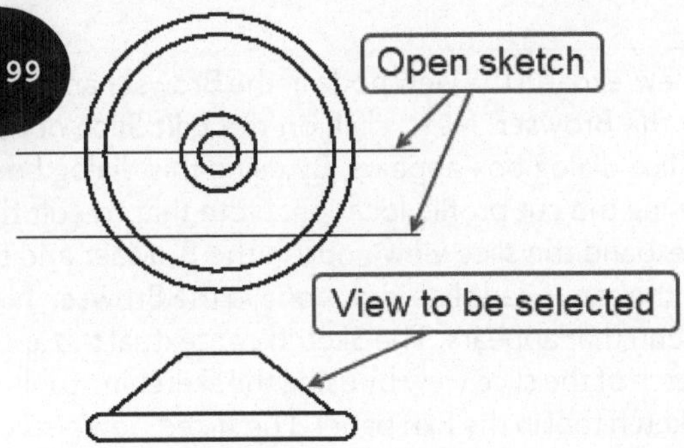

2. Click on the **Slice** tool in the **Modify** panel and then select a drawing view for creating the slice view, see Figure 14.99. The **Slice** dialog box appears, see Figure 14.100. Also, you are prompted to select an open sketch.

14.100

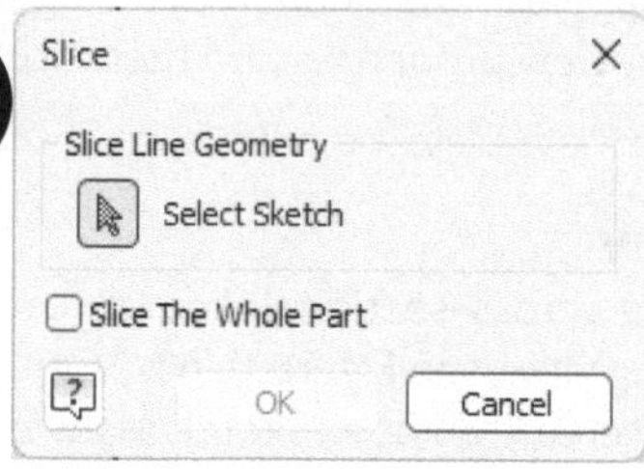

3. Select an open sketch created on a source view and then select the **Slice The Whole Part** check box in the dialog box.

   Slice The Whole Part: On selecting the **Slice The Whole Part** check box, the default section participation setting that is configured for each part in the **Browser** gets overridden. As a result, all parts in the selected view get sliced.

4. Click on the **OK** button in the dialog box. The slice view gets created, see Figures 14.101 and 14.102. Note that Figure 14.102 shows the projected view of the slice for your reference.

14.101

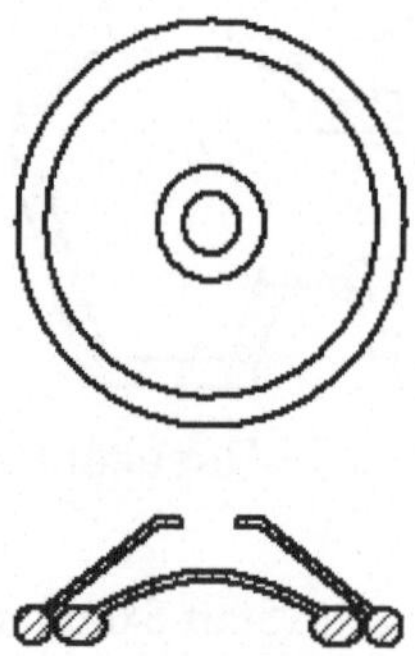

14.102

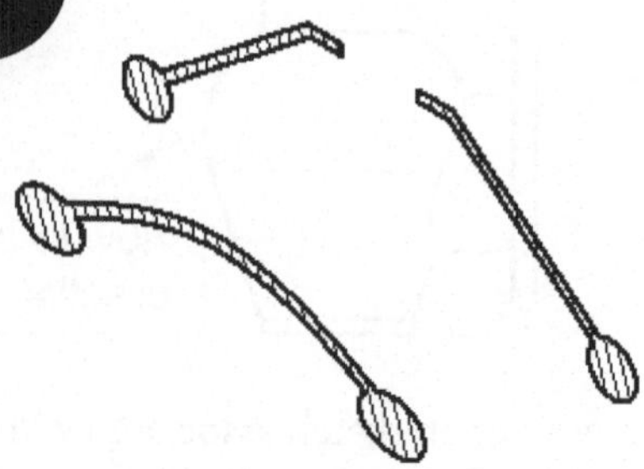

Tip: To edit a slice view, expand the view node in the **Browser** and then right-click on the slice view to be edited in the **Browser**. Next, click on the **Edit Slice** option in the shortcut menu that appears. The **Slice** dialog box appears. By using this dialog box, you can select a new open sketch for defining the cut profile location. Note that to edit the existing selected sketch of the slice view, expand the slice view node in the **Browser** and then right-click on the sketch that appears in the expanded slice view node in the **Browser**. Next, click on the **Edit** option in the shortcut menu that appears. The **Sketch** contextual tab appears in the **Ribbon**. Now, you can edit the sketch of the slice view by using the sketching tools. After editing the sketch, click on the **Finish Sketch** tool in the **Exit** panel. The sliced view gets updated on the drawing sheet.

Creating a Crop View

A crop view is created by cropping an existing view using a closed sketch in such a way that only the portion that is lying inside the closed sketch is retained in the view, see Figure 14.103. You can create a crop view by using the **Crop** tool. Note that you can create an irregular shaped closed sketch associated with a view before invoking the **Crop** tool or a rectangular shaped sketch after invoking the **Crop** tool. The method for creating a crop view is discussed below:

14.103

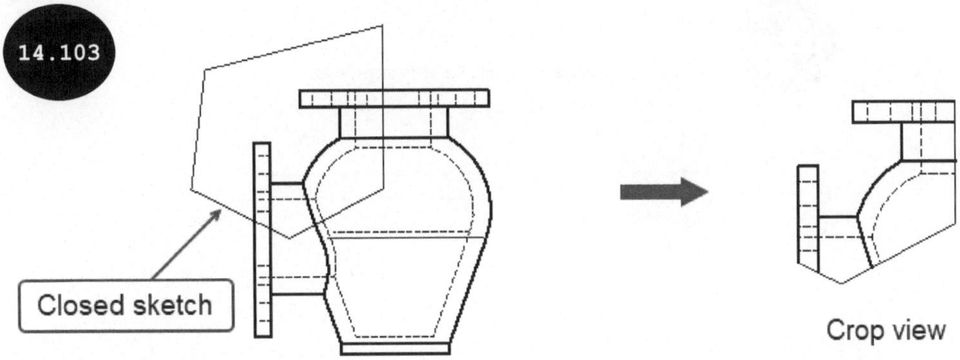

1. Click on the **Crop** tool in the **Modify** panel of the **Place Views** tab. You are prompted to select a view or a closed sketch associated with the view.
2. Select an existing view. You are prompted to specify the first corner of a rectangle. Note that instead of selecting an existing view, if you select a closed associated sketch of the view, then the crop view gets created by retaining only the portion that lies inside the sketch.
3. Create a rectangle by specifying its two opposite corners on the selected view. The crop view is created by retaining only the portion that lies inside the drawn rectangle.

Tip: You can edit the sketch of an already created crop view. For doing so, expand the view node in the **Browser** and then expand the crop view node. The sketch used for creating the crop view appears in the expanded crop view node. Next, right-click on the sketch in the expanded crop view node and then click on the **Edit** option in the shortcut menu that appears. The **Sketch** contextual tab appears in the **Ribbon**. Now, you can edit the sketch of the crop view by using the sketching tools. After editing the sketch, click on the **Finish Sketch** tool in the **Exit** panel. The crop view gets updated.

Deleting a Drawing View

You can delete unwanted drawing views from the drawing sheet. For doing so, select a drawing view to be deleted in the drawing sheet or in the **Browser** and then press the DELETE key. The **Autodesk Inventor Professional 2026** dialog box appears which confirms whether you want to delete the selected view. Click on the **OK** button. The selected view gets deleted from the drawing sheet. Note that if the selected view has its dependent or child views, then the **Delete View** dialog box appears on pressing the DELETE key. This dialog box confirms whether you want to delete the selected view and its dependents. Click on the double arrows >> at the lower right corner of the **Delete View** dialog box to display a list of all the dependent views, if not expanded by default, see Figure 14.104. By default, the

Yes status is defined for each dependent view in the **Delete** column of the expanded dialog box. As a result, all the dependent views get deleted on deleting the selected view. Click on the **Yes** status of a dependent view in the **Delete** column, the **Yes** status gets replaced with **No** status. Note that the dependent view with **No** status will not be deleted on deleting the selected view (parent view). Next, click on the **OK** button in the **Delete View** dialog box. The selected view and its dependent views with **Yes** status get deleted from the drawing sheet.

14.104

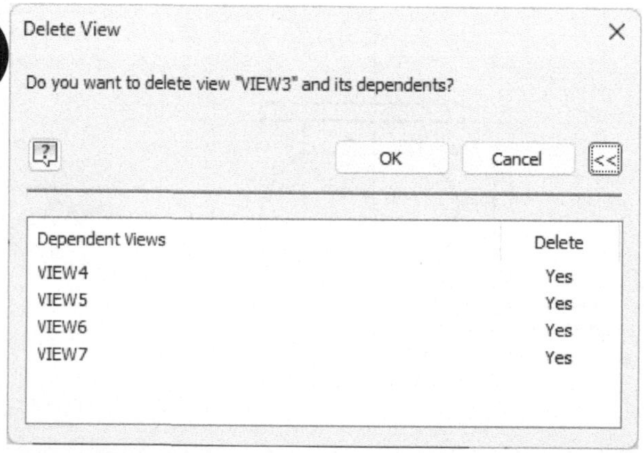

Applying Dimensions

After creating various drawing views of a part or an assembly, you need to apply dimensions to them. In Autodesk Inventor, you can apply two types of dimensions: drawing dimensions and model dimensions. Drawing dimensions are applied manually on the drawing views by using the dimension tools such as **Dimension**, **Baseline**, **Ordinate**, and **Chain**, whereas the model dimensions are generated automatically by retrieving the dimensions that are applied while creating the model. The methods for applying both types of dimensions are discussed next.

Applying Drawing Dimensions

You can apply drawing dimensions by using the dimension tools such as **Dimension**, **Baseline**, **Ordinate**, and **Chain** available in the **Dimension** panel of the **Annotate** tab, see Figure 14.105.

14.105

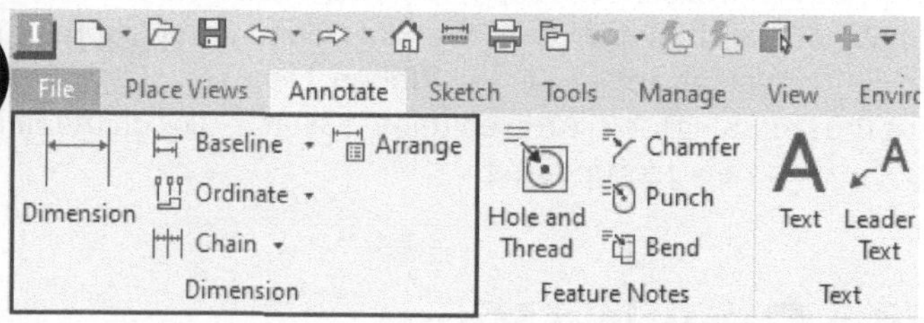

The method for applying dimensions to a drawing view by using the **Dimension** tool is the same as discussed in the Sketching environment while dimensioning sketch entities. For example, to apply dimension to a linear edge in a view, click on the **Dimension** tool in the **Dimension** panel of the **Annotate** tab and then select the edge. The dimension value of the selected edge is attached to the cursor. Next, place the dimension to the required location in the drawing sheet. The **Edit Dimension** dialog box appears. Click on the **OK** button in this dialog box to exit the dialog box. The dimension gets applied to the selected edge of the view.

Tip: In the **Edit Dimension** dialog box, you can edit some of the dimension properties such as precision, tolerance, and inspection. You can also override the dimension value by selecting the **Override Displayed Value** check box in the **Precision and Tolerance** tab of the dialog box and then entering an override value in the field that is enabled in front of this check box. After editing the dimension properties, exit the dialog box.

Note: To edit or modify the text font, height, and properties of the drawing dimensions, click on the **Manage** tab in the **Ribbon** and then click on the **Styles Editor** tool in the **Styles and Standards** panel. The **Style and Standard Editor** dialog box appears. In this dialog box, expand the **Text** node on the left panel of the dialog box and then select the **Note Text** option that appears in the expanded **Text** node. Next, edit the text font, text height, and other properties of the text by using the options that appear on the right panel of the dialog box. After editing the text properties of the dimensions, click on the **Save and Close** button in the dialog box. The dimension text properties get modified.

The methods for applying baseline dimensions, ordinate dimensions, and chain dimensions by using the respective tools are discussed next.

Applying Baseline Dimensions

Baseline dimensions are a series of parallel linear dimensions that are measured from a base line (origin), see Figure 14.106. The baseline dimensions are used for eliminating cumulative errors that can occur due to the rounded dimension values between consecutive adjacent dimensions or due to the upper and lower dimension limits. You can apply baseline dimensions by using the **Baseline** and **Baseline Set** tools in the **Dimension** panel of the **Annotate** tab, see Figure 14.107. The method for applying baseline dimensions is discussed below:

14.106

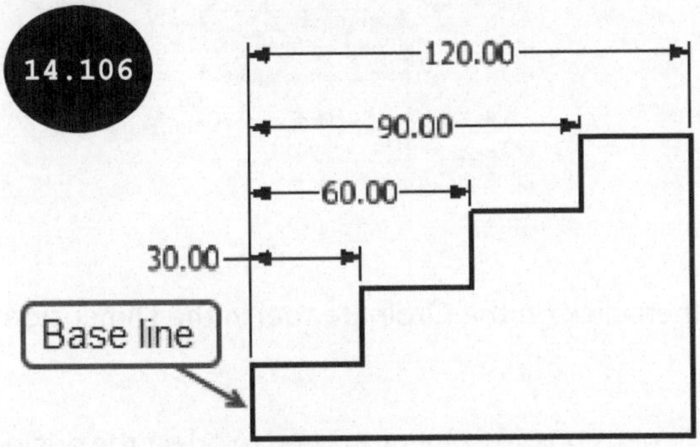

14.107

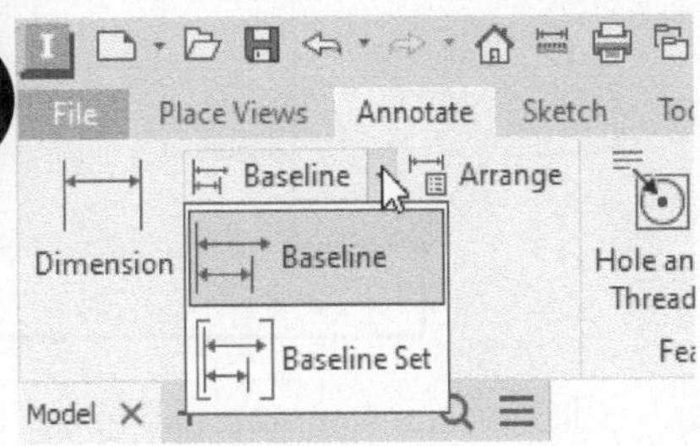

1. Click on the **Annotate** tab in the **Ribbon**. The tools of the **Annotate** tab appear.

2. Click on the **Baseline** tool in the **Dimension** panel of the **Annotate** tab. You are prompted to select drawing view edges for applying baseline dimensions.

3. Click to select a linear edge of a drawing view as the base entity (origin) for measuring the baseline dimensions, refer to Figure 14.106.

4. After selecting the base entity, you can select the remaining linear edges of the drawing view for applying the baseline dimensions. Next, right-click on the drawing sheet and then click on the **Continue** tool in the Marking Menu that appears. The preview of the baseline dimensions appears attached to the cursor.

5. Move the cursor to the required location on the drawing sheet and then click to define the placement point for the attached baseline dimensions on the drawing sheet. The baseline dimensions are applied measuring from the first selected entity (base entity). Next, right-click on the drawing sheet and then click on the **Done** (ESC) in the Marking Menu that appears to exit the tool.

Note: Similar to applying baseline dimensions by using the **Baseline** tool, you can apply baseline dimensions by using the **Baseline Set** tool. The baseline dimensions applied by using the **Baseline** tool act as individual dimensions, whereas the baseline dimensions applied by using the **Baseline Set** tool act as a group of dimensions.

Applying Ordinate Dimensions

Ordinate dimensions are used for dimensioning machine parts for maintaining accuracy. The ordinate dimensions measure the perpendicular distance from a specified origin, see Figure 14.108. You can apply ordinate dimensions by using the **Ordinate** and **Ordinate Set** tools in the **Dimension** panel of the **Annotate** tab, see Figure 14.109. The method for applying ordinate dimensions is discussed below:

14.108

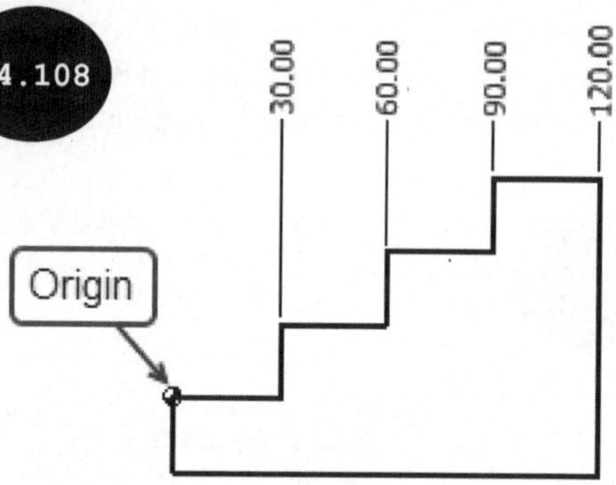

14.109

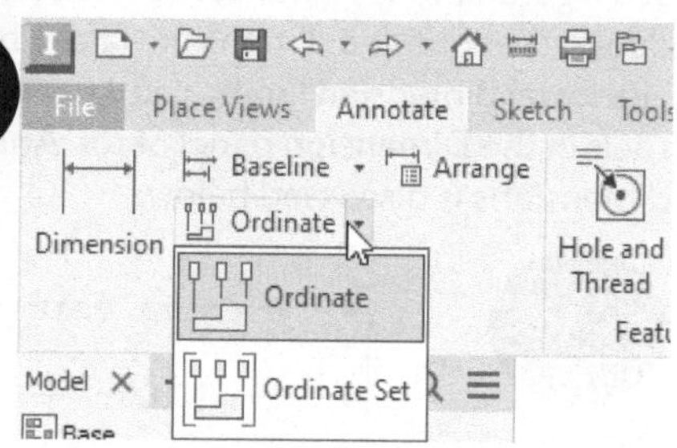

1. Click on the **Annotate** tab in the **Ribbon** and then click on the **Ordinate** tool in the **Dimension** panel. You are prompted to select a view.

2. Click on the drawing view to apply the ordinate dimensions. You are prompted to select the origin location.

3. Click to specify the origin location on the drawing view for measuring the ordinate dimensions, refer to Figure 14.108.

4. After specifying the origin location, select the linear edges of the drawing view for applying the ordinate dimensions. You can also draw a window around the edges of the drawing view to be selected for applying the ordinate dimensions.

5. Right-click on the drawing sheet and then click on the **Continue** tool in the Marking Menu that appears. The preview of the ordinate dimensions appears attached to the cursor.

6. Move the cursor to the required location on the drawing sheet and then click to define the placement point for the attached ordinate dimensions on the drawing sheet. The ordinate dimensions are applied measuring from the specified origin. Next, right-click on the drawing sheet and then click on the **OK** in the Marking Menu that appears to exit the tool.

Note: Similar to applying ordinate dimensions by using the **Ordinate** tool, you can apply ordinate dimensions by using the **Ordinate Set** tool. The ordinate dimensions applied by using the **Ordinate** tool act as individual dimensions, whereas the ordinate dimensions applied by using the **Ordinate Set** tool act as a group of dimensions.

Applying Chain Dimensions

Chain dimensions are a chain of linear dimensions that are placed end to end such that the second extension line of the first linear dimension is used as the first extension line for the next linear dimension, see Figure 14.110. You can apply chain dimensions by using the **Chain** and **Chain Set** tools in the **Dimension** panel of the **Annotate** tab, see Figure 14.111. The method for applying chain dimensions is discussed below:

14.110

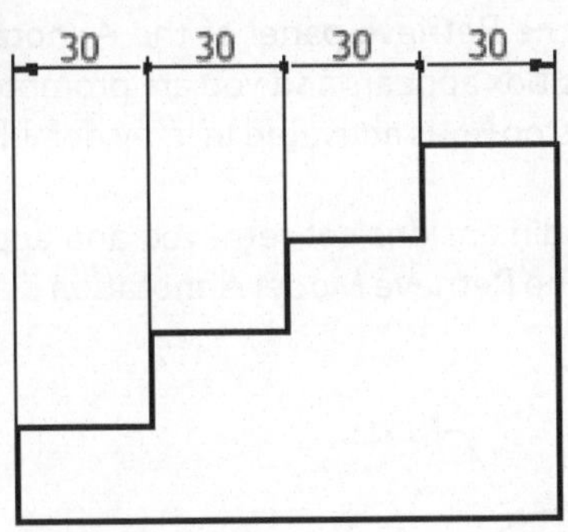

14.111

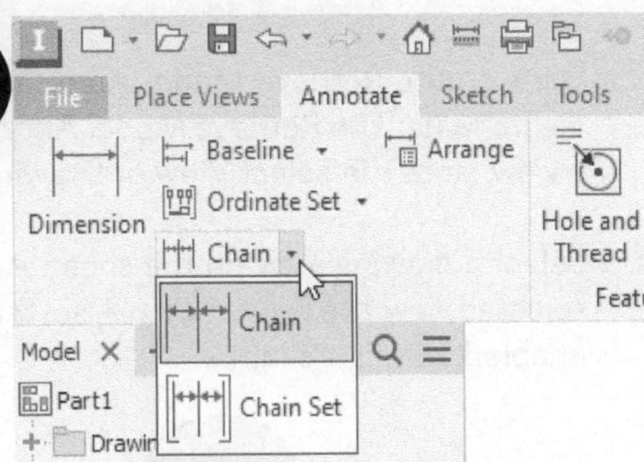

1. Click on the **Annotate** tab in the **Ribbon** and then click on the **Chain** tool in the **Dimension** panel.

2. Click to select linear edges of a drawing view one by one for applying the chain dimensions. You can also draw a window around the edges of the drawing view to be selected for applying the chain dimensions.

3. After selecting linear edges, right-click on the drawing sheet and then click on the **Continue** tool in the Marking Menu that appears. The preview of the chain dimensions appears attached to the cursor.

4. Move the cursor to the required location on the drawing sheet and then click to define the placement point for the attached chain dimensions on the drawing sheet. The chain dimensions get applied. Next, right-click on the drawing sheet and then click on the **Done** (ESC) in the Marking Menu that appears to exit the tool.

Note: Similar to applying chain dimensions by using the **Chain** tool, you can apply chain dimensions by using the **Chain Set** tool. The chain dimensions applied by using the **Chain** tool act as individual dimensions, whereas the chain dimensions applied by using the **Chain Set** tool act as a group of dimensions.

Applying Model Dimensions

Model dimensions are applied automatically in drawing views by retrieving the dimensions, which are applied in the sketches and features of the model. You can retrieve and apply model dimensions by using the **Retrieve Model Annotations** tool in the **Retrieve** panel of the **Annotate** tab, see Figure 14.112. The method for retrieving and applying model dimensions is discussed below:

14.112

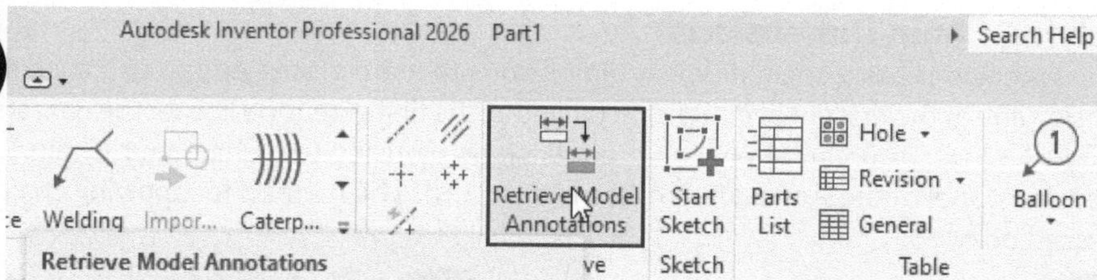

1. Click on the **Retrieve Model Annotations** tool in the **Retrieve** panel of the **Annotate** tab, see Figure 14.112. The **Retrieve Model Annotation** dialog box appears and you are prompted to select a view, since the **Select View or Drawing Sketch** button is activated in it, by default.

2. Select a drawing view on the sheet. All the model dimensions get retrieved and appear on the selected view, see Figure 14.113. Also, the options in the **Retrieve Model Annotation** dialog box get enabled, see Figure 14.114.

14.113

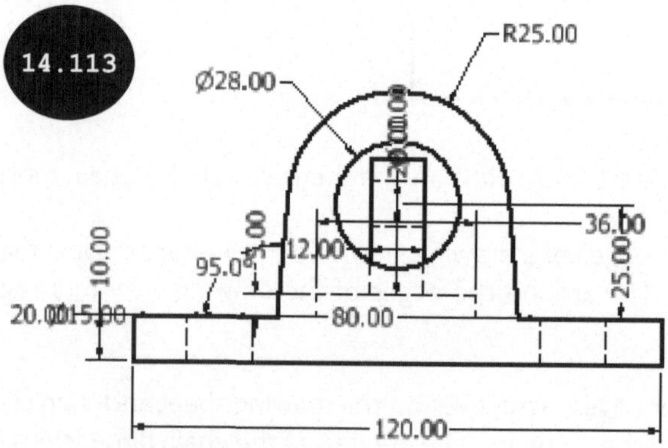

14.114

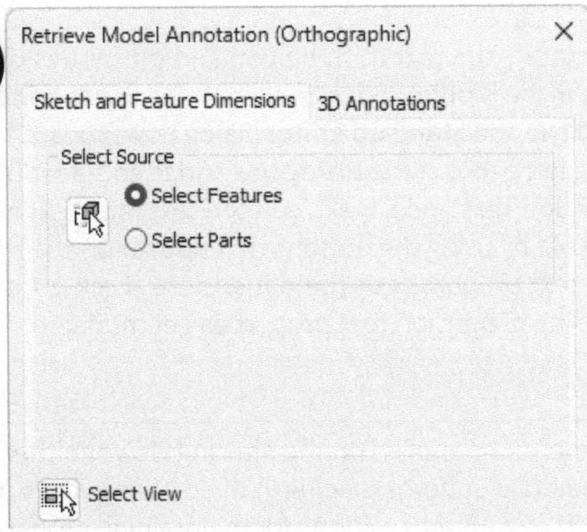

Select Source: The **Select Source Features** radio button in the dialog box is used for retrieving and displaying the dimensions of only the selected features on the view. For doing so, select this radio button and then click on the **Select Dimension Source** button in the dialog box. Next, click to select a feature in the selected view. Only the dimensions of the selected feature appear on the view. Similarly, you can select multiple features one by one to display the respective dimensions on the selected view. The **Select Parts** radio button is used for retrieving the dimensions of the selected parts of an assembly on the selected view. After selecting the features and parts, click on the **Select Dimension Source** button again to exit the selection mode.

Once the model dimensions appear, you can choose the dimensions to be applied the selected view.

3. Select the dimensions to be applied one by one on the selected view by clicking the left mouse button. You can also draw a window around the dimensions to be applied on the selected view. Note that if you did not select any dimensions, then all the dimensions that appear will be applied on the selected view.

14.115

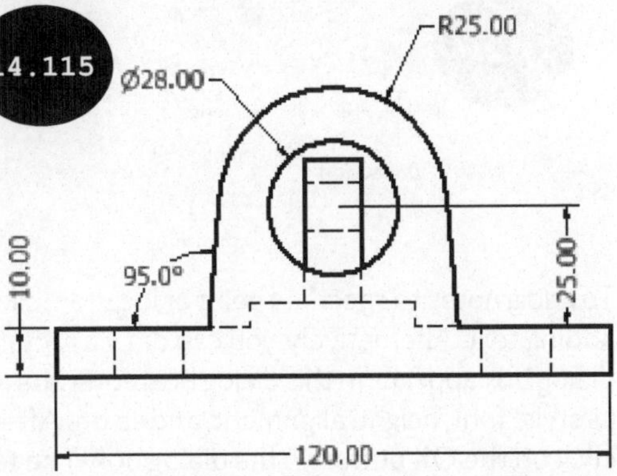

4. Click on the **OK** button in the dialog box. The selected dimensions get applied on the view, see Figure 14.115.

5. Similarly, you can apply model dimensions on the other drawing views by using the **Retrieve Model Annotations** tool. Note that the dimensions that are already applied on a drawing view will not be displayed on the other drawing views.

Note: To edit or modify the text font, height, and properties of model dimensions, click on the **Manage** tab in the **Ribbon** and then click on the **Styles Editor** tool in the **Styles and Standards** panel. The **Style and Standard Editor** dialog box appears. In this dialog box, expand the **Text** node on the left panel of the dialog box and then select the **Note Text** option that appears in the expanded **Text** node. Next, edit the text font, text height, and other properties of the dimension text by using the options that appear on the right panel of the dialog box. After editing the text properties of the dimensions, click on the **Save and Close** button in the dialog box. The dimension text properties get modified.

Tip: The model dimensions applied on the drawing views neither appear in the required positions, nor do they maintain uniform spacing in the drawing views. You can drag the dimensions and place them in the required positions for maintaining proper spacing between them. You can also arrange the dimensions by using the **Arrange** tool of the **Dimension** panel in the **Annotate** tab. For doing so, click on the **Arrange** tool and then select all the dimensions of the view by drawing a window around the dimensions. After selecting the dimensions, right-click and then click on the **OK** button. The selected dimensions get arranged.

Adding a Text/Note

Adding notes in drawings is used for conveying or providing additional information that is not available in the drawing views. In Autodesk Inventor, you can add notes in a drawing sheet by using the **Text** and **Leader Text** tools of the **Text** panel, see Figure 14.116. The **Text** tool is used for adding a note at a point specified in the drawing sheet and the **Leader Text** tool is used for adding a note with a leader.

14.116

To add a note at a specified point or location, click on the **Text** tool and then click to specify a location for adding text. Alternatively, you can draw a rectangular window by dragging the cursor. The **Format Text** dialog box appears. In this dialog box, enter the required text, specify text attributes and properties such as style, font, height, alignment, and so on. After writing the required text and specifying its properties, click on the **OK** button in the dialog box. The text gets added at the specified location on the drawing sheet. Note that to edit an existing text, double-click on the text to be edited. The **Format Text** dialog box appears. In this dialog box, you can edit the text, as required.

To add a note with a leader, click on the **Leader Text** tool in the **Text** panel. You are prompted to specify a location for the leader. Click to specify the leader location over an entity of a drawing view or anywhere in the drawing sheet. The leader arrow gets attached to the specified location. Next, click to specify the endpoint of the first segment of the leader. You can continue to specify endpoints for creating a multi-segments leader. Next, right-click on the drawing sheet and then click on the **Continue** tool in the Marking Menu that appears. The **Format Text** dialog box appears. In this dialog box, enter the required text, and specify text properties such as style, font, height, alignment, and so on. Next, click on the **OK** button in the dialog box. The note with leader gets added at the specified location on the drawing sheet.

Adding a Surface Finish Symbol

In Autodesk Inventor, you can add a surface finish symbol to specify the surface texture/finish for face of a model. A surface finish symbol has three components: surface roughness, waviness, and lay, see Figure 14.117. Specifications for the surface finish given in a surface finish symbol are used to machine the respective surface of the object. You can add a surface finish symbol to an edge or a face in a drawing view by using the **Surface** tool.

14.117

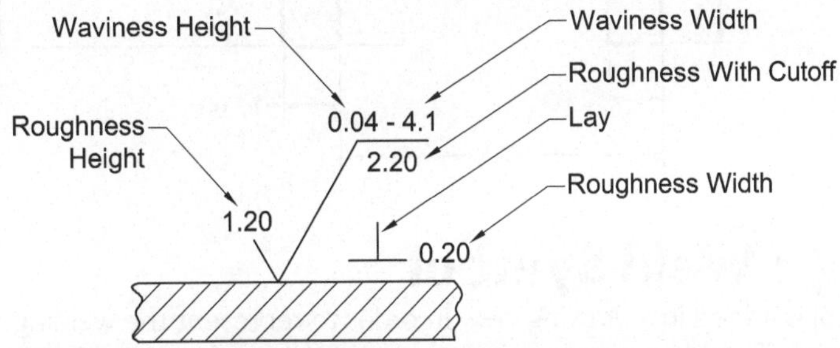

To add a surface finish symbol, click on the **Surface** tool in the **Symbols** panel of the **Annotate** tab. The default surface finish symbol gets attached to the cursor and you are prompted to specify the location. Click to specify the location of the surface symbol over an entity of a drawing view or anywhere on the drawing sheet. The leader arrow of the surface finish symbol gets attached to the specified location. Note that you can continue to specify points in the drawing sheet for adding a surface finish symbol with a single or multi-segments leader. Next, right-click on the drawing sheet and then click on the **Continue** tool in the Marking Menu that appears. The surface finish symbol gets attached to the specified location. Also, the **Surface Texture** dialog box appears, see Figure 14.118. In this dialog box, you can specify the required specifications for the surface finish (roughness, waviness, and lay) in the respective fields. Next, click on the **OK** button in the dialog box. The surface finish symbol is added and attached to the selected edge of the model, refer to Figure 14.119.

14.118

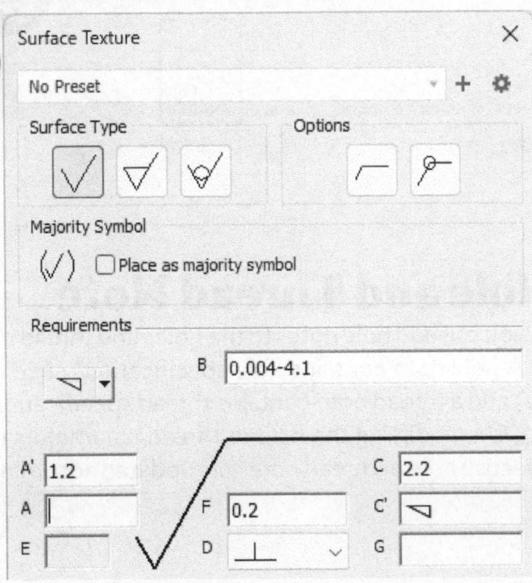

14.119

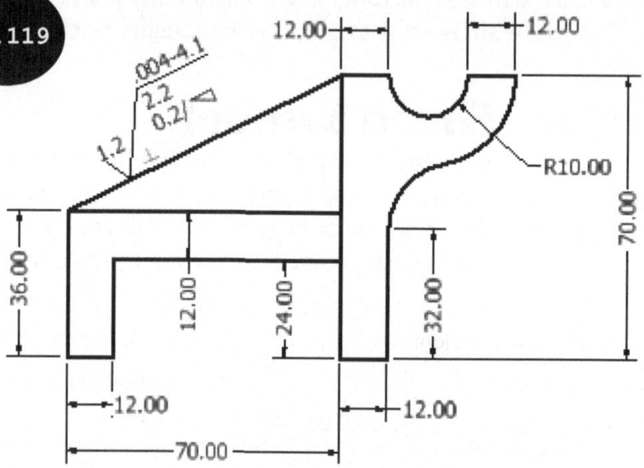

Adding a Weld Symbol

A weld symbol is added in a drawing view in order to represent the welding specification used while welding two parts. To add a weld symbol, click on the **Welding** tool in the **Symbols** panel of the **Annotate** tab, see Figure 14.120. The default weld symbol gets attached to the cursor and you are prompted to specify the location. Click to specify the location of the weld symbol over an entity of a drawing view or anywhere on the drawing sheet. The leader arrow of the weld symbol gets attached to the specified location. Note that you can continue to specify points in the drawing sheet for adding a weld symbol with a single or multi-segments leader. Next, right-click on the drawing sheet and then click on the **Continue** tool in the Marking Menu that appears. The weld symbol gets attached to the specified location. Also, the **Welding Symbol** dialog box appears. In this dialog box, you can specify the welding properties to be included in the weld symbol. Next, click on the **OK** button. The weld symbol gets added and attached to the selected edge of the model, refer to Figure 14.121.

14.120

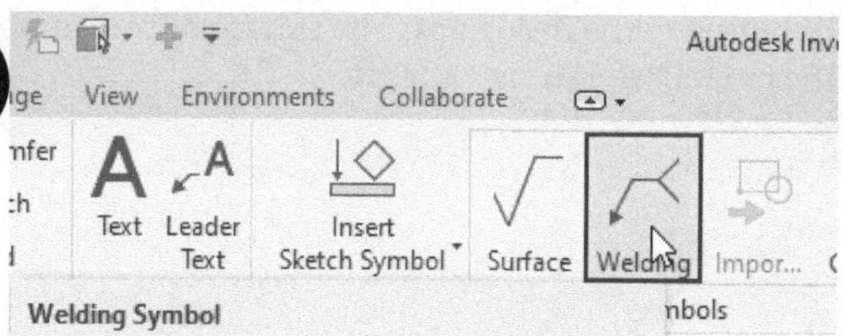

14.121

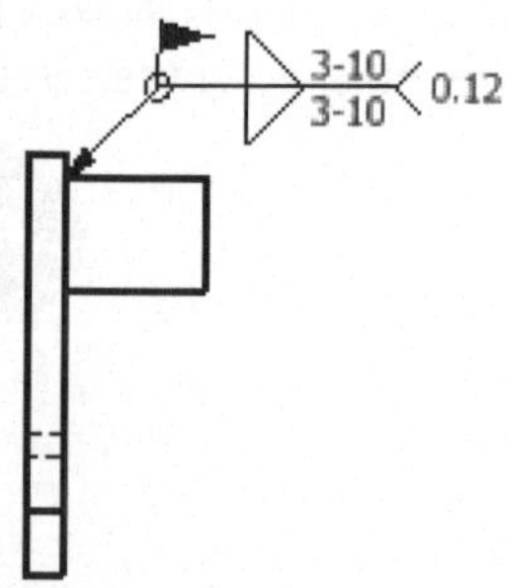

Adding a Hole and Thread Note

In Autodesk Inventor, you can add hole notes to the holes and thread notes to the threads of the model in the drawing views. A hole note contains hole specifications such as diameter, depth, and type of hole (see Figure 14.122) and a thread note contains thread specifications such as thread type, size, and class, see Figure 14.123. On modifying the hole or thread parameters of a model in the Part modeling environment, the respective hole or thread note gets updated accordingly in the Drawing environment.

14.122

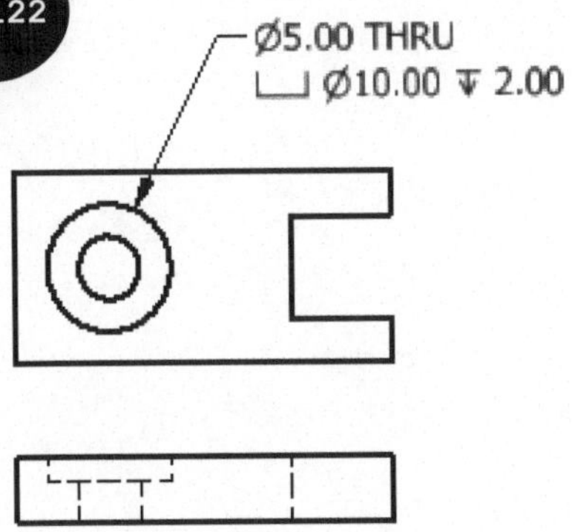

14.123

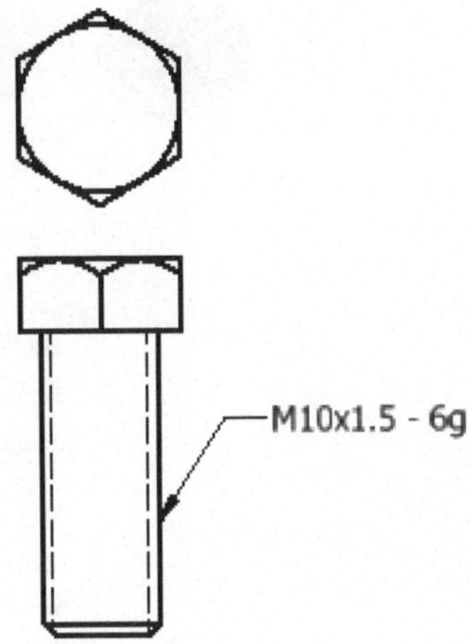

To add a hole or a thread note on a drawing view, click on the **Hole and Thread** tool in the **Feature Notes** panel of the **Annotate** tab, see Figure 14.124. You are prompted to select a hole or thread feature edge. Click on an edge of the hole or thread feature in a drawing view. The hole or thread note gets attached to the cursor with a leader, respectively. Next, click to specify the placement point for the attached note on the drawing sheet. The hole or thread note gets added, respectively. Also, the tool is still activated and you can continue to add remaining hole or thread notes in the drawing views. After adding the required hole or thread notes, press the ESC key to exit the tool.

14.124

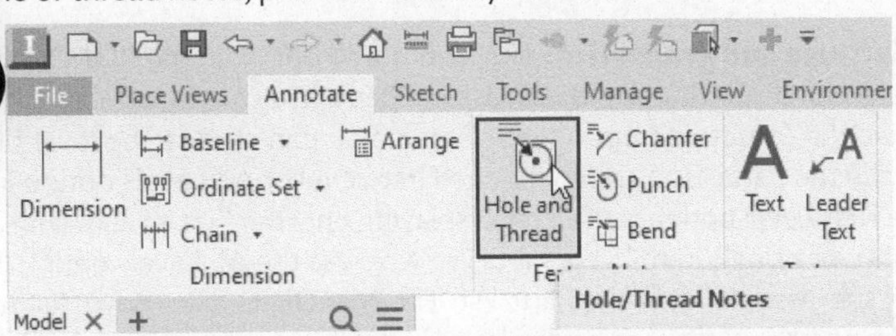

Adding the Parts List / Bill of Materials (BOM)

After creating all the required drawing views of an assembly in the Drawing environment, you need to add the Parts list (Bill of Materials). The Parts list contains all the required information such as the number of parts used in an assembly, part number, quantity of each part, and material. Since the Parts list contains all the information, it serves as a primary source of communication between the manufacturer and the vendors as well as the suppliers. The method for adding the Parts list is discussed below:

1. Click on the **Parts list** in the **Table** panel of the **Annotate** tab, see Figure 14.125. The **Parts List** dialog box appears, see Figure 14.126. Also, you are prompted to select a view.

14.125

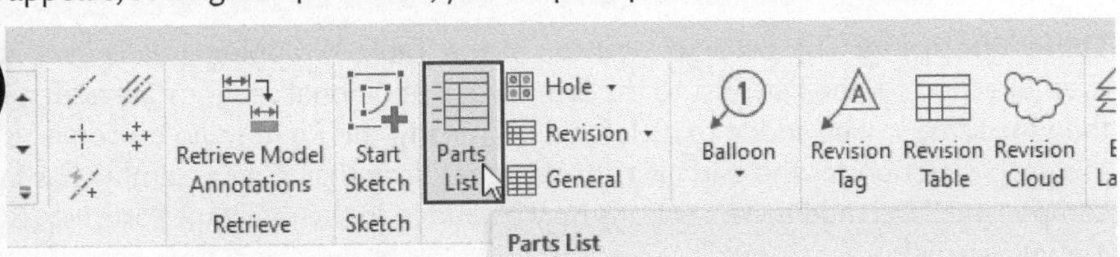

14.126

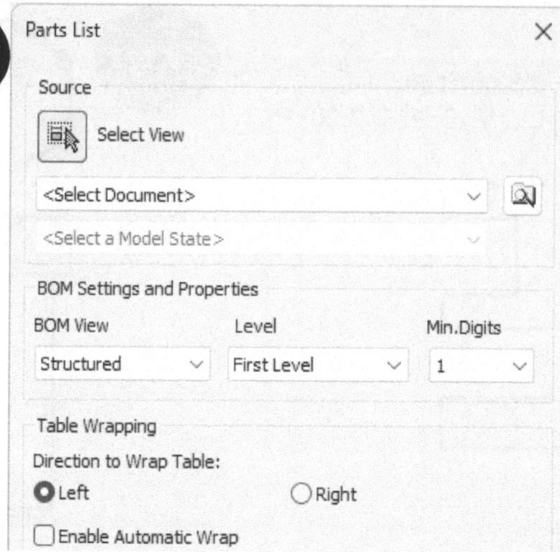

Select View : The **Select View** button is activated in the **Source** area of the **Parts List** dialog box, by default. As a result, you can select a view of an assembly in the drawing sheet for creating its Parts list (BOM). Alternatively, you can also click on the **Browse** button in the **Source** area of the dialog box and then select an assembly file for creating its Parts list in the **Open** dialog box that appears. If the selected assembly file has multiple model states, you can select a model state whose Parts list (BOM) is to be created.

BOM Settings and Properties: The **Structured** option in the **BOM View** drop-down list in this area is used for displaying all the sub-assemblies of the main assembly as a single item in the Parts list. When the **Structured** option is selected, you can choose the level of sub-assemblies to be included in the Parts list by selecting the **First Level** or **All Levels** option in the **Level** drop-down list. The **First Level** option is used for displaying only the first level of sub-assemblies of the main assemblies as a single item in the Parts list, whereas the **All Levels** option is used for displaying all levels of sub-assemblies in the Parts list. The **Min.Digits** drop-down list is used for selecting the minimum number of digits to be displayed in the item numbering of the Parts list. This drop-down list is available when the **First Level** option is selected in the **Level** drop-down list. The **Delimiter** drop-down list is used for selecting a delimiter for the item numbering of the sub-assemblies in the Parts list. This option restarts numbering for each level of sub-assemblies and is available when the **All level** option is selected in the **Level** drop-down list.

The **Parts Only** option in the **BOM View** drop-down list is used for displaying all components of the sub-assemblies of the main assembly as individual components in the Parts list. When the **Parts Only** option is selected in the **BOM View** drop-down list, you can choose the display of item numbering as numerical or alphabetical in the **Numbering** drop-down list.

Table Wrapping: The **Left** radio button in the **Table Wrapping** area is used for defining the wrap direction for the Parts list to the left. Also, if additional sections are added in the Parts list, then the same will be added to its left side. Similarly, the **Right** radio button is used for defining the wrap direction for the parts list to the right. Note that if an assembly has large number of components, then additional sections may be added in the resultant Parts list (BOM) to reduce its overall length.

On selecting the **Enable Automatic Wrap** check box in the **Parts List** dialog box, the **Maximum Rows** and **Number of Sections** radio buttons get enabled in the dialog box. On selecting the **Maximum Rows** radio button, you can specify maximum number of rows to be displayed in a section of the Parts list (BOM). For example, if the assembly has a total of 20 components and the maximum number of rows is specified as 10, then the resultant Parts list will be created with 2 sections (10 rows in each section). On selecting the **Number of Sections** radio button, you can specify number of sections to be added in the resultant Parts list (BOM).

2. Select the drawing view of the assembly for creating the Parts list (BOM).

3. Specify the required options in the **BOM Settings and Properties** area of the dialog box or accept the default selected options.

4. Click on the **OK** button in the dialog box. A rectangular box representing the Parts list (BOM) appears attached to the cursor.

Note: If the **BOM View Disable** dialog box appears on clicking the **OK** button in the **Parts List** dialog box, then click on the **OK** button to enable the display of Parts list (BOM). The **BOM View Disable** dialog box appears if the selected BOM view (**Structured** or **Parts Only**) is disabled for the assembly. To enable the BOM view for the assembly, expand the view node in the **Browser** and then right-click on the name of the assembly, see Figure 14.127. Next, click on the **Bill of Materials** option in the shortcut menu that appears. The **Bill of Materials** dialog box appears. In this dialog box, right-click on the **Structured** or **Parts Only** tab to enable the respective BOM view (Bill of materials), see Figure 14.128. Next, click on the **Enable BOM View** option in the shortcut menu that appears. The respective BOM view gets enabled and displayed in the dialog box. Next, click on the **Done** button to accept the change and exit the dialog box.

14.127

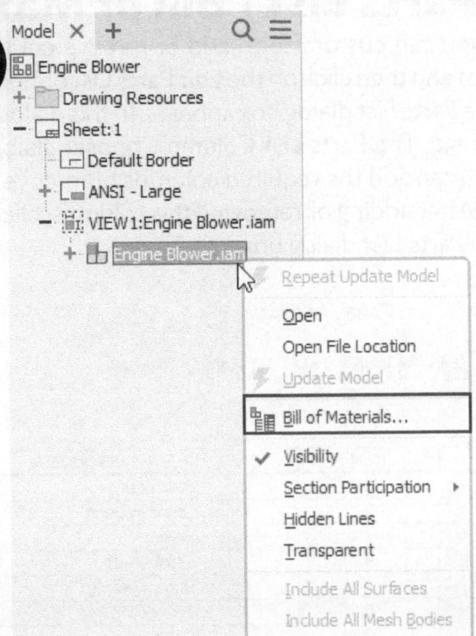

14.128

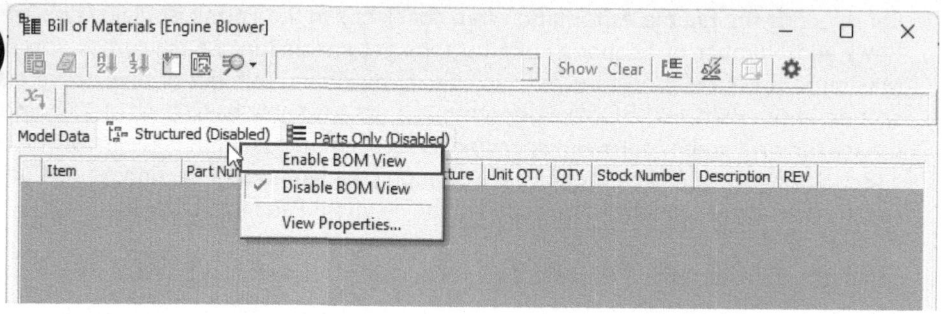

5. Click on the required location on the drawing sheet to define the placement of the Parts list (BOM). The Parts list gets added to the specified location on the drawing sheet, see Figure 14.129.

14.129

PARTS LIST			
ITEM	QTY	PART NUMBER	DESCRIPTION
1	1	Base Frame	
2	1	Lower Housing	
3	1	Blower	
4	1	Crank Shaft	
5	1	Upper Housing	
6	1	Connecting Rod	
7	1	Piston	
8	1	Engine Block	
9	1	Engine Cover	
10	1	Engine Head	

Editing the Parts List / Bill of Materials (BOM)

In Autodesk Inventor, you can customize to add or remove columns in the Parts list. For doing so, right-click on the Parts list and then click on the **Edit Parts List** option in the shortcut menu that appears or double-click on it. The **Parts List** dialog box appears. In this dialog box, click on the **Column Chooser** button, see Figure 14.130. The **Parts List Column Chooser** dialog box appears, see Figure 14.131. By using this dialog box, you can add the required columns or remove the columns that are not required in the Parts list (BOM). After adding or removing the columns, click on the **OK** button and then click on the **OK** button in the **Parts List** dialog box.

14.130

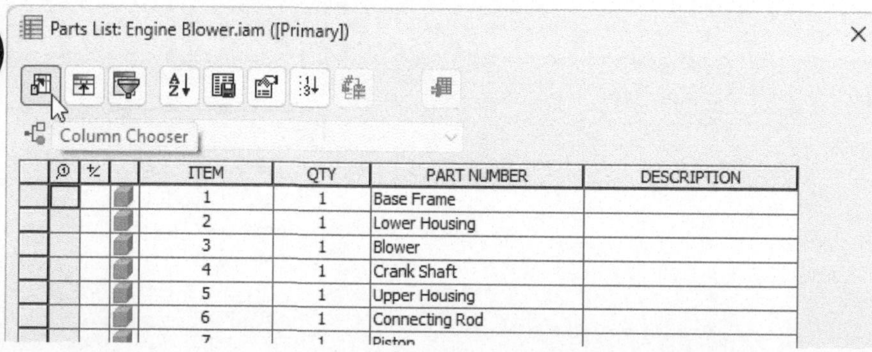

14.131

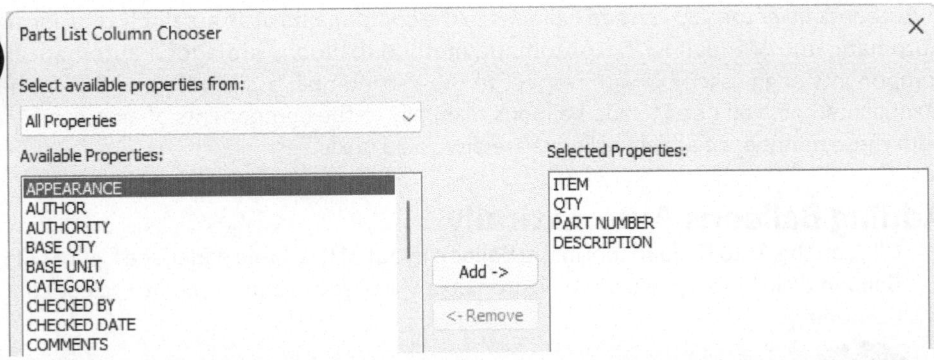

Tip: You can exit the Parts list style by using the **Style and Standard Editor** dialog box. For doing so, right-click on the Parts list on the drawing sheet and then click on the **Edit Parts List Style** option in the shortcut menu that appears. The **Style and Standard Editor** dialog box appears with the **Parts List** option selected on the left panel of the dialog box. Also, the options for editing the Parts list style appears on the right panel of the dialog box. By using these options, you can edit the Parts list style, as required and then close the dialog box by clicking on the **Save and Close** button. To edit the text height of the Parts list, expand the **Text** node in the **Style and Standard Editor** dialog box and then select the **Note Text** option in the expanded **Text** node. The options to edit text properties such as text height and font appear on the right panel of the dialog box. After editing the text properties, click on the **Save and Close** dialog box.

Adding Balloons

A Balloon is attached to a component with a leader line and displays the respective part (item) number assigned in the Parts list (Bill of Materials), see Figure 14.132. In drawings, balloons are added to the individual components of an assembly in order to identify them easily with respect to the part number assigned in the Bill of Materials (BOM).

14.132

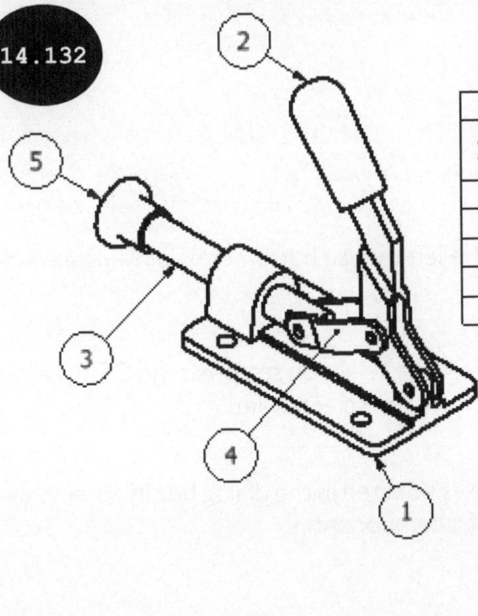

PARTS LIST			
ITEM	QTY	PART NUMBER	DESCRIPTION
1	1	Base	
2	1	Clamp Arm	
3	1	Connecting Rod	
4	2	Link	
5	1	Socket	

In Autodesk Inventor, you can add balloons to the components of an assembly by using two methods: Automatic and Manual. In the Automatic method, balloons are added automatically to all the components of an assembly with respect to the part number assigned in the BOM whereas, in the Manual method, you need to add balloons manually to the components of an assembly one by one. Both these methods of adding balloons are discussed next.

Adding Balloons Automatically

1. Click on the **Auto Balloon** tool in the **Balloon** flyout of the **Table** panel, see Figure 14.133. The **Auto Balloon** dialog box appears, see Figure 14.134. Also, you are prompted to select components for ballooning.

14.133

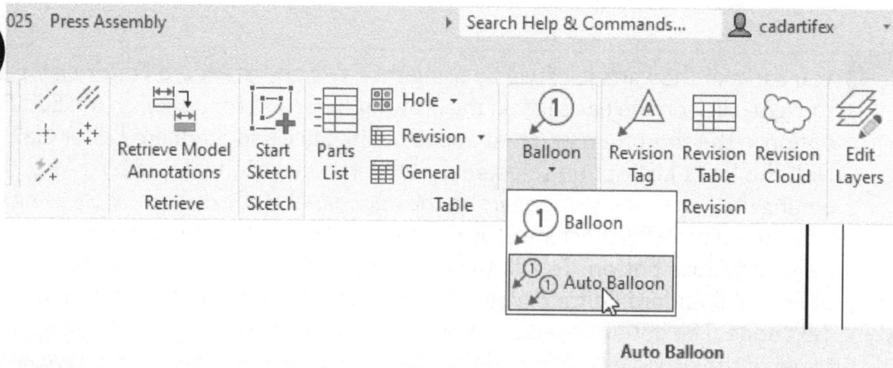

14.134

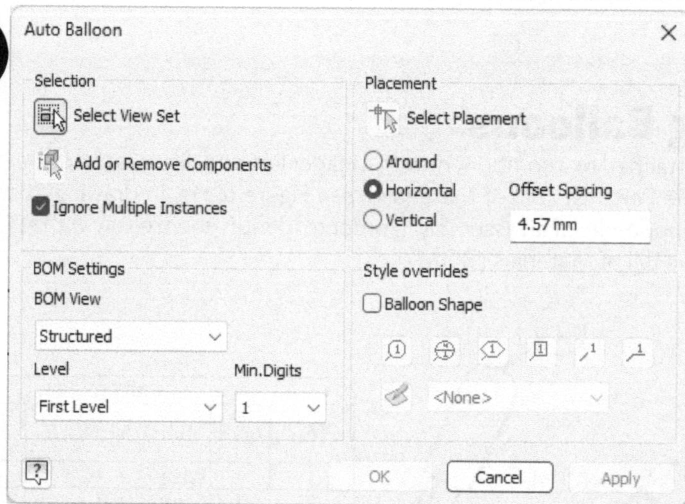

2. Select the components for ballooning by clicking the left mouse button or by drawing a window around the components to be selected.

Note: To remove an already selected component from the selection set, press the CTRL key and then click on the component to be removed from the selected set.

3. Ensure that the **Ignore Multiple Instances** check box is selected in the dialog box in order to avoid duplicates by not adding balloons to all instances of a component.

4. Select the required radio button (**Around**, **Horizontal**, or **Vertical**) in the **Placement** area of the dialog box for arranging balloons in the drawing sheet, accordingly.

5. Select the **Balloon Shape** check box in the **Style overrides** area of the dialog box to override the default circular shape of the balloon. On selecting this check box, all buttons representing different balloon shapes such as circular with 2 entities, hexagon, and rectangular get enabled in this area and you can choose the one, as required.

6. Select the required options in the **BOM Settings** area of the dialog box or accept the default selected options.

7. After selecting the components for ballooning and defining the required settings, right-click on the drawing sheet and then click on the **Continue** tool in the Marking Menu that appears. The preview of the balloons appears on the drawing sheet. Note that you can still define the arrangement of balloons (around, horizontal, or vertical), balloon shape, and so on by using the options in the dialog box.

   Now, you need to define the placement of the balloons on the drawing sheet.

8. Click on the drawing sheet to define the placement of the balloons. The balloons get placed at the specified location and attached to the respective components of the assembly with leaders.

9. Click on the **OK** button in the dialog box. The balloons get added to each selected component of the assembly in the drawing view.

Tip: After adding the balloons, you can change the location of a balloon by dragging it to the required location on the drawing sheet.

Adding Balloons Manually

1. Click on the **Balloon** tool in the **Table** panel of the **Annotate** tab, see Figure 14.135. Alternatively, press the **B** key. You are prompted to select a component.

14.135

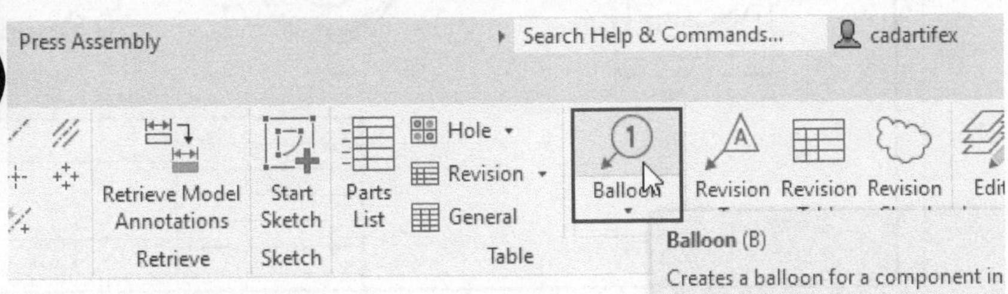

2. Click on a component of an assembly in a drawing view. The preview of a balloon appears attached to the selected component with a leader.

3. Click to specify the placement point for the attached balloon on the drawing sheet.

4. Right-click on the drawing sheet and then click on the **Continue** tool in the Marking Menu that appears. The balloon gets attached to the selected component.

5. Similarly, you can add balloons to the remaining components of the assembly in the drawing view.

Tutorial 1

Open the model created in Tutorial 2 of Chapter 7 and then create different drawing views: front, top, side, isometric, section, and detail, as shown in Figure 14.136 by using the ANSI (mm) standard drawing sheet of A3 size. You need to customize the drafting standard for dimensioning as given below:

Dimension Units	mm
Dimension linear precision	0
Dimension Terminator Size (X)	5 mm
Dimension Terminator Height (Y)	2 mm
Text Height	6 mm

14.136

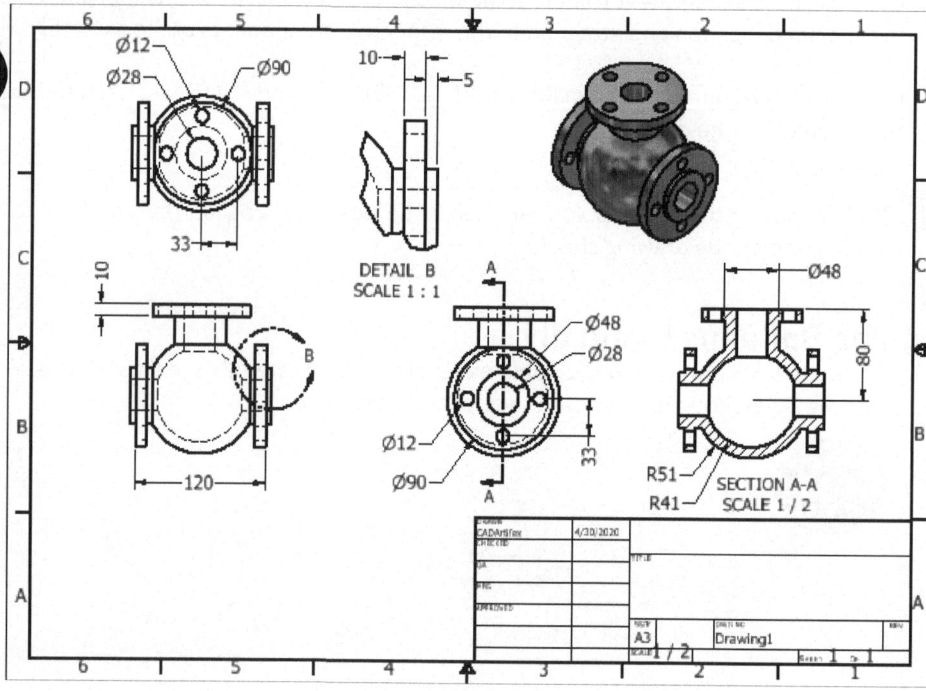

Section 1: Opening and Saving Model Created in Tutorial 2 of Chapter 7

1. Start Autodesk Inventor and then open the model created in Tutorial 2 of Chapter 7, see Figure 14.137.

14.137

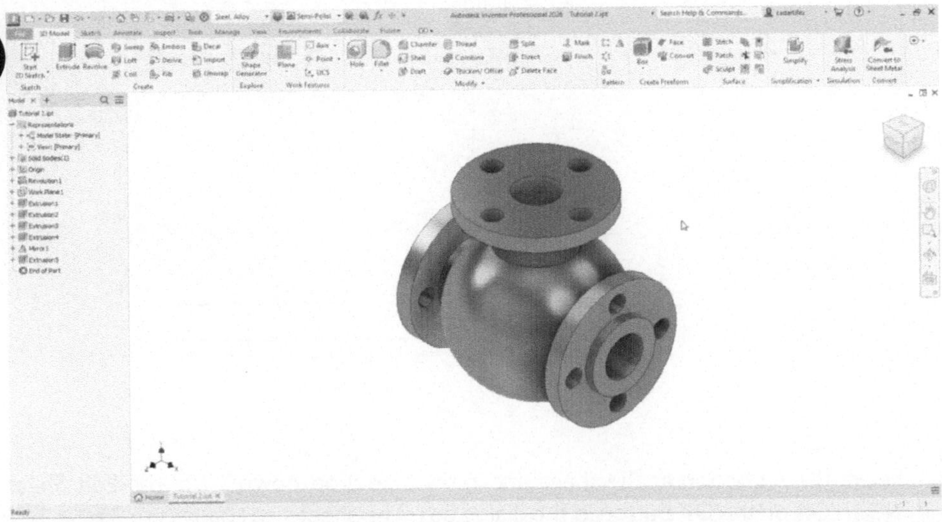

Now, you need to save the model with the name "Tutorial 1" in **Chapter 14** folder of the **Autodesk Inventor** folder.

2. Click on **File > Save As > Save As** in the **File Menu**, and then save the model with the name **Tutorial 1** inside the **Tutorial** folder of the **Chapter 14** folder. Note that you need to create these folders inside the **Autodesk Inventor** folder.

Section 2: Invoking Drawing Environment

1. Click on the **New** tool in the **Quick Access Toolbar** or press the **CTRL + N** keys. The **Create New File** dialog box appears.

2. Click on the **Metric** template folder on the left panel of the dialog box and then double-click on the **ANSI (mm).idw** template in the **Drawing** rollout that appears on the right panel of the dialog box. The Drawing environment gets invoked. Note that *.idw* is the file extension of a drawing file.

Section 3: Setting the Sheet Size and Drafting Standard

Now, you need to define the A3 sheet size and customize the drafting standard, as mentioned in the tutorial description.

1. Right-click on the **Sheet** node in the **Browser**, see Figure 14.138 and then click on the **Edit Sheet** option in the shortcut menu that appears. The **Edit Sheet** dialog box appears.

14.138

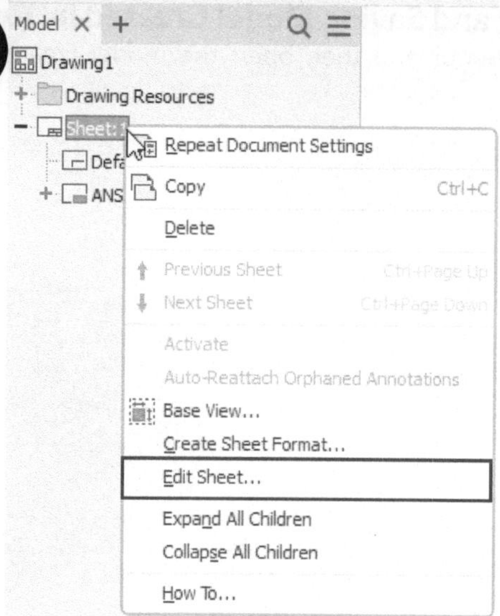

2. Select the **A3** option as the sheet size in the **Size** drop-down list of the **Edit Sheet** dialog box. Next, click on the **OK** button in the dialog box. The sheet size changes to A3.

   Now, you need to customize the drafting standard, as mentioned in the tutorial description.

3. Click on the **Manage** tab in the **Ribbon** and then click on the **Styles Editor** tool in the **Styles and Standards** tab, see Figure 14.139. The **Style and Standard Editor** dialog box appears.

14.139

4. Expand the **Dimension** node in the left panel of the dialog box and then select the **Default - mm (ANSI)** option in the expanded **Dimension** node, see Figure 14.140.

14.140

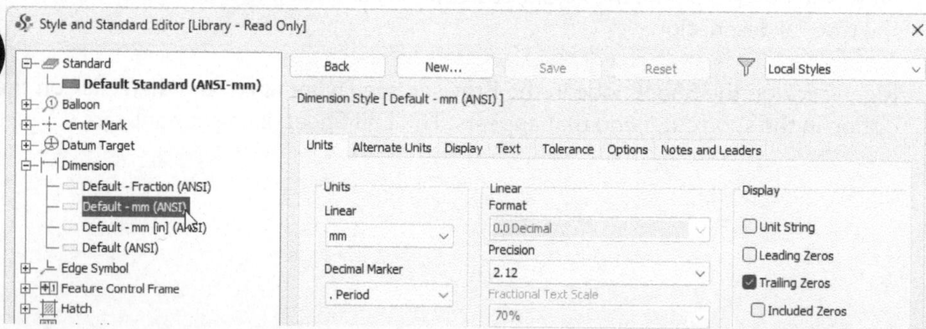

5. Ensure that **mm** is selected as the unit in the **Linear** drop-down list of the **Units** area on the right panel of the dialog box.

6. Select **0** as the precision value in the **Precision** drop-down list of the **Linear** area.

7. Click on the **Display** tab on the right panel of the dialog box, see Figure 14.141.

8. Enter **5 mm** in the **Size (X)** field and **2 mm** in the **Height (Y)** field of the **Terminator** area of the dialog box.

14.141

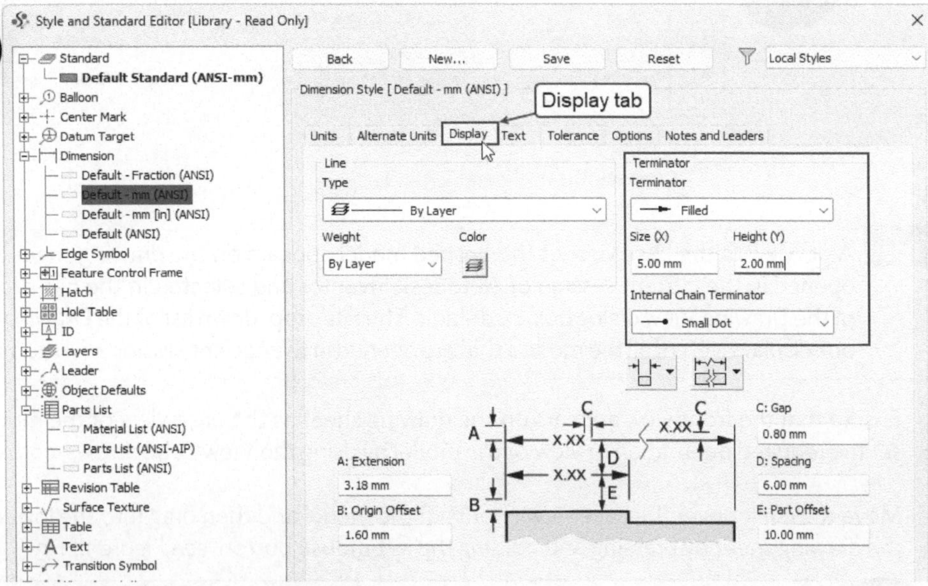

Now, you need to define the text height for dimensions.

9. Expand the **Text** node on the left panel of the dialog box and then select the **Note Text (ANSI)** option on the expanded Text node. The **Autodesk Inventor Professional 2026** dialog box appears. Click on the **Yes** button in this dialog box to save the changes made and continue with the editing process.

10. Enter **6 mm** in the **Text Height** field of the **Character Formatting** area of the dialog box.

11. Click on the **Save and Close** button in the dialog box to save the changes made and close the dialog box. The drafting standard gets modified.

Section 4: Creating Front, Top, and Right Views

Now, you can create the front view of the model as the base view, and then its projected views (top and right).

1. Click on the **Base** tool in the **Create** panel of the **Place Views** tab, see Figure 14.142. The **Drawing View** dialog box appears. Also, the preview of a base view appears at a default location on the drawing sheet with the display of ViewCube, refer to Figure 14.143.

14.142

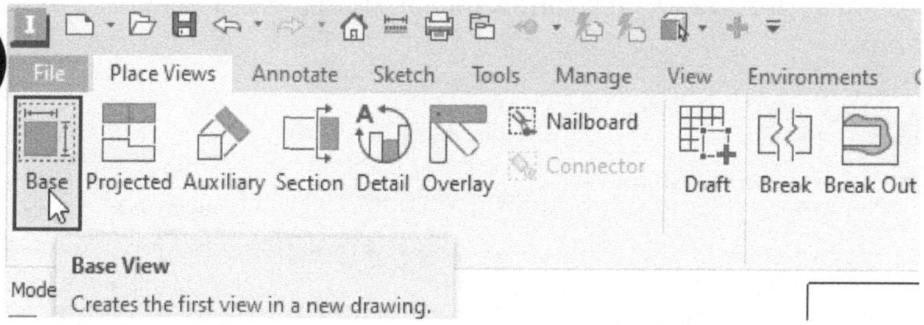

Tip: A preview of the base view of the desired model appears on the drawing sheet because it is opened in the current session of Autodesk Inventor and selected in the **File** drop-down list of the **Drawing View** dialog box, by default. The **File** drop-down list of the **Drawing View** dialog box displays a list of all the models that are opened in the current session of Autodesk Inventor.

2. Ensure that the front view appears on the drawing sheet as the base view of the model. You can set the required orientation or view of the model by using the ViewCube arrows, corners, or faces.

3. Move the cursor over the base view (front) of the model and then drag it to the lower left side of the drawing sheet by pressing and holding the left mouse button, see Figure 14.143.

14.143

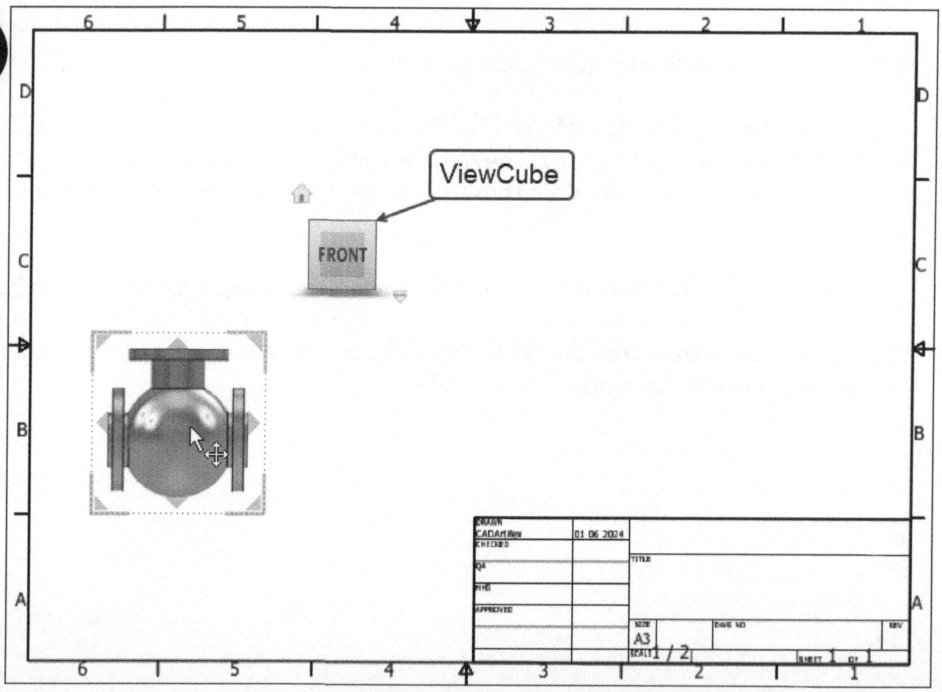

4. Ensure that the **Hidden Line** button is selected in the **Style** area of the **Drawing View** dialog box as the display style of the base view of the model.

5. Enter **1/2** as the scale value in the **Scale** field of the dialog box.

   After defining the position, style, and scale for base view of the model, you can create its projected views (top and right).

6. Move the cursor vertically upward. A rectangular box, representing the projected view (top view) of the model, appears attached to the cursor.

7. Click on the drawing sheet to specify the position of the top view on the drawing sheet, refer Figure 14.144. The preview of the top view appears in the specified position.

   Now, you need to create the right side view of the model.

8. Move the cursor horizontally toward the right of the base view. A rectangular box, representing the projected view (right view) of the model, appears attached to the cursor.

9. Click on the drawing sheet to specify the position for the right side view of the model, refer to Figure 14.144.

10. After specifying the position of all views, click on the **OK** button in the **Drawing View** dialog box. The front, top, and right side views are created, see Figure 14.144.

14.144

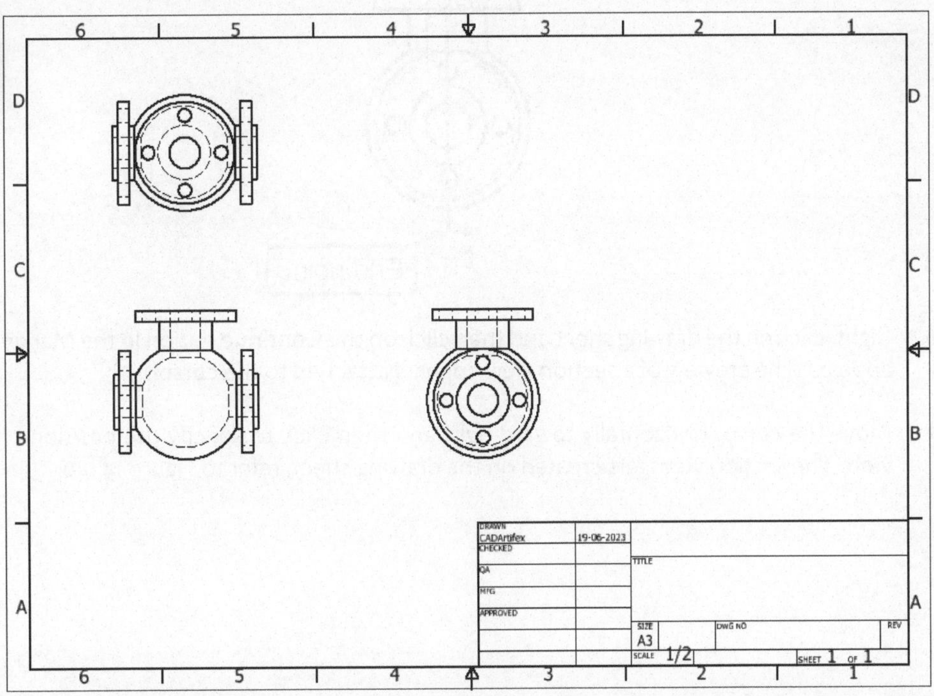

Tip: After creating views, you can further change their position. To change the position of a view, drag it to the required location by pressing and holding the left mouse button.

Section 5: Creating the Section View

1. Click on the **Section** tool in the **Create** panel of the **Place Views** tab. You are prompted to select a view.

2. Select the right side view of the model to create the section view. You are prompted to specify points for creating the section line on the right side view.

3. Move the cursor toward the center of the right side view and then move the cursor vertically upward outside a small distance from the top edge of the view.

4. Click to specify the start point of the section line outside a small distance from the top edge of the right side view, when a reference dotted line originating from the center appears, refer to Figure 14.145. You are prompted to specify the endpoint of the section line.

5. Move the cursor vertically downward and then click to specify the endpoint of the section line outside a small distance from the bottom of the view, refer to Figure 14.145.

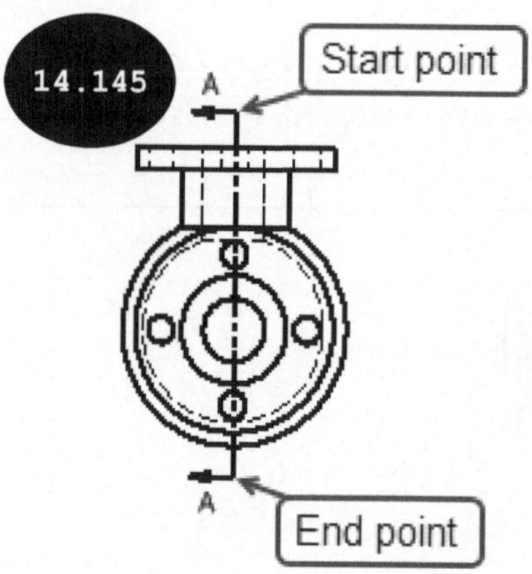

6. Right-click on the drawing sheet and then click on the **Continue** option in the Marking Menu that appears. The preview of a section view appears attached to the cursor.

7. Move the cursor horizontally toward right and then click to specify the position of the section view. The section view gets created on the drawing sheet, refer to Figure 14.146.

14.146

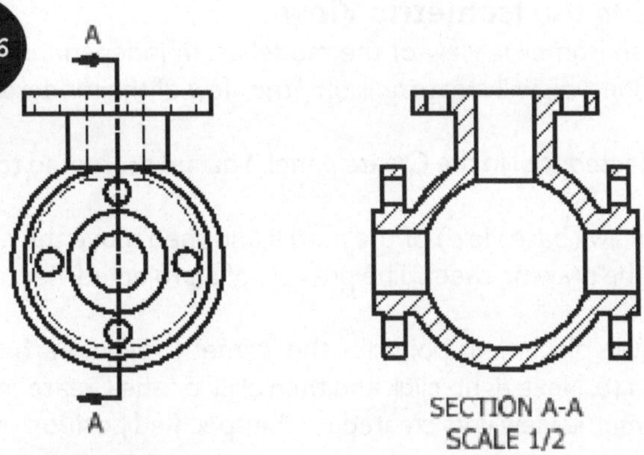

Section 6: Creating the Detail View

1. Click on the **Detail** tool in the **Create** panel of the **Place Views** tab. You are prompted to select a view.

2. Click on the front view for creating the detail view. The **Detail View** dialog box appears and you are prompted to select the center point of the fence.

3. Move the cursor over the top right most vertex of the front view and then click to specify the center point of the circle, see Figure 14.147. You are prompted to specify the endpoint of the fence.

14.147

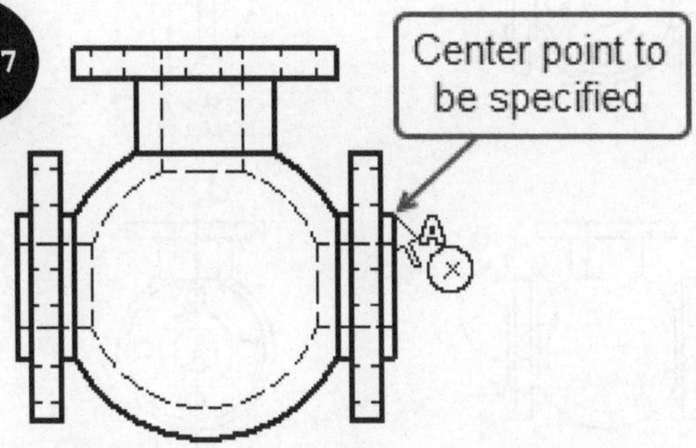

4. Move the cursor toward the right and click to specify the endpoint of the fence (circle), refer to Figure 14.148. The preview of a detailed view gets attached to the cursor.

5. Click to specify the placement point for the detailed view on the sheet, see Figure 14.148.

Section 7: Creating the Isometric View

You can create an isometric view of the model as an independent base view or as a projected view. In this section, you will create an isometric view of the model as a projected view.

1. Click on the **Projected** tool in the **Create** panel. You are prompted to select a view.

2. Select the front view (base view) of the model and then move the cursor at an angle toward the top right side of the drawing sheet. The preview of a projected view (isometric) appears.

3. Click to specify the placement point for the isometric view on the top right side of the sheet, refer to Figure 14.148. Next, right-click and then click on the **Create** tool in the Marking Menu that appears. The isometric view gets created on the specified position on the sheet.

   Now, you need to change the display style of the isometric view.

4. Double-click on the isometric view to display the **Drawing View** dialog box. Next, click on the **Shaded** button in the **Style** area and then click on the **OK** button. The display style of the isometric view gets changed to shaded. Figure 14.148 shows the sheet after creating all views.

14.148

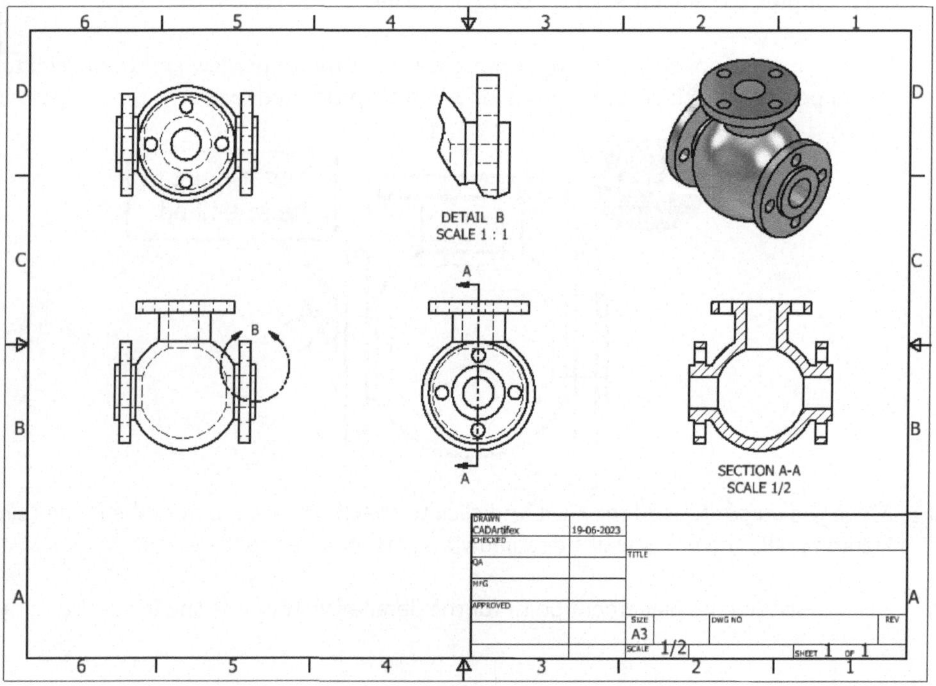

Section 8: Applying Drawing Dimensions

Now, you need to apply drawing dimensions to the drawing views.

1. Apply dimensions to the drawing view one by one by using the **Dimension** tool of the **Dimension** panel in the **Annotate** tab of the **Ribbon**. Figure 14.149.

14.149

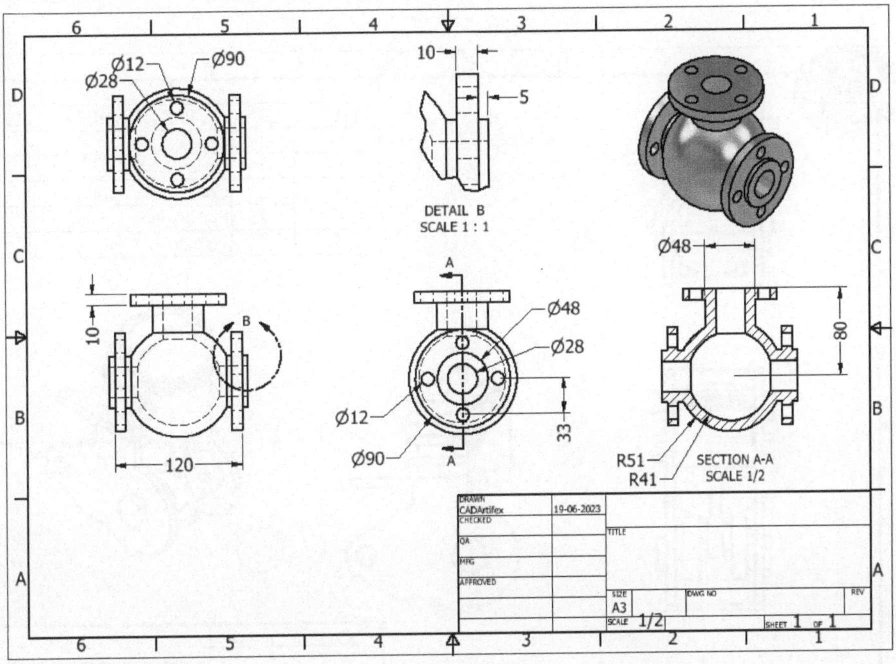

Tip: The method for applying a dimension is same as discussed earlier. After applying a dimension, you may need to change its position by dragging it to the new position.

Section 9: Saving the Model

1. Click on the **Save** tool in the **Quick Access Toolbar**. The **Save As** dialog box appears.

2. Browse to the **Tutorial** folder of **Chapter 14** folder and then save the drawing with the name Tutorial 1.

Hands-on Test Drive 1

Open the model created in Tutorial 1 of Chapter 11 and then create different drawing views: front, top, side, and isometric of the assembly at scale 1:3, as shown in Figure 14.150. You need to customize the text height for the Parts list, as required. Note that you need to use the ANSI (mm) standard drawing sheet of A3 size.

14.150

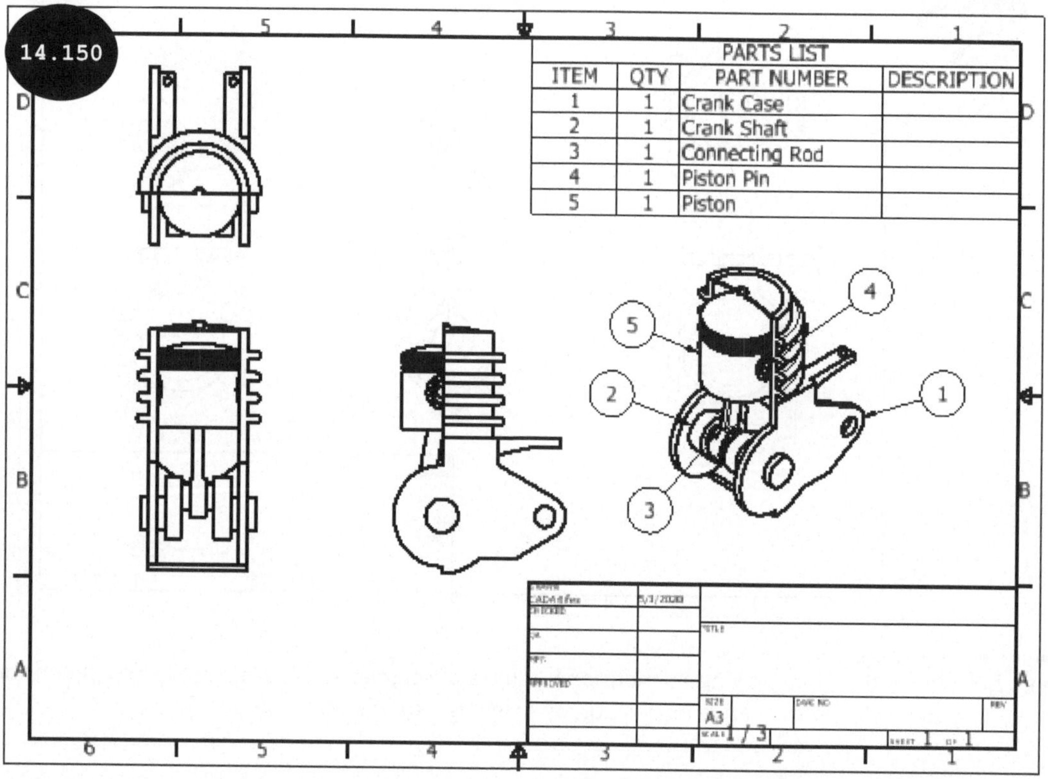

Hands-on Test Drive 2

Open the presentation file (*.ipn*) of the assembly created in Tutorial 1 of Chapter 13 and then create different drawing views (top, section, and right) of the unexploded snapshot view of the assembly at scale 1:2, as shown in Figure 14.151. Also, you need to create an exploded view by using the exploded snapshot view of the assembly at scale 1:4. Note that you need to use the ANSI (mm) standard drawing sheet of A2 size.

14.151

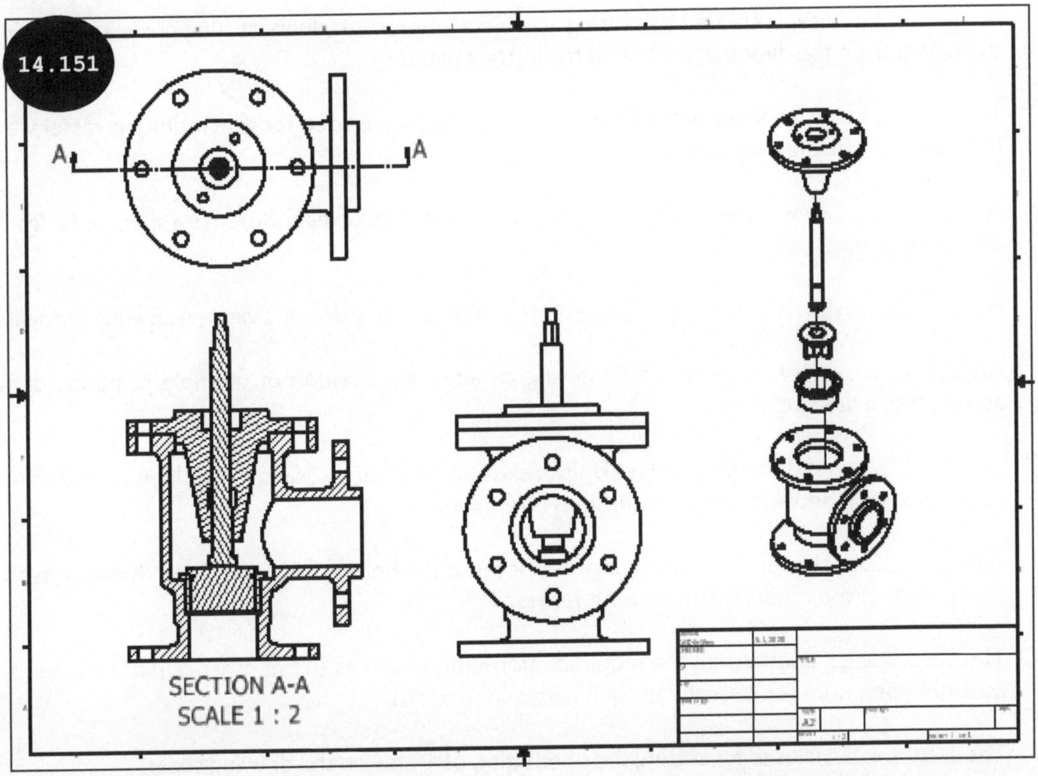

Summary

In this chapter, you have learned how to create various types of drawing views such as base views, projected views, section views, detail view, and crop view for creating 2D drawings of parts and assemblies. The chapter introduced the concepts of angles of projections, editing sheet size, title block, drafting standards, applying dimensions, text/note, surface finish symbol, weld symbol, hole and thread note, Parts list (BOM), and balloons. It also discussed methods for editing Parts list and deleting and editing drawing views.

Questions

Complete and verify the following sentences:

- In the _________ environment of Autodesk Inventor, you can generate error-free 2D drawings of a component or an assembly.
- _________ and _________ are the file extensions of a drawing file.
- Engineering drawings follow the _________ and the _________ angle of projections.
- A _________ view is an independent first drawing view.

- A _________ view is created by cutting an object with an imaginary cutting plane and viewing the object from the direction normal to the cutting plane.
- The _________ check box in the **Drawing View** dialog box is used for generating the raster view of a model in the drawing sheet.
- An _________ view is created by projecting the edges of an object normal to a specified edge of an existing view.
- A _________ view is used for showing a portion of an existing drawing view on an enlarged scale.
- An _________ view is created by showing an alternate position or multiple positions of an assembly in a drawing view.
- A _________ view is created by breaking an existing view using a pair of break lines such that the portion existing between the breaking lines is removed.
- The _________ tool is used for adding hole notes to the holes of the model and thread notes to the threads of the model in the drawing views.
- The _________ contains all the required information such as the number of parts used in an assembly, part number, quantity of each part, and material.
- The _________ is used for setting the orientation of a view on the drawing sheet.
- A surface finish symbol has three components: _________, _________, and _________.
- In Autodesk Inventor, you can add balloons by using automatic and manual methods. (True/False)
- You can edit or create the title block of a sheet as per the standard format of your company. (True/False)
- You cannot edit the default sheet size for creating drawing views. (True/False)
- In a section view, you can exclude some of the components like fasteners from the section cut. (True/False)

INDEX

Other Publications by CADArtifex

Some of the other Publications by CADArtifex are given below:

AutoCAD Textbooks

AutoCAD 2026: A Power Guide for Beginners and Intermediate Users
AutoCAD 2025: A Power Guide for Beginners and Intermediate Users
AutoCAD 2024: A Power Guide for Beginners and Intermediate Users
and more

AutoCAD For Architectural Design Textbooks

AutoCAD 2023 for Architectural Design: A Power Guide for Beginners and Intermediate Users
AutoCAD 2022 for Architectural Design: A Power Guide for Beginners and Intermediate Users
AutoCAD 2021 for Architectural Design: A Power Guide for Beginners and Intermediate Users
and more

Autodesk Fusion 360 Textbooks

Autodesk Fusion 360: A Power Guide for Beginners and Intermediate Users (7th Edition)
Autodesk Fusion 360: A Power Guide for Beginners and Intermediate Users (6th Edition)
Autodesk Fusion 360: A Power Guide for Beginners and Intermediate Users (5th Edition)
and more

Autodesk Fusion 360 Surface and T-Spline Textbooks

Autodesk Fusion 360 Surface Design and Sculpting with T-Spline Surfaces (7th Edition)
Autodesk Fusion 360 Surface Design and Sculpting with T-Spline Surfaces (6th Edition)
and more

Autodesk Inventor Textbooks

Autodesk Inventor 2026: A Power Guide for Beginners and Intermediate Users
Autodesk Inventor 2025: A Power Guide for Beginners and Intermediate Users
Autodesk Inventor 2024: A Power Guide for Beginners and Intermediate Users
and more

FreeCAD Textbooks

FreeCAD 1.0: A Power Guide for Beginners and Intermediate Users
FreeCAD 0.21: A Power Guide for Beginners and Intermediate Users

Onshape Textbooks

Onshape 2025: A Power Guide for Beginners and Intermediate Users

PTC Creo Parametric Textbooks

Creo Parametric 11.0: A Power Guide for Beginners and Intermediate Users
Creo Parametric 10.0: A Power Guide for Beginners and Intermediate Users
Creo Parametric 9.0: A Power Guide for Beginners and Intermediate Users
and more

SOLIDWORKS Textbooks

SOLIDWORKS 2025: A Power Guide for Beginners and Intermediate User
SOLIDWORKS 2024: A Power Guide for Beginners and Intermediate User
SOLIDWORKS 2023: A Power Guide for Beginners and Intermediate User
and more

SOLIDWORKS Sheet Metal and Surface Design Textbooks

SOLIDWORKS Sheet Metal and Surface Design 2025 for Beginners and Intermediate Users
SOLIDWORKS Sheet Metal and Surface Design 2024 for Beginners and Intermediate Users
and more

SOLIDWORKS Simulation Textbooks

SOLIDWORKS Simulation 2025: A Power Guide for Beginners and Intermediate User
SOLIDWORKS Simulation 2024: A Power Guide for Beginners and Intermediate User
SOLIDWORKS Simulation 2023: A Power Guide for Beginners and Intermediate User
and more

Exercises Books

Some of the exercises books are given below:

100 AutoCAD Exercises - Learn by Practicing (2 Edition)
Autodesk Inventor Exercises - Learn by Practicing
Autodesk Fusion 360 Exercises Learn by Practicing (2023-24)
SOLIDWORKS Exercises - Learn by Practicing (3 Edition)

Project-Based Video Courses by CADArtifex

- SOLIDWORKS for Beginners and Intermediate Users
- Learn SOLIDWORKS Sheet Metal: From Concept to Creation
- Complete Fusion 360 All-in-One Course for Beginners (2025)
- Learn Fusion 360 with Real-World Mechanical Projects
- Fusion 360 Surface Design & T-Spline Sculpting
- Mastering AutoCAD 2D & 3D for Beginners
- Complete Onshape for Beginners: Project-Based Approach
- Complete FreeCAD for Beginners – No Experience Needed

For full course details, visit: cadartifex.com